Introduction to Women's, Gender & Sexuality Studies

Introduction to Women's, Gender & Sexuality Studies

Interdisciplinary and Intersectional Approaches

Edited by

L. Ayu Saraswati, Barbara L. Shaw,
and Heather Rellihan

New York   Oxford
OXFORD UNIVERSITY PRESS

Oxford University Press is a department of the University of Oxford. It furthers the University's objective of excellence in research, scholarship, and education by publishing worldwide. Oxford is a registered trade mark of Oxford University Press in the UK and certain other countries.

Published in the United States of America by Oxford University Press
198 Madison Avenue, New York, NY 10016, United States of America.

© 2018 by Oxford University Press

Library of Congress Cataloging-in-Publication Data

CIP data is on file at the Library of Congress
9780190266066

9 8 7 6 5 4 3 2 1
Printed by LSC Communications Harrisonburg

Table of Contents

SECTION THREE   ## CULTURAL DEBATES IN WOMEN'S, GENDER AND SEXUALITY STUDIES   **201**

Rethinking the Family

Gender and Sexuality in the Labor Market

Reproductive Politics

Gendered Violence

Preface

Women's studies departments and programs are undergoing rapid transformation at all levels of higher education, transitioning from women's studies and feminist studies to women's and gender studies, and most recently to women's, gender and sexuality studies. With this transformation comes the need for a comprehensive and accessible introductory textbook that addresses the current state of the field. *Introduction to Women's, Gender & Sexuality Studies: Interdisciplinary and Intersectional Approaches* is the first text to reflect these exciting changes.

Introduction to Women's, Gender & Sexuality Studies is designed to appeal to a full range of programs and departments. Our core mission as teachers and scholars in creating this text is to be accessible yet represent the rigor in the field. We present complex interdisciplinary feminist and queer concepts and theories that are approachable for first- and second-year students entering a women's, gender and sexuality studies classroom, and supply pedagogical scaffolding crafted to engage a new generation of learners. Truly innovative in the field, *Introduction to Women's, Gender & Sexuality Studies* is a comprehensive mix of anthology and textbook that provides thorough overviews that begin each section; robust and engaging pedagogy that encourages students to think critically and self-reflexively as well as take action; and supplemental online resources for instructors (see Online Resources, below, for further information).

Introduction to Women's, Gender & Sexuality Studies offers students a strong foundation that teaches them to think in and across disciplines. We include key primary historical sources that represent broad social movements that helped shape the field; debates on contemporary issues to demonstrate the connections and tensions between individuals and social institutions; and recent work in science, technology, and digital cultures to emphasize the importance of truly interdisciplinary approaches to women's, gender and sexuality studies. In the sections that follow, we integrate new work from established scholars and emerging voices alongside key foundational creative and critical readings to introduce learners to multiple perspectives. Finally, we provide a range of genres (including poetry, short stories, interviews, op-eds, and feminist magazine articles) to complement the scholarly selections and acknowledge the roots of creative and personal expression in the field.

Introduction to Women's, Gender & Sexuality Studies emphasizes interdisciplinarity and intersectionality. This edited collection represents women's, men's, intersex, nonbinary and/or genderqueer, transgender, asexual, lesbian, gay, bisexual, and pansexual identities and experiences through scholarship in traditional disciplines and those that emerge from interdisciplinary fields. We proceed from the recognition that all identities are multifaceted social categories that require deep and contextual examinations in order to understand power dynamics that create sociocultural inequalities, hierarchies, oppressions, and privileges that shape our lives. Intersectionality is critical because it recognizes that universal and stabilized understandings of "women," "gender," and "queer" marginalize or exclude the voices, experiences, interests, and struggles of those who live their lives within material contexts of race, class, nationality, abilities, religion, and age.

For example, we include readings that allow learners to comprehend "gay men" or "Asian women" through the prism of skin color, religion, and/or body image. Other articles emphasizing the history of race, class, and ability call into question how "reproductive rights" have been exclusively positioned as empowering white, middle-class women in order to underscore how people in indigenous, black, gay, lesbian, and/or disabled communities must fight for the right to have children. Intersectionality requires framing any experience/ issue from standpoints based on complex identity formations and within hierarchical social structures. *Introduction to Women's, Gender & Sexuality Studies* takes this theoretical cornerstone as its conceptual framework and brings it to life with accessible and rigorous perspectives.

Please note that some of the readings may evoke certain (uncomfortable) feelings in the readers. Yet, as Saraswati argues in her book, *Seeing Beauty Sensing Race in Transnational Indonesia*, "sensing is . . . an epistemic apparatus" (2013, 3). Hence, it is important to be mindful of whatever feelings that may arise because they will, if addressed critically and mindfully, provide us with a mode of knowing and understanding the issue and the world better.

A NOTE ABOUT TERMINOLOGY

This reader purposefully uses a variety of racial/ethnic terminologies (e.g. Native American/American Indian/indigenous; black/African-American; Latino/Latina/ Latinx and Chicano/a; and Asian/Asian diaspora/Pacific islander) depending on the context, and as a way to honor certain individuals' and groups' preferences. For example, whereas "African-American" may be used to refer to people of African descent who are living in the United States, "black" may be deployed as a political and cultural term in reference to "black lives matter." It is important that students are exposed to these various terms and understand the different ways in which they are used to allow students to grapple with the complexity of race and ethnicity rather than providing privileged terms that affix and stabilize their meaning in a fluid world.

ORGANIZATION

Introduction to Women's, Gender & Sexuality Studies is divided into six sections. Each section begins with an introductory essay that frames the fields of study, contextualizing the selected readings and concluding with discussion questions that reinforce comprehension of key concepts while prompting critical thinking and self-reflection.

- Section I, "Mapping the Field: An Introduction to Women's, Gender and Sexuality Studies," engages concepts that serve as cornerstones of the field: social constructions that move beyond the dualities of sex and gender; the complexity of patriarchy as well as the categories of "women," "gender," and "queer" through intersectional approaches; the interlocking systems of oppression and privilege; how interdisciplinary approaches are critical to addressing complex contemporary socio-political issues; and the centrality of praxis and self-reflexivity in writing, oral communication, and activism.
- Section II, "Historical Perspectives in Women's, Gender and Sexuality Studies," traces the development of identity politics and social movements in the field. Beginning with nineteenth and early twentieth-century organizing around abolition, suffrage, lynching, and working conditions and moving through to the present day, this section follows the evolving questions over how to define "women's issues" or "queer issues" and how intersectional identities complicate notions of what counts as women's and queer activism. This section allows students to engage with primary sources that both contextualize and complicate the critical and creative texts in other sections.
- Section III, "Cultural Debates in Women's, Gender and Sexuality Studies," sets up some of the key contemporary issues in the field and challenges students to understand the power relations embedded in everyday experiences of family, work, reproduction, violence, and popular culture and media representations from multiple perspectives.
- Section IV, "Epistemologies of Bodies," examines the production of knowledge surrounding bodies and the cultural politics and social stratifications of embodiment, representation, and identity construction. The essays in this section critically analyze how labels (such as feminine, masculine, fat, queer, trans, disabled, racialized, reproductive, sexual, and aging) are attached to and provide meanings for how bodies *can* and *should* be experienced.
- Section V, "Science, Technology, and the Digital World," includes essays that map out the changes afforded by sciences and technologies, and the challenges of living as gendered, sexualized, racialized, and classed people in a digital age.

- Section VI, "Activist Frontiers: Agency and Resistance," emphasizes the roots of the field: activism. The readings in this section provide models of feminist and queer activism and avenues for understanding the interplay of agency and social change.

KEY FEATURES

Dynamic Approach *Introduction to Women's, Gender & Sexuality Studies* combines the best features of both traditional textbooks and anthologies. The standard single-voice textbook approach is useful because it succinctly summarizes key events or issues, provides context, and presents information in accessible language. However, part of the ethos of women's, gender and sexuality studies as a field is to engage multiple and contested ideas, accomplished most effectively through an anthology of diverse readings. *Introduction to Women's, Gender & Sexuality Studies* provides the best of both worlds by featuring in-depth introductory narratives for each section *and* a range of readings from canonical to emerging voices.

The section introductions provide the social and historical context for the selected readings that follow. Depending on the section, this may include an overview of important developments in the field, a historiography of pivotal debates, biographical information about influential thinkers, definitions of key vocabulary terms, and other background information necessary for understanding how the readings that follow are in conversation with one another. The selected pieces include both primary and secondary sources. The primary texts encourage critical thinking skills by providing the opportunity to engage with subjective narratives; secondary texts ask learners to interpret, evaluate, and synthesize while modeling scholarly writing. Many selections are included in their entirety; we also feature robust excerpts from longer sources. This allows for a balance between depth and breadth.

Interdisciplinary and Intersectional *Introduction to Women's, Gender & Sexuality Studies* encourages interdisciplinary analysis of United States-based and transnational cultural identities through critical and creative works. Each section includes multiple perspectives and genres, encouraging students to develop broad-based and multifaceted understandings of the complex issues surrounding "women," "gender," and "sexuality." A unique section emphasizing science, technology, and digital cultures adds to our understanding of women's, gender and sexuality studies as an interdisciplinary field.

New Works While the majority of selections included in this anthology are foundational texts–either frequently published or cited materials–*Introduction to Women's, Gender & Sexuality Studies* also includes new scholarship (critical essays as well as creative work) to expand current debates with new voices. Rather than relying only on where the field has been, *Introduction to Women's,*

Gender & Sexuality Studies points to future directions that actualize the emerging field of women's, gender and sexuality studies.

Pedagogy *Introduction to Women's, Gender & Sexuality Studies* includes pedagogical tools designed to facilitate learning and develop critical thinking skills. Each section introduction includes one of each of the following boxed features:

- **Intersectional Analysis** Students will be presented with a case study that is related to the theme of each section. This case study is followed by a series of questions that specifically prompt students to critically think about the issue from an intersectional perspective. By doing this exercise, students will have an opportunity to apply the concept of intersectionality to a thoughtfully-chosen topic, giving them a better understanding of both "intersectionality" as a mode of analysis and the rich content of the section's topic. These case studies will illustrate to students why intersectional analysis is complicated but necessary for better understanding the world around them.
- **Engaged Learning** This pedagogical tool features an engaging activity that allows students to further explore the topic of each section. It encourages students to make connections between the concepts presented in each section and their everyday lives. This exercise guides students through a "hands-on" activity with focused questions designed to further their understanding of the materials through application, analysis, and self-reflection.
- **Activism and Civic Engagement** Students will be presented with a brief description of either an activist, activist group, or activist method followed by reflection, or a suggestion for a civic engagement activity designed to encourage students to take an active role in making changes in their communities and to illustrate the connection between the theories they learn in class and activism.
- **Transnational Connections** By analyzing a case study or doing an activity, students will learn the transnational aspect of the topic discussed in each section. These cases studies and activities will emphasize the interconnectedness of our world and how decisions we make in our lives not only affect people in other parts of the world and vice versa, but also are shaped by transnational conditions.

Additional pedagogical resources to enhance student learning and engagement include:

- **Learning Objectives** In light of the current focus on learning outcomes assessment, each section introduction begins with specific learning objectives to guide students towards an understanding of key topics and overarching themes.
- **Marginal Glosses** This feature in the section introductions provides quick definitions for key terms and concepts as soon as students first encounter them in the text. These key terms are collected again in an alphabetized list

at the end of each section introduction (to allow for quick review); a glossary at the end of the book collects all of the key terms and definitions for general reference.

- **Headnotes** Introducing each reading selection, these narratives provide brief biographies of the authors, information about the historical context, and/or information about the original publishing context.

- **Critical Thinking Questions** Listed at the end of each section, these questions provide an opportunity to assess understanding and encourage self-reflection in developing arguments and perspectives.

- **Online Resources** In addition to the printed text, a website will be maintained that provides supplementary learning materials. Links will be provided for further readings including both primary and secondary sources that may be used for understanding the context surrounding any given topic, inspire debate around a particular issue, or allow for the application of a theoretical premise to a real-life example. The site will also contain suggested activities that can be developed either in the traditional face-to-face classroom or in an online learning environment. The site will collate and organize links to multimedia content that could be incorporated into a lecture, used as a prompt for classroom discussion or online discussion forums, or provided to students as supplementary classroom preparation.

Acknowledgements

The editors would like to thank Claire Moses for her insightful feedback as we developed the reader during the early stages. We would also like to thank Lynn Bolles who has been an important guide for each of us in our understandings of interdisciplinarity and intersectionality. We are also grateful for the meticulous and helpful editing from Meg Botteon and Sherith Pankratz. We would like to sincerely thank them. Saraswati would also like to thank Margaret Carnegie for her research assistance. Shaw thanks the librarians at Allegheny College and especially Linda Ernst, the interlibrary loan specialist, as well as Kelly Pohland '16 for her careful reading and research assistance. Rellihan thanks her colleagues Suzanne Spoor, Carolin Woolson, and Susan Kilgard for their feedback and suggestions and Kelley Squazzo for her insights around textbook publishing.

The feedback from kind and generous anonymous reviewers have helped the formation of this reader:

Heying Jenny Zhan, Georgia State University
Ann Fuehrer, Miami University
Tara Jabbaar-Gyambrah, Niagara University
Jill Hersh, Montclair State University
Matthew B. Ezzell, James Madison University
Amanda Koontz Anthony, University of Central Florida
Rebecca Tolley-Stokes, East Tennessee State University
Lauren Weis, American University
Kathleen Turkel, University of Delaware
Beth Sertell, Ohio University
Ariella Rotramel, Connecticut College
Julietta Hua, San Francisco State University
Laura Harrison, Minnesota State University
Avery Tompkins, Transylvania University
Elizabeth A. Hubble, University of Montana
Sujey Vega, Arizona State University

Lynn Comella, University of Nevada
Julianne Guillard, University of Richmond
Margaret Ann Harrison, City College of San Francisco
Alison Hatch, Armstrong State University
Kristan Poirot, Texas A&M University
Emily Burrill, University of North Carolina at Chapel Hill
Nicole Carter, Wright State University
Patricia Ackerman, The City College of New York
Barbara A. Barnes, University of California
Harleen Singh, Brandeis University
Jennifer A. Wagner-Lawlor, Pennsylvania State University
Sarah E. Dougher, Portland State University
Jerilyn Fisher, Hostos Community College
Dynette I. Reynolds, Weber State University
Racheal Stimpson, Alamance Community College
Dahlia Valle, Kingsborough Community College
Cheryl Waite, Community College of Aurora
Miranda Miller, Gillette College
Leandra Preston-Sidler, University of Central Florida
Rachel A. Lewis, George Mason University
Ann Schofield, University of Kansas

ABOUT THE EDITORS

L. Ayu Saraswati is an associate professor in the women's studies department at the University of Hawai'i, Manoa. Prior to her current position, she had been an assistant professor at the University of Kansas and a postdoctoral fellow at Emory University. She is the award-wining author of *Seeing Beauty, Sensing Race in Transnational Indonesia* (University of Hawai'i Press, 2013)—winner of the 2013 National Women's Studies Association (NWSA) Gloria Anzaldúa book prize. Saraswati also has published numerous articles in *Feminist Studies, Meridians, Feminist Formations,* and *Sexualities.*

Barbara L. Shaw is an assistant professor in women's, gender and sexuality studies at Allegheny College. She has experience transforming women's studies curricula to women's, gender and sexuality studies at undergraduate liberal arts institutions, leads workshops on curriculum transformation, and participates in national institutes on W/G/S undergraduate curriculum. She is completing a book-length manuscript, *Decolonizing Sexual Violence: Social Justice in Caribbean Women's Everyday Lives.*

Heather Rellihan is professor and coordinator of gender and sexuality studies at Anne Arundel Community College (AACC). She is assistant director of AACC's Curriculum Transformation Project, an initiative that encourages attention to diversity and equity issues in curriculum and pedagogy. She was a recipient of the 2014 John & Suanne Roueche Excellence Award for her achievements in community college teaching. She is co-editor of the forthcoming book, *Theory and Praxis: Women's and Gender Studies at Community Colleges.*

SECTION ONE

Mapping the Field: An Introduction to Women's, Gender and Sexuality Studies

TABLE OF CONTENTS

LEARNING OBJECTIVES

By the end of this section, you will have a better understanding of:

1. The connection between social movements and the field of women's, gender and sexuality studies.

2. How the contested meanings of feminist and queer are central to the academic field of women's, gender and sexuality studies.

3. Key terms and concepts in women's, gender and sexuality studies emphasizing oppression and privilege.

4. Intersectionality and how it is foundational to understanding the complexity of women, men, nonbinary, genderqueer, and transgender people and structures of power in US society.

5. Interdisciplinarity and its centrality to understanding the field.

Women's, gender and sexuality studies is an interdisciplinary field of study and emerges as part of a long history of feminist, queer, antiracist, anticapitalist, and anticolonial movements. As an academic field it is concerned with issues of gender, sexuality, race, ethnicity, class, nationality, abilities, age, body size, and religion. It also provides lenses or ways of seeing how sociocultural dynamics of power craft our understanding of gender, transgender, and queer and its effect on our daily life. Scholars, artists, and activists in women's, gender and sexuality studies (1) question what we know and how we know it, (2) craft theories and practices that work to end oppression and inequality and pursue social justice and change, (3) empower individuals who are marginalized, and (4) generally agree that there is no single or "correct" feminist or queer way of being, doing, and living. In the remainder of this introduction, you will learn key concepts (feminism, queer, gender, transgender, oppression, privilege, intersectionality, and interdisciplinarity) that provide the foundation for understanding women's, gender and sexuality studies.

WHAT DOES FEMINISM AND QUEER HAVE TO DO WITH IT?

In the English language, using the "f-word" is considered obscene; it shows anger, contempt, and disrespect to whoever (or whatever) is on the receiving end. Feminism seems to have similar cultural meanings. By now many of us have heard the stereotypes of feminists: angry, unshaven, dykes, bitchy, man-hating, and aggressive. bell hooks in her piece "Feminist Politics" (included in this section) makes the simple statement that feminism is "a movement to end sexism, sexist exploitation, and oppression" and uses this definition because it "implies that all sexist thinking and action is the problem," regardless of who is doing it (p 20). When asked, most individuals will readily tell you that people should not be exploited or oppressed. How is it then that when feminists come together to fight against individual and institutional sexism for protections, rights, social justice, and freedom, feminism becomes a dirty word? How or when do you think this sentiment emerged in our lives? bell hooks suggests that all of us learn antifeminism through US patriarchal mass media because it seeks to undermine gender justice, which for her moves beyond equality to include "the freedom to have abortions, to be lesbians, to challenge rape and domestic violence" (p 20).

Feminism has a long and contentious history in which its strongest advocates did not always agree with one another on the goals of the movement or the strategies for social change. As you will learn in more detail in Section II, women (and some men) were inspired by women's personal narratives and public speeches as well as abolition movements in the mid-nineteenth century to begin advocating for women's equality with men while others sought liberation from subjugation. Demanding everything from the right to vote to sexual autonomy, early feminists challenged the cultural belief that white, middle-class, and wealthy men innately deserved respect and dignity that was materially accompanied by access to education, work, and citizenship, while white, middle-class, and wealthy women were expected to be pious, pure, submissive, and domestic, thus best suited to be mothers and wives (Welter 152). Women's, gender and sexuality studies also traces its roots to movements such as the turn-of-the-twentieth-century anti-lynching movement led in part by African American journalist, newspaper owner, and grassroots activist Ida B. Wells; the labor movement organized by working class, Jewish immigrant women in the early twentieth century; and mid-twentieth-century women's groups such as Radicalesbian, WITCH (Women's International Conspiracy from Hell), and the Red Stockings who made it clear that eradicating patriarchal culture and crafting a women's centered one was the only means to liberation. The crucial questions that beget grassroots movements for change form the backbone of feminist and queer inquiry in women's, gender and sexuality studies. As Marilyn Boxer notes in *When Women Ask the Questions*, "From the beginning, the goal of women's studies was not merely to study women's position in the world but to change it" (13). Given the expansiveness of feminist politics today, it is critical to understand how the last century and a half of movements for civil rights and social justice fundamentally shaped the field and that **patriarchy** remains a central feature that reinforces racism, classism, homophobia, transphobia, nationalism, ageism, and ableism in our daily lives.

Some people often assume that patriarchy is the idea that all men dominate and control all women. As Allan Johnson explains in "Patriarchy, the System: An It, Not a He, a Them, or an Us" (included in this section), this oversimplified approach emphasizes individual actions and reactions rather than seeing patriarchy as a system in which we all—men, women, nonbinary, genderqueer, and transgender people—participate. Patriarchy is cultural—knit into the fabric of US society—and upheld by individuals *and* **social institutions** through the law, media, family, education, and religion. Johnson provides an example that makes this very clear: if we think about patriarchy as the actions of individuals, "we might ask why a particular man raped, harassed, or beat a woman. We wouldn't ask however what kind of society would promote persistent patterns of such behavior" (p. 24). If one in four women experience rape on college campuses, social change will depend on getting to the roots that condone the violence; this means looking closely at campus policies, language, and our assumptions about the behaviors of young people. If these favor men's experiences, it will silence and oppress women though some people may not see it as such. As Johnson argues, if society is oppressive, then people who grow up and live in it, accept, identify with, and participate in it as 'normal'. Feminist and queer inquiry intervenes in systems of subjugation and injustice, and, while there is significant overlap between feminist and queer studies, they are not synonymous.

Patriarchy: Cultural system in which men hold power and are the central figures in the family, community, government, and larger society.

Social institutions: rule-governed social arrangements that have survived across time and appear natural and normal but in fact represent one way of being in the world, e.g., the nuclear family, a well-armed military, and a capitalist economy.

Queer: Once a pejorative term, it has been reclaimed to describe sexual identities and political issues in lesbian, gay, bisexual, pansexual, polyamorous, transgender, questioning, asexual, and intersexed communities; used to push back against oversimplified and assumed definitions of lesbian and gay identity.

LGBTQPAI+: An acronym used to identify and politically unite lesbian, gay, bisexual, transgender, questioning and queer, pansexual and polyamory, asexual, and intersexed communities. The plus indicates that the acronym is fluid; as more queer identities are named, they can be added. The plus can also signify that people identify with more than one of these categories.

Trans: Shortened form of the term "transgender" and used to signify a diverse group of people who do not identify with the gender they were assigned at birth and/or traditional cultural definitions of woman and man. Trans may include but is not limited to trans woman, trans man, transsexual, nonbinary, genderfluid, genderqueer, genderless, agender, third gender, and two-spirited.

Genderqueer: Individuals who self-identify outside of the woman/man gender binary.

In her essay "Queer," Jennifer Purvis posits that women's, gender and sexuality studies "is always already queer," which she defines as "twisting" and "making strange" (190). In this context, feminism is intended to be inclusive of **queer.** Once a derogatory term hurled at lesbians and gay men, "queer" has been reclaimed by **LGBTQPAI+** communities as a term of self-identification as lesbian, gay, bisexual, transgender, questioning, pansexual, polyamorous, asexual, and intersexual. "Queer" is an umbrella term used to bring together people (1) who have been marginalized in US society because of their sexuality and gender expression and (2) whose descriptions and feelings do not fit easily within and may resist categories of lesbian, gay, bisexual, or **trans.** In the latter case, it becomes an inclusive term for those who self-identify as **genderqueer.** Queer can also be its own sexual identity (in some acronyms it can be the "Q"), and it can signify someone's politics. For scholars, practitioners, artists, and activists who fight for the political and legal protections, rights, and freedoms of all queer people, the phrase "queer nation" can represent the need for a continued national political voice. It is also important to note that when "queer" is deployed in the struggle for social justice, it assumes solidarity, which does not always exist between the various groups of people under its purview. For example, the queer community won a significant victory when the Supreme Court ruled in July 2015 that states must allow same-sex marriage. It is also true that this milestone is limited to those who want to participate in marriage—a historically **heteronormative** institution. As such, gay marriage unites and divides the queer community.

Purvis's statement that women's, gender and sexuality studies "is always already queer" is a bold one, particularly for some feminists. It *still* matters that lesbians, bisexual/pansexual, transgender, and asexual people who identify as women do not have the same privileges and rights as gay men because of sexism *and* have a history of exclusion in feminism. This was true in the late 1960s when the cofounder of the National Organization of Women, Betty Friedan, named lesbians as the "lavender menace" (which will be examined closely in Section II) and happening today as trans women fight for acceptance and inclusion in the women's movement, colleges, and other social institutions. When feminism excludes queer people, it replicates the power relations of patriarchy. Therefore, if feminism is to be queer it will mean that scholars, practitioners, artists, and activists will need to challenge the social norms that define womanhood and manhood—indeed, the binary of gender itself. And if queer communities are feminist, it will require consistent and public challenges to sexism and patriarchy. This matters so that all people's voices and experiences, especially those who have been marginalized, are valued and included in movements, laws, social institutions, creative communities, and scholarship.

LEARNING AND UNLEARNING GENDER AND SEXUALITY

Learning gender begins before any of us can even process it. In the United States, when a baby is born, many doctors still announce, "It's a healthy baby girl!" or "It's a healthy baby boy!" This simple act of looking at the baby's genitals and announcing their sex begins the process of assigning children a **gender status.** If it is a girl, friends may purchase gifts of pink or pastel clothing, exclaim how beautiful she is going to be when she grows up, and comment that she is such a good, quiet baby. If it is boy, he may receive blue or brightly colored clothing and told that he is smart, active, or will be the next star athlete. Knowing the sex of the baby sets the stage for how the child will be socialized into their **gender identity** and treated as a girl/woman and boy/man.

As this scenario demonstrates, there is an easy and unconscious slippage between sex and gender. We readily accept that female and male represent the biological differences between men and women and that two sexes exist. In "The Five Sexes Revisited" (included in this section), Anne Fausto-Sterling, a biologist and gender studies scholar, provides evidence that there is a wide variation of sexes in the natural world—including amongst humans. The concept that there are *only* two sexes is a **social construction** and has been institutionalized as a scientific fact through medicine, education, family, and religion. If, as Fausto-Sterling estimates, 1.7 percent of all births are people with varying degrees of intersexed development, what are the implications for the meaning of gender (*Sexing the Body*, 51)?

While gender may *appear* to be a natural and simple outgrowth of sex, it is a social process "constantly created and re-created out of human interaction, out of social life, and is the texture and order of that social life" (Lorber 99–100). We enact gender every day without paying much attention to it, yet it is one of the central ways we organize our lives. From deciding what to wear to how we sit, talk, and generally take up public space to what kinds of labor we perform, gender arrangements shape our lives. They are not built on individual efforts, hard work, or ability but on hierarchies of power that socialize men/boys to be dominant and women/girls to be subordinate and finds its legitimization through the social constructions of family, religion, law, media, education, work, and language. In her very personal piece, "Because You're a Girl," Ijeoma A. recounts experiences being raised in a family that embraced traditional customs characteristic of villages in eastern Nigeria. She spent her childhood in Lagos living under her family's Four Commandments that taught her how to become a good woman prepared for marriage: (1) her "office" is the kitchen, (2) she is responsible for all the chores in the home, (3) she is accountable for the children and their actions, and (4) of course, she must pledge complete and total allegiance to the man in charge first, before herself (p. 38). Angered by the patriarchal constrictions, Ijeoma finds pathways through education to resist always "being a good girl" as she empowers herself.

Without thinking twice about it, gender makes sense because it is systematized and reflected in our everyday lives: girls play with dolls and boys with toy soldiers; young women major in the humanities and young men in the physical sciences; nurses are women and engineers are men; and collectively women are valued for their looks and nurturing personalities and men for their intelligence, leadership, and ability to provide an income for households. "Gender is such a familiar part of daily life, it usually takes a deliberate disruption of our expectations of how women and men are supposed to act to pay attention to

Heteronormative: A worldview or ideology that assumes and promotes heterosexuality as a preferred sexual orientation and expression.

Gender status: The gender assigned to children and used to socialize them into boy/man and girl/woman; may also be referred to as gender assignment.

Gender identity: An individual's gendered sense of self.

Social constructionism: Theory that our knowledge of gender, race, class, sexuality, ethnicity, body size, ability, religion, and nationality are tied to social processes and therefore constantly being created and recreated by human beings within specific cultural contexts.

ACTIVISM AND CIVIC ENGAGEMENT

Log on to Twitter or access #GrowingUpAGirl through an Internet search. If the hashtag is not active, search Twitter and Instagram for a similar community talking about what it means to grow up female. If you cannot find this hashtag or one similar, start one as a class. Participants use #GrowingUpAGirl to raise awareness of how young women walk through the world experiencing patriarchal culture. It can range from detailing street harassment (when/where/what took place) to what it means to be a part of the punk community in Los Angeles. Read the entries and make two lists. The first should detail how girls experience daily life within patriarchal culture; for the second, write down how girls use the hashtag to empower themselves. Reflect on your own experiences of what it was like to grow up in your town/city and contribute to or start a conversation on what it means to grow up a girl. Think carefully about family life, experiences in school, what you learned through the media, how religion shaped your worldview, and how romance and attraction mattered as you grew up.

QUESTIONS

1. Examine your two lists carefully. Do you see any patterns that indicate what girls generally face in their daily life? What dominates each list? Why do you think these two things are at the top of the list? What role does sexism and patriarchy play in girls' lives?
2. Do the issues girls face cut across cultural differences, or do you see additional patterns based on race, class, sexuality, ability, and religious beliefs?
3. What did you contribute and why?
4. Name one thing that all of us could collectively do to empower girls and share it with your class. How might it affect girls' lives?
5. As a class, translate your suggestion for change into a community action such as (1) implementing a week (or month or year!) at school where no one can use the word "fat" or "slut" as a way of shaming a girl or (2) working with your professor and a teacher at a local elementary school to create a Girls' Empowerment Day. Whether real or hypothetical, what would you include and why?

how it is produced" (Lorber 100). A social system based on hierarchies of power is recognizable if when any of these examples are reversed they no longer make sense. For example, how are boys perceived if they want to play with dolls and not toy soldiers, or young women when they want to play professional sports rather than be cheerleaders?

In "Making Masculinity" (included in this section), C. J. Pascoe begins by narrating a scene that may sound familiar: at an annual high school assembly the most popular boy will be crowned "Mr. Cougar" to the loud cheers of his classmates. In this particular case, when the two highest vote-getting candidates run onto the floor, they are dressed like nerds and proceed to perform a skit in which they save their girlfriends from "gangstas" (young black men who volunteered to be run off the stage) and transform into handsome, rugged, all-American guys. This scene illustrates that "[t]his masculinizing process happens through a transformation of bodies, the assertion of racial privilege, and a shoring up of heterosexuality and is a stark reminder of how limiting masculinity is for boys and men" (p. 45). If adolescent boys are perceived as tough, in control, focused on sports and girls, and not to care about others, they will be rewarded for their gender performances (see Gardiner; hooks; Kimmel; Kimmel and Messner; Messner; Segal; Halberstam; Wiegman). If a young man steps outside these narrow bounds, his peers will police and control his behavior by publicly ridiculing him as a "fag," which, as Pascoe learned during her field research, is the worst insult possible for adolescents. She argues in this piece "how heteronormative and homophobic discourses, practices, and interactions (among students, teachers, and administrators) . . . produce masculine identities" (Pascoe 8).

Since gender is socially constructed and performed by us every day, we collectively can and do change the ways gender stereotypes circulate to uphold structures of inequality. Students enter women's, gender and sexuality courses telling their own personal narratives of how their fathers stay at home and do the cooking, cleaning, and laundry while their mothers pursue careers or how they were the only girl on their town's youth soccer team and excelled. In Judith Gardiner's "Friendship, Gender Theories, and Social Change" (included in this section), she argues that the insufficiently studied concept of "friendship" reveals paradoxes about gender as it continues to shift culturally. She writes, "On the one hand, Americans experience friendship as a realm of freedom from the restrictions of [gender in] families and workplaces. On the other . . . friendships usually reinforce gender binaries and so reassure individuals that they are performing gender appropriately" (p. 53). By looking closely at television shows such as *Friends* and *Girls* and films such as *The Hangover* and *Bridesmaid*, Gardiner identifies moments where (1) men and women share similar characteristics of historically defined masculinity and femininity (such as bonding over sports and spending time shopping) *and* (2) gender differences are reinforced to ensure masculinity and femininity are being performed properly. While individuals may redefine what gender means in their lives, whether through their friendships and/or on their own accord, until this paradox is addressed consistently across social institutions (from families, religion and the law to media and language), fundamental change will remain elusive.

BEYOND THE GENDER BINARY

In 1990, gender studies scholar Judith Butler argued that our understandings of gender are too closely mapped to how we understand the body. Rather than think of the body as constituting sex and gender, she and others suggest that it is more productive to understand gender performances as a fluid, social process based on repetition and reinforcement (see Halberstam; Muñoz). Gender flexibility disrupts the static equation that to be born male equals being a man/masculine/attracted to women and that to be born female means being a woman/feminine/attracted to men. It also challenges the concept that "masculine" and "feminine" have universal meanings. This shift away from the certainty of the social construction of gender is both embraced and challenged by feminists and queer scholars. It is liberating for those who understand gender binaries as too limiting yet of great concern for those who see structural inequalities still tied to the bodies of women, lesbians, gay men,

Transgender: An umbrella term that describes people whose gender identity and/or gender expression differs from the gender they were assigned at birth.

Cisgender: A term that describes when an individual's gender assigned at birth aligns with their gender identity and gender expression.

bisexuals, pansexuals, trans, and asexual women and men. It is also important to note that gender fluidity and flexibility come at a personal cost ranging from possible teasing and being outcast, to bullying and being disowned, to discrimination and physical violence.

In *Transgender History*, Susan Stryker uses the term **transgender** "to refer to people who move away from the gender they were assigned at birth, people who cross over (*trans-*) the boundaries constructed by their culture to define and contain that gender" (Stryker 1). The term describes the spectrum of someone's gender identity and expression, not their sexuality, while "transsexual" specifically is used in reference to people who desire medical interventions to transition from one sex to another. The term **cisgender** is used to describe an individual whose gender assignment and gender identity match. Its use as an adjective before "woman" or "man" is necessary "to resist the way that 'woman' or 'man' can mean 'nontransgendered woman' or 'nontransgendered man' by default, unless the person's transgender status is explicitly named" (Stryker 22). And while these terms and their attending politics have received media attention, activists such as Sylvia Rivera and Marsha P. Johnson were pioneers of the transgender movement in the mid-1960s, demanding rights and protections through political and legal change.

Entire books, courses, academic programs, blogs, and activist platforms are dedicated to the history and complexity of studying transgenderism and the struggle for justice in the transgender community. Paisley Currah's article "Stepping Back, Looking Outward: Situating Transgender Activism and Transgender Studies" (included in this section) allows us to see how activism and scholarship are bridged in the transgender movement as well as how the struggle for transgender rights is connected to other social movements. The article, which features a conversation between Kris Hayashi, a member of the Youth United for Community Action in California, Matt Richardson, a professor of English at the University of Texas, Austin, and affiliated with the Center for African and African American Studies and the Center for Gender and Women's Studies, and Susan Stryker, now a professor of gender and women's studies at the University of Arizona, consider "the broader outlines of activism . . . that has challenged the state's enforcement of the gender binary but also its power to do so" (p. 57). The work done here is significant because it takes aim at state policies that erase the identities and experiences of transgender individuals. The conversation also provides a unique opportunity to consider the pitfalls and promises of crafting an academic field dedicated to the recuperation of transgender biographies, histories, and issues. Some of the critical questions raised are: Whose stories are told and whose are left out in academe and the popular press; does the media convey violence more often than triumphs; and how can cisgender individuals work ethically alongside transgender activists? Learning the terms and their meanings in people's everyday lives is one of the best starting places to do this solidarity work.

Tables 1.1 and 1.2, adapted from the Southern Poverty Law Center, provide an overview of the gender spectrum.

Table 1.1. The Basics

Birth Sex/Biological Sex	A specific set of genetic, chemical, and anatomical characteristics that we are either born with or that develop as we mature. Types of birth/biological sex include female, male, and intersex.
Gender Identity	One's internal, personal sense of his or her own gender. Many people believe in a more fluid gender identity that simply correlates to "male" and "female."
Gender Expression	The external manifestation of one's gender identity, usually expressed through behavior, clothing, haircut, voice, or body characteristics.
Sexual Orientation	The nature of an individual's physical, romantic, emotional, and/or spiritual attraction to another person. Gender identity and sexual orientation are not the same. Trans and gender-variant people may identify with any sexual orientation, and their sexual orientation may or may not change before, during, or after gender transition.
Transgender	An umbrella term that describes people whose gender identity and/or gender expression differs from the sex they were assigned at birth. This group includes, but is not limited to, transsexuals, cross-dressers, and other gender-variant people. Transgender people may or may not choose to alter their bodies hormonally and/or surgically.

Table 1.2. The Full Spectrum

Assigned Sex	The sex/gender one is considered to be at birth based on a cursory examination of external genitalia.
Asexual	In its broadest sense, asexual describes individuals who are not sexually attracted to others or are not interested in sex. Those who identify as asexual may still be romantically attracted to others.
Bigendered	Describes individuals who identify as having both a "male" and a "female" side to their personalities.
Bisexual	Describes a person who is attracted to both men and women. Because bisexual assumes a binary, male/female paradigm, many individuals now use the term "pansexual."
Cisgender	Describes when an individual's biological sex matches his or her gender identity and gender expression.
Closeted or In the Closet	Hiding one's sexual orientation.
Coming Out	The processes by which lesbians, gay men, and bisexual people recognize, acknowledge, accept, and typically appreciate their sexual identities.
Gay	Describes a person whose emotional, romantic, and sexual attractions are primarily for individuals of the same sex, typically in reference to men and boys, sometimes used as a general term for gay men and lesbians.
LGBT	An acronym that stands for "lesbian, gay, bisexual, and transgender." Other versions may add "Q" for queer or questioning, "I" for intersex, or "A" for allied or asexual. Some may prefer to list the acronym as TBLG to place trans people in a position of importance and to rectify the way trans has historically been omitted, devalued, or excluded.
Genderqueer	Describes individuals who possess identities that fall outside of the widely accepted sexual binary.
Gender Role	Clothing, characteristics, traits, and behaviors culturally associated with masculinity and/or femininity.

Continued

Table 1.2. Continued

Gender Variant	A term that describes individuals who stray from socially accepted gender roles.
Heterosexism	The societal/cultural, institutional, and individual beliefs and practices that privilege heterosexuals and subordinate and denigrate lesbians, gay men, and bisexual/pansexual people. The critical element that differentiates heterosexism (or any other "-ism") from prejudice and discrimination is the use of institutional power and authority to support prejudices and enforce discriminatory behaviors in systematic ways with far-reaching outcomes and effects.
Heterosexual Ally	Heterosexual people who confront heterosexism in themselves and others out of self-interest; a concern for the well-being of lesbians, gay men, and bisexual/ pansexual people; and a belief that heterosexism is a social injustice.
Heterosexual Privilege	The benefits and advantages that heterosexuals receive in a heterosexist culture. Also the benefits that lesbians, gay men, and bisexual/pansexual people receive as a result of claiming a heterosexual identity and denying a lesbian, gay, or bisexual/pansexual identity.
Homophobia	Literally, the fear of homosexuals and homosexuality; however, this term is generally applied to anyone who dislikes LGBTIQ people, who uses derogatory sexuality- or gender-based terms, or who feels that LGBTIQ people want "special rights" and not "equal rights." Homophobic behavior can range from telling jokes about lesbians and gay men to verbal abuse and even acts of physical violence.
Intersex	Intersex people are born with physical sex markers (genitals, hormones, gonads, or chromosomes) that are neither clearly male nor female.
Lesbian	A woman or girl whose emotional, romantic, and sexual attractions are primarily for other women or girls.
Out or Out of the Closet	To be openly lesbian, gay, bisexual/pansexual, transgendered, queer, or intersex.
Outing	When someone discloses information about another's sexual orientation or gender identity without that person's knowledge and/or consent.
Queer	A term that has been reclaimed by members of the gay, lesbian, bisexual, and transgender communities to describe people who transgress culturally imposed norms of heterosexuality and gender traditionalism. Although still often an abusive epithet when used by bigoted heterosexuals, many queer-identified people have taken back the word to use it as a symbol of pride and affirmation of difference and diversity.
Sex Reassignment Surgery (SRS)	A procedure that physically transforms the genitals using plastic surgery. SRS is a single surgical alteration and is only one small part of a transition. Not all transgender people choose to, or can afford to, have SRS. While this procedure is often referred to as a "sex-change operation" in popular culture, SRS is the preferred term.
Sexism	The societal/cultural, institutional, and individual beliefs and practices that privilege men and subordinate and denigrate women.
Straight	Slang term for "heterosexual."
Trans	An umbrella term that describes people who permanently or periodically disidentify with the sex they were assigned at birth.
Transfriendly	Describes organizations or institutions that are open, affirming, and accepting of trans people and their social, political, and cultural needs.

Table 1.2. Continued

Gender Transition	The period of time in which a person begins to live in a gender role that is in accordance with his or her internal gender identity. Transition is not a one-step procedure; it is a complex process that occurs over a long period of time. Transition may include some or all of the following cultural, legal, and medical adjustments: informing one's family, friends, and/or coworkers; changing one's name and/or sex on legal documents; undergoing hormone therapy; and/or seeking surgical alteration (see *Sex Reassignment Surgery*).
Transphobia	The irrational fear and hatred of all those individuals who do not conform to dominant gender categories.

Source: "A Gender Spectrum Glossary." *Teaching Tolerance: A Project of the Southern Poverty Law Center.* http://www.tolerance.org/LGBT-best-practices-terms

Knowing that sex and gender exist on a spectrum helps us to unlearn limiting and harmful stereotypes. This is not just a matter of philosophical or political debate but has material consequences for people's equality, freedom, safety, and well-being and the social justice they seek.

OPPRESSION, PRIVILEGE, AND INTERSECTIONALITY

Oppression is the primary force that keeps marginalized people from achieving full equality and social justice. It is best understood as a system of barriers that operate socially and institutionally to disempower groups of people based on their gender, race, class, ethnicity, sexuality, ability, religion, body size, and/or nationality. "Oppression" can also refer to how individual people can suppress and control one another psychologically. In Marilyn Frye's classic essay, "Oppression" (included in this section), she argues that in patriarchal cultures *all* women are oppressed and men are not. Women are "caught . . . by networks of forces and barriers that expose one to penalty, loss, or contempt whether one works outside the home or not, is on welfare or not, bears children or not, marries or not, stays married or not, is heterosexual, lesbian, both or neither" (pp. 68–69). Frye makes clear that women universally are affected by the **double binds** that oppression creates.

While it is true that women face similar oppressions—such as the stigma tied to menstruation or being told never to walk alone at night or wear revealing clothing to "prevent" rape (rather than insisting that boys/men not rape)—**women of color** (and people of color) may experience oppression differently than white women (and white men) and in multiple ways. In Deborah King's "Multiple Jeopardy and Multiple Consciousness: The Context of a Black Feminist Ideology," she points out that black women recognize that "the interactive oppressions that circumscribe our lives provide a distinctive context for black womanhood" (42). While white people may experience oppression based on

Oppression: A social system of barriers that operate institutionally and interpersonally to disempower people because of their gender, race, class, sexuality, ethnicity, religion, body size, ability, and/or nationality.

Double bind: When a person faces two problematic choices as the only ones socially available (e.g., a woman can be labeled as a "slut" if sexually active and a "tease" or "prude" if not).

Women of color: A sociopolitical term used in the United States to describe African American/black, Asian American, Latina/x, and Native American/indigenous women.

INTERSECTIONAL ANALYSIS

Gina Metallic, coming out as two-spirit native womyn. Growing up in a small indigenous community in Canada that she describes as both homophobic and transphobic because of colonization and Christianity, Metallic now identifies as a cisgender, feminist, two-spirit Mi'kmaq womyn deeply connected to her family and community. She told her story to *The Montreal Gazette* in August 2015 so that others might know that it is possible to be both queer and native and that there is support.

A Case Study: Gina Metallic grew up in Listuguj, a small Mi'Kmaq community on the Gaspé Peninsula in Quebec, Canada. In her own words in the online version of the *Montreal Gazette*, she identifies as "a granddaughter, daughter, sister, aunt and a soon-to-be-wife. I also identify as a cisgender two-spirit Mi'kmaq womyn—a biological female inhabited at once by spirits of both male and female gender. I'm also a feminist who chooses to identify as 'womyn' rather than 'woman.'" In 1990 at the Third Annual First Nations Conference in Winnipeg, Canada, the term "two-spirited" was defined as "an Aboriginal who identifies with both male and female gender roles." When asked what identifying as two-spirited means to her, she discusses it historically and in her own life. According

to her community elders and family members, two-spirited people held respected positions in indigenous communities: marriage counselors, medicine people, and visionaries. When Europeans arrived in the Americas, they enforced Christianity, and two-spirited people were either exiled or killed. Today, Metallic openly embraces her identity and has found support through the maternal side of her family though still experiences rejection from her father's side, which she attributes to the lasting effects of colonialism. Through ongoing work with a traditional healer, Metallic better understands her own history and has found a community of two-spirited womyn. In coming out, she writes, "I have realized that 'gay pride' and 'native pride' can co-exist. Being two-spirit empowers me to take agency over my body, sexuality, my gender and my culture."

QUESTIONS

1. Do some further investigations into what "two-spirited" means, take notes, and in a paragraph describe it in your own words, making clear how it is similar to and different from identifying as gender fluid.
2. Why is it important to know the indigenous history of two-spirited people?
3. Is it possible for someone who does not identify as indigenous to be two-spirited? Why or why not?
4. How does Gina Metallic's story of identifying as indigenous, cisgender, womyn, feminist, and two-spirited add to your understanding of queer? How does it help you think through how people live in the world as they embody and inhabit many communities? Why is personal narrative a crucial tool for understanding how people identify?

Privilege: Cultural benefits and power granted to people through social and institutional inequalities.

class, sexuality, body size, age, religion, and abilities, whiteness is not marked as a racial category in the United States. Therefore, white people experience unearned cultural privileges *because* they are not black, Latino/a/x, Native American, and/or Asian American. More broadly speaking, **privilege** is deeply connected to oppression and defined as a set of advantages enjoyed by those who are empowered by US social hierarchies (e.g., male, Christian, heterosexual, able-bodied, and young adults). It can be differentiated from sexism, racism, homophobia, classism, ableism, ageism, and prejudice because people with privilege may be unconscious of it and not acting overtly to subordinate others. Peggy McIntosh's reading in this section, "White Privilege: Unpacking the Invisible Knapsack," examines this social process and provides a compelling list of examples that detail the white privilege she personally experiences and the male privilege she does not.

Intersectionality references the two-fold idea that people's identities are complex, often not fitting easily into distinct social categories of gender, race, class, and sexuality, *and* that sexism, racism, classism, homophobia, ableism, religious persecution, and nationalism are interlocking systems of oppression that shape our lives and social institutions (Collins and Bilge 2016). People are members of various identity groups *simultaneously,* and their position in each of these groups may bring them more or less power based on US social hierarchies. Beginning in the early 1980s with the publication of bell hooks's *Ain't I a Woman?* (1981); Hazel Carby's "White Woman Listen!" (1982); Cherríe Moraga and Gloria Anzaldúa's edited volume *This Bridge Called My Back* (1983); Angela Davis's *Women, Race & Class* (1981); Barbara Smith's edited collection *Home Girls* (1983); Alice Walker's *In Search of Our Mother's Gardens* (1983); Audre Lorde's *Sister Outsider* (1984); and Barbara Christian's *Black Feminist Criticism* (1985), scholarly and creative writers responded to white, middle-class feminist assumptions that all women experience oppressions similarly. Women on the margins of US society—black women, women of color, lesbians of color, working poor women, and **third world women**— argued that feminism and queer communities must grapple with how cultural differences shape people's everyday lives if they are to be inclusive and work together for social change.

In 1988, Kimberlé Crenshaw coined the term "intersectionality" as a way for scholars and practitioners to describe these intricacies as well as make clear the impossible "choice" women, lesbians of color, and poor women face in being asked to fight for their rights as women *or* as black, Chicana/Latina/x, Asian American, Native American, third world *or* queer *or* poor (Allen 1986; Anzaldúa, 1990; Asian Women United of California 1989; García 1989; Mohanty, Russo, and Torres 1991; Moraga 1983). Audre Lorde poignantly and personally eluci- dates this point in her essay "There Is No Hierarchy of Oppressions" (included in this section) with this statement: "I simply do not believe that one aspect of myself can possibly profit from the oppression of any other part of my identity" (p. 76). She goes on to point out that, in the lesbian community, she is both black and a lesbian, and in the black community, she is both black and a les- bian. How then can she fight against racism and not homophobia and sexism? This question and the insights based on the lived experiences of US women of color now form the intersectional approaches that are foundational in under- standing women's, gender and sexuality studies.

Intersectionality: Theoretical term used to discuss the interlocking systems of oppression of gender, race, class, sexual- ity, age, ability, religion, and nationality that shape people's experience and access to power.

Third world women: Women who inhabit or whose (familial) origins reflect Asian, African, and Latin American geogra- phies; used as a political term to reflect the colo- nial power relations be- tween the first world (the West or Global North) and the third world (or Global South).

Engaged Learning

In Peggy McIntosh's "White Privilege: Unpacking the Invisible Knapsack" she notes that many of the privileges she experiences as a white woman and a professor are based on not being racially profiled by the police. Imagine how significant this is when we consider the brutality that people of color disproportionately experience in the United States. If you are not familiar with examples of this violence perpetuated by the state, do a quick Google search for Trayvon Martin, Michael Brown, Eric Garner, Allen Locke, Freddi Gray, Paul Castaway, and Samuel DuBose. Do the same search through the archives of *Al Jazeera* and/or the online magazine *The Root* or *Colorlines*. Two of the men named here identified as Native American. According to the Lakota People's Law Project, Native Americans are most likely to be killed by law enforcement (Agorist). Expand the search to see what other names of people emerge and what communities they represent.

QUESTIONS

1. Why were each of the (young) men named previously in contact with the police? How does a mainstream media source such as CNN tell this story? And *Al Jazeera, The Root,* or *Colorlines*? How do you know what is closest to the truth? What do you trust and why?

2. In one month alone (July 2015), five black women died in police custody. Did your search yield any names of women of color? If not, why do you suppose this is so? Read carefully "Black Women Speak Out about Experiences with Police Brutality" (http://everydayfeminism .com/2015/07/black-women-police-brutality/). Take note of what you learn about how police brutality affects women and bring two points to class that you wish to discuss in more detail.

3. What does this exercise reveal about objectivity, reporting, and white privilege?

4. Reflect on your personal experiences and write down what you feel and how it makes you think as you learn this information.

Intersectionality matters in a global context too. Ashley Currier and Thérèse Migraine-George's article "Queer/African Identities: Questions, Limits, Challenges" (included in this section), examines antigay violence that specific African states perpetuate against the people in these countries. In asking us to think carefully about what constitutes a nation and its people and how this intersects with queer identity, they argue that violent backlashes most certainly negatively affect gay, lesbian, bisexual, and transgender people *and* it does not "predetermine the content and contours of queer African identities." While the US popular media only presents specific African nations as open hostility toward queer communities, the authors interview activists in Liberia, Malawi, and South Africa and draw on a queer African literature and films to provide more "complicated dimensions of generating, representing, and nurturing queer identities" (pp. 77–78). Rather than only showing African queer communities as victims of the stigma and violence in their homelands (which by itself only serves to reinforce oversimplified and sensational media constructions), Currier's and Migraine-George's research honors the voices of people who are working to make a difference.

Pride in Global Spaces. LGBTQ+ pride rallies take place all over the world and help us to understand that the movement to end discrimination and marginalization of queer-identified people is transnational. Participants here hold posters in support of the LGBTQ+ community in Manila during the twenty-first Pride Parade on June 27, 2015. The press reported that thousands marched through main streets to celebrate the queer community.

In her poem "Before Intersectionality" (included in this section), M. Soledad Caballero reminds us that while "intersectionality" is a relatively new term in academia, immigrant women and men of color have always lived complicated lives. Her poem names the violence immigrants face, gives voice to the pain, isolation, and invisibility of young people living in between English- and Spanish-speaking cultures and reaches out to anyone who may feel like they do not belong. It also speaks to the dimensions of what it means to care, empathize, and work toward social change.

To fully understand intersectionality, it is important to acknowledge that whiteness *is* a racial category—but one that has privilege and therefore can remain unmarked. Just as oppression must be understood in relation to privilege, social constructions of blackness and brown-ness are deeply connected to whiteness, and we cannot understand the empowerment of one without the disempowerment of the other. Second, while no one person is *responsible* for this way of thinking, guilt as a response to sexism, racism, classism, homophobia, and transphobia does very little to contribute to efforts toward social change as it recenters whiteness. Audre Lorde writes powerfully in *Sister Outsider,* "Guilt is not a response to anger; it is a response to one's own actions or lack of action. If it leads to change, then it can be useful, since it is then no longer guilt but the beginning of knowledge" (Lorde 130). It is only through **self-reflexivity**, careful listening, and understanding identity,

Self-reflexivity: The deliberate examination of how and why people come to their beliefs, ideas, and knowledge in the context of broader (gender, race, class, sexuality, abilities, age, religion, and nationalities) power relations; a necessary step in pursuing feminist and queer scholarship, activism, and institutional practices.

TRANSNATIONAL CONNECTIONS

A photographer and self-identified visual activist, Zanele Muholi was born in 1972 in South Africa. She has dedicated her life's work to telling the stories of lesbians, transgender, and intersexed people in South Africa through images. In her series, *Faces and Phases, 2006–2014*, Muholi creates portraits of more than two hundred individuals in the lesbian community, which as an archive makes a political statement on how South African lesbians exist and thrive in the midst of stigma and violence. The "Isibonelo/Evidence" exhibition at the Elizabeth A. Sackler Center for Feminist Art at the Brooklyn Museum (2015) featured eighty-seven of Muholi's works from *Faces and Phases*, *Weddings*, and the video *Being Scene* that incorporates firsthand accounts of what it is like to live in places where LGBTQPAI+ rights are constitutionally protected but often not defended. Her thought-provoking and sensitive photography also makes a point of focusing on love, intimacy, and daily life in close-knit lesbian and transgender communities. In Muholi's own words, she does this work because "it heals me to know that I am paving the way for others who, in wanting to come out, are able to look at the photographs, read the biographies, and understand that they are not alone" (qtd in Schwiegershausen). Do an Internet search on "Zanele Muholi" and choose a comprehensive website that provides her biography and images of her work. We recommend https://www.artsy.net/artist/zanele-muholi.

QUESTIONS

1. Muholi uses the term "visual activist" (instead of "visual artist") to describe her work. What does this mean to you as you read her biography and look at her photography?
2. The people in Muholi's photographs look back at the people who are looking at them. This is a central feature of portraiture. Why is it important that many of her photographs of the South African LGBTQPAI+ community are done in this style?
3. Both Muholi and Currier and Migraine-George discuss love and empowerment in African queer communities. How does this focus help you rethink what it means to be queer and transgender in Africa? Why is this important?
4. Zanele Muholi's work is affirming and empowering of queer and transgender people. How might you use this approach to think through LGBTQPAI+ issues in your home town/city?

cultural power, and social structures through intersectional lenses that we can understand, protest, and address systematic inequalities more fully and accurately.

INTERDISCIPLINARITY

Given the expansive landscape of the field, you may be wondering, "What does *not* count as women's, gender and sexuality studies?" Indeed, the field encompasses the study of all people and the social dynamics that shape their lives. To tell the stories of people's complex lives, especially of individuals and groups that are marginalized and invisible or hypervisible in the dominant culture, researchers must be self-reflexive about the kinds of questions they ask as well as how they go about collecting information. To do this, practitioners value the integration of research, theory, and **praxis**, which is a unique feature of the field according to Michele Tracy Berger and Cheryl Radeloff in "Claiming an Education: Your Inheritance as a Student of Women's and Gender Studies" (included in this section). Interdisciplinary work draws on a range of primary and secondary sources to make knowledge claims and frame political issues. Primary sources may include personal narratives, historical archives (official collections and those that are more intimate, such as diaries), quantitative research, ethnographies, art, literature, television and film, newspapers and online sources, scientific experiments, and critical legal analysis. Secondary sources, or those written by other scholars in the field, provide historical and cultural context for framing arguments. Both are necessary for analyzing subject matter.

Praxis: The integration of learning theoretical concepts with social justice actions so that one's own behaviors in the world reflect the liberatory philosophies of feminism and queer approaches.

Naming women's, gender and sexuality studies as an interdisciplinary field of study means that there is no one framework, no one method, and no one theory that explains feminist and queer cultures. Rather, it requires multiple modes of knowing and doing to produce the most accurate and politically engaged work possible. The reading selections included here draw extensively from traditional disciplines (such as English, political science, and sociology) as well as the humanistic interdisciplinary fields that also emerged from twentieth-century social movements (such as Africana studies, ethnic studies, Latino/a/x studies, Asian American studies, Native American studies, Puerto Rican studies, postcolonial studies, and cultural studies) to show you the exciting and engaging possibilities for doing interdisciplinary work.

Critical Thinking Questions

1. Marilyn Frye argues that girls' and women's lives are constricted by oppressive double binds. For example, if a young woman chooses to be sexually active, she is labeled a whore; if she chooses to not be sexually active, she is labeled a tease or prude. What other double binds do you see and/or experience? Think critically about your answers through an intersectional approach.

2. Read through Peggy McIntosh's list of white privilege that she personally experiences again. Think critically about this list through an intersectional approach. What would this list look like? How might we move beyond acknowledging privilege and toward dismantling oppression? What might be one of the next steps?

3. Reflect on your experiences learning about sexuality—whether it was through a sex education class, from your parents, with your friends, or from reading on your own. What did you learn? How was it gendered? What do you think it should include for the next generation?

4. Given what you have learned about intersectionality, what do you think it means for you as a student to be self-reflexive when talking about feminist and queer issues, cultural identities, and power?

GLOSSARY

Asexual 9	Gender variant 10	Queer 4
Assigned sex 9	Heteronormative 5	Self-reflexivity 15
Bigendered 9	Heterosexism 10	Sex reassignment surgery
Birth sex/Biological sex 9	Heterosexual ally 10	(SRS) 10
Bisexual 9	Heterosexual privilege 10	Sexism 10
Cisgender 8	Homophobia 10	Sexual orientation 9
Closet 9	Intersectionality 13	Social constructionism 5
Closeted/In the closet 9	Intersex 10	Social institutions 3
Coming out 9	Lesbian 10	Straight 10
Double bind 11	LGBTQPAI+ 4	Third world women 13
Gay 9	Oppression 11	Trans 4
Gender expression 9	Out/Out of the closet 10	Transfriendly 10
Gender identity 5	Outing 10	Transgender 8
Gender role 9	Patriarchy 3	Transphobia 11
Genderqueer 4	Praxis 17	Women of color 11
Gender status 5	Privilege 12	

WORKS CITED

"A Gender Spectrum Glossary." Teaching Tolerance: A Project of the Southern Poverty Law Center, Aug. 2015, www.tolerance.org/LGBT-best-practices-terms.

Agorist, Matt. "Police Are Killing Native Americans at Higher Rate Than Any Race, and Nobody is Talking about It." *The Free Thought Project.com*, 2 August 2015, thefreethoughtproject.com/police-killing-native-americans-higher-rate-race-talking/.

Allen, Paula Gunn. *The Sacred Hoop: Recovering the Feminine in American Indian Traditions*. Beacon Press, 1986.

Anzaldúa, Gloria. *Borderlands/La Frontera: The New Mestiza*. Aunt Lute Books, 1987.

———. *Making Face, Making Soul: Creative and Critical Perspectives by Women of Color*. Aunt Lute Books, 1990.

Asian Women United of California, editors. *Making Waves: An Anthology of Writings by and about Asian American Women*. Beacon Press, 1989.

Boxer, Marilyn. *When Women Ask Questions: Creating Women's Studies in America*. Johns Hopkins UP, 1998.

Butler, Judith. *Gender Trouble: Feminism and the Subversion of Identity*. Routledge, 1990.

Carby, Hazel. "White Woman Listen! Black Feminism and the Boundaries of Sisterhood." *The Empire Strikes Back: Race and Racism in 70s Britain*, edited by the Centre for Contemporary Cultural Studies, Routledge, 1982.

Christian, Barbara. *Black Feminist Criticism: Perspectives on Black Women Writers*. Teachers College P, 1985.

Collins, Patricia Hill. *Black Feminist Thought: Knowledge, Consciousness, and the Politics of Empowerment*. Routledge, 1990.

Collins, Patricia Hill and Sirma Bilge. *Intersectionality*. Polity, 2016.

Crenshaw, Kimberlé. "Mapping the Margins: Intersectionality, Identity Politics, and Violence Against Women of Color." *Stanford Law Review*, vol. 43, no. 124, 1993, pp. 1241–99.

Davis, Angela. *Women, Race & Class*. Vintage Books, 1981.

Fausto-Sterling, Anne. *Sexing the Body: Gender Politics and the Construction of Sexuality*. Basic Books, 2000.

García, Alma. "The Development of Chicana Feminist Discourse, 1970–1980." *Gender & Society*, vol. 3, no. 2, 1989, pp. 217–38.

Gardiner, Judith Kegan. *Masculinity Studies and Feminist Theory*. Columbia UP, 2002.

Ginsberg, Alice. *The Evolution of American Women's Studies: Reflections on Triumphs, Controversies, and Change*. Palgrave Macmillan, 2008.

Halberstam, Judith. *Female Masculinity*. Duke UP, 1998.

hooks, bell. *Ain't I a Woman? Black Women and Feminism*. South End Press, 1981.

———. *Black Looks: Race and Representation*. South End Press, 1992.

———. *Feminism Is for Everybody: Passionate Politics*. Pluto Press, 2000.

———. *Feminist Theory: From Margin to Center*. South End Press, 1984.

———. *We Real Cool: Black Men and Masculinity*. Routledge, 2003.

Hull, Gloria T., et al., editors. *But Some of Us Are Brave: All the Women Are White, All the Men Are Black: Black Women's Studies*. Feminist Press, 1993.

Kimmel, Michael. *Angry White Men*. Nation Books, 2013.

———. *Guyland*. Harper Collins, 2008.

———. *Misframing Men: The Politics of Contemporary Masculinities*. Rutgers UP, 2010.

———. *The Guys Guide to Feminism*. Seal Press, 2011.

Kimmel, Michael, and Michael Messner. *Men's Lives*. Macmillan, 1995.

King, Deborah. "Multiple Jeopardy, Multiple Consciousness: The Context of a Black Feminist Ideology." *Signs: Journal of Women in Culture and Society*, vol. 14, no. 1, 1988, pp. 42–72.

Launius, Christie and Holly Hassel. *Threshold Concepts in Women's and Gender Studies: Ways of Seeing, Thinking, and Knowing*. Routledge, 2015.

Lorber, Judith. "'Night to His Day': The Social Construction of Gender." *Paradoxes of Gender*, Yale UP, 1994.

Lorde, Audre. *Sister Outsider*. Crossing Press, 1984.

Messner, Michael. *Politics of Masculinities: Men in Movements*. Sage Publications, 1997.

Metallic, Gina. "My Coming Out: Finding My True Identity Meant Re-Connecting with My Culture." *Montreal Gazzette*, 5 August 2015, montrealgazette.com/life/ my-coming-out-finding-my-true-identity-meant-re-connecting-with-my-culture.

Mohanty, Chandra Talpade, et al., editors. *Third World Women and the Politics of Feminism*. Indiana UP, 1991.

Moraga, Cherríe. *Loving in the War Years: Lo Que Nunca Pasó Por Sus Labios*. South End Press, 1983.

Moraga, Cherríe, and Gloria Anzaldúa, eds. *This Bridge Called My Back: Writings by Radical Women of Color*. Kitchen Table, Women of Color Press, 1983.

Muholi, Zanele. *Faces and Phases, 2006–2014*. Steidl Verlag, 2014.

Muñoz, José Esteban. *Cruising Utopia: The Then and There of Queer Futurity*. New York UP, 2009.

Purvis, Jennifer. "Queer." *Rethinking Women's and Gender Studies*, edited by C. Orr, A. Braithwaite, and D. Lichtenstein, Routledge, 2012.

Reis, Elizabeth. *Bodies in Doubt: An American History of Intersex*. Reprinted ed. Johns Hopkins UP, 2012.

Rich, Adrienne. *Blood, Bread and Poetry*. Virago, 1978.

Schwiegershausen, Erica. "See Zanele Muholi's Powerful Portraits of the LGBTI Experience in South Africa." *The Cut*, New York Media, 7 January 2015, nymag. com/thecut/2015/01/powerful-portraits-of-queer-life-in-south-africa.html

Segal, Lynne. *Slow Motion: Changing Masculinities, Changing Men*. Virago, 1990.

Smith, Barbara, ed. *Home Girls: A Black Feminist Anthology*. Kitchen Table, Women of Color Press, 1983.

Stryker, Susan. *Transgender History*. Seal Press, 2008.

Walker, Alice. *In Search of Our Mother's Gardens*. Harcourt Brace Jovanovich, 1983.

Welter, Barbara. "The Cult of True Womanhood: 1820–1860." *American Quarterly*, vol. 18, no. 2, 1966, pp. 151–74.

Wiegman, Robyn. "Unmaking: Men and Masculinity in Feminist Theory." *Masculinity Studies and Feminist Theory*, edited by Judith Gardiner, Columbia UP, 2002.

Williams, Patricia. *The Alchemy of Race and Rights: Diary of a Law Professor*. Harvard UP, 1992.

1. • *bell hooks*

FEMINIST POLITICS:
Where We Stand (2000)

Born Gloria Jean Watkins, award-winning feminist scholar and cultural critic bell hooks is the author of over three dozen books and has contributed original work to seven collections and numerous periodicals. Her writing explores the intersections of race, class, gender, sexuality, spirituality, teaching, and the media and spans several genres including nonfiction, poetry, memoir, and children's literature. She has been an acclaimed and outspoken social justice activist throughout her career and the bell hooks Institute in Berea, Kentucky is dedicated to documenting her life and work. The Institute's mission is to end exploitation and oppression through critical thinking, teaching, and dialogue. "Feminist Politics: Where We Stand" is a chapter in her text *Feminism Is for Everybody*, an accessible and lively introduction to feminism designed for students and the general public.

Simply put, feminism is a movement to end sexism, sexist exploitation, and oppression. This was a definition of feminism I offered in *Feminist Theory: From Margin to Center* more than 10 years ago. It was my hope at the time that it would become a common definition everyone would use. I liked this definition because it did not imply that men were the enemy. By naming sexism as the problem it went directly to the heart of the matter. Practically, it is a definition which implies that all sexist thinking and action is the problem, whether those who perpetuate it are female or male, child or adult. It is also broad enough to include an understanding of systemic institutionalized sexism. As a definition it is open-ended. To understand feminism it implies one has to necessarily understand sexism.

As all advocates of feminist politics know, most people do not understand sexism, or if they do, they think it is not a problem. Masses of people think that feminism is always and only about women seeking to be equal to men. And a huge majority of these folks think feminism is anti-male. Their misunderstanding of feminist politics reflects the reality that most folks learn about feminism from patriarchal mass media. The feminism they hear about the most is portrayed by women who are primarily committed to gender equality—equal pay for equal work, and sometimes women and men sharing household chores and parenting. They see that these women are usually white and materially privileged. They know from mass media that women's liberation focuses on the freedom to have abortions, to be lesbians, to challenge rape and domestic violence. Among these issues, masses of people agree with the idea of gender equity in the workplace—equal pay for equal work.

Since our society continues to be primarily a "Christian" culture, masses of people continue to believe that god has ordained that women be subordinate to men in the domestic household. Even though masses of women have entered the workforce, even though many families are headed by women who are the sole breadwinners, the vision of domestic life which continues to dominate the nation's imagination is one in which the logic of male domination is intact, whether men are present in the home or not. The wrongminded notion of feminist movement which implied it was anti-male carried with it the wrongminded assumption that all female space would necessarily be an environment where patriarchy and sexist thinking would be absent. Many women, even those involved in feminist politics, chose to believe this as well.

There was indeed a great deal of anti-male sentiment among early feminist activists who were responding to male domination with anger. It was that anger at injustice that was the impetus for creating a women's liberation movement. Early on most feminist activists (a majority of whom were white) had their consciousness raised about the nature of male domination when they were working in anti-classist and anti-racist settings with men who were telling the world about the importance of freedom while subordinating the women in their ranks. Whether it was white women working on behalf of socialism, black women working on behalf of civil rights and black liberation, or Native American women working for indigenous rights, it was clear that men wanted to lead, and they wanted women to follow. Participating in these radical freedom struggles awakened the spirit of rebellion and resistance in progressive females and led them towards contemporary women's liberation.

As contemporary feminism progressed, as women realized that males were not the only group in our society who supported sexist thinking and behavior—that females could be sexist as well—anti-male sentiment no longer shaped the movement's consciousness. The focus shifted to an all-out effort to create gender justice. But women could not band together to further feminism without confronting our sexist thinking. Sisterhood could not be powerful as long as women were competitively at war with one another. Utopian visions of sisterhood based solely on the awareness of the reality that all women were in some way victimized by male domination were disrupted by discussions of class and race. Discussions of class differences occurred early on in contemporary feminism, preceding

discussions of race. Diana Press published revolutionary insights about class divisions between women as early as the mid-'70s in their collection of essays *Class and Feminism.* These discussions did not trivialize the feminist insistence that "sisterhood is powerful"; they simply emphasized that we could only become sisters in struggle by confronting the ways women—through sex, class, and race—dominated and exploited other women, and created a political platform that would address these differences.

Even though individual black women were active in contemporary feminist movement from its inception, they were not the individuals who became the "stars" of the movement, who attracted the attention of mass media. Often individual black women active in feminist movement were revolutionary feminists (like many white lesbians). They were already at odds with reformist feminists who resolutely wanted to project a vision of the movement as being solely about women gaining equality with men in the existing system. Even before race became a talked-about issue in feminist circles it was clear to black women (and to their revolutionary allies in struggle) that they were never going to have equality within the existing white supremacist capitalist patriarchy.

From its earliest inception feminist movement was polarized. Reformist thinkers chose to emphasize gender equality. Revolutionary thinkers did not want simply to alter the existing system so that women would have more rights. We wanted to transform that system, to bring an end to patriarchy and sexism. Since patriarchal mass media was not interested in the more revolutionary vision, it never received attention in mainstream press. The vision of "women's liberation" which captured and still holds the public imagination was the one representing women as wanting what men had. And this was the vision that was easier to realize. Changes in our nation's economy, economic depression, the loss of jobs, etc., made the climate ripe for our nation's citizens to accept the notion of gender equality in the workforce.

Given the reality of racism, it made sense that white men were more willing to consider women's rights when the granting of those rights could serve the interests of maintaining white supremacy. We can never forget that white women began to assert their need for freedom after civil rights just at the point when racial discrimination was ending and black people, especially black males, might have attained equality in the workforce with white men. Reformist feminist thinking focusing primarily on equality with men in the workforce overshadowed the original radical foundations of contemporary feminism which called for reform as well as overall restructuring of society so that our nation would be fundamentally anti-sexist.

Most women, especially privileged white women, ceased even to consider revolutionary feminist visions, once they began to gain economic power within the existing social structure. Ironically, revolutionary feminist thinking was most accepted and embraced in academic circles. In those circles the production of revolutionary feminist theory progressed, but more often than not that theory was not made available to the public. It became and remains a privileged discourse available to those among us who are highly literate, well-educated, and usually materially privileged. Works like *Feminist Theory: From Margin to Center* that offer a liberatory vision of feminist transformation never receive mainstream attention. Masses of people have not heard of this book. They have not rejected its message; they do not know what the message is.

While it was in the interest of mainstream white supremacist capitalist patriarchy to suppress visionary feminist thinking which was not anti-male or concerned with getting women the right to be like men, reformist feminists were also eager to silence these forces. Reformist feminism became their route to class mobility. They could break free of male domination in the workforce and be more self-determining in their lifestyles. While sexism did not end, they could maximize their freedom within the existing system. And they could count on there being a lower class of exploited subordinated women to do the dirty work they were refusing to do. By accepting and indeed colluding with the subordination of working-class and poor women, they not only ally themselves with the existing patriarchy and its concomitant sexism; they give themselves the right to lead a double life, one where they are the equals of men in the workforce and at home when they want to be. If they choose lesbianism they have the privilege of being equals with men in the workforce while using class power to create domestic lifestyles where they can choose to have little or no contact with men.

Lifestyle feminism ushered in the notion that there could be as many versions of feminism as there were women. Suddenly the politics was being slowly removed from feminism. And the assumption prevailed that no matter what a woman's politics, be she conservative or liberal, she too could fit feminism into her existing lifestyle. Obviously this way of thinking has made feminism more acceptable because its underlying assumption is that women can be feminists without fundamentally challenging and changing themselves or the culture. For example, let's take the issue of abortion. If feminism is a movement to end sexist oppression, and depriving females of reproductive rights is a form of sexist oppression, then one cannot be anti-choice and be feminist. A woman can insist she would never choose to have an abortion while affirming her support of the right of women to choose and still be an advocate of feminist politics. She cannot be anti-abortion and an advocate of feminism. Concurrently there can be no such thing as "power feminism" if the vision of power evoked is power gained through the exploitation and oppression of others.

Feminist politics is losing momentum because the feminist movement has lost clear definitions. We have those definitions. Let's reclaim them. Let's share them. Let's start over. Let's have T-shirts and bumper stickers and postcards and hip-hop music, television and radio commercials, ads everywhere and billboards, and all manner of printed material that tells the world about feminism. We can share the simple yet powerful message that feminism is a movement to end sexist oppression. Let's start there. Let the movement begin again.

2. • *Allan Johnson*

PATRIARCHY, THE SYSTEM:
An It, Not a He, A Them, or an Us (2014)

Allan Johnson is a cultural critic, novelist, sociologist, public speaker, and blogger interested in social justice through unraveling privileges tied to gender, race, and class. He is the author of eight books and several essays that span nonfiction, memoir, and fiction. Following the publication of *The Gender Knot*, from which this article is excerpted, he transitioned from academe to public speaking working as a diversity trainer in corporations, including IBM, GE, and BankBoston.

"When you say patriarchy" a man complained from the rear of the audience, "I know what you *really* mean—me!" A lot of people hear "men" whenever someone says "patriarchy," so that criticism of male privilege and the oppression of women is taken to mean that all men—each and every one of them—are oppressive people.

Some of the time, men feel defensive because they identify with patriarchy and its values and do not want to face the consequences these produce or the prospect of giving up male privilege. But defensiveness can also reflect a common confusion about the difference between patriarchy as a kind of society and the people who participate in it. If we are ever going to work toward real change, it is a confusion we will have to clear up.

To do this, we have to begin by realizing that we are stuck in a model of social life that views everything as beginning and ending with individuals, Looking at things in this way, the tendency is to think that if bad things happen in the world and if the bad thing is something big, it is only because there are bad people who have entered into some kind of conspiracy. Racism exists, then, because white people are racist bigots who hate members of racial and ethnic minorities and want to do them harm. The oppression of women happens because men want and like to dominate women and act out hostility toward them. There is poverty and class

oppression because people in the upper classes are greedy, heartless, and cruel.

The flip side of this individualistic model of guilt and blame is that race, gender, and class oppression are actually not oppression at all but merely the sum of individual failings on the part of people of color, women, and people living in poverty, who lack the right stuff to compete successfully with whites, men, and others who know how to make something of themselves.

What this kind of thinking ignores is that we are all participating in something larger than ourselves or any collection of us. On some level, most people are familiar with the idea that social life involves us in something larger than ourselves, but few seem to know what to do with that idea. Blaming everything on 'the system' strikes a deep chord in many people,[1] but it also touches on a basic misunderstanding of social life, because blaming the system (presumably society) for our problems doesn't take the next step to understanding what that might mean. What exactly is a system and how could it run our lives? Do we have anything to do with shaping *it*, and if so, how? How do we participate in patriarchy, and how does that link us to the consequences? How is what we think of as normal life related to male privilege, women's oppression, and the hierarchical, control-obsessed world in which everyone's lives are embedded?

Without asking such questions, not only can we not understand gender fully, but we also avoid taking responsibility either for ourselves or for patriarchy. Instead, 'the system' serves as a vague, unarticulated catch-all, a dumping ground for social problems, a scapegoat that can never be held to account and that, for all the power we think it has, cannot talk back or actually *do* anything.

[. . .]

If we see patriarchy as nothing more than men's and women's individual personalities, motivations, and behavior, then it won't occur to us to ask about larger contexts—such as institutions like the family, religion, and the economy—and how people's lives are shaped in relation to them. From an individualistic perspective, for example, we might ask why a particular man raped, harassed, or beat a particular woman. We would not ask, however, what kind of society would promote persistent *patterns* of such behavior in everyday life, from wife-beating jokes to the routine inclusion of sexual coercion and violence in mainstream movies. We would be quick to explain rape and battery as the acts of sick or angry men, but without taking seriously the question of what kind of society would produce so much male anger and pathology or direct it toward sexual violence rather than something else. We would be unlikely to ask how gender violence might serve other more normalized ends such as masculine control and domination and the proving of manhood. . . .

In short, the tendency in this patriarchal society is to ignore and take for granted what we can least afford to overlook in trying to understand and change the world. Rather than ask how social systems produce social problems such as men's violence against women, we obsess over legal debates and titillating but irrelevant case histories soon to become made-for-television movies. If the goal is to change the world, this will not help. We need to see and deal with the social roots that generate and nurture the *social* problems that are reflected in and manifested through the behavior of individuals. We cannot do this without realizing that we all participate in something larger than ourselves, something we did not create but that we now have the power to affect through the choices we make about *how* to participate.

Some readers have objected to describing women as 'participating' in patriarchy. The objection is based on the idea that participation, by definition, is something voluntary, freely chosen, entered into as equals, and that it therefore makes no sense that women might participate in their own oppression. But that is not my meaning here, and it is not a necessary interpretation of the word. To participate is to have a *part* in what goes on, to do something (or not) and to have that choice affect the consequences, regardless of whether it is conscious or unconscious, coerced or not. Of course, the *terms* of women's participation differ dramatically from those that shape men's, but it is participation, nonetheless.

This is similar to the participation of workers in the system of capitalism. They do not participate as equals to the capitalists who employ them or on terms they would choose if they could. Nevertheless, without workers, capitalism cannot function as a system that oppresses them.

The importance of participation can be seen in the many ways that women and working-class people respond to oppression—all the forms that fighting back or giving in can take. To argue that women or workers do not participate is to render them powerless and irrelevant to patriarchy's and capitalism's past, present, and future, for it is only as participants that people can affect anything. Otherwise, women and workers would be like pieces of wood floating down a river, which, as history makes clear, has never been the case.

[. . .]

Even more so, we cannot understand the world and our lives in it without looking at the dynamic relationship between individual people and social systems. Nor can we understand the countless details—from sexual violence to patterns of conversation to unequal distributions of power—that make up the reality of male privilege and the oppression of women.

As Figure 2 shows, this relationship has two parts. The arrow on the right side represents the idea that as we participate in social systems, we are shaped as individuals. Through the process of socialization, we learn how to participate in social life—from families, schools, religion, and the mass media, through the examples set by parents, peers, coaches, teachers, and public figures—a continuing stream of ideas and images of people and the world and who we are in relation to them.

Through all of this, we develop a sense of personal identity—including gender—and how this positions us in relation to other people, especially in terms of inequalities of power. As I grew up watching movies and television, for example, the message was clear that men are the most important people because they are the ones who do the most important things, as defined by patriarchal culture. They are the strong ones who build; the heroes and superheroes who fight the good fight; the geniuses, writers, and artists; the bold leaders; and even the evil—but always interesting—villains.

[. . .]

Invariably, some of what we learn through socialization turns out not to be true and then we may have to deal with that. I say "may" because powerful forces encourage us to keep ourselves in a state of denial, to rationalize what we have been taught. It is a way to keep it safe from scrutiny, if only to protect our sense of who we are and ensure our being accepted by other people, including family and friends. In the end, the default is to adopt the dominant version of reality and act as though it's the only one there is.

In addition to socialization, participation in social systems shapes our behavior through paths of least resistance, a concept that refers to a feature of social systems that guides the conscious and unconscious choices we make from one moment to the next. When a young male college student at a party, for example, observes another man taking sexual advantage of a young woman who is clearly so drunk that she has little idea of what is happening, there are many things he could do. The options vary, however, in how much social resistance they are likely to provoke. They range from asking to join in or standing by to watch as if it were some kind of entertainment to walking away and pretending he doesn't know what is happening or stepping in to intervene before it goes any further. And, of course, as a human being he could do plenty of other things—sing, dance, go to sleep, scratch his nose, and so on. Most of these possibilities won't even occur to him, which is one of the ways that social systems limit our options. But of those that do occur to him, usually one will risk provoking less social resistance than all the rest. The path of least resistance in such a situation is to go along and not make any trouble, to not get in the way of another man making use of a woman, to not risk being accused of siding with a woman against a man and thereby appearing to be less of a man himself, and unless he is willing to deal with the greater resistance that would follow, that is the choice he is most likely to make.

[. . .]

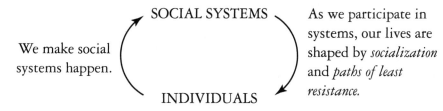

Figure 2 Individuals and systems

This brings us to the arrow on the left side of the figure, which represents the fact that human beings are the ones who make social systems happen. A classroom, for example, does not happen as a social system unless and until students and teachers come together and, through their choices from moment to moment, *make* it happen in one way or another. Because people make systems happen, then people can also make systems happen differently. And when systems happen differently, the consequences are different as well. In other words, when people step off paths of least resistance, they have the potential not simply to change other people but to alter the way the system itself happens.

Given that systems shape people's behavior, this kind of change can be powerful. When a man objects to a sexist joke, for example, it can shake other men's perception of what is socially acceptable and what is not so that the next time they are in this kind of situation, their perception of the social environment itself—not just of other people as individuals, whom they may or may not know personally—may shift in a new direction that makes old paths (such as telling sexist jokes) more difficult to choose because of the increased risk of social resistance.

The dynamic relationship between people and social systems represents a basic sociological view of the world at every level of human experience, from the global capitalist economy to casual friendships to the patriarchal system in which women and men participate. Thus, patriarchy is more than a collection of women and men and cannot be understood by understanding *them*. *We* are not patriarchy, no more than people who believe in Allah *are* Islam or Canadians *are* Canada. Patriarchy is a kind of society organized around certain kinds of social relationships and ideas that shape paths of least resistance. As individuals, we participate in it as we live our lives. Paradoxically, our participation both shapes our lives and gives us the opportunity to be part of changing or perpetuating it. But *we are not it*, which means patriarchy can exist without men having oppressive personalities or actively conspiring with one another to defend male privilege.

THE SYSTEM

In general, a system is any collection of interrelated parts or elements that we can think of as a whole. A car engine, for example, is a collection of parts that fit together in certain ways to produce a whole that is culturally identified as serving a particular purpose. A language is a collection of parts—letters of the alphabet, words, punctuation marks, and rules of grammar and syntax—that fit together in certain ways to form something we identify as a whole. In the same way, a family or a society qualify as systems that differ in what they include and how those elements are organized.

[. . .]

In spite of all the good reasons not to use individual models to explain social life, doing so constitutes a path of least resistance because personal experience and motivation are what we know best. As a result, we tend to see something like patriarchy as the result of poor socialization through which men learn to act dominant and masculine and women learn to act subordinate and feminine. While there is certainly some truth to this, it fails to explain patterns of privilege and oppression. It is no better than trying to explain war as simply the result of training men to be warlike, without looking at economic systems that equip armies at huge profits and political systems that organize and hurl armies at each other. . . . Socialization is merely a process, a mechanism for training people to participate in social systems. Although it tells us how people learn to participate, it does not illuminate the systems themselves. Accordingly, it can tell us something about the *how* of a system like patriarchy but very little of the *what* and the *why*.

[. . .]

Patriarchy is a way of organizing social life through which such wounding, failure, and mistreatment are bound to occur. If fathers neglect their sons, it is because fathers move in a world that makes pursuit of goals other than deeply committed fatherhood a path of least resistance.[2] If heterosexual intimacy is prone to fail, it is because patriarchy is organized in ways that set women and men fundamentally at odds with one another in spite of all the good reasons they otherwise have to get along together and thrive. And men's use of coercion and violence against women is a pervasive pattern only because force and violence are supported in patriarchal society, because women are designated as desirable and legitimate objects of male control, and because in a society organized around control, force and violence *work.*

We cannot find a way out of patriarchy or imagine something different without a clear sense of what patriarchy is and what it's got to do with us. Thus far, the alternative has been to reduce our understanding of gender to an intellectual gumbo of personal problems, tendencies, and motivations. Presumably, these will be solved through education, better communication skills, consciousness raising, heroic journeys and other forms of individual transformation, and the mere passage of time. Since this is not how social systems actually change, the result is widespread frustration and cycles of blame and denial, which is precisely where most people in this society seem to have been for many years.

We need to see more clearly what patriarchy is about as a system. This includes cultural ideas about men and women, the web of relationships that structure social life, and the unequal distribution of power, rewards, and resources that underlies privilege and oppression. We need to see new ways to participate by forging alternative paths of least resistance, for the system does not simply run us like hapless puppets. It may be larger than us, it may not be us, but it does not happen except *through* us. And that is where we have the power to do something about it and about ourselves in relation to it.

PATRIARCHY

The key to understanding any system is to identify its various aspects and how they are arranged to form a whole. To understand a language, for example, we have to learn its alphabet, vocabulary, and rules for combining words into meaningful phrases and sentences. A system like patriarchy is more complicated because there are many different aspects, and it can be difficult to see how they are connected.

Patriarchy's defining elements are its male-dominated, male-identified, male-centered, and control-obsessed character, but this is just the beginning. At its core, patriarchy is based on a set of symbols and ideas that make up a culture embodied by everything from the content of everyday conversation to the practice of war. Patriarchal culture includes ideas about the nature of things, including women, men, and humanity, with manhood and masculinity most closely associated with being human and womanhood and femininity relegated to the marginal position of other. It is about how social life is and what it is supposed to be, about what is expected of people and about how they feel. It is about standards of feminine beauty and masculine toughness, images of feminine vulnerability and masculine protectiveness, of older men coupled with younger women, of elderly women alone. It is about defining women and men as opposites, about the 'naturalness' of male aggression, competition, and dominance on the one hand and of female caring, cooperation, and subordination on the other. It is about the valuing of masculinity and manhood and the devaluing of femininity and womanhood. It is about the primary importance of a husband's career and the secondary status of a wife's, about child care as a priority in women's lives and its secondary importance in men's. It is about the social acceptability of anger, rage, and toughness in men but not in women, and of caring, tenderness, and vulnerability in women but not in men.

Above all, patriarchal culture is about the core value of control and domination in almost every area of human existence. From the expression of emotion to economics to the natural environment, gaining and exercising control is a continuing goal. Because of this, the concept of power takes on a narrow definition in terms of 'power over'—the ability to control others, events, resources, or oneself in spite of resistance—rather than alternatives such as the ability to cooperate, to give freely of oneself, or to feel and act in harmony with nature.[3] To have power over and to be prepared to use it are culturally defined as good and desirable (and characteristically masculine), and to lack such power or to be reluctant to use it is seen as weak if not contemptible (and characteristically feminine).

[. . .]

The main use of any culture is to provide symbols and ideas out of which to construct a sense of what is real. Thus, language mirrors social reality in sometimes startling ways. In contemporary usage, for example, the words 'crone,' 'bitch,' and 'virgin' describe women as threatening or heterosexually inexperienced and thus incomplete. In their original meanings, however, these words evoked far different images.[4] The crone was the old woman whose life experience gave her insight, wisdom, respect, and the power to enrich people's lives. The bitch was Artemis-Diana, goddess of the hunt, most often associated with the dogs who accompanied her. And the virgin was merely a woman who was unattached, unclaimed, and unowned by any man and therefore independent and autonomous. Notice how each word has been transformed from a positive cultural image of female power, independence, and dignity to an insult or a shadow of its former self, leaving few words to identify women in ways both positive and powerful.

Going deeper into patriarchal culture, we find a complex web of ideas that define reality and what is considered good and desirable. To see the world through patriarchal eyes is to believe that women and men are profoundly different in their basic natures, that hierarchy is the only alternative to chaos, and that men were made in the image of a masculine God with whom they enjoy a special relationship. It is to take as obvious the ideas that there are two and only two distinct sexes and genders; that patriarchal heterosexuality is natural and same-sex attraction is not; that because men neither bear nor breastfeed children, they cannot feel a compelling bodily connection to them; that on some level every woman, whether heterosexual, lesbian, or bisexual, wants a 'real man' who knows how to take charge of things, including

her; and that females cannot be trusted, especially when they're menstruating or accusing men of abuse.

In spite of all the media hype to the contrary, to embrace patriarchy still is to believe that mothers should stay home and that fathers should work outside the home, regardless of men's and women's actual abilities or needs.[5] It is to buy into the notion that women are weak and men are strong and that women and children need men to support and protect them, despite the fact that in many ways men are not the physically stronger sex, that women perform a huge share of hard physical labor in many societies (often larger than men's), that women's physical endurance tends to be greater than men's over the long haul, and that women tend to be more capable of enduring pain and emotional stress.[6]

[. . .]

To live in a patriarchal culture is to learn what is expected of men and women—to learn the rules that regulate punishment and reward based on how individuals behave and appear. These rules range from laws that require men to fight in wars not of their own choosing to the expectation that mothers will provide child care. Or that when a woman shows sexual interest in a man or merely smiles or acts friendly, she gives up her right to say no and to control her own body from that point on. And to live under patriarchy is to take into ourselves ways of feeling—the hostile contempt for women that forms the core of misogyny and presumptions of male superiority, the ridicule that men direct at other men who show signs of vulnerability or weakness, or the fear and insecurity that every woman must deal with when she exercises the right to move freely in the world, especially at night and by herself in public places.

[. . .]

The prominent place of misogyny in patriarchal culture, for example, doesn't mean that every man and woman consciously hates all things that are culturally associated with being female. But it does mean that to the extent that we do not feel such hatred, it is *in spite of* prevailing paths of least resistance. Complete freedom from such feelings and judgments is all but impossible. It is certainly possible for heterosexual men to love women without mentally fragmenting them into breasts, buttocks, genitals, and other variously desirable parts. It is possible for women to feel good about their bodies, to not judge themselves as being too big, to not abuse themselves to one degree or another in pursuit of impossible male-identified standards of beauty and sexual attractiveness.

All of this is possible, but to live in patriarchy is to breathe in misogynist images of women as objectified sexual property valued primarily for their usefulness to men. This finds its way into everyone who grows up breathing and swimming in it, and once inside us it remains, however unaware of it we may be. When we hear or express sexist jokes and other forms of misogyny, we may not recognize it, and even if we do, we may say nothing rather than risk other people thinking we're too sensitive or, especially in the case of men, not one of the guys. In either case, we are involved, if only by our silence.

The symbols and ideas that make up patriarchal culture are important to understand because they have such powerful effects on the structure of social life. By 'structure,' I mean the ways privilege and oppression are organized through social relationships and unequal distributions of power, rewards, opportunities, and resources. This appears in countless patterns of everyday life in family and work, religion and politics, community and education. It is found in family divisions of labor that exempt fathers from most domestic work even when both parents work outside the home, and in the concentration of women in lower-level pink-collar jobs and male predominance almost everywhere else. It is in the unequal distribution of income and all that goes with it, from access to health care to the availability of leisure time. It is in patterns of male violence and harassment that can turn a simple walk in the park or a typical day at work or a lovers' quarrel into a life-threatening nightmare. More than anything, the structure of patriarchy is found in the unequal distribution of power

that makes male privilege possible, in patterns of male dominance in every facet of human life, from everyday conversation to global politics. By its nature, patriarchy puts issues of power, dominance, and control at the center of human existence, not only in relationships between men and women but among men as they compete and struggle to gain status, maintain control, and protect themselves from what other men might do to them.

[. . .]

THE SYSTEM IN US IN THE SYSTEM

One way to see how people connect with systems is to think of us as occupying social positions that locate us in relation to people in other positions. We connect, for example, to families through positions such as mother, daughter, and cousin; to economic systems through positions such as vice president, secretary, or unemployed; to political systems through positions such as citizen, registered voter, and mayor; and to religious systems through positions such as believer and clergy.

How we perceive the people who occupy such positions and what we expect of them depend on cultural ideas—such as the belief that mothers are naturally better than fathers at child care. Such ideas are powerful because we use them to construct a sense of who we and other people are. When a woman marries a man, for example, how people (including her) perceive and think about her will change as cultural ideas about what it means to be a wife come into play—ideas about how wives feel about their husbands, what is most important to wives, what is expected of them, and what they may expect of others.

From this perspective, *who* we and other people think we are has a lot to do with *where* we are in relation to social systems and all the positions we occupy in them. We would not exist as social beings without our participation in one social system or another. It is hard to imagine just who we would be and what our existence would consist of if we took away all of our connections to the symbols, ideas, and relationships that make up social systems. Take away language and all that it allows us to imagine and think, starting with our names. Take away all the positions that we occupy and the roles that go with them—from daughter and son to occupation and nationality—and with these all the complex ways our lives are connected to other people. Not much would be left over that we would recognize as ourselves.[7]

We can think of a society as a network of interconnected systems within systems, each made up of social positions and their relations to one another. To say, then, that I am white, male, college educated, nondisabled, and a nonfiction author, novelist, sociologist, U.S. citizen, heterosexual, husband, father, grandfather, brother, and son identifies me in relation to positions which are themselves related to positions in various systems, from the entire world to the family of my birth.

In another sense, the day-to-day reality of a society exists only through what people actually do as they participate in it. Patriarchal culture, for example, places a high value on control and manhood. By themselves, these are just abstractions. But when men and women actually talk and men interrupt women more than women interrupt men, or men ignore topics introduced by women in favor of their own or in other ways control conversation,[8] or when men use their authority to harass women in the workplace, then the reality of patriarchy as a kind of society and people's sense of themselves as gendered beings within it actually happen in a concrete way.

In this sense, like all social systems, patriarchy exists only through people's lives. Through this dynamic relationship, patriarchy's various aspects are there for us to see over and over again. This has two important implications for how we understand the system. First, to some extent people will experience patriarchy as external to them. This does not mean the system is a distinct and separate thing, like a house in which we live. Instead, by participating in patriarchy we are *of* patriarchy and it is *of* us. Both exist *through* the other, and neither exists without the other.

Second, patriarchy is not static. It is an ongoing *process* that is continually shaped and reshaped. Since the thing we are participating in is patriarchal, we tend to behave in ways that create a patriarchal world from one moment to the next. But we have some freedom to break the rules and construct everyday life in different ways, which means the paths we choose to follow can do as much to change patriarchy as they can to perpetuate it.

We are involved in patriarchy and its consequences because we occupy social positions in it, which is all it takes. Because patriarchy is, by definition, a system of inequality organized around culturally created gender categories, we cannot avoid being involved in it. *All* men and *all* women are therefore involved in this oppressive system, and none of us can control *whether* we participate, only *how*. As Harry Brod argues, this is especially important in relation to men and male privilege:

> We need to be clear that there is no such thing as giving up one's privilege to be "outside" the system. One is always *in* the system. The only question is whether one is part of the system in a way which challenges or strengthens the status quo. Privilege is not something I *take* and which I therefore have the option of *not* taking. It is something that society *gives* me, and unless I change the institutions which give it to me, they will continue to give it, and I will continue to *have* it, however noble and egalitarian my intentions.[9]

Because privilege is conferred by social systems, people do not have to *feel* privileged to *be* privileged. When I do presentations, for example, I usually come away feeling good about how it went and, therefore, about myself and my work. If anyone were to ask me to explain why things went so well, I would probably mention my ability, my years of experience in public speaking, the quality of my ideas, and the interest and contributions of the audience. The last thing that would occur to me, however, would be that my success was aided by my gender, that if I had performed in exactly the same way but was perceived to be a woman, research shows quite clearly that I would have been taken less seriously, evaluated less positively along many dimensions, and have less of my success attributed to my own efforts and ability.

The difference between the two outcomes is a measure of male privilege, and there is little I can do to get rid of it, because its authority rests not in me but in society itself, especially in cultural images of gender. The audience does not know it is conferring male privilege on me, and I may not be aware that I'm receiving it. But the privilege is there nonetheless. That all of this may feel natural and nonprivileged only deepens the system's hold on all who participate in it.

[. . .]

NOTES

1. Sam Keen, *Fire in the Belly: On Being a Man* (New York: Bantam Books, 1991), 207.
2. For a history of American fatherhood, see Robert L. Griswold, *Fatherhood in America: A History* (New York: Basic Books, 1993).
3. For a thorough discussion of this distinction, see Marilyn French, *Beyond Power: On Men, Women, and Morals* (New York: Summit Books, 1985).
4. For discussions of language and gender, see Jane Caputi, *Gossips, Gorgons, and Crones* (Santa Fe, NM: Bear, 1993); Mary Daly, *Gyn/Ecology: The Metaethics of Radical Feminism* (Boston: Beacon Press, 1978); Margaret Gibbon, *Feminist Perspectives on Language* (New York: Longman, 1999); Dale Spender, *Man Made Language* (London: Pandora, 1980); Robin Lakoff, *Language and Woman's Place,* rev. ed. (New York: Harper and Row, 2004); Barbara G. Walker, *The Women's Encyclopedia of Myths and Secrets* (San Francisco: Harper and Row, 1983); and Barbara G. Walker, *The Woman's Dictionary of Symbols and Sacred Objects* (San Francisco: Harper and Row, 1988). For a very different slant on gender and language, see Mary Daly (in cahoots with Jane Caputi), *Webster's First New Intergalactic Wickedary of the English Language* (Boston: Beacon Press, 1987).
5. See Arlie Hochschild, *The Second Shift: Working Parents and the Revolution at Home,* rev. ed. (New York: Viking/Penguin, 2012).
6. See, for example, Rosalyn Baxandall, Linda Gordon, and Susan Reverby, eds., *America's Working Women: A Documentary History—1600 to the Present,* rev. ed. (New York: Norton, 1995); Ashley Montagu, *The Natural Superiority of Women* (New York: Collier, 1974); Robin Morgan, ed., *Sisterhood Is Global* (New York: Feminist Press, 1996); and Marilyn Waring, *If Women Counted: A New Feminist Economics* (San Francisco: HarperCollins, 1990).
7. Some would no doubt argue, with good reason, that our social selves mask more essential selves, but that's another argument for another place.
8. There is a substantial research literature documenting such genderized patterns of conversation. See, for example, Laurie P. Arliss, *Women and Men Communicating: Challenges and Changes,* 2nd ed. (Prospect Heights, IL: Waveland Press, 2000); N. Henley, M. Hamilton, and B. Thorne, "Womanspeak and Manspeak: Sex Differences and Sexism in Communication," in *Beyond Sex Roles,* edited by A. G. Sargent (New York; West, 1985), 168–85; P. Kollock, P. Blumstein, and P. Schwartz, "Sex and Power in Interaction, *American Sociological Review* 50, no. 1 (1985): 34–46; L. Smith-Lovin and C. Brody "Interruptions in Group Discussions: The Effect of Gender and Group Composition, *American Sociological Review* 51, no. 3 (1989): 424–35; and Mary M. Talbot, *Language and Gender. An Introduction,* 2nd ed. (Cambridge, UK: Polity Press, 2010).
9. Harry Brod, "Work Clothes and Leisure Suits: The Class Basis and Bias of the Men's Movement," in *Men's Lives,* edited by Michael S. Kimmel and Michael A. Messner (New York: Macmillan, 1989), 280.

3. • *Anne Fausto-Sterling*

THE FIVE SEXES, REVISITED (2000)

Anne Fausto-Sterling is the Nancy Duke Lewis Professor Emerita of Biology and Gender Studies at Brown University, the founder and director of the Science & Technology Studies Program at Brown, and fellow of the American Association for the Advancement of Science. Author of three books and more than sixty scholarly articles, her work strives to dismantle conversations that depend on either/or ways of seeing the world (e.g., nature/nurture and male/female) to develop theories that demonstrate interconnectedness. In "The Five Sexes, Revisited," Fausto-Sterling challenges us to interrogate how dualities found in cultural and gender differences become bodily differences despite scientific evidence that there are more than two sexes.

As Cheryl Chase stepped to the front of the packed meeting room in the Sheraton Boston Hotel, nervous coughs made the tension audible. Chase, an activist for intersexual rights, had been invited to address the May 2000 meeting of the Lawson Wilkins Pediatric Endocrine Society (LWPES), the largest organization in the United States for specialists in children's hormones. Her talk would be the grand finale to a four-hour symposium on the treatment of genital ambiguity in newborns, infants born with a mixture of both male and female anatomy, or genitals that appear to differ from their chromosomal sex. The topic was hardly a novel one to the assembled physicians.

Yet Chase's appearance before the group was remarkable. Three and a half years earlier, the American Academy of Pediatrics had refused her request for a chance to present the patients' viewpoint on the treatment of genital ambiguity, dismissing Chase and her supporters as "zealots." About two dozen intersex people had responded by throwing up a picket line. The Intersex Society of North America (ISNA) even issued a press release: "Hermaphrodites Target Kiddie Docs."

It had done my 1960s street-activist heart good. In the short run, I said to Chase at the time, the picketing would make people angry. But eventually, I assured her, the doors then closed would open. Now, as Chase began to address the physicians at their own convention, that prediction was coming true. Her talk, titled "Sexual Ambiguity: The Patient-Centered Approach," was a measured critique of the near-universal practice of performing immediate, "corrective" surgery on thousands of infants born each year with ambiguous genitalia. Chase herself lives with the consequences of such surgery. Yet her audience, the very endocrinologists and surgeons Chase was accusing of reacting with "surgery and shame," received her with respect. Even more remarkably, many of the speakers who preceded her at the session had already spoken of the need to scrap current practices in favor of treatments more centered on psychological counseling.

What led to such a dramatic reversal of fortune? Certainly, Chase's talk at the LWPES symposium was a vindication of her persistence in seeking attention for her cause. But her invitation to speak was also a watershed in the evolving discussion about how to treat children with ambiguous genitalia. And that discussion, in turn, is the tip of a biocultural iceberg—the gender iceberg—that continues to rock both medicine and our culture at large.

Chase made her first national appearance in 1993, in these very pages, announcing the formation of ISNA in a letter responding to an essay I had written for *The Sciences*, titled "The Five Sexes" [March/April 1993]. In that article I argued that the two-sex system embedded in our society is not adequate to encompass the full spectrum of human sexuality. In its place, I suggested a five-sex system. In addition to males and females, I included "herms" (named after true hermaphrodites, people born with both a testis and an ovary); "merms" (male pseudohermaphrodites, who are born with testes and some aspect of female genitalia); and "ferms" (female pseudohermaphrodites, who have ovaries combined with some aspect of male genitalia).

I had intended to be provocative, but I had also written with tongue firmly in cheek. So I was surprised by the extent of the controversy the article unleashed. Right-wing Christians were outraged, and connected my idea of five sexes with the United Nations–sponsored Fourth World Conference on Women, held in Beijing in September 1995. At the same time, the article delighted others who felt constrained by the current sex and gender system.

Clearly, I had struck a nerve. The fact that so many people could get riled up by my proposal to revamp our sex and gender system suggested that change—as well as resistance to it—might be in the offing. Indeed, a lot has changed since 1993, and I like to think that my article was an important stimulus. As if from nowhere, intersexuals are materializing before our very eyes. Like Chase, many have become political organizers, who lobby physicians and politicians to change current treatment practices. But more generally, though perhaps no less provocatively, the boundaries separating masculine and feminine seem harder than ever to define.

Some find the changes under way deeply disturbing. Others find them liberating.

Who is an intersexual—and how many intersexuals are there? The concept of intersexuality is rooted in the very ideas of male and female. In the idealized, Platonic, biological world, human beings are divided into two kinds: a perfectly dimorphic species. Males

have an X and a Y chromosome, testes, a penis and all of the appropriate internal plumbing for delivering urine and semen to the outside world. They also have well-known secondary sexual characteristics, including a muscular build and facial hair. Women have two X chromosomes, ovaries, all of the internal plumbing to transport urine and ova to the outside world, a system to support pregnancy and fetal development, as well as a variety of recognizable secondary sexual characteristics.

That idealized story papers over many obvious caveats: some women have facial hair, some men have none; some women speak with deep voices, some men veritably squeak. Less well known is the fact that, on close inspection, absolute dimorphism disintegrates even at the level of basic biology. Chromosomes, hormones, the internal sex structures, the gonads and the external genitalia all vary more than most people realize. Those born outside of the Platonic dimorphic mold are called intersexuals.

In "The Five Sexes" I reported an estimate by a psychologist expert in the treatment of intersexuals, suggesting that some 4 percent of all live births are intersexual. Then, together with a group of Brown University undergraduates, I set out to conduct the first systematic assessment of the available data on intersexual birthrates. We scoured the medical literature for estimates of the frequency of various categories of intersexuality, from additional chromosomes to mixed gonads, hormones and genitalia. For some conditions we could find only anecdotal evidence; for most, however, numbers exist. On the basis of that evidence, we calculated that for every 1,000 children born, seventeen are intersexual in some form. That number—1.7 percent—is a ballpark estimate, not a precise count, though we believe it is more accurate than the 4 percent I reported.

Our figure represents all chromosomal, anatomical and hormonal exceptions to the dimorphic ideal; the number of intersexuals who might, potentially, be subject to surgery as infants is smaller—probably between one in 1,000 and one in 2,000 live births. Furthermore, because some populations possess the relevant genes at high frequency, the intersexual birthrate is not uniform throughout the world.

Consider, for instance, the gene for congenital adrenal hyperplasia (CAH). When the CAH gene is inherited from both parents, it leads to a baby with masculinized external genitalia who possesses two X chromosomes and the internal reproductive organs of a potentially fertile woman. The frequency of the gene varies widely around the world: in New Zealand it occurs in only forty-three children per million; among the Yupik Eskimo of southwestern Alaska, its frequency is 3,500 per million.

Intersexuality has always been to some extent a matter of definition. And in the past century physicians have been the ones who defined children as intersexual—and provided the remedies. When only the chromosomes are unusual, but the external genitalia and gonads clearly indicate either a male or a female, physicians do not advocate intervention. Indeed, it is not clear what kind of intervention could be advocated in such cases. But the story is quite different when infants are born with mixed genitalia, or with external genitals that seem at odds with the baby's gonads.

Most clinics now specializing in the treatment of intersex babies rely on case-management principles developed in the 1950s by the psychologist John Money and the psychiatrists Joan G. Hampson and John L. Hampson, all of Johns Hopkins University in Baltimore, Maryland. Money believed that gender identity is completely malleable for about eighteen months after birth. Thus, he argued, when a treatment team is presented with an infant who has ambiguous genitalia, the team could make a gender assignment solely on the basis of what made the best surgical sense. The physicians could then simply encourage the parents to raise the child according to the surgically assigned gender. Following that course, most physicians maintained, would eliminate psychological distress for both the patient and the parents. Indeed, treatment teams were never to use such words as "intersex" or "hermaphrodite"; instead, they were to tell parents that nature intended the baby to be the boy or the girl that the physicians had determined it was. Through surgery, the physicians were merely completing nature's intention.

Although Money and the Hampsons published detailed case studies of intersex children who they said had adjusted well to their gender assignments, Money thought one case in particular proved his theory. It was a dramatic example, inasmuch as it did not involve intersexuality at all: one of a pair of identical twin boys lost his penis as a result of a circumcision accident. Money recommended that "John" (as he came to be known in a later case study) be surgically turned into "Joan" and raised as a girl. In time, Joan grew to love wearing dresses and having her hair done. Money proudly proclaimed the sex reassignment a success.

But as recently chronicled by John Colapinto, in his book *As Nature Made Him*, Joan—now known to be an adult male named David Reimer—eventually rejected his female assignment. Even without a functioning penis and testes (which had been removed as part of the reassignment) John/Joan sought masculinizing medication, and married a woman with children (whom he adopted).

Since the full conclusion to the John/Joan story came to light, other individuals who were reassigned as males or females shortly after birth but who later rejected their early assignments have come forward, so, too, have cases in which the reassignment has worked—at least into the subject's mid-twenties. But even then the aftermath of the surgery can be problematic. Genital surgery often leaves scars that reduce sexual sensitivity. Chase herself had a complete clitoridectomy, a procedure that is less frequently performed on intersexuals today. But the newer surgeries, which reduce the size of the clitoral shaft, still greatly reduce sensitivity.

The revelation of cases of failed reassignments and the emergence of intersex activism have led an increasing number of pediatric endocrinologists, urologists and psychologists to reexamine the wisdom of early genital surgery. For example, in a talk that preceded Chase's at the LWPES meeting, the medical ethicist Laurence B. McCullough of the Center for Medical Ethics and Health Policy at Baylor College of Medicine in Houston, Texas, introduced an ethical framework for the treatment of children with ambiguous genitalia. Because sex phenotype (the manifestation of genetically and embryologically determined sexual characteristics) and gender presentation (the sex role projected by the individual in society) are highly variable, McCullough argues, the various forms of intersexuality should be defined as normal. All of them fall within the statistically expected variability of sex and gender. Furthermore, though certain disease states may accompany some forms of intersexuality, and may require medical intervention, intersexual conditions are not themselves diseases.

McCullough also contends that in the process of assigning gender, physicians should minimize what he calls irreversible assignments: taking steps such as the surgical removal or modification of gonads or genitalia that the patient may one day want to have reversed. Finally, McCullough urges physicians to abandon their practice of treating the birth of a child with genital ambiguity as a medical or social emergency. Instead, they should take the time to perform a thorough medical workup and should disclose everything to the parents, including the uncertainties about the final outcome. The treatment mantra, in other words, should be therapy, not surgery.

I believe a new treatment protocol for intersex infants, similar to the one outlined by McCullough, is close at hand. Treatment should combine some basic medical and ethical principles with a practical but less drastic approach to the birth of a mixed-sex child. As a first step, surgery on infants should be performed only to save the child's life or to substantially improve the child's physical well-being. Physicians may assign a sex—male or female—to an intersex infant on the basis of the probability that the child's particular condition will lead to the formation of a particular gender identity. At the same time, though, practitioners ought to be humble enough to recognize that as the child grows, he or she may reject the assignment—and they should be wise enough to listen to what the child has to say. Most important, parents should have access to the full range of information and options available to them.

Sex assignments made shortly after birth are only the beginning of a long journey. Consider, for instance, the life of Max Beck: Born intersexual, Max was surgically assigned as a female and consistently raised as such. Had her medical team followed her into her early twenties, they would have deemed her assignment a success because she was married to a man. (It should be noted that success in gender assignment has traditionally been defined as living in that gender as a heterosexual.) Within a few years, however, Beck had come out as a butch lesbian; now in her mid-thirties, Beck has become a man and married his lesbian partner, who (through the miracles of modern reproductive technology) recently gave birth to a girl.

Transsexuals, people who have an emotional gender at odds with their physical sex, once described themselves in terms of dimorphic absolutes—males trapped in female bodies, or vice versa. As such, they sought psychological relief through surgery. Although many still do, some so-called transgendered people today are content to inhabit a more ambiguous zone. A male-to-female transsexual, for instance, may come out as a lesbian. Jane, born a physiological male, is now in her late thirties and living with her wife, whom she married when her name was still John. Jane takes hormones to feminize herself, but they have not yet interfered with her ability to engage in intercourse as a man. In her mind Jane has a lesbian relationship with her wife, though she views their intimate moments as a cross between lesbian and heterosexual sex.

It might seem natural to regard intersexuals and transgendered people as living midway between the poles of male and female. But male and female, masculine and feminine, cannot be parsed as some kind of continuum. Rather, sex and gender are best conceptualized as points in a multidimensional space. For some time, experts on gender development have distinguished between sex at the genetic level and at the cellular level (sex-specific gene expression, X and Y chromosomes); at the hormonal level (in the fetus, during childhood and after puberty); and at the anatomical level (genitals and secondary sexual characteristics). Gender identity presumably emerges from all of those corporeal aspects via some poorly understood interaction with environment and experience. What has become increasingly clear is that one can find levels of masculinity and femininity in almost every possible permutation. A chromosomal, hormonal and genital male (or female) may emerge with a female (or male) gender identity. Or a chromosomal female with male fetal hormones and masculinized genitalia—but with female pubertal hormones—may develop a female gender identity.

The medical and scientific communities have yet to adopt a language that is capable of describing such diversity. In her book *Hermaphrodites and the Medical Invention of Sex,* the historian and medical ethicist Alice Domurat Dreger of Michigan State University in East Lansing documents the emergence of current medical systems for classifying gender ambiguity. The current usage remains rooted in the Victorian approach to sex. The logical structure of the commonly used terms "true hermaphrodite," "male pseudohermaphrodite" and "female pseudohermaphrodite" indicates that only the so-called true hermaphrodite is a genuine mix of male and female. The others, no matter how confusing their body parts, are really hidden males or females. Because true hermaphrodites are rare—possibly only one in 100,000—such a classification system supports the idea that human beings are an absolutely dimorphic species.

At the dawn of the twenty-first century, when the variability of gender seems so visible, such a position is hard to maintain. And here, too, the old medical consensus has begun to crumble. Last fall the pediatric urologist Ian A. Aaronson of the Medical University of South Carolina in Charleston organized the North American Task Force on Intersexuality (NATFI) to review the clinical responses to genital ambiguity in infants. Key medical associations, such as the American Academy of Pediatrics, have endorsed NATFI. Specialists in surgery, endocrinology, psychology, ethics, psychiatry, genetics and public health, as well as intersex patient-advocate groups, have joined its ranks.

One of the goals of NATFI is to establish a new sex nomenclature. One proposal under consideration replaces the current system with emotionally neutral terminology that emphasizes developmental processes rather than preconceived gender categories. For example, Type I intersexes develop out of anomalous virilizing influences; Type II result from some interruption of virilization; and in Type III intersexes the gonads themselves may not have developed in the expected fashion.

What is clear is that since 1993, modern society has moved beyond five sexes to a recognition that gender variation is normal and, for some people, an arena for playful exploration. Discussing my "five sexes" proposal in her book *Lessons from the Intersexed,* the psychologist Suzanne J. Kessler of the State University of New York at Purchase drives this point home with great effect:

> The limitation with Fausto-Sterling's proposal is that . . . [it] still gives genitals . . . primary signifying status and ignores the fact that in the everyday world gender attributions are made without access to genital inspection. . . . What has primacy in everyday life is the gender that is performed, regardless of the flesh's configuration under the clothes.

I now agree with Kessler's assessment. It would be better for intersexuals and their supporters to turn everyone's focus away from genitals. Instead, as she suggests, one should acknowledge that people come in an even wider assortment of sexual identities and characteristics than mere genitals can distinguish. Some women may have "large clitorises or fused labia," whereas some men may have "small penises or misshapen scrota," as Kessler puts it, "phenotypes with no particular clinical or identity meaning."

As clearheaded as Kessler's program is—and despite the progress made in the 1990s—our society is still far from that ideal. The intersexual or transgendered person who projects a social gender—what Kessler calls "cultural genitals"—that conflicts with his or her physical genitals still may die for the transgression. Hence legal protection for people whose cultural and physical genitals do not match is needed during the current transition to a more gender-diverse world. One easy step would be to eliminate the category of "gender" from official documents, such as driver's licenses and passports. Surely attributes both more visible (such as height, build and eye color) and less visible (fingerprints and genetic profiles) would be more expedient.

A more far-ranging agenda is presented in the International Bill of Gender Rights, adopted in 1995 at the fourth annual International Conference on Transgender Law and Employment Policy in Houston, Texas. It lists ten "gender rights," including the right to define one's own gender, the right to change one's physical gender if one so chooses and the right to marry whomever one wishes. The legal bases for such rights are being hammered out in the courts as I write and, most recently, through the establishment, in the state of Vermont, of legal same-sex domestic partnerships.

No one could have foreseen such changes in 1993. And the idea that I played some role, however small,

in reducing the pressure—from the medical community as well as from society at large—to flatten the diversity of human sexes into two diametrically opposed camps gives me pleasure.

Sometimes people suggest to me, with not a little horror, that I am arguing for a pastel world in which androgyny reigns and men and women are boringly the same. In my vision, however, strong colors coexist with pastels. There are and will continue to be highly masculine people out there; it's just that some of them are women. And some of the most feminine people I know happen to be men.

4. • *Ijeoma A.*

BECAUSE YOU'RE A GIRL (2002)

Ijeoma A. was born and raised in West Africa. Her first trip to the United States was to attend college in Ohio. Her essay included here grew out a column she contributed to a popular student publication in which she shared what it was like growing up in West Africa as well as her experiences as a migrant negotiating US culture. Since graduation, she has worked in Washington, DC.

It was a Sunday night in Lagos during the African Cup series. In these parts, we lived by soccer. Often, you'd hear the tale of the lover who threatened his sweetheart because she walked past the television, obstructing his vision for a precious second while the Nigerian Eagles were playing. Indeed, soccer was serious business.

This year, Nigeria had made it to the finals, and tonight's game was going to be watched by *everybody* who was *anybody* that knew *somebody*. I couldn't miss this game for the world. We had an earlier-than-recommended dinner, and before long, all of us—two brothers, five cousins and myself—littered ourselves around the miniature TV screen to witness this lifetime event. It was then that the unmistakable voice of my mother burst through the bustle,

with a distinctly familiar hint of irritation: "Ijeoma, when exactly did you intend to clean up?"

"Only me?" I responded. "Could one of the boys help this time? I don't want to miss the game. *Please!*"

"Ije! You're a girl and we're raising you to become a woman some day. Now, stop being stubborn and go clean that kitchen up!"

My heart ached. Ten people were a lot to clean up after, especially on a finals night. As I dug through a bottomless sink of dirty dishes, the boys and my parents were in the living room, screaming, yelling and cheering. I felt so small. I was alone, with filthy mountains of blackened pots and kettles surrounding me in that small, somber kitchen. Once in a while, one of the boys would stop by and ask me where he might place an empty glass he had just used so that I wouldn't forget to wash it. I would use such opportunities to ask "Who's winning?!" Then I was alone again, sulking at soccer ball-shaped saucers that constantly reminded me I would be spending the core of the Eagles' game cleaning up in the kitchen; because I was a girl.

Although I was raised in Nigeria's capital city of Lagos, most of my guardians (my parents, uncles, aunts and older cousins) were raised in the rural villages of Eastern Nigeria. As a result, my upbringing was not as diluted of traditional customs as is typical in the big and populated cities of Nigeria. My parents, uncles and aunts had Four Commandments incorporating what a woman's responsibilities were to her family:

1. Her office is the kitchen.
2. She is responsible for all the chores in the home.
3. She is accountable for the children and their actions.
4. And, of course, she must pledge complete and total allegiance to the man in charge first, before herself.

I know my guardians believed that they were looking out for my best interests by molding me in accordance with these ideas. Frankly, I can understand why. In our society, it is considered every woman's destiny to be married one day and have children. Deviations from that fate usually ended up in an unhappy everafter of spite and loneliness. Being a woman in her late twenties with no suitors to pop the Question seemed the greatest shame a woman could endure. Thus, by raising me in accordance with these Four Commandments, my guardians hoped to ensure that I would not have to endure the mockery or the pain of being an old unmarried woman. However, despite their good intentions, I was never able to appreciate this way of life wholeheartedly.

Everything in my childhood substantiated the need for women to submit. The stability of our society depended heavily on it. Fairytales were laden with morals of submission, as well as forewarnings against the girl who talked back, or the wife who

tried to be the second captain on a ship that demanded just one. Before long, like other girls I was convinced that something bad would happen to me if I rocked the boat. I decided that I would dutifully execute anything my family demanded, since I didn't want the same fate as the girls in those tales who dared to go against our customs. My family's approval was all that I lived for, and I wanted my parents to be proud of me. But, whenever I was alone, I'd often catch myself wishing that I were born a boy.

As I observed my family's dynamics, it became evident that my brothers and cousins didn't have the same "duties to the family" as I did. Every morning, I had to get up early to dust and sweep. I would get in trouble if breakfast weren't ready by the time the boys got hungry. It was also my responsibility to ensure that my younger brother bathed and dressed himself appropriately for the day. Of course, I had to do the dishes when everyone was done and *then* get myself ready in time for school or church, depending on what day it was.

I really wanted to be a good daughter, but at night I would dream that I could wake up a little later the next morning, and like a boy find my breakfast already waiting for me. I would take off my slippers and tease my toes with the fresh feel of a dustless floor that had already been swept and mopped . . . just like the boys did each morning. At times I would gather the courage to inquire about the discrepancies in the division of labor, but would be silenced with an abrupt: "It's a woman's job to do those things." Whenever I persisted, I became the subject of corrosive criticism that was sometimes accompanied by some form of punishment. Thus, I learned to conform and embrace the life that had been carved out for me.

On the surface I was the good girl that my family wanted me to be. I grew content with my predicament as I got older and even impressed my parents with my devotion to serve. Deep down, however, I despised my submission. I hated taking orders and cleaning after people. I usually had to consciously press my lips firmly together, so I wouldn't say "inappropriate" things whenever I was assigned a chore, or if one of the boys complained about his meal. One night, I was doing the dishes while the rest of the family enjoyed a sitcom in the living room. A cousin then came into the kitchen, slightly irritated that there were no clean glasses available for him to take a drink. He then instructed me to hurry up with the dishes when I suddenly snapped at him, "Well maybe if you learned to wash your own dirty dishes I wouldn't ever have to listen to you whine like that over a glass!" Neither of us could believe what I had just said. As expected, I was reported, and then punished for my impudence.

On another occasion, I had just baked some chicken to accompany the Sunday lunch my mother had prepared. According to our customs, the heart was a part of the chicken that could only be eaten by the oldest man at the table. As I placed the poultry pieces neatly in a serving dish, something made me swiftly snatch the heart from the dish and toss it into my mouth. It tasted really, really good, but suddenly I became afraid. How would I account for the missing heart? What was going to happen to me? I promptly decided that I would blame the merchant who sold us the chicken. At the table, I swore that he must have taken the heart out before selling the bird to us, because I didn't recall seeing it with the rest of the chicken. Fortunately, everyone believed me.

In my day-to-day experiences school became my refuge, an oasis in the midst of all the mindless house cleaning and cooking. In the classroom I didn't feel so passive. Despite my gender, my teachers often sought my insight in resolving problems that they used to test the students. I was encouraged to develop my own ideas, since productive class discussions depended highly on the individuality and diversity of the students. Something about school made me feel "great" about myself. I would suddenly become more talkative and would volunteer my opinions in various situations without the fear of reproach. It seemed my teachers were not as focused on gender as my family, and I often wondered about that irregularity. They were more interested in a student's ability to absorb their teachings and then

use them in productive ways, irrespective of gender. They made me believe that being a girl wasn't really a factor in my ability to answer a test question, and I found this new way of thinking rather refreshing. In the classroom, gender didn't rank the boys higher than the girls. Instead, it was your academic excellence that earned you your respect and the teacher's favor. If you had an interest in student leadership, or if you wanted membership in exclusive school organizations, your grades were inspected, and it was those grades that earned you your rank.

For me, this was ample incentive to excel. Although I had little power over my predicament at home, I had a magnitude of control over my school performance, and fortunately my efforts didn't go unnoticed. Before too long, I was appointed Class Captain in primary-3 (equivalent to the third grade in American schools). As a Class Captain, I was in charge of the classroom's cleanliness, but in very different capacity than at home. In the classroom, I *supervised* the cleaning, and I *assigned* the different chores to my fellow classmates. In school, I had the ability to enforce the change that I was powerless at creating in my own home. I made sure that the boys worked just as hard as the girls, and I ensured that their hands got just as dirty from sweeping and scrubbing the floors. Thereafter, I would take my shoes off and indulge my feet in that nice feeling you get from walking on a really clean floor.

As Class Captain, it was also my responsibility to enforce the School Rules on my peers. Since I was in charge, I would momentarily forget about my family's ideals of Woman's submission to Man. Whenever I spoke, my words had to be obeyed since I embodied the school authorities in the classroom. As a result of my position, I was always the first in line for school assemblies and field trips, the first to be seated at important school functions, and even the first to receive my report card at the end of each trimester. At home my place had always been after the boys. But in the classroom, I was Number One; ahead of the other girls, and of course before the boys. I valued my relationship with the other girls, however, given my background, male respect had a closer resemblance to the "forbidden fruit" and so I tended to focus more of my efforts on obtaining it. This taste of power made me feel that I could potentially transcend my fate of becoming a family Cook and Maid in my future husband's house. I suddenly felt like I could achieve more with my life: do great things, make a lasting difference.

As I became an adolescent, the demands on my time seemed to increase exponentially, especially in conjunction with my academic obligations. Since I received little help, I often found myself grumbling about all the "because-you're-a-girl" rhetoric. Whenever I lamented openly, my mother and aunts would try to comfort me: "You're a big girl now and you may marry soon. These are the things your husband and his family will expect of you, and we're only preparing you to handle them." I really hated to hear that. If my forty-eight-hour days were indicative of my life with a husband, then I didn't ever want to get married. Of course, the family hated to hear that. Still, as a minor I had to fulfill the demands of my family.

By my senior year of high school, my resources were stretched as thin as they could get. I pressured myself to do well in school because I was very addicted to the prominence my previous grades had earned me in the student government. My father also pressured me to score only the highest grades. He had gotten so accustomed to my excellent performance in earlier years that he was unwilling to accept anything less during my senior year. Nonetheless, I was still expected to fulfill all my "duties to the family." No one seemed to understand that in order to keep stellar grades, it would be helpful to have fewer chores at home. "If you don't do them, who will?" was their response. I believe my situation was exacerbated simply because I was the "only" girl in a large family of men. Perhaps if I had a sister or two, one of them could have covered for me while I studied for exams. Maybe then, my sessions slaving in the kitchen while the boys watched the TV would not have been so lonely and harrowing.

During this year my father revealed his plans to educate me abroad. To gain admission to an American college, I had to satisfy several other academic requirements in addition to my schoolwork. No one seemed to empathize with me, and so I began to see my father's intention to send me to the United States as my ticket out of these stressful conditions and an escape from my future as a "good wife." This thought motivated me to excel academically despite the odds and to earn admission and a scholarship to attend Oberlin College in Ohio.

* * *

After arriving in America, I was not quite sure how to proceed with my life. For the past seventeen years I had become accustomed to someone else telling me how and when to live. Now, I was suddenly answerable to only myself—a role I had never learned to play. I found myself waiting for someone to tell me my chores. After living in a cage all my life, I guess I found this new environment a little too big to live in. Despite the liberating utopia that America represented, it took me a long time to let go of my previous life. How could the world suddenly expect me to take initiative when it had always trained me to receive my opinions from others? Sometimes I felt the sudden urge to do something really outrageous, like sleeping in for a couple of extra hours in the morning. "Would someone come to scold me and yank me out from under my blanket?" I would wait and see. If nothing happened, I would get up and leave my bed unmade indefinitely. Then I would wait again. Would my roommate report me? Perhaps my parents would be notified of my misbehavior and then force me to return to Nigeria. I would then become afraid and return to my room to make the bed.

I was taken aback as I learned that my roommate was messier than I was; she claimed she had always been that way. How could her parents tolerate that? Didn't they worry that she would never find a good husband? As I opened up to her, I was stunned by everything she shared about herself. She had never had to clean her brother's room. "He does that his damned self," she said, a bit surprised that I had thought that she had ever waited on him. Also, she had never cooked in her life. She probably couldn't even tell you how to boil water, yet she wasn't ashamed.

Slowly I fell in love with America. Sometimes I would hang out with the boys, just so I could say "No" to them. Whenever I felt really bold, I'd say, "Do it your damned self," just like my roommate. Once, I cooked an African meal for some of my American friends. I didn't make anything complicated, simply because I didn't want to generate too many dirty dishes. I wasn't sure I could handle the same loads as I used to in Nigeria. To my surprise, however, one of the boys offered to do the dishes when we were done eating. I paused and then said, with my accent, "Yeah, do it your damned self!" He thought that was funny and so we laughed about it.

Gradually I found myself saying and doing things I wouldn't have dared to in the past, in West Africa. I finally felt light and free. I was able to focus on my studies without needing to rush home and cook lunch. I now had "leisure" time to sit around and chat with people from all over the world. I could sleep in longer, and I could experience "idle" moments when I simply did nothing. I could make boys clean after themselves, and I could do it with authority. And sometimes, just to be cheeky, I would even make them clean up after me. I really loved this new life that I was allowed to live.

Whenever I returned home for the holidays, I always underwent psychological conflicts within myself. My family had missed my cooking. They missed me too, however they had also missed my services. After two semesters of being my own master, I had to readjust to being the passive daughter they had been used to in previous years. Once, I told a cousin to do something "his damned self." I was very frustrated. It wasn't easy reassuming my domestic role, especially after a whole year of retirement. He was livid. Before long, the rest of the family clamored around me, inquiring about what possessed me to say something like that. I remained quiet and listened to them answer the question for themselves: "She's gone to America, and now she has forgotten about her heritage." "Why did they send her there?

Now look at what she is becoming." "She thinks she is American." My father returned home from work and, of course, I was spoken to sternly. I was never to repeat that behavior again.

But had America really changed me? I vehemently oppose that theory. It is true that as I progressed through college, my relationship with my family clearly experienced a metamorphosis. Although I was still respectful of my elders, I gradually became less restrained in expressing my true sentiments in various situations. I no longer followed orders passively as I had in the past, and little by little, I acquired the audacity to question them. Of course, I didn't always have my way, but at least I made it known that I was not always happy with the kind of life that they felt was right for me. This perceived impudence was not always welcomed, and I was repeatedly accused of disregarding my homeland's traditions and thinking that I was now an American.

But my theory is that America introduced me to Me. Growing up, I had numbed myself to the dissatisfactions I felt in a society that favored boys. My only option was to conform, so I brainwashed myself into thinking that I was happy. That was the only way I knew to keep a level head. I lived an emotionally uncomfortable life plagued with internal conflicts. It was always my reflex to suppress my true opinions on the gender inequalities for the fear of reproach from a conservative society that I loved more than myself. Each time I felt violated because one of the boys was being treated like a first-class citizen at my expense, a voice inside me affirmed that I was being treated unjustly, but I would dismiss it as the voice of a wayward extremist. America helped me realize that all that time, I had been dismissing myself, choosing instead to embrace the beliefs of a society that taught me that I was inferior to my male counterparts. American society was conducive to nurturing that part of me that didn't believe that I was weaker by virtue of my gender. America didn't change me, but rather it simply allowed me to discover myself.

As I continued to enjoy this growing sense of empowerment, I became acquainted with American feminism. Quite frankly, I didn't know what to make of it. It surprised me that any American woman could be discontent with the gender conditions of the same country I credited for liberating me. America felt like the Promised Land, and I wondered what else an American feminist could want. In my patriarchal background, women were considered the property of the male breadwinner. My aunt's husband, for instance, would use her as a punching bag without compunction after say, a stressful day at work. As a young woman I choked on these realities; my hands were tied when it came to protesting how my uncle handled my aunt, whom he considered his "property." At least in the United States my aunt could have been shielded from battery since her husband might have feared the threat of arrest. Thus, from my first perspective, America was surely the feminist's paradise.

It was interesting to learn later that many years ago, America's situation was quite similar to the current one in my natal country. I find this encouraging since it indicates that my people may one day embrace some of the values I now enjoy in America. Therefore, I do support the feminist and womanist movements in the United States, simply because these were forces that drove the change in America. I may eventually participate in the U.S. feminist struggles; perhaps I will gain some insight into what it would take to effect change in my country. For now, however, I am still living my American dream. I am so addicted to the freedoms I have enjoyed here, and I hope I can keep them, irrespective of the country in which I finally decide to settle down.

Today I am an independent woman working in the United States. I am very happy with my life, and I feel more fulfilled than I ever have. Occasionally, however, I find myself missing home. There are many aspects of the Nigerian society, besides the gender inequalities, that I failed to appreciate until I came to America. I miss the Nigerian sense of community; the security of knowing that I can depend on my next-door neighbor to worry if she doesn't see me for several days. Here in the United States, my neighbor of two years still isn't sure whether or not I have children. Come to think of it, we don't even know each other's names. I also miss Nigerian food, the obstinate devotion to family, and the festive celebrations. I miss home. However, irrespective of how nostalgic I get, I know deep inside that America is the best option for me right now. I have deviated so much from my childhood's domestic and subservient lifestyle that I don't think it will ever be possible for me to adopt it again. The only way I could return to that life would be to erase the past six years I spent in America. Without those years I would never have tasted the sweet wine of independence that has gotten me drunk and addicted today.

I think that my family is gradually coming to terms with the person that I have become. I wouldn't say that my relatives are thrilled, but they recognize the futility of compelling me to marry a man from my community who is attached to its "good wife" values. They know that I will probably tell him to do his cooking and laundry his damned self, just like I have already told some members of my family to date. However, I wouldn't necessarily conclude that an American would make the perfect companion for me either, since he may not embody the Nigerian values that I love and miss.

It is difficult to predict what the future holds for me, since I am very much in the middle of the two worlds that have molded me into who I am today. I have decided that I will go anywhere destiny takes me, provided that I have primary control over my life and that my opinions count, despite my gender. Anything less would not be a life for me. I have worked and struggled very hard to become the intelligent, independent and strong woman that I am today. I absolutely cannot ignore all that I have endured and achieved by settling for a passive life as Adam's Rib. Some may choose to call me a rebel, but I am simply a woman searching for a happier life. One in which I am allowed to love myself, and not sacrifice that love in favor of a society's values.

5. • *C. J. Pascoe*

MAKING MASCULINITY:
Adolescence, Identity, and High School (2011)

C. J. Pascoe, a professor of sociology at the University of Oregon, researches the constructions of gender, sexuality, and inequalities in youth culture and is the award-winning author of *Dude You're a Fag: Masculinity and Sexuality in High School* excerpted here. Her research has been featured in *The New York Times*, *The Wall Street Journal*, *The Toronto Globe and Mail*, *American Sexuality Magazine*, and *Inside Higher Ed*. Pascoe's most recent book, coauthored with Tristan Bridges, is *Exploring Masculinities: Identity, Inequality, Continuity, and Change* (2015). She is a public advocate for anti-bullying and harassment policies, and her most recent projects investigate youth culture, sexuality, homophobia, and new media.

REVENGE OF THE NERDS

Cheering students filled River High's gymnasium. Packed tightly in the bleachers, they sang, hollered, and danced to loud hip-hop music. Over their heads hung banners celebrating fifty years of River High's sports victories. The yearly assembly in which the student body voted for the most popular senior boy in the school to be crowned Mr. Cougar was under way, featuring six candidates performing a series of skits to earn student votes.

Two candidates, Brent and Greg, both handsome, blond, "all-American" water polo players, entered the stage dressed like "nerds" to perform their skit, "Revenge of the Nerds." They wore matching outfits: yellow button-down shirts; tight brown pants about five inches too short, with the waistbands pulled up clownishly high by black suspenders; black shoes with white kneesocks; and thick black-rimmed glasses held together with white tape. As music played, the boys started dancing, flailing around comically in bad renditions of outdated dance moves like the Running Man and the Roger Rabbit. The crowd roared in laughter when Brent and Greg rubbed their rear ends together in time to the music. Two girls with long straight hair and

matching miniskirts and black tank tops, presumably the nerds' girlfriends, ran out to dance with Brent and Greg.

Suddenly a group of white male "gangstas" sporting bandannas, baggy pants, sports jerseys, and oversized gold jewelry walked, or, more correctly, gangsta-limped, onto the stage. They proceeded to shove Brent and Greg, who looked at them fearfully and fled the stage without their girlfriends. The gangstas encircled the two girls, then "kidnapped" them by forcing them off the stage. After peering timidly around the corner of the stage, Brent and Greg reentered. The crowd roared as Brent opened his mouth and, in a high-pitched feminine voice, cried, "We have to get our women!"

Soon a girl dressed in a sweat suit and wearing a whistle around her neck carried barbells and weight benches onto the stage. Greg and Brent emerged from behind a screen, having replaced their nerd gear with matching black and white sweat pants and T-shirts. The female coach tossed the barbells around with ease, lifting one with a single hand. The audience hooted in laughter as the nerds struggled to lift even the smallest weight. Brent and Greg continued to work out until they could finally lift the weights. They ran up to the crowd to flex their newfound muscles as the audience cheered. To underscore how strong they had become, Brent and Greg ripped off their pants. The crowd was in hysterics as the boys revealed, not muscled legs, but matching red miniskirts. At first Greg and Brent looked embarrassed; then they triumphantly dropped the skirts, revealing matching shorts, and the audience cheered.

Brent and Greg ran off stage as stagehands unfurled a large cloth sign reading "Gangstas' Hideout." Some of the gangstas who had kidnapped the girlfriends sat around a table playing poker, while other gangstas gambled with dice. The nerds, who had changed into black suits accented with ties and fedoras, strode confidently into the hideout. They threw the card table in the air, causing the gangstas to jump back as the cards and chips scattered. Looking frightened at the nerds' newfound strength, the gangstas scrambled out of their hideout. After the gangstas had fled, the two miniskirted girlfriends ran up to Brent and Greg, hugging them gratefully. Several African American boys, also dressed in suits and fedoras, ran onto the stage, dancing while the former nerds stood behind them with their arms folded. After the dance, the victorious nerds walked off stage hand in hand with their rescued girlfriends.

I open with this scene to highlight the themes of masculinity I saw during a year and a half of fieldwork at River High School. The Mr. Cougar competition clearly illuminates the intersecting dynamics of sexuality, gender, social class, race, bodies, and institutional practices that constitute adolescent masculinity in this setting. Craig and Brent are transformed from unmasculine nerds who cannot protect their girlfriends into heterosexual, muscular men. This masculinizing process happens through a transformation of bodies, the assertion of racial privilege, and a shoring up of heterosexuality.

The story line of the skit—Brent and Craig's quest to confirm their heterosexuality by rescuing their girlfriends—posits heterosexuality as central to masculinity. Brent and Craig's inability to protect "their women" marks their physical inadequacy. Their appearance—tight, ill-fitting, outdated clothes—codes them as unmasculine. Their weakness and their

high-pitched voices cast them as feminine. Their homoerotic dance moves position them as homosexual. By working out, the boys shed their weak, effeminate, and possibly homosexual identities. Just in case they didn't get their message across by bench-pressing heavy weights, the boys shed their last remnants of femininity by ripping off their matching miniskirts. They become so physically imposing that they don't even have to fight the gangstas, who flee in terror at the mere hint of the nerds' strength.

This skit lays bare the ways racialized notions of masculinity may be enacted through sexualized tropes. The gangstas symbolize failed and at the same time wildly successful men in their heterosexual claim on the nerds' women. Their "do-rags," baggy pants, shirts bearing sports team insignias, and limping walks are designed to invoke a hardened inner-city gangsta style, one portrayed on television and in movies, as a specifically black cultural style. In representing black men, the gangstas symbolize hypersexuality and invoke a thinly veiled imagery of the black rapist (A. Davis 1981), who threatens white men's control over white women. But in the end, the gangstas are vanquished by the white, middle-class legitimacy of the nerds, turned masculine with their newfound strength. The skit also portrays black men as slightly feminized in that they act as cheerleaders and relieve the white heroes of the unmasculine practice of dancing.

Markers of femininity such as high voices and skirts symbolize emasculation when associated with male bodies. The girlfriends also signal a relationship between femininity and helplessness, since they are unable to save themselves from the gangstas. However, the female coach symbolizes strength, a sign of masculinity the nerds initially lack. The students in the audience cheer her as she engages in a masculinized practice, lifting weights with ease, and they laugh at the boys who can't do this. Male femininity, in this instance, is coded as humorous, while female masculinity is cheered.

[. . .]

My findings illustrate that masculinity is not a homogenous category that any boy possesses by virtue of being male. Rather, masculinity—as constituted and understood in the social world I studied—is a configuration of practices and discourses that different youths (boys and girls) may embody in different ways and to different degrees. Masculinity, in this sense, is associated with, but not reduced or solely equivalent to, the male body. I argue that adolescent masculinity is understood in this setting as a form of dominance usually expressed through sexualized discourses.[1]

Through extensive fieldwork and interviewing I discovered that, for boys, achieving a masculine identity entails the repeated repudiation of the specter of failed masculinity. Boys lay claim to masculine identities by lobbing homophobic epithets at one another. They also assert masculine selves by engaging in heterosexist discussions of girls' bodies and their own sexual experiences. Both of these phenomena intersect with racialized identities in that they are organized somewhat differently by and for African American boys and white boys. From what I saw during my research, African American boys were more likely to be punished by school authorities for engaging in these masculinizing practices. Though homophobic taunts and assertion of heterosexuality shore up a masculine identity for boys, the relationship between sexuality and masculinity looks different when masculinity occurs outside male bodies. For girls, challenging heterosexual identities often solidifies a more masculine identity. These gendering processes are encoded at multiple levels: institutional, interactional, and individual.

[. . .]

WHAT DO WE MEAN BY MASCULINITY?

Sociologists have approached masculinity as a multiplicity of gender practices (regardless of their content) enacted by men whose bodies are assumed to be biologically male. Early in the twentieth century, when fears of feminization pervaded just about every sphere of social life, psychologists became

increasingly concerned with differentiating men from women (Kimmel 1996). As a result, part of the definition of a psychologically "normal" adult came to involve proper adjustment to one's "gender role" (Pleck 1987). Talcott Parsons (1954), the first sociologist to really address masculinity as such, argued that men's "instrumental" role and women's "expressive" role were central to the functioning of a well-ordered society. Deviations from women's role as maternal caretakers or men's role as breadwinners would result in "role strain" and "role competition," weakening families and ultimately society.

With the advent of the women's movement, feminist gender theorists examined how power is embedded in these seemingly neutral (not to mention natural) "gender roles" (Hartmann 1976; Jaggar 1983; Rosaldo and Lamphere 1974; Rubin 1984). Psychoanalytic feminist theorists explicitly addressed masculinity as an identity formation constituted by inequality. Both Dorothy Dinnerstein (1976) and Nancy Chodorow (1978) argued that masculinity, as we recognize it, is the result of a family system in which women mother. Identification with a mother as the primary caregiver proves much more problematic in the formation of a gender identity for a boy than for a girl child, producing a self we understand as masculine characterized by defensive ego boundaries and repudiation of femininity. Feminist psychoanalytic theorists equate contemporary masculinity with a quest for autonomy and separation, an approach that influences my own analysis of masculinity.

Recognizing the changes wrought for women by feminist movements, sociologists of masculinity realized that feminism had radical implications for men (Carrigan, Connell, and Lee 1987). Frustrated with the paucity of non-normative approaches to masculinity, and what they saw (a bit defensively) as feminist characterizations of masculinity as "unrelieved villainy and all men as agents of the patriarchy in more or less the same degree" (64), these sociologists attempted to carve out new models of gendered analysis in which individual men or men collectively were not all framed as equal agents of patriarchal oppression.

The emergent sociology of masculinity became a "critical study of men, their behaviors, practices, values and perspectives" (Whitehead and Barrett 2001, 14). These new sociologists of masculinity positioned themselves in opposition to earlier Parsonian theories of masculinity, proffering, not a single masculine "role," but rather the idea that masculinity is understandable only in a model of "multiple masculinities" (Connell 1995). Instead of focusing on masculinity as the male role, this model asserts that there are a variety of masculinities, which make sense only in hierarchical and contested relations with one another. R. W. Connell argues that men enact and embody different configurations of masculinity depending on their positions within a social hierarchy of power. *Hegemonic masculinity,* the type of gender practice that, in a given space and time, supports gender inequality, is at the top of this hierarchy. *Complicit masculinity* describes men who benefit from hegemonic masculinity but do not enact it; *subordinated masculinity* describes men who are oppressed by definitions of hegemonic masculinity, primarily gay men; *marginalized masculinity* describes men who may be positioned powerfully in terms of gender but not in terms of class or race. Connell, importantly, emphasizes that the content of these configurations of gender practice is not always and everywhere the same. Very few men, if any, are actually hegemonically masculine, but all men do benefit, to different extents, from this sort of definition of masculinity, a form of benefit Connell (1995) calls the "patriarchal dividend" (41).

This model of multiple masculinities has been enormously influential, inspiring countless studies that detail the ways different configurations of masculinity are promoted, challenged, or reinforced in given social situations. This research on how men do masculinity has provided insight into practices of masculinity in a wide range of social institutions, such as families (Coltrane 2001), schools (Francis and Skelton 2001; Gilbert 1998; Mac an Ghaill 1996; Parker 1996), the workplace (Connell 1998; Cooper 2000), the media (Craig 1992; Davies 1995), and sports (Curry 2004; Edley and Wetherell 1997; Majors 2001; Messner 2002). This focus on masculinity as what men do has spawned an industry of cataloguing "types" of masculinity: gay, black, Chicano, working class, middle class, Asian, gay

black, gay Chicano, white working class, militarized, transnational business, New Man, negotiated, versatile, healthy, toxic, counter, and cool masculinities, among others (Messner 2004b).

While Connell intends this model of masculinities to be understood as fluid and conflictual, the multiple masculinities model is more often used to construct static and reified typologies such as the ones listed by Michael Messner. These descriptions of masculinity are intended to highlight patterns of practice in which structure meets with identity and action, but they have the effect of slotting men into masculinity categories: a hegemonic man, a complicit man, a resistant man (or the multitude of ever-increasing types of masculinities catalogued above). While these masculinities may be posited as ideal types, they are sometimes difficult to use analytically without lapsing into a simplistic categorical analysis. Because of the emphasis on masculinities in the plural, a set of types some men can seemingly step in and out of at will, this model runs the risk of collapsing into an analysis of styles of masculinity, thereby deflecting attention from structural inequalities between men and women. In other words, we must always pay attention to power relations when we think in pluralities and diversities; otherwise we are simply left with a list of differences (Zinn and Dill 1996). Additionally, the category of "hegemonic masculinity" is so rife with contradictions it is small wonder that no man actually embodies it (Donaldson 1993). According to this model both a rich, slim, soft-spoken businessman and a poor, muscular, violent gang member might be described as hegemonically masculine. At the same time neither of them would really be hegemonically masculine, since the businessman would not be physically powerful and the poor gang member would lack claims on institutional gendered power. Because of some of these deployment problems, those studying masculinities have for some time called for a more sophisticated analysis of masculinity (Messner 1993; Morgan 1992).

To refine approaches to masculinity, researchers need to think more clearly about the implications of defining masculinity as what men or boys do. This definition conflates masculinity with the actions of those who have male bodies. Defining masculinity as "what men do" reifies biologized categories of male and female that are problematic and not necessarily discrete categories to begin with (Fausto-Sterling 1995). In the end, masculinity is framed as a social category based on an assumed biological difference that in itself is constituted by the very social category it purports to underlie. This is not to say that sociologists of masculinity are biological determinists, but by assuming that the male body is the location of masculinity their theories reify the assumed biological basis of gender. Recognizing that masculinizing discourses and practices extend beyond male bodies, this book traces the various ways masculinity is produced and manifested in relation to a multiplicity of bodies, spaces, and objects. That is, this book looks at masculinity as a variety of practices and discourses that can be mobilized by and applied to both boys and girls.

BRINGING IN SEXUALITY

Heeding the admonition of Carrigan, Connell, and Lee (1987) that "analysis of masculinity needs to be related as well to other currents in feminism" (64), I turn to interdisciplinary theorizing about the role of sexuality in the construction of gender identities. Building on studies of sexuality that demonstrate that sexuality is an organizing principle of social life, this book highlights intersections of masculinizing and sexualizing practices and discourses at River High.

Thinking about sexuality as an organizing principle of social life means that it is not just the property of individuals. Sexuality, in this sense, doesn't just indicate a person's sexual identity, whether he or she is gay or straight. Rather, sexuality is itself a form of power that exists regardless of an individual's sexual identity. Thinking about sexuality this way can be initially quite jarring. After all, usually we discuss sexuality as a personal identity or a set of private practices. However, researchers and theorists have increasingly argued that sexuality is a quite public part of social life (Foucault 1990). Though sexuality was initially studied as a set of private acts, and

eventually identities, by physicians and other medical professionals intent on discerning normal from abnormal sexuality, social theorists are now documenting the ways institutions, identities, and discourses interact with, are regulated by, and produce sexual meanings.

In this sense, *sexuality* refers to sex acts and sexual identities, but it also encompasses a range of meanings associated with these acts and identities. The meanings that vary by social class, location, and gender identity (Mahay, Laumann, and Michaels 2005) may be more important than the acts themselves (Weeks 1996). A good example of this is heterosexuality. While heterosexual desires or identities might feel private and personal, contemporary meanings of heterosexuality also confer upon heterosexual individuals all sorts of citizenship rights, so that heterosexuality is not just a private matter but one that links a person to certain state benefits. Similarly contemporary meanings of sexuality, particularly heterosexuality, for instance, eroticize male dominance and female submission (Jeffreys 1996, 75). In this way what seems like a private desire is part of the mechanisms through which the microprocesses of daily life actually foster inequality.

Interdisciplinary theorizing about sexuality has primarily taken the form of "queer theory." Like sociology, queer theory destabilizes the assumed naturalness of the social order (Lemert 1996). Queer theory moves the deconstructive project of sociology into new areas by examining much of what sociology sometimes takes for granted: "deviant" sexualities, sexual identities, sexual practices, sexual discourses, and sexual norms (Seidman 1996). In making the taken-for-granted explicit, queer theorists examine sexual power as it is embedded in different areas of social life and interrogate areas of the social world not usually seen as sexuality—such as the ways heterosexuality confers upon an individual a variety of citizenship rights (A. Stein and Plummer 1994). The logic of sexuality not only regulates intimate relations but also infuses social relations and social structures (S. Epstein 1994; Warner 1993).

. . . Queer theory draws on a postmodern approach to studying society that moves beyond traditional categories such as male/female, masculine/feminine, and straight/gay to focus instead on the instability of these categories. That is, we might think of "heterosexual" and "homosexual" as stable, opposing, and discrete identities, but really they are fraught with internal contradictions (Halley 1993). To this end, queer theory emphasizes multiple identities and multiplicity in general. Instead of creating knowledge about categories of sexual identity, queer theorists look to see how those categories themselves are created, sustained, and undone.

One of the ways a queer theory approach can bring studies of masculinity in line with other feminist theorizing is to uncouple the male body from definitions of masculinity. The masculinities literature, while attending to very real inequalities between gay and straight men, tends to look at sexuality as inherent in static identities attached to male bodies, not as a major organizing principle of social life (S. Epstein 1994; Warner 1993). As part of its deconstructive project, queer theory often points to disjunctures between pairings thought of as natural and inevitable. In doing so queer theorists may implicitly question some of the assumptions of the multiple masculinities model—specifically the assumption that masculinity is defined by the bodily practices of boys and men—by placing sexuality at the center of analysis. Eve Sedgwick (1995), one of the few theorists to address the problematic assumption of the centrality of the male body to academic discussions of masculinity, argues that sometimes masculinity has nothing to do with men and that men don't necessarily have anything to do with masculinity. As a result "it is important to drive a wedge in, early and often and if possible conclusively, between the two topics, masculinity and men, whose relation to one another it is so difficult not to presume" (12).

Assuming that masculinity is only about men weakens inquiries into masculinity. Therefore it is important to look at masculinizing processes outside the male body, not to catalogue a new type of masculinity, but to identify practices, rituals, and discourses that constitute masculinity. Doing so indicates the centrality of sexualized meanings to masculinity in relation to both male and female bodies.

Dislodging masculinity from a biological location is a productive way to highlight the social constructedness of masculinity and may even expose a latent sexism within the sociological literature in its assumption that masculinity, as a powerful social identity, is only the domain of men. Judith Kegan Gardiner (2003) points out in her review of gender and masculinity textbooks "the very different investments that men, including masculinity scholars, appear to have in preserving masculinity as some intelligible and coherent grounding of identity in comparison to the skepticism and distance shown by feminists towards femininity" (153). Indeed, gender scholars who study women have not been nearly as interested in femininity as scholars of men have been in masculinity.

It is not that bodies are unimportant. They are. Bodies are the vehicles through which we express gendered selves; they are also the matter through which social norms are made concrete. What is problematic is the unreflexive assumption of an embodied location for gender that echoes throughout the masculinities literature. Looking at masculinity as discourses and practices that can be mobilized by female bodies undermines the conflation of masculinity with an embodied state of maleness (Califia 1994; Halberstam 1998; Paechter 2006). Instead, this approach looks at masculinity as a recognizable configuration of gender practices and discourses.

Placing sexuality at the center of analysis highlights the "routinely unquestioned heteronormative expectations and proscriptions that exist as background context in contemporary U.S. culture," assumptions that "emerge when traditional normative gender boundaries are crossed" (Neilsen, Walden, and Kunkel 2000, 292). Examining these heteronormative structures and how masculine girls and feminine boys challenge them gets at contemporary constructions of masculinity in adolescence. Studying gender transgressions in adolescence provides empirical evidence to bolster and extend some of the claims of queer theory, an approach that often relies on literary or artistic examples for its data (Gamson and Moon 2004, 49).

RETHINKING MASCULINITY, SEXUALITY, AND BODIES

Attending to sexuality and its centrality to gendered identities opens insight into masculinity both as a process (Bederman 1995) and as a field through which power is articulated (Scott 1999) rather than as a never-ending list of configurations of practice enacted by specific bodies. My research indicates that masculinity is an identity that respondents think of as related to the male body but as not necessarily specific to the male body. Interviews with and observations of students at River High indicate that they recognize masculinity as an identity expressed through sexual discourses and practices that indicate dominance and control.[2]

As scholars of gender have demonstrated, gender is accomplished through day-to-day interactions (G. Fine 1989; Hochschild 1989; Thorne 2002; West and Zimmerman 1991). In this sense gender is the "activity of managing situated conduct in light of normative conceptions of attitudes and activities appropriate for one's sex category" (West and Zimmerman 1991, 127). People are supposed to act in ways that line up with their presumed sex. That is, we expect people we think are females to act like women and males to act like men. People hold other people accountable for "doing gender" correctly.

The queer theorist Judith Butler (1999) builds on this interactionist approach to gender, arguing that gender is something people accomplish through "a set of repeated acts within a highly rigid regulatory frame that congeal over time to produce the appearance of substance, of a natural sort of being" (43). That is, gender is not just natural, or something one is, but rather something we all produce through our actions. By repeatedly acting "feminine" or "masculine" we actually create those categories. Becoming gendered, becoming masculine or feminine, is a process.

Butler argues that gendered beings are created through processes of repeated invocation and repudiation. People constantly reference or invoke a gendered norm, thus making the norm seem like a timeless truth. Similarly, people continually repudiate a "constitutive outside" (Butler 1993, 3) in which is contained all that is cast out of a socially recognizable gender category. The "constitutive outside" is inhabited by what she calls "abject identities," unrecognizably and unacceptably gendered selves. The interactional accomplishment of gender in a Butlerian model consists, in part, of the continual iteration and repudiation of an abject identity. The abject identity must be constantly named to remind individuals of its power. Similarly, it must be constantly repudiated by individuals or groups so that they can continually affirm their identities as normal and as culturally intelligible. Gender, in this sense, is "constituted through the force of exclusion and abjection, one which produces a constitutive outside to the subject, an abjected outside, which is, after all, 'inside' the subject as its own founding repudiation" (Butler 1993, 3). This repudiation creates and reaffirms a "threatening specter" (3) of failed gender, the existence of which must be continually repudiated through interactional processes.

Informed by this interactionist approach to gender, in which gender is not just a quality of an individual but the result of interactional processes, this study examines masculinity as sexualized processes of confirmation and repudiation through which individuals demonstrate mastery over others. Building on the insights of the multiple masculinities literature, I emphasize that this definition of masculinity is not universal but local, age limited, and institutional and that other definitions of masculinity may be found in different locales and different times. Examining masculinity using Butler's theory of interactional accomplishment of gender indicates that the "fag" position is an "abject" position and, as such, is a "threatening specter" constituting contemporary American adolescent masculinity at River High. Similarly, drawing on Butler's concept of the constitution of gender through "repeated acts within a highly rigid regulatory frame" elucidates how seemingly "normal" daily interactions of male adolescence are actually ritualized interactions constituting masculinity. These repeated acts involve demonstrating sexual mastery and the denial of girls' subjectivity. The school itself sets the groundwork for boys' interactional rituals of repudiation and confirmation, like those illustrated in the opening vignette.

Butler also suggests ways to challenge an unequal gender order. Individuals who deliberately engage in gender practices that render them culturally unintelligible, such as practices that are at odds with their apparent sex category, challenge the naturalness and inevitability of a rigid gender order. Some girls at River High engage in precisely this sort of resistance by engaging in masculinizing processes. While challenging an unequal gender order at the level of interactions does not necessarily address larger structural inequalities, it is an important component of social change. That said, doing gender differently by engaging in gender practices not "appropriate" for one's sex category, such as drag, also runs the risk of reifying binary categories of gender. Resistance, in this model, is fraught with danger, since it is both an investment in gender norms and a subversion of them. Sometimes it challenges the gender order and sometimes it seems to bolster it.

[. . .]

NOTES

1. This is not to say that women don't possess this sort of subjectivity, but these qualities are what students at River High associate with masculinity.
2. While trying to retain the insight that there are multiple masculinities that vary by time and place, I self-consciously use the singular *masculinity* in this text because students at River talk about masculinity as a singular identity that involves practices and discourses of sexualized power and mastery.

REFERENCES

Bederman, Gail. 1995. *Manliness and Civilization: A Cultural History of Gender and Race in the United States, 1880–1917.* Chicago: University of Chicago Press.

Butler, Judith. 1993. *Bodies That Matter: On the Discursive Limits of "Sex."* New York: Routledge.

Butler, Judith. 1999. *Gender Trouble: Feminism and the Subversion of Identity.* New York: Routledge.

Califia, Pat. 1994. "Butch Desire." In *Dagger: On Butch Women,* edited by L. Burana and L. Roxie Due, 220–24. San Francisco: Cleis Press.

Carrigan, T., B. Connell, and J. Lee. 1987. "Towards a New Sociology of Masculinity." In *The Making of Masculinities: The New Men's Studies,* edited by H. Brod, 63–102. Boston: Allen and Unwin.

Chodorow, Nancy. 1978. *The Reproduction of Mothering: Psychoanalysis and the Sociology of Gender.* Berkeley: University of California Press.

Coltrane, Scott. 2001. "Selling the Indispensable Father." Paper presented at the conference "Pushing the Boundaries: New Conceptualizations of Childhood and Motherhood," Temple University, Philadelphia.

Connell, R. W. 1995. *Masculinities.* Berkeley: University of California Press.

Connell, R. W. 1998. "Masculinities and Globalization." *Men and Masculinities* 1, no. 1:3–23.

Cooper, Marianne. 2000. "Being the 'Go-to Guy': Fatherhood, Masculinity and the Organization of Work in Silicon Valley." *Qualitative Sociology* 23, no. 4:379–405.

Craig, Steve. 1992. *Men, Masculinity, and the Media.* Research on Men and Masculinities Series 1. Newbury Park, CA: Sage Publications.

Curry, Timothy Jon. 2004. "Fraternal Bonding in the Locker Room: A Profeminist Analysis of Talk about Competition and Women." In *Men's Lives,* edited by Michael Messner and Michael Kimmel, 204–17. Boston: Pearson.

Davies, Jude. 1995. "'I'm the Bad Guy?' *Falling Down* and White Masculinity in Hollywood." *Journal of Gender Studies* 4, no. 2:145–52.

Davis, Angela. 1981. *Women, Race and Class.* New York: Vintage Books, 1981.

Dinnerstein, Dorothy. 1976. *The Mermaid and the Minotaur: Sexual Arrangements and Human Malaise.* New York: Harper Perennial.

Donaldson, Mike. 1993. "What Is Hegemonic Masculinity?" *Theory and Society* 22, no. 5:643–57.

Edley, Nigel, and Margaret Wetherell. 1997. "Jockeying for Position: The Construction of Masculine Identities." *Discourse and Society* 8, no. 2:203–17.

Epstein, Steven. 1994. "A Queer Encounter." *Sociological Theory* 12:188–202.

Fausto-Sterling, Ann. 1995. "How to Build a Man." In *Constructing Masculinity,* edited by Maurice Berger, Brian Wallis, and Simon Watson, 127–34. New York: Routledge.

Fine, Gary Alan. 1989. "The Dirty Play of Little Boys." In *Men's Lives,* edited by Michael Kimmel and Michael Messner, 171–79. New York: Macmillan.

Foucault, Michel. 1990. *The History of Sexuality.* Vol. 1. Translated by Robert Hurley. New York: Vintage Books.

Francis, Becky, and Christine Skelton. 2001. "Men Teachers and the Construction of Heterosexual Masculinity in the Classroom." *Sex Education* 1, no. 1:9–21.

Gamson, Joshua, and Dawne Moon. 2004. "The Sociology of Sexualities: Queer and Beyond." *Annual Review of Sociology* 30:47–64.

Gardiner, Judith Kegan. 2003. "Gender and Masculinity Texts: Consensus and Concerns for Feminist Classrooms." *NWSA Journal* 15, no. 1:147–57.

Gilbert, Rob. 1998. *Masculinity Goes to School.* New York: Routledge.

Halberstam, Judith. 1998. *Female Masculinity.* Durham: Duke University Press.

Halley, Janet E. 1993. "The Construction of Heterosexuality." In *Fear of a Queer Planet: Queer Politics and Social Theory,* edited by Michael Warner, 82–102. Minneapolis: University of Minnesota Press.

Hartmann, Heidi. 1976. "Capitalism, Patriarchy and Job Segregation by Sex." *Signs* 1:137–70.

Hochschild, Arlie Russell. 1989. *The Second Shift.* New York: Avon.

Jaggar, Alison. 1983. *Feminist Politics and Human Nature.* Totowa, NJ: Rowman and Allanheld.

Jeffreys, Sheila. 1996. "Heterosexuality and the Desire for Gender." In *Theorising Heterosexuality,* edited by Diane Richardson, 75–90. Buckingham: Open University Press.

Kimmel, Michael S. 1996. *Manhood in America: A Cultural History.* New York: Free Press.

Lemert, Charles. 1996. "Series Editor's Preface." In *Queer Theory/Sociology,* edited by Steven Seidman, vii–xi. Cambridge: Blackwell.

Mac an Ghaill, Martain. 1996. "What about the Boys? Schooling, Class and Crisis Masculinity." *Sociological Review* 44, no. 3:381–97.

Mahay, Jenna, Edward O. Laumann, and Stuart Michaels. 2005. "Race, Gender and Class in Sexual Scripts." In *Speaking of Sexuality: Interdisciplinary Readings,* edited by J. Kenneth Davidson Sr. and Nelwyn B. Moore, 144–58. Los Angeles: Roxbury.

Majors, Richard. 2001. "Cool Pose: Black Masculinity and Sports." In *The Masculinities Reader,* edited by Stephen Whitehead and Frank Barrett, 208–17. Cambridge: Polity Press.

Messner, Michael. 1993. "'Changing Men' and Feminist Politics in the United States." *Theory and Society* 22, no. 5:723–27.

Messner, Michael. 2002. *Taking the Field: Women, Men and Sports.* Minneapolis: University of Minnesota Press.

Messner, Michael. 2004b. "On Patriarchs and Losers: Rethinking Men's Interests." Paper presented at the Berkeley Journal of Sociology Conference: Rethinking Gender, University of California, Berkeley, March.

Morgan, David. 1992. *Discovering Men.* New York: Routledge.

Neilsen, Joyce McCarl, Glenda Walden, and Charlotte A. Kunkel. 2000. "Gendered Heteronormativity: Empirical Illustrations in Everyday Life." *Sociological Quarterly* 41, no. 2:283–96.

Paechter, Carrie. 2006. "Masculine Femininities/Feminine Masculinities: Power, Identities and Gender." *Gender and Education* 18, no. 3:253–63.

Parker, Andrew. 1996. "The Construction of Masculinity within Boys' Physical Education." *Gender and Education* 8, no. 2:141–57.

Parsons, Talcott. 1954. *Essays in Sociological Theory.* New York: Free Press.

Pleck, Joseph H. 1987. "The Theory of Male Sex-Role Identity: Its Rise and Fall, 1936 to the Present." In *The Making of Masculinities: The New Men's Studies,* edited by Harry Brod, 21–38. Boston: Allen and Unwin.

Rosaldo, Michelle, and Louise Lamphere. 1974. "Introduction." In *Woman, Culture and Society,* edited by Michelle Rosaldo and Louise Lamphere. Stanford: Stanford University Press.

Rubin, Gayle. 1984. "Thinking Sex: Notes for a Radical Theory of the Politics of Sexuality." In *Pleasure and Danger: Exploring Female Sexuality,* edited by Carol Vance, 267–319. London: Pandora.

Scott, Joan Wallach. 1999. *Gender and the Politics of History.* New York: Columbia University Press.

Sedgwick, Eve Kosofsky. 1995. "'Gosh, Boy George, You Must Be Awfully Secure in Your Masculinity!'" In *Constructing Masculinity,* edited by Maurice Berger, Brian Wallis, and Simon Watson, 11–20. New York: Routledge.

Seidman, Steven. 1996. "Introduction." In *Queer Theory/Sociology,* edited by Steven Seidman, 1–29. Oxford: Blackwell.

Stein, Arlene, and Ken Plummer. 1994. "'I Can't Even Think Straight': Theory and the Missing Sexual Revolution in Sociology." *Sociological Theory* 12, no. 2:178–87.

Thorne, Barrie. 2002. "Gender and Interaction: Widening the Conceptual Scope." In *Gender in Interaction: Perspectives on Femininity and Masculinity in Ethnography and Discourse,* edited by Bettina Baron and Helga Kotthoff, 3–18. Philadelphia: John Benjamins.

Warner, Michael. 1993. "Introduction." In *Fear of a Queer Planet: Queer Politics and Social Theory,* edited by Michael Warner, vii–xxxi. Minneapolis: University of Minnesota Press.

Weeks, Jeffrey. 1996. "The Construction of Homosexuality." In *Queer Theory/Sociology,* edited by Steven Seidman, 41–63. Cambridge: Blackwell.

West, Candace, and Don Zimmerman. 1991. "Doing Gender." In *The Social Construction of Gender,* edited by Judith Lorber, 102–21. Newbury Park, CA: Sage Publications.

Whitehead, Stephen, and Frank Barrett. 2001. "The Sociology of Masculinity." In *The Masculinities Reader,* edited by Stephen Whitehead and Frank Barrett, 1–26. Malden, MA: Blackwell.

Zinn, Maxine Baca, and Bonnie Thornton Dill. 1996. "Theorizing Difference from Multiracial Feminism." *Feminist Studies* 22, no. 2:321–31.

6. • *Judith Kegan Gardiner*

FRIENDSHIP, GENDER THEORIES, AND SOCIAL CHANGE (NEW)

Judith Kegan Gardiner is a professor of English and of gender and women's studies, emerita, at the University of Illinois at Chicago. Her publications include two monographs, three edited collections of critical essays, and more than one hundred essays and chapters. Recent publications, including the one written specifically for this collection, discuss feminist theories, masculinity studies, contemporary women writers, popular culture, and pedagogy. She is a member of the editorial collective of the interdisciplinary journal *Feminist Studies* and the editor of the forthcoming volume *Approaches to Teaching Alison Bechdel's* Fun Home, to be published by the Modern Language Association.

A contemporary online cartoon pictures three young white women facing each other across a table. They say, "Oh my God I love you guys." The caption reads: "Girl friendship: lasts 2–3 years." The accompanying illustration shows two young white men sitting side by side with video game controllers in their hands. One says, "asshole," and the other says, "bitch," presumably to each other. The caption reads: "Guy friendships: lasts forever" ([sic] funsubstance. com). Despite its inaccuracy, the cartoon reinforces long-standing ideas that men and women, and their same-sex friendships, are not only different but opposite, with contrasting emotions as well as physical expressions. In Geoffrey Greif's terms, men's friendships are "shoulder to shoulder" while women's are "face to face" (134).

Today masculinity studies scholars still polarize men's and women's friendships according to twentieth-century theories of gender and psychology influenced by Freudian psychoanalysis (Kimmel).

Much current ethnography and sociology continues to endorse these gendered oppositions, echoed by contemporary popular culture (Felmlee et al.). However, recent research shows convergences between men's and women's friendships, particularly for young adults. Looking at American men's and women's friendships in the contexts of gender theory and social change, I describe some paradoxical developments. On the one hand, Americans experience friendship as a realm of freedom from the restrictions of families and workplaces. On the other, I claim that friendships usually reinforce gender binaries and so reassure individuals that they are performing gender appropriately. Thus while friendships seem freer than other social connections, they flourish chiefly through what social scientists call *homophily*—between people freely choosing to associate with those of similar race, ethnicity, religion, social class, gender, and sexual orientation. Despite this familiar picture, significant changes are indeed taking place concerning who forms friendships with whom, how friendships reinforce or disrupt gender binaries, what emotions are involved, and how friendships are depicted in popular culture.

Twentieth-century cultural feminist theorists, who see men and women as deeply different, described male psychology as autonomous, competitive, and defensive, in contrast to interdependent and empathic women's psychologies. In 1978 Nancy Chodorow argued that mother-dominated childrearing in households of stay-at-home mothers and employed fathers produced these asymmetries. Girls identified with their nurturing mothers while boys struggled to separate from them in order to gain masculine independence. Dual parenting in which both parents shared, she proposed, would produce more autonomous women and more empathic men. In 1980 Adrienne Rich claimed that all women exist on a "lesbian continuum," whatever their sexual preferences, so that women naturally bond with other women, while men are loyal to other men and masculine institutions. Such theories created a framework for understanding women's relationships with other women as different from men's friendships with men.

Family structures in the United States have changed dramatically since the post–World War II norm of white breadwinner fathers and housewife mothers, and male and female personalities have converged in some respects, as predicted by theorists like Chodorow. Some women of color are raising children without a father present. Later marriage and childbearing, a divorce rate of almost 50 percent, and longer life expectancies have led to over 27 percent of Americans now living in single person households ("Marriage and Divorce"). As more Americans stay single longer, these demographic changes may encourage sexual relationships outside of marriage; open lifestyles for lesbian, gay, and transgender individuals; and desires for community and friendship outside traditional nuclear families—all changes supported by those feminists who believe men and women are fundamentally similar.

Most research on American friendships is based on college students, so scholarship is skewed toward middle-class, well-educated, predominantly white youth. For many, college relationships continue into years of relative freedom from family obligations but also into precarious working lives. Racial, ethnic, and class differences also affect friendship choices. For example, working-class African American men form closer, more mutually supportive ties than their upwardly mobile peers (Franklin). For masculinities scholar Michael Kimmel, homophobia crucially inhibits men's friendships: "The single cardinal rule of manhood, the one from which all the other characteristics—wealth, power, status, strength, physicality—are derived is to offer constant proof that you are not gay" (50). In contrast, Eric Anderson contends that men's friendships today are less homophobic. As more people openly identify as gay or lesbian, gay/straight friendships have also increased, a change that may inspire greater emotional intimacy in friendships between heterosexual men (Nardi). Aging also affects friendships. As life expectancies lengthen, there are more lonely old men, while elderly women socialize more. "Doing gender" also means "doing friendship," and friendship becomes a way of doing gender (West and Zimmerman).

Changes in technology and workplaces are re-shaping friendships for both men and women. Fewer Americans work in settings like factories with large numbers of fellow workers, while more people face screens on which they can develop online friendships and find groups with similar tastes (Gardiner). Online, dominant tendencies to associate only with one's own demographic may be countered by cross-gendered avatars or reinforced by niche-targeted websites. Alison Winch claims that for the social network Facebook, friendships are "its content, its market, and its worth," reinforcing the connections between friendship and traditional gender categories (Winch 191).

Cross-culturally, friendships are bound by fewer constraints than marriage and kinship, although some societies have strong conventions for friendships shaped by blood brotherhood or the mutual aid expected by Chinese urban immigrants from the same villages (Bell and Coleman). In some situations friendships overlap with sexual relations, from American "friends with benefits" to Caribbean "Mati work," in which working-class Afro-Caribbean women are sexually intimate with women friends (Wekker). Friendships may also overlap with kinship structures, as with Mexican "comadres" (López). And Americans often agree with political theorist Robert Putnam, who says, "everyone needs a best friend; I am blessed to be married to mine." (213). All these varying aspects of friendship tend to reinforce traditional gender boundaries.

Using a materialist feminist analysis, Winch asserts that women's friendships in the US and the UK now incorporate attitudes shaped by contemporary capitalism as women bond in consumer activities like shopping and succumb to the commercial "thinspiration" that says that losing weight "empowers" "girlfriend culture" (50). Men, in turn, bond through sports, cars, and videogames, all parts of the capitalist marketplace. Popular advice books claim friendships boost people's health and well-being but also describe conflict and betrayal in women's friendships, and competition in men's, while both genders seek loyalty and intimacy (Bertsche). Girls' friendships provide spaces to try out feelings and shape identities. Boys' friendships reveal stress through joking and sports, while younger boys are more intimate than homophobic teens (Way). Such differences in friendship patterns become built into people's emotional makeup.

In the late twentieth century, US popular culture paid fresh attention to mixed-sex groups of young adult friends, as in the television programs *Seinfeld* (1989–1998) and *Friends* (1994–2004). These programs exposed the unstable, often comically immature romances of both male and female characters, yet the supportive, mixed-sex friendship groups remained intact. In these programs, families moved to the margins and friendships to the center of what it means to be a man or woman in the city. A more recent television trend features female-centric sitcoms like *Girls* and *Broad City*, where the central women oscillate between responsibility—looking out for one another—and irresponsibility—like swiping strangers' ice cream cones—in behavior previously attributed mostly to young men.

Two postmillennial movie comedies illustrate changing representations of men's and women's friendships and of continuing gender binaries in popular culture: the male buddy film *The Hangover* (2009) and the "chick flick" *Bridesmaids* (2011). Both films shape their plots around difficulties preceding a friend's wedding, but marriage is not the movies' main goal or even shown as desirable. Both films revel in regression to childish messes, spontaneity, and rebellions against middle-class propriety shown in swearing, drug and alcohol use, and extramarital sexual behavior. Neither movie prioritizes families or heterosexual relationships, instead emphasizing the importance of same-sex friendship, so anchoring a sense of gender cohesion at the same time that women try out traditionally male behavior and men get to bond intimately.

For men more than women, marriage popularly represents the end of boyhood camaraderie and the taking on of adult responsibility. *The Hangover* begins with the perfect alibi for bad behavior—drug-induced amnesia following a night of partying during which the groom gets lost. The three groomsmen bond more closely as they improbably defeat Asian gangsters, find a tiger, and win big in Las Vegas casinos. One man tenderly straps a found baby to his chest, casually taking on a traditionally feminine nurturing role. In *Bridesmaids*, similarly, heterosexual relationships are subordinate to same-sex friendships and rivalries. The main character, Annie, a single woman, loses her bakery business to economic recession and then loses her job in a jewelry store. She is envious of the coming wedding of her best friend Lillian, then disappointed when Lillian replaces her as maid of honor with the rich wife of her fiancé's boss. Annie and the boss's wife vie for best friend status with the bride, establishing the emotional core of the film. The richer woman arranges designer dresses and lavish travel for the bridesmaids, but Annie's noncommercial worth is shown by her homemade gift of a photo album picturing her childhood adventures with Lillian. Finally, the wedding proceeds without a hitch, and all three women unite in friendship.

Thus the films portray their characters as subject to the emotionally intense female friendships and competitive male friendships predicted by cultural feminist theory. However, whereas former gender theories contrasted men's and women's friendships in accordance with supposedly opposing psychologies, here the women are also competitive and the men nurturing. Both movies showcase young adults of both sexes united by friendship loyalties and sharing feelings of envy and competition as well as triumphs and pleasures.

Friendship remains more important in many contemporary lives than current gender theories attest, and these changes have been little studied. Friendship continues to be only slightly theorized even though friendships in fact provide significant emotional support, especially for young adults undergoing the stresses of insecure economies, more mobile relationships, and confusing identity issues related to gender and sexuality. Raewyn Connell reminds us that because "dichotomous gender symbolism" is still so strong globally, it is "not surprising that when researchers look at sex and gender, what they see is difference, even now when the differences are minor, decreasing, and variable in their social contexts and emotional reverberations" (44). Although people of all ages benefit from friendships, friendship is increasingly associated with youth, leisure, same-sex bonding, and experiences of consumption within shared markets of sports, travel, and shopping. While friendships bless people with the pleasures of similarity and comradeship, I argue that a major function of the institution of friendship is that it reassures individuals that they are performing gender appropriately and so reinforces society's established gender binaries and other social boundaries. On the other hand, contemporary friendships are indeed changing shape. Peter Nardi claims that for gay men friendships "mean more and last longer" than romantic relationships (3). More LGBT people are openly enjoying each other's company and also forming gay/straight friendships. Ideals for friendship are converging for both genders, and cross-gender friendships are increasing (Felmlee, et al.). The convergence in male and female psychologies, personalities, and life experiences that some feminist theorists seek has only partly occurred (Lorber). Young women swear and drink more like their male peers, and young men may be more comfortable than previously with physical intimacy and self-disclosure between friends. Thus today's social forces simultaneously expand liberatory possibilities for American friendships and also conservatively reinforce established gender hierarchies.

Current research shows that men's and women's friendships are not as polarized as the cartoon beginning this essay pronounced, while such popular representations continue both to inhibit social change and to hide those changes that have in fact occurred. Friendships among both men and women may be diminishing somewhat in number and duration as people move more often, change employers, grow dispirited when unemployed or cheerfully overextended juggling childcare and work (Putnam).

Liberal feminists may welcome the convergence in gendered lifestyles; cultural feminists may mourn the loss of female-specific activities; materialist feminists and theorists of color point out the economic and cultural contexts shaping such changes.

American friendships cushion the constraints of more structured institutions like the workplace and the family. They support American ideologies of individual freedom, autonomy, and freedom of association and play a large part in individual happiness. Through the tendency of people to form friendships mostly with people situated like themselves, they consolidate social hierarchies of power and privilege and the emotions that accompany them, including envy, competitiveness, and affection. Yet friendships are now becoming less polarized between the sexes and more encouraging of flexible attitudes toward gender and sexuality.

WORKS CITED

Anderson, Eric. *Inclusive Masculinity: The Changing Nature of Masculinities*. Routledge, 2009.

Bell, Sandra, and Simon Coleman, editors. *The Anthropology of Friendship*. Bloomsbury Academic, 1999.

Bertsche, Rachel. *MWF Seeking BFF: My Yearlong Search for a New Best Friend*. Ballantine Books, 2011.

Chodorow, Nancy. *The Reproduction of Mothering: Psychoanalysis and the Sociology of Gender*. U of California P, 1978.

Connell, Raewyn. *Gender in World Perspective*. 2nd ed., Polity Press, 2009.

Felmlee, Diane, Elizabeth Sweet, and H. Colleen Sinclair. "Gender Rules: Same- and Cross-Gender Friendship Norms," *Sex Roles*, vol. 66, 2012, pp. 518–29.

Franklin, Clyde. "'Hey Home –Yo, Bro': Friendship among Black Men." *Men's Friendships*, edited by Peter M. Nardi, Sage Publications, 1992, pp. 201–14.

Gardiner, Judith Kegan. "South Park, Blue Men, Anality, and Market Masculinity." *Men and Masculinities*, vol. 2, no. 3, Jan. 2000, pp. 251–71.

"Friendship: Men vs. Women." Funsubstance, funsubstance.com/fun/7943/friendship-men-vs-women/. Accessed 7 July 2015.

Greif, Geoffrey L. *Buddy System: Understanding Male Friendships*. Oxford UP, 2009.

Kimmel, Michael. *Guyland: The Perilous World where Boys Become Men*. HarperCollins, 2008.

López, Adriana, editor. *Count on Me: Tales of Sisterhoods and Fierce Friendships*. Atria Books, 2012.

Lorber, Judith. *Breaking the Bowls: Degendering and Feminist Change*. W. W. Norton, 1995.

"Marriage and Divorce." American Psychological Association, 2015, www.apa.org/marriage.

Nardi, Peter M. *Gay Men's Friendships: Invincible Communities*. Chicago UP, 1999.

Putnam, Robert D. *Bowling Alone: The Collapse and Revival of American Community*. Simon and Schuster, 2000.

Rich, Adrienne. "Compulsory Heterosexuality and Lesbian Existence." *Signs*, vol. 5, no. 4, 1980, pp. 631–60.

Way, Niobe. *Deep Secrets: Boys' Friendships and the Crisis of Connection*. Harvard UP, 2011.

Wekker, Gloria. "What's Identity Got to Do with It? Rethinking Identity in Light of Mati Work in Suriname." *Female Desires: Same-Sex and Transgender Practices across Cultures*, edited by Evelyn Blackwood and Saskia E. Wieringa. Columbia UP, 1999, pp. 119–38.

Winch, Alison. *Girlfriends and Postfeminist Sisterhood*. Palgrave Macmillan, 2013.

West, Candace, and Don H. Zimmerman. "Doing Gender." *Gender & Society*, vol. 1, no. 2, 1987, pp. 125–51.

7. • *Paisley Currah*

STEPPING BACK, LOOKING OUTWARD:
Situating Transgender Activism and Transgender Studies (2008)

Paisley Currah, a professor of political science at Brooklyn College and the City University of New York, is a founding editor of *Trans Studies Quarterly* (Duke University Press); the coauthor of two articles that explore the intersections of gender, sexuality, law, and LGBT studies, and coeditor of two books *Transgender Rights* (University of Minnesota Press, 2006) and *Corpus: An Interdisciplinary Reader on Bodies and Knowledge* (Palgrave, 2011). His current book, *The United States of Sex: Legislating, Litigating, and Regulating (Trans)Gender Identities*, is forthcoming with New York University Press. The reading included here was published in *Sexuality Research and Social Policy* (2008) and brings together leading voices in the field to ask some of the most pressing questions about the connections between transgender scholarship and activism.

. . . With this roundtable, . . . we step back and consider the broader outlines of the activism—usually branded in LGBT communities and, increasingly, in the popular press as the transgender rights movement—that has challenged not only the state's enforcement of the gender binary but also its power to do so. My coeditor and I were interested in eliciting a dialogue that contemplated this movement relationally: How does this movement articulate with other movements for social justice, such as antiracist work? Can it be framed in relation to analogous struggles for gender self-determination in locations outside the United States without merely exporting the Western notion of *transgender*? Have the notions that gender is also racialized, that racial categories are also enforced through gender norms, influenced the policy goals of the movement and, if so, how? How might the relationship between the movement's past, its present, and its future be understood?

Finally, we wanted to take this opportunity to reflect on the relation between the newly emerging academic field of transgender studies and its central object of study—the challenges by gender-nonconforming people to traditional gender normativities. . . . The last decade has witnessed the materialization of this interdisciplinary field with conferences, special issues of journals, and the publication of *The Transgender Studies Reader* (Stryker & Whittle, 2006) and Transgender Rights (Currah, Juang, & Minter, 2006). Despite these inroads, the place of transgender studies, especially work outside of the humanities that does not construct trans subjects as pathological, remains tenuous in academia.

[. . .]

Nonetheless, the field is destined to grow. We hope that growth will be in locations that provide more permanent institutional support; even without that support, however, transgender studies practitioners will continue to carve out spaces for themselves to research and write about transgender communities. The configuration of the relationship between transgender studies and transgender activism, then, is of central concern. How immediately responsive should this academic area of inquiry be to the needs of those located in the midst of activists' struggles? Who should frame the research questions? What can be learned from the relationship between other areas—such as ethnic studies and disability studies—that have sprung largely from social movements?

[. . .]

This roundtable conversation with Kris Hayashi, Matt Richardson, and Susan Stryker took place in structured e-mail exchanges between January and March 2007. Responses are presented in the order they were written. Kris Hayashi was unable to respond to the third question.

What does the emerging trans rights movement—if it is a movement—look like and how does it fit into a broader struggle for social justice domestically and globally? What key coalitional opportunities are yet to be exploited by trans activists and our allies?

Susan Stryker: As a historian, I tend to look to the past as a way of situating myself in the present. Glancing into the rearview mirror to survey the twentieth century, it certainly appears that we have a trans movement today—however polyvocal, multidirectional, and contradictory it might appear when we are involved with it on a day-to-day basis.

Figuring out when a movement for trans rights begins is a tricky proposition, a question perhaps of interest primarily to historians. People who do not fit currently conventional and dominant patterns of relating a gendered sense of self to a sexed embodiment are pervasive throughout history and across cultures; the visibility of such people to us, however, as well as our desire to connect with them as ancestors and kindred spirits, is better evidence of what Eurocentric modernity perceives as noteworthy than of essential, transhistorical, transcultural, transgender identities. Not all of those who have been in social locations we're tempted to call transgendered have had oppositional relationships to their conventional culture. Still, researchers have turned up many historical examples of such gender-variant people pushing back, sometimes with inspiring levels of success, both individually and collectively, against the cultural gender norms that marginalize them from fully and freely participating in the benefits and responsibilities of social life. But to what extent can this episodic resistance be construed as a movement? When, and under what circumstances, can we start talking about *trans* people?

Personal identities rooted in notions of transness, crossing, inversion, and reversal start turning up in subcultural and medicolegal discourses around the middle of the nineteenth century, often in relation to overlapping categories of homosexuality and intersexuality. It's not clear exactly when large numbers of people began to organize their experiences of self and the world through these trans categories, when they began to think of themselves as specific and peculiar kinds of persons who had an interest in coming together as a community, or when they started to think of their identity-based social groups as a basis for political action. Answering these questions requires further research into the shift from acts to identities, but it's pretty clear that the enabling conditions for a political movement advocating for the civil rights of a significantly disenfranchised minority of trans people were beginning to coalesce by the late nineteenth and early twentieth centuries.

[. . .]

By the 1960s, the fledgling transgender movement was beginning to diversify. . . . By the middle of the decade, socially marginalized transgender women in San Francisco, who routinely experienced discrimination and harassment from the police when they gathered at a favorite late-night hangout in the Tenderloin neighborhood where many of them worked as prostitutes, were sufficiently politicized to band together and fight back against their oppression. This uprising, the Compton's Cafeteria Riot of August 1966, was part of a wave of increasingly militant resistance on the part of transgender street people that included street-fighting outside Cooper's Donut Stand in Los Angeles in 1959 and the Dewey's Lunch Counter sit-ins and picketing in Philadelphia in 1965.

The Compton's Riot stands out from these other instances because the resistance there was sparked by the formation of a political group, Vanguard, composed of queer street kids, hustlers, and queens, and also because it resulted in the formation of the first transsexual advocacy and support groups—Conversion Our Goal (COG), California Advancement for Transsexuals (CATS), the National Sexual-Gender Identification Council, the National Transsexual Counseling Unit, and the Transsexual Counseling Service—all formed before 1973. These San Francisco groups, which worked to change polices, practices, and public opinion, as well as provide peer support, were soon joined by similar groups in New York and Los Angeles, such as the Street Transvestite Action Revolutionaries (STAR), and the Transsexual Activist Organization (TAO). By the middle of the 1970s, as female-to-male (FTM) individuals became more involved in social-change activism, a new cohort of organizations and publications had emerged that included the FTM-oriented Labyrinth Foundation in New York, *Metamorphosis* in Toronto, and the Renaissance group in Southern California. By the end of the 1970s, in spite of increasing estrangement between transgender groups and gay, lesbian, and feminist movements, the groundwork had been established for a transgender movement. Due to the devastating impact of the AIDS epidemic in the 1980s, however, and because of transphobia within progressive political moments, it would be another decade before the foundation laid in the 1960s and 1970s would sustain a larger movement.

Since the early 1990s, the trans movement has undergone a growth spurt of historic proportions. A more single-issue political focus on transgender-specific needs, such as changing gender designation on personal identification documents or gaining access to medical and psychological services related to changing sex, has blossomed into a multifaceted movement, one that increasingly addresses structural social inequalities and finds powerful and creative ways of linking transgender issues with those of other groups. A favorite example of how transgender issues can be articulated differently in the present than they typically have been in the past has to do

with identification documents—without appropriate identification, people who live in a gender other than the one they were assigned to at birth become undocumented workers who experience greater difficulties crossing borders, are subject to higher levels of surveillance, and are more at risk for state-initiated personal violence. People in the United States who cross gender borders, regardless of where they were born and how they make their living, have a common stake with other sorts of migrants who work without documentation. They have a common stake with those who are profiled, whose movements are restricted, and who become targets of border control for reasons other than gender. It is the same power of state that has deployed itself against us all, a power that attempts to limit our access to the means of life, that gives us a motive for resistance.

Contemporary transgender activism also presents new opportunities at a global level for resisting homonormative, neoliberal strategies that collaborate with global capital. Transgender activism in decades past, particularly when it has been self-consciously queer-identified, has typically sought to ally with gay and lesbian political causes—understandably so, given the long history of interrelated sociocultural formation and the greater resources and political clout of the gay and lesbian organizations. But as gay liberation drifts (seemingly inexorably) toward a consumerist quietism that accepts a gay place at the table of capitalist abundance without asking why so many of the hungry people in the streets are there because they are classed as deviant, the transgender movement should carefully reassess how closely it wants to be associated with such a homosexual agenda. The exclusion in late 2007 of transgender people from the proposed federal Employment Non-Discrimination Act (2007), which was revised to cover sexual orientation only rather than also including gender identity or expression, serves to highlight this potential rift. Gay and lesbian politics are not necessarily synonymous with progressive politics. What are the underlying norms, manners, modes of comportment, and dispositions that allow certain kinds of ostensibly queer expression to appear respectable and acceptable while other forms remain abject? Such phrases as *socioeconomic class, physical ability and appearance, skin color,* and *transgender status,* among others, spring to mind.

Transgender activism can function as a vital critique of this new homonormativity. It brings into visibility at least one incipient norm present in U.S. gay and lesbian political movements since the 1950s—that is, the extent to which these gay and lesbian social formations have predicated their minority sexual-orientation identities on the gender-normative notions of *man* and *woman* that homosexual subcultures tend to share with the heteronormative societies of Eurocentric modernity. When this gender-normative, assimilationist brand of homosexuality circulates internationally with the privileges of its first-world point of origin, it all too readily becomes the primary template through which human rights are secured, or resources for living are accessed, by people rooted in nonheteronormative formations of sex-gender-sexuality that have developed from non-Eurocentric traditions in diverse locations around the world—*gay,* in other words, has the power to colonize. *Transgender* poses a similar risk, but to the extent that transgender activism can distinguish itself from homonormative neoliberalism, it can help create a different set of openings for resisting the homogenizing forces of global capital than those that have circulated through the categories lesbian, gay, or homosexual.

Kris Hayashi: I appreciate Susan starting us off with the history of our communities' activism and organizing; I also believe it's important to recognize, remember, and honor that our communities as trans and gender-nonconforming (TGNC) people have organized and fought back against injustice throughout history—individually and collectively, as part of trans movements and as part of many other movements both within and outside of the United States. . . .

The trans movement in the United States today is, as are most movements, diverse, multifaceted, and continually changing and shifting. If we are looking at an overall picture of those working individually and collectively to meet the needs of TGNC communities and fight for justice for TGNC communities, this picture is broad. It encompasses a wide range of

structures and organization including, but not limited to groups and projects that are part of larger organizations such as TransJustice, a TGNC organizing project for people of color; LGBT organizations with strong TGNC leadership reflected in the work of the organization, such as the Center for Lesbian and Gay Studies, FIERCE!, and Q-TEAM (the latter two are both organizing projects for lesbian, gay, bisexual, two-spirit, transgender, and queer youth of color); various grassroots groups such as Transsistahs and Transbrothas, a group of African American transgender people in Kentucky who organize a national conference; communities within the House Ball scene; local nonprofits, such as the Sylvia Rivera Law Project, the Transgender, Gender Variant, and Intersex Justice Project; and a few national nonprofits, such as the National Center for Transgender Equality. Additionally, this picture includes the countless numbers of individual TGNC people who fight injustice and discrimination through daily interaction with institutions and communities and the various web-based forums and electronic mailing lists. These organizations, groups, and individuals engage in multiple strategies including direct services, community building, advocacy, education, academics, leadership development, cultural work, legal services, and organizing.

Yet, the need of TGNC communities is much greater than the resources that exist. Funding for TGNC work is limited because few funders include TGNC communities within their funding. LGBT organizations in general have not prioritized the needs of TGNC communities and, within other social justice organizations, the needs of TGNC communities are often invisible.

Moreover, it is still the case that our communities are pathologized and viewed as in need of services, not as leaders and organizers. Thus, there is a clear lack of programs focused on organizing and leadership development. Furthermore, there are only a handful of efforts that prioritize the leadership of TGNC people with the least access to resources, such as communities of color, low-income communities, immigrants, youth, elders, rural communities, differently abled individuals, and so forth.

The answer to the question of how the trans movement fits into a broader struggle for social justice domestically and globally is affected by the ways in which racism, patriarchy, economic injustice, ageism, ableism, and geography have shaped our priorities. TGNC communities include communities of color, immigrants, youth, elders, rural communities, and differently abled communities. Thus, how a trans movement fits into a broader struggle is clear. For example, as TGNC communities of color, we view our struggles as one and the same as broader struggles for social justice domestically and directly connected—if not the same as—struggles for social justice globally. Members of TransJustice, a community organizing group led and run by TGNC people of color that is part of ALP, stated in its *Points of Unity,* a document written for the 2006 Trans Day of Action in New York City:

> As Trans and Gender Non-Conforming (TGNC) people of color, we see that our struggle today is directly linked to many struggles here in the US and around the world. We view The 2nd Annual Trans Day of Action for Social and Economic Justice on June 23, 2006, as a day to stand in solidarity with all peoples and movements fighting against oppression and inequality. We view this action as following the legacy of our Trans People of Color warriors, such as Sylvia Rivera and Marsha P. Johnson, and others who with extreme determination fought not only for the rights of all trans and gender non-conforming people, but also were on the frontlines for the liberation of all oppressed peoples.

> (TransJustice, 2006)

[. . .]

The Transgender, Gender Variant and Intersex Justice Project (TGIJP) is a legal services and community-organizing project that is primarily led and run by TGNC people of color and that prioritizes the leadership of TGI prisoners and former prisoners. According to its mission statement, TGIJP seeks to

challenge and end the human rights abuses committed against transgender, gender variant/ genderqueer and intersex (TGI) people in California prisons and beyond. Recognizing that poverty borne from profound and pervasive discrimination and marginalization of TGI people is a major underlying cause of why TGI people end up in prison, TGIJP addresses human rights abuses against TGI prisoners through strategies that effect systemic change. . . .

> (TGIJP, 2007)

During a period of time when U.S. imperialism and corporate power continue to destroy communities and lives on a global scale, as TGNC people within the United States, we have a responsibility to act in solidarity with global struggles and act in solidarity or as a part of broader domestic struggles for social and economic injustice.

Matt Richardson: . . . I will contribute to this dialogue by foregrounding the part of the question about struggles for social justice in a U.S. racial context, which I hope will inform discussion of coalitional opportunities. I am very interested in how the Black body in particular comes into Western thought and material reality as the marker for sexual aberrance and deviance. By *sexual* I mean both the physical body and the act of sex. Often, where biology and behavior meet is in the (social) scientific study of Black people. It is through the study of the Black as a scientific object that Black genders have been constructed as *pathological,* to use a term from Daniel Patrick Moynihan (1967); the effects of this construction cascade globally because they have helped set the standards for what is considered normal in Eurocentric modernity, as Susan describes. For this reason, it is crucial to think about the ways in which trans discourses are implicated in struggles surrounding dehumanization (even when they are invested in gender normativity).

Let me clarify what I mean by considering how comparative anatomy set the stage for the racial construction of biological sex. Slavery positioned people of African heritage as quasihuman in the great chain of being. There were many attempts to prove racial hierarchy through systematic investigation, many arguments resting on observations of the physical difference in biological sex that could then be used to explain imagined abnormal sexual degenerate behavior—all of which, of course, was fodder for anti-Black violence. For eighteenth- and nineteenth-century scientists such as Johann Blumenbach and Georges Cuvier or philosophers and politicians such as Thomas Jefferson, this less-than-human designation left open questions surrounding the difference in Black sex organs (e.g., the famed extended labia minora, called the *Hottentot apron*, of South African women), igniting Western imaginations of bestiality and excessive lascivious desires. (See, for example, Thomas Jefferson's ruminations on African women copulating with orangutans in his 1787 volume *Notes on the State of Virginia*). To this end, the gendered expressions of those whom Havelock Ellis (1897/2007) called the "lower human races" (p. 17) became a fascination for a variety of scholars of anthropology, sociology, sexology, psychology, and anatomy. The desire to quantify the difference in Black female sex organs came from the assertion that the genitals of Black female objects of study was, as an article from the 1867 inaugural volume of the *Journal of Anatomy and Physiology* put it, "well marked to distinguish these parts at once from any of the ordinary varieties of the human species" (Flowers & Murie, p. 208). Claims of physiological excesses rendered Black people ideal for excessive labor and torture, well beyond what would be considered acceptable for any so-called civilized man or true woman. These early attempts to congeal racist taxonomies of difference through anatomical investigation and ethnographic observation produced the Black body as always already variant and Black people as the essence of gender aberrance, thereby defining the norm by making the Black its opposite.

[. . .]

Any trans rights movement that successfully emerges from Black people or incorporates Black people as partners in struggles against violence and exploitation needs to look at how the historical conditions of slavery and colonialism set the stage for the ways in which gender is assigned and lived. What would be useful is recognizing that in the contemporary United States, for example, the Black population comprises a multitude of populations across the African diaspora. The immigration of Black people from Latin America, the Caribbean, and Africa, among other places, produces a complex and multifaceted set of communities. It would then make sense to take into consideration how people of different genders are designated before they are transported or come to the United States and what happens to genders once they arrive. Important questions to ask are: What was the impact of slavery and colonialism on gender categories before arrival and after? How does this impact differ according to skin color, class, and age and ability? . . .

How has the framing of trans rights changed in the last 10–20 years with its increasing visibility and legislative gains? What should be the central political and policy objectives of this movement? How can we build a successfully antiracist movement for trans justice?

Kris Hayashi: At ALP, we believe in multi-issue organizing and caution against single-issue movements. We believe that single issue movements often leave behind the very communities, which are most vulnerable. . . .

[. . .]

At ALP, we also believe that in order to build a successful movement for justice for all oppressed communities, it is critical to place at the forefront the needs, perspectives, and leadership of those within our communities who are most vulnerable, are most lacking in access to resources, and face the greatest barriers to survival. We believe that these communities should determine the key issues and problems our movement seeks to address. Due to the systemic oppression on which U.S. society and, thus, our movements within the United States are based, often the exact opposite occurs. If we take a look at organizations and movements led by TGNC people facing some of the greatest barriers to survival, the issues that those communities have prioritized do not often receive the greatest visibility and resources—and thus are often not within our movements' or other movements' thinking in regard to trans issues. These issues range from justice for TGNC prisoners, to police brutality and violence, to gentrification, to the U.S.-led war on terrorism both within the United States and abroad, to immigrant rights, to welfare, to unemployment, to education access. For example, in addition to the Transgender, Gender Variant, Intersex Justice Project, other organizations have also placed the needs of the most disempowered at the forefront. In New York City, TGNC youth of color and low-income youth in the West Village neighborhood face ongoing violence and harassment at the hands of the police, as well as from residents who are primarily White and middle-class to upper class. As a result, FIERCE!, an organization led and run primarily by TGNC low-income and homeless youth of color, prioritizes issues of police brutality and violence, as well as gentrification. TransJustice, a project of ALP that is led and run by TGNC people of color, has prioritized issues of unemployment and education access due to high rates of unemployment (60%–70%) facing TGNC people of color. Also in New York, a coalition of organizations and groups including TransJustice, Welfare Warriors, and the LGBT Community Center's Gender Identity Project have prioritized efforts to end the regular harassment and discrimination faced by TGNC people seeking to gain access to public assistance. Finally, many TGNC groups led primarily by people of color and low-income communities have also prioritized ending the U.S war on terrorism, both in the United States and abroad. As trans movements progress it's important that we look critically at which issues are prioritized and adequately resourced, which issues are not, and how those choices have been shaped by systems of oppression.

With regard specifically to building a successful antiracist movement for trans justice, I think it's important to reflect on the current state of trans activism and organizing in relation to a few key questions. Are our organizations and groups structured in ways that support the leadership and involvement of people of color? Is the leadership of our organizations and movements majority White? Are the people who decide what issues the trans movement should focus on majority White? Are the people and organizations who receive the greatest amount of resources majority White? Are the people, organizations, and individuals who receive the greatest amount of visibility within the general public and the movement majority White?

Building a successful antiracism movement requires White allies to challenge the ways in which racism is perpetuated within trans movements—both when it occurs on a day-to-day basis and when it occurs in the building of groups and institutions. White allies also need to understand the importance of spaces for people of color and support leadership and organizing by and for trans and gender-nonconforming people of color. Specifically, it's important for White allies to look toward White antiracist leaders and organizers within trans communities for models of antiracist work. . . .

Matt Richardson: . . . Building an antiracist trans movement in the United States requires recognition that not all trans people are the same, especially in relation to state power. This misrecognition of all gender-nonconforming people as being the same before the law fuels an emphasis on legal means to help alleviate the problem of trans discrimination. Changes in law do not necessarily produce the same benefit for everyone. To focus on legislative gains is to rely on a dictum of equal protection, a focus that overlooks the experience of those of us who are not recognized by the state as full citizens no matter what our passports say and whether or not we were born in the United States.

[. . .]

The lived experience of contemporary Black trans people in the United States demonstrates the incongruity between the promise of state protection and the practice of regulation, surveillance, and brutality. In 1999, during the Creating Change Conference in Oakland, California, a group of African American trans women were attacked in downtown Oakland. When the police arrived on the scene, they attacked the assault victims as well. One officer was quoted as saying, "I am tired of having to do all this paperwork. You guys have been told not be on the corner of 14th and Broadway. I am tired of your shit" (GenderPAC, 1999). A demonstration by the conference attendees happened that night at the Oakland police headquarters. I was at the demonstration, as were other members of this roundtable. The original attack and the subsequent verbal police assault are part of a larger continuation of a refusal to protect and serve that has implications specifically about police brutality toward trans people and about a history of state-mandated racist violence. What did not happen that night in most of the speeches I heard was a connecting the incident to the everyday racial violence that happens to many members of the same community.

[. . .]

Any antiracist movement—trans or otherwise—must contend with the everyday life of people who are vulnerable to racism in all of its forms. After the 1999 attack on the transgender women, it was recommended that the police undergo sensitivity training on trans issues. This is a fine proposal, but it does not touch the much more structural conditions that prompted the assault or the police response. Echoing Kris's questions about trans organizational leadership, the more that trans organizations are led by people who are affected by racism and class oppression, the more multilayered strategies will be enacted, including working together with other organizations that are already tackling connected issues.

Susan Stryker: I have seen a great deal of change in how transgender issues have been framed since I first started getting involved at a personal level in the trans community in the late 1980s; it seems hard to believe that it's been almost 20 years. Back then, it was very difficult for me to find another trans person who thought in political terms. Most everybody I met was focused on survival; trans support groups were pretty gloomy affairs, and there were very few resources of any kind. What activism existed was focused almost exclusively on educating medical and psychotherapeutic service providers in order to create better access for surgery, hormones, and counseling. There was a lot of talk about us as a medically colonized people; a lot of talk about hormones and surgery on demand; a lot of talk about the transsexual witch hunts in gay, lesbian, and progressive movements in the 1970s; and a lot of talk about turning tricks and AIDS risk—but that was it for political discourse, as far as I could see. Except for the folks who were active on AIDS issues, I didn't see a lot of political activism at all.

[. . .]

It took me a few years to realize that, in the late 1980s, it wasn't necessarily true that trans folks were apolitical by choice. The fact of the matter was that there wasn't a lot of opportunity to do much of anything at that point except tell other people that—hey, really, just because I'm transgendered it doesn't mean I'm psychotic, or need to go to a feminist consciousness raising group, or come out as the gay man I really am by liberating myself from the oppressive gender stereotypes that made me want to mutilate my body. Transgender issues were pretty effectively contained by countervailing cultural tendencies; opportunities to do political work were meager; and it took a lot of strength and determination just to make it from day to day as a trans person.

[. . .]

The exhilaration of watching a new transgender dialogue begin to take shape is hard to reduce to words. It was glorious to finally be able to speak with some nontrans people and not have to educate them first about the fact that you were a viable human being. My awareness of the profound difference between not having a speaking position at all and having disagreements among trans people about the best thing to say is what allows me to take a very long view on what the trans movement needs to be doing. I'm still a little amazed that we are doing anything at all and that so much has been done in such a relatively short period of time. The biggest change in framing has been that we have the opportunity to create multiple possible frames.

[. . .]

How well does transgender studies, as it has been framed academically, fit the needs and agendas of trans activists? What kinds of academic work are most needed? Which are the least helpful?

Matt Richardson: . . . I would like to see a turn in the future of trans studies that takes its direction from the most vulnerable trans populations. For example, Kris mentioned the TGIJP, which is based in the San Francisco Bay Area. What might be of most use for the people that TGIJP serves—those who are mass incarcerated, which is also majority people of color—are scholars who are themselves activists. Scholars who value praxis would be involved in the hands-on work of struggle that actually informs their scholarship. Angela Davis is a prime example: Her service to the struggle over 4 decades is well documented as is her related academic writing, including her recent book, *Are Prisons Obsolete?* (Davis, 2003). Another case in point is someone such as Ruth Wilson Gilmore who, in addition to directing the Program in American Studies and Ethnicity at the University of Southern California, Los Angeles, is a founding member of the collective Critical Resistance, one of the most important national antiprison organizations in the United States. Gilmore is also active in the Prison Moratorium Project and California Prison Focus and has just published *Golden Gulag: Prisons, Surplus, Crisis and Opposition in Globalizing California* (Gilmore, 2007). Few of us, myself included, could ever live up to the dizzying career of Angela Davis and Ruth Wilson Gilmore;

however, they provide models to which we can all aspire, at least in the spirit of their commitments to being personally invested in trying to change the material conditions that they write about.

[. . .]

Susan Stryker: I really resist framing transgender studies as a field structured by the demands, on the one hand, of activist strategies and, on the other hand, of academic concerns. It suggests that academics are not activists, or that activists are not academics, and that the proper role of academic trans studies should be to provide content and tools for nonacademic activists to then use out in the real world. When you ask, "What kind of academic work is most needed?", the answer needs to be qualified by another question: Needed by whom? Likewise with the question about what is least helpful: least helpful to whom? Knowledges and their utility are quite specific to their situations.

This activist versus academic conflict is a familiar way to frame the internal politics of interdisciplinary fields of study that have their roots in minoritarian critiques of knowledge, power, and social structure, and I don't think it is ever very productive. This same debate says that feminist theory has no value for women's struggles, that critical race theory has nothing to do with Black struggles, and that queer theory has nothing to do with gay rights.

[. . .]

I think we need to be more nuanced in our thinking about the role of the academy in the production of trans knowledges and about the relationship of this knowledge to transgender social justice movements. The university, after all, is just another place to work, and it has its own peculiar workplace issues. Bringing trans politics into the politics of the academic workplace—for students, staff, and faculty alike—is one important way to channel some of the financial resources and symbolic capital of academe toward the trans struggle for social justice. Part of this work involves legitimating trans concerns in the language of academe. This is specialized work, requiring expert knowledge and technical, sometimes jargon-riddled language. Institutionalizing transgender studies in the academy is one strategy for using the considerable resources of the academic institution while keeping the issues on the table. It becomes part of educating the rising generation of trans youth who have been fortunate enough to gain college admission and of creating a safe and empowering educational experience for them, part of creating secure working conditions for trans people on staff, and part of transforming disciplinary academic knowledge in ways that will have unforeseen consequences. This sort of transgender intellectual work, which is specific to the academic workplace, should not be seen as intrinsically useless to a broader trans social justice movement even if it is very arcane, because this sort of academic work performs the queer labor of refashioning the relationship of trans issues to social power. If nothing else, it helps make visible the means through which trans concerns have been rendered invisible and marginal. At best, it situates

the kind of knowledges that come from trans embodiment and experience at the very heart of the academic enterprise.

[. . .]

What this boils down to for me is a question about how transgender studies in the academy and transgender social activism work together. Even very abstract kinds of academic knowledge can be inspiring for activist practices beyond the ivory tower, in the same way that music can be inspiring even if you can't say in words how music moved you to do something. However, even the most rigorous kinds of intellectual analysis will be nothing but dead formalism without an enlivening engagement with the broader material conditions that the analysis seeks to apprehend. Let's all be more patient with the various kinds of work we each do, more curious, more connected across our differences—and more creative in the ways we draw inspiration from the work others do in locations that are not our own.

REFERENCES

Bailey, M. M., Kandaswamy, P., & Richardson, M. U. (2004). Is gay marriage racist? In M. B. Sycamore (Ed.), *That's revolting! Queer strategies for resisting assimilation* (pp. 87–96). Brooklyn, NY: Soft Skull Press.

BeyondMarriage.org. (2006, July 26). *Beyond same-sex marriage: A new strategic vision for all our families & relationships.* Retrieved May 23, 2007, from http://www.beyondmarriage.org/full_statement. html

Chess, S., Kafer, A., Quizar, J., & Richardson, M. U. (2004). Calling all restroom revolutionaries! In M. B. Sycamore (Ed.), *That's revolting! Queer strategies for resisting assimilation* (pp. 189–206). Brooklyn, NY: Soft Skull Press.

Currah, P., Juang, R. M., & Minter, S. P. (Eds.). (2006). *Transgender rights.* Minneapolis: Minnesota University Press.

Davis, A. (2003). *Are prisons obsolete?* New York: Seven Stories Press.

Dred Scott v. Sandford, 60 U.S. 393 (1857).

Ellis, H. (1897/2007). *Studies in the psychology of sex, volume II: Sexual inversion.* Charleston, NC: BiblioBazaar.

Employment Non-Discrimination Act of 2007, H.R. 3685, 110th Cong. (2007).

Flowers, W. H., & Murie, J. (1867). Account of the dissection of a Bushwoman. *Journal of Anatomy and Physiology*, 1, 189–208.

GenderPAC. (1999). 1,500 at Creating Change protest police harassment. Retrieved November 9, 2007, from http://www.gpac.org/archive/news/notitle. html?cmd=view&archive=news&msgnum=0197

Gilmore, R. W. (2007). *Golden gulag: Prisons, surplus, crisis, and opposition in globalizing California.* Berkeley: University of California Press.

Hirschfeld, M. (1910). *Die Transvestiten: Eine Untersuchung über den erotischen Verkleidungstrieb* [The transvestites: An investigation of the erotic drive to cross dress]. Berlin: Pulvermacher.

Hirschfeld, M. (1914). *Jahrbuch für sexuelle Zwischenstufen* [Yearbook for sexual intermediaries]. Leipzig, East Germany: Max Spohr.

Jefferson, T. (1787/2002). *Notes on the state of Virginia.* New York: Palgrave MacMillan.

Moynihan, D. P. (1967). The Negro family: The case for national action. In L. Rainwater & W. Yancy (Eds.),

The Moynihan Report and the politics of controversy (pp. 39–124). Cambridge, MA: MIT University Press.

Richardson, M. (2003). No more secrets, no more lies: Compulsory heterosexuality and African American history. *Journal of Women's History, 15*(3), 63–76.

Silverman, S. (Writer/Director), & Stryker, S. (Writer/Director). (2005). *Screaming queens: The riot at Compton's Cafeteria* [Motion picture]. United States: Frameline.

Stryker, S. (2001). *Queer pulp: Perverted passions from the golden age of the paperback.* San Francisco: Chronicle Books.

Stryker, S. (2006). (De)subjugated knowledges: An introduction to transgender studies. In S. Stryker & S. Whittle (Eds.), *The transgender studies reader* (pp. 1–17). New York: Routledge.

Stryker, S. (2008, winter). Homonormativity, disciplinarity, and transgender history. *Radical History Review, 100,* 145–157.

Stryker, S., & Van Buskirk, J. (1996). *Gay by the bay: A history of queer culture in the San Francisco Bay Area.* San Francisco: Chronicle Books.

Stryker, S., & Whittle, S. (Eds.). (2006). *The transgender studies reader.* New York: Routledge.

Sycamore, M. B. (Ed.). (2004). *That's revolting! Queer strategies for resisting assimilation.* Brooklyn, NY: Soft Skull Press.

Transgender, Gender Variant, and Intersex Prison Project. (2007). Mission. Retrieved May 23, 2007, from http://www.tgijp.org/mission.html

TransJustice. (2005). *Trans Day of Action Points of Unity.* Manuscript on file with the author.

TransJustice. (2006). *Points of Unity.* Manuscript on file with the author.

8. • *Marilyn Frye*

OPPRESSION (1983)

Marilyn Frye, a University Distinguished Professor in the department of philosophy at Michigan State University, is the author of two books of essays in feminist theory, *The Politics of Reality* (1983) and *Willful Virgin* (1992), both published by the Crossing Press. She has authored several articles that address sexism, racism, oppression, and lesbian identity and was honored in 2001 as the Distinguished Woman Philosopher of the Year. The article included here is a part of *The Politics of Reality* collection and was reprinted in *Feminist Theory: A Philosophical Anthology* (Blackwell, 2005).

It is a fundamental claim of feminism that women are oppressed. The word 'oppression' is a strong word. It repels and attracts. It is dangerous and dangerously fashionable and endangered. It is much misused, and sometimes not innocently.

The statement that women are oppressed is frequently met with the claim that men are oppressed too. We hear that oppressing is oppressive to those who oppress as well as to those they oppress. Some men cite as evidence of their oppression their much-advertised inability to cry. It is tough, we are told, to be masculine. When the stresses and frustrations of being a man are cited as evidence that oppressors are oppressed by their oppressing, the word 'oppression' is being stretched to meaninglessness; it is treated as though its scope includes any and all human experience of limitation or suffering, no matter the cause, degree or consequence. Once such usage has been put over on us, then if ever we deny that any person or group is oppressed, we seem to imply that we think they never suffer and have no feelings. We are accused of insensitivity; even of bigotry. For women, such accusation is particularly intimidating, since sensitivity is one of the few virtues that has been assigned to us. If we are found insensitive, we may fear we have no redeeming traits at all and perhaps are not real women. Thus are we silenced before we begin: the name of our situation drained of meaning and our guilt mechanisms tripped.

But this is nonsense. Human beings can be miserable without being oppressed, and it is perfectly consistent to deny that a person or group is oppressed without denying that they have feelings or that they suffer.

We need to think clearly about oppression, and there is much that mitigates against this. I do not want to undertake to prove that women are oppressed (or that men are not), but I want to make clear what is being said when we say it. We need this word, this concept, and we need it to be sharp and sure.

The root of the word 'oppression' is the element 'press'. *The press of the crowd; pressed into military service; to press a pair of pants; printing press; press the button.* Presses are used to mold things or flatten them or reduce them in bulk, sometimes to reduce them by squeezing out the gasses or liquids in them. Something pressed is something caught between or among forces and barriers which are so related to each other that jointly they restrain, restrict or prevent the thing's motion or mobility. Mold. Immobilize. Reduce.

The mundane experience of the oppressed provides another clue. One of the most characteristic and ubiquitous features of the world as experienced by oppressed people is the double bind—situations in which options are reduced to a very few and all of them expose one to penalty, censure or deprivation. For example, it is often a requirement upon oppressed people that we smile and be cheerful. If we comply, we signal our docility and our acquiescence in our situation. We need not, then, be taken note of. We acquiesce in being made invisible, in our occupying no space. We participate in our own erasure. On the other hand, anything but the sunniest countenance exposes us to being perceived as mean, bitter, angry or dangerous. This means, at the least, that

we may be found "difficult" or unpleasant to work with, which is enough to cost one one's livelihood; at worst, being seen as mean, bitter, angry or dangerous has been known to result in rape, arrest, beating and murder. One can only choose to risk one's preferred form and rate of annihilation.

Another example: It is common in the United States that women, especially younger women, are in a bind where neither sexual activity nor sexual inactivity is all right. If she is heterosexually active, a woman is open to censure and punishment for being loose, unprincipled or a whore. The "punishment" comes in the form of criticism, snide and embarrassing remarks, being treated as an easy lay by men, scorn from her more restrained female friends. She may have to lie and hide her behavior from her parents. She must juggle the risks of unwanted pregnancy and dangerous contraceptives. On the other hand, if she refrains from heterosexual activity, she is fairly constantly harassed by men who try to persuade her into it and pressure her to "relax" and "let her hair down"; she is threatened with labels like "frigid," "uptight," "man-hater," "bitch" and "cocktease." The same parents who would be disapproving of her sexual activity may be worried by her inactivity because it suggests she is not or will not be popular, or is not sexually normal. She may be charged with lesbianism. If a woman is raped, then if she has been heterosexually active she is subject to the presumption that she liked it (since her activity is presumed to show that she likes sex), and if she has not been heterosexually active, she is subject to the presumption that she liked it (since she is supposedly "repressed and frustrated"). Both heterosexual activity and heterosexual nonactivity are likely to be taken as proof that you wanted to be raped, and hence, of course, weren't *really* raped at all. You can't win. You are caught in a bind, caught between systematically related pressures.

Women are caught like this, too, by networks of forces and barriers that expose one to penalty, loss or contempt whether one works outside the home or not, is on welfare or not, bears children or not, raises children or not, marries or not, stays married or not, is heterosexual, lesbian, both or neither. Economic necessity; confinement to racial and/or sexual job ghettos; sexual harassment; sex discrimination; pressures of competing expectations and judgments about *women*, *wives* and *mothers* (in the society at large, in racial and ethnic subcultures and in one's own mind); dependence (full or partial) on husbands, parents or the state; commitment to political ideas; loyalties to racial or ethnic or other "minority" groups; the demands of self-respect and responsibilities to others. Each of these factors exists in complex tension with every other, penalizing or prohibiting all of the apparently available options. And nipping at one's heels, always, is the endless pack of little things. If one dresses one way, one is subject to the assumption that one is advertising one's sexual availability; if one dresses another way, one appears to "not care about oneself" or to be "unfeminine." If one uses "strong language," one invites categorization as a whore or slut; if one does not, one invites categorization as a "lady"—one too delicately constituted to cope with robust speech or the realities to which it presumably refers.

The experience of oppressed people is that the living of one's life is confined and shaped by forces and barriers which are not accidental or occasional and hence avoidable, but are systematically related to each other in such a way as to catch one between and among them and restrict or penalize motion in any direction. It is the experience of being caged in: all avenues, in every direction, are blocked or booby trapped.

Cages. Consider a birdcage. If you look very closely at just one wire in the cage, you cannot see the other wires. If your conception of what is before you is determined by this myopic focus, you could look at that one wire, up and down the length of it, and be unable to see why a bird would not just fly around the wire any time it wanted to go somewhere. Furthermore, even if, one day at a time, you myopically inspected each wire, you still could not see why a bird would have trouble going past the wires to get anywhere. There is no physical property of any one wire, *nothing* that the closest scrutiny could discover,

that will reveal how a bird could be inhibited or harmed by it except in the most accidental way. It is only when you step back, stop looking at the wires one by one, microscopically, and take a macroscopic view of the whole cage, that you can see why the bird does not go anywhere; and then you will see it in a moment. It will require no great subtlety of mental powers. It is perfectly *obvious* that the bird is surrounded by a network of systematically related barriers, no one of which would be the least hindrance to its flight, but which, by their relations to each other, are as confining as the solid walls of a dungeon.

It is now possible to grasp one of the reasons why oppression can be hard to see and recognize: one can study the elements of an oppressive structure with great care and some good will without seeing the structure as a whole, and hence without seeing or being able to understand that one is looking at a cage and that there are people there who are caged, whose motion and mobility are restricted, whose lives are shaped and reduced.

The arresting of vision at a microscopic level yields such common confusion as that about the male door-opening ritual. This ritual, which is remarkably widespread across classes and races, puzzles many people, some of whom do and some of whom do not find it offensive. Look at the scene of the two people approaching a door. The male steps slightly ahead and opens the door. The male holds the door open while the female glides through. Then the male goes through. The door closes after them. "Now how," one innocently asks, "can those crazy womenslibbers say that is oppressive? The guy *removed* a barrier to the lady's smooth and unruffled progress." But each repetition of this ritual has a place in a pattern, in fact in several patterns. One has to shift the level of one's perception in order to see the whole picture.

The door-opening pretends to be a helpful service, but the helpfulness is false. This can be seen by noting that it will be done whether or not it makes any practical sense. Infirm men and men burdened with packages will open doors for able-bodied women who are free of physical burdens. Men will impose themselves awkwardly and jostle everyone in order to get to the door first. The act is not determined by convenience or grace. Furthermore, these very numerous acts of unneeded or even noisome "help" occur in counterpoint to a pattern of men not being helpful in many practical ways in which women might welcome help. What *women* experience is a world in which gallant princes charming commonly make a fuss about being helpful and providing small services when help and services are of little or no use, but in which there are rarely ingenious and adroit princes at hand when substantial assistance is really wanted either in mundane affairs or in situations of threat, assault or terror. There is no help with the (his) laundry; no help typing a report at 4:00 a.m.; no help in mediating disputes among relatives or children. There is nothing but advice that women should stay indoors after dark, be chaperoned by a man, or when it comes down to it, "lie back and enjoy it."

The gallant gestures have no practical meaning. Their meaning is symbolic. The door-opening and similar services provided are services which really are needed by people who are for one reason or another incapacitated—unwell, burdened with parcels, etc. So the message is that women are incapable. The detachment of the acts from the concrete realities of what women need and do not need is a vehicle for the message that women's actual needs and interests are unimportant or irrelevant. Finally, these gestures imitate the behavior of servants toward masters and thus mock women, who are in most respects the servants and caretakers of men. The message of the false helpfulness of male gallantry is female dependence, the invisibility or insignificance of women, and contempt for women.

One cannot see the meanings of these rituals if one's focus is riveted upon the individual event in all its particularity, including the particularity of the individual man's present conscious intentions and motives and the individual woman's conscious perception of the event in the moment. It seems sometimes that people take a deliberately myopic view and fill their eyes with things seen microscopically in order not to see macroscopically. At any rate,

whether it is deliberate or not, people can and do fail to see the oppression of women because they fail to see macroscopically and hence fail to see the various elements of the situation as systematically related in larger schemes.

[. . .]

It seems to be the human condition that in one degree or another we all suffer frustration and limitation, all encounter unwelcome barriers, and all are damaged and hurt in various ways. Since we are a social species, almost all of our behavior and activities are structured by more than individual inclination and the conditions of the planet and its atmosphere. No human is free of social structures, nor (perhaps) would happiness consist in such freedom. Structure consists of boundaries, limits and barriers; in a structured whole, some motions and changes are possible, and others are not. If one is looking for an excuse to dilute the word 'oppression,' one can use the fact of social structure as an excuse and say that everyone is, oppressed. But if one would rather get clear about what oppression is and is not, one needs to sort out the sufferings, harms and limitations and figure out which are elements of oppression and which are not.

From what I have already said here, it is clear that if one wants to determine whether a particular suffering, harm or limitation is part of someone's being oppressed, one has to look at it *in context* in order to tell whether it is an element in an oppressive structure: one has to see if it is part of an enclosing structure of forces and barriers which tends to the immobilization and reduction of a group or category of people. One has to look at how the barrier or force fits with others and to whose benefit or detriment it works. . . .

[. . .]

The boundary that sets apart women's sphere is maintained and promoted by men generally for the benefit of men generally, and men generally do benefit from its existence, even the man who bumps into it and complains of the inconvenience. That barrier is protecting his classification and status as a male, as superior, as having a right to sexual access to a female or females. It protects a kind of citizenship which is superior to that of females of his class and race, his access to a wider range of better paying and higher status work, and his right to prefer unemployment to the degradation of doing lower status or "women's" work.

If a person's life or activity is affected by some force or barrier that person encounters, one may not conclude that the person is oppressed simply because the person encounters that barrier or force; nor simply because the encounter is unpleasant, frustrating or painful to that person at that time; nor simply because the existence of the barrier or force, or the processes which maintain or apply it, serve to deprive that person of something of value. One must look at the barrier or force and answer certain questions about it. Who constructs and maintains it? Whose interests are served by its existence? Is it part of a structure which tends to confine, reduce and immobilize some group? Is the individual a member of the confined group? Various forces, barriers and limitations a person may encounter or live with may be part of an oppressive structure or not, and if they are, that person may be on either the oppressed or the oppressor side of it. One cannot tell which by how loudly or how little the person complains.

Many of the restrictions and limitations we live with are more or less internalized and self-monitored, and are part of our adaptations to the requirements and expectations imposed by the needs and tastes and tyrannies of others. I have in mind such things as women's cramped postures and attenuated strides and men's restraint of emotional self-expression (except for anger). Who gets what out of the practice of those disciplines, and who imposes what penalties for improper relaxations of them? What are the rewards of this self-discipline?

Can men cry? Yes, in the company of women. If a man cannot cry, it is in the company of men that he cannot cry. It is men, not women, who require this restraint; and men not only require it, they reward it. The man who maintains a steely or tough or laid-back

demeanor (all are forms which suggest invulnerability) marks himself as a member of the male community and is esteemed by other men. Consequently, the maintenance of that demeanor contributes to the man's self-esteem. It is felt as good, and he can feel good about himself. The way this restriction fits into the structures of men's lives is as one of the socially required behaviors which, if carried off, contribute to their acceptance and respect by significant others and to their own self-esteem. It is to their benefit to practice this discipline.

Consider, by comparison, the discipline of women's cramped physical postures and attenuated stride. This discipline can be relaxed in the company of women; it generally is at its most strenuous in the company of men.* Like men's emotional restraint, women's physical restraint is required by men. But unlike the case of men's emotional restraint, women's physical restraint is not rewarded. What do we get for it? Respect and esteem and acceptance? No. They mock us and parody our mincing steps. We look silly, incompetent, weak and generally contemptible. Our exercise of this discipline tends to low esteem and low self-esteem. It does not benefit us. It fits in a network of behaviors through which we constantly announce to others our membership in a lower caste and our unwillingness and/or inability to defend our bodily or moral integrity. It is degrading and part of a pattern of degradation.

Acceptable behavior for both groups, men and women, involves a required restraint that seems in itself silly and perhaps damaging. But the social effect is drastically different. The woman's restraint is part of a structure oppressive to women; the man's restraint is part of a structure oppressive to women.

---

* Cf. *Let's Take Back Our Space: "Female" and "Male" Body Language as a Result of Patriarchal Structures,* by Marianne Wex (Frauenliteratureverlag Hermine Fees, West Germany, 1979), especially p. 173. This remarkable book presents literally thousands of candid photographs of women and men, in public, seated, standing and lying down. It vividly demonstrates the very systematic differences in women's and men's postures and gestures.

One is marked for application of oppressive pressures by one's membership in some group or category. Much of one's suffering and frustration befalls one partly or largely because one is a member of that category. In the case at hand, it is the category, *woman*. Being a woman is a major factor in my not having a better job than I do; being a woman selects me as a likely victim of sexual assault or harassment; it is my being a woman that reduces the power of my anger to a proof of my insanity. If a woman has little or no economic or political power, or achieves little of what she wants to achieve, a major causal factor in this is that she is a woman. For any woman of any race or economic class, being a woman is significantly attached to whatever disadvantages and deprivations she suffers, be they great or small.

None of this is the case with respect to a person's being a man. Simply being a man is not what stands between him and a better job; whatever assaults and harassments he is subject to, being male is not what selects him for victimization; being male is not a factor which would make his anger impotent—quite the opposite. If a man has little or no material or political power, or achieves little of what he wants to achieve, his being male is no part of the explanation. Being male is something he has going *for* him, even if race or class or age or disability is going against him.

Women are oppressed, *as women.* Members of certain racial and/or economic groups and classes, both the males and the females, are oppressed *as* members of those races and/or classes. But men are not oppressed *as men.*

> . . . and isn't it strange that any of us should have been confused and mystified about such a simple thing?

---

9. • *Peggy McIntosh*

WHITE PRIVILEGE:
Unpacking the Invisible Knapsack (1988)

Peggy McIntosh is the former associate director of the Wellesley Center for Women, founder of the National SEED (Seeking Education Equity & Diversity) Project on Inclusive Curriculum, and director of the Gender, Race, and Inclusive Education Project. In addition to working with college and university faculty to include women's, gender and sexuality studies materials in a wide range of courses, she is a recipient of the Klingenstein Award for Distinguished Educational Leadership from Columbia Teachers College. "White Privilege: Unpacking the Invisible Knapsack" is a classic essay that first articulated unearned white advantages and rights within a feminist context.

Through work to bring materials from Women's Studies into the rest of the curriculum, I have often noticed men's unwillingness to grant that they are over-privileged, even though they may grant that women are disadvantaged. They may say they will work to improve women's status, in the society, the university, or the curriculum, but they can't or won't support the idea of lessening men's. Denials which amount to taboos surround the subject of advantages which men gain from women's disadvantages. These denials protect male privilege from being fully acknowledged, lessened or ended.

Thinking through unacknowledged male privilege as a phenomenon, I realized that, since hierarchies in our society are interlocking, there was most likely a phenomenon of white privilege that was similarly denied and protected. As a white person, I realized I had been taught about racism as something that puts others at a disadvantage, but had been taught not to see one of its corollary aspects, white privilege, which puts me at an advantage.

I think whites are carefully taught not to recognize white privilege, as males are taught not to recognize male privilege. So I have begun in an untutored way to ask what it is like to have white privilege. I have come to see white privilege as an invisible package of unearned assets that I can count on cashing in each day, but about which I was "meant" to remain oblivious. White privilege is like an invisible weightless knapsack of special provisions, maps, passports, codebooks, visas, clothes, tools and blank checks.

Describing white privilege makes one newly accountable. As we in Women's Studies work to reveal male privilege and ask men to give up some of their power, so one who writes about white privilege must ask, "Having described it, what will I do to lessen or end it?"

After I realized the extent to which men work from a base of unacknowledged privilege, I understood that much of their oppressiveness was unconscious. Then I remembered the frequent charges from women of color that white women whom they encounter are oppressive.

I began to understand why we are justly seen as oppressive, even when we don't see ourselves that way. I began to count the ways in which I enjoy unearned skin privilege and have been conditioned into oblivion about its existence.

My schooling gave me no training in seeing myself as an oppressor, as an unfairly advantaged person, or as a participant in a damaged culture. I was taught to see myself as an individual whose moral state depended on her individual moral will. My schooling followed the pattern my colleague Elizabeth Minnich has pointed out: whites are taught to think of their lives as morally neutral, normative, and average, and also ideal, so that when we work to benefit others, this is seen as work which will allow "them" to be more like "us."

I decided to try to work on myself at least by identifying some of the daily effects of white privilege in my life. I have chosen those conditions which I think in my case *attach somewhat more to skin-color privilege* than to class, religion, ethnic status, or geographic location, though of course all these other factors are intricately intertwined. As far as I can see, my African American coworkers, friends, and acquaintances with whom I come into daily or frequent contact in this particular time, place and line of work cannot count on most of these conditions.

1. I can if I wish arrange to be in the company of people of my race most of the time.
2. If I should need to move, I can be pretty sure of renting or purchasing housing in an area which I can afford and in which I would want to live.
3. I can be pretty sure that my neighbors in such a location will be neutral or pleasant to me.
4. I can go shopping alone most of the time, pretty well assured that I will not be followed or harassed.
5. I can turn on the television or open to the front page of the paper and see people of my race widely represented.
6. When I am told about our national heritage or about "civilization," I am shown that people of my color made it what it is.
7. I can be sure that my children will be given curricular materials that testify to the existence of their race.
8. If I want to, I can be pretty sure of finding a publisher for this piece on white privilege.
9. I can go into a music shop and count on finding the music of my race represented, into a supermarket and find the staple foods that fit with my cultural traditions, into a hairdresser's shop and find someone who can cut my hair.
10. Whether I use checks, credit cards or cash, I can count on my skin color not to work against the appearance of financial reliability.

11. I can arrange to protect my children most of the time from people who might not like them.

12. I can swear, or dress in secondhand clothes, or not answer letters, without having people attribute these choices to the bad morals, the poverty, or the illiteracy of my race.

13. I can speak in public to a powerful male group without putting my race on trial.

14. I can do well in a challenging situation without being called a credit to my race.

15. I am never asked to speak for all the people of my racial group.

16. I can remain oblivious of the language and customs of persons of color who constitute the world's majority without feeling in my culture any penalty for such oblivion.

17. I can criticize our government and talk about how much I fear its policies and behavior without being seen as a cultural outsider.

18. I can be pretty sure that if I ask to talk to "the person in charge," I will be facing a person of my race.

19. If a traffic cop pulls me over or if the IRS audits my tax return, I can be sure I haven't been singled out because of my race.

20. I can easily buy posters, postcards, picture books, greeting cards, dolls, toys, and children's magazines featuring people of my race.

21. I can go home from most meetings of organizations I belong to feeling somewhat tied in, rather than isolated, out-of-place, outnumbered, unheard, held at a distance, or feared.

22. I can take a job with an affirmative action employer without having coworkers on the job suspect that I got it because of race.

23. I can choose public accommodations without fearing that people of my race cannot get in or will be mistreated in the places I have chosen.

24. I can be sure that if I need legal or medical help, my race will not work against me.

25. If my day, week, or year is going badly, I need not ask of each negative episode or situation whether it has racial overtones.

26. I can choose blemish cover or bandages in "flesh" color and have them more less match my skin.

I repeatedly forgot each of the realizations on this list until I wrote it down. For me, white privilege has turned out to be an elusive and fugitive subject. The pressure to avoid it is great, for in facing it I must give up the myth of meritocracy. If these things are true, this is not such a free country; one's life is not what one makes it; many doors open for certain people through no virtues of their own.

In unpacking this invisible knapsack of white privilege, I have listed conditions of daily experience that I once took for granted. Nor did I think of any of these perquisites as bad for the holder. I now think that we need a more finely differentiated taxonomy of privilege, for some of these varieties are only what one would want for everyone in a just society, and others give license to be ignorant, oblivious, arrogant and destructive.

I see a pattern running through the matrix of white privilege, a pattern of assumptions that were passed on to me as a white person. There was one main piece of cultural turf; it was my own turf, and I was among those who could control the turf. *My skin color was an asset for any move I was educated to want to make.* I could think of myself as belonging in major ways and of making social systems work for me. I could freely disparage, fear, neglect, or be oblivious to anything outside of the dominant cultural forms. Being of the main culture, I could also criticize it fairly freely.

In proportion as my racial group was being made confident, comfortable, and oblivious, other groups were likely being made unconfident, uncomfortable, and alienated. Whiteness protected me from many kinds of hostility, distress and violence, which I was being subtly trained to visit, in turn, upon people of color.

For this reason, the word "privilege" now seems to me misleading. We usually think of privilege as being a favored state, whether earned or conferred by birth or luck. Yet some of the conditions I have described here work systematically to overempower certain groups. Such privilege simply *confers dominance* because of one's race or sex.

I want, then, to distinguish between earned strength and unearned power conferred systemically. Power from unearned privilege can look like strength when it is in fact permission to escape or to dominate. But not all of the privileges on my list are inevitably damaging. Some, like the expectation that neighbors will be decent to you, or that your race will not count against you in court, should be the norm in a just society. Others, like the privilege to ignore less powerful people, distort the humanity of the holders as well as the ignored groups.

We might at least start by distinguishing between positive advantages, which we can work to spread, and negative types of advantage, which unless rejected will always reinforce our present hierarchies. For example, the feeling that one belongs within the human circle, as Native Americans say, should not be seen as privilege for a few. Ideally it is an *unearned entitlement*. At present, since only a few have it, it is an *unearned advantage* for them. This paper results from a process of coming to see that some of the power that I originally saw as attendant on being a human being in the United States consisted in unearned advantage and conferred dominance.

I have met very few men who are truly distressed about systemic, unearned male advantage and conferred dominance. And so one question for me and others like me is whether we will be like them, or whether we will get truly distressed, even outraged, about unearned race advantage and conferred dominance, and, if so, what will we do to lessen them. In any case, we need to do more work in identifying how they actually affect our daily lives. Many, perhaps most, of our white students in the U.S. think that racism doesn't affect them because they are not people of color, they do not see "whiteness" as a racial identity. In addition, since race and sex are not the only advantaging systems at work, we need similarly to examine the daily experience of having age advantage, or ethnic advantage, or physical ability, or advantage related to nationality, religion, or sexual orientation.

Difficulties and dangers surrounding the task of finding parallels are many. Since racism, sexism, and heterosexism are not the same, the advantages associated with them should not be seen as the same. In addition, it is hard to disentangle aspects of unearned advantage which rest more on social class, economic class, race, religion, sex, and ethnic identity than on other factors. Still, all of the oppressions are interlocking, as the Combahee River Collective Statement of 1977 continues to remind us eloquently.

One factor seems clear about all of the interlocking oppressions. They take both active forms, which we can see, and embedded forms, which as a member of the dominant group one is taught not to see. In my class and place, I did not see myself as a racist because I was taught to recognize racism only in individual acts of meanness by members of my group, never in invisible systems conferring unsought racial dominance on my group from birth.

Disapproving of the systems won't be enough to change them. I was taught to think that racism could end if white individuals changed their attitudes. But a "white" skin in the United States opens many doors for whites whether or not we approve of the way dominance has been conferred on us. Individual acts can palliate, but cannot end, these problems.

To redesign social systems, we need first to acknowledge their colossal unseen dimensions. The silences and denials surrounding privilege are the key political tool here. They keep the thinking about equality or equity incomplete, protecting unearned advantage and conferred dominance by making these taboo subjects. Most talk by whites about equal opportunity seems to me now to be about equal opportunity to try to get into a position of dominance while denying that systems of dominance exist.

It seems to me that obliviousness about white advantage, like obliviousness about male advantage, is kept strongly inculturated in the United States so as to maintain the myth of meritocracy, the myth that democratic choice is equally available to all. Keeping most people unaware that freedom of confident action is there for just a small number of people props up those in power and serves to keep power in the hands of the same groups that have most of it already.

Although systemic change takes many decades, there are pressing questions for me and I imagine for some others like me if we raise our daily consciousness on the perquisites of being light-skinned. What will we do with such knowledge? As we know from watching men, it is an open question whether we will choose to use unearned advantage to weaken hidden systems of advantage, and whether we will use any of our arbitrarily awarded power to try to reconstruct power systems on a broader base.

10. • *Audre Lorde*

THERE IS NO HIERARCHY OF OPPRESSIONS (1983)

Audre Lorde, born in New York in 1934 to Caribbean immigrant parents Frederic Byron and Linda Belmar Lorde, self-identified as a "black feminist lesbian mother poet." She dedicated her life and creative work to the struggle for liberation of all oppressed people, elucidating how racism, sexism, and homophobia work together to create injustices. Among her eighteen publications is the highly acclaimed collection of poetry, *The Black Unicorn* (1978), that deals with lesbian relationships and love in accessible and affective ways. Her essays in *The Cancer Journals* (1980), *I Am Your Sister: Black Women Organizing Across Sexualities* (1985), *Sister Outsider: Essays and Speeches* (1984), and *Zami: A New Spelling of My Name* (1982) are required reading for anyone interested in feminist, queer, antiracist social justice work. It was a great loss to so many communities when she died in 1992 of cancer.

I was born Black, and a woman. I am trying to become the strongest person I can become to live the life I have been given and to help effect change toward a liveable future for this earth and for my children. As a Black, lesbian, feminist, socialist, poet, mother of two including one boy and a member of an interracial couple, I usually find myself part of some group in which the majority defines me as deviant, difficult, inferior or just plain "wrong."

From my membership in all of these groups I have learned that oppression and the intolerance of difference come in all shapes and sexes and colors and sexualities; and that among those of us who share the goals of liberation and a workable future for our children, there can be no hierarchies of oppression. I have learned that sexism and heterosexism both arise from the same source as racism.

"Oh," says a voice from the Black community, "but being Black is NORMAL!" Well, I and many Black people of my age can remember grimly the days when it didn't used to be!

I simply do not believe that one aspect of myself can possibly profit from the oppression of any other part of my identity. I know that my people cannot possibly profit from the oppression of any other group which seeks the right to peaceful existence. Rather, we diminish ourselves by denying to others what we have shed blood to obtain for our children. And those children need to learn that they do not have to become like each other in order to work together for a future they will all share.

Within the lesbian community I am Black, and within the Black community I am a lesbian. Any attack against Black people is a lesbian and gay issue, because I and thousands of other Black women are part of the lesbian community. Any attack against lesbians and gays is a Black issue, because thousands of lesbians and gay men are Black. There is no hierarchy of oppression.

I cannot afford the luxury of fighting one form of oppression only. I cannot afford to believe that freedom from intolerance is the right of only one particular group. And I cannot afford to choose between the fronts upon which I must battle these forces of discrimination . . . wherever they appear to destroy me. And when they appear to destroy me, it will not be long before they appear to destroy you.

11. • *Ashley Currier and Thérèse Migraine-George*

QUEER/AFRICAN IDENTITIES:
Questions, Limits, Challenges (new)

Ashley Currier, an associate professor of women's, gender and sexuality studies at the University of Cincinnati, researches lesbian, gay, bisexual, transgender, and queer (LGBTQ) organizing in southern and West Africa. Her first book, *Out in Africa: LGBT Organizing in Namibia and South Africa* (2012), was a finalist for the 2013 Lambda Literary Book Award. Her research has appeared in leading feminist studies journals, including *Feminist Formations*, *Gender & Society*, *Signs: Journal of Women in Culture and Society*, and *Women's Studies Quarterly*. With Thérèse Migraine-George, she is working on a series of articles on queer African studies, the first of which will be published in *GLQ* in 2016.

Thérèse Migraine-George is a professor of romance languages and literatures and women's, gender and sexuality studies at the University of Cincinnati. She is the author of *African Women and Representation: From Performance to Politics* (2008), *From Francophonie to World Literature in French: Ethics, Poetics, and Politics* (2013), two novels, and a book of essays.

"Queer Africanness" has been associated with hardship and violent realities over the past twenty years. The now-infamous homophobic statement made by Zimbabwean President Robert Mugabe in 1995 that homosexuals are "worse than pigs and dogs" generated visibility for queer African movements, communities, and identities and a political backlash against African gender and sexual dissidents that continues today (Aarmo 262). By "gender and sexual dissidence," we mean both lived gender and sexual variance and gender and sexual minorities' organized resistance. The backlash instigated by Mugabe's comments constrains how African gender and sexual dissidents express "queer" identities. For instance, Sarah, a lesbian who volunteers at a Liberian HIV/AIDS activist organization that works with lesbian, gay, bisexual, and transgender (LGBT) persons, explains in an interview that passersby who observe people entering the organization's office in Monrovia would assume that visitors were lesbian or gay. In light of the organization's reputation as the "office of lesbians" and gay men, lesbian, bisexual, and transgender (LBT) women are reluctant to participate in activities the organization sponsors. Sarah explains that some LBT women "don't want to be seen" associating with the organization. When Sarah tried to recruit LBT women to join an LGBT rights campaign, they asked her, "'Are we coming to be put on television? Are we going to be put [in the] newspaper?'" (Currier, Interview). These women feared being outed as gender and/or sexual minorities and becoming victims of anti-LGBT prejudice.

Although the continuing antigay backlash affects how, when, and why queer Africans articulate gender and sexual minority identities and claims, it does not completely predetermine the content and contours of queer African identities. In this essay, we consider the complicated dimensions of generating, representing, and nurturing queer identities in African countries hostile to gender and sexual diversity. We marshal insights derived from original fieldwork conducted with LGBT activists in Liberia, Malawi, and South Africa and analyses of literary and cultural depictions of African queerness.

SCRUTINIZED IDENTITIES

Queer African communities respond not only to local opponents but also to a legacy of scientific racism, sexism, and homophobia. In the nineteenth century, scientific racism and ethnocentrism pervaded investigations of African sexualities. Exemplified by European fascination with the bodies of African women like Saartjie "Sara" Baartman, scientific and colonial racism distorted Euro-American perceptions of African sexual practices and bodies, as research by Clifton Crais and Pamela Scully and Siobhan Somerville shows. Such views promoted racist, heteronormative views of African women as temptresses who lured white men into adulterous relationships and African men as sexual predators who raped white women. Scholars, including Signe Arnfred and Sylvia Tamale, work to dispel racist and ethnocentric misconceptions of African sexualities, just as African LGBT activists confront the lingering effects of colonial constructions of race, gender, and sexuality. Such effects include the notions that "homosexuality is un-African" and that Western governments use LGBT rights to undermine African sovereignty (Msibi 68).

Over the past ten years, African antigay opponents have attempted to constrain how queer African communities portray themselves and to limit the political claims they can make. In 2006, a white South African lesbian couple, Engelina de Nysschen and Hannelie Botha, stood trial for abusing and murdering their son (Ndaba). At the time, South Africa was one of the few countries in the world with legislation prohibiting discrimination on the basis of sexual orientation, and the Constitutional Court had recently issued a ruling asking lawmakers to legalize same-sex marriage. Members of the African Christian Democratic Party (ACDP) viewed the trial as a chance to argue that lesbians were violent and should not have access to the same rights and protections as heterosexual South Africans. Reverend Kenneth Meshoe, the ACDP leader, used the case to denounce same-sex marriage and to call on lawmakers not to legalize same-sex marriage. Meshoe stated, "Parliament must do more to protect children who are exposed to such sinful relationships" (Xaba 4). The fact that the lesbian women were white bolstered claims underlying Meshoe's opposition that same-sex sexualities were un-African, white phenomena. It was precisely this type of misrepresentation against which South African LGBT activists had been working. Although Meshoe's call to deny queer South Africans access to marriage equality went unheeded, it was one of many homophobic assertions intended to limit the social and political space queer Africans could safely claim. Ultimately, the court sentenced De Nysschen to 25 years and Botha to 20 years in prison (Ndaba).

BISEXUALS' SECONDARY MARGINALIZATION

In light of antiqueer sentiments, one might expect that queer African communities are safe spaces for all gender and sexual dissidents. Yet not all queer constituents—specifically, bisexual persons—receive a warm embrace in queer African community spaces. For some black South African lesbians, bisexuality was a term laden with perilous connotations. Black lesbian activists with the Forum for the Empowerment for Women (FEW) sponsored "antiviolence training" workshops intended to educate black lesbians about "corrective rape," a term black South African lesbian activists devised to describe the punitive intentions of antilesbian sexual violence (Currier 64, 2). At one such workshop in 2006, FEW addressed antilesbian violence and intimate partner violence in lesbian relationships. The workshop leader provocatively asked if anyone in the audience believed that there was an instance in which a woman deserved to be beaten. One lesbian woman bluntly stated that she "hated bisexuals" and that bisexual women needed punishment because, after sleeping with men, they sleep with women, exposing lesbians to HIV/AIDS. The workshop leader disapproved and advised women that if they were in a relationship with someone who held similar views, their partners would eventually become physically abusive, implying a close connection between beliefs about gender and sexual norms and violent action. Within this workshop setting, no woman who identified as bisexual likely felt comfortable disclosing her sexual identity. Such marginalization, which Cathy J. Cohen names "secondary marginalization," involves marginalized members within disenfranchised groups experiencing "the denial of access not only to dominant resources and structures, but also to many of the indigenous resources and institutions needed for their survival" (70, 75). Such ostracism can alienate and make less privileged queers feel unsafe and unwelcome in LGBT communities.

Bisexuality also acquired a negative valence for some LGBT and HIV/AIDS activists in Liberia and Malawi. In interviews, some activists derided married, bisexually active men for putting their wives at risk for contracting HIV and sexually transmitted infections (STIs) and for not being liberated enough, even in a homophobic society, to acknowledge what activists assumed to be an overriding sexual desire for men. These views resonate with the stereotype of some US men of color who have sex with men as being "on the down low," a category that portrays these men as endangering heterosexual women of color (Snorton 122). Arthur, a gay man and HIV/AIDS activist in Liberia, pitied married, bisexually active men whom he assumed were too insecure to live exclusively as gay men and embrace their sexual attractions to men as a step toward gay authenticity.

> There are some people even living complicated lives because you want to cover up so you get married to a woman, but you're not satisfied [sexually]. You call your friend: "Can I bring my friend to your house?" Why can't people be who they're supposed to be? (Currier, Interview)

Activists' disapproval of married men's bisexual activity was premised on a sense of sexual agency and liberation. The logic went like this: if men could be secure in their sexual desires for men in societies like Liberia and Malawi where antihomosexual sentiments suffused political debate, they could commit to one partner. For such activists, gay authenticity—the alignment of sexual desires, behaviors, and identity in a linear fashion—would serve as the social substrate on which LGBT activist organizations could advance their political projects.

ACTIVISM, AGENCY, AND QUEER IDENTITIES

Although insistence on gender and sexual "authenticity" could result in unreasonable demands on African LGBT persons, narratives of authenticity produced an unexpected variant of the sexual liberation logic in some movements, which involved expressing sexual agency. For instance, some Malawian gay men involved with LGBT organizing spontaneously disclosed in interviews that an older boy or man had raped them when they were younger. Both men were in their twenties and worked as HIV/AIDS peer educators at a Malawian LGBT movement organization. Although, when recounting these sexual encounters, these men did not label them as "rape," they clearly conveyed that they did not want to have sex (Currier and Manuel 295). Both men's HIV/AIDS educational training and experiences working as peer educators counseling men who have sex with men transformed their sense of sexual agency. Just as they advised men to turn down sex with men they did not desire, these two men became aware that they could reject sex with men who propositioned them, a possibility that did not occur to their younger selves. By articulating the principles of sexual consent that were important to them, these peer educators confirmed how LGBT activism resulted in the reorganization of their sexual agency and identities.

Such renewed sexual agency has also translated into wider representations of same-sex desire in African literatures and cultures, which had afforded little space to such representations. African "homosexualities" have usually not been depicted as an expression of identity politics, which in Western countries were borne out of gay and lesbian liberation movements, but rather have been submerged in subtext. While transgressing sociocultural norms, the female homoeroticism illustrated in the works of postcolonial Francophone African novelists, such as Calixthe Beyala and Ken Bugul, registers the prohibition associated with such desires in patriarchal African cultures (Etoke 176–177, 186). Considered to be the first feature film about homosexuality in sub-Saharan Africa, Mohamed Camara's 1997 film *Dakan* broke new ground by portraying the irrepressible attraction and love between two Guinean male high school students. Although the film celebrates their relationship as an authentic alternative to heteronormativity, it closes on the protagonists' forced departure for an unknown place and future (Migraine-George 46). Recent documentaries, such as *Born This Way* (and *Call Me Kuchu*, similarly focus on the ostracism experienced by queer Africans in Cameroon and Uganda.

However, literary and cultural representations of African same-sex sexualities treat queer relationships as legitimate modes of pleasure and commitment. The Nigerian writer Chimamanda Ngozi Adichie, now a high-profile figure in US media (she was notably quoted by pop star Beyoncé in one of her songs), broached the topic of same-sex desire in a collection of short stories, *The Thing around Your Neck* (2009). In an op-ed, "Why Can't He Just Be Like Everyone Else?" Adichie publicly opposes the antigay law passed in January 2014 by the Nigerian government, declaring: "If anything, it is the passage of the law itself that is 'unafrican.' It goes against the values of tolerance and 'live and let live' that are part of many African cultures." Another example is the photographer and activist Zanele Muholi, whose internationally exhibited work focuses on black South African lesbians. While documenting homophobic violence, Muholi's photographs illustrate a multifaceted sensuality. A BBC journalist described one of her pictures of two women kissing as one of "art history's greatest kisses," alongside famous artworks by European artists, such as Auguste Rodin and Gustav Klimt. Such representations capture the complexity of the public and private lives of queer Africans.

While examining queer African identities, one needs to account for how colonial homophobia, scientific racism, local forms of stigmatization, and perceived Western meddling in African sovereign affairs fuel anti-LGBT discrimination in Africa (Ekine and Abbas). Despite the looming threat of antiqueer violence and discrimination, queer persons, whether in Africa or elsewhere, manifest resilience and creativity in determining their lives and futures. Online social media enable them to network within a global queer community in which people increasingly view identities as fluid and borderless. Activists and gender and sexual dissidents throughout Africa and cultural depictions of queer Africans defy easy categorization, insisting that observers consider cultural, economic, social, and political similarities and distinctions when discussing queerness on the African continent.

ACKNOWLEDGMENTS

Funding from the National Science Foundation (SES-0601767) supported Ashley Currier's fieldwork in South Africa, and funding from the American Sociological Association Fund for the Advancement for the Discipline supported her research in Liberia.

WORKS CITED

Aarmo, Margrete. "How Homosexuality Became 'Un-African': The Case of Zimbabwe." *Female Desires: Same-Sex Relations and Transgender Practices across Cultures.* Edited by Evelyn Blackwood and Saskia E. Wieringa. Columbia UP, 1999, pp. 255–80.

Adichie, Chimamanda Ngozi. *The Thing around Your Neck.* Alfred A. Knopf, 2009.

———. "Why Can't He Just Be Like Everyone Else?" *The Scoop*, 18 Feb. 2014, www.thescoopng.com/chimamanda-adichie-why-cant-he-just-be-like-everyoneelse/.

Arnfred, Signe, editor. *Re-Thinking Sexualities in Africa*. Nordic Africa Institute, 2004.

Camara, Mohamed, director. *Dakan*. Les Films du 20ème et La Sept Cinéma/California Newsreel, 1997.

Cohen, Cathy J. *The Boundaries of Blackness: AIDS and the Breakdown of Black Politics*. U of Chicago P, 1999.

Crais, Clifton C., and Pamela Scully. *Sara Baartman and the Hottentot Venus: A Ghost Story and a Biography*. Princeton UP, 2009.

Currier, Ashley. Interview by Thérèse Migraine-George. Monrovia, Liberia, 10 July 2013.

Currier, Ashley. *Out in Africa: LGBT Organizing in Namibia and South Africa*. U of Minnesota P, 2012.

Currier, Ashley, and Rashida A. Manuel. "When Rape Goes Unnamed: Gay Malawian Men's Responses to Unwanted and Nonconsensual Sex." *Australian Feminist Studies*, vol. 81, 2014, pp. 289-305. *MasterFILE Complete*, doi:10.1080/08164649.2014.959242.

Ekine, Sokari, and Hakima Abbas, editors. *Queer African Reader*. Pambazuka Press, 2013.

Etoke, Nathalie. "Mariama Barry, Ken Bugul, Calixthe Beyala, and the Politics of Female Homoeroticism in Sub-Saharan Francophone African Literature." *Research in African Literatures*, vol. 40, no. 2, 2009, pp. 173–89.

Call Me Kuchu. Directed by Katherine Fairfax Wright and Malika Zouhali-Worrall. Docurama, 2013.

Farago, Jason. "Art History's Greatest Kisses." *Culture*, BBC, 13 Feb. 2015, www.bbc.com/culture/story/20150213-art-historys-greatest-kisses.

Kadlec, Shaun, and Deb Tullmann, dirs. *Born This Way*. Good Docs, 2014.

Migraine-George, Thérèse. "Beyond the 'Internalist' vs. 'Externalist' Debate: African Homosexuals' Local-Global Identities in Two Films, *Woubi Chéri* and *Dakan*." *Journal of African Cultural Studies*, vol. 16, no. 1, 2003, pp. 45–56.

Murray, Stephen, and Will Roscoe. *Boy-Wives and Female Husbands: Studies in African Homosexualities*. St. Martin's Press, 1998.

Msibi, Thabo. "The Lies We Have Been Told: On (Homo) Sexuality in Africa." *Africa Today*, vol. 58, no. 1, 2011, pp. 55-77. *Project MUSE*, doi:10.2979/africatoday.58.1.55.

Ndaba, Baldwin. "Mom, Lesbian Lover Imprisoned for Boy's Death." *The Star*, 28 November 2006, www.iol.co.za/news/south-africa/mom-lesbian-lover-imprisoned-for-boy-s-death-1.305130#.VbY2FXhjqS0.

Snorton, C. Riley. *Nobody Is Supposed to Know: Black Sexuality on the Down Low*. U of Minnesota P, 2014.

Somerville, Siobhan B. *Queering the Color Line: Race and the Invention of Homosexuality in American Culture*. Duke UP, 2000.

Tamale, Sylvia, editor. *African Sexualities: A Reader*. Pambazuka Press, 2011.

Xaba, Phindile. "Same-sex Sin Blamed for Child's Murder." *Sowetan*, 24 March 2006, p. 4.

12. • *M. Soledad Caballero*

BEFORE INTERSECTIONALITY (NEW)

M. Soledad Caballero, a professor of English at Allegheny College, researches British Romanticism, travel writing, and Gothic literature. Her published scholarship focuses on British women's travel narratives about South America, in particular those by Maria Dundas Graham and Frances Calderón de la Barca. Her more recent research interests include an interdisciplinary study of emotion, work she does with a colleague in cognitive psychology. Her poems have appeared in journals including *The Missouri Review*, the *Mississippi Review*, and the *Pittsburgh Poetry Review*, among others. The following poem is part of a larger body of work titled "Immigrant Confessions," which focuses on the complex and paradoxical intersections between memory, language, loss, identity, and immigration.

After school, you hid in the bathroom
examining the day's insults
stuck to your face. You punched
lockers. You slammed bedroom
doors. I tried books. I tried invisibility. We
lived our sadness through each other. We
lived our silence too. We straddled
emptiness. Spanish in whispers,
our parents' accents, their immigrant fears.
South Carolina 1986. There were
only two colors, only two histories
to choose. We were neither.

13. • *Michele Tracy Berger and Cheryl Radeloff*

CLAIMING AN EDUCATION:
Your Inheritance as a Student of Women's and Gender Studies (2015)

Michele Tracy Berger is a professor of women's studies and the director of the Faculty Fellows Program for the Institute for the Arts and Humanities at the University of North Carolina, Chapel Hill. She was awarded the Best Book Award by the American Political Science Association for *Workable Sisterhood: The Political Journey of Stigmatized Women with HIV/AIDS* (Princeton, 2004) and coedited *Gaining Access: A Practical and Theoretical Guide for Qualitative Researchers* (Altamira, 2003) and *The Intersectional Approach: Transforming the Academy through Race, Class, and Gender* (University of North Carolina, 2010).

Cheryl Radeloff is a disease investigation and intervention specialist with the Southern Nevada Health District and an adjunct professor of women's studies at the College of Southern Nevada. Her work has focused on HIV testing laws and policies in Nevada's sex industry. For this piece, they surveyed over 900 women's and gender studies graduates (1995–2010) from around the globe regarding their career paths, and it remains the largest data set on the subject.

In one of your WGST classes you have probably read the well-known and anthologized essay by poet, essayist, and feminist Adrienne Rich that discusses "claiming an education." In this inspiring essay, Rich highlights the importance of being an active participant in the process of becoming educated. This piece stirred an entire generation of students, both women and men, to apply themselves to their interests, to take ownership of their education, to question what they were taught and how it was relevant to them. . . . One way to do that is to understand Women's and Gender Studies' unique history and to be able locate yourself within it. Most students have some knowledge of the early history of Women's Studies, but this cursory understanding often eludes you when someone pointedly asks, "What is Women's Studies? Isn't Women's Studies just a response to oppression?" Questions about the goals and roots of Women's Studies can often be surprising to students. The foundation about WGST that we provide here will enhance your current understanding of the politics and debates surrounding the role of WGST in higher education and its public perception. . . .

. . . We look at how Women's Studies evolved into Women's and Gender Studies. We take you behind the scenes to help you understand that what happens in a Women's and Gender Studies classroom is an outgrowth of activism, debate, and rich intellectual tradition. We also provide a contemporary picture of Women's and Gender Studies—who your professors are, and who is likely to sit next to you in the classroom (or share a virtual classroom). You will also hear from graduates about what they have considered valuable in their training.

[. . .]

QUIZ: HOW MUCH DO YOU KNOW ABOUT THE HISTORY OF WOMEN'S AND GENDER STUDIES?

How much do you know about the birth of Women's and Gender Studies? See how many of the following questions you can answer.

1. What was the first Women's Studies program in the United States?
2. True or false: Most professors in the 1970s who taught Women's Studies did not get paid for their classes.
3. What is feminist pedagogy?
4. Why does Women's and Gender Studies value research, theory, and praxis?
5. What is the National Women's Studies Association?
6. Where were the first Women's Studies courses offered in the United States?
7. What is the relationship between the civil rights movement, the women's rights movement, and student activism for the discipline of Women's Studies in the US?
8. How many countries around the world offer WGST degrees?
9. True or false: Community colleges play a vital role in training students in WGST.
10. What topics might you have covered in one of the first Women's Studies classes on women's health?

You will discover the answers as you keep reading! But they are also at the end of the chapter.

"BACK IN THE DAY": THE BIRTH OF WOMEN'S STUDIES

Today you stand as some of the latest in a long line of students who paved the way for Women's and Gender Studies on campuses across the US and now the world. Women's Studies has its roots and origins in the social movements of the 1960s and 1970s, specifically the civil rights and women's rights movements. Women's Studies courses, and other interdisciplinary studies (e.g. American Studies), were born largely due to student activism and demand. This was a time when more women in the United States were attending colleges and universities than ever before!

While many students attending college during the late 1960s and early 1970s were "traditional" in age and pre-college education, many others were nontraditional (e.g. veterans, married or divorced women, those of different socio-economic strata, racial/ethnic backgrounds, and sexual orientations). This generation of new students (and new professors) creates a unique culture in higher education that challenged the status quo as we describe below. Feminist activism spilled onto college campuses, forcing new questions about academic study. The earliest integrated Women's Studies programs at major universities were founded around 1970, although there were a few courses in Women's Studies (and/ or courses on "women" or "feminism") that were offered at some colleges and universities before this time. While acknowledging the importance of individual and group-level change in the classroom, the first Women's Studies educators knew they had to change the very structure and curriculum of higher education. At many of the newly coeducational colleges and universities of the 1970s, Women's Studies developed as part of the process of incorporating and integrating women into their campus communities. Often the first Women's Studies professors taught new courses unpaid out of their absolute commitment to this academic endeavor!

[. . .]

CREATING CHANGE AND THE IMPORTANCE OF RESEARCH, THEORY, AND PRAXIS

Early Women's Studies faculty were innovative pioneers in creating this new academic endeavor. They wrote their own textbooks, compiled and shared reading lists, developed new curricula, organized conferences, and established academic journals. Their courses provided the first opportunity for women's lives and experiences to be studied seriously in higher education from a gender-inclusive perspective. Previously most scholarship was male dominated. The advances made by these innovators were in concert with the skills and knowledge they had gained as members of civil rights, liberal, and radical women's groups and organizations. The early twin goals of Women's Studies as an academic enterprise were: (1) to document and redress the exclusion of women's experiences from the traditional male-defined curriculum; and (2) to pose interdisciplinary questions and analyses across the social sciences, arts, humanities, and sciences. Early on, scholars realized that no single discipline could answer or address women's experiences. Therefore, a commitment to multiple approaches and perspectives from a variety of disciplinary communities in addressing women's lives

took root. Faculty emphasized acknowledging and studying women's lives through women's own diverse experiences. Early founders believed that Women's Studies needed to stay connected and relevant to the everyday issues that women faced, and to work on challenging the myriad of persisting inequalities.

From the beginning of the institutionalization of Women's Studies in the academy, the concept of integrating research, theory, and praxis became central. This "triad" (the concept of research, theory, and praxis as being equally valued) is a unique feature of Women's Studies in higher education, and you will hear it mentioned as you progress through coursework. . . .

RESEARCH

In the academy, one of the primary ways that knowledge is advanced and legitimated is through the publication of scholarly articles and books based on original research. In the early phases of the movement Women's Studies faculty contributed to the academic knowledge base that had been primarily androcentric, or male-centered, in nature. Scholars during 1970s and 1980s spent much of their time documenting the ways women's experiences were left out of various types of research projects and priorities, and one aspect of this inquiry was to question the stereotypes about women that were pervasive in research (Hesse-Biber and Leavy 2007). These stereotypes were prevalent in science and other seemingly "neutral" forms of empirical research. Hesse-Biber and Leavy discuss a well-known example by anthropologist Emily Martin, who pioneered a critique of gendered bias in the sciences:

[. . .]

Martin shows that so-called truthful and objective medical textbooks were infused with nonobjective stereotypes, shaping both the medical and cultural understanding of natural events. . . . She argues that medical textbooks were depicting gender stereotypes through scientific language that had little basis in reality.

Researchers began to ask new questions when women were included in the center of analysis. This meant rejecting the idea that women could simply be "stirred" into disciplines without a serious rethinking of research and theoretical approaches. Scholars looked everywhere for answers in the social sciences and humanities. They examined culture, systems of representation, the analysis of literary texts, creative expression, and the ways in which institutions are shaped by and reflect ideas about gender and society.

Researchers also used multiple methods to explore new questions about women and gender, including: experiments, oral histories, historical analysis, surveys, textual analysis, ethnographies, and other qualitative data gathering.

THEORY

Theory, the second piece to the conceptual triad, is an important component in Women's Studies. It is grounded in experience, critical reflection, and interaction with the larger world. In many disciplines, ideas, concepts, frameworks, and perspectives that had been defined as normal, universal, and centrally important were revealed to focus on a small number of people—usually upper middle-class, heterosexual, able-bodied white men. The development of theory as a vital tool with which to challenge oppression and domination has become central in Women's Studies. Early Women's Studies scholars sought new theoretical concepts to explore the features of women's lives that had yet to be fully understood (e.g. sexual violence, prostitution, motherhood). Scholars in Philosophy and Political Science took up central concepts of citizenship, political participation, and democratic rights, and rethought them by looking at women's experiences. Scholars in Theology began questioning the interpretation of foundational works of organized religion, and questioned the very language that is used in religion and faith-based communities to marginalize women (see Christ 1992; Daly 1993).

We think it is important to stress that many Women's Studies scholars were also making changes in their own disciplines, and creating groups within their professional organizations that would make scholarship on women a priority. For example, in Sociology, the foremothers of Sociologists for Women in Society (SWS, an organization within Sociology dedicated to supporting and promoting gender scholars and research through conferences and their own publication) were making changes within Sociology, as well as in Women's Studies. Thus, Women's Studies emerged in concert with changes happening in established disciplines by the very women (and men) who were also shaping it.

PRAXIS

Finally, we turn to the concept of praxis. Praxis is about the integration of learning with social justice. As a term, it means that seeking knowledge for knowledge's sake will not change structures of domination and oppression in women's lives.[1] Praxis is about applying one's knowledge to challenge oppressive systems and unequal traditions. It is related to the well-known phrase "the personal is political" espoused by many advocates of the second-wave women's movement. Over time, for those in Women's Studies, it has meant training students to think and learn about inequalities beyond the borders of the classroom. This integrated triad of concepts helps to distinguish Women's Studies' intellectual goals from other disciplines. Women's Studies as an academic endeavor seeks to weigh all three of these concepts equally in teaching, research, and engagement outside of the academy. This emphasis speaks to the way in which the field is informed by and engaged in activism and advocacy that in turn shape the creation of new knowledge.

NWSA—PROFESSIONAL OUTCOME OF AN ACADEMIC MOVEMENT

Every academic discipline has its own professional organization, and the field of WGST is no different. The National Women's Studies Association (NWSA) was formed in 1977, and signaled an important moment for Women's Studies. NWSA's emergence as a key player in the academic landscape, with the members to prove it, suggested to the larger academic community that there was enough interest in teaching and research among people who considered themselves committed to

Women's Studies to form an official association. NWSA continues to be the premier organization for scholars and students of Women's Studies. It holds an annual conference with over 1,600 attendees, in past years including K–12 teachers, college professors, undergraduate students, graduate students, higher education administrators (such as deans, etc.), and women's center directors.

[. . .]

TRANSFORMATION OF THE CLASSROOM

Another part of your inheritance is the Women's and Gender Studies classroom.

You have probably heard of, or read about, the social unrest of the late twentieth century. During the 1960s and 1970s, student activists in the US protested not only the war and government policy, but also the very knowledge that was being taught and produced in establishments of higher learning or post-secondary educational institutions. Students and faculty alike were experimenting with the structure and style of teaching, ranging from consciousness-raising sessions in the classroom, changing the physical structure of the classroom itself (such as seating, moving the classroom from inside to outdoors), and emphasizing student participation rather than the passive learning model of the "banking concept of education" (see Friere 2001). People experimented with class design to provide a better format for engaging students. This time of transition had a profound effect on the development of the Women's Studies classroom and teaching practices. You might have noticed that you are often seated in a circle that creates a space where everyone faces everyone. It might seem strange to you that a simple change such as this—seating students in a circle where they can see and hear one another—was unique and transformative. But it was! This new arrangement allowed for a greater accountability for each student, the possibility for rapport to form more deeply between

students and faculty, and a more level playing field in which the distance between professor "knowers" and student "learners" was decreased. This arrangement also served as a type of "container" when strong emotions were expressed.

Faculty members in the 1960s and 1970s drew upon a new teaching style that was more participatory and personal, which later became known as "feminist pedagogy."[2] They helped to develop the concept of "student-centered learning." The new courses offered faculty and students the opportunity to conduct in-depth scholarly work on subjects that had previously not been a part of the college curriculum, or were at the margins of more traditional disciplines, such as domestic violence, women's roles in historical periods, and women's literature. By listening to and valuing the experiences of students, topics that may have been largely ignored rose to prominence, as they reflected the everyday concerns and interests of students. Rather than being the objects of study (such as wife and mother in nuclear family structures, as challenged by Betty Friedan in *The Feminine Mystique,* deviant career woman, and/or over-sexualized prostitute or woman of color), Women's Studies was able to do more than just "add women" superficially to traditional curricula. Women's Studies courses allowed students to choose what subjects to study, to question how subjects would be studied, to challenge ideas of objectivity and power within research, and to create knowledge that would support the changes occurring on local, state, and national levels due to feminist organizing (including rape laws, domestic violence, women's health advocacy, women entering nontraditional occupations, wages for housework).

[. . .]

UNDERSTANDING THE LEGACY

Activist and political roots are part of Women's Studies history, which it shares with Chicano Studies, American Studies, Peace and Justice Studies,

Native American Studies, Environmental Studies, and African and African American Studies. Not surprisingly, these interdisciplinary fields are sometimes attacked as less scholarly because of their political origins. Traditional disciplines, without seemingly overt activist beginnings, by comparison, look neutral and unbiased. . . . One hundred years ago, a person studying the field of Politics was just as likely to read literature and study languages as he (or she) was to learn statistics. Political Science, as a discipline, went through major shifts post–World War II, and then again in the early 1980s. The truth is that the boundaries of what a discipline encompasses are ones of constant change and development. Knowledge, and what is perceived as important in the make-up of a discipline, shifts and changes. In 100 years, we can assume that Women's Studies will be configured very differently than it is now. . . .

. . . As you can see, Women's Studies, as a distinct academic interdisciplinary field, would not have been possible without the social movements that preceded its founding. Moreover, given its origins in social movements, Women's Studies was, from its beginnings, activist in orientation. Professors and students saw Women's Studies as committed to transforming women's roles in the world, and not simply understanding such stratified roles. Its goal was not "disinterested" academic inquiry, rather, Women's Studies focused on ending gender oppression and challenging traditional paradigms. Indeed, the relationship of Women's Studies to the women's movement was crucial in establishing and developing the field. The women's movement, in particular, helped pressure colleges and universities to establish Women's Studies programs and helped establish the study of women and gender as a worthy endeavor.

Practitioners of Women's and Gender Studies have also worked as allies in supporting the growth of student services on college campuses and universities, including centers of diversity and multicultural affairs, LGBTQ offices, and women's centers, thus affecting the overall quality of contemporary student life.

FOR YOUR LIBRARY

We encourage you to do further reading about the history, debates, and development of Women's and Gender Studies. You will feel more informed when you talk to your professors (always a plus!) and various publics, and it will help you understand the larger patterns that have shaped the knowledge that you are learning.

Jane Aaron and Sylvia Walby (Eds.) (1991). *Out of the Margins: Women's Studies in the Nineties.* Bristol, PA: Falmer Press.

Marilyn Jacoby Boxer and Catherine R. Stimpson (2001). *When Women Ask the Questions: Creating Women's Studies in America.* Baltimore, MD: Johns Hopkins University Press.

Ann Braithwaite, Susan Heald, Susanne Luhmann, and Sharon Rosenberg (Eds.) (2005). *Troubling Women's Studies: Pasts, Presents, and Possibilities* Toronto: Sumach Press.

Florence Howe (Ed.) (2000). *The Politics of Women's Studies: Testimony from the Thirty Founding Mothers.* New York: The Feminist Press.

Ellen Messer-Davidow (2002). *Disciplining Feminism: From Social Activism to Academic Discourse.* Durham, NC: Duke University Press.

Joan Wallach Scott (Ed.) (2008). *Women's Studies on the Edge.* Durham, NC: Duke University Press.

Robyn Weigman (Ed.) (2002). *Women's Studies on its Own: A Next Wave Reader in Institutional Change.* Durham, NC: Duke University Press.

YOUR WOMEN'S AND GENDER STUDIES PROFESSOR

If we were to rely solely on media images of a category called "Women's and Gender Studies professors," it would be slim pickings. In the past 50 years, it was unusual to even see a woman *portrayed* as a college professor. Typically, stereotyped images of college professors included rumpled, white, older befuddled men (i.e. the absent-minded professor) who pontificated to a classroom (often of other men), or lecherous, leather-patch-and-tweed white men who used their position and influence to seduce naive coeds (have you ever seen *Animal House?*). If female students of Women's Studies were represented at all in the movies, they were portrayed as ethnic print-wearing, Birkenstock-shoed, vegetarian, cheerless, angry, man-hating women in films such as *PCU (1994)*. These characters were one-dimensional misrepresentations of women who often "only needed a man" in order to become happy.

Recently, however, media representations have begun to challenge these stereotypes of students and professors. In films such as *Nutty Professor II: The Klumps* (2000) and *Something's Gotta Give* (2003), Janet Jackson and Frances McDormand are portrayed as smart, witty women who challenge the main male character's ideas about love and life. In fact, at the end of the previous decade, HBO (a major cable network in the US) made news by initiating conversations about developing a comedy series entitled *Women's Studies,* which would follow the day-to-day life issues experienced by a Women's Studies professor (Andreeva 2009).

Witty, complicated, and even problematic depictions of feminism and Women's Studies now populate airwaves, including the horror film *Women's Studies* (2010), the satire *The Dictator* (2012), the comedy *Girls* (2011), and the online series *Vag Magazine* (2010–) and *Portlandia* (2011–). With the rise of increasing numbers of female filmmakers working across various digital media, we believe that we will continue to see more diverse and complicated depictions of both second- and third-wave feminism(s) and Women's and Gender Studies students and professors.

Women's and Gender Studies professors come from a diversity of intellectual backgrounds and training. Historically, people who were known as Women's Studies professors were activists and academics from other fields who were interested in women's lives. Many of the faculty members we trained with in college, for example, might have claimed the title of feminist or Women's Studies academic, but were not formally trained in Women's Studies. They typically advocated and fought to have Women's Studies on their campuses, supported the advancement of female faculty, and took on equity issues. But their main intellectual work continued to be in their home discipline and department. In their disciplines, they put questions about gender

front and center and published research in discipline-specific journals. Many women and men who pioneered Women's and Gender Studies are considered baby boomers (i.e. people who were born between 1945 and 1964). Soon, this group will be retiring from the discipline, and those of us who will inherit their legacy are women and men who have advanced degrees (such as MAs and PhDs) or graduate certificates in Women's and Gender Studies.

[. . .]

Women's and Gender Studies, as an interdisciplinary field, has paid attention to issues of underrepresentation of groups, and is committed to promoting a diverse faculty, particularly promoting the visibility and advancement of women of color. So how are we doing in the US? A recent National Women's Studies Association (NWSA) report, "Mapping Women's and Gender Studies," which partnered with the Ford Foundation and the National Opinion Research Center, found that 30.4 percent of Women's Studies faculty are faculty of color, compared with 19 percent of faculty nationally in other disciplines (National Women's Studies Association 2007).[3] This is a good trend for Women's and Gender Studies, but it still requires institutional commitment and effort to maintain and/or improve these numbers. There are, however, fewer data available to critically assess how Women's and Gender Studies, as a field, is faring in hiring individuals from other marginalized groups, including lesbians and other members from the LGBT community, physically challenged individuals, or men.

WOMEN'S AND GENDER STUDIES STUDENTS—WHO ARE THEY?

[. . .]

. . . There are lots of reasons why students come to Women's and Gender Studies. Think, for example, about your own learning path. What made you switch from, say, a Business major to Women's and Gender Studies? What identities do you have as a Women's and Gender Studies student and why? Although there is no existing comprehensive international database about Women's and Gender Studies students, we wanted to touch on who might be in the classroom with you (or who has been in the classroom with you). You may have been exposed to some of the ideas discussed in your Women's Studies class through one of your parent's involvement in women's and gender equality movements, your own experience with activism, or from classes in middle or high school. We are seeing more and more students who have had some positive contact with Women's and Gender Studies prior to taking our courses. Some students enter Women's Studies already familiar with the key perspectives of the field. We think this trend is the fruition of the hard work of activists, educators, and many in the nonprofit sector who are committed to gender equity and the promotion of Women's Studies. Still, for many students, finding Women's Studies is an unanticipated discovery and an area of study with which they had not previously been familiar (unlike English, History, Education, Business, Communication, etc.).

[. . .]

YOUR WOMEN'S AND GENDER STUDIES CLASSROOM: DATA FROM GRADUATES

Women's and Gender Studies majors and minors at the undergraduate level are predominantly composed of female students,[4] although not all students identify as either "women" or "men." As gender and transgender politics have become more visible on college campuses, the gendered composition of our students has reflected this. Ideally, biological determinism should not play a role in who can major in Women's Studies, but as evidenced in the works of feminist scholars such as Emi Koyama (2003), debates still erupt in feminist academic and activist communities about whether men can be feminists and the role of transmen and transwomen in "female-centered" spaces.

Yet, the preponderance of females in Women's Studies should not be surprising, given the history of the field. Women's and Gender Studies offers the opportunity to study issues of power and gender dynamics in a way that supports many young women's learning trajectories. However, in the past several years, the male participation has risen, and we think that several factors are responsible for this. Due to the women's movement, more men have been raised in egalitarian households over the past three decades, and are generally interested in women's lives. Some male students come to view classes in Women's Studies as an extension of their interests shaped by family dynamics. Women, men, and transgendered students take Women's and Gender Studies courses and enjoy them enormously, and see that they can study in this interdisciplinary field. Additionally, male, female, and intersex students often take an Introduction to Women's Studies course as part of fulfilling general educational requirements and decide that they wish to take more. They may also find classes on masculinity and gender that are of interest. Many learn how the construction of gender cannot be seen in isolation, and therefore the study of masculinity is important for men, as well as for women, to understand the construction of gender for their own lives, and those of their peers.

According to our study, the overwhelming majority of Women's and Gender Studies students identify as biologically "female" (95 percent) followed by "male" (4 percent), with the rest identifying as "intersex" or "other." Even though many of our respondents did identify with traditional classifications of sex in the survey, the nature and placement of the question was raised as an issue by several participants:

> I'm a trans man, and I know you want me to say "female," but really, this question is worded awfully. And it sucks that the sex I was assigned at birth is regarded as more important than how I identify (which I assume you consider it to be, based on this being the second question in the survey).

Contemporary Women's and Gender Studies scholars have sought to question and challenge binary sex classifications; therefore, it is not surprising that some respondents do not identify with ascribed or traditional sex or gender categories.

The majority of the graduates who answered our survey were born in the United States (82 percent), with about 9 percent born in Canada Other graduates hail from a variety of countries, including Germany, South Korea, Brazil, Australia, Kenya, Russia, Scandinavia, Japan, and China. After graduating with their degree in Women's and Gender Studies, the majority of those surveyed now live in the United States (83 percent), with about 2 percent residing in either the UK or Canada. Other places your fellow classmates may reside after graduation include Germany, Scandinavia, the Netherlands, South Korea, Spain, Italy, Trinidad and Tobago, or Ghana.

As for race and ethnic identities, the majority of Women's and Gender Studies graduates marked "white" (82 percent). About 5 percent of the graduates marked "black/African American," 3 percent identified as Hispanic/Latino, 4 percent claimed an Asian or Pacific Islander heritage, 1.5 percent claimed a Native American or Alaska Native ancestry, and less than 1 percent claimed a Middle Eastern identity. About 6 percent of those surveyed claimed a multiracial/multiethnic heritage, along with a few respondents who identified as Roma and Jewish. Survey respondents were given the opportunity to claim as many ethnic identities as they felt appropriate, as well as describing their racial/ethnic heritage in the "other" category. However, the classification system used also reflects the traditional "big five" categories commonly used in the United States by survey researchers and government entities. As the majority of Women's and Gender Studies graduates either were born or raised in the United States, these racial/ethnic categories may be familiar; yet, as recent debates over the census—and as raised in Women's and Gender Studies classrooms—have shown, these classifications do not capture the complex heritage of our graduates in the United States or Canada, nor in the world.

In addition to the mix of students in the Women's and Gender Studies classroom in terms of biological sex, racial/ethnic classifications, and countries of origin, the age of graduates varies as well. The majority of those in our survey (who all graduated between 1995 and 2010) were 23–26 years of age (31 percent) at the time of their graduation. Another 29 percent were 27–31 years of age, with 18 percent being 32–36 years of age at graduation. By comparison, the most prevalent range in which our graduates started their Women's and Gender Studies degree program is 18–22 years of age (84 percent). Therefore, more "traditional" aged undergraduate students are actively choosing Women's and Gender Studies as part of their degree selection process.[5]

[. . .]

As the number of Women's and Gender Studies departments and programs have increased since its inception, we found that the majority of graduates surveyed were majors (61 percent), with minors comprising almost one-quarter (24 percent) of the sample. About 7.2 percent of the respondents indicated that they had a concentration in Women's and Gender Studies. We also acknowledge that internationally, a major or minor may not have an equivalent.

Many Women's and Gender Studies programs emphasize a global or multicultural perspective, and this is reflected in the fact that one-third of our respondents participated in an international studies or study-abroad experience. Of those who participated in undergraduate study abroad, 36.7 percent had some Women's and Gender Studies courses as part of their overseas curriculum.

While about one-third of Women's and Gender Studies graduates experienced an international studies program, 45 percent of graduates completed an internship during the course of the undergraduate experience. Of those who completed an internship, 58.5 percent received college credit for their internship.

[. . .]

After completing an undergraduate degree in Women's and Gender Studies, a notably high 57 percent of those who responded to the survey completed some graduate or professional degree courses.

During the past two decades, many Women's and Gender Studies departments and programs have been instrumental in supporting the development of Queer and Sexuality Studies (or allies of new interdisciplinary perspectives). Many biologically identified or transgendered men find Women's and Gender Studies to be compatible with their sexual identities and interests. For example, many men participate in campus organizations and events directed by LGBT centers and/or women's centers. On many campuses, these entities have long-standing cooperative working relationships in which students gain internship or volunteer experience while simultaneously receiving credit in their Women's Studies units.

Ultimately, the Women's and Gender Studies classroom is a global classroom. In our experience, we have seen that our classes have become increasingly diverse in terms of social class, nationality, ethnicity, and sexual orientation. Over the course of your academic career, you are likely to be taking classes with students who have been shaped by a variety of experiences and social contexts.

A NEW KIND OF STUDENT

The work that you have committed to in Women's and Gender Studies has a rich intellectual and social history. For the past four decades, the university has been producing a new type of student in higher education. We believe Women's and Gender Studies students are emerging as a type of educational pioneer (Luebke and Reilly 1995; Boxer and Stimpson 2001). What do we mean by this? Women's Studies' early twin goals of reaching across the disciplines to answer questions about gender and challenging the status of women were innovative in higher education. Since that time, Women's and Gender Studies has developed classroom practices and pedagogical styles that have been adopted by many other disciplines. It has broadened the traditional liberal arts education to encompass a specific focus on inequality, power, and advocacy that continues to be distinctive. The student–professor relationship has also

been rethought—moving from an expert–student relationship to a relationship of co-collaborators. Women's and Gender Studies has pushed for curricula transformation, and that translates into students who have been trained to learn multiple perspectives and to demonstrate the application of knowledge in pursuit of a more equitable society. It encourages students to evaluate their goals and values, as well as synthesize knowledge. The emphasis on synthesizing knowledge and applying it in new contexts is exciting to students, and encourages them to become involved in issues they care deeply about. . . .

Our research and framing about the unique role of Women's and Gender Studies students in higher education is complemented by discussions of how Women's and Gender Studies students view themselves. Narratives and vignettes can be found in the scholarly articles, magazines, online discussions, and several introductory textbooks in Women's Studies that have emerged over the past two decades.[6] One Women's Studies graduate, reflecting on applying her Women's Studies training now as an obstetrician and gynecologist, says that de-masking "unspoken assumptions" was an important lesson that she now uses in her work environment:

> Being realistic and intelligent about power relationships and inequities is another lesson of Women's Studies. Being a student of Women's Studies did not influence my career choice, [but] it helped shape my values, how I see the world, and what I see as my role in it as an African American woman. I value women as full members of society in whatever roles they choose. However, I recognize the world as gendered and unequal. I feel that I have a responsibility to change that status quo wherever possible. . . . These values are neither objective nor neutral. But the fallacy of objectivity is another lesson of Women's Studies.

> (Thompson 2002: 634)

Another Women's Studies graduate has found that the training to examine how assumptions about gender shape the world has been useful after college: "I left the Women's Studies program at SUNY [State

University of New York] New Paltz with energy and enthusiasm to go out into the world and make a difference in the lives of women." She joined the Peace Corps and discusses how her Women's Studies training led her to think critically about the challenges of working with women and children on health literacy, given many of the structural dimensions of their lives:

> My Women's Studies education gave me an understanding of the problems that women living in the Third World face. It also gave me insights into how grassroots level initiatives work. It was with these things in mind that I was able to reach as well as be taught by the women of The Gambia. I learned in Women's Studies the importance of listening and learning from women of different cultures. I knew that what I needed to do was to join the women in their work.

> (Rivera 2006: 634)

Her Women's Studies education allowed her to consider working in a participatory way with the women, to begin to understand the complexity of their lives as both distinctive and similar to her own. It also allowed her to re-evaluate what she thought about "women's work" and how underappreciated it was. Her training, she says, "enhanced my appreciation for the work women do and enabled me to bring to the world of women's work insights and ideas that will somewhat ease women's burdens" (Rivera 2006: 635).

[. . .]

. . . Women's Studies situates civic engagement in a unique curricular context. With the discipline's historical roots in activist movements, its social justice mandate, and its reflective approach to its own knowledge production, Women's Studies offers students a distinctive method for learning how to grapple with the tensions between theory and practice in civic engagement contexts. By encouraging critical reflection on, say, the values of "the community" or "the good citizen," a Women's Studies approach to

civic engagement demands that students *analyze the historical and cultural foundations that create the need for their service in the first place,* as well as *interrogate their own motivations* to "help others."

[. . .]

In addition to bringing analytical concepts to bear on what the student encounters in any community-based context, civic engagement in Women's Studies requires some amount of personal reflection, in which the student is asked to consider how his or her own historical and cultural location (e.g. gender expression, racialized identity, regional bias, class interests, sexual orientation, professional experience, level of education, age, etc.) has an impact on what he or she is able to learn from and do for others in any given context. Without such self-awareness on the part of students, differences of race, culture, class, etc. can too often disrupt their best efforts to "do good." In this way, Women's Studies teaches students entering communities that are not their own that: (1) they are products of historical and cultural forces; (2) these forces form both their sense of selves and differences among individuals but are neither neutral nor simply chosen; and (3) the students themselves are responsible for attempting to negotiate as best they can the impacts of these differences in that community-based context.

[. . .]

THE GLOBAL PRESENCE OF WOMEN'S AND GENDER STUDIES

Women's and Gender Studies is flourishing in many places around the world. In the above section, we drew heavily on how majors, minors, etc. are organized in the U.S. system. When we look outside the US, we see some differences in how "undergraduates" are trained globally. In many parts of the world (such as the UK), undergraduate education is post-secondary education up to the level of a master's degree. Below, we provide a snapshot of both established programs and programs that have emerged more recently.

- The Institute for Women's Studies in the Arab World (IWSAW) at the Lebanese American University offers six courses that address the topic of Women's and Gender Studies: "Introduction to Gender Studies," "Representations of Women in the Arts and the Media," "Women and Economic Power," "Women in the Arab World: Sociological Perspectives," "Psychology of Women: A Feminist Perspective," and "Issues and Debates in Feminist Theory." They are in the process of preparing a graduate program (MA) in Gender Studies (see http://iwsaw.lau.edu.lb).

[. . .]

- The University of Auckland's Women's Studies program has been reorganized into a more streamlined Gender Studies program. It is run under the auspices of the Anthropology Department and consists mostly of Social Sciences courses with a few Literature courses available on a less-regular basis. It became available for a major, minor, BA honors (this is a graduate degree in New Zealand), MA, and Ph.D. in 2011. The undergraduate programmer consists of eight courses (see University of Auckland 2014).
- Women's and Gender Studies is offered through the Institute for Gender and Development Studies at the University of the West Indies, St. Augustine Unit. This is an autonomous multidisciplinary and interdisciplinary unit located in the Office of the Vice-Chancellor of the University. Currently, a minor in Gender Studies or a minor in Gender and Development are offered. Many of the students enroll in the graduate program and pursue a postgraduate diploma in Gender—or do a master's or a Ph.D., or go to law school. Others find work in the nonprofit sector, work in local and regional nongovernmental organizations (NGOs), work for international organizations such as the UN, UNDP, IDRC, UNIFEM, and UNICEF, or enter into public service, getting employment in

government ministries that deal with gender and gender affairs (see http://sta.uwi.edu/igds).

[. . .]

GRADUATES SPEAK TO YOU

. . . You are committed to Women's and Gender Studies but may be wondering, "How will this training help and support my interests overall?" You might feel daunted or overwhelmed at the possible ways to apply your interest in WGST. You may not be receiving positive support for your choice. We thought this might be a good time for you to hear how graduates from our survey reflect on their choices. If you ever face doubts or feel challenged, you are not alone! In our survey, we asked graduates: "What advice would (or do) you tell other students or friends considering a course of study or degree in Gender and/or Women's Studies?" While we received many emphatic responses that said "Do it!" and "Go for it!" below we highlight some of our longer and more detailed answers:

> It's a fantastic interdisciplinary degree that gives you the communication skills employers need. You'll use these skills the rest of your life. Put it together with a foreign language, internships and study abroad and you can't be beat. Do what you love. Follow your bliss. . . . A Women's Studies degree is a fabulous, well-rounded liberal arts course of study, and I would do it again in a heartbeat.
>
> (2003, WMST major, Hollins University)

[. . .]

I have talked to a few undergraduate students who worry about the employability of Women's Studies graduates (or whose parents worry about this). I tell people that from my own experience and perspective, employers (and grad school admissions committees) in many arenas are less interested in what someone's undergrad major was, and more interested in skills like critical thinking, writing, communicating with people of diverse backgrounds and perspectives, etc. Women's Studies courses provide a lot of opportunities to develop these kinds of skills, and can prepare students for a range of future career paths.

(2003, Gender and WMST double major,
Oberlin College)

I found it personally interesting, but I also knew I was going to law school after I completed my undergraduate degree. Thus, for me, it was a good forum for learning critical analysis, researching, and writing, as well as developing an understanding of multiple perspectives of an issue or topic. No doubt there are more opportunities to do interesting work or further studies in this space now than there were 15 years ago.

From a more personal perspective, my mother was Chinese, and came from an arranged marriage in which my grandmother was an object and who could only speak when spoken to. My father was from a very traditional patriarchal Scandinavian household who favored sons over daughters. It was eye-opening for me to realize I could do and be so much more than what I had grown up to believe. I loved challenging traditional ideas, rules, and norms! The Women's Studies curriculum was great for me—it was in my undergraduate studies that I began what has been a lifelong journey of self-discovery, trying to understand who I am, what I have been told is me, what and who society expects me to be, and what and who I'd like to be going forward. I would probably have undergone a similar journey of exploration in any case, but a Women's Studies degree gave me the space and frame of reference in which to structure my thinking in more meaningful ways.

In addition to changing the way I view myself as a woman, it has changed the way I view other women in all walks of life. I do a lot of international travel for my work, with a focus on environmental and social issues in emerging markets. I am particularly sensitive to the role of women in their communities and thinking about how women are a vastly underserved segment of the population in terms of access to capital and banking. . . .

I would further add that by challenging traditional notions of what it means to be a woman, and what we understand about sexuality, my Women's Studies courses opened my mind to alternative approaches to gender roles and sexuality. This has made me generally a more open and accepting person over the years. Coming from a small, very close-minded, conservative, provincial town in Michigan, this was an important step for me in recognizing, being more sympathetic to, and accepting "nontraditional" lifestyles. I am so much richer for opening my world to different people with different views, value systems, and lifestyles. I take this into my personal and professional life and, given the international nature of my work and extensive travel I have done on a personal level, I have found that I am intellectually interested in and curious about people everywhere and what makes them who they are—nature/nurture, cultural norms and influences, geography, race, creed, origins, sexuality, etc. This makes me a better person, a better professional, a better advocate.

(1995, WMST major, University of Michigan)

We think that the last respondent captures a frame of mind the Women's and Gender Studies education strives for—supporting students to live their lives fully, take on meaningful employment, and speak up on issues that they care about. The benefits of Women's Studies continuing to thrive in higher education include creating students who are ready for deep civic engagement and a vibrant community of scholars that contribute cutting-edge knowledge to the most pressing societal problems.

ANSWERS FOR QUIZ: HOW MUCH DO YOU KNOW ABOUT THE HISTORY OF WOMEN'S STUDIES?

1. San Diego State University.
2. True. Most professors in the 1970s who taught Women's Studies did not get paid for their classes.

3. Feminist pedagogy is a set of theoretical assumptions about how to interact with students, and encourages a participatory and personal approach to how knowledge is produced in the classroom.
4. Women's and Gender Studies, as a field, believes that research, theory, and practice are interconnected and important for developing new knowledge, both inside and outside the academy.
5. The National Women's Studies Association is the professional organization of scholars and practitioners who teach and research in the field of Women's and Gender Studies.
6. San Diego State University.
7. Many early Women's Studies professors were involved in social protest movements of the 1960s and 1970s. Also, more female students began attending colleges and universities during the 1970s and brought social justice questions to the classroom.
8. Over 50 countries have colleges and universities that offer Women's and Gender Studies degrees.
9. True. Community colleges play a vital role in training students in Women's and Gender Studies.
10. Topics in one of the first Women's Studies classes on women's health might have included: women's experience of discrimination in the medical system, the history of midwives in the sixteenth and seventeenth centuries, and the lack of female doctors.

NOTES

1. Praxis has its roots in ancient philosophy and the writings of Aristotle. Later it was associated with nineteenth-century Marxist thought, as well as with twentieth-century neo-Marxist writers such as Georg Lukács and Paulo Freire.
2. The term "pedagogy" refers to theories about teaching and learning; "feminist pedagogy" has been the preferred term in Women's Studies.
3. This figure is based on a National Center for Education Statistics (NCES) report published in 2003 on post-secondary faculty at degree-granting institutions (see National Women's Studies Association 2007).
4. The use of the word "female" is intentional here.
5. Unfortunately, we did not inquire on the survey as to whether students declared their major/minor/concentration prior to attending college or university, after their first Women's and Gender Studies course, or during their matriculation process.
6. See the work of Australian Women's Studies researcher MaryAnn Dever (2004), *Ms.* magazine's ongoing collecting of responses by Women's and Gender Studies graduates to the question "What has women's studies meant to your life? And what are you currently doing with your women's studies degree?" (available at www.ms-magazine.com), Luebke and Reilly (1995), and vignettes from various Women's Studies students presented in Kesselman, McNair, and Schniedewind (2008).

SECTION TWO

Historical Perspectives in Women's, Gender and Sexuality Studies

TABLE OF CONTENTS

History and activism are inextricably intertwined: if want equality today, we have to understand the past. Chandra Talpade Mohanty notes that "[f]eminist analysis has always recognized the centrality of rewriting and remembering history . . . not merely as a corrective to the gaps, erasures, and misunderstandings of hegemonic masculinist history, but because the very practice of remembering and rewriting leads to the formation of politicized consciousness and self-identity" (34). For most of American history, narratives that chronicled politics, work, medicine, religion, and other aspects of life focused largely, if not exclusively, on privileged men. However, our knowledge of women's lives developed rapidly after the 1970s as an increasing number of historians started writing about women. The very decision to *focus* on women, to see women as *historical actors*, was itself a revolutionary political act. Historians worked to recover the stories of women who had made significant contributions to their society but who were then overlooked, and therefore devalued, by the mostly male historians who recorded the stories of their times. The same process has been true for LGBTQPAI+ history and the histories of other marginalized groups; the stories of the subordinate group were often absent or misperceived in histories written by the dominant group. Telling the stories of subordinate groups gives us a richer—and more accurate—understanding of American history.

Feminist and queer activism need not focus exclusively, or even primarily, on gender or sexual identity. Focusing on gender discrimination only, for example, is a luxury usually only afforded to women who are privileged by other categories of identity. For example, as we discussed in Section I, for women of color the fight against race-based discrimination has often been just as pressing as the fight against sexism. Furthermore, as historian Elsa Barkley Brown explains, the differences between women are *relational*—one is always affecting the other. So it's not only that race and class-based differences alter the experience of being a woman; it's that "middle-class women live the lives they do precisely *because* working-class women live the lives they do. White women and women of color not only live different lives but white women live the lives they do in large part *because* women of color live the ones they do"

(Barkley Brown [emphasis ours], 298). To explore these issues of relational differences, this section focuses on three interconnected subjects within US history: (1) Examples of women and LGBTQPAI+ people organizing for progressive change in their communities; (2) activism to advance the interests of women and LGBTQPAI+ communities and seek justice and equity around race, class, gender, sexual orientation, and other identities; and (3) activism to expose, challenge, and destabilize social hierarchies where one identity group is given more access to social, political, and/or economic power.

The scope of this section is necessarily modest. Restricting ourselves to the past two hundred years, and focusing on the United States, the narrative is grounded in an intersectional approach that highlights the relational aspects of privilege and oppression. This does not mean that feminist and queer activism are limited to the United States or that there aren't earlier examples. Furthermore, while the sections move in chronological order, this is not to suggest a linear narrative but rather to group events in ways that allow for intersectional analysis within a historical context. Meant to supplement and contextualize the primary documents that follow, this introduction is *a* history of organizing in the United States, but it is not *the* history. Indeed, one way in which the following narrative diverges from more traditional feminist histories is in its move away from the "wave" metaphor that has commonly been used to structure and canonize the history of feminism into three distinct periods: the First Wave, the Second Wave, and the Third Wave. This wave model has been criticized for focusing mostly on the activism of more privileged women. Even as the following history challenges the wave model, it *will* privilege certain stories over others. While feminist and queer historians challenge dominant narratives, they are not immune from the bias of their own experience. Therefore, it is common for

LEARNING OBJECTIVES:

By the end of this section, you will have a better understanding of:

1. The connections between the abolitionist movement, anti-lynching campaigns, and the suffrage movement.

2. How women's labor organizing helped regulate the workplace and fight inequalities of class and gender.

3. How housewives organized in women's auxiliaries and as consumers, and how the limitations of the post–World War II constructions of women's roles affected some housewives.

4. How differences of race and class affected women's demands around reproductive control.

5. How the medical community's constructions of sexuality affected women, lesbians, and gay men and how the articulation of lesbian and gay rights changed over time.

6. The role of intersectional analysis in the evolution of feminist and queer activism.

feminist and queer historians to point out the limitations in another historian's work, perhaps noting, for example, the ways in which the historian's class privilege causes them to reproduce a class-biased narrative even while they are trying to dismantle a male-biased narrative. Feminist and queer scholarship is dynamic and ever-changing, and the ethic of the field of women's, gender and sexuality studies encourages these types of critiques, understanding that everyone's knowledge is "situated" (Haraway). Part of becoming an active learner with strong critical thinking skills is imagining what stories are left out and why. We encourage you to do that with this history, as with all histories.

Engaged Learning

In a group, compare and contrast different histories to understand how subjectivity, bias, and power affect one's version of events.

QUESTIONS

1. Write a one-page history of your course since the beginning of the semester.
2. Read your classmates' histories and read your professor's history.
3. Analyze the collection of histories by asking: What did each person include in their version of events? What did they leave out? What accounts for the differences between various histories of the same events? Are there places where two or more histories are saying conflicting things? If so, how do you decide which version to use?
4. Think about the narrative you wrote. Are there ways in which your subjectivity affected what you wrote? For example, did you talk about the lectures because you really like the professor? Did you talk more about what happened in the classroom because you didn't complete all of the reading assignments? Why do you think you didn't mention some of the things that your classmates talked about?
5. Consider your fellow classmates and the professor. Which of these class historians has the most power? If the president of your college came to your class and asked for the "official history" of the course, whose narrative do you think she would take? Why? What would be forgotten if that was the only story recorded?

THE ABOLITIONIST MOVEMENT, ANTI-LYNCHING CAMPAIGNS, AND THE SUFFRAGE MOVEMENT, 1830–1920

Frederick Douglass, a man born into slavery who became a leader in both the abolitionist movement and the suffrage movement, said, "When the true history of the anti-slavery cause shall be written, women will occupy a large space in its pages, for the cause of the slave has been peculiarly women's cause" (qtd. in Davis 30). One reason white women—poor young women working in factories as well as wealthier social reformers—were so active in the abolitionist movement was because many drew connections between women's oppression and slavery. For example, Sarah and Angelina Grimké, white sisters from a wealthy family who had grown up on a plantation in South Carolina where they witnessed firsthand the horrors of slavery, moved to Philadelphia after converting to Quakerism and began speaking out publicly against slavery. Even among the progressive Quakers, many found the idea of women lecturing about political issues "unnatural" and therefore objectionable, but, despite strong opposition, Sarah and Angelina continued to voice their opinions lecturing for the American Anti-Slavery Society and writing on the subjects of gender and race.

Abolitionists gather to oppose Fugitive Slave Act. Angelina Grimké stands in the background with other abolitionists including Frederick Douglass (seated, left of center) at the Fugitive Slave Law Convention in Cazenovia, New York on August 22, 1850. The convention, attended by over two thousand people including many former slaves like Emily and Mary Edmonson (standing row, left of center and right of center, dressed in plaid), was called to protest the proposal of the Fugitive Slave Act of 1850. © The Art Archive / Alamy Stock Photo

We might ask whether it was fair for white women to compare themselves to slaves. After all, women like the Grimké sisters were able to advocate for abolition because they had education and leisure time, both of which were a result of the wealth from their family's slave-holding plantation. This strategy was effective, though, in getting white women to see their affinity with black women, as demonstrated by Angelina's "An Appeal to the Christian Women of the South" (included in this section) in which she challenges the religious arguments used to support slavery and tells Southern women that ending slavery is part of their Christian duty.

Women's experiences in the abolitionist movement helped develop their political consciousness and provided crucial activist training. Lucretia Mott, an abolitionist who helped with the Underground Railroad, was one of the organizers of the first US conference on women's rights, the 1848 Seneca Falls Convention, envisioned by Mott and other organizers as "the inauguration of a rebellion such as the world had never before seen" (Stanton et al. 68). Indeed, the attendees made many radical statements, articulated in the document that emerged out of the convention, the "Declaration of Sentiments" (included in this section). This document shows the influence of the abolitionist movement, as many of the ideas highlighted in the "Declaration of Sentiments" echoed those made years earlier in Quaker meetings and antislavery organizations (Hewitt 18).

Unfortunately, male journalists at the time represented the convention as "excessively silly" (Hulin and Avery). Referring to the convention as "the most shocking and unnatural incident in the history of womanity," the *Oneida Whig* asked, "If our ladies will insist on voting and legislating, where, gentlemen, will be our dinners and our elbows? where our domestic firesides and the holes in our stockings?" With similar disdain, *The Mechanic's Advocate* reported: "The women who attend these meetings, no doubt at the expense of their more appropriate duties . . . affirm, as among their rights, that of unrestricted franchise, and assert that it is wrong to deprive them of the privilege to become legislators, lawyers, doctors, divines, etc. etc. . . . Now it requires no argument to prove that this is all wrong. Every true-hearted female will instantly feel that it is unwomanly."

The newspaper comments foreshadowed many of the arguments against women's suffrage: women were weak, in need of men's protection, and best suited to taking care of the house and children. Sojourner Truth, a gifted orator, challenged these arguments in her 1851 speech (included in this section) by calling attention to the intersections of gender and race. Truth had been born a slave and had done hard manual labor and therefore observed, "I have plowed and reaped and husked and chopped and mowed, and can any man do more than that?" (p. 124). Exposing the conflict between gendered ideology and the treatment of poor and enslaved women, Truth asks: If women are inherently weak, why was she able to do the same work as a man?

The relationship between the abolitionist movement and those working for women's rights was severely damaged after the Civil War when the Fourteenth and Fifteenth Amendments to the Constitution were passed to raise the status of formerly enslaved black men, giving them the right to vote. Outraged that black men would vote while women remained disenfranchised, some activists believed that black leaders should withhold their support for the amendments in solidarity with women. This issue was so divisive that in 1869 activists for women's rights divided into two organizations, the National Woman Suffrage Association (NWSA), who opposed the Fifteenth Amendment because it didn't include women, and the American Woman Suffrage Association (AWSA), who supported the amendment. The organizations didn't reunite until 1890. Although many in the NWSA had been abolitionists, after the Civil War they ignored issues important to black women like lynching and interracial rape, seeing them as "'race questions,' irrelevant to the . . . goal of 'political equality of women'" (Newman 6). Therefore, while the Suffragist slogan "Votes for Women" suggests advocacy for *all* women, some activists privileged white women's lives at the expense of black women.

Despite the lack of support from some suffrage circles, black women like Ida B. Wells launched campaigns to address racial discrimination in the post-slavery era. Her 1895 pamphlet, "A Red Record" (included in this section), exposed the horror of lynching. Lynching was a form of domestic terrorism used to maintain white supremacy, but "before lynching could be consolidated as a popularly accepted institution . . . its savagery and its horrors had to be convincingly justified" (Davis 185). The myth of the black male rapist who preyed on white women became this justification as evidenced in the following statement by South Carolina Senator Ben Tillman: "When stern and sad-faced white men put to death a creature in human form who has deflowered a white woman, they have avenged the greatest wrong, the blackest crime" (qtd. in Davis 187). Wells exposed the image of the black male rapist as a racist myth, thereby helping to turn the public against lynching.

Some activists argued that the Fourteenth and Fifteenth Amendments *did* give women the right to vote because the Fourteenth Amendment made *all* persons born or naturalized in the United States citizens and the Fifteenth Amendment gave *all citizens* the right to vote. In 1872, Susan B. Anthony attempted to vote

Ida B. Wells, journalist and activist. Wells, imaged here at around 31 years of age, documented and exposed the motivations underlying lynching. Her work was an influential part of the anti-lynching movement. © Pictorial Press Ltd / Alamy Stock Photo

using this justification, but she was arrested. While her attempt to vote was unsuccessful, her trial helped undermine a key argument against women's suffrage: that women didn't have the intellectual capacity to understand politics. Pointing out the hypocrisy of a democracy that denies half of its citizens the right to vote, Anthony's testimony (included in this section) demonstrates her knowledge of the Constitution and US history.

Suffragists focused on two primary strategies in the late nineteenth century. First, they began to focus on getting women the right to vote at the state level; second, they introduced a new constitutional amendment that stated: "The right of citizens of the United States to vote shall not be denied or abridged by the United States or any State on account of sex." The Nineteenth Amendment was first introduced in Congress in 1878 but not ratified until 1920—forty-two years later. It took many new and daring strategies to change public opinion. To this end, under the leadership of Alice Paul and Lucy Burns, suffragists picketed outside the White House. In 1917, after months of picketing, 218 suffragists were arrested. In prison, some of them went on a hunger strike, risking their lives for the cause. Although the passing of the Nineteenth Amendment was a major victory, it was not a complete victory because, in practice, suffrage was only afforded to certain women (Hewitt 31): African American women were barred from voting by local discriminatory measures, most of which weren't successfully removed until the 1965 Voting Rights Act. The Chinese Exclusion Act restricted citizenship, and thus voting, for Chinese women and men until 1943. Many Native Americans were not considered citizens until 1924, and even then some states didn't allow Native Americans to vote.

ACTIVISM AND CIVIC ENGAGEMENT

Voting is a not just a right but a responsibility. Your vote is one of the most powerful tools for making social change. To be an effective voter, you must educate yourself about the issues. Sharing your knowledge can be an effective way to influence others.

QUESTIONS

1. Divide into groups. Each group should research one local, state, or federal office (i.e., school board president, attorney general, senator, etc.). Determine who holds the position or, if there is an upcoming election, who is competing for the position. Research the individual(s), looking at things like their policy statements, biography, voting history, and any news coverage.

2. Based on your findings, discuss with your group members whether you think the individual(s) are strong or weak on social justice issues. Be sure to explain what information you used to form your opinion.

3. Discuss how important social justice issues should be in determining whether you should vote for a candidate and say whether you would support the individual(s) you researched.

4. Share your information with the class and take notes on the information the other groups offer so that you have them as a reference for upcoming elections.

LABOR ORGANIZING AND THE EQUAL RIGHTS AMENDMENT, 1870–1930

Labor organizing was a major area of women's activism in the late nineteenth and early twentieth centuries. For example, beginning in 1903, the Women's Trade Union League (WTUL) brought together women across racial, ethnic, class, and religious differences and successfully mobilized factory workers, suffragists, college students, and their affluent allies (Boris and Orleck 34). With leadership from immigrant women, especially Jewish women who immigrated from eastern Europe bringing with them Socialist ideals, these activists helped bring about new laws regulating the extremes of capitalism that emerged with the Industrial Revolution: ending child labor, creating a minimum wage, restricting the length of work days, and creating basic safety standards. Theresa Serber Malkiel's 1910 *Diary of a Shirtwaist Striker* (included in this section) gives us insight into the lives of women labor activists who fought both class and gender discrimination.

On March 25, 1911, a devastating fire at the Triangle Shirtwaist Factory demonstrated the need for basic safety protections. The New York City factory employed many young immigrant girls and women who worked long hours for low pay. An article in *The New York Times* (included in this section) reported more than 140 workers were killed in the fire. Most, if not all, of these deaths

Factory Fire kills 146 in New York City on March 25, 1911. The Triangle Shirtwaist Fire is an infamous moment in the history of worker rights. One hundred and forty six victims, most of them young immigrant women, died because of the lack of sufficient fire exits and other basic safety standards. Here victims are seen in coffins on the sidewalk where many jumped nine stories to their death to avoid the flames. © Everett Collection Historical / Alamy Stock Photo

would have been prevented with basic safety precautions. The factory owners were not convicted of manslaughter, a charge many thought they deserved, but the Triangle Shirtwaist fire was a turning point in labor regulation. Prior to this, the government had resisted workers' calls to regulate private business. However, after the fire, public outrage and women's organizing spurred government officials to act, creating some of the basic safety regulations that we take for granted today.

Despite the many victories for women labor activists, ethnic, racial, and class differences created and reinforced divisive hierarchies within wage-earning women, detracting from their organizing power. For example, women who worked in department stores considered themselves above "factory girls" even though their wages were often lower (Kessler-Harris 135-7). Similarly, factory workers saw themselves as superior to domestic workers, despite the fact that domestic workers often earned higher wages (135-6). A worker in 1915 explained: "Intelligent people set no stigma on factory workers who are well bred and ladylike. These girls are received in good circles anywhere. . . . But no one has ever invited someone's maid or cook to their home for afternoon tea or any other social affair" (qtd. in 136). Black women created divisions within the bottom tier of the labor market, where they preferred laundry and domestic work over agricultural field work which had associations with slavery (137). Employers exploited these hierarchies to control wages. If the workplace was more "genteel"—as defined by the race and ethnicity of its workers—women would choose to work there even if the wages were lower than other employment. Thus racial and ethnic discrimination hurt even the white, native-born women who were at the top of the social hierarchy because it depressed wages for all women.

Women workers also had to contend with male workers who saw women's increasing role in the labor market as competition for scarce resources. As men began to unionize in larger numbers, they were effective in using gender ideology to discourage women's advancement in the workforce (Kessler-Harris 142). Organizing around demands like an eight-hour day and equal pay, the Boston Working Women's League was created in 1869 by Jennie Collins, Aurora Phelps, and Elizabeth Daniels and serves as an example of how women fought against gender and class discrimination (Vapnek 311, 320). Collins also used her writing to advocate for change. In 1871, she wrote *Nature's Aristocracy: A Plea for the Oppressed,* becoming one of the first working-class women to publish her own book. In it she criticizes class inequality and explains the relational aspect between wealthy women's privilege and poor women's oppression, noting that while some wealthy women give to charity, they are simultaneously producing the *need* for charity by exploiting those that they employ with low wages.

The class struggle between working-class women and wealthy women can be seen in the conflict over the Equal Rights Amendment (ERA), a proposed constitutional amendment (first introduced into Congress in 1923) that aimed to ensure that men and women were treated equally under the law. The amendment read: "Equality of rights under the law shall not be denied or abridged by the United States or by any state on account of sex." The language of the amendment immediately worried women labor activists in groups like the WTUL and the National Consumer's League (NCL) that had been lobbying for protective laws for women: limiting the amount of hours women worked, increasing women's wages, and protecting women from unsafe working conditions (Orleck 32). Because the ERA was intended to remove any legal differentiation based on sex, women labor activists feared that, if it passed, the laws protecting women workers would be lost. ERA supporters, however, believed that any legal differentiation between the sexes—even in terms of laws benefiting women—undermined feminist progress. The idea that women needed special protective laws, they argued, positioned women as inferior to men. Attempts at compromise between the two groups failed. Congress didn't pass the ERA until 1972. The next phase required ratification by thirty-eight states, but the amendment failed to reach that mark before time expired in 1982.

Both sides of the early ERA debate wanted to improve women's lives, but their different positions exposed a major issue for feminist activism that still resonates today: Is it possible to create a women's coalition if various groups of women will have different, and sometimes opposing, interests around a particular issue?

INTERSECTIONAL ANALYSIS

A Case Study: In 2013, the chief operating officer of Facebook, Sheryl Sandberg, published *Lean In: Women, Work, and the Will to Lead*, in which she discusses gender equality in the workforce and what women can do to increase their success. Sandberg's approach has been criticized by feminist scholars like Susan Faludi and bell hooks, who argue that Sandberg's approach is a cooptation of feminism that undermines gender equality and female solidarity. Watch Sandberg's TED Talk, "Why We Have Too Few Women Leaders" (http://www.ted.com/talks/sheryl_sandberg_why_we_have_too_few_women_leaders?language=en), where she summarizes some of the main points from her book.

QUESTIONS

1. What are Sandberg's main strategies for producing more women leaders?
2. Using intersectional analysis, which women do you think Sandberg is talking about?
3. How does she propose to address structural sexism?
4. Why do you think feminist critics say Sandberg is coopting feminism?

HOUSEWIVES REVOLT! 1930–1970

While wage-earning women used unions to organize and affect change, women who weren't in the labor market also played important roles through women's auxiliaries. These support organizations were affiliated with a union and made up of workers' wives and family members. The story of the working-class, Mexican American women in the Mine-Mill Ladies Auxiliary 209 is a great example. In 1950 in New Mexico, Mexican American mine workers went on strike to protest wage policies and hiring practices that paid Mexican American workers less than white workers at the Empire Zinc mine (Orleck 62). After the Empire Zinc owners won a court order to prevent the men from picketing outside the mine, Virginia Chacón, the wife of the mine's local union president, suggested that the wives and children of the miners picket in the men's place (62). The women, part of Mine-Mill Ladies Auxiliary 209, continued the picketing. They were harassed and ultimately jailed for their actions. Those arrested were told they would be released from jail if they would go home and not return to the picket line, but they refused (Cargill 208–9). Even once the men returned to the picket line, many women continued to strike, and their efforts remained important to the overall union strategy.

Although women's participation in the strike won the respect of male Mexican American activists, it did not result in substantive changes to women's subordinate status in the union or in their families (Cargill 243–46). Despite the fact that the male miners were able to recognize inequalities based on race, ethnicity, and class, they had not developed the same level of consciousness around gender. The women's most important demand—indoor plumbing in the company-owned housing—was not made a priority during the strike and few women maintained influence in the union organizations after the strike (244–46).

Housewives also entered into collective action as buyers. In the 1930s, 1940s, and 1950s, poor and working-class women across the country "staged anti-eviction protests, consumer boycotts, rent strikes and protests for better education and affordable public housing . . . Echoing the language of trade unionism, [housewives] asserted that housing and food, like wages and hours, could be regulated by organizing and applying economic pressure" (Orleck 44). Building on their experiences as labor activists, organizers of the housewives' movement like Clara Lemlich Shavelson, Rose Schneiderman, and Pauline Newman recognized that while working-class women held little power in the workforce, they could use their power as *consumers* to effectively pressure businesses to lower prices and government to increase regulation and address price gouging (45–48).

The 1935 meat boycott in Hamtramck, Michigan, is a good example. In light of the pervasive unemployment around the country, a large increase in the cost of meat drove women to organize. On July 27, 1935, the Hamtramck Women's Committee picketed the local shopping district demanding a 20 percent cut in the price of meat and blocking the entrance to food stores (White 114). When shoppers exited the stores, the picketers searched their bags, taking and destroying any meat they found (114). The first day alone, the picketers were credited with a loss of $65,000 in sales (114–15). These women activists were successful not only in cutting the prices of meat and other food staples but in creating a new consumer consciousness that lives on until today (Orleck 48).

Perhaps the most well-known story of housewife revolt was spurred by Betty Friedan's 1963 book, *The Feminine Mystique*, which chronicles the stories of middle-class, white women who found the role of housewife unfulfilling. Friedan describes the problem: "As she made the beds, shopped for groceries, matched slipcover material, ate peanut butter sandwiches with her children, chauffeured Cub Scouts and Brownies, lay beside her husband at night—she was afraid to ask even of herself the silent question—'Is this all?'" (15). Friedan explains that while these women felt empty, dissatisfied, and depressed, they didn't have the words to describe their situation. It was "the problem that has no name." Women were too ashamed to tell their friends and family about it. After all, they said, what could they complain about? According to the images of the "happy housewife" presented on TV and in women's magazines, they had a perfect life. If they weren't happy, the women reasoned, there must be something wrong with *them*. The power of *The Feminine Mystique* was that in making these stories public, women began to realize that it was not an *individual* problem. The problem was in the culture's expectations: the post–World War II construction of femininity created unrealistic and unfulfilling roles for women.

It's important to understand Friedan's critique within the historical context of the 1950s. For the women Friedan described, their identity was defined as *relational*: they were someone's wife and someone's mother. The idea that they "could be a person in [their] own right, in addition to being a wife and mother, seemed completely new to many women" (Coontz xxi). Books and magazines regularly encouraged women to be better wives by being more self*less*. If she worked outside the home, she was told to make sure it didn't "take priority in her life" or "become more important to her than his" work (qtd. in 16). Women were also encouraged to submit to their husbands, to become "the perfect follower" making her husband "feel that he is the boss at home," and never to "appear to know more than [her husband] does" (qtd. in 15, 16).

The Feminine Mystique is an important marker in the history of feminist organizing—both for what it said and what it didn't say. Despite its usefulness in providing a language to discuss female subordination, Friedan makes concerning generalizations about women. While her account did reflect the lives of many middle-class, white women, it did not represent *all* women. Indeed, the book makes the stories of women of color and other less privileged women all but invisible. For example, because racial discrimination usually prevented black men from making enough money to support their families, it was common for black women to work outside the home. These women would not have identified with the stories told in Friedan's book. Historian Stephanie Coontz notes the way in which the exclusion of black women's stories limited the book: "In ignoring the experience of African-American women in *The Feminine Mystique*, Friedan missed an opportunity to prove that women could indeed combine family commitments with involvement beyond the home" (126). Because *The Feminine Mystique* became such a well-known example of feminism in the 1960s, and because it privileged the stories of white, middle-class women while claiming to speak for all women, this book is often pointed to as an example of the ways in which the feminist movement reproduced hierarchies of race and class while challenging them in terms of gender.

THE PERSONAL IS POLITICAL: HOUSEWORK AND REPRODUCTIVE CHOICE, 1960–1980

In the 1960s and 1970s, the feminist slogan "the personal is political" challenged the idea that social and family concerns were "private" matters and therefore outside of the realm of politics. For example, in her 1970 article, "The Politics of Housework" (included in this section), Pat Mainardi argues that the unequal distribution of housework is based on the subordination of women. Because men are seen as superior, they are excused from housework; because men don't do housework, it is not valued. Housework is unpaid and it depletes women's leisure time, time that women could use to improve their status through increased education and more political activism.

The recognition that individual problems in the home, in marriages, and in the family were connected to larger structures of inequality encouraged women to mobilize on a number of fronts. For example, many feminist activists argued for the widespread availability of birth control and access to abortion (this is discussed more in Section III).

However, often poor women and women of color viewed the issues of birth control and abortion differently than white, middle- and upper-class women. While "the personal is political" mantra encouraged privileged feminists to recognize that male controls over female reproduction were tools of patriarchy, there wasn't the same recognition that the regulation of minority women's reproduction advanced racial oppression. For example, in the 1960s and 1970s, when the civil rights movement was challenging white supremacy, coerced sterilization of women of color became commonplace. Presented as anti-poverty initiatives, women of color were routinely sterilized by state authorities without informed consent or through coercion. African American girls like Minnie Lee (age fourteen) and Mary Alice Relf (age twelve) were sterilized without their parents' informed consent "on the grounds that they were 'at risk' of early sexual activity" (Gordon 114). In other cases women were told they would lose their welfare benefits if they didn't agree to be sterilized (114). One woman, Mexican American Helena Orozco, testified that her doctor said that if she "did not consent to the tubal ligation that the doctor repairing [her] hernia would use an inferior type of stitching material" (qtd. in 115). The effects of sterilization programs on women of color are shocking: in Puerto Rico, a third of women of child-bearing age were sterilized by 1968 (Roberts 94). Similarly, between 1970 and 1976, the Indian Health Services clinics had sterilized between 25 percent and 42 percent of Native American women of child-bearing age (Orleck 99).

Women of color activists organized to end these practices. Dr. Helen Rodriguez-Trias, who founded the Coalition to End Sterilization Abuse (CESA) and cofounded the Committee for Abortion Rights and Against Sterilization Abuse (CARASA), successfully lobbied New York City to provide information about sterilization in a woman's native language and require a waiting period between childbirth and sterilization (Orleck 98). Women of All Red Nations (WARN), a Native American women's organization that organized around this issue, cites ending the forced sterilization of Native women as one of their major accomplishments. However, while women of color were organizing to prevent forced sterilization, white, middle-class feminists advocated for unfettered access to *all* methods of birth control including sterilization, seeing this as tied to women's liberation. Therefore, groups like the National Abortion Rights Action League (NARAL) and Planned Parenthood *opposed* sterilization restrictions. Dorothy Roberts argues, "Focusing on the obstacle the regulations would pose to middle-class white women, they ignored the ravages on minority women's bodies the new law would help to prevent" (96).

ACTIVISM AROUND SEX AND SEXUALITY, 1950–1980

Anatomy textbooks from the early nineteenth century defined the clitoris as "passive and unimportant to female sexual expression," but at least the clitoris was discussed (Gerhard 452). By the twentieth century the clitoris wasn't even labeled in most anatomy textbooks (452). Therefore, it shouldn't be surprising that when Freud published *Three Essays on the Theory of Sexuality* in 1905, he defined the clitoral orgasm as "immature," while he positioned the vaginal orgasm as the "normal" response to sexual intercourse. Women who didn't experience vaginal orgasm through intercourse were pathologized as "frigid." This figuring of women's sexuality both assumed and legitimated heterosexuality as the only healthy orientation.

Writing in the 1950s and 1960s, sex researchers like Alfred Kinsey, William Masters, and Virginia Johnson presented a very different view of women's sexuality. They rejected the claim that a clitoral orgasm was somehow deficient or inferior; indeed, they presented it as central to female sexual pleasure. Anne Koedt's 1970 article, "The Myth of the Vaginal Orgasm" (included in this section), helped to redefine women's sexuality with a focus on the clitoris. As one scholar observes, "When Koedt attacked [the vaginal orgasm] as a myth, or more pointedly, as a fraudulent misinformation campaign that created a host of psychological problems for women, she appeared to challenge the very foundation of heterosexuality as it was understood in psychoanalytic, medical, and popular discourse" (Gerhard 449).

In her 1980 essay "Compulsory Heterosexuality and Lesbian Existence," Adrienne Rich examines the ways in which heterosexual norms have been constructed in the interest of patriarchy. She says that **compulsory heterosexuality** naturalizes opposite-sex attraction as normal and universal and pressures people to conform. Like Koedt, Rich sees the construction of sexuality as about power. She argues that compulsory heterosexuality perpetuates male privilege and marks lesbians as deviant. As with the anatomy textbooks discussed previously, an examination of the treatment of homosexuality in the field of medicine helps demonstrates how our understanding of sexuality is connected to larger social issues.

Beginning in the late nineteenth century, most in the medical community saw homosexuality as a "sickness," a perversion of "normal" sexuality that required treatment (Frank 9). This representation of homosexuality supported and legitimated large-scale discrimination, which was heightened by the Cold War fervor in the 1950s. The argument went something like this: because homosexuals were "sick," most homosexuals were "in the closet." This meant they could be blackmailed—and if they could be blackmailed, they could be motivated to take actions against the United States. Therefore, gays were seen as an inherent threat to the safety and security of the nation. While the blackmail argument was conveniently overblown to support discriminatory measures, being outed did have consequences. As gay activist Harry Hay explains, "The moment a person was listed as a homosexual [following arrest], his name appeared on the front page of the newspaper. The moment that happened you lost your job, you lost your insurance, you lost your credit" (qtd. in Frank 10).

The legitimation that the medical community gave to gay discrimination helps explain the strategies of early LGBT activists. Often referred to as part of the homophile movement, activists organizations like the Mattachine Society, founded in 1950, and the Daughters of Bilitis, founded in 1955, laid the foundation for the challenges to social and legal discrimination that would come later. However, from today's vantage point they don't seem radical because they largely focused on assimilationist strategies, emphasizing the commonalities between homosexuals and heterosexuals and encouraging gays and lesbians to conform to heterosexual norms and behaviors. For example, the "Statement of Purpose" for the Daughters of Bilitis (included in this section) encourages the lesbian to "make her adjustment to society" as opposed to demanding that society change its treatment of lesbians (p. 140). While these organizations have been criticized for their strategies of accommodation, the incredible persecution of gays and lesbians during the Cold War era may have made this feel like the only realistic alternative (Adam 70).

Compulsory heterosexuality: A term coined by Adrienne Rich meaning that patriarchal institutions and social norms create and enforce the expectation that all women are heterosexual.

In the 1960s, in conjunction with other social movements, gay and lesbian activists began to question the accommodation strategies of the homophile movement and began to take a more militant approach (Adam 75). The Stonewall riots of 1969 are perhaps the most noted marker of this transition from assimilation to liberation. On the night of June 27–28, 1969, police raided a New York City bar that LGBT folks patronized called the Stonewall Inn. This was nothing new. Police often raided gay bars. However, as Sylvia Rivera describes in her interview with Leslie Feinberg, "I'm Glad I Was in the Stonewall Riot" (included in this section), this time the patrons rebelled. Unbiased contemporaneous first-person accounts of Stonewall are limited. Reporting from mainstream publications of the time are imbued with homophobia and transphobia. Indeed, gay rights activist Dick Leitsch's 1969 account, published in the newsletter of the New York Mattachine Society, provides a rare glimpse of the Stonewall uprising written from the activists' point of view at the time. Leitsch describes how "an almost solid mass of people—most of them gay" chanted "'Gay Power,' 'We Want Freedom Now,' and 'Equality for Homosexuals'" as they blocked traffic on "Christopher Street, from Greenwich to Seventh Avenue." While the overall significance of Stonewall is debated by scholars—did it really represent *the* turning point for gay rights?—what we know is that "Stonewall and aftermath gave something to the gay community, particularly its younger generation, that it had never had: it transformed a shared narrative of oppression into a new narrative of rebellion" (Frank 38).

A group gathers outside the boarded-up Stonewall Inn in New York City after June 1969 uprising. Stonewall patrons rebelled against police harassment igniting mass protest that became an important turning point in the gay rights movement. Fred W. McDarrah / Getty Images

After Stonewall we start to see a shift in the tenor of queer activism. For example, the Gay Liberation Front (GLF) was founded in 1969 and was markedly different from the earlier homophile organizations in that it attacked "the consumer culture, militarism, racism, sexism, and homophobia" and emphasized "coming out" as necessary to gay liberation (Rimmerman 23). After the GLF broke up, the Gay Activists Alliance (GAA) became more visible (24). The GAA focused on the single issue of gay rights and was less radical that the GLF; however, the GAA adopted a focus on political elections which proved to be a very effective strategy and it was successful at establishing institutional structures (24–26).

One of the most visible early successes of post-Stonewall activism was the removal of homosexuality from the American Psychiatric Association's *Diagnostic and Statistical Manual of Mental Disorders* in 1973. The Chicago Gay Liberation Front handed out leaflets (included in this section) to doctors at the American Medical Association's 1970 convention. They demanded an end to the pathologizing of homosexuality as a "sickness," arguing that the problem didn't lie in the individual psychology and behavior of gays and lesbians but rather in the social system that discriminates against them.

By the 1970s, feminist and queer activists shared many connections. By exposing the socially constructed nature of gender, feminists had implicitly challenged all "natural" identities; by challenging the connection between sex and procreation, emphasizing and encouraging a valuing of sex for pleasure, some antigay arguments were weakened. However, there were those within the women's movement who feared that incorporating the issues of the queer community would hurt them politically. Indeed, in 1969 National Organization for Women (NOW) leader Betty Friedan referred to the lesbians within the women's movement as a "lavender menace." In protest to her comment but also in recognition of the larger issues around the silencing of lesbians in the women's movement, a group of lesbian feminists called the Radicalesbians distributed a manifesto called "The Woman-Identified Woman" (included in this section), which argued that lesbians should be central to the women's movement. By 1971, Friedan changed her opinion on lesbians and NOW adopted a resolution supporting gay rights (Gordon 91). Despite the progress around sexual orientation, writers like Tina Vasquez, in her article "It's Time to End the Long History of Feminism Failing Transgender Women" (included in this section), suggest that trans women continue to be marginalized within feminist activism.

IDENTITY POLITICS AND PRIVILEGE: CROSSING BORDERS AND QUEER IDENTITIES, 1970–PRESENT

In the 1980s, the question of identity politics and privilege came to the forefront of many feminist debates. Many less privileged women (working-class women, women of color, and lesbians) argued that they were marginalized within the women's movement of the 1960s and 1970s. These critiques noted that publicly recognized feminist leaders were white, middle-class, straight women and that the platforms of many feminist organizations focused on issues that reflected the lived experiences of white, middle-class, straight women. For example, as bell hooks points out, "[w]omen in lower-class and poor groups, particularly those who are non-white, would not have defined women's libera- tion as woman gaining equality with men . . . Knowing that men in their groups do not have social, political, and economic power, they would not deem it liberatory to share their social status" (19). Less privileged women may not have been intentionally excluded, but, in large and small ways, they were made to feel like second-class citizens within the movement. This debate caused many more privileged women to reflect on the ways in which they were simultaneously *perpetuating* hierarchies of race, class, and sexual orienta- tion even while they were *challenging* hierarchy in terms of gender. Many of the white, middle-class, straight women had previously seen themselves as oppressed, and having to accept that they were also the oppressor was often difficult to acknowledge.

As discussed in Section I, in the 1980s and 1990s many scholars explored the role of simultaneous oppression and intersectional identities. For example, Benita Roth notes that black feminists challenged their marginalization in both the women's movement and the civil rights movement simultaneously, chal- lenging "white feminist movements for ignoring economic and survival issues common to the Black community, and for failing to examine personal racism" and challenging "the Black Civil Rights movement as it shifted into a Black liberation/nationalist movement that seemed to be recreating its gender politics along white middle class patriarchal lines" (49). Born of this marginalization, black feminist activism incorporated an intersectional perspective that looked at race, class, and gender simultaneously, positioning these social hierarchies as mutually reinforcing. Angela Davis's "Masked Racism: Reflections on the Prison Industrial Complex" (included in this section) exemplifies the legacy of this type of scholarship. Here she looks at how the **prison industrial complex** relies on concepts of criminality that both emerge from and reinforce the sub- ordination of the poor and people of color.

Prison industrial complex: The industry and its supporters who promote institutional punishment as the solu- tion for social problems in order to further political and financial self-interest.

While black feminists had been vocal about the intersections of race, class, and gender, they were sometimes silent on issues of heterosexual privilege. To address this, the Combahee River Collective, a black lesbian feminist organi- zation in the 1970s, issued "A Black Feminist Statement" (included in this section). In it they emphasize that racial, sexual, heterosexual, and class oppres- sions are all interconnected, and they argue for an alternative "to universalistic visions of sisterhood that erased differences between women" (Roth 52). Part of the legacy of this era of black feminism is an understanding that systems of oppression work together: the idea that some people should be accorded more rights and privileges because of socially constructed ideas around difference is the underlying premise in *all* social hierarchies. Therefore, if one's work

Third world feminism:
Feminist activism that emerges from the lived experiences of women from the geographical third world and from women of color living in powerful countries like the United States.

implicitly or explicitly supports this premise in regard to race, class, or sexual orientation, the argument for gender equality is weakened. Consequently, all efforts to promote gender equality must simultaneously address other social hierarchies.

Using Benedict Anderson's idea of "imagined communities," Chandra Talpade Mohanty defines **third world feminism** as an alliance of women "with divergent histories and social locations, woven together by the *political* threads of opposition to forms of domination that are not only pervasive but also systemic" (emphasis original, 4). Therefore, she positions this alliance based not on essentialist identities, not on biology or culture, but on consciousness: "the *way* we think about race, class, and gender—the political links we choose to make among and between struggles" (emphasis original, 4). For Mohanty, it is the "common context of struggle" that creates a "potential commonality" for "the peoples of Africa, Asia, Latin America, and the Middle East, as well as 'minority' populations (people of color) in the United States and Europe" (7, 2).

Many third world feminists critiqued what they saw as mainstream US (white) feminism's "narrow conception of feminist terrain as an almost singularly antisexist struggle" (Johnson-Odim 315). While third world feminists support the fight for gender equality, they also face discrimination based on factors like race, class, and nation. Therefore, for feminism to improve the lives of third world women, activists must address other social hierarchies as well as *"the position of the societies* in which Third World women find themselves" (emphasis ours, Johnson-Odim 320). This means that privileged women in the United States and Europe must interrogate their complicity in the imperialist relationships that bring their own countries wealth at the expense of others. As Jo Carrillo's poem, "And When You Leave, Take Your Pictures With You" (included in this section) represents, many third world women see feminism's superficial inclusion of women of color as more for show than for substance.

In the introduction to their influential 1981 book, *This Bridge Called My Back: Writings by Radical Women of Color,* Cherríe Moraga and Gloria Anzaldúa say their motivation "began as a reaction to the racism of white feminists," but soon "became a positive affirmation of the commitment of women of color to our own feminism" (xxiii). The lived experiences of women of color have given rise to transformative concepts like Gloria Anzaldúa's *mestiza* consciousness. In "La Conciencia de la Mestiza/Towards a New Consciousness" (included in this section), Anzaldúa champions the liberatory potential of "borderlands" as a space which can embrace ambiguity and contradictions and can challenge binaries.

Mestiza **consciousness:**
A term coined by Gloria Anzaldúa that emerges out of her lived experience as a Chicana and means a sense of self that embraces borders and ambiguity and challenges dualistic thinking.

Historian Susan Stryker notes the connections between Anzaldúa's articulation of hybrid and intersectional identities and queer theory (124). Reclaiming the previously pejorative word "queer," activists now use the term to refer to empowering concepts of identity that resist traditional categorizations. As discussed in Section I, queer identity refers to fluidity in terms of gender and

---

TRANSNATIONAL CONNECTIONS

The question of how to define women's issues has been at the heart of debates around feminist activism. Choose three countries and do an Internet search for women's organizations based in that country. Decide the criteria you will use to define "women's organizations" and select at least one women's organization from each country. Read about the work of each organization and look for their mission statement or a list of their goals.

QUESTIONS

1. Compare and contrast the women's organizations from different countries. How does each organization define its focus?

2. How is the organization funded? Who is the audience for the organization's website? How might the funding source affect the framing of women's issues?

3. What narratives about women travel across these countries? Are there certain themes that structure a transnational discourse around women's issues? What tensions might there be in a definition of women's issues from a transnational perspective?

---

sexuality but can also be used to mean any identity that is nonnormative or outside of traditional boundaries.

Debates about privilege, intersectionality, and alliances have also examined the role of men in feminist activism. In bell hooks's "Men: Comrades in Struggle" (included in this section) she observes that viewing men as the enemy emerges from a gender-only focus. If one's vantage point is informed by understandings of intersectionality, men become part of the struggle. And indeed, men benefit from feminism. For example, challenging rigidly defined definitions of masculinity has created new definitions of fatherhood, encouraging men to spend more time with their children. Men have also become increasingly involved in activism around gender roles and violence against women, both as allies to women and to improve the lives of boys and men. In "Guilty Pleasures: Pornography, Prostitution, and Stripping" (included in this section), Jackson Katz talks about men's role in addressing **rape culture**. Katz insists that in addition to the harm the pornography industry does to women, it hurts men.

In her 2012 article, "'What's in a Name?' On Writing the History of Feminism," historian Claire Goldberg Moses asks, "what is at stake in naming a particular form of women's collective action 'feminism'?" (p. 190). She asks questions that have been central to this section introduction: How do we define feminist activism? What stories do we tell about feminism? Who benefits from particular histories? Why are some people's contributions less visible than others? These questions are important because how we remember the past, and how we understand the limitations of our histories, will influence our strategies around current issues.

Rape culture: An environment that normalizes sexual violence against women through a number of cultural practices, including misogynistic social norms, victim blaming, rape myths, and sexual objectification.

Critical Thinking Questions

1. How have differences in race, class, and sexual orientation created conflict within women's activism?

2. What strategies have been used to advocate for women and queer communities?

3. When the Equal Rights Amendment was first proposed, women labor activists were against it because they supported protective legislation for women, legislation that relied on a legal differentiation between the sexes. Today we still have protections for women written into our laws. For example, only men can be drafted for war. Do you think protective legislation undermines arguments for gender equality?

4. Compare the "Statement of Purpose" of the Daughters of Bilitis with the Front's "A Leaflet for the American Medical Association." What are the assumptions that inform each document? How do they differ?

5. How does Gloria Anzaldúa's concept of the *mestiza* challenge social hierarchies?

GLOSSARY

Compulsory heterosexuality 112   Prison industrial complex 115   Third world feminism 116
Mestiza consciousness 116   Rape culture 117

WORKS CITED

Adam, Barry. *The Rise of a Gay and Lesbian Movement.* Twayne Publishers, 1995.

Anderson, Benedict. *Imagined Communities: Reflections on the Origin and Spread of Nationalism.* Rev. ed., Verso, 2006.

Barkley Brown, Elsa. "'What Has Happened Here': The Politics of Difference in Women's History and Feminist Politics." *Feminist Studies*, vol. 18, no. 2, 1992, pp. 295–312.

"Bolting Among the Ladies." *Oneida Whig*, 1 Aug. 1848. https://www.loc.gov/exhibits/treasures/images/vc006199.jpg

Boris, Eileen, and Annelise Oleck. "Feminism and the Labor Movement: A Century of Collaboration and Conflict." *New Labor Forum*, vol. 20, no. 1, 2011, pp. 33–41.

Cargill, Jack. "Empire and Opposition: The 'Salt of the Earth' Strike." *Labor in New Mexico: Unions, Strikes, and Social History since 1881,* edited by Robert Kern, U of New Mexico P, 1983.

Collins, Jenni, and Judith Ranta. *Nature's Aristocracy or, Battle Wounds in the Time of Peace: A Plea for the Oppressed.* Edited by Russell H. Conwell. Lee and Shepard Publishers, 1871.

Coontz, Stephanie. *A Strange Stirring: The Feminine Mystique and American Women at the Dawn of the 1960s.* Basic Books, 2011.

Davis, Angela Y. *Women, Race & Class.* Vintage Books, 1981.

Frank, Walter. *Law and the Gay Rights Story: The Long Search for Equal Justice in a Divided Democracy.* Rutgers UP, 2014.

Friedan, Betty. *The Feminine Mystique.* W.W. Norton, 1963.

Gerhard, Jane. "Revisiting 'The Myth of the Vaginal Orgasm': The Female Orgasm in American Sexual Thought and Second Wave Feminism." *Feminist Studies*, vol. 26, no. 2, 2000, pp. 449–76.

Gordon, Linda. "The Women's Liberation Movement." *Feminism Unfinished: A Short, Surprising History of American Women's Movements.* Liveright Publishing, 2014, pp. 69–145.

Haraway, Donna. "Situated Knowledges: The Science Question in Feminism and the Privilege of Partial Perspective." *Feminist Studies*, vol. 14, no. 3, 1988, pp. 575–99.

Hewitt, Nancy A. "From Seneca Falls to Suffrage? Reimagining a 'Master' Narrative in U.S. Women's History." *No Permanent Waves: Recasting Histories of U.S. Feminism,* edited by Nancy Hewitt. Rutgers, 2010, pp. 15–38.

hooks, bell. *Feminist Theory: From Margin to Center.* South End Press, 2000.

Hulin, G. H., and J. A. Avery, editors. "The Recorder [Syracuse]." *The Recorder {Syracuse},* 3 Aug. 1848. https://www.loc.gov/exhibits/treasures/images/vc006198.jpg

Johnson-Odim, Cheryl. "Common Themes, Different Contexts: Third World Women and Feminism." *Third World Women and the Politics of Feminism,* edited by Chandra Talpade Mohanty et al., Indiana UP, 1991, pp. 314–27.

Kessler-Harris, Alice. *Women Have Always Worked: A Historical Overview.* Feminist Press, 1981.

Leitsch, Dick "Police Raid on N.Y. Club Sets off First Gay Riot" (1969). http://www.advocate.com/society/activism/2012/06/29/our-archives-1969-advocate-article-stonewall-riots

Mohanty, Chandra Talpade. "Cartographies of Struggle: Third World Women and the Politics of Feminism." *Third World Women and the Politics of Feminism,* edited by Chandra Talpade Mohanty, et al. Indiana UP, 1991, pp. 1–47.

Moraga, Cherríe, and Gloria Anzaldúa. Introduction. *This Bridge Called My Back: Writings by Radical Women of Color,* edited by Cherríe Moraga and Gloria Anzaldúa. Kitchen Table: Women of Color Press, 1983, pp. xxii–xxvi.

Newman, Louise Michele. *White Women's Rights: The Radical Origins of Feminism in the United States.* Oxford UP, 1999.

Orleck, Annelise. *Rethinking American Women's Activism.* Routledge, 2015.

Rich, Adrienne. "Compulsory Heterosexuality and Lesbian Existence." *Women: Sex and Sexuality, Signs: Journal of Women in Culture and Society,* special issue, vol. 5, no. 4, 1980, pp. 631–60.

Rimmerman, Craig. *The Lesbian and Gay Movement: Assimilation or Liberation.* 2nd ed. Westview Press, 2015.

Roberts, Dorothy. *Killing the Black Body: Race, Reproduction, and the Meaning of Liberty.* Vintage Books, 1997.

Roth, Benita. "Second Wave Black Feminism in the African Diaspora: News from New Scholarship." *African Feminisms III, Agenda: Empowering Women for Gender Equity,* special edition, no. 58, 2003, pp. 46–58. doi:10.1080/10130950.2003.9674493.

Stanton, Elizabeth Cady, et al. *History of Woman Suffrage (1848–1861).* Vol. 1, 1881.

Stryker, Susan. *Transgender History.* Seal Press, 2008.

Tanner, John. "Women out of Their Latitude." *The Mechanic's Advocate,* 12 Aug. 1848. https://www.loc.gov/exhibits/treasures/images/vc006200.jpg

Vapnek, Lara. "Staking Claims to Independence: Jennie Collins, Aurora Phelps, and the Boston Working Women's League, 1865–1877." *No Permanent Waves: Recasting Histories of U.S. Feminism,* edited by Nancy Hewitt. Rutgers UP, 2010, pp. 305–28.

White, Ann Folino. *Plowed Under: Food Policy Protests and Performance in New Deal America.* Indiana UP, 2014.

14. • *Angelina Emily Grimké*

AN APPEAL TO THE CHRISTIAN WOMEN OF THE SOUTH (1836)

Angelina Emily Grimké and her sister Sarah were influential abolitionists and women's rights activists. Born in 1805 to a slave-holding family in South Carolina, Grimké had first-hand experience with the institution of slavery. Leaving her parents' home and rejecting their lifestyle, Grimké became a Quaker and moved to Philadelphia. In 1835 she sent a letter to abolitionist William Lloyd Garrison condemning slavery. He published the letter in his antislavery newspaper, *The Liberator*, and afterward Grimké began giving speeches against slavery. Because she spoke to audiences of both men and women, she faced strong criticism for stepping outside the bounds of appropriate female behavior. While her initial focus was on abolition, Grimké came to see that, in order to be a strong abolitionist, she had to advocate for women's rights as well. In "An Appeal to the Christian Women of the South," Grimké uses religious rhetoric and biblical references to argue that slavery is a sin and that it is women's Christian duty to end the practice.

Respected Friends,

It is because I feel a deep and tender interest in your present and eternal welfare that I am willing thus publicly to address you. Some of you have loved me as a relative, and some have felt bound to me in Christian sympathy, and Gospel fellowship; and even when compelled by a strong sense of duty, to break those outward bonds of union which bound us together as members of the same community, and members of the same religious denomination, you were generous enough to give me credit, for sincerity as a Christian, though you believed I had been most strangely deceived. I thanked you then for your kindness, and I ask you *now*, for the sake of former confidence, and former friendship, to read the following pages in the spirit of calm investigation and fervent prayer. It is because you have known me, that I write thus unto you.

[. . .]

. . . "The *supporters* of the slave system," says Jonathan Dymond in his admirable work on the Principles of Morality, "will *hereafter* be regarded with the *same* public feeling, as he who was an advocate for the slave trade *now is*." It will be, and that very soon, clearly perceived and fully acknowledged by all the virtuous and the candid, that in *principle* it is as sinful to hold a human being in bondage who has been born in Carolina, as one who has been born in Africa. All that sophistry of argument which has been employed to prove, that although it is sinful to send to Africa to procure men and women as slaves, who have never been in slavery, that still, it is not sinful to keep those in bondage who have come down by inheritance, will be utterly overthrown. We must come back to the good old doctrine of our forefathers who declared to the world, "this self evident truth that *all* men are created equal, and that they have certain *inalienable* rights among which are life, *liberty*, and the pursuit of happiness." It is even *sarcasm*

a greater absurdity to suppose a man can be legally born a slave under *our free Republican* Government, than under the petty despotisms of barbarian Africa. If then, we have no right to enslave an African, surely we can have none to enslave an American; if it is a self evident truth that *all* men, every where and of every color are born equal, and have an *inalienable right to liberty*, then it is equally true that *no* man can be born a slave, and no man can ever *rightfully* be reduced to *involuntary* bondage and held as a slave, however fair may be the claim of his master or mistress through wills and title-deeds. . . .

[. . .]

But perhaps you will be ready to query, why appeal to *women* on this subject? *We* do not make the laws which perpetuate slavery. *No* legislative power is vested in *us; we* can do nothing to overthrow the system, even if we wished to do so. To this I reply, I know you do not make the laws, but I also know that *you are the wives and mothers, the sisters and daughters of those who do;* and if you really suppose *you* can do nothing to overthrow slavery, you are greatly mistaken. You can do much in every way: four things I will name. 1st. You can read on this subject. 2d. You can pray over this subject. 3d. You can speak on this subject. 4th. You can *act* on this subject. I have not placed reading before praying because I regard it more important, but because, in order to pray aright, we must understand what we are praying for; it is only then we can "pray with the understanding and the spirit also."

[. . .]

The *women of the South can overthrow* this horrible system of oppression and cruelty, licentiousness and wrong. Such appeals to your legislatures would be irresistible, for there is something in the heart of man which *will bend under moral suasion.* There is a swift witness for truth in his bosom, *which will respond to truth* when it is uttered with calmness and dignity. If you could obtain but six signatures to such a petition in only one state, I would say, send up that petition, and be not in the least discouraged

by the scoffs and jeers of the heartless, or the resolution of the house to lay it on the table. It will be a great thing if the subject can be introduced into your legislatures in any way, even by *women,* and *they* will be the most likely to introduce it there in the best possible manner, as a matter of *morals* and *religion,* not of expediency or politics. You may petition, too, the different ecclesiastical bodies of the slave states. Slavery must be attacked with the whole power of truth and the sword of the spirit. You must take it up on *Christian* ground, and fight against it with Christian weapons, whilst your feet are shod with the preparation of the gospel of peace. And *you are now* loudly called upon by the cries of the widow and the orphan, to arise and gird yourselves for this great moral conflict, with the whole armour of righteousness upon the right hand and on the left.

[. . .]

Sisters in Christ, I have done. As a Southerner, I have felt it was my duty to address you. I have endeavoured to set before you the exceeding sinfulness of slavery, and to point you to the example of those noble women who have been raised up in the church to effect great revolutions, and to suffer for the truth's sake. I have appealed to your sympathies as women, to your sense of duty as *Christian women.* I have attempted to vindicate the Abolitionists, to prove the entire safety of immediate Emancipation, and to plead the cause of the poor and oppressed. I have done—I have sowed the seeds of truth, but I well know, that even if an Apollos were to follow in my steps to water them, "*God only* can give the increase." To Him then who is able to prosper the work of his servant's hand, I commend this Appeal in fervent prayer, that as he "hath *chosen the weak things of the world*, to confound the things which are mighty," so He may cause His blessing, to descend and carry conviction to the hearts of many Lydias through these speaking pages. Farewell—Count me not your "enemy because I have told you the truth," but believe me in unfeigned affection,

Your sympathizing Friend,
Angelina E. Grimkè.

15. • *Seneca Falls Convention*

DECLARATION OF SENTIMENTS (1848)

The Seneca Falls Convention took place on July 19–20, 1848, bringing together around three hundred men and women in Seneca Falls, New York, for the first women's rights convention in US history. Prior to the convention, a document called the "Declaration of Sentiments" was drafted by Elizabeth Cady Stanton with help from other organizers. The document, which was modeled after the Declaration of Independence, was a statement of principles and a list of injustices that resulted in women's oppression. The convention voted on a series of resolutions that they believed would help remedy the injustices outlined in the "Declaration of Sentiments," among which was a statement that women should have the right to vote. While the other resolutions including those demanding equality in law and opportunity were unanimously approved, the suffrage resolution barely passed and only after a fervent plea for support from Frederick Douglass. Asking for women's right to vote was seen as too extreme by many of the convention attendees.

When, in the course of human events, it becomes necessary for one portion of the family of man to assume among the people of the earth a position different from that which they have hitherto occupied, but one to which the laws of nature and of nature's God entitle them, a decent respect to the opinions of mankind requires that they should declare the causes that impel them to such a course.

We hold these truths to be self-evident: that all men and women are created equal; that they are endowed by their Creator with certain inalienable rights; that among these are life, liberty, and the pursuit of happiness; that to secure these rights governments are instituted, deriving their just powers from the consent of the governed. Whenever any form of government becomes destructive of these ends, it is the right of those who suffer from it to refuse allegiance to it, and to insist upon the institution of a new government, laying its foundation on such principles, and organizing its powers in such form, as to them shall seem most likely to effect their safety and happiness. Prudence, indeed, will dictate that governments long established should not be changed for light and transient causes; and accordingly all experience hath shown that mankind are more disposed to suffer, while evils are sufferable, than to right themselves by abolishing the forms to which they are accustomed. But when a long train of abuses and usurpations, pursuing invariably the same object, evinces a design to reduce them under absolute despotism, it is their duty to throw off such government, and to provide new guards for their future security. Such has been the patient sufferance of the women under this government, and such is now the necessity which constrains them to demand the equal station to which they are entitled.

The history of mankind is a history of repeated injuries and usurpations on the part of man toward woman, having in direct object the establishment of an absolute tyranny over her. To prove this, let facts be submitted to a candid world.

He has never permitted her to exercise her inalienable right to the elective franchise.

He has compelled her to submit to laws, in the formation of which she had no voice.

He has withheld from her rights which are given to the most ignorant and degraded men—both natives and foreigners.

Having deprived her of this first right of a citizen, the elective franchise, thereby leaving her without representation in the halls of legislation, he has oppressed her on all sides.

He has made her, if married, in the eye of the law, civilly dead.

He has taken from her all right in property, even to the wages she earns.

He has made her, morally, an irresponsible being, as she can commit many crimes with impunity, provided they be done in the presence of her husband. In the covenant of marriage, she is compelled to promise obedience to her husband, he becoming, to all intents and purposes, her master—the law giving him power to deprive her of her liberty, and to administer chastisement.

He has so framed the laws of divorce, as to what shall be the proper causes, and in case of separation, to whom the guardianship of the children shall be given, as to be wholly regardless of the happiness of women—the law, in all cases, going upon a false supposition of the supremacy of man, and giving all power into his hands.

After depriving her of all rights as a married woman, if single, and the owner of property, he has taxed her to support a government which recognizes her only when her property can be made profitable to it.

He has monopolized nearly all the profitable employments, and from those she is permitted to follow, she receives but a scanty remuneration. He closes against her all the avenues to wealth and distinction which he considers most honorable to himself. As a teacher of theology, medicine, or law, she is not known.

He has denied her the facilities for obtaining a thorough education, all colleges being closed against her.

He allows her in Church, as well as State, but a subordinate position, claiming Apostolic authority for her exclusion from the ministry, and, with some exceptions, from any public participation in the affairs of the Church.

He has created a false public sentiment by giving to the world a different code of morals for men and women, by which moral delinquencies which exclude women from society, are not only tolerated, but deemed of little account in man.

He has usurped the prerogative of Jehovah himself, claiming it as his right to assign for her a sphere of action, when that belongs to her conscience and to her God.

He has endeavored, in every way that he could, to destroy her confidence in her own powers, to lessen her self-respect, and to make her willing to lead a dependent and abject life.

Now, in view of this entire disfranchisement of one-half the people of this country, their social and religious degradation—in view of the unjust laws above mentioned, and because women do feel themselves aggrieved, oppressed, and fraudulently deprived of their most sacred rights, we insist that they have immediate admission to all the rights and privileges which belong to them as citizens of the United States.

[. . .]

16. • *Sojourner Truth*

1851 SPEECH

Sojourner Truth was an African American abolitionist and women's rights activist born into slavery circa 1797 under the name Isabella Baumfree. She escaped from slavery in 1826 and renamed herself Sojourner Truth in 1843. Truth was illiterate but dictated her memoir, *The Narrative of Sojourner Truth: A Northern Slave*, which was published in 1850. After the Civil War, Truth advocated for land grants for former slaves and desegregation. She continued her activist work until her death in 1883. Truth's 1851 speech was presented at the Ohio Women's Rights Convention.

May I say a few words? Receiving an affirmative answer, she proceeded; I want to say a few words about this matter. I am a woman's rights. I have as much muscle as any man, and can do as much work as any man. I have plowed and reaped and husked and chopped and mowed, and can any man do more than that? I have heard much about the sexes being equal; I can carry as much as any man, and can eat as much too, if I can get it. I am as strong as any man that is now. As for intellect, all I can say is, if woman have a pint and man a quart—why can't she have her little pint full? You need not be afraid to give us our rights for fear we will take too much, for we can't take more than our pint'll hold. The poor men seem to be all in confusion, and don't know what to do. Why children, if you have woman's rights give it to her and you will feel better. You will have your own rights, and they won't be so much trouble. I can't read, but I can hear. I have heard the bible and have learned that Eve caused man to sin. Well if woman upset the world, do give her a chance to set it right side up again. The Lady has spoken about Jesus, how he never spurned woman from him, and she was right. When Lazarus died, Mary and Martha came to him with faith and love and besought him to raise their brother. And Jesus wept—and Lazarus came forth. And how came Jesus into the world? Through God who created him and woman who bore him. Man, where is your part? But the women are coming up, blessed be God, and a few of the men are coming up with them. But man is in a right place, the poor slave is on him, woman is coming on him, and he is surely between a hawk and a buzzard.

17. • *Susan B. Anthony*

SENTENCING SPEECH IN THE CASE OF *UNITED STATES VS. SUSAN B. ANTHONY* (1873)

While Susan B. Anthony was involved in other reform movements, she is most well known as an activist for women's suffrage. Along with Elizabeth Cady Stanton, she published a newspaper focused on women's rights called *The Revolution*. In 1872,

Anthony, along with other women, tried to register to vote in Rochester, New York. While she was initially refused, Anthony argued with the male election inspectors insisting that the Fourteenth Amendment gave her the right to vote. The inspectors eventually approved her registration, and Anthony cast her ballot four days later on Election Day. On November 14, an arrest warrant was issued for Anthony alleging that she violated the Enforcement Act, which prohibited illegal voting. Anthony's case went to trial on June 17, and Judge Ward Hunt found her guilty. Before sentencing, Judge Hunt gave Anthony the opportunity to speak, which she used to rail against the guilty verdict and the fact that she was denied her ability to exercise her rights as a citizen. The Nineteenth Amendment, which gave women the right to vote, was known as the Anthony Amendment and was ratified in 1920, fourteen years after Anthony's death.

Judge Hunt- (Ordering the defendant to stand up), "Has the prisoner anything to say why sentence shall not be pronounced?"

Miss Anthony- Yes, your honor, I have many things to say; for in your ordered verdict of guilty, you have trampled under foot every vital principle of our government. My natural rights, my civil rights, my political rights, my judicial rights, are all alike ignored. Robbed of the fundamental privilege of citizenship, I am degraded from the status of a citizen to that of a subject; and not only myself individually, but all of my sex, are, by your honor's verdict, doomed to political subjection under this, so-called, form of government.

Judge Hunt- The Court cannot listen to a rehearsal of arguments the prisoner's counsel has already consumed three hours in presenting.

Miss Anthony- May it please your honor, I am not arguing the question, but simply stating the reasons why sentence cannot, in justice, be pronounced against me. Your denial of my citizen's right to vote, is the denial of my right of consent as one of the governed, the denial of my right of representation as one of the taxed, the denial of my right to a trial by a jury of my peers as an offender against law, therefore, the denial of my sacred rights to life, liberty, property and—

Judge Hunt- The Court cannot allow the prisoner to go on.

Miss Anthony- But your honor will not deny me this one and only poor privilege of protest against this high-handed outrage upon my citizen's rights. May it please the Court to remember that since the day of my arrest last November, this is the first time that either myself or any person of my disfranchised class has been allowed a word of defense before judge or jury—

Judge Hunt- The prisoner must sit down—the Court cannot allow it.

Miss Anthony- All of my prosecutors, from the 8th ward corner grocery politician, who entered the complaint, to the United States Marshal, Commissioner, District Attorney, District Judge, your honor on the bench, not one is my peer, but each and all are my political sovereigns; and had your honor submitted my case to the jury, as was clearly your duty, even then I should have had just cause of protest, for not one of those men was my peer; but, native or foreign born, white or black, rich or poor, educated or ignorant, awake or asleep, sober or drunk, each and every man of them was my political superior; hence, in no sense, my peer. Even, under such circumstances, a commoner of England, tried before a jury of Lords, would have far less cause to complain than should I, a woman, tried before a jury of men. Even my counsel, the Hon. Henry R. Selden, who has argued my cause so ably, so earnestly, so unanswerably before your honor, is my political sovereign. Precisely as no disfranchised person is entitled to sit upon a jury, and no woman is entitled to the franchise, so, none but a regularly admitted lawyer is allowed to practice in the courts, and no woman can gain admission to the bar—hence, jury, judge, counsel, must all be of the superior class.

Judged Hunt- The Court must insist—the prisoner has been tried according to the established forms of law.

Miss Anthony- Yes, your honor, but by forms of law all made by men, interpreted by men, administered by men, in favor of men, and against women; and hence, your honor's ordered verdict of guilty; against a United States citizen for the exercise of "that citizen's right to vote," simply because that citizen was a woman and not a man. But, yesterday, the same man-made forms of law, declared it a crime punishable with $1,000 fine and six months' imprisonment, for you, or me, or any of us, to give a cup of cold water, a crust of bread, or a night's shelter to a panting fugitive as he was tracking his way to Canada. And every man or woman in whose veins coursed a drop of human sympathy violated that wicked law, reckless of consequences, and was justified in so doing. As then, the slaves who got their freedom must take it over, or under, or through the unjust forms of law, precisely so, now, must women, to get their right to a voice in this government, take it; and I have taken mine, and mean to take it at every possible opportunity.

Judge Hunt- The Court orders the prisoner to sit down. It will not allow another word.

Miss Anthony- When I was brought before your honor for trial, I hoped for a broad and liberal interpretation of the Constitution and its recent amendments, that should declare all United States citizens under its protecting egis—that should declare equality of rights the national guarantee to all persons born or naturalized in the United States. But failing to get this justice—failing, even, to get a trial by a jury *not* of my peers—I ask not leniency at your hands—but rather the full rigors of the law:

Judge Hunt- The Court must insist—

(Here the prisoner sat down.)

Judge Hunt- The prisoner will stand up.

(Here Miss Anthony arose again.)

The sentence of the Court is that you pay a fine of one hundred dollars and the costs of the prosecution.

Miss Anthony- May it please your honor, I shall never pay a dollar of your unjust penalty. All the stock in trade I possess is a $10,000 debt, incurred by publishing my paper—*The Revolution*—four years ago, the sole object of which was to educate all women to do precisely as I have done, rebel against your man-made, unjust, unconstitutional forms of law, that tax, fine, imprison and hang women, while they deny them the right of representation in the government; and I shall work on with might and main to pay every dollar of that honest debt, but not a penny shall go to this unjust claim. And I shall earnestly and persistently continue to urge all women to the practical recognition of the old revolutionary maxim, that "Resistance to tyranny is obedience to God."

Judge Hunt- Madam, the Court will not order you committed until the fine is paid.

18. • *Ida B. Wells*

A RED RECORD (1895)

Ida B. Wells (later Wells-Barnett) was born into slavery in 1862 but received a strong education and became a successful member of the new black middle class working first as a schoolteacher and later becoming a journalist. Wells was active in both the civil rights movement and the suffrage movement. She became known for her writing on race and became an editor of the antisegregationist Memphis newspaper *Free Speech and Headlight*. After three black businessmen who were friends of Wells were lynched by a white mob, she began a campaign to expose the injustice and horror of lynching. The following excerpt from her pamphlet, "A Red Record," demonstrates how Wells challenged the underlying arguments that legitimated lynching.

Beginning with the emancipation of the Negro, the inevitable result of unbridled power exercised for two and a half centuries, by the white man over the Negro, began to show itself in acts of conscienceless outlawry. During the slave regime, the Southern white man owned the Negro body and soul. It was to his interest to dwarf the soul and preserve the body. Vested with unlimited power over his slave, to subject him to any and all kinds of physical punishment, the white man was still restrained from such punishment as tended to injure the slave by abating his physical powers and thereby reducing his financial worth. While slaves were scourged mercilessly, and in countless cases inhumanly treated in other respects, still the white owner rarely permitted his anger to go so far as to take a life, which would entail upon him a loss of several hundred dollars. The slave was rarely killed, he was too valuable; it was easier and quite as effective, for discipline or revenge, to sell him "Down South."

But Emancipation came and the vested interests of the white man in the Negro's body were lost. The white man had no right to scourge the emancipated Negro, still less has he a right to kill him. But the Southern white people had been educated so long in that school of practice, in which might makes right, that they disdained to draw strict lines of action in dealing with the Negro. In slave times the Negro was kept subservient and submissive by the frequency and severity of the scourging, but, with freedom, a new system of intimidation came into vogue; the Negro was not only whipped and scourged; he was killed.

Not all nor nearly all of the murders done by white men, during the past thirty years in the South, have come to light, but the statistics as gathered and preserved by white men, and which have not been questioned, show that during these years more than ten thousand Negroes have been killed in cold blood, without the formality of judicial trial and legal execution. And yet, as evidence of the absolute impunity with which the white man dares to kill a Negro, the same record shows that during all these years, and for all these murders only three white men have been tried, convicted, and executed. As no white man has been lynched for the murder of colored people, these three executions are the only instances of the death penalty being visited upon white men for murdering Negroes.

Naturally enough the commission of these crimes began to tell upon the public conscience, and the

Southern white man, as a tribute to the nineteenth-century civilization, was in a manner compelled to give excuses for his barbarism. His excuses have adapted themselves to the emergency, and are aptly outlined by that greatest of all Negroes, Frederick Douglass, in an article of recent date, in which he shows that there have been three distinct eras of Southern barbarism, to account for which three distinct excuses have been made.

The first excuse given to the civilized world for the murder of unoffending Negroes was the necessity of the white man to repress and stamp out alleged "race riots." For years immediately succeeding the war there was an appalling slaughter of colored people, and the wires usually conveyed to northern people and the world the intelligence, first, that an insurrection was being planned by Negroes, which, a few hours later, would prove to have been vigorously resisted by white men, and controlled with a resulting loss of several killed and wounded. It was always a remarkable feature in these insurrections and riots that only Negroes were killed during the rioting, and that all the white men escaped unharmed.

From 1865 to 1872, hundreds of colored men and women were mercilessly murdered and the almost invariable reason assigned was that they met their death by being alleged participants in an insurrection or riot. But this story at last wore itself out. No insurrection ever materialized; no Negro rioter was ever apprehended and proven guilty, and no dynamite ever recorded the black man's protest against oppression and wrong. It was too much to ask thoughtful people to believe this transparent story, and the southern white people at last made up their minds that some other excuse must be had.

Then came the second excuse, which had its birth during the turbulent times of reconstruction. By an amendment to the Constitution the Negro was given the right of franchise, and, theoretically at least, his ballot became his invaluable emblem of citizenship. In a government "of the people, for the people, and by the people," the Negro's vote became an important factor in all matters of state and national politics. But this did not last long. The southern white man would not consider that the Negro had any right which a white

man was bound to respect, and the idea of a republican form of government in the southern states grew into general contempt. It was maintained that "This is a white man's government," and regardless of numbers the white man should rule. "No Negro domination" became the new legend on the sanguinary banner of the sunny South, and under it rode the Ku Klux Klan, the Regulators, and the lawless mobs, which for any cause chose to murder one man or a dozen as suited their purpose best. It was a long, gory campaign; the blood chills and the heart almost loses faith in Christianity when one thinks of Yazoo, Hamburg, Edgefield, Copiah, and the countless massacres of defenseless Negroes, whose only crime was the attempt to exercise their right to vote.

But it was a bootless strife for colored people. The government which had made the Negro a citizen found itself unable to protect him. It gave him the right to vote, but denied him the protection which should have maintained that right. Scourged from his home; hunted through the swamps; hung by midnight raiders, and openly murdered in the light of day, the Negro clung to his right of franchise with a heroism which would have wrung admiration from the hearts of savages. He believed that in that small white ballot there was a subtle something which stood for manhood as well as citizenship, and thousands of brave black men went to their graves, exemplifying the one by dying for the other.

The white man's victory soon became complete by fraud, violence, intimidation and murder. The franchise vouchsafed to the Negro grew to be a "barren ideality," and regardless of numbers, the colored people found themselves voiceless in the councils of those whose duty it was to rule. With no longer the fear of "Negro Domination" before their eyes, the white man's second excuse became valueless. With the Southern governments all subverted and the Negro actually eliminated from all participation in state and national elections, there could be no longer an excuse for killing Negroes to prevent "Negro Domination."

Brutality still continued; Negroes were whipped, scourged, exiled, shot and hung whenever and wherever it pleased the white man so to treat them, and as the civilized world with increasing persistency held the white people of the South to account for its outlawry, the murderers invented the third excuse—that Negroes had to be killed to avenge their assaults upon women. There could be framed no possible excuse more harmful to the Negro and more unanswerable if true in its sufficiency for the white man.

Humanity abhors the assailant of womanhood, and this charge upon the Negro at once placed him beyond the pale of human sympathy. With such unanimity, earnestness and apparent candor was this charge made and reiterated that the world has accepted the story that the Negro is a monster which the Southern white man has painted him. And today, the Christian world feels, that while lynching is a crime, and lawlessness and anarchy the certain precursors of a nation's fall, it can not by word or deed, extend sympathy or help to a race of outlaws, who might mistake their plea for justice and deem it an excuse for their continued wrongs.

[. . .]

If the Southern people in defense of their lawlessness, would tell the truth and admit that colored men and women are lynched for almost any offense, from murder to a misdemeanor, there would not now be the necessity for this defense. But when they intentionally, maliciously and constantly belie the record and bolster up these falsehoods by the words of legislators, preachers, governors and bishops, then the Negro must give to the world his side of the awful story.

A word as to the charge itself. In considering the third reason assigned by the Southern white people for the butchery of blacks, the question must be asked, what the white man means when he charges the black man with rape. Does he mean the crime which the statutes of the civilized states describe as such? Not by any means. With the Southern white man, any mésalliance existing between a white woman and a colored man is a sufficient foundation for the charge of rape. The Southern white man says that it is impossible for a voluntary alliance to exist between a white woman and a colored man, and therefore, the fact of an alliance is a proof of force. In numerous instances where colored men have been lynched on the charge of rape, it was positively known at the time of lynching, and indisputably proven after the victim's death, that the relationship sustained between the man and woman was voluntary and clandestine, and that in no court of law could even the charge of assault have been successfully maintained.

[. . .]

In his remarkable apology for lynching, Bishop Haygood, of Georgia, says: "No race, not the most savage, tolerates the rape of woman, but it may be said without reflection upon any other people that the Southern people are now and always have been most sensitive concerning the honor of their women—their mothers, wives, sisters and daughters." It is not the purpose of this defense to say one word against the white women of the South. Such need not be said, but it is their misfortune that the chivalrous white men of that section, in order to escape the deserved execration of the civilized world, should shield themselves by their cowardly and infamously false excuse, and call into question that very honor about which their distinguished priestly apologist claims they are most sensitive. To justify their own barbarism they assume a chivalry which they do not possess. True chivalry respects all womanhood, and no one who reads the record, as it is written in the faces of the million mulattoes in the South, will for a minute conceive that the southern white man had a very chivalrous regard for the honor due the women of his own race or respect for the womanhood which circumstances placed in his power. That chivalry which is "most sensitive concerning the honor of women" can hope for but little respect from the civilized world, when it confines itself entirely to the women who happen to be white. Virtue knows no color line, and the chivalry which depends upon complexion of skin and texture of hair can command no honest respect.

[. . .]

19. • *Theresa Serber Malkiel*

DIARY OF A SHIRTWAIST STRIKER (1910)

Theresa Serber Malkiel was a Jewish immigrant who arrived in New York in 1891 at the age of seventeen. Like many other female immigrants at that time, she began working in a sweatshop in the garment industry. She quickly became active in the labor movement and joined the Socialist Labor party. Her marriage to a lawyer allowed her to leave the factory, but she remained involved in politics and began her work as a journalist. She wrote for the *New York Call,* a socialist newspaper, and the *Jewish Daily Forward,* where she wrote a women's column. While her socialist beliefs made her suspicious of middle-class suffragists, Malkiel believed strongly in women's right to vote. *Diary of a Shirtwaist Striker* is a fictionalized account of the New York City Shirtwaist Strike of 1909–1910. With twenty thousand strikers, most of them young, Jewish, immigrant women, this was, at the time, the largest strike of women workers in American history. The excerpt below presents the evolving political consciousness of one striker.

November 23, 1909

Ha, ha, ha! that's a joke. By Jove, it is. I'm a striker. I wonder what Jim'll have to say to this?

I must say I really don't know why I became one—I went down just because everybody else in the workroom did. . . .

[. . .]

I guess Jim wouldn't mind my being a striker if he knew what fun I'm getting out of it. But I know better, he's that strict about all such things. I can just hear him call me an anarchist. And yet, it's a good thing, this strike is; it makes you feel like a real grown-up person. But I wish I'd feel about it like them Jew girls do. Why, their eyes flash fire as soon as they commence to talk about the strike— and the lot of talk they can Put up—at times they make a body feel like two cents.

I simply can't get over the way little Ray Goldovsky jumped on a chair and suddenly, without a minute's notice, stopped the electricity. I must say, it's nothing but her bravery that took us all. Why, we were simply stunned. And Mr. Hayman, too, was taken off his feet. Before you could say Jack Robinson we all rose, slipped on our duds and marched down the stairs, shouting, yelling and giggling about our walkout, as they called it.

[. . .]

I'm surprised that Mr. Hayman didn't show up this afternoon; they were all so sure that he'd settle within a few hours. I guess it has been the girls' own imagination. It makes me smile when I think of being labeled; but what was I to do? Everybody gave in their name, so I had to give mine and a dime with it. They warned me that I can't get my union book unless I pay in the rest, $1.15 in all. As if a body cares for their old book. What in the world do I want with a union? My mother and grandmother have gone through life without belonging to one and I guess I, too, can get along without it.

The only thing that keeps me with them is that it may help those poor devils who have to work for three and four dollars a week. It's but very few of the girls that make such wages as I do. And I believe they must have a real hard time of it. They look it. It was enough to break one's heart to see some of them. Perhaps it will be over tomorrow.

November 24

Well, well, I think this strike is a more serious business than I thought, otherwise the papers wouldn't make so much of it. Why, every one of them is full of the strike and strikers; we are made so much of. It really feels good to be somebody. It even gave me courage to tell ma that I, too, am a striker. Of course I had to give her a whopper—had to tell her that Mr. Hayman closed up shop when the girls went out. He's just the one to do it. He's sure to keep it up, if only for spite. I wonder why he hates the union so much?

[. . .]

It's simply amazing what a difference one day may make. I think a complete change has come over me, and no wonder! It is enough to make any one mad the way they treat the girls, as if a body mustn't talk to anybody on the street. That's just why they've arrested Ray. It's ridiculous, their saying that she wanted to hit big Moe, as if that ruffian would be afraid of her. Poor kid, I'm real sorry for her, she has a hard lot with that whole family upon her frail shoulders, an' I don't see how she can do it. Here am I that ain't got any board to pay, for ma don't need my money. Pa makes enough to keep the whole lot of us, so whatever I make is my own, but a body needs a whole lot these days and I don't get much left out of my wages.

[. . .]

And then again, one can't really help standing up for the girls. I went down to see Minnie; she's down

in bed; some hoodlum hit her last night. God! how those people do live! I don't see how she can afford to stop for a single day.

Her brother Mack is out of work, her father never works, Minnie and her sister, Sarah, are out on strike. Talk about nerve, I really think them Jew girls have it all. I'd like a share of it myself, but somehow I ain't of the brave kind. Ray said she'd rather starve to death than be a scab and take some one else's bread out of their mouths. I'm sure I couldn't have that much courage, but I'd hate to go back on the girls.

One of these talking women was trying to tell us girls that we ought to be glad of the opportunity to be idle for awhile—it gives us a chance to see and learn things that we could have never known anything about. She may be right, after all; what I've learned in these last two days is enough to put me wise to many a wrong. Only a little while ago I would have laughed had somebody told me that I would take this strike in earnest, but this afternoon, listening to the stories of assault upon the girls, watching the poor, miserable creatures that don't earn enough to keep body and soul together, I believe I was as much excited as the rest of them.

[. . .]

November 25

Another day spent in that dingy, smelly hall and still no end. Mr. Hayman don't come around and I'm pretty sure he won't come, either. The crowds increase every hour. Just like the ocean tide, their number grew higher and yet they said down at the headquarters that forty-one bosses have settled already and seven thousand girls are back to work. But then there are still four times seven thousand out and if the bosses will be settling at the rate of seven thousand in three days it will take almost two weeks before this big strike is settled. I think it's terrible. Why, some of the girls can't wait a day!

They asked me to go picketing, but I refused, of course. The idea of walking around the street corner as if I was a watch dog! They ought to be glad that I come down to their meetings every day. . . .

[. . .]

. . . Jim was up here a little while ago. It's just as I had expected; why, he is just wild at my having mixed myself up with the strike. He said that I'd better quit and I said I won't, and before long we were having a tongue lashing and came pretty near having a falling out. That never happened to us since we have been going together.

The idea of his saying that a strike is good enough for these East Side girls, but he can't see the sense of my going into it. As if I was something better, made of different clay, perhaps. No, the speaker justly said that it makes no difference to what nationality we girls belong, or of what religion we are, so long as we have to work one is as good as the other, for all have one and the same interest—to make life a bit easier.

I'm mighty glad I had the courage to tell Jim just what I thought of his words. I'm sure he'll mind his business after this and I'll try to mind my own. It's a bit too much, him acting as if he is my boss already. Not by a long shot! There's many a slip between the cup and the lip.

[. . .]

November 26

[. . .]

It ain't only our girls that are out doing the job, there is a lot of college women, members of the Woman's Trade Union League, who spend their days watching our factories. And a fine lot of women they are at that. I've come to know quite a number of them. What sets me a-thinking is the fact that these women could go on living to their heart's content. They needn't come downtown among us if they don't want to, and why should they do it? It can't be for the sake of what's in it, for there ain't much fun in standing around the bleak, cold corners, being arrested by the cops and taken to the station house and police court.

I shouldn't wonder that their conscience pricks them a bit—they must be ashamed of being fortune children while so many of the girls have never known what a good day means. The rich women seem to be softer than the men; perhaps it's because they ain't making the money—they're only spending it. Or is it that women, as a rule, are better natured than their men folk? The saying has it that there is nothing so bad as a bad woman, nor anything better than a good one. I must admit the league women are the goodest of the good. And the Woman's Trade Union League in general is a mighty good thing for us girls.

[. . .]

November 27

I felt a bit shaky when I came down town this morning. But picketing ain't half as bad as I thought it would be. And another thing—it's enough to get down in that neighborhood and see the way these cops handle our girls, to be mad through and through; there ain't no thought of shame in them.

To tell the truth—it's only false pride—this imaginary shame is. There is nothing dishonest in standing up for one's bread. We must warn the newcomers that us girls are out on strike because our boss is paying starvation wages. To be sure, this is a business of much consequence, and so far as I can see the union is really the one to help us out. Then why be ashamed to belong to it and fight for it? In fact, we're all union people, only we don't seem to remember it. This land is one big union, and us children were taught very early that united we stand and divided we fall, and that's just what we girls are demanding—the right to be united.

[. . .]

. . . Jim is just set on seeing me leave the strike, and I'm just as set on sticking to it. He even went so far as to threaten me—said that I'd have to make my choice. And suppose I will, I'm sure it's better to suffer than turn traitor, and this is just what I would be were I to leave the girls now, when they are abused the most, and treated worse than street dogs. . . .

[. . .]

November 28

I stayed home today; thought I'd rest up a bit, but nothing doing—had more trouble than I've bargained for. Pa didn't have a chance to say much to me during the week; in fact, we hardly see him at all except Sundays and holidays. And I guess he had it in for me all along. At any rate, I got all that's a-coming to me today.

"See here," was the first thing he said to me this morning. "I've never been very strict with you girls; you've always had enough rope to run about, but not too much. I won't stand for it. I wouldn't have my neighbors point their finger at me. I ain't the kind to be pitied. You've been fooling around long enough with that strike business of your 'n, and now it's high time to quit. I don't give a snap about the money you've lost during the week. It ain't that. It's just because I don't think it's a woman's place to be hangin' around street corners, fighting with rowdies and be taken to jail. Union is all good and well by itself, but it was never meant for the women."

His words just set my blood a boiling—as if it is woman's place to go out of the home in order to be the breadwinner for the family. If she's good enough to spend her days in some of the shops that ain't fit for pig stys, she may as well stand up on the corners and fight for her rights. I'm sure it's much better than standing on the corner for other purposes, which some women are compelled to do. And if woman is to go on submitting to the love-making of every rowdy that's got some power over her, she may as well teach others that she, too, can stand up for herself. I wouldn't have minded him so much, if he hadn't been a union man himself. People laugh at woman's reason, but, honestly, I think man's beats it all to pieces. Where's the difference between man and woman when it comes to work? They're both anxious to earn an honest living and have the right to protect themselves as best they can.

[. . .]

December 2

[. . .]

Everybody tried to make love to the little coal stove when we got back to the meeting rooms. But I wouldn't be a bit surprised if many of the girls will be laid up with sore throats by tomorrow. It is terrible; they go down like flies. There's scarcely a shop but has a number of girls sick in bed. This makes it so much harder for those who are still up. Poor Ray, her teeth were just rattling when she got back this afternoon; even the cup of hot water we gave her didn't help much. She ain't fit to work or strike, either. It's a sanitarium and good care that she needs, but where is she to get it, and what will the others do without her?

[. . .]

December 4

[. . .]

Stopped on the square this afternoon and listened to them that talks votes for women. It's all very true. I also say that a woman is every bit as good as a man and should have the same rights with him. But us girls have something else to think of just now. We must see to it that we win the strike for bread and then we can start one for the ballot.

As I was leaving the square I met a girl going to the headquarters; her face was all swollen, one of her teeth knocked out, her clothes in tatters and she running around since early this morning unable to find a policeman willing to arrest the brute who beat her so terribly. I wonder if this is what our good Mayor is doing for us?

As I said, we have our hands full just at present—a number of girls went back on us. The fools got scared because Hayman told them that he'd rather go out of business than give in to us girls. I don't believe a word he says—what else would he do if not be in business unless he turned dog catcher? But it wouldn't pay as well as the waist making business does.

The pity of it is that us working people don't really realize what a power we are. I fully agree with that speaker who said that in spite of all their money our bosses couldn't get along without us working people. For if they had even a hundred times as many machines, and the whole world built of factories, they couldn't deliver a single order unless the working people chose to make them up.

[. . .]

December 8

[. . .]

The judges and police make the mistake of their lives if they hope to stop us by keeping up this jail business—every new arrest makes a firm convert to the cause. The girls' sense of justice becomes sharpened by the fact that they are persecuted for telling the truth. Helen tried to assure us that they'll impeach the judges—I'd like to know who'll be brave enough to do it. But anything is good, so long as it quiets the girls.

Some of the League women rushed off in a hurry, they said, to hold a conference with the bosses. I do hope they'll come to some understanding this time, for this strike is just killing many of the girls. But some of them labor leaders needn't think that they can bunco us into any tom fool settlement, for we won't stand for it. Us girls have come to realize that the welfare of one means the welfare of all, and this is likewise true about the hardships. Annie and Rosie don't amount to anything as long as they remain only hands and stand up each one for herself and let the devil take the hindmost.

[. . .]

December 12

[. . .]

"Why, Jim, what are you cursing about, and on Sunday at that?" "I'm cursing that blame strike of yourn," says he. "Before that nuisance took place you were perfectly satisfied with your lot, obeyed your father and cared and believed in me as every good woman should do, and now you seem so changed that I often wonder what has come over you."

"Why, Jim, my boy," I said, quietly. "I've grown up since then and learned a thing or two. A tin rattle and a funny man can't satisfy me any longer. I've come to understand that, until I left the workbench on that Tuesday morning, I had lived in a trance without really knowing why I kept it up from day to day. I was no better than the cow in the stall—as long as I had enough to eat I was satisfied. But I'm sure, Jim, that even you wouldn't want me to remain a cow."

"I—I don't know what I'd want; I'd want you to be a woman and not a freak," blurted out Jim at last.

"I wonder what a man means when he says he'd want you to be a woman? If to believe in everything that's right, to sorrow for the needy, to help the weak, to censure the wicked, to refuse being stepped upon, used and abused, means not being a woman, then I don't want to be a woman. Honestly, I don't. My Ma is considered a good woman—she wakes up long before sunrise and she works and works until we are all in bed. And she never has her say, but does what Pa wants her to do."

"Mary!" exclaimed Jim in anger. "I'm sure you'll rue the day you've mixed yourself up with those darn anarchists. They'll be the ruin of you," and with this he left me standing near the house and rushed off.

[. . .]

December 17

[. . .]

They've brought me to their fashionable clubhouse to hear about our misery. To tell the truth, I've no appetite to tell it to them, for I've almost come to the conclusion that the gulf between us girls and these rich ladies is too deep to be smoothed over by a few paltry dollars; the girls would probably be the better off in the long run if they did not take their money. They would the sooner realize the great contrast and the division of classes; this would teach them to stick to their own. But say and think what I please, we simply have to go to them for the present and accept as little or as much as they're willing to give. The lines down at Clinton Street are growing daily. And it ain't for curiosity that they come there and shove and push, only to get a bit nearer to the sacred door behind which sits Mr. Shindler. No, it's nothing but merciless hunger that brings them there.

The women gave us a thousand dollars, but what does this amount to? Not even a quarter a piece for each striker, and I know of many that need at least a ten-dollar bill to drive the wolf away from the door. And can there be a worse wolf than the landlord when there's two months' rent due him?

Only this morning as I was leaving home I walked past an evicted family. It almost broke my heart to see their pitiful faces. Can they be blamed for insisting that their daughters give up the strike and go back to work? Some of these people hadn't a cent to their name when the strike first started and one can imagine the state they're in after almost four weeks of idleness.

I can't understand somehow where in this world the justice comes in as it is arranged just now— here's us that work hard and steady and must face starvation as soon as we cease to work, while them that's idle have more money and good things than they really know what to do with.

I think it's foolish of us working people to accept our fate so quietly. It can't be that we are doomed to go through life in misery and darkness, without a ray of natural light in the shop, without a bit of sunshine at home. Can't the working people realize that we are at the complete mercy of selfishness and greed? I did to-day when I was brought face to face with all those riches; if they'd know what's good for them they wouldn't bring us in their midst, for, if anything will, this is sure to arouse the spirit of rebellion. I know it did in me. I felt sore for the rest of the day.

[. . .]

December 23

[. . .]

When I got there Jim was waiting for me, and, by the way he acted, I'm beginning to believe he has changed his opinion about us girls. I tried to be as jolly as I possibly could under the circumstances— I don't believe of sniffling before anybody, especially Jim—I wasn't going to show him how bad I felt. What's the use? And yet, I'd be more than happy if I could turn him to my way of looking upon life. Not that I'd want to boss over him. I wouldn't want that for anything in the world—no more than I'd want him to boss over me.

[. . .]

December 24

It just struck me this morning that this is the second month since we are out on strike. It seems easy to say the second month. But Lord! Thirty-two whole days, 7248 hours since Clara said to us girls down at that big meeting: "Come, girls, let's go out on strike." And all those hours were hours of suffering, agony and growth. Yes, growth—whatever else we'll gain from this strike it certainly was an eye-opener to some of us, myself especially.

[. . .]

December 25

[. . .]

Silently, for the first time in this holy morning, I delivered a prayer to the Lord. The Jim I disliked was slipping away and a new one, nobler and more generous, was entering into my life.

We left the barracks after a while, had a bite and, I leading the way, started up Fifth avenue. I thought it was a good policy to let him note the difference. And, sure enough, he did.

"Mary," says he, "it seems to be a shame that these people gorge themselves with all good stuff, while most of the others have to stand in line in order to get their leavings. I—I really think you're about right in trying to help make things as they should be, for it seems a grievous sin to live amid all the misery without lifting a finger to help."

And so I've succeeded in awakening another human heart. I know Jim, and am sure that he won't shrink from the trials he is sure to meet on this new path of life.

[. . .]

December 27

[. . .]

In the afternoon there were five mass meetings held in different halls in order to give all the girls a chance to vote on the latest proposition. I made it my business to have a peep at all of them, and I must say it was the greatest sight I've met yet. Girls with sore throats and girls with broken noses; girls with wet, torn shoes and girls without hats or coats, shivering from cold and faint from hunger; they were all on hand; their condition didn't matter a bit. Their vote was wanted and they came. Tired, half starved and almost dropping from weakness, they stood up on the tables, clung to the banisters, steadied themselves on window sills and hung onto the balcony railings. Their deep, thoughtful eyes wide open, their lips parted, they tried not to miss a single word uttered from the platform and the expression of their worn faces was even more eloquent than words.

Like a numberless army of bees they rose in a body against those who were trying to mar their future. "We're sick of all these assurances," shouted Fanny. "This is the time to strike them while the iron is red hot and we're going to get what we want or die in the attempt."

To listen to the numerous individual expressions one would have thought that us girls must be positive of a near victory, and yet this very morning many of the girls deserted our ranks and went back to work, but it doesn't seem to matter; somehow we've become so desperate that we look upon the whole thing this way: We don't die twice and don't live on forever, and us girls are resigned to accept whatever comes along. At any rate, it's better to die fighting than being fought with your hands tied behind your back.

"We ain't going back!" yelled Molly, jumping from a nearby table onto the platform. "I move that we remain out unless the bosses sign an agreement with the union." I'm happy to say her motion was accepted unanimously.

[. . .]

December 28

Spent this morning in the office of the union and, honestly, it pretty near did me up—the lines of applicants for strike benefits grow hourly; as it is they already extend from the fourth 'way down to the ground floor, standing four abreast. It's enough to break one's heart to witness their misery, even for a little while. People are dying with hunger, and this, coupled with the horrible brutalities practiced upon our girls, reaches a point where description becomes impossible.

We in the office had to listen to their tales of unbearable cold, of starvation and sickness that reigns in their gloomy homes. The truth of their words could easily be verified by the careworn expression of their pale faces. God! where do we get the power to stand it all? I myself often go for days with just a bit of dry bread, but somehow a body's insides get so dried up that one don't mind it any longer—only that our strength is giving out bit by bit.

[. . .]

January 13

[. . .]

"Mary," said Jim to me after we had talked a while about our future life, "I don't know as I could be called a woman's rights man, but it seems to me that these women ought to try and wake up us men as well. I know this little woman," pointing at me, "did wake me up. I've come to believe that us men do not understand the make-up of you girls. For we would know better if we did. It's silly talk; we can't live without one another; there can't be no man's nor woman's world, Mary, there must be a human world."

I just wonder what pa would say if he heard Jim talk. Lord! . . .

January 19

[. . .]

God! what a terrible, bloodless tragedy this strike of ours turned out to be! Yes, I'm right in saying bloodless, for there ain't a bit of blood left in the girls. I don't know, but I had a funny day and can't help seeing everything from the dark side. I guess it's because Jim didn't come 'round.

Strange as it may seem, in spite of my moods and thoughts, I ain't a bit sorry for having struck. For the last few years things have been getting steadily worse. Wages decreasing and the cost of living getting higher. Many of the people that I've met since the strike have lost half of their families through nothing but starvation. Why, even the charities reported that this year is the worst ever. It was about time that somebody should protest and I'm glad that us girls were brave enough to do it, even if many will have to pay with their life for it. I'm willing to forfeit mine.

[. . .]

January 21

[. . .]

Some blame us girls for having started this whole affair. They claim that it's going to hurt everybody and won't help us. Well, I beg to differ. It helped us already—twenty-one thousand people enrolled on the union books, about seventeen thousand back to work under agreements with the bosses, the remainder still fighting and at the same time being molded into types that will withstand any fire.

[. . .]

January 23

All comes to him who works for it! All hail to us girls—we got what we wanted—Mr. Hayman had to sign the agreement after all. Oh, I begged and coaxed them and they took me along on the committee—just wanted to see for myself how he behaved. Well, well, he made me think of the animals at the circus—jumped and kicked and gnawed his teeth to the very last moment—but us girls had the strong whip over him—he must send out his orders and pride must go. Ours went long ago—we needed bread to keep up our life. And why should we alone suffer all the time?

I know that it has been going on that way for a long, long while—the poor worked and suffered and watched their children growing pale from lack of food and ill health. But still they went on uncomplaining—it's all because there's a dark curtain hung over their tired eyes and they don't see natural things in their natural light. And yet—the contrast is getting too great. I know it's nothing but the terrible contrast that helped open my eyes and Jim's.

[. . .]

I know, I've promised Jim to marry him on the day Mr. Hayman settles with us girls. I shall keep my promise; in fact, I'm happy to do it—I'm perhaps as anxious for the event as he himself. . . .

[. . .]

. . . I mean to bring myself to the point where I could be a real friend and companion to Jim. I shall be with him in the hour of joy and in the hour of sorrow. I shall soothe and comfort him, consult and advise. For one thing—I know Jim will meet me exactly on the same grounds—we will be, we must be, happy.

141 MEN AND GIRLS DIE IN WAIST FACTORY FIRE (1911)

Despite the gains achieved through the New York Shirtwaist Strike of 1909, working conditions in the garment industry remained dangerous. The Triangle Shirtwaist Factory was one of the largest garment companies in Manhattan and employed mostly immigrant women as factory workers. *The New York Times'* account of the fire describes the deaths of 141 workers (later found to be 146) and the horror of onlookers. This tragedy demonstrated the inadequacies of existing worker protections and became a rallying cry for improved government regulation and increased unionization.

Three stories of a ten-floor building at the corner of Greene Street and Washington Place were burned yesterday, and while the fire was going on 141 young men and women—at least 125 of them mere girls—were burned to death or killed by jumping to the pavement below.

The building was fireproof. It shows now hardly any signs of the disaster that overtook it. The walls are as good as ever; so are the floors; nothing is the worse for the fire except the furniture and 141 of the 600 men and girls that were employed in its upper three stories.

Most of the victims were suffocated or burned to death within the building, but some who fought their way to the windows and leaped met death as surely, but perhaps more quickly, on the pavements below.

[. . .]

The victims who are now lying at the Morgue waiting for some one to identify them by a tooth or the remains of a burned shoe were mostly girls from 16 to 23 years of age. They were employed at making shirtwaists by the Triangle Waist Company, the principal owners of which are Isaac Harris and Max Blanck. Most of them could barely speak English. Many of them came from Brooklyn. Almost all were the main support of their hard-working families.

There is just one fire escape in the building. That one is an interior fire escape. In Greene Street, where the terrified unfortunates crowded before they began to make their mad leaps to death, the whole big front of the building is guiltless of one. Nor is there a fire escape in the back.

[. . .]

LEAPED OUT OF THE FLAMES.

At 4:40 o'clock, nearly five hours after the employees in the rest of the building had gone home, the fire broke out. The one little fire escape in the interior was never resorted to by any of the doomed victims. Some of them escaped by running down the stairs, but in a moment or two this avenue was cut off by flame. The girls rushed to the windows and looked down at Greene Street, 100 feet below them. Then one poor, little creature jumped. There was a plate glass protection over part of the sidewalk, but she crashed through it, wrecking it and breaking her body into a thousand pieces.

Then they all began to drop. The crowd yelled "Don't jump!" but it was jump or be burned—the proof of which is found in the fact that fifty burned bodies were taken from the ninth floor alone.

They jumped, they crashed through broken glass, they crushed themselves to death on the sidewalk. Of those who stayed behind it is better to say nothing—except what a veteran policeman said as he gazed at a headless and charred trunk on the Greene Street sidewalk hours after the worst cases had been taken out:

"I saw the Slocum disaster, but it was nothing to this."

"Is it a man or a woman?" asked the reporter.

"It's human, that's all you can tell," answered the policeman.

It was just a mass of ashes, with blood congealed on what had probably been the neck.

Messrs. Harris and Blanck were in the building, but they escaped. They carried with them Mr. Blanck's children and a governess, and they fled over the roofs. Their employees did not know the way, because they had been in the habit of using the two freight elevators, and one of these elevators was not in service when the fire broke out.

[. . .]

"It's the worst thing I ever saw," said one old policeman.

Chief Croker said it was an outrage. He spoke bitterly of the way in which the Manufacturers' Association had called a meeting in Wall Street to take measures against his proposal for enforcing better methods of protection for employees in cases of fire.

NO CHANCE TO SAVE VICTIMS.

[. . .]

It may convey some idea too, to say that thirty bodies clogged the elevator shaft. These dead were all girls. They had made their rush there blindly when they discovered that there was no chance to get out by the fire escape. Then they found that the elevator was as hopeless as anything else, and they fell there in their tracks and died.

The Triangle Waist Company employed about 600 women and less than 100 men. One of the saddest features of the thing is the fact that they had almost finished for the day. In five minutes more, if the fire had started then, probably not a life would have been lost.

Last night District Attorney Whitman started an investigation—not of this disaster alone but of the whole condition which makes it possible for a firetrap of such a kind to exist. Mr. Whitman's intention is to find out if the present laws cover such cases, and if they do not to frame laws that will.

GIRLS JUMP TO SURE DEATH. FIRE NETS PROVE USELESS— FIREMEN HELPLESS TO SAVE LIFE.

[. . .]

How the fire started no one knows. On the three upper floors of the building were 600 employees of the waist company, 500 of whom were girls. The victims—mostly Italians, Russians, Hungarians, and Germans—were girls and men who had been employed by the firm of Harris & Blanck, owners of the Triangle Waist Company, after the strike in which the Jewish girls, formerly employed, had become unionized and had demanded better working conditions. The building had experienced four recent fires and had been reported by the Fire Department to the Building Department as unsafe on account of the insufficiency of its exits.

The building itself was of the most modern construction and classed as fireproof. What burned so quickly and disastrously for the victims were shirtwaists, hanging on lines above tiers of workers, sewing machines placed so closely together that there was hardly aisle room for the girls between them, and shirtwaist trimmings and cuttings which littered the floors above the eighth and ninth stories.

Girls had begun leaping from the eighth story windows before firemen arrived. The firemen had trouble bringing their apparatus into position because of the bodies which strewed the pavement and sidewalks. While more bodies crashed down among them, they worked with desperation to run their ladders into position and to spread firenets.

[. . .]

Five girls who stood together at a window close to the Greene Street corner held their places while a fire ladder was worked toward them, but which stopped at its full length two stories lower down. They leaped together, clinging to each other, with fire streaming back from their hair and dresses. They struck a glass sidewalk cover and crashed through it to the basement. There was no time to aid them. With water pouring in upon them from a dozen hose nozzles the bodies lay for two hours where they struck, as did the many others who leaped to their deaths.

One girl, who waved a handkerchief at the crowd, leaped from a window adjoining the New York University Building on the westward. Her dress caught on a wire, and the crowd watched her hang there till her dress burned free and she came toppling down.

[. . .]

---

21. • *Daughters of Bilitis*

STATEMENT OF PURPOSE (1955)

The Daughters of Bilitis (DOB) was the first lesbian civil rights organization in the United States. It formed in San Francisco in 1955 and later opened up chapters across the country. While initially functioning as more of a social club where lesbians could meet and interact safely, DOB quickly grew into an activist organization. In 1956 DOB began publishing *The Ladder,* the first nationally distributed lesbian publication, which became an important source of information for lesbians across the country and created a sense of community. The goals of DOB seem modest by today's standards and, along with others that were part of the homophile movement, they are often criticized for their assimilationist rhetoric. However, the pioneering work of the DOB laid the groundwork for more radical activism.

A WOMEN'S ORGANIZATION FOR THE PURPOSE OF PROMOTING THE INTEGRATION OF THE HOMOSEXUAL INTO SOCIETY BY:

1. Education of the variant, with particular emphasis on the psychological, physiological and sociological aspects, to enable her to understand herself and make her adjustment to society in all its social, civic and economic implications—this to be accomplished by establishing and maintaining as complete a library as possible of both fiction and non-fiction literature on the sex deviant theme; by sponsoring public discussions on

pertinent subjects to be conducted by leading members of the legal, psychiatric, religious and other professions; by advocating a mode of behavior and dress acceptable to society.

2. Education of the public at large through acceptance first of the individual, leading to an eventual breakdown of erroneous taboos and prejudices; through public discussion meetings aforementioned; through dissemination of educational literature on the homosexual theme.

3. Participation in research projects by duly authorized and responsible psychologists, sociologists and other such experts directed towards further knowledge of the homosexual.

4. Investigation of the penal code as it pertains to the homosexual, proposal of changes to provide an equitable handling of cases involving this minority group, and promotion of these changes through due process of law in the state legislatures.

22. • *Leslie Feinberg, interview with Sylvia Rivera*

I'M GLAD I WAS IN THE STONEWALL RIOT (1998)

Sylvia Rivera was a long-time activist for the LGBTQPAI+ community, particularly for genderqueer and other groups who felt marginalized within the gay rights movement. She was an influential member of several activist organizations including the Gay Liberation Front (GLF), Gay Activists Alliance (GAA), and the Street Transvestite Action Revolutionaries (STAR). While other readings in this section provide contemporaneous historical accounts, most of the reports of the Stonewall Riot written at the time reflect a heavily-biased, heteronormative, cisgender perspective. Therefore, to include a first-person, queer history of the uprising, we have chosen a retrospective piece, written three decades after the riots, and positioned it chronologically in terms of the time period it discusses rather than the year it was published. In this interview, Rivera tells her story of the Stonewall Riot and discusses her other activist work.

I left home at age 10 in 1961. I hustled on 42nd Street. The early 60s was not a good time for drag queens, effeminate boys or boys that wore makeup like we did.

Back then we were beat up by the police, by everybody. I didn't really come out as a drag queen until the late 60s.

When drag queens were arrested, what degradation there was. I remember the first time I got arrested, I wasn't even in full drag. I was walking down the street and the cops just snatched me.

We always felt that the police were the real enemy. We expected nothing better than to be treated like we were animals—and we were.

We were stuck in a bullpen like a bunch of freaks. We were disrespected. A lot of us were beaten up and raped.

When I ended up going to jail, to do 90 days, they tried to rape me. I very nicely bit the shit out of a man.

I've been through it all.

In 1969, the night of the Stonewall riot, was a very hot, muggy night. We were in the Stonewall [bar] and the lights came on. We all stopped dancing. The police came in.

They had gotten their payoff earlier in the week. But Inspector Pine came in—him and his morals squad—to spend more of the government's money.

We were led out of the bar and they cattled us all up against the police vans. The cops pushed us up against the grates and the fences. People started throwing pennies, nickels, and quarters at the cops.

And then the bottles started. And then we finally had the morals squad barricaded in the Stonewall building, because they were actually afraid of us at that time. They didn't know we were going to react that way.

We were not taking any more of this shit. We had done so much for other movements. It was time.

It was street gay people from the Village out front—homeless people who lived in the park in Sheridan Square outside the bar—and then drag queens behind them and everybody behind us. The Stonewall Inn telephone lines were cut and they were left in the dark.

One *Village Voice* reporter was in the bar at that time. And according to the archives of the *Village Voice*, he was handed a gun from Inspector Pine and told, "We got to fight our way out of there."

This was after one Molotov cocktail was thrown and we were ramming the door of the Stonewall bar with an uprooted parking meter. So they were ready to come out shooting that night.

Finally the Tactical Police Force showed up after 45 minutes. A lot of people forget that for 45 minutes we had them trapped in there.

All of us were working for so many movements at that time. Everyone was involved with the women's movement, the peace movement, the civil-rights movement. We were all radicals. I believe that's what brought it around.

You get tired of being just pushed around.

STAR came about after a sit-in at Weinstein Hall at New York University in 1970. Later we had a chapter in New York, one in Chicago, one in California and England.

STAR was for the street gay people, the street homeless people and anybody that needed help at that time. Marsha and I had always sneaked people into our hotel rooms. Marsha and I decided to get a building. We were trying to get away from the Mafia's control at the bars.

We got a building at 213 East 2nd Street. Marsha and I just decided it was time to help each other and help our other kids. We fed people and clothed people. We kept the building going. We went out and hustled the streets. We paid the rent.

We didn't want the kids out in the streets hustling. They would go out and rip off food. There was always food in the house and everyone had fun. It lasted for two or three years.

We would sit there and ask, "Why do we suffer?" As we got more involved into the movements, we said, "Why do we always got to take the brunt of this shit?"

Later on, when the Young Lords [revolutionary Puerto Rican youth group] came about in New York City, I was already in GLF [Gay Liberation Front]. There was a mass demonstration that started in East Harlem in the fall of 1970. The protest was against police repression and we decided to join the demonstration with our STAR banner.

That was one of first times the STAR banner was shown in public, where STAR was present as a group.

I ended up meeting some of the Young Lords that day. I became one of them. Any time they needed any help, I was always there for the Young Lords. It was just the respect they gave us as human beings. They gave us a lot of respect.

It was a fabulous feeling for me to be myself—being part of the Young Lords as a drag queen—and my organization [STAR] being part of the Young Lords.

I met [Black Panther Party leader] Huey Newton at the Peoples' Revolutionary Convention in Philadelphia in 1971. Huey decided we were part of the revolution—that we were revolutionary people.

I was a radical, a revolutionist. I am still a revolutionist. I was proud to make the road and help change laws and what-not. I was very proud of doing that and proud of what I'm still doing, no matter what it takes.

Today, we have to fight back against the government. We have to fight them back. They're cutting back Medicaid, cutting back on medicine for people with AIDS. They want to take away from women on welfare and put them into that little work program. They're going to cut SSI.

Now they're taking away food stamps. These people who want the cuts—these people are making millions and millions and millions of dollars as CEOs.

Why is the government going to take it away from us? What they're doing is cutting us back. Why can't we have a break?

I'm glad I was in the Stonewall riot. I remember when someone threw a Molotov cocktail, I thought: "My god, the revolution is here. The revolution is finally here!"

I always believed that we would have a fight back. I just knew that we would fight back. I just didn't know it would be that night.

I am proud of myself as being there that night. If I had lost that moment, I would have been kind of hurt because that's when I saw the world change for me and my people.

Of course, we still got a long way ahead of us.

---

23. • *Pat Mainardi*

THE POLITICS OF HOUSEWORK (1970)

Pat Mainardi belonged to a radical feminist group called the Redstockings, which was formed in New York in 1969. One of the activist strategies of the group was consciousness-raising, a practice that used group discussion to make links between individual experiences and larger structures of exploitation and discrimination. Mainardi's article illustrates the feminist slogan "the personal is political" by demonstrating how housework, something that seemed trivial and apolitical, was really connected to the undervaluing of women's work and therefore to women's oppression more generally.

. . . Liberated women—very different from Women's Liberation! The first signals all kinds of goodies, to warm the hearts (not to mention other parts) of the most radical men. The other signals— HOUSEWORK. The first brings sex without marriage, sex before marriage, cozy housekeeping arrangements ("I'm living with this chick") and the self-content of knowing that you're not the kind of man who wants a doormat instead of a woman. That will come later. After all, who wants that old commodity anymore, the Standard American Housewife, all husband, home and kids. The New Commodity, the Liberated Woman, has sex a lot and has a Career, preferably something that can be fitted in with the household chores—like dancing, pottery, or painting.

On the other hand is Women's Liberation—and housework. What? You say this is all trivial? Wonderful! That's what I thought. It seemed perfectly reasonable. We both had careers, both had to work a couple of days a week to earn enough to live on, so why shouldn't we share the housework? So I suggested it to my mate and he agreed—most men are too hip to turn you down flat. You're right, he said. It's only fair.

Then an interesting thing happened. I can only explain it by stating that we women have been brainwashed more than even we can imagine. Probably too many years of seeing television women in ecstasy over their shiny waxed floors or breaking down over their dirty shirt collars. Men have no such conditioning. They recognize the essential fact of housework right from the very beginning. Which is that it stinks.

Here's my list of dirty chores: buying groceries, carting them home and putting them away; cooking meals and washing dishes and pots; doing the laundry; digging out the place when things get out of control; washing floors. The list could go on but the sheer necessities are bad enough. All of us live to do these things, or get someone else to do them for us. The longer my husband contemplated these chores, the more repulsed he became, and so proceeded the change from the normally sweet considerate Dr. Jekyll into the crafty Mr. Hyde who would stop at nothing to avoid the horrors of housework. As he felt himself backed into a corner laden with dirty dishes, brooms, mops and reeking garbage, his front teeth grew longer and pointier, his fingernails haggled and his eyes grew wild. Housework trivial? Not on your life! Just try to share the burden.

So ensued a dialogue that's been going on for several years. Here are some of the high points:

- "I don't mind sharing the housework, but I don't do it very well. We should each do the things we're best at." MEANING: Unfortunately I'm no good at things like washing dishes or cooking. What I do best is a little light carpentry, changing light bulbs, moving furniture (how often do *you* move furniture?) ALSO MEANING: Historically the lower classes (black men and us) have had hundreds of years experience doing menial jobs. It would be a waste of manpower to train someone else to do them now. ALSO MEANING: I don't like the dull stupid boring jobs, so you should do them.

- "I don't mind sharing the work, but you'll have to show me how to do it." MEANING: I ask a lot of questions and you'll have to show me everything every time I do it because I don't remember so good. Also don't try to sit down and read while I'M doing my jobs because I'm going to annoy hell out of you until it's easier to do them yourself.

- "We used to be so happy!" (Said whenever it was his turn to do something.) MEANING: I used to be so happy. MEANING: Life without housework is bliss. No quarrel here. Perfect Agreement.

- "We have different standards, and why should I have to work to your standards? That's unfair." MEANING: If I begin to get bugged by the dirt and crap I will say, "This place sure is a sty" or "How can anyone live like this?" and wait for your reaction. I know that all women have a sore called "Guilt over a messy house" or "Household work is ultimately my responsibility." I know that men have caused that sore—if anyone visits and the place *is* a sty, they're not going to leave and say, "He sure is a lousy housekeeper." You'll take the rap in any case. I can outwait you. ALSO MEANING: I can provoke innumerable scenes over the housework issue. Eventually doing all the housework yourself will be less painful to you than trying to get me to do half. Or I'll suggest we get a maid. She will do my share of the work. You will do yours. It's women's work.

- "I've got nothing against sharing the housework, but you can't make me do it on your schedule." MEANING: Passive resistance. I'll do it when I damned well please, if at all. If my job is doing dishes, it's easier to do them once a week. If taking out laundry, once a month. If washing the floors, once a year. If you don't like it, do it yourself oftener, and then I won't do it at all.

- "I hate it more than you. You don't mind it so much." MEANING: Housework is garbage work. It's the worst crap I've ever done. It's degrading and humiliating for someone of *my* intelligence to do it. But for someone of *your* intelligence. . . .
- "Housework is too trivial to even talk about." MEANING: It's even more trivial to do. Housework is beneath my status. My purpose in life is to deal with matters of significance. Yours is to deal with matters of insignificance. You should do the housework.
- "This problem of housework is not a man–woman problem. In any relationship between two people one is going to have a stronger personality and dominate. MEANING: That stronger personality had better be *me*.
- "In animal societies, wolves, for example, the top animal is usually a male even where he is not chosen for brute strength but on the basis of cunning and intelligence. Isn't that interesting?" MEANING: I have historical, psychological, anthropological and biological justification for keeping you down. How can you ask the top wolf to be equal?
- "Women's Liberation isn't really a political movement." MEANING: The Revolution is coming too close to home. ALSO MEANING: I am only interested in how I am oppressed, not how I oppress others. Therefore the war, the draft and the university are political. Women's Liberation is not.
- "Man's accomplishments have always depended on getting help from other people, mostly women. What great man would have accomplished what he did if he had to do his own housework?" MEANING: Oppression is built into the system and I, as the white American male, receive the benefits of this system. I don't want to give them up.

* * *

Participatory democracy begins at home. If you are planning to implement your politics, there are certain things to remember:

1. He *is* feeling it more than you. He's losing some leisure and you're gaining it. The measure of your oppression is his resistance.

2. A great many American men are not accustomed to doing monotonous repetitive work which never issues in any lasting, let alone important, achievement. This is why they would rather repair a cabinet than wash dishes. If human endeavors are like a pyramid with man's highest achievements at the top, then keeping oneself alive is at the bottom. Men have always had servants (us) to take care of this bottom strata of life while they have confined their efforts to the rarefied upper regions. It is thus ironic when they ask of women—where are your great painters, statesmen, etc.? Mme Matisse ran a millinery shop so he could paint. Mrs. Martin Luther King kept his house and raised his babies.

3. It is a traumatizing experience for someone who has always thought of himself as being against any oppression or exploitation of one human being by another to realize that in his daily life he has been accepting and implementing (and benefiting from) this exploitation; that his rationalization is little different from that of the racist who says "Black people don't feel pain" (women don't mind doing the shitwork); and that the oldest form of oppression in history has been the oppression of 50% of the population by the other 50%.

4. Arm yourself with some knowledge of the psychology of oppressed peoples everywhere, and a few facts about the animal kingdom. I admit playing top wolf or who runs the gorillas is silly but as a last resort men bring it up all the time. Talk about bees. If you feel really hostile bring up the sex life of spiders. They have sex. She bites off his head.

The psychology of oppressed peoples is not silly. Jews, immigrants, black men and all women have employed the same psychological mechanisms to survive: admiring the oppressor, glorifying the oppressor, wanting to be like the oppressor, wanting the oppressor to like them, mostly because the oppressor held all the power.

5. In a sense, all men everywhere are slightly schizoid—divorced from the reality of maintaining life. This makes it easier for them to play games with it. It is almost a cliché that women feel greater grief at sending a son off to a war or losing him to that war because they bore him, suckled him, and raised him. The men who foment those wars did none of those things and have a more superficial estimate of the worth of human life. One hour a day is a low estimate of the amount of time one has to spend "keeping" oneself. By foisting this off on others, man has seven hours a week—one working day more to play with his mind and not his human needs. Over the course of generations it is easy to see whence evolved the horrifying abstractions of modern life.

6. With the death of each form of oppression, life changes and new forms evolve. English aristocrats at the turn of the century were horrified at the idea of enfranchising working men—were sure that it signaled the death of civilization and a return to barbarism. Some workingmen were even deceived by this line. Similarly with the minimum wage, abolition of slavery, and female suffrage. Life changes but it goes on. Don't fall for any line about the death of everything if men take a turn at the dishes. They will imply that you are holding back the Revolution (their Revolution). But you are advancing it (your Revolution).

7. Keep checking up. Periodically consider who's actually *doing* the jobs. These things have a way of backsliding so that a year later once again the woman is doing everything. After a year make a list of jobs the man has rarely if ever done. You will find cleaning pots, toilets, refrigerators and ovens high on the list. Use time sheets if necessary. He will accuse you of being petty. He is above that sort of thing (housework). Bear in mind what the worst jobs are, namely the ones that have to be done every day or several times a day. Also the ones that are dirty—it's more pleasant to pick up books, newspapers, etc., than to wash dishes. Alternate the bad jobs. It's the daily grind that gets you down. Also make sure that you don't have the responsibility for the housework with occasional help from him. "I'll cook dinner for you tonight" implies it's really your job and isn't he a nice guy to do some of it for you.

8. Most men had a rich and rewarding bachelor life during which they did not starve or become encrusted with crud or buried under the litter. There is a taboo that says women mustn't strain themselves in the presence of men—we haul around 50 lbs of groceries if we have to but aren't allowed to open a jar if there is someone around to do it for us. The reverse side of the coin is that men aren't supposed to be able to take care of themselves without a woman. Both are excuses for making women do the housework.

9. Beware of the double whammy. He won't do the little things he always did because you're now a "Liberated Woman," right? Of course he won't do anything else either. . . .

I was just finishing this when my husband came in and asked what I was doing. Writing a paper on housework. Housework? he said. *Housework?* Oh my god how trivial can you get. A paper on housework.

THE MYTH OF THE VAGINAL ORGASM (1970)

Anne Koedt was a founding member of the New York Radical Feminists. "The Myth of the Vaginal Orgasm" was first published in the feminist journal, *Notes from the Second Year* and quickly became a seminal text in feminist scholarship by arguing that contemporary understandings of female pleasure were inaccurate because they were produced in a male-dominated society. Koedt argues that women achieve orgasms through their clitoris and that the focus on vaginal orgasms is a mischaracterization of female pleasure that has caused many women to be sexually deprived while blaming themselves.

Whenever female orgasm and frigidity is discussed, a false distinction is made between the vaginal and the clitoral orgasm. Frigidity has generally been defined by men as the failure of women to have vaginal orgasms. Actually the vagina is not a highly sensitive area and is not constructed to achieve orgasm. It is the clitoris which is the center of sexual sensitivity and which is the female equivalent of the penis.

I think this explains a great many things: First of all, the fact that the so-called frigidity rate among women is phenomenally high. Rather than tracing female frigidity to the false assumptions about female anatomy, our "experts" have declared frigidity a psychological problem of women. Those women who complained about it were recommended psychiatrists, so that they might discover their "problem"—diagnosed generally as a failure to adjust to their role as women.

The facts of female anatomy and sexual response tell a different story. There is only one area for sexual climax, although there are many areas for sexual arousal; that area is the clitoris. All orgasms are extensions of sensation from this area. Since the clitoris is not necessarily stimulated sufficiently in the conventional sexual positions, we are left "frigid."

Aside from physical stimulation, which is the common cause of orgasm for most people, there is also stimulation through primarily mental processes. Some women, for example, may achieve orgasm through sexual fantasies, or through fetishes. However, while the stimulation may be psychological, the orgasm manifests itself physically. Thus, while the cause is psychological, the *effect* is still physical, and the orgasm necessarily takes place in the sexual organ equipped for sexual climax—the clitoris. The orgasm experience may also differ in degree of intensity—some more localized, and some more diffuse and sensitive. But they are all clitoral orgasms.

All this leads to some interesting questions about conventional sex and our role in it. Men have orgasms essentially by friction with the vagina, not the clitoral area, which is external and not able to cause friction the way penetration does. Women have thus been defined sexually in terms of what pleases men; our own biology has not been properly analyzed. Instead, we are fed the myth of the liberated woman and her vaginal orgasm—an orgasm which in fact does not exist.

What we must do is redefine our sexuality. We must discard the "normal" concepts of sex and create new guidelines which take into account mutual sexual enjoyment. While the idea of mutual enjoyment is liberally applauded in marriage manuals, it is not followed to its logical conclusion. We must begin to demand that if certain sexual positions now defined as "standard" are not mutually conducive to orgasm, they no longer be defined as standard. New techniques must be used or devised which transform this particular aspect of our current sexual exploitation.

FREUD—A FATHER OF THE VAGINAL ORGASM

Freud contended that the clitoral orgasm was adolescent, and that upon puberty, when women began having intercourse with men, women should transfer the center of orgasm to the vagina. The vagina, it was assumed, was able to produce a parallel, but more mature, orgasm than the clitoris. Much work was done to elaborate on this theory, but little was done to challenge the basic assumptions.

To fully appreciate this incredible invention, perhaps Freud's general attitude about women should first be recalled. Mary Ellman, in *Thinking About Women,* summed it up this way:

> Everything in Freud's patronizing and fearful attitude toward women follows from their lack of a penis, but it is only in his essay *The Psychology of Women* that Freud makes explicit . . . the deprecations of women which are implicit in his work. He then prescribes for them the abandonment of the life of the mind, which will interfere with their sexual function. When the psychoanalyzed patient is male, the analyst sets himself the task of developing the man's capacities; but with women patients, the job is to resign them to the limits of their sexuality. As Mr. Rieff puts it: For Freud, "Analysis cannot encourage in women new energies for success and achievement, but only teach them the lesson of rational resignation."

It was Freud's feelings about women's secondary and inferior relationship to men that formed the basis for his theories on female sexuality.

Once having laid down the law about the nature of our sexuality, Freud not so strangely discovered a tremendous problem of frigidity in women. His recommended cure for a woman who was frigid was psychiatric care. She was suffering from failure to mentally adjust to her "natural" role as a woman. Frank S. Caprio, a contemporary follower of these ideas, states:

> . . . whenever a woman is incapable of achieving an orgasm via coitus, provided her husband is an adequate partner, and prefers clitoral stimulation to any other form of sexual activity, she can be regarded as suffering from frigidity and requires psychiatric assistance. (*The Sexually Adequate Female,* p. 64.)

The explanation given was that women were envious of men—"renunciation of womanhood." Thus it was diagnosed as an anti-male phenomenon.

It is important to emphasize that Freud did not base his theory upon a study of woman's anatomy, but rather upon his assumptions of woman as an inferior appendage to man, and her consequent social and psychological role. In their attempts to deal with the ensuing problem of mass frigidity, Freudians created elaborate mental gymnastics. Marie Bonaparte, in *Female Sexuality*, goes so far as to suggest surgery to help women back on their rightful path. Having discovered a strange connection between the non-frigid woman and the location of the clitoris near the vagina,

> it then occurred to me that where, in certain women, this gap was excessive, and clitoridal fixation obdurate, a clitoridal-vaginal reconciliation might be effected by surgical means, which would then benefit the normal erotic function. Professor Halban, of Vienna, as much a biologist as surgeon, became interested in the problem and worked out a simple operative technique. In this, the suspensory ligament of the clitoris was severed and the clitoris secured to the underlying structures, thus fixing it in a lower position, with eventual reduction of the labia minora. (p. 148.)

But the severest damage was not in the area of surgery, where Freudians ran around absurdly trying to change female anatomy to fit their basic assumptions.

The worst damage was done to the mental health of women, who either suffered silently with self-blame, or flocked to the psychiatrists looking desperately for the hidden and terrible repression that kept from them their vaginal destiny.

LACK OF EVIDENCE?

One may perhaps at first claim that these are unknown and unexplored areas, but upon closer examination this is certainly not true today, nor was it true even in the past. For example, men have known that women suffered from frigidity often during intercourse. So the problem was there. Also, there is much specific evidence. Men knew that the clitoris was and is the essential organ for masturbation, whether in children or adult women. So obviously women made it clear where they thought their sexuality was located. Men also seem suspiciously aware of the clitoral powers during "foreplay," when they want to arouse women and produce the necessary lubrication for penetration. Foreplay is a concept created for male purposes, but works to the disadvantage of many women, since as soon as the woman is aroused the man changes to vaginal stimulation, leaving her both aroused and unsatisfied.

It has also been known that women need no anesthesia inside the vagina during surgery, thus pointing to the fact that the vagina is in fact not a highly sensitive area.

Today, with extensive knowledge of anatomy, with Kinsey, and Masters and Johnson, to mention just a few sources, there is no ignorance on the subject. There are, however, social reasons why this knowledge has not been popularized. We are living in a male society which has not sought change in women's role.

ANATOMICAL EVIDENCE

Rather than starting with what women *ought* to feel, it would seem logical to start out with the anatomical facts regarding the clitoris and vagina.

The Clitoris is a small equivalent of the penis, except for the fact that the urethra does not go through it as in the man's penis. Its erection is similar to the male erection, and the head of the clitoris has the same type of structure and function as the head of the penis. G. Lombard Kelly, in *Sexual Feeling in Married Men and Women,* says:

> The head of the clitoris is also composed of erectile tissue, and it possesses a very sensitive epithelium or surface covering, supplied with special nerve endings called genital corpuscles, which are peculiarly adapted for sensory stimulation that under proper mental conditions terminates in the sexual orgasm. No other part of the female generative tract has such corpuscles. (Pocketbooks; p. 35.)

The clitoris has no other function than that of sexual pleasure.

The Vagina—Its functions are related to the reproductive function. Principally, 1) menstruation, 2) receive penis, 3) hold semen, and 4) birth passage. The interior of the vagina, which according to the defenders of the vaginally caused orgasm is the center and producer of the orgasm, is:

> like nearly all other internal body structures, poorly supplied with end organs of touch. The internal entodermal origin of the lining of the vagina makes it similar in this respect to the rectum and other parts of the digestive tract. (Kinsey, *Sexual Behavior in the Human Female,* p. 580.)

The degree of insensitivity inside the vagina is so high that "Among the women who were tested in our gynecologic sample, less than 14% were at all conscious that they had been touched." (Kinsey, p. 580.)

Even the importance of the vagina as an *erotic* center (as opposed to an orgasmic center) has been found to be minor.

Other Areas—Labia minora and the vestibule of the vagina. These two sensitive areas may trigger off a clitoral orgasm. Because they can be effectively stimulated during "normal" coitus, though infrequent, this kind of stimulation is incorrectly thought to be vaginal orgasm. However, it is important to distinguish between areas which can stimulate the clitoris, incapable of producing the orgasm themselves, and the clitoris:

> Regardless of what means of excitation is used to bring the individual to the state of sexual climax, the sensation is perceived by the genital corpuscles and is localized where they are situated: in the head of the clitoris or penis. (Kelly, p. 49.)

Psychologically Stimulated Orgasm—Aside from the above mentioned direct and indirect stimulations of the clitoris, there is a third way an orgasm may be triggered. This is through mental (cortical) stimulation, where the imagination stimulates the brain, which in turn stimulates the genital corpuscles of the glans to set off an orgasm.

WOMEN WHO SAY THEY HAVE VAGINAL ORGASMS

Confusion—Because of the lack of knowledge of their own anatomy, some women accept the idea that an orgasm felt during "normal" intercourse was vaginally caused. This confusion is caused by a combination of two factors. One, failing to locate the center of the orgasm, and two, by a desire to fit her experience to the male-defined idea of sexual normalcy. Considering that women know little about their anatomy, it is easy to be confused.

Deception—The vast majority of women who pretend vaginal orgasm to their men are faking it to, as Ti-Grace Atkinson says, "get the job." In a new bestselling Danish book, *I Accuse* (my own translation), Mette Ejlersen specifically deals with this common problem, which she calls the "sex comedy." This comedy has many causes. First of all, the man brings a great deal of pressure to bear on the woman, because he considers his ability as a lover at stake. So as not to offend his ego, the woman will comply with the prescribed role and go through simulated ecstasy. In some of the other Danish women mentioned, women

who were left frigid were turned off to sex, and pretended vaginal orgasm to hurry up the sex act. Others admitted that they had faked vaginal orgasm to catch a man. In one case, the woman pretended vaginal orgasm to get him to leave his first wife, who admitted being vaginally frigid. Later she was forced to continue the deception, since obviously she couldn't tell him to stimulate her clitorally.

Many more women were simply afraid to establish their right to equal enjoyment, seeing the sexual act as being primarily for the man's benefit, and any pleasure that the woman got as an added extra.

Other women, with just enough ego to reject the man's idea that they needed psychiatric care, refused to admit their frigidity. They wouldn't accept self-blame, but they didn't know how to solve the problem, not knowing the physiological facts about themselves. So they were left in a peculiar limbo.

Again, perhaps one of the most infuriating and damaging results of this whole charade has been that women who were perfectly healthy sexually were taught that they were not. So in addition to being sexually deprived, these women were told to blame themselves when they deserved no blame. Looking for a cure to a problem that has none can lead a woman on an endless path of self-hatred and insecurity. For she is told by her analyst that not even in her one role allowed in a male society—the role of a woman—is she successful. She is put on the defensive, with phony data as evidence that she better try to be even more feminine, think more feminine, and reject her envy of men. That is, shuffle even harder, baby.

WHY MEN MAINTAIN THE MYTH

1. *Sexual Penetration is Preferred*—The best stimulant for the penis is the woman's vagina. It supplies the necessary friction and lubrication. From a strictly technical point of view this position offers the best physical conditions, even though the man may try other positions for variation.

2. *The Invisible Woman*—One of the elements of male chauvinism is the refusal or inability to see women as total, separate human beings. Rather, men have chosen to define women only in terms of how they benefited men's lives. Sexually, a woman was not seen as an individual wanting to share equally in the sexual act, any more than she was seen as a person with independent desires when she did anything else in society. Thus, it was easy to make up what was convenient about women; for on top of that, society has been a function of male interests, and women were not organized to form even a vocal opposition to the male experts.

3. *The Penis as Epitome of Masculinity*—Men define their lives greatly in terms of masculinity. It is a *universal,* as opposed to racial, ego boosting, which is localized by the geography of racial mixtures.

   The essence of male chauvinism is not the practical, economic services women supply. It is the psychological superiority. This kind of negative definition of self, rather than positive definition based upon one's own achievements and development, has of course chained the victim and the oppressor both. But by far the most brutalized of the two is the victim.

   An analogy is racism, where the white racist compensates his feelings of unworthiness by creating an image of the black man (it is primarily a male struggle) as biologically inferior to him. Because of his power in a white male power structure, the white man can socially enforce this mythical division.

   To the extent that men try to rationalize and justify male superiority through physical differentiation, masculinity may be symbolized by being the *most* muscular, the most hairy, the deepest voice, and the biggest penis. Women, on the other hand, are approved of (i.e., called feminine) if they are weak, petite, shave their legs, have high soft voices, and no penis.

   Since the clitoris is almost identical to the penis, one finds a great deal of evidence of men

in various societies trying to either ignore the clitoris and emphasize the vagina (as did Freud), or, as in some places in the Mideast, actually performing clitoridectomy. Freud saw this ancient and still practiced custom as a way of further "feminizing" the female by removing this cardinal vestige of her masculinity. It should be noted also that a big clitoris is considered ugly and masculine. Some cultures engage in the practice of pouring a chemical on the clitoris to make it shrivel up into proper size.

   It seems clear to me that men in fact fear the clitoris as a threat to their masculinity.

4. *Sexually Expendable Male*—Men fear that they will become sexually expendable if the clitoris is substituted for the vagina as the center of pleasure for women. Actually this has a great deal of validity if one considers *only* the anatomy. The position of the penis inside the vagina, while perfect for reproduction, does not necessarily stimulate an orgasm in women because the clitoris is located externally and higher up. Women must rely upon indirect stimulation in the "normal" position.

   Lesbian sexuality could make an excellent case, based upon anatomical data, for the extinction of the male organ. Albert Ellis says something to the effect that a man without a penis can make a woman an excellent lover.

   Considering that the vagina is very desirable from a man's point of view, purely on physical grounds, one begins to see the dilemma for men. And it forces us as well to discard many "physical" arguments explaining why women go to bed with men. What is left, it seems to me, are primarily psychological reasons why women select men at the exclusion of women as sexual partners.

5. *Control of Women*—One reason given to explain the Mideastern practice of clitoridectomy is that it will keep the women from straying. By removing the sexual organ capable of orgasm, it must be assumed that her sexual drive will

diminish. Considering how men look upon their women as property, particularly in very backward nations, we should begin to consider a great deal more why it is not in the men's interest to have women totally free sexually. The double standard, as practiced for example in Latin America, is set up to keep the woman as total property of the husband, while he is free to have affairs as he wishes.

6. *Lesbianism and Bisexuality*—Aside from the strictly anatomical reasons why women might equally seek other women as lovers, there is a fear on men's part that women will seek the company of other women on a full, human basis. The establishment of clitoral orgasm as fact would threaten the heterosexual *institution*. For it would indicate that sexual pleasure was obtainable from either men *or* women, thus making heterosexuality not an absolute, but an option. It would thus open up the whole question of *human* sexual relationships beyond the confines of the present male-female role system.

BOOKS MENTIONED IN THIS ESSAY

Sexual Behavior in the Human Female, Alfred C. Kinsey, Pocketbooks

Female Sexuality, Marie Bonaparte, Grove Press

Sex Without Guilt, Albert Ellis, Grove Press

Sexual Feelings in Married Men and Women, G. Lombard Kelly, Pocketbooks

I Accuse (Jeg Anklager), Mette Ejlersen, Chr. Erichsens Forlag (Danish)

The Sexually Adequate Female, Frank S. Caprio, Fawcett Gold Medal Books

Thinking About Women, Mary Ellman; Harcourt, Brace & World

Human Sexual Response, Masters and Johnson; Little, Brown

Also see:

The ABZ of Love, Inge and Sten Hegeler, Alexicon Corp.

25. • *Radicalesbians*

THE WOMAN-IDENTIFIED WOMAN (1970)

"The Woman-Identified Woman" was distributed at the Second Congress to Unite Women on May 1, 1970, a conference sponsored by the National Organization for Women (NOW). The manifesto came about specifically as a response to the comment made by NOW president Betty Friedan that lesbians were a "lavender menace" that detracted from the credibility of the women's movement but also more generally to the feeling on the part of many lesbians that their issues weren't being taken seriously within feminist circles. To call attention to this silencing and to respond to Friedan's comments, a group of women wearing t-shirts that said "lavender menace," who came to be known as the Radicalesbians, took over the conference, voicing anger over their exclusion and challenging the idea that lesbianism was a threat to the women's movement. "The Woman-Identified Woman" articulates a lesbian-feminist politics that positioned lesbianism as a form of resistance to patriarchy.

What is a lesbian? A lesbian is the rage of all women condensed to the point of explosion. She is the woman who, often beginning at an extremely early age, acts in accordance with her inner compulsion to be a more complete and freer human being than her society—perhaps then, but certainly later—cares to allow her. These needs and actions, over a period of years, bring her into painful conflict with people, situations, the accepted ways of thinking, feeling and behaving, until she is in a state of continual war with everything around her, and usually with herself. She may not be fully conscious of the political implications of what for her began as personal necessity, but on some level she has not been able to accept the limitations and oppression laid on her by the most basic role of her society—the female role. The turmoil she experiences tends to induce guilt proportional to the degree to which she feels she is not meeting social expectations, and/or eventually drives her to question and analyze what the rest of her society more or less accepts. She is forced to evolve her own life pattern, often living much of her life alone, learning usually much earlier than her "straight" (heterosexual) sisters about the essential aloneness of life (which the myth of marriage obscures) and about the reality of illusions. To the extent that she cannot expel the heavy socialization that goes with being female, she can never truly find peace with herself. For she is caught somewhere between accepting society's view of her—in which case she cannot accept herself—and coming to understand what this sexist society has done to her and why it is functional and necessary for it to do so. Those of us who work that through find ourselves on the other side of a tortuous journey through a night that may have been decades long. The perspective gained from that journey, the liberation of self, the inner peace, the real love of self and of all women, is something to be shared with all women—because we are all women.

It should first be understood that lesbianism, like male homosexuality, is a category of behavior possible only in a sexist society characterized by rigid sex roles and dominated by male supremacy. Those sex roles dehumanize women by defining us as a supportive/serving caste in relation to the master caste of men, and emotionally cripple men by demanding that they be alienated from their own bodies and emotions in order to perform their economic/political/military functions effectively. Homosexuality is a by-product of a particular way of setting up roles (or approved patterns of behavior) on the basis of sex; as such it is an inauthentic (not consonant with "reality") category. In a society in which men do not oppress women, and sexual expression is allowed to follow feelings, the categories of homosexuality and heterosexuality would disappear.

But lesbianism is also different from male homosexuality, and serves a different function in the society. "Dyke" is a different kind of put-down from "faggot," although both imply you are not playing your socially assigned sex role—are not therefore a "real woman" or a "real man." The grudging admiration felt for the tomboy and the queasiness felt around a sissy boy point to the same thing: the contempt in which women—or those who play a female role—are held. And the investment in keeping women in that contemptuous role is very great. Lesbian is the word, the label, the condition that holds women in line. When a woman hears this word tossed her way, she knows she is stepping out of line. She knows that she has crossed the terrible boundary of her sex role. She recoils, she protests, she reshapes her actions to gain approval. Lesbian is a label invented by the man to throw at any woman who dares to be his equal, who dares to challenge his prerogatives (including that of all woman as part of the exchange medium among men), who dares to assert the primacy of her own needs. To have the label applied to people active in women's liberation is just the most recent instance of a long history; older women will recall that not so long ago, any woman who was successful, independent, not orienting her whole life about a man, would hear this word. For in this sexist society, for a woman to be independent means she can't be a woman—she must be a dyke. That in itself should tell us where women are at. It says as clearly as can be said: woman and person are contradictory terms. For a lesbian is not considered a "real woman." And yet, in popular thinking, there is really only one essential difference between a lesbian and other women: that of sexual orientation—which is to say, when you strip off all the packaging, you must finally realize that the essence of being a "woman" is to get fucked by men.

"Lesbian" is one of the sexual categories by which men have divided up humanity. While all women are dehumanized as sex objects, as the objects of men, they are given certain compensations: identification with his power, his ego, his status, his protection (from other males), feeling like a "real woman," finding social acceptance by adhering to her role, etc. Should a woman confront herself by confronting another woman, there are fewer rationalizations, fewer buffers by which to avoid the stark horror of her dehumanized condition. Herein we find the overriding fear of many women toward exploring intimate relationships with other women: the fear of her being used as a sexual object by a woman, which not only will bring no male-connected compensations, but also will reveal the void which is woman's real situation. This dehumanization is expressed when a straight woman learns that a sister is a lesbian; she begins to relate to her lesbian sister as her potential sex object, laying a surrogate male role on the lesbian. This reveals her heterosexual conditioning to make herself into an object when sex is potentially involved in a relationship, and it denies the lesbian her full humanity. For women, especially those in the movement, to perceive their lesbian sisters through this male grid of role definitions is to accept this male cultural conditioning and to oppress their sisters much as they themselves have been oppressed by men. Are we going to continue the male classification system of defining all females in sexual relation to some other category of people? Affixing the label lesbian not only to a woman who aspires to be a person, but also to any situation of real love, real solidarity, real primacy among women is a primary form of divisiveness among women: it is the condition which keeps women within the confines of the feminine role, and it is the debunking/scare term that keeps women from forming any primary attachments, groups, or associations among ourselves.

Women in the movement have in most cases gone to great lengths to avoid discussion and confrontation with the issue of lesbianism. It puts people up-tight. They are hostile, evasive, or try to incorporate it into some "broader issue." They would rather not talk about it. If they have to, they try to dismiss it as a "lavender herring." But it is no side issue. It is absolutely essential to the success and fulfillment of the women's liberation movement that this issue be dealt with. As long as the label 'dyke' can be used to frighten women into a less militant stand, keep her separate from her sisters, keep her from giving primacy to anything other than men and family—then to that extent she is controlled by the male culture. Until women see in each other the possibility of primal commitment which includes sexual love, they will be denying themselves the love and value they readily accord to men, thus affirming their second-class status. As long as male acceptability is primary—both to individual women and to the movement as a whole—the term lesbian will be used effectively against women. Insofar as women want only more privileges within the system, they do not want to antagonize male power. They instead seek acceptability for women's liberation, and the most crucial aspect of the acceptability is to deny lesbianism—i.e., deny any fundamental challenge to the basis of the female role.

It should also be said that some younger, more radical women have honestly begun to discuss lesbianism, but so far it has been primarily as a sexual "alternative" to men. This, however, is still giving primacy to men, both because the idea of relating more completely to women occurs as a negative reaction to men, and because the lesbian relationship is being characterized simply by sex, which is divisive and sexist. On one level, which is both personal and political, women may withdraw emotional and sexual energies from men, and work out various alternatives for those energies in their own lives. On a different political/psychological level, it must be understood that what is crucial is that women begin disengaging from male-defined response patterns. In the privacy of our own psyches, we must cut those cords to the core. For irrespective of where our love and sexual energies flow, if we are male-identified in our heads, we cannot realize our autonomy as human beings.

But why is it that women have related to and through men? By virtue of having been brought up in a male society, we have internalized the male culture's definition of ourselves. That definition views us as relative beings who exist not for ourselves, but for the servicing, maintenance and comfort of men. That definition consigns us to sexual and family functions, and excludes us from defining and shaping the terms of our lives. In exchange for our psychic servicing and for performing society's non-profit-making functions, the man confers on us just one thing: the slave status which makes us legitimate in the eyes of the society in which we live. This is called "femininity"or "being a real woman" in our cultural lingo. We are authentic, legitimate, real to the extent that we are the property of some man whose name we bear. To be a woman who belongs to no man is to be invisible, pathetic, unauthentic, unreal. He confirms his image of us—of what we have to be in order to be—as he defines it, in relation to him—but cannot confirm our personhood, our own selves as absolutes. As long as we are dependent on the male culture for this definition, for this approval, we cannot be free.

The consequence of internalizing this role is an enormous reservoir of self-hate. This is not to say the self-hate is recognized or accepted as such; indeed most women would deny it. It may be experienced as discomfort with her role, as feeling empty, as numbness, as restlessness, a paralyzing anxiety at the center. Alternatively, it may be expressed in shrill defensiveness of the glory and destiny of her role. But it does exist, often beneath the edge of her consciousness, poisoning her existence, keeping her alienated from herself, her own needs, and rendering her a stranger to other women. Women hate both themselves and other women. They try to escape by identifying with the oppressor, living through him, gaining status and identity from his ego, his power, his accomplishments. And by not identifying with other "empty vessels" like themselves, women resist relating on all levels to other women who will reflect their own oppression, their own secondary status, their own self-hate. For to confront another woman is finally to confront one's self—the self we have gone to such lengths to avoid.

And in that mirror we know we cannot really respect and love that which we have been made to be.

As the source of self-hate and the lack of real self are rooted in our male-given identity, we must create a new sense of self. As long as we cling to the idea of "being a woman," we will sense some conflict with that incipient self, that sense of I, that sense of a whole person. It is very difficult to realize and accept that being "feminine" and being a whole person are irreconcilable. Only women can give each other a new sense of self. That identity we have to develop with reference to ourselves, and not in relation to men. This consciousness is the revolutionary force from which all else will follow, for ours is an organic revolution. For this we must be available and supportive to one another, give our commitment and our love, give the emotional support necessary to sustain this movement. Our energies must flow toward our sisters not backwards towards our oppressors. As long as women's liberation tries to free women without facing the basic heterosexual structure that binds us in one-to-one relationship with a man, how to get better sex, how to turn his head around—into trying to make the "new man" out of him, in the delusion that this will allow us to be the "new woman." This obviously splits our energies and commitments, leaving us unable to be committed to the construction of the new patterns which will liberate us.

It is the primacy of women relating to women, of women creating a new consciousness of and with each other which is at the heart of women's liberation, and the basis for the cultural revolution. Together we must find, reinforce and validate our authentic selves. As we do this, we confirm in each other that struggling incipient sense of pride and strength, the divisive barriers begin to melt, we feel this growing solidarity with our sisters. We see ourselves as prime, find our centers inside of ourselves. We find receding the sense of alienation, of being cut off, of being behind a locked window, of being unable to get out what we know is inside. We feel a realness, feel at last we are coinciding with ourselves. With that real self, with that consciousness, we begin a revolution to end the imposition of all coercive identifications, and to achieve maximum autonomy in human expression.

26. • *Chicago Gay Liberation Front*

A LEAFLET FOR THE AMERICAN MEDICAL ASSOCIATION (1970)

After the 1969 Stonewall Riots, queer activist groups formed under the name the Gay Liberation Front (GLF). Emboldened with a new revolutionary fervor, these activists challenged the prevailing social norms around homosexuality including the belief that homosexuals were "sick." Up until the mid-twentieth century, the consensus within the medical and psychiatric communities was that homosexuality was an illness that should be treated. However, influenced by Alfred Kinsey and other pioneering researchers in the 1950s and 1960s, an increasing number of doctors began to question this view. Gay activists like those in the GLF argued that the pathologization of homosexuality encouraged antigay attitudes and that to the extent that homosexuals experienced psychological problems, the cause was the discrimination they faced, not something intrinsic to their sexual orientation. Activists in the Chicago GLF distributed "A Leaflet for the American Medical Association" to doctors attending the 1970 convention of the American Medical Association. Three years later the American Psychiatric Association removed homosexuality from its list of psychiatric disorders.

The establishment school of psychiatry is based on the premise that people who are hurting should solve their problems by "adjusting" to the situation. For the homosexual, this means becoming adept at straight-fronting, learning how to survive in a hostile world, how to settle for housing in the gay ghetto, how to be satisfied with a profession in which homosexuals are tolerated, and how to live with low self-esteem.

The adjustment school places the burden on each individual homosexual to learn to bear his torment. But the "problem" of homosexuality is never solved under this scheme; the anti-homosexualist attitude of society, which is the cause of the homosexual's trouble, goes unchallenged. And there's always another paying patient on the psychiatrist's couch. Dr. Socarides claims, "A human being is sick when he fails to function in his appropriate gender identity, which is appropriate to his anatomy." Who determined "appropriateness"? The psychiatrist as moralist? Certainly there is no scientific basis for defining "appropriate" sexual behavior. In a study of homosexuality in other species and other cultures, Ford and Beach in *Patterns of Sexual Behavior* conclude, "Human homosexuality is not a product of hormonal imbalance or 'perverted heredity.' It is the product of the fundamental mammalian heritage of general sexual responsiveness as modified under the impact of experience."

Other than invoking moral standards, Dr. Socarides claims that homosexuality is an emotional illness because of the guilt and anxieties in homosexual life. Would he also consider Judaism an emotional illness because of the paranoia which Jews experienced in Nazi Germany?

We homosexuals of gay liberation believe that the adjustment school of therapy is not a valid approach to society.

We refuse to adjust to our oppression, and believe that the key to our mental health, and to the mental health of all oppressed peoples in a racist, sexist, capitalist society, is a radical change in the structure and accompanying attitudes of the entire social system.

Mental health for women does not mean therapy for women—it means the elimination of male supremacy. Not therapy for blacks, but an end to racism. The poor don't need psychiatrists (what a joke at 25 bucks a throw!)—they need democratic distribution of wealth. OFF THE COUCHES, INTO THE STREETS!

We see political organizing and collective action as the strategy for effecting this social change. We declare that we are healthy homosexuals in a sexist society, and that homosexuality is at least on a par with heterosexuality as a way for people to relate to each other (know any men that don't dominate women?).

Since the prevalent notion in society is that homosexuality is wrong, all those who recognize that this attitude is damaging to people, and that it must be corrected, have to raise their voices in opposition to anti-homosexualism. Not to do so is to permit the myth of homosexual pathology to continue and to comply in the homosexual's continued suffering from senseless stigmatization.

A psychiatrist who allows a homosexual patient—who has been subject to a barrage of anti-homosexual sentiments his whole life—to continue in the belief that heterosexuality is superior to homosexuality, is the greatest obstacle to his patient's health and well-being.

We furthermore urge psychiatrists to refer their homosexual patients to gay liberation (and other patients who are victims of oppression to relevant liberation movements). Once relieved of patients whose guilt is not deserved but imposed, psychiatrists will be able to devote all their effort to the rich—who do earn their guilt but not their wealth, and can best afford to pay psychiatrists' fees.

We are convinced that a picket and a dance will do more for the vast majority of homosexuals than two years on the couch. We call on the medical profession to repudiate the adjustment approach as a solution to homosexual oppression and instead to further homosexual liberation by working in a variety of political ways (re-educating the public, supporting pickets, attending rallies, promoting social events, etc.) to change the situation of homosexuals in this society.

Join us in the struggle for a world in which all human beings are free to love without fear or shame.

---

27. • *The Combahee River Collective*

A BLACK FEMINIST STATEMENT (1977)

The Combahee River Collective (CRC) was an activist group who wanted to draw attention to the intersecting oppressions of race, class, gender, and sexual orientation. After attending a meeting of the National Black Feminist Organization in 1973, members of the Collective saw the need for a new organization, one with a more radical vision and that would better address issues that were important to black lesbians.

They named their new group the Combahee River Collective to honor Harriet Tubman, who led the 1863 Union raid that freed 750 slaves along the Combahee River in South Carolina during the American Civil War. In the mid-1970s, the Collective used meetings and retreats to articulate a politics of black feminism out of which emerged "A Black Feminist Statement." This document is regarded as a seminal text in the critique of white feminists' gender-only focus and helped trigger an increased emphasis on intersectionality within the field of women's, gender and sexuality studies.

We are a collective of Black feminists who have been meeting together since 1974. During that time we have been involved in the process of defining and clarifying our politics, while at the same time doing political work within our own group and in coalition with other progressive organizations and movements. The most general statement of our politics at the present time would be that we are actively committed to struggling against racial, sexual, heterosexual, and class oppression, and see as our particular task the development of integrated analysis and practice based upon the fact that the major systems of oppression are interlocking. The synthesis of these oppressions creates the conditions of our lives. As Black women we see Black feminism as the logical political movement to combat the manifold and simultaneous oppressions that all women of color face.

We will discuss four major topics in the paper that follows: (1) the genesis of contemporary Black feminism; (2) what we believe, i.e., the specific province of our politics; (3) the problems in organizing Black feminists, including a brief herstory of our collective; and (4) Black feminist issues and practice.

1. THE GENESIS OF CONTEMPORARY BLACK FEMINISM

Before looking at the recent development of Black feminism we would like to affirm that we find our origins in the historical reality of Afro-American women's continuous life-and-death struggle for survival and liberation. Black women's extremely negative relationship to the American political system (a system of white male rule) has always been determined by our membership in two oppressed racial and sexual castes. As Angela Davis points out in "Reflections on the Black Woman's Role in the Community of Slaves," Black women have always embodied, if only in their physical manifestation, an adversary stance to white male rule and have actively resisted its inroads upon them and their communities in both dramatic and subtle ways. There have always been Black women activists—some known, like Sojourner Truth, Harriet Tubman, Frances E. W. Harper, Ida B. Wells Barnett, and Mary Church Terrell, and thousands upon thousands unknown—who had a shared awareness of how their sexual identity combined with their racial identity to make their whole life situation and the focus of their political struggles unique. Contemporary Black feminism is the outgrowth of countless generations of personal sacrifice, militancy, and work by our mothers and sisters.

A Black feminist presence has evolved most obviously in connection with the second wave of the American women's movement beginning in the late 1960s. Black, other Third World, and working women have been involved in the feminist movement from its start, but both outside reactionary forces and racism and elitism within the movement itself have served to obscure our participation. In 1973, Black feminists, primarily located in New York, felt the necessity of forming a separate Black feminist group. This became the National Black Feminist Organization (NBFO).

Black feminist politics also have an obvious connection to movements for Black liberation, particularly those of the 1960s and 1970s. Many of us were active in those movements (Civil Rights, Black nationalism, the Black Panthers), and all of our lives were greatly affected and changed by their ideologies, their goals, and the tactics used to achieve their goals. It was our experience and disillusionment within these liberation movements, as well as experience on the periphery of the white male left, that led to the need to develop a politics that was antiracist, unlike those of white women, and antisexist, unlike those of Black and white men.

There is also undeniably a personal genesis for Black Feminism, that is, the political realization that comes from the seemingly personal experiences of individual Black women's lives. Black feminists and many more Black women who do not define themselves as feminists have all experienced sexual oppression as a constant factor in our day-to-day existence. As children we realized that we were different from boys and that we were treated differently. For example, we were told in the same breath to be quiet both for the sake of being "ladylike" and to make us less objectionable in the eyes of white people. As we grew older we became aware of the threat of physical and sexual abuse by men. However, we had no way of conceptualizing what was so apparent to us, what we *knew* was really happening.

Black feminists often talk about their feelings of craziness before becoming conscious of the concepts of sexual politics, patriarchal rule, and most importantly, feminism, the political analysis and practice that we women use to struggle against our oppression. The fact that racial politics and indeed racism are pervasive factors in our lives did not allow us, and still does not allow most Black women, to look more deeply into our own experiences and, from that sharing and growing consciousness, to build a politics that will change our lives and inevitably end our oppression. Our development must also be tied to the contemporary economic and political position of Black people. The post-World War II generation of Black youth was the first to be able to minimally partake of certain educational and employment options, previously closed completely to Black people. Although our economic position is still at the very bottom of the American capitalistic economy, a handful of us have been able to gain certain tools as a result of tokenism in education and employment which potentially enable us to more effectively fight our oppression.

A combined antiracist and antisexist position drew us together initially, and as we developed politically we addressed ourselves to heterosexism and economic oppression under capitalism.

2. WHAT WE BELIEVE

Above all else, our politics initially sprang from the shared belief that Black women are inherently valuable, that our liberation is a necessity not as an adjunct to somebody else's but because of our need as human persons for autonomy. This may seem so obvious as to sound simplistic, but it is apparent that no other ostensibly progressive movement has ever considered our specific oppression as a priority or worked seriously for the ending of that oppression. Merely naming the pejorative stereotypes attributed to Black women (e.g. mammy, matriarch, Sapphire, whore, bulldagger), let alone cataloguing the cruel, often murderous, treatment we receive, indicates how little value has been placed upon our lives during four centuries of bondage in the Western hemisphere. We realize that the only people who care enough about us to work consistently for our liberation are us. Our politics evolve from a healthy love for ourselves, our sisters and our community which allows us to continue our struggle and work.

This focusing upon our own oppression is embodied in the concept of identity politics. We believe that the most profound and potentially most radical politics come directly out of our own identity, as opposed to working to end somebody else's oppression. In the case of Black women this is a particularly repugnant, dangerous, threatening, and therefore revolutionary concept because it is obvious from looking at all the political movements that have preceded us that anyone is more worthy of liberation than ourselves. We reject pedestals, queenhood, and walking ten paces behind. To be recognized as human, levelly human, is enough.

We believe that sexual politics under patriarchy is as pervasive in Black women's lives as are the politics of class and race. We also often find it difficult to separate race from class from sex oppression because in our lives they are most often experienced simultaneously. We know that there is such a thing as racial-sexual oppression which is neither solely racial nor solely sexual, e.g., the history of rape of Black women by white men as a weapon of political repression.

Although we are feminists and lesbians, we feel solidarity with progressive Black men and do not advocate the fractionalization that white women who are separatists demand. Our situation as Black people necessitates that we have solidarity around the fact of race, which white women of course do not need to have with white men, unless it is their negative solidarity as racial oppressors. We struggle together with Black men against racism, while we also struggle with Black men about sexism.

We realize that the liberation of all oppressed peoples necessitates the destruction of the political-economic systems of capitalism and imperialism as well as patriarchy. We are socialists because we believe that work must be organized for the collective benefit of those who do the work and create the products, and not for the profit of the bosses. Material resources must be equally distributed among those who create these resources. We are not convinced, however, that a socialist revolution that is not also a feminist and antiracist revolution will guarantee our liberation. We have arrived at the necessity for developing an understanding of class relationships that takes into account the specific class position of Black women who are generally marginal in the labor force, while at this particular

time some of us are temporarily viewed as doubly desirable tokens at white-collar and professional levels. We need to articulate the real class situation of persons who are not merely raceless, sexless workers, but for whom racial and sexual oppression are significant determinants in their working/economic lives. Although we are in essential agreement with Marx's theory as it applied to the very specific economic relationships he analyzed, we know that his analysis must be extended further in order for us to understand our specific economic situation as Black women.

A political contribution which we feel we have already made is the expansion of the feminist principle that the personal is political. In our consciousness-raising sessions, for example, we have in many ways gone beyond white women's revelations because we are dealing with the implications of race and class as well as sex. Even our Black women's style of talking/testifying in Black language about what we have experienced has a resonance that is both cultural and political. We have spent a great deal of energy delving into the cultural and experiential nature of our oppression out of necessity because none of these matters has ever been looked at before. No one before has ever examined the multilayered texture of Black women's lives. An example of this kind of revelation/conceptualization occurred at a meeting as we discussed the ways in which our early intellectual interests had been attacked by our peers, particularly Black males. We discovered that all of us, because we were "smart" had also been considered "ugly," i.e., "smart-ugly." "Smart-ugly" crystallized the way in which most of us had been forced to develop our intellects at great cost to our "social" lives. The sanctions in the Black and white communities against Black women thinkers is comparatively much higher than for white women, particularly ones from the educated middle and upper classes.

As we have already stated, we reject the stance of lesbian separatism because it is not a viable political analysis or strategy for us. It leaves out far too much and far too many people, particularly Black men, women, and children. We have a great deal of criticism and loathing for what men have been socialized to be in this society: what they support, how they act, and how they oppress. But we do not have the misguided notion that it is their maleness, per se—i.e., their biological maleness—that makes them what they are. As Black women we find any type of biological determinism a particularly dangerous and reactionary basis upon which to build a politic. We must also question whether lesbian separatism is an adequate and progressive political analysis and strategy, even for those who practice it, since it so completely denies any but the sexual sources of women's oppression, negating the facts of class and race.

3. PROBLEMS IN ORGANIZING BLACK FEMINISTS

During our years together as a Black feminist collective we have experienced success and defeat, joy and pain, victory and failure. We have found that it is very difficult to organize around Black feminist issues, difficult even to announce in certain contexts that we *are* Black feminists. We have tried to think about the reasons for our difficulties, particularly since the white women's movement continues to be strong and to grow in many directions. In this section we will discuss some of the general reasons for the organizing problems we face and also talk specifically about the stages in organizing our own collective.

The major source of difficulty in our political work is that we are not just trying to fight oppression on one front or even two, but instead to address a whole range of oppressions. We do not have racial, sexual, heterosexual, or class privilege to rely upon, nor do we have even the minimal access to resources and power that groups who possess any one of these types of privilege have.

The psychological toll of being a Black woman and the difficulties this presents in reaching political consciousness and doing political work can never

be underestimated. There is a very low value placed upon Black women's psyches in this society, which is both racist and sexist. As an early group member once said, "We are all damaged people merely by virtue of being Black women." We are dispossessed psychologically and on every other level, and yet we feel the necessity to struggle to change the condition of all Black women. In "A Black Feminist's Search for Sisterhood," Michele Wallace arrives at this conclusion:

> We exists as women who are Black who are feminists, each stranded for the moment, working independently because there is not yet an environment in this society remotely congenial to our struggle—because, being on the bottom, we would have to do what no one else has done: we would have to fight the world.[1]

Wallace is pessimistic but realistic in her assessment of Black feminists' position, particularly in her allusion to the nearly classic isolation most of us face. We might use our position at the bottom, however, to make a clear leap into revolutionary action. If Black women were free, it would mean that everyone else would have to be free since our freedom would necessitate the destruction of all the systems of oppression.

Feminism is, nevertheless, very threatening to the majority of Black people because it calls into question some of the most basic assumptions about our existence, i.e., that sex should be a determinant of power relationships. Here is the way male and female roles were defined in a Black nationalist pamphlet from the early 1970s:

> We understand that it is and has been traditional that the man is the head of the house. He is the leader of the house/nation because his knowledge of the world is broader, his awareness is greater, his understanding is fuller and his application of this information is wiser . . . After all, it is only reasonable that the man be the head of the house because he is able to defend and protect the development of his home . . . Women cannot do the same things as men—they are made by nature to function differently. Equality of men and

women is something that cannot happen even in the abstract world. Men are not equal to other men, i.e. ability, experience or even understanding. The value of men and women can be seen as in the value of gold and silver—they are not equal but both have great value. We must realize that men and women are a complement to each other because there is no house/family without a man and his wife. Both are essential to the development of any life.[2]

The material conditions of most Black women would hardly lead them to upset both economic and sexual arrangements that seem to represent some stability in their lives. Many Black women have a good understanding of both sexism and racism, but because of the everyday constrictions of their lives, cannot risk struggling against them both.

The reaction of Black men to feminism has been notoriously negative. They are, of course, even more threatened than Black women by the possibility that Black feminists might organize around our own needs. They realize that they might not only lose valuable and hardworking allies in their struggles but that they might also be forced to change their habitually sexist ways of interacting with and oppressing Black women. Accusations that Black feminism divides the Black struggle are powerful deterrents to the growth of an autonomous Black women's movement.

Still, hundreds of women have been active at different times during the three-year existence of our group. And every Black woman who came, came out of a strongly-felt need for some level of possibility that did not previously exist in her life.

When we first started meeting early in 1974 after the NBFO first eastern regional conference, we did not have a strategy for organizing, or even a focus. We just wanted to see what we had. After a period of months of not meeting, we began to meet again late in the year and started doing an intense variety of consciousness-raising. The overwhelming feeling that we had is that after years and years we had finally found each other. Although we were not doing political work as a group, individuals continued their involvement in Lesbian politics, sterilization abuse and abortion rights work, Third World Women's International Women's Day activities, and support activity for the trials of Dr. Kenneth Edelin, Joan Little, and Inéz García. During our first summer when membership had dropped off considerably, those of us remaining devoted serious discussion to the possibility of opening a refuge for battered women in a Black community. (There was no refuge in Boston at that time.) We also decided around that time to become an independent collective since we had serious disagreements with NBFO's bourgeois-feminist stance and their lack of a clear political focus.

We also were contacted at that time by socialist feminists, with whom we had worked on abortion rights activities, who wanted to encourage us to attend the National Socialist Feminist Conference in Yellow Springs. One of our members did attend and despite the narrowness of the ideology that was promoted at that particular conference, we became more aware of the need for us to understand our own economic situation and to make our own economic analysis.

In the fall, when some members returned, we experienced several months of comparative inactivity and internal disagreements which were first conceptualized as a Lesbian-straight split but which were also the result of class and political differences. During the summer those of us who were still meeting had determined the need to do political work and to move beyond consciousness-raising and serving exclusively as an emotional support group. At the beginning of 1976, when some of the women who had not wanted to do political work and who also had voiced disagreements stopped attending of their own accord, we again looked for a focus. We decided at that time, with the addition of new members, to become a study group. We had always shared our reading with each other, and some of us had written papers on Black feminism for group discussion a few months before this decision was made. We began functioning as a study group and also began discussing the possibility of starting a Black feminist publication. We had a retreat in the late spring which provided a time for both political discussion and working out interpersonal issues. Currently we are planning to gather together a collection of Black feminist writing. We feel that it is absolutely essential to demonstrate the reality of our politics to other Black women and believe that we can do this through writing and distributing our work. The fact that individual Black feminists are living in isolation all over the country, that our own numbers are small, and that we have some skills in writing, printing, and publishing makes us want to carry out these kinds of projects as a means of organizing Black feminists as we continue to do political work in coalition with other groups.

4. BLACK FEMINIST ISSUES AND PROJECTS

During our time together we have identified and worked on many issues of particular relevance to Black women. The inclusiveness of our politics makes us concerned with any situation that impinges upon the lives of women, Third World and working people. We are of course particularly committed to working on those struggles in which race, sex, and class are simultaneous factors in oppression. We might, for example, become involved in workplace organizing at a factory that employs Third World women or picket a hospital that is cutting back on already inadequate heath care to a Third World community, or set up a rape crisis center in a Black neighborhood. Organizing around welfare and daycare concerns might also be a focus. The work to be done and the countless issues that this work represents merely reflect the pervasiveness of our oppression.

Issues and projects that collective members have actually worked on are sterilization abuse, abortion

rights, battered women, rape and health care. We have also done many workshops and educationals on Black feminism on college campuses, at women's conferences, and most recently for high school women.

One issue that is of major concern to us and that we have begun to publicly address is racism in the white women's movement. As Black feminists we are made constantly and painfully aware of how little effort white women have made to understand and combat their racism, which requires among other things that they have a more than superficial comprehension of race, color, and Black history and culture. Eliminating racism in the white women's movement is by definition work for white women to do, but we will continue to speak to and demand accountability on this issue.

In the practice of our politics we do not believe that the end always justifies the means. Many reactionary and destructive acts have been done in the name of achieving "correct" political goals. As feminists we do not want to mess over people in the name of politics. We believe in collective process and a nonhierarchical distribution of power within our own group and in our vision of a revolutionary society. We are committed to a continual examination of our politics as they develop through criticism and self-criticism as an essential aspect of our practice. In her introduction to *Sisterhood is Powerful* Robin Morgan writes:

> I haven't the faintest notion what possible revolutionary role white heterosexual men could fulfill, since they are the very embodiment of reactionary-vested-interest-power.

As Black feminists and Lesbians we know that we have a very definite revolutionary task to perform and we are ready for the lifetime of work and struggle before us.

NOTES

1. Wallace, Michele. "A Black Feminist's Search for Sisterhood," *The Village Voice*, 28 July 1975, pp. 6–7.

2. Mumininas of Committee for Unified Newark, *Mwanamke Mwananchi (The Nationalist Woman)*, Newark, N.J., ©1971, pp. 4–5.

28. • *Jo Carrillo*

AND WHEN YOU LEAVE, TAKE YOUR PICTURES WITH YOU (1981)

Jo Carrillo is a professor at University of California Hastings College of the Law. Her poem, "And When You Leave, Take Your Pictures With You," was published in an influential anthology of feminist writings called *This Bridge Called My Back: Writings by Radical Women of Color*. The poem criticizes the romanticized image of a global sisterhood and the appropriation of third world women and their struggle by white, privileged feminists.

Our white sisters
radical friends
love to own pictures of us
sitting at a factory machine
wielding a machete
in our bright bandanas
holding brown yellow black red children
reading books from literacy campaigns
holding machine guns bayonets bombs knives
Our white sisters
radical friends
should think
again.

Our white sisters
radical friends
love to own pictures of us
walking to the fields in hot sun
with straw hat on head if brown
bandana if black
in bright embroidered shirts
holding brown yellow black red children

reading books from literacy campaigns
smiling.
Our white sisters radical friends
should think again.
No one smiles
at the beginning of a day spent
digging for souvenir chunks of uranium
of cleaning up after
our white sisters
radical friends

And when our white sisters
radical friends see us
in the flesh
not as a picture they own,
they are not quite as sure
if
they like us as much.
We're not as happy as we look
on
their
wall.

MEN: COMRADES IN STRUGGLE (1984)

bell hooks is the pen name of Gloria Jean Watkins, an influential feminist scholar whose work uses intersectional analysis to interrogate social inequality. hooks is a prolific writer with more than thirty books including *Ain't I a Woman: Black Women and Feminism, Teaching to Transgress: Education as the Practice of Freedom*, and *Feminism Is for Everybody: Passionate Politics*. She founded the bell hooks Institute in Berea, Kentucky in 2014. In "Men: Comrades in Struggle," hooks illustrates the importance of intersectionality arguing that the binary view of women as oppressed and men as oppressor overlooks the ways in which race and class also confer or restrict privilege. She contends that anti-male feminist rhetoric and separatist ideology alienates women of color as well as poor and working-class women because these women feel connected to men in their communities through the recognition of a common struggle.

Feminism defined as a movement to end sexist oppression enables women and men, girls and boys, to participate equally in revolutionary struggle. So far, contemporary feminist movement has been primarily generated by the efforts of women—men have rarely participated. This lack of participation is not solely a consequence of anti-feminism. By making women's liberation synonymous with women gaining social equality with men, liberal feminists effectively created a situation in which they, not men, designated feminist movement "women's work." Even as they were attacking sex-role divisions of labor, the institutionalized sexism which assigns unpaid, devalued, "dirty" work to women, they were assigning to women yet another sex-role task: making feminist revolution. Women's liberationists called upon all women to join feminist movement, but they did not continually stress that men should assume responsibility for actively struggling to end sexist oppression. Men, they argued, were all-powerful, misogynist, oppressor—the enemy. Women were the oppressed—the victims. Such rhetoric reinforced sexist ideology by positing in an inverted form the notion of a basic conflict between the sexes, the implication being that the empowerment of women would necessarily be at the expense of men.

As with other issues, the insistence on a "woman only" feminist movement and a virulent anti-male stance reflected the race and class background of participants. Bourgeois white women, especially radical feminists, were envious of and angry at privileged white men for denying them an equal share in class privilege. In part, feminism provided them with a public forum for the expression of their anger as well as a political platform they could use to call attention to issues of social equality, demand change, and promote specific reforms. They were not eager to call attention to the fact that men do not share a common social status, that patriarchy does not negate the existence of class and race privilege or exploitation, that all men do not benefit equally from sexism. They did not want to acknowledge that bourgeois white women, though often victimized by sexism, have more power and privilege, are less likely to be exploited or oppressed, than poor, uneducated, non-white males. At the time, many white women's liberationists did not care about the fate of oppressed groups of men. In keeping with the exercise of race and/or class privilege, they deemed the life experiences of these men unworthy of their attention, dismissed them, and simultaneously deflected attention away from their support of continued exploitation and oppression. Assertions like "all men are the enemy" and "all men hate women" lumped all groups of men in one category, thereby suggesting that they share equally in all forms of male privilege. One of the first written statements that endeavored to make an anti-male stance a central feminist position was the "Redstockings Manifesto." Clause III of the manifesto reads:

> We identify the agents of our oppression as men. Male supremacy is the oldest, most basic form of domination. All other forms of exploitation and oppression (racism, capitalism, imperialism, etc.) are extensions of male supremacy: men dominate women, a few men dominate the rest. All power situations throughout history have been male-dominated and male-oriented. Men have controlled all political, economic, and cultural institutions and backed up this control with physical force. They have used their power to keep women in an inferior position. All men receive economic, sexual, and psychological benefits from male supremacy. All men have oppressed women.

Anti-male sentiments have alienated many poor and working-class women, particularly non-white women, from feminist movement. Their life experiences have shown them that they have more in common with men of their race and/or class group than with bourgeois white women. They know the sufferings and hardships women face in their communities; they also know the sufferings and hardships men face, and they have compassion for them. They have had the experience of struggling with them for a better life. This has been especially true for black women. Throughout our history in the United States, black women have shared equal responsibility in all struggles to resist racist oppression. Despite sexism, black women have continually contributed equally to anti-racist struggle, and frequently, before contemporary black liberation effort, black men recognized this contribution. There is a special tie binding people together who struggle collectively for liberation. Black women and men have been united by such ties. They have known the experience of political solidarity. It is the experience of shared resistance struggle that led black women to reject the anti-male stance of some feminist activists. This does not mean that black women were not willing to acknowledge the reality of black male sexism. It does mean that many of us do not believe we will combat sexism or woman-hating by attacking black men or responding to them in kind.

Bourgeois white women cannot conceptualize the bonds that develop between women and men in liberation struggle and have not had as many positive experiences working with men politically. Patriarchal white male rule has usually devalued female political input. Despite the prevalence of sexism in black communities, the role black women play in social institutions, whether primary or secondary, is recognized by everyone as significant and valuable. In an interview with Claudia Tate, black woman writer Maya Angelou explains her sense of the different role black and white women play in their communities:

> Black women and white women are in strange positions in our separate communities. In the social gatherings of black people, black women have always been predominant. That is to say, in the church it's always Sister Hudson, Sister Thomas, and Sister Wetheringay who keep the church alive. In lay gatherings it's always Lottie who cooks, and Mary who's going to Bonita's where there is a good party going on. Also, black women are the nurturers of children in our community. White women are in a different position in their social institutions. White men, who are in effect their fathers, husbands, brothers, their sons, nephews, and uncles, say to white women or imply in any case: "I don't really need you to run my institutions. I need you in certain places and in those

places you must be kept—in the bedroom, in the kitchen, in the nursery, and on the pedestal." Black women have never been told this.

Without the material input of black women as participants and leaders, many male-dominated institutions in black communities would cease to exist; this is not the case in all white communities.

Many black women refused participation in feminist movement because they felt an anti-male stance was not a sound basis for action. They were convinced that virulent expressions of these sentiments intensify sexism by adding to the antagonism which already exists between women and men. For years black women (and some black men) had been struggling to overcome the tensions and antagonisms between black females and males that is generated by internalized racism (i.e., when the white patriarchy suggests one group has caused the oppression of the other). Black women were saying to black men, "We are not one another's enemy," "We must resist the socialization that teaches us to hate ourselves and one another." This affirmation of bonding between black women and men was part of anti-racist struggle. It could have been a part of feminist struggle had white women's liberationists stressed the need for women and men to resist the sexist socialization that teaches us to hate and fear one another. They chose instead to emphasize hate, especially male woman-hating, suggesting that it could not be changed. Therefore no viable political solidarity could exist between women and men. Women of color from various ethnic backgrounds, as well as women who were active in the gay movement, not only experienced the development of solidarity between women and men in resistance struggle, but recognized its value. They were not willing to devalue this bonding by allying themselves with anti-male, bourgeois white women. Encouraging political bonding between women and men to radically resist sexist oppression would have called attention to the transformative potential of feminism. The anti-male stance was a reactionary perspective that made feminism appear to be a movement that would enable white women to usurp white male power, replacing white male supremacist rule with white female supremacist rule.

Within feminist organizations, the issue of female separatism was initially separated from the anti-male stance; it was only as the movement progressed that the two perspectives merged. Many all-female, sex-segregated groups were formed because women recognized that separatist organizing could hasten female consciousness-raising, lay the groundwork for the development of solidarity among women, and generally advance the movement. It was believed that mixed groups would get bogged down by male power trips. Separatist groups were seen as a necessary strategy, not as a way to attack men. Ultimately, the purpose of such groups was integration with equality.

The positive implications of separatist organizing were diminished when radical feminists, like Ti-Grace Atkinson, proposed sexual separatism as an ultimate goal of feminist movement. Reactionary separatism is rooted in the conviction that male supremacy is an absolute aspect of our culture, that women have only two alternatives: accepting it or withdrawing from it to create subcultures. This position eliminates any need for revolutionary struggle, and it is in no way a threat to the status quo. . . .

[. . .]

During the course of contemporary feminist movement, reactionary separatism has led many women to abandon feminist struggle, yet it remains an accepted pattern for feminist organizing, e.g., autonomous women's groups within the peace movement. As a policy, it has helped to marginalize feminist struggle, to make it seem more a personal solution to individual problems, especially problems with men, than a political movement that aims to transform society as a whole. To return to an emphasis on feminism as revolutionary struggle, women can no longer allow feminism to be another arena for the continued expression of antagonism between the sexes. The time has come for women active in feminist movement to develop new strategies for including men in the struggle against sexism.

All men support and perpetuate sexism and sexist oppression in one form or another. It is crucial that feminist activists not get bogged down in intensifying our awareness of this fact to the extent that we do not stress the more unemphasized point, which is that men can lead life-affirming, meaningful lives without exploiting and oppressing women. Like women, men have been socialized to passively accept sexist ideology. While they need not blame themselves for accepting sexism, they must assume responsibility for eliminating it. It angers women activists who push separatism as a goal of feminist movement to hear emphasis placed on men being victimized by sexism; they cling to the "all men are the enemy" version of reality. Men are not exploited or oppressed by sexism, but there are ways in which they suffer as a result of it. This suffering should not be ignored. While it in no way diminishes the seriousness of male abuse and oppression of women, or negates male responsibility for exploitative actions, the pain men experience can serve as a catalyst calling attention to the need for change. Recognition of the painful consequences of sexism in their lives led some men to establish consciousness-raising groups to examine this. Paul Hornacek explains the purpose of these gatherings in his essay "Anti-Sexist Consciousness-Raising Groups for Men":

> Men have reported a variety of different reasons for deciding to seek a C-R group, all of which have an underlying link to the feminist movement. Most are experiencing emotional pain as a result of their male sex role and are dissatisfied with it. Some have had confrontations with radical feminists in public or private encounters and have been repeatedly criticized for being sexist. Some come as a result of their commitment to social change and their recognition that sexism and patriarchy are elements of an intolerable social system that needs to be altered.

Men in the consciousness-raising groups Hornacek describes acknowledge that they benefit from patriarchy and yet are also hurt by it. Men's groups, like women's support groups, run the risk of overemphasizing personal change at the expense of political analysis and struggle.

Separatist ideology encourages women to ignore the negative impact of sexism on male personhood. It stresses polarization between the sexes. According to Joy Justice, separatists believe that there are "two basic perspectives" on the issue of naming the victims of sexism: "There is the perspective that men oppress women. And there is the perspective that people are people, and we are all hurt by rigid sex roles." Many separatists feel that the latter perspective is a sign of co-optation, representing women's refusal to confront the fact that men are the enemy—they insist on the primacy of the first perspective. Both perspectives accurately describe our predicament. Men do oppress women. People are hurt by rigid sex-role patterns. These two realities co-exist. Male oppression of women cannot be excused by the recognition that there are ways men are hurt by rigid sex roles. Feminist activists should acknowledge that hurt—it exists. It does not erase or lessen male responsibility for supporting and perpetuating their power under patriarchy to exploit and oppress women in a manner far more grievous than the psychological stress or emotional pain caused by male conformity to rigid sex-role patterns.

Women active in feminist movement have not wanted to focus in any way on male pain so as not to deflect attention away from the focus on male privilege. Separatist feminist rhetoric suggested that all men share equally in male privilege, that all men reap positive benefits from sexism. Yet the poor or working-class man who has been socialized via sexist ideology to believe that there are privileges and powers he should possess solely because he is male often finds that few, if any, of these benefits are automatically bestowed on him in life. More than any other male group in the United States, he is constantly concerned about the contradiction between the notion of masculinity he was taught and his inability to live up to that notion. He is usually "hurt," emotionally scarred because he does not have the privilege or power society has taught him "real men" should possess. Alienated, frustrated, pissed off, he may attack, abuse, and oppress an individual woman or women, but he is not reaping positive benefits from his support and perpetuation of sexist ideology. When he beats or rapes women, he is not exercising privilege or reaping positive rewards; he may feel satisfied in exercising the only form of domination allowed him. The ruling-class male power structure that promotes his sexist abuse of women reaps the real material benefits and privileges from his actions. As long as he is attacking women and not sexism or capitalism, he helps to maintain a system that allows him few, if any, benefits or privileges. He is an oppressor. He is an enemy to women. He is also an enemy to himself. He is also oppressed. His abuse of women is not justifiable. Even though he has been socialized to act as he does, there are existing social movements that would enable him to struggle for self-recovery and liberation. By ignoring these movements, he chooses to remain both oppressor and oppressed. If feminist movement ignores his predicament, dismisses his hurt, or writes him off as just another male enemy, then we are passively condoning his actions.

The process by which men act as oppressors and are oppressed is particularly visible in black communities, where men are working-class and poor. In her essay "Notes for Yet Another Paper on Black Feminism, or, Will the Real Enemy Please Stand Up?" black feminist activist Barbara Smith suggests that black women are unwilling to confront the problem of sexist oppression in black communities:

> By naming sexist oppression as a problem it would appear that we would have to identify as threatening a group we have heretofore assumed to be our allies—Black men. This seems to be one of the major stumbling blocks to beginning to analyze the sexual relationships/sexual politics of our lives. The phrase "men are not the enemy" dismisses feminism and the reality of patriarchy in one breath and also overlooks some major realities. If we cannot entertain the idea that some men are the enemy, especially white men and in a different sense Black men, too, then we will never be able to figure out all the reasons why, for example, we are beaten up every day, why we are sterilized against our wills, why we are being raped by our neighbors, why we are pregnant at age twelve, and why we are at home on welfare with more children

than we can support or care for. Acknowledging the sexism of Black men does not mean that we become "man-haters" or necessarily eliminate them from our lives. What it does mean is that we must struggle for a different basis of interaction with them.

Women in black communities have been reluctant to publicly discuss sexist oppression, but they have always known it exists. We too have been socialized to accept sexist ideology, and many black women feel that black male abuse of women is a reflection of frustrated masculinity—such thoughts lead them to see that abuse is understandable, even justified. The vast majority of black women think that just publicly stating that these men are the enemy or identifying them as oppressors would do little to change the situation; they fear it could simply lead to greater victimization. Naming oppressive realities, in and of itself, has not brought about the kinds of changes for oppressed groups that it can for more privileged groups, who command a different quality of attention. The public naming of sexism has generally not resulted in the institutionalized violence that characterized, for example, the response to black civil rights struggles. (Private naming, however, is often met with violent oppression.) Black women have not joined feminist movement not because they cannot face the reality of sexist oppression; they face it daily. They do not join feminist movement because they do not see in feminist theory and practice, especially those writings made available to masses of people, potential solutions.

So far, feminist rhetoric identifying men as the enemy has had few positive implications. Had feminist activists called attention to the relationship between ruling-class men and the vast majority of men, who are socialized to perpetuate and maintain sexism and sexist oppression even as they reap no life-affirming benefits, these men might have been motivated to examine the impact of sexism in their lives. Often feminist activists talk about male abuse of women as if it is an exercise of privilege rather than an expression of moral bankruptcy, insanity, and dehumanization. For example, in Barbara

Smith's essay, she identifies white males as "the primary oppressor group in American society" and discusses the nature of their domination of others. At the end of the passage in which this statement is made she comments: "It is not just rich and powerful capitalists who inhibit and destroy life. Rapists, murderers, lynchers, and ordinary bigots do, too, and exercise very real and violent power because of this white male privilege." Implicit in this statement is the assumption that the act of committing violent crimes against women is either a gesture or an affirmation of privilege. Sexist ideology brainwashes men to believe that their violent abuse of women is beneficial when it is not. Yet feminist activists affirm this logic when we should be constantly naming these acts as expressions of perverted power relations, general lack of control over one's actions, emotional powerlessness, extreme irrationality, and, in many cases, outright insanity. Passive male absorption of sexist ideology enables them to interpret this disturbed behavior positively. As long as men are brainwashed to equate violent abuse of women with privilege, they will have no understanding of the damage done to themselves or the damage they do to others, and no motivation to change.

Individuals committed to feminist revolution must address ways that men can unlearn sexism. Women were never encouraged in contemporary feminist movement to point out to men their responsibility. Some feminist rhetoric "put down" women who related to men at all. Most women's liberationists were saying, "Women have nurtured, helped, and supported others for too long—now we must fend for ourselves." Having helped and supported men for centuries by acting in complicity with sexism, women were suddenly encouraged to withdraw their support when it came to the issue of "liberation." The insistence on a concentrated focus on individualism, on the primacy of self, deemed "liberatory" by women's liberationists, was not a visionary, radical concept of freedom. It did provide individual solutions for women, however. It was the same idea of independence perpetuated by the imperialist patriarchal state which equates independence with narcissism,

and lack of concern with triumph over others. In this way, women active in feminist movement were simply inverting the dominant ideology of the culture—they were not attacking it. They were not presenting practical alternatives to the status quo. In fact, even the statement "men are the enemy" was basically an inversion of the male supremacist doctrine that "women are the enemy"—the old Adam and Eve version of reality.

In retrospect, it is evident that the emphasis on "man as enemy" deflected attention away from focus on improving relationships between women and men, ways for men and women to work together to unlearn sexism. Bourgeois women active in feminist movement exploited the notion of a natural polarization between the sexes to draw attention to equal-rights effort. They had an enormous investment in depicting the male as enemy and the female as victim. They were the group of women who could dismiss their ties with men once they had an equal share in class privilege. They were ultimately more concerned with obtaining an equal share in class privilege than with the struggle to eliminate sexism and sexist oppression. Their insistence on separating from men heightened the sense that they, as women without men, needed equality of opportunity. Most women do not have the freedom to separate from men because of economic interdependence. The separatist notion that women could resist sexism by withdrawing from contact with men reflected a bourgeois class perspective. In Cathy McCandless's essay "Some Thoughts about Racism, Classism, and Separatism," she makes the point that separatism is in many ways a false issue because "in this capitalist economy, none of us are truly separate." However, she adds:

> Socially, it's another matter entirely. The richer you are, the less you generally have to acknowledge those you depend upon. Money can buy you a great deal of distance. Given enough of it, it is even possible never to lay eyes upon a man. It's a wonderful luxury, having control over who you lay eyes on, but let's face it: most women's daily survival still involves face-to-face

contact with men whether they like it or not. It seems to me that for this reason alone, criticizing women who associate with men not only tends to be counterproductive; it borders on blaming the victim. Particularly if the women taking it upon themselves to set the standards are white and upper- or middle-class (as has often been the case in my experience) and those to whom they apply these rules are not.

Devaluing the real necessities of life that compel many women to remain in contact with men, as well as not respecting the desire of women to keep contact with men, created an unnecessary conflict of interest for those women who might have been very interested in feminism but felt they could not live up to the politically correct standards.

Feminist writing did not say enough about ways women could directly engage in feminist struggle in subtle, day-to-day contacts with men, although they have addressed crises. Feminism is politically relevant to the masses of women who daily interact with men both publicly and privately if it addresses ways that interaction, which usually has negative components because sexism is so all-pervasive, can be changed. Women who have daily contact with men need useful strategies that will enable them to integrate feminist movement into their daily life. By inadequately addressing or failing to address the difficult issues, contemporary feminist movement located itself on the periphery of society rather than at the center. Many women and men think feminism is happening, or happened, "out there." Television tells them the "liberated" woman is an exception, that she is primarily a careerist. Commercials like the one that shows a white career woman shifting from work attire to flimsy clothing exposing flesh, singing all the while "I can bring home the bacon, fry it up in the pan, and never let you forget you're a man," reaffirm that her careerism will not prevent her from assuming the stereotyped sex-object role assigned women in male supremacist society.

Often men who claim to support women's liberation do so because they believe they will benefit by no longer having to assume specific, rigid sex roles they find negative or restrictive. The role they are most willing and eager to change is that of economic provider. Commercials like the one described above assure men that women can be breadwinners or even "the" breadwinner, but still allow men to dominate them. . . .

[. . .]

Men who have dared to be honest about sexism and sexist oppression, who have chosen to assume responsibility for opposing and resisting it, often find themselves isolated. Their politics are disdained by anti-feminist men and women, and are often ignored by women active in feminist movement. Writing about his efforts to publicly support feminism in a local newspaper in Santa Cruz, Morris Conerly explains:

> Talking with a group of men, the subject of Women's Liberation inevitably comes up. A few laughs, snickers, angry mutterings, and denunciations follow. There is a group consensus that men are in an embattled position and must close ranks against the assaults of misguided females. Without fail, someone will solicit me for my view, which is that I am 100% for Women's Liberation. That throws them for a loop and they start staring at me as if my eyebrows were crawling with lice.
>
> They're thinking, "What kind of man is he?" I am a black man who understands that women are not my enemy. If I were a white man with a position of power, one could understand the reason for defending the status quo. Even then, the defense of a morally bankrupt doctrine that exploits and oppresses others would be inexcusable.

Conerly stresses that it was not easy for him to publicly support feminist movement, that it took time:

> Why did it take me some time? Because I was scared of the negative reaction I knew would come my way by supporting Women's Liberation. In my mind I could hear it from the brothers and sisters. "What kind of man are you?" "Who's wearing the pants?" "Why are you in that white shit?" And on and on.

Sure enough the attacks came as I had foreseen but by that time my belief was firm enough to withstand public scorn.

With growth there is pain . . . and that truism certainly applied in my case.

Men who actively struggle against sexism have a place in feminist movement. They are our comrades. Feminists have recognized and supported the work of men who take responsibility for sexist oppression—men's work with batterers, for example. Those women's liberationists who see no value in this participation must rethink and re-examine the process by which revolutionary struggle is advanced. Individual men tend to become involved in feminist movement because of the pain generated in relationships with women. Usually a woman friend or companion has called attention to their support of male supremacy. Jon Snodgrass introduces the book he edited, *For Men Against Sexism: A Book of Readings,* by telling readers:

> While there were aspects of women's liberation which appealed to men, on the whole my reaction was typical of men. I was threatened by the movement and responded with anger and ridicule. I believed that men and women were oppressed by capitalism, but not that women were oppressed by men. I argued that "men are oppressed too" and that it's workers who need liberation! I was unable to recognize a hierarchy of inequality between men and women (in the working class) nor to attribute it to male domination. My blindness to patriarchy, I now think, was a function of my male privilege. As a member of the male gender caste, I either ignored or suppressed women's liberation.
>
> My full introduction to the women's movement came through a personal relationship. . . . As our relationship developed, I began to receive repeated criticism for being sexist. At first I responded, as part of the male backlash, with anger and denial. In time, however, I began to recognize the validity of the

accusation, and eventually even to acknowledge the sexism in my denial of the accusations.

Snodgrass participated in the men's consciousness-raising groups and edited the book of readings in 1977. Towards the end of the 1970s, interest in male anti-sexist groups declined. Even though more men than ever before support the idea of social equality for women, like women they do not see this support as synonymous with efforts to end sexist oppression, with feminist movement that would radically transform society. Men who advocate feminism as a movement to end sexist oppression must become more vocal and public in their opposition to sexism and sexist oppression. Until men share equal responsibility for struggling to end sexism, feminist movement will reflect the very sexist contradictions we wish to eradicate.

Separatist ideology encourages us to believe that women alone can make feminist revolution—we cannot. Since men are the primary agents maintaining and supporting sexism and sexist oppression, they can only be successfully eradicated if men are compelled to assume responsibility for transforming their consciousness and the consciousness of society as a whole. After hundreds of years of anti-racist struggle, more than ever before non-white people are currently calling attention to the primary role white people must play in anti-racist struggle. The same is true of the struggle to eradicate sexism—men have a primary role to play. This does not mean that they are better equipped to lead feminist movement; it does mean that they should share equally in resistance struggle. In particular, men have a tremendous contribution to make to feminist struggle in the area of exposing, confronting, opposing, and transforming the sexism of their male peers. When men show a willingness to assume equal responsibility in feminist struggle, performing whatever tasks are necessary, women should affirm their revolutionary work by acknowledging them as comrades in struggle.

30. • *Gloria Anzaldúa*

LA CONCIENCIA DE LA MESTIZA/ TOWARDS A NEW CONSCIOUSNESS (1987)

Gloria Anzaldúa was a queer Chicana writer and scholar whose use of the terms *mestizaje* and "the new *mestiza*" were significant contributions to the fields of queer, feminist, Chicana, and postcolonial scholarship. *Mestizaje* is a rejection of traditional dualistic and hierarchical identity constructions, and the embracing of this concept is what gives the new *mestiza* an ability to use her multiple identities as a source of strength and vision. Anzaldúa's writing is grounded in her lived experience as a Chicana who grew up on the Texas–Mexico border, and she used the ambiguity of borderlands to rethink traditional concepts of race, gender, sexuality, and nation. Moving between English and Spanish, her writing style reflected her theoretical work. "La Conciencia de la Mestiza/Towards a New Consciousness" is a section from *Borderlands/La Frontera: The New Mestiza*, one of Anzaldúa's most well-known works.

*Por la mujer de mi raza
hablará el espíritu.*[1]

José Vasconcelos, Mexican philosopher, envisaged *una raza mestiza, una mezcla de razas afines, una raza de color—la primera raza síntesis del globo.* He called it a cosmic race, *la raza cósmica,* a fifth race embracing the four major races of the world.[2] Opposite to the theory of the pure Aryan, and to the policy of racial purity that white America practices, his theory is one of inclusivity. At the confluence of two or more genetic streams, with chromosomes constantly "crossing over," this mixture of races, rather than resulting in an inferior being, provides hybrid progeny, a mutable, more malleable species with a rich gene pool. From this racial, ideological, cultural and biological cross-pollination, an "alien" consciousness is presently in the making—a new *mestiza* consciousness, *una conciencia de mujer.* It is a consciousness of the Borderlands.

UNA LUCHA DE FRONTERAS/ A STRUGGLE OF BORDERS

Because I, a *mestiza,*
continually walk out of one culture
and into another,
because I am in all cultures at the same time,
*alma entre dos mundos, tres, cuatro,
me zumba la cabeza con lo contradictorio.
Estoy norteada por todas las voces que me hablan
simultáneamente.*

The ambivalence from the clash of voices results in mental and emotional states of perplexity. Internal strife results in insecurity and indecisiveness. The *mestiza's* dual or multiple personality is plagued by psychic restlessness.

In a constant state of mental nepantilism, an Aztec word meaning torn between ways, *la mestiza* is a product of the transfer of the cultural and spiritual values of one group to another. Being tricultural, monolingual, bilingual, or multilingual, speaking a patois, and in a state of perpetual transition, the *mestiza* faces the dilemma of the mixed breed: which collectivity does the daughter of a darkskinned mother listen to?

El choque de un alma atrapado entre el mundo del espíritu y el mundo de la técnica a veces la deja entullada. Cradled in one culture, sandwiched between two cultures, straddling all three cultures and their value systems, *la mestiza* undergoes a struggle of flesh, a struggle of borders, an inner war. Like all people, we perceive the version of reality that our culture communicates. Like others having or living in more than one culture, we get multiple, often opposing messages. The coming together of two self-consistent but habitually incompatible frames of reference[3] causes *un choque,* a cultural collision.

Within us and within *la cultura chicana,* commonly held beliefs of the white culture attack commonly held beliefs of the Mexican culture, and both attack commonly held beliefs of the indigenous culture. Subconsciously, we see an attack on ourselves and our beliefs as a threat and we attempt to block with a counterstance.

But it is not enough to stand on the opposite river bank, shouting questions, challenging patriarchal, white conventions. A counterstance locks one into a duel of oppressor and oppressed; locked in mortal combat, like the cop and the criminal, both are reduced to a common denominator of violence. The counterstance refutes the dominant culture's views and beliefs, and, for this, it is proudly defiant. All reaction is limited by, and dependent on, what it is reacting against. Because the counterstance stems from a problem with authority—outer as well as inner—it's a step towards liberation from cultural domination. But it is not a way of life. At some point, on our way to a new consciousness, we will have to leave the opposite bank, the split between the two mortal combatants somehow healed so that we are on both shores at once and, at once, see through serpent and eagle eyes. Or perhaps we will decide to disengage from the dominant culture,

write it off altogether as a lost cause, and cross the border into a wholly new and separate territory. Or we might go another route. The possibilities are numerous once we decide to act and not react.

A TOLERANCE FOR AMBIGUITY

These numerous possibilities leave *la mestiza* floundering in uncharted seas. In perceiving conflicting information and points of view, she is subjected to a swamping of her psychological borders. She has discovered that she can't hold concepts or ideas in rigid boundaries. The borders and walls that are supposed to keep the undesirable ideas out are entrenched habits and patterns of behavior; these habits and patterns are the enemy within. Rigidity means death. Only by remaining flexible is she able to stretch the psyche horizontally and vertically. *La mestiza* constantly has to shift out of habitual formations; from convergent thinking, analytical reasoning that tends to use rationality to move toward a single goal (a Western mode), to divergent thinking,[4] characterized by movement away from set patterns and goals and toward a more whole perspective, one that includes rather than excludes.

The new *mestiza* copes by developing a tolerance for contradictions, a tolerance for ambiguity. She learns to be an Indian in Mexican culture, to be Mexican from an Anglo point of view. She learns to juggle cultures. She has a plural personality, she operates in a pluralistic mode—nothing is thrust out, the good the bad and the ugly, nothing rejected, nothing abandoned. Not only does she sustain contradictions, she turns the ambivalence into something else.

She can be jarred out of ambivalence by an intense, and often painful, emotional event which inverts or resolves the ambivalence. I'm not sure exactly how. The work takes place underground—subconsciously. It is work that the soul performs. That focal point or fulcrum, that juncture where the *mestiza* stands, is where phenomena tend to collide. It is where the possibility of uniting all that is separate occurs. This assembly is not one where severed or separated pieces merely come together. Nor is it a balancing of oppos-ing powers. In attempting to work out a synthesis, the self has added a third element which is greater than the sum of its severed parts. That third element is a new consciousness—a *mestiza* consciousness—and though it is a source of intense pain, its energy comes from continual creative motion that keeps breaking down the unitary aspect of each new paradigm.

En unas pocas centurias, the future will belong to the *mestiza.* Because the future depends on the breaking down of paradigms, it depends on the straddling of two or more cultures. By creating a new mythos—that is, a change in the way we per-ceive reality, the way we see ourselves, and the ways we behave—*la mestiza* creates a new consciousness.

The work of *mestiza* consciousness is to break down the subject-object duality that keeps her a prisoner and to show in the flesh and through the images in her work how duality is transcended. The answer to the problem between the white race and the colored, between males and females, lies in healing the split that originates in the very foundation of our lives, our culture, our languages, our thoughts. A massive uprooting of dualistic thinking in the individual and collective consciousness is the beginning of a long struggle, but one that could, in our best hopes, bring us to the end of rape, of violence, of war.

LA ENCRUCIJADA/THE CROSSROADS

A chicken is being sacrificed
    at a crossroads, a simple mound of earth
a mud shrine for *Eshu,*
    Yoruba god of indeterminacy,
who blesses her choice of path.
    She begins her journey.

Su cuerpo es una bocacalle. La mestiza has gone from being the sacrificial goat to becoming the officiating priestess at the crossroads.

As a *mestiza* I have no country, my homeland cast me out; yet all countries are mine because I am every woman's sister or potential lover. (As a lesbian I have no race, my own people disclaim me; but I am all races because there is the queer of me in all races.) I am cultureless because, as a feminist, I chal-lenge the collective cultural/religious male-derived beliefs of Indo-Hispanics and Anglos; yet I am cul-tured because I am participating in the creation of yet another culture, a new story to explain the world and our participation in it, a new value system with images and symbols that connect us to each other and to the planet. *Soy un amasamiento,* I am an act of kneading, of uniting and joining that not only has produced both a creature of darkness and a creature of light, but also a creature that questions the defini-tions of light and dark and gives them new meanings.

We are the people who leap in the dark, we are the people on the knees of the gods. In our very flesh, (r)evolution works out the clash of cultures. It makes us crazy constantly, but if the center holds, we've made some kind of evolutionary step forward. *Nuestra alma el trabajo,* the opus, the great alchemi-cal work; spiritual *mestizaje,* a "morphogenesis,"[5] an inevitable unfolding. We have become the quicken-ing serpent movement.

Indigenous like corn, like corn, the *mestiza* is a product of crossbreeding, designed for preservation under a variety of conditions. Like an ear of corn—a female seed-bearing organ—the *mestiza* is tenacious, tightly wrapped in the husks of her culture. Like kernels she clings to the cob; with thick stalks and strong brace roots, she holds tight to the earth—she will survive the crossroads.

Lavando y remojando el maíz en agua de cal, despo-jando el pellejo. Moliendo, mixteando, amasando, haci-endo tortillas de masa.[6] She steeps the corn in lime, it swells, softens. With stone roller on *metate,* she grinds the corn, then grinds again. She kneads and moulds the dough, pats the round balls into *tortillas.*

We are the porous rock in the stone *metate*
squatting on the ground.
We are the rolling pin, *el maíz y agua,*
la masa harina. Somos el amasijo.

Somos lo molido en el metate.
We are the *comal* sizzling hot,
the hot *tortilla,* the hungry mouth.
We are the coarse rock.
We are the grinding motion,
the mixed potion, *somos el molcajete.*
We are the pestle, the *comino, ajo, pimienta,*
We are the *chile colorado,*
the green shoot that cracks the rock.
We will abide.

EL CAMINO DE LA MESTIZA/ THE MESTIZA WAY

Caught between the sudden contraction, the breath sucked in and the endless space, the brown woman stands still, looks at the sky. She decides to go down, digging her way along the roots of trees. Sifting through the bones, she shakes them to see if there is any marrow in them. Then, touching the dirt to her forehead, to her tongue, she takes a few bones, leaves the rest in their burial place.

She goes through her backpack, keeps her journal and address book, throws away the muni-bart metromaps. The coins are heavy and they go next, then the greenbacks flutter through the air. She keeps her knife, can opener and eyebrow pencil. She puts bones, pieces of bark, *hierbas,* eagle feather, snakeskin, tape recorder, the rattle and drum in her pack and she sets out to become the complete *tolteca.*

Her first step is to take inventory. *Despojando, desgranando, quitando paja.* Just what did she inherit from her ancestors? This weight on her back—which is the baggage from the Indian mother, which the baggage from the Spanish father, which the baggage from the Anglo?

Pero es difícil differentiating between *lo heredado, lo adquirido, lo impuesto.* She puts history through a sieve, winnows out the lies, looks at the forces that we as a race, as women, have been a part of. *Luego bota lo que no vale, los desmientos, los desencuentos, el*

embrutecimiento. Aguarda el juicio, hondo y enraízado, de la gente antigua. This step is a conscious rupture with all oppressive traditions of all cultures and religions. She communicates that rupture, documents the struggle. She reinterprets history and, using new symbols, she shapes new myths. She adopts new perspectives toward the darkskinned, women and queers. She strengthens her tolerance (and intolerance) for ambiguity. She is willing to share, to make herself vulnerable to foreign ways of seeing and thinking. She surrenders all notions of safety, of the familiar. Deconstruct, construct. She becomes a *nahual,* able to transform herself into a tree, a coyote, into another person. She learns to transform the small "I" into the total Self. *Se hace moldeadora de su alma. Según la concepción que tiene de sí misma, así será.*

QUE NO SE NOS OLVIDEN LOS HOMBRES

"Tú no sirves pa' nada—
you're good for nothing.
Eres pura vieja."

"You're nothing but a woman" means you are defective. Its opposite is to be *un macho.* The modern meaning of the word "machismo," as well as the concept, is actually an Anglo invention. For men like my father, being "macho" meant being strong enough to protect and support my mother and us, yet being able to show love. Today's macho has doubts about his ability to feed and protect his family. His "machismo" is an adaptation to oppression and poverty and low self-esteem. It is the result of hierarchical male dominance. The Anglo, feeling inadequate and inferior and powerless, displaces or transfers these feelings to the Chicano by shaming him. In the Gringo world, the Chicano suffers from excessive humility and self-effacement, shame of self and self-deprecation. Around Latinos he suffers from a sense of language inadequacy and its accompanying discomfort; with Native Americans he suffers from a racial amnesia which ignores our common blood, and from guilt because the Spanish part of him took their land and oppressed them. He has an excessive compensatory hubris when around Mexicans from the other side. It overlays a deep sense of racial shame.

The loss of a sense of dignity and respect in the macho breeds a false machismo which leads him to put down women and even to brutalize them. Coexisting with his sexist behavior is a love for the mother which takes precedence over that of all others. Devoted son, macho pig. To wash down the shame of his acts, of his very being, and to handle the brute in the mirror, he takes to the bottle, the snort, the needle, and the fist.

Though we "understand" the root causes of male hatred and fear, and the subsequent wounding of women, we do not excuse, we do not condone, and we will no longer put up with it. From the men of our race, we demand the admission/acknowledgment/ disclosure/testimony that they wound us, violate us, are afraid of us and of our power. We need them to say they will begin to eliminate their hurtful put-down ways. But more than the words, we demand acts. We say to them: We will develop equal power with you and those who have shamed us.

It is imperative that *mestizas* support each other in changing the sexist elements in the Mexican-Indian culture. As long as woman is put down, the Indian and the Black in all of us is put down. The struggle of the *mestiza* is above all a feminist one. As long as *los hombres* think they have to *chingar mujeres* and each other to be men, as long as men are taught that they are superior and therefore culturally favored over *la mujer,* as long as to be a *vieja* is a thing of derision, there can be no real healing of our psyches. We're halfway there—we have such love of the Mother, the good mother. The first step is to unlearn the *puta/ virgen* dichotomy and to see *Coatlalopeuh-Coatlicue* in the Mother, *Guadalupe.*

Tenderness, a sign of vulnerability, is so feared that it is showered on women with verbal abuse and blows. Men, even more than women, are fettered to gender roles. Women at least have had the guts to break out of bondage. Only gay men have had the courage to expose themselves to the woman inside them and to challenge the current masculinity. I've encountered a few scattered and isolated gentle straight men, the beginnings of a new breed, but they are confused, and entangled with sexist behaviors that they have not been able to eradicate. We need a new masculinity and the new man needs a movement.

Lumping the males who deviate from the general norm with man, the oppressor, is a gross injustice. *Asombra pensar que nos hemos quedado en ese pozo oscuro donde el mundo encierra a las lesbianas. Asombra pensar que hemos, como femenistas y lesbianas, cerrado nuestros corazónes a los hombres, a nuestros hermanos los jotos, desheredados y marginales como nosotros.* Being the supreme crossers of cultures, homosexuals have strong bonds with the queer white, Black, Asian, Native American, Latino, and with the queer in Italy, Australia and the rest of the planet. We come from all colors, all classes, all races, all time periods. Our role is to link people with each other—the Blacks with Jews with Indians with Asians with whites with extraterrestrials. It is to transfer ideas and information from one culture to another. Colored homosexuals have more knowledge of other cultures; have always been at the forefront (although sometimes in the closet) of all liberation struggles in this country; have suffered more injustices and have survived them despite all odds. Chicanos need to acknowledge the political and artistic contributions of their queer. People, listen to what your *jotería* is saying.

The *mestizo* and the queer exist at this time and point on the evolutionary continuum for a purpose. We are a blending that proves that all blood is intricately woven together, and that we are spawned out of similar souls.

[. . .]

NOTES

1. This is my own "take off" on José Vasconcelos' idea. José Vasconcelos, *La Raza Cósmica: Misión de la Raza Ibero-Americana* (México: Aguilar S.A. de Ediciones, 1961).
2. Vasconcelos.
3. Arthur Koestler termed this "bisociation." Albert Rothenberg, *The Creative Process in Art, Science, and Other Fields* (Chicago, IL: University of Chicago Press, 1979), 12.
4. In part, I derive my definitions for "convergent" and "divergent" thinking from Rothenberg, 12–13.
5. To borrow chemist Ilya Prigogine's theory of "dissipative structures." Prigogine discovered that substances interact not in predictable ways as it was taught in science, but in different and fluctuating ways to produce new and more complex structures, a kind of birth he called "morphogenesis," which created unpredictable innovations. Harold Gilliam, "Searching for a New World View." *This World* (January, 1981), 23.
6. *Tortillas de masa harina:* corn tortillas are of two types, the smooth uniform ones made in a tortilla press and usually bought at a tortilla factory or supermarket, and *gorditas,* made by mixing *masa* with lard or shortening or butter (my mother sometimes puts in bits of bacon or *chicharrones*).

---

31. • *Angela Davis*

MASKED RACISM: REFLECTIONS ON THE PRISON INDUSTRIAL COMPLEX (1998)

Angela Davis is distinguished professor emerita in the history of consciousness and feminist studies departments at the University of California, Santa Cruz. A scholar, activist, and author, her work demonstrates a commitment to fighting oppression based on race, class, and gender. She has published numerous books, including *Women, Race, and Class* and *Are Prisons Obsolete?* and she is a founding member of Critical Resistance, a grassroots organization calling attention to racism in the criminal justice system and working to end the prison industrial complex. In "Masked Racism: Reflections on the Prison Industrial Complex," Davis analyzes the growing prison population, the privatization of the corrections system, and the use of racist narratives to justify the exploitation of prison populations for corporate profit.

Imprisonment has become the response of first resort to far too many of the social problems that burden people who are ensconced in poverty. These problems often are veiled by being conveniently grouped together under the category "crime" and by the automatic attribution of criminal behavior to people of color. Homelessness, unemployment, drug addiction, mental illness, and illiteracy are only a few of the problems that disappear from public view when the human beings contending with them are relegated to cages.

Prisons thus perform a feat of magic. Or rather the people who continually vote in new prison bonds and tacitly assent to a proliferating network of prisons and jails have been tricked into believing in the magic of imprisonment. But prisons do not disappear problems, they disappear human beings. And the practice of disappearing vast numbers of people from poor, immigrant, and racially marginalized communities has literally become big business.

The seeming effortlessness of magic always conceals an enormous amount of behind-the-scenes work. When prisons disappear human beings in order to convey the illusion of solving social problems, penal infrastructures must be created to accommodate a rapidly swelling population of caged people. Goods and services must be provided to keep imprisoned populations alive. Sometimes these populations must be kept busy and at other times—particularly in repressive super maximum prisons and in INS detention centers—they must be deprived of virtually all meaningful activity. Vast numbers of handcuffed and shackled people are moved across state borders as they are transferred from one state or federal prison to another.

All this work, which used to be the primary province of government, is now also performed by private corporations, whose links to government in the field of what is euphemistically called "corrections" resonate dangerously with the military industrial complex. The dividends that accrue from investment in the punishment industry, like those that accrue from investment in weapons production, only amount to social destruction. Taking into account the structural similarities and profitability of business-government linkages in the realms of military production and public punishment, the expanding penal system can now be characterized as a "prison industrial complex."

THE COLOR OF IMPRISONMENT

Almost two million people are currently locked up in the immense network of U.S. prisons and jails. More than 70 percent of the imprisoned population are people of color. It is rarely acknowledged that the fastest growing group of prisoners are black women and that Native American prisoners are the largest group per capita. Approximately five million people—including those on probation and parole—are directly under the surveillance of the criminal justice system.

Three decades ago, the imprisoned population was approximately one-eighth its current size. While women still constitute a relatively small percentage of people behind bars, today the number of incarcerated women in California alone is almost twice what the nationwide women's prison population was in 1970. According to Elliott Currie, "[t]he prison has become a looming presence in our society to an extent unparalleled in our history—or that of any other industrial democracy. Short of major wars, mass incarceration has been the most thoroughly implemented government social program of our time."

To deliver up bodies destined for profitable punishment, the political economy of prisons relies on racialized assumptions of criminality—such as images of black welfare mothers reproducing criminal children—and on racist practices in arrest, conviction, and sentencing patterns. Colored bodies constitute the main human raw material in this vast experiment to disappear the major social problems of our time. Once the aura of magic is stripped away from the imprisonment solution, what is revealed is racism, class bias, and the parasitic seduction of capitalist profit. The prison industrial system materially and morally impoverishes its inhabitants and devours the social wealth needed to address the very problems that have led to spiraling numbers of prisoners.

As prisons take up more and more space on the social landscape, other government programs that have previously sought to respond to social needs—such as Temporary Assistance to Needy Families—are being squeezed out of existence. The deterioration of public education, including prioritizing discipline and security over learning in public schools located in poor communities, is directly related to the prison "solution."

PROFITING FROM PRISONERS

As prisons proliferate in U.S. society, private capital has become enmeshed in the punishment industry. And precisely because of their profit potential, prisons are becoming increasingly important to the U.S. economy. If the notion of punishment as a source of potentially stupendous profits is disturbing by itself, then the strategic dependence on racist structures and ideologies to render mass punishment palatable and profitable is even more troubling.

Prison privatization is the most obvious instance of capital's current movement toward the prison industry. While government-run prisons are often in gross violation of international human rights standards, private prisons are even less accountable. In March of this year, the Corrections Corporation of America (CCA), the largest U.S. private prison company, claimed 54,944 beds in 68 facilities under contract or development in the U.S., Puerto Rico, the United Kingdom, and Australia. Following the global trend of subjecting more women to public punishment, CCA recently opened a women's prison outside Melbourne. The company recently identified California as its "new frontier."

Wackenhut Corrections Corporation (WCC), the second largest U.S. prison company, claimed contracts and awards to manage 46 facilities in North America, U.K., and Australia. It boasts a total of 30,424 beds as well as contracts for prisoner health care services, transportation, and security.

Currently, the stocks of both CCA and WCC are doing extremely well. Between 1996 and 1997, CCA's revenues increased by 58 percent, from $293 million to $462 million. Its net profit grew from $30.9 million to $53.9 million. WCC raised its revenues from $138 million in 1996 to $210 million in 1997. Unlike public correctional facilities, the vast profits of these private facilities rely on the employment of non-union labor.

THE PRISON INDUSTRIAL COMPLEX

But private prison companies are only the most visible component of the increasing corporatization of punishment. Government contracts to build prisons have bolstered the construction industry. The architectural community has identified prison design as a major new niche. Technology developed for the military by companies like Westinghouse is being marketed for use in law enforcement and punishment.

Moreover, corporations that appear to be far removed from the business of punishment are intimately involved in the expansion of the prison industrial complex. Prison construction bonds are one of the many sources of profitable investment for leading financiers such as Merrill Lynch. MCI charges prisoners and their families outrageous prices for the precious telephone calls which are often the only contact prisoners have with the free world.

Many corporations whose products we consume on a daily basis have learned that prison labor power can be as profitable as third world labor power exploited by U.S.-based global corporations. Both relegate formerly unionized workers to joblessness and many even wind up in prison. Some of the companies that use prison labor are IBM, Motorola, Compaq, Texas Instruments, Honeywell, Microsoft, and Boeing. But it is not only the hi-tech industries that reap the profits of prison labor. Nordstrom department stores sell jeans that are marketed as "Prison Blues," as well as t-shirts and jackets made in Oregon prisons. The advertising slogan for these clothes is "made on the inside to be worn on the outside." Maryland prisoners inspect glass bottles and jars used by Revlon and Pierre Cardin, and schools throughout the world buy graduation caps and gowns made by South Carolina prisoners.

"For private business," write Eve Goldberg and Linda Evans (a political prisoner inside the Federal Correctional Institution at Dublin, California) "prison labor is like a pot of gold. No strikes. No union organizing. No health benefits, unemployment insurance, or workers' compensation to pay. No language barriers, as in foreign countries. New leviathan prisons are being built on thousands of eerie acres of factories inside the walls. Prisoners do data entry for Chevron, make telephone reservations for TWA, raise hogs, shovel manure, make circuit boards, limousines, waterbeds, and lingerie for Victoria's Secret—all at a fraction of the cost of 'free labor.'"

DEVOURING THE SOCIAL WEALTH

Although prison labor—which ultimately is compensated at a rate far below the minimum wage—is hugely profitable for the private companies that use it, the penal system as a whole does not produce wealth. It devours the social wealth that could be used to subsidize housing for the homeless, to ameliorate public education for poor and racially marginalized communities, to open free drug rehabilitation programs for people who wish to kick their habits, to create a national health care system, to expand programs to combat HIV, to eradicate domestic abuse—and, in the process, to create well-paying jobs for the unemployed.

Since 1984 more than twenty new prisons have opened in California, while only one new campus was added to the California State University system and none to the University of California system. In 1996-97, higher education received only 8.7 percent of the State's General Fund while corrections received 9.6 percent. Now that affirmative action has been declared illegal in California, it is obvious that education is increasingly reserved for certain people, while prisons are reserved for others. Five times as many black men are presently in prison as in four-year colleges and universities. This new segregation has dangerous implications for the entire country.

By segregating people labeled as criminals, prison simultaneously fortifies and conceals the structural racism of the U.S. economy. Claims of low unemployment rates—even in black communities—make sense only if one assumes that the vast numbers of people in prison have really disappeared and thus have no legitimate claims to jobs. The numbers of black and Latino men currently incarcerated amount to two percent of the male labor force. According to criminologist David Downes, "[t]reating incarceration as a type of hidden unemployment may raise the

jobless rate for men by about one-third, to 8 percent. The effect on the black labor force is greater still, raising the [black] male unemployment rate from 11 percent to 19 percent."

HIDDEN AGENDA

Mass incarceration is not a solution to unemployment, nor is it a solution to the vast array of social problems that are hidden away in a rapidly growing network of prisons and jails. However, the great majority of people have been tricked into believing in the efficacy of imprisonment, even though the historical record clearly demonstrates that prisons do not work. Racism has undermined our ability to create a popular critical discourse to contest the ideological trickery that posits imprisonment as key to public safety. The focus of state policy is rapidly shifting from social welfare to social control.

Black, Latino, Native American, and many Asian youth are portrayed as the purveyors of violence, traffickers of drugs, and as envious of commodities that they have no right to possess. Young black and Latina women are represented as sexually promiscuous and as indiscriminately propagating babies and poverty. Criminality and deviance are racialized. Surveillance is thus focused on communities of color, immigrants, the unemployed, the undereducated, the homeless, and in general on those who have a diminishing claim to social resources. Their claim to social resources continues to diminish in large part because law enforcement and penal measures increasingly devour these resources. The prison industrial complex has thus created a vicious cycle of punishment which only further impoverishes those whose impoverishment is supposedly "solved" by imprisonment.

Therefore, as the emphasis of government policy shifts from social welfare to crime control, racism sinks more deeply into the economic and ideological structures of U.S. society. Meanwhile, conservative crusaders against affirmative action and bilingual education proclaim the end of racism, while their opponents suggest that racism's remnants can be dispelled through dialogue and conversation. But conversations about "race relations" will hardly dismantle a prison industrial complex that thrives on and nourishes the racism hidden within the deep structures of our society.

The emergence of a U.S. prison industrial complex within a context of cascading conservatism marks a new historical moment, whose dangers are unprecedented. But so are its opportunities. Considering the impressive number of grassroots projects that continue to resist the expansion of the punishment industry, it ought to be possible

to bring these efforts together to create radical and nationally visible movements that can legitimize anti-capitalist critiques of the prison industrial complex. It ought to be possible to build movements in defense of prisoners' human rights and movements that persuasively argue that what we need is not new prisons, but new health care, housing, education, drug programs, jobs, and education. To safeguard a democratic future, it is possible and necessary to weave together the many and increasing strands of resistance to the prison industrial complex into a powerful movement for social transformation.

---

32. • *Jackson Katz*

GUILTY PLEASURES: PORNOGRAPHY, PROSTITUTION, AND STRIPPING (2006)

Jackson Katz is an antiviolence activist whose work focuses around the social construction of American masculinity. He is an award-winning filmmaker well known for his films *Tough Guise* and *Tough Guise 2*, which examine what he sees as a crisis in masculinity. He argues that cultural norms encourage a style of manhood steeped in misogyny, homophobia, and violence. Katz works with boys and men in schools, sports organizations, and the military to change the definition of manhood as a way to address the social problems of bullying, sexual assault, and domestic violence. In "Guilty Pleasures: Pornography, Prostitution, and Stripping," Katz analyzes the effect of the sex industry on heterosexual men and how it shapes their view of girls and women.

[. . .]

It has long been understood that what people do for entertainment—and sexual pleasure—can be shockingly revealing. But until recently, most discussions about pornography, prostitution, and stripping have

focused on the women and girls in those industries— who they are, how they got into that life, and what happens to them once they do. These are important areas of discussion, and over the past couple of decades activists and researchers have learned a great deal about the reality of women's and girls' lives in the commercial "sex industry"—largely as a result of the courageous testimonies of women who have survived it. But if we hope to *prevent* sexual violence and other forms of sexual exploitation, we must begin to ask another set of questions: How does heterosexual men's use of pornography as a masturbatory aid help to shape not only their view of women and girls, but their own manhood and sexuality? What is the influence on boys' sexuality of early and repeated exposure to the pornography industry's particular representation of "normal" sex? Is it possible to discuss sexual violence in our society and not talk about the influence in male culture of the $10 billion pornography industry? What is the relationship between the sexual abuse of children and the proliferation of media products that deliberately sexualize young girls—and in some cases boys? How do men treat prostitutes, and what impact does this have on the way they treat their wives, girlfriends, female coworkers, and fellow students? As strip culture seeps ever more visibly into the mainstream, what effect does this have on men's and boys' attitudes toward women? What can be done about what seems to be a steady movement away from the idea of sex as mutually respectful? Short of creating our own version of a Taliban-like theocracy, is it possible to reverse the seemingly inexorable societal trend toward the pornographic fantasy of men using women like blow-up dolls?

These are uncomfortable questions, and what makes them even more difficult is that not everyone wants to know the answers. Men have an obvious incentive to change the subject. But it is also true that many women are not eager to find out about what goes on in certain parts of male culture that historically have been off-limits to them, especially when it gets personal and involves men close to them. And who can blame them? The "truth" about some men's callousness, cruelty, and need for sexual dominance that is revealed in pornography, prostitution, and strip culture is a lot to stomach. Some women carry the added burden of having done things sexually with men to accommodate a man's pornographic fantasy, which in another context they might feel compromised their integrity. It also must be painful

for women to admit to themselves that their fathers, brothers, sons, and lovers are often the very same men who rent videos with titles like *A Cum-Guzzling Slut Named Kimberley,* pay twenty-year-old strippers for lap dances at "gentlemen's clubs" on the way home from work, get blow jobs from prostitutes at friends' bachelor parties, and in some cases travel abroad to have cheap sex with twelve-year-old girls.

REVOLUTIONARY HONESTY

The writer John Stoltenberg once said that pornography tells lies about women, but it tells the truth about men. I think Stoltenberg is only partially right. Unless it can be proven that male infants are born hard-wired for sexism, the only truth about men that pornography reveals is that they are products of their environment. Thus if we want to reduce the level of sexual violence perpetrated by boys and men, we need to critically examine the environment in which we socialize boys and establish norms in male culture. This will not be easy, especially since so many men have conscious or unconscious feelings of guilt about how they have objectified women, or perpetuated their oppression through their treatment of them as purchasable commodities. But in order for men to transform their feelings of guilt into something more constructive, they need to do something about the underlying problem. They need to move beyond defensiveness and ask themselves how they can help to change the sexual rituals and norms in male culture that are harmful to women and children. A good place to start this process would be to commit—in private and public—what Stoltenberg calls acts of "revolutionary honesty" about their lives, loves, and guilty pleasures.

In this spirit of revolutionary honesty, I want to come clean about some of my own guilty pleasures. At the very least, I want to make sure that I am not self-righteous or moralizing in this discussion. I do not characterize myself as a "good guy" while other guys who use porn or pay prostitutes are "bad guys," or irredeemably sexist. I have never had non-consensual sex or sex with a prostitute, but I am far from prudish. In my teens and twenties, before I was politically conscious about the sexist exploitation at the heart of the "sex industry," I went to strip clubs and used pornography. But I never saw myself as oppressing women. I denied any connection between my private pleasure and the perpetuation of rape culture. At first I did not know, and then I did not want to know, how badly some men (and women) treat the women and girls in those industries. It was only as I came to hear and read about their life experiences—and reflect on the feminist idea that the high incidence of rape and sexual harassment in the U.S. is linked to the pervasive sexual objectification of women in our society—that I consciously refused to support or condone the commercial sex industry. Still, the effects of my earlier conditioning have stayed with me to this day. For example, I am sometimes aroused by images that I know are sexist and degrading to women. I appreciate the complexity of the human erotic imagination, but I wonder how much my fantasy life—and the fantasy life of tens of millions of my fellow men—has been shaped by the increasingly angry and misogynistic porn that has flooded the culture and our psyches in recent decades. I would never hold other men to a standard which I do not hold for myself. Any man who wants to fight gender violence—and all forms of sexism—needs to be careful not to condemn in others what he refuses to acknowledge about himself. The solution I have found is simply to be honest about my own self-doubts and contradictions. In my work with men, I have found that most of them respect and appreciate this, even if they do not agree with all of my interpretations or conclusions.

ANTI-SEXIST MEN AND THE PORN WARS

Pornography is usually thought of as a women's issue. But as the sociologist Gail Dines bluntly states, "Men make, distribute, and get rich on porn. They jerk off to it. Tell me why it's a women's issue."[1] Although men are overwhelmingly the producers

and consumers of porn, they are nonetheless dramatically underrepresented among the people who take the time to reflect on and discuss its societal function. In fact, millions of men use pornography, but I suspect very few have ever had a serious conversation about it. (Pornography marketed to gay men is a huge industry itself, and many feminist critics—gay and straight—have called attention to the ways in which much of gay porn eroticizes power and control and sexual violence. For the purpose of this discussion, I am focusing on by far the largest segment of the pornography market: heterosexual men and boys.) I know that countless men with whom I have worked over the past twenty years report they had never even heard—much less discussed—thoughtful critiques of the role of porn in men's lives, and the possible negative affect it has had on their sexuality and ability to connect with real women. Some men avoid this sort of introspection because it is still awkward to talk honestly about sex in this culture, and they are embarrassed. Other men like to shift the conversation about pornography into political arguments about free speech and censorship and away from questions about how boys and men use it, what types of porn they find pleasurable and why, and what effect heavy porn use might have on their feelings about women's bodies and sexuality. I am certain that part of their motivation for these evasions is personal: if they engaged in serious discussions about pornography, men might have to ask themselves troubling questions about what effect pornography has on how they view *themselves*, their bodies, and their desires for intimate connections with women.

The debate in this country about hot-button issues like pornography and the sexualization of children in advertising has become so polarized that to the casual observer, there are only two positions: either you are for porn or against it, with no thought given to the complexity of the subject. In real life, people tend to have much more nuanced views of these matters. People in the movements to end sexual and domestic violence are often falsely accused of prudery by the self-described "sex positive" advocates and of being "in bed with the Christian right" if they dare to critique the behavior of "consenting adults." In fact, over the past couple of decades, pornography has even been a divisive issue among people who call themselves feminists. There are two major camps. Anti-porn feminists take the position that pornography sexualizes women's subordination, and is a critical factor in maintaining gender inequality. It might not directly cause men's violence against women, but it portrays men's domination and control of women as sexy. In practice, the porn industry is also a heartless corporate enterprise which can be quite brutal and exploitative of the largely working-class women (and men)—many of them in their late teens and early twenties—whose bodies provide the main attraction, but whose careers in the unforgiving adult film business—Jenna Jameson notwithstanding—are nasty, brutish, and short.

Pro-porn feminists, by contrast, argue that unbridled sexual expression—even if much of it is sexist and produced by and for men—is in women's self-interest because one of the cornerstones of women's oppression is the suppression of their sexuality. True emancipation requires the celebration of women's right to do whatever they want with their bodies—which includes their right to appear in pornography, strip, and sell sex.

Notably, these arguments about pornography have largely taken place between women.

Until recently, men who have a public voice about pornography tended to fall into one of two categories: conservative Christians or pro-porn enthusiasts.[2] In the former category are men like the Reverend Jerry Falwell and Dr. James Dobson, who publicly chastise the purveyors of "obscenity" and "filth," and who also oppose women's reproductive freedom, readily available contraception for young people, and school-based sex education. In the latter category are libertarians like Howard Stern who talk endlessly about how much they love porn, along with men in the porn industry itself who write and speak about its positive effects and savagely attack its right-wing and feminist critics.

But as a growing number of men enter the sexual violence prevention field, a new men's conversation about pornography is beginning to take shape.[3] These men frequently bring an "insider" perspective on the role of pornography in the lives of boys and men. They do not have to debate in the abstract about whether they think the pornography industry is harmful to women. For many of them, the answer flows out of their lived experience and observations of the men around them. There are no formal studies on this topic, but my sense is that a sizable majority of men who have worked in college and community-based anti-rape organizations over the past fifteen or twenty years share the anti-porn feminist view that pornography contributes to the problem of sexual violence, and at the very least desensitizes men to women's sexual subordination. There is by no means unanimity of opinion among these men about what can be done to counteract the popularity and influence of the porn industry in boys' and men's lives. And there are ongoing debates on college campuses and email Listservs about whether all pornography is objectification, and hence bad, or whether the real problem is the misogynistic vision of women's sexuality and men's power that the multi-billion dollar porn industry has sold to the public as normal and even liberating. (Note: There are competing definitions of pornography. But to simplify matters, consider the definition Gail Dines uses in her work. Pornography, she says, consists of those materials that are produced by the multi-billion dollar pornography industry. "The industry knows exactly what it is producing," she says.)

It is also important to note that the vast majority of men in the rape prevention world who are critical of the pornography industry do not object because they think public displays of sex are obscene, but because of the harm inflicted on women and children by sexist displays of women's and men's sexuality. In fact, I would bet that most of these men would celebrate uninhibited expressions of women's sexuality. Their opposition to pornography stems from their belief that most of the magazines and videos produced by the pornography industry actually *limit* women's sexual freedom, while setting women up to be sexually victimized by men. The problem is not only that a high percentage of women in porn are sexual abuse survivors, some of whom were coerced into the business when they were troubled or naïve teenagers by predatory pimps and other abusive older men. It is not only the reduction of women to what University of Texas journalism professor Robert Jensen, writing in the *Sexual-Assault Report,* painfully describes as "three holes and two hands."[4] It is the way the pornography industry helps to define heterosexual *men's* sexuality. Every time a video portrays a scene where a woman asks to be penetrated by a succession of men who ejaculate all over her face as they contemptuously call her a "cum-guzzling whore," it also portrays men getting pleasure from the sight of that "cum-guzzling whore" getting what she wants, and deserves. It normalizes the men's pleasure-taking as it sexualizes the woman's degradation. The idea that consumers of porn can masturbate and have orgasms to that kind of treatment of women and not have it affect their attitudes toward the women and girls in their lives is more a fantasy than anything the most creative porn writers can conjure up.

✳ ✳ ✳

Mainstream pornography has changed a lot in the past couple of decades. People of a certain age who still associate heterosexual porn with "girlie magazines" and air-brushed photos of big-breasted women shot in soft light on luxurious beds with big pillows would be shocked by the brutality, outright contempt for women, and racism that is common in today's product. One need not search out the extremist fringe of porn culture to find this. A simple Google search will suffice to see some of the "adult" titles readily available: *A Cum-Sucking Whore Named Francesca, Rectal Reamers, Brianna Banks aka Filthy Whore #1, Love Hurts,* and *Ride 'em and Wreck 'em.* There are thousands of porn videos that sexualize some of the most racist caricatures of women and men of color, with titles like *Big Black Beast, Slaves on Loan, Asian Fuck Sluts,*

and *Three Black Dicks and a Spanish Chick.* The Web is full of porn sites that advertise not just "sex," but the sexual degradation of women. One such site is called *Violated Teens: Cum in and use them,* which boasts of "Teens forced to fuck, exploited for hard cash: we do what we want to them and they have to love it." Consider one of the most popular porn sites on the Internet, called BangBus. Since its debut in 2001, this site has pioneered what has been called "reality porn," a new genre of "humilitainment" that features what Shauna Swartz in *Bitch* magazine calls "some of the most violent and degrading porno scenes to hit the mainstream." BangBus consists of a couple of average guys who drive around southern Florida in a van, "in search of every girl's inner slut." What they are looking for—the viewer is led to believe—are young women who will agree to go for a ride with them on the promise that they will be paid a few hundred dollars to do something sexual on camera. The videotape documents the initial pick-up on the side of the road, followed by a brief conversation inside the moving van, where the men convince the seemingly naïve woman to take off her clothes. As the handheld camera rolls, the woman has vaginal or anal sex with one of the guys, or she performs oral sex on him. He then withdraws and ejaculates on her face, as the narrator with the camera shrieks in delight. Then after the sex act, the men figure out some way to get the woman out of the van, in one instance to let her pee, in another so she can wash off in a lake. Once she is outside, they hit the gas and race away without paying her. The men laugh and congratulate each other on another successful "drop off," as the young woman's face registers disbelief and then shame as she realizes she has been duped and literally kicked to the curb. The success of this site—which in recent years has drawn huge crowds at the porn industry's major convention in Las Vegas—has predictably spawned a series of imitators, including a site called Trunked, which boasts, "It's simple. Throw the bitch in the trunk. If she doesn't like it, she can get out. Oh yeah. We're goin' 55 mph."

✳ ✳ ✳

The word "pornography" translates from Greek to mean "writing about prostitutes," and there is no doubt that just as women's bodies are the center of attention in heterosexual pornography, most of the people who have written about pornography as a cultural phenomenon have written about how it affects women's lives. This is understandable and appropriate, because it is primarily the bodies of women and girls that pornography producers use and abuse for profit. But if our goal is to dramatically reduce the incidence of sexual violence, we must turn our attention to the demand side of the pornography question and begin to look critically at the role of pornography in the lives of boys and men.

. . . The concept of rape culture . . . starts with the premise that sexual violence is common in our society not because there are so many sick men, but because we socialize *normal* boys to be sexually dominant and *normal* girls to be sexually subordinate. The pornography industry is clearly a key area in the culture where "normal" boys learn to objectify and dehumanize girls and women. For example, Diane Rosenfeld, who teaches gender violence at Harvard Law School, says that her students worry about whether the male judge who watched a porn movie last night is taking her seriously at all.

But sexual objectification notwithstanding, Robert Jensen has written that people are mistaken in assuming that pornography is such a difficult and divisive issue because it is about sex. On the contrary, Jensen maintains that our culture struggles unsuccessfully with pornography because it is really about men's cruelty to women, and the pleasure men sometimes take in that cruelty. Like, many women in the anti-rape movement who have studied pornography, Jensen has spent thousands of hours coding and analyzing the content of mainstream porn videos and magazines. His research focuses on men's use of pornography, and how that might shape their attitudes toward women or their own sexuality. In his prolific popular writings on the subject, he cites numerous examples as evidence, realizing that people who are not familiar with contemporary heterosexual porn—especially women—can

be skeptical about feminist claims that porn is less about naked bodies and "sex," and more about the eroticization of men's dominance and control of women. The following extended quotation is from an article by Jensen that was published in 2004 in the *Sexual-Assault Report*.

> One of the ten scenes in the film *Gag Factor* #10, a 2002 release from J. M. Productions, begins with a woman and man having a picnic in a park. He jokes about wanting to use the romantic moment to make love to her mouth, and then stands and thrusts into her mouth while she sits on the blanket. Two other men who walk by join in. Saying things such as "Pump that face, pump that fucking face," "All the way down, choke, choke," and "That's real face fucking," they hold her head and push harder. One man grabs her hair and pulls her head into his penis in what his friend calls "the jackhammer." At this point she is grimacing and seems in pain. She then lies on the ground, and the men approach her from behind. "Eat that whole fucking dick. . . . You little whore, you like getting hurt," one says, as her face is covered with saliva. "Do you like getting your face fucked?" one asks. She can't answer. "Open your mouth if you like it," he says, and she opens her mouth. After they all ejaculate into her mouth, the semen flows out onto her body. After the final ejaculation, she reaches quickly for the wine glass, takes a large drink, and looks up at her boyfriend and says, "God, I love you baby." Her smile fades to a pained look of shame and despair.

Jensen recounts several similar scenes from a variety of bestselling porn videos, and then concludes that because the vast majority of people who rent or buy these sorts of videos are men, "we have to ask why some men find the infliction of pain on women during sexual activity either (1) Not an obstacle to their ability to achieve sexual pleasure, or (2) A factor that can enhance their sexual pleasure." The *optimistic* way to read the contemporary market demand for cruelty in pornography is that men and boys have been so desensitized to women's suffering that they are not bothered by the cruelty. This is a frightening development by itself, with serious implications for the present and future of relations between the sexes. If present trends continue, heterosexual sex—at least that which is represented as such in the commercial sex industry—would seem to be growing increasingly impersonal, and men's pleasure increasingly linked to displays of masculine power and dominance. In other words, transforming the rape culture could become even more of a difficult challenge than it is at present.

The more pessimistic assessment is that some men's sexual pleasure is actually enhanced by the mistreatment and degradation of women. Sadly, there is a wealth of documentary evidence which suggests that the producers of porn are quite conscious in their attempt to provide men with an outlet for their anger and feelings of sexual aggression. Consider the words of Max Hardcore, a popular porn director and actor whose name calls up over one million hits on Google. In an interview with *Hustler* magazine that is recounted by Robert Jensen and Gail Dines in their book *Pornography: The Production and Consumption of Inequality,* Hardcore said, "There's nothing I love more than when a girl insists to me that she won't take a cock in her ass, because—oh yes she will!"[5] He described his trademark as being able to "stretch a girl's asshole apart wide enough to stick a flashlight in it," and went on to say that he doesn't hate all women, just "stuck-up bitches." The porn performer Amanda McGuire told this story about him in *Icon* magazine: "He has made girls cry and lots of girls puke—that's not unusual. I was there once when he throat-fucked a girl so hard she puked and started bawling." Hardcore, whose work has been referred to by porn reviewers as "pseudo-pedophilia" because of how he dresses up his "actresses" to look like young girls, explained the challenges he faces making his films. "It's pretty easy to get a slut to spread solo for the camera," he said. "And quite a different matter to get her to take it up the ass and puke up piss."

In spite of these sorts of statements by men in the industry, its defenders—including women such as the "thinking man's porn star" Nina Hartley—downplay or even deny that porn culture is saturated with misogyny and sexism.[6] They point to the small percentage of porn written and produced by women, or they emphasize the growing popularity of "couples porn," which is typically less misogynistic and abusive than the majority of products that are aimed at the predominantly male market. However, veteran porn director and actor Bill Margold comes right out and admits what he and so many other pornographers are trying to do:

> I'd like to really show what I believe the men want to see: violence against women. I firmly believe that we serve a purpose by showing that. The most violent we can get is the cum shot in the face. Men get off behind that, because they can get even with the women they can't have. We try to inundate the world with orgasms in the face.

Examples like this of the sort of open misogyny and woman-hatred that comes out of the mainstream pornography industry still have the potential to shock young women, because due to the segmentation of the porn market, many of them have never been exposed to it. Dines says that her women students who think they know what's out there in porn are often devastated to learn what their boyfriends consider "normal." This is because the guys are more likely to use the "gonzo" porn referenced above to masturbate by themselves—with effects on their sexuality that we have not yet even begun to understand.

[. . .]

Girls and women suffer the most harm from a culture awash in misogynist pornography, but boys and men are hurt, too. It is important to discuss this hurt both for pragmatic reasons, and out of genuine concern for these boys and men. In order to stem the tide of cruelty, callousness, and brutality toward girls and women that is now mainstream fare from the porn industry, men and boys in sufficient numbers will need to make the decision to stop paying for porn magazines, videos, and Internet porn sites. Some men will be motivated to give up their porn habits as they develop a greater sensitivity to the damage that eroticized cruelty does to girls and women—inside and outside the porn industry. But altruistic concern for harm done to women cannot motivate anywhere near as many men and boys as enlightened self-interest. In other words, if they can be shown that porn hinders rather than facilitates a healthy sex life for *men,* there is at least a chance that enough men will reject it to truly make a difference. But unless heterosexual men perceive that they have a personal stake in a sexual culture that is not dominated by the cartoonish version of sexual fulfillment created by middle-aged businessmen in windowless studios in the San Fernando Valley outside Los Angeles, it is hard to see how the current trend toward greater acceptance of sexualized brutality will be reversed in coming generations.

[. . .]

NOTES

1. *"Men make, distribute, and get rich on porn."*: From personal conversation with Gail Dines.
2. *Until recently, men who have a public voice about pornography*: One notable and powerful exception to this is John Stoltenberg's 1989 collection of essays *Refusing to Be a Man: Essays on Sex and Justice.* Another thoughtful contribution to men's writing about pornography—pro and con—is Michal Kimmel's 1990 book *Men Confront Pornography,* a groundbreaking and highly readable collection of essays from men about various ways that pornography functions in men's lives.
3. *A new men's conversation about pornography is beginning to take shape:* Feminists who criticize the pornography industry are often characterized by "pro-porn feminists" as "prudes" and "Victorian moralists" who do not like the sexual or erotic choices some women make and hence seek to couch their discomfort in language about women's exploitation. Anti-porn feminists are also often accused of being anti-male, or of caricaturing heterosexual men's sexuality. As a heterosexual man who takes—in this book and elsewhere—a strong stance against the pornography industry for its misogyny and contribution to rape culture, I want to make it clear that I preemptively reject any attempt to characterize me as prudish or moralizing. Since my years in college when I led student opposition to the New Right and groups such as the Moral Majority, organized banned book displays, distributed contraceptive information to women and men, and participated in a pioneering peer sexuality education program at the University of Massachusetts, I have fought for women's sexual and reproductive freedom and will continue to do so for the rest of my life. Criticism of the pornography industry is NOT criticism of women's fundamental right to sexual expression, nor is it inherently anti-male. In fact, as I have argued in this book, in spite of some people's efforts to produce "nonviolent, non-exploitative, non-sexist" erotic porn, I believe the pornography industry as a whole over the past generation has done incalculable damage to both women's and men's sexuality.
4. *Robert Jensen . . . painfully describes as "three holes and two hands"*: See Jensen, 2004.
5. *"There's nothing I love more than when a girl insists to me"*: From Dines, Jensen, and Russo, p. 81.
6. *Its defenders—including women such as the "thinking man's porn star" Nina Hartley:* For a fascinating left/feminist response to Nina Hartley's defense of pornography that links opposition to the porn industry's exploitation of women (and men) to other forms of class exploitation, see Stan Goff's piece, entitled "The Porn Debate: Wrapping Profit in the Flag," available at: www.notforsalebook.org/Articles/Goff_Hartley.html

33. • *Claire Goldberg Moses*

'WHAT'S IN A NAME?' ON WRITING THE HISTORY OF FEMINISM (2012)

Claire Goldberg Moses is professor emerita of women's studies at the University of Maryland, College Park. She is the author of *French Feminism in the Nineteenth Century* and coeditor of *U.S. Women in Collective Struggle: A Feminist Studies Anthology* and *Feminism, Socialism, and French Romanticism.* From 1977 to 2011 Moses served as the editorial director for *Feminist Studies*, the oldest scholarly journal in the field of women's studies. "'What's in a Name?' On Writing the History of Feminism" was originally written as a keynote address for a 1998 international conference in Beijing and then published by *Feminist Studies* in 2012. In the article, Moses analyzes the use of the term "feminism" as a unifying term for activism focused on improving the lives of women. She asks what's at stake in using a common identifier, and what's lost if we don't.

[. . .]

In my work as a historian, I focus on women's collective activities in the West, especially in the United States and Europe, and especially those activities that are intended to further the interests of women.[1] This presentation is intended to share a small part of that work with you and also to explore my most recent interest, which is to examine the names we use for this kind of collective activity—by women and on behalf of women—and then to question the significance of our naming practices.[2] In other words, what is at stake in naming a particular form of women's collective action "feminism"? When is it not called "feminism"? What happens when this distinction is parsed too carefully? What does the history of the scope of the term "feminism" tell us about its political successes and shortcomings?

[. . .]

Do women's historians in the United States claim that all women's groups are "feminist"? If not, what makes some groups "feminist" and others not? . . . In Western Europe and the Americas, historians typically use the word "feminist" to describe women's collective activities to advance women's condition; but the meaning of "feminism" is neither stable nor fixed. As a historian, I know for example that the word is often assigned to women's collective actions that occurred before the word even existed. But if the word did not yet exist, how do historians decide which activities are to be labeled "feminist"? And if we label some activities "feminist" and not others, are we not constructing—rather than identifying—feminism?

For example, when studying the history of nineteenth-century women's collective activities, if we historians of the twentieth century choose to look at the activities of nineteenth-century women of the privileged classes only—perhaps because they wrote books about their activities and therefore make our research easy for us—and in fact look at only some of their activities (for example, their organizational activity to win voting rights for women—perhaps because it is easy to study organizational records), then we would be defining as "feminist" something that is narrow in class interest.[3] But since the word "feminist" did not actually exist, and it is therefore we—as historians—and not those women, nor any other women, who actually use the word to label their activities, what would happen to our understanding of the meaning of the word "feminism" if historians used it for another group of women who also worked collectively to advance women's development? For example, if historians used it for Black women who, in the years following their emancipation from slavery, created organizations intended to overcome the indignities of racism? Their efforts were also collective: in their Black women's clubs they organized separately from men, they also focused on advancing women's development, and they challenged standard notions of permissible "womanly" actions both within and beyond the community of Black women and men. Would not this make them "feminists"? What would happen to our understanding of the word "feminism" if we attached it to the efforts of women industrial workers to improve their conditions of work—efforts that directly challenged men who were either their employers or their coworkers (who thought that all working-class organizing should be by and for men)? What would happen to our understanding of the word "feminism" if we attached it to the power exercised by American Indian women in tribal councils? Recent histories, for example, have now identified close personal connections between Seneca Indians and famous voting rights activists, and we now know that Indian women played an important role in shaping the goals of what we have labeled US feminism.[4]

In other words, *history* is not simply *the past;* rather it is the way we construct a narrative of the past. Historians do not simply uncover history; they construct it in the way in which we assign meanings and make sense of the mass of materials that we find from the past. In the practice of women's history in the United States and Western Europe today, the very word "feminist" is hotly debated, and these debates tell us as much about disagreements concerning present-day politics as they do about the past.

[. . .]

It is interesting for us today to reflect on the broad usage of the term "feminist" in the late nineteenth century and the narrowing of its usage in the early twentieth century, because this history might tell us something about the present. In recent decades in the United States, we have witnessed, first, a recuperation of the word "feminist" (for many whose knowledge of women's history was limited, it seemed like a newly invented word). We then watched as the term became very widely used among all those engaged in an increasingly popular agenda for women's development. But at some point in the 1980s, and increasingly so in the 1990s, we once again witnessed the narrowing of the term's usage. What explains this? Does it prove a lessening of commitment to gender equality? Is it simply a matter of semantics—a desire to change the name but not the commitment to equality? What do people who continue to call themselves "feminists" mean when they apply the term to themselves? What do people who disparage the term intend to disparage? To examine these questions, we should look at feminism's most recent history, from the 1970s to the present.

The recuperation of the word "feminist" for activities on behalf of women's development happened in the West in the 1970s, a full decade at least after the reemergence of a visible and effective movement for women's equality and development. Following the election of the progressive Democrat John Kennedy in 1960, women who had ties to his administration and to members of the Democratic Congress were able to use their influence to advance women's development. They focused on employment and education, and (not surprisingly, given that their influence was based on their ties to government leaders) their strategy was to press for new laws in these areas. And they were successful: a 1963 law insisted that women be paid the same as men when they worked in the same jobs; a 1964 law stated that all employment must be open to women and men alike; and a 1972 law made unequal treatment of women and men in education illegal.

At the same time, a different group of women, younger (many were only students in universities) and not yet established in professional careers, were also beginning to agitate for women's development. This group's politics, however, were to the left of the Democrats in power. Like the earliest nineteenth-century voting-rights advocates, they came to political consciousness in male-led emancipatory movements. In the 1960s, these were the civil rights movement for equal rights for Black people and the movement against the United States war in Vietnam. And like nineteenth-century voting-rights advocates, they came to an awareness of women's oppression both because of the emancipatory rhetoric of these other movements, but also because they found themselves disparaged—even in these progressive movements—simply because they were women.

At first, these women named themselves—in the language of international, anticolonial struggles—the Women's Liberation Movement. And they organized quite differently from the ways that the women with connections to the Democratic Party leadership had organized—in informal and small groups where consciousness raising was a central activity. Most importantly, they turned their attention to a host of questions that were not likely to be addressed simply by passing laws: questions concerning the private relationships between women and men. "The personal is political" was the slogan that best summed up their politics. Their goal was to point out that the questions that Western governments traditionally refused to address—questions, according to these governments, that were "private" matters (such as violence against women in families)—were the very basis of male power.

It was the women of the Women's Liberation Movement who first reclaimed the term "feminist" for their politics: perhaps because the name "Women's Liberation Movement" was unwieldy; perhaps also because the name identified them with other radical liberatory movements—including the Chinese Cultural Revolution—and they recognized that the majority of US women were unlikely to use those words for themselves; and perhaps, too, because the first books in the renewed practice of women's history had recovered women's earlier struggles and

had named these struggles "feminism."[5] By the 1970s, the new women's studies scholarship may have encouraged their desire to connect to a historical tradition that was widely acceptable. (Who, after all, in the 1970s, still thought it was wrong that women had the right to vote alongside men?)

However it happened, though, by the mid-1970s US women advocating women's equality—whether they were closely connected to the liberals in the Democratic Party or were aligned with more left-wing groups, whether they advocated a legal strategy or were organizing in small consciousness-raising groups, or whether they focused on education and work or on sharing housework and child rearing with men—had all come to agree on the term "feminist" for their work. This was the moment in history when use of the term "feminist" was perhaps the most widespread and seemed acceptable to the largest group of advocates for women's equality, even though their views often differed sharply.

Feminism, so broadly accepted, was a term, then, that encompassed many different views about womanhood and many different strategies. Some people identified the differences among feminists by speaking of "liberal feminists," "socialist feminists," "radical feminists," "cultural feminists," "spiritual feminists," "lesbian separatist feminists," "Black feminists," "multicultural feminists," "Christian feminists," "Jewish feminists," and more. In their strategies, some feminists gave priority to sexuality or issues of reproduction; some gave priority to work-related issues; some called for a socialist revolution; some defended capitalism, but noted that reforms were necessary to include women in capitalism's benefits; some stressed the necessity for a new psychology of women if women were to empower themselves; and some stressed that state and economic structures had to change. On the theoretical level, some believed that women had been socialized differently from men and in ways that disempowered them. Some stressed that women were naturally different from and perhaps even superior to men, especially in their capacity for interpersonal relationships.

The gains for women during this period when feminism was so broadly construed were enormous. Laws intended to equalize work opportunities were not only passed, but were supervised by government administrations to assure that they were implemented. Laws equalized women's access to bank credit and their right to own and control property and earnings. Laws also guaranteed women's equal access to higher education, and for the first time in US history, women entered universities in numbers equal to men. Problems that had never been identified as problems before were now named: the double standard that punished women for sexual behavior that was approved of for men was challenged; rape was identified as a crime of violence by men against women, no longer as deserved behavior for women's sinful ways; wife battering was identified as a crime against women, no longer as a husband's prerogative; women's "double day" as wage worker and home worker was challenged and men learned that they, too, could cook and clean and care for children alongside their wives who now worked as many hours outside the home as men did. It was no longer considered appropriate to represent women as stupid or clumsy or as existing solely to satisfy men's sexual needs on television and in other forms of media. Women writers, women's experiences in history, and women's social issues became respected topics for academic research.

Women who learned to proudly name themselves feminists in the 1970s are quick to point out that all of these successes are partial and that our goals have not yet been met. Worse, there are new problems emerging out of the social revolution of the sexes. For example, with most women now fully employed in the waged workforce, the lack of government assistance for childcare has become a truly acute problem in the United States. Also, nearly three decades of legislation favoring corporate interests over workers' interests has resulted in an absolute decline in the standard of living of very poor Americans—women and men alike. The gains for women, in other words, are increasingly leaving behind poor women. Moreover, the gains for women

in education are happening at the same time that government funds for education have been cut back so that schooling for women and men alike is worsening. In other words, the transformation of women's lives since the mid-1960s has been enormous, but it is neither complete nor all encompassing.

That brings us to the present moment when, as I said above, the use of the term "feminism" in the United States is narrowing once again. Since the 1990s, my undergraduate students in the university have, for the most part, ceased to call themselves feminists. This always surprises me because they have not disavowed feminist views, only the name that is given to these views. For example, when I would ask them if they believe that women and men should be treated equally in the law, they would overwhelmingly answer affirmatively. If I were to ask them if women should have an equal chance to be educated, they would all respond "yes." I could push them for more detail by asking if they believe that women should be limited to only five percent of any class of medical students (as used to be the case before Title IX of the Education Amendments of 1972 made this illegal), they would cry out against what they considered a grave injustice. They would respond in similar outrage to the suggestion that women should be ineligible for scholarships or even that parents might expect their daughters to leave school for work at age eighteen so that they, the daughters, could pay for their brothers to attend university (as happened with my mother and most of her women friends). If I asked if they wished to prepare themselves for professional careers, they would answer "yes." And I know that they would find it unacceptable if a potential employer told them he only hired men for management-level positions or if the employer had two separate pay scales for the same jobs—one for men, the other for women.

These gains are, of course, what women calling themselves "feminists" struggled to obtain. In the 1970s and 1980s, there were many people who were not feminists, who did not wish women to have equal rights, and who opposed the changes noted above. My students would not agree with these opponents. So why was their naming different from mine? What do they think that a "feminist" is that they are not?

In questioning them I have found that there are many different answers to this question—sometimes different for each one of my students. Some of them are unaware of the meanings I assign to the term "feminism," and they have little understanding of the history of women's advances. Rather, they reject the distorted version of feminism that has grown increasingly common on television shows and in movies. In these depictions, feminists—or oftentimes simply strong and proud women—are more and more represented as evil (sometimes even murderers), unfeeling, or "losers" who are never able to find personal happiness.[6] Rarely are feminists presented as just ordinary women, as ordinary as I am, for example. Many of my students are convinced by media representations of what feminism is and have actually come to believe that the caricature is true. Who then can blame them for their desire to distance themselves from these portrayals of mean, crazy, or ridiculous women? Unfortunately, feminists do not control the major corporations who, in turn, control the media.

Others of my students, however, know that feminists are actually pretty ordinary women, as ordinary as I am—and as their mothers are. For them, feminism is old fashioned, appropriate maybe for the 1970s, but not for young women today. They wish to invent something original—different from what their mothers have already invented. For them, feminist struggles against rape and representations of women as sexual objects make us seem as old fashioned as our grandmothers probably seemed to me and my friends. Some of these students are my most radical students, but they have also often associated feminism with racism and prejudice. There is a literature, of course, by antiracists that critiques feminism's historical insensitivity to issues of race that would prove the point. Many of these same students call themselves "womanist," adopting the term Alice Walker invented to convey the special power and perspectives of Black women. But these students are

not always aware of scholarship that also names as "feminist" the activities of Black women and other women of color, both in the nineteenth century and from the 1960s to the present day (for example, histories by Rosalyn Terborg-Penn and Carla Peterson and the anthology *Words of Fire* edited by Beverly Guy-Sheftall).[7] The 2001 anthology of writings from the Women's Liberation Movement, *Dear Sisters*, collected by Rosalyn Baxandall and Linda Gordon, is especially rich in material documenting the feminist activities of Black radical women in the 1960s and 1970s.[8] These students are often even unaware that Alice Walker, in describing her "womanist" woman, defined her as a "feminist," seeking to adjoin feminism to a feisty tradition of Black female rebelliousness rather than to oppose it.[9]

Finally, in discussing this issue with my students, I have discovered another reason that they dissociate themselves from feminism—their alienation from politics, of any kind, but especially progressive politics. Even those students who are progressive—and vote that way—disdain political activism. . . .

[. . .]

Does any of this matter? If my students agree with feminist values, does it matter that they disavow the name? Perhaps you might think not: what, after all, is in a name? But I look back on feminism's history and women's history and find that the periods in which our gains were most striking were when we used the word "feminism" most broadly, imbuing it with multiple meanings, and thereby created the largest sense of belonging, a shared aspiration for women's empowerment. During the periods when the meaning and usage of feminism narrowed, we became suspicious of those who spoke for women's equality but argued for different strategies from ours. The result was never more perfect strategies; rather, it was diminished energy. We turned against each other instead of turning against the forces oppressing women.

Over the past several years, I have been discussing this issue with different audiences, particularly in other countries. This question has become an important one, especially since the 1985 and 1995 United Nations world conferences on women, in Nairobi and in Beijing respectively. At those conferences, I met women from all over the world who are joined together by the shared desire to better women's condition, although their priorities and strategies may differ. They are struggling right now with just this question. In their countries, also, "feminism" and "feminists" have been disparaged. Feminism is viewed as another form of cultural imperialism whose associations with the capitalist and imperialist West make it virtually useless in the analysis of women's experiences outside of the United States and Europe. It is caricatured as a movement that makes all men the enemy in a sexual and political struggle, forcing women (always) to choose between the struggle for women's equality and national liberation movements or socialism. This is in spite of the fact that feminist history has most often been one of coalition with movements of national liberation, with socialism, with antiracist struggles—and with men as leaders of these movements. . . .

[. . .]

Again I ask: does it matter how we name ourselves? After all, the struggle for women's equality could continue by a multitude of other names. I'd like to suggest it does matter. It matters because our history matters. It matters because those who distort our history are not motivated by a concern for women's equality. It matters because, in this increasingly globalized world, women are strengthened by also belonging to a global movement and reflecting their commitment to a global movement in their naming. It matters, in other words, for us to believe ourselves joined in a common vision of women's empowerment.

But for this vision of an international women's movement to be achieved, we must learn these lessons from the history of feminism: that "feminism" has had different meanings to different people in different times and places; that we must allow these different meanings to emerge to address the needs and priorities of women in their context; that feminism can never define sexism as the only oppressive force in women's lives. Since such things as class relations, structural poverty, illiteracy, hunger, racism, ethnocentrism, and imperialism figure prominently in the oppression of women, feminism must be inclusive, flexible, and willing to accept contradiction. But if we learn these lessons, the benefits will be great. However our strategies, our priorities, our views might differ, we shall know that we are joined in support of each other, in support of women, and in support of women's empowerment.

NOTES

1. My reference to the West in this article reflected, specifically, that the lecture was originally presented in China (and thereafter in Korea) where an East/West divide is a common point of reference.
2. On feminism in France, see my *French Feminism in the Nineteenth Century* (New York: SUNY Press, 1984); and Claire Goldberg Moses and Leslie Wahl Rabine, *Feminism, Socialism, and French Romanticism* (Bloomington: Indiana University Press, 1993). For feminism in the United States, see Claire Goldberg Moses and Heidi Hartmann, eds., *U.S. Women in Struggle: A Feminist Studies Anthology* (Urbana: University of Illinois Press, 1995). On the political stakes of "naming" feminisms,

see especially Claire Goldberg Moses, "Debating the Present/Writing the Past: 'Feminism' in French History and Historiography," *Radical History Review* 52 (Winter 1992): 79–94; and "Made in America: 'French Feminism' in Academia," *Feminist Studies* 24, no. 2 (Summer 1998): 241–74.
3. An example of this construction of history is the anthology, edited by Miriam Schneir, *Feminism: The Essential Historical Writings* (New York: Random House, 1972). For many years, this anthology served to teach students what was the so-called First Wave, and therefore it is an important historical document. I believe it is crucial that students of feminism understand the origin of our

"knowledge" of feminism's history and recognize the limited sources upon which this "knowledge" is based. In Schneir's case, the source was primarily Susan B. Anthony, Elizabeth Cady Stanton, and Mathilda Gage's *The History of Woman Suffrage*—a source that constructed a history that placed Stanton and Anthony at the center of that history and limited the range of feminist activities and writings to those written by them or presented in their presence. Although most present-day faculty would shun an anthology such as Schneir's as both out of date and racist, I consider it an important historical artifact in and of itself and especially useful as a starting point to discuss the concept of "constructions of historical narratives." Interestingly, Schneir also included a few documents written by famous nineteenth-century European (mostly male) socialists—thereby presenting a narrative of a historical feminism that united socialists with—in the lingo of early twentieth-century socialists—"bourgeois feminists." Given Schneir's leftist background, and that of so many other radical feminist women in the late 1960s and early 1970s, this narrative presented a history that met our then needs, indicating the interplay of present-day politics with historical constructions.

4. In a course I taught for several years before retiring, Feminist Theories and Women's Movements: Genealogies, I assign selections from Sally Wagner, *The Untold Story of the Iroquois Influence on Early Feminists: Essays* (Aberdeen, SD: Sky Carrier Press, 1996).

5. In the 1960s—with the renewal of interest in women's equality and civil rights—a number of high quality books on the nineteenth-century movement were published, among which were Eleanor Flexner, *A Century of Struggle: The Woman's Rights Movement in the United States* (New York: Atheneum, 1968); and Aileen Kraditor, *Ideas of the Woman Suffrage Movement, 1890–1920* (New York: Columbia University Press, 1965). Note, however, that neither used the term "feminism" for the movement. Only with the emergence of the women's liberation movement is the link made back

to feminism. Several books that connected the women's movement of the nineteenth century to feminism and popularized this relationship as they became widely used in women's studies classrooms were William O'Neill, *Everyone Was Brave: The Rise and Fall of Feminism in America* (New York: Quadrangle, 1969); and in 1973, two published anthologies, Miriam Schneir's *Feminism: The Essential Historical Writings;* and Alice Rossi, *The Feminist Papers: From Adams to de Beauvoir* (New York: Columbia University Press, 1973). Also important was Ellen Carol Dubois, *Feminism and Suffrage: The Emergence of an Independent Women's Movement in America, 1848–1869* (Ithaca, NY: Cornell University Press, 1978).

6. Popular culture representations of feminists may always have been ambivalent, but I'm thinking here about a particularly sharp shift that I saw occurring in the late 1980s with films such as *Fatal Attraction,* starring Glenn Close ("liberated woman" and murderer), and *Broadcast News,* with Holly Hunter ("liberated woman," condemned to loneliness).

7. Rosalyn Terborg-Penn, *African American Women in the Struggle for the Vote, 1850–1920* (Bloomington: Indiana University Press, 1978); Carla Peterson, *"Doers of the Word": African-American Woman Speakers and Writers in the North, 1830-1880* (New Brunswick, NJ: Rutgers University Press, 1995); and Beverly Guy-Sheftall, *Words of Fire: An Anthology of African-American Feminist Thought* (New York: New Press, 1995).

8. Rosalind Baxandall and Linda Gordon, *Dear Sisters: Dispatches from the Women's Liberation Movement* (New York: Basic Books, 2001).

9. See the first of Alice Walker's four-part definition for "womanist": "A black feminist or feminist of color. From the black folk expression of mothers to female children, 'You acting womanish,' i.e., like a woman. Usually referring to outrageous, audacious, courageous or *willful* behavior." Alice Walker, *In Search of Our Mothers' Gardens* (San Diego: Harcourt Brace Javonovich, 1983), xi.

34. • *Tina Vasquez*

IT'S TIME TO END THE LONG HISTORY OF FEMINISM FAILING TRANSGENDER WOMEN (2014)

Tina Vasquez is a writer whose work focuses on issues related to gender, sexuality, and race. She was formerly the associate editor of *Black Girl Dangerous* and has written for blogs and websites like Jezebel, Bitch Media, and Everyday Feminism. Her article "It's Time to End the Long History of Feminism Failing Transgender Women" won a 2015 Impact Award from The Media Consortium. The article analyzes the use of feminist discourse to discriminate against the trans community.

[. . .]

In her 2013 article "Unpacking Transphobia in Feminism" on the website The TransAdvocate, writer Emma Allen explained that radical feminists such as [Cathy] Brennan assert that trans women are a problem because they perpetuate the idea that "gender roles are biologically determined rather than socially constructed" is the antithesis of feminism. "Radical feminists claim that gender oppression can only be abolished by getting rid of the whole concept of gender and they view transgender people as a threat to that ideal," Allen wrote.

Janice Raymond's 1979 book *The Transsexual Empire: The Making of the She-Male* shaped the notion that transgender rights have no place in feminism. Max Wolf Valerio reflected on the book in his 2006 memoir *The Testosterone Files: My Hormonal and Social Transformation from Female to Male,* writing that "Raymond postulated that all transsexuals were dupes of the patriarchy, 'mutilating' their bodies in order to live out stereotyped sex roles instead of changing those roles through a rigorously applied program of radical feminism." Other feminist writing of the 1970s also hit on the anti-transgender ideas. Mary Daly's 1978 book *Gyn/Ecology* compared

the drag queen "phenomenon" to blackface and included assertions such as: "The surgeons and hormone therapists of the transsexual kingdom . . . can be said to produce feminine persons. They cannot produce women."

Drawing from that history, Brennan, fellow attorney Elizabeth Hungerford, and other modern-day feminists continue to actively question the inclusion of trans people in women's spaces. These feminists refer to themselves as "radical feminists" or "gender critical feminists." In 2008, trans women and trans advocates started referring to this group as "transexclusionary radical feminists" or TERFs, a term Brennan considers a slur. Cristan Williams, managing editor of The TransAdvocate and founder of Houston's Transgender Center and the Transgender Archive, asserts that TERFs should be recognized as a hate group by the Southern Poverty Law Center. (To that end, a petition calling for the Southern Poverty Law Center to track the activities of the Gender Identity Watch website as a hate group was recently circulated and garnered nearly 7,000 signatures.)

This debate is not just feminist-theory inside baseball. Though outspoken, politically active trans-exclusionary radical feminists are relatively few in number, their influence on legislation and mainstream perceptions of transgender people is powerful and real.

For example, transgender people were able to readily obtain government-funded healthcare prior to 1980. That year, Janice Raymond wrote a report for the Reagan administration called "Technology on the Social and Ethical Aspects of Transsexual Surgery" which informed the official federal position on medical care for transgender people. The paper's conclusion reads, "The elimination of transsexualism is not best achieved by legislation prohibiting transsexual treatment and surgery, but rather by legislation that limits it and by other legislation that lessens the support given to sex-role stereotyping." In her book *Transgender History*, Susan Stryker says that the government curtailed transgender access to government social services under Reagan, "In part in response to anti-transgender feminist arguments that dovetailed with conservative politics."

[. . .]

The belief that transgender women are "not really women" sadly finds traction among many people—not just conservative politicians, but some mainstream feminists. However, few people use the tactics of the most outspoken trans-exclusionary activists to promote their ideas.

"TERFs do a good job of colonizing feminist discourse by framing their hate as a 'feminist critique of gender,' thereby representing the hate that follows as the feminist position. It's not," says Trans-Advocate editor Williams.

The problem is that when trans-exclusionary feminists speak, a lot of people listen. Take the Michigan Womyn's Festival for example which takes place each August and attracts performers like Le Tigre and the Indigo Girls. Since its inception in 1976, the feminist music festival has asked that only "womyn-born-womyn" attend. In 2006, the festival's founder, Lisa Vogel, defended her stance, writing, "As feminists, we call upon the transwomen's community to help us maintain womyn-only space, including spaces created by and for womyn-born womyn."

In response to a 2013 petition opposing the festival's ongoing exclusion of trans women, Vogel continued to defend the festival's stance, writing, "The Festival, for a single precious week, is intended for womyn who at birth were deemed female, who were raised as girls, and who identify as womyn. I believe that womyn-born womyn is a lived experience that constitutes its own distinct gender identity."

This idea that "women-born-women" need space away from transgender women impacts not just music festivals, but legislation. As policies promoting the creation of gender-neutral bathrooms continue to gain traction around the country, Brennan and other trans-exclusionary feminists have devoted time to arguing that trans women are somehow dangerous to cisgender women in public restrooms. In 2011, Brennan and Elizabeth Hungerford teamed up to write a letter to the United Nations urging opposition to laws prohibiting discrimination based on gender identity and gender expression. In her interview with Bustle, Brennan explained her thinking:

Our whole lives we are raised very much aware of our vulnerability as women, so I don't understand why when a man says he's a woman, all of a sudden the penis is no longer (an issue) . . . Men rape women and girls in bathrooms all the time, so it's not like women's concerns about that aren't reasonable. And these laws are broadly enough written to justify the entry of anyone into a (women-only) space.

To imply that trans women pose a threat to cisgender women in restrooms is misinformation that preys on unfounded fears. I searched for news stories in which transgender women have assaulted cisgender women in bathrooms, coming across nothing but news stories detailing the attacks on transgender women themselves.

Indeed, if anyone is in harm's way in public restrooms, it's trans people, who can face abuse or assault no matter which restroom they choose. A 2011 survey of 6,000 transgender Americans found that more than half of the people surveyed reported experiencing harassment in public accommodations, including bathrooms, restaurants, and hotels. This is why there has been a push to make public restrooms a little safer for those who are trans, including legislation in Philadelphia that requires all new or renovated city-owned buildings to include gender-neutral bathrooms. There's also California's School Success and Opportunity Act, which mandates that transgender students must be included in school activities on the basis of their identified gender rather than their assigned sex. This extends to using bathrooms and locker rooms consistent with their gender. The Transgender Law Center heralded the law, which passed in August 2013, as a change that will save lives.

In contrast to that positive, progressive narrative around gender-neutral bathrooms, there was one story about the "dangers" of trans girls in girl's restrooms that popped up in the fall. In October, the right-wing organization Pacific Justice Institute altered press that a transgender teenager was harassing students in the girls' restroom at Florence High School in Colorado. The *Daily Mail*, Fox Nation, and at least one local TV station picked up the story, with Fox posting a short piece including the misgendering line, "When parents complained, school officials said the boy's rights as a transgender trumped their daughters' privacy rights." While some outlets referred to the minor as Jane Doe, Gender Identity Watch posted the name of the teen in question, describing her as a "male student" who "claims to be transgender."

It turns out, the story was false. The TransAdvocate's Cristan Williams quickly called the school's superintendent to inquire about the story and was told that the story was based on the complaint of one parent who was opposed to allowing the transgender student to use the girl's restroom; there were no actual reported incidents of harassment.

After this incident, the teen's mom said her daughter was struggling with harassment because of the story and was in such bad shape, the family had her on suicide watch.

It's clear from this example that trans-exclusionary feminists don't just spend their days making waves on social media—some get mainstream attention and hold successful, powerful positions. Cathy Brennan has used her skills as a lawyer to threaten legal action against a magazine that published an article critical of her. She also served as a liaison

to the American Bar Association's Commission on Sexual Orientation and Gender Identity from 2008-2009. She appeared on Roseanne Barr's weekly radio program specifically to discuss her radical feminism and beliefs on female biology and gender identity. Trans-exclusionary feminists Janice Raymond and Mary Daly worked as well-respected, tenured professors. Like-minded feminist thought leader Sheila Jeffreys is still an established professor in Australia. Her forthcoming book *Gender Hurts*, from major publisher Routledge, will argue that "the ideology and practice of transgenderism" is harmful.

This approach to feminism is beyond troubling—it's downright dangerous, considering that the transgender community is one of the nation's most vulnerable. According to a 2011 study from the Anti-Violence Project, 40 percent of anti-LGBT murder victims were transgender women. A report from the National Transgender Discrimination Survey conducted by the National Gay & Lesbian Task Force and the National Center for Transgender Equality, found that transgender people faced double the rate of unemployment of the general population, with 63 percent of the transgender people surveyed reporting they experienced a serious act of discrimination that majorly affected their ability to sustain themselves. These numbers are even worse for trans people of color, especially trans women of color, the deaths of whom have been deemed a "state of emergency."

For these reasons, the concern these feminists elicit among trans women is serious. Trans blogger and womanist Monica Roberts has been blogging as TransGriot for years, discussing the intersections between race and the violence experienced by trans women of color and writing about the importance of knowing black trans history. Roberts routinely writes about how closely white privilege is tied to radical feminists' ability to incite scorn toward a vulnerable minority and not only get away with it, but remain gainfully employed in the process.

[. . .]

It has been said that feminism has failed the transgender community. It's hard to disagree. Trans women have been weathering a storm of hate and abuse in the name of feminism for decades now and for the most part, cisgender feminists have failed to speak out about it or push against it.

[. . .]

. . . It seems the tide is turning. People in queer communities are demanding that the silencing of trans women be addressed. Cisgender feminists are speaking out about Brennan's activism. Radical feminists like Julie Bindel are distancing themselves from trans-exclusionary groups. Healthcare is becoming more accessible for trans people, including the removal of health exclusions. Workplace discrimination bills are being expanded to encompass gender identity and as discussed previously, gender-neutral bathrooms are becoming law. "Transphobic" is now in the *Oxford English Dictionary* and even Facebook now has the option to set your gender to "custom."

Though change has been far too slow and painful, trans pioneer Autumn Sandeen, who was the first to be officially recognized by the Pentagon as a transgender service member, expresses hope that transphobia is becoming less acceptable.

"Every major gay-rights organization includes trans people in their mission statements. Trans people are more public than ever before and the media is moving beyond telling transition stories. Even though we've experienced so much hate from certain feminists, the real support is coming from feminist and queer circles," Sandeen said. "Transphobia is no longer acceptable in the name of feminism, so while people like Brennan are free to express their anti-trans sentiments and meet with like-minded feminists while excluding trans women, there is now a cost for expressing those viewpoints."

[. . .]

Trans women have been saddled with the responsibility of taking on trans-exclusionary feminists for far too long—but it's not their issue to deal with alone. Cisgender feminists, such as myself, have to make it clear that our feminism loves and supports trans women and that we will fight against transphobia. As Williams said, it's time to expose trans-exclusionary feminists for who they really are.

[. . .]

SECTION THREE

Cultural Debates in Women's, Gender and Sexuality Studies

TABLE OF CONTENTS

LEARNING OBJECTIVES

By the end of this section, you will have a better understanding of:

1. How historical constructions of family and work are connected and significant to understanding contemporary formations of gender and sexuality.

2. How social constructions of gender, race, class, sexuality, age, and nationality stratify the labor market.

3. How intersectional approaches to reproductive politics crafts contested meanings about reproductive choice and reproductive justice.

4. How gender-based violence is tied to structures of race, class, sexuality, age, and nationality.

5. How popular culture and media representations play an integral role in understanding gender, race, class, sexuality, religion, age, ability, and nationality.

Feminist and queer scholars, activists, and practitioners do not all agree on how to address and analyze topics examined in women's, gender and sexuality studies. This dynamic nature of interdisciplinarity gives the field its breadth, depth, and vibrancy. In this section, readings about gender, sexuality, and the family; labor market; reproductive politics; gendered violence; and popular culture and media representations ask you to consider multiple points of view. Social, political, and deeply human issues are full of tensions, and as Audre Lorde so eloquently evokes in *Sister Outsider*, our intellectual, political, and creative work is required in order to find multiple paths toward social change and justice.

RETHINKING THE FAMILY

Families or kinship systems are central organizing structures of people globally. As sites of both reproduction and production, they take care of our basic human needs as well as provide love, care, and discipline (and sometimes neglect and abuse); teach us about who we are as gendered and sexualized beings as well as shape our belief systems and perspectives on social issues; and prepare us for the public worlds of school, work, and, if we choose, to have our own families. Early feminist scholars Louise Tilly and Joan Scott argue in *Women, Work & Family* that the gendered labor within families is deeply tied to economic structures. While it matters that (some, not all) women bear children, the cultural meanings ascribed to motherhood, fatherhood, the role of children, and what "counts" as work are social constructions woven into socioeconomic systems and dominant political ideologies. This section briefly analyzes the social institutions of marriage and family as they shifted from home-based agriculture to industrialization and again under postindustrial neoliberalism.

Prevailing ideas about marriage and families are deeply tied to relations of power. In the United States, it may appear as though the **nuclear family** is "normal" and has been central to development of the society, yet this view is oversimplified and historically inaccurate, especially from an intersectional approach. From historians' marking of their arrival in Jamestown, Virginia, in 1607 to the end of the colonial period in 1763, the labor of white, Christian **settler-colonials** in the New World was gendered, but the work was valued for its contributions to the family and community. In this context, family is defined more as an extended kinship network since it required having as many children as possible to produce needed goods for exchange, sale, and use.

Dominant constructions of marriage and family were (and are) deeply tied to property ownership, social constructions of race and gender, and religious beliefs that shape what constitutes moral behavior. The ideal marriage of white, wealthy men and women meant that the household was a combination of opposite but complementary gender roles. Men dominated the public sphere, while women's domain was in the home. Men were understood to be strong, rational, and provide for the family, while "[t]he attributes of True Womanhood, by which a woman judged herself and was judged by her husband, her neighbors, and society were piety, purity, submissiveness, and domesticity" (Welter 152). Women's responsibilities were to love, honor, and obey their husbands and rear the children. Christianity and nineteenth-century law anchored men's superiority by naming women as property—first of their fathers and later their husbands. While this may seem like a far cry from how marriage is practiced today, Rebecca Barrett-Fox makes clear in "Constraints and Freedoms in Conservative Christian Women's Lives" (included in this section) that "gender fundamentalism" is alive and well in the Fundamentalist Church of Jesus Christ of Latter Day Saints (FDLS) Church, Quiverfull, and other conservative religious groups. Men continue to exercise power and control over women in the name of religious practices; in the case of the FDLS, this includes polygamy.

The modern idea of gendered division of labor was further solidified with American industrialist Henry Ford's introduction of the Five Dollar Day in 1914. When the Ford Motor Company proposed its higher standard of living, the intention was to stabilize, standardize, and control its male workforce while creating an economically comfortable American middle class. By offering men a livable wage, it meant

Nuclear family: social construction that crafts the family as a married man and woman living together with at least one child.

Settler-colonials: white Europeans who immigrated to the Americas; the term is used to emphasize how indigenous peoples inhabited the nation now called the United States.

that more married working-class and immigrant women could stay home in greater numbers. The legacy of this paradigm is that men emerged as the culturally appropriate "breadwinner" for the family, and it provided the foundation for what would become the gender wage gap (discussed in detail in the Gender and Sexuality in the Labor Market section). Moreover, wage work associated with the domestic sphere—jobs that include cleaning, working with children, and caregiving—retain less cultural value and today disproportionately affect low-income women of color and immigrant women. In her essay "Love, Labor, and Lorde: The Tools My Grandmother Gave Me" (included in this section), Jessica Birch considers a feminist response to the devaluing of domestic and care work.

Despite the concerted efforts of religion, government, and industry to secure the nuclear family as the dominant ideological and organizing structure in the United States, family structures and relationships have varied greatly historically and today. As historian Stephanie Coontz argues, the nuclear family in the United States is a heteronormative cultural construction representing a nostalgic past that never really existed the way we might imagine. In "It's All in the Family," Patricia Hill Collins names family as "an imagined traditional family ideal . . . and a privileged exemplar of intersectionality" (62-3). This section explores the multiple ways the state exerts control over kinship ties and specifically the ways in which family was and is torn apart through colonization, slavery, mass incarceration, and immigration; historically denied to lesbian and gay people because of heteronormative definitions of marriage; and is configured in contemporary US households.

Prior to contact with settler-colonials, family structures in Native American populations were more accurately described as small communities within specific tribes. They drew on the strength of extended kinship ties, where elders taught the young. The earth, the sky, objects, animals, and activities (such as hunting, fishing, and weaving) crafted meaning in people's lives and were not to be conquered and controlled. As poet and novelist Paula Gunn Allen (1939–2008), a Laguna Pueblo descendent, explains in "Where I Come From Is Like This," in such an environment gender was fluid: "women" and "men" did not hold the same meanings as they do in white settler traditions. Because they were perceived as "uncivilized" and a threat to the expanding United States, many Native American children were removed from their communities by the Bureau of Indian Affairs and Christian missionaries and placed in boarding schools and adoptive families to enforce assimilation. This included socializing children to adhere to rigid white US constructions of gender (see Briggs; Smith).

Beginning with the colonial era in the New World, African, African Caribbean, and African American enslaved populations were forced by plantation owners to become Christian and live in rudimentary family dwellings. Yet slaveholding white men and women did not recognize the marriage of black men and women and sold children into slavery across the South. Scholars know through collected oral histories and literature that extended kinship networks provided people with strength, resilience, and the means to resist the brutal conditions. Because slavery left a legacy of poverty, after Emancipation (1863)

INTERSECTIONAL ANALYSIS

In 2013, the Supreme Court heard arguments in *Adoptive Family v. Baby Girl* in which a white family in South Carolina sued for permanent custody of "Baby Veronica" after the birth father, Dusten Brown, and the Cherokee Nation alleged that she was unlawfully taken from them in Oklahoma. The birth mother, Christina Maldonado, and Brown never married; soon after the birth of Veronica and unbeknownst to Brown, Maldonado relinquished the child to Nightlife Christian Adoption Agency. Subsequently, a couple in South Carolina—a state whose laws are unfavorable to birth fathers—adopted the baby. Brown is Cherokee, and according to the Indian Child Welfare Act (ICWA) of 1978, all efforts must be made to keep American Indian children with American Indian families. Therefore, Brown's attorney successfully argued that the ICWA applied to the case and Brown should gain custody of Baby Veronica. However, the adoptive couple's counsel, Paul Clement, was able to produce arguments so that the Supreme Court of the United States (SCOTUS) was willing to hear the case. In a 5–4 decision, SCOTUS handed down the verdict that the noncustodial parent (Brown) could not invoke the ICWA to win custody of his child when the custodial parent, who was not Cherokee, voluntarily and legally initiated the adoption process.

QUESTIONS

1. The birth mother told the Nightlife Christian Adoption Agency that there might be difficulties because Brown is Cherokee and could invoke ICWA for custodial rights. Look online to learn more about the case. How did the adoption agency circumvent the law?

2. Given the history of removing American Indian children from their homes to socialize them to be Christian—what scholar Andrea Smith (2015) names as a mode of genocide in *Conquest*—why is it important that Brown and his attorneys invoked ICWA to argue for the birth father's rights in this case?

3. The Baby Veronica case was sensationalized in US media, and many supporters launched "Save Baby Veronica" websites. Look specifically at http://www.saveveronica.org/. Take notes on the language and images that are used throughout the site. What patterns do you perceive, and what are the messages that are telegraphed?

4. What relations of power are at work in this specific case? Do you think it was an injustice to the father? Did the adoptive parents receive justice?

5. Is this case relevant to feminism? How so or why not?

many black women needed to work to sustain themselves and/or their families and kinship networks. Being the "true woman" was not available to women of color or immigrant women, including those considered free black women and/or who could trace their ancestry through substantial economic means. "True womanhood" was a social production of white femininity.

American immigration laws over the past two centuries have separated families. Historically, one of the most restrictive policies focused on Chinese immigration The Page Act (1875) denied entrance to anyone considered "undesirable." It was specifically used to bar all Asian women (regardless of their country of origin) from entering the United States even if their fathers, husbands, sons, and extended family members had been working for the railroads and other industries in the western United States for over twenty years. Established in 1882 and propelled by fear and **xenophobia**, the Chinese Exclusion

Xenophobia: Irrational and intense dislike of people from other countries.

Act prohibited men and women from entering the country and gave the US government power to repatriate workers and their families. This act was law until Congress drafted a measure to rescind it in 1943.

In today's global economy, it is necessary to think about family, labor, and immigration under the regimes of **neoliberalism**. As corporations receive tax breaks, CEOs post record salaries, social programs become privatized, workers fear losing their jobs and must work twice as hard for less wages and fewer benefits, a toxic environment is created for documented and undocumented immigrants alike. Economic precarity fuels xenophobia. While very few US American citizens actually will do the work associated with immigrant labor (e.g., seasonally picking fruits and vegetables or working as a live-in domestic), the phrase "they are taking our jobs" circulates easily through US media and at kitchen tables and informs electoral politics. Economic policies not only shape family structures; they also craft competition among middle- and low-income people by establishing social hierarchies of who is "deserving" of employment and wealth and who must provide the labor for others to acquire profit, governing power, and influence over social policies—all of which undercut the middle and working classes. Thus neoliberal policies have both created the low-paying, backbreaking work climate *and* the pervasive "us versus them" rhetoric that feeds xenophobia.

In her essay "'Broken Hearts, Broken Families': The Political Use of Families in the Fight Against Deportation" (included in this section), Monisha Das Gupta explains that since September 11, 2001, Congress has crafted laws that target and incarcerate immigrants suspected of drug, weapon, and/or terrorism and expedited their deportation. With Congress debating immigration laws and the perceived need for tighter borders, immigrants from Latin America, the Caribbean, Asia, and Africa experience the effects most directly. Das Gupta examines the representational strategies of the New York–based group Freedom for Families, which features fathers as caregivers and integral members of normative family structures, to make the cultural and legal case for immigrant families to remain together in the United States.

It is important to note that while documented and undocumented immigrant households fight to stay together, lesbian, gay, and transgender couples successfully have argued for their right to marry and be recognized as a family under state and federal law. In addition to being recognized by the state and the general public as loving couples, advocates insist that the financial and health benefits tied to marriage must be extended to gay and lesbian couples. For example, the rate of taxation is lowered for a couple who files jointly; families receive the Child Tax Credit based on how many children are in a state-recognized household; and married couples pay less for health insurance, can make healthcare decisions in the event the other is incapacitated, and can be named as the beneficiaries of retirement and other funds. While the Defense of Marriage Act (1996) circumvented gay marriage recognizing same-sex partnerships, legal marriage for gays and lesbians received its first victory in Massachusetts in 2004. However, other states did not have to acknowledge its legality, and advocates pushed for a comprehensive federal law. On June 26, 2015, in

Neoliberalism: Set of economic policies that shape social formations and people's lived experiences by favoring a free market economy, deregulation of industry, and the privatization of government social programs that erodes the middle class and emphasizes individual responsibility.

Latinas protest deportation. As political rhetoric and immigration policies tighten US and European borders, women take to the streets in protest to keep families together. In the United States, "illegal" immigration is not just about people crossing to find safety, security, and economic opportunity; it is also widely supported by corporations and big agricultural conglomerates that demand cheap labor.

a 5–4 ruling in *Obergefell vs. Hodges*, the Supreme Court proclaimed same-sex marriage a right under the US Constitution.

The fight for marriage equality divides the LGBTQPAI+ community. Some question if it really gets us any closer to equality since marriage favors state-sanctioned lesbian and gay couples over other people (regardless of their sexuality) who choose to be single or live in domestic partnerships (see Duggan; Muñoz; Spade). Collectively written, "Beyond Same-Sex Marriage: A New Strategic Vision for All Our Families and Relationships" (included in this section) contends that there are significant costs to extending rights only to those who embrace a heteronormative institution. The authors argue that we will come closer to equality only when we "reflect and honor the diverse ways in which people find and practice love, form relationships, create communities and networks of care and support, establish households, bring families into being and build innovative structures to support and sustain community" (p. 244).

Love has no bounds. Feminist and queer scholars, activists and practitioners celebrate and advocate for families and communities across gender, sexuality, racial, class, and national divides. While gay marriage allows people to marry who they choose, it does not guarantee a world free of housing discrimination, employment discrimination, microaggressions, and violence. How might emphasizing love rather than social divisions help us make these changes?

While marriage and restrictive definitions of "family" allow the state and religious institutions to shape "normal" and "desirable" nuclear families, statistics from the US Census Bureau tell a different story about what is happening to the family as an institution. From 1967 to 2014, there has been a steady decline in the nuclear family, from 70 percent to approximately 50 percent of US households (US Census Current Population Survey). Economic struggles brought on by neoliberal policies, combined with women pursuing higher education and entering the workforce in increased numbers, divorce rates, and more people opting for flexible and cooperative living arrangements, including crafting families that are chosen, means that as a social institution our everyday experiences of family have changed, though ideology and political rhetoric about the family have been slow to follow.

GENDER AND SEXUALITY IN THE LABOR MARKET

In a patriarchal capitalist society, women's independence is tied to their ability to earn money. When we look at women's employment rates over the past fifty years, it is not surprising that we see significant change. Today, the US

Department of Labor website reports that 57 percent of women participate in the labor force and 70 percent of women with children under the age of eighteen work; these numbers are matched only when women entered the workforce during World War II. Not only have more women entered the paid work force, they are also moving into positions where they have real decision-making power. While some women advance, it is clear that progress is not evenly distributed. Most gains in the past few decades have been experienced by middle- and upper-class women, while women in low-wage jobs, who are more likely to be women of color, have experienced little improvement in their overall employment outlook (Boushey 50). Nearly two-thirds of minimum-wage workers are women (Boushey 45). These jobs pay low wages, have low job security, rarely offer paid sick leave, and often come with schedules that change from week to week, making it difficult to plan childcare, pursue more education, or hold a second job. Moreover, gains have not been evenly distributed across the range of professions, with traditionally male-dominated fields like science, technology, engineering, and math showing little improvement for women (51).

Because women's labor force participation has increased but social institutions have not adapted, many women in the paid labor force experience the **second shift**. These hours of household, childcare, and eldercare work that women complete in addition to their paid employment are often overlooked as work because the labor is supposed to be done out of love. Yet housework and caretaking are both vital to a capitalist economy, and when women take on a disproportionate amount of this unpaid labor, they have less leisure time, less time to devote to their education or career advancement, and less time to participate in civic activities.

Second shift: A term coined by sociologist Arlie Hochschild (1989) referring to the household and caregiving labor performed by women in addition to their wage work.

While recent years have seen progress around LGBTQPAI+ rights, workplace discrimination remains an issue. Because there is no federal law, and twenty-nine states do not have laws protecting the queer community, workers can be legally denied employment or fired based on their sexual orientation or gender identity. While there is limited data regarding LGBTQPAI+ unemployment, what we know suggests that lesbian, gay, and bisexual workers experience a higher unemployment rate than the heterosexual population and that gay and bisexual men receive lower wages—between 10 percent to 32 percent lower—than their heterosexual counterparts (*A Broken Bargain* 7, 34). In the US, transgender workers have an unemployment rate twice the national average. For transgender people of color, the situation is even bleaker with their unemployment numbers as much as *four times* the national average (*A Broken Bargain*, 2013, 7). Employment discrimination, higher rates of unemployment, hostile work environments, and wage penalties all contribute to the fact that queer communities are more likely to experience poverty (*A Broken Bargain* 8).

THE GENDER PAY GAP

The pay differential between men's and women's average earnings is referred to as the **gender pay gap**. These lost wages affect women's economic power, but

Gender pay gap: The average difference between men's and women's earnings.

it's not only women who are affected. Because women make up a large share of breadwinners and co-breadwinners, these lost wages affect *families*.

When we compare the median incomes for full-time, year-round, male and female workers in the United States, women earn only about 79 percent of what men earn. (Hill 5). However, while 79 percent is the median difference, this number varies depending on several factors, including region, race, and national origin. For example, women in the District of Columbia make about 90 percent of what their male counterparts earn, whereas in Louisiana, that number drops to 65 percent (7). In every racial and ethnic group, women earn less than men, but there is significant variation. For example, African American women earn about 90 percent of what African American men earn, while white women earn 78 percent of what white men earn (*The Simple Truth* 10). When we use white men's salary as the benchmark (they have the highest average earnings and make up the largest demographic group in the workforce), we find that Latinas make only 54 percent of their salary, American Indian and Alaska Native women make 59 percent, Native Hawaiian and Pacific Islander women make 62 percent, and African American women make 63 percent. Asian American women experience the smallest gap compared to white men, earning 90 percent of their earnings (*The Simple Truth* 11).

Because the pay gap is caused in part by how women act in the labor market, a superficial analysis of the problem, indeed a neoliberal one, might lead us to blame women for their lower pay. However, research tells us that it is more accurate to see choices in labor force participation as "constrained" because there are structural variables that limit or influence the options afforded to women, queer people, people of color, and immigrants.

Occupational segregation: The division of men and women in the workforce.

Women are socialized by their families, religion, and/or the media and may feel social pressure to *choose* gendered professions causing **occupational segregation**, and there are two types: horizontal and vertical segregation. Horizontal segregation occurs when men and women staff certain career fields disproportionately. For example, teachers are overwhelmingly female while construction workers are overwhelmingly male. Horizontal segregation matters because the jobs staffed by women tend to pay less. This raises the question: Do we as a society value certain jobs less? In attempting to answer that question, it is interesting to note that the pay gap exists even when men hold traditionally "female" jobs or women hold traditionally "male" jobs. In 2013, full-time female registered nurses earned only 88 percent of the median weekly earnings of their male counterparts. The gap was wider in the traditionally male field of computer programming, where females earned only 81 percent compared to their male peers (*The Simple Truth* 16).

Horizontal segregation is particularly damaging for women employed in occupations with lower educational requirements. While men without college degrees tend to work in industries that are heavily unionized, we find women without college degrees disproportionately in industries that are *not* unionized. Unionized workers receive higher wages and better benefits, and there is a lower pay gap between male and female employees. An analysis of 2012 data found that full-time, unionized female workers earned 90 percent of what their male coworkers did (Boushey 52; Corbett and Hill 32). The unionization of domestic care workers in places like California and Hawai'i demonstrate that union organizing can bring about important gains for women in female-segregated jobs.

Vertical segregation refers to gender stratification *within* an occupation or career field. For example, women now make up about one-third of doctors and lawyers in the United States, which represents a significant change from the 1970s when these jobs were overwhelmingly male. However, women are poorly represented at the top of these professions. Women make up about 50 percent of law school graduates and about 45 percent of law firm associates, for example, but only 28 percent of nonequity partners and only 18 percent of equity partners (Rikleen 2). When we look more closely at *which* women hold top positions, we find that women of color are significantly less likely than their white counterparts to make it into leadership positions. Of LGBTQPAI+ lawyers, only 2 percent of female and 1 percent of male equity partners identify as queer (Rikleen 6). Horizontal and vertical segregation matter because these divisions solidify gender, racial, sexual, and class hierarchies.

Women who have children may face added barriers. First, they may opt for an occupation that allows them more flexibility to enter and exit the labor market during prime reproductive years. Often these jobs do not require advanced education and are low paying. Second, since women are still expected to be the primary caretakers, they are much more likely to leave the workforce for longer periods of time or work part-time if they can afford to do so. The **mother pay penalty** refers to the wages women lose once they become mothers. Conversely, men experience wage increases in their jobs and advancement in their career, referred to as the **fatherhood bonus** if they have children. According to sociologist Michelle Budig in "The Fatherhood Bonus and the Motherhood Penalty," the pay gap related to parenthood seems to be increasing while the gender pay gap seems to be eroding very slowly over time. Women's sacrifice becomes particularly problematic in the case of divorce. A married stay-at-home mother who returns to the workforce will lose future earnings because of her leave of absence, but if she stays married, those lost wages will be shared with her spouse. In the case of divorce, the woman bears the brunt of those lost wages. This does not mean that women should not be stay-at-home parents, work part-time, or stay in a marriage for economic reasons. It does suggest that when our culture pressures women to make those sacrifices, we end up with gender-based economic inequality.

Another cause of the pay gap is that women are less likely to negotiate their salaries, ask for a raise, or ask for a promotion. In *Women Don't Ask: Negotiation and the Gender Divide*, Babcock and Laschever provide a useful example of how much is at stake in not understanding the art of negotiation. A twenty-two-year-old man and an equally qualified twenty-two-year-old woman are each offered a job for $25,000 a year. If the man negotiates his salary to $30,000 but the woman accepts the original offer, and each receives a 3 percent cost of living increase every year for thirty-eight years, at the end of his career the man's salary will be $92,243 while the woman's salary will be $76,870 (Babcock and Laschever 5).

Mother pay penalty: Lost wages that mothers experience in comparison to non-mothers.

Fatherhood bonus: Increased wages and career advancement that fathers experience when being a part of a family structure because they are perceived as needing to provide for people and fulfilling their responsibilities as citizens within patriarchy and capitalism.

Glass ceiling: Invisible barriers structurally tied to gender, race, class, sexuality, age, ability, and nationality that prevent job and career advancement for women, queer-identified people, and people of color.

Workers from marginalized groups are more vulnerable to the glass ceiling, sexual harassment, and wage theft in the labor market. The **glass ceiling** refers to the phenomenon whereby women, LGBTQPAI+ people, and people of color move into professional positions but then for reasons that are invisible but deeply structural, they have difficulty advancing. The reason it is referred to as a *glass* ceiling is because subtle things, like prejudice in hiring and promotion, micro-aggressions in the workplace, and lack of mentoring do more to hold workers back than earlier practices of denying them employment. Hostile work environments also affect people's ability to do their best work and advance. Unwelcome sexual advances, requests for sexual favors, and offensive comments cause emotional distress and physical health problems and can push people out of jobs even though it is the workplace climate that should be changing. Women across racial, ethnic, and class differences have been the most commonly acknowledged victims of sexual harassment, but, according to the website for Catalyst, an organization dedicated to changing workplace culture "nearly one in ten LGBTQPAI+ employees left a job because the environment was unwelcoming." Wage theft refers to employer violations of minimum wage and overtime laws, forced unpaid "off-the-clock" work, erasing work hours on time cards, stealing tips, and issuing paychecks. A 2010 report on workers in Chicago, Los Angeles, and New York City found that women and immigrant workers were most likely to experience minimum wage violations and that African Americans had three times as many violations as whites (Berhnardt 43). In cases where employees are undocumented, abuse is rampant because wages are unregulated.

Popular initiatives to address gender-based inequalities in the labor market tend to fall under three general strategies that aim to reform the existing system: (1) make all salary information public; if workers see the discrepancies, they have better footing to demand equal pay for equal work; (2) give women and LGBTQPAI+ equal access and equal opportunities in the paid workforce; and (3) value and reward care work. In "Policies to End the Gender Wage Gap in the United States" (included in this section), Marlene Kim discusses six specific initiatives: using existing laws to prosecute discrimination, adopting family-friendly policies like paid parental leave and publicly funded childcare, establishing comparable worth standards to ensure that jobs that require similar skills and responsibilities are rewarded equitably, increasing unionization, prohibiting pay secrecy, and focusing on change at the state level.

To ensure progress is equitable, we must look at how race, ethnicity, class, sexualities, citizenship status, disability, and age affect the gendered experience of work. For example, the United States is the only industrialized country in the world that does not provide paid leave for new mothers. The US Family and Medical Leave Act (FMLA) allows for twelve weeks of *un*paid leave. For working poor, low-income, and even many middle-class women, taking unpaid leave is not an option. At best, FMLA is a safety net for some people, but overall the policy is designed to benefit industries and institutions, not employees.

For LGBTQPAI+ workers, federal nondiscrimination legislation is needed to ensure that workers cannot be treated unfairly based on sexual orientation, gender identity, or gender expression and that workplace benefits can be extended to domestic partners. However, as Dean Spade contends in "Compliance Is Gendered: Struggling for a Gendered Self-Determination in a Hostile Economy" (included in this section), "[a]ccess to participation in the U.S. economy has always been conditioned on the ability of each individual to comply with norms of gendered behavior and expression, and the U.S. economy has always been shaped by explicit incentives that coerce people into normative gender and sexual structures, identities, and behaviors" (p. 257). Nonbinary, agender, genderqueer, and transgender people face barriers that the law cannot address because transphobia is deeply enmeshed in how people think. Feminist and queer movements interested in social change must focus on finding just, intersectional approaches to alleviate the violence of poverty and the US economic system itself, not reforming a broken system that was never meant to protect trans and genderqueer people, and especially trans and genderqueer people of color.

SEX WORK AS LABOR

Sex work and **sex trafficking** are not synonymous. Sex work represents a paid industry that can include pornography, street prostitution, indoor prostitution (such as escort services, massage parlors, and brothels), phone sex, exotic dancing, and online nude modeling. Most collected data focus on prostitution, in which it is estimated by investigative reporter Stephanie Chen of CNN that 1 million to 2 million women in the United States and 40 million to 42 million women globally participate. These figures do not account for the number of LGBTQPAI+ people in sex work industries. Sex trafficking refers to those victims who are forced into the industry against their will and mostly without pay. Feminist, queer, and human rights scholars and organizations use the term "sex work" to emphasize that, regardless of its legal status, women, men, genderqueer, and LGBTQPAI+ individuals make constrained economic choices to enter sex work. Since it is an intricate (and largely an underground) commercial economy, workers do not benefit from international, federal, and state regulations. Therefore, sex workers' rights are framed as human rights. They need protection from pimps and syndicates stealing their money; protection from violence, discrimination, and social marginalization; and access to health services and housing. It is particularly unjust that sex workers are frequently criminalized while the men involved (whether a consumer or those who control labor) are not prosecuted. Feminist and queer scholars, activists, and practitioners disagree on whether to decriminalize, legalize, and/or unionize sex work, though all agree that social constructions of gender, race, class, age, sexuality, and nationality create the economic conditions that allow sex work to persist within violent patriarchal and capitalist paradigms.

In "Women Work, Men Sponge and Everyone Gossips: Macho Men and Stigmatized/ing Women in a Sex Tourist Town" (included in this section), Denise Brennan makes clear that sex workers have agency and power within a stigmatized occupation. In her field research in Sosúa, Dominican Republic,

Sex work: Paid work within the sex industry.

Sex trafficking: Forced work against people's wills within the sex industry and often as the result of being made vulnerable due to poverty, refugee status, and as women/girls and LGBTQPAI+ youth/ adults.

TRANSNATIONAL CONNECTIONS

It is relatively easy to find international organizations that work to eliminate sex trafficking (see humantrafficking.org). With transnational feminism's recent interest in naming sex work as a form of labor that is tied to political, economic, and social global systems of gender, migration, race, class, and neocolonialism, and neoliberalism, spend time individually locating feminist and/or queer organizations that advocate sex workers rights. We suggest starting with International Union of Sex Workers and Amnesty International, though see if you can find organizations in specific countries that advocate for inclusion in women's, civil, human, and labor rights.

QUESTIONS

1. Why do you think it is easier to find organizations that seek to end sex trafficking compared to advocate for safe conditions for sex work, and how might this be tied to assumptions about gender, race, class, and nationalities?

2. If sex work (not trafficking) was seen as a form of labor, what kinds of rights and protections would workers need?

3. In global locations where sex work is illegal and not regulated, for example, in parts of Africa, South Asia, and the United States, rates of sexually transmitted infections, including HIV/AIDS, are high and disproportionately affect the working poor and homeless. How might health outcomes be tied to cultural issues, including the stigmatizing of sex work? What could be one intervention for lowering disease and the stigma?

4. Sex work is also tied to sex tourism in places such as the Dominican Republic, as shown in Denise Brennan's article. With 41 percent of the population living below the national poverty lines and the general economic prospects above that of other Caribbean nations, why might state and local governments on this small island be uninterested in regulating sex work and protecting the workers?

a sex tourist destination for mostly German men, Brennan notes how women sex workers are the breadwinners of their families providing better housing, education, and opportunities for their children compared to their neighbors. Yet because of the way the town gossips about sex work, the social constructions of gender are unchanged. In her award-winning book, *Taste of Brown Sugar: Black Women in Pornography*, Mirelle Miller-Young argues that while black women have stereotypical roles in the adult film industry, they wield economic power both as workers and producers. These findings both substantially reframe sex workers as agents within, and not victims of, an industry. What remains unchanged is how harshly the broader public may judge people who earn a living through sex work.

REPRODUCTIVE POLITICS

Reproductive issues have played a role in US politics since the turn of the twentieth century. The origin of the movement is historically attributed to Margaret Sanger (1879–1966). A nurse by profession, she was a public advocate for contraception after watching her mother suffer because she bore eleven children

Margaret Sanger, birth control advocate and supporter of eugenics. Sanger is widely known as the founder of the modern birth control movement advocating for working-poor mothers struggling under deplorable living conditions in the early twentieth century. Archival evidence, such as this photograph taken March 23, 1925 at the annual Neo-Malthusian and Birth Control Conference and her writing for the *Birth Control Review*, tie her to eugenics organizations.

and had seven miscarriages. As a nurse, Sanger witnessed women dying from unregulated abortions. She devoted her life to making birth control legal by challenging the state and federal **Comstock Laws** and providing it to all women, especially struggling, poor mothers. "She knew that women could not achieve full equality unless they had control over their reproductive lives" (May 14). This popular narrative hides contested histories of the movement. First, as historians Linda Gordon in *The Moral Property of Women: A History of Birth Control Politics in America*, and Kathy Ferguson in her article "Birth Control" (included in this section) conclude, its radical roots in anarchism and socialism are largely unknown and ignored, and it fails to acknowledge that Sanger's advocacy among low-income immigrant women, black women, and disabled women was linked to the **eugenics movement** (See Davis; Roberts; Washington).

The legacies of these divisions in reproductive politics can be seen today. Generally, advocates agree that people across the spectra of race, ethnicity, class, and abilities benefit from comprehensive sex education; affordable birth control (and its availability through health insurance); a robust, federally funded Planned Parenthood; available and affordable abortion options; and reproductive technologies (such as sperm and egg donation, IVF, and surrogacy). What matters greatly are the conditions under which birth control is enforced and procedures (such as abortion, sterilization and surrogacy) are performed. Next we look more closely at contemporary feminist and queer perspectives on what reproductive "choice" and "justice" mean.

Comstock Laws: Federal act passed in 1873 criminalizing the use of the US Postal Service to exchange materials and information the government deemed obscene, such as pornography, contraceptives, and information on abortion.

Eugenics movement: In the late nineteenth and early twentieth century, the belief that a superior human race is possible by controlling the reproduction of those deemed incapable or inferior by those who considered themselves superior in terms of race, looks, and intelligence found popular support as well as generous funding from organizations such as the Carnegie Institution and Rockefeller Foundation.

REPRODUCTIVE CHOICE

The slogan "My Body, My Choice" was a rallying cry for many women across the United States throughout the 1960s and 1970s and continues to be an integral part of today's political landscape. Pro-choice positions emphasize that *all* women inherently have the right to control their fertility and if/when they will carry a pregnancy to term. While it may seem for some like common sense to argue for access to safe and effective birth control, the protection of legal abortion procedures, and women's rights to their bodies, for others it remains highly contested. Conservative religious institutions (as Rebecca Barrett-Fox illustrates in "Constraints and Freedom in Conservative Christian Women's Lives") teach that sex is between a husband and wife, and while it can and should be pleasurable, birth control is unnecessary. Moreover, pro-life advocates have restricted access to care in a handful of states by arguing that abortion providers (who often work out of free-standing clinics or doctor's offices) must provide facilities and standards equivalent to those of full hospitals. Ultimately, pro-life activists, policymakers, and lawmakers would like to see *Roe v. Wade* overturned by the Supreme Court and birth control fully privatized.

In the 1960s, federal approval of the birth control pill coincided with feminists' call for a sexual revolution. As historian Elaine Tyler May makes clear in *America and the Pill: A History of Promise, Peril, and Liberation*, there was momentum for women "to pursue sex, education, work and marriage when and how they liked it . . . [and while] the pill encouraged this trend, it did not create it" (May 71). Women themselves did. The pill's form assisted. It was discreet; she did not need to rely on her partner to agree to it; it required no interruption immediately before sex (unlike the diaphragm, cervical cap, sponge, and spermicide); and at the time it was considered safer than the IUD. The pill represented freedom and independence.

Birth control and the legalization of abortion in *Roe v. Wade* (1973) were and still are largely framed politically as "health initiatives"—not women's rights—and purposefully so because it is an effective political strategy for ensuring both are available. It is important to note that for women to secure certain forms of birth control (such as an IUD), they must see a doctor. This simple step makes women's reproductive "choice" a constrained one. "A variety of scholars and activists have critiqued the choice paradigm because it rests on essentially individualistic, consumerist notions of 'free choice' that do not take into consideration all the social, economic, and political conditions that frame the so-called choices women are supposed to make" (Smith 127).

REPRODUCTIVE JUSTICE

When it comes to issues of reproduction, one person's freedom or choice can be another's oppression. This is especially clear in thinking about the difference between reproductive choice and reproductive justice. Marginalized communities, including low-income, immigrant, and women of color in the United

States, including Puerto Rico, have a long history of not having a "choice" when it comes to reproduction.

The historical legacy of slavery, colonization, and immigration policies has been coercive abuse. Black feminist scholars, such as Angela Davis in *Women, Race & Class* and Dorothy Roberts in *Killing the Black Body: Race, Reproduction and the Meaning of Liberty,* have written extensively on how black women were forced—and frequently raped—to produce children for slave owners to sell. In the 1980s, low-income women of color seeking state assistance ("welfare") were forced to use the implantable contraceptives Norplant and Depo Provera in exchange for money and food. What the women did not know at the time, and as Roberts reveals in *Killing the Black Body*, was that they were the test subjects for these new birth control methods. Barbara Gurr's research in *Reproductive Justice: The Politics of Health Care for Native American Women* documents how indigenous women were sterilized without their consent through National Indian Health Services. Spanish-speaking Puerto Rican women in New York and Latinas in Los Angeles report signing consent forms but not being able to understand what they signed because it was never translated. Between 1929 and 1976, North Carolina forcibly sterilized more than 7,000 men, women, and children, many of whom were poor, black, and/or mentally challenged. According to Eric Mennel of National Public Radio in "Payments Start for N.C. Eugenics Victims," the state set aside $10 million in reparations in 2013 to be dispersed through the Office of Justice for Sterilization Victims, though many will not qualify given bureaucratic stipulations or may never see the money because they are quite elderly and the process of reparations is slow.

In Alexandra DelValle's first-person narrative "From the Roots of Latina Feminism to the Future of the Reproductive Justice Movement" (included in this section), she argues that "the mainstream reproductive rights movement has done a poor job of including the voices and concerns of people of color and . . . that Latino organizations are often wary of including reproductive health issues in their platforms" (p. 280). The National Latina Institute for Reproductive Health, where DelValle worked from 2003 to 2006, advocates "everyone should be able to decide when (if ever) and how to be pregnant, give birth, and parent . . . that everyone deserves the right to engage sexually and/or lovingly as they please" (p. 281).

In "Birth Control" (included in this section), Kathy Ferguson suggests studying the radical philosophies of nineteenth- and twentieth-century anarchists and socialists will help us find pathways to winning the war against repressive and unjust forces that seek to control women's bodies. They understood that birth control was one tenet of a larger struggle for freedom and that all members of society would not be free, including those who engage in sex outside of heterosexual, procreative marriage, if one member experienced control exercised by the state, churches, and families. By adjusting the frame, Ferguson asks us to understand that history does not march steadily toward progress. If we continue to react to contemporary politics by rolling our eyes and silently wondering "isn't this the twenty-first century?", the ideological forces that insist sex is

ACTIVISM AND CIVIC ENGAGEMENT

Loretta Ross is the national coordinator of the SisterSong Women of Color Reproductive Health Collective, whose mission is to "strengthen and amplify the collective voices of indigenous women and women of color to achieve reproductive justice by eradicating reproductive oppression and securing human rights" (sistersong.net). Ross has written extensively on the history of abortion in the black community, editing *Undivided Rights* and contributing "The Color of Choice: White Supremacy and Reproductive Justice" to the *Color of Violence: The Incite! Anthology*. She was an honors student throughout her education and found her way to reproductive justice and antiviolence work after being raped by a stranger at age eleven, a victim of incest at the age of fifteen, becoming pregnant while at Radcliffe College and losing her scholarship, and left infertile by the Dalkon Shield, an IUD that led to serious infections, sterility, and death in thousands of women in the 1970s.

QUESTIONS

1. Visit SisterSong's website. Why is it important to have a reproductive justice organization crafted by and for indigenous women and women of color?

2. What does it mean to "mobilize women around our lived experiences," and why is this integral to understanding intersectional approaches to reproductive rights?

3. SisterSong contends that reproductive justice is a human right and draws on the internationally accepted United Nations Declaration of Human Rights to claim that women's reproductive decisions must be protected. Why do they ground their work in human rights?

4. Why is it important to add "comprehensive sexual education, alternate birth options, prenatal care, domestic violence assistance, adequate wages, and safe homes" to the definition of reproductive justice?

5. Is there a group in your community that serves a similar mission to SisterSong? If not, can you find one in your state? Does it provide an intersectional framework for understanding reproductive choice or justice? If so, what does it emphasize? If not, how might you and your class advocate for more racial, class, genderqueer, and transgender awareness within your community?

heteronormative, tied to marriage, and procreative will also continue to erode women's access to birth control, abortion, and other reproductive health care.

When we act in the name of reproductive freedom globally, US-based scholars, activists, and practitioners must be knowledgeable about and respectful of the specific histories of gender, class, ethnicity, and religion in any given community as well as recognize that the issues in the United States do not necessarily shape the lives of women in other countries. In "The Industrial Womb" (included in this section), France Winddance Twine analyzes the global politics of surrogacy and argues that our actions in the West directly harm poor women in the Global South. Since the "outsourcing of the womb" is a largely unregulated multibillion-dollar industry, it preys upon impoverished women for their reproductive labor, especially in India and Bangladesh, so that expectant parents (whether heterosexual or within the LGBTQPAI+ community) can have children. Reproductive freedom entails a full spectrum of possibilities for all women and acknowledges the economic, political, and social structures that shape our interconnected lives.

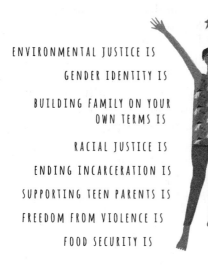

ENVIRONMENTAL JUSTICE IS

GENDER IDENTITY IS

BUILDING FAMILY ON YOUR
OWN TERMS IS

RACIAL JUSTICE IS

ENDING INCARCERATION IS

SUPPORTING TEEN PARENTS IS

FREEDOM FROM VIOLENCE IS

FOOD SECURITY IS

IMMIGRATION JUSTICE IS

ACCESSIBLE ABORTION IS

SUPPORTING BIRTHPARENTS IS

PAID LEAVE IS

DISABILITY JUSTICE IS

QUEER FAMILIES ARE

SAFE COMMUNITIES ARE

DECOLONIZATION IS

REPRODUCTIVE JUSTICE.

REPEAL HYDE ART PROJECT

Reproductive Justice, an intersectional movement for social change. Reproductive justice movements are deeply interested in women's access to birth control, abortion clinics, repealing the Hyde Amendment, and supporting *Roe v. Wade*. Started by women of color, it also makes clear how the well being of all marginalized people is deeply connected to justice within all social systems—whether it is living in communities with lead-free water or the abolition of the prison system.

GENDERED VIOLENCE

The statistics are startling. According to the National Organization of Women's website, three women are killed per day in the United States, a third of them murdered by an intimate partner; one in five women on US college campuses will experience rape and sexual assault; and 4.8 million women in the United States experience physical assaults and rape within a domestic partnership. The United Nations through its UN Women website reports that 70 percent of women have experienced violence from an intimate partner, 120 million girls experience forced or coerced intercourse or other forced sex acts, and 88% of women have experienced verbal sexual harassment; 133 million girls and women in twenty-nine countries experience some form of female genital mutilation; and women and girls account for 70 percent of all sex trafficking victims. While the United Nations World's Women 2015 Report celebrates women's abilities to live longer, healthier lives and that more girls are receiving formal education, violence against women and girls darkens these advances.

Gendered violence has reached pandemic levels. Yet these stark numbers do not sufficiently address the **interpersonal sexual violence** that women of color and LGBTQPAI+ communities experience. Moreover, this privatized violence

Interpersonal sexual violence: Intimate-partner violence or domestic violence, rape, and emotional or psychological violence within privatized relationships.

State violence: Harm that government, social institutions, industry, and individual members of society perpetuate based on stereotypical and interlocking ideas about gender, race, class, sexuality, religion, and nationality; also referred to as structural violence.

does not address **state violence** that women, men, queer, and trans people experience. These acts of bodily and psychological harm are largely unseen by the broader public for two reasons. First, the very institutions meant to protect LGBTQPAI+ and racial/ethnic communities, such as the US Justice Department, the police, and the State Department, can perpetuate it. Specific examples include police brutality and murder, racial profiling and mass incarceration, xenophobia linked to anti-Arab and anti-Muslim violence, and hate crimes and homelessness in LGBTQPAI+ communities. Second, misogyny colludes with culturally accepted practices that harm and kill women, such as sex trafficking, female genital mutilation, and femicide. Although instances of systemic violence may appear to be isolated events, when investigated carefully, it becomes clear how historical processes and the social meanings ascribed to gender, race, class, sexuality, religion, and nationality create an atmosphere where the unthinkable becomes a daily reality.

INTERPERSONAL AND SEXUAL VIOLENCE ACROSS THE GENDER SPECTRUM

Antiviolence scholars, activists, and practitioners argue that private incidents of intimate partner violence and rape must be understood as public acts that require political attention; physical violence, abuse, and coercive sex are acts of power tied to toxic enactments of gender; and shelter systems and the law must be seen as safety nets and not solutions to addressing, preventing, and eliminating sexual violence. By proclaiming that violence can and does happen to anyone, feminists have consistently (and to some degree successfully) pushed US state and federal legislatures to craft laws that punish perpetrators found guilty of rape, sexual assault, and domestic violence. Yet, according to the statistics on the Rape, Abuse and Incest Network (RAINN) website, 68 percent of sexual assaults are not reported to the police, and 98 percent of rapists will not spend a day in jail or prison. SafeHorizon, the largest nonprofit victim services agency in the United States, notes that "most domestic violence incidents are *never* reported."

In the United States, we live in a rape culture. This explains why women do not use the structures for reporting sexual violence available to them through schools, the military, workplaces, or the police and why so few cases are successfully prosecuted through the US justice system. Knowing that one in five women experiences sexual assault on college campuses and only 2 percent of victims report to police and 4 percent to campus authorities, the authors of "Friends of Survivors: The Community Impact of Unwanted Sexual Experiences" (included in this section) wanted to know in whom victims/survivors confided. They discovered that most tell their friends about the assault and that it is critical for campus communities (professionals and students) to work together to address and prevent violence so that students are not burdened with this care work.

From a young age, girls are taught that they must keep themselves safe—through modest dress, monitoring when and with whom they consume alcohol,

Engaged Learning

In 2013, the magazine *The Nation* suggested ten ways to participate in ending rape culture: (1) name the problem as violent masculinity and victim blaming; (2) re-examine and re-imagine masculinity; (3) get enthusiastic about consent and engaging in sexual contact after hearing "yes!"; (4) speak up for what you really want even if it feels difficult; (5) recognize and ask critical questions about media cultures that promote rape culture; (6) read/think/discuss how rape culture is a global issue; (7) understand US history as one that sanctions state violence; (8) use your knowledge about intersectionality to reimagine gender-based violence; (9) practice what you think: if you see rape culture around you, do not participate in it and if you hear rape jokes, do not laugh at them; and (10) lobby your college and social media communities not to tolerate gender-based violence (http://www.thenation.com/article/ten-things-end-rape-culture/). Read the article independently and work in small groups to think through a strategy that might be most effective in your community for addressing violence. What role might **bystander intervention** play? Discuss as a large group and develop an action plan, keeping in mind that there is no one "blueprint" in how to end rape culture and it requires creative and inclusive thinking.

being careful on social media, and never walking alone at night. Rape culture curtails women's freedom; patriarchy, racism, classism, homophobia, transphobia, and xenophobia insist that women are responsible and therefore to blame if men (or anyone else) assault them. In "Hooking Up with Healthy Sexuality: The Lessons Boys Learn (and Don't) about Sexuality and Why a Sex Positive Rape Prevention Paradigm Can Benefit Everyone Involved" (included in this section), Brad Perry suggests that gender-based violence, in part, can be prevented by building smarter national sexual education curricula that purposefully set out to change toxic masculinities by introducing humor and pleasure into how boys learn about gender and sexuality.

Scholars, activists, and practitioners acknowledge that we do not know enough about sexual violence perpetuated against women of color, men, and LGBTQPAI+ communities for at least four reasons: (1) we do not invest as many resources into collecting this data nationally and internationally; (2) given the harsh realities of racism, xenophobia, homophobia, and transphobia some victims/survivors choose to protect members of their communities at their own personal cost; (3) members of the LGBTQPAI+ community may not be out and therefore do not feel like they can disclose violence in their relationships; and (4) others do not feel safe reporting to campus personnel and/or the police because of possible police brutality. In "A Black Feminist Reflection on the Antiviolence Movement" (included in this section), Beth Richie critiques the feminist antiviolence movement for not including racial and class analyses in its approach. She argues that "a reassessment of the responses that have been central to antiviolence work—in particular, the reliance on law enforcement as the principal provider of women's safety" is central to creating change and bringing justice into the lives of black women (p. 312).

Bystander intervention: A strategy for preventing violence, including gender-based violence, by training individuals to disrupt social norms that perpetuate victim blaming and the privatization of violence.

For the first time in its history, the Centers for Disease Control and Prevention produced a press release in 2013 detailing the data it collected on interpersonal and sexual violence based on sexual orientation. According to its website, the agency found that "lesbians and gay men reported IPV and SV over their lifetimes at levels equal to or higher than those of heterosexuals . . . and bisexual women (61.1%) report a higher prevalence of rape, physical violence, and/or stalking by an intimate partner compared to both lesbian and heterosexual women." The report suggests that the LGBTQPAI+ community "suffer[s] a heavy toll of sexual violence and stalking" and that sexism and homophobia are deeply connected such that bisexual women experience a disproportionate amount of harm. If intimate partner violence and sexual violence continue to be perceived only as heterosexual crimes linked to toxic straight masculinity, violence in the LGBTQPAI+ community will remain invisible and violence against straight men will be virtually absent.

STATE VIOLENCE

According to the authors of "False Promises: Criminal Legal Responses to Violence against LGBT People" (included in this section), there has been a notable spike in stranger and intimate violence in the LGBTQPAI+ community. In 2008, the National Coalition of Anti-Violence Programs "reported over 2,000 instances of homophobic and transphobic violence . . . representing a 26 percent increase over 2006 figures" (p. 314). Mitch Killaway and Sunnivie Brydum in the online magazine *The Advocate*, report that twenty-one trans women of color were murdered in 2015. While many incidents are supposed to be investigated as a **hate crime**, the authors argue that "the same criminalizing archetypes that permeate treatment of queers in other contexts also profoundly inform police approaches to LGBT victims of crime" (Mogul, Ritchie, and Whitlock 120). In the United States, justice is tied to the thoroughness of police work. If LGBTQPAI+ community members experience gender, racial, and sexual discrimination and bias in that very process, people distrust authorities and stop reporting crimes. As the authors contend, so long as we focus on violence as individual acts and not "dismantling the systemic forces that promote, condone, and facilitate homophobic and transphobic violence," we will continue to see continued violence and systemic protection of perpetrators (p. 317).

Following the terrorist attacks of September 11, 2001, and President George W. Bush's decision to wage war in the Middle East under false claims that Iraq was producing weapons of mass destruction, the Southern Poverty Law Center reported a dramatic increase in anti-Arab and anti-Muslim hate groups in the United States. **Islamophobia** is fueled by government promises to fight "terrorism" in the name of US national security and the repeated media construction of Muslims as "anti-American jihadists." As Isis Nusair argues in "Making Feminist Sense of Torture at Abu-Ghraib" (included in this section), facile ideologies that misrepresent one of the oldest and the most practiced religions

Hate crime: Violence motivated by race, color, religion, ethnicity, national origin, sexual orientation, gender, gender identity or expression, or disability.

Islamophobia: Prejudice produced by fear of Islam or Muslims.

The complexity of "Muslim women." In today's world, some media outlets and politicians drawing ties between Muslim communities and terrorism have incited violence and amplified cultural divides. Muslim women are at home in countries across Asia, Africa, the Middle East, Europe, and the Americas and cannot be reduced to oversimplified and deliberately crafted stereotypes. Here, women march in the Annual Muslim Day Parade in New York City (2013) demanding better from the dominant culture.

in the world does the cultural work of condoning war, justifying torture, and violating human and women's rights.

It can be overwhelming to take all this in at once *and* it is necessary to understand how interpersonal and structural violence are linked before we can even begin addressing gender, sexual, and racial violence with the goal of prevention and elimination. Violence is all around us, perhaps so much so that collectively we become desensitized, tune it out, or grow numb to it. However, one of the first steps in combatting this scourge is to become aware of its depth and dimensions and discuss violence openly.

POPULAR CULTURE AND MEDIA REPRESENTATIONS

In 1975, feminist film theorist Laura Mulvey argued that the structures of Hollywood films represented women through the **male gaze** for all audience members. The male gaze crafted women on screen as passive, helpless, and in need of rescue; sexualized but not sexual; and available for men's pleasure. Since 1975, feminist and queer scholars have debated how much agency marginalized

Male gaze: How the production of visual arts is crafted by and through patriarchal interpretations of the world, and therefore film, television, and art represents women as objects rather than subjects.

communities have in popular culture and the ways in which representations of women and LGBTQPAI+ people either reinforce harmful stereotypes or allow the boundaries of gender, race, social class, sexuality, abilities, religion, and nationalities to be challenged.

Pop culture is among the most readily accessible and easily digestible cultural texts. As an "agent of socialization" and a pedagogical tool, it teaches us how to see, live, and be in this world (D'Enbeau 17; Kellner 7; Lindner 409). How feminism and queer identity is represented *in* pop culture matters because many people may first learn about gender, race, sexuality, feminism, and LGBTQPAI+ communities through pop culture (Hollows and Moseley 1). In Sut Jhally's film *Stuart Hall: Representations and the Media*, cultural theorist and sociologist Stuart Hall argues that representation is constitutive of reality, and it is through representations that we make sense of the world. Skewed media representations undoubtedly contribute to a distorted perception of reality. Psychological research has shown, for example, that when people are exposed to sexually explicit advertisements, they tend to show "greater gender role stereotyping, rape myth acceptance, and acceptance of sexual aggression against women" (Lindner 410).

Would a solution to this problem then be to have more "accurate" representations of people the world? The answer to this question may not be that simple. Wanting to see an "authentic" representation of a social group is in itself troubling because it is often based on the assumption that there is an essence to what is being represented. For example, it assumes that the creative minds of any given media product have access to knowing what a wealthy heterosexual Muslim woman's life *really* looks like. With different histories and fluid experiences even within the same group of people, any attempt to construct *a* representation of anything or anyone will be fraught with some form of misrepresentation. It is thus important to be critical of how a cultural text is produced, circulated, and consumed; to be aware of the relations of power within these media agents and agencies; and to understand how certain politics and ideologies limit and shape the production of texts (Kellner 11). The first step to analyzing any media representation requires us to ask, "[w]ho does visibility benefit, and on what terms is it offered? For whose purposes, and under whose control do media artifacts circulate?" (Mann 293).

Sociologist Patricia Hill Collins argues in *Black Feminist Thought* that the dominant media representations of black Americans function as "controlling images." These representations usually deploy the stereotypical figures of the mammy, matriarch, welfare mother, and jezebel. Working-class black men are often represented as "athletes" or "criminals" (being "inherently violent and/ or hyper-heterosexual") and middle-class black men as "sissies and sidekicks" (being "friendly and deferential; . . . loyal both to dominant societal values such as law and order as well as to individuals who seemingly uphold them; . . . a safe, nonthreatening Black identity") (Collins, "Booty Call," 320, 323–324). Hence, representations of black people in US media do not necessarily challenge racial hierarchy; they may even do the cultural work of further cementing inequalities.

Esra Özcan draws on this argument in her essay "Who Is a Muslim Woman?": Questioning Knowledge Production on 'Muslim Woman'" (included in this section) and makes clear that the representations of Muslim women (and men) have also been very limited and limiting. Her essay traces how **Orientalist** knowledge about Muslim women is produced in and through media and how these technologies craft how US citizens think they understand a very diverse group of people. Hip-hop artist and author Anaya McMurray (stage name: Anaya Alimah) resists Western constructions of Muslim women as passive and oppressed by circulating empowered images that defy existing racial, religious, and gender stereotypes. Alimah shows how black Muslim women artists "improvise" hip-hop to produce nonmisogynistic lyrics that address spirituality and Islam; she even makes references to the Qur'an in her music (McMurray 85).

It is challenging to find representations that empower women and LGBTQPAI+ communities. In contemporary media, **postfeminism** appears to do this work. However, when we apply a critical lens to its mode of representation, we can see that it functions as another way of limiting how we interpret gender, race, class, sexuality, abilities, age, and nationalities in and the *only* way in which we have access to feminism in mass-circulated media (Tasker and Negra 2). Postfeminism is both a popular and academic term. It circulates in much the same way that postracial does by suggesting that we have moved beyond the need for feminism because gender equality and justice have been realized. One of the primary reasons it has popular traction is because Hollywood films and television shows (such as *Sex in the City* and *Scandal*) feature independent and empowered women who appear to no longer need broader sociopolitical changes to achieve their personal goals. It is important to note that women in these shows often are simultaneously sexualized and interpreted as in control of their sexuality. What such critique ignores is how creating individual characters who may claim to be successful and empowered still exist within patriarchal, racist, classist, homophobic, transphobic, and xenophobic social structures and that their self-proclaimed liberation is not *all* women's liberation.

As a scholarly term, postfeminism first was conceptualized within feminist media studies and has two identifiable strategies (Hollows and Moseley 7). First, it refers to a form of subjectivity (or being) that values "agency, freedom, sexual pleasure, fashion, consumer culture, hybridism, humor, and the renewed focus on the female body" (Adriaens and Bauwel 191). Second, it flags an economically independent subject that "promote[s] an aesthetic of wealth, to display privileged whiteness, heterosexuality, normative Western beauty ideals and individualism" (Wilkes 18). In this way, it suggests that feminism is an individualistic pursuit that can be reflected in what we buy (which ultimately reflects how others see and produce goods for us) rather than bell hooks's definition in Section I that emphasized feminism as a movement for social change.

Postfeminist television shows and movies often represent feminism *as* history (something that happened in the past, i.e., in the 1960s and 1970s) rather than embedded *in* an ongoing history. In the 1980s, there was an increase in the number of women and girls seen on television, but any sense of their political

Orientalist: The historical and contemporary constructions of people from the Middle and Far East through Western ideology; such representations have cultural and material effects because of the relations of power between East and West.

Postfeminism: How everyday people assume that gender equality and justice has been achieved and, within feminist media studies, the ways in which media appropriates feminism to sell ideas, images, and products to consumers.

and social progress was not represented. This phenomenon cannot be separated from how major television networks contributed to a return to conservative values in US society and a "backlash against feminism" (see Faludi; Kellner).

For example, television featured more young female characters (Ivins-Hulley 1198). However, as Kristen Myers found in her study of forty-five episodes of four TV series targeted at preteen girls (*Hannah Montana, Suite Life on Deck, Wizards of Waverly Place*, and *iCarly*), these shows circulate "antifeminist" messages. They "celebrated beauty and heterosexual coupling, demonized strong and unattractive women, and valorized antisocial girls" (Myers 198–199, 203). These programs featured "strong girl characters" that seemed to defy traditional notions of femininity, but when analyzed carefully, they were simply "heterosexy bullies, not feminists" (Myers 201). Indeed, in recent media, girls have been represented as bullies, more violent than ever before (and "meaner" than boys). Yet, as Meda Chesney-Lind shows in "Mean Girls, Bad Girls, or Just Girls: Corporate Media Hype and the Policing of Girlhood" (included in this section), this story is far more complicated. She deflates this media hype by providing context and statistics that show why girls only *seem* to be more violent or meaner than boys.

Girls, women, and LGBTQPAI+ people are not passive consumers of pop culture in their everyday lives. With the relatively recent boom of social media, people's engagement with pop culture has been reconfigured. New digital media provide alternative spaces for marginalized voices and forces us to rethink old notions of "expertise, authority, and communication skills" (Mann 295). The participation of black women media makers in social media such as Twitter and Tumblr "far outweighs their participation in other media channels" (Mann 294). Feminist zines and fan fiction challenge problematic gender ideologies and find new outlets online (Spiers 9). As Susan Driver shows in her book *Queer Girls and Popular Culture: Reading, Resisting, and Creating Media,* pop culture becomes a "process through which queer girls creatively imagine possibilities, forge connections, make meanings, and articulate relations" (14). New media provides an outlet to experiment with nonheteronormative identities.

Although changes have occurred in media as they broadcast shows that focus on same-sex couples or transgender people, heterosexuality still remains the hegemonic norm. Often, when LGBTQPAI+ identities are represented in media, they further perpetuate rather than challenge existing stereotypes. In the case of bisexual identities of celebrities such as Angelina Jolie and Lindsay Lohan that Ian Capulet observes in "With Reps Like These: Bisexuality and Celebrity Status" (included in this section), bisexuality is used as a "source of social status or publicity, rather than a potential avenue for empowerment and greater visibility" (p. 337). That is, it is only included in media when the media can profit from it and because "young heterosexual males . . . 'get a rise' out of reading that hot, young star hook-up with women on the side" (p. 342).

Could fetishizing bisexual celebrities for heterosexual males' fantasies or transgender celebrities for voyeuristic media consumption by the general public be another form of the male gaze that Mulvey theorized over forty years ago?

Perhaps it more accurately reflects straight and queer men and women's participation in crafting meanings ascribed to gender and sexuality in popular culture? Might we need a more structural analysis of how media institutions use sex—and a very particular version of sex—to sell their products? Regardless of how we answer these questions, it is clear we need more than just representations of difference; it matters greatly *how* gender, race, social class, age, abilities, and nationalities are constructed. The next time you hear someone say with ease that "sex sells"—whether it is in reference to products in advertisements or how a film is promoted to draw in an audience—you may want to ask which kind of sex they are referring to, because it appears as though only the bodies of young, white, slim women who wear sexy outfits and pose in submissive and seductive positions for heterosexual men sell. If we expand the notion of "sex" to include bodies of people of color and/or with disability and in different sizes, older women, or same-sex couples, then perhaps sex does not sell. By asking these kinds of critical questions, we can engage with popular culture and media representations in productive ways so that we might one day see a full range of empowered feminist and queer identities reflected back to us.

This section has asked you to think about a range of issues central to feminist and queer studies, from the social constructions of family and work to intersectional representations of straight and queer communities in popular culture. In each section, you have seen how some people's freedom might be others' oppressions and how this is yoked to our understandings of gender, race, social class, sexuality, religion, age, abilities, and nationality; you have also learned that feminist and queer scholars, activists, and practitioners do not always agree on how to address inequalities. Rather, as bell hooks argues in *Feminism Is for Everybody,* they offer ideas for social change based on philosophies of reform or revolution. As you reflect on the social issues debated in this section, ask yourself: Can equality and social justice be approached—perhaps even achieved—by working within the existing system? Will it require rethinking and new political initiatives that reconfigure gender, race, social class, sexuality, abilities, age, religion, and nationality so that social institutions are rebuilt on new foundations?

Critical Thinking Questions

1. How is the history of the social construction of families integral to our understanding of occupational segregation, the gender pay gap, sexual harassment, and discrimination in the contemporary labor market? How do intersectional approaches shed light on your answers to this question?

2. Why is it important to frame sex work as labor and not just as an extension of patriarchy and global capitalism?

3. In your own words, what are the philosophical and political differences between reproductive choice and reproductive justice? What role does intersectionality play?

4. In his essay included in this section, Brad Perry argues that sex education curricula—one that is robust and reflects our lives—is the key to building healthy sexualities and preventing gender-based violence in the future. Reflect on your own sex education. Do you agree with his statement? Why or why not?

5. Can you think of media texts that construct an empowered feminist or queer gaze? If so, what are they, where are they found, and how does it resist controlling images? If not, why do you think this is the case?

GLOSSARY

Bystander intervention 221
Comstock Laws 215
Eugenics movement 215
Fatherhood bonus 211
Gender pay gap 209
Glass ceiling 212
Hate crime 222
Interpersonal sexual violence 219

Islamophobia 222
Male gaze 223
Mother pay penalty 211
Neoliberalism 206
Nuclear family 203
Occupational segregation 210
Orientalist 225
Postfeminism 225

Second shift 209
Settler-colonials 203
Sex work 213
Sex trafficking 213
State violence 220
Xenophobia 205

WORKS CITED

Adriaens, Fien, and Sofie Van Bauwel. *"Sex and the City*: A Postfeminist Point of View? Or How Popular Culture Functions as a Channel for Feminist Discourse." *The Journal of Popular Culture*, vol. 47, no. 1, 2014, pp. 174–95.

Allen, Paula Gunn. *The Sacred Hoop: Recovering the Feminine in American Indian Traditions*. Reissued ed., Beacon Press, 1992.

Amott, Teresa, and Julie Matthaei. *Race, Gender and Work: A Multicultural Economic History of Women in the United States*. Revised ed., South End Press, 1999.

Babcock, Linda and Sara Laschever. *Women Don't Ask: Negotiation and the Gender Divide*. Princeton UP, 2003.

Bernhardt, Annette, et al. "Broken Laws, Unprotected Workers: Violations of Employment and Labor Laws in America's Cities." *Unprotected Workers Organization*, 2010, www.unprotectedworkers.org/index.php/broken_laws/index.

Boushey, Heather. "A Woman's Place is in the Middle Class." *The Shriver Report: A Woman's Nation Pushes Back from the Brink*, edited by Olivia Morgan et al., 2014, pp. 45–73.

Briggs, Laura. *Somebody's Children: The Politics of Transracial and Transnational Adoption*. Duke UP, 2012.

A Broken Bargain: Discrimination, Fewer Benefits and More Taxes for LGBT Workers. Movement Advancement Project/Center for American Progress/Human Rights Campaign, June 2013, www.lgbtmap.org/file/a-broken-bargain-full-report.pdf.

Budig, Michelle, "The Fatherhood Bonus and the Motherhood Penalty: Parenthood and the Gender Gap in Pay." *Third Way Fresh Thinking*, 2 Sept. 2014, content.thirdway.org/publications/853/NEXT_-_Fatherhood_Motherhood.pdf.

"CDC Releases Data on Interpersonal and Sexual Violence by Sexual Orientation." 2013. *CDC Newsroom*, United States Centers for Disease Control and Prevention, 25 Jan. 2013, www.cdc.gov/media/releases/2013/p0125_NISVS.html.

Chen, Stephanie. "'John Schools' Try to Change Attitudes about Paid Sex." *CNN*, 28 Aug. 2009, www.cnn.com/2009/CRIME/08/27/tennessee.john.school/index.html?eref=rss_us.

Collins, Patricia Hill. *Black Feminist Thought: Knowledge, Consciousness, and the Politics of Empowerment*. 10th Anniversary ed., Routledge, 2000.

———. "Booty Call: Sex, Violence, and Images of Black Masculinity." *Media and Cultural Studies Keyworks*, edited by Meenakshi Gigi Durham and Douglas M. Kellner, 2nd ed., Wiley-Blackwell, 2012, pp. 318–37.

———. "It's All in the Family: Intersections of Gender, Race, and Nation." *Hypatia*, vol. 13, no. 3, 1998, pp. 62.82.

Corbett, Christianne, and Catherine Hill. *Graduating to a Pay Gap: The Earnings of Men and Women One Year after College Graduation*. American Association of University Women, 2012, www.aauw.org/files/2013/02/graduating-to-a-pay-gap-the-earnings-of-women-and-men-one-year-after-college-graduation.pdf.

Davis, Angela. *Women, Race & Class*. Vintage Books, 1983.

D'Enbeau, Suzy. "Feminine and Feminist Transformation in Popular Culture: An Application of Mary Daly's Radical Philosophies to Bust Magazine." *Feminist Media Studies*, vol. 9, no. 1, 2009, pp. 17–36.

"Domestic Violence: Statistics and Facts." *SafeHorizon*, 2015, www.safehorizon.org/page/domestic-violence-statistics--facts-52.html.

Driver, Susan. *Queer Girls and Popular Culture: Reading, Resisting, and Creating Media*. Peter Lang, 2007.

Duggan, Lisa. *Twilight of Equality: Neoliberalism, Cultural Politics, and the Attack on Democracy*. Beacon Press, 2004.

"Facts and Figures: Ending Violence against Women." *UN Women*, Oct. 2015, www.unwomen.org/en/what-we-do/ending-violence-against-women/facts-and-figures.

Faludi, Susan. *Backlash: The Undeclared War against American Women*. Crown Publishing, 1991.

Gordon, Linda. *The Moral Property of Women: A History of Birth Control Politics in America*. U of Illinois P, 2007.

Gurr, Barbara. *Reproductive Justice: The Politics of Health Care for Native American Women*. Rutgers UP, 2014.

Hill, Catherine. *The Simple Truth About the Gender Pay Gap*. American Association of University Women, Fall 2015, www.aauw.org/research/the-simple-truth-about-the-gender-pay-gap/.

Hochschild, Arlie. *The Second Shift*. Avon Books, 1989.

Hollows, Joanne, and Rachel Moseley. *Feminism in Popular Culture*. Berg, 2006.

hooks, bell. *Feminism Is for Everybody*. Pluto Press, 2000.

Ivins-Hulley, Laura. "Narrowcasting Feminism: MTV's *Daria*." *The Journal of Popular Culture*, vol. 47, no. 6, 2014, pp. 1198–212.

Jhally, Sut, director. *Stuart Hall: Representation and the Media*. Media Education Foundation, 1997.

Kellner, Douglas. "Cultural Studies, Multiculturalism, and Media Culture." *Gender, Race, and Class in Media*, edited by Gail Dines and Jean M. Humez, 4th ed., Sage Publications, 2015, pp. 7–19.

Killaway, Mitch and Sunnivie Brydum. "These are the U.S. Transwomen Killed in 2015." *Advocate*, www.advocate.com/transgender/2015/12/11/these-are-trans-women-killed-in-2015.

Lindner, Katharina. "Images of Women in General Interest and Fashion Magazine Advertisements from 1955 to 2002." *Sex Roles*, vol. 51, no. 7/8, 2004, pp. 409–21.

Mann, Larisa. "What Can Feminism Learn from New Media?" *Communication and Critical/Cultural Studies*, vol. 11, no. 3, 2014, pp. 293–97.

May, Elaine Tyler. *America and the Pill*. Basic Books, 2010.

McMurray, Anaya. "Hotep and Hip-Hop: Can Black Muslim Women Be Down with Hip-Hop?" *Meridians*, vol. 8, no. 1, 2008, pp. 74–92.

Mennel, Eric. "Payments Start for N.C. Eugenics Victims, But Many Won't Qualify. *Shots: Health News*, National Public Radio, 5 Nov. 2014, www.npr.org/sections/health-shots/2014/10/31/360355784/payments-start-for-n-c-eugenics-victims-but-many-wont-qualify.

Miller-Young, Mirelle. *A Taste for Brown Sugar: Black Women in Pornography*. Duke UP, 2014.

Muñoz, José Esteban. *Cruising Utopia: The Then and There of Queer Futurity*. New York UP, 2009.

Myers, Kristen. "Anti-Feminist Messages in American Television Programming for Young Girls." *Journal of Gender Studies*, vol. 22, no. 2, 2013, pp. 192–205.

Quick Take: Lesbian, Gay, Bisexual, and Transgender Workplace Issues. Catalyst, 2015, http://www.catalyst.org/knowledge/lesbian-gay-bisexual-transgender-workplace-issues.

Rikleen, Lauren Stiller. "Women Lawyers Continue to Lag Behind Male Colleagues: Report of the Ninth Annual NAWL Survey on Retention and Promotion of Women in Law Firms." *National Association of Women Lawyers*, 2013. heinonline.org/HOL/LandingPage?handle=hein.journals/wolj100&div=32&id=&page=.

Roberts, Dorothy. *Killing the Black Body: Race, Reproduction and the Meaning of Liberty*. Vintage Books, 1998.

Ruiz, Vicki, and Ellen Carol DuBois, editors. *Unequal Sister: An Inclusive Reader in U.S. Women's History*. 4th ed., Routledge, 2007.

Smith, Andrea. "Beyond Pro-Life versus Pro-Choice: Women of Color and Reproductive Justice. *NWSA Journal*, vol. 17, no. 1, 2005, pp. 119–40.

———. *Conquest: Sexual Violence and American Indian Genocide*. Duke UP, 2015.

Spade, Dean. *Normal Life: Administrative Violence, Critical Trans Politics & the Limit of the Law*. Duke UP, 2015.

Spiers, Emily. "'Killing Ourselves Is Not Subversive': Riot Grrrl From Zine to Screen and the Commodification of Female Transgression." *Women: A Cultural Review*, vol. 26, no. 1/2, 2015, pp. 1–21.

"Statistics." *RAINN: Rape, Abuse, and Incest National Network*, 2009, rainn.org/statistics.

Tasker, Yvonne and Diane Negra. "Introduction: Feminist Politics and Postfeminist Culture." *Interrogating Post-Feminism*, edited by Yvonne Tasker and Diane Negra, Duke UP, 2007, pp. 1–26.

Tilly, Louise A., and Joan W. Scott. *Women, Work & Family*. Routledge, 1989.

United States Department of Labor. *Data and Statistics*. Jan. 2015, www.dol.gov/wb/stats/stats_data.htm.

"Violence Against Women in the United States: Statistics." *National Organization of Women,* 2015, now.org/resource/violence-against-women-in-the-united-states-statistic/.

Washington, Harriet. *Medical Apartheid: The Dark History of Medical Experimentation on Black Americans from Colonial Times to the Present.* Reprint ed., Anchor Books, 2008.

Welter, Barbara. "The Cult of True Womanhood: 1820-1860." *American Quarterly*, vol. 18, no. 2, 1966, pp. 151–74.

Wilkes, Karen. "Colluding with Neo-Liberalism: Post-Feminist Subjectivities, Whiteness and Expressions of Entitlement." *Feminist Review*, vol. 110, 2015, pp. 18–33.

Zinn, Maxine Baca, and Bonnie Thornton Dill, editors. *Women of Color in U.S. Society*. Temple UP, 1993.

---

35. • *Rebecca Barrett-Fox*

CONSTRAINTS AND FREEDOM IN CONSERVATIVE CHRISTIAN WOMEN'S LIVES (NEW)

Rebecca Barrett-Fox is a professor of sociology at Arkansas State University, where she directs women and gender studies. Her research focuses on conservative Christian movements in the United States, particularly the links between gender, sex, theology, and politics. She is the author of *God Hates: Westboro Baptist Church, American Nationalism, and the Religious Right* (University Press of Kansas, 2016), as well as numerous articles about religion, politics, and hate groups. The following piece was written specifically for this collection.

Hannah (who shared her story over a course of interviews but requested that her real name and identifying information not be shared) hoists her toddler daughter into the swing on the playground as her older daughter climbs the slide. Her friend Rachel should arrive soon with her own preschoolers, and Hannah is anxious. Rachel is pregnant again, as Hannah should be now, too—except that her third pregnancy ended a month ago in the stillbirth of a yearned-for baby boy. She attends a two hundred–person independent fundamentalist church—a congregation that interprets the Bible literally and espouses conservative political and social views and has no official ties to any other church. She loves her church and values the intergenerational mentoring of other women. They model for her Proverbs 31 womanhood, a template of femininity drawn from a Biblical passage describing the ideal wife and mother as both beautiful and hardworking. Broadly rejecting what they see as government interference, they homeschool their own many children. Despite their busy lives, after her stillbirth, members of the church provided several weeks' worth of meals and babysitting for the girls so that Hannah and her husband could focus on the funeral. Now, Hannah is not sure she can bear to see Rachel. She is blessed to have Quiverfull friends—families who believe that any form of birth control is a sin. As Psalm 127:4–5 in the King James Version (KJV) of the Bible states, "As arrows are in the hand of a mighty man; so are children of the youth. Happy is the man that hath his quiver full of them." However, she sometimes feels that the other wives in her church have made childbearing a competition—one in which a stillbirth is a sign of failure. She worries that her feelings may be rooted in jealousy and resolves to devote more prayer to the issue.

For conservative and fundamentalist Christians like Hannah, gender identities and roles are informed by orthodoxy ("right belief"), which tells participants what they should *believe* about gender, sex, and sexuality, and orthopraxis ("right practice"), which tells them what they should *do*. Hannah's beliefs about fertility shape her hopes about childbearing; her beliefs about gender shape her ideas about mothering. Though many women find such constraints oppressive, others find them empowering—a paradox that has often puzzled observers. In *You Can Be the Wife of a Happy Husband*, self-help author and motivational speaker Darien B. Cooper explains the liberating effects of constraints that she experienced in her own life-long marriage to her husband, saying, "Submission never means that our personalities, abilities, talents, or individuality should be buried. Rather, they are to be directed so they can be maximized and reflect the goodness and glory of God" (Cooper 23). Though there are many varieties of conservative Christianity, each stresses submission of the individual's life to the will of God, a will that is committed to gender *complementarianism*—the idea that God created everyone with a sex that aligns with a masculine or feminine gender and that God values and loves men and women equally but has created them for different roles (Council on Biblical Manhood and Womanhood). Strife, unhappiness, and inequality are not the result of gender distinctions but of people's fight against them. Christian

gender manuals, such as *The Total Woman*, *The Power of a Praying Wife*, *Raising a Modern-Day Knight*, and *Wild at Heart: Discovering the Secrets of a Man's Soul*, stress that marital harmony comes from embracing the limitations that conservative belief places on our lives and then excelling within those limits. While the details of orthopraxis vary among conservative Christian groups, three domains of women's lives, explored in this essay, are the targets of religious control: sexuality, bodies, and marriage and reproduction.

SEXUALITY

As the sexual revolution began to reshape mainstream American culture, many conservative Christians, such as Tim and Beverly LaHaye in *The Act of Marriage* (1976), argued for sexual passion in marriage. In their handbook, the LaHayes explained how new couples could achieve sexual pleasure—including orgasms for the bride, an explicit recognition that women deserve sexual pleasure. More recently, some conservative churches have tried pro-sex programming. Sermon series about sex's importance, along with ad campaigns promoting these series, are especially popular in nondenominational megachurches known for recruiting new members. Books such as *Holy Sex!* and *Intended for Pleasure* suggest that sex is created by God for human pleasure, not just procreation, and that heterosexual married partners have a mutual obligation to have great sex. Pastor Ed Young and his wife Lisa encourage a seven-day "sexperiment" (also the title of their book) in which congregants commit to having sex every day for a week. Pastor Mark Driscoll, coauthor with his wife Grace Driscoll of *Real Marriage*, has gone further, listing all the kinds of sex that the figures in the Bible's Song of Solomon had that Christians, too, should be having: fellatio, cunnilingus, "sacred stripping" (erotic dance for one's partner alone), and outdoor sex.

Yet these explicit commands for Christians to have sex are still presented within the narrow confines of married monogamous heterosexuality. Hebrews 13:4 of the KJV admonishes that "marriage be held in honor by all, and the bed undefiled" and warns that that "fornicators and adulterers God will judge." This verse is often used to explain that *only* heterosexual, cisgender marital sex is honorable; even if LGBTQ+ people are legally married, sex is sinful. Additionally, among more conservative groups, divorce is sinful (though being the victim of a divorce is not), and any remarriage, even between opposite-sex partners, may be considered adultery.

Within conservative Christian culture, as in secular culture, women are seen as less interested in sex's physical aspects and more interested in emotional connection, whereas men are depicted as primarily interested in physical sensation. Explains Juli Slattery of Focus on the Family, a conservative Christian media organization:

> A woman's sexual desire is far more connected to emotions than her husband's sex drive is.

> A man can experience sexual arousal apart from any emotional attachment. He can look at a naked woman and feel intense physical desire for her, while *at the same time* he may be completely devoted to and in love with his wife. For most women, this just doesn't compute. (para. 5)

Christian gender manuals consistently frame sex as *resulting from* emotional connection for women and *causing* emotional connection for men—giving women, who control access to sex, an inherent power advantage. In this view, men do not seek emotional connection to women, though women *need* emotional connection for sex. In contrast, because men are attracted to women's physical bodies, men are inherently tempted by women. Indeed, writers often coach men on how to express, within a range of acceptable "masculine" styles, those emotions that will connect them to women—and lead to holy sex. In contrast, because women are not attuned to men's physical desire, both married and unmarried women must be frequently reminded that their bodies tempt men; their appearances must be policed to protect men they encounter. The American Decency Association, a conservative Christian organization that opposes "indecent" media, ranging from pornography

to lingerie catalogues, reminds women of their duty in one of their radio spots:

> Ladies, God calls you to walk in this world as a candle among straw or gunpowder. A fire can injure and destroy many lives. Are you aware of how powerful your dress affects men? Does your style of dress help or hinder men? Bring glory to God as you honor God by your modesty. (Johnson)

First, women must recognize normative standards of sexual attractiveness, such as exposed knees and cleavage, then must refuse to adopt them for men's sake. In this way, every woman must morally guard men's spirituality and sexuality with her own body.

BODIES

Gender embodiment varies across conservative Christian subcultures, but modesty, however, defined, is valued highly, as is gender difference. In many groups, modesty and gender distinctiveness mean unisex dress is prohibited. Amish, conservative Mennonites, FLDS, and River Brethren, some Pentecostals and Baptists, and others require women to wear dresses that cover the majority of the leg and hide the outline of breasts. FLDS dress codes, for example, never allow women to show ankles, and both Amish and conservative Mennonites wear "cape dresses," which include an apron-like top to de-emphasize breasts. Among the most conservative groups, cosmetics are forbidden, as is hair cutting because 1 Corinthians 11:15 of the KJV declares that "if a woman have long hair, it is a glory to her: for her hair is given her for a covering." Some groups mandate long or uncut hair, sometimes in combination with head coverings such as the *kapp* (Amish), *Mitz* (Hutterite), or scarf or bonnet to indicate submission to the God-ordained hierarchy described in 1 Corinthians 11:3: "that the head of every man is Christ; and the head of the woman is the man; and the head of Christ is God." For groups that adopt head coverings, it is evidence of a woman's agreement with male leadership in the family and church and her willingness to be under the authority of men.

Among evangelical churches that are theologically and politically conservative while still engaging mainstream culture more than sects such as the Amish, women have to negotiate more ambiguous standards. Southern Baptists, Covenant Evangelicals, members of the Church of Christ, women in nondenominational churches, and many others must be simultaneously modest and attractive to their husbands without tempting other men. They must also put enough effort into their appearance that their husbands and others know that they care about being attractive to and therefore respectful of their husbands without prompting lust in other men or allowing such effort to interfere with other wifely duties. They face a double bind: if they fail to comply with these codes, they are either slovenly or vain, either disrespectful of their husbands' needs to have an attractive wife or disrespectful of other husbands (and their wives) by tempting men.

MARRIAGE AND REPRODUCTION

Because marriage is so highly valued (and perhaps because premarital sex is prohibited), conservative Christians tend to marry and have children (and more of them) at a younger age than their peers. While most Protestants have long accepted birth control methods and most Catholics who reject artificial birth control still use natural family planning (tracking fertility and abstaining from sex during ovulation), the most conservative groups do not. Families involved in the Quiverfull Movement, which reaches across denominations, reject all efforts to control family size or the spacing between births, including periodic abstinence within marriage. In this view, children are *always* a blessing from God, and therefore contraceptives or abstaining during times of female fertility is a rejection of God's blessing and, by extension, God's plan and God's authority. Pregnancy avoidance is thus a rejection of the hierarchy of authority over women's lives: God, then husband.

Men, like women, must accept their place in this hierarchy: the head of the family—a term often

reviled outside of conservative Christian subculture but one that proponents insist makes sense. Male "headship" means taking responsibility for the family, eschewing laziness and controlling behaviors and, for Quiverfull families, openness to large families. They can only do this, though, when women give them respect—something that may be difficult for women (Smith 95). In this model, men need respect and women need love, and only when they give each other what they require will marriage be happy (Eggerichs 5).

FREEDOM IN CONSTRAINT

Not every woman yields all domains of her life easily or fully to the doctrines and practices of her conservative Christian religion. Even when such groups thrive, women are not simply doing what they are told. They innovate, pushing beliefs to allow new practices. Religion has been a place where women lead before they can do so in other domains, such as politics or the workplace. The Salvation Army, a group organized around the masculine metaphor of the military, allowed nineteenth-century women to travel to cities, an opportunity they would have likely not had otherwise, to evangelize. Pentecostalism's somatic focus allows women's bodies to be inhabited by the Holy Spirit, giving them spiritual authority at least sometimes. Amish sects carefully proscribe women's dress, including the type and color of cloth, the style of dress, and the process for creating clothing, but within those confines, women express themselves with pride. Women who live in religious enclaves find support and community in them absent in the secular world, even if they must sometimes negotiate the rules of those communities carefully and creatively, as the story of Hannah, profiled at the beginning of this essay, suggests.

Hannah suffered eight miscarriages before undergoing a partial hysterectomy. Even as she mourned the loss of her fertility, she felt relieved not to have to suffer further pregnancy losses. During her fertility struggles, she had internalized implication that her "closed womb" was due to weak faith or unconfessed sin, but when biological children were no longer the measure of God's love for her, Hannah was able to approach her husband about alternatives to achieving her dream of motherhood. They soon adopted two children from Belarus, and they hope to adopt through domestic foster care. In this way, Hannah's body continues to rear, if not bear, children, cementing her place under her husband's headship and thus indicating her willingness to submit to God's gendered will for her life. Keeping her focus on maintaining that hierarchal relationship, rather than obsessing about fertility, has, Hannah shares, made her more available to God's directions for her life and brought two wonderful children into it. Like many women who willingly remain in their conservative tradition, she has found that the narrow confines of her faith have allowed her a deeper experience of it. Only by listening to women's own stories and their interpretations of their experiences can scholars hope to understand what, on the surface, seems like a paradox between women's subjugation and their liberation.

WORKS CITED

Cooper, Darien B. *You Can Be the Wife of a Happy Husband: Discovering the Keys to Marital Success.* Rev. ed., Destiny Image, 2010.

Driscoll, Mark and Grace. *Real Marriage: The Truth about Sex, Friendship, and Life Together.* Thomas Nelson, 2013.

Eggerichs, Emerson. *Love and Respect: The Love She Most Desires, the Respect He Desperately Needs.* Thomas Nelson, 2004.

Focus on the Family, www.focusonthefamily.com/marriage/sex-and-intimacy/understanding-your-husbands-sexual-needs/sex-is-a-physical-need.

The Holy Bible. King James Version, Zondervan, 1984.

Johnson, Bill. "Decency Minute." *American Family Minute*, 3 Sept. 2015, www.americandecency.org/decency_minute/AFR/decencyminute1.08.26.15.mp4.

LaHaye, Tim, and Beverly LaHaye. *The Act of Marriage: The Beauty of Sexual Love.* Zondervan, 1998.

Slattery, Juli. "Sex Is a Physical Need." *No More Headaches*, Tyndale House, 2009.

Smith, Leslie Durrough. *Righteous Rhetoric: Sex, Speech, and the Politics of Concerned Women for America.* Oxford UP, 2014.

Young, Ed, and Lisa Young. *Sexperiment: 7 Days to Lasting Intimacy with Your Spouse.* FaithWords, 2012.

36. • *Jessica E. Birch*

LOVE, LABOR, AND LORDE (NEW)

Jessica E. Birch is a lecturer in the general education SAGES program at Case Western University. Her teaching and research focus on how cultural narratives justify and perpetuate social inequality, using the theoretical lenses of feminist theory, critical race theory, critical pedagogy, multiethnic literature analysis, and cultural studies; she is particularly interested in the intersections among these areas. She is the area chair for race and ethnicity, as well as for popular culture and pedagogy, for the Midwest Popular Culture Association and has done a series of workshops on pedagogical inclusivity at the National Women's Studies Association Conference. Recent publications include contributions in *Gothic and Racism* (Universitas

Press, 2015), *Race and the Vampire Narrative* (Sense Publishers, 2015), *The Supernatural Revamped: From Timeworn Legends to 21st Century Chic* (Fairleigh Dickinson University Press, forthcoming), and *The Wiley-Blackwell Encyclopedia of Gender and Sexuality Studies* (Wiley-Blackwell, 2016). Her current research project examines the vampire in literature within the paradigm of dominant neoliberal discourse. The following piece was written specifically for this collection.

At the National Women's Studies Association Annual Conference, a button proclaims, "This is a recipe for success, not cookies."

Feminist theorists describe that idea as the public/private distinction: Men's lives are public, because men participate politically and economically. Women's lives are private, focusing on care work—childrearing, cleaning, and cooking. This is the story society discursively tells about women (because, for society, women are all the same): On one side lies success: financial gain, career advancement, and societal impact; on the other, mixing bowls derail women from success.

Care work is unpopular in the contemporary neoliberal US. Neoliberalism is an ideology—a set of narratives that shape society—that operates "to re-establish the conditions for capital accumulation and to restore the power of economic elites" (Harvey 19). One of the ways it does this is by demanding individualism, telling us that society is composed of a set of individuals, each of whom has an obligation only to herself, rather than community members who have obligations to care for each other.

Personal responsibility is the driving theme of neoliberalism. American society prizes independence and self-sufficiency, so we assume the powerful have earned their rewards. Each person sinks or swims on her own merits—and the only actions that matter are the ones in the job market.

This is why I bake cookies for my students.

❊ ❊ ❊

My grandmother's funeral: Someone is talking about my grandmother's biscuits. After the sermon, delivered by a man with hair like Don King's, a sweaty forehead, and the rolling cadence that differentiates preachers from ministers, come the eulogies. A man from the church group replaces biscuit woman. Leaning heavily on the podium, he fixes the congregation with a watery, sharp eye.

"I'm talking about some FRIED CHICKEN." I've never heard anyone address poultry with such vehemence. Wiping his forehead with a purple-striped handkerchief that matches his tie, he sighs heavily. "Anna made some damned fine fried chicken. Her fried chicken was so good, it made hot sauce cry! You hear me?"

Behind me to the left, a reflexive "Amen, brother" bursts out.

❊ ❊ ❊

On the campaign trail in 1992, Hillary Rodham Clinton says, "I could have stayed home and baked cookies and had teas, but what I decided to do was fulfill my profession" (Swinth 1).

Clinton has a profession. My grandmother had a job. My grandmother did not have teas. She did not stay home. She scrubbed white women's toilets, took care of white women's children, and washed white women's clothes. After working a full day, her hat still pinned perfectly, her dress still starched, her white gloves still perfectly clean, Anna Roberson came home to the house paid for by the blistered, calloused hands the gloves hid. There she scrubbed her own toilet, took care of her own children, and washed her own clothes in the bathtub.

We who are "poor, who are lesbians, who are Black, who are older," we are the women who know, as Audre Lorde says, "that survival is not an academic skill" (112). Survival in a world that tries to smother us before we can breathe, much less speak, is an act of resistance, an act that matters. My grandmother did more than survive. She had plans.

Later in life, she married the man I knew as my grandfather, a man who had a good job working for the city. Sometimes, then, she stayed home. She worked on her plans. When he entered high school—she herself had never gone to high school—she bought my father a violin. As a black boy in Pittsburgh in the 1950s, he took violin lessons, playing in the orchestra of the newly desegregated high school. He learned how to box, because he had to, and he was good at it, because he had to be to survive. And every Sunday, every holiday, my grandmother laid out a spread of food like the Baby Jesus Himself was coming down for dinner.

✳ ✳ ✳

I am nine. My aunts and uncles and cousins are all there when my grandmother drags me by the wrist into her bathroom. She is slender, skin dark and smooth like rye bread, tiny birdlike hands, and smoothly coiffed hair. Next to her, I look like a loaf of bread left out in the rain: pale, puffy, and unwanted.

The scale says I am 120 pounds. I step off the scale. She steps on: 92 pounds. She waits until we are again sitting on the beds with the red satin spreads—there is no space for couches—to say, "You're fat. Sloppy. Look at your thighs."

I look. When the tears well up in my eyes, I pick up my book, pretending to read.

✳ ✳ ✳

In 1972, Shirley Chisholm was the first black person and the first woman to run for the US presidency. She ran under the slogan, "unbought and unbossed" (392), as Carole Boyce Davies explains, contrasting Chisholm with Condoleeza Rice's loyalty to the George W. Bush administration. When a "black and/or female subject" gains power, and with that power begins "working publicly against the larger interests of the group to which s/he belongs," that is "condification" (395). That's what Davies calls

it when women work against the interests of other women. Condification is another word for women who internalize oppression so hard they lose everything, including their knowledge of who they are, where they've been, and how they got there.

When women with professions pay minimal wages to Anna Robersons to clean their homes, to cook their meals, to care for their children, they are engaging in condification. The narrative of family as a free choice disregards the material circumstances of women's lives and their interconnectedness. As Elsa Barkley Brown points out, these women "live the lives they do . . . because working class women live the lives they do . . . [and] white women live the lives they do . . . because women of color live the ones they do" (287). Some women support the status quo because it gives them a free pass into the privilege club. As members, they promote individualism to justify their insistence that they belong in the club.

Condification creates women who, "day by day," accept "tyrannies" that they "attempt to make [their] own," and perhaps one day, as Audre Lorde suggests, they may "sicken and die of them, still in silence" (41)—but I hope they do not. I am not a religious woman, but I pray that they may someday realize that their silence is imposed upon them by those who feed their fear like my grandmother fed her family. May they remember the defiant taste of their deeply buried words. May they remember themselves. May they remember that they are us.

✳ ✳ ✳

I am eleven. I ask my grandmother how to make apple pie. She stares at me for a long moment. I think she's going to tell me I'm fat. Instead, she says, "Watch."

She peels three McIntoshes, her small hands curving the paring knife around them, each peel coming off in one long spiral. Then she hands me an apple and waits. The family's running joke is that if my grandmother met God, she'd have a list of instructions ready. Now, my grandmother the talker says nothing.

My peels are choppy little hunks, wasting apple flesh. I cringe, trying to make them match hers, but then I'm slow. I know too well that when the Lord gave out patience, my grandmother didn't wait in line to get hers. At the twelfth apple, she shifts her weight, and I lay down the knife. She picks it up, slices one of the apples into quarters, puts it down.

When I put the second pie in the oven and look at my grandmother, she gives me a small nod. One movement of her head, down and then up.

For the rest of the visit, she does not tell me I'm fat.

❋ ❋ ❋

When my grandmother dies, we learn that she was born December 14, 1906, not December 24, 1916. Every year, we carefully wrapped a birthday present in birthday paper and a Christmas present in Christmas paper. She saved the paper from both. Gave it back to us as we left so we could reuse it. What kind of person lies to her family about her age and her birthday? The kind of person my grandmother was, I guess.

I wonder if I know what kind of person my grandmother was at all.

❋ ❋ ❋

The first year of my Ph.D. program, in a feminist theory course, one of my classmates says, "If you're not going to stay home to take care of your children, you don't deserve to have them."

No one disagrees with her, including our professor. I am the only person in this room who was in daycare as a child.

I know now that feminism, unlike survival, is often academic, because "the convenient omission of household works' problems from the programs of 'middle class' feminists past and present has often turned out to be a veiled justification . . . of their own exploitative treatment of their maids" (Davis 96). The "contemporary American culture" that Betty Friedan describes in *The Feminine Mystique* applies only to a specific set of women— women who, like Clinton, had a choice.

If the Devil had opened her screen door, Anna Roberson would have looked him in the eye and told

him, in the voice she used for white people, debt collectors, disrespectful children, and catcalling men, that he was not welcome in her home. There were— and are—thousands of Anna Robersons. Many of them do not get college degrees, or even high school diplomas. Most of them are strong, physically and emotionally. Some, like my grandmother, are what my father calls "a hard woman": a woman who takes no disrespect and gives no compliments.

These women are not Friedan's housewives, whose days involved "smiling as they ran the new electric waxer over the spotless kitchen floor . . . [and] kept their new washing machines and dryers running all day" (Friedan 61). Women of color and working class women "have rarely been offered the time and energy to become experts at domesticity" (Davis 232), because becoming an expert at domesticity has generally required the support of a (white) man with a (middle- to upper-class) stable income.

The work of women who had no choices except whether to survive provided choices to my classmates' mothers. I got my determination from women like my grandmother, who stepped up to vote knowing that they might be beaten and would be jailed. We are not the same, my classmates and I—and I do not want to be like them. Audre Lorde writes, "[The] master's tools will never dismantle the master's house. They may allow us temporarily to beat him at his own game, but they will never enable us to bring about genuine change" (Lorde 112). Succeeding by standing on the necks of others is the master's game, not mine.

My face is hot, but the voice that comes out of my mouth is my grandmother's, her ice-cold, diamond-sharp voice, girded by the hardness of Pittsburgh steel forged in the mills we can smell from her house when the wind is strong: "I don't believe I heard you correctly."

❋ ❋ ❋

As I begin teaching my first class, I must decide what to do when students fail assignments. My preliminary syllabus says that major assignments can be revised for partial credit. Colleagues tell me, "Some of them just don't want to work—save your time and energy. Failing is failing."

I think of my grandmother, who gave me the freedom to find my way in the kitchen, knowing that if I failed, I'd waste what precious little food we had. I remember those who came before me, who fought the first, most dangerous steps of the same battle I fight: my grandmother, Angela Davis, Shirley Chisholm, Mary McLeod Bethune, Audre Lorde, Fannie Lou Hamer, Rose Parks, Ella Baker, and all those whose names history has forgotten but whose actions live on. They did not save their time and energy. Unlike food, time and energy are free. They are mine to give, and I have a debt that will always be owed.

I revise my syllabus: *All assignments may be revised and resubmitted for full credit. Learning is a process, and we will figure it out together. No failure is final.*

* * *

After the funeral, we go to my grandmother's house, except that it's not my grandmother's house anymore. The church brings food: green beans, macaroni and cheese, collard greens, ham. Fried chicken. Everyone tells stories as they fill their plates. I sit on the red satin bedspread. The chicken is dry, and the hot sauce I pour on it doesn't even whimper, much less sob.

* * *

In my Introduction to Gender Studies course, my student bites into a butterscotch-oatmeal cookie, saying, "I thought feminists would laugh at me if I said I baked with my son on weekends. But my grandmother taught me how. Who taught you?"

I see my grandmother's hands, putting Sunday dinner on the table set with the blue and white china she'd acquired, piece by piece. And I realize something: I know what kind of person my grandmother was. She was unbought and unbossed, her whole life. She helped make a world in which I don't always have to be a hard woman, taught me how to survive when I do have to be. She was a woman whose pride in care work was a form of love.

To my student, I say, "My grandmother taught me."

WORKS CITED

Brown, Elsa Barkley. "'What Has Happened Here': The Politics of Difference in Women's History and Feminist Politics." *Feminist Studies*, vol. 18, no. 2, 1992, pp. 295–312.

Collins, Patricia Hill. *Black Feminist Thought: Knowledge, Consciousness, and the Politics of Empowerment.* 2nd ed., Routledge, 2000.

Davies, Carol Boyce. "'Con-di-fi-cation': Black Women, Leadership, and Political Power." *Still Brave: The Evolution of Black Women's Studies.* Edited by Stanlie M. James et al., Feminist Press at CUNY, 2009.

Davis, Angela. *Women, Race, and Class.* Random House, 1983.

Friedan, Betty. *The Feminine Mystique.* W.W. Norton, 1997.

Harvey, David. *A Brief History of Neoliberalism.* Kindle ed., Oxford UP, 2005.

Lorde, Audre. *The Black Unicorn: Poems.* Reissue ed., W.W. Norton, 1995.

———. *Sister Outsider: Essays and Speeches.* Reprint ed., Crossing Press, 2007.

Swinth, Kirsten. "Hillary Clinton, Cookies, and the Rise of Working Families." *CNN*, 16 Mar. 2012, www.cnn.com/2012/03/16/opinion/swinth-hillary-clinton/.

37. • *Monisha Das Gupta*

"BROKEN HEARTS, BROKEN FAMILIES":
The Political Use of Families in the Fight Against Deportation (new)

Monisha Das Gupta is professor of ethnic studies and women's studies at the University of Hawai'i at Mānoa. Among numerous articles and books in chapters, she published the award-winning *Unruly Immigrants: Rights, Activism, and Transnational South Asian Politics in the United States* (Duke 2006) and has an article forthcoming in *Latino Studies* titled "Mexican Migration to Hawai'i and U.S. Settler Colonialism." The piece that follows was written specifically for inclusion in this collection. It has been adapted from the author's article "'Don't Deport Our Daddies': Gendering State Deportation Practices and Immigrant Organizing." *Gender & Society,* vol. 28, no. 1, 2014, pp. 83–109.

In the course of my involvement in the immigrant rights movement since it was reenergized in 2006, when documented and undocumented migrants poured out on the streets of cities across the United States to protest anti-immigrant federal legislation, I joined an anti-deportation rally in Manhattan at the invitation of Families for Families in the summer of 2009. I was in New York for a few weeks to learn about migrant organizing, and was curious about Families for Freedom (FFF), which had been formed in 2002 in the wake of escalating deportations post-9/11. From its inception, it has been made up entirely of deportees and their loved ones. Those not directly affected by deportation are allies but not members. The organization represents migrants from the Caribbean, Latin America, Asia and Africa. The members have a range of immigration status—some are undocumented, others legal permanent residents (LPRs), and still others asylum seekers. Many of them live in mixed-status families with members who are US citizens.

The rally that day in front of the Federal Plaza, which houses the immigration court, was for a FFF organizer, the then fifty-two-year-old Brooklyn resident, Roxroy Salmon, a Jamaican national and a LPR. He was appearing before an immigration judge for a hearing on his deportation case. Many of us who had gathered that morning held signs that read "Broken Hearts, Broken Families. Stop Deportation Now," "Help Keep Children Safe. Stop Deportation," and "A Family United Is a Happy Family." During the several hours we waited for Roxroy, we sang and chanted about the attentiveness with which Roxroy cared for his mother and his children, three of whom lived with him; we communicated to all those who passed us on that busy street that we were standing up against a state practice that separated children from their parents. Hours later, Roxroy, who had been building the campaign against his deportation for two years, emerged to tell us that the judge had ordered his deportation for two minor drug convictions over twenty years ago.

As I examined FFF's representational strategies, I wondered what would make criminalized men of color, like Roxroy, sympathetic figures. Reading member testimonies on its older website,[1] I found that the emphasis on Roxroy's caregiving in his family was not exceptional. It was a theme that ran through the narratives of and about other men who had been deported or were in deportation proceedings. Was the portrayal of these men as loving and caring fathers a move on their part to represent themselves in the public eye as migrants deserving of reprieve? As a feminist, I wanted to find out how the organization mobilized families, the public appeal to which made me wary because "the family" and family values have been appropriated by the Right to push a conservative white heteropatriarchal agenda to promote sexual, economic, and political control over women, measures that are particularly punitive for poor women.

What set FFF apart from many others, which appealed to normative ideas of the family in fighting deportation, was its unwavering commitment to publicly advocating the rights of criminalized members, most of whom, mirroring the prison population, were men of color. Its entry point—the role of deportation in tearing apart families—helps us piece together how deportation, working hand in hand with mass incarceration, reorganizes kinship arrangements as well as the division of labor within families. The testimonies that were carried on its older website and my interviews with organizers reveal the ways in which the state intrudes in the lives of migrants of color to put not only their economic viability at risk but also their ability to do carework in the private sphere. This type of state violence, feminist theorists of color have reminded us, have historically shaped communities of color, which are not allowed to shield their private lives from state intervention (Cohen).

Migrants, who often share the same inner-city neighborhoods with African Americans and Chicanos, are subject to heavy policing and racial profiling, which have led to the mass incarceration of the minoritized citizenry in the United States. But for noncitizens the consequences of encounters with the criminal legal system are somewhat different from those suffered by citizens. Under current law, they are barred for their lifetime from returning to the United States regardless of the lives they built and of their intimate ties to US-born spouses, children, and siblings.

The legal grounds for the permanent removal of lawfully present immigrants and undocumented migrants with criminal convictions had been consolidated in 1996. With the passage of the Illegal Immigration Reform and Immigrant Responsibility Act (IIRIRA) in 1996, immigration judges lost the discretion they had exercised from 1976 onward to waive the removal of long-term LPRs with criminal records by taking into account the hardship to US-born or LPR family members (Hing 58–64). The IIRIRA expanded the definition of aggravated felony to misdemeanors and low-level offenses for noncitizens. Those with such convictions are subject to mandatory detention and removal. The changes to the law have been applied zealously in the twenty-first century. In this period, several federal programs authorized local police to find out whether arrested noncitizens had immigration (civil) violations. This federal–local law enforcement cooperation enhanced the ability of immigration authorities to identify deportable migrants. In 2014, the Immigration and Customs Enforcement removed 315,943 people and reported that 85 percent of the 102,224 individuals removed from the interior (i.e., not at the border) had criminal convictions (United States). These numbers show that the criminal legal system has become a key partner in the business of deporting migrants who lived in the United States.

The removal of "criminal aliens" as an immigration priority has broad public support fed by racialized discourses about criminality and the need for law and order. The division this discourse creates between "good" migrants, who deserve legalization, and "bad" criminal migrants, who need to be expelled permanently, is so powerful that it has also entrenched itself in immigrant activism. A FFF organizer at the time, Manisha Vaze, pointed out the pervasiveness of this divisive argument in the movement when she observed, "I hear it all over—we want to keep the hardworking undocumented family-oriented immigrants in this country. But those criminals should be deported. And there is no real analysis of what it means to be a criminal for immigration purposes" (Vaze). The importance of FFF's work lies in offering an analysis of how criminalization works in the lives of migrants of color and in situating the deportation crisis in the daily struggles of these migrants.

The FFF members, many of whom had criminal convictions, faced a difficult task, akin to that shouldered by those who advocate prisoners' rights, because the public perceives them as lawbreakers and deadbeat dads who are unable to financially and emotionally support their families. These racialized expectations about normative fatherhood were codified into law in 1996 as part of restructuring welfare and reducing public assistance for single mothers, whose benefits were tied to stringent child support collection and paternity establishment requirements (Curran and Abrams). The FFF men's accounts as well as those of their partners and children directly counter the stereotypical casting of men who have criminal convictions as uncaring and irresponsible (see Pallares on the emergence of the family as a political subjectivity and site of racial resistance in the immigrant rights movement). They present in loving detail the work they did in caring not only for their biological children but also stepchildren from their partners' previous marriages as well as elderly parents. They eloquently express the ways in which their indefinite separation from their children or their constant fear of deportation interfered with their ability to be good fathers.

Howard, a FFF member deported to Jamaica for not complying with a prior deportation order, described his feelings on being separated from his US citizen wife, who sponsored him for residency, and three children: "Even though I'm not locked up, it feels like prison. I worry about time I used to spend with kids. We spent precious time together. I don't want my kids to grow up without a father" ("Barbara and Howard"). From his wife's testimony, we learn that Howard used to "pick up the children from school; take them to the library,

park and McDonalds." After Howard's deportation, his wife, who worked at a drug store, had difficulty picking up one of their children from school on time because of her work schedule and was told that the school would notify the Office of Children and Family Services for neglect if she were repeatedly late. Like Howard's wife, who remarked, "Life has turned upside down since our husbands were taken away," Carol, whose Guyanese husband was arrested for marijuana possession, expressed her frustration with her new role as a single mother as a result of her husband's nine-month-long incarceration at an immigration detention center. In her testimony, she confessed, "Raising a daughter without any help is a struggle. . . . Natasha got sick last week. . . . No matter how much it hurt, I had to send her to school and go to work as a home health aide" ("Carol and Linden"). Carol's narrative points to an irony that is typical of a society where commodified and paid carework is done by women of color for other, better-off families while struggling to take care of their own. In this racialized and gendered division of labor, families that lose a caregiver to deportation do not have the resources to replace the emotional and physical labor. Jani, an African American woman, in asking for sanctuary for her Haitian husband, Jean, who had a criminal record, recounted the crucial role he played in her life by taking care of their children so that she could attend college and earn her bachelor's degree.

Joe, an asylum seeker from China, in his testimony to the congregants of St. Paul of the Apostle Church, expressed his and his wife's constant anxiety of being separated from their small children. He said, "As parents facing deportation, we feel helpless to protect our own children. . . . We love our children's smiles. We want to see them grow. We want to be in their daily life. . . . I have been working in a restaurant for 10 years. . . . Today I am 28. I am a young father. I want to be a good father. . . . My daughter here—she is the oldest child. She is 2 now. I take her to the playground, even if I am tired. She has a lot of energy. She deserves the best." Both Howard and Joe articulate what they consider to be the qualities of good fatherhood; both emphasize time spent with their children and focus on everyday tasks of taking care of them and the daily, mundane pleasures of fatherhood. Similarly, when testifying with her nine-year-old son, Joshua, to the United Nations Special Rapporteur, Kathy McArdle, who continues to sit on FFF's board, shared an ordinary but tender domestic moment while recounting the horrors of Calvin's arrest at their home early one morning by eight armed immigration agents. Recalling the interactions Calvin had with their son, she said, "Their greatest joy was probably the tickle fights they used to have, and just quiet moments together that can never be duplicated by phone calls." In the magazine *Colorlines*, an older Joshua is quoted as remembering his father's cooking: "I miss his cooking. I really liked his rice that he used to make. It had coconut milk in it" (Wessler). Calvin, a LPR, had lived in the United States for thirty-three years at the time of his arrest and deportation in 2004.

Janis Rosheuvel, former executive director of FFF, attributes the focus on men's caregiving in their households to the lived experience of these families. Fathers struggling to find work often become the primary caretakers, cooking their children dinner, taking them to the park, and helping them with their homework. FFF, she noted, represents men and women who jointly care for their children and elderly to survive in decaying urban areas while working low-paying jobs without adequate benefits (Rosheuvel). These inner city men of color have few prospects of gainful employment, especially if they have a criminal record or are undocumented. Roxroy, for example, could not financially support his family. Instead, he took on the role of the person who took care of his children, his mother, who suffered from Alzheimer's disease, and his infant grandchild. This work ensured that his eighteen-year-old daughter could attend a local university. His life story, Rosheuvel points out, is not an exception when it comes to members of the organization.

The testimonies from FFF members challenge us to apply the feminist insights about kinship arrangements in communities of color where men's place in their families cannot be read straightforwardly

through the hegemonic scripts about masculinity that is contingent on breadwinning. The emotional content of the testimonies of FFF members sheds light on the reorganization of kinship and the everyday caregiving tasks in migrant and mixed-status families through immigration enforcement. Deportation not only serves to deprive migrants of their livelihood, discipline them for their activism, and target their biological reproduction (Chavez; Buff) but also impacts their ability to care for their family members and households.

In the application of deportation policy, we can discern a set of codes that appeal to morality to devalue the relationships of criminalized migrants to their loved ones. The folding together of law enforcement, national security, and immigration enforcement constantly remind FFF that their members and their loved ones are under attack because they fall outside of nationally and racially marked familial arrangements considered normative. In this context, Rosheuvel's insistence that "Our *family* is valuable; our family deserves justice; our family should have access to relief and justice like any other family" rests on the recognition that deportees' kinship ties are devalued because they do not conform to dominant ideologies that govern the family as an institution (Rosheuvel). The revaluation renders visible the emotional and material labor of migrant men in their households. The stories of domesticity, intimacy, and tenderness under social and economic circumstances that strain heteronormative versions of these affective states counteract the dehumanizing portrayals of these men as dangerous criminals, terrorists, and men who flout the "rule of law," a concept that reifies the state's sovereignty exercised through its right to deport. Deportation practices that mandate lifetime separation of family members themselves create new configurations of nonnormative kinship, desire, and intimacy. These split families may signal a restructuring of heterosexuality by unmooring it from heteronormativity, as feminist scholar Jasbir Puar suggests (146). The long-distance arrangements raise afresh questions about what it means to negotiate heterosexuality as well as affective and caregiving structures in an era of deportation.

Simply put, FFF's narratives of good fathering are not just a strategic choice to cast these men as respectable, domesticated, and deserving of public sympathy. They confront us with the ways in which deportation becomes an instrument through which the state continues to define "the family." However, in the immigrant rights movement, discussions about the relationship between immigration regulation and the regulation of gender and sexuality are rare outside of feminist and queer spaces. As an immigrant feminist who is involved in the movement, the process of interrogating my skepticism about FFF's mobilization of "families" and attending to FFF's analysis of the intersection between the criminal legal system and immigration enforcement underlines the importance of recognizing that the organization of gender and sexuality lies at the heart of immigration policy and, thus, addressing state control over our intimate lives needs to be central to visions of justice for migrants and their loved ones.

NOTES

1. The older version of the FFF Web page is archived at wayback.archive.org/ and can be accessed by searching for www.familiesforfreedom.org/index.htm. Some of the personal narratives quoted here can be accessed by clicking on the Truth Commission link. The testimonies of Jean and Jani, Joe and Mei, and Josh and Kathy used here are no longer online, but the stories about Joe and Mei and Josh and Kathy can be accessed at familiesforfreedom.org/families/kathy-josh-calvin and familiesforfreedom.org/families/chen-family.

WORKS CITED

"Barbara and Howard." *Families for Freedom,* familiesforfreedom.org/families/barbara-howard. Accessed 11 Sept. 2015.

Buff, Rachel Ida. "The Deportation Terror." *American Quarterly*, vol. 60, no. 3, 2008, pp. 523–51.

"Carol and Linden." *Families for Freedom,* familiesforfreedom.org/families/carol-linden. Accessed 11 Sept. 2015.

Chavez, Leo R. *The Latino Threat: Constructing Immigrants, Citizens, and the Nation.* Stanford UP, 2008.

Cohen, Cathy. "Deviance as Resistance: A New Research Agenda for the Study of Black Politics." *Du Bois Review*, vol. 1, no. 1, 2004, pp. 27–45.

Curran, Laura, and Laura Abrams. "Making Men into Dads: Fatherhood, the State and Welfare Reform." *Gender & Society*, vol. 14, no. 5, 2000, pp. 662–78.

Hing, Bill Ong. *Deporting Our Souls: Values, Morality, and Immigration Policy.* Cambridge UP, 2006.

Paralles, Amalia. *Family Activism: Immigrant Struggles and the Politics of Noncitizenship.* Rutgers UP, 2014.

Puar, Jasbir. *Terrorist Assemblage: Homonationalism in Queer Times.* Durham, NC: Duke UP, 2007.

Rosheuvel, Janis. Personal Interview. 2010.

United States, Department of Homeland Security, Immigration and Customs Enforcement. *FY 2014 ICE Immigration Removals.* 2014, www.ice.gov/removal-statistics.

Vaze, Manisha. Personal Interview. 10 July 2009.

Wessler, Seth. "Double Punishment." *Colorlines*, 9 Oct. 2009, www.colorlines.com/articles/double-punishment.

ADDITIONAL RESOURCES

Detention Watch Network. www.detentionwatchnetwork.org/.

Families for Freedom. familiesforfreedom.org/.

BEYOND SAME-SEX MARRIAGE:
A New Strategic Vision for All Our Families and Relationships (2008)

Founded in 2006, beyondmarriage.org is a collective of LGBTQPAI+ activists. Their cooperative work was generated following a two-day workshop and the statement is intended to offer political strategies that intervene in heteronormative constructions of marriage and inform public policy. The following article originally was published in *Gender and Sexuality* (2008).

We, the undersigned—lesbian, gay, bisexual, and transgender (LGBT) and allied activists, scholars, educators, writers, artists, lawyers, journalists, and community organizers—seek to offer friends and colleagues everywhere a new vision for securing governmental and private institutional recognition of diverse kinds of partnerships, households, kinship relationships, and families. In so doing, we hope to move beyond the narrow confines of marriage politics as they exist in the United States today.

We seek access to a flexible set of economic benefits and options regardless of sexual orientation, race, gender/gender identity, class, or citizenship status.

We reflect and honor the diverse ways in which people find and practice love, form relationships, create communities and networks of caring and support, establish households, bring families into being, and build innovative structures to support and sustain community.

In offering this vision, we declare ourselves to be part of an interdependent, global community. We stand with people of every racial, gender, and sexual identity, in the United States and throughout the world, who are working day-to-day—often in harsh political and economic circumstances—to resist the structural violence of poverty, racism, misogyny, war, and repression and to build an unshakable foundation of social and economic justice for all, from which authentic peace and recognition of global human rights can at long last emerge.

WHY THE LGBT MOVEMENT NEEDS A NEW STRATEGIC VISION

The struggle for same-sex marriage rights is only one part of a larger effort to strengthen the security and stability of diverse households and families. LGBT communities have ample reason to recognize that families and relationships know no borders and will never slot narrowly into a single existing template.

All families, relationships, and households struggling for stability and economic security will be helped by separating basic forms of legal and economic recognition from the requirement of marital and conjugal relationship.

U.S. census findings tell us that a majority of people, whatever their sexual and gender identities, do not live in traditional nuclear families. Recognizing the diverse households that already are the norm in this country is simply a matter of expanding upon the various forms of legal recognition that already are available. The LGBT movement has played an instrumental role in creating and advocating for domestic partnerships, second parent adoptions, reciprocal beneficiary arrangements, joint tenancy/

home-ownership contracts, health care proxies, powers of attorney, and other mechanisms that help provide stability and security for lesbian, gay, bisexual, and heterosexual individuals and families. During the height of the AIDS epidemic, our communities formed support systems and constructed new kinds of families and partnerships in the face of devastating crisis and heartbreak. Both our communities and our HIV organizations recognized, respected, and fought for the rights of nontraditionally constructed families and nonconventional partnerships. Moreover, the transgender and bisexual movements, so often historically left behind or left out by the larger lesbian and gay movement, have powerfully challenged legal constructions of relationship and fought for social, legal, and economic recognition of partnerships, households, and families, which include members who shatter the narrow confines of gender conformity.

To have our government define as "legitimate families" only those households with couples in conjugal relationships does a tremendous disservice to the many other ways in which people actually construct their families, kinship networks, households, and relationships. For example, who among us seriously will argue that the following kinds of households are less socially, economically, and spiritually worthy?

- Senior citizens living together, serving as each other's caregivers, partners, and/or constructed families
- Adult children living with and caring for their parents
- Grandparents and other family members raising their children's (and/or a relative's) children
- Committed, loving households in which there is more than one conjugal partner
- Blended families
- Single-parent households
- Extended families (especially in particular immigrant populations) living under one roof, whose members care for one another
- Queer couples who decide to jointly create and raise a child with another queer person or couple, in two households
- Close friends and siblings who live together in long-term, committed, nonconjugal relationships,

serving as each other's primary support and caregivers
- Caregiving and partnership relationships that have been developed to provide support systems to those living with HIV/AIDS

Marriage is not the only worthy form of family or relationship, and it should not be legally and economically privileged above all others. Although we honor those for whom marriage is the most meaningful personal— for some, also a deeply spiritual-choice, we believe that many other kinds of kinship relationship, households, and families must also be accorded recognition.

AN INCREASING NUMBER OF HOUSEHOLDS AND FAMILIES FACE ECONOMIC STRESS

Our strategies must speak not only to the fears but also to the hopes of millions of people in this country— LGBT people and others–who are justifiably afraid and anxious about their own economic futures.

Poverty and economic hardship are widespread and increasing. Corporate greed, draconian tax cuts and breaks for the wealthy, and the increasing shift of public funds from human needs into militarism, policing, and prison construction are producing ever greater wealth and income gaps between the rich and the poor in this country and throughout the world. In the United States, more and more individuals and families (disproportionately people of color and single-parent families headed by women) are experiencing the violence of poverty. Millions of people are without health care, decent housing, or enough to eat. We believe a LGBT vision for the future ought to accurately reflect what is happening throughout this country. People are forming unique unions and relationships that allow them to survive and create the communities and partnerships that mirror their circumstances, needs, and hopes. Although many in the LGBT community call for legal recognition of same-sex marriage, many others–heterosexual and/ or LGBT–are shaping for themselves the relationships, unions, and informal kinship systems that validate and support their daily lives, the lives they are actually living, regardless of what direction the current ideological winds might be blowing.

The Right's "Marriage Movement" is Much Broader Than Same-Sex Marriage

LGBT movement strategies must be sufficiently prophetic, visionary, creative, and practical to counter the Right's powerful and effective use of "wedge" politics—the strategic marketing of fear and resentment that pits one group against another.

Right-wing strategists do not merely oppose same-sex marriage as a stand-alone issue. The entire legal framework of civil rights for all people is under assault by the Right, coded not only in terms of sexuality but also in terms of race, gender, class, and citizenship status. The Right's anti-LGBT position is only a small part of a much broader conservative agenda of coercive, patriarchal marriage promotion that plays out in any number of civic arenas in a variety of ways—all of which disproportionately impact poor, immigrant, and people-of-color communities. The purpose is not only to enforce narrow, heterosexist definitions of marriage and coerce conformity but also to slash to the bone governmental funding for a wide array of family programs, including childcare, health care and reproductive services, and nutrition, and transfer responsibility for financial survival to families themselves.

Moreover, as we all know, the Right has successfully embedded "stealth" language into many anti-LGBT marriage amendments and initiatives, creating a framework for dismantling domestic partner benefit plans and other forms of household recognition (for queers and heterosexual people alike). Movement resources are drained by defensive struggles to address the Right's issue-by-issue assaults. Our strategies must engage these issues head-on, for the long term, from a position of vision and strength.

"Yes!" to Caring Civil Society and "No!" to the Right's Push for Privatization

Winning marriage equality in order to access our partners' benefits makes little sense if the benefits that we seek are being shredded.

At the same time same-sex marriage advocates promote marriage equality as a way for same-sex couples and their families to secure Social Security survivor and other marriage-related benefits, the Right has mounted a long-term strategic battle to dismantle all public service and benefit programs and civic values that were established beginning in the 1930s, initially as a response to widening poverty and the Great Depression. The push to privatize Social Security and many other human needs benefits, programs, and resources that serve as lifelines for many, married or not, is at the center of this attack. In fact, all but the most privileged households and families are in jeopardy as a result of a wholesale right-wing assault on funding for human needs, including Medicare, Medicaid, welfare, HIV-AIDS research and treatment, public education, affordable housing, and more.

This bad news is further complicated by a segment of LGBT movement strategy that focuses on same-sex marriage as a stand-alone issue. Should this strategy succeed, many individuals and households in LGBT communities will be unable to access benefits and support opportunities that they need because those benefits will be available only through marriage, if they remain available at all. Many transgender, gender queer, and other gender-nonconforming people will be especially vulnerable, as will seniors. For example, an estimated 70–80% of LGBT elders live as single people, yet they need many of the health care, disability, and survivorship benefits now provided through partnerships only when the partners are legally married.

Rather than focus on same-sex marriage rights as the only strategy, we believe the LGBT movement should reinforce the idea that marriage should be one of many avenues through which households, families, partners, and kinship relationships can gain access to the support of a caring civil society.

The Longing for Community and Connectedness

We believe LGBT movement strategies must not only democratize recognition and benefits but also speak to the widespread hunger for an authentic and just community.

So many people in our society and throughout the world long for a sense of caring community and connectedness and for the ability to have a decent standard of living and pursue meaningful lives free from the threat of violence and intimidation. We seek to create a movement that addresses this longing.

So many of us long for communities in which there is systemic affirmation, valuing, and nurturing of difference, and in which conformity to a narrow and restricting vision is never demanded as the price of admission to caring civil society. Our vision is the creation of communities in which we are encouraged to explore the widest range of nonexploitive, nonabusive possibilities in love, gender, desire, and sex–and in the creation of new forms of constructed families without fear that this searching will potentially forfeit for us our right to be honored and valued within our communities and in the wider world. Many of us, too, across all identities, yearn for an end to repressive attempts to control our personal lives. For LGBT and queer communities, this longing has special significance.

We who have signed this statement believe it is essential to work for the creation of public arenas and spaces in which we are free to embrace all of who we are, repudiate the right-wing demonizing of LGBT sexuality and assaults upon queer culture, openly engage issues of desire and longing, and affirm, in the context of caring community, the complexities and richness of gender and sexual diversity. However we choose to live, there must be a legitimate place for us.

THE PRINCIPLES AT THE HEART OF OUR VISION

We, the undersigned, suggest that strategies rooted in the following principles are urgently needed:

- Recognition and respect for our chosen relationships, in their many forms
- Legal recognition for a wide range of relationships, households, and families and for the children in all of those households and families, including same-sex marriage, domestic partner benefits, second-parent adoptions, and others

- The means to care for one another and those we love
- The separation of benefits and recognition from marital status, citizenship status, and the requirement that "legitimate" relationships be conjugal
- Separation of church and state in all matters, including regulation and recognition of relationships, households, and families
- Access for all to vital government support programs, including but not limited to affordable and adequate health care, affordable housing, a secure and enhanced Social Security system, genuine disaster recovery assistance, and welfare for the poor
- Freedom from a narrow definition of our sexual lives and gender choices, identities, and expression
- Recognition of interdependence as a civic principle and practical affirmation of the importance of joining with others (who may or may not be LGBT) who also face opposition to their household and family compositions, including older people, immigrant communities, single parents, battered women, prisoners and former prisoners, people with disabilities, and poor people

We must ensure that our strategies do not help create or strengthen the legal framework for gutting domestic partnerships (LGBT and heterosexual) for those who prefer this or another option to marriage, reciprocal beneficiary agreements, and more. LGBT movement strategies must never secure privilege for some while foreclosing options for many. Our strategies should expand the current terms of debate, not reinforce them.

A WINNABLE STRATEGY

No movement thrives without the critical capacity to imagine what is possible.

Our call for an inclusive new civic commitment to the recognition and well-being of diverse households and families is neither utopian nor unrealistic. To those who argue that marriage equality must take strategic precedence over the need for relationship recognition for other kinds of partnerships, households, and families, we note that same-sex marriage (or close approximations thereof) were approved in Canada and other countries only after civic commitments to universal or widely available health care and other such benefits. In addition, in the United States, a strategy that links same-sex partner rights with a broader vision is beginning to influence some statewide campaigns to defeat same-sex marriage initiatives.

A Vision for All Our Families and Relationships is Already Inspiring Positive Change

We offer a few examples of the ways in which an inclusive vision, such as we propose, can promote practical, progressive change and open up new opportunities for strategic bridge-building.

- **Canada**
  Canada has taken significant steps in recent years toward legally recognizing the equal value of the ways in which people construct their families and relationships that fulfill critical social functions (such as parenting, assumption of economic support, provision of support for aging and infirm persons, and more).
  - In the 1990s, two constitutional cases heard by that country's Supreme Court extended specific rights and responsibilities of marriage to both opposite-sex and same-sex couples. Canada's federal Modernization of Benefits and Obligation Act (2000) then virtually erased the legal distinction between marital and non-marital conjugal relationships.
  - In 2001, in consideration of its mandate to "consider measures that will make the legal system more efficient, economical, accessible, and just," the Law Commission of Canada released a report, *Beyond Conjugality,* calling for fundamental revisions in the law to honor and support all caring and interdependent personal adult relationships, regardless of whether or not the relationships are conjugal in nature.

[. . .]

- **South Carolina**
  The South Carolina Equality Coalition (www.scequality.org) is fighting a proposed constitutional amendment with an organizing effort emphasizing "Fairness for All Families." This coalition is not only focused on LGBT-headed families but also is intentionally building relationships with a broad multiconstituency base of immigrant communities, elders, survivors of domestic violence, unmarried heterosexual couples, adopted children, families of prisoners, and more. As we write this statement, the coalition's efforts to work in this broader way are being further strengthened by emphasis on the message "Families have no borders. We all belong."

- **Utah**
  In September 2005, Salt Lake City Mayor Ross Anderson signed an executive order enabling city employees to obtain health insurance benefits for their "domestic partners." A few months later, trumping the executive order, the Salt Lake City Council enacted an ordinance allowing city employees to identify an "adult designee" who would be entitled to health insurance benefits in conjunction with the benefits provided to the employee. The requirements included living with the employee for more than a year, being at least 18 years old, and being economically dependent or interdependent. Benefits extend to children of the adult designee as well. Although an employee's same-sex or opposite-sex partner could qualify, this definition is broad enough to encompass many other household configurations. The ordinance has survived both a veto by the mayor (who wanted to provide benefits only to "spousal like" relationships) and a lawsuit launched by antigay groups. The judge who ruled in the lawsuit wrote that "single employees may have relationships outside of marriage, whether motivated by family feeling, emotional attachment or practical considerations, which draw on their resources to provide the necessaries of life, including health care." We advocate close attention to such

efforts to provide material support for the widest possible range of household formations.

[. . .]

A Bold, New Vision Will Speak to Many Who Are Not Already With Us

At a time when an ethos of narrow self-interest and exclusion of difference is ascendant, and when the Right asserts a scarcity of human rights and social and economic goods, this new vision holds long-term potential for creating powerful and vibrant new relationships, coalitions, and alliances across constituencies—communities of color, immigrant communities, LGBT and queer communities, senior citizens, single-parent families, the working poor, and more—hit hard by the greed and inhumanity of the Right's economic and political agendas.

At a time when the conservative movement is generating an agenda of fear, retrenchment, and opposition to the very idea of a caring society, we need to claim the deepest possibilities for interdependent social relationships and human expression. We must dare to dream the world that we need, the world that has room for us all, even as we also do the painstaking work of crafting the practical strategies that will address the realities of our daily lives. The LGBT movement has a history of being diligent and creative in protecting our families. Now, more than ever, is the time to continue to find new ways of defending all our families and to fight to make same-sex marriage just one option on a menu of choices that people have about the way they construct their lives.

We invite friends everywhere to join us in ensuring that there is room, recognition, and practical support for us all, as we dream together a new future where all people will truly be free.

---

39. • *Marlene Kim*

POLICIES TO END THE GENDER WAGE GAP IN THE UNITED STATES (2013)

Marlene Kim, a professor of economics at the University of Massachusetts, Boston, specializes in discrimination of the working poor and wrote *Race and Economic Opportunity in the Twenty-first Century* (Routledge 2007) as well as numerous articles. She is the recipient of the first Rhonda Williams Prize from the International Association of Feminist Economics (2002). The following article originally was published in the *Review of Radical Political Economics* (2013).

Women continue to earn less than men in the United States. Among full-time workers, on average women earned 82 percent of men's wages in 2011. Gender wage gaps are pervasive among all races and ethnicities: Asian women earned 23 percent, white women 18 percent, and black and Hispanic women 9 percent less than men of the same race (U.S. Bureau of Labor Statistics 2012). Thus, although women's wages have increased over the past thirty years, they remain stubbornly below men's.

Much of the explanation for these wage differentials is that women work in different jobs than men, and these are lower paid. Although women have made some progress over the past thirty years in some professional occupations such as law and medicine, women work in the lower-paying specialties of these fields, and they remain in the same low-paid jobs in which they had always worked, such as office support and service occupations (England 2010). Little progress has been made in traditionally male blue collar jobs such as construction (England 2010). Research continues to show that entry into high-paid top executive jobs remains difficult for women (Smith 2012). Thus, over-representation in lower-paid jobs and underrepresentation in higher-paid ones continue to reduce women's pay.

There is a lively debate about the cause of these occupational differences. Neoclassical economists believe that women are less productive and that they choose lower-paying jobs in order to care for their families. Women work fewer years than men, and if they work at all, women with young children are more likely to work part-time compared to men with young families (O'Neill 2004). Anticipating their family needs, women choose occupations that allow them flexibility in the hours they work, such as nursing and teaching, and they avoid jobs that require highly specific skills and knowledge that become quickly outdated, such as in physics, knowing that they may take time off to raise families (O'Neill 2004; O'Neill and O'Neill 2005).

Critics of these neoclassical explanations control for factors that can explain productivity differences, including education level, hours worked, working part-time, having young children at home, and being married. These studies generally find that even with these controls, women earn less than men (Blau and Kahn 2007). To counter the argument that women are less career-focused or motivated, scholars find that even after adding controls for job aspirations and occupational preferences, women earn less than men (Blau and Ferber 1991). Finally, to dispute the argument that women major in less remunerative

areas, such as the liberal arts rather than engineering or sciences, Weinberger and Joy (1997) add controls for college major, the university attended, and grade point average. They find that even when attending the same college and having the same college major and GPA, women earn less than men.

Audit and correspondence studies in hiring indicate that men are favored over women, even with the same qualifications. David Neumark (1996) found that when resumés for similarly-qualified women and men were left in restaurants, men received higher call-back rates in higher-paid restaurants, while women were favored in the lower-paid ones. Other studies find that women's qualifications are often overlooked, while men's qualifications are often used to justify their higher pay (Bergmann 1996). Mothers are perceived as less competent and less committed to working and consequently are recommended for lower salaries. They are also less likely to be recommended to be hired or to be promoted into management (Corell et al. 2007).

Thus, given that gender disparities in wages may result from bias, policies are needed to remedy these. Such policies can be divided into two strategies: increasing access to higher-paying jobs, and increasing pay in the jobs in which women already work.

1. ENFORCING EXISTING EQUAL OPPORTUNITY STATUTES

If women are less likely to be hired into higher-paying jobs because of discrimination, enforcing existing statutes would help alleviate this. In a cross-country analysis, Doris Weichselbaumer and Rudolf Winter-Ebmer (2007) find that laws mandating equal treatment in workplaces reduce the gender wage gap. Indeed, Title VII of the 1964 Civil Rights Act in the United States, which mandates non-discrimination regarding gender in the workplace, has been very successful in mitigating discrimination when this law is enforced (Leonard 1989).

In addition, enforcing affirmative action mandates can also increase women's employment and pay (Leonard 1989). Affirmative action requires that companies that receive government contracts examine the gender and racial composition of their workplaces in broad occupational categories and compare this with the composition of workers available to work. When workplaces are deficient in their representation of women or minorities, employers must use voluntary goals and timetables and take affirmative steps so that the gender and racial composition in their workplace reflects the composition of the workers available. Affirmative steps include publicizing the availability of jobs, recruiting underrepresented workers, and training and mentoring them. In egregious cases of discrimination, courts can mandate hiring quotas so that employers are forced to hire underrepresented workers.

Affirmative action has been successful in increasing the proportion of women in jobs, but it has been dismantled by the courts (Leonard 1989). Despite critics' allegations, it does not lead to weaker candidates being hired or a loss in productivity in the firm (Holzer and Neumark 1999; Leonard 1989).

2. FAMILY-FRIENDLY POLICIES

Family friendly policies allow women to work so that they do not have to choose between their careers and their families. Many countries that have family-friendly policies have higher labor participation rates among women than in the United States, since women in these countries can have both a job and a family. Parental leave, especially paid leave, as well as part-time work and child care policies, increase the proportion of mothers who work (Hofferth 1996; Joech 1997; Gornick et al. 1998), and moderate length paid parental leave and publicly-funded child care can increase earnings for mothers (Budig et al. 2012).[1] Thus, adopting paid family leave and child care policies that are available in many industrialized countries can reduce the gender wage gap.

One must ensure that family-friendly policies do not reinforce the gendered division of labor, however (Bergmann 1997; Singley and Hynes 2005). Allowing part-time work only in low-paid female jobs, paid parental leave for women but not men (e.g. women receive disability payments for childbirth in some U.S. states), and higher pay for men ensures that women rather than men will care for families. Thus, part-time work should be available in high-paying fields, both parents should be required to take alternating periods of "use or lose" paid parental leave, and families should not forfeit the higher pay of fathers who take such leave (Singley and Hynes 2005).

3. COMPARABLE WORTH

Besides increasing access to higher-paying jobs, another strategy to improve women's earnings is to increase pay in the jobs in which women work. Comparable worth, also known as pay equity, is one such strategy. To comprehend it, one must understand that employers' compensation systems meet three different goals: to adequately recruit and retain workers, they pay market wages (hence they perform or purchase salary surveys); to pay more for occupations that are evaluated as having greater worth (often measured as having greater duties and responsibilities), they conduct job evaluations; and to motivate hard work, they pay more for more productive workers even within occupations (hence they use performance appraisals). (See Milkovich et al. 2010.)

Comparable worth addresses the second of these goals. It advocates that when employers conduct job evaluations, they should not underpay jobs simply because women are employed. Occupations evaluated as having the same value to the employer should be paid the same, whether women or men perform the work.

This is not the case in the United States. The greater the proportion of women in an occupation, the lower the pay, and even employers' own job evaluations often indicate that women's occupations should receive higher pay (England 1992). In addition, there is much historical evidence that employers commonly paid less to occupations filled by women. For example, in 1945, Westinghouse and General Electric paid 70.5 cents per hour for women's jobs having 50–62 job evaluation points, but 84.5 cents per hour for men's occupations with the same number of points (Newman 1976). Kim (1999) similarly shows that when the State of California established its pay system in the 1930s, it paid occupations primarily held by women less than those primarily held by men, where otherwise the duties and responsibilities were the same. Because the employer maintains the existing salary relationships among occupations, this underpayment to female-dominated occupations continues into the present, even when market wages are accounted for.

Thus scholars believe that employers should re-evaluate their job evaluation systems to ensure that women's occupations are no longer underpaid. Indeed, research indicates that when comparable worth is implemented at the state level (for public sector workers), the wage gap is reduced (Hartmann and Aaronson 1994) once these inequities are remedied.

4. UNIONIZATION

Unionized workers earn ten to thirty percent more than non-union workers (Freeman and Medoff 1986), and the union wage premium is higher among women than among men in public sector jobs (Freeman and Leonard 1987). The result is that unionization decreases the gender wage gap (Cho and Cho 2011). Thus, unionizing workers in typically female jobs and industries can reduce the gender wage gap.

Women are less likely to belong to unions, however, even though they are more likely to favor them, because historically organizing drives occurred in manufacturing and blue collar jobs, where men typically worked (Freeman and Medoff 1986). Given the decline of these jobs and the rise of the service sector, including health care, education, and other sectors in which women work, unionizing women is critical to revitalizing union density in the nation. However, this will require changes in the law so that organizing drives can occur without union-busting tactics of employers (Freeman and Medoff 1986).

5. PAY SECRECY

An interesting strategy to close the gender pay gap is to prohibit pay secrecy. Pay secrecy includes rules, policies, and practices that forbid workers from sharing information on their earnings. Even though the National Labor Relations Act (NLRA) of 1935 mandates that employees have the right to share information on wages, most employers either formally or informally forbid this (Institute for Women's Policy Research 2010). Feminists are concerned that women may be underpaid because they do not know that they are paid less than men, as in the case of Lilly Ledbetter. Ledbetter worked as a manager for Goodyear Tire for twenty years before receiving an anonymous note that the male managers in her position were paid more than she.

Six states (California, Vermont, Michigan, Colorado, Illinois, and Maine) forbid employers from retaliating against employees for sharing information about their earnings (Kim 2012). These laws are important because the NLRA does not cover supervisors; hence Lilly Ledbetter could have been fired had she inquired about the pay of male managers. In addition, because the remedies under the NLRA are mild, limited to back wages minus any earnings in other jobs, employers commonly ignore this law (Freeman and Medoff 1986).

Research indicates that in states that outlaw pay secrecy, wages are higher for women, even when accounting for standard human capital controls as well as state effects. In other words, wages for women increased in the same state after such laws were passed compared to similar women in the state before these laws were in effect (Kim 2012). Thus expanding pay secrecy laws to other states would benefit women, increasing their pay and lowering the gender wage gap.

6. POLICIES TO END THE GENDER WAGE GAP

Because the wage gap results from multiple causes, no single policy can end it, and multiple remedies are required. Title VII and affirmative action address the problem of women being employed in low-paying jobs and being overlooked for higher-paid ones. Family-friendly policies would ensure that women can work and retain their jobs. Comparable worth, unionization, and pay secrecy laws can allow women to increase their pay in the jobs in which they already work. Research indicates that all of these policies improve women's wages and lower the gender wage gap.

But national legislation has been introduced many times in these areas. The Paycheck Fairness Act has been introduced by Congress 20 times, most recently in 2012. This legislation proposed to increase the remedies and penalties under Title VII and also outlaw pay secrecy. Comparable worth and family-friendly laws have also been introduced but never passed by Congress. Labor law reform that would make it easier to elect unions and that would increase the penalties to employers and remedies to employees under the NLRA also has failed in Congress.

Given this political reality, advocates should follow the very successful political strategy of the radical right. The right failed to pass federal legislation outlawing abortions, so it took its campaign to the states. Over the years, it has limited abortions with state laws mandating parental consent, waiting periods, and other conditions so that in many states abortions are effectively unavailable. A similar campaign is now being waged over unions, with Michigan recently becoming a Right to Work state.

Let us follow this example. Individual states have passed stronger laws on non-discrimination, pay secrecy, comparable worth, and paid family leave. States should continue to take this lead. Advocates can assess and target the states most likely to pass such legislation, and researchers can study and disseminate the effects of these policies on the gender wage gap, leading to more support for these policies. In addition, states can be pro-active in identifying and remedying unequal pay for women. The Attorney General's Office in Vermont, for example, explicitly asks during every intake of any complaint (including minimum wage or maximum hour violations) whether women are underpaid at work, and if women answer affirmatively, they initiate and investigate a pay discrimination complaint. In this way, they proactively uncover and resolve problems that women encounter in their workplaces. States can use this as a model to uncover, investigate, and remedy underpayment to women. Instead of attempting to pass the same legislation that continues to fail on a national level, women can reap the rewards of higher pay through targeted state and local initiatives and legislation that can remedy the problem of unequal pay that women face.

ACKNOWLEDGMENTS

Arsenia Reilly provided excellent research assistance. Joya Misra provided useful feedback. The errors in this paper remain the author's.

[. . .]

REFERENCES

Bergmann, B. R. 1997. Work-family policies and equality between women and men. In *Gender and family issues in the workplace*, ed. F. D. Blau and R. G. Ehrenberg. New York: Russell Sage.

Bergmann, B. R. 1996. *In defense of affirmative action*. New York: Basic Books.

Blau, F. D., and M. A. Ferber. 1991. Career plans and expectations of young women and men: The earnings gap and labor force participation. *Journal of Human Resources* 26: 581–607.

Blau, F. D. and L. M. Kahn. 2007. The gender pay gap: Have women gone as far as they can? *Academy of Management Perspectives* 21: 7–23.

Budig, M. J., J. Misra, and I. Boeckmann. 2012. The motherhood penalty in cross-national perspective: The importance of work-family policies and cultural attitudes. *Social Politics* 19: 163–193.

Cho, D., and J. Cho. 2011. How do labor unions influence the gender earnings gap? A comparative study of the US and Korea. *Feminist Economics* 17: 133–157.

Correll, S. J., S. Benard, and I. Paik. 2007. Getting a job: Is there a motherhood penalty? *American Journal of Sociology* 112: 1297–1339.

England, P. 2010. The gender revolution: Uneven and stalled. *Gender and Society* 24(2): 149–166.

England, P. 1992. *Comparable worth: Theories and practice.* New York: Aldine de Gruyer.

Freeman, R., and J. S. Leonard. 1985. Union maids: Unions and the female workforce. NBER Working Paper 1652.

Freeman, R. and J. Medoff. 1986. *What do unions do?* New York: Basic Books.

Gornick, J. C., M. K. Meyers, and K. E. Ross. 1998. Public policies and the employment of mothers: A cross-national survey. *Social Science Quarterly* 79: 35–54.

Hartmann, H. I., and S. Aaronson. 1994. Pay equity and women's wage increases: Success in the states, a model for the nation. *Duke Journal of Gender Law and Policy* 1: 69–87.

Hofferth, S. L. 1996. Effects of public and private policies on working after childbirth. *Work and Occupations* 23: 378–404.

Holzer, H., and D. Neumark. 1999. Assessing affirmative action. NBER Working Paper 7323.

Joech, J. M. 1997. Paid leave and timing of women's employment before and after birth. *Journal of Marriage and the Family* 59: 1008–21.

Institute for Women's Policy Research. 2010. Pay secrecy and paycheck fairness.

Kim, M. 1999. Inertia and discrimination in the California State civil service. *Industrial Relations* 38: 46–68.

Kim, M. 2012. Pay secrecy and the gender wage gap. Mimeo.

Leonard, J. 1989. Women and affirmative action. *Journal of Economic Perspectives* 3: 6175.

Milkovich, G., G. Newman, and B. Gerhart. 2010. *Compensation.* New York: McGraw-Hill.

Newman, W. 1976. Presentation III. In *Women and the workplace: The implications of occupational segregation,* ed. B. B. Reagan and M. Blaxall, 265–272. Chicago: University of Chicago Press.

Neumark, D. 1996. Sex discrimination in restaurant hiring: An audit study. *Quarterly Journal of Economics* 111: 915–941.

O'Neill, J. E. 1994. The gender gap in wages, circa 2000. *American Economic Review* 93: 309–314.

O'Neill, J. E. and D. M. O'Neill. 2005. What do wage differentials tell us about labor market discrimination? NBER Working Paper 11240.

Singley, S. G., and K. Hynes. 2005. Transitions to parenthood: Work-family policies, gender, and the couple context. *Gender and Society* 19: 376–397.

Smith, R. 2012. Money, benefits and power: A test of the glass ceiling and glass escalator hypotheses. *The Annuals of the American Academic of Political and Social Science* 639: 149–172.

U.S. Bureau of Labor Statistics. 2012. Highlights of women's earnings in 2011. Report 1038. www.bls.gov/cps/cpswom2011.pdf.

Weichselbaumer, D., and R. Winter-Ebmer. 2007. International gender wage gaps. *Economic Policy*: 237–287.

Weinberger, C., and L. Joy. 2007. Relative earnings of black college graduates. In *Race and economic opportunity in the twenty-first century,* ed. M. Kim, 50–72. London: Routledge.

NOTES

1. Extensively long paid leaves for mothers may relegate them to low-paid jobs after they return from their long absence (Budig et al. 2012).

40. • *Dean Spade*

COMPLIANCE IS GENDERED:
Struggling for Gendered Self-Determination in a Hostile Economy (2006)

Dean Spade, a professor at the Seattle University School of Law, founded the Sylvia Rivera Law Project, a nonprofit collective that provides free legal services to transgender, intersex, and nonconforming people who are low income and/or people of color. Spade is currently the coeditor of the online journal *Enough* and originally published *Normal Life: Administrative Violence, Critical Trans Politics, and the Limits of the Law* with South End Press; it was reissued with Duke University Press in 2015. The public can access multimedia talks, additional writing, and teaching information at http://www.deanspade.net. The following article originally appeared in *Transgender Rights* edited by P. Currah, R. Juang, and S. Price Minter (Minnesota 2006).

[. . .]

Since the emergence of poor-relief programs in sixteenth-century Europe, governments have developed varying strategies of social welfare to quell resistance among those who inhabit the necessary lowest level of the capitalist economy: the pool of unemployed whose presence keeps wages low and profit margins high.[1] Throughout their history, relief systems have been characterized by their insistence on work requirements for recipients, their vilification of recipients of relief, and their ability to paint the necessary failures of the economic systems they prop up as moral failures of the individuals who are most negatively affected by those systems.[2]

Feminist theorists have provided vital insight into how public relief systems have also operated through moralistic understandings of sexuality and family structure to force recipients into compliance with sexist and heterosexist notions of womanhood and motherhood. The creation of coercive policies requiring this compliance have usually been mobilized by appeals to white supremacist notions of white motherhood and racial purity, as well as depictions of black women as oversexualized, lazy, and morally

loose. Feminist theorists have provided a picture of how the day-to-day surveillance of low-income people and the rigid and punitive rule systems used in social services create a highly regulated context for the gender expression, sexuality, and family structure of low-income women who often rely on these systems to get out of economically dependent relationships with men. This fits into a broader analysis of how gendered models of citizenship, and gender and race hierarchies in the economy, operate to dominate the lives of low-income people most forcefully and directly affect the ability of all people to determine and express our gender, sexuality, and reproduction.

Unfortunately, this analysis has not yet been applied to examine how gender regulation of the poor applies to those who face some of the most dire consequences of a coercive binary gendered economy, those who transgress the basic principles of binary gender. Much feminist analysis of binary gender transgression has focused on the pathologizing medical discourses that have defined popular understandings of gender role distress to reinscribe meaning into rigid notions of "male" and "female."[3] However, as transgender liberation movements proliferate, and feminist analysis of gender transgression becomes more nuanced and sophisticated, it is essential that we bring along the feminist analysis of gender regulation in work and public assistance systems in order to account for the extreme economic consequences that gender-transgressive people face because of our gender identities and expressions.

Similarly, many lesbian, gay, and bi activists and theorists have tended to miss the vital connection between economic and anticapitalist analysis and the regulation of sexual and gender expression and behavior. The most well-publicized and well-funded LGB organizations have notoriously marginalized low-income people and people of color, and framed political agendas that have reflected concern for economic opportunity and family recognition for well-resourced and disproportionately white LGB populations. Feminist, anticapitalist, and antiracist analysis has been notably absent from mainstream discourses about LGBT rights, and low-income people, people of color, and gender-transgressive people have been notoriously underrepresented from leadership and decision-making power in these movements.[4]

This is particularly distressing given the economic realities that people who transgress gender norms face. Economic and educational opportunity remain inaccessible to gender transgressive people because of severe and persistent discrimination, much of which remains legal,[5] but for low-income people caught up in the especially gender-regulating public relief systems and criminal justice systems that dominate the lives of the poor, the gender regulation of the economy is felt even more sharply.

Many trans people start out their lives with the obstacle of abuse or harassment at home, or being kicked out of their homes because of their gender identities or expressions. Some turn to foster care, but often end up homeless when they experience harassment and violence at the hands of staff and other residents in foster care facilities (most of which are sex segregated and place trans youth according to birth sex designation).[6] The adult homeless shelter system, similarly, is inaccessible because of the fact that most facilities are sex segregated and will either turn down a trans person outright or refuse to house them according to their lived gender identity.[7] Similarly, harassment and violence against trans and gender nonconforming students is rampant in schools, and many drop out before finishing or are kicked out. Many trans people also do not pursue higher education because of fears about having to apply to schools and having their paperwork reveal their old name and birth sex because they have not been able to change these on their documents. Furthermore, trans people face severe discrimination in the job market and are routinely fired for transitioning on the job or when their gender identities or expressions come to their supervisors' attention.[8]

Trans people also have a difficult time accessing the entitlements that exist, though in a reduced and diminished format, to support poor people. Discrimination on the basis of gender identity occurs in welfare offices, on workfare job sites, in Medicaid offices, in Administrative Law Hearings for welfare, Medicaid, and Social Security Disability benefits. These benefit programs have been decimated in the last ten years and are generally operated with a punitive approach that includes frequent illegal termination of benefits and the failure to provide people their entitlements. For most people seeking to access these programs consistently during a time of need, the availability of an attorney or advocate to help navigate the hearings process has been essential to maintaining benefits. Unfortunately, most poverty attorneys and advocacy organizations are still severely lacking in basic information about serving trans clients and may reject cases on the basis of a person's gender identity or create such an unwelcoming environment that a trans client will not return for services. Based on community awareness of this problem, many trans people will not even seek these services, expecting that they will be subjected to humiliating and unhelpful treatment. The resulting lack of access to even the remaining shreds of the welfare system leaves a disproportionate number of trans people in severe poverty and dependent on criminalized work such as prostitution or the drug economy to survive. This, in turn, results in large numbers of trans people being entangled in the juvenile and adult criminal justice systems where they are subjected to extreme harassment and violence.

Given these conditions, the need for an understanding of the operations of gender regulation on gender-transgressive people in the context of poverty is urgent. . . . I want to begin to suggest how we could reexamine what we know from feminist and LGB analysis of gender, sexual, and reproductive regulation, to see how this applies to the lives of low-income transgender, transsexual, intersex, and other gender-transgressive people. I come to these questions as a poverty lawyer working for these populations, and I want to use feminist, queer, and anticapitalist analysis of the operation of poverty alleviation programs and other methods of controlling and exploiting poor people to contextualize case studies from the day-to-day lives of my clients. I want to begin a conversation about what it means that almost all, of the institutions and programs that exist to control and exploit poor people and people of color in the United States are sex segregated, especially in a context where membership in a sexual category is still determined with regard to access to medical technologies that are prohibitively expensive to all but the most well-resourced gender-transgressive people. . . .

Now is the time to recognize that no project of gender and sexual self-determination will be meaningful if it fails to engage resistance to an inherently violent and hierarchical capitalist economic system that grounds its control over workers and the poor in oppressive understandings of race, sex, gender, ability, and nationality.[9] To address homophobic and transphobic domination in pursuit of a better world, we need to start from an understanding of the experiences of those who face the intersection of multiple oppressions, centralize the analysis that this intersectionality fosters, and think concretely about what strategies a movement dedicated to these principles would engage.

CAPITALISM, ACCESS TO INCOME, AND THE USE OF SOCIAL WELFARE POLICIES TO REGULATE GENDER AND SEXUALITY AND PROMOTE WHITE SUPREMACY

Access to participation in the U.S. economy has always been conditioned on the ability of each individual to comply with norms of gendered behavior and expression, and the U.S. economy has always been shaped by explicit incentives that coerce people into normative gender and sexual structures, identities, and behaviors. At the same time the U.S. economy has, since its inception, been structured to recognize and maintain access to wealth for white people and to exploit the labor, land, and resources of native people, immigrants, and people of color. Property ownership itself has been a raced and gendered right throughout U.S. history, and an individual's race, gender, and sexuality have operated as forms of property themselves.[10] Similarly, interventions that would appear to seek to remedy the exploitative and damaging outcomes of our economic system have often been structured to control gendered behavior and expression and incentivize misogynist and heterosexist family norms. These interventions have typically been mobilized by white supremacy and the desire to benefit white workers and families to the disadvantage of people of color and immigrants. For example, the first wage and hour laws in the United States were passed under a notion of protectionism for women, the logic being that since women really did not belong in the workplace anyway, if they had to work outside the home, it was the states' role to intervene in their labor contracts to protect them from exploitation.[11] Similarly, since the inception of poor relief in the United States, programs have been structured to support gendered divisions of labor and promote heterosexual family structure and have been mobilized by discourses of racial purity.[12] . . .

[. . .]

Anyone who has lived through the last ten years of "welfare reform" rhetoric in the United States will notice that racist and sexist rhetoric and policy in the realm of welfare is still strongly with us. Such rhetoric is still being used to formulate welfare policies that control the gender and sexual behavior and expression of women and firmly tie economic survival and advantage to racial status. The most recent well-publicized massive overhaul of the welfare system, the "welfare reform" of the mid-1990s, was motivated, structured, and sold to the American public through racist and sexist understandings of poverty, work, and family structure. Its results have lived up to its intentions, with poor women of color suffering horribly under the new system.[13] Holloway Sparks writes about how the changes in welfare policy in the mid-1990s were based on a concept of contractual citizenship in which low-income people needed to be obligated to work and meet certain moral standards in order to earn their rights to public benefits.[14] Public benefits recipients were cast in the media as pathological, amoral people caught in a "cycle of dependency." Welfare mothers were depicted as people who couldn't stop having more and more children and committing welfare fraud.[15] The media uproar focused on racist and sexist images of black "welfare queens" and irresponsible teenage mothers. The mobilization of these images was an essential part of the creation of the Personal Responsibility and Work Opportunity Reconciliation Act of 1996 (PRWORA).[16]

The purpose and result of vilifying welfare recipients and focusing on sexual morality and gender role transgression is the creation of coercive policies designed to force poor people to obey rigid gender and family norms. Marriage incentives and requirements that mothers disclose the paternity of their children are only the most explicit examples of how the moral performance on which benefit receipt is conditional is fundamentally a requirement that poor women rigidly obey conservative notions of gender role and family structure. As countless critics have pointed out, these requirements create horrendous obstacles to women struggling with domestic violence who cannot safely disclose paternity or comply with other aspects of the "maintenance and sustenance

of two-parent families" dictated by welfare policy.[17] Additionally, for lesbian mothers the rigidity with which family structure is viewed and regulated by welfare policies and rules makes benefits inaccessible or dependent on remaining closeted.[18]

[. . .]

The example of the PRWORA passage, as well as more recent activity around reauthorizing PRWORA, which has included increasing discussion of "healthy marriage promotion,"[19] demonstrates that social welfare programs are explicitly designed to promote oppressive and racialized understandings of gender, sexuality, and family structure. The depiction of the lives of poor women that motivated the PRWORA, and behind which both Democrats and Republicans rallied, made it clear that poor women were responsible for their poverty and that the only remedy was to coerce them into marriage and work. These morality-based understandings of poverty play out in the day-to-day operation of social services programs that emphasize surveillance and gender regulation of poor people.

FAILING TO COMPLY

The climate of vilification of the poor and pathologization of the conditions and consequences of poverty produce and operate through day-to-day punitive and coercive structures within poverty service provision. These programs often focus on notions of "compliance" and "noncompliance" among participants. Feminist theorists have provided helpful analysis in this area, examining the ways that access to homeless and domestic violence shelters is mediated through punitive processes where those looking for assistance are treated as morally and intellectually deficient and subjected to humiliating violations of privacy as an integral part of the disincentification of receiving services.[20] Navigating benefits systems, shelter systems, essential medical services, and entanglement with the criminal justice system that is now a central aspect of low-income existence in order to survive is increasingly tied to the ability of each person to meet highly gendered and raced behavioral and expression requirements.[21] While feminist analysis has exposed the hidden agendas of poverty policies to shape women's work and family structure and inhibit the ability of women to be economically independent and escape violent relationships, this analysis has not extended to examine the effects of this system on poor people who also transgress the coercive binary gender system that maintains sexism.

The following two stories from my work with low-income gender-transgressive people illustrate the particular ways in which the incorporation of rigid binary gender expectations into social service provision and the criminal justice system operate in the lives of gender-transgressive people.

JIM'S STORY

Jim is an intersex person.[22] He was raised as a girl, but during adolescence began to identify as male. To his family, he remained female identified, but in the world he identified as male. The stress of living a double life was immense, but he knew it was the only way to maintain a relationship with his family, with whom he was very close. When Jim was nineteen, he was involved in a robbery for which he received a sentence of five years' probation. During the second year of that probation period, Jim was arrested for drug possession and was sentenced to eighteen months of residential drug treatment. Jim was sent to a male residential facility. In a purportedly therapeutic environment, Jim discussed his intersex status with his therapist. His confidentiality was broken, and soon the entire staff and residential population were aware that Jim was intersex. Jim was facing such severe rape threat with no support or protection from staff that he ultimately ran away from the facility. I met Jim after he had turned himself in, wanting to deal with his criminal justice status so that he could safely apply to college and get on with his life. Jim was in a Brooklyn men's jail, again facing severe rape threat because the jail refused to continue his testosterone

treatments, which caused him to menstruate, and when he was strip-searched while menstruating other inmates and staff learned of his status. Jim and I worked together to try to convince the judge in his case that Jim could safely access drug treatment services only in an outpatient setting because of the rape threat he continually faced in residential settings. Even when we had convinced the judge of this, though, we faced the fact that most programs were gender segregated and would not be a safe place for Jim to be known as intersex. When I contacted facilities to find a place for Jim, staff at all levels would ask me questions like "Does he pee sitting or standing?" and "Does he have a penis?" indicating to me that Jim would be treated as a novelty and his intersex status would be a source of gossip. Even the few lesbian and gay drug treatment programs I identified seemed inappropriate because Jim did not identify as gay and was, in fact, quite unfamiliar with gay and lesbian communities and somewhat uncomfortable in queer spaces. Eventually, the judge agreed to let Jim try outpatient treatment, but on a "zero tolerance" policy, where a single relapse would result in jail time. Jim was under enormous stress, engaged in treatment where he was always afraid he might be outed and where his participation in the daily hours of group therapy required hiding his identity. He relapsed and was sentenced to two years in state prison. When I went before the judge to request that Jim be placed in women's prison because of his well-founded fear of sexual assault in men's facilities, the judge's response was "He can't have it both ways." Once again, Jim's intersex status, and his inability to successfully navigate the gender requirements of the extremely violent system in which he was entangled because of involvement in nonviolent poverty-related crimes, was considered part of his criminality and a blameworthy status.

BIANCA'S STORY

Bianca is a transgender woman. In 1999 she was attending high school in the Bronx. After struggling with an internal understanding of herself as a woman for several years, Bianca eventually mustered the courage to come out to her peers and teachers at school. She and another transgender student who were close friends decided to come out together, and arrived at school one day dressed to reflect their female gender identities. They were stopped at the front office and not allowed to enter school. Eventually, they were told to leave and not come back. When their parents called the school to follow up and find out what to do next, their calls were never returned. They were given no referrals to other schools, and no official suspension or expulsion documents. Because of their families' poverty and language barriers, they were never able to successfully get documentation or services from the schools. I met Bianca three years later. She had been trying to find an attorney to take the case and had never found one, and when I met her and began investigating the possibility of bringing a lawsuit, I discovered that the statute of limitations had run out, and she no longer had a claim. When I met Bianca, she was homeless and unemployed and was trying to escape from an abusive relationship. She was afraid to go to the police both because of the retaliation of her boyfriend and because she rightly feared that the police would react badly to her because of her transgender status. Her IDs all said her male name and gender, and there would be no way for her to seek police protection without being identified as transgender. As we searched for places for Bianca to live, we ran up against the fact that all the homeless shelters would only place her according to birth gender, so she would be a woman in an all-men's facility, which she rightly feared would be unsafe and uncomfortable. Women's shelters for domestic violence survivors were unwilling to take her because they did not recognize her as a woman. When Bianca went to apply for welfare she was given an assignment to attend a job center to be placed in a workfare program. When she tried to access the job center, she was severely harassed outside, and when she entered she was outed and humiliated by staff when she attempted to use the women's restroom. Ultimately, she felt too unsafe to return, and her benefits were terminated. Bianca's total lack of income also meant that she had no access

to the hormone treatments that she used to maintain a feminine appearance, which was both emotionally necessary for her and kept her safe from some of the harassment and violence she faced when she was identifiable as a trans woman on the street. Bianca felt that her only option for finding income sufficient to pay for the hormones she bought on the street (it would have been more expensive from a doctor, since Medicaid would not cover it even if she could successfully apply for Medicaid) was to engage in illegal sex work. This put her in further danger of police violence, arrest, and private violence. Additionally, because she was accessing injectable hormones through street economies, she was at greater risk of HIV infection and other communicable diseases.

These two cases are typical of my clients in that almost everyone who comes to the Sylvia Rivera Law Project for services is facing serious consequences of failing to fit within a rigid binary gender structure in multiple systems and institutions: welfare, adult or juvenile justice, public education, voluntary or mandated drug treatment, homeless services, and mental and physical health care. Compliance is a central issue that my clients face in these systems. They are unable to comply or "rehabilitate" because to do either means to match stereotypes associated with their birth genders. Some are kicked off welfare because they fail to wear birth-gender appropriate clothing to "job training" programs that require them to.[23] Others are labeled "sex offenders" in juvenile justice simply because of their transgender identities despite the fact that their criminal offenses were not sex-related, and forced to wear sex offender jumpsuits while locked up and attend sex offender therapy groups. If they cannot or will not remedy their gender transgressions, they cannot complete the rehabilitation process required for release. Some clients lose housing at youth or adult shelters because staff argue that their failures to dress according to birth gender means they are not seriously job hunting, a requirement of the program to maintain housing. The ways that these systems, apply rigid gendered expectations to poor people, which are notably not applied to nonpoor people, are manifold, because these systems operate through detailed surveillance coupled with extensive discretion on the part of individual caseworkers and administrators. I find my clients serving the role of example, particularly in adult and juvenile justice contexts, by being humiliated, harassed, or assaulted because of their gender transgressions in a way that communicates clearly to others entangled in those systems exactly what is expected of them. For many transgender, transsexual, or intersex people, this violence results in long-term severe injuries and in death.[24]

The other vitally important component to the inability of gender-transgressive poor people to access benefits and services is the fact that gender segregation remains a central organizing strategy of systems of social control. Employed people with stable housing are subjected to far fewer gender-segregated facilities on a daily basis than poor or homeless people. While we all must contend with bathrooms or locker rooms that are gender segregated, those of us with homes and jobs may even be able to avoid those a good deal of the time, as opposed to homeless people who must always use public facilities that are likely to be segregated and highly policed. Additionally, all the essential services and coercive control institutions (jails, homeless shelters, group homes, drug treatment facilities, foster care facilities, domestic violence shelters, juvenile justice facilities, housing for the mentally ill) that increasingly dominate the lives of poor people and disproportionately of people of color use gender segregation as a part of the gendered social control they maintain.[25] For the most part, these institutions recognize only birth gender, or rely on identity documents such as birth certificates to determine gender. In every state in the United States that allows people to change their gender markers on their birth certificates, evidence of sex reassignment surgery is required.[26]

As I have written elsewhere,[27] the reliance on medical evidence in all legal contexts in which transgender and other gender-transgressive people struggle for recognition or rights is highly problematic. Whether seeking to prove our marriages valid so that we can keep our parental rights or access our spouse's estate,[28] or attempting to change our names and gender on our identity documents so that we can apply for educational or employment opportunities,[29] or when attempting to access sex-segregated facilities of various kinds,[30] medical evidence remains the defining factor in determining our rights. This is problematic because access to gender-related medical intervention is usually conditioned on successful performance of rigidly defined and harshly enforced understandings of binary gender,[31] because many gender-transgressive people may not wish to undergo medical intervention, and because medical care of all kinds, but particularly gender-related medical care, remains extremely inaccessible to most low-income gender-transgressive people.[32]

[. . .]

ASKING FOR MORE

The most well-funded organizations in the lesbian and gay movement do not provide direct legal services to low-income people, but instead focus their resources on high-profile impact litigation cases and policy efforts. Most of these efforts have traditionally focused on concerns central to the lives of nonpoor lesbian and gay people and have ignored the most pressing issues in the lives of poor people, people of color, and transgender people. The "gay agenda" has been about passing our apartments to each other when we die, not about increasing affordable housing or opposing illegal eviction. It has been about getting our partnerships recognized so our partners can share our private health benefits, not about defending Medicaid rights or demanding universal health care. It has been about getting our young sons into Boy Scouts, not about advocating for the countless/uncounted queer and trans youth struggling against a growing industry of youth incarceration. It has been about working to put more punishment power in the hands of an overtly racist criminal system with passage of hate crimes laws, not about opposing the mass incarceration of a generation of men of color, or fighting the abuse of queer and trans people in adult and juvenile justice settings.

The debates about gender identity inclusion in the federal Employment Non-Discrimination Act (ENDA)[33] or the exclusion of gender identity protection from New York States Sexual Orientation Non-Discrimination Act (SONDA)[34] are only the most blatant examples of the mainstream lesbian and gay movement's lack of commitment to gender-transgressive populations, but the failure of "LGBT" dollars, services, and resources to reach the lives of low-income people is even more widespread. What it means in the lives of low-income gender-transgressive people is that not only do they lack essential legal protections, they cannot find effective advocacy to access the fair treatment, services, or benefits they are entitled to. Unfortunately, the trend in gender rights litigation toward the recognition of gender identity change only in the context of medicalization maintains this imbalance. The history of gender rights litigation seems to be progressing with increasing recognition of membership in the "new" gender category, but only for those transgender people who have undergone medical intervention. The vast majority of gender-transgressive people who will either not want or not be able to afford such intervention remain unprotected. . . .

On a broader level, though, the distribution of resources (services, policy and legislative advocacy, direct representation) is something that our movements can be more responsible about than they have been. Transgender and gender-transgressive movements are at a moment of building and expansion, and in some senses institutionalization. We are increasingly forming organizations, we are seeking funding, and we are forming a growing national and international conversation seeking an end to the inequality and oppression we have struggled against. It is in this moment that it is most urgent for us to examine where our resources have been going, and what unintentional consequences may result from following the model of the lesbian and gay rights movement. Inevitably, given the context of capitalism in which transliberation activism occurs, and

the economic/educational privilege that usually accompanies the ability to secure paid "movement leader" jobs in nonprofits and to raise money to start and maintain movement organizations, the voices of low-income people and people of color will remain underincluded without a serious commitment to intervention.[35] . . .

[. . .]

The notion that we should put our movement resources into a struggle for gender identity nondiscrimination in employment, but not concern ourselves with the fact that there is no one to represent struggling gender-transgressive people being harassed on workfare jobsites or raped in prisons or falsely arrested for prostitution, indicates a problem in terms of the depth and breadth of liberation we are seeking. LGBT movement activists have the power to determine whether the liberation we pursue will follow a tolerance model, making room for those who can access private employment and housing to not experience discrimination there because of their gender identities (and possibly conditioned on medical intervention), or we can quest for a broader liberation that demands gender self-determination for all people regardless of their positions in capitalist economies. To make the latter real, we need to strategize beyond a notion that if we win rights for the most sympathetic and normal of our lot first, the others will be protected in time. Instead, we should be concerned that the breadth of our vision will determine the victories we obtain. If we want to end oppression on the basis of gender identity and expression for all people, we need to examine how the rigid regulation of binary gender is a core element of participation in our capitalist economy, how the hyperregulation of poor peoples' gender and sexuality has propped up that system, and how this has resulted in disproportionate poverty and incarceration for poor, gender-transgressive people. Starting from that analysis, we can undertake strategies to combat these problems and make sure that our activism does not further entrench this regulation by relying on pathologization and medicalization to articulate gender rights.

[. . .]

NOTES

Many people generously provided editorial advice for this chapter. Thanks to Craig Willse, Paisley Currah, Danny McGee, Franklin Romeo, Jenny Robertson, Bridge Joyce, and Richard M. Juang for their help. The asterisks that appear with page numbers in these notes refer to screen page numbers from a database.

1. Frances Fox Piven and Richard Clower, *Regulating the Poor* (New York: Vintage, 1993).
2. Ibid.
3. Janice Raymond, *The Transsexual Empire* (New York: Teachers College Press, 1994); Dwight B. Billings and Thomas Urban, "The Socio-Medical Construction of Transsexualism: An Interpretation and Critique," *Social Problems* 29 (1982): 266, 276. Billings and Urban are engaged in an anticapitalist critique of the gender-regulating process of sex reassignment therapy and the adoption of norm-supporting narratives by patients seeking medical interventions. However, rather than focusing on the problems of a coercive system that demands the performance of rigid gender norms by people seeking body alteration, they vilify transgender people for performing these narratives. The resulting analysis paints trans subjects as clueless gender upholders, who are buying our way out of our gender distress and ruining any radical potential for disrupting gender norms. For more on the strategic uses of medical narratives by trans subjects, and the attribution of oppressive medical understandings of gender to trans people, see Dean Spade, "Mutilating Gender," *makezine* (spring 2002), http://makezine.org/mutilate.html.
4. Theorists and activists who produce intersectional and multi-issue queer and trans analysis and activism continually critique these failures. See, for example, Eli Clare, *Exile and Pride* (Cambridge, MA: South End, 1999); Amber Hollibaugh, "Queers without Money," *Village Voice,* June 2001; Cathy Cohen, "Punks, Bulldaggers, and Welfare Queens: The Radical Potential of Queer Politics?" *GLQ* 3 (1997): 437; Craig Willse and Dean Spade, "Confronting the Limits of Gay Hate Crimes Activism: A Radical Critique," *Chicano-Latino Law Review* 21 (2000): 38–49; Sylvia Rivera, "Queens in Exile, the Forgotten Ones," in *Genderqueer: Voices from Beyond the Binary,* ed. Joan Nestle et al. (New York: Alyson, 2002),

67-85; Richard E. Blum, Barbara Ann Perina, and Joseph Nicholas DeFilippis, "Why Welfare Is a Queer Issue," *NYU Review of Law and Social Change* 26 (2001): 207.
5. According to the National Gay and Lesbian Task Force, 76 percent of the U.S. population lives in jurisdictions that are not covered by antidiscrimination laws that include prohibitions on gender identity discrimination. See L. Mottet, "Populations of Jurisdictions with Explicitly Transgender Anti-Discrimination Laws" (Washington, DC: National Gay and Lesbian Task Force, 2003), http://ngltf.org/downloads/TransIncPops.pdf. Even those who are covered may find these laws ineffectual when they try to enforce their rights before biased judges. See *Goins v. West Group,* 635 N.W.2d 717 (Minn. 2001) (finding that an employer's refusal to allow a transgender employee access to the women's bathroom was not gender identity discrimination); *Hispanic AIDS Forum v. Bruno,* 792 N.Y.S. 2d 43 (2005). Further, even for those who live in jurisdictions where gender identity discrimination is prohibited, seeking redress may be difficult because of a lack of attorneys willing to take cases with transgender plaintiffs and because of the failure of city governments to enforce these provisions. See *Local Laws of the City of New York* 3, 2002, http://www.council.nyc.ny.us/pdf_files/bills/law02003.pdf; Duncan Osborne, "Trans Advocates Allege Foot-Dragging," *Gay City News,* June 17, 2004; Cyd Zeigler Jr., "Trans Protection Compromised?" *New York Blade,* May 28, 2004.
6. *Doe v. Bell,* 2003 WL 355603 at *1–2 (N.Y. Sup. Ct. 2003) (finding that group home's policy forbidding transgender youth from dressing in skirts and dresses was illegal).
7. L. Mottet and J. Ohle, *Transitioning Our Shelters: A Guide to Making Homeless Shelters Safe for Transgender People* (Washington, DC: National Gay and Lesbian Task Force, 2003). In 2006 transgender advocates succeeded in winning a written policy in the Department of Homeless Service of New York City addressing the rights of transgender people seeking shelter in the city's facilities. The policy explicitly states that transgender people may not be placed in shelters that do not comport with their self-identified gender and may not be forced to wear clothing associated with their birth gender. Years of advocacy were required to put this policy, which is not yet being enforced as of this writing, in place. A handful of cities in North America, including Boston, San Francisco, and Toronto, have policies addressing the discrimination and exclusion transgender people face in shelter systems. For more information on these policies, see www.srlp.org.

8. *Oiler v. Winn-Dixie Louisiana, Inc.*, 2002 WL 31098541 at *1 (September 16, 2002) (where a grocery store loader and truck driver was fired for cross-dressing off the job).

9. I use the term *gender self-determination* throughout this chapter, and more broadly in my political work, as a tool to express opposition to the coercive mechanisms of the binary gender system (everything from assignment of birth gender to gender segregation of bathrooms to targeting of trans people by police). I use this term strategically while also recognizing that any notion of self-determination is bound up in understandings of individuality that support capitalist concepts like individual freedom to sell labor" that obscure the mechanisms of oppression we are seeking to overcome. While I want to think past and reconceptualize articulations of individuality and replace them with understandings of community-centered change, mobilizing around ending coercive gender within a political framework where we still experience ourselves through heavily entrenched concepts of individuality and freedom requires strategic employment of ideas like self-determination.

10. See Cheryl I. Harris, "Whiteness as Property," in *Critical Race Theory Reader,* ed. Kimberlé Crenshaw, Neil Gotanda, Garry Peller, and Kendall Thomas (New York: New Press, 1996), 276-91. Harris traces the racial origins of property ownership, both in terms of how race has defined, property status with one's ability to own property or to be property of another determined by race—and in terms of how racial identity itself has been attributed a property status through libel and slander laws. She argues that racial identity still has property value recognized and protected by American law. Gender and sexual orientation have also, at times, had property status protected in various ways in the law. In the case of gender, clearly the right to own property has at times been a gender-based right, and, additionally, we see value being assigned to sexuality in tort claims of Loss of Consortium, typically brought by spouses claiming that they have been damaged by the loss of sexual service from their spouses because of whatever tort was committed. Additionally, defamation cases regarding false accusations of homosexuality similarly indicate a legal protection of heterosexual identity. See E. Yatar, "Defamation, Privacy, and the Changing Social Status of Homosexuality: Re-Thinking Supreme Court Gay Rights Jurisprudence," *Law and Sexuality* 12 (2003): 119–56.

11. The court decisions establishing protection for women laborers are based on this protectionist logic: "It is manifest that this established principle is peculiarly applicable in relation to the employment of women in whose protection the state has a special interest. That phase of the subject received elaborate consideration in *Muller v. Oregon* (1908) 208 U.S. 412, 28 S.Ct. 324, 326, 52 L.Ed. 551, 13 Ann.Cas. 957, where the constitutional authority of the state to limit the working hours of women was sustained. We emphasized the consideration that 'woman's physical structure and the performance of maternal functions place her at a disadvantage in the struggle for subsistence' and that her physical well being 'becomes an object of public interest and care in order to preserve the strength and vigor of the race.' We emphasized the need of protecting women against oppression despite her possession of contractual rights. We said that 'though limitations upon personal and contractual rights may be removed by legislation, there is that in her disposition and habits of life which will operate against a full assertion of those rights. She will still be where some legislation to protect her seems necessary to secure a real equality of right.' Hence she was properly placed in a class by herself, and legislation designed for her protection may be sustained, even when like legislation is not necessary for men, and could not be sustained'" (*West Coast Hotel v. Parrish,* 57 S.Ct. 578, at 583 [upholding Washington State's minimum wage law for women]).

12. Gwendolyn Mink, "The Lady and the Tramp: Gender, Race, and the Origins of the American Welfare State," in *Women, the State, and Welfare,* ed. Linda Gordon (Madison: University of Wisconsin Press, 1990), 92–122.

13. *See J. Heinz and N. Folbre, The Ultimate Field Guide to the U.S. Economy: A Compact and Irreverent Guide to Economic Life in America (New York: New Press, 2000).*

14. Holloway Sparks, "Queens, Teens, and Model Mothers: Race, Gender, and the Discourse of Welfare Reform," in *Race and the Politics of Welfare Reform,* ed. Sanford F. Schram, Joe Soss, and Richard C. Fording (Ann Arbor: University of Michigan Press, 2003), 188–89.

15. See Susan James and Beth Harris, "Gimme Shelter: Battering and Poverty," in *For Crying Out Loud: Women's Poverty in the United States,* ed. Diane Dujon and Ann Withorn (Boston: South End, 1996), 57–66.

16. Sparks, "Queens, Teens, and Model Mothers," 171. Then senator John Ashcroft utilized the contractual view of citizenship described by Sparks during one of the final debates on welfare reform in the 104th Congress: "I think it is time for us to limit the amount of time that people can be on welfare. It is time for us to provide disincentives to bear children out of wedlock. It is time

for us to provide powerful incentives for people to go to work. It is time for us to say that, if you are on welfare, you should be off drugs. It is time for us to say that, if you are on welfare, your children should be in school . . . You have to be responsible for what you are doing. We are not going to continue to support you in a way in which you abdicate, you simply run from, you hide from, your responsibility as a citizen" (quoted in Sparks, "Queens, Teens, and Model Mothers," 190).

17. Sparks, "Queens, Teens, and Model Mothers," 189.

18. See Blum, Perina, and DeFilippis, "Why Welfare Is a Queer Issue," 207.

19. Current Republican proposals for the reauthorization include an increase in work requirements to forty hours a week and $200 million in federal grants plus $100 million in state matching grants for marriage promotion programs. See Jonathan Riskind, "House Set to Revisit Welfare Reform This Week: Legislators to Vote on Bill Very Similar to One Passed in May," *Columbus Dispatch,* February 12, 2003. See also Sharon Tubbs and Thomas C. Tobin, "When Government Wants Marriage Reform," *St. Petersburg Times,* February 8, 2003; Sharon Lerner, "Marriage on the Mind: The Bush Administration's Misguided Poverty Cure," *The Nation,* July 5, 2004.

20. See Roofless Women's Action Research Mobilization, "A Hole in My Soul: Experiences of Homeless Women," ed. Marie Kennedy, in Dujon and Withorn, *For Crying Out Loud,* 41–56.

21. I recently participated in a bar association panel about queer and trans youth in juvenile justice and foster care at which a youth service provider smilingly described continued efforts to not let the transgender youth leave the residence she supervised looking like "hos." Her determination that an aspect of receiving housing at her facility should include compliance with particular expressions of femininity, and her use of a racialized term to indicate the prohibited expression, exemplifies the type of race/gender expression management that typically becomes the concern of poverty service providers measuring compliance.

22. Intersex people are people who have physical conditions that make their bodies difficult to classify under current medical understandings of what constitutes a "male" or "female" body. Intersex activists are working to stop the infant and childhood surgeries that intersex people are frequently subjected to as doctors attempt to bring their bodies into line with medical expectations of what a male or female body should look like. For more information on intersex conditions and intersex activism, see the Web site of the Intersex Society of North America, www.isna.org.

23. Blum, Perina, and DeFilippis, "Why Welfare Is a Queer Issue," 213.

24. See Remembering Our Dead, http://www.rememberin gourdead.org.

25. A common response to questions about the wisdom of sex segregation in jails, prisons, shelters, and other contexts is a concern for women's safety and a suggestion that sex segregation exists to prevent violence against women. While women's safety should be of paramount concern to service providers and corrections staff, there is not sufficient evidence that sex segregation policies are motivated by concern for women's safety or that women are safe in these institutions. In fact, systemic sexual assault and violence against women are more often than not a fundamental part of the coercive control exercised over poor women in these institutions. Examining the violence against women and gender-transgressive people in these settings should be a project that advocates for women's safety are deeply engaged in with advocates for gender self-determination, as these two populations are frequently targets for related violence. The first step may be to acknowledge that control of low-income people, not safety, is the aim of these institutions. See R. Ralph, "Nowhere to Hide: Retaliation against Women in Michigan State Prisons," *Human Rights Watch* 10 (1998), http://hrw.org/reports98/women/.

26. See *Ala. Code* § 22–9A-19 (2002) (order of court of competent jurisdiction and surgery required); *Artz. Rev. Stat.* § 36–326 (2001) (change may be made based on sworn statement from licensed physician attesting to either surgical operation or chromosomal count, although registrar may require further evidence); *Ark. Code Ann.* § 20–18–307 (2002) (order of court of competent jurisdiction and surgery required); *Cal. Health & Safety Code* § 103425, 103430 (2002 Supp.) (court order and surgery apparently required); *Colo. Rev. Stat. Ann.* § 25–2–115 (2002) (same); *D.C. Code Ann.* § 7–217 (2002) (same); *Ga. Code Ann.* § 31–10–23 (2002) (same); *Haw. Rev. Stat.* § 338–17.7 (2002) (physician affidavit and surgery required; registrar can require additional information); 410 *Ill. Comp. Stat.* 535/17 (2002) (same); *Iowa Code* § 144.23 (2002) (physician affidavit and surgery "or other treatment"); *La. Rev. Stat. Ann.* § 40: 62 (2002) (order of court of competent jurisdiction and surgery required); *Mass. Ann. Laws* chap. 46, § 13 (2002) (same); *Mich. Comp. Laws* § 333.2831 (2002) (affidavit of physician certifying

sex reassignment surgery); *Miss. Code Ann.* § 41-57-21 (2001) (registrar may correct certificate that contains incorrect sex on affidavit of two persons having personal knowledge of facts; not clear whether restricted to initial error in certificate or includes gender change); *Mo. Rev. Stat* § 193.215 (2001) (order of court of competent jurisdiction and surgery required); *Neb. Rev. Stat.* § 71–604.1 (2002) (affidavit of physician as to sex reassignment surgery and order of court of competent jurisdiction changing name required); *N.J. Stat. Ann.* 26:8–40.12 (2002) (certificate from physician attesting to surgery and order of court of competent jurisdiction changing name); *N..M. Stat. Ann.* § 24–14–25 (2002) (same); *N.C. Gen. Stat.* 130A-118 (2001) (affidavit of physician attesting to sex reassignment surgery); *Or. Rev. Stat.* § 432.235 (2001) (order of court of competent jurisdiction and surgery required); *Utah Code Ann.* § 26–2–11 (2002) (order of Utah District Court or court of competent jurisdiction of another state required; no specific requirement of surgery); *Va. Code Ann.* § 32.1-269 (2002) (order of court of competent jurisdiction indicating sex has been changed by "medical procedure"); *Wis. Stat.* § 69.15 (2001) (order of court or administrative order) cited in *Matter of Heilig,* 2003 WL 282856 at *15 n.8 (Md. 2003). See also. Lambda Legal Defense and Education Fund, Resources: Transgender Issues, http://www.lambdalegal.org/cgi-bin/iowa/documents/record?record=1162 (November 12, 2002) (accessed March 30, 2003).

27. Dean Spade, "Resisting Medicine, Re/modeling Gender," *Berkeley Women's Law Journal* 18 (2003): 16–26.

28. *In re Estate of Gardiner, 42* P.3d 120 (Kan. 2002); *Kantaras v. Kantaras,* Case No. 98–5375CA (Circuit Court of the Sixth Judicial Circuit, Pasco County, Florida, February 19, 2003).

29. See, for example, *In re Rivera,* 165 Misc.2d 307, 627 N.Y.S,2d 241 (Civ. Ct. Bx. Co. 1995); *Application of Anonymous,* 155 Misc.2d 241, 587 N.Y.S.2d 548 (N.Y.City Civ.Ct, August 27, 1992); *Matter of Anonymous,* 153 Misc.2d 893, 582 N.Y.S.2d 941 (N.Y.City Civ.Ct., March 27, 1992); but see, *In re Guido,* 2003 WL 22471153, 2003 NY. Slip Op. 23821 (NY. Civ.Ct, October 24, 2003).

30. See Jody Marksamer and Dylan Vade, "Gender Neutral Bathroom Survey," http://www.transgenderlawcenter .org/documents/safe_WC_survey_results.html (2001) (accessed March 30, 2003). See Dean Spade, "2 Legit 2

Quit, Piss & Vinegar," http://www.makezine.org/21egit .html (accessed March 14, 2003).

31. See Spade, "Resisting Medicine," 16–26, for a broader discussion of the gender regulation accomplished by medical approaches to gender role distress.

32. Most states in the United States still explicitly exclude "sex reassignment related care" from Medicaid coverage, and most medical insurance companies still exclude this care from coverage. See *Smith v. Rasmussen,* 249 F.3d 755 (8th Cir. 2001) (reversing district court's ruling and holding that Iowa's rule denying coverage for SRS was not arbitrary or inconsistent with the Medicaid Act); *Rush v. Parham,* 625 F.2d 1150 (5th Cir. 1980) (reversing district court's ruling that Georgia's Medicaid program could not categorically deny coverage for SRS); 18 NYCRR § 505.2(1). See N.Y. St. Reg. (March 25, 1998) at 5; Ill. Admin. Code tit. 89 at 140.6(1); 55 Pa. Code at 1163.59(a)(1); Alaska Admin. Code tit 7, at 43.385(a)(1); Medicare Program: National Coverage Decisions, 54 Fed. Reg. 34555, 34572 (August 21, 1989); 32 C.F.R. at 199.4(e)(7) (excluding sex reassignment surgeries from the Civilian Health and Medical Program of the Uniformed Services); but see *J.D. v. Lackner,* 80 Cal. App. 3d 90 (Cal. Ct. App. 1978).

33. See L. Mottet, *Partial Equality* (Washington, DC: National Gay and Lesbian Task Force, 2003), http:// www.ngltf.org/library/partialeq.htm.

34. H. Humm, "Unity Eludes SONDA Advocates, Gender Identity Divides Duane, Pride Agenda," *Gay City News,* December 13, 2002, http://www.gaycitynews. com/gcn29/unity.html; K. Krawchuk, "SONDA Bill Heads to Senate," *Capital News 9* (Albany, NY), 2002, http://www.capitalnews9.com/content/ headlines/?SecID=33&ArID=7580.

35. Significant inequalities in access to education persist. In 1997 less than 75 percent of African Americans and less than 55 percent of Latinos had completed four years of high school, and less than 14 percent of either group had completed four years of college. Cuts in financial aid for college students have reinforced a decline in the percentage of low-income high school graduates going to college (Heinz and Folbre, *Ultimate Field Guide to the US. Economy,* 74). Further, the end of affirmative action policies in higher education and new rules making people with drug convictions ineligible for federal financial aid have reduced access to higher education for poor communities and communities that are overexposed to police enforcement.

41. • *Denise Brennan*

WOMEN WORK, MEN SPONGE, AND EVERYONE GOSSIPS:
Macho Men and Stigmatized/ing Women in a Sex Tourist Town (2004)

Denise Brennan, a professor in the department of anthropology at Georgetown University, is author of two critically acclaimed books, *What's Love Got to Do with It: Transnational Desires and Sex Tourism in the Dominican Republic* (Duke 2004) and *Life Interrupted: Trafficking into Forced Labor in the United States* (Duke 2014). Her current research focuses on how families manage detention in and deportation from the United States to their countries of origin. Her work has been supported by the Woodrow Wilson International Studies for Scholars, the Guggenheim Foundation, the American Association for University Women, and the Fulbright Program. Brennan has served as a board member of Different Avenues and Helping Individual Prostitutes Survive and is the founder of Survivor Leadership Training Fund. The following reading originally appeared in *Anthropological Quarterly* (2004).

Carlos's wife worked in Europe.[1] Everyone gossiped that she worked in the sex trade and Carlos admitted as much to his close friends. In his wife's absence he and his sons lived relatively well. Surrounded by wooden shacks, their house was constructed with cement, they always wore pressed shirts and the latest belts and jeans, and they—especially Carlos—wore many gold chains and rings. The biggest symbol of Carlos's wife success overseas, however, was his motorcycle—which set him apart from other men in town who putted around on mere motor scooters. Carlos worked hard, as a manager of a small hotel, but it is unlikely his salary alone—without his wife's remittances—would have allowed for such extravagances. His wife's remittances gave him and his two sons more disposable income than they could earn working (legally) in Sosúa's tourist economy on the north coast of the Dominican Republic.

[. . .]

Examination of Sosúans' gossip about sex work and money—money earned either in the sex industry overseas[2] or in Sosúa's sex-tourist industry—reveals three interrelated issues: women's capacity for power, control, and opportunity in a globalized economy; the effect of women's earning power on gender relations and expectations; and women's role in not only challenging traditional gender ideologies through their earning capacity, but also in perpetuating them through their gossip about other women. This article focuses on gossip about Dominican women's sexual labor as an entry point into documenting shifting gender relations and ideologies in Sosúa, a sex tourist destination frequented primarily by German tourists.[3] It examines how Sosúa's sex workers create and hold one another to a restrictive "code of behavior," essentially operating like the "village eye" described by Mahler. Even though these particular internal migrants have freed themselves from the constraints of traditional gender ideologies and practices in their home communities, they find themselves nevertheless ensnared within a new set of gender-based expectations. What is of interest to me is that a comparable set of expectations and pressures does not exist for men in Sosúa—specifically sex workers' new boyfriends who are also migrants to Sosúa.[4] While sex workers in Sosúa are subject to new kinds of expectations—within their own community of sex workers—men in Sosúa experience a kind of loosening of expectations (among other migrant men) on their behavior. They become the envy of other migrant men in town, not stigmatized objects of their gossip. We will see that sex workers are criticized for giving money to boyfriends and for not working enough, while men are praised for sponging off of women and for working less.

The women's lives I write about here are more marked by continuity than change, and thus demonstrate the endurance of gender ideologies. However, the reversal of breadwinner status in Sosúa combined with some sex workers' use of sex tourism with European clients as a way to migrate to Europe are also significant challenges to traditional gender practices. I am reluctant, therefore, to write that the ethnographic stories here signal either the wholesale endurance or transformation of traditional gender ideologies. Rather, I see gender ideologies in this sex tourist town as both changing and continuing to inform peoples' self-image, performance, and life choices. Of course, assessing changes in gender thinking and doing is difficult while the forces of change—in this case foreign capital, new migration circuits to Europe, and a thriving sex industry—are relatively new and still unsettling. Moreover, fissures in gender ideologies may appear in one sex worker's life but not in another's, just as the power dynamics of one relationship might look different from another, and the decision-making in one household might look different from the next. And, ethnographers face the inevitable tension of how to adequately attend to both agency and constraints, without presenting one-dimensional portraits of women as victims of persistent machismo or as innovators of bold new gender scripts. . . .

. . . As the old world of men as breadwinners changes, and women turn to sex work not just to make ends meet but also as a stepping stone to international migration, women's gossip about one another reflects their efforts to hold on to traditional constructions of gender roles, motherhood, and sexuality. These attachments to old understandings of gender roles operate as a kind of drag on the changes tourism and sex tourism introduced, as well as on the possibilities of benefitting from the appearance of foreign capital and new migration choices to Europe. Meanwhile, as women might choose to hold on to past conceptualizations of gender roles (even though their practices indicate otherwise), men benefit from a re-working of the old notions of men as breadwinners, as they still remain macho without actually working.

PART I. SEX WORK IN SOSÚA

SEX WORKERS AS EXPLOITED AND EXPLOITING

Sosúa's sexual economy shapes its gender relations and ideologies around earning, spending, and saving money. With its constant flow of Afro-Dominican and Afro-Haitian migrants for work in the sex and tourist trades, and of white European tourists for play, as well as of a large foreign-resident community (primarily German) living there year-round, Sosúa has become a transnational sexual meeting ground. The transnational process of *sex tourism* has quickly and flamboyantly changed daily life in Sosúa in different ways than has *tourism*—especially for Dominican women who can out-earn most Dominican men. Because sex tourism has played a critical role in the town's transformation, I see it as a space intextricably tied up with transactional sex—it has become of sexscape of sorts.[5] As sites in the developing world become known as sexscapes, sex-for-sale can come to define these countries—and the women who live there—in North American and European imaginations. The association between nationality, race, and sexual prowess draws sex tourists to sexscapes in the developing world where they not only buy sex more cheaply than in their home countries, but they also can live out their racialized sexual fantasies. . . . In the Dominican Republic it is . . . common for European men to seek long-term relationships with Dominican women as a break from the "demands" of "liberated" European women. They have fantasies not only of 'hot' and "fiery" sex, but also of greater control and power than they might have in their relationships with European women. . . .

. . . The growth of the sex trade in the developing world and poor women's participation in it are consequences of not only the restructuring of the global economy, but also of women's central role in the service sector of tourism, a "hospitality" industry (Sinclair 1997, Kinnaird and Hall 1994, Swain 1995). Women perform the majority of this "service-oriented" labor, and since they often are paid less than men, their relatively cheap labor has assured that destinations—such as Sosúa—are affordable to even the most budget-conscious travelers. But sex tourism can be different and in Sosúa it is. It pays considerably more than cleaning hotel rooms (a typical job for women in Sosúa) or driving a motor scooter taxi (a typical job for men in Sosúa). While a sex worker can earn 500 pesos *a client*, these other tourist-related jobs yield around 1000—1500 pesos *a month*.

Women in Sosúa's sex trade not only out-earn Dominican men in Sosúa but also control much of their working conditions in their daily work lives since they do not have pimps or any other intermediaries. I should note that except for Maria, whose story I tell below, this article analyzes men's role as opportunists who try to sponge off of women's sexual labor and not as sex industry entrepreneurs. Sosúa's sex workers use the sex tourist trade as an advancement strategy, not just as a survival strategy. This strategy hinges on their performance of "love" as they try to marry their European clients-turned-suitors and migrate to these men's home countries. Their earning power, retention of earnings, and the migration strategies they weave into the sex trade, are examples of how women

struggle to take advantage of the foreign men who are in Sosúa to take advantage of them.

As Sosúa's sex-tourist trade grew, particularly since the early 1990's, poor Dominican women—all single mothers—were drawn into Sosúa's sex trade and new migration patterns were set in motion. Like feminist ethnographers who explore larger structural forces that contribute to poor women's oppression while also highlighting how these women try to improve their lives (Constable 1997), I too not only consider structures of inequality in sex workers' lives—such as limited educational opportunities for poor women, and the relationship between consensual unions and female headed households—but also their creative responses to them. I see a great deal of what Ortner calls "intentionality" in these women's use of the sex trade.[6] Their creative strategizing presents an important counter-example to claims that *all* sex workers in *all* contexts are powerless victims of violence and exploitation.[7] Rather, women enter sex work for diverse reasons and have greatly varying experiences within it. Even within Sosúa, sex workers' experiences are highly differentiated. In Sosúa there are Dominican and Haitian sex workers; women who work with foreign or Dominican clients; women who receive money wires from European and Canadian clients; women who receive financial help from local Dominican *clientes fijos* (regular clients); women who live with or separated from their children; women who have AIDS, and/or have been raped and/or battered in the sex trade; and, the focus of this article, women who give money to Dominican boyfriends and women who are careful to not give any money to any men. These differences are crucial to shaping a woman's capacity for choice and control in Sosúa's sex trade.

Consequently, rather than lumping all sex workers in all places together as victims with no control over their lives, I suggest a nuanced understanding of women's room to maneuver (agency) within the sex trade—at least within the context of Sosúa,[8] especially since I propose that Dominican women use Sosúa's sex trade as an *advancement* strategy through marriage and migration. . . .

SOSÚA'S SEX WORKERS LOOK TO MIGRATE OFF THE ISLAND

. . .The quest for a visa, to Canada, the United States, or Europe, is virtually a national pastime. Dominican musician, Juan Luis Guerra, captures this preoccupation with *fuera* (outside/off the island) and the visas necessary to get there in his hit song "Visa para un Sueño" (Visa for a Dream).[9] Whereas tourists can enter the Dominican Republic without a visa, Dominican citizens must jump through hoops to travel abroad and often undertake elaborate and dangerous schemes to do so. Since the benefits of working abroad can prove transformative for extended families left behind (through remittances), a variety of legitimate means to get *fuera*, as well as scams, abound. Some are so desperate to get off the island, that they willingly risk their lives. Dominicans perish in *yolas* (small boats or rafts used to travel to Puerto Rico),[10] professional line-waiters are paid to hold places in the visa line at the United States consulate, and there is a lively industry in false papers, including passports and visas, some of which cost thousands of dollars.

This preoccupation, with getting *fuera* plays a significant role in shaping women's expectations that Sosúa's sex trade with foreign tourists might be an exit from the island. As a transnational space, Sosúa represents a land of opportunity within the Dominican Republic and a point of departure to other countries. Many often migrate internally to Sosúa since it the closest they can get to the "outside." Consequently, when women move to Sosúa to enter into sex work, they are able to see themselves as taking the first step toward entering another country with more and greater possibilities. Sex tourism links the two forms of migration in a powerfully gendered and racialized way as it relies on and perpetuates sexualized and racialized stereotypes of Afro-Caribbean women.

PERFORMING LOVE AND SELLING SEX FOR VISAS

Dominican sex workers not only pretend that they desire their clients and enjoy the sex—a charade sex workers the world over undertake—but they also pretend to be in love. Sex workers in Sosúa, make a distinction between marriage *por amor* (for love) and marriage *por residencia* (for visas). After all, why waste a marriage certificate on romantic love when it can be transformed into a visa to a new land and economic security? Theirs is a high-stakes performance that, if successful, could catapult their families out of poverty. Sex workers correspond by fax with four or five clients at the same time (it costs under a dollar to send or receive a fax at Codetel, the national phone company) and dropping by the Codetel office to see if they have received any faxes is a daily ritual for these women. The lucky ones receive faxes instructing them to pick up money at the Western Union office. Others, such as the women whose stories I tell below, receive word that their European clients-turned-boyfriends are planning return visits to Sosúa, or have news about the women's visas and travel arrangements to visit or to move to Europe with the men. However, even though I distinguish between sex work as an advancement or survival strategy, as a feminist scholar I walk a tightrope between calling attention to marginalized women's attempts *progesar* (to get ahead) and highlighting the role of both local and global forces that constrain them. Relationships with foreign men inevitably fall short of mutual exploitation since white male sex tourists are better positioned than Afro-Caribbean female sex workers to leave Sosúa satisfied with their experiences there. Sex workers in Sosúa are at once independent and dependent, exploiters and exploited by foreign men—and as the stories below indicate—by Dominican men as well.

PART II: REWRITING THE GENDER "SCRIPT" IN SOSÚA

SOSÚA'S SEX WORKERS' CODE OF BEHAVIOR

While men in Sosúa enjoy a re-writing of gender-based expectations that praise them for sponging rather than earning, women in Sosúa's sex trade risk being subjected to stigmatizing gossip if they stray too far from a different set of gender-based expectations. . . . In the case of Sosúa's sex workers, it is not just their talent for expressive storytelling that makes their self-descriptions and gossip compelling. Another striking feature is that a diverse group of women with vastly different experiences in sex work adhere to the same themes as if their stories were scripted. Of course the themes in sex workers' gossip and self-descriptions might not have anything to do with the values and beliefs that women hold dear or actually live by; rather the values and beliefs women publicly claim to embrace reveal the pressures sex workers are under to appear to live in a certain way. Within days of arriving in Sosúa, sex workers learn the "code of behavior" to which they are expected to adhere. Newcomers quickly catch on to the major themes their coworkers expect them to stress: Motherhood and the suffering and sacrifice it demands, safe sex, and frustration with Dominican men's infidelity. This code undergirds their idealized construct of the self-sacrificing mother who is not *really* a sex worker. By setting up these expectations, sex workers pit themselves against other sex workers. In so doing, they preserve their self-esteem in the face of public scrutiny and stigma, and also try to avoid being the object of gossip themselves.

GOSSIP'S FUNCTION: UNIFIES AND DIVIDES

Since my field notes are bursting with sex workers' gossip about one another, I turn to their gossip as a guidepost to their perceptions of their social obligations both to their families and in their daily experiences in sex work. Gossip can bring people together as well as pull them apart. When it takes the form of what Patricia Meyer Spacks calls "serious" gossip "in private, at leisure, in a context of trust, usually among no more than two or three people," it functions as a sign of "intimacy" and it "provides a resource for the subordinated. . . . a crucial means of self-expression, a crucial form of solidarity" (1985:5). Although "intimate" discussions are essential to the friendships sex workers forge in the bars and boarding houses, the distinctions that sex workers draw among themselves also clearly divide them. At the

other extreme, gossip "manifests itself as distilled malice. It plays with reputations, circulating truths and half-truths and falsehoods about the activities, sometimes about the motives and feelings of others. Often it serves serious (possibly unconscious) purposes for the gossipers, whose manipulations of reputation can further political or social ambitions by damaging competitors or enemies, gratify envy and rage by diminishing another, generate an immediate sense of power" (Spacks 1985:4). As sex workers compete with one another for clients, especially sober, clean, and generous customers, the atmosphere in the bars and boarding houses is ripe for gossip and back-biting.

I'M NOT LIKE 'OTHER' SEX WORKERS

The central image Sosúan sex workers overwhelmingly use in their self-descriptions and in their gossip about one another is that of the "good mother." Within a matrix of maternal responsibility and morality, sex workers depict themselves as selfless, responsible and caring mothers. By using the themes of family obligation and sacrifice, sex workers liken themselves and their concerns to those of other poor mothers. "We poor women suffer a lot" is a phrase Sosúan sex workers frequently employ in daily conversation. In fact some women adamantly do not identify as sex workers, such as Helena, who explained: "In my head I don't see myself as a prostitute." In sex workers' self-descriptions *prostitutas* (prostitutes) or *putas* (whores) are set in opposition to good mothers.[11] Just as in his book on manhood, Gilmore (1990) examines what makes a man "good at being a man," Dominican sex workers rely on dominant discourses about gender relations and roles—especially about motherhood—to determine not only what makes a woman *good at being a woman*, but also what makes a woman who sells sex to meet her financial obligations as a single mother *good at not really being a sex worker*.

Insistence that they are not like "other" sex workers pervades Sosúan sex workers' self-descriptions and gossip about co-workers. Simultaneously their gossip about "other" sex workers mirrors the criticism and rumors that Sosúan residents, angered by rapid commercial development and the influx of sex tourists, circulate about them. Although sex workers help and support their co-workers, they also actively castigate one another by strategically and selectively appropriating the dominant discourse of women's sexuality as dangerous and uncontrollable. Sosúa's sex workers often describe "other" sex workers as dangerous (transmitters of AIDS and petty thieves who prey on unsuspecting, or drunk, tourists); untrustworthy (liars about their HIV status); and manipulative (opportunists when it comes to men and money). Ani, for example, singles out sex workers who steal from tourists, and she imagines that their plunder has made them wealthy and enables them to live well in "two-story houses surrounded by lots of land." . . .

. . . Rita (who entered Sosúa's sex trade to pay for a leg operation her daughter needed as well as to save money to buy a house) carefully distanced herself, for example, from other sex workers by elaborating on what characterized other women as *putas* while emphasizing that she was "not of the street." She explained, "I'm different from other *prostitutas*. I'm not used to this life. I don't like the Anchor (the main tourist bar), and I am embarrassed with tourists. I don't approach them—that's shameful. I sit and wait and order a beer myself. And I'm afraid of AIDS so I always use condoms unlike other women." She continued, "I stay with one man a night, while some women go with four or five" and remarked that she was a discriminating seller and unwilling to have sex with anyone willing to pay. "I make sure they are clean—their hair and teeth." She also refused to go out with clients during the day; that was *her* time. Rita saw herself as worlds apart from the other, more "aggressive" women in the tourist bars, so much so that she did not consider herself a *prostituta* at all. Rather, she explained, "My style is different—I always dress like a *señora*. I sit and wait to be invited for a drink. I would rather go home alone than throw myself at a man like some of the other girls." . . .

[. . .}

PART III: BOYFRIENDS SPONGE WHILE WOMEN ARE SUBJECT OF GOSSIP

NEW MEANINGS OF MASCULINITY

Beyond new spatial arrangements, this section explores other examples of challenges to traditional gender ideologies and practices in Sosúa. One Nineteen-year-old sex worker from the capital, Santo Domingo, was shocked at the inversion of gender relations in Sosúa: "Here in Sosúa women take care of men, and give them money. In Santo Domingo (the capital city) it is men who take care of women." Honor and manhood long have been associated in Latin America and the Caribbean with protecting and financially providing for one's family (Gutmann 1996, Safa 1995). Contrary to these myths of manhood, Dominican men in Sosúa who siphon money from their Dominican girl-friends—even from women who have sex with other men for a living—are not seen as any less macho. In the context of Sosúa's sexscape/sex-tourist economy, depending on a woman—as Carlos does—is, in fact, macho. Carlos's financial dependence on his wife (through her remittances) affirmed his machismo rather than compromised it.

With women's new-found earning power through the sex trade with foreign men, men in Sosúa such as Carlos openly—even flamboyantly—rely on their wives'[12] or girlfriends' participation in Sosúa's or the overseas sex trade, or their migration to Europe to live with the European men they met while working in Sosúa's sex trade. New meanings of masculinity emerge in Sosúa that allow men to be *tígueres* (tigers),[13] the ultimate Dominican machos, without out-earning the women in their lives—or in some cases without earning at all.[14] Tígueres, Christian Kohn-Hansen argues, is "a type who acts according to the situation, is cunning, and has a gift for improvisation . . . the image of the *tíguere* represents both an everyday hero and a sort of trickster." Even though sex workers harshly criticize men who sponge off of fellow sex workers' hard-earned money and call them *chulos* (pimps), these men—this new brand of *tígueres*—at the same time, are admired by the other migrant men in town. In the process, while men try to reap the benefits, women assume all the stress, risks, and possible dangers associated with the experiences of sex work and migration—as well as with having to "perform" at being in love with their European clients/suitors.

DRAINS ON SEX WORKERS' EARNINGS

While saving money is not possible in factory or domestic work (where women earn around or under 1,000 pesos a month), sex workers whose clients are foreign tourists, in theory at least, make enough money to build up modest savings. In practice, however, it is costly to live in Sosúa. Many sex workers earn just enough to cover their daily expenses in Sosúa while sending home remittances for their children. Even though poor women earn more money in sex work than they can in other jobs available to them, they end up spending most of it picking up the financial obligations abandoned by absentee fathers. Realizing this, and missing their children, most women return to their home communities in less than a year, just as poor when they first arrived. Those who manage to save money use it to buy or build homes back in their home communities. Alternatively, they might try to start small businesses, such as *colmados* (small grocery stores), out of their homes. But first, soon after they arrive in Sosúa, women must learn how to guard their earnings since their new-found economic power invites exploitation. The police (through extortion), Dominican boyfriends, family, friends, and shop and restaurant owners all hope to profit from women's participation in the sex trade. These women's Dominican male lovers' attempts to siphon their earnings, in particular, can severely jeopardize women's financial independence and few are able, for example, to put enough money aside to start a small business, something to move on to after sex work. However, Dominican men in their lives, in some cases, benefit considerably. In the remaining parts of this article I explore examples of men who sponge off of women who earn in the sex trade. Throughout these ethnographic examples I also weave instances of women's gossip.

BOYFRIENDS BENEFIT FROM SEX WORKERS' TRANSNATIONAL RELATIONSHIPS

[. . .]

Luisa's Boyfriend

Luisa is another sex worker who received money wires from a German client and whose Dominican boyfriend also rode on her good fortune. In fact he moved in with Luisa (who paid for the rent), and even stopped working while he sponged off Luisa's money wires from the German client as well as her earnings in the sex trade. Quite remarkably, she had received US$500 every two weeks over a six-month period from her German client who had wanted her to leave sex work and to start her own clothing store (most money wires sex workers receive are $100-200 and less frequent). She told him she had stopped working the tourist bars, and that she used the money he was sending her to buy clothes for the store. Months later, when he found out that she was still working as a sex worker (although not as much as before the money wires), had not opened a store, and was living with a Dominican boyfriend, he stopped wiring money. The way he found out testifies to the increasing efficiency of the transnational networks linking Sosúa and Germany, as well as the critical role of fax machines in the building and maintenance of these transnational social networks. Carla, another sex worker and a friend of Luisa's, also had an ongoing fax and money-wire relationship with a German man, who knew Luisa's German boyfriend. This is not uncommon, since the men in the tourist bars often are on vacation with other male friends from Europe and they go out to the bars together to pick up sex workers. Luisa believes Carla faxed her (Carla's) boyfriend in Germany, who then told Luisa's boyfriend, essentially "blowing the whistle" on Luisa's infidelity and her phantom clothing store. After this revelation, the money wires dried up and Luisa's German boyfriend stopped returning to Sosúa to visit Luisa. At this juncture, Luisa's expenses soon outpaced her dwindling resources. She had not saved any money— in part because the house she had been renting was twice the size and double the rent of friends' apartments—and in part because she had been supporting her boyfriend. She also sent money home to her mother in Santo Domingo, who cared for her twelve-year-old son (who, tragically, later died in Hurricane George when his Grandmother's house collapsed).

When her Dominican boyfriend did not get a job during this financial crisis, but, rather, Luisa increased her time working in the sex trade—and hocked some of her necklaces and rings in a pawn shop—it fueled other sex workers' gossip. They called her Dominican boyfriend a *chulo* (pimp), since he lived off of Luisa's earnings and money wires, and thought Luisa had been foolish for bankrolling him. However, while Luisa was castigated by fellow sex workers—for spending too much on herself (rather than her son) and for bankrolling a man (especially one who is not the father of her son)—her boyfriend was admired by other Dominican men in town. While other sex workers worked to distinguish themselves from Luisa, other men hoped to replicate and envied the good fortune of her financially dependent boyfriend.

GOSSIP ABOUT BANKROLLING A BOYFRIEND

Although it is difficult to know what motived Luisa's friend to snitch on her, she might not have if Luisa's son had appeared to be the main beneficiary of the money instead of her Dominican boyfriend. "Luisa is crazy," her friends gossiped, "She spends all her money on her *chulo* (pimp) who does not even work." Women who receive money from men overseas are

enviable, but how they spend it determines their reputation. Even though many depend on money from regular clients, and look forward to marrying so that their new husbands can financially "take care of" them, Sosúa's sex workers also are proud of their ability to earn money to raise their children without the help of their children's fathers. Since their earnings are so hard won, some sex workers go to great lengths to protect their money from men in their lives. . . .

Within the sex-work community's code of acceptable behavior, sex workers often see certain lies that they tell men in faxes, letters, and phone calls— such as that they love them and miss them—as a necessary part of sex work. But sex workers also harshly criticize women who tell too many lies. Although within the sex-work community it is expected that women build relationships with foreign men not for love but for money and *residencia*, Luisa's friends told me Luisa had been overly greedy. When Luisa's German boyfriend stopped sending her money, her friends were not surprised, nor sad for Luisa. It is difficult to pinpoint what tarnished Luisa's reputation within the community of sex workers—her bankrolling of her Dominican boyfriend, her squandering of such large money wires, or her too-comfortable living arrangements (instead of spending the money on her son). Moreover, since it was not just mere bad luck that dried up her money wires, but deliberate sabotage by her friend Carla, Luisa's stigmatization by other sex workers is a far cry from the uncritical admiration that her Dominican boyfriend enjoyed in his community of friends (comprised of men like him who had migrated internally to Sosúa to make money off the tourist trade). It did not help that, unlike some sex workers who generously buy drinks for their friends, or share new clothes— as Andrea did with the money her German boyfriend wired her—Luisa had a reputation for being stingy.

GOSSIP ABOUT WOMEN WHO SPEND TOO MUCH MONEY ON THEMSELVES

Whereas Carlos's open display (with his gold chains and expensive motorcycle) of his financial dependence on his wife's participation in the sex trade enhanced his reputation in town, sex workers' reputations were damaged by flashy displays of spent income. Sex workers cannot appear to live too well, otherwise their invocation of motherhood as a justification for selling sex will not ring true. Of course no sex worker can be sure how much their co-workers earn, what portion of their earnings they send home, or what they spend on themselves, unless there are material indicators (such as Luisa's large house). Or they might witness women spending money: Carmen admonished a sex worker, for example, with whom she had worked and lived at a bar, who was "in debt to vendors who go to the bars selling women's clothes, lingerie, jewelry and hair clips." Carmen observed that "Every time they come by, she buys things." Moreover, gossip began to circulate among the "old-timers" in the sex trade, about some of the newer—and younger (in their early twenties)—sex workers, who, as regulars in the restaurants, and the main patrons in the stores, became a focus of other—older (in their late twenties and early thirties)—sex workers' censure. The more seasoned and older sex workers explained that the behavior and stylish—and, at times, provocative—dress of their younger, flashier counterparts reflected their young age. Carmen thought that they were dressing "the way they think prostitutes should dress. They don't know any better. It's as if they are young girls play acting."

Sex workers seem to reserve their most serious criticisms, however, for older sex workers such as Luisa. These criticisms, of sex workers' diversion of earnings from their children, echoed complaints sex workers make of Dominican men's spending patterns as draining family income. Women certainly did not want to be seen as irresponsible as the men who left them. Whereas Carmen forgave the younger sex workers since they "don't know any better," Luisa's co-workers relentlessly scrutinized the way she lived. "At age 32," Carmen complained, "Luisa should have known to live less extravagantly and to save money." Most especially for someone like Carmen who cautiously guarded her earnings from the Dominican

men in her life, Luisa's spending on her Dominican boyfriend was synonymous with wasted income.

[. . .]

Maria's Boyfriend

Dominican men in Sosúa have tried to elbow in on sex workers' transnational ties.[15] Juan even went so far as to push Maria, his girlfriend, into a transnational relationship with a German man (whom she had met as a sex worker). In a way, this was Juan's transnational "fantasy," not Maria's. Even though the German man wanted to marry Maria, the goal of many Sosúan sex workers, she was clearly reluctant. Maria was not in love with her German boyfriend and dreaded going to Germany to visit him. Her German boyfriend had been quite generous with her, and had sent enough money on a regular basis that she was able to quit the sex trade and to bring her children to Sosúa to live with her. It is at this point when Maria rented a house that Juan moved in with her; soon after, he started physically abusing her. Juan greatly enjoyed the material benefits of Maria's ongoing transnational liaison and pressured her to continue the relationship. Extremely shy, Maria replied to her German boyfriend's faxes only at Juan's urging. He knew her transnational ties could prove to be a gold mine, and he was right. From the money wires the German boyfriend sent, he bought an impressive stereo system, a large color television, and a stove. He moved from a one-room wooden shack into a concrete house.[16] Juan had worked only sporadically before the money wires, but gave up looking for jobs altogether once the wires started.

When Maria finally moved to Germany, she returned only weeks later. She had not liked it there: It was too cold, she missed her children and, most of all, she was not in love. As it turned out, *residencia* was not enough for her. When she returned without the windfall of money Juan had hoped for, his beatings escalated. She eventually left him, however, and moved into her mother's home with her children. Afraid to bring along the things bought with the money wires, she left them behind with Juan. While Juan benefitted from Maria's transnational relationship, she ended up back where she financially had started off before she had ever been involved with a foreign man. In Maria's case, her greater earning power over Juan's translated into exploitation and abuse.

[. . .]

CONCLUSION

As Carlos swaggers around town in clothes and jewelry purchased with money his wife has remitted, he, and other migrant men who benefit financially from women's overseas or local sexual labor, challenge traditional understandings of gender roles and ideologies. In Sosúa's sexscape, new meanings of masculinity have emerged alongside women's earning capacity. While sex workers must temper their displays of monetary gains so as to not compromise their reputations as mothers sacrificing for their children, men openly enjoy freedom from gender ideologies that make demands on them to appear as hard working and sacrificing fathers. In this sexual economy, men even can flaunt their unemployment. Their laziness and/or dependency—such as Luisa's and Maria's boyfriends—are recast as macho. Only a savvy macho could cook up a way to make money—in some cases a lot of money—without actually working. Only fools would work in low-paying jobs; real men sponge off of women.

As men are freed from expectations to be households' main breadwinners (or to earn at all), women find themselves working more than men. At the same time, women face intense scrutiny and possible criticism by their coworkers. Here is one industry where poor Dominican women have the opportunity to make significant earnings and to jump out of poverty, yet their migration and labor strategies do not necessarily ensure a reconfiguration of gender roles and ideologies that works in their favor. Rather, migrant men in Sosúa enjoy such a reworking that lowers expectations for them, while women are caught in a set of increased expectations. In order to keep their images as "good mothers" intact while selling sex, these successful entrepreneurs must appear to live frugally. As "good mothers," they cannot risk swaggering around town.

ENDNOTES

1. I have changed all the names of Sosúans, including sex workers, their boyfriends, husbands, and clients. I also have changed the name of bars and nightclubs. This article draws from field research that I conducted in Sosúa in the summer of 1993, 1994-1995, the summer of 1999, and January and July of 2003. I owe a great debt to the Dominican HIV/AIDS outreach and education non-governmental organization CEPROSH, particularly to its peer educators (known as *mensajeras de salud*)

2. The remainder of this article, however, focuses on sexual labor in Sosúa. For a discussion on Dominican women's experiences in the sex trade overseas—as well as on their experiences living in Europe as the wives or girlfriends of European men—see Brennan 2004.

3. Other tourists and sex tourists include Canadians and other Europeans such as Austrians, Dutch, English, Italians, and Spaniards.

4. I want to be clear: The women who migrate to Sosúa to work in its sex trade do not have husbands or boyfriends in their home communities, but are entering the sex trade because men have abandoned them and their responsibilities to their children. The boyfriends I write about as sponging, are Dominican men these women met once in Sosúa. These women's children usually remain in the women's home communities, far from the knowledge of their mothers' work, and cared for by female relatives such as grandmothers and aunts.

5. I use the term "sexscape" to refer to both a new kind of sexual landscape and the sites within it. The word sexscape builds on the five terms Arjun Appadurai has coined to describe landscapes that are the "building blocks" of "imagined worlds:" "The multiple worlds which are constituted by the historically situated imaginations of persons and groups spread around the globe"

(1990: 4). He uses the suffix "*-scape*" to allow "us to point to the fluid, irregular shapes of these landscapes" (with such terms as *ethnoscape, mediascape, technoscape, finanscape,* and *ideoscape*) as he considers the relationship among these five dimensions of global cultural flows (1990: 6-7). Sex-for-sale is one more dimension of global cultural flows, and Sosúa is one site within a global economy of commercialized sexual transactions.

6. Since I argue that Dominican sex workers' opportunity for agency is highly nuanced, Ortner's discussion of "partial hegemonies" in her "subaltern version of practice theory" helps to conceptualize the thorny territory of agency in the sex trade. Her analysis which looks for the "slippages in reproductions," the "disjunctions" in the "loop in which structures construct subjects and practices" and "subjects and practices reproduce structures," allows for seeing how Dominican women try to find ways in the sex trade *progesar* (to get ahead) (1996: 17-18).

7. In light of debates over whether sex work can by anything but exploitative, ethnographic accounts of Dominican women's experiences in Sosúa help demonstrate that there is a wide range of experiences within the sex trade, some beneficial and some tragic. The debate on how to conceive of women's sexual labor centers on issues of agency and victimization, as well as of economic empowerment and powerlessness. Some scholars, activists, and sex workers assert that women who are forced to choose sex work because of their race, class, nationality, colonial status and gender are not exercising "choice." To them, all forms of sex work are exploitative and oppressive, which is why they usually employ the terms prostitute and prostitution rather than sex worker and sex work. The latter terminology recognizes that selling one's body is a form of labor that—under certain contexts—women can *choose*. While grappling with the thorny issue of whether sex work is inherently oppressive, McClintock's warning against conflating agency with context in discussions about sex work is helpful: "Depicting all sex workers as slaves only travesties the myriad, different experiences of sex workers around the world. At the same time, it theoretically confuses social *agency* and identity with social *context*" (1993).

8. Feminist scholars' contribution to "transnational feminist theory" is particularly valuable since it emphasizes the particularized, historical contexts of women's experiences (Grewal and Kaplan 1995). This contextualizing has profound consequences for the question of agency/choice in sex work since consideration of sex workers' experiences in various contexts throughout the globe

challenges the view that sex workers experience a monolithic set of oppressions in the sex trade.

9. On account of this preoccupation Pessar named her book on Dominican migration after Guerra's popular song, *A Visa for a Dream: Dominicans in the United States* (1995).

10. The U.S. Coast Guard interdicted 5,430 Dominicans at sea in 1996; 1,143 in 1997; 831 in 1998; 531 in 1999; 781 in 2000; 270 in 2001; and 801 in 2002 (U.S. Coast Guard 2003).

11. These dichotomies (good-bad women, selfless mothers as Madonnas, selfish mothers as *putas*) engage notions of honor and shame that have been analyzed in studies on the Mediterranean. These writings explore how a woman's (and, by extension, her family's) reputation rests on her chastity, whereas a man's status is derived from his success in business and with women (Davis 1977; Herzfeld 1980 and 1985).

12. Unless I indicate otherwise, the "marriages" I write about between Dominican men and women are consensual unions, a common practice among the poor in the Dominican Republic of living together but not marrying.

13. Christian Krohn-Hansen describes the meaning of *tíguere* in the Dominican Republic: "the Dominican mythology of the *tíguere* has shaped, and continues to shape, a man who is both astute and socially intelligent; both courageous and smart; both cunning and convincing; and a gifted talker who gets out of most situations in a manner that is acceptable to others, while he himself does not at any time step back, stop chasing, or lose sight of his aim (be it women, money, a job, a promotion, etc.)" (1996: 108-9).

14. Sosúa's twist on what qualifies as "macho" or on who is a *tíguere,* dismantles hegemonic and unitary notions of "the Latin American male." Gutmann (1996) explores the varied and diverse interpretations and expectations of maleness and machismo in Mexico City. In contrast to Dominican men in Sosúa who often embrace the term *tíguere* and revel in being perceived as traditional machos, Gutmann found that Mexican men are resistant to being typecast as the "typical" Mexican macho.

15. Elsewhere I write about Dominican men who try to use romance and sex with foreign women as a way to build their own transnational ties that also can yield money wires, return visits with gifts, as well as marriage and migration overseas to the women's home countries (Brennan 2004). Sosúans and other Dominicans pejoratively refer to these men as "sanky-pankies," which evolved from a Spanglish term "los hanky-pankies."

16. When Maria's German boyfriend came to visit her on several occasions, Juan moved out temporarily.

REFERENCES CITED

Appadurai, Arjun. 1990. "Disjuncture and Difference in the Global Cultural Economy." *Public Culture* 2(2): 1-24.

Bowman, Glenn. 1986. "Fucking Tourists: Sexual Relations and Tourism in Jerusalem's Old City." *Critique of Anthropology* 9(2): 77-93.

Bunster, Ximena and Elsa M. Chaney. 1985. *Sellers and Servants: Working Women in Lima, Peru*. New York: Praeger.

Cohen, Erik. 1982. "Thai Girls and Farang Men: The Edge of Ambiguity." *Annals of Tourism Research* 9(3): 403-28.

Constable, Nicole. 1997. *Maid to Order in Hong Kong: Stories of Filipina Workers*. Ithaca, New York: Cornell University Press.

Davis, John. 1977. *People of the Mediterranean*. London: Routledge and Kegan Paul.

Enloe, Cynthia. 1989. *Bananas, Beaches and Bases: Making Feminist Sense of International Politics*. Berkeley: University of California Press.

Fernández-Kelly, María Patricia. 1983. *For We Are Sold, I and My People: Women and Industry in Mexico's Frontier*. Albany: State University of New York.

Gilmore, David D. 1990. *Manhood in the Making: Cultural Concepts of Masculinity*. New Haven: Yale University Press.

Glick Schiller, Nina, Linda Basch, and Cristina Blanc-Szanton. 1992. "Towards a Transnationalization of Migration: Race, Class, Ethnicity, and Nationalism Reconsidered." In *Towards a Transnational Perspective on Migration: Race, Class, Ethnicity, and Nationalism Reconsidered*. N. Glick Schiller, L. Basch, and C. Blanc-Szanton, eds. pp. 1-24. New York: New York Academy of Sciences.

Glick Schiller, Nina, Linda Basch, and Cristina Szanton-Blanc. 1994. *Nations Unbound: Transnational Projects, Postcolonial Predicaments and Deterritorialized Nation-States*. Langhorne, PA: Gordon and Breach Science Publishers.

Glick Schiller, Nina. 1999. "Transmigrants and Nation-States: Something Old and Something New in the U.S. Immigrant Experience." In *The Handbook of International Migration: The American Experience*. C. Hirschman, P. Kasinitz, and J. DeWind, eds. pp. 94-119. New York: Russell Sage Foundation.

Greenberg, H.R. 1991. "Rescrewed: Pretty Woman's Co-opted Feminism" *Journal of Popular Film and Television* 19(1): 9-13.

Grewal, Inderpal and Caren Kaplan, eds. 1995. *Scattered Hegemonies: Postmodernity and Transnational Feminist Practices*. Minneapolis: University of Minnesota Press.

Gutmann, Mathew C. 1996. *The Meanings of Macho: Being a Man in Mexico City*. Berkeley: University of California Press.

Hamilton, Annette. 1997. "Primal Dream: Masculinism, Sin and Salvation in Thailand's Sex Trade." In *Sites of Desire, Economics of Pleasure: Sexualities in Asia and the Pacific*. Lenore Manderson and Margaret Jolly, eds. pp. 145-65. Chicago: University of Chicago Press.

Herzfeld, Michael. 1985. *The Poetics of Manhood: Contest and Identity in A Cretan Mountain Village*. Princeton: Princeton University Press.

———. 1980. "Honour and Shame: Some Problems in the Comparative Analysis of Moral Systems." *Man* 15:339-51.

———. 1994. *Gendered Transitions: Mexican Experiences of Immigrants*. Berkeley: University of California Press.

Kempadoo, Kamala and Jo Doezema, eds. 1998. *Global Sex Workers: Rights, Resistance and Redefinition*. New York: Routledge.

Kinnaird, Vivian and Derek Hall, eds., 1994. *Tourism: A Gender Analysis*. New York: John Wiley & Sons, 1994.

Krohn-Hansen, Christian. 1996. "Masculinity and the Political among Dominicans: 'The Dominican Tiger'," in *Machos, Mistresses, Madonnas: Contesting the Power of Latin American Gender Imagery*, Marit Melhuus and Kristi Anne Stølen, eds. pp. 108-9. London: Verso.

Mahler, Sarah. 2001. "Transnational Relationships: The Struggle to Communicate across Borders." *Identities*. 7(4): 583-619.

Mahler, Sarah and Patricia Pessar. 2001. "Gendered Geographies of Power: Analyzing Gender Across Transnational Spaces." *Identities* 7(4):441-459.

McClintock Anne. 1993. "Sex Workers and Sex Work: An Introduction" *Social Text*. 11(4): 1-10.

Mills, Mary Beth. 1999. *Thai Women in the Global Labor Force*. New Brunswick, N.J.: Rutgers University Press.

Nelson, Nici. 1978. "'Women Must Help Each Other': The Operation of Personal Networks Among Buzaa Beer Brewers in Mathare Valley, Kenya." In *Women United, Women Divided: Cross-Cultural Perspectives on Female Solidarity*. Janet Burja and Patricia Caplan, eds. New York: Tavistock Publications.

Ong, Aihwa. 1987. *Spirits of Resistance and Capitalist Discipline: Factory Women in Malaysia*. Albany: State University of New York.

Ortner, Sherry. 1996. *Making Gender: The Politics and Erotics of Culture*. Boston: Beacon Press.

Pessar, Patricia. 1995. *A Visa for a Dream: Dominicans in the United States*. Needham Heights, MA: Allyn and Bacon.

Phongpaichit, Pasuk. 1982. *From Peasant Girls to Bangkok Masseuses*. Geneva: International Labor Office.

Rouse, Roger. 1992. "Making Sense of Settlement: Class Transformation, Cultural Struggle, and Transnationalism among Mexican Migrants in the United States." In *Towards a Transnational Perspective on Migration*, Nina Glick Schiller, Linda Basch, and Cristina Szanton-Blanc, eds. pp. 25-52. New York: New York Academy of Sciences.

Safa, Helen. 1995. *The Myth of Breadwinner: Women and Industrialization in the Caribbean*. Boulder: Westview Press.

Sassen, Saskia. 1998. *Globalization and Its Discontents*. New York: New Press.

Seabrook, Jeremy. 1996. *Travels in the Skin Trade: Tourism and the Sex Industry*. London: Pluto.

Sinclair, Thea M., ed. 1997. *Gender, Work, and Tourism*. London: Routledge.

Sorenson, Ninna Nyberg. 1998. "Narrating Identity across Dominican Worlds." *Transnationalism from Below*. M.P.

Smith and L.E. Guarnizo, eds. pp. 241-269. New Brunswick, N.J.: Transaction Publishers.

Smith, Michael Peter, and Luis Eduardo Guarnizo. 1998. "The Locations of Transnationalism." In *Transnationalism From Below*. M.P. Smith and L.E. Guarnizo, eds. pp. 3-34. New Brunswick, N.J.: Transaction Publishers.

Spacks, Patricia Meyer. 1985. *Gossip*. New York: Alfred A. Knopf.

Sturdevant, Saundra Pollock and Brenda Stoltzfus, eds. 1992. *Let the Good Times Roll*. New York: New Press.

Swain, Margaret Byrne 1995. "Gender in Tourism." *Annals of Tourism Research*. 22(2): 247-66.

Thorbek, Susanne and Bandana Pattanaik, eds. 2002. *Transnational Prostitution: Changing Global Patterns*. New York: Zed Books.

U.S. Coast Guard. 2003. Alien Migrant Interdiction: Migrant Interdiction Statistics, 1982-present.

Vollman, William. 1993. "Sex Slave." *Spin*. 9(9).

42. • *Alexandra DelValle*

FROM THE ROOTS OF LATINA FEMINISM TO THE FUTURE OF THE REPRODUCTIVE JUSTICE MOVEMENT (2006)

Alexandra DelValle is the program director at Groundswell Fund and graduate of the Columbia University Mailman School of Public Health specializing in reproductive, adolescent, and children's health. In 2006 she was awarded the Choice USA's Generation Award for Commitment to Leadership. The following article originally appeared in *We Don't Need Another Wave* edited by M. Berger (Seal Press 2006).

My mom likes to tell this story to explain to confused family and friends why I work in reproductive justice for a living: When I was very young, so young that my father was still around, there was an "incident." I was in the back seat of my dad's car; my parents were listening to NPR. A story came on about abortion, and as they began to talk about abortion rights, I stuck my head between their two seats and declared that women should have the right to do whatever they want with their bodies. I think my father tried to send me to counseling shortly thereafter.

I was raised in a very feminist home—just me and my working, independent mom. Her feminism ranged from magnets on the fridge that announced female superiority to her decision to get pregnant with me when she was thirty-six, single, and dating a married man. Pretty cool for the Bronx in the '80s, no? I grew up, wore feminist pins on my turtlenecks, dyed my hair pink, and soon enough went away to college at Oberlin—that infamous bastion of hippie liberal Midwestern barefoot glory. On campus, I had two major political revelations: (1) The world is racist (I must have known this before, but my segregated campus, the shock of being one of maybe four Puerto Ricans on campus, and the dirty looks I got at local stores made this even clearer); and (2) much of the world treats women like shit, and this happens in a very oppressive, racist, complex way. I started thinking about legacies of colonialism and imperialism, and how women's lives and bodies are sites where all these battles are fought.

I went to my first women's studies class, where my radical Cypriot teacher challenged us to stop using mirrors and watches, and, upon asking the class who it was that benefited from the capitalist patriarchy (or the "c-p" as we liked to call it), wrote the answer—Big White Men—on the board. I almost peed my pants it was so exciting. I wrote papers about the little white men on campus and how they oppressed me and my people. It all seemed very simple and clear to me. I was on my way to becoming a radical woman of color feminist/womanist activist.

I interned at an antigun violence organization, at NOW, at NARAL, and spent a month one summer organizing with a union. On campus, I organized within the Latina/o student community and became a peer sexual health counselor. And upon graduation, I found myself back in New York, knee-deep in the search for the perfect social justice, low-paying, radical activist job.

Two months later, I was hired (yes!) at the National Latina Institute for Reproductive Health (NLIRH). I felt immediately at home working with a mission to ensure the fundamental human right to reproductive healthcare for Latinas, their families, and their communities. The organization was in the middle of its comeback year (after having been shut down for a couple of years), and I was one of two staff people responsible for reestablishing NLIRH on the national scene and implementing new programs. My twin passions of reproductive and sexual health and racial-justice organizing had come together in an organization I would have wanted to create had it not already existed. I was thrilled to be a part of something so revolutionary.

My main work at NLIRH has been organizing Latinas across the country for demonstrations such as the 2004 March for Women's Lives, developing and running our Latinas Organizing for Leadership and Advocacy (LOLA) training series, and supporting our local Latina Advocacy Networks. We know that the mainstream reproductive rights movement has done a poor job of including the voices and concerns of people of color, and we also know that Latino organizations are often wary of including reproductive health issues in their platforms. Our work seeks to change the faces and agendas of both of these vitally important movements by finding and supporting progressive Latina leadership in doing work for reproductive justice. This work has taken me to states as diverse in need as North Carolina, Arizona, and California; in each state, I have the fantastic job of identifying fierce Latina leaders who are committed to fighting for their rights, as well as those of their friends, families, and neighbors.

Let's make one thing clear: There is no shortage of Latinas who care about these issues. Every single day, I see the myth of Latinas as monolithically religious, conservative, and opposed to abortion and choice debunked. Our activists include:

- A woman in her sixties who goes dancing at the hip Latino spots on the weekends and believes music videos can serve as tools for progressive education and outreach;
- A student in his twenties who worked with his state Democratic party to get a reproductive-justice statement included in its platform;
- A woman waiting impatiently to hit the streets in the armed revolution, but who, for now, will settle for doing progressive research;

- Mothers, daughters, sons, men, women, trans and genderqueer people, students, doctors, service providers, nurses, organizers, lawyers, South Americans, Caribbeans, Central Americans, immigrants, first-, second-, and third-generation Americans, Chicanos, multiracial and multilingual folks, and so on.

Point being, we are diverse, we are powerful, we are angry, and we care about every person's right to live free, safe, and informed sexual and reproductive lives. We believe that everyone should be able to decide when (if ever) and how to be pregnant, give birth, and parent. We believe that everyone deserves the right to engage sexually and/or lovingly as they please. We believe that these rights are integral to achieving social justice and ending oppression in this world. And we're organizing, across this country, and across the world.

People—specifically non-Latinos—always want to know why there needs to be a separate organization for Latinos, or why we prioritize Latino participation at our events. Part of me feels like we shouldn't even have to answer those questions—after hundreds of years of continual oppression. Why can't we just have our own thing, if only 'cause we feel like it? I guess this is scary and wrong to some people: Watch out! Those crazy brown people are talking and planning and may try to dismantle racism! Or. It's "reverse racism," and there is no value in safe spaces for marginalized peoples. Whatever.

But the real answer to the question of why we need separate spaces is that the best and most real and true organizing comes when it's led by and for a community of people. Nobody can speak for me and my experiences—as a woman, as a Bronx-bred Latina—but me. We need to be the ones advocating for change on local, state, national, and global levels. It *is* important that we have our own spaces where we can have even a little understanding of shared experience: language barriers, immigration and migration stories, and lack of access to healthcare, to name a few. I feel tremendously empowered when I sit in our trainings and feel the company of so many other strong, powerful, progressive, and change-making Latinas. I know they share this sense of empowerment and use it as momentum for their work.

This work is not without complications. We are so diverse, so different, that it can be hard to agree on what we believe in and how we want to do the work. We don't all look alike, we don't all speak the same language, some of us have money and some don't, some of us menstruate and some don't, some of us are American citizens and some of us aren't. Racism, classism, ageism, heterosexism, and every other possible ism plays out in our communities. We're also busy and don't necessarily have the time to meet and plan and run big fat campaigns. And time has shown me that, unfortunately, people of color and other women are not always interested in solidarily, and can be just as oppressive in the work as the BIG WHITE MEN I was always so angry at.

We think that's okay. We promote real and honest dialogues about tensions in our communities and use them as a starting place for developing campaigns. We encourage continual evaluation and evolution of our work, taking into account the holistic experiences and multiple identities we all have. We have a lot of work to do, and we're not giving up until we know that our sisters and daughters won't have to have children when they're not ready, and that they'll have access to daycare and support when they are ready to parent. We won't give up until we know that when one of our moms goes to the doctor she will be insured, and that when she gets there, she will be treated with respect and get the best possible care.

What makes this work so meaningful and critical for me is that I can see myself in it. This is about me end what I deserve as much as it is about anyone else. I also find safety and strength in this fantastic and growing community of Latina activists. The media love to make a big deal about how Latinos are taking over, how we're growing so fast, blah blah blah. I say, *hell yeah!* (Never mind that half this land was ours to begin with) We are here to stay, and united, we will fight to make (this country and this world a better place.

43. • *Kathy E. Ferguson*

BIRTH CONTROL (NEW)

Kathy Ferguson, a professor of political science and women's studies at the University of Hawai'i is currently writing a book on the activism of anarchist women advocating for reproductive and sexual freedom, labor rights, and an end to war. She has received several teaching, research, and service awards from the University of Hawai'i and from the field of political science, most recently for scholarship that directly benefits local communities. An earlier version of this essay first appeared in the blog *The Contemporary Condition* on July 14, 2015.

The second decade of the twenty-first century is witnessing significant political attacks on women's ability to use birth control—the Supreme Court case *Burwell v. Hobby Lobby* (2014), the presidential campaigns of Mitt Romney, Ted Cruz, and Rick Santorum, and a plethora of state-level initiatives from conservative and religious sources: such assaults often elicit disbelief from progressive women. We thought those battles were over. We thought we had won. A Planned Parenthood ad reminds us that it's not the 1950s anymore: "It is unbelievable that in 2014 we are still fighting about women's access to basic health care like birth control." Progressive women often ask, sarcastically, if this is 1915, not 2015, as if the passage of a hundred years were a guarantor of progress.

However, a stronger grasp of the history of the birth control movement suggests otherwise: the anarchists and socialists who fought those battles in the early twentieth century would not, I think, be surprised that the issue is still with us. I imagine that Emma Goldman, Alexander Berkman, Marie Equi, Ida Rauh, Crystal Eastman, Eugene Debs, Walter Adolphe Roberts, and many, many others working for access to contraception would know better, because they understood birth control as a central tenet of a larger struggle. Rather than looking at opposition to birth control as a lingering remnant of an otherwise settled past, the earlier radicals encourage us to see birth control as inextricably woven into

other ongoing struggles for freedom and community. Rather than assuming progress and being repeatedly surprised at its absence, we could learn from earlier struggles to locate our understanding of birth control in a more radical frame.

The anarchists and socialists who fought for birth control in the late nineteenth and early twentieth centuries did not think they were winning a definitive war but that they were engaging in a prolonged and messy set of battles in which victories came at significant costs. They understood that if women did not control their own reproduction, someone else would control it, since states, capitalists, churches, and families have serious investments in controlling women's bodies. It wasn't just attitudes that needed to be changed but also institutions. They fought for birth control, not as a private decision between a woman and her doctor but as a potentially revolutionary practice that radically challenged prevailing power arrangements, including that of men over women, capitalists over workers, militaries over soldiers, and churches over parishioners.

The Supreme Court decision in *Burwell v. Hobby Lobby* offers an unwelcome opportunity to think about birth control through an appreciation of its radical past. Many good questions have been asked regarding the *Hobby Lobby* ruling—why do for-profit corporations have religious rights? Why is men's sexuality unproblematic, so that insurance coverage for Viagra and vasectomies is uncontested, while women's sexuality is subject to scrutiny? Why are straightforward medical distinctions between preventing conception and aborting a fetus ignored or confused? Why do many conservatives decry recreational sex on the part of women but seem unconcerned that men might have sex for fun?

While recognizing the legitimacy of these queries, I want to raise a different question: Why are we surprised? Why is our indignation tinged with disbelief: "How could this happen in this day and age?" Critics routinely call the decision "hopelessly backward" and accuse critics of wanting to "turn back the clock," as though there were a single historical timeline that carries us forward unless someone pushes us back. This is an utterly inadequate view of history. Instead, we need to locate both our victories and our defeats within multidirectional and open-ended historical processes, not steps in a single unfolding drama. We won't understand the tenacity of efforts to control women's sexuality until we give up the comforting assumption that history is a story of progress, and look more closely at the stakes and the terms of political struggle.

RECLAIMING OUR RADICAL PAST

Linda Gordon rightly points out, in her landmark study *Woman's Body, Woman's Right*, that the radical roots of the struggle for birth control are largely unknown today. The situation faced by women in the United States in the early twentieth century with regard to controlling their reproduction was dire. The main problem was not a lack of known birth control technology, since, as Gordon documents, ancient, effective forms of birth control were selectively available, but in the United States it had been largely forced underground. In 1873 the passage of the Comstock Law, which criminalized sending "obscene" material through the mail, gathered birth control, sexuality, and radical ideas in general into its elastic net of prohibitions. During this time, various barrier and suppository methods, called pessaries, were known and available to wealthy women through their doctors but largely unknown or

unavailable to the poor. Diaphragms and condoms had to be smuggled into the United States from Europe. Politics, rather than technology, made birth control unavailable to most American women, and to change that situation political struggle was required.

From a contemporary point of view, it is startling to realize that many anarchists and socialists placed women's access to birth control at the heart of social revolution. We are accustomed to seeing the medicalized perspective—the claim that reproductive choices are questions of women's health and should be left to women and their doctors—as the feminist position, the position we must defend. Yet, there is another set of feminist voices, radical voices, voices that aimed to free women as well as liberate workers, end war, and transform society. Jamaican writer Walter Adolphe Roberts championed birth control both to enhance women's freedom and to advance the cause of social revolution (Roberts 7). Emma Goldman and Alexander Berkman located women's control over their reproduction as a central aspect of workers' struggles and antiwar activism. Emma Goldman's journal *Mother Earth* devoted its April 1916 issue to birth control. Alexander Berkman's journal *The Blast* concentrated on birth control in its February 12, 1916, issue and mentioned it in several others. While they supported Margaret Sanger in her early activism, they objected to Sanger's later strategy, which legitimized the birth control movement by aligning it with (mostly male) doctors. The radicals felt this approach removed birth control from the larger political context while giving power over women (including midwives) to doctors rather than to women themselves. Understanding these arguments can help feminists today learn from our own movement's past and perhaps shape current reproductive struggles as steps toward more radical political change.

Anarchists and socialists who embraced birth control framed it as a revolutionary demand to include sexual and reproductive freedom as necessary aspects of social justice and individual autonomy. Controlling one's own reproduction was part of transforming society. These progressive women and men integrated the liberation of women's sexuality into their vocal anticapitalist, antiwar mass movements. Just as capitalism sought to control the laboring bodies of workers and militaries sought to control the fighting bodies of soldiers, so did patriarchal families, churches, professions, and governments seek to control the reproductive bodies of women. Restrictions on birth control, they concluded, served the interests of states by producing an endless supply of cannon fodder for imperial wars, the interests of capital by generating a reserve army of labor to keep wages down, and the interests of organized religion by maintaining women's subservience and vulnerability within families and communities. A free society would be a society in which workers control their own labor, soldiers control their own fighting, and women control their own wombs. The radicals watched with dismay as their vision of a transformed society was displaced by the rise of a coalition between feminists, doctors, and the state to privatize contraception as an issue "between a woman and her doctor." Understanding the potentially radical implications of women's reproductive freedom, they also saw that some kinds of birth control reform could reinforce patriarchy rather than challenge it.

Attention to these struggles can reframe contemporary debates over birth control. The *Hobby Lobby* decision and other contraceptive losses for women are not temporary backsliding or inexplicable throwbacks to an earlier era but instead indicate ongoing and predictable unrest over proper standards of sexuality and of women's place. It would not surprise earlier anarchist and socialist feminists that the current Gilded Age, driven by neoliberal values and global corporate priorities, includes a resurgent war on women's reproductive autonomy. These radicals would, however, likely recoil from the pallid notion that birth control is a "women's issue" rather than a central aspect of a larger system of exploitation and control. A fuller grasp of our radical past can help us think of history as a dynamic network of shifting relations, operating at different paces in response to various challenges. The birth control movement then becomes a site of struggle, not an unfolding of a telos of development. We can look for the forgotten

victories and lost possibilities of human freedom recorded there and bring those minoritarian views back into contemporary discussions.

HOW CAN BIRTH CONTROL BE MORE RADICAL?

How might a greater appreciation of birth control's radical past change feminism's present and future? Perhaps it could give us an alternative to being on the defensive: rather than asking for healthcare, we might demand freedom. Rather than seeing doctors as our main partners, we might see unions, antiwar groups, civil rights organizations, environmental groups, alternative spiritual movements, and other radical communities as coalition partners. There is a vibrant history of such coalitions: the early years of the journal *The Birth Control Review* brought together labor leaders like Eugene Debs, antiwar activists such as John Haynes Holmes, and civil rights activists including W. E. B. Dubois to endorse women's access to birth control as a central aspect of freedom for all oppressed people. Today, we could make common cause with others who are similarly disadvantaged by, for example, judicial rulings granting corporations personhood, defining money as speech, and attributing religious identity to for-profit businesses. We might become bolder, not more cautious, in our thinking and acting.

For example, feminists often stress the difference between preventing and terminating pregnancy in order to use opposition to abortion to promote acceptance of birth control. Abortion and contraception are two separate issues, we say. Hobby Lobby's court arguments are invalid because they confuse technologies that prevent fertilization with technologies that remove fertilized eggs, we point out. We invite people who oppose abortion to agree with us about birth control because, if all women had access to birth control, there would be fewer abortions. These are very old arguments: birth control activist Mary Ware Dennett made the exact same claims in her 1926 book advocating the removal of contraception from the category of obscenity (12). Perhaps we need to stop concentrating on these arguments. Even though these claims are accurate, they don't appear to be working. I suspect they give up too much. While clearly abortion and contraception are different, it is their common value to women who want to control their fertility that makes both birth control and abortion into targets of conservative wrath.

Also, feminists often stress the priority of the relationship "between a woman and her doctor" to discredit other possible relations, say, between a woman and her employer, a woman and her husband, a woman and her Supreme Court justices. Perhaps we need to stop doing that too. Medicalization of contraception has come to be the progressive position, the position we have to defend. But that only happened because more radical, more feminist perspectives were sidelined. Maybe it's time to stress women's freedom—and access to affordable and high quality healthcare would surely be an aspect of that freedom—rather than women's health as our primary goal. When Sandra Fluke bravely testified before Congress in 2012 about the importance of oral contraception for treating health issues other than pregnancy, she was vilified as a slut and a prostitute anyway (Moorhead). So perhaps it's time to demand access to the birth control techniques that we want rather than parsing our desires to downplay sexual freedom. Calling on the courts to consider the "plight" of women who use contraception for non-sexual purposes implicitly suggests that those uses are somehow more legitimate, that women who have a "plight" are more worthy of consideration than women who have a cause. If contraceptives were sold over-the-counter at affordable prices or distributed for free at accessible clinics, then women's reasons for wanting them would be irrelevant and the opportunities to judge women's sexuality might diminish.

Further, feminists sometimes speak of opposition to birth control as psychological, a question of men's fears of women's sexual autonomy. Joan Walsh of Salon.com writes of a deep fear of women's freedom on the Right; Dan Savage writes on *Slog,* "it's sex for pleasure that they hate." I don't disagree with either of these claims, but I want to push them further—opposition to women's reproductive freedom is not primarily a bad attitude or emotional hang-up. The interests of material structures and institutions that distribute resources, organize labor, conduct war, and administer spirituality are fully in play. Birth control keeps coming back as an issue not just because men don't get it but because capitalism, the state, empire, war, and patriarchal religions are still in power, and those institutions have an enormous stake in controlling women's sexuality. Controlling access to physical pleasure, managing demographic change, disciplining labor, and ensuring inheritance, among other outcomes, are at issue.

Finally, feminists need to give up the comforting idea that history is on our side, that progress toward fuller rights and greater equality is written into the order of things, once we dispense with those irrational, wrong-thinking obstructionists. History, I think, isn't on anyone's side; more importantly, there are many histories, many trajectories, and many different futures past. When feminists assure us, as Joan Walsh recently did, that "the right's crippling panic over women's autonomy will eventually doom it to irrelevance," or, as Amanda Marcote commented, "the anti-sex argument is a losing argument," we should question the implicit progress narrative folded into such guarantees. We are neither doomed nor blessed—rather, we have multiple opportunities to struggle for a better world and we should think carefully about their possibilities.

NOTE

1. My thanks to Nicole Sunday Grove, Jairus Grove, and Lori Marso for their help on this essay. An earlier version appeared in *The Contemporary Condition*, 14 July 2014.

WORKS CITED

Bauman, Nick. "The Republican War on Contraception." *Mother Jones*, 9 Feb. 2012, www.motherjones.com/politics/2012/02/republican-war-birth-control-contraception.

Dennett, Mary Ware. *Birth Control Laws: Shall We Keep Them, Change Them or Abolish Them*. Grafton Press/Frederick H. Hitchcock, 1926.

Gordon, Linda. *Woman's Body, Woman's Right: The History of Birth Control in America*. Penguin Books, 1976.

Marcote, Amanda. "The Religious Right's No. 1 Obsession: Policing Women's Sex Lives by Any Means Necessary." *Salon*, 3 July 2014, www.salon.com/2014/07/03/the_religious_rights_1_obsession_policing_womens_sex_lives_by_any_means_necessary_partner/.

Moorhead, Molly. "In Context: Sandra Fluke on Contraceptives and Women's Health." *Tampa Bay Times*, 6 Mar. 2012, www.politifact.com/truth-o-meter/article/2012/mar/06/context-sandra-fluke-contraceptives-and-womens-hea/.

Roberts, Walter Adolphe. "Birth Control and the Revolution." *The Birth Control Review*, June 1917, p. 7.

Savage, Dan. "Republicans in Colorado Vote for More Abortions," *Slog*, Stranger, 1 May 2015, www.thestranger.com/blogs/slog/2015/05/01/22147727/republicans-in-colorado-vote-for-more-abortions.

Walsh, Joan. "GOP's Culture War Disaster: How This Week Highlights a Massive Blindspot." *Salon*, 3 July 2014, www.salon.com/2014/07/03/gops_culture_war_disaster_how_this_week_highlighted_a_massive_blind_spot/.

44. • *France Winddance Twine*

THE INDUSTRIAL WOMB (2011)

France Winddance Twine is a professor of sociology and feminist studies at the University of California, Santa Barbara. She has authored and coedited numerous books and articles, including *Geographies of Privilege* (Routledge 2013), *Girls with Guns* (Routledge 2013), *Retheorizing Race and Whiteness in the Twenty-First Century* (Routledge 2012), and *Outsourcing the Womb* (Routledge 2011) from which the following is excerpted. Winddance Twine is also the recipient of a number of grants and awards from the National Science Foundation, Stanford University, The Rockefeller Foundation, and the Andrew Mellon Foundation and is enrolled in the Creek (Muskogee) Nation of Oklahoma.

On January 3, 2008, Judith Warner published "Outsourced Wombs" in a blog in *The New York Times*. Warner raises ethical questions about the complexities of transnational gestational surrogacy, a growing segment of the reproductive tourism industry. Increasingly women and couples from the United States and Europe have begun traveling to India to hire women at discount rates to gestate and deliver babies for a fraction of what it would cost in the United States. They are, like companies that outsource labor to other countries, traveling to purchase a cheaper source of reproductive labor. In this blog Warner made references to the dystopic fiction of Aldous Huxley's *Brave New World* and Margaret Atwood's *A Handmaid's Tale* in which reproduction is imagined as an industrial or outsourced procedure.

The print version of the *American Heritage Dictionary* defines outsourcing as "To farm out (work) for example to an outside provider or manufacturer to cut costs" (1996: 1287). In recent years, the term outsourcing has been increasingly used by feminists and others to refer to the reproductive labor performed by pregnant women who are providing a form of contract labor—renting their wombs out to women whom they may not even meet to gestate babies to whom they have no genetic tie. Gestational surrogacy is a form of industrial labor that has not been previously considered by economists or economic sociologists in their discussions of outsourcing yet it represents a growing segment of the reproductive tourism or medical tourism market.

Women, typically the mothers of young children and from poor or lower middle class backgrounds, are selling their reproductive labor on an increasingly competitive global market. The comments of the hundreds of people who responded to Warner's blog reflect the mixture of ambivalence, anxiety, genetic entitlement, and a range of competing ethical attitudes towards this form of commercial pregnancy in the fertility industry.

On April 8, 2008, the cover story for *Newsweek* magazine featured the pregnant belly of an anonymous White woman. The cover read, "Womb for Rent: The Complex World of Surrogate Mothers." We learn that military wives are targeted by agencies as potential surrogates: "Surrogate agencies target the population by dropping leaflets in the mailboxes of military housing complexes such as those around San Diego's Camp Pendleton and placing ads in on-base publications such as *Military Times* and *Military Spouse* (Ali and Kelley 2008: 48). The *Newsweek* article addressed an issue that is central to sociologists interested in new family formations and social inequality.[1]

"Are there any ethical limits on what one person may pay another to do? It is a question that rarely arises in the world of normal commerce, even in the

modern service economy," wrote Roger Rosenblatt in 1987. Rosenblatt raised questions that remain the subject of controversy in academic, legal, public policy, and ethical debates about surrogacy and assisted reproductive technologies (ART). Although profound ambivalence and anxieties continue to surround the practice of commercial surrogacy in the United States, a laissez-faire capitalist consumer culture has enabled surrogacy to become a major industry attracting a global clientele. What is surprising is not that surrogacy has generated controversy, but that it has generated less controversy than abortion, contraception and same sex marriage—all issues used by politicians during every campaign season to generate support, raise financing and to negotiate their image. Surrogacy has yet to become a high-profile campaign issue. How can we understand the ethical debates around surrogacy?

What role should the state play in providing individuals and families with access to reproductive technologies? What criteria should be used to determine who "deserves" to have assisted conception? What role, if any, should private for-profit agencies play in assisted conception? Do unmarried women have a right to in vitro fertilization (IVF), assisted reproductive technology and to purchase sperm? What restrictions should be placed on ART? What role should religious beliefs play in access to and utilization of these assistive reproductive technologies? Should the U.S. pass federal legislation to protect the bodily integrity and rights of commercial surrogates?

Why does commercial surrogacy generate anxieties, ambivalence, controversy and hostility, yet remain legal in many countries? Why is surrogacy banned in most countries? A critical analysis of gestational surrogacy requires an analysis of the ways that the moral, social, political, legal, and religious contexts shape its interpretation and implementation.

This [reading] provides an introduction to the global industry of commercial surrogacy. The gestational surrogacy industry, a growing segment of the global medical tourism industry, assists individuals and families in conceiving and acquiring children to form families. This transnational profit-driven industry has generated controversy, legislation, and a

---

1. According to this article, "Military wives who do decide to become surrogates can earn more with one pregnancy than their husbands' annual base pay (with ranges for new enlistees from $16,080 to $28,900)" (Ali and Kelley 2008: 48). Military wives are also "attractive candidates because of their health insurance, Tricare, which is provided by three different companies—Humana, TriWest and Health Net Federal Services. And it has some of the most comprehensive coverage for surrogates in the industry" (2008: 48).

number of ethical questions that are troubling for sociologists of race, gender, and class inequality. Who should have access to these technologies? Should the state provide funding for ART to families who lack the resources to pay for them? How are racial, class, social, and other inequalities reinforced, reinscribed, and reproduced via these technologies? How do religious beliefs inform the transfer and utilization of these technologies? How do these technologies reinforce racial and ethnic boundaries? How is the problem of infertility conceptualized? Is it a personal problem? A public health problem? What are the competing frames? How do these interpretative frames reflect power inequities?

. . . .The ethical, moral, legal, religious, and policy debates surrounding the practice of gestational surrogacy are analyzed using the concept of stratified reproduction. Shellee Colen introduced the concept of stratified reproduction in her analysis of the relationships between West Indian migrant women working as childcare workers for U.S.-born White employers in New York. Colen defines stratified reproduction thus:

> By stratified reproduction, I mean that physical and social reproductive tasks are accomplished differentially according to inequalities that are based on hierarchies of class, race, ethnicity, gender, place in a global economy . . . The reproductive labor of bearing, raising, and socializing children . . . is differentially experienced, valued and rewarded according to inequalities of access to material and social resources in particular historical and cultural contexts.

(quoted in Ginsburg and Rapp 1995: 78)

Building upon the research of Shellee Colen, who conducted research among Black Caribbean domestic servants working on the upper West Side of Manhattan for New York White elites, I argue that gestational surrogacy is embedded in a transnational capitalist market that is structured by racial, ethnic, and class inequalities and by competing nation-state regulatory regimes. Consequently the same women who sell their reproductive labor and become reproductive service workers carrying pregnancies to term

under labor contracts may not be able to afford basic health care for themselves or their own children once their labor contract expires. There is unequal access to assisted reproductive technologies in most countries because the cost is prohibitive and if it is not state funded then only elites and the upper middle classes can afford to purchase these services.

Do women have the right to rent out their wombs on a short-term basis? This is an area of controversy. Most industrialized countries either ban commercial surrogacy or highly regulate it. The United States is an exception. Poor women, underemployed women or women who want to supplement their income may rent their wombs out for a fee. However, the state plays a crucial role in the way the gestational surrogates and the intended parents experience this process. . . .

There is a sparse but growing body of empirical literature on gestational surrogacy. Although vigorous debates have surrounded surrogacy, and the Baby M trial of the late 1980s generated media frenzy and resulted in a series of public debates that led to legislation restricting commercial surrogacy on the East coast, there are very few sociological studies of gestational surrogacy. The vast majority and most rigorous research has been done by anthropologists. There is a regional imbalance in that we have extensive participant observation and ethnographic research in the Middle East including Israel (Kahn 2000; Teman 2010) and Egypt (Inhorn 1995, 2003) and much less in the United States and Europe. A related body of literature has been focused upon the egg and sperm donation market, which is central to the assisted reproductive technology market (Ameling 2008). . . .

THE SHIFT FROM ADOPTION TO ASSISTED REPRODUCTION

The decriminalization of abortion at the federal level dramatically altered the adoption market in the United States. After the 1973 Supreme Court case *Roe v. Wade* which legalized abortion and redefined it as a constitutional right to "privacy," the number of unmarried White women who gave birth to children declined. Abortion became more accessible, safer, and less stigmatized. The demand for White babies increased while the supply decreased. In other words, the supply chain was affected not only by abortion but also by the increasing refusal of White women to relinquish their children for adoption. A decade later, innovations in biomedicine increased the chances that people with resources could use in vitro fertilization to reproduce a child that had a genetic link. This altered expectations because now infertile couples who could afford it could seek IVF rather than adoption.

FROM TEST-TUBE BABIES TO GESTATIONAL SURROGATES

Aldous Huxley introduced the term "test-tube" babies in his 1932 novel *Brave New World,* in which he described a world where children were fertilized and incubated in artificial wombs. The term "test-tube" baby refers to fertilization that takes place outside of the womb. In vitro which literally means "in glass" refers to a biological process that ordinarily takes place within the body but occurs in a Petri dish or a glass laboratory receptacle.

On July 25, 1978, Louise Brown, the first "test-tube" baby was born in Oldham, England. Her parents were from working class backgrounds and had struggled to form a family for years. Three decades have passed since the first "test-tube" baby was born. At that time, this was still the stuff of science fiction novels and only barely believable. Today, according to the Center for Disease Control (2006), 1 percent of U.S. live births involved some assisted reproductive technologies. Embryos can be produced by in vitro fertilization using sperm and/or eggs from third parties (sellers or donors) and then transferred to a woman who is the gestational surrogate but may not be the intended parent. IVF has made it possible for same sex lesbian and gay male couples to have children biologically related to them. An embryo contains the full and unique genome of a potential human being, with all of his or her traits. Embryos

are often frozen and stored for later use because the retrieval of eggs is an invasive and risky procedure. Consequently, doctors prefer to use hormones to overstimulate the ovaries to produce more eggs. Then multiple eggs (between 10 and 15 eggs) can be harvested in one procedure. Embryos withstand the **cryopreservation** process much better than eggs do.

THE LEGACY OF THE BABY M TRIAL

On March 27, 1986, Mary Beth Whitehead, a 28-year-old White mother of two children, gave birth to a daughter whom she and her husband named Sara Elizabeth Whitehead. The baby was the biological daughter of Mary Beth Whitehead, a surrogate, and the biological child of William Stern, a 38-year-old biochemist. Ms. Whitehead had signed the surrogacy contract prior to being impregnated with the sperm of Mr. Stern. She had agreed to relinquish the child for adoption and give up her rights as the mother so that Mrs. Elizabeth Stern could adopt the child. She changed her mind after the birth and fought for custody. Prior to this high-profile custody battle, few Americans were aware of this technology and it was relatively uncommon. Because Mary Beth Whitehead had a genetic tie to the child and was the mother as well as the surrogate, there was ambiguity surrounding the issue of whether she could be forced to give up her maternal status. She had not yet signed the adoption papers so she was technically still the legal guardian. Her name and that of her husband were listed on the birth certificate.

When Ms. Whitehead refused to sign the adoption papers and relinquish her rights as the legal mother, a custody dispute ensued that would mesmerize the nation. Whitehead had signed a surrogacy contract with William and Elizabeth Stern in February of 1985. According to this agreement, in exchange for $10,000 she would surrender the baby to Mr. Stern and relinquish all parental rights thus allowing him to be adopted by Elizabeth Stern who had no genetic tie to the child. After giving birth and seeing her daughter Mary Beth Whitehead changed her mind and decided to keep the baby whom she breastfed for 40 days. A custody battle ensued and they went to court to fight for Sara Elizabeth, who was named Melissa Elizabeth Stern by the Sterns and became known as "Baby M" by the press. This case raised a number of issues involving surrogacy, contract law, parental rights, and ultimately led to the State of New Jersey banning commercial surrogacy. An analysis of the media coverage provides insights into the ways that class and power played out in the treatment of Mary Beth Whitehead. The judge granted custody to Mr. Stern but also allowed Mary Beth Whitehead to retain her material rights and gave her limited visitation privileges.

In 1987 the New Jersey Court ruled that surrogacy contracts are unenforceable and then awarded custody of Baby M to Mr. William Stern, her biological father and his wife Elizabeth Stern while giving limited visitation rights to Mary Beth Whitehead, who remained the legal mother. Unlike today, this case occurred in a period when the gestational surrogate was also the genetic mother. Since William Stern's wife was unable to carry a pregnancy to term and would not be able to bear a child to whom she had a genetic tie, and Mary Beth Whitehead already had two children, the court compromised. They supported one portion of the contract, which gave Mr. Stern custody, but they refused to allow his wife to have her name put on the birth certificate thus upholding Mary Beth Whitehead's legal status as the mother. . . .

[. . .]

This case divided feminists into two camps. Feminists who supported a woman's right to rent out her womb or uterus as part of a contract supported the Sterns while those who argued that commercial surrogacy is a form of baby-selling that commodifies women and their bodies opposed this decision. Kelly Oliver criticizes the liberal framework used by the courts to conceal social inequalities. Oliver argues that, "Within a liberal framework all people are considered equal with equal rights. They all operate autonomously and have the freedom to exercise their

rights as long as they don't interfere with the rights of others. In this framework, the surrogacy contract is seen as an agreement between two or more equal partners" (Oliver 1989: 98–99).

In the decades since the Baby M case, gestational surrogacy has replaced what is called "traditional" surrogacy for most individuals contracting. Gestational surrogacy enables the intended mother or parent to sever the "genetic tie" between the birth mother and the infant. In other words it enables women and men who are the intended parents to retain their genetic tie to the child even though they do not gestate it. In the case of women whose eggs are too old or not viable for other reasons, they can purchase anonymous ova and still sever the tie between the gestational surrogate and the child so that the genetic tie occurs between a woman who does not carry the child and has merely sold her genetic material to the intended parents.

Innovations in biomedicine have dramatically increased the fertility treatments available and made it possible for women who have no genetic relations to the fetuses they carry to serve as surrogates, also referred to as "gestational carriers." The tie between genetics and gestation has been severed. This has radically transformed the experience of family formation for women and men with fertility problems, particularly the group between the ages of 35 and 45.

In *The Baby Business,* Deborah Spar, a former faculty member of the Harvard Business School, provides a comprehensive analysis of the economic, legal, and technological foundations of the commercial surrogacy market. In her summary of the debates in the 1980s Spar outlines the ideological divisions between opponents and supporters of commercial surrogacy:

[S]upporters of surrogacy framed their arguments in terms of either parental desperation (those who turned to surrogacy had no other means of producing a muchwanted child) or the freedom to contract (if individuals were allowed to procreate and to contract, then surely they should be able to procreate under contract). These arguments played out in both academic and public forums, pitting market advocates against the defenders of women's rights. Interestingly, most feminists aligned with traditional conservatives in this debate, arguing that women's rights did not include the right to sell procreative services. More libertarian feminists, by contrast, sided with the more radical free marketers, insisting that freedom for women included the freedom to contract for labor, be it working in a factory or bearing a child.

(Spar 2006: 77)

These arguments continue to be recycled and resurrected into today's media accounts and tabloid docudramas involving surrogacy. What is missing in most of these debates and media representations and what was disappointingly lacking in Spar's analysis is the role of race, racism, and class inequalities in structuring the market logics. Who can enter into these contracts as a commissioning parent? And why are Blacks, Hispanics, Latinos, and poor women overrepresented as gestational surrogates?

Control over one's reproductive labor remains a privilege rather than a right in the United States. Whether one is discussing access to abortion, contraception, or IVF fertility treatments, services related to the reproductive functions of women are highly stratified along racial, ethnic, class, and religious lines. In the United States assisted reproductive technologies are not accessible to the poor, working class, and many members of racial and ethnic minorities. Access to fertility treatments is available primarily to the wealthy, upper middle class, or those able and willing to borrow the money required. In other words, commercial surrogacy is limited to the economically privileged. (The price for the cost of hiring a gestational surrogate including the costs of IVF, legal, travel, gifts, and related expenses can range from $50,000–100,000 depending on the number of live births, experience of surrogate, and region.)

Spar's analysis, although an important intervention into this debate, is limited by its failure to consider carefully the ways that racial inequalities and class inequalities structure the surrogacy industry in the United States and abroad. Black feminists and critical race scholars have opposed commercial surrogacy and have expressed skepticism about the meaning of consumer "choice" and "free" markets in a nation whose early economy was built on enslaved labor and slave-produced crops (for example, cotton sugar, rice, indigo, tobacco).

For almost 300 years women of African ancestry worked as slave laborers and produced children who were commodities in a stratified system. As the mothers of children who constituted a form of wealth for their owners (and sometimes their biological fathers) they did not possess what Dorothy Roberts call reproductive liberty. They did not have control over their reproductive labor. They could not choose when to have children, or how many children to bear, and their children were commodities that did not belong to them. Critics might argue that non-slave women during this same period (i.e. White women) also possessed limited, if any, control over their reproductive lives as married women due to the lack of availability of contraception; however, there was one difference. Children born to non-slave mothers were not commodities that generated wealth or could be traded and sold like livestock. Moreover, their fathers, who were often Europeans or European-Americans, did not have to acknowledge any genetic ties they might have to these children who were born under slavery.

The significance of the legacies of racialized slavery, class inequalities, and the exploitation of the reproductive labor of Black women is not considered in Spar's analysis. This inattention to race (and racism) is characteristic of much of the academic and media accounts of surrogacy. In striking contrast, the Black feminist legal scholars see U.S. slavery and the lack of reproductive liberty as having structured and continuing to structure the experiences of large segments of the U.S. population including poor White women, immigrant women and women of obvious African ancestry.

In the United States there are no federal laws regulating surrogacy. Consequently, in contrast to Israel there have been a small number of controversial and high-profile court cases involving surrogacy contract disputes. The federal government's failure to regulate this industry has left it up to individual states to regulate. Consequently we have a patchwork of laws and competing and contradictory legislation in the United States. Some states, such as Arizona and the District of Columbia, ban all commercial surrogacy contracts, while others ban payments but allow for services (Florida, Nevada, New York, New Hampshire, Virginia, Washington), while others like California have become interstate and international destinations of choice for couples wishing to purchase reproductive services and hire surrogates.

Imagine that you can hire someone to carry a pregnancy to term for around the cost of a mid-sized car. And you can be insured that the woman's medical condition is monitored during the entire pregnancy. You are relieved because she is receiving adequate nutrition and under continual medical supervision. There are no opportunities for your gestational surrogate to consume alcohol, use recreational drugs, or smoke. If you have donated the eggs and the sperm, then the child also has a genetic tie to you. In other words, it belongs to you "genetically" because the genetic material (ovum, sperm) belongs to you or a sibling.

In the first of a three-part series of reports, after outlining the systematic corruption and economic coercion in the adoption or what some called the "baby trade" in Guatemala, one of the poorest countries in the Americas, Karen Smith Rotabi reveals that demand for babies is so great and the supply so low that surrogacy is now replacing adoption.

> Desperately poor Guatemalan women will inevitably find themselves offered an opportunity to earn a wage to birth a baby in this dollar-a-day-nation . . . The financial payment for surrogacy in Guatemala is unclear but inter-country adoption experts estimate that some women earned approximately $1,500 for child relinquishment signatures in the old adoption system which amounts to just over $5 a day for a normal 280 day gestational period. For a woman of privilege in the United States looking for fertility alternatives, this is a bargain basement price, but extreme poverty is the only reason why any Guatemalan women would agree to such an arrangement.
>
> (Rotabi 2010)

Today a growing number of children enter families via surrogates and surrogacy contracts. These contracts are essentially pre-conception legal agreements in which a woman agrees to rent her womb to another individual or couple for the purpose of gestating a fetus to which she may or may not have a genetic tie. The majority of women who provide gestational services are poor or members of racial or ethnic minority groups.

On November 30, 2008 *The New York Times Magazine* published "Her Body, My Baby," a cover story by Alex Kucyznski in which she reports on her own experiences of hiring a gestational surrogate. The magazine cover shows Alex Kucyysnki standing next to a pregnant White woman. Inside the magazine the article is accompanied by a photograph of Alex Kucyznski, a White upper middle class woman holding her baby while a Black baby nurse stands behind her at attention. She is poised in front of her home in South Hampton, an elite residential enclave on Long Island. As a White, married, upper middle class, economically secure woman with fertility problems Kucyznski symbolically represents women who have the financial resources to purchase the reproductive services of a surrogate. Supporters of commercial surrogacy would argue that Kucyznski had suffered enough, deserved to become a mother and had the right to "assistance." Opponents of commercial surrogacy would argue that this is a form of "baby brokering" and that a capitalist culture in the United States has generated a cult of genetic entitlement that has trained upper middle class women who near the end of their childbearing clock to feel that they must have (and deserve) a child with whom they have genetic tie. In the past these women would have adopted a child.

This issue has divided public policy makers and legislators in the United States. The result is a patchwork of divergent regulatory regimes in which some states completely ban commercial surrogacy, while others allow surrogacy but restrict payments to a third party and yet other states like California are surrogacy-friendly and allow all forms of commercial surrogacy without restrictions. Some feminists have argued in support of commercial surrogacy because they argue that women have the right or "freedom" to enter into surrogacy contracts, while others have compared surrogacy to "sex work"—a form of denigrated labor that exploits poor women. We must understand the economic, legal, global, and racial context of these decisions. Women do not make decisions in isolation from factors that structure their options. Their class position, race, nationality, maternal status, marital status, and legal condition shape their ability to exercise agency. These structures shape what constitutes a desirable option.

The 1990s marked a period of rapid innovations in assistive reproductive technologies. These medical technologies further severed the ties between the intended parents and the birth mother, or what is now typically referred to as the "gestational carrier" or "gestational surrogate." Commercial surrogacy splits the function of the mother into three components: 1) genetic, 2) gestational (biological), and 3) social. Gillian Goslinga-Roy argues that these distinctions are not

> "stable" and have to be constantly enacted. For example, she notes that "The professional language of assisted reproduction firmly upholds these divisions [between genetic, biological and social]: surrogates are referred to as "carriers" or "womb donors" pointing to their instrumentality in the arrangement while "intended" or "recipient" couples are referred to as the genetic (a.k.a. "real") parents.
>
> (Goslinga-Roy 2000: 113)

1. **Gestational surrogate:** This is the most common form of commercial surrogacy today. A woman who gestates a fetus (allows herself to be impregnated and carries the pregnancy to term) but has no genetic tie to the child she births. She is not the "intended" parent but is a paid laborer working on a nine-month commercial contract. There is an embryo transfer and she carries a child of which she is not the biological mother. Higher-income infertile couples who can afford the costs of paying someone to be a gestational carrier contract with a surrogate. This form of commercial surrogacy is illegal in Australia, Canada, Egypt, Mexico, and most of Europe.

2. **Traditional surrogate:** The birth mother is both the "gestational" surrogate and the biological mother (contributes the genetic material—the ovum). Like a gestational surrogate she is selling her reproductive labor, that is, renting her womb out for a fee. In contrast to "gestational" surrogates she has a genetic tie to the child she is carrying. In traditional case law she is the legally recognized mother until she relinquishes the child for adoption.

3. **Intended mother:** This is the woman who, either alone or with a male or female partner, commissions the pregnancy and enters into a commercial contract with another woman who agrees to be implanted with an embryo that consists of her ovum or donated ovum. The "intended" mother is understood to be the "commissioning mother" and typically custody of the baby is turned over to her upon the birth. Her name, not the gestational surrogate's, is listed on the birth certificate.

Since 1997 private clinics have been required to report their IVF statistics to the Center for Disease Control. However, accurate national data does not exist about the number of *private* arrangements because birth certificates are not required to list how a baby came to be fertilized. In 2005 the Center for Disease Control recorded 1,012 gestational surrogacy/ IVF surrogacy/IVF attempts using non-donor embryos (Center for Disease Control 2006: 3). In 2008 the Center for Disease Control published a national report on outcomes of their AVF cycles. According to the 2006 CDC National Report on Fertility 10 percent of the 62 million women of childbearing age in the United States have received some infertility services at some time in their lives (2006: 3-4).

BIBLIOGRAPHY

Ali, Lorraine, and Raina Kelley. 2008. "'The Curious Lives of Surrogates." Cover story for *Newsweek* (April 7): 45–51.

Almeling, Rene. 2008. Selling Genes, Selling Gender: Egg Donation, Sperm Donation, and the Medical Market in Genetic Material," unpublished Ph.D. dissertation, University of California at Los Angeles (UCLA).

American Heritage Dictionary of the English Language, 3rd edition. 1996 (1992). Boston/New York: Houghton Mifflin Company.

Center for Disease Control. 2006. *Assisted Reproductive Technology Success Rates.* Atlanta, GA: US Department of Health and Human Services, Center for Disease Control and Prevention. Available online (www.cdc.gov/art/ART2006/PDF/2006ART.pdf).

Colen, Shellee. 1995. "Like a Mother to Them: Stratified Reproduction and West Indian Childcare Workers and Employers in New York." Pp. 78–102 in *Conceiving the New World Order: The Global Politics of Reproduction,* eds. Faye D. Ginsburg and Rayna Rapp. Berkeley and Los Angeles: University of Chicago Press.

Ginsburg, Faye, and Rayna Rapp, eds. 1995. *Conceiving the New World Order: The Global Politics of Reproduction.* Berkeley/Los Angeles/London: University of California Press.

Goslinga-Roy, Gillian. 2000. "Body Boundaries, Fiction of the Female Self: An Ethnography of Power, Feminism and the Reproductive Technologies." *Feminist Studies* 26(1) (Spring): 113-40.

Inhorn, Marcia. 1995. *Infertility and Patriarchy: The Cultural Politics of Gender and Family Life in Egypt.* Philadelphia: University of Pennsylvania Press.

_____. 2003. *Local Babies, Global Science: Gender, Religion and In Vitro Fertilization.* New York: Routledge.

Krucoff, Carol. 1983. "The Surrogate Baby Boom." *Washington Post* (January 25): Section C: 5. Kuczynski, Alex. 2008. "Her Body, My Baby: My Adventures with a Surrogate Mom." *The New York Times Magazine* (November 20): 42.

Oliver, Kelly. 1989. "Marxism and Surrogacy." *Hypatia 4(3)* (Fall): 95–115.

Roberts, Dorothy. 1998. *Killing the Black Body: Race, Reproduction and the Meaning of Liberty.* New York: Vintage Books.

Rosenblatt, Roger. 1987. "Baby M—Emotions for Sale." *Time* magazine (Monday, April 6).

Rotabi, Karen Smith. 2010. "Human Rights and the Business of Reproduction: Surrogacy Replacing International Adoption from Guatemala." Retrieved May 20, 2010 (www.rhrealitycheck.org/blog/).

Spar, Deborah. 2006. *The Baby Business: How Money, Science and Politics Drive the Commerce of Conception.* Boston, MA: Harvard Business School Press.

Teman, Ely. 2010. *Birthing the Mother: The Surrogate Body and the Pregnant Self.* Berkeley: University of California Press.

Warner, Judith. 2008. "Outsourced Wombs." *The New York Times* (January 3).

45. • *Victoria Banyard, Mary M. Moynihan, Wendy A. Walsh, Ellen S. Cohn, and Sally Ward*

FRIENDS OF SURVIVORS:
The Community Impact of Unwanted Sexual Experiences (2010)

The following piece originally was published in the *Journal of Interpersonal Violence,* and the coauthors are either professors or fellows at the University of New Hampshire. Victoria Banyard is in psychology with an affiliation with justice studies and conducts research on mental health and resilience of survivors of interpersonal violence. Mary Moynihan is a professor of women's studies and justice studies and co-coordinator of Prevention Innovations, a research center dedicated to eliminating gender-based violence. Wendy Walsh is a sociologist in the Crimes Against Children Research Center, and her research focuses on community response systems. Ellen Cohn specializes in social psychology of law and researches rape and dating violence attitudes and behaviors. Sally Ward is a sociologist and codirector of the Masters in Public Policy Program at the Casey School of Public Policy; her research interests focus on the role of social policy in effecting social change.

Unwanted sexual experiences are an epidemic on college campuses leading to calls for increased prevention and intervention efforts (see Adams-Curtis & Forbes, 2004, for a review; Gross, Winslett, Roberts, & Gohm, 2006; Karjane, Fisher, & Cullen, 2005). Yet, support systems for survivors and criminal justice responses to deal with perpetrators are predicated on the initiative and courage of survivors who must first come forward and tell someone what has happened to them. Thus, a growing body of research examines issues of disclosure (e.g., Arata, 1998; Filipas & Ullman, 2001; Ullman & Filipas, 2001). To date, however, most of this work has centered on survivors—whether they tell, whom they tell, and what responses they receive. Less examined are the experiences of those to whom survivors disclose—most often their friends. How do they perceive being on the receiving end of this information? Do they know how to respond in a supportive way? Understanding the experiences of these informal helpers is an important next step in research on this issue. The current study aims to do this in an exploratory way.

DO SURVIVORS TELL AND WITH WHAT EFFECT?

In examining whether survivors disclose their unwanted sexual experiences, Fisher, Daigle, Cullen, and Turner's (2003) national study of college women found that only 2% of victims of sexual violence reported to police and only 4% disclosed to campus authorities. A majority of victims (70%) did tell someone else, usually a friend. Banyard et al. (2005) found that about 1 in 5 women who self-reported

an unwanted sexual experience during part of 1 academic year in college also reported that they told no one about it. The nearly 80% of women who did disclose were most likely to have told a friend or roommate. Feelings of shame, fear, and embarrassment, feeling that what happened is a private matter, or concern that what happened was not "really rape" are all reasons why survivors may choose not to come forward (Filipas & Ullman, 2001).

Several studies have gone further to examine the consequences for survivors of telling others. For example, Ahrens (2006) documented the silencing effect that negative reactions from others can have on survivors who disclose. Ahrens, Campbell, Ternier-Thames, Wasco, and Sefl (2007) documented the array of impacts that a first disclosure can have on survivors, ranging from healing responses (feeling comforted and supported) to hurtful responses (creating further distress and anger in survivors). Filipas and Ullman (2001) also discussed the range of reactions survivors receive when they do decide to disclose. They found that although women told on average 2.67 people about their assault, they found the average number of support sources who were helpful to be 1.86. Women also reported a variety of negative social reactions to telling others, including being stigmatized or hearing rape myths from others. Some were even revictimized by those they told. Ullman, Filipas, Townsend, and Starzynski (2007) and Ullman and Filipas (2001) examined models of post-traumatic stress symptoms (PTSD) among sexual assault survivors and found clear links between negative social reactions received to telling about the assault specifically and higher levels of PTSD. This finding is echoed in work by Campbell, Sefl, and Barnes (1999), who found significant effects on PTSD symptoms among adult sexual assault survivors who received negative reactions from community professionals (lawyers, medical professionals, police). They term these effects *secondary traumatization*.

Survivors have also been asked about responses that are helpful. Filipas and Ullman (2001) reported that survivors appreciated emotional support from others as well as instrumental help and hearing from other survivors about their own experiences. They noted,

> Most women wished they had received more emotional support, validation/belief, and tangible aid such as being taken to the police or the hospital or being allowed to stay at a friend's home. Another important response that survivors wished for was not being distracted or discouraged from talking about their experiences. (p. 682)

Mahlstedt and Keeny (1993) also found such responses in their sample of college women who reported dating violence.

THE VIEWPOINT OF INFORMAL HELPERS

To date, however, the majority of research on disclosure and unwanted sexual experiences focuses on the vantage point of survivors. Much less is known about the viewpoints of those to whom survivors disclose. This is a notable omission in the literature given the growing view of the important role of friends as potential helpful bystanders and allies for survivors found in the research. A recent innovation in sexual violence prevention highlights the role that all community members can play in ending sexual violence (e.g., Banyard, Plante, & Moynihan, 2004). Community members are taught skills for being prosocial and active bystanders before, during, or after an incident of sexual violence (e.g., Banyard, Moynihan, & Plante, 2007). Research in support of this prevention framework shows that individuals want to be helpful but often lack the confidence, knowledge, or skills to do so effectively (Opinion Research Corporation,

n.d.; Peter D. Hart Research Associates, 2007). Yet, to date, we know little about how individuals feel when they have received a disclosure from a friend.

A few studies to date have surveyed college students, with some suggesting that a third of samples have received disclosures (Dunn, Vail-Smith, & Knight, 1999). Qualitatively, these participants report feeling shock and surprise, not knowing what to do, giving advice, challenging the victim (why didn't she do anything to stop it?), or expressing disbelief in the victim in response. In relation to physical intimate partner violence, college students as informal helpers are more likely to have given helpful intervention responses if they were female and if they endorse lower levels of victim blaming attitudes toward domestic violence survivors assessed using hypothetical vignettes (West & Wandrei, 2002).

Ahrens and Campbell (2000) examined responses to survivors by friends in more detail using victimization perspective theory (e.g., Silver, Wortman, & Crofton, 1990, cited in Ahrens & Campbell, 2000), which posits that informal helpers deal with the stress of those who disclose to them with a conflict of wanting to help and yet feeling helpless and powerless when what they try to do does not seem to help. Ahrens and Campbell tested this theory by developing and researching a quantitative measure of friends' own reactions to receiving a disclosure about sexual assault from a friend. Their small sample of college students indicates that for the most part participants do not often feel distressed by the disclosure and most feel that they are able to be helpful to their friend. They also find interesting moderating variables, including gender, own sexual assault history, and length of friendship. In particular, men are less empathic, blamed survivors more, are more confused, and feel less effective in helping friends. Friends who have their own sexual assault history feel that the assault has more of an impact on their friend, engage in less victim blame, and see more positive changes and fewer negative changes on the relationship postdisclosure. Friendships with a longer history prior to disclosure are related to more positive changes in the friendship postdisclosure.

CURRENT STUDY

Given the increasing focus on informal helpers as targets of prevention efforts and as agents of intervention who can both prevent risky situations from escalating into sexual assaults and provide solid safety nets for survivors after an assault has happened, there is still much to be learned about friends' perceptions of the disclosure experience. Even though Ahrens and Campbell's (2000) study is instructive, their sample included only 60 participants. Although a variety of other studies have examined how informal helpers generally feel about disclosure, less is known about more specific aspects of how they react to the disclosure. Thus, the current study aimed to replicate and extend the findings of Ahrens and Campbell by gathering a larger and more representative sample of students on a campus. We hypothesized that overall friends would feel positively about the disclosure. We hypothesized that there would be gender differences—with men being less certain about their helpfulness to friends and women being more likely to have their friends' disclosure trigger their own safety concerns. We also examined whether victimization history was associated with how a student reacted to a friend's disclosure of an unwanted sexual experience.

METHOD

OVERVIEW

This study is the result of an ongoing research collaboration at the University of New Hampshire (UNH) funded by the UNH Office of the President. It presents findings from the most recent study conducted in 2006 on a range of unwanted sexual experiences among undergraduates on the UNH campus. The main aim of the study has been to examine the incidence and prevalence of unwanted sexual experiences among undergraduate students at UNH (Banyard, Cohn, et al., 2007; Banyard et al., 2005).

PARTICIPANTS

The current analyses are based on data from 1,241 students. The mean age was 19.95 (*SD* = 2.48). More than half (60.7%) were female. The sample was distributed among years in college (38.8% first-year students, 22.8% sophomores, 20.1% juniors, 17.3% seniors). Compared to university enrollments for that semester, the sample slightly overrepresents women (58% for the university) and first-year students (24% at the university) and underrepresents seniors (28% at the university). It should be noted that deliberate oversampling of courses with first-year students was done given that previous research has indicated that this may be a particularly at-risk group in college communities.

MEASURES

Participants were asked if a friend ever told them that she/he had been the victim of an unwanted sexual experience since they had been at college. They were then asked to list how many male friends and how many female friends had told them this. The survey provided definitions of unwanted sexual contact and sexual intercourse to insure overall consistency of answers.

Participants who indicated that a friend had disclosed to them were asked to complete a shortened version of Ahrens and Campbell (2000) Impact on Friends measure. We used 22 items from the scale across four of the subscales developed by Ahrens and Campbell. Factor analysis of current study data produced a solution similar to that reported by Ahrens and Campbell, thus we decided to use a number of their subscales. In particular, we used four items from the Confusion subscale (e.g., "I didn't know what to do to help"; Cronbach's alpha for the current sample was .76, *M* = 10.42, *SD* = 3.64) and seven items from the Validating subscale (indicating participants felt positive about their response to the disclosure: "I felt appreciated" or "I felt at ease dealing with her/his experience"; Cronbach's alpha = .66, *M* = 22.43, *SD* = 3.85). We also used four items from the Ineffectiveness subscale (with items such as "I felt that I wasn't supportive enough"; Cronbach's alpha = .76, *M* = 9.32, *SD* = 3.28) and seven items from the Emotional Distress subscale (e.g. "I became afraid to do things that never bothered me before") producing a Cronbach's alpha of .87, *M* = 16.98, *SD* = 3.85. Given the high intercorrelation between the Ineffectiveness and Confusion subscales ($r = .57$), a decision was made to combine these two into one subscale for further analyses.

Three questions from the Sexual Experiences Survey (Koss & Gidycz, 1985) were used to assess lifetime experience of sexual victimization ("How many times in your life have you ever had sexual intercourse against your wishes because someone used force?" "Because someone threatened to harm you?" "When you were so intoxicated that you were unable to consent?").

[. . .]

RESULTS

A total of 354 (28.9%) students said that a friend had disclosed to them while they were attending the university (more than half of those who had friends disclose to them, 206 students or 58%, revealed that more than one friend had disclosed to them). Of students who had a friend disclose to them, 96.5% were told by a female friend that this had happened and 19.7% were told by a male friend. Female students (33.7%) were much more likely to say that a friend had disclosed to them than were male students (21.4%), $x^2 = 21.58$, $p < .001$. Nonetheless, this suggests that 1 in 3 female undergraduates and 1 in 5 male students will be told by a friend that he or she was a victim.

Participants were then asked about their reaction to their friend's disclosure. Table 1 shows student responses based on the percentage that indicated "agree" or "strongly agree" to each item. Nearly two thirds of students felt that they were a good source of support for their friend. However, it is important to point out that about the same percentage of students felt upset as felt that they were doing a good job helping their friend.

Sex Comparisons

Analyses were performed based on data from the subsample of the 354 students who reported that a friend had disclosed to them about an unwanted sexual experience. A MANOVA was conducted using the 22 individual items from the Impact on Friends Scale as dependent measures and sex as the independent variable. We found a significant main effect of sex, $F(22, 254) = 5.38$, Wilks' Lambda = .68. Table 2 presents the mean differences by sex.

Across the 22 items on the Impact on Friends measure, there were sex differences in 12 items. Overall, men reported higher levels of discomfort talking to disclosing friends, greater concerns they were causing harm to their friend, greater worries they were not supportive enough, and greater sense that they felt burdened by their friend's disclosure. Women were more likely to report agreeing that they became more afraid for their own safety and afraid they would be assaulted, were angry at society for the problem of rape, being fearful of doing things they used to do, and feeling greater loss of a sense of security than did men. Women were also more likely to agree that as a result of the disclosure they felt they were a good source of support for their friend, felt more knowledgeable about the issue, and felt they did a good job helping. Two items approached significance ($p < .10$), with men more likely to agree that they felt their efforts were not helpful and women more likely to have felt upset dealing with their friend's experience.

In addition, a MANOVA was performed on the three composite indices of responses to friends (confusion/ineffectiveness, positive response, emotional distress). Again, there were significant sex differences with a main effect for sex, $F(3, 273) = 16.89$, $p < .001$, Wilks' Lambda = .84, partial $\eta^2 = .16$. Table 3 presents these findings. Women reported greater emotional distress in response to a friend's disclosure, greater positive responses, and lesser-perceived confusion/ineffectiveness about what to do when a friend disclosed that they had had an unwanted sexual experience. Effect sizes were small.

Victimization History Comparisons

An additional MANOVA was performed using victimization history as the independent variable and the three subscales indicating positive and negative reaction by friends as the dependent variables (see Table 4). There was a significant main effect for victimization history, $F(3, 258) = 4.28$, $p < .01$, Wilks' Lambda = .95, partial $\eta^2 = .05$. Interestingly, the one scale on which there was a significant difference was

Table 1 Descriptive Statistics of Responses to Disclosure for Full Sample Who Reported Disclosure *(N = 354)*

Response to Disclosure	Percentage of Students (Disclosed to) Who Agreed or Strongly Agreed
1. Didn't know what to do	20.0
2. Didn't know enough	20.0
3. Felt uncomfortable talking to him/her	16.1
4. Felt appreciated	44.8
5. Unsure what they needed	37.7
6. Felt efforts didn't help	21.5
7. Need to become involved in efforts to deal with broader problem	37.2
8. Felt afraid was causing more harm	14.3
9. Felt wasn't supportive enough	15.3
10. Felt burdened by friend's needs	9.2
11. Felt good about myself for helping	45.9
12. Became angry at society for rape	46.6
13. Became afraid for own safety	21.8
14. Felt I was good source of support for friend	64.5
15. Became afraid to do things I did before	11.7
16. Became afraid of being assaulted	18.0
17. Felt loss of sense of security	17.3
18. No longer felt world was safe place	17.3
19. Felt more knowledgeable about this problem	42.2
20. Felt upset dealing with friend's experience	43.1
21. Felt at ease dealing with friend's experience	16.0
22. Felt I was doing a good job helping friend	44.5

for emotional distress, with participants who had a history of their own victimization reporting higher levels of emotional distress in response to hearing a friend's disclosure of an unwanted sexual experience. The effect size was small.

DISCUSSION

The current study examines the prevalence of friends' disclosures of unwanted sexual experiences among college students and students' reactions to such disclosures, an understudied question in the growing literature on social support and unwanted sexual experiences. Although a significant minority of participants to whom a friend had disclosed reported being unsure about what to do, nearly half reported that they felt they were able to be supportive and helpful, and most found it a positive experience that they were able to help or to be supportive when a friend disclosed to them. These results are consistent with earlier work by Ahrens and Campbell (2000), who noted many positive reactions by friends who worked to support survivors who disclosed to them. It replicates these findings using a larger sample, a sample representative of students on the campus where the current study took place. Also significant are responses indicating that participants felt anger and distress related to the disclosure, reminding us that unwanted sexual experiences have consequences for people beyond individual survivors and that communities ought to provide education and support to recipients of disclosure about unwanted sexual experiences.

Table 2 Sex Differences in Perceived Responses to Friend's Disclosure

Item Description	Male (*n* = 77)	Female (*n* = 200)	F
Didn't know what to do	2.79 (1.07)	2.61 (1.14)	1.47
Didn't know enough to help	2.65 (1.10)	2.45 (1.25)	1.51
Felt uncomfortable	2.43 (1.24)	1.85 (1.03)	15.68***
Felt appreciated	3.27 (1.00)	3.43 (0.99)	1.31
Felt unsure what friend needed	3.05 (1.00)	3.02 (1.07)	0.05
Felt efforts didn't help	2.81 (0.93)	2.56 (1.05)	3.22
Felt need to get involved in efforts to solve this problem	2.99 (1.04)	3.23 (1.10)	2.69
Felt afraid was causing more harm	2.52 (1.05)	2.15 (1.05)	7.10**
Felt not supportive enough	2.57 (1.06)	2.20 (1.05)	7.07**
Felt burdened by friend's needs	2.22 (1.11)	1.78 (0.99)	10.33***
Felt good about self for helping	3.38 (0.84)	3.46 (0.99)	0.43
Angry at society for rape	3.05 (1.39)	3.41 (1.22)	4.31*
Afraid for own safety	1.73 (0.90)	2.78 (1.25)	45.10***
Felt I was good source of support	3.26 (0.92)	3.87 (0.80)	29.44***
Afraid to do things that didn't bother in past	1.94 (0.94)	2.31 (1.12)	6.60**
Afraid might also be assaulted	1.56 (0.85)	2.51 (1.25)	37.72***
Felt lost sense of security	1.77 (0.94)	2.51 (1.17)	24.75***
No longer felt world was fair or safe	2.18 (1.10)	2.40 (1.12)	2.02
Felt more knowledgeable about this problem	2.95 (0.97)	3.28 (1.03)	5.97*
Felt upset dealing with friend's experience	2.92 (1.21)	3.20 (1.08)	3.42
Felt at ease dealing with friend	2.42 (0.91)	2.60 (1.05)	1.84
Felt did good job helping	3.04 (0.82)	3.47 (0.90)	13.05***

*$p < .05$. **$p < .01$. ***$p < .001$.

Table 3 MANOVA of Sex Differences in Subscale Scores of Reactions to Disclosure

Scale	Male (n = 77)	Female (n = 200)	F	Partial η^2
Emotional distress	15.14 (5.02)	19.10 (6.35)	$(1, 277) = 24.08***$	.08
Positive reaction	21.30 (3.59)	23.33 (3.89)	$(1, 277) = 15.75***$	.05
Confusion/Ineffectiveness	21.04 (5.62)	18.61 (5.72)	$(1, 277) = 10.13**$	.04

**$p < .01$. ***$p < .001$.

Table 4 MANOVA of Differences in Reactions to Friend's Disclosure by Victim Status

	Victim (*n* = 87)	Nonvictim (*n* = 175)	F	Partial η^2
Emotional distress	19.57 (6.18)	17.01 (6.05)	$(1, 262) = 10.34***$	.04
Positive reaction	23.07 (4.22)	22.49 (3.88)	$(1, 262) = 1.24$	.01
Confusion/Ineffectiveness	18.79 (5.61)	19.41 (5.94)	$(1, 262) = .65$	.00

***$p < .001$.

These findings alert us to the need for programming as well as widespread education on campuses. One promising form of programming that has become more widespread on college campuses is the focus on bystanders and allies. For example, a number of programs focus particularly on men's roles as allies in preventing sexual violence or in supporting survivors after an unwanted sexual experience has occurred (Berkowitz, 2002; Fabiano, Perkins, Berkowitz, Linkebach, & Stark, 2003; Foubert, 2000; Foubert & Cowell, 2004; Foubert & Newberry, 2006; Katz, 1995; Kilmartin & Berkowitz, 2005). Increasingly such programs are also being tailored for women and all community members (e.g. Ahrens, 2006; Banyard, Moynihan, et al., 2007; Edwards & Sexton, 2006). Social marketing strategies with these messages also appear (Potter et al., 2008; Virginia Sexual Assault and Domestic Violence Action Alliance, 2007). The results of the current study are important for this new line of prevention programming and research. Effective prevention efforts that specifically target bystanders need to be built on a more thorough understanding of bystanders' experiences. To date research has focused importantly on survivors' perceptions of social supports and disclosure reactions. We still know little about how friends feel about receiving disclosures. Furthermore, while bystander-focused prevention programs have been created for both men and women, to date nearly all of them are conducted using single sex groups. The current research provides support for such a model, suggesting that male and female friends of survivors may need to focus on different issues related to being a bystander and ally. Male bystanders may need to build confidence in their abilities to be supportive to friends, whereas female bystanders may need assistance with their own feelings of vulnerability and anxiety that may arise from the bystander role.

The current study has a number of limitations including its cross-sectional design, the sample's limited ethnic and racial diversity, and its focus on a college sample. Future research is needed to examine the process of disclosure in more detail. For example, how do friends' reactions to a disclosure match survivors' perceptions of their friends' reactions? Friends may indicate that they felt they were supportive, but do survivors' perceptions mirror this? Do survivors actually find these friends helpful? How does the disclosure process unfold? How do the reactions of friends unfold over time? Do friends help survivors connect with more formal support systems, such as crisis centers or the criminal justice system?

[. . .]

Our findings along with those of others (e.g., Ahrens et al., 2007; Ahrens & Campbell, 2000; Filipas & Ullman, 2001) indicate the need to develop and implement educational materials and programming that give friends and other informal helpers greater knowledge, specific information, and concrete suggestions about appropriate or helpful language to use or things to do when a friend discloses to them. Equally important, friends need to learn about ways of taking care of themselves and their feelings in the aftermath of a disclosure. In particular, they need information about where to go or whom they can talk to in confidence about their feelings. Dunn et al.'s (1999) "Guidelines" for helping when a friend discloses date/acquaintance rape adapted from Hall (1995) is a practical list of suggestions for helping friends who disclose as well as for ways of seeking self-care for the recipient of disclosure. Campus administrators could easily and economically broadcast these throughout their university communities.

REFERENCES

Adams-Curtis, L. E., & Forbes, G. B. (2004). College women's experiences of sexual coercion: A review of cultural, perpetrator, victim, and situational variables. *Trauma, Violence, & Abuse, 5,* 91-122.

Ahrens, C. (2006). Being silenced: The impact of negative social reactions on the disclosure of rape. *American Journal of Community Psychology, 38,* 263-274.

Ahrens, C. E., & Campbell, R. (2000). Assisting rape victims as they recover from rape: The impact on friends. *Journal of Interpersonal Violence, 15,* 959-986.

Ahrens, C. E., Campbell, R., Ternier-Thames, N. K., Wasco, S. M., & Sefl, T. (2007). Deciding whom to tell: Expectations and outcomes of rape survivors' first disclosures. *Psychology of Women Quarterly 31,* 38-49.

Arata, C. M. (1998). To tell or not to tell: Current functioning of child sexual abuse survivors who disclose their victimization. *Child Maltreatment, 3,* 63-71.

Banyard, V. L., Cohn, E. S., Moynihan, M. M., Walsh, W., & Ward, S. (2007). *Unwanted sexual experiences at UNH: Incidences and prevalence 2006.* Durham: University of New Hampshire.

Banyard, V. L., Moynihan, M. M., & Plante, E. G. (2007). Sexual violence prevention through bystander education: An experimental evaluation. *Journal of Community Psychology, 35,* 463-481.

Banyard, V. L., Plante, E., & Moynihan, M. M. (2004). Bystander education: Bringing a broader community perspective to sexual violence prevention. *Journal of Community Psychology, 32,* 61-79.

Banyard, V. L., Plante, E., Ward, S., Cohn, E., Moorehead, C., & Walsh, W. (2005). Revisiting unwanted sexual experiences on campus: A twelve-year follow-up. *Violence Against Women, 11,* 426-446.

Banyard, V. L., Ward, S., Cohn, E. S., Moorhead, C., & Walsh, W. (2007). Unwanted sexual contact on campus: A comparison of women's and men's experiences. *Violence and Victims, 22,* 52-70.

Berkowitz, A. D. (2002). Fostering men's responsibility for preventing sexual assault. In P. A. Schewe (Ed.), *Preventing violence in relationships: Interventions across the lifespan* (pp. 163-196). Washington, D.C.: American Psychological Association.

Campbell, R., Sefl, T., & Barnes, H. E. (1999). Community services for rape survivors: Enhancing psychological well-being or increasing trauma? *Journal of Consulting and Clinical Psychology, 67,* 847-858.

Dunn, P. C., Vail-Smith, K., & Knight, S. M. (1999). What date/acquaintance rape victims tell others: A study of college student recipients of disclosure. *Journal of American College Health, 47,* 213-218.

Edwards, D., & Sexton, M. (2006). *SEEDS: Students educating and empowering to develop safety* (University of Kentucky Violence Intervention and Prevention Center). Retrieved April 24, 2009, from http://www.uky.edu/StudentAffairs/VIPCenter/

Fabiano, P. M., Perkins, H. W., Berkowitz, A., Linkenbach, J., & Stark, C. (2003). Engaging men as social justice allies in ending violence against women: Evidence for a social norms approach. *Journal of American College Health, 52,* 105-112.

Filipas, H. H., & Ullman, S. E. (2001). Social reactions to sexual assault victims from various support sources. *Violence and Victims, 16,* 673-692.

Fisher, B., Daigle, L., Cullen, F., & Turner, M. (2003). Reporting sexual victimization to the police and others: Results from a national-level study of college women. *Criminal Justice and Behavior, 30,* 6-38.

Foubert, J. D. (2000). The longitudinal effects of a rape-prevention program on fraternity men's attitudes, behavioral intent, and behavior. *Journal of American College Health, 48,* 158-163.

Foubert, J. D., & Cowell, E. A. (2004). Perceptions of a rape prevention program by fraternity men and male student athletes. *NAPSA Journal, 42,* 1-20.

Foubert, J. D., & Newberry, J. T. (2006). Effects of two versions of an empathy-based rape prevention program on fraternity men's survivor empathy, attitudes, and behavioral intent to commit rape or sexual assault. *Journal of College Student Development, 47,* 133-148.

Gross, A. M., Winslett, A., Roberts, M., & Gohm, C. L. (2006). An examination of sexual violence against college women. *Violence Against Women, 12,* 288-300.

Karjane, H. M., Fisher, B. S., & Cullen, F. T. (2005). *Sexual assault on campus: What colleges and universities are doing about it* (NIJ Research for Practice Report; NCJ 205521). Washington, DC: U.S. Department of Justice.

Katz, J. (1995). Reconstructing masculinity in the locker room: The Mentors in Violence Prevention Project. *Harvard Educational Review, 65,* 163-174.

Kilmartin, C. & Berkowitz, A. D. (2005). *Sexual assault in context: Teaching college men about gender.* Mahwah, NJ: Lawrence Erlbaum Associates.

Koss, M. P., & Gidycz, C. A. (1985). Sexual experiences survey: Reliability and validity. *Journal of Consulting and Clinical Psychology, 53,* 422-423.

Mahlstedt, D., & Kenny, L. (1993). Female survivors of dating violence and their social networks. *Feminism & Psychology, 3,* 319-333.

Opinion Research Corporation. (n.d.). *It's time to talk.* Retrieved April 24, 2009, from www.loveisnotabuse.com/itstimetotalk

Peter D. Hart Research Associates. (2007). *Fathers' day poll 2007: A survey among men* (Family Violence Prevention Fund and Verizon Wireless). Retrieved April 24, 2009, from www.endabuse.org/07menspoll/files/Hart_Research_Poll_Report-6.5.07.pdf

Potter, S. J., Moynihan, M. M., Stapleton, J. G., & Banyard, V. L. (2008). Empowering bystanders to prevent campus violence against women: A preliminary evaluation of a poster campaign. *Violence Against Women, 15,* 106-212.

Stefanski, S. (2005). *The effect of No Zebras bystander education on attitudes and awareness.* Retrieved March 6, 2007, from http://www.sapa.cmich.edu/Page/P_NZ.htm

Ullman, S. E., & Filipas, H. H. (2001). Gender differences in social reaction to abuse disclosures, post-abuse coping and PTSD of child sexual abuse survivors. *Child Abuse & Neglect, 29,* 767-782.

Ullman, S. E., Filipas, H. H., Townsend, S. M., & Starzynski, L. L. (2007). Psychosocial correlates of PTSD symptom severity in sexual assault survivors. *Journal of Traumatic Stress, 20,* 821-831.

Virginia Sexual and Domestic Violence Action Alliance. (2007). *The Red Flag campaign.* Retrieved on May 15, 2007, from http://www.theredflagcampaign.org

West, A., & Wandrei, M. L. (2002). Intimate partner violence: A model for predicting interventions by informal helpers. *Journal of Interpersonal Violence, 17,* 972-986. Available from www.theredflagcampaign.org

46. · *Brad Perry*

HOOKING UP WITH HEALTHY SEXUALITY:
The Lessons Boys Learn (and Don't Learn) about Sexuality and Why a Sex Positive Rape Prevention Paradigm Can Benefit Everyone Involved (2008)

Brad Perry served as the statewide Prevention Coordinator for Virginia Sexual & Domestic Violence Action Alliance from 2000 to 2011. His work in the community focused on the promotion of healthy sexuality and healthy sexual behaviors across the gender spectrum. In his written publications and recorded podcasts, he defines healthy sexuality as the capacity to understand, enjoy, and control one's own sexual and reproductive decisions and discusses why education is the key to ending violence and living enriched social lives that respect and value men, women, gender non-conforming people, and trans* individuals. This work was originally published in Jaclyn Friedman and Jessica Valenti's edited collection *Yes Means Yes: Visions of Female Sexual Power and a World Without Rape* (2008).

Steal the beer, meet the girls, get them drunk, and try to get some—that was the plan. I was thirteen years old, and my friend Jon and I were sleeping over at our buddy Zach's house. What we heard that night made every cell of our newly pubescent bodies crackle with electricity. Zach's older brother informed us that he had recently experienced the most mysterious and most desired pinnacle of male teen-age existence—ejaculation caused not by his own hands, but by a real live girl. He "got some."

Tellingly, the specifics of exactly how Zach's brother was able to achieve this milestone were far more interesting to us than hearing what "getting some" was actually like. We'd all learned about the wonders of masturbation by this time, so we thought we had a decent reference point for the physical rewards. The fact that girls could like sex hadn't even crossed our minds. We knew sex was supposed to involve some type of mutual appreciation for each other's genitals, but we didn't understand why—after all, it was us boys who were doing the "getting" of the "some" right? And growing up in white-bread, middle-class, suburban Virginia, we no doubt received plenty of messages in our social environment casting sex with girls (and *only* with girls) as a one-sided affair where the boy makes the moves and calls the shots. We were intent on learning these moves. So most of what Zach's brother told us about his encounter—and all we really wanted to know—revolved around *how* the pre-ejaculatory events unfolded.

Zach's brother was a fifteen-year-old punk-rock skateboarder, and was totally badass as far as I was concerned, since I aspired to be a similar brand of aloof cool guy. Through this lens of awe, I listened to him recount key events over the previous few months. It seems that one afternoon Zach's brother stole a twelve-pack of beer from a neighbor's garage and invited his neighbor Cheryl over to drink it while his parents were out of town. At some point they started making out. Zach's brother told us he thought the beer had made her really "into it," so he started taking off her clothes. He then recounted a litany of sexual acts in which they engaged, culminating in that most cherished of naked heterosexual activities: actual penile/vaginal intercourse. This same scenario played itself out several more times over the weeks following the first encounter, usually with the aid of beer or pot.

We listened to Zach's brother with rapt stares and took copious mental notes. All three of us came to basically the same set of conclusions: 1) It is possible for girls to actually want to do "sexual stuff" with you; 2) Getting a girl to do sexual stuff with you usually requires some "loosening agents," such as

alcohol or pot; 3) The guy usually has to make the first move.

I wanted so badly to be convinced that Zach's brother—along with innumerable commercials, TV shows, movies, pop songs, church sermons, and strong opinions from adults and peers—had given me the final clue I would need to reveal the secret of how to get some. I wanted to be comforted that this whole romance-with-girls thing wasn't as staggeringly mysterious as I had initially feared. A host of anxieties were stirring in my hormonal tween psyche around this time. Adolescence was upon me, and with it a host of powerful new pressures and rules that made no sense—especially the stuff about gender and sexuality. My parents at least had the insight to have several "talks" with me, and they even sent me to "sex-ed camp" for a weekend, so I was certainly more knowledgeable about the basics than many of my peers. But none of that information could help me negotiate the demands of manhood and emerge as a well-adjusted man with a positive and organically formed view of sexuality. Back in 1988, like now, there were very few places in America where young people could receive the knowledge, skills, and opportunities to gradually develop their own unique feelings about gender, sexuality, and intimate relationships. Thus, we all looked—and continue to look—for oversimplified answers like those provided by men's magazines, church-based abstinence-only programs, and Zach's brother.

As it turned out, Zach's brother's "insights" were timely, because we had already planned to meet up with three girls from our class later that very night. We couldn't get any pot, so we'd have to use beer. Zach assured us he knew how to break into the neighbor's garage (a.k.a. beer lending library), and since it was on the way to the construction site where we were meeting the girls, everything seemed to be coming together. The only thing left to do was figure out which girl each of us was going to attempt to "seduce." I don't remember how, but I actually got my first pick: Janice. Once we were sure Zach's parents were asleep, we snuck out into the night. We stopped at the neighbor's house, and I kept lookout while Jon and Zach broke into the garage. A few minutes later they returned with beaming smiles and a cold case of Nasty-Brau.

We arrived at the construction site, and after sitting there for about fifteen minutes, we cracked open some beers. We started to think we might just be getting drunk by ourselves—though I didn't even know what getting drunk felt like, as this was the first time I'd ever attempted to drink alcohol. Nevertheless, I resolved to act natural so no one would sense my rampant inexperience. When the girls finally showed, Jon, Zach, and I enacted the pièce de résistance of our plan. We'd each stowed unopened beers next to us, and when the girls walked up, we each nonchalantly (at least, *we thought* we were being nonchalant) called "our" girl's name and offered her a beer in order to get her next to us. When I said, "Hey, Janice, you want a beer?" she at least humored me and replied, "Sure," sitting down next to me, just as I had hoped.

After my first beer, I decided I really didn't want to drink much more because, like most cheap beer, it tasted like cat piss smells. Janice, however, seemed to not have this aversion to cat piss, and put away three beers in the time it took me to force down half of my second can. I think I might have been aware that I was supposed to feel like less of a man for being outchugged by a girl, but before I could castigate myself, a new masculine archetype popped into my head. He looked a lot like Zach's older brother—complete with a detached confidence and a vibe of unfathomable sexual prowess. Without even removing the cigarette from his imaginary lips, he breezed, *Hey, man, it's cool if she gets drunk quicker than you. After all, you already know you want to get some, but she needs the alcohol to realize that she wants to help you out with that.* It seemed like good advice at the time, so I put my arm around her waist to see what would happen. Amazingly, she didn't recoil. In fact, she actually seemed to relax and lean into me a bit. At this point, all of the three couples had started talking between themselves more than with the entire group. It was really dark, so I couldn't see what was going on with everyone else, but I naturally assumed that, given my inexperience, I was probably not as "far along."

In my anxious, overly literal, and self-centered thirteen-year-old mind, all I had to do was give the beer a few more minutes to work and then bust my move. In no time Janice would happily come with me behind one of the parked bulldozers to engage in all sorts of naked pawing. I don't think I even wanted to have sexual intercourse. I just wanted to see and touch a naked girl, and experience a naked girl touching me (and my penis). When she opened her fourth beer, I busted said move, which first consisted of trying to stroke one of her breasts. She sat up straight as soon as I did it, but she kept talking with me as if everything was okay, and so I, in all of my single-minded self-absorption, interpreted that to mean, *Go for it!* I began to slip my hand under the waistband of her pants and underwear.

Fortunately for all involved, Janice knew what she was and was not comfortable with, despite having pounded four beers. She promptly removed my hand from under the waistband of her underwear. Confused, but still foolishly hoping that Zach's brother's advice was *the key,* I tried once more. Again, Janice removed my hand, stopped midsentence, and quietly but assertively said, "Stop it." I mumbled, "Sorry . . . I . . . I don't know why I . . ." but no words would come. Then I realized: I had been acting like a dick. I set down my unfinished beer, put my hands in my lap, and tried not to make Janice more ill at ease than she already was. Janice didn't move away from me, probably because she didn't want to make a scene, or maybe because she realized I meant her no harm and was just deluded and clueless. Maybe both. In any case, I was responsible for the awkward silence between us. We sat there a while longer and listened to the others whisper to each other several yards away. Eventually it got late, and everyone just kind of went home.

I, like most people in our sexually myopic culture, wanted one quick and easy answer to a host of profound questions that are best considered over the course of many years. It is this drive to oversimplify and distort the intricacies of gender and sexuality that enables us to minimize the existence of sexual violence, while simultaneously blocking healthy affirmations of human sexuality and oppressing people with nontraditional sexual and gender identities. It is crucial that young people be empowered to explore their own experiences of gender and sexuality with the help of their schools and families, yet such developmental opportunities are rarely present in the form or amount needed. For example, in our educational systems, language and math skills are taught at every achievement level, every school day. But navigating the gender/sexuality pressures of adolescence is equally complex as, if not more complex than, understanding transitive property or the use of animal imagery in *Madame Bovary.* Most educational systems in the United States devote a minimal amount of hours per year (and for only a few years) to gender and sexuality. Likewise, the relatively small amount of quality education that does exist has been artificially divided into two camps: sexual violence prevention and sexual health promotion. If we can bridge these disciplines and saturate our culture with their messages and methods, then we might have a shot at realizing a grand vision: a culture where people experience sexuality in a state of well-being—a culture incompatible with sexual violence because of a deeply shared belief that sexuality is a precious part of everyone's humanity.

If there's one conclusion I've drawn in more than twelve years of doing sexual violence–prevention work, it is this: Rapists are created, not born. While female sexual empowerment is an important factor in the struggle to end rape, it will not succeed without corresponding shifts in how boys are taught to experience sexuality and gender. My insights are, admittedly, limited by my relatively narrow experience of the world as a straight, white, middle-class, male U.S. citizen, though I strive to offer ideas that are as generally applicable as I can muster. . . .

[. . .]

BOY MEETS RAPE CULTURE

[. . .]

Thankfully, I learned my lesson from Janice and abandoned the notion that sexuality should be reduced to a boys-versus-girls, winner-takes-all game,

but I still struggled with the day-to-day boys-will-be-boys stuff. While I like to think I avoided the overtly harmful extremes of that mindset, I was also a chronically horny young man, . . . and other dudes were playing the get-some game as intensely as they knew how. It wouldn't have been a big deal, except that most of the girls I knew were hot for the guys rocking some type of badboy/meathead/dickbag persona. I'll never forget hearing this from a girl I really liked: "You're sweet . . . you're like the kind of guy I might marry, but you're not the kind of guy I want to have sex with." I suppose I just wanted an "I can be respectful *and* make you come" option that simply didn't exist in this stud/husband dichotomy. Of course, had my senses been less clogged with an omnipresent cloud of teenage angst, I might have realized that girls are pressured to play their side of this craptastic get-some game, too. It was in trying to make sense of these frustrations that I started seeing the bigger picture of what drives this madness. Understanding how boys are socialized to view sexuality can show us where to blend the approaches of sexual violence prevention and sexual health promotion, and how to enhance the effectiveness of programs rooted in these fields. But first we have to pull back the curtain on our unhealthy sexual status quo.

At the heart of countless American neuroses is the nonsensical, pervasive belief that sexuality is derived from a weakness in humanity. . . . In other words, we've been taught to objectify sexuality itself, and see it only as a "thing" to act upon, or that acts upon us. We don't recognize it as integral to our own humanity, nor as a beautiful and important link among all humanity. This detachment shames us out of embracing our sexuality as a positive part of ourselves, and constrains sexual expression to certain "permissible" *physical* acts.

Consider how this objectification of sexuality plays out with the socialization of boys in the United States. My friends and I learned quickly that our sexuality was to be characterized by action, control, and achievement—certainly, familiar themes to us by the time we hit puberty. We ascertained that sexuality is tied to a boy's ability to play and win the get-some game. Sexual violence is one of many inevitable negative outcomes in this adversarial climate, which also gives rise to unwanted pregnancies, STIs, and an abundance of shitty sexual encounters that can unfavorably impact the way any of us experience sexuality in general.

This game places special emphasis on boys' learning to control every possible variable surrounding sexual interactions, and thereby sends the clear message that sexuality should be expressed and enjoyed only in the context of a power dynamic. (Note: This is not a new idea, and has been the topic of numerous feminist-authored books and articles over the past forty years.[1, 2]). My account of the night with Janice is replete with examples of this push to control. We had a plan accounting for every detail our thirteen-year-old brains could conjure. Our attention to detail in trying to dictate the progression of the sexual interaction—and our assumption that there was going to be sexual interaction in the first place—was not uncommon. During adolescence it became as clear as a bottle of cheap vodka that a lot of guys seemed to have an angle on how they could control the situation and get some.

Boys' control strategies seem to become only more elaborate as we pass through adolescence and into our twenties. Domination over the sexual autonomy of others can almost become fetishized, and operates from a societal level (e.g., restrictions on reproductive freedoms, forced sterilization policies, inadequate laws against rape, etc.) down through the interpersonal (e.g., a greater concern for the number of bedpost notches than for the people involved in the experiences, or the experiences themselves). Feminist activists realized this a long time ago, which is why they created the concept of rape culture(s), and pointed out that rape is as much about power as it is about sex. Some fascinating research by Dr. David Lisak[3] supports this observation.

Lisak found that acquaintance rapists tend to be men who buy strongly into "the game," usually targeting women they perceive to be younger, more naive, and easier to manipulate. Dr. Lisak's subjects also demonstrate an utter lack of awareness that this entitled, self-centered system and its potential results are problematic, or are anything other than "the usual" manner in which men seduce. These men firmly believe "no" means "try harder," and never think of themselves as rapists, despite a self-admitted pattern of ignoring and suppressing verbal/physical resistance, and forcing intercourse on semiconscious women. Of course, not all men buy into "the game" to such an extent that they commit rape. But follow public reaction to rape cases for a few years—especially acquaintance-rape cases—and you'll quickly realize that Lisak's subjects have a lot of support for their shared belief that women shouldn't be allowed any sexual autonomy. Most of us have inherited enough shares in the rape culture(s) to perpetuate the disastrous results from previous generations.

The good news is that there are some promising strategies that can impact the whole of our rape-supportive, sexually unhealthy landscape. As previously mentioned, I propose playing matchmaker with two disciplines that have always seemed to be like ships passing in the night: sexual health promotion and sexual violence prevention. They're the perfect couple—philosophically complementary, yet with their own things going. Whether they're engaged in stimulating research comparisons over dinner, flirting about the REAL Act[4] on a walk through the park, or making sweet, back-arching, toe-curling collaboration at home with the lights on, our society can only benefit.

CHEMISTRY BETWEEN TWO GREAT BODIES (OF WORK)

Sexual health promotion is usually known by its most visible component here in the United States: sex education. And *effective* sexual health promotion—that is, the kind that actually leads to low rates of STIs, abortions, accidental pregnancies, and so on—is medically accurate and based on science, rather than on one group's version of morality. Unfortunately for U.S. citizens, former senator John Ashcroft (yes, *that* John Ashcroft) smuggled a sneaky little amendment into some mid-1990s welfare "reform" legislation, ensuring precisely the opposite of effective sexual health promotion. Some call it abstinence-only-until-marriage (AOUM) education, but I prefer to call it a goddamned travesty.

AOUM programs reinforce many of the harmful norms about gender and sexuality that perpetuate "the game." They shame girls who choose to engage in premarital sex, and blame survivors of sexual violence through an obsessive contention that just saying no is the solution for everything—there is no consideration of what happens when no is ignored. Meanwhile, male volition is left largely unexamined. Fanning this growing inferno of outrage are findings released in April 2007 by a nonpartisan policy-evaluation firm.[5] This congressionally commissioned, decade-spanning report concluded that kids who received AOUM education were just as likely to have sex as kids who didn't.

[. . .]

The Netherlands, France, and Germany all use a similar model of sexual health promotion, and Advocates for Youth, a Washington, D.C., based non-profit, compiled the elements that have allowed these countries to be so effective. Among these keys to success are:

- Governments support massive, consistent, long-term public education campaigns [that are] far more direct and humorous than in the U.S, and focus on safety and pleasure.
- Sexuality education is not necessarily a separate curriculum and may be integrated across school subjects and at all grade levels. Educators provide accurate and complete information in response to students' questions.
- Families have open, honest, consistent discussions with teens about sexuality and support the role of educators and health care providers in making sexual health information and services available for teens.
- The morality of sexual behavior is weighed through an individual ethic that includes the values of responsibility, respect, tolerance, and equity.
- [All programs] work to address issues around cultural diversity in regard to immigrant populations and their values that differ from those of the majority culture.

- Research is the basis for public policies . . . political and religious interest groups have little influence on public health policy.[6]

[. . .]

The fields of sexual health promotion and primary sexual violence prevention are clearly complementary, which is why we should root for these two to fall in love and get married in Massachusetts or California—or at least become BFFs. Happily, both fields do seem to be borrowing from a similar set of methods and incorporating parallel program content. Consistent with the elements of the effective European sexual health promotion model, primary sexual violence-prevention strategies have become savvier by learning to engage multiple levels of our social environment (e.g., policies, community institutions, and parents). Both fields in the United States are also gradually recognizing the importance of avoiding one-size-fits-all models, opting instead for the more flexible and pluralistic "community mobilization" approach. And as for content, proponents of sexual health promotion have integrated issues of respect, coercion, gender roles, and healthy relationships into their work (e.g., the International Planned Parenthood Federation's "Framework for Comprehensive Sexuality Education"[7]), while sexual violence-prevention specialists (e.g., Care For Kids[8], and statewide anti-rape coalitions in Virginia[9] and Vermont[10]) have started tinkering with the idea that promoting "healthy sexuality" can foster—among numerous other positive outcomes—safe, respectful sexual relationships.

Such a "healthy sexuality" program would counter our society's superficial, achievement-obsessed framing of sexuality by helping people to make a deeper connection with all of our sexual domains: emotional, intellectual, spiritual, social, and physical. These five areas of sexuality correspond to the ways in which we exist as human beings in this world. Experiencing sexuality across these various domains helps us form our sense of who we are and who we want to be. Segmenting our experiences of sexuality to only the physical realm constrains us to an artificially rote understanding of humanity in ourselves and others. It's like trying to connect with music by listening only to top 40 songs. Sure, there can be a pleasurable aspect to it, but you're missing out on other worlds of sonic delight, and you're sure as shit not gaining any deeper insights into your own musical proclivities.

Connecting more deeply with these various aspects of our individual sexualities also benefits anyone with whom we might be sharing a sexual experience. Thus, healthy sexuality programs would facilitate the viewing of sexual interactions as things adults share with one another, instead of do to one another. This means teaching people the value of—and how to practice—honest, proactive communication about one another's likes, dislikes, and expectations, and respect for sexual expression in any consensual, subjectively affirming form it takes. These programs would also exhibit all of the previously described methods and content elements currently in use by the two disciplines.

So how would a healthy sexuality program have been experienced by guys like me and my friends? By men like the ones in Lisak's study? I suppose we won't know for sure until we're able to realize some approximation of this vision. However, I'm confident that we would see the rates of sexual violence plummet if we, as a society, committed to teaching boys the aforementioned values and skills in developmentally relevant ways throughout the first twenty years of their life. To realize this vision, our government has to get with it and allocate money and mandates for this type of work, and key corporations and community institutions have to put human welfare first and support these efforts through their policies and practices. Parents, teachers, and older siblings have to learn how to become allies in modeling and teaching these values, and all schools have to provide the corresponding knowledge and skills throughout all grades and curricula. At the moment, many of these forces are either disengaged or actively working against healthy sexuality. Boys learn little about sexuality that is accurate or affirming, and this void is filled by ignorant teammates, MTV's *Next,* and sexually abusive politicians and their often detrimental policies concerning sexuality. We must work to pull these levers of influence in our direction.

A society in which everyone is allowed and encouraged to become genuinely connected to a complete experience of their own sexuality will naturally facilitate a widespread understanding of sexuality's vital status in everyone's humanity. It is a society incompatible with sexual violence, but ripe for positive human experience. It is the society I hope we'll build.

NOTES

1. P. R. Sanday, "The Socio-cultural Context of Rape: A Cross-cultural Study," *Journal of Social Issues* 37 (1981): 5–27.
2. M. S. Kimmel, *The Gendered Society* (New York: Oxford University Press, 2000).
3. D. Lisak and P. M. Miller, "Repeat Rape and Multiple Offending among Undetected Rapists," *Violence and Victims* 17 (2002): 73–84.
4. See www.advocatesforyouth.org/real.htm for more information.
5. See www.mathematica-mpr.com/publications/PDFs/impactabstinence.pdf for more information.
6. Advocates For Youth, "Adolescent Sexual Health in Europe and the U.S.—Why the Difference?" 2nd ed. (Washington, D.C.: Advocates For Youth, 2001). See www.advocatesforyouth.org/publications/factsheet/fsest.pdf for more information.
7. International Planned Parenthood Federation, "IPPF Framework for Comprehensive Sexuality Education," (London: IPPF, 2006).
8. See www.healthunit.org/carekids/default.htm for more information.
9. See www.vsdvalliance.org/secPublications/Moving%20Upstream%204-l.pdf for more information.
10. See www.vtnetwork.org/newsletter/2004_04/joyfullarticle.html for more information.

47. • Beth Richie

A BLACK FEMINIST REFLECTION ON THE ANTIVIOLENCE MOVEMENT (2000)

Beth Richie, professor of African American studies and criminology, law, and justice at the University of Illinois at Chicago, is the author of *Arrested Justice: Black Women, Violence, and America's Prison Nation* (NYU Press 2012) and *Compelled to Crime: The Gender Entrapment of Black Battered Women* (Routledge 1995). The short list of her awards includes the Audre Lorde Legacy Award from the Union Institute, the Advocacy Award from the US Department of Health and Human Services, and the Visionary Award from the Violence Intervention Project. Richie serves on the board of numerous organizations and is a founding member of Incite! Women of Color against Violence. The following article originally appeared in *Signs* (2000).

For the feminist-based antiviolence movement in the United States, the new millennium marks the beginning of an interesting third decade that poses particular challenges and concerns for Black feminist activists and our work to end violence against women. The mainstream social movement, organized over twenty years ago in response to an emerging consciousness that regarded gender violence as the most extreme point along the continuum of women's oppression, can claim numerous victories, such as legal reforms that protect the rights of battered women and sexual assault survivors, the criminalization of sexual harassment, and legislative moves to call attention to the needs of children who witness domestic violence. In addition, an elaborate apparatus of social services has been developed to provide emergency shelter, crisis intervention counseling, medical and legal advocacy, and ongoing assistance with housing, employment, and custody issues that women who experience violence need. African-American and other women of color have been at the forefront of the most radical dimensions of this work.

Services and support at the individual level have been matched with an array of academic and public policy initiatives designed to address violence against women. There are several journals dedicated to presenting new research and intervention discussions related to gender violence, and at least four university-based research centers focus on violence against women. Each year witnesses a growing number of national conferences on issues related to gender violence, which attract a range of audiences, some with more activist goals and others with more professional and bureaucratic interests. The National Institute for Justice, the Centers for Disease Control, the Departments of Housing and Urban Development and Health and Human Services, and—paradoxically—even the Department of Defense have established federal initiatives that attempt to reduce or respond to violence against women in this country. The feminist campaign at the grassroots level has influenced government and public policy to a considerable extent, which has resulted in a significant influx of public funding for victim services, law enforcement training, and prevention services. This growth, due in no small part to the grassroots activism of survivors and other women, has deeply influenced the mainstream consciousness. Evidence of this influence appears in several recent public awareness campaigns and opinion polls that suggest that tolerance for gender-based violence has decreased significantly in the past ten years. Feminist activism has paid off; we have witnessed a considerable shift in public consciousness with regard to the problem of violence against women.

Arguably, a critical dimension of the public awareness campaign that has led to this expansion in resources for, and the credibility of, the antiviolence movement in this country is the assertion that violence against women is a common experience, that any woman or child can be the victim of gender violence. In fact, many of us who do training, public speaking, teaching, and writing on violence against women traditionally begin our presentations by saying, "It can happen to anyone." This notion has become a powerful emblem of our rhetoric and, some would argue, the basis of our mainstream success. Indeed, many people in this country finally understand that they and their children, mothers, sisters, coworkers, and neighbors can be victimized by gender violence— that it really *can* happen to anyone.

The ideas that any woman can be a battered woman and that rape is every woman's problem were part of a strategic attempt by early activists to avoid individualizing the problem of domestic and sexual violence, to focus on the social dimensions of the problem of gender violence, and to resist the stigmatization of race and class commonly associated with mainstream responses to social problems. This approach was based not only on the empirical data available at the time but also on the lived experiences of most women who—at many points in our lives—change our behavior to minimize our risk of assault. This generalized construction helped to foster an analysis of women's vulnerability as both profound and persistent, rather than as particular to any racial/ethnic community, socioeconomic position, religious group, or station in life. As a result, from college campuses to private corporations, from

public housing complexes to elite suburban communities, and in all manner of religious institutions progress has been made in increasing awareness that violence against women is an important social problem that requires a broad-based social response.

And yet, as a Black feminist activist committed to ending violence against women, something seems terribly wrong with this construction at this point in time, something that leaves many African-American women and other women of color still unsafe and renders our communities for the most part disconnected from the mainstream antiviolence movement. I would even argue that the notion that every woman is at risk—one of the hallmarks of our movement's rhetorical paradigm—is in fact a dangerous one in that it has structured a national advocacy response based on a false sense of unity around the experience of gender oppression. For, as the epistemological foundation of the antiviolence movement was institutionalized, the assumption of "everywoman" fell into the vacuum created by a white feminist analysis that did not very successfully incorporate an analysis of race and class.

In the end, the assumed race and class neutrality of gender violence led to the erasure of low-income women and women of color from the dominant view. I contend that this erasure, in turn, seriously compromised the transgressive and transformative potential of the antiviolence movement's potentially radical critique of various forms of social domination. It divorced racism from sexism, for example, and invited a discourse regarding gender violence without attention to the class dimensions of patriarchy and white domination in this country.

Put another way, when the national dialogue on violence against women became legitimized and institutionalized, the notion that "It could happen to anyone" meant that "It could happen to those in power." Subsequently, the ones who mattered most in society got the most visibility and the most public sympathy; those with power are the ones whose needs are taken most seriously. When mainstream attention to the needs of victims and survivors was gradually integrated into the public realm of social service and legal protection and became visible in research studies, "everywoman" became a white middle-class woman who could turn to a private therapist, a doctor, a police officer, or a law to protect her from abuse. She consumed the greater proportion of attention in the literature, intervention strategies were based on her needs, she was featured in public awareness campaigns, and she was represented by national leaders on the issue of violence against women.

So what began as an attempt to avoid stereotyping and stigma has resulted in exactly that which was seen early in the antiviolence movement as a threat to the essential values of inclusion, equality, and antioppression work. The consequence of this paradigmatic problem is that victimization of women of color in low-income communities is invisible to the mainstream public, at best. Worse yet, when poor African-American, Latina, Native American women and other women of color are victimized, the problem is cast as something other than a case of gender violence.

Similarly, scholarship and activism around racial/ethnic and class oppression often ignores gender as an essential variable. This argument is supported by the growing body of research on women who use drugs, women in prison, women who live in dangerous low-income neighborhoods, lesbians of color, or young women who are involved with street gangs. Where women and girls are included in these studies or activist campaigns, they are seen as "special cases" within those populations rather than as women per se. Gender is not considered a central, defining part of their identity, and their experiences are subsumed by other master categories, typically race and class. They are essentially de-gendered, which renders them without access to claims of gender oppression and outside the category of individuals at risk of gender violence.

It is here, at a critical crossroads, that I ponder my work in the antiviolence movement as a Black feminist activist and academic. From here I offer critical observations and make recommendations for the future. First, it seems that to continue to ignore the race and class dimensions of gender oppression will seriously jeopardize the viability and legitimacy of the antiviolence movement in this country, a dangerous development for women of color in low-income communities, who are most likely to be in both dangerous intimate relationships and dangerous social positions. The overreliance on simplistic analyses (as in the case of "everywoman") has significant consequences for the potential for radical social change. I suggest that we revisit our analytic frame and develop a much more complex and contextualized analysis of gender violence, one rooted in an understanding of the historical and contemporary social processes that have differentially affected women of color.

I argue for a reassessment of the responses that have been central to antiviolence work—in particular, the reliance on law enforcement as the principal provider of women's safety. For over a decade, women of color in the antiviolence movement have warned against investing too heavily in arrest, detention, and prosecution as responses to violence against women. Our warnings have been ignored, and the consequences have been serious: serious for the credibility of the antiviolence movement, serious for feminist organizing by women of color, and, most important, serious for women experiencing gender violence who fall outside of the mainstream.

The concern with overreliance on law enforcement parallels a broader apprehension about the expansion of state power in the lives of poor women of color in this country. Just as the antiviolence movement is relying on legal and legislative strategies to criminalize gender violence, women in communities of color are experiencing the negative effects of conservative legislation regarding public assistance, affirmative action, and immigration. And, while the antiviolence movement is working to improve arrest policies, everyday safety in communities of color is being threatened by more aggressive policing, which has resulted in increased use of force, mass incarceration, and brutality. The conflict between the antiviolence movement's strategy and the experiences of low-income communities of color has seriously undermined our work as feminists of color fighting violence against women.

Obviously, leadership emerges as central to this dilemma. While there is a renewed call for unity and diversity from some corners of our movement, others (women of color who have dedicated years to this work) are appalled at the persistent whiteness of the nationally recognized leadership. As the bureaucratic and institutional apparatus of the antiviolence movement grows—bringing more funding, more recognition, and also more collaborations with partners who do not share our radical goals—there is little evidence of increasing racial/ethnic and class diversity. Despite some notable exceptions, the lack of women of color in leadership roles in antiviolence programs is startling and contrasts sharply with the rhetoric of inclusion, diversity, and commitment to antioppression work. While there may be structural excuses for this, the fact that so few national organizations (even feminist ones) have successfully promoted the leadership of women of color is almost a mockery of the values on which the movement was built. Given the similar invisibility of women of color as leaders in struggles for racial justice (again, with some exceptions), the situation can seem dire as we face the new millennium.

Yet, for better or worse, the solutions are not enigmatic; they exist within our core values and the principles on which the antiviolence movement was organized. Feminist women of color need to step forward as never before, reclaiming our place as leaders both in the antiviolence movement and in struggles for gender equality in our communities. The antiviolence movement needs only to acknowledge the contradictions between its rhetoric and practice and to deal honestly with the hypocrisy in its work. As members of a social justice movement committed to ending oppression, we must reconsider the complexity of rendering justice by paying attention to specific vulnerabilities of race and class. As we claim victories on some very important fronts, our understanding of gender oppression must be broadened to include state-sanctioned abuse and mistreatment of women. If we are prepared to go there, we can begin the millennium ready to face the really hard, radical work of ending violence against women—for each and any woman.

48. • *Joey L. Mogul, Andrea J. Richie, and Kay Whitlock*

FALSE PROMISES:
Criminal Legal Responses to Violence against LGBT People (2011)

The following piece, excerpted from *Queer (In)Justice: Criminalization of LGBT People in the U.S.* (Beacon 2011), was collective written by the three authors. Joey Mogul is a partner at the People's Law Office where he fights for justice for people who have suffered from police and other state torture, abuse, and misconduct. He also directs a clinic at DePaul University's College of Law. Andrea Richie is a leading Black lesbian police misconduct attorney who has written extensively on the profiling and policing of women of color and litigated *Tikkun v. City of New York*, a groundbreaking case that challenged unlawful searches of trans people in policy custody. In 2014 she was awarded a Senior Soros Justice Fellowship to continue her work. Kay Whitlock is an activist and writer committed to dismantling structural violence. She coauthored *Considering Hate* (with Michael Bronski, Beacon 2015) and is the cofounder and coeditor (with Nancy Heitzeg) of the Criminal Injustice Series on the blog *Critical Mass Progress*.

In March 2002 April Mora, a lesbian teen of African American and Native American descent, was walking to a store in Denver, Colorado, to get a soft drink. A car pulled up behind her and the driver called out, referring disparagingly to Mora as a "dyke." Two other men jumped from the car, attacked her, and pinned her to the ground. When Mora screamed, one man with a knife cut her tongue, causing blood to gather in her throat. He held a knife to her neck while the other used a razor blade to carve the word "dyke" on her left forearm and "R.I.P." into the flesh of her stomach. Choking, she fought to get free. The man with the razor cut her face. Before leaving her on the street, both men kicked her in the ribs, telling her she was lucky they hadn't raped her, and that next time, they would.

Dazed, injured, and bloodied, Mora walked back home and called her girlfriend, Dominicque Quintana, at school. When Quintana arrived, they called an ambulance and the police. The scene that unfolded when the police arrived both compounded and complicated the homophobic ferocity of the original attack. According to Quintana's mother, who lived with the two young women, the police immediately wanted to know if Mora and her girlfriend had been fighting, and if they were on drugs. They did not search for the men who attacked Mora, instead insisting that she take a polygraph to prove she was telling the truth.

After the young women were finally allowed to leave for the hospital, officers remaining on the scene focused their investigation on a "self-infliction of injury" theory. Quintana's mother later recounted that "the police went into my house and looked for a razor and the tee shirt April had been wearing. The police trashed April and Dominicque's bedroom in the basement and went through the freezer, too." Though the health care providers who treated Mora offered to confirm in writing that the injuries she suffered could not have been self-inflicted, the police nevertheless insisted on focusing on Mora rather than on investigating her account of events, thereby foreclosing any opportunity to locate her attackers.[1]

Violence against LGBT people at the hands of strangers on the streets and family members in our homes continues to be reported at alarming rates across the country. According to the National Coalition of Anti-Violence Programs (NCAVP), a national network of thirty-five local organizations providing services to and advocating on behalf of LGBT people, in 2008 there were over two thousand instances of homophobic and transphobic violence reported to just thirteen local organizations across the country, representing a 26 percent increase over 2006 figures.[2] Homophobic and transphobic violence spans a spectrum from brutal physical attacks such as that experienced by Mora, to pervasive verbal abuse and harassment. While commonplace, physical assaults make up the minority of reported incidents. Nevertheless, the viciousness and impunity of the violence in many instances shocks the conscience, prompts outrage, and spurs demands for action.

[. . .]

Unfortunately, but perhaps not surprisingly given the central role played by the criminal legal system in policing sexual and gender nonconformity, April Mora's experience with seeking protection and accountability from the police is also not unique. LGBT people across the country consistently report that police often focus on them, rather than their assailants, when they are victims of violence, by questioning their account or blaming them for bringing violence upon themselves. With appalling frequency, LGBT victims of violence are subjected to further homophobic or transphobic verbal or physical abuse at the hands of law enforcement authorities that are charged with protecting them. Often, police refuse to take reports, neglect to classify violence as motivated by anti-LGBT sentiment or as domestic violence, or fail to respond altogether.[3] For many LGBT people, and particularly LGBT people of color, immigrants, youth, and criminalized queers, reliance on the police and criminal legal system for safety is simply not an option because of the risk of adverse consequences.

[. . .]

VIOLENCE AGAINST LGBT PEOPLE

The virulently homophobic and transphobic assault April Mora experienced constitutes what is generally understood to be a *hate crime,* a term used to describe violence motivated, in whole or in part, by actual or perceived race, color, religion, ethnicity, national origin, sexual orientation, gender, gender identity or expression, or disability. According to the FBI, the majority of identity-related violence is motivated by race, followed by violence based on religion, homophobia, and national origin.[4] Indeed, the grisly 1998 murder of James Byrd, Jr., who was beaten and then dragged behind a truck to his death by three white supremacists in Jasper, Texas, remains foremost among iconic representations of present-day manifestations of hate crimes in the United States.

Recognizing that many forms of violence are motivated by a range of intentions and hostilities, the terms *racist, sexist, anti-Semitic, anti-Muslim,* and *homophobic and transphobic violence* are used here in an effort to more accurately describe the phenomena under discussion: the terms *bias* or *hate crime* suggest that such violence is motivated entirely by prejudice (presumably irrational) and not informed by historical patterns of dominance and subordination that produce tangible political, social, and economic benefits for majority groups. Regardless of the terminology used or its targets, there is no question that such violence is abhorrent, structural, and pervasive.

Where violence against LGBT people is concerned, the problem is difficult to quantify for a variety of reasons. Like many forms of gender and sexuality-based violence, it is underreported across the board, and particularly to law enforcement officials.[5] Numerous factors may contribute to LGBT individuals' reluctance to report violence they experience, including fear of retribution by their attackers, and of disclosure of sexual orientation, gender identity, or immigration status, perceptions that police will not take the report seriously, or will blame them for the violence, and participation in informal or criminalized economic activity, including sex work.[6] According to the NCAVP, "Because anti-LGBT violence has historically been poorly addressed by law enforcement (and because law enforcement officials remain one of the prime categories of offenders documented by NCAVP each year), it is very often underreported to police even in jurisdictions where relationships between law enforcement and the LGBT population have improved." As a result, LGBT antiviolence activists and service providers generally agree that much—perhaps even most—harassment and violence against queers is never reported.[7]

Moreover, official figures do not even accurately depict the number of incidents that *do* come to the attention of law enforcement, due to police officers' failure to adequately and appropriately respond to, classify, document, and report such instances.[8] While the FBI issues an annual report that includes data on incidents reported to law enforcement where a motive based on sexual orientation and, more recently, gender identity or expression has been ascribed, it relies on inconsistent, voluntary reporting by a small and unrepresentative number of local law enforcement agencies. In 2007, for example, only 2,025 out of nearly 17,000 law enforcement agencies reported hate crime data to the federal Uniform Crime Reporting Program.[9] The most reliable source of national data on anti-LGBT violence is compiled annually by the NCAVP. Although limited by resources and the fluctuating capacity of its member organizations to consistently collect and report data, the NCAVP's reports document incidents of homophobic and transphobic violence reported directly to its member organizations, including incidents in which victims have declined to report to the police, or where law enforcement refused classification as a hate crime.

The NCAVP's 2008 report paints a sobering picture. In addition to an increase of 26 percent over 2006 figures in incidents of vandalism, verbal abuse, and physical abuse, the incidence of sexual assaults reported to be motivated by homophobia and transphobia rose sharply for the third consecutive year. While murders represent only a small fraction of violence experienced by LGBT people, their numbers increased by 28 percent from 2007 to 2008, and, according to the NCAVP, constituted "the highest number of deaths since 1999."[10]

Since racially motivated violence makes up the majority of reported hate crimes, it is not surprising that LGBT people of color are overrepresented among those targeted for homophobic and transphobic violence.[11] Transgender people also experience high levels of violence: 12 percent of the total number of reported incidents of violence targeted transgender people, and transgender and gender-nonconforming people report some of the most pervasive and egregious forms of harassment and abuse.[12] Even among LGB people who do not identify as transgender, gender nonconformity has been found to be a predictor of both "every day discrimination" and violence.[13] Finally, despite the prevailing perception that gay men are "the natural and most frequent targets of homophobic hate crime," some estimate that one in five lesbians have been assaulted in an antilesbian incident in their lifetimes.[14]

No matter which numbers or populations we look at, homophobic and transphobic violence against LGBT people in the United States clearly demands a response. The question is whether responses rooted in a criminal legal system invested in policing and punishing sexual and gender deviance, rather than in community-based accountability and systemic change, are effective in actually preventing and protecting queers from violence.

THE "HATE CRIME" FRAMEWORK

The predominant response to violence against LGBT people over the past decade has focused on enactment of legislation against hate crimes. In almost all cases,

the underlying violation—criminal mischief, harassment, malicious intimidation or threat, vandalism, arson, assault, battery, rape, or murder—is already subject to criminal penalties.[15] The addition of provisions specific to motivations for already-criminalized activity is intended to ensure harsher punishment of such offenses and promote law enforcement measures intended—at least in theory—to deter and prevent such violence.

[. . .]

In 1981, the Anti-Defamation League (ADL)[16] developed a "model" template for hate crime laws, promoted as an effective response to the problem of harassment, intimidation, and violence based on a victim's actual or perceived race, religion, or national origin. Sexual orientation and gender were later added to the ADL model. The core feature of the ADL approach is "a 'penalty-enhancement' concept: criminal activity motivated by hate is subject to a stiffer sentence" on the grounds that the harm extends beyond the individual, affecting the entire community.[17]

The model is based on the theoretical swift and harsh "retribution" for violence directed at any member of a particular group, without reference to historical context, the complexities of intersecting power relations, or consequences to members of other oppressed groups. The powerful appeal of such an approach rests in its implied promise that, by framing communities historically targeted for ongoing harassment and violence as "crime victims," law enforcement will "be on our side."

[. . .]

In 1982, the National Gay Task Force initiated the first national antiviolence organizing project to document and increase public awareness of violence against lesbian and gay people, and mobilize "community indignation about hate crimes [in order to] finally end the long-ignored epidemic of anti-LGBT violence." The primary policy tool for bringing about an end to this violence would be "the passage of state and federal laws that recognize LGBT vulnerability to crimes motivated by anti-LGBT hate and prejudice."[18] Other national, state, and local groups representing LGBT communities also quickly embraced the hate crime framework. State hate crime legislation rapidly proliferated, particularly as advocates worked to expand the original list of protected categories to include actual or perceived ethnicity, sexual orientation, mental or physical disability, gender, and gender identity or expression. By late 2009, forty-five states had legislation addressing bias-motivated harassment and violence. Laws vary with regard to protected categories, though most include race, religion, ethnicity, and national origin. Twelve states and the District of Columbia include both gender identity and sexual orientation, while eighteen states only include sexual orientation.[19]

[. . .]

New federal hate crime laws passed as well, beginning with the 1990 Hate Crimes Statistics Act. Sentencing enhancements were tucked into the much broader 1994 Violent Crime Control and Law Enforcement Act.[20] In 2009, the Local Law Enforcement Enhancement Act (LLEEA), also known as the Matthew Shepard and James Byrd, Jr. Hate Crimes Prevention Act, authorized the Department of Justice to assist or, where local authorities are unwilling or unable, take the lead in state and local investigations and prosecutions.

A push for the creation of specialized law enforcement units to investigate and prosecute hate crimes accompanied the rapid spread and expansion of these laws, a call taken up by many LGBT organizations. Such units now exist in a growing number of locales. In many more community liaisons are charged with educating law enforcement officers about affected communities and facilitating appropriate responses to hate crimes.[21]

[. . .]

Closer examination of the hate crime framework reveals substantive flaws in this approach. A central shortcoming is its exclusive focus on individual acts

of violence rather than on dismantling the systemic forces that promote, condone, and facilitate homophobic and transphobic violence. Hate or bias-related violence is portrayed as individualized, ignorant, and aberrant—a criminal departure by individuals and extremist groups from the norms of society, necessitating intensified policing to produce safety. The fact is many of the individuals who engage in such violence are encouraged to do so by mainstream society through promotion of laws, practices, generally accepted prejudices, and religious views. In other words, behavior that is racist, homophobic, transphobic, anti-Semitic, anti-Muslim, and anti-immigrant, and violence against disabled people, does not occur in a political vacuum. And it is not always possible to police the factors that encourage and facilitate it.

For instance, violence against LGBT people generally increases in the midst of highly visible, homophobic, right-wing political attacks. Michigan saw the largest increase (207 percent) in anti-LGBT incidents reported to NCAVP in 2007, as the state's attorney general was concluding a three-year campaign against domestic partnership benefits.[22] In 2008, during the volatile backlash that accompanied the statewide Yes on Proposition 8 campaign to reverse a California Supreme Court decision permitting same-sex couples to marry, Community United Against Violence (CUAV) reported a large increase in reported anti-LGBT violence.[23] Other tensions also produce notable increases in violence against LGBT people who are immigrants or people of color. For example, attacks against South Asian and Middle Eastern LGBT people surged in the aftermath of the anti-Arab and anti-Muslim rhetoric following 9/11.[24]

Because they fail to address larger social forces influencing individual acts of violence, and instead focus on harsher punishment of individuals rather than prevention, there is no proactive "protection" in hate crime laws, despite the claims of supporters.[25] While the presumed deterrent value of enhanced penalties is advanced as a central argument for the laws, the hate crime statutes currently in place in thirty states and the District of Columbia do not appear to deter much, if any, harassment and violence. More than two decades after the first LGBT embrace of hate crime laws, as NCAVP figures illustrate, violence directed against queers remains a serious problem.

[. . .]

LGBT people of color do not escape the problematic effects of the hate crime framework. Police profile LGBT people of color, particularly youth, as potential perpetrators of hate crimes in predominantly white, gay urban enclaves. Given prevailing perceptions of LGBT people as predominantly, if not exclusively, white, people of color are perceived by police and residents to be criminally "out of place" in these neighborhoods. Archetypes framing people of color as inherently dangerous and more violently homophobic than whites further contribute to law enforcement targeting, aggressively harassing, stopping, and questioning LGBT people of color about the "legitimacy" of their presence in LGBT-identified areas. . . .

[. . .]

LAW ENFORCEMENT RESPONSES TO ANTI-LGBT VIOLENCE

The hate crime framework is further compromised by placing primary responsibility for preventing violence in the hands of a criminal legal system that is itself responsible for much of the LGBT violence. As journalist Richard Kim has noted, "It seems improbable that the passage of hate crimes laws would suddenly transform the state into a guardian of gay and lesbian people."[26] Recent NCAVP data underscores the point: the 2008 report concludes that "law enforcement officers remain one of the prime categories of offenders documented by NCAVP each year."[27] Over the past three decades LGBT people have increasingly turned to police and prosecutors for protection, only to be met with responses that further devalue queer lives, sometimes placing victims in greater jeopardy. Nevertheless, resources allocated by hate crime legislation for responding to and reducing violence continue to be directed almost

exclusively to the expansion of policing, prosecution, and punishment.

But instances in which law enforcement–based approaches have failed to address or further contributed to the problem abound. For example, the Anti-Violence Project (AVP) of the Los Angeles Gay and Lesbian Center reported a case in which several youth in a car saw a Latina transgender woman, stopped, and proceeded to beat and stab her. Los Angeles Police Department officers responding to the scene demanded the victim's driver's license, which identified her as female, refused to accept it, and insisted that paramedics on the scene examine her genitals. The paramedics did not comply with the demand. Witnesses to the attack alleged the officers inquired in an intimidating fashion about their immigration status.[28] As in April Mora's case, criminalizing archetypes framing transgender and gender-nonconforming people as inherently deceptive and unworthy of protection drove police response, which in turn led the victim and witnesses to refuse to speak further to the police, even though they had information that could have helped identify the assailants.

Unfortunately, such responses do not appear to be the product of an aberrant few insensitive, untrained officers. Researchers studying police response to violence against LGBT people in Minnesota over a ten-year period described numerous instances of 911 operators failing to send assistance, police mocking and laughing at victims, and officers blaming victims for the violence they experienced. Overall, police engaged in verbal harassment of victims of homophobic and transphobic violence in 32 percent of all incidents in which police responded, although this percentage decreased over time.[29]

[. . .]

The Minnesota researchers found that "there continues to be a significant percentage of incidents where officers refuse to file a report indicating that a crime has occurred. Over the course of the nine years, on average, officers refused in 31 percent of the cases to file a general incident report."[30] More recent figures compiled by the NCAVP indicate a

27 percent rate of refusal to classify violence against LGBT people as motivated by sexual orientation or gender identity.[31]

The Minnesota study also found that, despite deliberate efforts on the part of local LGBT antiviolence activists to build strong relationships with local police departments through education, outreach, sharing information about specific incidents, and advocating on behalf of victims of crime, negative interactions with police continued. More than half of the incidences of violence reported by LGBT people over this period were met with "negative" responses by law enforcement, compared to 20 percent positive responses. Although negative responses decreased by 50 percent over a nine-year period, they still made up the bulk of police-related incidents reported. The authors concluded, "While Minnesota has a reputation as one of the best states in the nation that offers protection against bias-motivated violence and intimidation, we still found low levels of reporting, refusal by police to indicate bias when requested by the victim, and police misconduct against those in the GLBT community."[32]

For almost thirty years, hate crime laws have existed as a kind of untouchable "third rail" of mainstream LGBT politics. In some respects debates around hate crime laws seem to powerfully distill all of the insult, harm, and fear born by queers for centuries. Many LGBT people—especially those who have little ongoing contact or engagement with policing and prison systems and their broader social and economic impacts—respond as if any challenge to these laws is an active betrayal of wounded gay people, an almost intentional reinfliction of murderous violence.

But it is also becoming apparent to at least some supporters of such legislation that, while data collection, civil remedies, and other provisions might be useful and important in particular contexts, penalty enhancements are largely ineffective. Three prominent transgender advocates hinted as much when they wrote, in 2006, "Including transgender people in hate crime laws does not create a change by enhancing penalties but by educating legislators, the media, the police, and the courts about the violence faced by trans people and by asking the public at large to side with the victims rather than the perpetrators of hate."[33] The NCAVP has distanced itself from penalty enhancements over a period of several years, and in 2008, NCAVP affirmed its opposition to enhanced penalties for those convicted of hate crimes.[34] In 2009, the Sylvia Rivera Law Project (SRLP), joined by FIERCE, INCITE! Women of Color Against Violence, Queers for Economic Justice (QEJ), Right Rides, the Transgender Intersex Justice Project (TGIJP), and the Transformative Justice Law Project (TJLP), declared their opposition to the Matthew Shepard and James Byrd, Jr. Hate Crimes Prevention Act. Placing their stand within a larger context of opposition to mass incarceration, militarization, and colonialism, they said, "The evidence . . . shows that hate crimes laws and other 'get tough on crime' measures do not deter or prevent violence. Increased incarceration does not deter others from committing violent acts motivated by hate, does not rehabilitate those who have committed past acts of hate, and does not make anyone safer."[35]

DOMESTIC VIOLENCE IN QUEER RELATIONSHIPS

Over the past two decades, in addition to demanding protection from homophobic and transphobic violence at the hands of strangers, LGBT individuals and communities have increasingly sought protection for violence in intimate relationships. Although historically even more invisible than its heterosexual counterpart, the existence of violence in the context of queer relationships is being brought to light by antiviolence advocates working to counter reluctance both within and outside queer communities to recognize it. In so doing they have come up against resistance on the part of LGBT people concerned about feeding negative perceptions of queers as well as resistance on the part of policymakers loathe to appear to be condoning homosexuality by providing protections to victims of violence in homosexual relationships.[36] Despite these challenges, by 2008, thirty-seven states provided for civil orders of protection against an intimate partner of the same sex under varying circumstances, although the availability of this remedy in reality varies from judge to judge and jurisdiction to jurisdiction.[37]

Fifteen organizations in fourteen jurisdictions across the country provide services to LGBT survivors of domestic violence (DV) and jointly report on the populations they serve in an annual report published by the NCAVP. They define domestic violence as "a pattern of behavior where one partner coerces, dominates, and isolates the other to maintain power and control over their partner."[38] While this is a welcome expansion beyond a domestic violence frame that encompasses only physical abuse in heterosexual relationships, it does not include violence queers experience in other intimate relationships, including at the hands of family members such as parents, siblings, and extended family members, as well as caregivers. A significant proportion of homophobic and transphobic violence takes place within or near our homes, and often represents some of the most brutal violence experienced by LGBT people.[39] The widely used term *same sex domestic violence,* which appears to reflect an effort to shoehorn queer lives into mainstream domestic violence discourse, similarly excludes these experiences of violence, as well as those of transgender people involved in heterosexual relationships. Recognizing that LGBT people, and particularly queer youth and elders, are vulnerable to violence in a multitude of intimate contexts beyond monogamous relationships that mirror heterosexual marriage, many LGBT anti-violence activists use the broader term *LGBT domestic violence* to reflect this reality and distinguish these experiences from violence experienced at the hands of strangers or public authorities.

A recent study found, based on a review of the literature, that police are less likely to intervene in domestic violence cases that involve gay or lesbian couples. The study's authors suggest that failure to do so may be based on homophobia, and on notions that "women cannot be abusers and men cannot be abused." They also note that such beliefs are likely held not only by law enforcement officers, but also by others who will determine survivors' success in obtaining safety

through in the criminal legal system, including witnesses, health care workers, attorneys, judges, and jurors. As a result, the researchers conclude, lesbian and gay people who experience domestic violence "may not receive equal protection under the law."[40]

[. . .]

In far too many cases, police heap harassment and abuse on top of that already experienced at the hands of an intimate. NCAVP data indicates that, of the 18 percent of cases of LGBT DV reported to affiliates across the country in which the police intervened, police misconduct, including verbal abuse, use of slurs, and physical abuse, was reported in 6 percent. Arrest of survivors in addition to or instead of abusers took place in an additional 6 percent. And, overall reports of police misconduct in DV cases increased by 93 percent in 2008. In Los Angeles, which consistently reports the largest number of LGBT DV cases per year, a misarrest was reported in over 97 percent of cases in 2007: "Frequently both parties are arrested or law enforcement officers threaten to arrest both."[41] . . .

[. . .]

In some cases, police failure to respond, combined with an absence of alternative community-based responses, can prove deadly. On March 28, 1998, Marc Kajs was shot by his former partner at the restaurant where he worked in Houston, Texas. A lawsuit brought by Kajs' mother alleged that, although he contacted police to report abuse by the former partner on at least six separate occasions, each time officers failed to file written reports or offer him assistance. On the last occasion Kajs sought help from the police, he ran into a police station at two thirty in the morning while being chased by his former partner, who threatened him in front of a police officer. Kajs told the officer he was frightened, that the man had threatened his life and that of his friends and family members, and asked for protection. The officer gave him an incident number and sent him back out on the street with his abuser, telling him to return the following Monday. Kajs was dead before Monday came around.[42]

In many more cases, as with hate crimes, queers feel unable to seek protection from the criminal legal system, fearing ineffective or homophobic responses, disclosure of their sexual orientation or gender identity, or arrest, deportation, loss of custody of children, or other adverse outcomes.[43] NCAVP suggests that this is particularly true for LGBT people of color and LGBT immigrants. It is also the case for a substantial number of transgender people. According to NCAVP, "Since police officers were perpetrators in almost half (48 percent) of the incidents of antitransgender violence [in 2000], transgender people are not likely to seek police protection from an abusive partner." The number of incidents reported to NCAVP member organizations in which police were called decreased by 41 percent in 2.008.[44]

[. . .]

Not surprisingly, the situation doesn't much improve once queer survivors of domestic violence reach the courts. As the National Resource Center on Domestic Violence notes, "In the overtly hierarchical structure of the legal system . . . survivors of violence in same-gender/gender variant relationships are not routinely afforded the same protections as those employed to protect privileged heterosexual victims of domestic violence."[45] Not only do queer survivors face generic and pervasive homophobic treatment, but in some jurisdictions courts continue to refuse to enforce existing protections for people who experience LGBT domestic violence on the grounds that they believe doing so would put gay relationships on equal legal footing with heterosexual marriage.[46] Further aggravating the situation, the STOP DV program of the Los Angeles AVP reports a lack of awareness among legal professionals regarding domestic partnership law and custody and visitation issues in LGBT relationships, which may lead to hesitation to offer assistance because the issues appear too complicated.[47]

[. . .]

For transgender women, the problem is endemic. Archetypes of transgender people as deceptive, mentally unstable, and sexually degraded permeate responses to domestic violence committed against them as much as they do other law enforcement activities. A San Antonio woman, who called the police for help when her boyfriend broke a window and some of her personal possessions, was arrested on the mere word of her abuser that she was "bipolar." A young African American transgender woman living in Los Angeles who repeatedly called police for assistance when her boyfriend was abusive was told each time that there was nothing the officers could do, despite the presence of visible bruises on her body. However, one morning two undercover officers knocked on her door and told her she was under arrest pursuant to an old warrant on a solicitation charge. In 2002, in Washington, DC, a transgender woman choked by her male partner managed to call police only to be arrested, handcuffed, pushed down the stairs, and referred to by male pronouns throughout her subsequent detention. Although charges against her were eventually dismissed, the message was clear: gender "deception" can be met with violence, with no recourse to the law.[48]

[. . .]

The challenge is to develop bolder justice visions and new frameworks for naming, analyzing, and confronting the myriad forms of individual and systemic violence that not only hurt individuals, but also destabilize entire communities—to shift our focus to our communities, to help them grow stronger, more just, more stable, and more compassionate. LGBT people need to deeply question whether institutions rooted in the control and punishment of people of color, poor people, immigrants, *and* queers can ever be deployed in the service of LGBT interests without abandoning entire segments of queer communities to continuing state violence. But how do we start to break out of the old frames, confront the inhumanity of criminal archetypes, and begin to open up what Angela Y. Davis calls "new terrains of justice"?[49]

NOTES

1. "CAVP Condemns Assault on Lesbian Youth," Colorado Anti-Violence Project, www.coavp.org/content/view/35/44/ (accessed September 13, 2009); and Amnesty International, *Stonewalled: Police Abuse and Misconduct against Lesbian, Gay, Bisexual and Transgender People in the U.S.* (New York: Amnesty International USA, 2005), 76.

2. National Coalition of Anti-Violence Projects, *Hate Violence against Lesbian, Gay, Bisexual, and Transgender People in the United States 2008,* 2009 Release Edition, www.ncavp.org/publications/NationalPubs.aspx (accessed September 5, 2009).

3. Kristina B. Wolff and Carrie L. Cokeley, "To Protect and Serve? An Exploration of Police Conduct in Relation to the Gay, Lesbian, Bisexual and Transgender Community," *Sex Cult* II (2007): 1–23; and Amnesty, *Stonewalled,* 67, 78.

4. Federal Bureau of Investigation, *Uniform Crime Report: Hate Crime Statistics 2008,* www.fbi.gov/ucr/hc2008/documents/abouthc.pdf (accessed February 11, 2010).

5. See U.S. Department of Justice, Bureau of Justice Statistics, *Criminal Victimization, 2004,* Office of Justice Programs, NCJ 210674 (Washington, DC, September 2005); U.S. Department of Justice, Bureau of Justice Statistics, *Rape and Sexual Assault: Reporting to Police and Medical Attention, 1992–2000,* Office of Justice Programs, NCJ 194530 (Washington, DC, August 2002); and Wolff and Cokeley, "To Protect and Serve?"

6. Wolff and Cokeley, "To Protect and Serve?"; Amnesty, *Stonewalled,* 67–68; and Suzanna M. Rose, "Community Interventions Concerning Homophobic Violence and Partner Violence Against Lesbians," *Journal of Lesbian Studies* 7, no. 4 (2003): 125–39.

7. NCAVP, *Hate Violence in 2008,* 16–17.

8. See, e.g., Wolff and Cokeley, "To Protect and Serve?" See also Amnesty, *Stonewalled,* 75–77.

9. U.S. Department of Justice, *Hate Crimes Statistics, 2007,* Uniform Crime Reporting Program, Federal Bureau of Investigation (Washington, DC, October 2008), www.fbi.gov/ucr/htm (accessed October 12, 2009).

10. NCAVP, *Hate Violence in 2008,* 5.

11. Ibid., 7; and FBI, *Uniform Crime Report.*

12. Amnesty, *Stonewalled,* 70.

13. Allegra R. Gordon and Ilan H. Meyer, "Gender Nonconformity as a Target of Prejudice, Discrimination, and Violence against LGB Individuals," *Journal of LGBT Health Research* 3, no. 3 (2007): 55–71.

14. Rose, "Community Interventions," 131.

15. James B. Jacobs and Kimberly Potter, *Hate Crimes: Criminal Law & Identity Politics* (New York: Oxford University Press, 1998), 29–44.

16. The ADL states that its mission is fighting "anti-Semitism and all forms of bigotry in the United States and abroad." The organization has been critiqued for its embrace of centrist/extremist theory, which fashions bigotry and violence as the product of extremism on the part of individuals while ignoring systemic forms of violence against marginalized groups by the state. See "Focus on Individual Aberration," www.publiceye.org/liberty/Repression-and-ideology-o6.html (accessed February 2, 2010). ADL has also been critiqued for its uncritical support of the policies and practices of the State of Israel, and its efforts to suppress dissenting voices. See, e.g., Edward W. Said and Christopher Hitchens, eds., *Blaming the Victims: Spurious Scholarship and the Palestinian Question* (New York: Verso, 1988), 10, 12. See also, e.g., Eric Alterman, "The Defamation League," *Nation,* February 16, 2009.

17. Anti-Defamation League, *ADL Model Legislation* (2003), www.adl.org/99hatecrime/penalty.asp (accessed September 15, 2009); Anti-Defamation League, *Hate Crimes Laws Introduction,* (2003), www.adl.org/99hatecrime/intro.asp (accessed September 15, 2009); and Levin, "Slavery to Hate Crime," 237.

18. National Gay and Lesbian Task Force Action Fund, *Hate Crimes Protections Historical Overview,* www.thetaskforce.org/issues/hate_crimes_ main_page/overview (accessed September 10, 2009).

19. National Gay and Lesbian Task Force Action Fund, *Map of Hate Crime Laws in the U.S.* (updated July 14, 2009), www.thetaskforce.org/reports_and_research/hate_crimes_laws (accessed September 8, 2009). Two states include sexual orientation in data collection laws/provisions only.

20. See Levin, "Slavery to Hate Crimes," 235-41. See also Jacobs and Potter, *Hate Crimes,* 29-44.

21. See, e.g., Amnesty, *Stonewalled*, 98–99.

22. National Coalition of Anti-Violence Programs, *Anti-Lesbian, Gay, Bisexual and Transgender Violence in 2007*

(2008), www.ncavp.org/publications/NationalPubs.aspx (accessed September 5, 2009).

23. NCAVP, *Hate Violence in 2008.*

24. See National Coalition of Anti-Violence Programs, *Anti-Lesbian, Gay, Bisexual and Transgender Violence in 2002* (2003), 5, www.ncavp.org/publications/NationalPubs .aspx (accessed February 5, 2010). See also American Friends Service Committee, *Is Opposing the War an LGBT Issue?,* produced in partnership with the National Youth Action Coalition (2003), www.afsc.org/lgbt/ht/display /ContentDetails/i/i8752 (accessed February 4, 2010).

25. Richard Kim, "The Truth about Hate Crimes Laws," *Nation,* July 12, 1999, www.thenation.com/article/ truth-about-hate-crimes-laws (accessed October 15, 2009).

26. Kim, "Truth about Hate Crimes."

27. NCAVP, *Hate Violence in 2008*, 16.

28. Amnesty, *Stonewalled,* 69.

29. Wolff and Cokeley, "To Protect and Serve?" 12, 18.

30. Wolff and Cokeley, "To Protect and Serve?" 13.

31. NCAVP, *Hate Violence in 2008, 13.*

32. Wolff and Cokeley, "To Protect and Serve?" 12, 19.

33. Paisley Currah, Richard Juang, and Shannon Minter, eds., *Transgender Rights* (Minneapolis: University of Minnesota Press, 2006), xxiii. See also Lee, "Prickly Coalitions," 110–11.

34. NCAVP, *Hate Violence in 2008, 86.*

35. See SLRP's Web site: http://srlp.org/fedhatecrimelaw (accessed February 2010).

36. National Coalition of Anti-Violence Programs, *Lesbian, Gay, Bisexual and Transgender Domestic Violence in the United States in 2007* (2008), 3, www.avp.org (accessed February 14, 2010); National Resource Center on Domestic Violence, *LGBT Communities and Domestic Violence: Information and Resources* (Pennsylvania, 2007), www.nrcdv.org (accessed February 14, 2010); and Amnesty, *Stonewalled,* 80.

37. Sheila M. Seelau and Eric P. Seelau, "Gender-Role Stereotypes and Perceptions of Heterosexual, Gay and Lesbian Domestic Violence," *Journal of Family Violence* 20, no. 6 (2005): 363-71, 363; and NCAVP, *Domestic Violence in 2007.*

38. National Coalition of Anti-Violence Programs, *Lesbian, Gay, Bisexual and Transgender Domestic Violence in the United States in 2008* (2009), 6, 11. NCAVP is moving toward the use of the term *intimate partner violence* to describe this phenomenon.

39. Ibid., 6, 11, 12. The NCAVP recognizes the existence of violence in these contexts, but nevertheless focuses its reporting on *intimate partner violence* and *domestic violence,* using these terms synonymously. Nearly one-third of all incidents reported to the NCAVP took place in or near a private residence.

40. Seelau and Seelau, "Gender-Role Stereotypes," 364–70.

41. NCAVP, *Domestic Violence in 2007,* 24, 19; and NCAVP, *Domestic Violence in 2008,* 2.

42. Harvey Rice, "Judge Again Dismisses Law Suit over Gay Domestic Violence Case," *Houston Chronicle,* February 4, 2004; Harvey Rice, "Expert Questions Police Report on Gay Man's Death," *Houston Chronicle,* December 19, 2003; Rosanna Ruiz, "Court Reinstates Mom's Suit over Death of Gay Son," *Houston Chronicle,* December 15, 2001; Wendy Grossman, "Bullets after Brunch," *Houston Press,* May 4, 2000; and Amnesty, *Stonewalled,* 82.

43. NCAVP, *Domestic Violence in 2007,* 19, 24; NRCDV, *LGBT Communities and Domestic Violence;* Danica R. Borenstein et al., "Understanding the Experiences of Lesbian, Bisexual and Trans Survivors of Domestic Violence: A Qualitative Study," *Journal of Homosexuality* 51, no. 1 (2006): 159-81, 162, 172; and Rose, "Community Interventions," 131.

44. NCAVP, *Domestic Violence in 2008,* 3; NCAVP, *Domestic Violence in 2007,* 16; and National Coalition of Anti-Violence Programs, *Lesbian, Gay, Bisexual and Transgender Domestic Violence in the United States in 2000,* www .avp.org (accessed February 14, 2010).

45. NRCDV, *LGBT Communities and Domestic Violence.*

46. NCAVP, *Domestic Violence in 2007, 35;* and NRCDV, *LGBT Communities and Domestic Violence.*

47. NCAVP, *Domestic Violence in 2007,* 25.

48. NRCDV, *LGBT Communities and Domestic Violence.*

49. Angela Y. Davis, *Are Prisons Obsolete?* (New York: Seven Stories, 2003), 21.

49. • *Isis Nusair*

MAKING FEMINIST SENSE OF TORTURE AT ABU-GHRAIB (NEW)

Isis Nusair is a professor of international studies and women's and gender studies at Denison University. She previously served as a researcher on women's human rights in the Middle East and North Africa at Human Rights Watch and at the Euro-Mediterranean Human Rights Network. She is the coeditor with Rhoda Kanaaneh of *Displaced at Home: Ethnicity and Gender among Palestinians in Israel.* She is completing a book on the effect of war and displacement on Iraqi women refugees in Jordan and the United States and is currently conducting research with Syrian refugees in Germany. The following piece was written for this collection; a longer, more theoretical examination of the subject can be found in *Feminism and War: Confronting U.S. Imperialism* edited by R. Riley, C. Mohanty, and M. Bruce Pratt (Zed Books, 2008).

I analyze in this essay how the essentializing and dichotomizing discourses of Orientalism justified, facilitated, and shaped gendered, racialized, and sexualized torture at the Abu-Ghraib prison outside Baghdad. The torture at Abu-Ghraib remains a sign of what constitutes Orientalist militarized hypermasculine domination and power over Iraq and by extension the Middle East and North Africa.

The *Taguba Report* on the treatment of Abu-Ghraib prisoners in Iraq states that the intentional abuse of detainees by American military police personnel at Abu-Ghraib post 2003 included the following acts: punching, slapping, and kicking detainees; jumping on their naked feet; videotaping and photographing naked male and female detainees; forcibly arranging detainees in various sexually explicit positions for photographing; forcing detainees to remove their clothing and keeping them naked for several days at a time; forcing naked male detainees to wear women's underwear; forcing groups of male detainees to masturbate themselves while being photographed and videotaped; arranging male detainees in a pile and then jumping on them; positioning a naked detainee on a MRE Box, with a sandbag on his head, and attaching wires to his fingers, toes, and penis to simulate electric torture; writing "I am a Rapest" (sic) on

the leg of a detainee alleged to have forcibly raped a fifteen-year old fellow detainee and then photographing him naked; placing a dog chain or strap around a naked detainee's neck and having a female soldier pose for a picture; a male MP guard having sex with a female detainee; and using military working dogs (without muzzles) to intimidate and frighten detainees, resulting in at least one case of a dog biting and severely injuring a detainee.

Orientalism, as a body of thought and system of representation, helps us frame these US military actions in Iraq. Orientalism splits the world into the Occident versus the Orient, positing essential differences between the two that are hard to overcome (Said). This binary opposition is not only a means to set boundaries but a representation that is interlocked with the will to rule over others. This was illustrated in the aftermath of the September 11, 2001, attacks when President George W. Bush's discourses on terrorism divided the world into "good versus evil" and "us against them." This representation reinforced an absolute view of the world without offering a way of understanding the economic and political contexts that contributed to them. Furthermore, on September 16, 2001, Bush made the association between the war on terrorism and the war against Islam and described it as a "crusade," giving the conflict a clear religious dimension (Hatem 84). The Bush doctrine, as it came to be called, argued that if you "harbor them, feed them, house them, you are just as guilty and you will be held accountable." This dispensed with legal niceties and embraced the lawless motif of the Old West: "get them dead or alive" and "smoke them in their caves/holes" (84). In a press conference on September 17, 2001, Bush explained that the United States faced a new enemy, one that has no borders and an extensive network. Yet his representation did not go beyond describing it as a barbarian whose objectives were incomprehensible.

Within Orientalism, the taming and civilizing mission of the "barbaric" Orient requires the dissemination of rational procedures of Western institutions of law and order and reorganization of Oriental cultures along the principles of the modern, progressive, and civilized West (Yegenoglu). In order to be able to construct the West and the Orient as different, the machinery of colonial discourse uses terms such as "primitive," "backward," and "traditional." This pushes the cultural other back in time, implying and inscribing an "articulation and ordering of cultural difference" that is gendered and racialized (96). This representation facilitated the conceptual gendered division between the nation (masculine) and the enemy other (feminine) and the successful reproduction of US intervention as a superior moral mission (Shepherd).

Manifest Orientalism refers to various stated views about Oriental society, languages, literatures, and history while latent Orientalism refers to an almost unconscious and untouchable act. Latent Orientalism achieves power through its everydayness and naturalness, its taken-for-granted authority (Said). It also encourages a peculiarly male and sexist conception of the world (Yegenoglu). The connection between latent and manifest Orientalism is illustrated in the military psychology assessment report indicating that "soldiers were immersed in Islamic culture, a culture with different worship and belief systems that they were encountering for the first time." It explains how the "association by soldiers of Muslims with terrorism could exaggerate difference and lead to fear and to a devaluation of people." Difference between US soldiers and Iraqi prisoners reached such a level that, according to a military dog-handler, even dogs "came not to like Iraqi detainees. They [*the dogs*] did not like

the Iraqi culture, smell, sound, skin-tone, hair-color or anything about them."

Orientalism constructs the Middle East as the place of sensuality, irrationality, corrupt despotism, mystical religiosity, and sexually unstable Arabs. It also makes Western inquiry into the nature of the "Islamic mind" and "Arab character" perfectly legitimate as a means to control that "other" (Yegenoglu). In a *New Yorker* May 14, 2004, article titled "How a Secret Pentagon Program Came to Abu-Ghraib," Seymour Hersh states that the notion that Arabs are particularly vulnerable to sexual humiliation became a talking point among prowar Washington conservatives in the months before the 2003 invasion of Iraq. "The Patai book [*The Arab Mind*], an academic told me, was 'the bible of the neocons on Arab behavior . . .' [where] two themes emerged—'one, that Arabs only understand force and, two that the biggest weakness of Arabs is shame and humiliation'" (Hersh).

Even though Islam's 'oppression' of women formed some element of the European narrative of Islam from early on, the issue of women only emerged as the centerpiece of the Western narrative of Islam in the nineteenth century as Europeans established themselves as colonial powers in Muslim countries (Ahmed). Fusion between women and culture and the idea that other men, men in colonized societies or societies beyond the borders of the civilized West, oppressed women was to be used, in the rhetoric of colonialism, "to render morally justifiable its project of undermining or eradicating the cultures of colonized people" (Ahmed 151). Accordingly, Islam was "innately and immutably oppressive to women, that the veil and segregation epitomized that oppression, and that these customs were the fundamental reasons for the general and comprehensive backwardness of Islamic societies" (Ahmed 152). Only "if these practices 'intrinsic' to Islam (and therefore Islam itself) were cast off could Muslim societies begin to move forward on the path of civilization" (152).

By posing and presupposing that the veil is hiding something, the subject turns the veil into a mask that needs to be penetrated, a mask behind which the other is suspected of hiding some dangerous secret threatening his unity and stability. The grand narrative of the colonial gaze is made up of tales of unveiling, fantasies of penetrating, domesticating, reforming, and thus controlling her (Yegenoglu). The aggressive, hostile, and violent act of unveiling, stripping, penetrating, and tearing apart Iraqi bodies at Abu-Ghraib where the body is left nude, exposed, and laid bare is a guarantee for the colonial power that the body and consequently the mind become knowable, observable, visible, and thereby manipulative. This gendered, racialized, and sexualized violence maintains discipline and secures the boundaries between the private and public and between community, nation and state. Within this context, they are all bodies to be disciplined. This is evident in Sherene Razack's (2005) analysis that what took place at Abu-Ghraib is part of a larger "national project of dominating racially inferior peoples" and that the violence in these photos is a sexualized colonial violence that "the soldiers understand to be one between conquerors and racially, morally and culturally inferior" others.

What took place at Abu-Ghraib is part of a constructed heterosexual, racialized, and gendered script that is firmly grounded in the colonial desires and practices of the larger social order (Richter-Montpetit). This construction of difference is laden with negative cultural, gendered, racial, and social connotations. It is associated with constructions of power and hierarchy in that the detainees, seen as "other," are sexually tortured and humiliated in ways that are most often associated with the violence inflicted on women's bodies. Sexual domination and national conquest are part of a militarist hypersexuality that endorses elements of masculinity, such as rigid gender roles, vengeful and militarized reactions, and obsession with order, power, and control (Burnham; Eisenstein; Enloe).

Photos of torture and abuse at Abu-Ghraib are evident of the violent act of unveiling, stripping, and penetration, the ultimate act of cultural and sexual domination over an emasculate Iraqi order. Male Iraqi prisoners were represented in the Abu-Ghraib photos as the opposite of what a US militarist and hypersexual soldier should be. The Iraqi prisoners were represented as helpless, obedient, and docile (read feminine) others. They were sexually dominated, degraded, and forced to simulate homosexual acts. Within this homophobic, militarized, racist, and sexist representation, US military were defining their position as well as the nature of their domination over Iraqi others.

Taking over 1,800 pictures of torture of Iraqi prisoners at Abu-Ghraib marks not only the difference between "us" and "them" in terms of sexuality, religion, belief system, and culture but makes these pictures available for the whole world to see. The act of taking a picture automatically implies distancing the self from its objectified other, and the process of reproducing these orchestrated images marked and recorded these representations of absolute and essential *difference from* and *domination over* those others.

Torture at Abu Ghraib was first exposed not by a digital photograph but by a letter that was smuggled out of the prison. A woman prisoner inside the jail managed to smuggle out a note in December 2003. The contents of the letter were so shocking that Amal Kadham Swadi and other Iraqi women lawyers who had been trying to gain access to the US jail found them hard to believe. The note claimed that US guards had been raping women detainees and that several of the women were now pregnant. The note added that women had been forced to strip naked in front of men, and it urged the Iraqi resistance to bomb the jail to spare the women further shame. Swadi, one of seven female lawyers who represented women detainees in Abu Ghraib, began to piece together a held without charge in various detention centers in Iraq (Harding).

The statement from the *Taguba Report* that "a male MP [Military Police] guard having sex with a female detainee," seems to be as far as US officials are willing to admit that actual rape of Iraqi women took place at Abu-Ghraib. Within the logic of Orientalist domination, male Iraqi prisoners are still men, although weak and emasculate others. Acknowledging the actual rape of Iraqi women would shatter the civilizing and rescuing rhetoric of the US military mission. Although the moral superiority and saving mission was severely damaged by the release of the photos of abuse and torture at Abu-Ghraib, the Bush administration blamed the torture in the pictures on a few "bad apples." This focus on the action of the few stands in stark opposition to Human Rights Watch's analysis that what created the climate for Abu-Ghraib was part of a larger continuum of torture and mistreatment of detainees during the US wars in Afghanistan and Iraq and in Guantanamo Bay (a US military prison in Cuba where detainees were held after 2002). Within the sexist and hierarchical logic of militarized hypermasculinity, penetration of and dominance over Iraqi male prisoners could still be justified as something to be resolved between men. After all, and despite women comprising about 15 percent of the US military, waging war is still constructed within the domain of the masculine.

Acknowledging the rape of Iraqi female prisoner exposes the undifferentiated power of penetration and control over not only the bodies of Iraqis but the land and its resources. This exposure, in turn, strips naked and tears apart the moral foundation of the US masculinized and militarized "liberation" mission in Iraq.

WORKS CITED

Ahmed, Leila. *Women and Gender in Islam*. Yale UP, 1992.

AR 15-6 Investigation – Allegation of Detainee Abuse at Abu-Ghraib: Psychological Assessment. American Civil Liberties Union, www.aclu.org/files/projects/foiasearch/pdf/DODDOA000309.pdf. Accessed 10 January 2005.

Brody, Reed. "The Road to Abu-Ghraib." *Human Rights Watch*, June 2004, www.hrw.org/reports/2004/usa0604/.

Burnham, Linda. "Sexual Domination in Uniform: An American Value." *CounterPunch,* 18 May 2004, www.counterpunch.org/2004/05/22/an-american-value/.

Eisenstein, Zillah. "Sexual Humiliation, Gender Confusion and the Horrors at Abu Ghraib." *ZNet,* 22 June 2004, zcomm.org/znetarticle/sexual-humiliation-gender-confusion-and-the-horrors-at-abu-ghraib-by-zillah-eisenstein/.

Enloe, Cynthia. *Maneuvers: The International Politics of Militarizing Women's Lives*. UC Press, 2000.

Harding, Luke. "The Other Prisoners." *The Guardian*, 19 May 2004, www.theguardian.com/world/2004/may/20/iraq.gender.

Hatem, Mervat. "Discourses on the 'War on Terrorism' in the US and its View of the Arab, Muslim, and Gendered 'Other.'" *Arab Studies Journal*, vol. 11, no. 2/12.1, 2003/2004, pp. 77–97.

Hersh, Seymour M. "The Gray Zone: How a Secret Pentagon Program Came to Abu-Ghraib." *The New Yorker*, 24 May 2004, www.newyorker.com/magazine/2004/05/24/the-gray-zone.

Patai, Raphael. *The Arab Mind*. Hatherleigh Press, 2002.

Razack, Sherene. "When is Prisoner Abuse Racial Violence?" *Selves and Others*, 24 May 2004.

Richter-Montpetit, Melanie. "Empire, Desire and Violence: A Queer Transnational Feminist Reading of the Prisoner 'Abuse' in Abu-Ghraib and the Question of 'Gender Equality.'" *International Feminist Journal of Politics*, vol. 9, no. 1, 2007, pp. 38–59. *Academic Search Premier*, doi:10.1080/14616740601066366.

Said, Edward. *Orientalism*. Vintage Books, 1979.

Shepherd, Laura. "Veiled References: Constructions of Gender in the Bush Administration Discourse on the Attacks on Afghanistan Post-9/11." *International Feminist Journal of Politics*, vol. 8, no. 1, 2006, pp. 19–41.

Yegenoglu, Meyda. *Colonial Fantasies: Toward a Feminist Reading of Orientalism* Cambridge UP, 1998.

50. • *Esra Özcan*

WHO IS A MUSLIM WOMAN?: QUESTIONING KNOWLEDGE PRODUCTION ON 'MUSLIM WOMAN' (NEW)

Esra Özcan is a communication studies scholar at Tulane University, Department of Communication in New Orleans, United States. She received her Ph.D. in communication science from Jacobs University Bremen in Germany and worked as an assistant professor at Kadir Has University in Istanbul. Her recent publications include

"Women's Headscarves in News Photographs: A Comparison between the Secular and Islamic Press during the AKP Government in Turkey" (*European Journal of Communication*, 2015) and "Lingerie, Bikinis, and the Headscarf: Visual Depictions of Muslim Female Migrants in German News Media" (*Feminist Media Studies*, 2013). She is a contributor to the alternative news network Bianet in Turkey and the author of the forthcoming book *Mainstreaming the Headscarf: Islamic Politics and Women in the Turkish Media* (I.B. Tauris). "Who Is a Muslim Woman?" was written specifically for this collection.

In political and popular media discourse "Muslim woman" has become the prime example of the oppression of women in the world. In a climate where Islam is constantly associated with extremism, violence and oppression of women, this article aims to give the students tools to critically engage with the category of "Muslim woman" and have a nuanced understanding of how we come to know Muslim women and the complexity of this category.

Let us start with an exercise: if somebody asked to name or to describe "Christian woman," what would you tell? Or maybe a better question is: which "Christian" woman would you think of—a white American evangelical who lives in Kansas, a Brazilian Catholic from the favelas or perhaps an African American Lutheran from Alabama? Would you think of yourself as a typical example of a Christian woman (if you were born into a Christian family)? You can probably already see how difficult it would be to say something about the broad category of "Christian woman."

The same is true with "Muslim woman." The term "Muslim woman" is an abstract category and it does not say anything about the complex lives of women living in societies where Islam is the predominant religion. Women who are lumped together under this term live in a vast geography that includes Asia-Pacific, North and Sub-Saharan Africa, the Middle East, Europe and Americas. They come from widely different historical, cultural, political, economic, sectarian, national, ethnic, linguistic and other backgrounds. According to Pew Research Center, 1.57 billion Muslims live in the world today. About 80 percent live in fifty Muslim-majority countries and 20 percent live as minorities. There are sizeable Muslim minorities in India (161 million), China (22 million) and Russia (16 million). In other words, except from being born into Muslim parents, there may be very little in common between a woman from Afghanistan and a woman from India.

WHO PRODUCES THE KNOWLEDGE ABOUT MUSLIM WOMAN? EXAMINING IMPERIAL POLITICS AND CORPORATE MEDIA

Power is critical to knowledge production and representations are not neutral, objective depictions of the world (Hall). The representations of Muslim women are not free from power dynamics and politics. Various scholars have shown how the representations of Muslim women in Europe (and later, the United States) have emerged in a particular historical context within a specific imperialist political paradigm (Abu-Lughod; Ahmed; Kahf).

European colonialism (from fifteenth-century to the end of World War II) had a huge impact on all countries where Muslims are a majority either by direct colonization or indirect influence and control. The borders in the Middle East were drawn by the British and French in their own interests during the First World War. Egypt and Pakistan were British colonies, Algeria a French colony, Indonesia a former Dutch colony, Malaysia a former British colony, to cite just a few. The imperial powers produced knowledge about these colonies and their populations in order to rule the natives and justify their domination of foreign lands. Knowledge about these countries was, thus, produced from the perspective of the imperial powers (Said; Kumar), leaving out local knowledges or modes of self-identification. One common way of justifying domination is to depict the colonized as lesser, morally and intellectually inferior people, and conversely the colonizer as civilized people at the higher stages of human progression with the burden to civilize the "primitive" people. The knowledge produced through travel writing (Mabro), postcards (Alloula), literary and artistic work (Kahf), photographs (Graham-Brown), novels and scientific accounts have depicted Muslim women from an imperial perspective, showing women either in need of emancipation and imperial intervention or exotic sex objects. In other words, the imperial power showed only one side of the picture and concealed its own role in disempowering women. For example, Lord Cromer, the British Consul-General of Egypt from 1883 to 1907, declared that Islam "degraded" women while Christianity "elevated" them. For him practice of veiling was the evidence of Islam's degradation of women. Yet, he did not invest in education and refused to fund the training of women doctors in Egypt, and at the same time opposed women's suffrage in England (Ahmed 30-32; qtd.in Abu-Lughod 33).

Little seems to have changed in the past century. Following the World War II, colonialism took on new forms as the US emerged as the new global imperial power. Scholars pointed to the US invasion of Afghanistan in 2001 as an example of justifying military intervention by deploying the old colonial language of liberating the Muslim women from their oppressive cultures (Abu-Lughod; Mahmood). Abu-Lughod notes how the language of "saving the Muslim women" makes women's own work toward gender equality in Muslim societies invisible and conceals the cultural oppression, violence and discrimination women experience in Western societies.

Today, television programs, news media, magazine articles, blogs, textbooks, academic articles, conferences, publishing houses, bookstores are all part of an immense process of producing knowledge about Muslim women. If the imperial politics is one filter through which knowledge is produced, corporate media and journalistic routines are another that shape the ways in which we learn about Muslim women. Furthermore, there is a substantial body of research that shows that the media coverage of international affairs align with US foreign policy interests (Andersen; Herman and Chomsky) that center on the control of oil in the Middle East.

In popular representations, Muslim women are seen in stereotypical stock photos of the veil, burqa and headscarf most of the time. The practices of headcovering are rarely contextualized within a specific location (village, city, region or country) or to a particular group (defined by ethnicity, denomination, and class background). The struggles and debates around these sartorial symbols in Muslim countries are not part of the picture; rather what we see is an essentialized image of Muslim women as the victims of culture and tradition. Yet in Turkey and Tunisia, some women have been fighting to uphold their rights to cover their hair, opposing their families and governments to freely express their religious observance. In Iran, they fight against forced headcover and take it off whenever the opportunity presents itself. There is no single meaning to the headscarf, veil or burqa.

In addition to the absence of multiple forms of dress worn by women in various geographies and demographic groups, accomplished women from Muslim countries rarely exist in the media and other popular representations. Stories about feminist activism in Muslim societies remain invisible leaving the impression that women's lives have remained unchanged throughout centuries. Yet, vibrant feminist movements, inspired both by secular or religious approaches, have been actively and passionately working to improve women's lives in Malaysia, Turkey, Egypt, Afghanistan, Morocco and Iran among others. Sisters in Islam (in Malaysia) and Revolutionary Association of the Women of Afghanistan (RAWA) are well known for their women's rights activism. These movements and organizations also have many male supporters.

Of course, oppression and its sources are multiple, including the histories of colonization, war, current neoliberal global economy, authoritarian regimes (some supported by the Western governments) and religious extremism. These are the sources of structural oppression that have deeply affected both women's and men's lives in both Muslim and non-Muslim societies all over the world.

WHO TO TURN TO FOR KNOWLEDGE ABOUT "MUSLIM WOMAN"?

If popular representations and the knowledge that we can gain from the mainstream media is filtered through imperial politics and commercial interests, who shall we then turn to if we want to learn about the lives of women in Muslim societies? Here, I would advocate that as long as we evaluate the information and its sources with a critical attitude, it does not matter who we turn to. The main challenge is to look for different perspectives, and critically analyze and contextualize these ideas.

Let us assume that you are interested in hearing what women born into Muslim parents think about Islam in the X city of Country Y, and you decide to go and ask women themselves. The Islam you will hear about from a professional or academic woman may be pretty different from what you will hear from a working class woman. You may be surprised to find out that some of the denigrating views about Islam and the Muslims are reproduced among Muslim women themselves. Some will own Islam wholeheartedly and tell you how politicians and extremists corrupt their religion for worldly gains. Others will be members of the extremist and fundamentalist movements. Some will tell you what they think you want to hear. Any answer that you will get will depend on the type of question you ask and the context of interaction. There is no single "Muslim" voice, and each Muslim woman will speak from their own social, cultural and political standpoint in society; as an example see the documentary *(Un)Veiled: Muslim Women Talk about Hijab*. Asking Muslim women is not about "finding authenticity." It is about making their perspectives visible and thereby disrupting the power relations in the current system of representations.

There are three yardsticks to evaluate the knowledge you encounter about Muslim women whether it is an academic book, a commentary, a documentary, a memoir, a novel, or an exhibition. First is contextualization. Look at the language and content. Is the language generalized to the vast majority of Muslim women without reference to any particular geographic location, or social or cultural group? How does the text sound if the terms "Islam" and "Muslims" are replaced with terms such as "Christianity/Christians," or "Judaism/Jews"? Is there any reference to the history of the region as well as domestic and international political contexts? What is included and what is left out?

Second, locate the author(s) within the network of competing arguments and politics. What do debates among different readers and scholars tell you about the political background or motivations of the author? Try to identify the main argument: what the author is trying to promote and how the "knowledge" is organized for that purpose. How is the work funded? Would the sponsors expect a certain kind of outcome or argument?

Finally, try to figure out your own position vis-à-vis the text by analyzing your own reading and response to it. Ask self-reflexive questions such as: Who am I according to this text? What does this text assume about me? Where do I stand in relation to the politics surrounding this work? If I have a strong response, where does it come from? What does my own culture tell me?

Contextualization, critical reading, and self-reflexivity are some of the best keys to process, evaluate and produce knowledge that come closest to doing justice to the complex lives of women and men living not only in Muslim majority societies but all around the world.

HOW TO CREATE KNOWLEDGE FOR BETTER COMMUNICATION AND PEACE?

In Europe and North America, most material about Muslim women (books, TV shows, news articles, exhibitions, and magazines) position their readers as the members of the "Western" culture and readers are rarely invited to critically engage with the binary between the "West" and the "non-West." In fact, the category of the "West" (or Western woman) is as problematic as the category of "Muslim woman" as it assumes a false commonality among people (or women) in the so-called Western world and masks the common problems that women both in the "West" and the "non-West" face. Identity categories such as Western, European, American, or Muslim are products of historical and political struggles. The categories, as well as their meanings, change when cultural contexts and time change. We should question not only the knowledge and discourse about "Muslim woman" and "Islamic culture" but also the discourse about "Western culture."

I propose that to relate to women living far away from us, we should focus on similarities. Irrespective of religion and culture, women face similar problems all over the world today. A woman working at minimum wage at Walmart and a woman working at a sweatshop (i.e. a textile factory) in Bangladesh face the same problems created by the neoliberal global economy and suffer from structural inequality and poverty in spite of their hard work. A fancy blouse that a woman wears in London, might be touched by the hands of a Bangladeshi woman worker. As Launius and Hassel put it "in order to understand how individual social locations are shaped, it is important to see how systems of privilege and oppression [based on nationality, gender, race and class among others] intersect (114).

Only when we see ourselves not as members of a certain society and culture (which we assume to be better than the others) but as life-long learners and members of a global community of equals, only then we can focus our attention to producing knowledge for better communication, peace and understanding; not for power, profit and domination. We can fight gender injustice together without creating cultural hierarchies among each other. Questioning the category of "Muslim woman" by contextualization, critical reading and self-reflexivity provides a good start to challenge the role of imperial politics and the corporate media in knowledge production.

WORKS CITED

Abu-Lughod, Lila. *Do Muslim Women Need Saving?* Harvard UP, 2013.

Alloula, Malek. *The Colonial Harem.* Translated by Myrna Godzich and Wlad Godzich, U of Minnesota P, 1986.

Ahmed, Leila. *A Quiet Revolution: The Veil's Resurgence, from the Middle East to America.* Yale UP, 2011.

Andersen, Robin. "The Power of Images at Times of War." *The Political Economy of Media and Power*, Edited by Jeffery Klaehn, Peter Lang, 2010, pp. 161–79.

Graham-Brown, Sarah. *Images of Women: The Portrayal of Women in the Photography of the Middle East, 1860-1950.* Quartet Books, 1988.

Hall, Stuart. Ed. *Representation: Cultural Representations and Signifying Practices.* Sage/Open University, 1997.

Herman, Edward S., and Noam Chomsky. *Manufacturing Consent: The Political Economy of the Mass Media.* Pantheon Books, 1988.

Kahf, Mohja. *Western Representations of the Muslim Woman: From Termagant to Odalisque.* U of Texas P, 1999.

Kumar, Deepa. *Islamophobia and the Politics of Empire.* Haymarket Books, 2012.

Lauinus, Christie and Holly Hassel. *Threshold Concepts in Women's and Gender Studies.* Routledge, 2015.

Mabro, Judy. *Veiled Half-Truths: Western Travellers' Perceptions of Middle Eastern Women.* I.B. Tauris, 1991.

Mahmood, Saba. "Religion, Feminism and Empire: The New Ambassadors of Islamophobia." *Feminism, Sexuality, and the Return of Religion*, Edited by Linda Martin Alcoff and John D. Caputo, Indiana UP, 2011, pp. 77–102.

Mapping the Global Muslim Population. Pew Research Center, 7 Oct. 2009, www.pewforum.org/2009/10/07/mapping-the-global-muslim-population/.

Said, Edward. *Orientalism.* Penguin Books, 1977.

(Un)veiled: Muslim Women Talk About Hijab. Directed by Ines Hofmann Kanna, Documentary Educational Resources, 2007.

51. • *Meda Chesney-Lind*

MEAN GIRLS, BAD GIRLS, OR JUST GIRLS:
Corporate Media Hype and the Policing of Girlhood (new)

Meda Chesney-Lind, a professor of women's studies at the University of Hawai'i, is nationally recognized for her work on women and crime; her testimony before Congress resulted in national support of gender-responsive programming for girls in the juvenile justice system. Her recent book on girls' use of violence, *Fighting for Girls* (coedited with Nikki Jones), won an award from the National Council on Crime and Delinquency for "focusing America's attention on the complex problems of the criminal and juvenile justice systems." The following article was written specifically for this collection.

It seems as though the bad news about American girls just keeps coming, at least if you watch television or read the papers. Girls are going "wild," girls are "mean" (and certainly meaner than boys), and girls are even getting as violent as boys. Current media coverage of modern girlhood, at least in the United States, is virtually all grim, and it is also clear as to the source of the problem—girls are getting more like boys and that is bad news for girls.

As an example, on June 2001, an ABC report on trends in gang membership maintained that girls are "catching up with boys in this one area," "joining gangs for the same reasons as boys," and doing the same activities as boys: selling drugs and committing murder (Gibbs). Likewise, on July 28, 2009, New Jersey Attorney General Anne Milgram announced that law enforcement officials dismantled an all female–led, gang-involved narcotics ring. Dubbing the investigation "Operation Bloodette," Milgram went on to state that she wished "this was not one [glass] ceiling women were breaking" and that "women are taking over dominant roles in traditionally male-dominated gangs" (Read). Finally, in March 2006, ABC's *Good Morning America* contributed to these stories with its series titled, "Why Girls

Are Getting More Violent: Violence Is on the Rise among High School Girls" (ABC). One segment was specifically labeled "Girls Are Beating and Bullying."

This last headline introduces a theme closely related to the news media's obsession with girls' violence—a focus on "mean" girls. The manipulative and damaging characteristics of girls' social worlds have been the subject of high-profile bestselling books like *Odd Girl Out* (Simmons), and *Queen Bees and Wannabes* (Wiseman). These, in turn, spawned hit movies, like *Mean Girls*, and also innumerable articles. *The New York Times Magazine* ran a cover story titled, "Girls Just Want to Be Mean" where the author noted "it is not just boys who can bully." (Talbot 24), and other media outlets quickly jumped on the bandwagon, running stories titled "Girl Bullies Don't Leave Black Eyes, Just Agony" (Elizabeth), "She Devils" (Metcalf), and "Just Between Us Girls: Not Enough Sugar, Too Much Spite" (*Pittsburgh Post-Gazette*).

Books like *Odd Girl Out* and *Queen Bees and Wannabes* all rely on recent psychological research on aggression, particularly what is called "relational," "covert," or "indirect" aggression (Underwood et al. 248). The concept of relational or covert aggression relates to a repertoire of passive and/or indirect behaviors (e.g., rolling eyes, spreading rumors, ostracizing, and ignoring), used with the "intent to hurt or harm others" (Crick and Grotpeter), and thus the concept expands the range of behaviors that are considered aggressive in nature.

By identifying a "relational," "covert," or "indirect" aggression, rather than physical type of aggression, researchers argued that they shattered the myth of the nonaggressive girl (Bjorkqvist and Niemela). These researchers note that girls are as aggressive as boys, when these indirect aggressions are considered. In fact, they claimed that they were not only shattering myths but that they were unraveling years of gender bias in which male researchers tended to only look at male problems. Bjorkqvist and Niemela argued that researchers, "the majority being males, . . . may, for personal reasons, find male aggression easier to understand and a more appealing object of study" (5).

While this characterization of the "discovery" has been widely accepted, there are reasons to be a bit more skeptical that this concept benefits girls. First, does this aggression really challenge stereotypes and myths about girls? Thinking about the behaviors included in relational aggression, this research is arguing that girls and women are manipulative, sneaky, mean-spirited, and backstabbing—hardly new ideas, which may, in fact, be one reason that the public and the media embraced them so quickly.

More importantly, the literature on relational aggression does not consistently support the notion that girls specialize in these forms of aggression while boys are more physically aggressive (Chesney-Lind et al.). For example, University of Georgia researchers randomly selected 745 sixth-graders from nine middle schools across six school districts in northeast Georgia. The student participants took computer surveys each spring semester for seven years, from sixth to twelfth grade (Orpinas et al.).

Key findings included the following. First, covert and relational aggression is extremely common; 96 percent of the students who participated in the study reported at least one act of relational aggression (meaning basically everyone is mean sometimes), and 92.3 percent of boys and 94.3 percent of girls said they'd been the victim of such an attack at one point during the study period. Second, they found that boys admitted to significantly more acts of relational aggression than girls did, and girls were more likely to be victims. Finally, and of the greatest significance, of the meanest kids (the ones who fell into the "high" relational aggression group), 66.7 percent were boys and 33.3 percent were girls (Orpinas et al.).

So while the media focuses on the "meanness" of girls, the reality is that boys might be meaner than girls. But what of the media hype regarding those "bad" girls who are using violence, including those in gangs? Are girls really seeking violent equality with their male counterparts, as the media insists? There is also an important racial element to this discussion. Stock media imagery of girls, particularly girls in gangs, tends to suggest that these girls are just as menacing as their male counterparts. *Newsweek* did this by using a stereotypical headline, "Girls Will Be Girls," while showing a picture of a black girl holding a gun and wearing a mask, with the subtitle "Some girls carry guns. Others hide razor blades in their mouths" (Leslie and Biddle 44). In essence, black and Latina violence is positioned in ways that invite a contrast to the assumed "nonviolence" of white girls.

Media accounts of this "problem" also are caused by girls trying to act like boys. There's nothing new about this argument, by the way. In the 1920s, opponents of women's suffrage fretted about increases in "intensely immoral" behavior among the "modern age of girls" and, in the 1930s, commentators contended that "women becoming more criminally minded" as a result of "the fight for Emancipation" (Pollock 84). By the 1970s, the argument was that the second wave of feminism had "caused" a surge in women's serious crimes (Chesney-Lind).

The current media backlash to efforts to improve both girls and women's lives, though, has settled on girls' commission of violent crimes, particularly but not always in gangs. Is this true that girls are more violent today than in decades past?

Certain data, which the media tend to rely on heavily, suggest that girls are getting in trouble more often than in the past and also that they are engaged in more serious delinquent behavior. In 1983, arrests of girls accounted for roughly one in five arrests (21.4 percent), but by 2013, girls accounted for nearly one in three juvenile arrests (28.8 percent) (United States, FBI). And while both male and female arrests have been declining in recent years, arrests of juvenile boys decreased far more steeply, decreasing 26.5 percent during the first decade of the twenty-first century compared to a decrease in girls' arrests of only 15.4 percent. The much vaulted "crime drop," at least among youth, was really a crime drop in just boys' official delinquency.

Data on juvenile courts suggest that the number of girls' cases referred to the court has also increased. The National Center for Juvenile Justice noted that most of the surge in male and female delinquency cases occurred between 1985 and 1997. During that time period, the reported increase in cases involving girls grew 97 percent versus a 52 percent increase for boys (Puzzanchera and Hockenberry 14). And the gendered pattern continues in the current period; between 1997 and 2011, the male delinquency caseload declined by 38 percent compared to a female caseload that decreased by only 22 percent. As a result, in 2011 females accounted for 28 percent of the delinquency caseload, up from only 19 percent in 1985 (Hockenberry and Puzzanchera). Much of this pattern is explained by soaring increases in arrests of girls for simple assault in over the past few decades. While these have recently leveled off, one study of court referrals found that "for females, the largest 1985–2002 increase was in person offense cases (202 percent)" (Snyder and Sickmund 160).

What about other data on girl's violence? The Centers for Disease Control and Prevention in Atlanta has monitored youthful behavior in a national sample of school-age youth in a number of domains (including violence) at regular intervals since 1991 in a biennial survey titled the Youth Risk Behavior Survey. As an example, a review of the data collected over the 1990s and into this century reveals that, although 34.4 percent of girls surveyed in 1991 said that they had been in a physical fight in the previous year; slightly over half (50.2 percent) of the boys reported fighting. Two decades later, 2011, 24.4 percent of girls and 40.7 percent of boys said they had been in a physical fight in the last year ("Youth Risk"). In essence, the data show that girls have always been more violent than their stereotype suggests but also that girls' violence, at least by their own accounts, has been decreasing, not increasing.

To further explore these issues about girl's self-reported violence and likelihood of arrest, Stevens et al. used several national self-report data sets to compare self-reported behavior with self-reported arrests in two different time periods (1980 and 2000) (Stevens et al.). This research found that girls who admitted to simple assault in 1980 had about a one-in-four chance of being charged with a crime, compared to girls in 2000, who had about a three-in-four chance of arrest. Furthermore, black girls in 2000 were nearly seven times more likely as their 1980 counterparts to be charged with a crime.

In short, while girls had long reported that they were acting out violently, their arrests, particularly in the 1960s and 1970s, did not necessarily reflect that reality. Instead, girls' arrests tended to emphasize petty and status offenses (like running away from home); by the 1990s, that had changed dramatically, as more girls were arrested, particularly for such seemingly "masculine" offenses as simple assault—and this pattern was particularly pronounced among black girls.

Research increasingly suggests that these shifts in girls' arrest patterns are not products of a change in girls' behavior, with girls getting "more" violent. Rather, girls are being more heavily policed, particularly at home and in school (Chesney-Lind and Irwin). Girls are being arrested for assault because of arguments with their parents, often their mothers (Buzawa and Hotaling), or for "other assault" for fighting in school because of new zero-tolerance policies enacted after the Columbine shootings (*Criminalizing*). In decades past, this violence would have been ignored or labeled a status offense, like being "incorrigible" or a "person in need of supervision." Now an arrest is made.

Taking a global look at the American obsession with bad, violent, and mean girls is also important. Consider that the work of two most recent recipients of the Nobel Peace Prize (Malala Yousafzai and Kallash Satyarthi) reflects a growing global focus on girls' rights, especially their right to education and to be safe from abuse, particularly physical abuse, sexual abuse, and early marriages ("Nobel Peace"). This international concern about the extensiveness of girl's victimizations and girls' rights stands in stark contrast to the discourse on girls in the past twenty-five years in the United States, where both media and policymakers have been expressing concern about the growing numbers of "bad" and "violent" girls coming into the juvenile justice system. Clearly, it is time to stop bashing girls in the United States and start entering the global conversation about improving their lives and futures. Our girls are not getting worse—they are getting short changed.

WORKS CITED

Bennett, Samantha. "Just Between Us Girls: Not Enough Sugar, Too Much Spite." *Pittsburgh-Post Gazette*, 5 June 2002, pp. 3–5.

Bjorkqvist, Kaj, and Pirkko Niemela. *Of Mice and Women: Aspects of Female Aggression.* Academic Press, 1992.

Buzawa, Eve S., and Gerald T. Hotaling. "The Impact of Relationship Status, Gender, and Minor Status in the Police Response to Domestic Assaults." *Victims and Offenders*, vol. 1, 2006, pp. 323–60.

Chesney-Lind, Meda. "Women and Crime: A Review of the Literature on the Female Offender." *Signs: Journal of Women in Culture and Society*, vol. 12, no. 1, 1986, pp. 78–96.

———, Merry Morash, and Katherine Irwin. "Policing Girlhood? Relational Aggression and Violence Prevention." *Youth Violence and Juvenile Justice*, vol. 5, no. 3, 2007, pp. 328–45.

Chesney-Lind, Meda, and Katherine Irwin. *Beyond Bad Girls: Gender, Violence and Hype.* Routledge, 2008.

Crick, Nicki R., and Jennifer K. Grotpeter. "Relational Aggression, Gender, and Social-Psychological Adjustment." *Child Development*, vol. 66, 1995, pp. 710–22.

Criminalizing the Classroom: The Over-Policing of New York City Schools. New York Civil Liberties Union/American Civil Liberties Union, 2007.

Elizabeth, Jane. "Girl Bullies Don't Leave Black Eyes, Just Agony." *Pittsburgh Post-Gazette*, 10 April 2002, p. A1.

Gibbs, B. "Number of Girls in Gangs Increasing." *ABC*, 19 June 2001, abclocal.go.com/wtvd/features/061901_CF_girlsgangs.html.

Hockenberry, S., and C. M. Puzzanchera. *Juvenile Court Statistics 2011.* National Center for Juvenile Justice, 2014.

Leslie, C., N. Biddle, D. Rosenberg, and J. Wayne. "Girls Will Be Girls." *Newsweek*, 2 Aug. 1993, p. 44.

Metcalf, F. "She Devils." *Courier Mail* [Queensland], 22 June 2002, p. L6.

"Nobel Peace Prize Winners Malala Yousufzai and Kailash Satyarthi Make South Asia Proud." *Pakistan*, UNICEF, www.unicef.org/pakistan/media_9026.htm.

Orpinas, P., et al. "Gender Differences in Trajectories of Relational Aggression Perpetration and Victimization from Middle to High School." *Aggressive Behavior*, vol. 41, 2014, pp. 401–12.

Pollock, Joycelyn. *Women's Crimes, Criminology, and Corrections.* Waveland, 2014.

Puzzanchera, C. M., and S. Hockenberry. *Juvenile Court Statistics 2010.* National Center for Juvenile Justice, 2013.

Read, Phillip. "'Operation Bloodette' Nets 43 Members of Female-Led Drug Ring." *The Star-Ledger*, New Jersey On-Line, 28 July 2009, www.nj.com/news/index.ssf/2009/07/operation_bloodette_nets_43_me.html.

Sikes, Gini. *8 Ball Chicks.* Anchor Books, 1997.

Simmons, Rachel. *Odd Girl Out: The Hidden Culture of Aggression in Girls.* Harcourt, 2002.

Snyder, H. N., and M. Sickmund. *Juvenile Offenders and Victims: 2006 National Report (NCJ 178257).* United States, Department of Justice, Office of Justice Programs, Office of Juvenile Justice and Delinquency Prevention, 2006.

Stevens, Tia, et al. "Are Girls Getting Tougher, or Are We Tougher on Girls? Probability of Arrest and Juvenile Court Oversight in 1980 and 2000." *Justice Quarterly*, vol. 28, no. 5, 2011, pp. 719–44.

Talbot, Margaret. "Girls Just Want to Be Mean." *The New York Times Magazine*, 24 Feb. 2002, pp. 24–64.

Underwood, Marion K., et al. "Top Ten Challenges for Understanding Gender and Aggression in Children: Why Can't We All Just Get Along?" *Social Development*, vol. 10, 2001, pp. 248–66.

United States Federal Bureau of Investigation. *Crime in the United States—2013.* Government Printing Office, 2014.

"Why Girls Are Getting More Violent: Violence is on the Rise Among High School Girls." *Good Morning America*, ABC, 11 Mar. 2006.

Wiseman, Rosalind. *Queen Bees and Wannabees: Helping Your Daughter Survive Cliques, Gossip, Boyfriends and other Realities of Adolescence.* Crown Publishers, 2002.

"Youth Risk Behavior Surveillance—1991–2001." *CDC Surveillance Summaries,* United States, Department of Health and Human Services, Centers for Disease Control, 1992–2012.

52. • *Ian Capulet*

WITH REPS LIKE THESE:
Bisexuality and Celebrity Status (2010)

Ian Capulet is the founder and editor-in-chief of CEFashion.net and a long-time blogger. The following article was published in the *Journal of Bisexuality* (2010).

Various forces of erasure continue to belittle the bisexual cause, promoting ignorance of and skepticism about the orientation. This antagonism ranges old-fashioned thick headedness to questionable research practices, a principal case being Gerulf Rieger and J. Michael Bailey's outrageous 2005 study, "Sexual Arousal Patterns of Bisexual Men."[1] The conclusions of such flawed studies and the rhetoric of bigots, though invalid, continually persuade people to doubt bisexuals.

Although awareness efforts performed by lesbian, gay, bisexual, trans-gender (LGBT) organizations undoubtedly help overcome the obstacles faced by homosexuals (gays and lesbians), such activism neglects to address bisexual-specific problems. To this day, many lack the very concept of bisexuality as a third sexual orientation. Even more seriously, others deny, with assuredness, the very existence of bisexuals. Dr. Ruth Westheimer, the famous radio and television personality, is a perfect example of such deniers: "There really is no such thing as being bisexual," she announced in a 2005 advice column (Keegan, 2005). Bisexuals cannot begin work on developing a political presence[2] as long as people continue to equate their ontological status with that of unicorns.

Pessimism about the future of bisexual causes might be tempered by a tepid hope coming from, of all places, the realm of popular culture. In the last 10 years, there has been a clear increase in chatter about bisexuality in Western, predominantly American popular culture. The impetus for such growing reference comes from the perceived increase of celebrities who find men and women sexually attractive. With the rising expectation of transparency to the lives of the famous, more celebrities are being identified, and self-identifying, as bisexuals than ever before. News of someone's bisexuality is not cornered off on page 9 or in idle gossip columns—celebrities unabashedly call themselves bisexuals. These self-identifications, in particular, tend to ignite media frenzy. For instance, Megan Fox's disclosure of her bisexuality in a June 2009 interview ("Megan Fox Interview," 2009) was subsequently reproduced and referred to in a dozen other magazines, hundreds of electronic news articles and thousands of posts on web forums and blogs. What once might have remained a private matter or secluded to Hollywood gossip circles now is an object of national discourse.

Without a doubt, then, this swell of publicity commits some level of presence to bisexuals. Our starlets and beauties have no truck with mythical unicorns: they breathe, pose and sleep with men and women. Short of contentiously arguing that self-proclaimed bisexuals are just gay people unable to "fully" come out,[3] one must admit bisexuals roam among us—at least in Manhattan and on Sunset Boulevard. Furthermore, because these celebrities carry allure and clout, one can imagine how other forces of erasure will soon lose their footing. Whether motivated by humanitarian goals or even purely selfish ones, these celebrities could easily bring bisexual concerns to the table of political discussion.

Unfortunately, the increase in celebrities identifying as bisexuals has yet to engender any noticeable political changes. None of these celebrities has so much as issued a press release, publicly lobbied or even marched alongside a group of bisexuals. This is alarming because celebrities today routinely endorse all kinds of political fronts, ranging from the call for a cure to breast cancer to entire political parties. Some even get their hands dirty: Sean Penn flying down to New Orleans just after Hurricane Katrina hit. In addition, a multitude of famous people consistently speak out against same-sex marriage discrimination, "Don't ask, Don't tell," and so on. Although these campaigns confer a message of "Love knows no boundaries" that applies to all sexualities, bisexuality included, no celebrity has yet endorsed a group whose focus is bisexuality, for example, the Bisexual Institute. The fact that no celebrity has yet to champion bisexual rights is glaring in light of all other endorsements.

[. . .]

Although one might argue that not enough time has passed for awareness about bisexual celebrities to positively influence policy, or for them to gather support themselves, there is reason to believe very little will politically ever come of these celebrities and their sexuality. From reading the almost daily reports of these celebrities' antics, analyzing their projected image in photos and video and examining what they say about being bisexual, I believe they actually damage the greater bisexual cause. This damage manifests as one of the greater erasive force challenging bisexuals today: stereotype reinforcement. To varying degrees, the celebrities listed below, and others left unlisted, contribute to public misconceptions of bisexual and therefore make bisexuals seem unworthy of serious political consideration.

The cascading response of the media only further cements these stereotypes in the minds of Americans. As is discussed, those at the helms of media and news outlets stand to profit by appealing to the interests of heterosexual males, not to promote progressive issues. The fact that their services in effect reinforce stereotypes about bisexuals will never faze these producers. In fact, as is shown, they very well profit from it. Furthermore, media frenzies themselves paint picture of bisexuality as source of social

status or publicity, rather than a potential avenue for empowerment and greater visibility. In recognizing who and what institutions exacerbate their political struggles, bisexual activists need to establish a contrast between everyday bisexuals and these self-identifying celebrities turned de facto representatives.

The celebrities the public has come to associate with bisexuality share a number of commonalities.[4] For one, as noted previously, the public associates these particular famous people with bisexuality as a result of a mass-media response to actions and statements regarding their sexuality, especially in the cases of succinct self-identifications.[5] This very response, which transcends the boundaries of print, digital publication and television, is responsible for fixing celebrities as referents for bisexuality in the public eye.

A second quality common to these celebrities is that they all work in show business; in other words, they are famous for being entertainers. To my knowledge, no politician, political activist, industrious entrepreneur, poet laureate, acclaimed author or Olympic athlete recently experienced such spotlighting for publicly disclosing their bisexuality.[6]

Another commonality is that they are all women. Although some famous male entertainers have indeed come out as bisexuals, their sexual status never becomes a subject of media frenzy. For instance, Billie Joe Armstrong of the alternative rock band Green Day admitted, "I always have been bisexual [despite never dating a man]" in a 1995 issue of *The Advocate*; it is safe to say that this detail about him rarely enters popular discussion today (Wieder, 1995, p. 3).[7] Recently, the more actively bisexual Alan Cummings stated without ambiguity that he always has labeled himself a bisexual (Walsh, 2007, p. 2). A Google search for *alan cummings oasis interview bisexual*, as of July 2009, retrieves a meager 7,000 hits (compared the more than 60,000 that comes from *megan fox esquire bisexual*).

[. . .]

Finally, all of the celebrities below are also popular sex symbols for heterosexual men's consumption. Each posed for model shoots featured in the likes of

Maxim, GQ, and so on, as well as assumed provocative roles in either music videos or film. They also often entertain questions during interviews where they openly discuss their sexual habits and experiences—in fact, the celebrities' self-identifications often come out in these conversations.

Succinctly then, the celebrities in question are female sex symbols in the entertainment industry who received a massive media response following their admission of bisexuality. These commonalities are not accidental: media and news outlets only stand to profit from sensationalist stories about women that already attract media attention. As anyone knows, being bisexual, for whatever reason, generates a lot of sensationalism. Before further investigating the connection between young starlets' sexual orientations, sensationalism and the media's interests, it is crucial to further appreciate the "brand" of bisexuality these celebrities promote through their actions and words. Unfortunately, as stated before, this brand often comprises stereotypes.

At a concert in Palms Springs, California, Joanne Angelina Germanotta, better known as Lady Gaga, revealed to the audience that her hit single "Poker Face" was a lyrical account of a real-life sexual encounter. She went on to explain how, on one occasion, she found herself in bed with a man but secretly wished she had been with a woman instead. She then donned her "poker face" to make it through the sex act—in other words, she faked interest. The crowd went wild upon hearing this ("Lady Gaga Entertains Thousands," 2009).

It was not until her interview for the May 2009 issue of *Rolling Stone* magazine that she discussed her sexuality more directly (Hiatt, 2009, p. 4). Her bisexuality is something that historically upsets her boyfriends: "The fact that I'm into women, they're all intimidated by it." Soon after the publication of her revealing interview, the music video for her following single "LoveGame" appeared. The video features several scenes where Lady Gaga lasciviously entrances a number of scantily clad male dancers before moving on to seduce a female police officer. Her interactions with the femme officer escalate inside a glass booth, the walls of which quickly fog up from all the restlessness inside. Needless to say, the video claimed more than five million views on YouTube within a couple of months of its drop ("LoveGame Music Video," 2006).

[. . .]

When paired with Lady Gaga's interpretation, the premise of the song is clear: a bisexual woman (Gaga) slept with a man, not because she wanted him sexually, but because she wants something from him. Pop song lyrics might not usually warrant such close analysis, but when they are among the few public statements on the bisexual experience, they gain significance. If we understand the song as an account of a past sexual situation, and assume Lady Gaga and the first-person subject of the song as the same, then it says something about Lady Gaga's character: she is not above using sex to squeeze someone. Needless to say, this is the oldest cliché about bisexuals in the book—Lady Gaga seems to pride herself in her ability to be manipulative.

"She don't got to love nobody," a line in the chorus of "Poker Face," speaks to Lady Gaga's own characterization of her bisexuality. In the *Rolling Stone* interview, Lady Gaga explains her attraction to women as "only physical" while admitting earlier she loved her current partner, a man. Coupled with the fact that she has never openly dated a woman, Lady Gaga appears happy to sleep around with women, but never lets the hook-ups develop into commitments. Any bisexual can vouch for how often homosexuals and heterosexuals refuse to get involved with a bisexual for fear of being "used for just sex." Stating she wants only sex from women, Lady Gaga adds to the image of bisexuals as being "slippery" and noncommittal.

[. . .]

Like Lady Gaga, the actress Megan Fox recently came out as a bisexual in a magazine interview. In the June 2009 issue of *Esquire*, Megan Fox announced her sexuality decisively, but then quickly qualified her situation. "I have no question in my mind about being bisexual," she starts boldly, "But

I'm also a hypocrite. I would never date a girl who was bisexual, because that means they also sleep with men, and men are so dirty that I'd never want to sleep with a girl who had slept with a man" (Katz, 2009, p. 3). Before the issue even hit the stands, this portion of the interview appeared in articles on TMZ.com, numerous tabloids and an innumerable amount of blogs.

Taken at face value, her qualification tells us that Megan Fox is only interested in dating lesbians—men are somehow "dirty" and their dirt brushes off onto the women they sleep with like some sort of sexually transmitted tinge. However, Megan Fox does not date only lesbians; in fact by almost all accounts Megan Fox dates exclusively men. Besides one occasion when she courted a female stripper, news about Megan Fox's dating habits primarily center on her wishy-washy relationship with actor Brian Austin Green. She has not dissuaded this impression.

This is not the first instance of Fox talking out of both sides of her mouth about her sexual preferences. In the July 2009 issue of *British GQ*, Fox suggests that "[p]eople assume I'm really overtly sexually aggressive and that I'm this wild child. And I'm not like that at all" (Kirby, 2009, p. 4). This statement flies in the face of what she said in an interview with *E! Online*: "I'm young and have a lot of hormones—I'm always in the mood!" (Finn, 2008, p. 2). It also contradicts an earlier 2008 interview where she confessed to repeated attempts to coax a stripper with gifts and sexual suggestions. Of course, Megan Fox also said in the 2008 interview that she could see herself "in a relationship with a girl,"[8] an idea she will no longer entertain.

By continuing to submit contradictory statements about her sexual preferences, Megan Fox makes it hard to trust anything she says as serious. Being that she received such attention for coming out definitively as a bisexual, her contradictions only serve to reinforce the stereotype of bisexuals as unreliable. Bisexuals should and do answer questions such as "Do you find both men and women sexually attractive?" not only with ease, but without stipulating bizarre qualifications let alone inconsistencies. As for the particular inconsistency about whether

Megan Fox constantly itches for sex, the various magazine covers and shoots featuring her topless and licking her lips certainly makes her seem far from sexually idle.

Interest in the bisexuality of Thien Thanh Thi Nguyen, better known by the Internet moniker Tila Tequila, was stoked in a different way. Rather than disclosing her orientation in flashy interviews, Tila Tequila has always worked to let her bisexuality be known; it is a crucial, implicit aspect of her image, as well as one of her strongest selling points.[9]

To Ms. Tequila's merit, she has been consistent in her advertisement of herself as a bisexual. Old copies of her web page on the MySpace Network, the social network she used to propel herself to fame, include several references to prior relationships of hers with men and women (Nguyen, 2006). In addition, since the premier of her reality television program *A Shot at Love*—itself a contest between men and women for Ms. Tequila's affections—several online entertainment news Websites regularly release reports of her dating men and women, albeit always of the famous variety. Despite accusations following the show's season finale that Tila faked her sexuality for fame, she continues to adamantly assert her love of men and women. "If you're faking bisexuality, then you'd be one of those Girls Gone Wild girls. I'm not one of those fake ones," as she put it bluntly in *King Mag* (Leu, 2007, p. 2). Finally, more can be said of her efforts in queer activism than of the likes of Megan Fox and Lady Gaga: she recently published an open letter to President Obama, urging him to repeal the "Don't Ask, Don't Tell" policy as it discriminates against queers (Nguyen, 2009).

[. . .]

The success of her reality program *A Shot at Love* largely relied on her image as an aggressive sexpot. The very premise of the show—put 16 heterosexual males and 16 lesbians in the same house and make them vie for a chance to date Tila—forces the audience to view Tila as an object of desire. Of course, she is no idle object: just from watching a few episodes, we see that Tila Tequila enjoys (or at least acts as if she does) watching the contestants fight each other and willingly demean themselves in stupid, often sexist challenges. Like a despot content to watch his or her servants running amuck to meet unreasonable orders, Tila Tequila leaves the impression that being hot and bisexual is license to toy with people.

In addition to disclosing details about her sexuality, Tila Tequila clearly wants to talk about her emotional instability and recklessness. In an early interview for *Import Tuner*, Ms. Tequila ("Up Close and Personal," 2006) admitted to joining a gang in her teens and spoke lightly of how she often engaged other girls in fistfights. She also abused drugs often during these years. . . . She describes herself as "very high strung and suffer from multiple personalities"; a few sentences later, she also admits to suffering from bi-polar disorder. Whether she suffers from mental illness or not, saying so serves Ms. Tequila by eliciting attention and promoting intrigue; the conflation with her bisexuality is an unavoidable consequence.

In a November 2007 interview with eTalk, Tila Tequila describes herself as a positive role model for queer kids who are otherwise scared to come out of the closet. "So many kids who write to me were afraid to come out . . . But now they feel really proud and they say 'So what. Tequila's bisexual, too.' Now it's like a cool thing" (Droganes, 2007, p. 2). Unfortunately, Ms. Tequila is yet another example of active self-promotion as a sexual object. And though sexually empowerment might be found in her selection of a mate from a very attractive pool of willing applicants, Tila Tequila also comes across as manipulative, perhaps even cruel. Finally, unless she openly admits to seeking therapy about the disorders she claims to have, then these disorders come to resemble inalterable character traits—again, ones often associated with bisexuals.

Lindsay Lohan most candidly discussed her sexuality in an interview featured in the December 2008 issue of *Bazaar*. When asked if she considers herself a bisexual, Lindsay Lohan plainly remarked, "Maybe. Yeah." She then clarified her position, "I don't want to classify myself." It was also in this interview where Ms. Lohan coyly admitted the rampant rumors of her dating female disc jockey Samantha Ronson (Heyman,

2009, p. 2). Although not a surprise to most, the confirmation nevertheless appeared on virtually every celebrity gossip blogs and was even referenced later in a *New York Times* article (Newman, 2008, p. 3).

The case for Lindsay Lohan reinforcing bisexual stereotypes is about as clear-cut as they come: she acts on par with a character straight out of a Bret Easton Ellis novel. Ms. Lohan's ex-boyfriend Riley Giles famously stated that Lohan "[is] definitely a nymphomaniac" as evidence of her "addictive personality" ("Ex Calls Lindsay," 2007). Several news reports further detail her rampant promiscuity and disastrous relationships.[10] The American public is well aware of Ms. Lohan's recidivism and notoriously delinquent work ethic, because it has frequently resulted in the delay of much-hyped studio movies ("Lindsay Lohan Arrested," 2007). The media coverage of her numerous vice-filled evenings rivals only that of Britney Spears and her personal catastrophes in 2008; Britney Spears has supposedly since recovered from her unsustainable lifestyle, whereas Lindsay Lohan continues to self-destruct.

[. . .]

One other celebrity comes to mind in discussing bisexuality: the movie star Angelina Jolie. However, I suspect the public hardly thinks of her as an example of the brand of bisexuality popular these days. That is not to say that her sexuality has never been the subject of sensationalism: Aside from her prolific work in Hollywood, where performed provocative and dramatic roles, Ms. Jolie's air of seductiveness ensnares all. Everyone lusts for Angelina—"if women had to choose a female lover, they would want to sleep with Angelina Jolie"—and Angelina lusts for everyone (Wolf, 2009, p. 2). Every biography about her, printed or otherwise, is sure to mention her attraction to "[b]oyish girls, girlish boys, the heavy and the skinny," her fling with Jenny Shimizu, and the numerous interviews where she discusses her love for the feminine and masculine forms ("'Tis the Season," 1997).

She is also, unlike the other bisexuals of Hollywood, an upstanding citizen of the world. Angelina's tally of charitable donations easily exceeds

$10 million. Her work in Pakistan, Uganda and Darfur is well documented, and she is an honored member of United Nations Refugee Agency as well a dozen other humanitarian organizations ("Look to the Stars," 2008). Her kindness appears bottomless, and her contribution to the advancement of human rights is unrivaled in the current Hollywood scene. Of course, neither her acting nor her humanitarianism prevents her from being a loving mother of seven children. She is also a recovered self-injurist (Susman, 2003, p. 2). Still, Angelina's explicit promotion of herself as a bisexual pales to her often discussed humanitarian ideals. As Sarah Warn pointed out in a 2003 AfterEllen.com article, though Angelina Jolie often talks about her "love" for men and women, rarely does she label herself a bisexual (Warn, 2003, p. 3). In fact, by Warn's research, as well as my own, Angelina has never been recorded using *bisexual* to apply to herself—she instead prefers circumlocutions even when asked if she labels herself one or not. The poignant example Warn gave is from the 2003 interview conducted by Barbara Walters: "I consider myself a very sexual person who loves who she loves, whatever sex they may be" (Warn, 2003, p. 3).

All her humanitarian accomplishments aside, Ms. Jolie very rarely supports queer-related organizations or movements, AIDs relief excluded ("Look to the Stars," 2008). Granted, queer issues might seem little more than a civil concern now, and therefore less pressing than tying together emergency funds for African refugees attempting to escape mass starvation and strife. However, Angelina also supports less urgent causes, like the aims of the Daniel Pearl Foundation to "promote cross-cultural understanding through journalism, music, and innovative communications."[11] Surely Ms. Jolie must know her clout and prestige from serving humanitarian causes would easily translate to fighting prejudice against queer individuals, especially her fellow lovers of boys and girls. . . .

[. . .]

Nevertheless, given her enthusiasm in other forms of activism, Ms. Jolie's minimal efforts toward supporting queer rights leave something to be desired. For her to even openly advocate some bisexual organization like the Kinsey Institute would undoubtedly cause a dramatic increase in discussion of bisexuality. However, again, Ms. Jolie seems to have moved away from her earlier, more controversial ways. Without question, Angelina Jolie is the enlightened queen of humanitarian advocacy in Hollywood—but when it comes to her serving as a de facto delegate for bisexuality, like David Bowie and Madonna before her, she has chosen a more conventional public life.

Among other undesirable qualities, the recorded statements and actions of these celebrities paint them collectively as sex-crazed, unstable, untrustworthy and manipulative. Various media and news outlets consistently profit from publishing stories or produced materials that support these impressions; in other words, for whatever reason, consumers love seeing, reading and hearing this kind trashy news and portrayals. Unfortunately, as stated earlier, these generalizations are also commonplace stereotypes of bisexuals. Hearing about bisexual celebrities behaving as drama queens or addicts undoubtedly cements existing stereotypes in the minds of the public.[12]

In most cases, I believe media and news see no special profit in publishing stories about bisexual celebrities who appear unstable, untrustworthy or manipulative. This is because stories about any famous individual behaving as such attract attention, especially publications that focus on criticizing and demeaning the famous. The power of *schadenfreude* (pleasure one derives from witnessing the misfortune of another) runs deep. A measure of envy inspires the popular desire for seeing the rich and famous get in trouble with the law or wear something hideous or scream at a coworker, and outlets like *What Would Tyler Durden Do?* aim to meet that demand. However, despite lacking a particular ambition to drag the label *bisexual* through more dirt, these outlets nevertheless augment bisexual stereotypes just by causing a stir when a female celebrity comes out as bisexual and then quickly return to throwing mud at her.

Unlike these other qualities of poor character, outlets deliberately profit from portraying bisexual celebrities as sex crazed. In running stories about these particular celebrities' sex scandals, or by sharing produced content with sexual overtones, these outlets knowingly provide heterosexual male consumers with masturbatory fodder. Consider this: in learning how the women they already fantasize about are bisexual and (seemingly) sex crazed, a whole slew of new sexual possibilities enters the imaginations of the heterosexual American male consumer. Although some males might have before dismissed the fantasy as entirely too unrealistic, in hearing now how Megan Fox is bisexual and sexually aggressive makes imagining themselves and Ms. Fox in a threesome with Portia de Rossi, a promiscuous female stripper, or even Lindsay Lohan seem slightly less fantastical.[13] More reports of scandal and more produced content accentuating celebrities' sexual appeal solicits more erotic possibilities for that ideal audience—the prized demographic of heterosexual males 13 to 35 years old—to envision.

[. . .]

What this retort misses, however, is the very basic question I have left unanswered throughout this entire essay: why is bisexuality so sensational, so prone to causing a mass-media response in the first place? No other explanation strikes me as more illuminating and plausible than because young heterosexual males, again that golden demographic, "get a rise" out of reading that hot, young star hook-up with women on the side. Perhaps if the widespread media response to these celebrities' self-identifications was denunciatory, that is, they badmouthed these celebrities for claiming to be bisexuals, a case could be made for these stories being just like the ones about celebrities harboring the qualities of poor character. The fact remains, however, that magazines never, and only occasionally in blogs for the sake of crass humor, belittle celebrities for coming out as bisexuals. Likewise, accounts of their sexual dalliances rarely meet open scorn or disapproval—in fact, the interviews discussed above seem designed to elicit as many sexual anecdotes as possible. What one learns from reading all the stories on TMZ or People.com

tagged "bisexual" and "celebrity" is how a young woman calling herself bisexual may be one strategy, when coupled with other ladder-climbing ones, to getting your face on the cover of *GQ* or *Maxim*. This is a familiar sounding motive no doubt, but one that additionally spreads misunderstanding and false representation of bisexuals at large.

[. . .]

In short, Hollywood, even with its command of the media's attention, is no place for bisexuals to look for political agency. Fortunately, in its exultation of people who epitomize perceived stereotypes, other, more commonplace bisexuals now have access to a clear and definite foil for themselves. The vast majority of bisexuals of the world are stable and trustworthy and never worry about what managers think they should do to better sell themselves or how their Q Score ranks on any given week. Put tersely, the bisexuals outside of the spotlight are nothing like those in it. This is an important distinction because in the past bisexuals and their allies could only speak against the clichés perpetuated in television and films which, although enforced common misconceptions of bisexualities, only were character portrayals. Now with celebrities promoting a stereotypical brand of bisexuality, the everyday bisexual has a person, rather than a projected or transmitted picture, they can point at and say, "I'm nothing like her."

The everyday bisexuals will need to be creative to challenge this publicized branding of their sexuality, especially because the media continues to profit from the brand's perpetuation. In hopes of providing a springboard of sorts, I humbly suggest bisexuals turn to the Internet. Although digital media and news outlets greatly surpass activist efforts like AfterEllen.com in terms of popularity, both still rely on a common source for viewer traffic: search engines. With enough grassroots Internet marketing and search engine optimization, any time someone searches Google for *Lady Gaga bisexual*, a simple, yet forceful blog title along the lines of "I am a bisexual, but I am not Lady Gaga" could result and easily grab their attention.

NOTES

1. Wherein the researchers took crudely elicited arousal patterns in self-identifying bisexual men to suggest the participants were confused about their sexuality.

2. What constitutes a bisexual concern, politic, problem, and so on is far from ambiguous. Broadly speaking, rallying points for specifically bisexuals might include better guided discussion of identity politics, acknowledgement of triadism and polyamory as alterative relational dynamics, and so on. Further discussion is warranted elsewhere.

3. Such theories, however ridiculous, still find supporters, for example, Benedict Cary of the *New York Times*.

4. It is a limitation of this article that I was unable to survey a significant sample population and methodologically determine the top five or six names that come to people's minds when asked about contemporary famous bisexuals. I instead relied on my own answers as well as those of a number of associates, bisexuals included.

5. Note that pithy statements like "I am bisexual" invariably make broadcast and reproduction easier.

6. This immediately raises another question: how often can and do poets, athletes and (especially) politicians reveal themselves as bisexuals? This tangential consideration need be explored, but not here.

7. Although Wikipedia and several Green Day fan Websites reference the relevant portion of the interview, there is no evidence of the topic ever arising again in the numerous interviews with him since.

8. Of note, she also trounced any suspicions of her like exclusively women with her blunt, "Look, I'm not a lesbian."

9. The common explanation for how Tila Tequila became famous to begin with is that once she made friends with over million people on MySpace, studios and agencies started to pay attention to her—how she got those friends probably rested on not only her willingness to be friends with anyone, but also on her appeal as sexy young Asian woman who also happens to be bisexual.

10. A search of her name on thehollywoodgossip.com elicits hundreds of articles, all with titles like "Sex and the City to Blame for Lindsay Lohan Looseness," "Police, Counselors Descend on Samantha Ronson's House After Huge Fight; Lindsay Lohan Not Arrested," and so on.

11. "The foundation's mission is to promote cross-cultural understanding through journalism, music, and innovative communications" www.danielpearl.org

12. Mickey Eliason discusses these and other bisexual stereotypes comprehensively (2001).

13. Of course, such consideration occurs in spite of the resounding improbability of ever meeting Megan Fox, Lindsay Lohan, and so on, let alone bedding them.

REFERENCES

Angelina Jolie bio. (2009, October 13). *Yahoo! Movies*. Retrieved October 13, 2009, from http://movies.yahoo.com/movie/contributor/1800019275/bio

Barnes, B. (2008, November 20). Angelina Jolie's carefully orchestrated image. *New York Times*. Retrieved October 13, 2009, from http://www.nytimes.com/2008/11/21/business/media/21angelina.html

Daniel Pearl Website. (2010, March). *Homepage*. Retrieved October 13, 2009, from http://www.danielpearl.org

Droganes, C. (2007, November 20). Sexy Tila Tequila, racy role model for bisexuals. *CTV Entertainment*. Retrieved October 13, 2009, from http://www.ctv.ca/CTVNews/SciTech/20071116/ENT_tilatequila

Eliason, M. (2001, May). Bi-negativity: The stigma facing bisexual men. *Journal of Bisexuality, 1*, 137–154.

Ex calls Lindsay sex addict in tell-all interview. (2007, December 26). *MSNBC*. Retrieved October 13, 2009, from http://today.msnbc.msn.com/id/22398878/

Finn, N. (2008, June 3). Megan a fox in heat. *E! Online*. Retrieved October 13, 2009, from http://www.eonline.com/uberblog/b1603_megan_fox_in_heat.html

Heyman, M. (2009, May). Lindsay Lohan: Myth vs. reality. *Bazaar*, p. 70.

Hiatt, B. (2009, May 27). The rise of Lady Gaga. *Rolling Stone*, pp. 41–42.

Katz, D. (2009, June). Megan Fox interview. *Esquire*, p. 84.

Keegan, A. (2005, November 4). Bisexuals need to choose, says Dr. Ruth. *Washington Blade*. Retrieved October 13, 2009, from http://www.washblade.com/2005/11-4/view/actionalert/

Kirby, M. (2009, July). All mouth and no trousers. *British GQ*, p. 55.

Lady GaGa entertains thousands at Palm Springs white party. (2009, April 14). *NBC Bay Area News*. Retrieved October 13, 2009, from http://www.accesshollywood.com/

lady-gaga-entertains-thousands-at-palm-springs-white-party_article_16715

Leu, L. (2007, June 16). Tequila sunrise. *King Mag*. Retrieved October 13, 2009, from http://www.king-mag.com/online/?p=6137

Lindsay Lohan arrested for DUI, drugs. (2007, July 24). *ABC News*. Retrieved October 13, 2009, from http://abcnews.go.com/Entertainment/story?id=3408314&page=2

Look to the stars: Angelina Jolie. (2008, January). *Look to the Stars*. Retrieved October 13, 2009, from http://looktothestars.org/celebrity/2-angelina-jolie

Lovegame Lovegamemusic video. (2006, June 2). *Youtube*. Retrieved October 13, 2009, from http://www.youtube.com/watch?v=1mB0tP1I-14

Newman, A. (2008, June 12). What women want (maybe). *New York Times*. Retrieved October 13, 2009, from http://www.nytimes.com/2008/06/12/fashion/12bisex.html

Nguyen, T. (2006, January 4). Tila Tequila's MySpace page!. *MySpace Network*. Retrieved October 13, 2009, from http://www.myspace.com/TilaTequila

Nguyen, T. (2008, June 4). Quick bio. *The Official Tila Nguyen Website*. Retrieved October 13, 2009, from http://www.tilashotspot.com/popups/short_biography.html

Nguyen, T. (2009, July 1). Yes we can, but only if you can Mr. President. *Global Grind*. Retrieved October 13, 2009, from http://globalgrind.com/channel/news/content/789351/tilas-letter-to-the-president/

Rader, D. (2009, August 5). Brad Pitt on gay marriage, smoking pot and "real love." *Parade Magazine*. Retrieved October 13, 2009, from http://www.parade.com/celebrity/celebrity-parade/2009/brad-pitt-on-real-love.html

Rieger, G., Chivers, M. L., & Bailey, J. M. (2005). Sexual arousal patterns of bisexual men. *Psychological Science, 16*, 574–584.

Susman, G. (2003, July 9). Blood ties. *EW Online*. Retrieved October 13, 2009, from http://www.ew.com/ew/report/0,6115,463669_7_0_,00.html

'Tis the season to be Jolie. (1997, December). *Girlfriends Magazine*, pp. 35–37. Todd, T. (2009, October 12). Twitter buzz: Lady GaGa speaks at National Equality March. *Examiner*. Retrieved October 13, 2009, from http://image.examiner.com/x-24390-Twitter-Entertainment-Examiner~y2009m10d12-Twitter-buzz-Lady-GaGa-speaks-at-National-Equality-March

Up close & personal: Tila Nguyen. (2006, June). *Import Tuner*. Retrieved October 13, 2009, from http://www.importtuner.com/models/archives/0211_cover_model_tila_nguyen/index.html

Walsh, J. (2007, November). Alan Cumming: Interview. *Oasis Journals*. Retrieved October 13, 2009, from http://www.oasisjournals.com/2007/11/alan-cumming-interview

Warn, S. (2003, July 13). Bi with a boyfriend. *AfterEllen.com*. Retrieved October 13, 2009, from http://www.afterellen.com/archive/ellen/People/bicelebs.html

Wieder, J. (1995, January 24). Coming clean. *The Advocate*, pp. 66–71.

Wolf, N. (2009, June 19). The power of Angelina. *Bazaar*, pp. 45–49.

SECTION FOUR

Epistemologies of Bodies: Ways of Knowing and Experiencing the World

TABLE OF CONTENTS

LEARNING OBJECTIVES

By the end of this section, you will have a better understanding of:

1. How we know what we know (the epistemology) about the body.

2. How the body becomes an important element in the process of identity formation and the limitations of such a construction.

3. How we inhabit the body influences how others respond to us and how we experience and therefore understand the world we live in.

4. How we need to be more critical of existing discourses (including the "real," medical, and other discourses) about the body in a neoliberal age.

5. How bodies become a medium through and with which we navigate, "talk back" to, and challenge the power hierarchy.

Epistemologies: Theories that are concerned with how knowledge is produced and circulated.

Does inhabiting a particular body influence how others treat you and how you experience the world? What is the relationship between your body and your identity? And why is it important to ask these questions? This introductory essay and the texts included in this section will help us address these questions and better understand the **epistemologies** of the bodies. Together, the voices collected here point to how labels (such as fit, fat, freaky, feminine, masculine, queer, trans, disabled, racialized, sexualized, and aging) are attached to and provide meanings for the body. Such labels are intersectional categories that both cement and create cultural scripts for how these bodies should be experienced and power hierarchies are maintained. Critically examining the body and its meanings is important because it allows us to peek into the changing constructions of gender, sex, and sexuality as cultural and historical shifts are often represented and "materially inscribed" on the body (Conboy et al. 8).

BEYOND REALNESS: DECONSTRUCTING ESSENTIALISM

Janet Mock's book *Redefining Realness: My Path to Womanhood, Identity, Love and So Much More* (excerpted here) opens this section with its captivating portrayal of a mixed-race transwoman from Hawai'i whose body does not reflect back the stereotypical postcard image of Hawaiian hula dance girls. Beginning with Mock's essay, this section disrupts the conventions of telling a story about the body, stories that often begin at the center: a young, white, cisgender, heterosexual, middle- and upper-class, abled body. Doing so also allows us to challenge the limited constructions of normative versus deviant bodies, move beyond **essentializing** *any* bodies, and destabilize any categories of identity that may originate in the body, such as gender, race, age, and so on. For example, when we talk about women's bodies, we have to ask *which women* are we talking about? What makes a body a *woman's* body? Who decides?

More important, we begin with an excerpt from Mock's memoir because it serves as a powerful critique that illuminates the disjuncture between the "real" and the represented/idealized bodies as well as the tension between the material and the discursive body. Her story of transitioning illustrates the instability of the body, from hormone therapy and sex-reassignment surgery to the ways in which others respond to her changing body. As the materiality of the body is reconfigured, it shifts not only the semantic and semiotic of the

Janet Mock and Laverne Cox, famous transwomen in American pop culture. Janet Mock became famous after the publication of her *New York Times* bestseller book *Redefining Realness: My Path to Womanhood, Identity, Love & So Much More*. She is also the TV host of "So POPular!" on MSNBC. Laverne Cox is the Emmy-nominated leading actress of the Netflix TV series *Orange Is the New Black*. She has received many awards including the Stephen Kolzak award, the Dorian Rising Star award, and the Courage award from the Anti-Violence Project, among many other things. Here they were seen attending the 26th Annual GLAAD Media Awards in New York in 2015.

Essentialism: A theory that there is an *essence* that defines a particular entity and makes it *innately* different from other groups. Bodies are perceived to be the determining factor for people's identities and behaviors. To argue that women's behavior is inherently different from men's because of their biological differences is to essentialize them.

body but also the somatic experience that is felt through and with that body (Prosser 6). Mock's insistence that we must move beyond "realness" (or, in her words, "redefine realness") reminds us that, as long as the "success" of a person's transition is measured by their ability to "pass" as a "real" woman or man, we will continue to reinscribe and reinforce the hierarchy of "realness" that leads to discrimination and even violence.

Why, one may wonder, is embracing (rather than challenging) "realness" problematic? Susan Pickard, in critically examining the issue of embodiment in "older" people, challenges the notion of the real by arguing that it is not that the real body does not exist. Rather, she invites us to ponder, "why it is that 'real' happens to take the form it does, physiologically as well as phenomeno-logically and symbolically" (Pickard 1283–84). Her query pushes us to think more critically about the problematic production of the real body: why the real body is deemed more desirable and whose body gets to be counted as real, and

INTERSECTIONAL ANALYSIS

A Case Study: Thomas Beatie was the first trans man who made his pregnancy public in 2008. An image of him naked at five months into his pregnancy appeared in the magazine *Advocate* alongside an article he wrote about the challenges and discriminations he had faced when trying to conceive a baby as a trans man (his wife, Nancy, had a hysterectomy that made it impossible for her to carry a child). When his news became widely known, people posted online comments that highlighted that he was really a "woman having a baby," not a man. His body became the locus of conversations about the anatomy and journey of a transgender body, medical technologies, and transphobia (fear of bodies that are marked deviant and challenge the continuity between bodies and identities).

QUESTIONS

1. What do you think of the online comments that Beatie was a woman, and not a man, having a baby? How do the comments reflect the notion of a "man" as a category of gender that is unstable and intersectional? How does the "real" body discourse affect how people view his body? Why are some people invested in the "real" discourse narrative (i.e., real body, real man, real beauty, etc.)?

2. How does his pregnant body shape how he experiences his gender, as an intersectional category, differently? What are the intersecting categories that are at work here? How does his trans identity intersect with and complicate his gender and sexuality?

3. What do the readers' responses to his story reveal about our society's assumption of the relationship between bodies and identities?

by whom. For example, as Riki Wilchins' article, "Angry Intersex People with Signs!" (in this section) shows, being born intersex does not count as embodying a "real" body. A compulsory surgery often takes place during infancy to reconstruct the gendered materiality of the intersex body, transforming it into what society considers more "real:" a body that fits neatly into either one of the two acceptable gender categories.

KNOWING AND EXPERIENCING BODIES

What do you know about female orgasms, female ejaculation, or women's sexual pleasures in general? According to Nancy Tuana and her article, "Coming to Understand: Orgasm and the Epistemology of Ignorance," probably not much. Tuana argues that epistemic ignorance about women's sexuality is not simply a "lack" of information but rather a systematic way in which this unknowingness is constructed. Not only by being structurally erased, knowledge about (heterosexual) women's sexual pleasure is also and often attached to "horror" narratives to prevent young women from getting pregnant (hooks 57). Even body practices such as female genital surgeries and foot binding are/were purposefully done to curb women's sexual pleasures (in the case of female genital surgeries) and to discipline women's bodies for the sake of men's sexual arousal (in the case of foot binding). Indeed, as Rose Weitz argues, repressing women's sexuality has been used as "an effective way to control women's lives" ("Introduction" 65).

Not suprisingly then, feminists and **sex-positive** activists have worked toward challenging this ignorance and repression of women's bodies, sexualities, and pleasures. The book *Our Bodies Ourselves*, first published in 1970 as *Women and Their Bodies*, was the first and perhaps best-known book to provide women with a comprehensive knowledge about women's health and bodies, allowing them to take control of their bodies. Activists such as Betty Dodson advocated and taught women to masturbate; her book *Liberating Masturbation: A Meditation on Self Love*, published in 1974, redefines women's sexual pleasure. In the midst of these celebrations of women's sexualities, that is, the "freedom to" do whatever one wants, Breanne Fahs reminds us that we need to reclaim the "freedom from" discourse (i.e., the freedom from having to be sexual). (Asexuals, for example, have been pathologized and minoritized.) Thus, in this section, No'u Revilla's and Tagi Qolouvaki's poems are queering and further complicating the notions of women's sexualities, sexual pleasures, and reproductive issues.

A different way of knowing about the body, as phenomenologists would argue, is through experiencing the body itself. Phenomenologists believe that the sensory apparatus of the body or the "lived body" provides us with an insight to knowing about the world (Hammers 69; McWeeny 275). In phenomenology, people are viewed "as embodied subjects who think, act, and know through their bodies"; they exercise their "epistemic agency" as they produce knowledge that stems from their everyday experiences (Davis 57, 59).

The body we inhabit and the identity that we project (whether or not it is in continuity with the body) help shape how we experience and therefore perceive and know ourselves, our bodies, and the world. When certain bodies are attached to specific meanings, however, how we experience these or other bodies will be "mediated" by these meanings (Conboy et al. 1). In other words, our experiences of, in, and with our bodies are always socially constructed (Bordo *Unbearable* 35). For example, when a person takes on a particular gender identity, there are scripts of how one *should* dress, talk, love, or live. In this case, meanings of gender, as it intersects with other categories of identity, matter because they prescribe how to live in our bodies (Halsema 159).

It is important to remember, however, that a person's gender does not have to follow their genitalia or the materiality of their body. If someone claims, or is seen to be performing, a particular gender, that person is expected to be familiar with and conform to these roles. In their article "What Her Body Taught (or, Teaching about and with a Disability): A Conversation," (this section), Brenda Jo Brueggemann, Rosemarie Garland-Thomson, and Georgina Kleege share their experiences of how expectations of gendered disabled bodies frame their critical and pedagogical encounters with their students.

Although the body we inhabit helps structure how we experience the world, it does not mean that everyone with the same body shape will share the same

Sex-positive: A view that a person can choose whether or not to express their sexuality and in a variety of ways. It highlights the pleasure rather than simply the procreative aspect of sex.

Colorism: A form of discrimination based on one's skin color that privileges people with light skin color.

experience. A light-skinned, thin woman, for example, may not experience the same intensity of **colorism** as another woman with a darker skin tone who is just as thin, because of their intersecting and complex historical, geographical, and other social locations. Thus in this section we include Aleichia Williams's essay, which brings the complexity of intersectionality to the fore by reflecting on her experience of being perceived as, to quote from the title of her essay, "Too Latina To Be Black, Too Black To Be Latina." Instead of choosing to be *either* black *or* Latina, however, she embraces her intersectional identities and even challenges the limited understanding of "Latina" as a homogenous category by sharing her story of being called a "Mexican," when her mother actually came from Honduras. Also framing intersectionality as a core issue, Dominique C. Hill's creative work, "(My) Lesbianism Is Not a Fixed Point," helps us rethink the fluidity of our own bodies and sexual desires and invites us to dive into this chaotic messiness of identity and sexual politics of the body.

Moreover, the spaces where these bodies exist and move through also matter in shaping experiences. Pat Gozemba's performance memoir piece in this section exposes the troubling ways in which racism works in the intimate sphere of one's (nonblack) family life. Black bodies are accepted as long as these bodies stay in "the theoretical realm" or outside of one's home and do not become one's daughter's romantic partner. Her creative writing throws us into a world where academic and everyday lives are in tension with each other, and where the person who is closest and dearest to us may be the person who says and displays racist behaviors. She also animates the everyday emotional injury caused by being associated with a person whose body is deemed undesirable.

Bodies matter in how we experience the world and what we know. However, relying simply on the body as a source of knowledge will necessarily limit our claim to the kinds of knowledge we can discern and the identities we can claim. This is why in the Cartesian tradition (the mind/body dualism), the body is considered "a site of epistemological limitation" (Bordo *Unbearable* 227). When a person with a vagina chooses to identify as a man, or **agender**, or advocates for the end of violence against men, for example, society might not readily accept and may even question his identity, credibility, and authority. This certainly speaks to the issue of essentialism and the need to critically rethink such sticky attachments between bodies, identities, and "lived experience"–based knowledge.

Agender: A person without gender. This gender-neutral category challenges the gender binary system.

MEDICALIZATION OF BODIES

In the present day, medical discourse is the dominant framework through which we understand our bodies. This, however, has not always been the case. Prior to the late eighteenth century, the scientific community viewed women's and men's bodies as having similar functions and structures, except women's genitalia were inverse while men's appeared outward (Laqueur 5; Lorber 12;

Martin "Medical" 18). By the late nineteenth century, people began to see women's and men's bodies as not only different but also as opposite, and the medical discourse had begun to take hold in society (Laqueur 5; Martin "Medical" 19).

Medical discourse provides a narrative with which we make sense of what happens to our bodies (i.e., a "medical diagnosis") and who we are in relation to the symptom (i.e., a patient with a disease) (Waples 59). Once we are diagnosed, we *become* a patient in need of a medical intervention, and therein lies the problem.

This process is known as medicalization. However, **medicalization** is not simply identifying symptoms or behaviors through medical discourses. It also involves categorizing certain behaviors or symptoms as "deviant" with the purpose of "eliminating or controlling" them (Riessman 47–48). In this section, Eunjung Kim's article "How Much Sex Is Healthy? The Pleasures of Asexuality" shows us how medical discourse pathologizes, or considers abnormal, asexuality. **Asexual** is defined by the Asexual Visibility and Education Network (AVEN) as "a person who does not experience sexual attraction" (qtd. in Cerankowski and Milks 651; Van Houdenhove et al. 179); people who are asexual make up approximately 0.6 to 5.5 percent of the population. Asexuality is not the same as antisexuality, which sees sexuality in a more negative light.

This pathologization by way of medical discourse certainly has negative effects on the materiality of the body. Transgender people, for example, have been discriminated against by the healthcare system, from not being able to be reimbursed by insurance companies for certain kinds of care to being retroactively denied insurance when the insurance company finds out the person's transgender status. Insurance companies are also very rigid and limited in understanding the human body; when a transgender woman identifies herself as a female, she may get health coverage related to female organs, that is, mammograms, but not for prostate problems (Gorton and Grubb 219). Medicalization thus limits how people understand and experience their own and others' bodies.

Let's use the childbirthing process as an example to understand the concept of medicalization. Until the nineteenth century in America, childbirth was experienced at home, attended by friends and family, who would help the midwife (many of whom were immigrant or black) deliver the baby. At that time, obstetrics was not a common field taught at medical schools (Riessman 51). By 1910, however, obstetricians (usually men from the "dominant class") became more popular as they claimed that "normal pregnancy" was a medical condition that needed a science-based intervention; this resulted in a significant decrease in childbirth assisted by midwives (Riessman 51). This shift was partly supported by the women themselves who wanted to lessen the pain of childbirth by getting the "twilight sleep" ("a combination of morphine and scopolamine") that the physicians used at the time (Riessman 52). Even Queen Victoria requested such a drug (in her case, "chloroform") to alleviate the pain of childbirth during the delivery of her eighth and ninth children. Indeed, physicians used drugs and childbirth technology to justify their presence and make them seem "indispensable."

Medicalization: The idea that physicians have the ultimate authority to diagnose a symptom and through this process a person becomes a patient in need of medical intervention.

Asexual: A person who does not experience sexual attraction.

This medicalization of women's bodies in the late nineteenth century also caused some women to undergo unnecessary and dangerous surgeries to have their healthy ovaries or clitorises removed, with up to 30 percent mortality rates (Weitz "A History" 7). These surgeries were linked to the class ideology at the time that considered middle-class women's bodies frail and thus in need of medical intervention (working-class women, regardless of their race, were seen as "more robust") (Riessman 53; Weitz "A History" 6–7). In addition to using medical discourses and class ideologies, these nineteenth-century doctors also used "Christian and Aristotelian" discourses that viewed women in contempt and as emotionally and physically weak, to discourage women, who at the time had begun to work part-time, from working outside the home and furthering their education (Weitz "A History" 6).

Even menstruation was used to keep middle-class women from pursuing work outside the home. Around this time, in the nineteenth century, the "process" of menstruation began to be seen as pathological and as having negative effects on women's lives (Martin "Medical" 20). After the beginning of World War II, various studies showed that menstruation wasn't responsible for women's "condition" (that made them unable to work) after all (Martin "Premenstrual" 224). It is clear that the negative meanings attached to menstruation reflected the dominant gender and political economy ideologies of the time. Indeed, as Gloria Steinem argues ("If Men Could Menstruate," in this section), the meanings of and practices involved in menstruation would change if, in this man-dominated world, men could menstruate.

Because the medicalization framework mediates women's experiences of their bodies, it becomes problematic if it is the *only* discourse through which women can understand their bodies. Hence, some scholars such as Catherine Kohler Riessman suggest that we demedicalize our relationships with our bodies while being selective about the benefits of medical knowledge (61). For her, "demedicalization" is about changing "the ownership, production, and use of scientific knowledge;" it is not about being opposed to the biological aspect of it (Riessman 60). Other strategies that women have used in resisting medicalization, according to Emily Martin's research, is how women, particularly working-class women, pay careful attention to their own body, how it "feels, looks, or smells" rather than referring to the medical model that may alienate women's experience (qtd. in Davis 58). What do *you* think is the best way to address the medicalization of the body?

CHOICE, CONTROL, AND COMMODITY: UNDERSTANDING BODIES IN A NEOLIBERAL AGE

Body work in today's society is often shaped by neoliberal politics. Michelle Leve offers a definition of neoliberalism that is useful here: "a political-economic ideology and practice that promotes individualism, consumerism, deregulation, and transferring state power and responsibility to the individual" (279). A neo-liberal economy rests on the assumption that individuals are responsible for improving themselves, preferably through consumption for their own (economic) benefit. The problem with this view is that any inequalities that an individual experiences are merely seen as personal rather than institutional issues (Stuart and Donaghue 101). To further explore this point and to shed light on how neoliberalism frames our relationship with our bodies as well as others', three popular discourses (choice, control, and commodity) are discussed next.

THE CHOICE DISCOURSE: BEAUTY IDEALS AND IMAGES OF THE BODY

One of the legacies of the second wave women's movement is a woman's right to choose, especially when it comes to her pregnancy. This feminist discourse, however, has been co-opted by various people and corporations that tell women (or all genders, for that matter) that they are now "free" to choose whatever products they want to buy.

This "free" choice, however, is a mere, if seductive, illusion. Various technologies, ideologies, and political economy conditions, including the neoliberal economy, enable as well as limit these choices. Some choices indeed hold more currency than others. If a woman "chooses" not to practice **body work** that emulates the dominant beauty standard, for example, she may be subjected to the "stigmatization and the loss of social capital" (Dolezal 357). In this sense, beauty practice is not a mere "choice," albeit framed in such a way. Rather, it functions to normalize and discipline women's bodies. As Naomi Wolf's now-classic book *The Beauty Myth* has shown, beauty is a systematic structure that keeps women subordinated.

> **Body work**: "an effort to create an alignment . . . between appearance and character, between identity and body" (Shapiro 144).

Decades after Wolf's book was published and the women's liberation movement protested against the beauty industry and beauty pageants, many women *still* practice body work. Satu Liimaka, referencing Rubin, Nemeroff, and Russo's research, argues that this persistence in doing body work is related to the fact that although feminism and feminist identity have helped some people to change their "thoughts" about beauty ideals, they have not changed how people "feel" about these beauty standards (812). Indeed, as L. Ayu Saraswati argues in her book *Seeing Beauty, Sensing Race in Transnational Indonesia*, beauty practice (in her case, skin-whitening), rather than simply reflecting women's desire to look beautiful, is a manifestation of how women *manage* their *feelings* about their body along gender lines, or what she calls as the "gendered management of affect." For example, women are supposed to feel bad when they show signs of aging, and hence in managing this bad feeling, they apply anti-aging cream that makes them feel good about their skin. Men, however, may manage their feelings about their body differently than women (due to the different social constructions between how men and women express and relate to their feelings). This explains why beauty practices are still more common for women. She thus suggests that we pay attention to these feelings (who feels what about which

Engaged Learning

Choose three parts of your body to focus on (i.e., hair, nose, skin color, stomach, thighs, etc.). As you focus on each body part, pay attention to how you feel at this exact moment. Do you feel good, bad, or indifferent about that body part? You may even have mixed, contradicting feelings. Name all of these feelings and write them down in Table 4.1.

Then trace where you might have learned to feel that way about this body part: think of any TV shows, films, or magazines that might have advertised such an idea; then think of any comments or praise your friends and family have uttered about this part of your body. Write as much as you can, and answer the questions in Table 4.1.

Table 4.1: Tracing Feelings about My Body

Body Part	Your Current Feelings	Media's Narrative	Friends' and Family's Comments

QUESTIONS

1. Examine the completed table carefully. Do you notice any patterns and connections between how you feel about your body and the media's narrative? What about your friends' and family's comments? Have you practiced any body work because you feel a certain way about your body? Are any of these practices gendered? Do they reflect your class position? What about your racial background or disabled body status? How do you relate these body works to neoliberalism?

2. If your feelings about these body parts have been mostly unhappy, do you think you might be able to change these feelings? How? What would this entail? How does shifting our feelings challenge the power hierarchy?

3. If your feelings have been mostly happy, satisfied, or indifferent, where did you learn to feel that way? Might you be able to identify anyone (or anything) that might have helped shape these feelings? How can we reimagine our relationship with our bodies as mindful, critical, and empowering while still being content in our bodies?

bodies, why, and what we do about these feelings) and even intervene and challenge the very production of these feelings, especially when they are attached to specific bodies and not others. Although these feelings may seem *natural* to us when we feel them, we need to question how these emotions are constructed and how they support the existing power hierarchy of bodies.

What feelings, for example, motivate many women, more than men, to shave their body? Indeed, more than 90 percent of women shave their legs and armpits (only 18 percent of men shave their legs and 30 percent shave their armpits) (Fahs "Shaving" 562). It is true, however, that a new and growing trend called "manscaping" (men who groom their body hair for aesthetic purposes) has become more popular. Nonetheless, it remains critical to be mindful of how certain beauty practices are manifestations of how people manage their feelings about their bodies based on gender.

A masculine beauty ideal has now become more accepted in and disseminated through popular culture. Susan Bordo's "Beauty (Re)Discovers the Male Body," also included in this section, argues that although homophobia and the fear of being perceived as gay had previously made heterosexual men reluctant to engage in body work that specifically aims to achieve a male beauty standard, designers such as Calvin Klein and celebrities such as Michael Jordan have paved the way in popularizing and shifting this view on male beauty practices—that is, men too are subjected to the rules and practices of being good neoliberal citizens who exercise their "freedom to choose" whatever products they want to express their masculinities.

Men also sculpt their bodies to conform to the masculine body ideal. Dan Sabo in his article, "Doing Time, Doing Masculinity: Sports and Prisons," in this section, looks at how men participate in sports in prison to "cultivate their bodies in order to send a variety of messages about masculinity to themselves and others" (65). Here, the notion of masculinity, as is true of femininity, can be seen as limiting, for it can only be articulated through a particular kind of (hard) body.

In addition to gender, skin color, race, body hair, and body shape, age also plays an important role in defining a beauty ideal. Prior to the 1950s, "older" women were expected to have a "mature" body figure and wear "mature" outfits (Dinnerstein and Weitz 191). Since then, however, the youthful (and slim) culture has become the beauty standard for all women. By the late 1970s, the "fitness craze" took over American culture and (older) women with "mature" figures were told that they were "a sign of social or even moral failure" (Dinnerstein and Weitz 191). Aging bodies become the repulsive "abject" bodies that people hope to escape by consuming various beauty products (Carter 235–36).

New discourses about aging have certainly been articulated. These discourses push for a healthy and "active aging" life, rather than simply aiming for a youthful appearance (Carter 232). In whatever discourse the process of aging has been articulated thus far (i.e., health, beauty, or both), it nonetheless clings to the neoliberal idea that it is the responsibility of the individual to choose a body project that can keep their body young and vibrant, which is considered the ultimate desirable body. Even contemporary media still continues to circulate advertisements for anti-aging products and represent older people as sexually inactive (or needing Viagra, for men, and Premarin, for women), "boring," "useless," and "old-fashioned" (Dickerson and Rousseau 308; Haboush et al. 669, 673).

The media has been one of the most prevalent means through which beauty ideals are circulated. Unfortunately, as some studies show, it has negatively affected people's body image across the globe (Warren 551). In the United

States, for example, Hollywood films have contributed to people's internalization of the thin ideal, leading to eating disorders (Fox-Kales). Another study shows that when women compare their bodies to models' bodies in the media, it lowers their self-esteem and exacerbates their body image issues (Haboush et al. 669). In Fiji and Japan, studies show that the exposure to Western media in these countries led to an increase in young women's body dissatisfaction and disordered eating (Jung and Forbes 382; Warren 551).

It is important to remember, however, that as we explore how the Western media negatively affects body image in non-Western countries, we do not judge *any* beauty practice as emulating the white beauty standard. In fact, this idea is in and of itself revealing of a racialized and Eurocentric frame of thinking. As L. Ayu Saraswati shows in her essay, "Cosmopolitan Whiteness: The Effects and Affects of Skin Whitening Advertisements in Transnational Indonesia" (included in this section), although skin-whitening practice does suggest a desire for white skin color, this desire is *not* the same as a desire for Caucasian whiteness. Rather, it is a desire for what she calls "Cosmopolitan whiteness," a whiteness that is not attached to any racial background (p. 413). Even the practice of skin-tanning that many people assume to show a desire for dark skin, according to Saraswati, actually exposes a desire for Cosmopolitan whiteness.

Skin-whitening cream, a lucrative industry. Skin-whitening cream is one of the top-selling products in the world. In Indonesia, it is dubbed as the crisis-proof industry whose sales remained steady even in the midst of economic crisis. Desire for whiteness, as L. Ayu Saraswati argues in this book, should not be seen as mere desire to emulate Caucasian whiteness, however. Rather, it is an expression of a new kind of whiteness that she calls "Cosmopolitan whiteness."

Table 4.2: Cosmetic Plastic Surgery by Race

Race	Number of People Undergoing Cosmetic Surgery
Caucasians	10.8 million
Hispanics	1.6 million
African Americans	1.3 million
Asian Americans	1.0 million

Chimamanda Ngozi Adichie's fictional story, excerpted from *Americanah* and included in this section, takes us further in examining the complexities of body and beauty norms through the issue of hair from the perspective of a Nigerian woman living in the United States. Her story allows us to peek into the troubling ways in which bodies are marked and read differently as they travel across different communities and how hair becomes a signifier for racialized and gendered beauty ideals and identities.

Beauty ideals may be unattainable. However, some people have used cosmetic surgeries to help them negotiate these standards. Unsurprisingly, then, cosmetic surgery, and the beauty industry as a whole, has become a multibillion-dollar business. (Note that calling it a "surgery" implies the medicalization process of this body work.) Based on 2014 data from the American Society of Plastic Surgeons, Americans spent approximately $12.9 billion on cosmetic surgery alone, and women had 92 percent of these surgeries. In this neoliberal age, however, this act of *choosing* to have surgery (or other body work) remains in the realm of one's personal responsibility, beautifully cloaked under the fraud discourse of "choice."

THE POLITICS OF CONTROL: BODY WEIGHT AND EATING DISORDERS

Eating disorders have become an epidemic in the Western world since the 1980s, although in the nineteenth century the medical world began to take note of how upper-class women were practicing "self-starvation" (Bordo "The Body" 93). In contemporary America, eating disorders have been reframed and understood as a form of self-control, a manifestation of being a good neoliberal subject. As M. Cristina Alcalde argues, although the discourse of control over

Table 4.3: Top Five Cosmetic Surgeries by Gender

The Top Five Cosmetic Surgeries for Women	The Top Five Cosmetic Surgeries for Men
1. Breast augmentation	1. Nose reshaping
2. Nose reshaping	2. Eyelid surgery
3. Liposuction	3. Breast reduction
4. Eyelid surgery	4. Liposuction
5. Facelift	5. Facelift

one's body has long been associated with the feminist movement, this is no longer the case. This practice now reflects a way of being in a neoliberal age (34). Maintaining an ideal body weight involves knowing what to consume (and purge) (Stokes 59).

However, because not having control over one's body is perceived to be a sign of a failed neoliberal subject, it therefore is used to justify discrimination against "fat" people. (Here, "fat" refers to being 20 percent over the height/weight ratio standard, which is the definition used in many studies [Fikkan and Rothblum 577]. This, of course, is another example of medicalization of bodies in which certain bodies are deemed "normal," whereas other bodies are "overweight." Fat is indeed a contentious concept, once used to marginalize people considered by societal and medical standards as "over" the "healthy" weight but that has since been reclaimed by various scholars and activists to challenge this problematic body norm.) Households headed by fat women, for example, have lower income than those headed by non-fat women—an average of 12 percent to 17.51 percent less. This is not the case for fat men, except in the small case of "obese black men," another example of how race, gender, and body weight intersect with

ACTIVISM AND CIVIC ENGAGEMENT

You will work in a group to create an online petition as a way to create change and end discrimination based on the body, its meanings and its social regulation.

1. With your classmates, brainstorm an issue related to the body that has affected many people. For example, you can focus on the discrimination against fat, transexuals, and/ or older people in the workplace or request gender-neutral or "all-gender" restrooms at your campus. The more specific the issue and the goal, the more effective the petition.
2. Then conduct thorough research to gather as much information as you can about the issue, including statistics and case studies that you can use to support your argu- ment. If possible, find an example from your community.
3. Craft a solid petition that describes the situation, backed up by solid data, and your goals. Think about the audience for your

petition and to whom you will submit your petition.
4. Choose an online petition website that you think will be the best medium to circulate your petition. Some examples include change.org or ipetitions.com. Post and circulate your petition.

QUESTIONS

1. Explain to the class the thought processes of creating your petition. What were the difficulties that your group experienced? What were the most exciting parts of the process? Why?
2. After one week of posting and circulating your petition, assess which group has the most signatures or is closest to reaching their goals. Why? How does this reflect the interest of the audience and the state of our society? What did you learn from working toward an end to body-based discrimination?

each other in creating different experiences of the body (Fikkan and Rothblum 577, 578). A 2003 study by Hebl and Mannix shows that men who were seen by their employer to have sat next to a fat woman before their job interview were treated more harshly during the interview than men who didn't sit next to a fat woman (qtd. in Fikkan and Rothblum 577). (This echoes Gozemba's story of injury that one experiences from being associated with someone with an undesirable body.) Regardless of this prevalent discrimination, there is no law that protect people against size discrimination, except in Madison, Wisconsin; Urbana, Illinois; Washington, DC; Binghamton, New York; six cities in California; and the state of Michigan.

Kimberly Dark's "Big Yoga Student" essay in this section creates an intriguing rupture to the dominant narrative about fat people. She makes visible how the normalized body is constructed through narratives of erasures, that is, bodies that don't belong, and disciplinary practices. She playfully animates her every-day experiences of being a fat yoga teacher whose body provokes a certain level of discomfort in her students—some even left the class after seeing her body. However, she insists that fat women keep showing up in yoga classes. Not par-ticipating means being subsumed by the very structure that erases fat women's bodies in these spaces. Nonetheless, showing up in yoga classes also requires that these women *invest* in fees for yoga sessions, mats, and clothes, as a way to invest in themselves, inadvertently turning them into neoliberal subjects.

RELATING TO BODIES THROUGH A COMMODITY DISCOURSE

Bodies are attached to a price tag, as in the adult entertainment industry. Bodies are even fragmented and sold, as in international organ trafficking cases. Bodies, women's bodies in particular, are also used to sell other products or ideas (Conboy et al. 8, 11). Simply turn to any form of popular culture to see how it relies heavily on the selling (and objectification) of women's bodies to keep the money flowing in.

It is not only the body that is sold as a commodity. Our experiences with and in our bodies have also been commodified. In this neoliberal age, women are expected to do the "third shift of body work"—the second shift revolves around housework (Hallstein 114). Women are bombarded with advice to "help" them achieve sexy postpregnancy bikini bodies, for example, by purchasing various weight-loss meal plans and exercise classes, and transforming themselves into a "yummy mummy" (Hallstein 122, 125).

Moreover, spending time, energy, and money on one's body, as we are told, is a reflection that we love our body. The mainstream "love your body" discourse is indeed a clear example of how all these three discourses merge, overlap, and are articulated through each other. The love your body discourse conveniently sits at the intersection of "neoliberal governmentality, emotional capitalism, the growth of social media and commodity feminism" (Gill and Elias 179). That is, people are taught that to feel good they need to improve and invest in them-selves by purchasing various products that are represented to have the ability to empower them. Social media further supports this behavior by functioning as a site where people can post images of the products they purchase or activities that they do (i.e., eating at a fancy restaurant or working out at a gym as a sign of self-love) as well as images of their "improved" bodies. This discourse incorporates "pseudo" feminist messages that tell women and girls that they are "incredible" and have the power to "redefine" beauty (Gill and Elias 180). Women are told that they are "worth it" and may now *choose* whatever color of lipstick they want. Although telling women and girls to love their body may seem harmless, Rosalind Gill and Ana Sodia Elias argue that this could be dangerous because now not only is the *physical* appearance of the body being disciplined but also women's "psychic life" is being oppressed (185). This love your body discourse is different, of course, from the ways in which women of color, with a long history of gendered, racialized, and sexualized oppression, exploitation, and discrimination, have reclaimed self-care and view it as "self-preservation, . . . an act of political warfare" rather than a mere "self-indulgence" (Lorde 131). That is, to care for one's own body when society deems it unworthy and actively marginalizes it is a necessary act, a survival technique, rather than a mere narcissism disguised as liberation (Douglas).

TRANSNATIONAL CONNECTIONS

Originating in India around the third century, Tantra is a dynamic mélange of Hindu, Jain, and Buddhist traditions that incorporates visualization, meditation, and circulation of energies. In its contemporary American incarnation (or perhaps as a form of cultural appropriation), widely popularized since the 1960s by celebrities such as Jimi Hendrix and Mick Jagger (and later by Sting), Tantra is now known in the United States mostly for its teachings that squarely locate sensual desire at the epicenter of liberation and regulate sexual pleasure through carefully choreographed body movements and sexual techniques and positions (see: White; Shaw; Urban). Tantra workshops around the world promise to teach singles and couples how to connect with their own body as well as their partner's, to be mindfully aware of their bodily sensations, and to have an "enlightened" love-making session.

QUESTIONS

1. How does Tantra as a (spiritual) body practice function as a transnational commodity?
2. How does a Tantra workshop exemplify how people's experiences with their bodies are mediated by the commodity discourse? How does neoliberalism work in encouraging people to take Tantra classes?
3. Who reaps the financial benefits from these Tantra classes? Would you consider "American Tantra" as a form of cultural appropriation? Why or why not? Are there any other forms of body work that would be considered as a cultural appropriation? What about yoga? Why or why not?
4. Have you ever been to a yoga or Tantra class? Did you notice how or if the teachers contextualize, historicize, and repackage the teachings of yoga or Tantra in their classes?

If you are not familiar with any Tantra or yoga classes, it may be helpful for you to do some (online) research about these classes.

BODY TALK, BODY HACK: AGENCY AND THE BODY AS A SITE OF RESISTANCE

Bordo argues that bodies are a "medium" of or a "metaphor" for culture. That is, what we eat, how we dress, and how we practice body rituals are informed by the culture within which we are a part. However, as she also points out, they are not simply a "tabula rasa, awaiting inscription by culture" (Bordo *Unbearable* 35, 165). We negotiate these (at times conflicting) cultures and in doing so transform our bodies into a dynamic site of contested meanings and practices. In a sense, then, the body becomes a battleground, a site where one can try out different ways of being and identifying with oneself, if not one's body, and talk back to power.

Catrina Brown, Shelly Weber, and Serena Ali call this mode of communicating with one's body a "body talk" (93, 94). Body talk, they argue, is different from body project. Whereas in body project women's relationship to their bodies is one of "control" and "repression," in body talk, women exercise their agency to talk back to the dominant body ideal using their bodies. For some "older women," for example, when they do beauty practice as a "coping technique" to help address an early-life trauma (i.e., experiencing rape, dysfunctional childhood, or divorce) they are talking back to and taking back their power (Clarke and Griffin 200, 205). These women no longer let their perpetrators, who once negatively influenced their body image, dictate how they treat their body.

Moreover, in various street protests, bodies have functioned as an instrument of resistance. These bodies stand in solidarity as they march together, or become a "human barricade," in cases such as in Tiananmen square in 1989, or occupying the building of the People's Consultative Assembly/the People's Representative Council in Jakarta, Indonesia, in 1998 that resulted in a change of government.

Beyond the physical world, activists also use cyberspace as a different way to incorporate the body as a medium of activism. The Egyptian women's rights activist Aliaa Magda Elmahdy, for instance, posts nude photos of herself on her blog to challenge racism, sexism, and violence. Not merely subscribing to existing ideologies of gender and sexuality, she creates a rupture in the convention of female nude protest by embodying an oppositional gaze and a political agency through her nonsubmissive poses (Eileraas 45–46).

Another form of resistance that uses the body as its medium is the practice of body modification. The body art movement, including tattoos and other forms of "body modification," expands our understanding of body talk by using a more extensive form of technology to create new meanings of the body in order to challenge existing categories of identity such as race, gender, and sexuality (Pitts 236). The practice of body hacking (biohacking), for example, is a form of non-mainstream body modification that became known in the 1990s through cyberpunk communities (Olivares 288). An example of a body hack is how Cheto Castellano, a performance artist, had (what look like) horns surgically inserted into his forehead. Because body hacking such as Castellano's aims to contest and decolonize the normative body (Olivares 292), it is what Victoria Pitts calls "social rebellion through the body" (qtd. in Olivares 288).

A woman at the body modification convention, in New York City. Body modification is often known as part of the body art movement that aims to challenge the fixity of the body or as a form of what Victoria Pitts calls "social rebellion through the body." In this picture, a woman is seen with tattoos, piercings, and her under-the-skin ring implants. The picture was taken during the fifth annual tattoo convention in New York City.

Bodies speak, whether we intend them to or not. As Aimee Rowe points out, "The body is on the table. It becomes the text of pedagogy. All bodies are teaching, whether White and male, queer and Black, South Asian, and foreign. The trick is to become aware of what lessons our bodies are teaching" (1051). It is therefore important to critically and perpetually examine: What stories does our body teach and tell? What knowledge does our body help produce and/or challenge? How can we complicate the stories that our bodies tell? Do these bodies "talk back" to power, or do they become the blank screen on which the dominant culture projects and makes visible its power? More important, who's listening? What kinds of bodies get to be heard, and which bodies can only be read in specific ways? What kind of embodiment would allow us to remain faithful to being critical of the dominance of power? We thus end this section with a poem by Christina Lux, "anticipation," that addresses some of these questions, as well as speaks to how women can embody resistance as they express their sexuality even under the institutional gaze of religion.

Critical Thinking Questions

1. How is knowledge about the body produced? Why do some people or agencies have more credibility and authority than others in constructing these knowledges?

2. How do dominant ideas about gendered bodies in your society (i.e., in media, religion, etc.) influence how you understand your body and help explain the relationship between your bodily practices and your identity?

3. How does the body influence how we experience the world and our understanding of the world?

4. What are some of the most effective ways to challenge dominant narratives about non-normative bodies?

GLOSSARY

Agender 350

Asexual 351

Colorism 350

Epistemologies 346

Essentialism 347

Medicalization 351

Sex-positive 349

WORKS CITED

Alcalde, M. Cristina. "Feminism and Women's Control over Their Bodies in a Neoliberal Context: A Closer Look at Pregnant Women on Bed Rest." *Feminist Formations*, vol. 25, no. 3, 2013, pp. 33–56.

American Society of Plastic Surgeons. *2014 Cosmetic Plastic Surgery Statistics*, 2015, www.plasticsurgery.org/news/plastic-surgery-statistics/2014-plastic-surgery-statistics.html

Bordo, Susan. "The Body and the Reproduction of Femininity." *Writing on the Body*, edited by Katie Conboy et al. Columbia UP, 1997, pp. 90–110.

———. *Unbearable Weight: Feminism, Western Culture, and the Body*. 1993. U of California P, 2003.

Boston Women's Health Book Collective. *Our Bodies Ourselves: A Book by and for Women*. Simon and Schuster, 1973.

Brown, Catrina, et al. "Women's Body Talk: A Feminist Narrative Approach." *Journal of Systemic Therapies*, vol. 27, no. 2, 2008, pp. 92–104.

Carter, Claire. "'Contemporary Ageing: 'Younger, Better, Fresher' How Does This Speak to Feminist Theories of the Body?" *Feminism and the Body: Interdisciplinary Perspectives*, edited by Catherine Kevin, Cambridge Scholars Publishing, 2009, pp. 228–45.

Case, Sue-Ellen. "Tracking the Vampire." *Writing on the Body: Female Embodiment and Feminist Theory*. Edited by Katie Conboy et al., Columbia UP, 1997, pp. 380–400.

Cerankowski, Karli, and Megan Milks. "New Orientations: Asexuality and Its Implications for Theory and Practice." *Feminist Studies*, vol. 36 no. 3, 2010, pp. 650–64.

Clarke, Laura, and Meridith Griffin. "Body Image and Aging: Older Women and the Embodiment of Trauma." *Women's Studies International Forum*, vol. 31, 2008, pp. 200–8.

Conboy, Katie, et al., editors. Introduction. *Writing on the Body: Female Embodiment and Feminist Theory*, Columbia UP, 1997, pp. 1–14.

Davis, Kathy. "Reclaiming Women's Bodies: Colonialist Trope or Critical Epistemology." *The Sociological Review*, vol. 55, no. 1, 2007, pp. 50–64.

Dickerson, Bette, and Nicole Rousseau. "Ageism through Omission: The Obsolescence of Black Women's Sexuality." *Journal of African American Studies*, vol. 13, 2009, pp. 307–24.

Dinnerstein, Myra, and Rose Weitz. "Jane Fonda, Barbara Bush, and Other Aging Bodies: Femininity and the Limits of Resistance." *The Politics of Women's Bodies: Sexuality, Appearance, and Behavior*, edited by Rose Weitz. Oxford UP, 1998, pp. 189–203.

Dodson, Betty. *Liberating Masturbation: A Meditation on Self Love*. Dodson, 1974.

Dolezal, Luna. "The (In)visible Body: Feminism, Phenomenology, and the Case of Cosmetic Surgery." *Hypatia*, vol. 25, no. 2, 2010, pp. 357–75.

Douglas, Susan. "Narcissism as Liberation." *The Gender and Consumer Culture Reader*, edited by Jennifer Scanlon. New York UP, 2000, pp. 267–82.

Eileraas, Karina. "Sex(t)ing Revolution, Femenizing the Public Square: Aliaa Magda Elmahdy, Nude Protest, and Transnational Feminist Body Politics." *Signs: Journal of Women in Culture and Society,* vol. 40, no. 1, 2014, pp. 40–52.

Fahs, Breanne. "'Freedom to' and 'Freedom from': A New Vision for Sex-Positive Politics." *Sexualities*, vol. 17, no. 3, 2014, pp. 267–90.

———. "Shaving it All Off: Examining Social Norms of Body Hair Among College Men in a Women's Studies Course." *Women's Studies*, vol. 42, 2013, pp. 559–77.

Fikkan, Janna, and Esther Rothblum. "Is Fat a Feminist Issue? Exploring the Gendered Nature of Weight Bias." *Sex Roles*, vol. 66, 2012, pp. 575–92.

Fox-Kales, Emily. *Body Shots: Hollywood and the Culture of Eating Disorders*. State U of New York P, 2011.

Gill, Rosalind, and Ana Elias. "'Awaken Your Incredible': Love Your Body Discourses and Postfeminist Contradictions." *International Journal of Media & Cultural Politics*, vol. 10, no. 2, 2014, pp. 179–88.

Gorton, Nick, and Hilary Maia Grubb. "General, Sexual, and Reproductive Health." *Trans Bodies, Trans Selves: A Resource for the Transgender Community*, edited by Laura Erickson-Schroth, Oxford UP, 2014, pp. 215–40.

Haboush, Amanda, et al. "Beauty, Ethnicity, and Age: Does Internalization of Mainstream Media Ideals Influence Attitudes Towards Older Adults?" *Sex Roles*, vol. 66, 2012, pp. 668–76.

Hallstein, D. Lynn. "She Gives Birth, She's Wearing a Bikini: Mobilizing the Postpregnant Celebrity Mom Body to Manage the Post–Second Wave Crisis in Femininity." *Women's Studies in Communication*, vol. 34, 2011, pp. 111–38.

Halsema, Annemie. "Reconsidering the Notion of the Body in Anti-Essentialism, with the Help of Luce Irigaray and Judith Butler." *Belief, Bodies, and Being: Feminist Reflections on Embodiment*, edited by Deborah Orr et al., Rowman and Littlefield, 2006, pp. 151–61.

Hammers, Corie. "Corporeality, Sadomasochism and Sexual Trauma." *Body and Society*, vol. 20, no. 2, 2014, pp. 68–90.

hooks, bell. *Wounds of Passion: A Writing Life*. Henry Holt, 1997.

Jung, Jaehee, and Gordon Forbes. "Body Dissatisfaction and Disordered Eating among College Women in China, South Korea, the United States: Contrasting Predictions from Sociocultural and Feminist Theories." *Psychology of Women Quarterly,* vol. 31, 2007, pp. 381–93.

Laqueur, Thomas. *Making Sex: Body and Gender From the Greeks to Freud*. Harvard UP, 1990.

Leve, Michelle. "Reproductive Bodies and Bits: Exploring Dilemmas of Egg Donation Under Neoliberalism." *Studies in Gender and Sexuality*, vol. 14, no. 4, 2013, pp. 277–88.

Liimaka, Satu. "Cartesian and Corporeal Agency: Women's Studies Students' Reflections on Women's Experience." *Gender and Education*, vol. 23, no. 7, 2011, pp. 811–23.

Lorber, Judith. "Believing is Seeing: Biology as Ideology." *The Politics of Women's Bodies: Sexuality, Appearance, and Behavior*, edited by Rose Weitz. Oxford UP, 1998, pp. 12–24.

Lorde, Audre. *A Burst of Light: Essays by Audre Lorde*. Firebrand, 1988.

Martin, Emily. "Medical Metaphors of Women's Bodies: Menstruation and Menopause." *Writing on the Body: Female Embodiment and Feminist Theory*, edited by Katie Conboy et al. Columbia UP, 1997, pp. 15–41.

———. "Premenstrual Syndrome, Work Discipline, and Anger." *The Politics of Women's Bodies: Sexuality, Appearance, and Behavior*, edited by Rose Weitz. Oxford UP, 1998, pp. 221–41.

McWeeny, Jennifer. "Topographies of Flesh: Women, Nonhuman Animals, and the Embodiment of Connection and Difference." *Hypatia*, vol. 29, no. 2, 2014, pp. 269–86.

Olivares, Lissette. "Hacking the Body and Posthumanist Transbecoming: 10,000 Generations Later as the Mestizaje of Speculative Cyborg Feminism and Significant Otherness." *Nanoethics*, vol. 8, 2014, pp. 287–97.

Pickard, Susan. "Biology as Destiny? Rethinking Embodiment in 'Deep' Old Age." *Ageing & Society*, vol. 34, 2014, 1279–91.

Pitts, Victoria. "Feminism, Technology and Body Projects." *Women's Studies*, vol. 34, 2010, pp. 229–47.

Prosser, Jay. *Second Skins: The Body Narratives of Transsexuality*. Columbia UP, 1998.

Riessman, Catherine. "Women and Medicalization: A New Perspective." *The Politics of Women's Bodies: Sexuality, Appearance, and Behavior*, edited by Rose Weitz. Oxford UP, 1998, pp. 46–63.

Rowe, Aimee. "Erotic Pedagogies." *Journal of Homosexuality*, vol. 59, 2012, pp. 1031–56.

Rubin, Lisa, et al. "Exploring Feminist Women's Body Consciousness." *Psychology of Women Quarterly*, vol. 28, 2004, pp. 27–37.

Saraswati, L. Ayu. *Seeing Beauty, Sensing Race in Transnational Indonesia.* U of Hawai'i P, 2013.

Shaw, Miranda. *Passionate Enlightenment: Women in Tantric Buddhism.* Princeton UP, 1994.

Shapiro, Eve. *Gender Circuits: Bodies and Identities in a Technological Age.* Routledge, 2010.

Stokes, Jasie. "Fat People of the World Unite!: Subjectivity, Identity, and Representation in Fat Feminist Manifestoes." *Interdisciplinary Humanities*, vol. 30, no. 3, 2013, pp. 50–62.

Stuart, Avelie, and Ngaire Donaghue. "Choosing to Conform: The Discursive Complexities of Choice in Relation to Feminine Beauty Practice." *Feminism and Psychology*, vol. 22, no. 1, 2011, pp. 98–121.

Tuana, Nancy. "Coming to Understand: Orgasm and the Epistemology of Ignorance." *Hypatia*, vol. 19, no. 1, 2004, pp.194–232.

Urban, Hugh. "The Cult of Ecstasy: Tantrism, the New Age, and the Spiritual Logic of Late Capitalism." *History of Religions*, vol. 39, no. 3, 2000, pp. 268–304.

Van Houdenhove, et al. "Asexuality: Few Facts, Many Questions." *Journal of Sex & Marital Therapy*, vol. 40, no. 3, 2014, pp. 175–92.

Waples, Emily. "Emplotted Bodies: Breast Cancer, Feminism, and the Future." *Tulsa Studies in Women's Literature*, vol. 32, no. 2 / vol. 33, no. 1, 2013, pp. 47–70.

Warren, Cortney. "Body Area Dissatisfaction in White, Black and Latina Female College Students in the USA: An Examination of Racially Salient Appearance Areas and Ethnic Identity." *Ethnic and Racial Studies*, vol. 37, no. 3, 2014, pp. 537–56.

Weitz, Rose. "A History of Women's Bodies." *The Politics of Women's Bodies: Sexuality, Appearance, and Behavior*, edited by Rose Weitz. Oxford UP, 1998, pp. 3–11.

———. Introduction. *The Politics of Women's Bodies: Sexuality, Appearance, and Behavior*, edited by Rose Weitz. Oxford UP, 1998, pp. 65–66.

White, David. *Kiss of the Yogini: 'Tantric Sex' in Its South Asian Contexts.* U of Chicago P, 2003.

Wolf, Naomi. *The Beauty Myth: How Images of Beauty are Used Against Women.* Anchor Books, 1992.

53. • *Janet Mock*

FROM *REDEFINING REALNESS*:
MY PATH TO WOMANHOOD, IDENTITY, LOVE & SO MUCH MORE (2014)

Janet Mock is an author, a transgender advocate, and a TV host. Her memoir *Redefining Realness* is a *New York Times* bestseller and winner of the 2015 Women's Way book prize. The excerpt from her memoir below speaks to the complexity and instability of the body and its relationship to one's identity.

[. . .]

What's difficult about being from Hawaii is that everyone has a postcard view of your home. Hawaii lives vividly in people's minds, like the orange and purple hues of the bird-of-paradise flower. It's a fantasy place of sunshine and rainbows, of high surf and golden boys with golden hair, of pigs on a spit and hula dancers' swaying hips, of Braddah Iz's "Somewhere Over the Rainbow" and the North Shore, of hapa goddesses with coconut bras and Don Ho's ukulele.

[. . .]

Ages before Hawaii's sugar boom, voyagers from Tahiti left their home to see what was beyond the horizon. Navigating the seas in handcrafted canoes with the mere guidance of the stars, they arrived in Hawaii and created new lives. Centuries later, I landed in 1995, and it was here, on the island of Oahu, that I would mirror my ancestors on my own voyage, one guided through a system of whispers, to reveal the person I was meant to be. I will forever be indebted to Hawaii for being the home I needed. There is no me without Hawaii.

[. . .]

Though we came from our native Hawaiian mother, Chad and I were perceived and therefore raised as black, which widely cast us as outsiders, nonlocals—and being seen as local in Hawaii was currency. When we first returned to Oahu, we spoke with a Texas twang that also got us teased. Chad has strong emotions surrounding those first few months: he was traumatized by his apparent blackness, which was a nonevent in Dallas and Oakland, where we were among many black kids. In Hawaii, we were some of the few mixed black kids around. And both our parents taught us that because the world would perceive us as black, we were black.

That didn't erase the unease I felt when the kids in the housing complex took notice of our darkness and kinky hair. Skin color wasn't necessarily the target as much as our blackness was the target for teasing. I say this because the kids who teased us were as brown as us, but we were black. There was a racial order that existed even in this group of tweens. They teased that Chad and I were *popolo*, Hawaiian slang for black people. *Popolo* are shiny berries that grow in clusters in the islands and are so black that they shine purple on branches. Hearing *popolo* on that playground didn't sound as regal as its namesake berries. It sounded dirty, like something that stuck on our bodies, like the red dirt of the playground. I craved belonging, especially to be reflected in my mother and her family, local-bred Hawaiian people, and spent my earlier years trying to separate

from my blackness. I've since learned that I can be both black and native Hawaiian despite others' perceptions and their assertion that I must choose one over the other.

Ethnicity is a common part of conversations in Hawaii. Two questions locals ask are: "What high school you went?" and "What you?" Your high school places you on the island, shedding light on your character and where you are from. "What you?" refers to your people, whom you come from, what random mixture has made you. Jeff, whose father was also black, was perceived as Hawaiian, taking after Mom's side, looking like those bronze-skinned local boys who surfed and threw shaka signs at Sandy Beach. Jeff later told me that he didn't even know he was black until he was about eight because he didn't look it and barely knew his father beyond the two-hundred-dollar monthly checks Mom received throughout his childhood.

[. . .]

Wendi's first words to me were "Mary! You *mahu?*"

I was sitting on a park bench as Jeff ran around with his friends on the lawn that separated my school from his. Wendi was passing by with her volleyball in hand, her backpack bouncing on her butt, and her drive-by inquiry in the air. Though there was definitely a question mark floating around, her direct yet playful approach made me internalize her words as a statement. *If she's asking—even kiddingly—then I must be suspect,* I thought.

Everyone took notice of Wendi. She was hard to miss, prancing around Kalakaua Intermediate School in super-short soccer shorts, with her green mop of hair vibrantly declaring her presence. Subtlety was not—and still isn't—her thing. Her irritated red skin, peppered with acne, glistened with sweat as she played volleyball on campus. I'd never been this close to her, and her scrutinizing stare was intimidating.

Jeff, whom I picked up every day after school while Chad was at basketball or baseball practice, wasn't paying attention, but I remember feeling self-conscious. I was afraid that if I got close to

Wendi or someone saw me interacting with her, I would be called *mahu*—a word that I equated to *sissy*. In my playground experience with the term, it was an epithet, thrown at any boy who was perceived to be *too* feminine. Until Wendi crossed paths with me, I was under the impression that I was doing a good job at being butch enough that such words wouldn't be thrown my way.

[. . .]

At the time, *mahu* was limited by our Western interpretation, mostly used as a pejorative. What I later learned in my Hawaiian studies classes in college was that *mahu* defined a group of people who embodied the diversity of gender beyond the dictates of our Western binary system. *Mahu* were often assigned male at birth but took on feminine gender roles in Kanaka Maoli (indigenous Hawaiian) culture, which celebrated *mahu* as spiritual healers, cultural bearers and breeders, caretakers, and expert hula dancers and instructors (or *Kumus* in Hawaiian). In the Western understanding and evolution of *mahu*, it translates to being transgender in its loosest understanding: to cross social boundaries of gender and/or sex. Like that of Hawaii's neighboring Polynesian islands, *mahu* is similar to the *mahu vahine* in Tahiti, *fa'afafine* in Samoa, and *fakaleiti* in Tonga, which comes from the Tongan word *faka* (meaning "to have the way of") and *leiti* (meaning "lady"). Historically, Polynesian cultures carved an "other" category in gender, uplifting the diversity, span, and spectrum in human expression.

To be *mahu* was to occupy a space between the poles of male and female in precolonial Hawaii, where it translated to "hermaphrodite," used to refer to feminine boys or masculine girls. But as puritanical missionaries from the West influenced Hawaiian culture in the nineteenth century, their Christian, homophobic, and gender binary systems pushed *mahu* from the center of culture to the margins. *Mahu* became a slur, one used to describe male-to-female transgender people and feminine men who were gay or perceived as gay due to their gender

expression. Despite *mahu's* modern evolution, it was one of the unique benefits of growing up in a diverse place like Hawaii, specifically Oahu (which translates to "the gathering place"), where multiculturalism was the norm. It was empowering to come of age in a place that recognized that diversity existed not only in ethnicities but also in gender. There was a level of tolerance regarding gender non-conformity that made it safer for people like Wendi and me to exist as we explored and expressed our identities.

The first person I met who took pride in being *mahu* was my hula instructor at school. Kumu Kaua'i was one of those *mahu* who reclaimed her place in society—specifically, being celebrated in the world of hula, where the presence and talent of *mahu* was valuable. Some trans women, who actively engaged in restoring native Hawaiian culture, reclaimed *mahu* at that time, choosing to call themselves *mahuwahine* (*wahine* is Hawaiian for "woman"), just as some people in marginalized communities reclaimed formerly derogatory words like *dyke, fag, nigger, queer,* and *tranny*. It was theirs to claim, use, and uplift. Kumu didn't call herself a woman or gay despite her femininity and preference for *she* and *her* as pronouns. She simply identified as *mahu* and had no qualms about the vessel she was given and nor any desire to change it.

[. . .]

Kumu bewildered me initially because I had been raised within the strict confines of male and female. This was a far cry from football Sundays with Dad in the projects. I was shaken by the dissonance of bright floral dresses and long hair on the form of a male-bodied person, someone who expressed her femininity proudly and visibly. Adding to that was the regular presence of Kumu's "husband," a tall, masculine man who appeared Samoan in stature and looks. He would pick up Kumu at the end of our practices, affectionately kissing her and helping her load the truck with the hula instruments—the *ipu* (a drum gourd) and *'ili'ili* (set of smooth black stones)—that she brought for us to dance with.

I now realize that my fascination with Kumu wasn't that she puzzled me; I was in awe. She resonated with me at age twelve as I yearned to explore and reveal who I was. With time, I accepted Kumu's own determination of gender and learned to evolve past my ironic need to confine her to the two boxes I had been raised to live within. Kumu Kaua'i, like *mahuwahine* who came before, staked a given righteous place in Hawaii by uplifting, breeding, and spreading many aspects of native Hawaiian culture, specifically through hula. Kumu taught me, this mixed plate of a kid, how to mirror the movements of my ancestors and give thanks for the island culture that respected various other identities.

Wendi similarly captivated me because she refused to be jailed by anyone's categories or expectations. There was no confining this girl. I noticed her everywhere after our brief exchange, during which she recognized something in me that I thought I had expertly hidden behind buzz cuts and polo shirts. I took note of her slamming her volleyball at recess, whipping her flamboyant bob around campus, carrying her black flute case as she sashayed to band practice. What still stuns me about Wendi is that no one tolerated her. She was not something to be tolerated. She was accepted as fact just as one would accept the plumpness of the lunch ladies or the way Auntie Peggy, the counselors secretary, would grab your palm as you waited for a meeting and read you your future (I recall her telling me, "You're going to get married in white!"). Wendi's changing hues, her originality, her audacity to be fully herself, was embraced and probably even more respected at an age when the rest of us were struggling and striving to fit in.

I refuse to pretend, though, that her uniqueness didn't make her a target. Wendi was called *faggot* at recess and asked when she was going to get her sex change. She used such ignorance as ammunition, threatening to kiss the boys who sought to humiliate her. I wasn't as daring as Wendi, and looking at her I was frightened by what I saw: myself. I told no one about her calling me *mahu* at the swings and avoided her as her long legs in her rolled-up shorts and knee-high socks glided past me in the halls.

Instead, I became all the more unwavering in my commitment to being the good son that year. I didn't put up a fight when it came to haircuts at the beauty school that offered barber discounts. I earned awards for my academic performance in class, was bumped into advanced courses, and even worked as an editor for the yearbook and the quarterly newspaper. My teachers praised and encouraged me, and in the spring of 1996, I was inducted into the National Junior Honor Society. I was the only boy from our class to be inducted. I loved the distinction of *only,* though the boy part I could've done without.

[. . .]

As I look back, what impresses me about my family is their openness. They patiently let me lead the way and kept any confusion or worry to themselves during a fragile period in my self-discovery. I recognize this as one of the biggest gifts they gave me. On some level, I knew they were afraid for me, afraid that I would be teased and taunted. Instead of trying to change me, they gave me love, letting me know that I was accepted. I could stop pretending and drop the mask. My family fortified my self-esteem, which I counted on as I embarked on openly expressing my rapidly evolving self.

Reflecting on this pivotal time in my life, I think of the hundreds of thousands of LGBTQ (lesbian, gay bisexual, transgender, queer or questioning) youth who are flung from intolerant homes, from families who reject them when they reveal themselves. Of the estimated 1.6 million homeless and runaway American youth, as many as 40 percent are LGBTQ, according to a 2006 report by the Task Force and the National Coalition for the Homeless. A similar study by the Williams Institute cited family rejection as the leading cause of the disproportionate number of homeless LGBT youth. These young people are kicked out of their homes or are left with no choice but to leave because they can't be themselves. That's something both Wendi and I fortunately never faced.

With an air of acceptance at home, it was fairly easy to approach my mother and declare my truth. Sitting at our kitchen table, I told Mom, with no extensive planning or thought, "I'm gay." I was thirteen years old and didn't know how to fully explain who I was, conflating gender identity and sexuality. What I remember about that brief exchange was Mom's warmth. She smiled at me, letting me know that it was okay. I felt loved and heard and, more important, not othered. From her lack of reaction—her brows didn't furrow, her brown irises didn't shift from side to side—I felt as if I had announced that I had on blue today, a simple fact that we were both aware of. Mom later told me that she remembers feeling afraid for me because she sensed that there was more I wanted to say but didn't know how to. "My love for you never diminished, but a part of me was scared that people would hurt you, and that is what I had a hard time with," she told me recently.

A part of me was scared, too. I couldn't acknowledge the gender stuff because I didn't have a full understanding of it. Saying "I think I am a girl" would have been absurd for many reasons, including my fear that it would be a lot for my mother to handle. I didn't know that trans people existed; I had no idea that it was possible for thirteen-year-old me to become my own woman. That was a fantasy.

[. . .]

It was in Wendi's room that I heard about hormones. She mentioned them as if discussing milk, something you had to drink in order to grow. She told me the older girls she knew ("These fierce, unclockable bitches!") went to a doctor in Waikiki who prescribed hormones for girls as young as sixteen. "I'm going to get my shots down when I turn sixteen," Wendi, who was fourteen at the time, said with excitement. "Trust."

I knew about hormones and puberty and safe sex from the handouts Coach Richardson gave us in health and physical education class. On Tuesdays and Thursdays, he'd lecture us about how we were raging with hormones, changing the shape and feel of our bodies. I felt nothing, barely five-two and a little chunky in the face and thighs: puberty hadn't really touched me. But I noticed the suppleness of the girls in class, the ones who seemed to be towering over

many of us in height and shape. They began to separate from the pack swimming way behind in the puberty kiddie pool.

"Your grandparents are going to let you do that?" I asked Wendi, stunned.

"They don't know what *that* is and can barely speak English," she said matter-of-factly. "My aunt's gonna take me."

I trusted that, she would do exactly as she said she would, and I admired her unstoppable determination. Wendi's friendship gave me the audacity to be noticed. One morning after one of our beauty experiments, I walked into student council homeroom with arched brows that framed my almond-shaped eyes, which were sparkling with a brush of silver eye shadow that Wendi said no one would really notice because it was "natural-looking." The girls in class, the ones who wore the white SODA platform wedge sneakers I so coveted, said, "I like your makeup." I remember tucking my short curls behind my ears, beaming under the gaze my new look warranted.

One early evening after playing volleyball, Wendi and I visited a group of her friends in a reserved room at the recreation center. They were rehearsing for a show they did at Fusions, a gay club on Kuhio Avenue in Waikiki. Most of them were drag queens, but a select few were trans women who performed as showgirls. Society often blurs the lines between drag queens and trans women. This is highly problematic, because many people believe that, like drag queens, trans women go home, take off their wigs and chest plates, and walk around as men. Trans womanhood is not a performance or costume. As Wendi likes to joke, "A drag queen is part-time for showtime, and a trans woman is all the time!"

The lines continue to be blurred due to the umbrella term *transgender,* which bundles together diverse people (transsexual, intersex, genderqueer, drag performers, crossdressers, and gender-nonconforming folks) living with gender variance. Unfortunately, the data on the transgender population is scarce. The U.S. Census Bureau doesn't ask about gender identity, how trans people self-identify varies, and many (if asked) may not disclose that they're trans. The National Center for Transgender Equality has estimated that nearly 1 percent of the U.S. population is transgender, while the Williams Institute has stated that 0.3 percent of adults in the United States (nearly seven hundred thousand) identify as transgender, with the majority having taken steps to medically transition. This number does not take into account the number of transgender children or individuals who have expressed an incongruity between their assigned sex and gender identity or gender expression.

Despite the misconceptions, I understood the distinction between a drag queen and a trans woman because I came of age in the mid-nineties, and drag queens were in vogue. There was the 1995 release of *To Wong Foo, Thanks for Everything! Julie Newmar.* I hated that movie because Wendi would tease that Noxeema Jackson—Wesley Snipes's drag character—was my "Queen Mother." Drag queens were on Cori's favorite talk shows, *Sally* and *Jerry Springer,* and then there was RuPaul, "Supermodel of the World." It was a time when a brown, blond, and glamorous drag queen was a household name, beaming on MAC Cosmetics billboards at the mall in shiny red latex.

Like RuPaul, the queens at the rec center staked their claim on a smaller scale in Hawaii, part of the fabric of Oahu's diverse trans community. Toni Braxton's "Unbreak My Heart" was blasting from a boom box, and they were huddled together, about ten of them, discussing their choreography. I watched, seated on the cold tile floor with my backpack and volleyball at my side. They soon reconfigured, gathering in a circle of arms as one woman knelt at the center, hidden by the fort of mostly rotund queens. With the tape rewound, each queen walked clockwise, slowly descending into a kneeling position as the lady in the center rose, lip-synching Toni's lyrics.

[. . .]

Lani, who wore a pair of knee-length denim shorts and a stretched white tank top with black bra straps visible on her shoulders, kissed Wendi on the cheek. I stood behind Wendi, looking at Lani's winged black eyeliner, which she had whipped all the way to a sharp point where it nearly intersected with her penciled-in brows. The other girls gathered around her when Wendi turned around to introduce me. They were the first trans women I had met outside of Wendi.

I extended my hand to Lani, and she pulled me to her fleshy chest and gave me a kiss on the cheek, which left a red lip print on my face. My heart was racing because they were staring at me. Tracy was standing off to the side, uninterested, brushing her hair. I could hear her raking through her mane, strands snapping with each stroke of her brush.

"Mary, she's fish, yeah," Lani said with a chuckle, holding me at arm's length by the biceps. The girls around her nodded. Then, looking directly into my eyes, she added, "You're going to be pretty, girl. Trust!"

I tried my best to smile, aware that she was giving me a compliment—blessing me, even. To Lani, my fishiness was something to boast about. To be called fish by these women meant that I was embodying the kind of femininity that could allow me access, safety, opportunity, and maybe happiness. To be fish meant I could pass as any other girl, specifically a cis woman, mirroring the concept of "realness," which was a major theme in *Paris Is Burning,* the 1990 documentary about New York City's ballroom community, comprising gay men, drag queens, and trans women of color. Ball legend Dorian Corey, who serves as the sage of the film, offering some of the most astute social commentary on the lived experiences of low-income LGBT people of color, describes "realness" for trans women (known in ball culture as femme queens) as being "undetectable" to the "untrained" or "trained." Simply, "realness" is the ability to be seen as heteronormative, to assimilate, to not be read as other or deviate from the norm. "Realness" means you are extraordinary in your embodiment of what society deems normative.

"When they can walk out of that ballroom into the sunlight and onto the subway and get home and still have all their clothes and no blood running off their bodies," Corey says in the film, "those are the femme *realness* queens."

Corey defines "realness" for trans women not just in the context of the ballroom but outside of the ballroom. Unlike Pepper LaBeija, a drag legend who said undergoing genital reconstruction surgery (GRS) was "taking it a little too far" in the film, a trans woman or femme queen embodies "realness" and femininity beyond performance by existing in the daylight, where she's juxtaposed with society's norms, expectations, and ideals of cis womanhood.

To embody "realness," rather than performing and competing "realness," enables trans women to enter spaces with a lower risk of being rebutted or questioned, policed or attacked. "Realness" is a pathway to survival, and the heaviness of these truths were a lot for a thirteen-year-old to carry, especially one still trying to figure out who she was. I was also unable to accept that I was perceived as beautiful because, to me, I was not. No matter how many people told me I was fish, I didn't see myself that way. My eyes stung, betraying me, and immediately I felt embarrassed by my visible vulnerability.

[. . .]

With Wendi at my side, I felt I could be bold, unapologetic, free. To be so young and aiming to discover and assert myself alongside a best friend who mirrored me in her own identity instilled possibility in me. I could be me because I was not alone. The friendship I had with Wendi, though, is not the typical experience for most trans youth. Many are often the only trans person in a school or community, and most likely, when seeking support, they are the only trans person in LGBTQ spaces. To make matters worse, these support spaces often only address sexual orientation rather than a young person's gender identity, despite the all-encompassing acronym. Though trans youth seek community with cis gay, lesbian, bisexual, or queer teens, they may have to educate their cis peers about what it means to be trans.

When support and education for trans youth are absent, feelings of isolation and hopelessness can worsen. Coupled with families who might be intolerant and ill equipped to support a child, young trans people must deal with identity and body issues alone and in secret. The rise of social media and online resources has lessened the deafening isolation for trans people. If they have online access, trans people can find support and resources on YouTube, Tumblr, Twitter, and various other platforms where trans folks of all ages are broadcasting their lives, journeys, and even social and medical transitions. Still, the fact remains that local trans-inclusive support and positive media reflections of trans people are rare outside of major cities like Los Angeles, New York, Portland, San Francisco, and Seattle.

Recently, the media (from the *New Yorker* and the *New York Times* to ABC's *20/20* and *Nightline*) has focused its lens on trans youth. The typical portrait involves young people grappling with social transition at relatively young ages, as early as four, declaring that they're transgender and aiming to be welcomed in their communities and schools as their affirmed gender. As they reach puberty, these youth—with the support and resources of their welcoming families—undergo medical intervention under the expertise of an endocrinologist who may prescribe hormone-blocking medications that suppress puberty before graduating to cross-sex hormones and planning to undergo other gender affirmation surgeries.

To be frank, these stories are best-case scenarios, situations I hope become the norm for every young trans person in our society. But race and class are not usually discussed in these positive media portraits, which go as far as erasing the presence of trans youth from low-income communities and/or communities of color. Not all trans people come of age in supportive middle- and upper-middle-class homes, where parents have resources and access to knowledgeable and affordable health care that can cover expensive hormone-blocking medications and necessary surgeries. These best-case scenarios are not the reality for most trans people, regardless of age.

[. . .]

54. • *Riki Wilchins*

ANGRY INTERSEX PEOPLE WITH SIGNS! (2013)

Riki Wilchins is an author and a gender activist. *Time* magazine named Wilchins as one of "100 Civic Innovators for the 21st Century." Most of Wilchins's writings focus on transgender issues. The following op-ed from *The Advocate* magazine exposes the problems and limitations of the ways in which the medical world reinforces gender binaries through practices of unnecessary surgeries that mold, quite literally, the genitalia to fit into its accepted norm and form.

When I first met Cheryl Chase 15 years ago, she was striking, to say the least: intense, charismatic, brilliant, and oh yeah . . . really, really angry.

Cheryl had been born Charlie, until doctors decided he was really she, and his small penis was her overly large clitoris.

So they operated; cut it down to better resemble "normal" girls. They told Cheryl's mom that she must never acknowledge any of this to her daughter, that she must, in fact, lie to her own child's face if she was ever asked about it. Because, they thought, a child knowing that his or her genital sex was in any way ambiguous would be so traumatic as to be devastating.

This was standard clinical practice at the time, and sadly, in too many places it is still followed.

Except as she grew, Cheryl realized something was wrong. How could she not?

For one thing, she had lost most of her genital sensation and couldn't experience sexual pleasure in that area.

And then there were also the pretty obvious signs that someone had operated upon her body.

But it took her years of searching to find out the truth of what had been done to her and why she felt so wrong and so different.

Eventually, understandably, she grew deeply depressed. By the time she was a world-class technology programmer who lived part-time in Japan, she was completely suicidal and only avoided taking her own life because she feared it would bring shame and cultural ostracism upon her hosts.

Part of what was slowly killing her was the sheer isolation and loneliness of being the only one in the world.

So Cheryl did what every accidental activist has done for centuries—she organized.

She founded the Intersex Society of North America, the world's first intersex advocacy organization. She told me at the time she did it mostly to find other people, to see if there was anyone else out there like her.

And this is a fine juncture for a sidebar on language. Although in the past Cheryl has tolerantly allowed me to refer to her as "The Head Herm," intersex people don't ever use the term *hermaphrodite,* which in any case was never accurate and actually derives from the Greek figure of Hermaphroditus, who had a female body with male genitals.

Most of us think of intersex as "people born with both sets of genitals," a condition so rare as to practically qualify as an urban myth.

Intersex—the new term is disorders of the sex development (DSD)—covers a cluster of conditions of chromosomal or anatomic sex at birth. Most of those conditions are nonthreatening and have little or no clinical or medical significance.

Cheryl used to talk about them as "unexpected genitals," but I think the really crucial thing about them is that these are genitals that make doctors uncomfortable. So they have to do something about it. Naturally, that means doing something to change the infant, not their own discomfort.

Current clinical standards still call for cutting up intersex kids, the earlier the better, so they have genitals that better resemble yours and mine.

Well, yours anyway.

Cheryl pithily defined DSD as a psychological emergency on the part of doctors treated by performing surgery on the body of the infant. That about sums it up.

It's done as compassionate surgery and even often for free. But that does nothing to ease its sheer awfulness and barbarity or the terrible waste of lives and young bodies.

Cheryl and I eventually started a protest group—yes, an intersex protest group—irreverently named after ISNA's occasional newsletter, Hermaphrodites With Attitude!

With Transexual Menace folks, we'd picket outside major urban hospitals—practically all of them perform intersex surgery—and big-name pediatric conventions. The doctors and medical staff simply didn't know what to make of us, looking on as if they felt under attack! By real live hermaphrodites! In matching T-shirts! With nasty picket signs!

Well, we knew then that the surgery—intrusive, unnecessary, irreversible, and utterly lacking in the most basic notions of informed patient consent—was ripe for medical malpractice suits. Cheryl and I would sometimes daydream about how things might be different for future DSD kids, if only there was a way to file lawsuits.

But the statute of limitations always had run out by the time children grew into (angry, aware) adults.

And parents never sued. And even if they wanted to, there was no national organization, with lawyers and funding and expertise, to back them up.

Now. There. Is.

With help from Advocates for Informed Choice, a South Carolina couple have filed a landmark lawsuit against state doctors and social workers for unnecessary genital surgery on their 16-month-old child. The Southern Poverty Law Center has joined the new group in the suit, and you can sign on to support the action here.

"We feel very strongly that these decisions to permanently alter somebody's genitalia and their reproductive ability for no medical reason whatsoever is an abhorrent practice and can't be continued," said Pamela Crawford, the mother.

"It is too late for our son. The damage has been done to him."

The child, identified to only as M.C., had been in the foster system when doctors noted the genital ambiguity and decided they would remake the genitalia—and the child—as female.

Alas, M.C., now 8, identifies as male and has been living as a boy. God only knows what awaits him as an adult with the body these doctors decided it was their right to create.

And M.C. is only one of multitudes. Dozens of these surgeries take place every day in U.S. hospitals. If this took place abroad, we'd call it by its real name: genital mutilation.

A U.S. District Court judge has already ruled that this unnecessary surgery on DSD kids could violate the Constitution, denying a state motion for dismissal.

The doctors and the state are refusing comment, supposedly because it's pending litigation. No doubt they feel . . . under attack! By real live hermaphrodites! With lawyers! Filing nasty lawsuits!

Well, here's hoping they do. And that this is only the start of many more nasty lawsuits. This dark, medieval corner of negligent malpractice needs to be pulled kicking and screaming into the light of day. Federal lawsuits have a way of doing that. They also will go a long way toward making doctor and hospitals—who believe it is their right to carve gender stereotypes into the bodies of uncomplaining infants—think twice before they operate.

The landmark actions of the Crawfords and Advocates for Informed Choice have brought that time one day closer. Here's hoping other parents follow. This practice must stop.

55. • *No'u Revilla*

HOW TO USE A CONDOM (2011)

No'u Revilla is a Native Hawaiian, *Kānaka Maoli* poet, and founder of Nolu 'Ehu: A Queer Nesian Creative Collective. She is the author of the chapbook *Say Throne*, from which the poem below is taken. In it, she addresses issues of indigeneity, sovereignty, and reproductive rights.

Pleasure Pack variety:
Her Pleasure.
Shared Pleasure.
Deep Impact.

We gotta stop

   Ultra ribbed

We gotta stop We gotta stop We gotta stop—
   TEAR HERE
   and concentrate.
   Substance interrupted

if used properly.
will reduce risk of transmission. In-and-out nothings
will eroticize motion and deeper spermicidal tendencies
will lead to murder.

Reproduction is not the problem.
Reproduction is the problem.
making children based on an image.
We gotta stop.

   Against highly effective pregnancy.

We are kissing in a picture in a frame on your shelf
(we intercoursed that night while your parents were home)
but the fluids stop there.
Our moments like wet hair in the cold: old stories
with low body temperatures, low resistance to virus.
Diminishing diminishing
until lubrication is a product.
For sale.
We gotta stop

I need connection to be source to be predicate to be don't stop
    don't stop don't stop—
will your lost erections ever find their way home?

    TEAR HERE.
    Unroll your barrier device.
    And leave space at the tip for collection.

56. • *Tagi Qolouvaki*

STORIES SHE SUNG ME (FOR KATALAINE) (NEW)

Tagi Qolouvaki is a queer indigenous writer, artist, and teacher. She is Fijian-Tongan through her mother's people and German-English American through her father's people. A student of indigenous Pacific literature and queer indigenous studies, Tagi is a Ph.D. candidate at the University of Hawai'i at Mānoa. When asked to bring a poem to a baby shower, she wrote this to honor her mother, whose unapologetic nonconformity to so many gender norms—but particularly those around mothering—taught her the strength and value of feminism.

"o o baua
lai vei iko tinamu
lai qoli keidaru

daru na mai tatavu
kemu na saku
qau na damu
o o baua"*

some women are made
for mothering
not you
nor me

you would let the sky
cradle me
baptized
in the choice of my
own gods

you would let the sun
clothe me
oiled down in bubu's
reliable brown hands
mokosoi and coconut
fragrant

you would let the earth
feed me
mouthfuls of ripened pawpaw
softened dalo
and fish you'd chewed

later you taught me
to love curried crab
so hot our skin sweat
tiny licks of flame

you would let the men
name me
my father choosing carefully
with his year-old fijian tongue
    tagi
while you called me
pumpkin-pie
your guji girl

you would let the rain
teach me lullabies
of the land
the humid air fill my lungs
and song
with loloma

"o o baua
lai vei iko tinamu
lai qoli keidaru

daru mai tatavu
kemu na saku
qau na damu
*o o baua"**

*Quoted text from Fijian lullaby

WHAT HER BODY TAUGHT (OR, TEACHING ABOUT AND WITH A DISABILITY):
A Conversation (2005)

Brenda Brueggemann is the director of composition and a professor of English at the University of Louisville. Her work focuses on disability and deaf studies. She is the author of *Deaf Subjects: Between Identities and Places*. Rosemarie Garland-Thomson is a professor of English at Emory University. She is a prominent figure in the field of feminist disability studies and has written many books on the topic, including *Staring: How We Look* and *Extraordinary Bodies: Figuring Physical Disability in American Culture and Literature*, which is considered an important work in the field. Georgina Kleege is professor of English at the University of California Berkeley. She is an author of many books including *Sight Unseen, Blind Rage: Letters to Helen Keller*, and *Home for the Summer* (a novel). Their collaborative work, which first appeared in *Feminist Studies*, is a conversation on what it means to teach about and with disability.

COMING INTO THE CLASSROOM

Georgina: Part of what our bodies teach in the classroom has to do with role modeling. Both students with disabilities and students without disabilities see a person with a disability in a position of authority, and, without having to say anything about it, it's a way of demonstrating that one can have authority and an intellectual life and a career and all these things. Over time the novelty of our otherness can disappear. In my case students know I can't see them, can't see their faces; I can't see them when they raise their hands so they have to speak up. After a while they sort of forget why that practice is imposed in my classroom, it just becomes a part of who I am as a teacher.

Brenda: I always have wondrously mixed feelings about that kind of different, but then naturalized,

interaction over disability. Mostly, I love it—because it keeps a kind of productive tension ongoing and that tension makes evident then how classrooms are extremely normalized. Public education in America has been all about that normalizing—from standardized testing to the whole notion of public schools, it's really about upholding a kind of normalized view that we all function and learn in the same way. And so in some ways I'm not surprised that happens, Georgina—that they begin to normalize you. In some ways I'm enchanted when students get to the point where they say that they have forgotten entirely about my difference, my "disability." And soon they don't even notice anymore the Frequency Modulated system I sometimes use—or how I make them repeat things that another one said or make them do all the writing on the board.[1] And yet, in the beginning of a class, the FM system is a new marker that really shakes them up, just having this little piece of hi-tech equipment on the table and they all stare at that the first day and then pretty soon they forget entirely. (Until the day someone says something a bit zany and then I pick it up, hold it to my mouth, and say "Beam me up, Scottie.")

And that makes me feel good that I can pass . . . but then it also makes me uneasy. And I've become more aware that I keep doing little things to keep bringing it back up in a classroom to keep *making* them notice and to not (over)normalize me. It's like wanting to erase difference, which is attractive but also a danger.

[. . .]

Rosemarie: Both of you are talking about how students can forget after a while that we have disabilities. And that such forgetting is both a good thing and a bad thing. It seems to me that what we want to try to achieve here is subtle in the sense that what we want is not for them to forget that we have disabilities and therefore to assume that we have normative bodies and to assume that we fit the standard expectation. We don't want them to forget that, but what we do want, I think, is for them to realize that our impairments no longer have the determining force of a master status. We want to redefine, to reimagine, disability—not make it go away. But also not have it remain with its stigmatic force. So we want it to go away in a way that *we* want it to go away.

Brenda: That's actually a really good one, Rosemarie, about the body and the classroom because I think that, in general, what we all don't know about is how *anyone* does *anything* in their lives or accomplishes anything. Yet we wonder. And that wonder is what makes us human. We fear that having a conversation about something like what Georgina can and can't see, what Brenda can and can't hear, what Rosemarie can and can't do is just too personal in a classroom space. Yet nothing should be more important in a classroom than that wonder.

[. . .]

Rosemarie: . . . I know that people don't ask—students don't ask me about my disability. Even when we're talking about disability. But then their papers come back. They write things like: "I never *thought* about disability before. I never thought how much people with disabilities must *suffer* and how difficult it must be and I find that I myself have all sorts of oppressive stereotypes and attitudes. And I'm really gonna be better about this." And I just kind of groan and think, "Well, that's good but somehow that isn't exactly what we wanted." It's not a *mea culpa* that I want out of them. And I get a lot of *mea culpas*. And, of course, part of it is that when you are teaching texts, a lot of the narratives are about how difficult it's been for the person with a disability. And I feel like a lot of those *mea culpas* and "I'm gonna be better" are directed toward me, but—

Georgina: As the representative of the group, right?

Rosemarie: Yeah. So I would like to have more moments like the one that you are talking about, but moments that we can kind of control and structure. Because I think of Carrie's point, if they were to really, *freely,* ask every single question that comes up about our difference or about what they imagine to be our differentness from them then it would be overwhelming, I think, or it could be. . . .

Georgina: What Brenda and I have in common is that we have to talk about our impairments on the first day of class because it affects certain behaviors in my classroom. I can't see them raise their hand, so we are going to have to figure out a different way to achieve that "normal" classroom behavior, if they have a question.

Brenda: Yes, it affects very core classroom functions.

Georgina: Yes, and it's going to affect in one way or the other how I read and respond to their papers and their exams. And so I have to explain that. And the awkwardness about that is, of course, it's the first day of class, it's the first time they have ever encountered me. They may be trying out this class, they don't know who I am, they don't know what the class is about. There are all those sort of first day of class intimidating, nervous-making things going on anyway. And there I am announcing that I'm blind. "Hey, I can't see what you are doing."

Rosemarie: And they must be thinking, "How in the hell is she going to teach this class?"

Georgina: Yeah, yeah, I've written about this, and the downside of this is I don't know if there are people who drop the class after that first moment for no other reason than the fact that they believe a blind woman can't teach and so they'll just go elsewhere. I think the ones who stay may form a different opinion and I've never had a student make any kind of statement about my blindness affecting my performance or how I evaluate their work or how I conduct the classroom.

[. . .]

Rosemarie: Do you get a lot of the admiration narrative? I get a lot of that. Not directed toward me, they never write papers where they say "Well I admire you," because of course we are always writing about a topic. So when you teach about disability, and you have one, what they are saying in their work about disability or a disabled character is in some ways a transference, because as Georgina just said, you become a representative. And so, I don't know what to do about that because it makes me uncomfortable because it's not, well, the point.

Georgina: I once had a student—and this ties into the role-modeling thing, but in a sort of uncomfortable way. We were walking to my office from the classroom, and first she asked me—it was sort of a neutral question that didn't really bother me—about how did I find my way. I talked a little bit about how you do that: it's a regular route that I do numerous times, so it's not hard. And then she made a comment about my appearance, something like, "And you always dress so nicely." And I knew that it was a compliment, and I knew that she was being nice, and I knew that she was a young woman, and I think probably appearance and clothes mattered to her. So she obviously took it into account, looking at other women—

Rosemarie: And surveying her own appearance.

Georgina: But at the same time there was that element that I think goes back in my own history to those patronizing remarks we all get like, "Isn't it marvelous that you can get your socks to match."

Rosemarie: Or that you care enough about your appearance, that you have enough self worth to bother.

Brenda and *Georgina*: Yeah, yeah.

Georgina: That you even bother getting nice clothes.

Brenda: Okay—here's one back at us—because the three of us always do dress really nicely. And in what ways we manage our stigma—work to unspoil our spoiled identities (as Erving Goffman would say) by making sure we dress the hypernormal part.[2] Especially because teaching is in and about performance. And because we are already aware of the stereotypes that culture places on what they think disabled people look like. So in some ways, are we managing the care of that "fact"?

Georgina: And that management and care is also a part of the rhetoric of rehabilitation. A lot of it seems to be about you as the spectacle, an awareness that people are going to look at us, and they are going to judge aspects of our appearance. It's what Rosemarie was saying this morning, about how you can't be anonymous and invisible as a disabled person out in the world.

OUT IN THE WORLD

Rosemarie: One of the things that I've always noticed about teaching that's different from what happens in the world at large—because I've been in the classroom since I was twenty-one years old, which is a *long* time—I've noticed all this stuff about staring. This is also something I'm writing on. Staring is a major response to my disability, because function is not so much the point with my disability, or the non-normative aspect is not such a functional issue, but it's a formal issue. I really look different from what people expect somebody to look like. So I'm always stared at. So one of the major occupations of my life, and it's a very subtle thread that runs all the way through, is to manage staring. It's a form of stigma management. Because my disability is right out there, right up front. It doesn't take very long for people to notice it in a way that with many other disabilities people are a little slower on the uptake. And so in some ways there's a kind of advantage to that; it's right there at the beginning, so there isn't that shock of discovery that I think some people experience when the person they are interacting with finally gets it, that they do have a disability. I don't have to worry about disclosure very often, although there's a little bit of that some of the time. Nevertheless, I've always found it really interesting that for the most part students don't stare as much at me in the classroom as people do on the street or in any other circumstance. And I've concluded that what it's about is that my authority as the teacher trumps the—

Brenda: Ah, the normalizing function of the classroom!

[. . .]

Rosemarie: So the problem with staring is not so much the staring. It's how nervous it makes the person. It's that they want to stare and don't want to stare, and they don't know how to not stare, and it's that ambivalence about the staring that's the problem almost more than the actual staring. So, somehow that's mitigated to some degree in the classroom.

[. . .]

Brenda: But you know, you are so right, Rosemarie. I was thinking about this a couple of weeks ago—one of the interesting things about disability is that the sphere of disability gets widened: being in a relationship with a person with a disability somehow can

make you disabled, too. It rubs off. I'll never forget running in Central Park in New York City with you, Rosemarie. It's kind of like the disabled fashion models that you have been researching and talking about in your presentation to the women's studies classroom at Ohio State yesterday—that while there's one element of the person that doesn't quite fit the norm, so much of the rest of you is so very attractive and fits a norm for what a very well-groomed woman should look like. And so, there we were, running side-by-side in Central Park that beautiful September Sunday. People would do a sort of glance at us; they would quickly and visually take us both in. I think you were even just in your little bra top and your little running shorts too. And then, whoa, they would see your arms, and they would do this sort of jump back thing with their eyes, eyebrows, and shoulders.

Rosemarie: Like you're clearing the sidewalk.

Brenda: Yes, people would jump back, and then their glance would go right over to me, and there would be a scope up and down *me* to look for what was wrong. And I told Georgina—and it has taken me eight years to figure this out—but this same kind of dynamic happens when I walk on campus or around town with Georgina. They do this looong stare—from Georgina's cane in front of her, up her arm, then way way up to her head. How tall are you, Georgina? 6'1"?

Georgina: 6'2."

[. . .]

Brenda: Yeah, and then so Georgina ran right home and asked her husband Nick about this halo effect, and he said, "Oh yeah, I get that all the time. It's a great babe magnet, actually."

Georgina: He says that attractive women give him that look.

Rosemarie: Because that's what women want.

Brenda: Exactly.

Rosemarie: The good, kind, generous man who will take care of you, instead of dominating you. I think the fact that he's shorter than you makes a lot of difference, too. In the sense that that probably makes him look less capable of dominating. It always gives me the creeps to see really big, hulking men with little, teeny, tiny wives and especially when they have them by the hand. It doesn't strike me as a gesture of affection, but rather as kind of coercive, or worse.

Brenda: Here's another interesting disability by association dynamic: when Georgina and I go out to eat together, the waiters never want to talk to Georgina, because they see the cane and they're mortified by her. So then they start yapping at me, and I'm totally lost, as I always am with waiter-speak. They'll say something to me and then I'll look across at Georgina and say to her, "What did he say?" And he's standing right there, and now he's totally freaked out. So Georgina translates waiter-speak for me and I read the menu to her.

[. . .]

ACCESSING THE ACADEMY

Rosemarie: Now I was saying that I thought that form and content came together when a person with a disability enters the classroom to talk about disability as a topic. Because it was a matter of integration and disability studies, at its most successful moments, has a two-pronged integration agenda: one is to integrate disability as a topic, as an idea, as a category of analysis, as a historical community into the subject matter of every single field and discipline across the entire academy, and to bring critical skills, critical analysis into the conversation about disability. But the other part of it is to integrate people with disabilities because the ultimate goal of critiquing disability is to critique the exclusion of people with disability from the public realm and from a

certain cultural valuing. And so when a person with a disability actually is in the classroom in a position of authority, that integration has taken place, because the stereotypes of disabled people would never place us in positions of authority, or even out in the public world, or educated, or knowledgeable, and we are usually what is talked *about*—

Georgina: By experts who are not disabled.

[. . .]

Brenda: Like wanting to be thought of as a writer first, but then that's not really what you want either because you don't want your disability, your identity to be taken away. But I think that's one of the provisions, because it's true—it's like there's literature's *here,* but then there's "literature about or by blind people" over *there.* And they are all too often separate categories.

Rosemarie: That conversation has gone on a long time about women who write, wanting to or not wanting to be called women writers. And a blind writer, that's even a more intensified version of that same problem.

[. . .]

Rosemarie: Yes, and there's also the way that disability complicates identity categories—the thing that has happened with women's studies. The evolution of women's studies has concerned itself with how identity operates and how identities intersect with one another. But now, women's studies has become much broader and sophisticated than just "this has to be about women and what women did." Certainly that is an important part of it, but on a theoretical level, women's studies or feminist theory or gender studies—depending on how you want to talk about it—concerns itself with the relationship between the body and identity. We are interested in how identity is formed, and how identity systems operate, and how identity systems interact.

And, of course, disability is an identity system that is very similar to race, gender, sexuality, but yet it has its own specificity and a tremendous number of interesting complications that get brought to the analysis. We say a lot in women's studies, "no woman is ever only a woman"—she also has all these other identities; she's always a disabled or nondisabled woman. She identifies, and is identified, in that way. So taking that into consideration, looking at how gender as a system operates in tandem with disability is implicit in women's studies.

Brenda: But sometimes—no make that, often—there is great tension, and arguments erupt. That's what happened yesterday when you showed all the slides, Rosemarie, and talked about the models with disabilities in high fashion. And the one student in the seminar pointed out that the problem with saying "hey, this is great—disabled people are being represented in high fashion now, too!" is that it also means disabled people are being commodified, fetishized, conformed, exploited in advertising now, too. Desiring to be in the mainstream of culture—and then actually being in and part of that "mainstream"—also means you have to deal with some of that yucky stuff floating around on the surface of the mainstream, too. Disability—as a concept and construct—keeps reminding us then of how complicated our bodies are, reminding us of the complicated, and often contradictory, "acceptance" and assessment and negotiation of our own (and others') bodies. That's what those young women were reminded of, and grappling with, when you gave them disabled fashion models in that seminar yesterday afternoon. It's part of what I think we all grapple with when faced with the figure or sense or face of disability.

NOTES

1. The FM system (or Frequency Modulated system) is a listening device that may be separate from, or also often adjoined to someone's hearing aid, that can help reduce the effective distance between the speaker and the hearing aid user while it also emphasizes one speaker/voice/noise at a time. Most movie theaters, for example, now carry FM systems that you can check out for use during a film. Working like specialized radio headphones, the FM system brings the speaker system more directly into the listener's ear (provided, however, that other patrons in the theater have their cell phones and other electronic devices, which often interfere with FM system reception, turned off). In aiding a hard-of-hearing student in the classroom, the teacher would wear the FM transmitter and a microphone in frequency with the student's hearing aid. The microphone is usually placed at chest level (about six inches away from the mouth) or at the level of the mouth (three inches from the mouth). In some situations a microphone may be used on a table as a conference microphone, allowing the FM user to hear voices all around a table. Some microphones also have a directional feature which lets the FM microphone "zoom in" on one specific speaker while it works to dampen a background of high noise. Directional microphones are often held by the FM user, who points the microphone toward the person who is talking.

2. Erving Goffman, *Stigma: Notes on the Management of a Spoiled Identity,* a classic book in sociology, examines the processes surrounding and creating "stigma," the ways and means or how we classify others and are, in turn, classified by them. Goffman's theory of stigma management is, like all of his theories, one of interaction and relationships. The process of interactive classification around the management of our own (and others') "discredit" or stigma is what Goffman called "normalization."

TOO LATINA TO BE BLACK, TOO BLACK TO BE LATINA

Aleichia Williams is a feminist writer, photographer, and artist. She has been blogging for *Huffington Post* and published her first book, *21 Ways to Live a Fulfilled Life According to a 21 Year Old,* based on her blog posts. She was born and raised in New York and currently lives in Texas.

I can remember the first time I had a 'race crisis.'

I was probably twelve or thirteen and I had just moved to the quiet state of North Carolina from my home state and city of New York. North Carolina was a lot different than New York. For one, there wasn't an enormous variety of culture and people. I didn't have class with any Russians. My professors weren't Puerto Rican and there wasn't a whole lot of mixing between kids of one race with kids of another. In fact, at my middle school you had three groups you could classify as; black, "Mexican", or white.

Unaware of this fact I walked into my second class on my first day of school and decided to sit next to a group of friendly looking Hispanic girls. As soon as I sat down the table was quiet. Then one girl snickered to another in Spanish "Why is she sitting here? I don't want her to sit here." Her friend, who had been in my previous class and had heard my class introduction, blushed and replied to her friend in English "She speaks Spanish."

That was the first time I could remember being aware of my skin color and the overwhelming implications it held. This was also my first 'race crisis.'

Now, I know what you're thinking. How could you grow up unaware that you were black? This isn't hard to answer. Growing up in an environment where it was normal to be colored and walk into a store and be spoken to in Spanish did not prepare me for how people in other places perceived my skin. My mom spoke Spanish. My grandmother spoke Spanish. Our family friends spoke Spanish. From the music we listened to, to the church we went to, to the food we ate, everything about me surrounded a Latin-American culture. This was a culture that I knew and belonged to but was excluded from it entirely when I left the melting pot that is New York City.

My crisis continued for years. When the violence broke out in middle school between the African-American gangs and the Hispanic gangs and the students spoke among themselves on who was best I could remember screaming "I don't know who to side with!" When I got into high school and a class mate told me "You're the most Mexican black girl I've ever met!" I could remember thinking 'Is that a compliment because my family is from Honduras?'

Even now as an adult I find people are constantly trying to restrict me into a specific mold and identity. My home language is Spanish so this must mean I eat tacos. I have kinky hair so this must mean I bang to Meek Mill. For many, I am too black to be Latin and too Latin to be black.

However, that's not how I see things. I currently live in Texas and my identity is unique because you don't have many dark skinned girls singing along to bachata around here. I've learned though, that just because I don't fit into one specific mold or the other doesn't mean I'm any less of who I am.

I'm learning to embrace every aspect of my identity and not let small minds put me in a box that just doesn't fit. I'm Latina. I'm black. Also, I'm human. No one can take that from me.

59. • *Dominique C. Hill*

(MY) LESBIANISM IS NOT A FIXED POINT (NEW)

Dominique C. Hill is a scholar-artist, auto/ethnographer, educator, and body lyricist. Her research employs the body as a site of inquiry, culture, and knowledge production. As a Blackgirl advocate/researcher, she has received recognition for her original contributions to the burgeoning interdisciplinary field of black girlhood studies. Highlights of these awards include the Gender and Women's Studies' 2014 Donald and Barbara Smalley Graduate Research Award at University of Illinois and the 2011 American Educational Research Association Minority Dissertation Award. She is currently an independent girhood studies scholar and artist in residence at the Oxford Community Arts Center.

I.

I've been scrolling through profiles for hours now. Blackplanet (the black and mostly hetero cyber community for dating) has *way* too many visitors. Why do I have to be in the middle of nowhere? Aside from myself there isn't a lesbian that I would date in sight! It would be a lot easier if I were home in Buffalo or New York City or even Syracuse, I surmise—anywhere but here. In this town of not quite 3,000 people, there are a few girls secretly interested in trying me but that s*** gets old. Don't get me wrong; it's thrilling, momentarily. I respect and understand being confused and/or disinterested in publicly declaring an interest in me, but I don't support performing the character "avid homophobe" in public so your friends who *know* about me (read: know I deal with women) remain unassuming about you. Nor am I moved by the church hugs to keep your distance while whispering in my ear, "You know I want you, right?" No! I want to be with another lesbian. Scratch that, a black lesbian. At the very least, I need someone whose default performance is not "avid homophobe." That means (sigh), that means I'm gonna keep scrolling through these damn profiles. One will jump out at me, I hope.

She wears dresses
Pumps and thongs
I like that.
She wants me,
fitted hat and baggy sweats
Not feeling it!

My lesbian packaging was (and remains) aberrant, to some. Committing to black community solidarity on campus situated me as a rising black nationalist. Working at the Women's Center and leading a women of color awareness and support group made me a strong candidate for the title A-rate black feminist. Somehow my lesbianism could be overlooked, misconstrued as "mannish" femininity. Either way, my sexuality was a craft, something I had to carve up and create for myself. Additionally, being black, female, involved in the black community on campus, interested in black women—with no car—made dating a bit difficult. I took to the Internet and found my first girlfriend—a black woman who, like me, loved wearing thongs and heels. Despite her meeting me through cyberspace as feminine presenting, my degree of femininity slightly bothered her. Maybe it was a predilection for my transgressive behavior or a foreshadowing of her return to men and heterosexuality. Nonetheless, it became abundantly clear that my performance of what it meant to be a lesbian wasn't rebellious enough.

II.

My mom insists on giving me money when going out with my feminine heterosexual friends. Also known as my femme friends. Also known as my ex-girlfriend and her friend who's slightly curious. No curfew. No questions. "Have fun!" she says, waving. Yet, when kickin' it with my masculine girlfriend, a dom, a soft stud as she called herself, there are *always* questions. Like, "Where are you going?" "When are you coming back?" Followed by the demand, "Don't be out all night!" And finally, "Do you have to go out with *those* people?!" I guess it didn't occur to her, I am one of *those* people. I guess I should've kept company with femmes only. Maybe then my lesbianism would remain less of a problem. That's just it—being a lesbian causes disruption.

> Dyke!, she yelled
> I don't want my son round'
> A bunch of dykes licking and kissing each
>   other!
> Merry Christmas!
> I'm a dyke,
> I guess

Identity involves performance. This epiphany broke me, only to put me back together again in 2003. The fact that my tomboyish ways as a child did not convert into baggy masculine clothing allowed my mother to dismiss my sexuality. Forget that I told her two years before in the local Pizza Hut near my university that I liked women. Forget that I labeled myself a lesbian. Up until this moment, I had not considered that my clothing could mark or in this case allow me to pass as heterosexual. Add my blackness to my style of dress and my sexuality could be disappeared altogether (see Harris-Perry, 2011; McCune, 2014)! While—prior to this unfortunate encounter with my mother—I deemed the labeling of myself as lesbian enough, I soon realized

labels function only as an initial conversation starter. The small talk ends when others begin reading and interpreting my performance.

How do I want to dress up my dykeness?

III.

Labels are flat. This is what I tell myself while sitting on my living room floor thinking about who I am and who I was. How else can I explain that my particular lesbianism includes no disdain for men? How do I call myself a lesbian when I'm attracted and the only things present are a man and his art (DJing/love for music)? I keep asking myself this question. Self? No answer. And how do I make sense of the burst of energy I get after making a man do things (sexual things) he said he would not? Power? A dent in patriarchy? What I know is that I'm ashamed, yet aroused. Overcome by an unsolicited and unjustifiable feeling as well as an intrinsic urge to be me, unapologetically, I—unafraid—go against the grain of what "normal" lesbians do and enter into a relationship with the opposite sex. Truth is, I feel like someone's gonna come and revoke my "lesbian" card.

> "Some Call Me a Misfit"
> Some call me a misfit because I say my home is
>   in my mind
> Every day I am trying to *trans*cend your limited
>   perception of me
> In college, I kissed a woman and smiled
>   afterward
>
> How could home be anywhere but where I am?
> Even as we speak I am *trans*itioning into some
>   place, some space
> Trying to take responsibility for once deeming
>   myself lesbian and now just ME
>
> Some call me confused because I refuse labels
> When I wake up my mind has already been in
>   *trans*it for a lifetime
> Last year I sexed a Black man
> Home is nestled in between my soul and spirit
>   *trans*forming in meaning

Some call people like me Black
Some call people like me Feminists
Some call people like me Weird
Some call people like me anything to crush my spirit
Some call people like me Ugly

I call people like me revolutionary
I am a living vessel of Revolution as process

I am a lesbian because I say I am!

IV.

I (silently and reluctantly) turned in my lesbian card for a queer one. Dating a man means you have to, right? Having sex with a man means you have to right? But why?! When I take my clothes off and we have sex, it's just that, sex. I am moved by the possibility of overtaking him, of inciting an earthquake in his body, of controlling him. There is no love in that! No love in control; at least not for me. And yet I stay. Proving (although unintentionally) two points to myself: (1) My sexual identity and its expression is fluid and not fixed; it can, and therefore should be, disruptive; and (2) I am a lesbian. I shoulda kept my lesbian card. Who said I had to turn that s*** in anyway?! And why did I listen to them?!

"Layered Living"
"Which do you put first?" they asked Aunt Barbara,

I'm sure she cringed.
Which do I put first?
Depends on the day and what you mean by first.
I suppose Black.
Seems I knew that space first,
Being black in the United States,
raised in highly segregated Buffalo.

Who benefits from me drawing lines around myself,
around my lesbianism,
with a separate circle around my blackness,
pretending they don't dance in the dark?
Aunt Cheryl considers my sexuality political.
Resist, she said.
Discourse.
Norms.
Power.
Contest these, she insisted.

Which do you put first,
how you see me or how I see me?
Behavior or labels?
Which do I put first?
Depends on the day and what you mean by first.
I am a blacklesbian,
with a queer aesthetic.
Trying to draw lines around that?
Don't bother.
Resist, I will.

WORKS CITED

Clarke, Cheryl. "Lesbianism: An Act of Resistance." *This Bridge Called My Back: Writings by Radical Women of Color.* Kitchen Table: Women of Color Press, 1981, pp. 128–37.

Harris-Perry, Melissa V. *Sister Citizen: Shame, Stereotypes, and Black Women in America.* Yale UP, 2011.

McCune Jr, Jeffrey Q. *Sexual Discretion: Black Masculinity and the Politics of Passing.* U of Chicago P, 2014.

Smith, Barbara. *The Truth That Never Hurts: Writings on Race, Gender, and Freedom.* Rutgers UP, 2000.

60. • *Patricia A. Gozemba*

THE LAST WORD:
A Performance Memoir on Mothers, Race, and Sexuality (new)

Patricia A. Gozemba is a writer, activist, and organizer who taught English and women's studies at Salem State University. She was a founding member of the National Women's Studies Association. *The Last Word* is part of her current writing/ performing her life project. Two of her books are *Pockets of Hope* (2002) and *Courting Equality* (2007).

MARCH 26, 1965

My dream job. White working-class students— mirror images of me. Salem State College, I'm a twenty-four-year-old beginning composition instructor. We're discussing the politics, rhetorical effectiveness, and message of Martin Luther King's 1963 "Letter from a Birmingham Jail."

Angie says, "Last night my parents and I watched the news about the Selma to Montgomery voting rights march and rally. A woman was murdered. I cried. My mother doesn't get it. I'd be embarrassed to tell you what she said. She sounds like the KKK." Student heads nod. I get Angie's point.

On days like today, discussing King with my students I feel grateful to Sister Marie, my old prof, social justice advocate, mentor who in 1959 brought me and a bunch of my freshman classmates to an ecumenical interracial weekend. We'd never met Negroes. Eaten with Negroes. Hung out, laughed, or talked with Negroes. Mutual hopes, fears, dreams. My eyes, my heart, my mind flew open. Ignominy of white and colored drinking fountains. Not being able to vote. Riding in the back of the bus.

A half hour after my composition class, I'm driving down Route 128, obligatory dinner at my mother, The Beak's house. Chance to collect my mail.

Beak loves riffling through my mail, beaking into my life. Doesn't approve of my interests: NAACP newsletters,

Catholic Interracial Conference bulletins . . . I'll probably hear, "Why the hell is this embarrassing stuff still coming? You don't live here."

As I buzz along, a flash bulletin comes on the radio. "President Lyndon Johnson will have a televised press conference within the hour, an important announcement regarding the killing of Viola Liuzzo."

I bust into the house, "Hi Beak, got to catch something on TV. Mind if I turn it on?"

"Suit yourself, Miss College Professor. Just don't get on the phone. I've got some bets to call in to my bookie."

"Mind if I sit next to you, Beak?"

"Your choice. What the hell is this on TV anyway?"

"Shhh, let's listen."

Beak sneers, "Oh that drawl of LBJ, it's a killer. Texas twang."

The president speaks, "After the tragic death of Mrs. Viola Liuzzo on a lonely road between Selma and Montgomery, Alabama, arrests were made a few minutes ago of four Ku Klux Klan members in Birmingham, Alabama, charging them with conspiracy to violate the civil rights of the murdered woman."

I cry. Beak's rattling her racing forms. "What the hell is he talking about?"

"Shhh, please, Beak."

"Mrs. Liuzzo went to Alabama to serve the struggle for justice. She was murdered by the enemies of justice."

I start crying. Again.

The newscaster wraps up: "Liuzzo, thirty-nine, white mother of five, social justice activist, murdered by the Ku Klux Klan. Just days ago, she delivered a check from her husband's Teamsters union supporting the march."

I wipe away tears.

Beak snarls, "What the hell are you crying about, Miss NAACP? Why wasn't she home with her five children instead of slutting around with n——— in Alabama? N——— lover."

My mouth hangs open. I remember Angie: "My parents don't get it."

I scream at Beak, "I hate hearing that word! You'll never, ever, use that word for a Negro under my roof. Ever."

She sputters as I bolt out of the house.

MONDAY, MAY 8, 1989

3 PM. I'm at Salem State chairing a women's studies meeting on improving our Introduction to Women's Studies syllabus. Great working with colleagues committed to social justice. I nudge them: "We need more on class, race, sexuality, and families." Exhausting, but we're being creative. Committed to justice.

5 PM. At home, glass of wine in hand, toasting with Congetta, my visiting ex-mother in law. My ex-partner Marilyn's mother. In women's studies, we discuss constructing families. Congetta, my mother of choice.

Riiinnnggg. Phone. Riiiinnnggg. Not answering. I need a little peace and quiet.

Riiiinnnng.

Suddenly Congetta's smile fades and she looks serious, asks, "Oh Pat, the Beak called earlier. Thinks we should all go to the race track on Wednesday. Could you do that Sweetie?"

Beak. My mother of birth. No choice there. She's a gambler. No jackpot for me. Beak thinks she's the big loser with a lesbian daughter. Congetta loves her lesbian daughter and gay son.

"Do you want to go, Congetta?"

Ring.

"Love to, Pat, if it's all right with you? But I know you work on Wednesday?"

Ring.

"That might be the Beak, Sweetie."

Love it when Congetta calls me, "Sweetie." Ring number 8. Beak. Who else lets the phone ring eight times? Nine times? Beaking in. Ten times.

I grab the phone. Click on speaker.

"What the hell takes you so long to pick up the phone?" Congetta puts her arm around me. I try to be charming and casual, neutralize Beak's condescending treatment of me.

Two hours ago professors listened to me, treated me, my ideas with respect. Now I'm being infantilized.

I choke out, "Oh, hi Beak."

"Don't give me any of that 'Oh hi Beak.' I'm your mother, Miss College Professor. Listen, clear your calendar. I'm coming over on Wednesday at 11. Congetta wants to go to the track with me. You're driving. This can be your Mother's Day gift to me."

Mother's Day gift? Wasn't planning on it. Maybe a card. Catholic guilt.

Beak knocks me out with her next line, "And listen. I want to meet that Jolene. Bring her. Congetta told me she likes her."

For the past six months, since Jolene, a nationally recognized African American scholar, and I have been together, I haven't breathed a word of our relationship to the Beak. I met Jolene's mother, Lizzie, in NYC. So nice. Smart. Fun. Had a great time with her and Jolene. To Beak, being black is worse than being a lesbian. If Jolene meets Beak, I'll be dropped like a hot potato.

MAY 9, 1989

Jolene and I are taking Congetta out to celebrate her seventieth birthday. Superb dinner Top of the Hub, mucho champagne, dancing at a gay club, fabulous. Everything Congetta requests. Jolene, 6'2" Grace

Jones look-alike, majestic African American icon and Congetta, 5' in her platform shoes, Carmen Miranda reincarnation. . . . quite the scene on the dance floor. Hot. I love watching them. They're a huge hit with all the gay guys. I'm crushed out on Jolene.

The DJ indulges me. "Nightclubbing," "Pull Up to the Bumper Baby," and then the song Jolene and I call our song, "I'm Not Perfect, But I'm Perfect for You." Jolene waves me over to join her and Congetta. I wave her off. I love to voyeur.

Jolene and Congetta bring everyone in the club to their feet—cheering them on. Jolene singing to the music looks like she is Grace Jones:

"I'm not perfect but I'm perfect for you . . ."

WEDNESDAY, MAY 10, 1989

I've taken the day off work to please Congetta. I casually told Jolene that I won't be at the college. Obligatory mother thing with Beak and Congetta at the track. Jolene apologizes too busy to join us. Didn't notice that I didn't invite her.

11 AM. Right on time. Gears grinding. Engine racing. CRASH—Beak customizing the driveway wall—again. I just had it repaired for $500 from her visit six months ago. Engine revving. She guns it. Rips off the capstone. Again. Decapitation. Again. Like she's knocking my block off. Slams her car door. Kicks in my back door. Well it feels like that. Like Grant taking Richmond.

"Jesus, Mary, and Joseph, Miss College Professor, I need a drink."

"Hi, Beak. Knew you were here. Heard your car hit the wall."

"What the hell are you talking about? Wall? What wall? You're imagining things."

11:10 AM. Clop, clop, clop. Congetta's Carmen Miranda wedgies clopping down the stairs.

Congetta coos, "Pat, sweetie, did you hear that crash?

"Oh, Mary. How good to see you. Was that your car? Are you okay?"

"Car? Come on, Congetta, have a Scotch. We're drinking the good stuff. Not her usual rotgut. I'm sure the professor got the good stuff for you. Where's Marilyn? If she has to be one of those L's—why isn't she with Marilyn?"

Beak ignores any reference to crashing her car. Refuses to say the word "lesbian." And the revisionist history! When I was with Marilyn, Beak hated her. Now that I'm not with Marilyn, she's great. Can't imagine what she'd say if she ever got to meet Jolene. But she'll never meet Jolene. Not if I can help it.

"What do you mean, Mary? What's an L?"

"Oh please, Congetta, that L word will never cross my lips. Miss Big Shot here, saying it on television, in the newspaper. I moved to Falmouth. No one there knows I'm her mother. Hey, where's that Jolene? You're a fool. Look at that nice Marilyn. Get rid of that Jolene. What do you think, Congetta?"

"Now, Mary, our kids make their own choices. I just want them to be happy. And you'll see, Jolene is very nice. Beautiful. Looks like Grace Jones."

"Who's Grace Jones?"

Noon. Congetta, Beak, and I are still sitting around the kitchen counter, cranking up our pre-luncheon cocktail festivities. Booze my defense, around The Beak. The doorbell. I peer out the window. Oh no, it's Jolene.

Beak. Jolene. Beak. Oh #**! What's she doing here?

"Hey what a surprise! What are you doing here?" *Oh my, Jesus.*

I give Jolene a peck on the cheek. I can see Beak craning her neck to see who it is.

Congetta runs over. Hugs Jolene. Gives her a kiss. Takes charge.

"Jolene, I'd like you to meet Pat's mother—the legend." Beak eyes Jolene. Gives me a disgusted look. Gives Jolene a smile.

Fake. I know Beak's fake smiles.

I try to ignore it, turning to Jolene. "Here honey, sit here, by me. What a surprise. How about some lunch."

"No, no, Pat. Got to go back to the college but wanted to drop by. Surprise you and Congetta. Wish you all luck at the track."

Congetta, rushes a glass of wine over to Jolene. Jolene gives her a thank you peck. Beak simmers.

I whip out lunch. Feign casual. "Got a big antipasto here and ham for sandwiches. What do you think, gang?"

Beak is eerily silent.

Jolene and Congetta dig into the antipasto.

Beak swallows the last of her second Scotch. Eyes me.

I'm solicitous. "Sandwich, Beak? Ham on rye, your favorite."

Congetta jumps in, "Looks great Pat. What do you think, Mary? Sandwich?"

Beak eyes me.

What the hell?

Beak silent.

Not a good sign.

Beak shifts in her seat. Stands up. Glares at me. Glances toward Jolene. Throws back her head. "Listen, Miss College Professor, cut the bull. Pour me a sandwich and make it a double. On the rocks."

Oh no, what's next? Ice in the air. Beak's frosty, snippy. Heads for the bathroom. I'm ten again. Scared. Not knowing what's going on with her. Wanting peace. Honor thy mother. Wanting everyone to get along. Wanting Beak to like Jolene.

Congetta and Jolene chatting it up. Quite the pair.

Congetta slides another Scotch to The Beak. Breaks in. Subject change. "Jolene is a wonderful dancer, Mary. Such fun the other night out dancing."

Beak scowls at Jolene and Congetta, "The two of you dancing together?"

"Yes, your darling daughter and Jolene took me to a gay bar for my seventieth birthday. Jolene and I brought the house down. Didn't we, sweetie?"

Beak shoots daggers, "Congetta, you need your head examined."

Jolene eyes me. She's picking up on Beak's vibe. Leans in and nuzzles Congetta. "Congetta, you're a fabulous dancer."

"Takes two to tango, Jolene. I'll go dancing with you anytime."

Beak sneers. Eyes Jolene. Oh, God, it's coming.

Jolene always amiable. A very tall and beautiful black woman's defense. Savvy. Grew up in Harlem projects. Went to Harvard. Writes about race and class. No pretense.

Beak from a Boston slum. Clawed out of there. Married a guy who got through seventh grade. Working-class stiff with a house and car. Nirvana. Beak, moving on up, marrying a union guy. College? Smart enough. But too poor.

Beak's doing a low boil looking at Jolene. Always measuring her life against others. Jealousy. Smirks. Throws back her head. Eyes her prey—again.

Coils back. Like a cobra.

"Now Jolene, wouldn't you really rather go out with Sidney Poitier? Remember him in *Guess Who's Coming to Dinner*? He's a nice-looking guy—kind of reminds me of you. Tall, handsome and . . . a . . ."

I spit out my drink. I fear it coming. "Beak, you know the rule. You're under my roof . . ."

Congetta senses danger, jumps off the bar stool, scurries out. "Gotta go change."

Jolene and I sitting across the kitchen counter from Beak.

"Beak, that's totally sick. Why the hell are you talking about Sidney Poitier?"

My head is exploding. Women's studies . . . intersection of race and sex . . . family dynamics. Guess Who's Coming to Dinner, 1967. Twenty-two years later. Beak still doesn't get it. But couldn't she keep it to herself? Congetta gets it. Jolene gets it.

Silence. Jolene looks right at The Beak, laughs, throwing back her head.

Maybe this is good. Maybe Jolene won't hold it against me? I'd like to kill The Beak. Shame washing over me.

Jolene putting her arm around my shoulder.

Oh, no. Too close.

Jolene leans toward The Beak. "No Mary, no Sidney Poitier for me, I'd rather go out with your darling daughter." Jolene kisses my cheek. I freeze.

One upping The Beak. Never a good idea. Beak doesn't lose. But please dear god don't let her win the ugly way. Not under my roof.

Beak glares at Jolene, shakes her head, blows a disgusted sigh, like she's auditioning for one of the ugly moments in *Guess Who's Coming to Dinner.*

Jolene pats my hand. Beak watches her.

Beak leans toward Jolene, hisses:

"You'd rather go out with my so-called darling daughter, than Sidney Poitier?"

Oh, damn it, Beak? No. Enough already.

"A good-looking girl like you, Jolene, going out with her?"

Mother love. Ever hear of it, Beak?

Beak's evil snake eyes slide toward me.

Don't say it, Beak.

She eyes her prey, "You know what you need, Jolene?" She gulps her scotch. Smirks. "You need a cold shower and a vinegar douche. That would do the trick."

The trick?

Race . . . Sex . . . Homophobia . . .

The KKK in all our families.

---

61. • *Eunjung Kim*

HOW MUCH SEX IS HEALTHY? THE PLEASURES OF ASEXUALITY (2010)

Eunjung Kim is assistant professor in the Department of Gender and Women's Studies at the University of Wisconsin-Madison. Her research spans the fields of disability, transnational disability theories, representations of asexuality, and US–South Korea humanitarian exchanges. The following article was first published in the anthology *Against Health: How Health Became New Morality.*

Physicians, public health practitioners, and "pro-sex" activists may agree that sexual drive is a natural, healthy, and essential aspect of the human. Health risks related to sexual activities are often highlighted by these individuals, but the idea that willingness and capability to have sex reflects and promotes a person's psychological and physiological health is widespread in Western contemporary culture. A popular news Website proclaims, "Want to get healthy? Have sex."[1] A *Newsweek* article elaborates, "Sex is good for adults. Indulging on a regular basis—at least once a week—is even better."[2] The health benefits of sex listed are increased immune strength in fighting off cold and flu, looking younger, burning calories, decreasing women's urinary incontinence, and reducing pain. While expressions of sexuality are regulated in society, the absence of sexual desires, feelings, and activities is seen as abnormal and reflective of poor health because of the explicit connection made between sexual activeness and healthiness. The way we understand desire and the relationship between sex and health are rarely simple. There lies the complexity of the cultural and social dimensions of sex beyond behavior, biological basis, sexual disorder, abstinence, religion, pleasure, and risk.

The public emergence of asexual people in the U.S., U.K., and Canadian media and in global online communities illustrates that some individuals understand their absence of sexual desire as an asexual identity or orientation, not as lack or dysfunction.[3] The Asexual Visibility and Education Network

(AVEN) describes an asexual person as someone who does not experience sexual attraction. Some asexual people may experience sexual desire but do not desire to engage with others sexually or desire only to engage in autoerotic practices. Others claim that they are born without sexual feelings entirely and never feel any kind of sexual desire.[4] AVEN asserts on its Website that "Asexuality is not a dysfunction, and there is no need to find a 'cause' or 'cure.'" A *New Scientist* article, "Glad to Be A," explains that some asexuals might simply have extremely low sex drives despite romantic orientation toward males or females. Other asexuals might be attracted to neither gender while they experience their sex drives. Kristin Scherrer, the author of several articles on asexual identity, adds that individuals who identify as asexual may also identify as lesbian, gay, bisexual, transsexual, queer, or heterosexual in their romantic orientation.[5] Many narratives of individuals demonstrate that asexuality escapes monolithic definition, simple behavior patterns, bodily characteristics, and identities despite some researchers' efforts to draw a clear boundary for the "condition." In other words, individuals who identify as asexual vary greatly in their explorations of identity to make sense of themselves as people who have other kinds of orientation outside of the sexual realm. For these reasons, my use of the term "asexuality" is meant to be broad and relatively and subjectively defined as an insufficient or absent willingness to engage in sexual activity with others. This descriptive and relative determination of asexuality is based on cultural assessments of "normal" frequency and level of desire.

Participants in asexual identity movements emphasize that their asexuality is not a problem in their experience and that they are healthy and happy.[6] They also argue that it is mainstream society that denies the existence of asexuality, marginalizes it, and stigmatizes it, and for that reason they are alienated and not recognized for who they are. I argue in this chapter that medical explanations of asexuality as an abnormality that has to be corrected constitute a large part of the stigmatization and marginalization experienced by asexual people.

However, the way that asexual activists use the claim of "being healthy" and seek legitimacy and normality in the name of health to counter the pathological charge significantly limits our understandings of diverse asexual lives. By closely analyzing two cultural texts that represent asexual lives from contrasting paradigms, I discuss how asexuality brings new ways of experiencing and understanding pleasure when considered outside of the framework of health and normality. This is not to say that all sexual or asexual practices are completely unrelated to one's health status and bodily events. However, health information and interpretations about sex are grounded too much in belief in universal sexual desire and give too much authority to health professionals to produce "cures" marketed by the sex therapy and pharmaceutical industries. Often, information about sexuality and health is equivocal, incoherent, and politically charged. I am "against health" as it is utilized by medical authorities to determine what is normal and to guard their professional territory, therefore shutting down new and creative understandings about how we might live with or without sex.

AGAINST PATHOLOGY, AGAINST FIGHTING STIGMA IN THE NAME OF HEALTH

I bring asexuality under the discussion of "against health" for two reasons. First, while sexual practices are heavily regulated in the United States in relation to gender, race, ethnicity, class, ability/disability status, religion, sexual orientation, and age, asexuality is subject to a pathologizing framework that demands a "cure" and "help" under the premise that sexual desire is universally and constantly present in adult life and that its absence reflects pathology or causes harm. As the AVEN Website explains, "In a world where sexuality is promoted as the norm, many asexuals grow up thinking that they're somehow sick, broken, or deficient." Absence of sexual desire may be alterable or not; it may coexist with physiological or psychological conditions; it may be present without any identifiable causes. Labeling all kinds of asexuality as ill-health obscures the diverse and ordinary aspects of asexual experience. According to Leonore Tiefer, the medical and pharmaceutical industries have taken an increasing interest in sex, using various strategies to create a disease of sexual inadequacy through which to market drug treatments.[7] This combination of medicalization of sexuality and market forces promotes the drive for a cure for asexuality. Medical diagnoses associated with asexuality such as Hypoactive Sexual Desire Disorder or Female Sexual Dysfunction may legitimize bodily difficulties that individuals experience as valid signs or serious causes of distress and interpersonal difficulties, but the medical model comes with a cost, solidifying norms and excluding other bodies that do not fit as exceptional and deviant.[8] In fact, distress and relationship difficulties may be caused by external factors such as social pressure, partner expectations, dominant gender role expectations, and stigma. Tiefer also claims that the medical model itself is severely limited in its ability to deal with problems of sexuality because of its separation between mind and body, its biological reductionism, its focus on disease rather than people as a whole, and its reliance on norms. She claims pharmacological research often oversimplifies the sexual difficulties of both men and women because it "promotes genital function as the centrepiece of sexuality and ignores everything else."[9] She further asserts that sexual life has become vulnerable to "disease mongering" because a long history of social and political control of sexual expression has created reservoirs of shame and ignorance, and popular culture has greatly inflated public expectations about sexual function and understandings of the importance of sex to personal and relationship satisfaction.[10]

Second, pathologizing asexuality puts asexual people on the defensive and leads them and some within the media to insist on their normality by using the language of their critics. Some asexual men emphasize the fact that their "plumbing works fine" in response to suspicious inquiries about their underlying problems which include physical abnormality, impotence, or lack of masculinity. Some asexuals argue that they are as normal as sexual persons except they do not desire to have sex with others. A reporter at *New Scientist* who interviewed a leading figure in the asexuality movement felt compelled to reassure readers that the asexual man was nonetheless physically attractive. The reporter describes the man's appearance and then concludes, "He is living proof that it is absolutely wrong to assume asexuals shun sex simply because they can't get any."[11] The seeming normalcy and healthiness of an asexual person operates as an entry toward public acceptance of asexuality. Although correcting the stereotypical image of an asexual person as undesirable or deviant by presenting the relevant "facts" is the goal of such endeavor, it is equally important to remember that being sexually desirable or healthy does not automatically lead to the recognition of asexuality as a legitimate difference. Just as with any other identity group with a significant range of diversity, many members of asexual communities acknowledge that they deal with various health issues as well as mental, physical, and psychological differences, some more common than others. The diversity within asexual groups makes the health claim of asexuality in order to fight pathologization more complicated. Is the claim that "we are not sick" a distancing strategy that erases other asexual people who have mental or physical illnesses, disabilities, and neurological differences? Claiming positive identity based on good health status and normalcy has the potential to ignore those people with various health issues, sexually related or not. Speaking of sex and its absence in the name of health easily falls into the moral and ableist binary of the *good body* and the *bad body*, and it relies on dominant able-bodied (hetero)sexual sex and gender expectations rather than presenting sex as composed of unpredictable and diverse practices, emotions, and reasons.

This is not to suggest that there is a unitary claim of healthiness and able-bodiedness in the asexuality movement that is employed by all asexual people. According to asexual activist David Jay, it is useful to mold the story of asexuality and health according to the audience at hand. To the general public, he emphasizes that he is happy and healthy, highlighting that asexuality is not correlated with any health issues. He explains that the medical conditions of the asexual individuals are not generally discussed with the press in order to avoid conjecture about possible correlations. To medical professionals, he says that asexuals' healthcare needs are not understood properly in medical communities and he emphasizes the need for more partnership. To the asexual community, he argues that asexuality is not a problem in itself but encourages medical consultation when individuals experience a sudden drop in sexual desire.[12] These maneuvers illustrate the multiple ways in which health is related with asexuality, but at the same time, how one has to notice the presence of the negative connection between them either by emphasizing healthiness or avoiding the topic.

Certainly, asexual people's recourse to identity politics and community-building does raise other important questions. Can one be asexual and claim asexuality as a positive identity within a society that understands asexuality not only as a sign of contempt but also as a naturalized trait for some people? What is it like to be asexual when one is not considered sexual at all or is somehow prohibited from being sexual? Many people are ordered into nonsexual and nonreproductive lives because of their age, disability, health, race, gender, class, or appearance. People in minority groups and those with oppressed sexualities have presented disagreements with the idea of asexuality when it is imposed as a stereotype or a mandate. People with disabilities, for example, dispute asexuality as stigma that denies them their basic right and access to sexual, intimate lives. Some Asian American men in the United States engage in online "anti-asexuality" communities that resist the stereotype of the sexually reserved, emasculated, and effete Asian American male (a stereotype that coexists with the highly sexualized yet submissive image of the Asian American female). This activity effectively erases the space for asexual Asian American men. Asexuality is a typical prejudice applied

to older persons and lesbians as well. To take this last example, scholars in the field of female sexuality studies challenge the pejorative connotation of inactive sexuality reflected in the term "lesbian bed death," a supposed "dropoff" in sexual activity in long-term lesbian relationships and alleged lower rates of sexual activity for lesbian couples in general. The stigma represented by the discourse of "lesbian bed death" creates a double bind: lesbians were once assumed to be "sick" when they were having sex, but now, according to some lesbian affirmative therapists, lesbians are "sick" when they are not having sex.[13] The activism of asexual people for recognition and respect of their asexual identity challenges the simplified understanding of asexuality only as a status of oppression, which ignores the presence of asexual people within desexualized groups. The discussion of asexuality should be positioned beyond the good (acceptable) body and the bad (unacceptable and therefore to be fixed) body binary; instead, the conundrum of asexuality invites considerations of multiple contestations among a positive identity politics, a medical framework, and labels of oppressed sexuality produced by desexualization, as well as their overlapping grounds. It is important that these examinations consider the possibilities of utilizing a diversity of health statuses and other differences in race, age, disability, religion, and other sexual orientations as a part of a larger asexual embodiment. Sexual rights and asexual rights are not at odds with each other but part of recognizing the intertwined construction of diversity.

"UNDER THE HOOD" AND SNOW CAKE: TWO DIFFERENT PARADIGMS

Authoritative medical explanations defining normal amounts of sex circulate beyond the clinical setting through the medium of popular cultural representations. First aired in 2005, the episode "Under the Hood," part of the Discovery Channel Canada's documentary series *Sexual Secrets*, offers an example of the contestation between medical authorities and individual narratives over the topic of a sexuality and sexual dysfunction. The episode deals with various sexual disorders including so-called persistent sexual arousal syndrome, male erectile dysfunction, female post-partum decrease of sexual desire, and sexual anorexia along with the topic of asexual identities. The documentary presents these presumably unknown sexual problems as serious disorders that cause a lot of suffering. The documentary also introduces sites of medical treatment, such as counseling, exercise, and therapies.

In order to introduce the absence of sexual desire as one of these problems, the film crew asks people in the street about not having sexual desire. "Do you think that's possible?" an interviewer asks. One woman says, "Yeah, I think they are called mothers," pointing out how frequently the absence of sexual desire is experienced by many women. Most people, however, characterize sex as necessary and natural, or as one man puts it, "I think people need to have sex to enjoy life." Another woman says, "I don't know [if] asexuality is a normal thing. I think sexuality is a good thing. I think it's a natural thing. And it's healthy. And it's good to be sexual." Through these interviews, the film sets up asexuality as a topic of public opinion that can be voted up or down.

The asexual individuals who address the audience describe their lack of interest in sex not as a problem but as a difference. The documentary rejects their perspective, interrupting each asexual individual's interview with sexual scenes of heterosexual couples in bed, therefore marking a sharp contrast between what these asexual people are saying and what the documentary presents as natural. The film's doubtful attitude toward asexual identity comes across clearly. After the interview with David Jay, the narrator poses a question. "David says he is perfectly content with his asexuality. But is there a dark side to saying no to sex?" The narrator continues, "Are some asexuals ignoring something traumatic from their pasts and denying their true feelings?"

The film focuses on pathological explanations for asexuality, though it does feature one scientist

who presents asexuality as an acceptable variation since asexual people pose no threat to society. The documentary highlights the fact that some asexual people are victims of sexual assault, suffer from post-traumatic stress disorder, or have religious guilt. The narrator says, "Asexuals declare that their lack of desire is normal. But some doctors argue that some asexuals are actually suffering deep emotional turmoil. They argue that being asexual is not a choice made from strength but from intense pain." An expert adds, "I hear people make the statement that 'I don't need sex and I'm not unhappy about it.' But I find them suicidal or they're depressed," thus assuming that these psychological difficulties are rooted in asexuality or are the cause of asexuality. What is problematic is that the film squelches diversity within asexual people, combining those who are untroubled by their asexuality and those who suffer and want to be sexual by conflating the two narratives. Moreover, it assumes that asexuality is not acceptable when it is brought by victimization without considering how individuals experience asexuality. This way, the presentation of asexual people as suffering subjects (exclusively due to asexuality) reframes the asexual identity narrative as a harmful coping mechanism that stands in denial of real "turmoil." It is important not to assume all asexual people are victims. Even if asexual people have been victimized, just as have many sexual people, this does not warrant the understanding of asexuality as a damaged sexuality. Asexual people experience their own struggles, experiment and question their sexual/asexual identity, and may want to come out as asexual and work toward developing senses of pride as asexual people. The film does provide access to asexual people's self-representation and its fluid nature, but goes on to present them as self-deceiving through the eyes of doubtful professionals.

To nail down the idea that asexuality is unnatural, the film makes a connection between sex and food, as if refusal of sex were a refusal of necessary sustenance. The analogy between sex and food defies the message of abstinence campaigns that assume that individuals can control and delay their sexual lives as long as they want with their willpower. "Searching for sex is a primal urge," the narrator claims, "almost as basic as hunting for food." The narrator asks viewers to imagine a life without food or sex, and this analogy leads quickly to the idea of sexual anorexia. Another expert on people who are repulsed by sex claims that "sexual anorexics" starve themselves and are full of self-loathing and hatred, and that, just as anorexic people deny themselves nourishment, sexually anorexic people deny themselves sexual contact.[14] Citing the case of a man who prefers a solitary life, the doctor makes the claim that when a man does not have enough male energy, he fears female energy and sees it as dangerous. Effectively converting fear and avoidance of sex into lack of dominant masculinity, the film once more presents an intimate scene of a man and a woman in bed as the ultimate goal in the healing of pathological asexuality. The repeated use of these types of sexual scenes in the documentary, contrasted with sad-looking, frustrated individuals alone in bed, creates a world divided between the sexual and the asexual. The medicalization of asexuality and the denial of asexual identity by health professionals turn individual bodies into medical facts, even though, as sexual scientists increasingly explain, there is neither evidence of psychic inhibition of libido in such individuals nor an effective treatment for people in a long-term state of asexuality.[15]

The film also presents the search for a medical cure for asexuality at a sexual treatment center in Chicago. The center recommends that women who do not want to have sex with their husbands maintain some kind of sexual relationship with their partner and think of it as a gift to them. Women exercise to increase their ability to orgasm and to fulfill their potential to enjoy sex. When a woman speaks with joy about meeting so many other women who experience no sexual desire, the idea is not that she has found a community to affirm her—an empowering experience shared by asexual people visiting online communities such as AVEN. Rather, the community attests to the severity of her problem. In fact, the documentary describes members of AVEN as

another group of patients in need of medical treatment and healing: "An essential element of any healing is asking out loud for help, understanding and hopefully finding a community to share a journey with." The journey of asexual people is, by implication, toward healing and the joy of sex, not toward a different identity and a respected difference.

As asexuality activists oppose the prevailing view that stigmatizes asexuality, their resistance can be assisted by cultural representations of asexuality outside of medically dominated discourse. My second example offers the possibility of resistance necessary to think critically about asexuality outside of the discourse of health and able-bodiedness, *Snow Cake* (2006), by British filmmaker Marc Evans, is a fictional film that depicts asexuality in a quite different way than the documentary "Under the Hood." It raises awareness about autism by focusing on the everyday life of an adult mother with autism living in Canada, but it also features asexuality as a main component of the highly verbal and autistic character's life. The film presents a compelling and vivid setting for asexuality beyond the realm of usual imperatives about asexuality as abnormality. The film's unusual quality comes from its presentation of an asexual woman who is not perfectly "normal" except for being asexual. Together with autism, asexual characteristics can be easily perceived as anti-social and anti-sexual attitudes. However, the film does not apply either moral or medical judgments to the main character. Rather, it depicts asexuality and autism as forms of human diversity and metaphorizes them as endlessly different kinds of snowflakes.

Aloof, middle-aged Englishman Alex Hughes (Alan Rickman) gives a ride to a teenage stranger, Vivienne (Emily Hampshire), who dies instantly when Alex's car is struck by a truck on the road. Mourning Vivienne's death, Alex visits her mother, Linda Freeman (Sigourney Weaver), and finds her actions strikingly non-reactive compared to those of a typical grieving mother. Puzzled by Linda's seeming indifference, Alex asks Linda's neighbor, Maggie (Carrie-Anne Moss), about this behavior, to which Maggie answers that Linda is autistic. To Alex, Linda does not appear to be grieving, especially when she describes the meaning of the death of Vivienne in functional terms of not having someone to carry out the garbage or with whom to have fun. Alex decides to stay with her until garbage day on Linda's request, thus temporarily solving the practical challenge that follows Vivienne's death.

Alex soon learns that Linda is not only autistic but asexual, although the term "asexual" is not used in the film. The next morning Alex discovers Linda lying down in the backyard, eating snow with increasing joy. Linda describes her feeling to Alex by referring to sexual orgasm. "Vivienne once described an orgasm to me," Linda says, "It sounds like an inferior version of what I feel when I have a mouthful of snow." On another occasion, Linda insists that Alex join her on the trampoline, and he jumps up and down while she lies on her back and enjoys the continuous bouncing. The snow-eating and trampoline scenes propose an equivalent to sexual pleasure experienced by the asexual Linda, giving the film a way for sexual and non-autistic audience members to imagine Linda's pleasure. In fact, the film carefully carves out Linda's asexuality to contrast her with her neighbor Maggie's sexual activeness (which also marginalizes her in the conservative community). The film presents the lives of two different women, mediated by the socially distant Alex, as two alternative lifestyles, each with its own hardships and joys. Having had a complicated past, Alex finds comfort in both the social, inquisitive, sexual Maggie and the asocial, indifferent, asexual Linda. Linda's asexuality is a characteristic related to her disability, but not—and this is of critical importance—a pathological condition to be examined. In an emblematic moment, Alex acknowledges the pleasure Linda takes in eating snow by leaving in her freezer a cake made of snow as a good-bye gift, perhaps providing her with the experience of an "orgasm,"[16] while neither problematizing her asexuality nor suggesting that asexuality is a state of deprivation.

The film also uses motherhood as another important reference point to prevent the audience from assuming that Linda's asexuality is either a pathology or an absolute condition caused by her autism. Given Linda's lack of interest in sex, Alex is puzzled as to how Vivienne "happened." Linda's father admits that no one knows the answer. The father tells Alex that he first suspected that the pregnancy was the result of a sexual assault. In fact, disabled women's sexual experience is often assumed to be the product of sexual violence not only because there is a high prevalence of sexual violence in women with disabilities, but also because the popular imagination cannot conceive of disabled women as exercising sexual agency. However, in this case, as her father further explains, Linda refused to answer questions about sexual violence and didn't seem to be upset. Her parents speculate that her pregnancy might have been a result of experimentation with her colleague at the community center. The film carefully avoids scripting the common image of a woman with a disability as an eternal child, an innocent angel, or a victim of sexual violence who needs protection. The film does not give any definite answer about how and why Linda engaged in sexual activity or whether or not she was sexually traumatized. The audience members are directed only to Linda herself and encouraged to move away from the desire to question or probe the apparent mismatch between motherhood and autism with asexuality.

Apart from characteristics unique to their different genres, "Under the Hood" and *Snow Cake* take thematically different courses in exploring lives without sex. With its authority of medical professionals and its dramatized sexual scenes, "Under the Hood" attempts to frame an exposé about a topic that is completely unknown to its general audience, thereby making asexuality exotic and unfamiliar. It imagines asexuality as a serious sign of health problems—despite its attempt to present asexual people's points of view—and creates hope for its audience when it proposes medical treatment for individuals struggling for a cure. *Snow Cake* proposes another point of view that does not make health a legitimizing or disapproving tool. It represents the imagined pleasures and heightened sensations of an asexual woman with autism experiencing a great pleasure that comes from other sensual activities.[17]

CONCLUSION

Medical knowledge about the topics of asexuality and sexuality circulates into public awareness in a way that privileges the professional point of view over individual experiences and their creative interpretations. "The power of medical ideology in the construction of sexual desire derives from its expansion, its authoritative voice," Janice Irvine explains.[18] In addition to medical ideology, Irvine also notes that popular representations associate "problems" of desire with disease, often adopting a language of dysfunction. I offered the text of "Under the Hood" as an example of popular culture's narration of sexual desire through the language of medical dysfunction based on normative gender expectations. Closely reading representations of asexual people with disabilities may be instructive as we look for more nuanced and less prescriptive ways of configuring sexual desire or its absence without erasing its diversity. The pathological framework for asexuality is symptomatic of a larger trend in which sexuality is tied up with the image of "normal" bodies. Understanding asexuality as a disorder that can and must be treated reveals anxiety about unstable aspects of sex, body functions, and sexual desire. By refusing to think about sexuality as a matter of health, I have argued that asexuality brings new ways of experiencing and understanding pleasure.

NOTES

1. Laura Berman, "Want to Get Healthy? Have Sex," *Today*, January 15, 2008, http://www.msnbc.msn.c0m/id/2265o19o.
2. Temma Ehrenfeld, "Six Reasons to Have Sex Every Week," *Newsweek*, December 10, 2007, http://www.newsweek.com/id/74575.
3. AVEN: The Asexuality Visibility and Education Network, http://www.asexuality.org.
4. Geraldine Levi Joosten-van Vilsteren, Edmund Fortuin, David Walker, and Christine Stone, *Nonlibidoism: The Short Facts* (Amsterdam: Lavender Publishers, 2005). Although the authors in this collection prefer to use the term "nonlibidoism" and not asexuality, I consider asexuality in a broader sense to include nonlibidoists, or people who are born without any sexual feelings.
5. Kristin Scherrer, "Asexuality: Understanding Sexual Diversities," in *Talk About It. National Coming Out Month Magazine 2007* (Ann Arbor: Office of LGBT Affairs and Division of Student Affairs, University of Michigan, 2007), 22–23.
6. Anonymous, "Is There an Asexual Closet?" Asexuality Visibility and Education Network, http://www.asexuality.org/en/lofiversion/index.php/t8569.html.
7. See Leonore Tiefer, "Female Sexual Dysfunction: A Case Study of Disease Mongering and Activist Resistance," *PLoS Medicine* 3, no. 4 (April 2006): 436–40. Ray Moynihan and Matthew Anderson are also concerned that pharmaceutical companies influenced the creation of female Hypoactive Sexual Desire Disorder (HSDD) as a disease in order to promote testosterone as a treatment. See Ray Moynihan, "The Making of a Disease: Female Sexual Dysfunction," *British Medical Journal* 326, no. 7379 (January 4, 2003): 45–47; "The Marketing of a Disease: Female Sexual Dysfunction," *British Medical Journal* 330, no. 7484 (January 22, 2005): 192–94; and Matthew Anderson, "Is Lack of Sexual Desire a Disease? Is Testosterone the Cure?" *Medscape Ob/Gyn and Women's Health* 10, no. 2 (2005).
8. Some researchers believe that asexuality and the medical diagnosis of HSDD are not the same thing, while others believe that they are undoubtedly connected.
9. Leonore Tiefer, "The Medicalization of Sexuality: Conceptual, Normative, and Professional Issues," *Annual Review of Sex Research* 7 (1996): 252–82.
10. Tiefer, "Female Sexual Dysfunction," 45–47.
11. Sylvia Pagan Westphal, "Glad to Be A," *New Scientist* 184, no. 2469 (October 14, 2004): 38–43.
12. Personal communication with David Jay, March 2009.
13. In order to disprove the asexuality label, some researchers argue that there is not sufficient data about the definition of lesbian sexual behavior itself. They further emphasize that lesbian sexuality is "healthier" and more "intimate" than typical genital activity. See Marny Hall, "Not Tonight Dear, I'm Deconstructing a Headache: Confessions of a Lesbian Sex Therapist," in *A New View of Women's Sexual Problems*, ed. Ellyn Kaschak and Leonore Tiefer (New York: Haworth Press, 2001).

14. Some media outlets present professional opinions of looking at asexuality as normal if it does not cause distress and conflict in a marriage or relationship, but they also quote sex therapists' dismissive attitudes of the legitimacy of asexual identity claims. A recent article in the *New York Times*, for example, quotes Dr. Leonard R. Derogatis as saying that "Sex is a natural drive, as natural as the drive for sustenance and water to survive. It's a little difficult to judge these folks as normal." See Mary Duenwald, "For Them, Just Saying No Is Easy," *New York Times*, June 9, 2005, http://www.nytimes.com/2005/06/09/fashion/thursdaystyles/o9asexual.html. Specialists appearing on television also worry that the resort to asexuality identity claims is a self-fulfilling prophecy because asexuals want to ignore real problems and possible treatments. These specialists sometimes refer to asexuals as "sexually neutered." See "Asexuals," 20/20 television program aired on ABC network, September 5, 2006.

15. See Elizabeth K. Ullery, Vaughn S. Milliner, and Heath A. Willingham, "The Emergent Care and Treatment of Women with Hypoactive Sexual Desire Disorder," *The Family Journal* 10, no. 3 (July 2002): 349; Helen Singer Kaplan, *The Sexual Desire Disorders. Dysfunctional Regulation of Sexual Motivation* (New York: Brunner/Mazel, 1995), 5; and Sandra R. Leiblum and Raymond C. Rosen, eds., *Sexual Desire Disorders* (New York: Guilford, 1988), 4.

16. Disability studies and film scholar Sally Chivers suggested this interpretation to me.

17. Linda's judgmental attitude toward Maggie for being sexually promiscuous and her hierarchical description of orgasm as being "inferior" to her own pleasures are troubling; however, they are a powerful way of affirming her own asexual life at an immediate level. Furthermore, the film ends with some hope that Linda and Maggie can coexist with difference. It is important that the hierarchy between asexuality and sexuality has to be challenged in both ways.

18. Janice M. Irvine, "Regulated Passions: The Invention of Inhibited Sexual Desire and Sexual Addiction," in *Deviant Bodies: Critical Perspectives on Difference in Science and Popular Culture*, ed. Jennifer Terry and Jacqueline Urla (Bloomington: Indiana University Press, 1995), 327.

---

62. • *Gloria Steinem*

IF MEN COULD MENSTRUATE (1978)

Gloria Steinem has been a well-known feminist activist and writer since the late 1960s. In 2005, with Jane Fonda and Robin Morgan, she cofounded the Women's Media Center that aims to make women more visible and powerful in media. She was a cofounder of the feminist *Ms. Magazine,* where the following essay was first published in 1978. Her works revolve around charting different ways to challenge patriarchy.

A white minority of the world has spent centuries conning us into thinking that a white skin makes people superior—even though the only thing it really does is make them more subject to ultraviolet rays and to wrinkles. Male human beings have built whole cultures around the idea that penis-envy is "natural" to women—though having such an unprotected organ might be said to make men vulnerable, and the power to give birth makes womb-envy at least as logical.

In short, the characteristics of the powerful, whatever they may be, are thought to be better than the characteristics of the powerless—and logic has nothing to do with it.

What would happen, for instance, if suddenly, magically, men could menstruate and women could not?

The answer is clear—menstruation would become an enviable, boast-worthy, masculine event:

Men would brag about how long and how much.

Boys would mark the onset of menses, that longed-for proof of manhood, with religious ritual and stag parties.

Congress would fund a National Institute of Dysmenorrhea to help stamp out monthly discomforts.

Sanitary supplies would be federally funded and free. (Of course, some men would still pay for the prestige of commercial brands such as John Wayne Tampons, Muhammad Ali's Rope-a-dope Pads, Joe Namath Jock Shields—"For Those Light Bachelor Days," and Robert "Baretta" Blake Maxi-Pads.)

Military men, right-wing politicians, and religious fundamentalists would cite menstruation ("menstruation") as proof that only men could serve in the Army ("you have to give blood to take blood"), occupy political office ("can women be aggressive without that steadfast cycle governed by the planet Mars?"), be priest and ministers ("how could a woman give her blood for our sins?") or rabbis ("without the monthly loss of impurities, women remain unclean").

Male radicals, left-wing politicians, mystics, however, would insist that women are equal, just different, and that any woman could enter their ranks if she were willing to self-inflict a major wound every month ("you MUST give blood for the revolution"), recognize the preeminence of menstrual issues, or subordinate her selfness to all men in their Cycle of Enlightenment. Street guys would brag ("I'm a three pad man") or answer praise from a buddy ("Man, you lookin' good!") by giving fives and saying, "Yeah, man, I'm on the rag!" TV shows would treat the subject at length. ("Happy Days": Richie and Potsie try to convince Fonzie that he is still "The Fonz," though he has missed two periods in a row.) So would newspapers. (SHARK SCARE THREATENS MENSTRUATING MEN. JUDGE CITES MONTHLY STRESS IN PARDONING RAPIST.) And movies. (Newman and Redford in "Blood Brothers"!)

Men would convince women that intercourse was more pleasurable at "that time of the month." Lesbians would be said to fear blood and therefore life itself—though probably only because they needed a good menstruating man.

Of course, male intellectuals would offer the most moral and logical arguments. How could a woman master any discipline that demanded a sense of time, space, mathematics, or measurement, for instance, without that in-built gift for measuring the cycles of the moon and planets—and thus for measuring anything at all? In the rarefied fields of philosophy and religion, could women compensate for missing the rhythm of the universe? Or for their lack of symbolic death-and-resurrection every month?

Liberal males in every field would try to be kind: the fact that "these people" have no gift for measuring life or connecting to the universe, the liberals would explain, should be punishment enough.

And how would women be trained to react? One can imagine traditional women agreeing to all arguments with a staunch and smiling masochism. ("The ERA would force housewives to wound themselves every month": Phyllis Schlafly. "Your husband's blood is as sacred as that of Jesus—and so sexy, too!" Marabel Morgan.) Reformers and Queen Bees would try to imitate men, and pretend to have a monthly cycle. All feminists would explain endlessly that men, too, needed to be liberated from the false idea of Martian aggressiveness, just as women needed to escape the bonds of menses envy. Radical feminists would add that the oppression of the nonmenstrual was the pattern for all other oppressions ("Vampires were our first freedom fighters!") Cultural feminists would develop a bloodless imagery in art and literature. Socialist feminists would insist that only under capitalism would men be able to monopolize menstrual blood. . . .

In fact, if men could menstruate, the power justifications could probably go on forever.

If we let them.

BEAUTY (RE)DISCOVERS THE MALE BODY (1999)

Susan Bordo is Otis A. Singletary Chair in the Humanities and professor of gender and women's studies at the University of Kentucky. She has published many important books in the field, including the now-classic *Unbearable Weight: Feminism, Western Culture, and the Body* (1993), which won Distinguished Publication Award from the Association for Women in Psychology and was nominated for a Pulitzer Prize. Her other book, *The Male Body: A New Look at Men in Public and in Private,* was also touted as a significant work in the field of masculinity studies, from which the following essay is excerpted.

MALE DECORATIVENESS IN CULTURAL PERSPECTIVE

Not all heterosexual men are as uptight about the pocket flaps on their pants as the Haggar executive would have us believe. Several weeks after the piece on khakis appeared in *The New Yorker,* a reader wrote in protesting that the idea "that men don't want to look like they're trying to be fashionable or sexy" was rather culture-bound. Maybe, this reader acknowledged, it applies to American, English, and Japanese men. "But are we really to believe that French, Italian, and Spanish men share this concern? And, when we expand the category 'male' beyond human beings, biologists have shown that the demonstration of male splendor is a key element in the vertebrate mating game. Are American males just an anomalous species?"

The letter reminds us that there are dangers in drawing broad conclusions on the basis of only those worlds with which one is familiar. And it's not just different international attitudes toward men and fashion that cast doubt on the universal applicability of the Dockers/Haggar view of masculinity. To look at the variables of race, class, and history is to produce a picture of male attitudes toward fashionable display that is far from consistently phobic.

First of all, for most of human history, there haven't been radically different "masculine" and "feminine" attitudes toward beauty and decorativeness. On farms, frontiers, and feudal estates, women were needed to work alongside men and beauty was hardly a priority for either. Among aristocrats, it was most important to maintain class privilege (rather than gender difference), and standards of elegance for both sexes (as Anne Hollander's fascinating *Sex and Suits* documents) were largely the same: elaborate headwear, cosmetics, nonutilitarian adornments, and accessories. Attention to beauty was associated not with femininity but with a life that was both privileged and governed by exacting standards. The constrictions, precarious adornments, elaborate fastenings reminded the elite that they were highly civilized beings, not simple peasant "animals." At the same time, decorativeness was a mode of royal and aristocratic competition, as households and courts would try to out-glam each other with jewels and furs. Hollander describes a sixteenth-century summit meeting between Francis I and Henry VIII, in which everyone wore "silver covered with diamonds, except when they were in cloth of gold and covered with rubies. Everything was lined with ermine and everything was 20 yards long, and there were plumes on everybody." Everybody—male or female—had to be as gorgeous as possible. It was a mode of power competition.

Until roughly the fourteenth century, men and women didn't even dress very differently. (Think of the Greeks and Romans and their unisex robes and togas.) Clear differences started to emerge only in the late Middle Ages and early Renaissance: women's breasts began to be exposed and emphasized in tight bodices, while their legs were covered with long skirts. Men's legs—and sometimes their genitals as well—were "fully articulated" and visible through pantaloons (what we call "tights"), with body armor covering the chest. While to our sensibilities, the shapely legs and genitals of men in tights (unless required by a ballet or historical drama) are either to be laughed at or drooled over, Hollander argues that in the Renaissance, to outline the male body was to make it more "real" and "natural," less a template for sexual fantasy (as women's bodies were becoming). This trend continued, with men's clothing getting progressively more unrestrictive, tailored, simple and women's more stiff, tightly fitted, decorative. Still, into the seventeenth century, fashionable gentleman continued to wear lace and silk, and to don powder and wigs before appearing in public. Hollander regards the nineteenth century as a "great divide," after which not only the styles of men's and women's clothing (trousers for me, increasingly romantic froufrou for women) would become radically different, but ideas about them as well. Men's clothing must now be "honest, comfortable, and utilitarian," while women's begins to develop a reputation for being "frivolous" and "deceptive." The script for "men act and women appear" was being written—right onto the male and female clothing.

Looking beyond fashion to the social world (something Hollander refuses to do, but I'll venture), it's hard not to speculate that these changes anticipated the emergence of the middle class and the nineteenth-century development of distinctively separate spheres for men and women within it. In the industrial era, men's sphere—increasingly the world of manufacturing, buying, selling, power brokering—was

performance-oriented, and demanded "no nonsense." Women, for their part, were expected not only to provide a comfortable, well-ordered home for men to return to but to offer beauty, fantasy, and charm for a man to "escape" to and restore himself with after the grim grind of the working day. As this division of labor developed, strong dualistic notions about "masculinity" and "femininity" began to emerge, with sanctions against the man or woman who dared to cross over to the side of the divide where they did not belong "by nature."

By the end of the nineteenth century, older notions of manliness premised on altruism, self-restraint, and moral integrity—qualities that women could have too—began to be understood as vaguely "feminine." Writers and politicians (like Teddy Roosevelt) began to complain loudly about the emasculating effects of civilization and the excessive role played by women teachers in stifling the development of male nature. New words like "pussyfoot" and "stuffed shirt"— and, most deadly, "sissy"—came into parlance, and the "homosexual" came to be classified as a perverse personality type which the normal, heterosexual male had to prove himself distinct from. (Before, men's relations with each other had been considerably more fluid, and even the heterosexual male was allowed a certain degree of physical intimacy and emotional connection—indeed, "heterosexuality" as such was a notion that hardly made sense at the time.) A new vogue for bodybuilding emerged. "Women pity weakly men," O. S. Fowler warned, but they love and admire "right hearty feeders, not dainty; sprightly, not tottering; more muscular than exquisite, and more powerful than effeminate, in mind and body." To be "exquisite," to be decorative, to be on display, was now fully women's business, and the man who crossed that line was a "fop."

From that time on, male "vanity" went into hiding, and when cosmetic products for men began to be marked (for men *did* use them, albeit in secret), they had to justify themselves, as Kathy Peiss documents, through the manly rhetoric of efficiency, rugged individualism, competitive advantage, autonomy. While Pompeian cream promises to "beautify and youthify" women, the same product for men will help them "win success" and "make promotion easier" on the job. Even that most manly of rituals (from our perspective), shaving, required special rhetoric when home shaving was first introduced early in the twentieth century. "The Gillette is typical of the American spirit," claimed a 1910 ad. "Its use starts habits of energy—of initiative. And men who *do* for themselves are men who *think* for themselves." Curley's Easy-Shaving Safety Razor claimed that "the first Roman to shave every day was no fop, but Scipio, conqueror of Africa." When it came to products used also by women—like scents and creams—manufacturers went out of the their way to reassure prospective customers of their no-nonsense "difference," through action names (Brisk, Dash, Vim, Keen, Zest) and other means. When Florian, a line of men's toiletries, was introduced in 1929, its creator, Carl Weeks, advised druggists to locate the products near cigar (again!) counters, using displays featuring manly accouterments like boxing gloves, pipes, footballs. This, he argued, "will put over the idea that the mascu-*line* is all *stag*. It's for he-men with no women welcome nohow."

This isn't to say that from the turn of the nineteenth century on, the drive to separate "masculine" and "feminine" attitudes toward self-beautification pushed forward relentlessly. For another, the history of gender ideology didn't end with the nineteenth century, as dramatic as its changes were. A century of mutations and permutations followed, as demanded by social, economic, and political conditions. Older ideals lingered too and were revived when needed. The Depression, for example, brought a love affair with (a fantasy of) aristocratic "class" to popular culture, and a world of Hollywood representations— as we've seen—in which sexual difference was largely irrelevant, the heroes and heroines of screwball comedy a matched set of glamorously attired cut-ups. In these films, the appeal of actors like Cary Grant, Fred Astaire, and William Powell was largely premised not on assertions of masculine performance but on their elegance, wit, and charm. Their male-ness wasn't thrown into question by the cut of their

suits. Rather, being fashionable signified that they led an enviable life of pleasure and play. Lauren, Valentino, Hugo Boss, and many others are crafted to appeal to the class consciousness of consumers; in that universe, one can never be too beautiful or too vain, whatever one's sex.

In the screwball comedies, it didn't matter whether you were a man or a woman, everyone's clothes sparkled and shone. Following the lead of the movies, many advertisements of the thirties promoted a kind of androgynous elegance. But others tried to have their cake and eat it too, as in a 1934 ad for Fougère Royale aftershave, which depicts a group of tony men in tuxedoes, hair slicked back, one even wearing a pince-nez, but with the caption "Let's *not* join the ladies!" We may be glamorous, even foppish—but *puh-lease! Ladies* we're not! I should note, too, that while the symbols of "class" can function to highlight equality between men and women, they can also be used to emphasize man's superiority over women—as in a contemporary Cutty Sark ad in which a glamorously attired woman relaxes, dream-ily stroking a dog, while the tuxedo-clad men stand-ing around her engage in serious conversation (about stocks, I imagine); these guys don't need to go off into the drawing room in order to escape the ladies; they can keep one around for a bit of decorativeness and sensual pleasure while she remains on her own, more languorous world within their own.

During World War II, movies and magazines continued to celebrate independent, adventurous women, to whom men were drawn "as much for their spirit and character as for their looks."* But when

---

* Not that women's beauty was dispensable. Concern for her looks symbolized that although she worked as hard as a man, a woman's mind was still on the *real* men who were fighting for her freedom. (An ad for Tangee lipstick describes "a women's lipstick [as] an instrument of personal morale that helps her to conceal heartbreak or sorrow; gives her self-confidence when it's badly needed...It symbolizes one of the reasons why we are fighting...the precious right of women to be feminine and lovely—under any circumstances.") The woman of this period was a creature of both "appearance" *and* "action"—a kind of forerunner to today's superwoman.

the fighting men returned, the old Victorian division of labor was revived with a new commercial avidity, and the world became one in which "men act" (read: *work*) and "women appear" (read: *decorate*—both themselves and their houses)—with a vengeance. Would Barbie get on a horse without the proper accessories? Would the Marlboro Man carry a mirror with him on the trail? By the late fifties and early sixties, the sexy, wisecracking, independent-minded heroine had morphed into a perky little ingenue. Popular actresses Annette Funicello, Connie Stevens, and Sandra Dee were living Barbie dolls, their femininity blatantly advertised on their shirtwaisted bodies. They had perfectly tended bouffant hairdos (which I achieved for myself by sleeping on the cardboard cylinders from the toilet tissue rolls) and wore high heels even when washing dishes (I drew the line at that). And what about the dashing, cosmopolitan male figure in fashionable clothes? He now was usually played as a sissy or a heel—as for example Lester (Bob Evans), the slick playboy of *The Best of Everything,* who seduces gullible April (Diane Baker) with his big-city charm, then behaves like a cad when she gets pregnant.

There have always been ways to market male clothes consciousness, however. Emphasizing neatness is one. Our very own Ronnie Reagan (when he was still a B-movie star) advertised Van Heusen shirts as "the neatest Christmas gift of all" because they "won't wrinkle...ever!!" Joining elegance with violence is another. James Bond could get away with wearing beautiful suits because he was ruthless when it came to killing and bedding. (A man's cologne, called 007, was advertised in the sixties with clips from *Thunderball,* the voice-over recommending: "When you use 007, be kind" because "it's loaded" and "licensed to kill...women.") The elegant male who is capable of killing is like the highly efficient secretary who takes off her glasses to reveal a passionate, gorgeous babe underneath: a species of tantalizing, sexy disguise.

When elegance marks one man's superior class status over another it gives him a competitive edge (as was the dominant function of elegance before the eighteenth century) rather than turning him into a fop. "We have our caste marks, too" ran a 1928 ad for Aqua Velva, which featured a clean-shaven, top-hatted young man, alongside a turbaned, bejeweled, elite Indian man. This ad, however, proved to be problematic, as Kathy Peiss points out. American men didn't like being compared with dark-skinned foreigners, even aristocratic ones. The more dominant tradition—among Europeans as well as Americans—has been to portray an order in which the clean, well-shaven white man is being served or serviced by the dark ones, as in an 1935 American ad for Arrow Shirts in which the black aid is so fashion-clueless that she doesn't even know what a manufacturer's label is, or in a German ad for shaving soap depicting the "appropriate" relation between the master race and the Others.

Such codes were clearly being poked fun at—how successfully I'm not sure—when a 1995 Arid Extra-Dry commercial depicted African-American pro basketball player Charles Barkley dressed up as a nineteenth-century British colonial, declaring that anything less than Arid "would be uncivilized." The commercial, however, is not just (arguably) a poke at the racist equation of civilization and whiteness. It's also, more subtly, a playful assertion of some distinctive African-American attitudes toward male display. "Primordial perspiration," Barkley says in the commercial, "shouldn't mess with your style." And "style" is a concept whose history and cultural meanings are very different for blacks and whites in this country. Among many young African-American men, appearing in high style, "cleaned up" and festooned with sparkling jewelry, is not a sign of effeminacy, but potency and social standing. Consider the following description, from journalist Playthell Benjamin's 1994 memoir, *Lush Life* (while you're reading it, you might also recall Anne Hollander's description of Henry VIII's summit meeting):

> [Fast Black] was dressed in a pair of white pants, white buck shoes, and a long-sleeve white silk shirt—which was open to his navel and revealed a 24-karat gold chain from which hung a gold medallion set

with precious stones: diamonds, rubies, and emeralds. His massively muscled body was strikingly displayed in a white see-through silk shirt, and the trousers strained to contain his linebacker thighs. His eyes were bloodshot and his skin was tight against his face, giving it the look of an ebony mask. He struck me right off as a real dangerous muthafucka; mean enough to kill a rock.

A "real dangerous muthafucka" in a white see-through silk shirt? For the white boys to whom the Dockers and Haggar ads are largely addressed, see-through silk is for girls, and showing off one's body—particularly with sensuous fabrics—is a "fag" thing. Thus, while a Haggar ad may play up the sensual appeal of soft fabrics—*"These clothes are very soft and they'll never wrinkle"*—it makes sure to include a parenthetical (and sexist) reference to a dreamed-of wife: *"Too bad you can't marry them."* But sartorial sensuality and decorativeness, as I've learned, do not necessarily mean "femininity" for African-American men.

When I first saw the Charles Barkley commercial, the word "style" slipped by me unnoticed, because I knew very little about the history of African-American aesthetics. An early paper of mine dealing with Berger's equation was utterly oblivious to racial differences that might confound the formula "men act and women appear." Luckily, an African-American male colleague of mine gently straightened me out, urging me to think about Mike Tyson's gold front tooth as something other than willful masculine defiance of the tyranny of appearance. Unfortunately, at that time not much of a systematic nature had been written about African-American aesthetics; I had to find illuminating nuggets here and there. Then, just this year, Shane White and Graham White's *Stylin'* appeared. It's a fascinating account of how the distinctive legacy of African aesthetics was maintained and creatively, sometimes challengingly, incorporated into the fashion practices of American blacks, providing a vibrant (and frequently subversive) way for blacks to "write themselves into the American story."

Under slavery, white ownership of blacks was asserted in the most concrete, humiliating way around the display of the body on the auction block. Slaves were often stripped naked and instructed to show their teeth like horses being examined for purchase. Women might have their hair cut off. Everyone's skin would be polished to shine, as apples are polished in grocery stores today. As a former slave described it:

"The first thing they had to do was wash up and clean up real good and take a fat greasy meat skin and run over their hands, face and also their feet, or in other words, every place that showed about their body so that they would look real fat and shiny. Then they would trot them out before their would-be buyers and let them look over us real good, just like you would a bunch of fat cows that you were going to sell on the market and try to get all you could for them."

It makes perfect sense that with the body so intimately and degradingly under the control of the slave owner, opportunities to "take back" one's own body and assert one's own cultural meanings with it would have a special significance. On Sundays, slaves would dress up for church in the most colorful, vibrant clothes they could put together—a temporary escape from and an active repudiation of the subservience their bodies were forced into during the week. Their outfits, to white eyes, seemed "clashing" and mismatched. But putting together unusual combinations of color, texture, and pattern was an essential ingredient of West African textile traditions, handed down and adapted by African-American women. Color and shape "coordination"—the tyranny of European American fashion until pretty recently—were not the ruling principles of style. "Visual aliveness," *Stylin'* reports, was. The visual aliveness of the slaves' Sunday best, so jangling to white sensibilities, was thus the child both of necessity they were forced to construct their outfits through a process of bricolage, putting them together from whatever items of clothing were available—and aesthetic tradition.

From the start, whites perceived there was something insubordinate going on when blacks dressed up—and they were not entirely wrong. "Slaves were only too keen to display, even to flaunt, their finery both to slaves and to whites"; the Sunday procession was, as I've noted, a time to reclaim the body as one's own. But at the same time, blacks were not just "flaunting," but preserving and improvising on vibrant African elements of style whose "flashiness" and "insolence" were largely in the eye of the white beholder, used to a very different aesthetic. The cultural resistance going on here was therefore much deeper than offended whites (and probably most blacks too) realized at the time. It wasn't simply a matter of refusal to behave like Stepin Fetchit, with head lowered and eyes down. A new culture of unpredictable, playfully decorative, visually bold fashion was being created—and it would ultimately (although not for some time) transform the world of mainstream fashion as much as Klein's deliberately erotic underwear and jeans.

After "emancipation," funeral marches and celebratory promenades were a regular feature of black city life, in which marchers, male and female alike, were "emblazoned in colorful, expensive clothes," the men in "flashy sports outfits: fancy expensive silk shirts, new pants, hats, ties, socks," "yellow trousers and yellow silk shirts," and "bedecked with silk-and-satin-ribboned streamers, badges." Apart from formal processions, streets like Memphis's Beale Street and New Orleans's Decatur Street were ongoing informal sites for "strolling" and display. The most dazzlingly dressed men, often jazz musicians, were known as "sports." As "Jelly Roll" Morton describes it, each "sport" had to have a Sunday suit, with coat and pants that did not match, and crisply pressed trousers as tight as sausage skins. Suspenders were essential and had to be "very loud," with one strap left provocatively "hanging down." These guys knew how to "use their walk" too. The sport would walk down the street in a "very mosey" style: "Your hands is at your sides with your index fingers stuck out and you kind of struts with it." Morton—by all accounts a particularly flashy sport—had gold on his teeth and a diamond in one of them. "Those days," he recalled, "I thought I would die unless I had a hat with the emblem Stetson in it and some Edwin Clapp shoes." Shades of Tony Manero. Or King Henry VIII.

In fact, the flashiest African-American male styles have partaken both of the African legacy and European notions of "class." Although the origin of the zoot suit—broad shoulders, long coats, ballooning, peg-legged trousers, usually worn with a wide-brimmed hat—is debated, one widely believed account says it was based on a style of suit worn by the Duke of Windsor. Another claims Rhett Butler in *Gone With the Wind* was the inspiration for the zoot suit (if so, it is a "deep irony," as the authors of *Stylin'* comment). But whatever its origins, the zoot suit, worn during the forties when cloth conservation orders ruled the use of that much fabric illegal, was a highly visible and dramatic statement in *disunity* and defiance of "American Democracy," a refusal to accede to the requirements of patriotism. Even more so than the slave's Sunday promenade, the zoot-suiter used "style" aggressively to assert opposition to the culture that had made him marginal to begin with—without his assent.

The use of high style for conspicuous display or defiance is still a big part of male street culture, as sociologist Richard Majors notes: "Whether it's your car, your clothes, your young body, your new hairdo, your jewelry, you style it. The word 'style' in [African-American] vernacular usage means to show off what you've got. And for teenagers with little money and few actual possessions, showing off what you do have takes on increased importance. As one youth puts it, 'It's identity. It's a big ego trip.'"

What's changed since Majors wrote these words in the early nineties is the increasing commercial popularity of hip-hop music and culture, which has turned the rebellious stylings of street youth into an empire of images and products, often promoted (and sometimes designed) by big-name stars. With postmodern sensibilities (grab what you like) ruling the fashion world, moreover, what once were signature elements of black street style have been incorporated—as gay styles have also been incorporated—in the fashions of other worlds, both "high" (designer clothing) and "low" (white high school boys with their pants slung low, trying to look so cool).

Despite the aggressive visibility of hip-hop culture, "showing off what you've got" has not been the only influential definition of style among African-Americans. In the late nineteenth and early twentieth century, several etiquette books were published, written by middle-class blacks, promoting a very different fashion ideal. The *National Capital Code of Etiquette,* published in 1889, warned young men to "avoid colors that do not blend with the remainder of your wearing apparel, and above all things shun the so-called 'loud' ties with colors that fairly shriek unto Heaven . . ." The young black men should also avoid "bright reds, yellows and light greens as you would the plague" and never, ever strut or swagger. Hortense Powdermaker, who studied black life in Indianola, Mississippi, in the late 1930s, noted that better-off African-Americans "deliberately avoided bright colors" and were offended when clerks, on the basis of "the Negroe's reputation for wearing gaudy clothes," assumed they wanted something "loud." Those who advocated a less ostentatious style were dismayed by the lower-class practice of adorning healthy front teeth with gold, while leaving bad back teeth unattended.

A recent *Essence* list of fashion "do's and don'ts" emphasizes this deliberately understated—and in today's world, "professional"—conception of black male style. "Yes" to well-groomed hands, well-fitting suit and a "definite sense of self." "No" to "glossy polished nails," "cologne that arrives before he does," "Mr. T jewelry (the T stands for tacky)," and "saggy jeans on anyone old enough to remember when 'Killing Me Softly' was *first* released." Even in their most muted variations, African-American styles have done a great deal to add color, playfulness, and unexpected, sexy little fillips to "tasteful," professional male clothing: whimsical ties, internationally inspired shirts and sweaters, and, in general, permission to be slightly dramatic, flirtatious, and ironic with one's clothes. The rule of always matching patterns, too, no longer holds in the world of high fashion, the result of a collaboration (not necessarily conscious, of course) between postmodern sensibilities and the slave legacy of bricolage.

Superstar Michael Jordan (his masculine credentials impeccable, his reputation as a family man solidly established over the years), a very effective spokesperson for style, has done a great deal to make fashionableness, even "feminine" decorativeness, congruous with masculinity. This year, he was named *GQ*'s "Most Stylish Man." "How stylish is Michael Jordan?" *GQ* asks. "Answer: So stylish he can get away with wearing five rings!" Of course, the fact that Jordan can "get away" with wearing five rings reveals *GQ*'s cultural biases. For the magazine, Jordan's stylishness resides in the "drape of his suits, in the plain gold hoop in his left ear, in the tempered, toned-down body language of his late career." For *GQ*, subtlety equals style. For Jordan too. But of course that plain gold hoop would not have been viewed as so tastefully subtle had Jordan not made it an acceptable item of male decorativeness.

Jordan, God bless him, is also unabashed in admitting that he shops more than his wife, and that he gets his inspiration from women's magazines. The night before he goes on the road, he tries on every outfit he's going to wear. He describes himself as a "petite-type person" who tries to hide this with oversize clothes and fabrics that drape. When questioned about the contradiction between the "manliness" of sports and his "feminine" love of fashion, Jordan replies that "that's the fun part—I can get away from the stigma of being an athlete." Saved by fashion from the "stigma" of being a sweaty brute—that's something, probably, that only an African-American man can fully appreciate. The fact that's it's being an athlete and not "femininity" that's the "stigma" to be avoided by Jordan—that's something a woman's got to love.

The ultimate affront to Dockers masculinity, however, is undoubtedly the Rockport ad with drag superstar RuPaul in a beautifully tailored suit. His feet and his stare are planted—virtually identically to Michael Jordan's posture in the feature I've just discussed—in that unmistakable (and here, ironic) grammar of face-off add masculinity. "I'm comfortable being a MAN." declares RuPaul. "I'm comfortable being a woman too," of course, is the unwritten subtext. Man, woman, what's the difference so long as one is "uncompromising" about style?

[. . .]

BIBLIOGRAPHY

Beauvoir, Simone de. (1952). *The Second Sex.* New York: Vintage Books.

Berger, John. (1972). *Ways of Seeing.* Great Britain: Penguin Books.

Blum, Deborah. (1997). *Sex on the Brain: The biological Differences Between Men and Women.* New York: Viking Penguin.

Boyd, Herbert, and Robert Allen (eds.). (1995). *Brotherman.* New York: Ballantine.

Clark, Danae. (1995). "Commodity Lesbianism." In Kate Meuhuron and Gary Persecute (eds.). *Free Spirits.* Englewood Cliffs, NJ: Prentice Hall, pp. 82–94.

Clarkson, Wensley. (1997). *John Travolta: Back in Character.* Woodstock: Over-look Press.

Ellenzweig, Allen. (1992). *The Homoerotic Photograph.* New York: Columbia University Press.

Farnharn, Alan. (1996). "You're So Vain," *Fortune,* September 9, pp 66–82.

Foucault, Michel. (1985). *The Use of Pleasure.* New York: Vintage Books,

Friday, Nancy. (1996). *The Power of Beauty.* New York: HarperCollins.

Gaines, Steven, and Sharon Churcher. (1994). *Obsession: The Lives and Times of Calvin Klein.* New York: Avon Books.

Gilmore, David. (1990). *Manhood in the Making.* New Haven: Yale University Press.

Gladwell, Anne. (1994). "Listening to Khakis," *The New Yorker,* July 28, pp. 54–58.

Hollander, Anne. (1994). *Sex and Suits: The Evolution of Modern Dress.* New York: Kodansha International.

Long, Ron. (1997). "The Fitness of the Gym," *Harvard Gay and Lesbian Review,* Vol. IV, No. 3, Summer, pp. 20–22.

Majors, Richard, and Janet Mancini Billson. (1992). *Cool Pose: The Dilemmas of Black Manhood in America.* New York: Lexington Books.

Peiss, Kathy. (1998). *Hope in a Jar: The Making of America's Beauty Culture.* New York: Metropolitan Books.

Pieterse, Jan Nederveen. (1990). *White on Black: Images of Africa and Blacks in Western Popular Culture.* New Haven: Yale University Press.

Plato. (1989). *Symposium.* Trans. Alexander Nehama. Indianapolis: Hackett Publishing.

Richmond, Peter. (1987). "How Do Men Feel About Their Bodies?" *Glamour,* April, pp. 312–313, 369–372.

Rotundo, E. Anthony. (1993). *American Manhood: Transformations in Masculinity from the Revolution to the Modern Era.* New York: Basic Books.

Sartre, Jean-Paul. (1966). *Being and Nothingness.* New York: Washington Square Press.

Shaw, Dan. (1994). "Mirror, Mirror," *New York Times,* May 29, Section 9, pp. 1, 6.

Sheets-Johnstone, Maxine. (1994). *The Roots of Power: Animate Form and Gendered Bodies.* Chicago: Open Court.

Spinder, Amy. (1996). "It's Face-Lifted Tummy-Tucked Jungle Out There," *New York Times,* June 9.

Taylor, John. (1995). "The Long Hard Days of Dr. Dick," *Esquire,* September, pp.120–130.

White, Shane, and Graham White. (1998). *Stylin'.* Ithaca: Cornell University Press.

---

64. • *Don Sabo*

DOING TIME, DOING MASCULINITY: SPORTS AND PRISONS (2001)

Don Sabo is professor emeritus of health policy in D'Youville and the founder and director of the Center for Research on Physical Activity, Sport & Health. He is known for his works on sports, men, and masculinities. The following essay is taken from a chapter in an anthology, *Prison Masculinities,* which he coedited with Terry A. Kupers and Willie London.

I am a white, male college professor in my forties, hunched over a table in Attica Correctional Facility. My heart is pounding, my upper body is locked taut and shaking, and I am gazing into the eyes of an African American prisoner who, like so many of the men in this New York State prison, comes from what sociologists call the "underclass." We are different in most respects, but right now we are alike. Like me, he's puffing and straining, trying not to show it, sometimes cursing, and returning my gaze. We are arm wrestling, and in this case he puts me down in about two minutes, which in arm wrestling can be a long, long time.

I started arm wrestling in the joint about five years ago. I enjoy the physical connection that the contest brings. The participants initially stalk one another over a period of days or weeks, keeping their distance, evaluating each other's strengths and weaknesses. There may be some playful bad-mouthing or boasting that leads up to an hour. Eventually, they make the necessary moves that bring each to the table hand-in-hand, eye-to-eye. Even though arm wrestling is overtly combative, it can breed a closer connection with another man than is allowed for in most aspects of men's lives. It allows me to climb outside the bourgeois husk of my life and join with somebody in a way that temporarily suspends the hierarchical distinctions between free man and inmate, white and black, privileged and underprivileged, and teacher and student.

Arm wrestling also lets me pull my athletic past into the present, to enjoin youthful masculine spirits and facades. At the same time that these manly juices are resurrected, though, I try to tell myself and others that I don't take the competition so seriously. I want to learn the lesson that it is OK to be vulnerable to defeat.

Sometimes I win; sometimes I lose. It still matters to me whether I win or lose. I try hard to win, but, when I lose, I get over it quickly, accept it, and even welcome it as inevitable. Part of me is happy for the man who beat me. When I win, I savor the victories for a few days, bragging to myself, sometimes others, soothing my middle-aging ego with transparently masculine rationalizations that I am still strong, not over the bloody hill yet. Arm wrestlers understand that nobody wins all the time. Beneath the grit and show, we know there is more to it than winning or losing. We also know that part of what makes arm wrestling more than just a contest or pastime is that it somehow speaks to our beliefs and feelings about being a man.

I have taught in prisons for fourteen years. My experiences, observations, and discussions with inmates have revealed that prison sports have different meanings for different men. I have learned that a great many motives, messages, and contradictions are crammed into the muscles and athletic pastimes of men in prison. Like men outside the walls, however, prisoners use sports as vehicles for creating and maintaining masculine identity.

DOING TIME, DOING SPORTS

Perhaps the most striking aspect of prison sports is their visibility. The yard is often a hub of athletic activity. Weight lifters huddle in small groups around barbells and bench press racks. Runners circle the periphery, while hoopsters spin and shoot on the basketball courts. There is the occasional volleyball game and bocce tournament. Depending on the facility and time of year, there may be football practices or games, replete with equipment and fans along the sidelines. Some prisons maintain softball leagues and facilities.

Inside the buildings, you will find a gym, basketball courts, and weight rooms. Power lifters struggle against gravity and insanity. Feats of strength produce heroes in the joint, sometimes even legends, or at least local legends. I have been told stories about Jihad Al-Sibbar, a man past his forties who weighs about 155 pounds. He is believed to be the strongest man in the New York State prison system, and I have heard it said more than once that, if given the opportunity, he could have competed at the Olympic level. I want and need to believe in these stories, not so much because they are tales of a strong man but because his triumphs say something about the potential of athletics to sustain sanity in an insane place.

Sports and fitness activities spill into the prison environment in other ways. An inmate may do daily calisthenics while in solitary. For example, Martin Sostre was an African American black power activist and inner-city bookstore owner who was framed by the police in 1967 and imprisoned for nine years. Sostre used physical exercise and yoga to survive long stints of solitary and to bolster his political struggles against prison and legal authorities (Copeland, 1970).

In almost any sector of the prison, fans may jabber about who will win the Super Bowl, the NBA finals, or the next heavyweight boxing match. The taunting, teasing, and betting that typify sports fans outside the walls are also rife among inmates and guards and other personnel. Some men gather in groups around television sets to watch the Final Four or "Monday Night Football," while others sit alone in their cells jabbing with George Foreman or soaring with Michael Jordan.

In short, sports and fitness activities in prison engage men's minds and bodies to varying degrees and, in the process, help them do their time. For some men, especially the young ones, athletics are no more than a fleeting pastime, a simple form of physical play, something to do to get to the end of another day. For others, sports and fitness activities are a crucial survival strategy, a life practice that is intended to create and maintain physical and mental health in a hostile, unhealthy place. For still others, working out or participating in sports helps them to displace anger and frustration, to get the rage out of their bodies and psyches before it explodes or turns in on them. And for some, the goal is to get big to be bad, to manufacture muscle and a jock presence in order to intimidate and dominate.

DOING MASCULINITY

The prison environment triggers a masculine awareness in me. I go on masculine alert. I don't walk around with biceps flexed and chest expanded, pretending to be a tough guy in front of anybody looking my way.

That kind of suck-in-your-belly-and-lower-your-voice stuff faded away with my twenties. The masculinity that surfaces in the prison is more an attitude, a hazy cluster of concerns and expectations that get translated into emotion and physical movement in ways that never quite come clear. Though there are a few women around (for example, an occasional female guard, some women teachers), I see and smell the prison as an all-male domain. I sense a greater potential for danger and a heightened need to protect myself. I could get caught in a bad situation. I have been told not to trust anybody—prisoners, guards, or bureaucrats. Nobody. It sounds crazy, but the tinges of distrust and paranoia almost feel good. Indeed, there are parts of me, call them "threads" or "echoes" of a masculine identity, that embrace the distrust and welcome the presumed danger and potential for violence.

These masculine prompts are seldom uppermost in my mind. They do not emanate from inside of me; they are more like visitors that come and go, moving in and out of me like tap water gushing through an overfilled glass. Arm wrestling allows me to play out masculinity in tune with other elements of jailhouse jock culture. At the same time, the wrestling breeds familiarity with prisoners, pushes toward closeness and trust, and subverts hierarchical distinctions based on class, race, and professional status.

Like me, many men in prison deploy sports and fitness activities as resources to do masculinity—that is, to spin masculine identities, to build reputations, to achieve or dissolve status. For the men in prison, as elsewhere, masculine identity is earned, enacted, rehearsed, refined, and relived through each day's activities and choices. I'm not saying that the gender scripts that men follow in prison are reinvented each day, from moment to moment, man to man. Masculinity does not unfold inside us as much as it flows through us. It is not a strictly individual or psychological process. In doing gender, each individual participates in the larger prison culture, which scripts masculinity by supplying direction, role models, props, motivations, rewards, and values (Messerschmidt, 1993; West and Zimmerman, 1987). For many men, sports are a part of the formula for shaping gender identity.

SOFTNESS AND HARDNESS

In prison, the manly injunction to be strong is evident not only in the bulk or bearing of many men's bodies but in everyday speech as well. I have often heard prisoners describe other men as "hard" or "soft." Over the years, I have learned that there are many guises of hardness, which, inside and outside the prison culture, illustrate a variety of masculine expressions that stretch between the honorable and the perverse.

Being hard can mean that the individual is toned, strong, conditioned, or fit, rather than weak, flabby, or out of shape. A hard man cares for and respects his body. Life in prison is extremely oppressive, and it is extraordinarily difficult to eke out a healthy lifestyle. Cigarette smoke is everywhere. The noise on the blocks can jam the senses. Most inmates will tell you that the chow stinks, and, for those who think about such matters, a nutritionally sound diet is impossible to scrape together from the available cafeteria fare. For some men, then, the pursuit of sports and fitness activity is a personal quest to create a healthy body in an unhealthy environment. Those who succeed build a sense of accomplishment and garner the respect of others. Some men strive to be hard in order to build self-esteem. Being in prison is a colossal reminder of personal failure. A regular fitness regimen helps some men center mind and identity in the undeniably tangible locus of the body. For others, getting good at basketball or being recognized as a leading athlete earns the respect of peers. Damaged egos and healing psyches drink in the recognition and repair themselves.

Being hard can also be a defense against prison violence. The hard man sends the message that he is somebody to contend with, not a pushover, not somebody to "fuck with." The sexual connotations of this last phrase take on particular significance in the prison subculture, where man-on-man rape is part of life. The act of prison rape is tied to maintaining the status order among a maze of male groups. Blacks may rape whites or vice versa in order to establish dominant status. Older prisoners may use rape to enslave newcomers. Guards or prison administrators

have been known to threaten to expose prisoners to greater threat of rape in order to evoke good behavior, to punish, or to squeeze out information. As Tom Cahill, himself a victim of prison rape, observed, "Once 'turned out'—prison parlance for raped—a survivor is caught in a bind. If an inmate reports a sexual assault, even without naming the assailant, he will be labeled a 'snitch,' a contract will automatically be placed on him, and his life expectancy will be measured in minutes from then" (1990:32).

Men's efforts to weave webs of domination through rape and physical intimidation *in prison* also reflect and reproduce men's domination of women in the social world beyond the walls. In the muscled, violent, and tattooed world of prison rape, woman is symbolically ever present. She resides in the pulpy, supple, and muted linguistic folds of the hardness/softness dichotomy. The prison phrase "make a woman out of you" means that you will be raped. Rape-based relationships between prisoners are often described as relationships between "men" and "girls" who are, in effect, thought of as "master" and "slave," victor and vanquished.

The hardness/softness split also echoes and fortifies stereotypes of masculinity and femininity (Bordo, 1999). To be "hard" means to be more manly than the next guy, who is said to be "soft" and more feminine. It is better to be hard than soft in prison. To be called hard is a compliment. To be labeled soft can be a playful rebuke or a serious put-down. The meanings around hardness and softness also flow from and feed homophobia, which is rampant in prison. The stigma of being labeled a homosexual can make a man more vulnerable to ridicule, attack, ostracism, or victimization.

CONCLUSION

Prison somehow magnifies the contradictions in men's lives, making them palpable, visible. For many prisoners, the pursuit of manhood was closely linked to their efforts to define masculine identity and worth—for example, robbing in order to be a good provider or husband, joining a gang in hopes of becoming a "big man" on the street, being a "badass" or "gangster" as a way of getting respect from peers, braving the violence of the drug trade, raping or beating on women in order to prove manly superiority, or embezzling to achieve financial success and masculine adequacy. The irony here is that these scripted quests for manly power led, in part, to incarceration and loss of freedom and dignity. For lots of prisoners, and countless men on the outside, adherence to the traditional pathways to masculinity turned out to be a trap.

Men's participation in prison sports is fused with yet another contradiction. On one hand, sports and exercise provide prisoners with vehicles for self expression and physical freedom. On the other hand, prison officials know that involvement in sports and exercise activities helps make inmates more tractable and compliant. Therefore, the cultivation of the body through sports and fitness activities is simultaneously a source of personal liberation and social control.

It is easy for men in prison or on the outside to get trapped by the cultural mandate of hardness. The image of the male athlete as a muscled, aggressive, competitive, and emotionally controlled individual dovetails the prevailing definition of masculinity in sexist culture. Conformity to this model for manliness can be socially and emotionally destructive. Muscles may remain *"the* sign of masculinity" (Glassner, 1988: 192) in the male-dominated culture and the gender hierarchies that constitute the North American prison system. And yet my observations tell me that prisoners' relationships to muscle and masculinity are not simple or one-sided. Men cultivate their bodies in order to send a variety of messages about the meaning of masculinity to themselves and others. Whereas conformity to the credo of hardness for some men feeds the forces of domination and subordination, for others athletics and fitness are forms of self-care. Whereas many prison jocks are literally playing out the masculine scripts they learned in their youth, others are attempting to attach new meanings to sports and exercise that affirm health, sanity, and alternative modes of masculinity.

Perhaps the greatest contradiction pervading prison sports is that, despite the diversity of gendered meanings and practices that prisoners attach to their bodies through sports and exercise, the cultural mandate for hardness and toughness prevails. Men's soft sides remain hidden, suppressed, and underground. The punitive and often violent structures of prison hierarchies persist, breathing aggression and fear into men's bodies and minds. The same tragic contradiction informs men's lives in sports outside the prison walls, where structured gender inequality and sexism constrain efforts to reform gender relationships toward equity and healthful affirmation of the body.

Arm wrestling teaches me that the cages in men's lives can be made of iron bars, muscles, or myths. The harder I wrestle, the more I dream of escape.

REFERENCES

Bordo, S. 1999. *The Male Body: A New Look at Men in Public and in Private.* New York: Farrar, Straus and Giroux.

Cahill, T. 1990. "Prison Rape: Torture in the American Gulag." In *Men and Intimacy: Personal Accounts Exploring the Dilemmas of Modern Male Sexuality,* ed. Franklin Abbott. Freedom, Calif.: Crossing Press.

Copeland, V. 1970. *The Crime of Martin Sostre.* New York: McGraw Hill.

Glassner, B. 1988. *Bodies: Why We Look the Way We Do (and How We Feel about It).* New York: Putnam.

Messerschmidt, James W. 1993. *Masculinities and Crime: Critique and Reconceptualization of Theory.* Lanham, Md.: Rowman and Littlefield.

West, Candace, and Don H. Zimmerman. 1987. "Doing Gender." *Gender and Society* 1(2): 125–51.

65. • *L. Ayu Saraswati*

COSMOPOLITAN WHITENESS:
The Effects and Affects of Skin Whitening Advertisements in Transnational Indonesia (2010)

L. Ayu Saraswati is associate professor in women's studies at the University of Hawai'i. Her book *Seeing Beauty, Sensing Race in Transnational Indonesia* won a National Women's Studies Association Gloria Anzaldúa book award for deftly using the lens of affect theories in exploring issues of race and gender in a transnational context. The following article, published in *Meridians: Feminism, Race, Transnationalism*, exposes the multiplicities of whiteness and introduces a new notion of whiteness as a virtual and affective construction: Cosmopolitan whiteness.

Skin-whitening advertisements dominate the landscape of Indonesian women's magazines. Often, these whitening advertisements appear on the first page of such magazines. In the June 2006 edition of the Indonesian *Cosmopolitan* (hereafter referred to as *Cosmo*), Estée Lauder's "Cyber White" ad appeared on the inside front-cover spread of the magazine. In the following issue of the Indonesian *Cosmo* (July 2006) Kosé's Sekkisei whitening ad with the slogan "Skin of Innocence" appeared as the front-cover gatefold. Neither of these transnational ads employs Indonesian models: a Caucasian woman models the "Cyber White" ad, and a Japanese woman models the Sekkisei ad. These skin-whitening ads, modeled by women of different racial backgrounds and facial features, beg the question: what kind of whiteness is being marketed in transnational women's magazine such as the Indonesian *Cosmo*?

Existing studies on skin-whitening phenomena in a variety of countries fall short of answering this question because these studies operate under the assumption that whiteness is an ethnic or racially based category, however marked it may be by biological,

social, and visual signifiers (Burke 1996; Peiss 1998; Kawashima 2002; Hall 2005; Hunter 2005; Rondilla and Spickard 2007; Pierre 2008; Glenn 2009; Parameswaran and Cardoza 2009). For example, when cultural studies scholar Radhika Parameswaran and journalist Kavitha Cardoza point out that whitening advertisements in contemporary Indian media do not necessarily reveal women's desire to be racially white, they are equating "white" with racially Caucasian people (Parameswaran and Cardoza 2009). Similarly, when historian Timothy Burke notes that women's consumption of skin whiteners in modern Zimbabwe was considered as a sign of (re)colonization and "selling-out" to the white regime, he also positioned "white" as a racial category (Burke 1996). Indeed, the term "white-privileging subject position" that Asian studies scholar Terry Kawashima coined in her analysis of contemporary anime, skin-whitening ads, and hair-coloring phenomena in Japan also rests on the same assumed white racial category: Caucasian (Kawashima 2002).

Other important studies on the racial politics of beauty that challenge body-altering practices as merely revealing people's desires for the white beauty norm nonetheless refer to Caucasian whiteness as a frame for referencing "whiteness." Kathleen Zane, although providing us with a different way of reading Asian women's eyelid surgeries that goes beyond Asian women's desire to "imitate a Caucasian appearance" (Zane 1998, 355), still attaches the category of "Caucasian" whiteness to the meaning of a "white" beauty norm. Kobena Mercer has demonstrated the complex "inter-culturation" of so-called "artificial" and "natural" techniques of hairstyling among black people (as well as among people in "white subcultures"), and asked "who in this postmodern mêlée of semiotic appropriation and counter-creolization, is imitating whom?" (Mercer 1987, 52). Yet he also refers to Caucasian whiteness when he highlights this complexity of whiteness as an embodied racial category. Thus, although critical scholarship on the racial politics of beauty convincingly debunks the myth of racially authentic bodies and points to the unstable quality of "looking white," these studies nonetheless still subscribe to the very notion of Caucasian whiteness as the point of theoretical reference in challenging such whiteness.

This article breaks away from these theoretical trajectories by arguing that desire for "whiteness" is not the same as desire for "Caucasian whiteness." By examining skin-whitening advertisements in the Indonesian *Cosmo*[1] published during the months of June, July, and August, 2006–2008,[2] I argue that in contemporary Indonesia it is what I am calling "cosmopolitan whiteness" that is being marketed through these whitening ads. By cosmopolitan whiteness, I refer to whiteness when represented to embody the "affective" and virtual quality of cosmopolitanism: transnational mobility. In using the term "affect," I am drawing on Teresa Brennan's definition of the term as "physiological shift accompanying a judgment" (Brennan 2004, 5). Here affect is understood as preceding emotions, yet also involving "sociality or social productivity" (Wissinger 2007, 232). In this article I position these ads as a socially productive site where affective qualities about white-skinned women are produced, represented, and circulated.

I propose the notion of cosmopolitan whiteness as a mode for rethinking whiteness beyond racial

and ethnic categories and for thinking about race, skin color, and gender as "affectively" constructed. To think about whiteness beyond a racial or ethnic category is not to argue that race and racialization are irrelevant in thinking about whiteness, of course. Rather, I argue that whiteness is also affectively constructed as cosmopolitan and that race and racialization operate in concert with cosmopolitanism in these whitening advertisements.

Redefining whiteness as cosmopolitan whiteness allows me to reveal yet another aspect of cosmopolitanness and whiteness that is not often discussed: its virtuality. Virtuality here is understood as occupying the space between the real and the unreal: the virtual. This notion of virtuality is important in understanding cosmopolitan whiteness because virtuality highlights the lack of "traditional physical substance" (Laurel 1993, 8). I argue that cosmopolitan whiteness is a signifier without a racialized, signified body. Cosmopolitan whiteness can and has been modeled by women from Japan to South Korea to the United States. There is no one race or ethnic group in particular that can occupy an authentic cosmopolitan white location because there has never been a "real" whiteness to begin with: whiteness is a virtual quality, neither real nor unreal.

[. . .]

TRANSNATIONAL CONTACTS AND *COSMO* CONTEXTS

THE RACIALIZED BEAUTY IDEAL IN TRANSNATIONAL INDONESIA

In Indonesia, a country of 300 ethnic groups, the formation of beauty ideals, articulated through racial, skin color, and gender discourses, has historically been transnational. As seen in some of the oldest surviving Indonesian literature, such as *Ramayana*, light-skinned women were the dominant beauty norm of the time. The Indonesian (or so-called *Old-Javanese*) version of *Ramayana* was adapted from its Indian origin in the late ninth century. In both the

Indian and Indonesian versions of *Ramayana*, beautiful women are described as having white, shining faces, like the full moon. This evidence suggests that: 1) preference for light-skinned women in Indonesia predates European colonialism; and 2) the light-skinned beauty standard in precolonial Indonesia should not be read as merely a "local" or "indigenous" construction. Rather, this idea of light skin color as beautiful is already a "transnational" construction, *avant la lettre*—from India to Indonesia.[3]

This transnational construction of beauty ideals has continued from Dutch and Japanese colonial times into the present day. During the early twentieth century, when Dutch colonialism fully matured in colonial Indonesia (then called the Indies) preference for light (decoded as Caucasian white) skin color was strengthened. Images of Caucasian white beauty represented the epitome of beauty in the beauty ads published in women's magazines during this time. When the Japanese took over as the new colonial power in Indonesia from 1942 to 1945, they propagated a new Asian beauty ideal: white was still the preferred color but not the preferred race. In postcolonial Indonesia, particularly since the late 1960s when the pro-American president Suharto reigned in Indonesia, American popular culture has become one of the strongest influences against which the Indonesian white beauty ideal is articulated and negotiated. . . .

[. . .]

THE COSMO POLITICS OF TRANSNATIONAL CIRCULATION: FROM THE UNITED STATES TO INDONESIA

U.S. popular culture, from its films and magazines to its consumer products, has become one of the most powerful "nodes" (Appadurai 1996) in shaping the terrain of contemporary Indonesian pop culture. Particularly since 1998,[4] there has been a major boom in Indonesian adaptations of American magazines such as *Cosmo*, *Good Housekeeping*, and *Esquire*. Hence,

although my focus in this article is on examining skin-whitening ads in the Indonesian *Cosmo*, in this section, I am also looking at U.S. *Cosmo* magazines during the same months (June–August of 2006–2008) to chart the circulation of beauty, racial, and gender discourses through this transnational magazine. Moreover, examining the United States as a site where whiteness is articulated as "desirable," my analysis makes visible how transnational circulations of whiteness from the United States to Indonesia depend on the ways in which whiteness is capable of maintaining its currency globally (hence the notion of cosmopolitan whiteness).

The magazine I examine here, *Cosmopolitan*, is one of the most popular transnational women's magazines in Indonesia. It originated in the United States in 1886 as a literary/fiction magazine. It underwent a significant transformation in 1965 when its new editor, Helen Gurley Brown, then the well-known author of *Sex and the Single Girl*, took a daring step by shifting the magazine's focus to women's sexuality and, as well as in, the workplace (McMachon 1990; Spooner 2001). With the slogan, "fun . . . fearless . . . female," U.S. *Cosmo*'s strategy of marketing to and advocating for sexually independent women saved it from almost certain bankruptcy. Prior to 1965, sexuality was rarely discussed in U.S. women's magazines, which at that time were focused more on women's place in the home (Nelson and Paek 2005). In Indonesia as well, when *Cosmo* (originally called *Kosmopolitan Higina*) first began publication in September 1997, promoting sexually assertive women (albeit in a much subtler way compared to the 2006–2008 editions that I analyzed for this article) meant breaking new ground. Although some Muslim groups in Indonesia sent letters to the editor protesting that the magazine was "helping Indonesian women love sex too much" (Carr 2002), nonetheless, the strategy of putting forth women's independence through sexuality was what made *Cosmo* one of the most successful magazines in the world. . . .

[. . .]

THE CONSTRUCTION OF COSMOPOLITAN WHITENESS IN SKIN-WHITENING ADS

Within its theoretical trajectories, the word "cosmopolitan" is understood to be rooted in the Greek "*kosmos*," which means "world," and "*polites*," meaning "citizen" (Cheah 1998, 22). It conveys the aura of a "citizen of the world." Eighteenth-century French philosophers used the term to highlight "an intellectual ethic, a universal humanism that transcends regional particularism" (Cheah 1998, 22). . . . Moreover, the way the magazine deploys the word "cosmopolitan" also falls within these theoretical trajectories insofar as the magazine seems to make meanings of cosmopolitan, as Bruce Robbins explains it: "the word *cosmopolitan* . . . evokes the image of a privileged person: someone who can claim to be a 'citizen of the world' by virtue of independent means, expensive tastes, and a globe-trotting lifestyle" (Robbins 1998, 248). Here, cosmopolitanism is framed within consumer culture to mean consuming the other's exoticized and commodified culture (Vertovec and Cohen 2002, 7). . . .

[. . .]

. . . The Indonesian *Cosmo*, like the U.S. *Cosmo*, circulates biased, gendered representations of skin color and race that privilege whiteness (oftentimes Caucasian white encoded as cosmopolitan white) in their magazines. Images of African Americans rarely appear in the Indonesian *Cosmo*. Even when African Americans' images appeared in the U.S. and Indonesian *Cosmo*, their numbers were significantly lower than those of Caucasians. For example, out of 308 pages in the August 2006 Indonesian *Cosmo*, only four pages have images of African Americans (1.5%). In comparison, out of 242 pages in the August 2006 U.S. *Cosmo*, only twenty-three pages (10%) contain images of African Americans. The numbers are significantly even lower for images of Asian Americans in the U.S. *Cosmo*. Indonesians or women with stereotypical Southeast Asian features rarely appear in the U.S. *Cosmo*. Indeed, in analyzing thirty-eight issues of U.S. *Cosmo* from 1976–1988, Kathryn McMachon pointed out how models, "if third-world, which is not often the case, are represented in codes which signify difference as the culturally exotic. Paradoxically, actual differences between third-world or minority women and white women in the United States are denied, while racial and ethnic stereotypes are exploited" (McMachon 1990, 383). Conversely, Caucasian women dominate advertisements and images that accompany editorial content in U.S. and Indonesian editions. Having Caucasian white women dominate the Indonesian *Cosmo* highlights the ways in which, within a transnational setting, not only do U.S. citizens travel elsewhere more freely, compared to Indonesian citizens, but their images (mostly of Caucasian Americans) are also circulated more frequently across the globe and therefore are thought to have more value than those of Indonesians.

[. . .]

LOOKING WHITE, FEELING GOOD: RACE, GENDER, AND COLOR AS AFFECTIVELY CONSTRUCTED

My argument that whiteness is cosmopolitan and transnationalized (transcending race and nation) leads us to this article's larger theoretical claim: gender, race, and skin color are "affectively" constructed. Cosmopolitan whiteness is more than just an embodiment of certain phenotypes and vaguely defined skin color, that is, Caucasian whites as having white skin color, big round eyes, and so on. It is also affectively constructed. . . .

At the heart of these ads lie powerful cultural narratives of how happiness is achieved by consuming specific products. As media scholar Sut Jhally argues, "Fundamentally, advertising talks to us as individuals and addresses us about how we can become happy. The answers it provides are all oriented to the marketplace, through the purchase of goods or services" (Jhally 2003, 251). Similarly, Kartajaya emphasizes that the "feel benefit," the benefit of reaching consumers' emotions and promising happiness over rational explanations, rather than the "think benefit," plays a significant role in helping consumers make their choices. As he succinctly points out, "people's actions are rooted in 'feelings'" (Kartajaya 2004, 34). . . .

In these whitening ads, happiness is offered via the route of whitening practices. Feminist cultural studies scholar Sara Ahmed argues, "some objects more than others embody the promise of happiness. In other words, happiness directs us to certain objects, as if they are the necessary ingredients for a good life" (Ahmed 2007, 127). In these skin-whitening ads, skin-whitening products become the objects necessary for a good life. Happiness is coded as cosmopolitan whiteness.

[. . .]

FACIALIZATION AND THE AFFECTIVE STRUCTURE

One of the most salient features of skin-whitening ads in the Indonesian *Cosmo* is its emphasis on the model's face. All but five whitening ads (Estée Lauder's "Re-Nutriv Ultimate White Lifting Serum," Lux's "White Glamour," Nivea's "Night Whitening Milk," SkinWhite's "Whitening Hand and Body Lotion," and Viva's "White") consist of close-up images of the model's face, which fill almost the entire page. This begs the question: what affective work does this magnification of the face in whitening ads do? I will answer this question by turning once again to the "Cyber White" ad.

In the version of the "Cyber White" ad published in the June 2007 issue of the Indonesian *Cosmo*, as in other whitening ads, the face is the focal point. The face of a blonde-haired, blue-eyed, stereotypical Nordic woman fills the left side of a two-page spread. Her close-up face is magnified. A large, ice-crystal necklace fits perfectly on her smooth, white neck. The neatly arranged light blue ice bricks provide a sense of cool aura to the ad's background. The spectator is invited to feel the "cool"-ness of the ad,

of the model, and of the product through the process of a transfer of meanings among these signs (a blue bottle with a white cap, blue ice bricks, a transparent ice-crystal necklace, and the model's blue eyes). She does not smile, which is often requisite in beauty ads. This lack of a smile, however, actually adds to her innocent presence. She peers deep into the spectator's eyes with her sharp and superior look. After all, she is a goddess, or is supposed to make us recall such a mythical figure.

[. . .]

Moreover, in this ad the model's face is represented as surreal in its state of "flawless," poreless, ultra-white brilliance. Here, the "Cyber White" ad positions whiteness as occupying the space in between real and unreal—the virtual. Thus, the invocation of the mythological Greek goddess who looks quite modern in the ad's rendition also makes visible the realness and the unrealness of her whiteness, "Cyber White."

Cyberdiscourse, according to cyber culture scholar Susanna Paasonen, "revolves around notions of mobility and freedom in terms of identity and self-expression" (Paasonen 2005, 2–3). This certainly reminds us of cosmopolitanism: the sense of a globe-trotting lifestyle and the luxury of making claims about multiple (virtual) homes. In this sense, the virtual and the cosmopolitan bleed into each other. However, as some cyberculture scholars have noted, cybercitizens have often been constructed as "white" (here, white usually refers to Caucasian white) (Kolko, Nakamura, and Rodman 2000; Ebo 2001; Nakamura 2002; Paasonen 2005; Nakamura 2008). Hence whiteness becomes one's access to experiencing cosmopolitanness (even if at times only virtually), and cosmopolitanness becomes one's access to experience whiteness.

Virtuality, as it reverberates with cosmopolitan whiteness, also brings to the surface the issue of "real" (authentic) vs. unreal (inauthentic). According to Brenda Laurel, "the adjective virtual describes things—worlds, phenomena, etc.—that look and feel like reality but lack the traditional physical substance" (Laurel 1993, 8). This provides us with yet another understanding of cosmopolitan whiteness: whiteness as lacking the traditional physical substance, traditionally (and discursively) known as Caucasian whiteness. Cosmopolitan whiteness can never be "real" or authentic, nor can any race occupy an authentic white location because there has never been a "real" whiteness to begin with.

Visual studies scholar Nicholas Mirzoeff points out that adding to this lack of authenticity, virtual space is a space that "is not real but appears to be" (Mirzoeff 1999, 91; emphasis mine). Thus, cosmopolitan whiteness is not about claiming a form of real whiteness. Rather, it is about appearing white—these creams can only make you *appear* white but cannot make you *become* a "real" white. The body can only be virtually white. The product's label, "Cyber White," therefore captures and exemplifies the cosmopolitanness of the whiteness that is being marketed in this ad. In some sense, this notion of virtuality—real but not real—bears a resemblance to postcolonial theorist Homi Bhabha's notion of colonial mimicry in which whiteness is read as white but not quite (Bhabha 1994).

The question, however, remains: why is the face emphasized in whitening ads? The term "face-to-face conversation" is used to signify the presence of bodies involved in the conversation. This hints at the importance of the face in relation to one's body and its subjectivity. In his analysis of webcam sex Dennis Waskul argues,

> Clearly the face occupies a supreme position in connecting or disconnecting the self with the body. One's face is the most identifiable feature of one's body and self; it is the single human physiological feature that concretely conjoins the corporeal with the self. (Waskul 2002/2004, 51)

Here, the face matters because it links the body and the self. The face becomes, to build on Deleuze and Guattari's argument, a "loc[us] of resonance" (Deleuze and Guattari 1987, 168) that allows us to make meanings out of forms of subjectivity played out in these ads. The face is a source of information through which we approximate the other's subjectivity. The wrinkled old face, the mad person's face, the evil face, the feminine face, the "Asian" face, or the beautiful face could tell us something about the person and how we would feel about them. The meanings of their faces seem so evident that we rarely question where or how these ideas arise, or why certain faces evoke particular feelings in us; that is, a beautiful face may evoke our desire or the mad person's face may incite our fear.

[. . .]

In this era of Photoshop, literally everything is up for alteration. Color is an option. Every pixel's color serves certain (affective, if not aesthetic) purposes. The easiest way to uncover the meanings of these images, according to media scholar Katherine Frith, is to alter the image of the ads and see what different meanings are produced (Frith 1997). For example, would we feel differently about the ad had the model's face been colored red and organized to look angry, that is, instead of having her lips represented as delicate, the model would show her clenched teeth to demonstrate her rage? Of course! These ads hence function as part of the faciality machine because they help the audience "rehearse" (Massumi 2002, 66) their perception of women with white skin color. Moreover, they also help maintain relations of power in which whiteness holds the supreme position. This ad feeds into the reconstruction of her white-skinned face as beautiful, desirable, and positive-affect generating. These are the faces we are "educated" to desire (Stoler 1995). This matters because the micromanagement of desire is central to the maintenance of power (Stoler 2002). In other words, whose face we desire is always implicated in the relations of power.

I do not argue, however, that when we look at a white-skinned face, we are *always* positively *affect*ed by it. This would rob the spectators of their own agency and discount the different degrees of "intensity" (Massumi 2002, 14) that the same face may evoke in different people. This is where I agree with Stoler, who argues that there is "a space for individual affect [to be] structured by power but not wholly subsumed by it" (Stoler 1995, 192). After all, as Terry Kawashima has pointed out, the work of labeling others based on established racial categories involves an active visual reading (Kawashima 2002). That is, readers often dismiss certain parts of the body and simultaneously privilege other parts to claim that a certain figure looks "white"—in this case the Japanese anime Sailor Moon (a blonde-haired, blue-eyed, small-nosed, petite, young girl). This is what she calls a "white-privileging subject position." (Note that once again, white here is assumed to be Caucasian white.) . . .

COSMOPOLITAN WHITENESS AND HEGEMONIC WHITE SUPREMACY

I wish to end this article with a twist. I would like to preempt a particular question, perhaps unnecessarily. However, it is a question that is almost always raised after I share my reading of these skin-whitening ads in conferences, seminars, or lectures: what about skin-tanning ads? Don't all of these ads simply expose the human desire to want what they don't have? My answer is no: skin-tanning ads actually perpetuate and further strengthen the notion of "cosmopolitan whiteness." Hence in this conclusion, I will provide a succinct reading of these tanning ads to demonstrate how both skin-whitening ads *and* skin-tanning ads function to provide positive affects toward white-skinned women and help construct "cosmopolitan whiteness."

Tanning ads published in the U.S. *Cosmo* during the months of June–August of 2006–2008 provide us with evidence that even in these tanning ads, the color "tan" is advertised *without* undermining the supremacy of the Caucasian white race. Instead, these ads merely affirm positive affects toward women with white skin color and "race," and, of course, their cosmopolitan whiteness. First, unlike whitening ads, none of these tanning ads use the word blackening or browning—words that have racial connotations in the U.S. context. Rather, ads for Banana Boat and

L'Oréal, for example, use the word "tan" or "bronze." "Deepest bronze," a surreal color—a color that is not often used to describe skin color—is used to describe the darkest skin tone that these women could achieve by using these tanning products. This suggests that these tanning ads do not even flirt with desires of racial transformation or desires to have black skin, let alone to be black.

Second, whereas none of the whitening ads hint at one's ability to take control of how white one's skin can be, these tanning ads explicitly employ the language of choice and control, an apparatus of white supremacy. Aveeno, for example, sells "moisturizer that lets you customize your color." Olay puts it even more strongly by advertising "the color you control." Hence here, the anxiety of getting too dark is eliminated because Caucasian women can control how "bronze" their skin can be. After all, as Sarita Sahay and Niva Piran found after surveying one hundred South-Asian Canadian undergraduate students and one hundred Euro-Canadian undergraduate students at the University of Toronto, even as Euro-Canadian women desire to have skin that is darker than their current skin color, this "darker skin" still falls within the "white-skin-color-category" (Sahay and Piran 1997, 165). This demonstrates that white skin is indeed the desired norm in North America.

Third, in these ads, tanning is represented within a specific temporal (and therefore contained) context. Most of these ads, such as Aveeno ("you choose the shade for the perfect summer radiance for you"), Dove ("gradually builds a beautiful summer glow in just one week"), and Jergens ("a gradual healthy summer glow, just by moisturizing"), use summer as the timeframe for their products. As such, tanning registers within the realm of postmodern playfulness. It invokes temporality, the changing nature of one's skin color, rather than the permanence of desire for darker skin tone. This certainly is not the normative convention of whitening ads that do not highlight any specific time frame in their ads.

Fourth, in these tanning ads, no one is advised to "detox" their white skin color. Whereas in whitening ads we are told that white is "perfect" and that it is a signifier for beauty, in tanning ads, one is advised to simply "enhance" one's skin color. L'Oréal, for example, offers a moisturizer that functions as a "natural skin tone enhancer." This is also the case for Jergens ("natural glow face") and Banana Boat ("natural looking color"). None of these ads insult the white-skinned audience because none of these ads tell them that brown is perfect and their white skin color is toxic.

Last, some of the tanning brands in these ads suggest that tanning is a form of cosmopolitan whiteness insofar as it articulates a sense of "imperialist nostalgia." Renato Rosaldo coined the term "imperialist nostalgia" to mark the colonial's "innocent yearning" for the native's precolonial life imagined as "pure" that had been transformed because of processes of colonialism (Rosaldo 1989). The imperialist nostalgia that haunts these ads can be seen through, for example, the "Hawaiian Tropic" ad, which at a glance resembles a tourism brochure. In this ad an almost fully-naked woman with medium-tanned skin stands seductively displaying her curves. We only see one half of her body, positioned on the right side of the ad, occupying only one third of the page. We see her lips, part of her nose, and one of her eyes, enough to sense that she's smiling coyly. In the background, there is a shadow of a man who is holding a surfboard and is seen walking on the beach. The gender narrative in this ad is too obvious: the man is surfing; the woman is posing for the audience. The colonial narrative, however, lingers subtly in the ad's text: "Hawaiian Tropic sunscreen pampers you with its luxurious tropical moisturizers, exotic botanicals and alluring island scent. . . . With protection up to SPF 70, you can embrace the sun and fully experience the pleasures of the Tropic." Here, tanning practices become a way for white female consumers to inhabit "the exotic other" (Williamson 1986). The Tropic, with a capital T, becomes a colonial site that

exists for the purpose of pampering cosmopolitan white consumers. This "going native," the glorification of the exotic other for the consumption of the white self, or "imperialist nostalgia," frames cosmopolitanism as a trope of "colonial modernity"—a mode of engaging the other in the colonizing context (Van der Veer 2002). Hence cosmopolitan whiteness, I argue, is at once a form of longing for the purity of the past and of belonging to the un-rooted and re-routed world culture simultaneously. Hence, I argue that although tanning ads register differently from whitening ads, they both have the same positive affective effects (that is, cosmopolitan, fun, fearless, and beautiful) toward women with white skin color. In whitening ads the English word "white" and foreign models function to infuse whiteness with a cosmopolitan flair. Skin-tanning ads in the U.S. *Cosmo*, by using the word "tanning" or "bronze" instead of "blackening," urge women to bask in the postmodern desires of playful color transformation while freeing them from the accusation of emulating blackness and hence still privileging (cosmopolitan) whiteness in its ability to travel and consume exoticized others.

In conclusion, in this article I argue that positive affective effects toward women with white skin color are the problematic effects of a transnational women's magazine that circulates within a racially saturated field of visibility. Rather than challenging any racial hierarchies, these skin-whitening (and tanning) ads simply affirm them even if in much more nuanced ways. Moreover, cosmopolitan whiteness illustrates that whiteness works in hegemonic ways. That is, whiteness adapts, mutates, and co-opts new forms of whiteness to maintain its supremacy. As Ahmed points out, "freedom involves proximity to whiteness" (Ahmed 2007, 130). I further argue that the freedom to move transnationally involves proximity to whiteness—and this is the essence of a non-essentialist, "virtual," cosmopolitan whiteness.

NOTES

1. *Cosmopolitan* costs Rp. 35,000 (US$4) and targets upper-middle-class Indonesian women. Class is a significant aspect that begs a more comprehensive analysis, which is beyond the scope of this article.

2. Whitening ads are published throughout the year in the Indonesian *Cosmo*. For this article, I focus on thirty-four whitening ads published in the summer months (June, July, and August) of 2006, 2007, and 2008. This is so because in the larger project from which this article stems, I also provide a comprehensive analysis of a total of nine tanning ads published in the U.S. *Cosmo* (usually published during the summer months).

3. For a thorough racial history of Indonesia from the precolonial to the postcolonial period, see Prasetyaningsih 2007.

4. In 1998, Suharto, who had been Indonesia's president for thirty-two years, voluntarily stepped down from his presidency following large-scale protests and the collapse of the economy. His decision was influenced in part because he lost the U.S. government's support. Since 1998 Indonesia has been undergoing a democratization process, one that includes a more open environment for various forms of expressive media that had been repressed under his regime.

WORKS CITED

Ahmed, Sara. 2000. *Strange Encounters: Embodied Others in Post-Coloniality*. London: Routledge.

———. 2007. "Multiculturalism and the Promise of Happiness." *New Formations* 63: 121–37.

Appadurai, Arjun. 1996. *Modernity at Large: Cultural Dimensions of Globalization*. Minneapolis: University of Minnesota Press.

Bhabha, Homi. 1994. "Of Mimicry and Man: The Ambivalence of Colonial Discourse." October 28: 125–33.

Brennan, Teresa. 2004. *The Transmission of Affect*. Ithaca, NY: Cornell University Press.

Burke, Timothy. 1996. *Lifebuoy Men, Lux Women: Commodification, Consumption, and Cleanliness in Modern Zimbabwe*. Durham, NC: Duke University Press.

Butler, Judith. 1993. "Endangered/Endangering: Schematic Racism and White Paranoia." In *Reading Rodney King: Reading Urban Uprising*, edited by Robert Gooding-Williams. New York: Routledge.

Carr, David. 2002. "Romance, in *Cosmo*'s World, is Translated in Many Ways." *New York Times*. May 26. http://tiny.cc/t12ks (accessed August 16, 2010).

Chang, Jui-Shan. 2004. "Refashioning Womanhood in 1990s Taiwan: An Analysis of the Taiwanese Edition of *Cosmopolitan* Magazine." *Modern China* 30, no. 3: 361–97.

Cheah, Peng. 1998. "Introduction Part II: The Cosmopolitical—Today." In *Cosmopolitics: Thinking and Feeling beyond the Nation*, edited by Peng Cheah and Bruce Robbins. Minneapolis: University of Minnesota Press.

Cosmopolitan (American). 2006–2008. (June, July, August)

Cosmopolitan (Indonesian). 2006–2008. (June, July, August)

Deleuze, Gilles, and Félix Guattari. 1987. *A Thousand Plateaus: Capitalism and Schizophrenia*. Trans. Brian Massumi. Minneapolis: University of Minnesota Press.

Dyer, Richard. 1997. *White*. New York: Routledge.

Ebo, Bosah, ed. 1998. *Cyberghetto or Cybertopia?: Race, Class, and Gender on the Internet*. Westport, CT: Praeger.

———. 2001. *Cyberimperialism?: Global Relations in the New Electronic Frontier*. Westport, CT: Praeger.

Fanon, Frantz. 1952/1967. *Black Skin White Masks*. Trans. Charles Markmann. New York: Grove Press.

Freeman, Carla. 2007. "Neo-liberalism and the Marriage of Reputation and Respectability: Entrepreneurship and the Barbadian Middle Class." In *Love and Globalization: Transformations of Intimacy*, edited by Mark Padilla and Jennifer Hirsch. Nashville, TN: Vanderbilt University Press.

Frith, Katherine, ed. 1997. *Undressing the Ad: Reading Culture in Advertising*. New York: Peter Lang.

Glenn, Evelynn, ed. 2009. *Shades of Difference: Why Skin Color Matters*. Stanford: Stanford University Press.

Gormley, Paul. 2005. *The New-Brutality Film: Race and Affect in Contemporary Hollywood Culture*. Bristol, UK: Intellect.

Grewal, Inderpal. 2005. *Transnational America: Feminisms, Diasporas, Neoliberalisms*. Durham, NC: Duke University Press.

Hall, Ronald. 2005. "The Euro-Americanization of Race: Alien Perspective of African Americans vis-à-vis Trivialization of Skin Color." *Journal of Black Studies* 36, no. 1: 116–29.

Harding, Jennifer, and E. Deidre Pribram, eds. 2009. *Emotions: A Cultural Studies Reader*. London: Routledge.

Hunter, Margaret. 2005. *Race, Gender, and the Politics of Skin Tone*. New York: Routledge.

Jhally, Sut. 2003. "Image-Based Culture: Advertising and Popular Culture." In *Gender, Race, and Class in Media*, edited by Gail Dines and Jean Humez. Thousand Oaks, CA: Sage.

Kartajaya, Hermawan. 2004. *Marketing in Venus*. Jakarta: Gramedia.

Kawashima, Terry. 2002. "Seeing Faces, Making Races: Challenging Visual Tropes of Racial Difference." *Meridians: Feminism, Race, Transnationalism* 3, no. 1: 161–90.

Kolko, Beth, Lisa Nakamura, and Gilbert Rodman, eds. 2000. *Race in Cyberspace*. New York: Routledge.

Laurel, Brenda. 1993. *Computer as Theater*. Reading, MA: Addison-Wesley.

Lindquist, Johan. 2009. *The Anxieties of Mobility: Migration and Tourism in the Indonesian Borderlands*. Honolulu: University of Hawaii Press.

Machin, David, and Joanna Thornborrow. 2003. "Branding and Discourse: The Case of *Cosmopolitan*." *Discourse and Society* 14, no. 4: 453–71.

Massumi, Brian. 2002. *Parables for the Virtual: Movement, Affect, Sensation*. Durham, NC: Duke University Press.

McMachon, Kathryn. 1990. "The *Cosmopolitan* Ideology and the Management of Desire." *Journal of Sex Research* 27, no. 3: 381–96.

Mercer, Kobena. 1987. "Black Hair/Style Politics." *New Formations* 3: 33–55.

Mirzoeff, Nicholas. 1999. *An Introduction to Visual Culture*. London: Routledge.

Nakamura, Lisa. 2002. *Cybertypes: Race, Ethnicity, and Identity on the Internet*. New York: Routledge.

———. 2008. *Digitizing Race: Visual Cultures of the Internet*. Minneapolis: University of Minnesota Press.

Nelson, Michelle, and Hye-Jin Paek. 2005. "Cross-Cultural Differences in Sexual Advertising Content in a Transnational Women's Magazine." *Sex Roles* 53, no. 5/6: 371–83.

Omi, Michael, and Howard Winant. 1994. *Racial Formation in the United States: From the 1960s to the 1990s*. New York: Routledge.

Ong, Aihwa. 1999. *Flexible Citizenship: The Cultural Logics of Transnationality*. Durham, NC: Duke University Press.

Paasonen, Susanna. 2005. *Figures of Fantasy: Internet, Women and Cyberdiscourse*. New York: Peter Lang.

Parameswaran, Radhika, and Kavitha Cardoza. 2009. "Melanin on the Margins: Advertising and the Cultural Politics of Fair/Light/White Beauty in India." *Journalism and Communication Monographs* 11, no. 3: 213–74.

Peiss, Kathy. 1998. *Hope in a Jar: The Making of America's Beauty Culture*. New York: Metropolitan Books.

Pierre, Jemima. 2008. "'I Like Your Colour!' Skin Bleaching and Geographies of Race in Urban Ghana." *Feminist Review* 90, no. 1: 9–29.

Prabasmoro, Aquarini. 2003. *Becoming White: Representasi Ras, Kelas, Femininitas dan Globalitas Dalam Iklan Sabun*. Yogyakarta: Jalasutra.

Prasetyaningsih, L. Ayu Saraswati. 2007. "The Maze of Gaze: The Color of Beauty in Transnational Indonesia." Ph.D. diss., Department of Women's Studies, University of Maryland, College Park.

Robbins, Bruce. 1998. "Comparative Cosmopolitanisms." In *Cosmopolitics: Thinking and Feeling beyond the Nation*, edited by Peng Cheah and Bruce Robbins. Minneapolis: University of Minnesota Press.

Rondilla, Joanne, and Paul Spickard. 2007. *Is Lighter Better?: Skin-Tone Discrimination among Asian Americans*. Lanham, MD: Rowman & Littlefield.

Rosaldo, Renato. 1989. *Culture and Truth: The Remaking of Social Analysis*. Boston: Beacon Press.

Sahay, Sarita, and Niva Piran. 1997. "Skin-Color Preferences and Body Satisfaction among South Asian-Canadian and European-Canadian Female University Students." *Journal of Social Psychology* 137, no. 2: 161–71.

Sarker, Sonita, and Esha Niyogi De, eds. 2002. *Trans-Status Subjects: Gender in the Globalization of South and Southeast Asia*. Durham, NC: Duke University Press.

Shohat, Ella, ed. 1998. *Talking Visions: Multicultural Feminism in a Transnational Age*. Cambridge, MA: MIT Press.

Spooner, Catherine. 2001. "Cosmo-Gothic: The Double and the Single Woman." *Women: A Cultural Review* 12, no. 3: 292–305.

Stoler, Ann. 1995. *Race and the Education of Desire: Foucault's History of Sexuality and the Colonial Order of Things*. Durham, NC: Duke University Press.

———. 2002. *Carnal Knowledge and Imperial Power: Race and the Intimate in Colonial Rule*. Berkeley: University of California Press.

Thiong 'O, Ngugi Wa. 1986. *Decolonizing the Mind: The Politics of Language in African Literature*. London: James Currey Ltd.

Van der Veer, Peter. 2002. "Colonial Cosmopolitanism." In *Conceiving Cosmopolitanism: Theory, Context, and Practice*, edited by Steven Vertovec and Robin Cohen. New York: Oxford University Press.

Vertovec, Steven, and Robin Cohen. 2002. "Introduction: Conceiving Cosmopolitanism." In *Conceiving Cosmopolitanism: Theory, Context, and Practice*, edited by Steven Vertovec and Robin Cohen. New York: Oxford University Press.

Waskul, Dennis. 2002/2004. "The Naked Self: Body and Self in Televideo Cybersex." In *Readings on Sex, Pornography, and the Internet*, edited by Dennis Waskul. New York: Peter Lang.

Wieringa, Saskia. 2008. "'If There is No Feeling': The Dilemma between Silence and Coming Out in a

Working-Class Butch/Femme Community in Jakarta." In *Love and Globalization: Transformations of Intimacy*, edited by Mark Padilla and Jennifer Hirsch. Nashville, TN: Vanderbilt University Press.

Williamson, Judith. 1986. "Woman is an Island: Femininity and Colonization." In *Studies in Entertainment: Critical Approaches to Mass Culture*, edited by Tania Modleski. Bloomington: Indiana University Press.

Winant, Howard. 1994. *Racial Conditions: Politics, Theory, Comparisons*. Minneapolis: University of Minnesota Press.

————. 2001. *The World is a Ghetto: Race and Democracy since World War II*. New York: Basic.

Wissinger, Elizabeth. 2007. "Always on Display: Affective Production in the Modeling Industry." In *The Affective Turn: Theorizing the Social,* edited by Patricia Clough with Jean Halley. Durham, NC: Duke University Press.

Zane, Kathleen. 1998. "Reflections on a Yellow Eye: Asian I(\Eye/)Cons and Cosmetic Surgery." In *Taking Visions: Multicultural Feminism in a Transnational Age*, edited by Ella Shohat. Cambridge, MA: MIT Press.

66. • *Chimamanda Ngozi Adichie*

FROM *AMERICANAH* (2013)

Chimamanda Ngozi Adichie is a novelist who has won many awards including the Commonwealth Writers' Prize, the Hurston/Wright Legacy Award, and Orange Prize. Her novel *Americanah*, excerpted here, won the National Book Critics Circle Award for Fiction and the Chicago Tribune Heartland Prize for Fiction. It critically addresses issues of gender, race, and transnationalism in the United States. She was born in Nigeria and divides her time between the United States and Nigeria.

Ifemelu came to love Baltimore—for its scrappy charm, its streets of faded glory, its farmers' market that appeared on weekends under the bridge, bursting with green vegetables and plump fruit and virtuous souls—although never as much as her first love, Philadelphia, that city that held history in its gentle clasp. But when she arrived *in* Baltimore knowing she was going to live there, and not merely visiting Curt, she thought it forlorn and unlovable. The buildings were joined to one another in faded slumping rows, and on shabby corners, people were hunched in puffy jackets, black and bleak people waiting for buses, the air around them hazed in gloom. Many of the drivers outside the train station were Ethiopian or Punjabi.

Her Ethiopian taxi driver said, "I can't place your accent. Where are you from?"

"Nigeria."

"Nigeria? You don't look African at all."

"Why don't I look African?"

"Because your blouse is too tight."

"It is not too tight."

"I thought you were from Trinidad or one of those places." He was looking in the rearview with disapproval and concern, "You have to be very careful or America will corrupt you." When, years later, she wrote the blog post "On the Divisions Within the Membership of Non-American Blacks in America," she wrote about the taxi driver, but she wrote of it as the experience of someone else, careful not to let on whether she was African or Caribbean, because her readers did not know which she was.

She told Curt about the taxi driver, how his sincerity had infuriated her and how she had gone to the station bathroom to see if her pink long-sleeved blouse *was* too tight. Curt laughed and laughed. It became one of the many stories he liked to tell friends. *She actually went to the bathroom to look at her blouse!* His friends were like him, sunny and wealthy people who existed on the glimmering surface of things. She liked them, and sensed that they liked her. To them, she was interesting, unusual in the way she bluntly spoke her mind. They expected certain things of her, and forgave certain things from her, because she was foreign. Once, sitting with them in a bar, she heard Curt talking to Brad, and Curt said "blowhard." She was struck by the word, by the irredeemable Americanness of it. Blowhard. It was a word that would never occur to her. To understand this was to realize that Curt and his friends would, on some level, never be fully knowable to her.

She got an apartment in Charles Village, a one-bedroom with old wood floors, although she might as well have been living with Curt; most of her clothes were in his walk-in closet lined with mirrors. Now that she saw him every day, no longer just on weekends, she saw new layers of him, how difficult it was for him to be still, simply still without thinking of what next to do, how used he was to stepping out of his trousers and leaving them on the floor for days, until the cleaning woman came. Their lives were full of plans he made—Cozumel for one night, London for a long weekend—and she sometimes took a taxi on Friday evenings after work to meet him at the airport.

"Isn't this great?" he would ask her, and she would say yes, it was great. He was always thinking of what else to *do* and she told him that it was rare for her, because she had grown up not doing, but being. She added quickly, though, that she liked it all, because she did like it and she knew, too, how much he needed to hear that. In bed, he was anxious.

"Do you like that? Do you enjoy me?" he asked often. And she said yes, which was true, but she sensed that he did not always believe her, or that his belief lasted only so long before he would need to hear her affirmation again. There was something in him, lighter than ego but darker than insecurity, that needed constant buffing, polishing, waxing. And

then her hair began to fall out at the temples. She drenched it in rich, creamy conditioners, and sat under steamers until water droplets ran down her neck. Still, her hairline shifted further backwards each day.

"It's the chemicals," Wambui told her. Do you know what's in a relaxer? That stuff can kill you. You need to cut your hair and go natural."

Wambui's hair was now in short locs, which Ifemelu did not like; she thought them sparse and dull, unflattering to Wambui's pretty face.

"I don't want dreads," she said.

"It doesn't have to be dreads. You can wear an Afro, or braids like you used to. There's a lot you can do with natural hair."

"I can't just cut my hair," she said.

"Relaxing your hair is like being in prison. You're caged in. Your hair rules you. You didn't go running with Curt today because you don't want to sweat out this straightness. That picture you sent me, you had your hair covered on the boat. You're always battling to make your hair do what it wasn't meant to do. If you go natural and take good care of your hair, it won't fall off like it's doing now. I can help you cut it right now. No need to think about it too much."

Wambui was so sure, so convincing. Ifemelu found a pair of scissors. Wambui cut her hair, leaving only two inches, the new growth since her last relaxer. Ifemelu looked in the mirror. She was all big eyes and big head. At best, she looked like a boy; at worst, like an insect.

"I look so ugly I'm scared of myself."

You look beautiful. Your bone structure shows so well now. You're just not used to seeing yourself like this. You'll get used to it," Wambui said.

Ifemelu was still staring at her hair. What had she done? She looked unfinished, as though the hair itself, short and stubby, was asking for attention, for something to be done to it, for *more*. After Wambui left, she went to the drugstore, Curt's baseball hat pulled over her head. She bought oils and pomades, applying one and then the other, on wet hair and then on dry hair, willing an unknown miracle to happen. Something, anything, that would make her like her hair. She thought of buying a wig, but wigs brought anxiety, the always-present possibility of flying off your head. She thought of a texturizer to loosen her hair's springy coils, stretch out the kinkiness a little, but a texturizer was really a relaxer, only milder, and she would still have to avoid the rain.

Curt told her, "Stop stressing, babe. It's a really cool and brave look."

"I don't want my hair to be *brave*."

"I mean like stylish, chic." He paused. "You look beautiful."

"I look like a boy."

Curt said nothing. There was, in his expression, a veiled amusement, as though he did not see why she should be so upset but was better off not saying so.

The next day she called in sick, and climbed back into bed.

"You didn't call in sick so we could stay a day longer in Bermuda but you call in sick because of your hair?" Curt asked, propped up by pillows, stifling laughter.

"I can't go out like this." She was burrowing under the covers as though to hide.

"It's not as bad as you think," he said.

"At least you finally accept that it's bad."

Curt laughed. "You know what I mean. Come here."

He hugged her, kissed her, and then slid down and began to massage her feet; she liked the warm pressure, the feel of his fingers. Yet she could not relax. In the bathroom mirror, her hair had startled her, dull and shrunken from sleep, like a mop of wool sitting on her head. She reached for her phone and sent Wambui a text: *I hate my hair. I couldn't go to work today.*

Wambui's reply came minutes later: *Go online. HappilyKinkyNappy.com. It's this natural hair community. You'll find inspiration.*

She showed the text to Curt. "What a silly name for the website."

"I know, but it sounds like a good idea. You should check it out sometime."

"Like now," Ifemelu said, getting up. Curt's laptop was open on the desk. As she went to it, she noticed a change in Curt. A sudden tense quickness. His ashen, panicked move towards the laptop.

"What's wrong?" she asked.

"They mean nothing. The e-mails mean nothing."

She stared at him, forcing her mind to work. He had not expected her to use his computer, because she hardly ever did. He was cheating on her. How odd, that she had never considered that. She picked up the laptop, held it tightly, but he didn't try to reach for it. He just stood and watched. The Yahoo mail page was minimized, next to a page about college basketball. She read some of the e-mails. She looked at attached photographs. The woman's e-mails—her address was SparklingPaola123—were strongly suggestive, while Curt's were just suggestive enough to make sure she continued. *I'm going to cook you dinner in a tight red dress and sky-high heels,* she wrote, *and you just bring yourself and a bottle of wine.* Curt replied: *Red would look great on you.* The woman was about his age, but there was, in the photos she sent, an air of hard desperation, hair dyed a brassy blond, eyes burdened by too much blue makeup, top too low-cut. It surprised Ifemelu, that Curt found her attractive. His white ex-girlfriend had been fresh-faced and preppy.

"I met her in Delaware," Curt said. "Remember the conference thing I wanted you to come to? She started hitting on me right away. She's been after me since. She won't leave me alone. She knows I have a girlfriend."

Ifemelu stared at one of the photos, a profile shot in black-and-white, the woman's head thrown back, her long hair flowing behind her. A woman who liked her hair and thought Curt would too.

"Nothing happened," Curt said. "At all. Just the e-mails. She's really after me. I told her about you, but she just won't stop."

She looked at him, wearing a T-shirt and shorts, so certain in his self-justifications. He was entitled in the way a child was: blindly.

"You wrote her too," she said.

"But that's because she wouldn't stop."

"No, it's because you wanted to."

"Nothing happened."

"That is not the point."

"I'm sorry. I know you're already upset and I hate to make it worse."

"All your girlfriends had long flowing hair," she said, her tone thick with accusation.

"What?"

She was being absurd, but knowing that did not make her any less so. Pictures she had seen of his ex-girlfriends goaded her, the slender Japanese with straight hair dyed red, the olive-skinned Venezuelan with corkscrew hair that fell to her shoulders, the white girl with waves and waves of russet hair. And now this woman, whose looks she did not care for, but who had long straight hair. She shut the laptop. She felt small and ugly Curt was talking. "I'll ask her never to contact me. This will never happen again, babe, I promise," he said, and she thought he sounded as though it was somehow the woman's responsibility rather than his.

She turned away, pulled Curt's baseball hat over her head, threw things in a bag, and left.

* * *

Curt came by later, holding so many flowers she hardly saw his face when she opened the door. She would forgive him, she knew, because she believed him. Sparkling Paola was one more small adventure of his. He would not have gone further with her, but he would have kept encouraging her attention, until he was bored. Sparkling Paola was like the silver stars that his teachers pasted on the pages of his elementary school homework, sources of a shallow, fleeting pleasure.

She did not want to go out, but she did not want to be with him in the intimacy of her apartment; she still felt too raw. So she covered her hair in a headwrap and they took a walk, Curt solicitous and full of promises, walking side by side but not touching, all the way to the corner of Charles and University Parkway, and then back to her apartment.

* * *

For three days, she called in sick. Finally, she went to work, her hair a very short, overly combed and overly oiled Afro. "You look different," her co-workers said, all of them a little tentative.

"Does it mean anything? Like, something political?" Amy asked, Amy who had a poster of Che Guevara on her cubicle wall.

"No," Ifemelu said.

At the cafeteria, Miss Margaret, the bosomy African-American woman who presided over the counter—and, apart from two security guards, the only other black person in the company—asked, "Why did you cut your hair, hon? Are you a lesbian?"

"No, Miss Margaret, at least not yet."

Some years later, on the day Ifemelu resigned, she went into the cafeteria for a last lunch. "You leaving?" Miss Margaret asked, downcast. "Sorry, hon. They need to treat folk better around here. You think your hair was part of the problem?"

* * *

HappilyKinkyNappy.com had a bright yellow background, message boards full of posts, thumbnail photos of black women blinking at the top. They had long trailing dreadlocks, small Afros, big Afros, twists, braids, massive raucous curls and coils. They called relaxers "creamy crack." They were done with pretending that their hair was what it was not, done with running from the rain and flinching from sweat. They complimented each other's photos and ended comments with "hugs." They complained about black magazines never having natural-haired women in their pages about drugstore products so poisoned by mineral oil that they could not moisturize natural hair. They traded recipes. They sculpted for themselves a virtual world where their coily, kinky, nappy woolly hair was normal. And Ifemelu fell into this world with a tumbling gratitude. Women with hair as short as hers had a name for it: TWA, Teeny Weeny Afro. She learned, from women who posted long instructions, to avoid shampoos with silicones, to use a leave-in conditioner on wet hair, to sleep in a satin scarf. She ordered products from women who made them in their kitchens and shipped them with clear instructions: BEST TO REFRIGERATE IMMEDIATELY, DOES NOT CONTAIN PRESERVATIVES. Curt would open the fridge, hold up a container labeled "hair butter," and ask, "Okay to spread this on my toast?" Curt thrummed with fascination about it all. He read posts on HappilyKinkyNappy.com. "I think it's great!" he said. "It's like this *movement* of black women."

One day, at the farmers' market, as she stood hand in hand with Curt in front of a tray of apples, a black man walked past and muttered, "You ever wonder why he likes you looking all jungle like that?" She stopped, unsure for a moment whether she had imagined those words, and then she looked back at the man. He walked with too much rhythm in his step, which suggested to her a certain fickleness of character. A man not worth paying any attention to. Yet his words bothered her, pried open the door for new doubts.

"Did you hear what that guy said?" she asked Curt.

"No, what did he say?"

She shook her head. "Nothing."

She felt dispirited and, while Curt watched a game that evening, she drove to the beauty supply store and ran her fingers through small bundles of silky straight weaves. Then she remembered a post by Jamilah1977—*I love the sistas who love their straight weaves, but I'm never putting horse hair on my head again*—and she left the store, eager to get back and log on and post on the boards about it. She wrote: *Jamilah's words made me remember that there is nothing more beautiful than what God gave me.* Others wrote responses, posting thumbs-up signs, telling her how much they liked the photo she had put up. She had never talked about God so much. Posting on the website was like giving testimony in church; the echoing roar of approval revived her.

On an unremarkable day in early spring—the day was not bronzed with special light, nothing of any significance happened, and it was perhaps merely that time, as it often does, had transfigured her doubts—she looked in the mirror, sank her fingers into her hair, dense and spongy and glorious, and could not imagine it any other way. That simply, she fell in love with her hair.

Why Dark-Skinned Black Women—Both American and Non-American—Love Barack Obama

Many American blacks proudly say they have some "Indian." Which means Thank God We Are Not Full-Blooded Negroes. Which means they are not too dark. (To clarify, when white people say dark they mean Greek or Italian but when black people say dark they mean Grace Jones.) American black men like their black women to have some exotic quota, like half-Chinese or a splash of Cherokee. They like their women light. But beware what American blacks consider "light." Some of these "light" people, in countries of Non-American Blacks, would simply be called white. (Oh, and dark American black men resent light men, for having it too easy with the ladies.)

Now, my fellow Non-American Blacks, don't get smug. Because this bullshit also exists in our Caribbean and African countries. Not as bad as with American blacks, you say? Maybe. But there nonetheless. By the way, what is it with Ethiopians thinking they are not that black? And Small Islanders eager to say their ancestry is "mixed"? But we must not digress. So light skin is valued in the community of American blacks. But everyone pretends this is no longer so. They say the days of the paper-bag test (look this up) are gone and let's move forward. But today most of the American blacks who are successful as entertainers and as public figures are light. Especially women. Many successful American black men have white wives. Those who deign to have black wives have light (otherwise known as high yellow) wives. And this is the reason dark women love Barack Obama. He broke the mold! He married one of their own. He knows what the world doesn't seem to know: that dark black women totally rock. They want Obama to win because maybe finally somebody will cast a beautiful chocolate babe in a big-budget rom-com that opens in theaters all over the country, not just three artsy theaters in New York City. You see, in American pop culture, beautiful dark women are invisible. (The other group just as invisible is Asian men. But at least they get to be super smart.) In movies, dark black women get to be the fat nice mammy or the strong, sassy, sometimes scary sidekick standing by supportively. They get to dish out wisdom and attitude while the white woman finds love. But they never get to be the hot woman, beautiful and desired and all. So dark black women hope Obama will change that. Oh, and dark black women are also for cleaning up Washington and getting out of Iraq and whatnot.

67. • *Kimberly Dark*

BIG YOGA STUDENT (2012)

Kimberly Dark is a writer, speaker, and performer. She has won five awards for her performance scripts and educational programs. Her writings often focus on gendered and racialized body, body size, beauty ideals, and ability. She is a lecturer at California State University, San Marcos. The following essay is her creative writing that speaks to her experience of being a yoga practitioner whose body is perceived to be "fat," published previously in an anthology, *Hot and Heavy: Fierce Fat Girls on Life, Love and Fashion*.

She was checking me out. No, really, you can feel that sort of thing, right? Her gaze lingered as I walked into the yoga studio—just that split second longer than a usual acknowledgement. She caught my eye as I rolled out my mat. She looked me up and down—quickly, not in a creepy way—and smiled broadly. Then, as I was picking up a blanket and a block, I could feel her eyes follow me.

So, was there some kind of come-on coming on? A budding yoga studio romance to ensue? I can tell you from experience that this glance likely had a different origin than erotic *tapas*.

We're fat women in a fitness setting.

I know the look—have experienced it for more than twenty years now at yoga studios, gyms, and aerobics classes. I'm accustomed to being looked at because I'm surprising—shocking even. I'm a large woman, and dare I say it—relatively fit, despite being more than one hundred pounds overweight by insurance chart standards. The woman who stared and smiled? She's fit and fat, too. And if she hadn't been so openly interested in looking at my body, I'd have been sneaking peeks at hers, catching glimpses of how her thighs appear in those stretch pants and how her belly or arm fat protrudes from her spandex tank top. The looking is better than the not looking. Sometimes a fat woman will avert her gaze from my flagrant display of largesse. But we were both at peace, happy to see each other. I can't guess what my admirer was thinking, but based on her smile, I will consider her kindred. Perhaps we were having the same thought: "How wonderful! She's living her life and using her body as she chooses, despite what others might think."

Part of why we find solidarity with one another is because we're scarce—at least at swank studios like that one. When I first started practicing yoga, twenty years ago, there was a range of bodies moving— sometimes struggling—through the postures. Yoga moves seemed a little eccentric and only the bold among us took them into daily life. Back then, I'd catch stares when practicing at the airport in hopes of finding some back-ease mid-flight. You know, those kind of "don't look now, but there's a fat woman doing freaky stuff just over your left shoulder" stares. Sometimes I'm so out-of-the-norm it's hard to tell which aspect of me is being gawked at. However, I receive some glances so frequently, I could make a study.

Nowadays it's easy to recognize the yoga-faithful in public places: the eagle arms in the park at noon on a Tuesday, a deliberate uttanasana at Gate 23, the Virabadrasana I on the beach. Yoga has expanded its reach, but in the process, it's left some of us behind. The great adjustments, clear instructions, and careful attention to detail of the better yoga studios come with a daunting environment of fitness fanaticism. It's no mystery why these studios market to the fitness faithful. They pay. And the rest of us just don't fit in.

Yes, yes, we're practicing *yoga,* so we should all just go within and release our self-judgments. Whoa now. We're working on that, but some have a steeper climb. Or do we? Perhaps it's just easier to look comfortable when one's ego attachment is to the perfect titibasana and the $100 recycled yak fur yoga mat. It's inevitable in a consumer culture that the people who can afford to pay a yoga teacher what she's worth will be interested in status. And "hot body" in America definitely equates status. Sometimes the noble fat person can sneak through—the beginner who's assumed to be fighting the good fight against her or his own flab. That person can be jovially accommodated and feel a little bit of love. But what of the average plodder who does a regular practice and never "looks" fit? Well, sometimes it's just not comfortable, so the group support and individual instruction offered by beautiful studios are forfeit.

And that's part of why I became a yoga teacher. Let me not sound too noble here—I love teaching; I've taught a lot of things in a variety of ways for years. And teaching deepens my practice. In addition to these common motivations, I also have a desire to model difference—to encourage others to live fuller lives and to love themselves with greater ease. And sometimes this is personally challenging in ways that it isn't for someone who looks the part, though surely personal doubts about credibility can assail anyone. I've had students at more fitness-oriented establishments see me, look aghast, and walk right out of the class. I've also subbed for classes where students see me and ask if it's going to be a "gentle" class today. To which I jovially respond, "Oh no! We're really gonna kick some ass!"

Ten years ago, I would make the effort to prove my fitness worthiness, but nowadays, I just make my own offering, flawed and brilliant as it can be. (And for pity's sake, if you can't focus on your own breath and asana through a 90-minute class that isn't what you thought you wanted, keep practicing baby. Just keep practicing.)

We need more fat yoga teachers and old yoga teachers and disabled yoga teachers and anyone with a different body than you think you want. That's what this mess is about, right? Most students want to think of the teacher's body as a goal, an attainable one because she got to look like that by doing this yoga thing. Well, it's not that simple, despite our desire to just pay, participate, and make it so. We want to hop on the yoga conveyor belt and plop off the end looking rested, flexing hot buns and deserving a martini (or a piece of chocolate cake—choose your poison). The bad news—and the good news— is that living a good life is more about acceptance than it is about attainment. Sure, change is possible, but it's not always the change you were taught to believe you should want.

So, are you thinking about going to a yoga class, but afraid you won't fit in? Chances are you don't. And go anyway. You and everyone else in the room will be better for it. And if you have a body that gets stares—and not always in a good way—and you want to teach, I encourage you. It really will deepen your experience to be the one demonstrating the beauty of a regular practice. Just remember, you may as well get up in front of the class to teach, they're looking at you anyway.

68. • *Christina Lux*

ANTICIPATION (NEW)

Christina Lux is a poet and literary scholar based at the University of California, Merced, where she is associate director of the Center for the Humanities. Her poetry has appeared on National Public Radio as well as in journals such as *Feminist Formations*, *Women's Studies Quarterly*, and *North Dakota Quarterly*. Her scholarship has appeared in *The Journal of Transnational American Studies* and the *International Journal of Francophone Studies*. The following poem explores sexuality and attachment in the context of religion.

bittersweet communion, on se rencontre
across this shadow-bitten table
carl dreyer gaze up: faux antique hook
crucifix accroché, loose vent's gaze

we, propulsed!
mary, gaze down:
pillows tossed,
brass base.

X backed, lines crossed
legs, legs, legs . . .
toes bent like ba's.

TRANSLATIONS:

on se rencontre = we meet
accroché = hooked/hung
ba = father-figure/compound head

SECTION FIVE

Science, Technology, and the Digital World

TABLE OF CONTENTS

Social egg freezing? Hormone injections? #Revolutions? What do inventions in technology, science, and the digital world such as these tell us about the ways in which feminist interventions reconfigure these fields and how these innovations affect our lives? Who gets to create what, for whose benefit, and at whose expense? This introductory essay and the readings that follow help us consider these questions and explore the many faces and facets of science, technology, and the digital world, and their relationships to women, gender, and sexuality issues.

SOCIAL CONSTRUCTION OF SCIENCE

While we often think of science, especially the "hard" sciences, as representing *the* absolute truth, a closer look at how scientists arrive at their findings reveals that dominant ideologies of race, gender, and sexuality shape the kinds of questions they ask, the methods they employ, and the conclusions they draw. Because science creates reality through narratives based on taxonomies and categories (ways of thinking that can be and have been used to justify discrimination), it is problematic to simply accept that whatever science tells us is "true." We need to always be critical of research findings, asking consistently: Who are the researchers? Where are they institutionally located, and who funds their research? What are their methods, and who benefits from these kinds of research?

Many ideas that we now find absurd were once considered "the truth" and circulated in scientific communities as well as the public. For example, in 1760 the Swiss physician Simon Tissot published *Onanism*, a treatise that warned people of the dangerous side effects of masturbation: pain, pimples, memory loss, and even organ failure. To address this issue, a professional society of physicians in Paris published a series of papers in 1864 suggesting chastity belts, cauterizations, infibulations, and amputation of the clitoris as possible methods to treat and deter people from masturbation (Kuefler 268–73).

Interestingly, around the same time, in late-nineteenth-century Austria, Sigmund Freud was diagnosing women with "hysteria" and enlisting a procedure akin to female masturbation to cure his patients. It was indeed these physicians who developed the electric technology of "anti-hysteria" devices, now known as "vibrators." (This is an example of how science informs technological invention.) Although the myth of masturbation as unhealthy finally came to an end around the mid-1950s when the American sexologist Alfred Kinsey published reports

Electric hand vibrator, circa 1909. In the late nineteenth-century, physicians began to create electric technology of "anti-hysteria" devices, which are now known as "vibrators." The woman shown in this picture is applying the device to her face. Indeed, around that time, the vibrator was advertised to beautify the skin, as well as to relieve pain. Today's vibrators come in different sizes, shapes, colors, and materials and are widely advertised to enhance sexual pleasure.

documenting that two-thirds of women and almost all men in the United States masturbated, all of these examples suggest that science, rather than representing the absolute truth, is socially constructed.

"Science as socially constructed" means that scientific knowledge cannot be regarded as merely an uncontested "fact." The social norms and values that the researchers hold will undoubtedly influence their research. During the 1980s and 1990s, feminist thinkers vigorously criticized the notion of science as "objective" and "value-free." Philosopher Sandra Harding was among the key feminist figures in this struggle. Her article, "Feminism Confronts the Sciences: Reform and Transformation," the first essay in this section, launches us into a conversation about women's positionality in science, how gender ideology infuses the sciences, and the transformations that happen when feminism confronts science. Harding and other feminist "**standpoint**" theorists call our attention to the importance of questioning science as value-free because the interests and values of the researcher will inevitably shape the research process (Harding and Norberg).

Standpoint theory: Theories that acknowledge how people's location of and relationship to power, or standpoint, shape one's worldview.

In her article, "The Egg and the Sperm: How Science Has Constructed a Romance Based on Stereotypical Male–Female Roles," also included in this section, anthropologist Emily Martin examines scientific textbooks used in undergraduate pre-med and medical school classes around the 1980s in the United States and finds that the narratives of the egg and the sperm in these textbooks follow existing gender ideologies: the female egg is considered passive and their reproductive process as negative, whereas male sperm is viewed as active, and the sperm production celebrated. She highlights research in the late 1980s and early 1990s that paints a more nuanced picture of the egg as being active and the reproductive process more complex.

It was also around this time, in 1986, that the diagnosis of "ego-dystonic homosexuality" was finally removed from the revised third edition of *Diagnostic and Statistical Manual of Mental Disorders* (DSM), published by the American Psychiatric Association. This came after a long fight, particularly in the 1970s when gay rights activists spoke against labeling homosexuality as a mental disorder (Drescher 427). In 1973 (ratified in 1974), homosexuality as a category was first removed from the DSM. However, this category was then replaced with the broader term "sexual orientation disturbance" (SOD). In 1980 a new diagnosis called "ego-dystonic homosexuality" replaced SOD in DSM-III. This process illustrates the back-and-forth struggle within the scientific community to remove homosexuality as a mental disorder.

Merging the fields of sexuality, gender, and race, Liam Lair's "Sexology, Eugenics, and Hirschfeld's Transvestites" in this section shows how the racist movement eugenics influenced the ways in which American sexologists in the early twentieth

Public domain

Transvestites at a congress in Berlin, 1921. These "transvestites" were standing at the First International Conference for Sexual Reform on a Scientific Basis in Berlin, in 1921. This conference was organized by Magnus Hirschfeld, the scholar known for coining the term "transvestite" and who was also the head of *Institut für Sexualwissenschaft* (Institute for Sexual Science).

century constructed the diagnoses of transvestite and transsexual as a separate category of pathology, a "degenerate," occupying a different category from homosexuality. Lair argues that "the present-day search for genetic or hereditary causes for transsexualism are rooted in this history of eugenics" (p. 473). His essay provides us with yet more evidence of how knowledge about transgender and cisgender bodies produced within the field of sexology as a branch of science is influenced by the dominant ideologies of eugenics, gender, race, sexuality, and the abled body—it thus also makes visible how the construction of knowledge in science (and technology) has been mostly "ableist" (Galis 825).

SITUATED KNOWLEDGES AND FEMINIST OBJECTIVITY

This evidence showing how science has been socially constructed should not deter us from conducting any scientific research or, worse, cause us to argue that all knowledge is falsely fabricated. An alternative and a feminist mode of addressing this issue, as Donna Haraway proposes, is to embody feminist objectivity in producing a "**situated knowledge**" and to avoid occupying the omniscient position of an all-knowing god. Instead, we should always be mindful of our situatedness and be accountable for what we know from that standpoint. This is why it is important to have women with various racial, sexuality, and class backgrounds participate actively as both researchers and research subjects. Including a diverse range of women who bring in their different lived experience and biological makeup in clinical trials shapes the research findings.

Situated knowledge: Knowledge is always produced from a specific disciplinary, ideological, and social location.

Unfortunately, based on recent statistics, the percentage of women in different branches of science is still relatively low, although some changes have been occurring (Table 5.1). In the workforce, women's participation in the sciences is also low (Table 5.2). Thus although women have made significant changes in the social sciences and medical sciences, the overall number of women participating in the sciences is still low. Inclusion of women in science therefore remains urgent and crucial, as it will change the face of science, from influencing the work culture in the field to producing different kinds of situated knowledges.

Table 5.1: Women Pursuing Undergraduate Degrees in the Sciences

Field	Percentage of Women Receiving Bachelor's Degrees	Percentage of "Minority" Women Receiving Bachelor's Degrees
Biological sciences	59.3	9.7
Computer sciences	18.2	4.8
Engineering	19.2	3.1
Mathematics and statistics	43.1	5.4
Social sciences	54.7	14.2

Source: National Science Foundation, *Women, Minorities, and Persons with Disabilities in Science and Engineering* 2012 data (published in 2013).

Table 5.2: Women in the Science Workforce

Occupation	Percentage of Women
Biological and medical sciences	48
Chemical engineers	17.7
Civil engineers	13.7
Electrical and electronics engineers	8.8
Environmental scientists and geoscientists	25.7
Industrial engineers	18.8
Mechanical engineers	4.5
Social scientists	58

Sources: US Department of Labor, Bureau of Labor Statistics, *Women in the Labor Force: A Databook* (2013) and National Science Foundation, *Science & Engineering Indicators* (2014).

TECHNOFEMINIST APPROACHES AND TECHNOLOGY AS GENDERED PRACTICES

What do you think of when you hear the word "technology"? Perhaps you might think of a computer, heavy machinery, or a sophisticated digital gadget. Although all of these certainly count as technology, there are other inventions that we do not often consider as such, for example, vitamins, shoes, and even books. Technology, according to Eve Shapiro, is "the wide variety of objects, knowledge, activities, and processes humans have developed to alter the material (and conceptual) world" (2). This definition is quite broad and alludes to how science, as a branch of knowledge, and technology may overlap with each other. In this section, when we use the word "science" we emphasize the *process* of knowledge production; the word "technology" is used to highlight the *tools* of production and reproduction.

Science, and the capitalistic market, provides a structure and a realm of possibilities for innovators to imagine new technologies that *can* and *need* to be invented. This means that if science is socially constructed and influenced by the ideologies, interests, and values held by researchers, the technology developed out of this scientific paradigm will inevitably reflect, or in other cases challenge, these dominant values.

As in the sciences, in technology feminists have also made critical interventions that affect our lives in significant ways. Feminist technology and science studies have expanded to move beyond seeing technology as either furthering patriarchal ideologies that are oppressive to women and aim to control women's bodies, such as in the case of reproductive technologies (Faulkner 80), or improving women's lives, such as better preventative healthcare technology for women. They have redefined what counts as technology, how to best engage with and influence the field, and how to use technology as a site for activism. For example, Clare Jen's essay in this section, "Feminist Hactivisms: Countering Technophilia and Fictional Promises," exposes how women still have limited

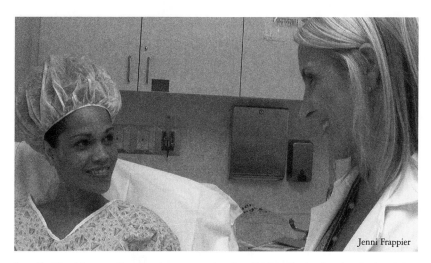

Jenni Frappier

Jennifer Frappier, egg-freezing documentarian. Jennifer Frappier is a Los-Angeles based documentary filmmaker whose 2016 film, *Chill*, critically examines the life-work balance for women and the demand to have it all, including family. In her film, Frappier documents her egg-freezing journey as a 39-year-old single woman, depicting a nuanced view of "the modern-day journey to motherhood." For more information about Frappier and her documentary, see her website: http://www.chillthedocumentary.com/

access to science, technology, and healthcare. She uses Apple Inc.'s "social egg freezing" as an example to reveal how neoliberal and technophilic approaches, which focus on the individual's responsibilities, are used to address institutional problems. She then provides alternative that she calls *feminist hactivism* as a way of intervening into existing "innovations that make lofty promises and misdirect focus from women's lived experiences in the present" (p. 478).

Women also intervene, as Joni Seager in her article, "Rachel Carson Died of Breast Cancer: The Coming of Age of Feminist Environmentalism" (included in this section) shows, in working to end the "destruction" of the earth. More specifically, she charts the significance of feminist environmentalism in various domains, including human and animal relationships, and, most important, on transforming how we view the relationship between health issues and social justice environmentalism. A prominent environmentalist who also connected health issues with environmentalism (and other matters as well) is Wangari Maathai. She was the first African woman to win a Nobel Peace Prize in 2004, in recognition of her taking "a holistic approach to sustainable development that embraces democracy, human rights and women's rights in particular" (Mjøs). Maathai founded the Green Belt Movement in 1977, employing women (about 900,000 of them) to plant trees to address the erosion issues in Kenya and across Africa. She passed away in 2011, also because of cancer.

Similarly, Judy Wajcman considers "technofeminist approaches" crucial in seeing how technology influences the materiality of women's lives in different ways. She argues that advantages for some women happen by exploiting other

© epa european pressphoto agency b.v. / Alamy Stock Photo

Wangari Maathai, Nobel Prize–winning environmental feminist. Wangari Maathai was the first woman in East and Central Africa to have received a doctoral degree in 1971, and was also the first African woman who won a Nobel Peace Prize in 2004 for taking "a holistic approach to sustainable development that embraces democracy, human rights and women's rights in particular." She founded the Green Belt Movement in 1977 to address the erosion issues in Kenya and across Africa. She was also named as a United Nations Messenger of Peace in 2009.

© Pictorial Press Ltd / Alamy Stock Photo

Rachel Carson, twentieth-century (1907-1964) scientist and ecologist. Rachel Carson was the author of *Silent Spring*, published in 1962, that was ahead of its time in warning us of the dangers of the use of chemical pesticides to our wellbeing. She thus challenged the direction that modern science was going to and was known as one of the most profound environmental activists of our time. She also wrote three other books on the issues of nature, the sea, and sea life.

TRANSNATIONAL CONNECTIONS

A Case Study: A twenty-one-year-old Thai woman became a surrogate mother for an Australian couple. However, when the twins were born, one of them (a boy), had Down syndrome and a congenital heart condition. The Australian couple took the baby girl but rejected the baby boy. The surrogate mother was supposed to receive 300,000 Thai baht ($9,300) for being a surrogate. She did not, however, get the full amount from the surrogate agency because of the baby's condition. An online campaign in 2014 succeeded in raising $200,000 for the surrogate, who ended up having to raise the baby boy herself.

QUESTIONS

1. How does reproductive technology shape the lives of both the surrogate mother in Thailand and the Australian couple?
2. How does disability matter in this case?
3. How do class, race, gender, and sexuality provide a structure for understanding this transnational dis/connection?
4. Who benefits from this transnational connection?
5. How can we use Wacjman's technofeminist approach to analyze this case?
6. How does technology perpetuate global inequality?

women (often of color or in other countries). She further reminds us to be critical of why certain technologies receive more funding and attention than others and how these technologies perpetuate global inequalities. In this sense, technology thus becomes "the critical surface for the writing and speaking of power and knowledge" (Masters 115).

Technological inventions also matter because they have the potential to challenge the fixity of and the fixation with existing gender, sexuality, able-bodied, and racial order. For example, Wendy Seymour in her article, "Putting Myself in the Picture: Researching Disability and Technology" (included in this section) shares how computer technology has helped her work with her disability. In the case of transgender bodies, hormone injections and surgery have made possible the transition from one gender to another (Alaimo). Other technologies such as birth control pills, available for women since the 1960s, have changed how heterosexual women experience and express their sexuality. In vitro fertilization has allowed people with the financial resources as well as reliable access to premium healthcare to access technology-assisted pregnancies. Dorothy Roberts in her book *Killing the Black Bodies: Race, Reproduction, and the Meaning of Liberty* illustrates the catastrophic ways in which technology has been used to violate black women's reproductive choices and freedom. These cases show how race, class, sexuality, ability, and gender are "constituted" in the "practices" of technoscience (Gill 100).

Gendered practices of technology can also be seen in other forms of everyday technology. The telephone as a form of technology, for instance, only became a profitable commodity after the companies changed strategy to specifically target women who used the telephone for social purposes, charging them for minutes used rather than for each connection they made. In the late nineteenth and early twentieth centuries, the telephone business failed to thrive because it

INTERSECTIONAL ANALYSIS

A Case Study: On Monday, September 29, 2014, Jennifer Cramblett and her partner filed a lawsuit against a fertility clinic in the Chicago area for mistakenly sending them sperm from a black donor. They claimed that they wanted to hold the clinic accountable for their error so that other people would not have to go through the suffering that they had to endure as a white couple raising a mixed-race child in a 97 percent white neighborhood in Uniontown, Ohio. This hardship includes, they attested, having to travel to an African American community to get a haircut for their daughter and feeling out of place while there. Their therapists advised them to move to a more racially diverse community.

The media draws specific attention to Jennifer's sexuality and quotes her saying that as a lesbian she knows what it feels like to be discriminated against and would not want her mixed-race daughter to experience what she had experienced. They sought justice by asking for $50,000 in damages.

QUESTIONS

1. What does it mean to think about "lesbian" as a category of identity that is *not* simply about sexuality but as it intersects with race, class, and parental status?
2. Look online for additional coverage of this case: How do the race, gender, class, and sexual identities of the couple influence the ways in which this story was reported by different news agencies? Why does the news coverage represent Jennifer Cramblett in such a way?
3. In what ways do science and technology affect women's lives (with "woman" as an intersectional category)?
4. In what ways do women engage with science and technology?

was primarily marketed to men for business purposes (Lubar 22). Similarly, it wasn't until Isaac Singer and his Singer sewing machine specifically adapted for home use came on the scene that the sewing machine took off in the United States (Lubar 22). As Ruth Schwartz Cowan shows in her book *More Work for Mother*, it was indeed the housewives of America that shaped the kinds of technologies invented and marketed in the United States.

Technology as gendered practices can also be seen from the gendered division of labor in this field. Skills associated with high technology are often delegated to men. Men's faces have, quite literally, become the face of innovative technology (think here of the late Steve Jobs of Apple or Mark Zuckerberg of Facebook). Many big tech companies are located in Silicon Valley, a place overpopulated by male tech workers (Hayer 1361). This, in turn, shapes its masculine work culture and the products and mobile apps they produce (Hayer 1361; Newton 73).

This is not to say, however, that women are absent in this field. Some women do work in big tech companies: 31 percent of Facebook employees are women (57 percent of their total employees are white); 30 percent of Twitter (29 percent are Asian); 30 percent of Apple (11 percent are Latino/as); and 30 percent of Google (2 percent are black) (McCandless). Women have also created mobile apps to help prevent violence against women, such as "Circle of 6," which won the 2011 White House/HHS Apps Against Abuse Technology

Courtesy of Tech 4 Good, 2015.

Circle of 6, app against sexual violence. Circle of 6 is an award-winning smartphone app—winner of 2011 White House Apps Against Abuse technology challenge. The app works by allowing the person with the app to ask for help by sending a prewritten message to one of the six friends in their "circle" just by clicking the phone twice. It thus aims to prevent rape and sexual violence.

Challenge and the 2012 Institute of Medicine/Avon Foundation for Women End Violence @Home Challenge. Technology, as Jen argues, can indeed be a critical site of activism.

CYBORGS

One of the most important metaphors in feminist technoscience studies is the figure of the "cyborg." In "A Cyborg Manifesto," an influential feminist text in the field first published in 1985, Haraway defines a cyborg as "a cybernetic organism, a hybrid of machine and organism, a creature of social reality as well as a creature of fiction" (149). The concept was first used in the aeronautics field in 1960 to refer to technologies that could improve and repair human bodies and their functions in outer space, although later it came to include everyday lives (Graham 423). Haraway positions "cyborg" as a figure that embraces the interconnections and relationships among human/animal/machines.

Conversations about cyborgs often lead to the binary thinking of technology versus "nature" that Haraway ironically attempted to move us away from. Women (more so than men) whose bodies have been touched by technology, specifically for cosmetic surgery, for instance, are perceived by society to have less integrity than those who embrace their natural bodies. However, if we are to pause and ask, whose body is *really* natural, we will find that everyone's body, with no exception, has benefitted from technologies that protect and prolong our lives: vaccines, shoes, medicines, food, eyeglasses, and cars, among other things. As Eve Shapiro eloquently argues, "technologies shape how we know, understand, and shape the body, and the body is always a product of historically and culturally specific transformative practices" (143).

Obviously, taking a painkiller is not the same as getting a breast augmentation or a prosthetic leg. The degree to which technology alters our bodies differs based on the form and intensity of that technology, the discourses surrounding the practice, and thence its consequences and meanings. In 2013 in the United States, women comprised 91 percent of cosmetic surgery patients (Hoffman 498). These surgeries and other beauty practices, from eyelid surgeries to applying whitening products, tend to affirm existing notions of racialized white femininity, although not necessarily of "Caucasian" whiteness, as Saraswati suggests in Section IV. These body alterations that conform to current societal beauty standards may create, to an extent, what Brenda Brasher calls the "homogenization of the human by the technological" (815).

CYBERSPACES

Perhaps we have all indeed turned into cyborgs. In the absence of a smartphone or, for the health-conscious person, a Fitbit wristband literally attached to the body, we can feel as if we're missing a limb. As Sue Thomas proclaims, "the Internet is my body. It's an extra set of senses, an additional brain, a second pair of eyes" (18). This "extended embodied awareness," or the ways in which the self is now a "networked" self, is what constitutes "posthuman" bodies (Nayar 8). Not simply an extension of our bodies providing us with a novel way to experience our bodies, cyberspace is also a space of dwelling. For some, it is literally the first place they visit, and stay, as soon as they open their eyes in the morning.

But what space is cyberspace? Although people often equate cyberspace with the Internet, they are not exactly the same. Susanna Paasonen considers cyberspace a narrative about, or a metaphor for, if you will, the Internet. For David Bell, cyberspace can be defined in terms of hardware: "as a global network of computers, linked through communications infrastructures, that facilitate forms of interaction between remote actors," or, symbolically, as an "imagined space between computers in which people might build new selves and new worlds" (7). Dennis Waskul and Mark Douglass define cyberspace as "a hyperreal technology of social saturation that dislocates space, time, and personal characteristics as variables of human interaction" (381). Thus, according to these scholars, cyberspace is a way to narrate stories about this imagined space of hyperreality, interactivity, "convergence" (how different forms of media, e.g., radio, books, TV, all come together in this space), and nonlinearity (we don't read websites from beginning to end; we only click on what we would like to see), where time and space are structured and experienced differently than in the offline world.

Seen in its early incarnation as "overly utopian" for having the potential to eliminate limitations set by and in the physical world, cyberspace is now

Engaged Learning

Circle of 6 is a smartphone app that aims to help prevent rape and sexual assaults on campus. It works by allowing the person with the app to ask for help by sending a prewritten message to one of the six friends in their "circle" just by clicking their phone twice. This app won the White House "Apps Against Abuse" technology challenge in 2011.

If you are comfortable with downloading this app, please feel free to do so. If not, simply learn more about this app or other similar "against abuse" apps from their websites. Explore how this app works and answer the following questions.

(Source: http://www.npr.org/2014/08/13/339888170/smartphone-apps-help-to-battle-campus-sexual-assaults)

QUESTIONS:

1. What technologies are available on your campus to help prevent rape and sexual assaults? Are these innovations efficient? Why or why not?

2. Why aren't more efficient technologies that could address issues of rape and sexual assaults on campus invented? How does this relate to ideas about gender and sexuality?

3. Although Circle of 6 is certainly a great app, it still puts rape and sexual assault prevention in the hands, quite literally, of women, asking *them* to protect themselves. How can we use innovations in science and technology to expand the responsibility of rape prevention to include everyone, not just women, and at the same time do not become another means of surveillance?

represented by various scholars as a more problematic space that allows for both change and perpetuation of the power structure. For example, Kim Williams's essay, "Women@Web: Cyber Sexual Violence in Canada," included in this section, provides an overview of how violence against women that happens in the physical world is now carried out in online spaces. Technology has at times indeed been used against women. Feminist surveillance studies scholars propose the term "white supremacist capitalist heteropatriachal surveillance" to describe "the use of surveillance practices and technologies to normalize and maintain whiteness, able-bodiedness, capitalism, and heterosexuality, practices integral to the foundation of modern state" (Dubrosfky and Magnet 7). Moreover, although it may seem that in the virtual world we have the freedom to click whatever we want, the organization of information, links, and advertisements, for instance, reveals the working of capitalism that may shape our choices (Gur-Ze'ev 447).

Capitalism and globalization played a major role in the development of the Internet. First, capitalism fostered the growth of the Internet. When the commercial Internet was introduced in the late 1980s and early 1990s in the United States, it allowed more people Internet access. Prior to that, in the 1970s, only universities/researchers and the military were using the network. This is because it was the US Department of Defense that launched the Advanced Research Projects Agency Network (the precursor of the Internet) in 1969.

Second, access to the Internet is made possible by the globalization process that has made the product and the labor that manufactures and transports these technologies less expensive, such as computers, laptops, modems, and so on.

This cheap labor is usually people of color who work at factories in other countries. Thus it is important to pay attention to issues of race and postcolonialism as we analyze cyberculture—these are indeed the focus of "digital humanities," a subfield in digital studies.

Interestingly, in the digital world, not only is the labor "cheap," but, in some cases, it is "free" (Terranova 33). Let's take Facebook as an example. Have you ever imagined discovering that suddenly none of your Facebook friends or the public pages you "like" post anything? How likely would it be for you to keep visiting the site the following day? Perhaps very unlikely. Yet people who attract these visitors on Facebook by posting statuses and images do it for free. Who benefits, then? Certainly many corporations, including Facebook, who turn these postings of information and images into commodities are the ones making the profit.

Why do people willingly become free laborers online? Perhaps it is because most people don't see their online activities in terms of labor and production, unless of course they are part of the new generation of entrepreneurs who use an online platform to sell their products. For example, in the specific case of black women porn stars that Mireille Miller-Young examines, because these women become their own agents and not only the porn stars on their websites, they are able to enjoy more financial profit for themselves; claiming power over one's own labor is a political act (214). Most of the time, however, when people go online and become active participants in social media without the intention to sell any product, their activity is driven by the need to manage their identity, seek social approval, or develop relationships (Livingstone 4). They too have their own self-interest in mind.

SEX, SEXUALITY, AND THE INTERNET

A couple of decades after it became available to the general public, the Internet continued to expand and transform itself into the next generation, known as Web 2.0. Now more people than ever, not only those in the Internet and computer professions, can participate in this world. For example, in the early days of the Internet, one had to learn HTML code to create a website; now users can easily build websites with existing templates, sell their merchandise online, and become authors, singers, and even celebrities using social media platforms and digital self-publishing. Because consumers can also be producers, the line between the two has been transgressed—hence the concept of "prosumers." Customizable information geared toward individual preference is also the feature of Web 2.0 (Nayar 4).

This advanced development of the Internet, as Lewis Perdue argues in his book *EroticaBiz: How Sex Shaped the Internet*, is heavily influenced by sexual activities (specifically pornography) that happen online. Secure online payment, for example, was born out of the need to conduct safe payment in purchasing access to pornographic materials; the faster download speed was developed to meet the demand of watching porn videos online at the lustful speed of light—imagine pleasuring ourselves to an image that would take five minutes to be completely downloaded, as was the case in the late 1990s.

Online pornography—unlike magazines and television that are predominantly white and heterosexual—also provides customers with more varied materials; digital technology enables the producers and users with different sexual fetishes, practices, and preferences to post various images and videos on their websites. It does not mean, however, that hetero/sexism and racism no longer exist in the online world. Shoshana Magnet analyzes suicidegirls.com, a nonconventional porn website that posts images of women with "alternative beauty" (with body modification, e.g., a tattooed body). Because on this website women stage their own photo shoots and become the "réalisateurs of their fantasies," visitors and feminists alike view this website as liberating and challenging the male gaze (Magnet 581). However, she argues, the site fails to bring down limiting notions of female sexuality because it prioritizes profit over women's sexuality and includes only a few women of color, and only when it is good for their business (577).

In theory, however, cybersex *can* be liberating. Sadie Plant sees cybersex as the "epitome of disembodied pleasure" because it gives women the autonomy of having sex without the physical touch and thus liberates (heterosexual) women from getting pregnant or contracting sexually transmitted infections (460). Cybersex that (hopefully?) leads to "cyberorgasm" also provides a space for talking about "female masturbation," a topic that is still not often discussed openly (Magnet 584).

The Internet can be a liberating space because the anonymity of the virtual world affords some women the possibility to try out a sexual orientation online before coming out in the offline world (Magnet 583). The Internet can also become a relatively safe space (some are safer than others) for LGBTQPAI+ people to meet each other online and learn what it means to be a part of the community (Bryson 249). For the transgender community, the Internet, specifically websites such as gendersanity.com, glamazon.net, and transgendercare.com, has been crucial in providing a space for "bodily transformation," from experimenting with identifying oneself to be of a different gender to learning about the transitioning process (Daniels 115). Jason Whitesel, whose essay "Gay Men's Use of Online Pictures in Fat-Affirming Groups" appears in this section, poses a crucial question: How do "emerging visual technologies reshape fat politics for gay men?" (p. 501). He examines "**subvertisements**" such as *Absolut Beefy* and the "fat morph" to show the gay culture's resistance against thinness and the process of negotiating desirable bodies within a gay community.

Subvertisements: A subversive form of reappropriating advertising images.

The ability for people to express and experience sex online necessarily raises the question of what happens when, for example, women have sex with men offline but have sex only with women when online. Would we call them heterosexual? Bisexual? Hetero-flexible? Saraswati proposes a new category of sexuality that she calls **wikisexuality** She defines wikisexuality as "a new formation

Wikisexuality: A collaborative- and interactive-based sexuality, not an essence-based sexuality.

of sexuality that takes into account the fluidity of sexuality as it traverses various layers of reality—the physical and virtual worlds. It is a collaborative- and interactive-based sexuality, rather than an essence-based sexuality. . . . It reflects the non-linear and chaotic formation of sexuality that moves us beyond the mono (i.e., homosexual, heterosexual) versus multiple (i.e., bisexual, pansexual) categories of sexuality and beyond the nature versus nurture debate by evoking the notion of sexuality as constantly shifting with every encounter" (Saraswati 588). In other words, as the Internet provides us with new ways of experiencing our sexuality, it calls for a new category of sexuality, more fluid, playful, interactive, and collaborative, that she calls wikisexuality.

Possible liberatory practices of the Internet do not always carry over to material fulfillment, however. Lisa Nakamura coins the term "identity tourism" to highlight how people can play with their identity online in ways that rely on and perpetuate racial stereotypes. Moreover, the concept of identity tourism allows us to understand how the values and ideas we have about race and gender in the physical world travel with us as we become tourists of identity in the virtual world.

The digital space itself still overrepresents narratives of men and white, able-bodied people. For example, Megan Paceley and Karen Flynn analyze American online news reports on bullying against queer youth and found that 97 percent of these articles focus on gay male victims and 94.3 percent on white victims (Paceley and Flynn 345). In addition to the race/gender/sexuality/age divide, there still exists the disability divide (Dobransky and Hargittai 314). This divide is partly due to the expensive "adaptive technology" that is not only hard to learn but also behind in technology compared to those for nondisabled netizens (Dobransky and Hargittai 329). All of these provide us with even more evidence that although changes have occurred, more work remains to be done in the virtual realm.

CYBERFEMINISMS

The digital world has not always been a welcoming place for women. In the online game world, for example, black and Asian women are often represented as hypersexualized (Nayar 380). In extreme sports online games, winning means having conquered the racialized others and dangerous/racialized urban spaces and having access to these hypersexualized female bodies (Leonard 113–16). As such, some online games become a space to imagine white masculinity that structures itself around notions of conquering the bodies and spaces of people of color.

Do women play video games? Of course! Women actually make up half of the PC gamers (Nielsen qtd. in Braithwaite 707). Some women players, the so-called "power gamers," are more active in the gaming world and tend to be more playful in expressing and experimenting with their gendered self.

ACTIVISM AND CIVIC ENGAGEMENT

Anita Sarkeesian is a feminist media critic who founded feministfrequency.com, a website of video webseries examining women's representation in pop culture. In 2012 she started a Kickstarter project to produce five (now twelve) video series of "Tropes vs. Women in Video Games," a critical analysis of women's representation in video games. Within twenty-four hours, she reached her goal of $6,000 and ended up with $158,922 (from 6,968 backers).

QUESTIONS

1. Explain how Kickstarter, an online platform, allows people to seek funding to support their projects or other forms of activism.
2. How has the Internet transformed activism? What are some of the creative ways in which people have used cyberspace as a site of activism?
3. Can you identify an urgent and important local issue or a local nongovernmental organization that needed funding and used a platform such as Kickstarter to raise money?

Other women, the "moderate gamers," play games simply to escape everyday life and tend to reinforce gender systems (Royse et al. 563–67).

Women who are integrated into the mainstream gaming world, however, often receive threats. Websites such as fatuglyorslutty.com collect and post comments sent to female players. Some digital corners of cyberspace, including the online gaming world, have indeed become another site for surveillance of and violence against women.

Against this backlash, feminists have been infiltrating the net in different domains such as in politics, economics, education, care, technology, and romance and transgressing these masculine and masculinized Internet spaces. This strand of feminism is called "cyberfeminism"—a term coined by Sadie Plant in the late 1990s (qtd. in Kuni 650). Jessie Daniels, referencing Mary Flanagan and Austin Booth, defines it as "a range of theories, debates, and practices about the relationship between gender and digital culture" (102).

An example of cyberfeminism is online activism. Elisabeth Jay Friedman argues that in the specific Latin American lesbian communities that she analyzes, the features of cyberspace such as emails, websites, and chat rooms provide an effective mode of organization and mobilization (791). Another example, Empowermentors Collective (empowermentors.org), an organization that provides a space for queer/trans/female/disabled people of color to share knowledge and produce free software and media, exemplifies the ways in which people have reclaimed cyberspace to challenge different forms of inequality (Gajjala 219). Farida Vis, Liesbet van Zoonen, and Sabina Mihelj's article, "Women Responding to the Anti-Islam Fitna: Voices and Acts of Citizenship on YouTube" (this section), points out how the young Muslim women from across the globe who responded to Geert Wilder's movie *Fitna* by uploading their videos to YouTube to challenge this movie and share their own interpretations of Islam show how women are transforming the net and using it to challenge patriarchy.

EMBODIMENT, DISEMBODIMENT, AND VIRTUAL/POSTHUMAN BODIES

Conversations about science, technology, and the digital world inevitably lead us to the notion of "posthumanism" and the kinds of bodies we can embody in this digital age. But first, let's clarify the meaning of embodiment. Eve Shapiro defines embodiment as "the lived body. A state of being in which the body is the site of meaning, experience, and expression of individuals in the world" (3). Thus, when people refer to cyberspace as a disembodied space, they think of how in this virtual world people can pretend to have the kinds of bodies (gender, race, sexuality, hair color, etc.) that do not correspond to their physical bodies and never have to reveal their offline identities. When some others argue that cyberspace *is* an embodied space, they insist that even when we are online we need our physical bodies to see the computer screen or use the computer keyboard, for example.

Certainly, with new technologies being invented, there are more ways to bring bodies into the digital world. Dianne Currier identifies two forms of virtual bodies. The first is the virtual body as "an informational representation" (526). In this sense, the virtual body can take the shape of whatever symbol or avatar one wishes and desires. Nonetheless, these virtual bodies become information, that other users can decode to gauge the identity of the person behind the virtual body. Second, as a virtual reality body, the physical body is literally brought into a virtual reality environment. For example, when we play bowling with Nintendo's Wii, we use our physical bodies to simulate the movement of "real" bowling in the physical world. This notion of the virtual reality body is also what drives the development of "teledildonic" sex toys and suits that allow people in different locations to have long-distance sex, which is another example of how technology shapes how we experience sex and sexuality.

Posthumanism: A way of being and living where technology, human, and nature seep into each other.

So what does **posthumanism** mean? Posthumanism refers to a "future in which the boundaries between humanity, technology and nature have become ever more malleable" (Graham 419). It does not mean that we simply leave our human bodies behind, at least not at this time. In this digital world, as Wajcman argues, "wetware —bodies, fluids, human agency" is just as important as "hardware and software" technologies (77).

Have you ever felt frustrated when clicking on your smartphone keyboard while wishing these buttons could be as convenient as your computer's? This is what Anna Everett is referring to in her "click theory" when she highlights the importance of the body's sense of tactility: the feeling of touching the keyboard that provides us with a certain kind of satisfaction (14). Her click theory thus reminds us to be aware of the apparatuses of the click, how our bodies emotionally respond, and how we rely on our physical bodies even when we are online. Thus, according to her, cyberspace is an embodied space, even in the age of posthumanism.

What would these posthuman bodies look like in the future? Of course, no one can accurately foretell the shape of these digitally infused cyborg bodies, or if there will be a homogenous version of a posthuman body at all, and how women, gender, and sexuality will be constructed then, when our bodies have been transformed. Aliette De Bodard's "Immersion," a work of science fiction with which we end this section, addresses these issues by provoking questions about culture, technology, and the virtual reality and futurity of identities, allowing us to play with our imaginations of what they may look like. After all, the digital world can be a productive and fun playground of identities.

Critical Thinking Questions

1. How do feminist interventions reconfigure the fields of science, technology, and cyber-culture studies? Give specific examples.

2. How do certain technological innovations affect our lives? Provide examples.

3. Who gets to create what technology? Who benefits from this particular technology? At whose expense is this technology invented?

4. How does the Internet reconfigure the *materiality* of our bodies?

5. How do we *experience* these new reconstructed bodies in cyberspace?

GLOSSARY

Posthumanism 448   Standpoint theory 433   Wikisexuality 445
Situated knowledge 435   Subvertisements 445

WORKS CITED

Alaimo, Stacy. "Cyborg and Ecofeminist Interventions: Challenges for an Environmental Feminism." *Feminist Studies*, vol. 20, no. 1, 1994, pp. 133–52.

Bell, David. *An Introduction to Cybercultures*. Routledge, 2001.

Braithwaite, Andrea. "'Seriously, Get Out': Feminists on the Forums and the War(craft) on Women." *New Media & Society*, vol. 16, no. 5, 2014, pp. 703–18.

Brasher, Brenda. "Thoughts on the Status of the Cyborg: on Technological Socialization and Its Link to the Religious Function of Popular Culture." *Journal of the American Academy of Religion*, vol. 64, no. 4, 1996, pp. 809–30.

Bryson, Mary. "When Jill Jacks In: Queer Women and the Internet." *Feminist Media Studies*, vol. 4, no. 3, 2004, pp. 239–54.

Cowan, Ruth S. *More Work for Mother: The Ironies of Household Technology from the Open Hearth to the Microwave*. Basic Books, 1983.

Currier, Dianne. "Assembling Bodies in Cyberspace: Technologies, Bodies, and Sexual Difference." *Reload: Rethinking Women and Cyberculture*, edited by Mary Flanagan and Austin Booth, Massachusetts Institute of Technology P, 2002, pp. 519–38.

Daniels, Jessie. "Rethinking Cyberfeminism(s): Race, Gender, and Embodiment." *WSQ: Women's Studies Quarterly*, vol. 37, no. 1/2, 2009, pp. 101–24.

Dobransky, Kerry, and Eszter Hargittai. "The Disability Divide in Internet Access and Use." *Information, Communication & Society*, vol. 9, no. 3, 2006, pp. 313–34.

Drescher, Jack. "Queer Diagnoses: Parallels and Contrasts in the History of Homosexuality, Gender Variance, and the Diagnostic and Statistical Manual." *Archives of Sexual Behavior*, vol. 39, no. 2, 2010, pp. 427–60.

Dubrofsky, Rachel, and Shoshana Magnet, editors. *Feminist Surveillance Studies*. Duke UP, 2015.

Everett, Anna. "Digitextuality and Click Theory: Theses on Convergence Media in the Digital Age." *New Media: Theories and Practices of Digitextuality*, edited by Anna Everett and John Caldwell, Routledge, 2003, pp. 3–28.

Faulkner, Wendy. "The Technology Question in Feminism: A View from Feminist Technology Studies." *Women's Studies International Forum*, vol. 24, no. 1, 2001, pp. 79–95.

Gajjala, Radhika. "Digital Media, Race, Gender, Affect, and Labor: Introduction to Special Section." *Television and New Media*, vol. 15, no. 3, 2014, pp. 215–22.

Galis, Vasilis. "Enacting Disability: How can Science and Technology Inform Disability Studies? *Disability & Society*, vol. 26, no. 7, 2011, pp. 825–38.

Gill, Rosalind. "Review: Technofeminism" *Science as Culture*, vol. 14, no. 1, 2005, pp. 97–101.

Graham, Elaine. "Cyborgs or Goddesses? Becoming Divine in a Cyberfeminist Age." *Information, Communication & Society*, vol. 2, no. 4, 1999, pp. 419–38.

Gur-Ze'ev, Ilan. "Cyberfeminism and Education in the Era of the Exile of Spirit." *Educational Theory*, vol. 49, no. 4, 1999, pp. 437–55.

Haraway, Donna. "A Cyborg Manifesto: Science, Technology, and Socialist-Feminism in the Late Twentieth Century." *Simians, Cyborgs and Women: The Reinvention of Nature*, Routledge, 1991, pp. 149–81.

———. "Situated Knowledges: The Science Question in Feminism and the Privilege of Partial Perspective." *Feminist Studies*, vol. 14, no. 3, 1988, pp. 575–99.

Hayer, Heike. "Segmentation and Segregation Patterns on 'Women-Owned High Tech Firms in Four Metropolitan Regions in the United States." *Regional Studies*, vol. 42, no. 10, 2008, pp. 1357–83.

Hoffman, Ginger. "The Self-Disrespect Objection to Bioenhancement Technologies: A Feminist Analysis of the Complex Relationship between Enhancement and Self-Respect." *Journal of Social Philosophy*, vol. 45, no. 4, 2014, pp. 498–521.

Horowitz, Roger, and Arwen Mohun, editors. *His and Hers: Gender, Consumption, and Technology*. UP of Virginia, 1998.

Kuefler, Matthew, editor. *The History of Sexuality: Sourcebook*. Broadview Press, 2007.

Kuni, Verena. "Cyborg—Communication—Code—Infection: 'How Do Cyborgs Communicate?' Re/Writing Cyberfeminism(s)." *Third Text*, vol. 21, no. 5, 2007, pp. 649–59.

Leonard, David. "To the White Extreme: Conquering Athletic Space, White Manhood, and Racing Virtual reality." *Digital Gameplay: Essays on the Nexus of Game and Gamer*, edited by Nate Garrelts, McFarland, 2005, pp. 110–29.

Livingstone, Sonia. "Taking Risky Opportunities in Youthful Content Creation: Teenagers' Use of Social Networking Sites for Intimacy, Privacy and Self-Expression. *New Media & Society*, vol. 10, no. 3, 2008, pp. 393–411.

Lubar, Steven. "Men/Women/Production/Consumption." *His and Hers: Gender, Consumption, and Technology*, edited by Roger Horowitz and Arwen Mohun. UP of Virginia, 1998, pp. 7–37.

Magnet, Shoshana. "Feminist Sexualities, Race and the Internet: An Investigation of suicidegirls.com." *New Media & Society*, vol. 9, no. 4, 2007, pp. 577–602.

Masters, Cristina. "Bodies of Technology: Cyborg Soldiers and Militarized Masculinities." *International Feminist Journal of Politics*, vol. 7, no. 1, 2005, pp. 112–32.

McCandless, David. "Diversity in Tech: Gender Breakdown of Key Companies." *The Guardian*, 25 Nov 2014, www.theguardian.com/news/datablog/ng-interactive/2014/nov/25/diversity-in-tech-gender-breakdown-of-key-companies.

Miller-Young, Mireille. "Sexy and Smart: Black Women and the Politics of Self-Authorship in Netporn." *C'Lick Me: A Netporn Studies Reader*, edited by Katrien Jacobs et al., Institute of Network Cultures and Paradiso, 2005, pp. 205–16.

Mjøs, Ole. "Award Ceremony Speech." Presented at the Nobel Peace Prize, 2004.

Nakamura, Lisa. "Race In/For Cyberspace: Identity Tourism and Racial Passing on the Internet." *Works and Days: Essays in the Socio-Historical Dimensions of Literature & the Arts,* vol. 25/26, 1995, pp. 181–93.

National Science Foundation. *Science and Engineering*. Jan. 2015, www.nsf.gov/statistics/2015/nsf15311/digest/.

——— *Women, Minorities, and Persons with Disabilities in Science & Engineering Indicators*, Feb. 2014, www.nsf.gov/statistics/seind14/.

Nayar, Pramod, editor. *The New Media and Cybercultures Anthology*. Wiley-Blackwell, 2010.

Newton, Stephen. "Breaking the Code: Women Confront the Promises and the Perils of High Technology." *Women's Studies Quarterly*, vol. 29, no. 3/4, 2001, pp. 71–79.

Paasonen, Susanna. *Figures of Fantasy: Internet, Women, and Cyberdiscourse*. Peter Lang, 2005.

Perdue, Lewis. *EroticaBiz: How Sex Shaped the Internet*. Writers Club Press, 2002.

Plant, Sadie. "Coming Across the Future." *The Cybercultures Reader,* edited by David Bell and Barbara Kennedy, Routledge, 2000, pp. 460–70.

Roberts, Dorothy. *Killing the Black Bodies: Race, Reproduction, and the Meaning of Liberty*. Pantheon Books, 1997.

Royse, Pam, et al. "Women and Games: Technologies of the Gendered Self." *New Media & Society*, vol. 9, no. 4, 2007, pp. 555–75.

Saraswati, L. Ayu. "Wikisexuality: Rethinking Sexuality in Cyberspace." *Sexualities*, vol. 16, no. 5/6, 2013, pp. 587–603.

Shapiro, Eve. *Gender Circuits: Bodies and Identities in a Technological Age*. Routledge, 2010.

Terranova, Tiziana. "Free Labor: Producing Culture for the Digital Economy." *Social Text*, vol. 63, no. 8.2, 2000, pp. 33–58.

Thomas, Sue. *Hello World: Travels in Virtuality*. Raw Nerve Books, 2004.

US Department of Labor, Bureau of Labor Statistics. *Women in the Labor Force: A Databook*. www.bls.gov/opub/reports/womens-databook/archive/women-in-the-labor-force-a-databook-2015.pdf.

Wajcman, Judy. *TechnoFeminism*. Polity Press, 2004.

Waskul, Dennis, and Mark Douglass. "Cyberself: The Emergence of Self in On-Line Chat." *The Information Society*, vol. 13, no. 4, 1997, pp. 357–97.

69. • *Sandra Harding*

FEMINISM CONFRONTS THE SCIENCES:
Reform and Transformation (1991)

Sandra Harding is a distinguished research professor in education and gender studies at the University of California, Los Angeles. In 1990, she was chosen as "Woman Philosopher of the Year, Eastern Division Society for Women in Philosophy." She also has received the John Desmond Bernal Prize of Society for the Social Studies of Science (4S), the highest award in 4S. Her works intersect feminism with science to question the scientific process of knowledge production, as is the essay included here. The essay included here is excerpted from her book, *Whose Science? Whose Knowledge? Thinking from Women's Lives.*

Only in the late 1970s did feminists begin to bring to bear on the theories and practices of science and technology the distinctive approaches that had been developing in the social sciences, the humanities, and, more generally, the women's movement. For many of us, it began to appear that in order to reform the sciences, as well as the philosophy, history, and social studies of science, there might have to be broad transformations of both science and society. Were reforms going to require revolutions? Were such revolutions going to be possible without further reforms?

[. . .]

WOMEN IN SCIENCE

First of all, among studies of women's lives within the social structure of science, there are at least four distinctive focuses. Each one has produced new understandings of women's situation, but taken alone, each one also limits our vision by its concentration on just one aspect of this issue. We need all four—and an analysis informed by the other concerns discussed below—to get a more comprehensive picture of the situation of women in the sciences.

WOMEN WORTHIES

Historical studies and biographies of contemporary scientists bring to our attention the "women worthies" in science: the many women who have made important contributions but who are ignored or devalued in the androcentric mainstream literature. . . .

Class and race played roles in creating opportunities for these women, as they did for their brothers. When scientific collecting and experimentation were primarily gentlemen's activities, daughters as well as sons could gain a scientific education in the laboratory out behind the kitchen. It is striking how many early women scientists were related to male scientists; they learned science from or were supported in their work by fathers or husbands who were also scientists. Indeed, it is difficult in many eras to find women scientists who were not mentored by male relatives. Class and race opportunities are obviously related: poor women and women of color were as unlikely as *their* brothers to have relatives who were scientists; however, occasionally—very occasionally— their brothers did succeed in gaining access to science education, even if not to the kinds of careers to which such an education provided entrance for white men in the elite class. There is a real "Black Apollo" in recent American science; but "Black Athena" apparently can be an image only for the (important but now unjustly devalued) science and knowledge of premodern and non-Western cultures.[1]

The consciousness of the women who did find a place in science was often not feminist. Indeed, even a *woman's* consciousness could hardly be permitted if the fiction were to be maintained that a woman scientist must be a contradiction in terms. In order to succeed as scientists, these women usually had to force their lives as closely as possible into life cycles

designed to accommodate the lives of men in patriarchal societies. Their possibilities for marriage and children were severely diminished in ways that never affected their brothers. Nevertheless, in both the nineteenth and twentieth centuries, many important scientists who were women have been active in projects everyone recognized as advanced by feminists. They have had to be, in order to open doors for themselves and their women students that were otherwise open only for male colleagues and their male students.

Moreover, we can ask whether "having a feminist consciousness" in the sense of overtly embracing feminism should really be regarded as a prerequisite for feminist activities: that is, for activities that have both the intention and the effect of specifically benefiting women. The term feminism is too radical for some people and too conservative for others. It is common today to find people struggling specifically to improve women's conditions but refusing to characterize their efforts as feminist, and to find different groups doing so for both progressive and conservative reasons. . . . Whether or not they took part in overtly feminist activities, simply surviving against the odds was a remarkable achievement. "Never Meant to Survive" is the title given to one African American woman's account of her life in science in order to emphasize the difficulties for her of simply enduring in this institution.[2] On the other hand, it trivializes feminism to insist that every success achieved by women in a male-dominant institution is a cause for feminist pride. Feminism must have principles for distinguishing between feminism and self-interest (does "advocating feminist capitalism" have any meaning?), and between feminisms associated with progressive politics and those that may be progressively feminist in some respects but are or become infused with regressive tendencies in other respects—for example, with racism or class privilege. Perhaps we can at least admire survival, if not always for feminist reasons.

There is much more to be learned about science and women's situation in it by examining the lives of these women who were doubly pioneers—as scientists and as women (and triply so if they were women of color).

With few exceptions they have been left out of the standard histories of science, engineering, mathematics, medicine, and the social sciences. There is much more to be done in restoring to historical awareness the record of these women's achievements and their struggles as women in the process. We do a disservice to our daughters and our sons—as well as to the historical record—in ignoring and undervaluing women's work. Yet far from being a phenomenon of the past, these exclusionary practices threaten to continue unless men as well as women are willing to speak up and fight against the androcentric biases that support such practices. After all, it was only twenty years ago that James Watson could devalue and ridicule in print—and with a macho hubris that signaled expected approval—the work of Rosalind Franklin in the discovery of the structure of DNA. It was Franklin's work as well as theirs that permitted Watson and Sir Francis Crick to win a Nobel Prize. Why was it not also awarded to her? Franklin was lucky enough to have a friend who was made so angry by Watson's account that she was willing to put in the time and energy to reconstruct the historical record and produce a book that corrected Watson's account.[3] Few of us—or our colleagues or daughters—will have friends with the knowledge available to Franklin's friend or the willingness to commit a significant part of their lives to that kind of effort on our behalf.

The studies of "women worthies" if taken by themselves, however, can distort our understanding of the situation of women in science. Exactly because they were so unusual in their own day, the lives and experiences of these women are not typical. They do not tell us what we need to know in order to understand the experiences of the majority of women who try to make it into science or who may achieve less distinguished careers than these few. . . .

Women's Contributions

Women's contributions to the history and practice of science are not limited to the achievements of a few extraordinary individuals. The new women's history and sociology have directed attention to the less public, less official, less visible, and less dramatic aspects of science in order to gain a better understanding of women's participation in these enterprises.[4] Salons organized and run by women enabled male scientists to find patrons to fund their laboratories and collecting trips in nineteenth-century France. In Europe and the United States, women's networks and more formally constituted women's clubs of botanists, biologists, and astronomers made important contributions to the collection of data. Some scientific fields, such as mathematics, have openly welcomed women in certain historical periods.[5] As elementary and secondary school teachers, women with advanced science training have provided a significant part of the preparation necessary for the subsequent pursuit of scientific careers by everyone in the scientific workforce, including the Nobel Prize winners. In their work as science and medical illustrators, editors, and popularizers, women have shaped perceptions that have made it possible to gather public support for scientific activity. Today, Nobel Prizes could not be won without the work of women as lab technicians and postdoctoral lab assistants, not to mention data analysts and computer programmers. Women have been active in the sciences in ways that are invisible if one focuses only on the public, official, visible, and dramatic figures and events that are favored in the conventional accounts.

[. . .]

Structural Obstacles

From the beginning, feminist observers of science have critically examined the structural obstacles to women's achievement in science. Historical studies of the formal barriers to women's equity reveal the vigorous campaigns that were usually necessary to allow women the access men had to scientific education, degrees, lab appointments, publication in journals, membership in scientific societies, jobs in universities or industry or the government, and scientific prizes.

Historical studies of the emergence, flourishing, and eventual decline of the formal barriers to women in the sciences have been complemented by sociological and psychological studies of informal barriers. Motivation and psychoanalytic studies have shown why boys and men more often want to enter and remain in science, engineering, and math than do girls and women.[6] For one thing, the very same personality traits that young males must take on to become masculine in the modern West are just those that are particularly valued for careers in science and related fields. . . .

[. . .]

One must emphasize that structural obstacles should be the focus here—not the purported biological or personality traits on which the sexist attempts to explain women's lack of equity in science have concentrated. Nor should the focus be primarily on the sexism of individual men or even precisely of men as a group. James Watson's treatment of Rosalind Franklin was certainly sexist, and he should be held responsible for that behavior. But of more interest for analyses of the structure of the sciences and attempts to change the future for women in the sciences is his correct perception that neither men nor women would criticize his behavior (at least, not until feminism came along). His bragging tone reveals the existence not just of one little sexist but, more important, of the entire institution of gender relations, including male supremacy, that he could depend upon to support his beliefs and behaviors.

[. . .]

An exclusive focus only on the structural obstacles to women's equity would give the impression that science as an institution as well as the individual men in science have been totally resistant to women's scientific activities, and that women have rarely succeeded in this institution. Of course, neither is the case. This kind of preoccupation with "victimology" must be balanced with the studies of women's resistance to marginalization and their achievements.

SCIENCE EDUCATION

Finally, attention to improved science, math, and engineering education for girls and women is one important concern of more general educational and curricular studies. This research is used to shape programs that try to create environments and learning processes that will encourage young women, and not just young men, to enter and remain in such fields.[7]

Another improvement in science education is less often discussed than it should be, both inside and outside feminist circles: what should we teach young—and not so young—men and women about how science functions? If "science education for girls" means the same kinds of educational opportunities and supportive environments available to their brothers, the implication is that boys' science education is just fine. . . .

[. . .]

Moreover, it is convenient to overlook the deep ties between science and warmaking. The new histories of science, such as Margaret Jacob's, bring these connections into sight, revealing that

> Western science at its foundations, as promoted by its most brilliant as well as its most ordinary exponents, never questioned the usefulness of scientific knowledge for warmaking. I know of no text from the early modern period which suggests that the scientist should withhold his knowledge from any government, at any time, but especially in the process of preparing for warmaking. Indeed most texts that recommend science also propose its usefulness in improving the state's capacity to wage war more effectively, to destroy more efficiently.[8]

Late twentieth-century physics, too, has been shaped by military control, as studies of U.S. science policy since World War II show.[9] Why should feminists want women or anyone else to be military researchers—or to engage in apparently valuable kinds of scientific or medical research whose results will be distributed only for profit? Neither the internal social structure of science nor science's involvement in exploitative politics is deeply challenged by the ways in which the equity issues are often formulated. Further, little attention has been given to the special achievements of and obstacles faced by women of color.[10]

There are good reasons to want more women in physics and other natural sciences . . . . But it is hard to discover them in much of the conventional literature intended to attract girls into science education and keep women in scientific jobs. Much of this recruitment literature has the numbing, depressing, and even alarming feel of U.S. military recruitment literature for the Vietnam war.

[. . .]

SEXIST MISUSE AND ABUSE OF SCIENCE AND TECHNOLOGY

Studies of the uses and abuses of biology, the social sciences, and their technologies show how they have been used in the service of sexism, racism, homophobia, and class exploitation. One important feminist focus in such research is on reproductive technologies and policies. Within this literature are studies of historical and contemporary aspects of the medicalization of birth, the introduction of reproductive technologies that often do not benefit women, sterilization and abortion policies, pronatalism, unsafe contraceptives, unnecessary gynecological surgery, and many other issues. But whatever the topic, common themes emerge. It is clear that the dominant culture has been willing to take far greater risks with women's reproductive systems than it would ever countenance for those of men—or, rather, for those of men in the dominant classes and races. This is just one way of saying that women's lack of power in the social order extends to their having far less control than do men in the dominant groups over what happens to their own bodies. Moreover, feminist analyses of reproductive issues again and again raise deeply disturbing questions for everyone about fundamental assumptions in Western thought, such as the inevitable benefits of greater knowledge and of greater choices.[11]

Not only technologies and applied sciences but also scientific theories have been used to move control of women's lives to those who exercise power in the dominant class, race, and culture.[12] Many egregiously sexist and androcentric misuses and abuses have been documented for workplace and domestic technologies.[13] And gender relations more generally—not just those that take the form of male supremacy—are implicated in the applications of science that result in ecological destruction and support militarism.[14]

[. . .]

These critiques can bring to the surface of the feminist science discussions the class, race, and imperialist projects of the West in which the sciences and their technologies have been and remain deeply implicated. Thus, they are radical in this way, too. They force feminist observers of science to notice that "women" are always women of a certain race, class, and culture. We are white as well as black; economically overprivileged as well as underprivileged; Western as well as Third World—and race supremacy, economic overprivilege, and Euro-centrism are problems that the sciences have helped to advance. That is, when race is the topic of discussion, white is at least as appropriate a focus as black. We replicate the oppression characteristic of androcentric discourses if we fail to observe that scientific and technological benefits accumulate for Westerners, whites, and the economically over-advantaged as the correlative disadvantages accumulate for Third World peoples, racial "minorities," and the poor.

Nevertheless, this focus, like that on women in the social structure of the sciences, can appear to leave the pure core of science untouched by feminist challenges. After all, the science enthusiast can say, these criticisms are applicable only to technologies and to the applications of science; pure science, the theoretical science that wins Nobel Prizes, is not implicated in the misuses and abuses of science and technology in the political realm. As this argument goes, we can have an easy conscience when we teach our students pure theoretical science. We and they are not responsible for what happens to the value-neutral information that is the result of pure scientific inquiry once it leaves the hands of scientists. After it is released into society, how it is used for good or bad purposes becomes others' responsibility.

The appropriate response to that kind of defense reveals yet another radical aspect of this feminist critique. The very language of "misuse and abuse," borrowed from conventional science studies, in fact gives away too much to the defenders of pure science. The sciences are part and parcel, woof and warp, of the social orders from which they emerge and which support them. "Science versus society" is a false and distorting image. First, social desires are frequently defined as technological needs, and as such they generate and legitimate scientific research for both individuals and institutions. Social desires have been defined as technological needs for better firearms, better navigation for sea voyages between Africa and the Americas, machines for large-scale and more cost-efficient industrial and agricultural production, and more effective means of controlling population growth. The "problematics" of science frequently arise from the translation of social agendas into technological ones.

Second, the technologies used to produce scientific information are not value-neutral. For example, the development of the telescope moved authority about the patterns of the heavens from the church to the secular world and supported the emerging importance of the authority of individual observation. Contemporary scientific technologies—computers, laboratory tests, nuclear accelerators—shift values in the sciences in other ways. [15]

Third, and most obvious, the sciences generate information that is used to produce technologies and applications that are not morally and politically neutral. The institution of science hides this fact in a variety of ways, most notably by constantly splitting off into what it conceptualizes as separate fields those sciences in which a focus on application has become obvious. (Is the moment of obviousness also the moment of redefinition as "separate"?) Thus electrical, mechanical, and civil engineering are "not really physics"; medicine, health policy, nursing, and the invention of reproductive technologies are "not really biology"; "applied mathematics" and "chemical engineering" have been sloughed off to separate disciplines, disciplinary organizations, journals, and university departments.

[. . .]

There is one problematic aspect of some feminist responses to the "misuse and abuse" critiques. We need to think about the possible positive effects for women of technologies that initially appear to offer only disasters and consider how to bring about these good effects. For example, it is certainly understandable that many feminists have been staunchly opposed to new reproductive technologies which, in the present misogynous cultures, threaten to decrease the already deteriorated control women have over their bodies and their reproductive choices. Moreover, the potential of these technologies for increasing class and race exploitation is clear. Nevertheless, we need to develop more discriminating responses to them because the chances of stopping them entirely are low, they do offer benefits to some women, and many of these women do not now have access to them: arguments against the hospital-centered delivery of health care are not especially appealing to women whose poverty and lack of insurance denies them and their children access to hospitals and doctors. . . .

SEXIST AND ANDROCENTRIC BIAS

Researchers have raised a variety of criticisms against the sexism and androcentrism that have shaped the results of research in biology and the social sciences. We can now see that females as well as males have made important contributions to the evolution of our species. Contrary to Darwinian and other interpretations of evolutionary theory, females too have evolved.[16] We can see that Woman the Gatherer played at least as significant a role as did Man the Hunter in ushering in the dawn of our species. Woman's moral development now appears different but just as necessary for the conduct of social relations—not immature, deviant, and a "problem" for the maintenance of social order.[17] Women's contributions to social life begin to appear once the paradigms of the social that seem natural to male sociologists and their male informants are enriched with understandings of women's less visible, dramatic, and public but nonetheless important activities.[18] In history, economics, and linguistics, too, much of what has passed for distinctively human activity and belief can now be seen to be only masculine activity and belief—and distinctively modern, Western, and upper-class at that.

What are some of the general conceptual issues that these criticisms raise about science and its dominant images?

Androcentric biases can enter the research process at every stage, as critics have shown.[19] They enter in the concepts and hypotheses selected, in the design of research, and in the collection and interpretation of data. The most radical implication of understanding how the structure of the institution of science structures the content of the science produced there, however, may be the recognition that whoever gets to define what counts as a scientific problem also gets a powerful role in shaping the picture of the world that results from scientific research.

[. . .]

. . . If the dominant gender perceives women's sexuality as problematic, we will get one view of human sexuality; if men's is perceived as the problem, we will get another. If explaining gender inequality without implicating powerful men or the rightness of male supremacy is implicitly defined as the scientific problem, one picture of human biology, history, and social life emerges; if the problem is to explain gender inequality and let the chips fall where they may, a different picture will emerge. If the problem is defined as overpopulation in the Third World, one scientific agenda will emerge; if it is the refusal of the West to permit Third World cultures to retain the resources they need to support their populations, a different agenda will seem appropriate. The sciences' methods of research will do little to eliminate social biases intrinsic to these conflicting definitions

as long as only one of the two problems is defined as a scientific one. And after centuries of primarily dominant groups defining what gets to count as scientific problems, do we need an equally long history of subordinated groups making the majority of such definitions? If not, how is our distorted picture of the world to be corrected?

One way to see this issue is to notice that though scientific methods are selected, we are told, exactly in order to eliminate all social values from inquiry, they are actually operationalized to eliminate only those values that differ within whatever gets to count as the community of scientists. If values and interests that can produce the most critical perspectives on science are silenced through discriminatory social practices, the standard, narrowly conceived conception of scientific method will have not an iota of a chance of maximizing either value-neutrality or objectivity.

[. . .]

THE SEXUAL MEANINGS OF NATURE AND INQUIRY

Science produces information, but it also produces meanings. Indeed, as even some conventional philosophers of science realize, the results of scientific research *are* information only if they have meaning for us; an undecipherable string of numbers or nonsense syllables is not yet information. Moreover, science produces meanings of its own activities which are intended to create resources for it. It leads us to think of its kind of method as a moral good, as the place where the inherently positive value of science is to be found—hence the term "positivism." Science produces meanings of itself as a "calling," as one of the most important supports of the rational life, as a heroic struggle, as the paradigm of a distinctively human activity, as the apogee of civilization, and so on and so on. It produces meanings of its methods of research as stripping the veils from nature, or torturing nature to reveal her secrets, or, more attractively, as attempting to defeat "might makes right" in the domain of empirical knowledge. And science delivers meanings for the nature it describes and explains—as something requiring domination or hiding its secrets, as a worthy opponent, even as the bride of the scientist.[20]

Hence, another focus of the feminist examination of science uses techniques of literary criticism, historical interpretation, and psychoanalysis to "read science as a text." The text is the whole of science: its formal statements, intellectual traditions, research practices, social formations, the scientific and popular beliefs about it, and so on. . . .

[. . .]

When we realize that the mechanistic metaphors that organized early modern science themselves carried sexual meanings, it is clear that these meanings are central to the ways scientists conceptualize both the methods of inquiry and models of nature. Restrained but clear echoes still appear even in a text that is clearly trying to keep science "buttoned up": "The laws of nature are not apparent in our everyday surroundings, waiting to be plucked like fruit from a tree. They are hidden and unyielding, and the difficulties of grasping them add greatly to the satisfaction of success."[21] Such metaphors and gender meanings of scientific methods, theories and objects of knowledge rescientize sex stereotypes as they simultaneously generate distortions of nature and inquiry.

These criticisms raise a number of important issues.[22] For one thing, it is important to see that the focus should not be on whether individuals in the history of science were sexist. Most of them were; in this they were like most men (and many women) of their day. Instead, the point is that the sexual meanings of nature and inquiry are used to express the anxieties of whole societies—or, at least, of the groups whose interests science was intended to advance. Cultural meanings, not individual ones, should be the issue here. Appeals to familiar sexual politics are used to allay anxieties about perceived threats to the social order.[23]

[. . .]

These sexist meanings are politically and morally obnoxious. But they also distort our understandings of nature in two ways. For one thing, if scientists tend to select (intentionally or not) certain kinds of methods of inquiry *because,* among other reasons, they are associated with distinctively masculine stereotypes—interventionist methods, for example—masculine stereotypes have become part of the *evidence* for the results of this research. Since we should be able to weigh all the evidence for a scientist's claims, this preference for certain methods on the grounds that they carry masculine meanings or avoid feminine ones should be presented as part of the evidence. (Imagine such a research report in a scientific journal!)[24]

[. . .]

Should we want these metaphors eliminated from science? Where possible, this would clearly appear to be desirable. But because these metaphors have become attractive in scientific work as a result of their social uses outside science, eliminating them from the language of science can be only part of the solution to the problem of how to degender the natural sciences. Doing so cannot in itself end the practice of drawing upon social meanings in the direction of research. Moreover, it raises the issue of how one should evaluate obviously sexist metaphors that have, nevertheless, contributed to the growth of scientific knowledge. How should feminism analyze, for instance, the fact that mechanistic metaphors drew on misogynous politics as a resource for the development of science?

In a certain sense, these are the wrong questions. Obviously, the sexist language of science is continuous with sexist thought in society in general. All thought and language both shapes and is shaped by the social order, its projects, and attempts to resolve conflicts within it. So solutions to this problem cannot be independent of more general struggles to end the subjection of women, racial "minorities," and the poor and to transform sciences into knowledge-seeking institutions *of, by,* and *for* these groups. We need to ask how to create the kinds of societies in which the dominant institutions of knowledge production are no longer so complicitous in benefiting the few to the detriment of the many. This critique is especially important however, because it shows that physics, chemistry, and abstract thought in every realm (including philosophy) can be deeply sexist or androcentric even when no humans at all appear in their domain of inquiry. Evidently, abstract thought is not quite as abstract as most have assumed. Perhaps even excessive preferences for the abstract themselves undercut the point of abstraction: these preferences, like all others, can be historically located.

ANDROCENTRIC EPISTEMOLOGIES

Finally, the preceding challenges to the natural and social sciences raise epistemological issues. One way to put the problem here is to note that in the humanities, biology, and the social sciences, it turned out to be impossible to "add women" without challenging the foundations of those disciplines. Similarly, the feminist science critics argue that when we try to "add women" as knowers within traditional theories of knowledge, we quickly discover how partial and distorted are those theories.

The issue is not whether individual women have gained scientific trainings and credentials and have made important contributions to the growth of knowledge; thousands and thousands of them have done so. The issue for the feminist epistemological critiques is a different one: "woman the knower" (like "woman scientist") appears to be a contradiction in terms. By "woman the knower" I mean women as agents of knowledge, as actors on the stage of history, as humans whose lives provide a grounding for knowledge claims that are different from and in some respects preferable to knowledge claims grounded in the lives of men in the dominant groups.

We can begin to sense the contradictions when we note that conventionally, what it means to be scientific is to be dispassionate, disinterested, impartial, concerned with abstract principles and rules; but what it means to be a woman is to be emotional, interested in and partial to the welfare of family and

friends, concerned with concrete practices and contextual relations. Feminists have argued that these features of womanliness are not the consequences of biology—let alone of inferior biology. Rather, they arise from a variety of social conditions that are more characteristic of women's lives than of the lives of men in the dominant groups. One argument is that men in the dominant groups assign to women (and other marginalized peoples) certain kinds of human activity that they do not want to do themselves. They assign to women the care of all bodies, including men's, and the local places where bodies exist (houses, offices, and so on), the care of young children, and emotional work—the processing of men's and everyone else's feelings. (Some men will do emotional labor only if they can charge psychiatrists' fees for it.) In short, most dominant-group men refuse to be responsible for daily life, their own or other people's.[25] Must women renounce what they can know about nature and social relations from the perspective of their daily lives in order to produce what the culture is able to recognize as knowledge? How can such socially situated knowledge be justified when the dominant epistemology assumes that since real knowledge is transcendental, the very idea of situated knowledge is a contradiction in terms?[26]

Distinctively feminist analyses of theories of scientific knowledge have begun to crystallize around three different and partially conflicting approaches. First, feminist empiricism attempts to bring the feminist criticisms of scientific claims into the existing theories of scientific knowledge by arguing that sexist and androcentric results of research are simply the consequence of "bad science." From this perspective, feminists are helping science to better follow its widely recognized procedures and to achieve its existing goals. Second, the feminist standpoint theorists argue that the problem is more extensive. The dominant conceptual schemes of the natural and social sciences fit the experience that Western men of the elite classes and races have of themselves and the world around them. Political struggle and feminist theory, they say, must be incorporated into the sciences if we are to be able to see beneath the partial and false images of the world that the sciences generate. By starting research from women's lives, we can arrive at empirically and theoretically more adequate descriptions and explanations—at less partial and distorting ones. Finally, a third approach argues that even these two feminist theories of knowledge are not radical enough. Both still adhere too closely to damaging Enlightenment beliefs about the possibility of producing one true story about a reality that is out there and ready to be reflected in the mirror of our minds. These postmodernist tendencies in feminist thought point to the far too intimate connections between science and power in the past. They ask whether feminist epistemology is to continue the policing of thought which characterizes the conventional epistemology-centered philosophies and sciences.

[. . .]

In *The Science Question in Feminism* I characterized the journey from issues about women in science to criticisms of theories of scientific knowledge as a shift from the "woman question in science" to the "science question in feminism." In its concern with equity issues, the woman question begins by asking, "What do women want from science?" It conceptualizes women as a special interest group—like, for instance, farmers or oil producers in their relationship to the government—who ask that their special needs and interests be fairly recognized in the institution of science. By the time we get to the epistemology discussions, both the issues and how women are conceptualized have radically shifted. The science question asks, "How can we use for emancipatory ends those sciences that are apparently so intimately involved in Western, bourgeois, and masculine projects?" And women appear not as a special interest group pleading for a hearing for their own interests alone but as thinkers expressing concerns about science and society that are echoed in the other "countercultures" of science—in antiracist and Third World movements, in anticapitalism movements, and in the ecology and peace movements. . . .

[. . .]

NOTES

1. See Kenneth Manning, *Black Apollo of Science: The Life of Edward Everett Just* (New York: Oxford University Press, 1983); Martin Bernal, *Black Athena: The Afroasiatic Roots of Classical Civilization* (New Brunswick, N.J.: Rutgers University Press. 1987). Chapters 8, 9, and 11 investigate the benefits of really trying to "add race" to the feminist science criticisms and the interesting challenges that result.

2. Aimée Sands, "Never Meant to Survive: A Black Woman's Journey," *Radical Teacher* 30 (1986); the phrase is from a poem of Audre Lorde's, "A Litany for Survival," in *The Black Unicorn* (New York: Norton, 1978).

3. James Watson, *The Double Helix* (New York: New American Library, 1969); Anne Sayre, *Rosalind Franklin and DNA: A Vivid View of What It Is Like to Be a Gifted Woman in an Especially Male Profession* (New York: Norton, 1975).

4. See Marcia Millman and Rosabeth Moss Kanter, eds., *Another Voice: Feminist Perspectives on Social Life and Social Science* (New York: Anchor Books, 1975), for pointed early arguments about the importance of such concerns to an understanding of the organization of social life; and Margaret Andersen, *Thinking about Women: Sociological Perspectives on Sex and Gender,* 2d ed. (New York: Macmillan, 1988), for a comprehensive literature review and critical analysis of how these concerns have transformed sociological understandings of social life. The new women's histories and sociologies are complementary, but it is primarily the new historical perspectives that have been brought to bear in extended analyses of the sciences.

5. Abir-Am and Outram, *Uneasy Careers;* Rossiter, *Women Scientists in America;* Schiebinger, *The Mind Has No Sex.*

6. See, e.g., Violet B. Haas and Carolyn C. Perrucci, eds., *Women in Scientific and Engineering Professions* (Ann Arbor: University of Michigan Press, 1984).

7. See Sue Rosser, *Teaching Science and Health from a Feminist Perspective* (New York: Pergamon Press, 1986); Sue Rosser, *Feminism in the Science and Health Care Professions: Overcoming Resistance* (New York: Pergamon Press, 1988); Joan Rothschild, *Teaching Technology from a Feminist Perspective* (New York: Pergamon Press, 1988).

8. Margaret Jacob, *The Cultural Meanings of the Scientific Revolution* (New York: Knopf, 1988), 251.

9. Paul Forman, "Beyond Quantum Electronics: National Security as the Basis for Physical Research in the U.S., 1940–1960," *Historical Studies in Physical and Biological Sciences* 18 (1987).

10. Exceptions can be found in the bibliography by Anne Fausto-Sterling and Lydia English, "Women and Minorities in Science: Course Materials Guide," 1982 (available from Fausto-Sterling, Division of Biology and Medicine, Brown University, Providence, RI 02912).

11. See, e.g., Rita Arditti, Renate Duelli-Klein, and Shelly Minden, eds., *Test-Tube Women: What Future for Motherhood?* (Boston: Pandora Press, 1984); Patricia Spallone and Deborah Steinberg, eds., *Made to Order* (New York: Pergamon Press, 1987).

12. Many critics make this argument. For one good recent analysis, see Ruth Hubbard, *The Politics of Women's Biology* (New Brunswick, N.J.: Rutgers University Press, 1990).

13. See Cynthia Cockburn, *Machinery of Dominance: Women, Men, and Technical Know-How* (Boston: Northeastern University Press, 1988); Barbara Ehrenreich and Deirdre English, *For Her Own Good: 150 Years of Experts' Advice to Women* (New York: Doubleday, 1979); Ruth Schwartz Cowan, *More Work for Mother: The Ironies of Household Technology from the Open Hearth to the Microwave* (New York: Basic Books, 1983); and critical studies of the situation of women in Third World development projects: e.g., Susan C. Bourque and Kay B. Warren, "Technology, Gender, and Development," *Daedalus* 116:4 (1987); Maria Mies, *Patriarchy and Accumulation on a World Scale: Women in the International Division of Labour* (Atlantic Highlands, N.J.: Zed Books, 1986); Maria Mies, Veronika Bennholdt-Thomsen, and Claudia von Werlhof, *Women: The Last Colony* (Atlantic Highlands, N.J.: Zed Books, 1988).

14. H. Patricia Hynes, *The Recurring Silent Spring* (New York: Pergamon Press, 1989); Sara Ruddick, *Maternal Thinking: Toward a Politics of Peace* (Boston: Beacon Press, 1989).

15. See, e.g., Stanley Reiser, *Medicine and the Reign of Technology* (Cambridge: Cambridge University Press, 1978); Sharon Traweek, *Beamtimes and Life Times: The World of High Energy Physicists* (Cambridge, Mass.: Harvard University Press, 1988).

16. Ruth Hubbard, "Have Only Men Evolved?" in Harding and Hintikka, *Discovering Reality.*

17. Carol Gilligan, *In a Different Voice: Psychological Theory and Women's Development* (Cambridge, Mass.: Harvard University Press, 1982).

18. Andersen, *Thinking about Women;* Millman and Kanter, *Another Voice.*

19. See, e.g., the analysis by Helen Longino and Ruth Doell, "Body, Bias, and Behavior: A Comparative Analysis of Reasoning in Two Areas of Biological Science," *Signs* 9:2 (1983).

20. See, e.g., Morris Berman, *The Reenchantment of the World* (Ithaca: Cornell University Press, 1981); Brian Easlea, *Witch Hunting, Magic, and the New Philosophy* (Brighton, Eng.: Harvester Press, 1980); Brian Easlea, *Fathering the Unthinkable* (London: Pluto Press, 1983); Keller, *Reflections;* Leiss, *Domination of Nature;* Carolyn Merchant, *The Death of Nature: Women, Ecology, and the Scientific Revolution* (New York: Harper & Row, 1980).

21. National Academy of Sciences, *On Being a Scientist,* 6.

22. See Harding, *The Science Question in Feminism,* 233–39.

23. See Merchant, *Death of Nature;* and Susan Bordo, *The Flight to Objectivity* (Albany: State University of New York Press, 1987).

24. For an illuminating discussion of how social and cultural values shape evidence, see Helen Longino, *Science as Social Knowledge: Values and Objectivity in Scientific Inquiry* (Princeton, N.J.: Princeton University Press, 1990).

25. Dorothy Smith, *The Everyday World as Problematic: A Feminist Sociology* (Boston: Northeastern University Press, 1987); Nancy Hartsock, "The Feminist Standpoint: Developing the Ground for a Specifically Feminist Historical Materialism," in Harding and Hintikka, *Discovering Reality;* Bettina Aptheker, *Tapestries of Life: Women's Work, Women's Consciousness, and the Meaning of Daily Life* (Amherst: University of Massachusetts Press, 1989).

26. See Donna Haraway, "Situated Knowledges: The Science Question in Feminism and the Privilege of Partial Perspective," *Feminist Studies* 14:3 (1988).

70. • *Emily Martin*

THE EGG AND THE SPERM:
How Science Has Constructed a Romance Based on Stereotypical Male–Female Roles (1991)

Emily Martin is an award-winning author and an anthropology professor at New York University. Her book *Bipolar Expeditions* won the 2009 Diana Forsythe prize for the best book of feminist anthropological research on work, science, and technology. She is also the founding editor of *Anthropology Now*. The following article, first published in *Signs: Journal of Women in Culture and Society*, is one of her most well-known and reprinted works. In it, Martin challenges how science views the female reproductive process.

The theory of the human body is always a part of a world-picture. . . .
The theory of the human body is always a part of a *fantasy*.
[James Hillman, *The Myth of Analysis*][1]

As an anthropologist, I am intrigued by the possibility that culture shapes how biological scientists describe what they discover about the natural world. If this were so, we would be learning about more than the natural world in high school biology class; we would be learning about cultural beliefs and practices as if they were part of nature. In the course of my research I realized that the picture of egg and sperm drawn in popular as well as scientific accounts of reproductive biology relies on stereotypes central to our cultural definitions of male and female. The stereotypes imply not only that female biological processes are less worthy than their male counterparts but also that women are less worthy than men. Part of my goal in writing this article is to shine a bright light on the gender stereotypes hidden within the scientific language of biology. Exposed in such a light, I hope they will lose much of their power to harm us.

EGG AND SPERM: A SCIENTIFIC FAIRY TALE

At a fundamental level, all major scientific textbooks depict male and female reproductive organs as systems for the production of valuable substances, such as eggs and sperm.[2] In the case of women, the monthly cycle is described as being designed to produce eggs and prepare a suitable place for them to be fertilized and grown—all to the end of making babies. But the enthusiasm ends there. By extolling the female cycle as a productive enterprise, menstruation must necessarily be viewed as a failure. Medical texts describe menstruation as the "debris" of the uterine lining, the result of necrosis, or death of tissue. The descriptions imply that a system has gone awry, making products of no use, not to specification, unsalable, wasted, scrap. An illustration in a widely used medical text shows menstruation as a chaotic disintegration of form, complementing the many texts that describe it as "ceasing," "dying," "losing," "denuding," "expelling."[3]

Male reproductive physiology is evaluated quite differently. One of the texts that sees menstruation as failed production employs a sort of breathless prose when it describes the maturation of sperm: "The mechanisms which guide the remarkable cellular transformation from spermatid to mature sperm remain uncertain. . . . Perhaps the most amazing characteristic of spermatogenesis is its sheer magnitude: the normal human male may manufacture several hundred million sperm per day."[4] In the classic text *Medical Physiology,* edited by Vernon Mountcastle, the male/female, productive/destructive comparison is more explicit: "Whereas the female *sheds* only a single gamete each month, the seminiferous tubules *produce* hundreds of millions of sperm each day" (emphasis mine).[5] The female author of another text marvels at the length of the microscopic seminiferous tubules, which, if uncoiled and placed end to end, "would span almost one-third of a mile!" She writes, "In an adult male these structures produce millions of sperm cells each day." Later she asks, "How is this feat accomplished?"[6] None of these texts expresses such intense enthusiasm for any female processes. It is surely no accident that the "remarkable" process of making sperm involves precisely what, in the medical view, menstruation does not: production of something deemed valuable.[7]

One could argue that menstruation and spermatogenesis are not analogous processes and, therefore, should not be expected to elicit the same kind of response. The proper female analogy to spermatogenesis, biologically, is ovulation. Yet ovulation does not merit enthusiasm in these texts either. . . .

[. . .]

But the texts have an almost dogged insistence on casting female processes in a negative light. The texts celebrate sperm production because it is continuous from puberty to senescence, while they portray egg production as inferior because it is finished at birth. This makes the female seem unproductive, but some texts will also insist that it is she who is wasteful.[8] In a section heading for *Molecular Biology of the Cell,* a best-selling text, we are told that "Oogenesis is wasteful." The text goes on to emphasize that of the seven million oogonia, or egg germ cells, in the female embryo, most degenerate in the ovary. Of those that do go on to become oocytes, or eggs, many also degenerate, so that at birth only two million eggs remain in the ovaries. Degeneration continues throughout a woman's life: by puberty 300,000 eggs remain, and only a few are present by menopause. "During the 40 or so years of a woman's reproductive life, only 400 to 500 eggs will have been released," the authors write. "All the rest will have degenerated. It is still a mystery why so many eggs are formed only to die in the ovaries."[9]

The real mystery is why the male's vast production of sperm is not seen as wasteful.[10] Assuming that a man "produces" 100 million (10^{11}) sperm per day (a conservative estimate) during an average reproductive life of sixty years, he would produce well over two trillion sperm in his lifetime. Assuming that a woman "ripens" one egg per lunar month, or thirteen per year, over the course of her forty-year reproductive life, she would total five hundred eggs in her lifetime. But the word "waste" implies an excess, too much produced. Assuming two or three offspring, for every baby a woman produces, she wastes only around two hundred eggs. For every baby a man produces, he wastes more than one trillion (10^{12}) sperm.

How is it that positive images are denied to the bodies of women? A look at language—in this case, scientific language—provides the first clue. Take the egg and the sperm.[13] It is remarkable how "femininely" the egg behaves and how "masculinely" the sperm.[14] The egg is seen as large and passive.[15] It does not *move* or *journey,* but passively "is transported," "is swept,"[16] or even "drifts"[17] along the fallopian tube. In utter contrast, sperm are small, "streamlined,"[18] and invariably active. They "deliver" their genes to the egg, "activate the developmental program of the egg,"[19] and have a "velocity" that is often remarked upon.[20] Their tails are "strong" and efficiently powered.[21]

Together with the forces of ejaculation, they can "propel the semen into the deepest recesses of the vagina."[22] For this they need "energy," "fuel,"[23] so that with a "whiplashlike motion and strong lurches"[24] they can "burrow through the egg coat"[25] and "penetrate" it.[26]

At its extreme, the age-old relationship of the egg and the sperm takes on a royal or religious patina. The egg coat, its protective barrier, is sometimes called its "vestments," a term usually reserved for sacred, religious dress. The egg is said to have a "corona,"[27] a crown, and to be accompanied by "attendant cells."[28] It is holy, set apart and above, the queen to the sperm's king. The egg is also passive, which means it must depend on sperm for rescue. Gerald Schatten and Helen Schatten liken the egg's role to that of Sleeping Beauty: "a dormant bride awaiting her mate's magic kiss, which instills the spirit that brings her to life."[29] Sperm, by contrast, have a "mission,"[30] which is to "move through the female genital tract in quest of the ovum."[31] One popular account has it that the sperm carry out a "perilous journey" into the "warm darkness," where some fall away "exhausted." "Survivors" "assault" the egg, the successful candidates "surrounding the prize."[32] Part of the urgency of this journey, in more scientific terms, is that "once released from the supportive environment of the ovary, an egg will die within hours unless rescued by a sperm."[33] The wording stresses the fragility and dependency of the egg, even though the same text acknowledges elsewhere that sperm also live for only a few hours.[34]

[. . .]

There is another way that sperm, despite their small size, can be made to loom in importance over the egg. In a collection of scientific papers, an electron micrograph of an enormous egg and tiny sperm is titled "A Portrait of the Sperm."[35] This is a little like showing a photo of a dog and calling it a picture of the fleas. Granted, microscopic sperm are harder to photograph than eggs, which are just large enough to see with the naked eye. But surely the use of the term "portrait," a word associated with the powerful and wealthy, is significant. Eggs have only micrographs or pictures, not portraits.

[. . .]

The more common picture—egg as damsel in distress, shielded only by her sacred garments; sperm as heroic warrior to the rescue—cannot be proved to be dictated by the biology of these events. While the "facts" of biology may not *always* be constructed in cultural terms, I would argue that in this case they are. The degree of metaphorical content in these descriptions, the extent to which differences between egg and sperm are emphasized, and the parallels between cultural stereotypes of male and female behavior and the character of egg and sperm all point to this conclusion.

NEW RESEARCH, OLD IMAGERY

As new understandings of egg and sperm emerge, textbook gender imagery is being revised. But the new research, far from escaping the stereotypical representations of egg and sperm, simply replicates elements of textbook gender imagery in a different form. The persistence of this imagery calls to mind what Ludwik Fleck termed "the self-contained" nature of scientific thought. As he described it, "the interaction between what is already known, what remains to be learned, and those who are to apprehend it, go to ensure harmony within the system. But at the same time they also preserve the harmony of illusions, which is quite secure within the confines of a given thought style."[36] We need to understand the way in which the cultural content in scientific descriptions changes as biological discoveries unfold, and whether that cultural content is solidly entrenched or easily changed.

In all of the texts quoted above, sperm are described as penetrating the egg, and specific substances on a sperm's head are described as binding to the egg. Recently, this description of events was rewritten in a biophysics lab at Johns Hopkins University—transforming the egg from the passive to the active party.[37]

Prior to this research, it was thought that the zona, the inner vestments of the egg, formed an impenetrable barrier. Sperm overcame the barrier by mechanically burrowing through, thrashing their tails and slowly working their way along. Later research showed that the sperm released digestive enzymes that chemically broke down the zona; thus, scientists presumed that the sperm used mechanical *and* chemical means to get through to the egg.

In this recent investigation, the researchers began to ask questions about the mechanical force of the sperm's tail. (The lab's goal was to develop a contraceptive that worked topically on sperm.) They discovered, to their great surprise, that the forward thrust of sperm is extremely weak, which contradicts the assumption that sperm are forceful penetrators.[38] Rather than thrusting forward, the sperm's head was now seen to move mostly back and forth. The sideways motion of the sperm's tail makes the head move sideways with a force that is ten times stronger than its forward movement. So even if the overall force of the sperm were strong enough to mechanically break the zona, most of its force would be directed sideways rather than forward. In fact, its strongest tendency, by tenfold, is to escape by attempting to pry itself off the egg. Sperm, then, must be exceptionally efficient at *escaping* from any cell surface they contact. And the surface of the egg must be designed to trap the sperm and prevent their escape. Otherwise, few if any sperm would reach the egg.

The researchers at Johns Hopkins concluded that the sperm and egg stick together because of adhesive molecules on the surfaces of each. The egg traps the sperm and adheres to it so tightly that the sperm's head is forced to lie flat against the surface of the zona, a little bit, they told me, "like Br'er Rabbit getting more and more stuck to tar baby the more he wriggles." The trapped sperm continues to wiggle ineffectually side to side. The mechanical force of its tail is so weak that a sperm cannot break even one chemical bond. This is where the digestive enzymes released by the sperm come in. If they start to soften the zona just at the tip of the sperm and the sides remain stuck, then the weak, flailing sperm can get oriented in the right direction and make it through

the zona—provided that its bonds to the zona dissolve as it moves in.

Although this new version of the saga of the egg and the sperm broke through cultural expectations, the researchers who made the discovery continued to write papers and abstracts as if the sperm were the active party who attacks, binds, penetrates, and enters the egg. The only difference was that sperm were now seen as performing these actions weakly.[39] Not until August 1987, more than three years after the findings described above, did these researchers reconceptualize the process to give the egg a more active role. They began to describe the zona as an aggressive sperm catcher, covered with adhesive molecules that can capture a sperm with a single bond and clasp it to the zona's surface.[40] In the words of their published account: "The innermost vestment, the *zona pellucida*, is a glycoprotein shell, which captures and tethers the sperm before they penetrate it. . . . The sperm is captured at the initial contact between the sperm tip and the *zona*. . . . Since the thrust [of the sperm] is much smaller than the force needed to break a single affinity bond, the first bond made upon the tip-first meeting of the sperm and *zona* can result in the capture of the sperm."[41]

[. . .]

SOCIAL IMPLICATIONS: THINKING BEYOND

All three of these revisionist accounts of egg and sperm cannot seem to escape the hierarchical imagery of older accounts. Even though each new account gives the egg a larger and more active role, taken together they bring into play another cultural stereotype: woman as a dangerous and aggressive threat. In the Johns Hopkins lab's revised model, the egg ends up as the female aggressor who "captures and tethers" the sperm with her sticky zona, rather like a spider lying in wait in her web.[42] The Schatten lab has the egg's nucleus "interrupt" the sperm's dive with a "sudden and swift" rush by which she "clasps the sperm and guides its nucleus to the center."[43]

Wassarman's description of the surface of the egg "covered with thousands of plasma membrane-bound projections, called microvilli" that reach out and clasp the sperm adds to the spiderlike imagery.[44]

These images grant the egg an active role but at the cost of appearing disturbingly aggressive. Images of woman as dangerous and aggressive, the femme fatale who victimizes men, are widespread in Western literature and culture.[45] More specific is the connection of spider imagery with the idea of an engulfing, devouring mother.[46] New data did not lead scientists to eliminate gender stereotypes in their descriptions of egg and sperm. Instead, scientists simply began to describe egg and sperm in different, but no less damaging, terms.

Can we envision a less stereotypical view? Biology itself provides another model that could be applied to the egg and the sperm. The cybernetic model—with its feedback loops, flexible adaptation to change, coordination of the parts within a whole, evolution over time, and changing response to the environment—is common in genetics, endocrinology, and ecology and has a growing influence in medicine in general.[47] This model has the potential to shift our imagery from the negative, in which the female reproductive system is castigated both for not producing eggs after birth and for producing (and thus wasting) too many eggs overall, to something more positive. The female reproductive system could be seen as responding to the environment (pregnancy or menopause), adjusting to monthly changes (menstruation), and flexibly changing from reproductivity after puberty to nonreproductivity later in life. The sperm and egg's interaction could also be described in cybernetic terms. J. F. Hartman's research in reproductive biology demonstrated fifteen years ago that if an egg is killed by being pricked with a needle, live sperm cannot get through the zona.[47] Clearly, this evidence shows that the egg and sperm *do* interact on more mutual terms, making biology's refusal to portray them that way all the more disturbing.

We would do well to be aware, however, that cybernetic imagery is hardly neutral. In the past, cybernetic models have played an important part in the imposition of social control. These models inherently provide a way of thinking about a "field" of interacting components. Once the field can be seen, it can become the object of new forms of knowledge, which in turn can allow new forms of social control to be exerted over the components of the field. During the 1950s, for example, medicine began to recognize the psychosocial *environment* of the patient: the patient's family and its psychodynamics. Professions such as social work began to focus on this new environment, and the resulting knowledge became one way to further control the patient. Patients began to be seen not as isolated, individual bodies, but as psychosocial entities located in an "ecological" system: management of "the patient's psychology was a new entrée to patient control."[48]

The models that biologists use to describe their data can have important social effects. During the nineteenth century, the social and natural sciences strongly influenced each other: the social ideas of Malthus about how to avoid the natural increase of the poor inspired Darwin's *Origin of Species*.[49] Once the *Origin* stood as a description of the natural world, complete with competition and market struggles, it could be reimported into social science as social Darwinism, in order to justify the social order of the time. What we are seeing now is similar: the importation of cultural ideas about passive females and heroic males into the "personalities" of gametes. This amounts to the "implanting of social imagery on representations of nature so as to lay a firm basis for reimporting exactly that same imagery as natural explanations of social phenomena."[50]

Further research would show us exactly what social effects are being wrought from the biological imagery of egg and sperm. At the very least, the imagery keeps alive some of the hoariest old stereotypes about weak damsels in distress and their strong male rescuers. That these stereotypes are now being written in at the level of the *cell* constitutes a powerful move to make them seem so natural as to be beyond alteration.

The stereotypical imagery might also encourage people to imagine that what results from the interaction of egg and sperm—a fertilized egg—is the result of deliberate "human" action at the cellular level. Whatever the intentions of the human couple, in this microscopic "culture" a cellular "bride" (or femme fatale) and a cellular "groom" (her victim) make a cellular baby. Rosalind Petchesky points out that through visual representations such as sonograms, we are given *"images of younger and younger, and tinier and tinier, fetuses being 'saved.'"* This leads to "the point of visibility being 'pushed back' *indefinitely.*"[51] Endowing egg and sperm with intentional action, a key aspect of personhood in our culture, lays the foundation for the point of viability being pushed back to the moment of fertilization. This will likely lead to greater acceptance of technological developments and new forms of scrutiny and manipulation, for the benefit of these inner "persons": court-ordered restrictions on a pregnant woman's activities in order to protect her fetus, fetal surgery, amniocentesis, and rescinding of abortion rights, to name but a few examples.[52]

Even if we succeed in substituting more egalitarian, interactive metaphors to describe the activities of egg and sperm, and manage to avoid the pitfalls of cybernetic models, we would still be guilty of endowing cellular entities with personhood. More crucial, then, than what *kinds* of personalities we bestow on cells is the very fact that we are doing it at all. This process could ultimately have the most disturbing social consequences.

One clear feminist challenge is to wake up sleeping metaphors in science, particularly those involved in descriptions of the egg and the sperm. Although the literary convention is to call such metaphors "dead," they are not so much dead as sleeping, hidden within the scientific content of texts—and all the more powerful for it.[53] Waking up such metaphors, by becoming aware of when we are projecting cultural imagery onto what we study, will improve our ability to investigate and understand nature. Waking up such metaphors, by becoming aware of their implications, will rob them of their power to naturalize our social conventions about gender.

NOTES

1. James Hillman, *The Myth of Analysis* (Evanston, Ill.: Northwestern University Press, 1972), 220.

2. The textbooks I consulted are the main ones used in classes for undergraduate premedical students or medical students (or those held on reserve in the library for these classes) during the past few years at Johns Hopkins University. These texts are widely used at other universities in the country as well.

3. Arthur C. Guyton, *Physiology of the Human Body*, 6th ed. (Philadelphia: Saunders College Publishing, 1984), 624.

4. Arthur J. Vander, James H. Sherman, and Dorothy S. Luciano, *Human Physiology: The Mechanisms of Body Function*, 3d ed. (New York: McGraw Hill, 1980), 483–84.

5. Vernon B. Mountcastle, *Medical Physiology*, 14th ed. (London: Mosby, 1980), 2:1624.

6. Eldra Pearl Solomon, *Human Anatomy and Physiology* (New York: CBS College Publishing, 1983), 678.

7. For elaboration, see Emily Martin, *The Woman in the Body: A Cultural Analysis of Reproduction* (Boston: Beacon, 1987), 27–53.

8. I have found but one exception to the opinion that the female is wasteful: "Smallpox being the nasty disease it is, one might expect nature to have designed antibody molecules with combining sites that specifically recognize the epitopes on smallpox virus. Nature differs from technology, however: it thinks nothing of wastefulness. (For example, rather than improving the chance that a spermatozoon will meet an egg cell, nature finds it easier to produce millions of spermatozoa.)" (Niels Kaj Jerne, "The Immune System," *Scientific American* 229, no. 1 [July 1973]: 53). Thanks to a *Signs* reviewer for bringing this reference to my attention.

9. Bruce Alberts et al., *Molecular Biology of the Cell* (New York: Garland, 1983), 795.

10. In her essay "Have Only Men Evolved?" (in *Discovering Reality: Feminist Perspectives on Epistemology, Metaphysics, Methodology, and Philosophy of Science,* ed. Sandra Harding and Merrill B. Hintikka [Dordrecht: Reidel, 1983], 45–69, esp. 60–61), Ruth Hubbard points out that sociobiologists have said the female invests more energy than the male in the production of her large gametes, claiming that this explains why the female provides parental care. Hubbard questions whether it "really takes more "energy" to generate the one or relatively few eggs than the large excess of sperms required to achieve fertilization." For further critique of how the greater size of eggs is interpreted in sociobiology, see Donna Haraway, "Investment Strategies for the Evolving Portfolio

of Primate Females," in *Body/Politics,* ed. Mary Jacobus, Evelyn Fox Keller, and Sally Shuttleworth (New York: Routledge, 1990), 155–56.

11. The sources I used for this article provide compelling information on interactions among sperm. Lack of space prevents me from taking up this theme here, but the elements include competition, hierarchy, and sacrifice. For a newspaper report, see Malcolm W. Browne, "Some Thoughts on Self Sacrifice," *New York Times* (July 5, 1988), C6. For a literary rendition, see John Barth, "Night-Sea Journey," in his *Lost in the Funhouse* (Garden City, N.Y.: Doubleday, 1968), 3–13.

12. See Carol Delaney, "The Meaning of Paternity and the Virgin Birth Debate," *Man* 21, no. 3 (September 1986): 494–513. She discusses the difference between this scientific view that women contribute genetic material to the fetus and the claim of long-standing Western folk theories that the origin and identity of the fetus comes from the male, as in the metaphor of planting a seed in soil.

13. For a suggested direct link between human behavior and purportedly passive eggs and active sperm, [see] Erik H. Erikson, "Inner and Outer Space: Reflections on Womanhood," *Daedalus* 93, no. 2 (Spring 1964): 582–606, esp. 591.

14. Guyton (n. 3 above), 619; and Mountcastle (n. 5 above), 1609.

15. Jonathan Miller and David Pelham, *The Facts of Life* (New York: Viking Penguin, 1984), 5.

16. Alberts et al., 796.

17. Ibid., 796.

18. See, e.g., William F. Ganong, *Review of Medical Physiology*, 7th ed. (Los Altos, Calif.: Lange Medical Publications, 1975), 322.

19. Alberts et al. (n. 9 above), 796.

20. Guyton, 615.

21. Solomon (n. 6 above), 683.

22. Vander, Sherman, and Luciano (n. 4 above), 4th ed. (1985), 580.

23. Alberts et al., 796.

24. All biology texts quoted above use the word "penetrate."

25. Solomon, 700.

26. A. Beldecos et al., "The Importance of Feminist Critique for Contemporary Cell Biology," *Hypatia* 3, no. 1 (Spring 1988): 61–76.

27. Gerald Schatten and Helen Schatten, "The Energetic Egg," *Medical World News* 23 (January 23, 1984): 51–53, esp. 51.

28. Alberts et al., 796.

29. Guyton (n. 3 above), 613.

30. Miller and Pelham (n. 15 above), 7.

31. Alberts et al. (n. 9 above), 804.

32. Ibid., 801.

33. Lennart Nilsson, "A Portrait of the Sperm," in *The Functional Anatomy of the Spermatozoon*, ed. Bjorn A. Afzelius (New York: Pergamon, 1975), 79-82.

34. Ludwik Fleck, *Genesis and Development of a Scientific Fact*, ed. Thaddeus J. Trenn and Robert K. Merton (Chicago: University of Chicago Press, 1979), 38.

35. Jay M. Baltz carried out the research I describe when he was a graduate student in the Thomas C. Jenkins Department of Biophysics at Johns Hopkins University.

36. Far less is known about the physiology of sperm than comparable female substances, which some feminists claim is no accident. Greater scientific scrutiny of female reproduction has long enabled the burden of birth control to be placed on women. In this case, the researchers' discovery did not depend on development of any new technology. The experiments made use of glass pipettes, a manometer, and a simple microscope, all of which have been available for more than one hundred years.

37. Jay Baltz and Richard A. Cone, "What Force Is Needed to Tether a Sperm?" (abstract for Society for the Study of Reproduction, 1985), and "Flagellar Torque on the Head Determines the Force Needed to Tether a Sperm" (abstract for Biophysical Society, 1986).

38. Jay M. Baltz, David F. Katz, and Richard A. Cone, "The Mechanics of the Sperm-Egg Interaction at the Zona Pellucida," *Biophysical Journal* 54, no. 4 (October 1988): 643–54. Lab members were somewhat familiar with work on metaphors in the biology of female reproduction. Richard Cone, who runs the lab, is my husband, and he talked with them about my earlier research on the subject from time to time. Even though my current research focuses on biological imagery and I heard about the lab's work from my husband every day, I myself did not recognize the role of imagery in the sperm research until many weeks after the period of research and writing I describe. Therefore, I assume that any awareness the lab members may have had about how underlying metaphor might be guiding this particular research was fairly inchoate.

39. Ibid., 643, 650.

40. Baltz, Katz, and Cone (n. 38 above), 643, 650.

41. Schatten and Schatten, 53.

42. Wassarman, "The Biology and Chemistry of Fertilization," 557.

43. Mary Ellman, *Thinking about Women* (New York: Harcourt Brace Jovanovich, 1968), 140; Nina Auerbach, *Woman and the Demon* (Cambridge, Mass.: Harvard University Press, 1982), esp. 186.

44. Kenneth Alan Adams, "Arachnophobia: Love American Style," *Journal of Psychoanalytic Anthropology* 4, no. 2 (1981): 157–97.

45. William Ray Arney and Bernard Bergen, *Medicine and the Management of Living* (Chicago: University of Chicago Press, 1984).

46. J. F. Hartman, R. B. Gwatkin, and C. F. Hutchison, "Early Contact Interactions between Mammalian Gametes *In Vitro*," *Proceedings of the National Academy of Sciences (U.S.)* 69, no. 10 (1972): 2767–69.

47. Arney and Bergen, 68.

48. Ruth Hubbard, "Have Only Men Evolved?" (n. 10 above), 51–52.

49. David Harvey, personal communication, November 1989.

50. Rosalind Petchesky, "Fetal Images: The Power of Visual Culture in the Politics of Reproduction," *Feminist Studies* 13, no. 2 (Summer 1987): 263–92, esp. 272.

51. Rita Arditti, Renate Klein, and Shelley Minden, *Test-Tube Women* (London: Pandora, 1984); Ellen Goodman, "Whose Right to Life?" *Baltimore Sun* (November 17, 1987); Tamar Lewin, "Courts Acting to Force Care of the Unborn," *New York Times* (November 23, 1987), A1 and B10; Susan Irwin and Brigitte Jordan, "Knowledge, Practice, and Power: Court Ordered Cesarean Sections," *Medical Anthropology Quarterly* 1, no. 3 (September 1987): 319–34.

52. Thanks to Elizabeth Fee and David Spain, who in February 1989 and April 1989, respectively, made points related to this.

71. • *Liam Lair*

SEXOLOGY, EUGENICS, AND HIRSCHFELD'S TRANSVESTITES (NEW)

Liam Lair is an instructor in women's and gender studies at Louisiana University. His recent publications include "Interrogating Trans* Subjectivities in the Archive" in *Out of the Closet, Into the Archive,* eds. Cantrell and Stone (Albany: SUNY Press, 2015) and "Embodied Knowledge and Accessible Community: An Oral History of Four Rehearsals and a Performance," *Oral History Review* 43 no.1 (2016). He was the John Money Fellow for Scholars of Sexology at the Kinsey Institute in 2014, where he conducted archival research for his larger project that examines the intersections of eugenics and sexology, of which the following article is a part.

I recently saw a new doctor for a cold. Included in the summary of my visit appeared the diagnosis: "Transsexualism with unspecified sexual history." At no point did I consent to having transsexualism on my record—my next insurer might understand this diagnosis as a "pre-existing condition"—yet the doctor took the liberty to label me this way.

The fact that my transsexualism is understood as a "condition" bespeaks a long history of pathologization, one that aligned transsexualism with mental disability. Transsexualism by definition indicates a deviation from the norm—a gender identity that can be *diagnosed* by medical experts. This diagnosis, and to whom it is applied, has historically dictated who can access medical care, whose identity is medicalized, and who is understood to have a "normal" gender. Thus it is important to explore how these diagnoses emerged, why they were created and by whom, and what are the effects of this history today.

Sexology, eugenics, and the ways in which they have intersected as disciplines, played a significant role in the history of gender diagnoses. Sexology is the study of human sexuality. Eugenics is the philosophical and scientific approach to managing the population through breeding a better *white* race. Historically, eugenics and sexology overlapped in part because many sexologists, including scientists, physicians, psychiatrists, and other professionals, also identified as eugenicists. Eugenicists, focused on the improvement and degradation of genes, believed that "degenerate conditions" like criminality or sexual deviance were inherited and that controlling reproduction would solve these social issues. People were labeled "degenerate" if they were seen as "deficient" or as individuals who "threatened to undermine established race and gender hierarchies" because of their "lesser" physical or mental constitution—the latter being an ableist construct that we might now refer to as a mental disability (Kline 2).

There are many dangers in the scientific justification for labeling people as "degenerate." Among these was the violation of basic human rights through involuntary institutionalization, sterilization, or imprisonment. As a concept, degeneracy was also problematic because its definitions were culturally specific and changed dramatically over time. For example, if a white, heterosexual, middle- or upper-class woman in the early 1900s was sexually active before marriage, she could be institutionalized with the diagnosis of "degenerate." Fifty years later this was virtually unheard of. Despite the inherent dangers of this diagnosis, eugenicists widely applied it, and by the 1910s, eugenics had grown from a small group of scientists researching genetic heredity to a broadly influential field of scientific and social theory.

The notion that transsexualism is *abnormal* emerges from this history of sexological and eugenical discourses and originated with the medical diagnosis of transvestism. American and European sexologists constructed the diagnosis of transvestism in the first decade of the 1900s. "Transvestite" referred to individuals who desired to dress in the clothes of the opposite sex as well as those who desired to *be* the opposite sex. It was a precursor to the term "transsexual," which emerged in the 1940s. While eugenicists applied the word "degenerate" to those deemed undesirable, so too did sexologists use it when constructing the diagnostic category of transvestite.

Yet the scholarship on transvestism typically focuses on how sexology intersected with popular culture, medicine, psychiatry, and politics and fails to explore eugenical influences within these fields or on the diagnosis (see Meyerowitz et al.). Likewise, most historical works about eugenics do not discuss transvestism (see Terry and Urla; Somerville; Ordover; McWhorter; Gilman). This essay addresses this oversight and reveals how eugenics intersected with sexology to significantly influence understandings of gendered abnormality.

In 1910, German physician Magnus Hirschfeld, credited with coining the term "transvestite," published his now-famous treatise *Transvestites: The Erotic Drive to Cross-Dress*. Hirschfeld's treatise provides insight into how transvestites, particularly those seeking medical intervention, were caught in a web of politics around the evolving norms of sexuality, race, and disability. Furthermore, tracing the impact of Hirschfeld's text up to our present historical context provides insight into the ways in which sexology and eugenics intersected at the site of trans*[1] diagnoses and shaped understandings of gendered abnormality, as well as how the vestiges of eugenics continue to be present in current-day figurations of transsexual diagnosis and identity.

THE RISE OF EUGENICS

In the decade prior to Hirschfeld's publication, eugenics began to command attention. Anthropologist Francis Galton, who coined the term "eugenics" in 1883, wanted eugenics "to become a new, guiding religion for a secular, rational age: namely knowledge of, and control over, human procreation" (Bland and

Doan 165). By the turn of the century, eugenicists unabashedly expressed desire to eliminate "degenerates," or the "unfit." In 1906, psychiatrist August Forel declared that "it is not our object to create a new human race of superior beings, but simply to cause gradual elimination of the unfit" (168). Those deemed unworthy of producing children varied over time, but several "categories" of individuals were consistently designated as "unfit." Among his "Types to Eliminate," Forel listed "criminals, lunatics, and imbeciles, and all individuals who are irresponsible, mischievous, quarrelsome or amoral" (512). Homosexuals, or "inverts," were closely associated with each label; sexual deviation was often believed to emerge from or lead to criminal behavior, lunacy, and imbecility (512).

As an ideology invested in the future of the "race" through genetic improvement, eugenics provided scientific support for notions of white racial superiority as well as the belief that nonwhite races were genetically inferior and polluting. Whiteness indicated superior intellect, mental health, and physicality, inflecting presumptions about who was "eugenically valuable" and could produce *normal* offspring. Eugenics perpetuated white supremacy under the guise of "scientific knowledge" as eugenicists promoted the creation of a fit, white race. Eugenics aligned degeneracy with disability, particularly psychiatric disability. In this way, "pure" whiteness necessitated able-mindedness, casting all others as degenerate. Eugenics was pervasive in the United States, and controlling reproduction, and thus sex and marriage, was key to its success, as was detecting, diagnosing, and controlling distinctions between normal and abnormal minds and bodies. Transvestism and transsexualism, as diagnoses of abnormality, are rooted in this history.

FROM INVERSION TO INTERMEDIARIES

By 1910, distinctions between gender, sex, and sexuality were beginning to take shape. It was in this context that Hirschfeld explored the "condition" of transvestism. Transvestism as a diagnosis would consolidate *ab*normal manhood and womanhood, further solidifying what it meant to be a "normal" man or woman. Hirschfeld's understanding of "normal" gender, his explanations of heredity and mental illness, his anxiety concerning marriage and reproduction, and his praise of eugenicists' assessment of transvestism all demonstrated the influence of eugenics in his writing.

Rather than focusing on sexual inversion, Hirschfeld understood transvestism within a framework of "intermediaries." He proposed four types of intermediaries, defined as individuals who failed to embody male masculinity or female femininity and deviated from the norm in at least one of these ways: (1) *sexual organs* (individuals known as hermaphrodites); (2) *other physical characteristics* (individuals with secondary sex characteristics of the opposite sex, i.e., men with gynecomastia or women with facial hair); (3) *sex drive* (those engaging in homosexual or nonnormative heterosexual sex acts); or (4) *other emotional characteristics* (individuals labeled as transvestites; Hirschfeld 220). This theory of intermediaries relied on a clear division between femininity and masculinity, both rooted in a white, middle-class, able-minded, and able-bodied norm. Hirschfeld never directly mentions race, but his explication of women's sexuality, that they should be "the receiver, responder . . . the more passive partner" to a man, mirrors cultural expectations based on understandings of white sexuality (216). Black women were constructed as "beyond the moral constraints of white sexuality codes" that included "purity, piety, domesticity, and submissiveness . . . the four ideals towards which (white) women should strive" (Maurer 39). Instead, black women were often portrayed as lascivious and hypersexual (Skidmore 292). Throughout his writings, Hirschfeld's understanding of "normal" femininity, therefore, mirrored that of white femininity.

Hirschfeld was among the first to suggest that transvestism was related to but distinct from homosexuality. This framed transvestism as gendered inversion rather than sexual inversion. However, just as with sexual inversion, he incorporated heredity and degeneracy into the diagnosis of transvestite.

In eleven of the seventeen cases discussed, Hirschfeld commented on degeneracy within the transvestite's families. He argued that in each case "a neurotic disposition . . . could be suggestive of a present degenerative constitution" (144). Commenting on degeneracy and heredity was not only a common eugenic practice of the time but was expected when discussing deviance. Hirschfeld's reliance on eugenic strategies reified the coconstitutive nature of transvestism and other "degenerate" conditions.

Hirschfeld's distinctions within "intermediary" categories are important to note. He categorized males who cross-dressed intermittently together with those whose sole desire was to *be* women. However, he distinguished transvestism from *metamorphosis sexualis paranoica,* a congenital "mental illness." He argued that most transvestites knew that they were not *really* women, even if they sometimes felt like one. Those who truly believed they *were* women, Hirschfeld believed, suffered from insanity or delusions. Hirschfeld's association of gendered abnormality and "congenital mental illness" was not uncommon. The terms describing "mental illness" varied, but they almost always included the "unfit" and sexual "perverts" and were more often applied to poor people and people of color. In line with eugenic goals of bettering the race, these individuals were either sterilized or strongly encouraged to *not* reproduce (235).

Hirschfeld's discussion of marriage and reproduction also revealed his reliance on eugenics. He asserted that heterosexual love was normal, even if one individual cross-dressed (327). However, Hirschfeld questioned the "suitability" of marriages between transvestites and their opposite-sex partners, despite his indication that many transvestites were in happy, heterosexual marriages. He was particularly doubtful about reproduction within these marriages. He believed that the transvestite's deviation could "lead to offspring who are psychologically disunified . . . [and] unstable, degenerated individuals" (235). He believed that transvestites were not "[fit] to enter into marriage" or to reproduce (235). Hirschfeld aligned himself with eugenics when he expressed anxieties concerning transvestites marrying and reproducing, two actions that eugenicists sought to control.

Last, Hirschfeld praised eugenicist August Forel's etiology of transvestism. Forel's examination of one transvestite provided "proof" that transvestism was a psychosexual condition "predetermined by heredity" (qtd. in Hirschfeld 321). Hirschfeld cited Forel as an expert source, supporting his hereditary explanation for transvestism as a degenerate condition, an explanation that was explicitly informed by eugenic logic. Aligning himself with Forel and this particular etiology of transvestism indicates Hirschfeld's belief in the accuracy of eugenic explanation for degenerative "conditions."

By the 1920s, it was impossible to discuss transvestism without also discussing eugenics, due in part to the wide influence of Hirschfeld's book. Eugenicist thinking remained central to the solidification of "transvestite" and "transsexual" as diagnoses over the next forty years. Reading Hirschfeld's text with this in mind, while also recognizing the discursive and historical context in which he wrote, makes visible how understandings of gender and eugenics were mutually productive.

A LASTING IMPACT

In the late 1800s, Francis Galton believed the body "told the truth about one's identity no matter how much one tried to disguise it" (qtd. in Serlin 12–13). Medical and legal classifications were, and continue to be, based on the "truth" of the body. Individuals who change the gendered presentation of their bodies are often accused of hiding this so-called "truth" of their bodies—their sex assigned at birth. This "truth" has haunted transsexuals for over a hundred years. Constructions of transsexualism are still rooted in ableist notions of psychiatric wellness, and most must undergo a year of therapy to access surgical intervention. Trans people are still seen as unfit parents, with trans people losing custody of children based solely on their gender identity (see

Cisek v. Cisek). Transsexual narratives from the 1910s are often still required for access to medical intervention today. Many trans* people must identify as a feminine woman or masculine man and be deemed "mentally healthy" in order to access care. For those like myself who have accessed medical intervention, the diagnosis can be forced upon us without consent and bespeaks an unequal power relationship between patients and doctors that mirrors those of the early twentieth century.

While current descriptions of transsexuals do not include terms like "degeneracy," its vestigial meanings remain. The present-day search for genetic or hereditary causes for transsexualism are rooted in this history of eugenics. Trans* diagnoses will always fail to describe the complexity of cross-gender identification. This does not minimize the ways in which they reflect and are inseparable from the histories from which they emerged, a history informed by a eugenic movement steeped in racist, ableist, and heterosexist discourses. Acknowledging this history is crucial for understanding what is at stake for inhabiting these diagnoses, as well as how trans* communities advocate for future healthcare access.

NOTE

1. Most individuals who identified as transvestites in 1910 now use the term "cross-dresser." "Transvestite" is often understood as a derogatory term, as is "hermaphrodite." Most individuals use the terms "cross-dresser" and "intersex," respectively. The "*" following "trans" indicates the terms beginning with the word "trans." Some examples include transgender or transfeminine. It is also important to note that not all trans people desire medical intervention.

WORKS CITED

Bland, Lucy, and Laura Doan, editors. *Sexology Uncensored: The Documents of Sexual Science.* U of Chicago P, 1998.

Cisek v. Cisek, 409 NW 2d 233. Minneapolis Court of Appeals, 1987.

Forel, August. *The Sexual Question: A Scientific, Psychological, Hygienic and Sociological Study.* 1906. Translated by C.F. Marshall. *Project Gutenberg,* 2009, gutenberg.polytechnic .edu.na/2/9/9/0/29903/29903-h/29903-h.htm.

Gilman, Sander L. *Difference and Pathology: Stereotypes of Sexuality, Race, and Madness.* Cornell UP, 1985.

Hirschfeld, Magnus. *Transvestites: The Erotic Drive to Cross Dress.* Translated by M. A. Lombardi, Prometheus Books, 1910.

King, Dave. *The Transvestite and the Transsexual: Public Categories and Private Identities.* Avebury Books, 1993.

Kline, Wendy. *Building a Better Race: Gender, Sexuality, and Eugenics from the Turn of the Century to the Baby Boom.* U of California P, 2001.

Maurer, Serena. "Embodied Public Policies: The Sexual Stereotyping of Black Women in the Design and Implementation of U.S. Policies." *Journal of Public and International Affairs,* vol. 11, 2000, pp. 36–51.

McWhorter, Ladelle. *Racism and Sexual Oppression in Anglo-America: A Genealogy.* Indiana UP, 2009.

Meyerowitz, Joanne. "Sex Change and the Popular Press." *GLQ: A Journal of Lesbian & Gay Studies,* vol. 4, no. 2, 1998, pp. 159–187.

Ordover, Nancy. *American Eugenics: Race, Queer Anatomy, and the Science of Nationalism.* U of Minnesota P, 2003.

Serlin, David. *Replaceable You: Engineering the Body in Postwar America.* U of Chicago P, 2004.

Skidmore, Emily. "Constructing the "Good Transsexual": Christine Jorgensen, Whiteness, and Heteronormativity in the Mid-Twentieth-Century Press." *Feminist Studies,* vol. 37, no. 2, 2011, pp. 270–300.

Somerville, Siobhan B. *Queering the Color Line: Race and the Invention of Homosexuality in American Culture.* Duke UP, 2000.

Stryker, Susan. *Transgender History.* Seal Press, 2008.

Terry, Jennifer, and Jacqueline Urla. *Deviant Bodies: Critical Perspectives on Difference in Science and Popular Culture.* Indiana UP, 1995.

72. • *Clare Jen*

FEMINIST HACTIVISMS:
Countering Technophilia and Fictional Promises (new)

Clare C. Jen is an assistant professor in the Women's and Gender Studies Program and the Department of Biology at Denison University. Her areas of inquiry are in feminist studies of science and technology, critical race and gender studies in public health, and cross-disciplinary approaches to feminist "laboratory" practices. Her works have been published in *Feminist Formations*, *Ethnic Studies Review*, *Rhizomes: Cultural Studies in Emerging Knowledge*, and *Knowing New Biotechnologies: Social Aspects of Technological Convergence* (2015). In the following essay, Jen challenges dominant narratives of technoscientific innovation and poses the concept of "feminist hacktivism."

Stories told about technological innovations have long held my curiosity. As a young girl, I didn't read the magazines my friends brought to school, like *Tiger Beat* and *YM*. I immersed myself in the latest issues of *Popular Mechanics* and *Discover* that littered our breakfast table. Tales about cutting-edge machines, tools, and the human-constructed world held me in awe. Thinking back, I would cast myself as a naive "technophile," not yet mindful of technology's capacity to harm and disrupt. Unlike "technophobes" who have aversions toward science and technology, technophiles are "unabashed technoscience enthusiast[s]" (Eglash 79). (Simply stated, "technoscience" refers to science and technology in society.)

My outlook as a technophile would be problematized in my first semester at college. I was enrolled in History of Science and Technology in Medicine. Due to a fluke (too many students, not enough books), I was assigned Audre Lorde's *The Cancer Journals* (1980) for a presentation. Neither the professor nor I was familiar with the text, so I read without expectations. At first, Lorde stunned—even rattled—me, then she roused me from my technophilic slumber. She details a hospital visit from American Cancer Society's Reach to Recovery program following her radical mastectomy. The volunteer visitor strongly advocated Lorde look on "the bright side of things" (56) and don a breast prosthesis—or an artificial breast form that mimics the appearance of breasts—with the promise that Lorde would "never know the difference" (42). To Lorde, this was clearly a fictional promise. Self-described as a "44 year old Black Lesbian Feminist" (56), she contends that prostheses mask breast loss, emphasize "physical pretense," and render silent a woman's feelings of loss and anger toward cancer's causative and correlative factors (57). Her refusal to wear the prosthesis—least of which defied gendered, sexualized, and classed rules of social decorum—challenged mainstream complacency in the political economy of breast cancer culture.

On my dorm room radio, third wave feminist icon Ani Difranco crooned "every tool is a weapon if you hold it right." This serendipitous mingling of Lorde and Difranco inspired my first semester thesis: context matters when appraising a technology's potential to help or harm. I define *technologies* here as objects, techniques, processes, or apparatuses designed to accomplish tasks. Technologies are not simply either "good" or "bad," yet they are not neutral. Promissory narratives conjure stories and anticipations about better futures made possible by technological innovations, but we should ask for whom is it a better future, by whom is it enacted, and who is left on the margins. Technologies also have genealogies and histories; their pasts bear legacies that ought not be forgotten, even if present-day usages, such as in "hacks," differ from their provenance (Jen). Now, years later, I regularly assign *The Cancer Journals* in my own courses, and I continue my scholarly interests in technoscience and feminist politics and activisms.

This essay's goal is to provide a brief—yet robust—entrée to some key conversations in the subfield of feminist science studies, including (1) the ways in which technological innovations are narrativized as magic bullet solutions to structural inequalities and social problems and (2) how feminists *hack*—or intervene into and reshape—economies of bodies, technoscience, and livelihoods. Attending to these goals, I consider the following questions: What can feminist thought and practice tell us about innovations in science, technology, and health? And, in turn, what can narratives about innovation tell us about feminist activisms? The premise underlying these questions is that only certain innovations are hailed as common goods, while feminist innovations—in the form of feminist technoscience activism—are often given short shrift. Here *feminist technoscience activism* refers to strategies, tactics, and acts of resistance that are grounded in the experiences, struggles, and knowledges of women, that engage with science and technology as artifacts and institutions that have historically excluded women and girls, and that challenge ideologies that legitimize inequalities (Jen).

MAGIC BULLET MISDIRECTION: COUNTERING TECHNOPHILIA'S FICTIONAL PROMISES

Nobel Prize winner Paul Ehrlich, known as the founder of chemotherapy, originated the magic bullet concept—defined as "targeted medicine . . . [that]

efficaciously attack[s] pathogens yet remain[s] harmless in healthy tissues" (Strebhardt and Ullrich 473). Doctors historically used mercury to treat syphilis patients, often inadvertently causing mercury poisoning, the effects of which included tooth loss and severe gastroenteritis (O'Shea 393). The "cure" itself was toxic to the body. However, with the development of salvaran, a synthetic drug with anti-syphilitic activity, and later on penicillin, doctors could treat syphilis with minimal side effects (O'Shea 394). This is a technophile's dream: magic bullets of innovation—typically seen as miraculous shots and pills—remarkably cure all that ails.

While the metaphor of magic bullets typically refers to medical therapies, I find it useful as an analytic tool. It facilitates queries such as: In what ways are technoscientific magic bullets or "cures" posed as deceptively simple solutions to complex, socially embedded problems? For example, Reach for Recovery deployed breast prostheses as a technique of, what I call, *magic bullet misdirection*. Its deployment is similar to a magician's technique of deception and misdirection of audience attention. The actual site of manipulation—or harm—remains out of view, unnoticed, and underexamined, while sleight of hand, smoke and mirrors—and in this case breast prostheses—"cure" the "problem" of breast loss while rendering its "scars" unseen. It is like an illusion—except instead of magically sawing a woman in half, women's breasts are literally incised and amputated. In her denunciation of breast prostheses, Lorde calls for a revolution: "what would happen if an army of one-breasted women descended on Congress and demanded that the use of carcinogenic fat-stored hormones in beef-feed be outlawed?" (116). She demands urgent attention to the ways women's lives are entangled with the technoscience of toxicity and agricultural management, with the flesh and hormones of other animals, and with the political-economic apparatuses of governance and capitalism. Technophilia as magic bullet misdirection comes wrapped in fictional promises.

In a second example, I shift focus to the narrativization of assisted reproductive technologies as magic bullets and again employ magic bullet misdirection as an analytic tool. We can ask: In what ways are technoscientific "cures" posed as deceptively simple solutions to complex, socially embedded inequalities? In October 2014, Apple Inc. ignited impassioned social media responses to its new family-planning benefits, specifically coverage up to $20,000 for "social egg freezing"—that is egg cell preservation and storage in sub-zero temperatures for nonmedical reasons (Farr). Medical reasons include fertility concerns related to cancer treatments, while social reasons typically involve healthy women who delay childbearing for "personal, professional, financial and psychological" reasons (Petropanagos et al. 666).

Egg freezing is narrativized as a technoscientific innovation in the service of women's empowerment. Apple stated, "We want to *empower* women at Apple to do the best work of their lives as they care for loved ones and raise their families" (my emphasis; qtd. in Farr). While a contingent of women expressed support for Apple's new policy, considering this benefit an additional, now more affordable option for delaying childbearing (Fox), others noted this policy announcement could be seen as a "PR Band-Aid" (Rosenblum). Apple's announcement arrived in the midst of Silicon Valley's dismal track record in hiring and retaining women and underrepresented minorities (Isaac). This new "benefit" misdirects attention away from resolving more substantive and costly reproductive and economic issues, such as lengthier paid parental leaves, on-site subsidized childcare, and the creation of more women-friendly and family-supportive educational and workplace environments. Delaying childbearing via egg freezing does not resolve gender, race, and class inequalities in STEM workplaces. Furthermore, addressing occupational health concerns remains imperative for the women, men, and children who labor in Chinese electronic manufacturing and Indonesian mineral mines in Apple's commodity chain (Blanding and White; Bilton). Egg freezing is magic bullet misdirection; its deployment by Apple does little to liberate its workers; instead, it insidiously obscures on-the-ground struggles. Its promises for women's empowerment ultimately ring false.

These illustrations challenge technophilic narrativizations of technoscientific innovations. Framed as magic bullet solutions, they misdirect needed attention and resources from interrogations of structural inequalities and social problems. I return to our first question: What can feminist thought and practice tell us about innovations in science, technology, and health? Scholarship and activisms in feminist science studies work toward breaking the magician's proverbial code—toward revealing magic bullet misdirection—in order to make visible underlying injustices along intersecting dimensions of gender, sexuality, race, class, and nation.

FEMINIST HACKTIVISMS AND PRESENT TENSE NARRATIVES

This essay's second question is: What can narratives about innovation tell us about feminist activisms? To *innovate* means "to change (a thing) into something new" and "to make changes *in* something established" (Oxford English Dictionary). Technological innovations are considered leading drivers of a nation's economic growth and global competitiveness (Pustovrh 40). Interested parties deploy promissory narratives about better futures made possible by innovations in technoscience in order to generate public interest and support. Investments in innovation percolate through governments, universities, and private technology firms and more recently encourage laypeople to "make" or innovate at home and in community spaces. Common maker activities include DNA extraction, robotics, soldering, circuitry, coding, and building whimsical contraptions like salad spinner centrifuges. Even the White House has jumped onto the "maker movement" bandwagon by proclaiming a National Week of Making and launching the Nation of Makers initiative (Office of Press Secretary).

Promises refer to moments in the future, but what about care for the present? Fictional promises require little concern for lived experiences in the present. Dominant promissory narratives about technoscientific innovation—like Reach for Recovery's stance on breast prostheses and Apple's possible interest in egg freezing as a way for female workers to delay childbearing—focus on abstract democratizations of the future. If social transformation is not an actual goal to be realized, then investments in understanding the struggles of the present are not necessary. Hence, it makes sense that fictional promises are built on sand and hold little emancipation potential. However, when promises are built on more solid foundations, what kinds of stories are told, and what kinds of potentials do they hold? This section addresses the ways feminists *hack* economies of bodies, technoscience, and livelihoods. I draw from the feminist hacktivist practices of three global feminist health groups—Women on Waves, Women on Web, and Team Code Gurus. I pose the concept of *present tense narratives*—stories grounded in concrete feminist struggles of the present—as more generative of social transformation than dominant promissory narratives about fictional futures.

To "hack" generally involves the modification or engagement of an object for reasons other than the object's intended usage. I use *feminist hacktivism* to describe oppositional endeavors that infiltrate and/or remake dominant technoscientific assemblages of people, objects, governance, and relations—all in order to meet on-the ground needs of women and children. These infiltrations and remixes work toward visions of social justice in their local and global particularities. This concept builds upon Ron Eglash's "oppositional technophilia"—that love for technology has "radical potential" (84)—and Morgan Meyer's "citizen biotech-economies" defined as "citizen economies of scientific equipment" that stand for "a material re-distribution, a democratization, and an alternative to established, technoscience."

Women on Waves and Women on Web facilitate medication abortions (till 6½ weeks pregnancy) for women living in countries where abortion is illegal or difficult to access (Vessel). Women on Waves states that it "trusts" women to do medical abortions themselves and that through "innovative strategies" it provides women with "tools" to ensure abortion access and information ("Who Are We?"). "Tools" include medication, information, support, and consultations with medical professionals. "Innovative

strategies," especially as documented in the film *Vessel* (2014), are numerous and include tactics such as hacking a shipping container into a sea-faring medical treatment room; commandeering a live television news interview into a how-to tutorial on abortion for viewers living in places where abortion is illegal; and appropriating maritime vehicles of international mobility—long the province of militarism, imperialism, and colonialism. Women on Waves sails its Dutch vessels to countries where abortion is illegal. These vessels operate in international waters (12 miles offshore), remaining under Dutch jurisdiction where abortion is legal. It has completed successful campaigns in Ireland, Poland, Portugal, Spain, and Morocco ("Ship Campaigns").

Women on Web started as a sister organization to work with women who may not have access to Women on Waves voyages. Women can get online personal consultations with doctors and are then mailed pills. Trained volunteers provide support throughout the entire process over email. Volunteers replied to over 100,000 emails from 135 countries in 2012. Medication abortions usually comprise two pills—mifepristone and misoprostol—and even the "discovery" of misoprostol as an abortion pill was a "hack" by Brazilian women in the 1990s who noticed a "may cause miscarriage" warning on over-the-counter ulcer medications (Vessel). Used safely and effectively to terminate pregnancies by millions of women worldwide, the medications are considered essential medicines by World Health Organization ("Ship Campaigns").

Furthermore, in June 2015, Women on Waves—in collaboration with women's groups in Germany, Poland, and Ireland—conducted and live-streamed their first successful Abortion Drone flight from Germany to Poland where abortion is illegal. The pilots successfully landed a drone with packets of pills taped to its sides ("Dutch campaigners fly abortion pills into Poland"). Two Polish women swallowed the termination pills before German police confiscated the aircraft ("First Abortion Drone"). This act of feminist hacktivism involved hacking a tool of the military-industrial complex to empower women in desperate need. Interested parties around the world watched the abortion drone mission in real time online and bore witness to transnational feminist health hacktivism in action.

Instead of pledging empty promises about a better future, Women on Waves and Women on Web actually "hack" a better present for more people through feminist technoscience activism. If not a promissory narrative to generate public buy-in, what is their present tense narrative? I paraphrase physician Rebecca Gompert who founded these organizations: many women around the world do not have the basic human right to determine what happens with their own bodies. Too many women are dying from unsafe abortions performed in countries where abortion is illegal or hard to access. To undermine restrictive legal constructs, individual women need to be empowered and trusted to do medical abortions (Vessel). Gompert's feminist hacktivism honors this narrative of the present and women's lived experiences.

A final example of feminist hacktivism focuses on Team Code Gurus, a Ugandan technology startup comprised of five women studying information technology and engineering at Makerere University (Bagorogoza). In June 2015, Team Code Gurus won Uganda Technovation—a technology, innovation, and entrepreneurship competition for women and girls. Participants submit prototypes of mobile applications designed to address community issues to digital technology professionals (Technovation). Technovation is a clear example of capitalism's entanglements with biotechnologies. Sunder Ranjan defines this new phase of capitalism as "biocapitalism" in which "biotechnology is a new form of enterprise inextricable from contemporary capitalism" (3, 149). Technovation is sponsored by corporations such as Google and Verizon, universities like the Massachusetts Institute of Technology, and intergovernmental organizations including United Nations (Technovation).

Team Code Guru's award-winning Her Health BVKit is a hardware-software prototype (pH sensor meter that communicates to a smartphone application) that helps women and girls detect urine pH levels and, in turn, determine their individualized likelihood of having bacterial vaginosis (a vaginal infection that can have serious reproductive health complications). The application also directs users to the nearest medical resources if necessary. From its funding "pitch" video, the women plan to market BVKit through nongovernmental organizations (NGOs), clinics, and pharmacies. The NGOs are significant because they can reach women who do not have access to medical facilities ("Vaginosis Her Health Video"). Uganda has one of the world's worst healthcare records; 51 percent of the population does not have contact with any public health facilities (Kelly). In an interview with *Fusion*, BVKit cocreator Nanyombi Margaret provides additional insight into their innovation's local exigency: women fear stigmatization around reproductive health issues and too frequently do not seek medical attention until their conditions are severe. The Gurus hope its technological innovation will empower women to engage in monthly self-care practices, especially in situations and locations where healthcare facilities are nonexistent or inaccessible ("Vaginosis Her Health Video"). In their present-tense narrative, these innovators want "women, mothers, and sisters around the world" to know that reproductive health is paramount (Hillin). They stress the underlying social, cultural, and structural conditions that constrict Ugandan women's livelihoods. Code Guru's feminist hacktivist project intervenes into existing biocapital economies and reshapes them into more equitable citizen biotech economies, in order to address women's limited access to science, technology, and healthcare.

I build a definition of feminist hacktivism from these cases. Feminist hacktivisms involve the hacking of objects—such as ulcer medications, military drones, pH meters, and mobile telephones—and the infiltration and remaking of technoscientific assemblages of people, objects, governance, and relations. They stand in contrast to magic bullet innovations that make lofty promises and misdirect focus from women's lived experiences in the present. Her Health BVKit is a digital update to the speculum and hand-mirror technologies of the 1970s US women's health movement, when feminists taught each other how to hack cervical exams. Similarly, Women on Waves is a transnational feminist update to Chicago-based

Jane Collective, and Women on Web is its digital media update. Between 1966 and 1972, women students at the University of Chicago taught themselves termination procedures, set up a network of volunteers and contacts, established clandestine methods to elude law enforcement, and ultimately provided over 12,000 safe, affordable, illegal abortions to women in need (Kirtz and Lundy). Women on Waves and Women on Web hack—or intervene into and reshape—complex technoscientific assemblages. These systems differ by country and region and involve numerous actants including activists, medical professionals, patients, consumers, medication, international and national laws and enforcement, information technologies, technologies of mobility, censorship, and social relations of control.

This essay sides with neither the technophile nor the technophobe. Contestations between camps actually bury important questions about the ways technoscientific innovations intersect with systems of power and oppression along dimensions of difference, geopolitical relations, feminisms, and women's bodies and lives. I return to our questions: What can feminist thought and practice tell us about innovations in science, technology, and health? And, in turn, what can narratives about innovation tell us about feminist activisms? This essay presents examples of magic bullet innovations employed by American Cancer Society and Apple that (mis)appropriate feminist "empowerment," that obscure systems of oppression and ignore gender stratifications across race, class, and nation. These ultimately fall short of their promissory narratives. Feminist hacktivisms, on the other hand, receive relatively little in financial investments and technogeek regard and do not trade fictional promises for public buy-in. Often driven by life-or-death necessities, feminist hacktivists like Women on Waves, Women on Web, and Team Code Guru transcend boundaries and literal borders to transform present-day possibilities for women and girls in need.

WORKS CITED

Bagorogoza, Victoria Mbabazi, compiler. "Uganda National Technovation Challenge Report." *U.S. Global Development Lab*, Resilient Africa Network, 5 June 2015, www.ranlab.org/uganda-national-technovation-challenge-report.

Bilton, Richard. "Apple 'Failing to Protect Chinese Factory Workers.'" *BBC Panorama*, 18 Dec. 2014, www.bbc.com/news/business-30532463.

Blanding, Michael, and Heather White. "How China Is Screwing Over Its Poisoned Factory Workers." *Wired*, 6 Apr. 2015, www.wired.com/2015/04/inside-chinese-factories/.

Difranco, Ani. "My I.Q." *Puddle Dive*. Righteous Babe, 1993.

"Dutch Campaigners Fly Abortion Pills into Poland." *BBC News*, 27 June 2015, www.bbc.com/news/world-europe-33299660.

Eglash, Ron. "Oppositional Technophilia." *Social Epistemology: A Journal of Knowledge, Culture and Policy*, vol. 23, no. 1, 2009, pp. 79–86.

Farr, Cynthia. "Apple, Facebook Will Pay for Female Employees to Freeze Their Eggs." *Reuters*, 14 Oct. 2014, www.reuters.com/article/us-tech-fertility-idUSKCN0I32KQ20141014.

"First Abortion Drone Flight a Success, Women in Poland Receive Medical Abortions." *Women on Waves*, www.womenonwaves.org/en/page/5832/first-flight-abortion-drone. Accessed 28 July 2015.

Fox, MeiMei. "Apple and Facebook Cover Egg Freezing Costs: Why Is This a Controversy?" *The Huffington Post*, 20 Oct. 2014, www.huffingtonpost.com/meimei-fox/apple-facebook-cover-egg_b_6015962.html.

Hillin, Taryn. "Five Ugandan Students Invented an App to Diagnose Vaginal Infections at Home." *Fusion*, 24 Aug. 2015, fusion.net/story/180574/how-the-bv-kit-app-could-help-millions/.

"Innovate." *Oxford English Dictionary*, 1989.

Isaac, Mike. "Behind Silicon Valley's Self-Critical Tone on Diversity, a Lack of Progress." *The New York Times*, 29 June 2015, p. B4.

Jen, Clare. "Feminist Technoscience Activism: A Double-Stranded Reading of Dr. Bodnar's Ig Nobel Striptease." *Rhizomes: Cultural Studies in Emerging Knowledge*, vol. 26, 2014, http://www.rhizomes.net/issue26/jen.html.

Kelly, Annie. "Healthcare a Major Challenge for Uganda." *The Guardian*, 31 Mar. 2009, www.theguardian.com/katine/2009/apr/01/healthcare-in-uganda.

Kirtz, Kate, and Nell Lundy. *Jane: An Abortion Service*. Independent Television Service, 1996.

Lorde, Audre. *The Cancer Journals*. Aunt Lute Books, 1980.

Meyer, Morgan. "Build Your Own Lab: Do-It-Yourself Biology and the Rise of Citizen Biotech-Economies." *Journal of Peer Production*, vol. 2, 2012, http://peerproduction.net/issues/issue-2/invited-comments/build-your-own-lab.

FACT SHEET: New Commitments in Support of the President's Nation of Makers Initiative. United States, The White House, Office of the Press Secretary, 2015, www.whitehouse.gov/the-press-office/2015/06/12/fact-sheet-new-commitments- support president%E2%80%99s-nation-makers-initiative.

O'Shea, JG. "'Two Minutes with Venus, Two Years with Mercury'—Mercury as an Antisyphilitic Chemotherapeutic Agent." *Journal of the Royal Society of Medicine*, vol. 83, 1990, pp. 392–95.

Petropanagos, Angel et al. "Social Egg Freezing: Risk, Benefits and Other Considerations." *Canadian Medical Association Journal*, vol. 187, no. 9, 2015, pp. 666–69. *MEDLINE Complete*, doi:10.1503/cmaj.141605.

Pustovrh, Toni. "Socially Responsible Science and Innovation in Converging Technologies." *Innovation in Socio-Cultural Context*. Edited by Frane Adam and Hans Westlund, Routledge, 2013, pp. 40–56.

Rosenblum, Emma. "Corporate Egg Freezing Offers May Send the Wrong Message." *All Things Considered,* hosted by Audie Cornish, NPR, 16 Oct. 2014, www.npr.org/2014/10/16/356728014/corporate-egg-freezing-offers-may-send-the-wrong-message.

"Ship Campaigns." *Women on Waves*, www.womenonwaves.org/en/page/2582/ship-campaigns. Accessed 28 July 2015.

Strebhardt, Klaus, and Axel Ullrich. "Paul Ehrlich's Magic Bullet Concept: 100 Years of Progress." *Nature Reviews,* vol. 8, 2008, pp. 473–80.

Sunder Rajan, Kaushik. *Biocapital: The Constitution of Postgenomic Life*. Duke UP, 2006.

Technovation Uganda. technovationug.blogspot.com/. Accessed 26 Aug. 2015.

"Vaginosis Her Health Video / BVkit." *YouTube,* uploaded by Margaret Nanyombi, 26 Mar. 2015, www.youtube.com/watch?v=d8CQ5UqhRV4.

Whitten, Diana, director. *Vessel*. Sovereignty Productions, 2014, vesselthefilm.com/#watch.

"Who Are We?" *Women on Waves*, www.womenonwaves.org/en/page/650/who-are-we. Accessed 28 July 2015.

73. • *Joni Seager*

RACHEL CARSON DIED OF BREAST CANCER:
The Coming of Age of Feminist Environmentalism (2003)

Joni Seager is professor of global studies at Bentley University. She is also an activist in global environmental policy. Her publications include *The Penguin Atlas of Women of the World* and *Earth Follies: Coming to Feminist Terms with the Global Environmental Crisis*. The essay included here first appeared in *Signs: Journal of Women in Culture and Society*.

Feminist environmentalism is shifting paradigms in public health, political economy, philosophy, science, and ecology. Feminist environmental theory and women's on-the-ground ecoactivism are challenging and transforming approaches to a breathtakingly wide range of issues, from animal rights to the environmental economy of illness and well-being, from exposing and theorizing complex processes such as global ecopiracy to interrogating the distortive privileging of "science" as an arbiter of the state of the environment. Feminist environmentalism is hot, and getting hotter.

But this may be news to most people outside the field. The one thing people typically seem to know about feminist environmentalism is that it involves something called *ecofeminism*, which they vaguely associate with spirituality and earth-loving women. From the outside looking in, feminist environmentalism can look like a large tent occupied by an elephant almost as large. Even from the inside it can look that way too. It is impossible to do work under the rubric of feminist environmentalism, or even to talk about it, without first explaining or positioning oneself in reference to ecofeminism.

ECOFEMINISM

Among scholars and activists closest to the project there is little agreement on what ecofeminism is or what its relationship is to the (presumptively) broader endeavor of feminist environmentalism. Browsing the literature we find *ecofeminism* variously described as a political stance, a take-it-to-the-streets movement, a feminist spiritual affirmation, an inspirational wellspring for women's activism, a retrieval of womanist earth wisdom, a feminist theory, an applied scholarship, a feminist rebellion within radical environmentalism (Sturgeon 1997, 31), an oppositional positionality, a praxis, and a remapping of women's relationship to place and ecology.

[. . .]

Despite this plasticity, the very term *ecofeminism* typically invokes strong reactions—and generally precipitates a rush to "for" or "against" camp making. There are three touchstone issues that separate ecofeminism-embracers from ecofeminism-distancers: the prominent association of eco-feminist thought with womanist spirituality, the (putative) essentialism of the ecofeminist affirmation of a meaningful nature-woman connection, and the old gown/town split between the presumptive sophistication of theory building and the presumptively atheoretical naïveté of social movement and activist practices.

[. . .]

As conceptualized by ecofeminist pioneers such as Ynestra King, ecological feminism held promise as a bridge across the analytical divide between radical cultural and socialist feminism. King identified ecofeminism as a "third direction," neither severing the connection between woman and nature (as socialist feminists would have it) nor reinforcing it (as many cultural feminists did): "the liberation of women is to be found neither in severing all connections that root us in nature nor in believing ourselves to be more natural than men" (1981, 15). Early articulations of the intersectional and interdependent oppressions of ecology, race, sex, and class (e.g., Reuther 1975) pointed to a path that transcended the dichotomous rendition of the human/nature relationship, the classic subject/object split at the heart of Western philosophical inquiry. By the late 1970s, then, ecofeminism was on a roll, full of promise and intellectual excitement.

The first discernibly coherent feminist environmentalism emerged in the United States through these broader feminist debates and explorations. In tandem with antimilitarist movements and a then-nascent environmental movement, feminist environmentalism emerged as a fusion of powerful analytical and paradigmatic challenges and activist energies.[1] Environmentalists provided baseline insights into the interdependence of human life and planet life and offered a systems analysis of the ways ecological destruction cascaded through intertwined social and ecological webs. Feminists honed these understandings with analyses of the ways the construction of social power, in its ineluctably gendered dimensions, produced those conditions of ecological threat.

[. . .]

For many women, the eco-focused feminism emerging in the 1980s was necessarily rooted in a reawakening of earth honoring and earth caring, involving a rehabilitation of nature-centered traditions and invoking anew the salience of earth goddess, women-wise spirituality. For these women, the central project of what they called ecofeminism was reclaiming the sacred and celebrating women's nurturing—and special—relationship with earth forces and life forces. Ecofeminism put spirituality, earth goddesses, nature/culture identities, and debates about essentialism, antiessentialism, and maternalism on the feminist front burner.

[. . .]

This meant that by the late 1980s, *ecofeminism* had become a fighting word. For every woman who reveled in the association of ecofeminism with earth goddesses, there was one who winced. Many women rejected ecofeminism, particularly academics in the social and biological sciences whose engagement with environmentalism was forged in a rationalist tradition, and who feared that talk of goddesses and life forces would undermine their hard-won but precarious professional credibility. For many political feminists, *ecofeminism* was a word to define *against*; the spiritual side of ecofeminism was derided as mystical bunk, dangerously apolitical and atheoretical. In 1993, Carol Adams calmly assessed the divide in this way: "There has been no one perspective on the place of spirituality in ecofeminism. . . . For some, the spiritual aspect of ecofeminism is integrally a part of their ecofeminism. For others spirituality is thought to derail the ecofeminist engagement with social conditions and political decisions that tolerate

environmental exploitation, encourage unbridled consumerism, and fail to rein in military spending" (4).

The contributions of ecofeminism to feminist environmentalism are myriad, and ecofeminism itself is clearly an enduring part of the feminist environmental mix. Spiritual engagement with the fate of the planet brings many women to the environmental table—and to the environmental barricades. Contemplation and contestation of the issues provoked by eco-feminism have produced a robust and challenging literature: on anthropomorphism, on the "sex-typing" of the planet, on encounters between feminism and deep ecology, on the nature of nature. The philosophy of ecofeminism is a well-developed field (see, e.g., Plumwood 1993; Salleh 1997; Warren 1997, 2000). . . .

[. . .]

ANIMAL RIGHTS AND FEMINIST ENVIRONMENTALISM

. . . Feminist work on animal rights builds on the foundational ecofeminist effort to understand linkages between environmental oppressions on the one hand (such as speciesist hierarchies, or the hierarchy of value established through the commodification of nature), and human social oppressions of many kinds (such as those based on class, or race, gender, and sexuality classifications; or judgments of "value" attributed to physical ability) on the other. At the same time, the serious contemplation of animal rights makes a considerable contribution to destabilizing identity categories and adds a new dimension to theorizing the mutability of identity.

Feminist environmental scholarship and grassroots activism on animals pivot around three concerns: elucidating the commonalities in structures of oppressions across gender, race, class, and species; developing feminist-informed theories of animal rights; and exposing the gendered assumptions and perceptions that underlie human treatment of nonhuman animals.

Like nineteenth-century racial and gender taxonomies that were constructed and then frantically repatched to keep pace with contravening evidence and with shifts in social and economic realities, efforts to fix a firm line between "us" (humans) and "them" (animals) are similarly becoming increasingly frenetic as the old standard-bearers of asserted human/animal difference topple. . . .

The myriad specific justifications for the oppression, enslavement, and exploitation of animals (which is occurring on a massive scale) are all rooted in dual assertions: of significant human/animal difference, and of the putatively scientifically provable "lesser" intellectual (or even emotional) capacities of animals. These are achingly close reprises of the conceptual bases for racial, sexual, and gender hierarchies. Echoing through the debates about animals are unmistakable invocations of familiar racist and sexist ideologies about "natural affinities," categories authorized by nature, destinies inscribed in biology, and "scientific proofs" of the limited capacities of the "other" that have rumbled through the centuries to justify slavery, the oppression of women, and ethnically and racially based holocausts and genocides. . . .

Out of struggles against the artifices of race, gender, and sex categories, feminists have developed sharp analyses of the distortions of binary dualisms and of the falsity of "science-based" identity categories. Furthermore, feminists have been in the forefront in exposing the sham of "universal" social hierarchies that are patently driven by culture-, gender-, and race-specific values. These insights are central to feminist reimaginings of animal rights.

Since animal exploiters rely on tropes about animals being "different from" humans (and thus not protected by human-like considerations or rights) and about animals being "lesser than" us in myriad ways, animal rights activists often start by arguing the opposite. Complacency about human exceptionalism is challenged by every report of parrots who can count, of whales with globe-spanning languages, of elephant mourning and memory, of gorillas who acquire extensive sign language vocabularies, of cephalopods who solve spatial problems, of cows who escape slaughterhouses with prodigious feats of athleticism and cunning, of lifelong devotional pairings between birds, of ants who form intentional alliances in supercolonies that stretch across hundreds of miles, of remarkable feats of dolphin intelligence. Recent discoveries that genetic differences between human and most nonhuman animals are slight (even negligible) have opened a new dimension in animal rights debates.

Such assertions of similitude between human and nonhuman animals are theoretically and philosophically congruent with the larger feminist project of destabilizing identity categories. Thus many animal rights feminists aver that the "line" between human animals and nonhuman animals is more of a broad, smudgy band than a sharp demarcation. Feminist and queer theorizing has blurred the line of "authorized by nature" identity categories. Feminist animal rights environmentalism queers the line even more. The "science"-based ideology that creates metrics of human/animal "difference" in its own image and then uses those metrics as if they were neutral analytical tools is the same value-laden universalizing science that puts gender, sex, and sexuality identity into discrete hierarchically stacked boxes—and it has been widely discredited, particularly in feminist theory. . . .

Calling into question the premise and measurement of the human/animal divide, though, is complicated by deeply theorized feminist political commitments to respecting and retaining the integrity of "difference." In this, feminists part company with prominent male animal rights advocates such as Peter Singer (1975) and Tom Regan (1983), who argue for an extension of the moral community to include animals primarily on the basis of their sameness to humans. The examples above, of animals learning to speak and count, that seem at first so unsettling, are, of course, yet another way of valuing animals only to the extent that they meet or mimic human tests of "intelligence" and behavior. In this light, I might reframe my prior point: an animal rights philosophy that creates metrics of human/animal sameness in its own human image and then uses those metrics as if they were neutral analytical tools is flawed by the same presumptive universalizing that has so distorted our understanding of sex, sexuality, and gender—and should therefore be rejected. Philosophers Karen Warren (1990), Deborah Slicer (1991), and Val Plumwood (1993) elaborate most clearly the importance of developing a feminist animal rights theory that does not sanctify the "erasure of difference," an erasure that almost always works primarily to the advantage of the dominant class. Internationally prominent environmentalist Vandana Shiva presents a key feminist assertion that "even the tiniest life form [must be] recognized as having intrinsic worth, integrity, and autonomy" (2000, 74).

[. . .]

The best of feminist animal rights theorizing does not simply resuscitate this overshadowed Western philosophical tradition of "care." Rather, it reimagines a human relationship to the nonhuman world by locating action and theory in the lived world and moral universe of women's identity and on the basis of feminist political insights. . . .

Some of this work returns us to ecofeminist discourses about women's "special kinship" with animals, an assertion that raises specters of essentialism again. However, most feminist animal rights theorists insist that developing a care-based ethic cannot rest on an appeal to a "natural(ized)" extension of women's affinities and experiences but rather must also reflect a honed political analysis.

[. . .]

PUBLIC HEALTH AND FEMINIST ENVIRONMENTALISM

Odd as it may seem to any woman who is living with cancer, or who worries about the likelihood of being diagnosed with breast cancer, or who worries about her child's asthma, "health" and "environment" issues until very recently were seldom linked, at least in mainstream and official channels. It has taken (and still takes) relentless pressure from environmental justice and women's health advocates to

shift paradigms—to put human health issues on the mainstream environmental movement agenda and to put environmental issues on the health map. Even now, virtually all assertions of causality between health disruptions and environmental assaults are fiercely contested, all the more so when women are the primary proponents of linkage.

Since the 1960s, women's health activists have forged sophisticated transnational coalitions to draw attention to the health needs and threats specific to women. The specificity of those needs and threats are sometimes a consequence of biology (women are "not just small men," as a popular book title proclaims [Goldberg 2002]) and sometimes due to social location, but averring the particularity of *women's* health was the first radical challenge. Beyond drawing attention to "women's issues," these movements simultaneously drew attention to the patriarchal, economic, and social structures that pose particular dangers to women's health and that keep women's health issues from being taken seriously. The recent history of women's health advocacy includes a long list of accomplishments: exposing international patterns of forced sterilization and other systematic reproductive rights abuses, drawing attention to the global epidemic of violence against women, tracing the emergence of the epidemic of breast cancer in Western countries, challenging the normative assumption of conventional health care and assessment practices that white men's health issues are generalizable and universal, and exposing the dumping of unsafe pharmaceuticals and devices in minority communities and "third world" countries.

On a parallel but separate track, throughout the 1980s and 1990s a growing chorus of voices from women's and social justice movements challenged the mostly male-led mainstream environmental movement on its bias in prioritizing wilderness, animal conservation, and wildlife protection and its concomitant neglect of urban and social environmental issues, including, prominently, human health issues. The human costs of environmental deterioration had always been on the agenda of local, community social justice, and women's groups; indeed, typically, health issues brought many women activists *to* environmentalism. But mainstream environmental groups were slow—and even resistant—to take up the challenge of human health (Taylor 1989; Bullard 1990; Seager 1993a).

Around the world, public awareness of the impact of environmental deterioration on human health was focused by a series of "discoveries" and spectacular environmental accidents in the 1970s and 1980s: discovery of the ozone hole, chemical disasters in Seveso in 1976 and Bhopal in 1984, nuclear catastrophes at Three Mile Island and Chernobyl among them. But while these hyperevents catalyzed public attention, the attention was usually temporary. The broader trend toward making a sustained connection between health and environmental movements was forged around more mundane and modest health issues that disproportionately affected women and that women were the first to "notice." In the United States and Europe, through sheer persistence and painstaking efforts to develop evidentiary support for their claims, women's health and environmental justice advocates were instrumental in forcing attention to the possible environmental sources of health problems such as escalating rates of asthma and lead poisoning in urban children, epidemics of breast cancer in women in Western countries, and rampant endocrine disruption and "estrogen mimicking" chemical derangement in animals and humans. At the same time, throughout the third world and particularly in South Asia, feminists were collaborating across gender and environmental movements to focus attention on the interlinkages of ecology, health, and "[mal]development."

In both North and South, women's involvement with health/environment issues typically started from concerns about the health of themselves and their families in daily life, an insistence on taking seriously the particularity of the impacts of environmental degradation on *women's* bodies and health (and particularly reproductive health), and a "personal" connection to "the environment." . . .

One of the most globally ubiquitous threats to human health is the saturation of the environment with "man-made" chemicals—developed and introduced with virtually no understanding of their singular let alone their synergistic impact on humans, animals, and ecosystems. Rachel Carson was not the first to suggest that the chemical fog produced by modern industry was carcinogenic. But her prodigious feat of synthesizing a jumble of scientific and medical information into an understandable, coherent argument about health and environment was transformative. In so doing, Carson pointed the way to the key paths of inquiry for contemporary feminist environmental public health interventions: the importance of persistence in accumulating evidence on chemical/carcinogenic linkages in the face of industry efforts to obfuscate the evidence and to hinder these efforts; foregrounding the synergistic effects of multiple chemical exposures, despite the inherently "unknowable" character of such effects; advocating precaution in the face of scientific uncertainty; and insisting on the necessity of intervening in the fight against cancer at the causal level, not merely the palliative.

[. . .]

Rachel Carson died from breast cancer. Surprisingly few people know this. Carson herself was resolutely unforthcoming about her diagnosis (most likely fearing that disclosure of her cancer would be used by her critics to call into question her integrity as a critic of the chemical industry). But Carson's dual legacy—as one of the most prominent whistleblowers on synthetic chemicals and as a casualty of a "women's" disease that was given short shrift by the male medical establishment—has sparked a remarkable effort to trace the linkages between chemical assaults and breast cancer.

In Carson's name and spirit, feminists who have insisted on bridging the health/environmental gap are transforming what we know about breast cancer in particular and human public health in general. National women's groups such as Breast Cancer Action (www.bcaction.org) and Silent Spring Institute (www.silentspring.org) track medical and environmental advances, releasing a steady stream of analyses and reports on topics as diverse as "Risk of Breast Cancer and Organochloride Exposure," or "Electromagnetic Exposure as a Potential Risk Factor for Breast Cancer," or "Awash in Atrazine: Herbicides, Hormones, and Cancer."[2]

Environmentalism has taken a radical movement—women's health—and made it even more so. It has propelled women's breast cancer support and activist groups well beyond the "pink ribbon" phase (Brenner and Ehrenreich 2001). The new wave of feminist health environmentalism is not a passive enterprise: groups such as Breast Cancer Action do not just "track" information, they are actively involved in the production of new knowledge. One of the central insights of community-based, social justice, and feminist environmental organizing is that the human costs of environmental destruction accrue differently across sexes, races, classes, ethnicities, and geographies. One repeated pattern manifested at scales from the local to the global is that the health "fallout" from environmental damage cascades down the social power gradient: people marginalized or stigmatized, people without a voice in the official expert and authority structures, people on the economic and social edges, feel the effects of environmental derangement first, longest, and most acutely. A related insight is that "place matters." Following these analytical bread crumbs, feminist environmentalists are on the leading edge of developing and deploying spatial proximity analysis.

Social justice environmentalism, including women's local activism on health and environment, has often been prompted by a local awareness of unusual distributions and odd geographic "clusters" of illness or of environmentally dangerous facilities and activities. In the last five or six years, activists have transformed this awareness into a powerful tool of environmental investigation. Using spatial analysis and particularly geographic information system (GIS) technologies, justice and health activists have started to develop sophisticated locational analyses of environmental correlations. Use of GIS allows the simultaneous mapping of layers of demographic, environmental, land use, historical, and social data, offering the ability to transpose maps of breast cancer incidence, for example, over maps of known chemical release sites. There is virtually no limit to the number of layers of data that can be accumulated and compared. Currently, two of the largest environmental health studies in the United States involve multidisciplinary research teams working with women's environmental health grassroots organizations in Massachusetts and New York to assess the elevated rates and distinctive geographic patterning of disproportionately high rates of breast cancer incidence found on Cape Cod and Long Island.[3]

This is a breakthrough adaptation of technology for feminist inquiry. In the environmental community, women's breast cancer researchers and activists have been in the lead in the adaptation of these technologies, and their efforts are already changing the broader nature of environmental investigation. Adoption (and adaptation) of this "scientific" approach has won for women and women's issues a new respect. Women's complaints about breast cancer (and other illness) clusters—previously dismissed as phantoms of overwrought female anxiety—are now being taken seriously.

But this engagement with mainstream science needs careful scrutiny. This is a good moment in feminist environmentalism to revisit Audre Lorde's caution about the use of the master's tools to dismantle the master's house. By entering into the environmental "big time" through the portal of mainline science, feminists risk losing their distinctive stance of oppositionality and their insistence that environmental knowledge comes in myriad forms. They also risk losing their way in what Sandra Steingraber has called the "miasma of uncertainty" (1997, 71). Breast cancer researchers using GIS technologies are entering into the "scientific proof" game on terms that they do not set, and on terms that are stacked against them.

Environmental investigation of all kinds is dogged by "scientific uncertainty"—the fact that it is almost impossible to "prove" direct environmental causes and effects. Ecological systems from the local to the global are complex and not fully comprehended by tools of scientific investigation; in the environmental domain, there is almost always room for (scientific) doubt, and the possibility of contravening evidence is always present. This uncertainty is particularly acute in matters of health: it is virtually impossible to establish scientifically certain "proof" that exposure to any given chemical at any given point in time "causes" cancer that may appear several years later and in people who may have moved to a new location far from the exposure site.

Scientific uncertainty serves as a refuge for scoundrels of all kinds. Chemical-producing and pollution-causing industries have relied for years on the "cover" that scientific uncertainty affords them. . . .

. . . In the last decade, the articulation of a principle of "precaution" is one of the most radical developments in global environmental thought. The most far-reaching implication of the "precautionary principle" may be that it offers an intervention against the closed loop of scientific uncertainty. The commonsensical and deceptively simple precautionary principle displaces the expectation that environmental action requires post facto scientific proof of harm. In a series of interlinked doctrines, the precautionary principle asserts that public and private interests have a positive obligation to act to prevent environmental/health harm before it occurs; that the indication of harm, rather than "proof" of harm, should be the trigger for action; that the burden of proof needs to be shifted to the front of the chain of production (the presumption of safety should be tested before potentially harmful substances are released into the environment rather than waiting to test for harm after the fact); and that all activities with potential health consequences should be guided by the principle of the least toxic alternative.[4]

[. . .]

GLOBAL POLITICAL ECONOMY AND FEMINIST ENVIRONMENTALISM

Feminist environmentalism digs deepest into structural explanations for the state of the earth in work done under the broad rubric of "feminist political ecology." This is not a coherent subfield in a disciplinary sense, but rather it describes practices and inquiries at a point of convergence of critical studies of science, global structural power, gender, and environment. Work in this domain ranges widely; much of it focuses on trans-national or international processes, and most feminist political ecology starts from a curiosity about the material conditions of lives rooted in specific environmental contexts. Much of this work includes a strong focus on the uneven distribution of access to and control over resources, and economies of uneven development (see, e.g., Rocheleau, Thomas-Slayter, and Wangari 1996; Sachs 1996); challenges to modernist inscriptions of resource-as-commodity relationships, especially the imposition of Western systems of the commodification of nature; and exposing environmental effects of the forced integration of local environments/communities into global capital flows, world trade regimes, and military webs.[5]

Gender is a particularly important explanatory variable in environmental relations of these kinds. Several axes of power define people's access to resources and to control over environments, but the particular foregrounding of gender, as well as race and class, across scales from the local to the global, produces potent analyses. The gendered nature of ecologically based power structures is often most apparent at moments of ecological change: when land is transferred from a commons system to private ownership, for example, or from forest to cropland, or from subsistence cropping to export cash cropping. Such shifts not only reveal patterns of gendered power but are also instrumental in the actual transference of power—typically away from women to men and away from local control to external control.

Feminist scholarship on the construction of science, much of which is built on the foundation set by Carolyn Merchant (1980), exerts a strong influence on the political ecology literature. The widespread export of Western technologies and ideologies of the "control of nature," whether as part of eighteenth-century colonialism or twenty-first century corporatist "development" strategies, is a strong determinant of the state of the global environment, and feminist political ecologists have been particularly attentive to the gendered import of the global spread of these ideologies (see, e.g., Shiva 1988, 1993, 2000; Agarwal 1992; Seager 1993b).

[. . .]

REFERENCES

Adams, Carol J. 1990. *The Sexual Politics of Meat: A Feminist-Vegetarian Critical Theory*. New York: Continuum.

———, ed. 1993. *Ecofeminism and the Sacred*. New York: Continuum.

Adams, Carol J., and Josephine Donovan, eds. 1995. *Animals and Women: Feminist Theoretical Explorations*. Durham, N.C.: Duke University Press.

Agarwal, Bina. 1992. "The Gender and Environment Debate: Lessons from India." *Feminist Studies* 18(1):119–58.

Bandarage, Asoka. 1997. *Women, Population and Global Crisis: A Political-Economic Analysis*. London: Zed.

Bordo, Susan. 1986. "The Cartesian Masculinization of Thought." *Signs: Journal of Women in Culture and Society* 11(3):439–56.

Brenner, Barbara, and Barbara Ehrenreich. 2001. "The Pink-Ribbon Trap." *Los Angeles Times*, December 23, M1.

Brown, Lester R., Gary Gardner, and Brian Halweil. 1999. *Beyond Malthus: Nineteen Dimensions of the Population Challenge*. New York: W. W. Norton.

Bullard, Robert D. 1990. *Dumping in Dixie: Race, Class, and Environmental Quality*. Boulder, Colo.: Westview.

Bunch, Charlotte. 1976. "Beyond Either/or Feminist Options." *Quest: A Feminist Quarterly* 3(1):2–17.

Carson, Rachel. 1962. *Silent Spring*. Boston: Houghton Mifflin.

Colborn, Theo, Dianne Dumanoski, and John Peterson Myers. 1996. *Our Stolen Future: Are We Threatening Our Fertility, Intelligence, and Survival? A Scientific Detective Story*. New York: Dutton.

Daly, Mary. 1978. *Gyn/Ecology: The Meta Ethics of Radical Feminism*. Boston: Beacon.

Donovan, Josephine. 1990. "Animal Rights and Feminist Theory." *Signs* 15(2):350–75.

———. 1994. "Attention to Suffering: Sympathy as a Basis for Ethical Treatment of Animals." In Donovan and Adams 1996, 34–59.

Donovan, Josephine, and Carol J. Adams, eds. 1996. *Beyond Animal Rights: A Feminist Caring Ethic for the Treatment of Animals*. New York: Continuum.

Doubiago, Sharon. 1989. "Mama Coyote Talks to the Boys." In *Healing the Wounds: The Promise of Ecofeminism*, ed. Judith Plant. Philadelphia: New Society Publishers.

Elder, Glen, Jennifer Wolch, and Jody Emel. 1998. "*Le pratique sauvage*: Race, Place, and the Human-Animal Divide." In *Animal Geographies: Politics, Race, and Identity in the Nature-Culture Borderlands*, ed. Jennifer Wolch and Jody Emel, 72–90. New York: Verso.

Emel, Jody. 1995. "Are You Man Enough, Big and Bad Enough? An Ecofeminist Analysis of Wolf Eradication in the United States." *Society and Space: Environment and Planning D* 13(6):707–34.

Gaard, Greta, ed. 1993. *Ecofeminism: Women, Animals, Nature*. Philadelphia: Temple University Press.

Garb, Yaakov. 1990. "Perspective or Escape? Ecofeminist Musings on Contemporary Earth Imagery." In *Reweaving the World: The Emergence of Ecofeminism*, ed. Irene Diamond and Gloria Orenstein. San Francisco: Sierra Club Books.

Goldberg, Nieca. 2002. *Women Are Not Small Men*. New York: Ballantine.

Griffin, Susan. 1978. *Woman and Nature: The Roaring Inside Her*. New York: Harper & Row.

Haraway, Donna. 2000. "A Manifesto for Cyborgs: Science, Technology and Socialist Feminism in the 1980s." In Kirkup et al. 2000, 50–57.

Harding, Sandra. 1986. *The Science Question in Feminism*. Ithaca, N.Y.: Cornell University Press.

Hartmann, Betsy. 1994. *Reproductive Rights and Wrongs*. Boston: South End Press.

Iglehart, Hallie. 1978. "The Unnatural Divorce of Spirituality and Politics." *Quest: A Feminist Quarterly* 4(3):12–24.

Keller, Evelyn Fox. 1978. "Gender and Science." *Psychoanalysis and Contemporary Thought* 1(3):409–33.

Kellert, Stephen, and Joyce Berry. 1987. "Attitudes, Knowledge, and Behaviors toward Wildlife as Affected by Gender." *Wildlife Society Bulletin* 15(3):363–71.

Kheel, Marti. 1995. "License to Kill: An Ecofeminist Critique of Hunters' Discourse." In Adams and Donovan 1995, 85–125.

King, Ynestra. 1981. "Feminism and the Revolt of Nature." *Heresies 13* 4(1): 12–16.

Kirkup, Gill, Linda Janes, Kathryn Woodward, and Fiona Hovenden, eds. 2000. *The Gendered Cyborg: A Reader*. London: Routledge, in association with the Open University.

Kurian, Priya A. 2000. *Engendering the Environment? Gender in the World Bank's Environmental Policies*. Aldershot: Ashgate.

Merchant, Carolyn. 1980. *The Death of Nature: Women, Ecology, and the Scientific Revolution*. San Francisco: Harper & Row.

Mies, Maria, and Vandana Shiva. 1993. *Ecofeminism*. London: Zed.

Ortner, Sherry B. 1974. "Is Female to Male as Nature Is to Culture?" In *Woman, Culture, and Society*, ed. Michelle Zimbalist Rosaldo and Louise Lamphere. Stanford, Calif.: Stanford University Press.

Plumwood, Val. 1993. *Feminism and the Mastery of Nature*. New York: Routledge.

Raffensperger, Carolyn. 2000. "The Precautionary Principle as Forecaring: Hopeful Work for the Environmental Health Movement." Plenary speech at the Taking Back Our Food conference, Mount Alverno Conference Center,

Redwood City, Calif., October. Available on-line at www
.sehn.org/forecaring.html.

Raffensperger, Carolyn, and Joel Tickner, eds. 1999. *Protecting
Public Health and the Environment: Implementing the
Precautionary Principle.* Washington, D.C.: Island Press.

Regan, Tom. 1983. *The Case for Animal Rights.* Berkeley:
University of California Press.

Reuther, Rosemary Radford. 1975. *New Woman, New Earth:
Sexist Ideologies and Human Liberation.* New York: Seabury.

Rocheleau, Dianne, Barbara Thomas-Slayter, and Esther
Wangari, eds. 1996. *Feminist Political Ecology: Global
Issues and Local Experiences.* London: Routledge.

Sachs, Carolyn E. 1996. *Gendered Fields: Rural Women,
Agriculture, and Environment.* Boulder, Colo.: Westview.

Salleh, Ariel. 1997. *Ecofeminism as Politics: Nature, Marx, and
the Postmodern.* New York: Zed.

Sardar, Ziauddin, ed. 1988. *The Revenge of Athena: Science,
Exploitation, and the Third World.* London: Mansell.

Seager, Joni. 1993a. *Earth Follies: Coming to Feminist Terms
with the Global Environmental Crisis.* New York and
London: Routledge.

———. 1993b. "A Not-So-Natural Disaster: Militaries,
Technology, and the Floods of 1993." *Ms. Magazine*
4(3):26–27.

———. 1999. "Patriarchal Vandalism: Militaries and the
Environment." In Silliman and King 1999, 163–88.

Shiva, Vandana. 1988. *Staying Alive: Women, Ecology and
Development.* London: Zed.

———. 1993. "Colonialism and the Evolution of
Masculinist Forestry." In *The "Racial" Economy of Science:
Toward a Democratic Future*, ed. Sandra Harding, 303–14.
Bloomington: Indiana University Press.

———. 1994. *Close to Home: Women Reconnect Ecology, Health,
and Development Worldwide.* Philadelphia: New Society.

———. 2000. *Stolen Harvest: The Hijacking of the Global
Food Supply.* Cambridge, Mass.: South End.

Silliman, Jael, and Ynestra King. 1999. *Dangerous
Intersections: Feminist Perspectives on Population, Environment
and Development.* Cambridge, Mass.: South End.

Singer, Peter. 1975. *Animal Liberation.* New York: Avon.

Slicer, Deborah. 1991. "Your Daughter or Your Dog? A
Feminist Assessment of the Animal Research Issue."
Hypatia: A Journal of Feminist Philosophy 6(1): 110–24.

Spiegel, Marjorie. 1988. *The Dreaded Comparison: Human and
Animal Slavery.* Philadelphia: New Society.

Steingraber, Sandra. 1997. *Living Downstream.* New York:
Vintage.

———. 2001. *Having Faith: An Ecologist's Journey to
Motherhood.* Cambridge, Mass.: Perseus.

Sturgeon, Noël. 1997. *Ecofeminist Natures: Race, Gender,
Feminist Theory, and Political Action.* New York:
Routledge.

Taylor, Dorceta. 1989. "Blacks and the Environment:
Toward an Explanation of the Concern and Action Gap."
Environment and Behavior 21(2):175–205.

Warren, Karen J. 1990. "The Power and Promise of
Ecological Feminism." *Environmental Ethics* 12(2):125–46.

———. 1997. *Ecofeminism: Women, Culture, Nature.*
Bloomington: Indiana University Press.

———. 2000. *Ecofeminist Philosophy: A Western Perspective on
What It Is and Why It Matters.* Lanham, Md.: Rowman &
Littlefield.

———, ed. 1991. "Ecological Feminism," special issue of
Hypatia: A Journal of Feminist Philosophy, vol. 6, no. 1.

Wingspread Statement on the Precautionary Principle.
1998. Available on-line at www.sehn.org/wing.html.

Wolch, Jennifer. 2001. "Attitudes toward Marine Wildlife
among Residents of Southern California's Urban Coastal
Zone." Unpublished manuscript, University of Southern
California.

Wolch, Jennifer, Alex Brownlow, and Unna Lassiter. 2000.
"Attitudes toward Animals among African American
Women in Los Angeles." In *Animal Spaces, Beastly Places:
New Geographies of Human-Animal Relations*, ed. Chris
Philo and Chris Wilbert. London: Routledge.

Women and Life on Earth. 1979. "Unity Statement."
Available on-line at www.womenandlife.org/WLOE-en/
background/unity-statem.html.

NOTES

1. One of the most comprehensive overviews of the emergence
   of ecofeminism in the United States is Sturgeon 1997.

2. These and related reports are available at: www.
   ourstolenfuture.org; www.silentspring.org; www.bcaction.org.

3. Health/GIS studies are also occurring elsewhere, but the
   Massachusetts and New York breast cancer studies are the
   largest. Information on these studies is available through
   www.silenstspring.org and www.healthgis-li.com.

4. The precautionary principle is now widely discussed.
   Some of the best articulations of it can be found in Steingraber 1997; Raffensperger and Tickner 1999; and
   the Web site of the Science and Environmental Health
   Network, www.sehn.org.

5. Sardar 1988; Agarwal 1992; Mies and Shiva 1993;
   Seager 1999; Silliman and King 1999; Kurian 2000;
   Shiva 2000.

PUTTING MYSELF IN THE PICTURE:
Researching Disability and Technology (2001)

Wendy Seymour is senior lecturer in the School of Social Work and Social Policy at the University of South Australia. She is the author of *Bodily Alterations: An introduction to the sociology of the body for health workers*. The following piece was first published in an anthology, *Technologies and Health: Critical Compromises*.

[. . .]

INTRODUCTION

[. . .]

In this chapter I interrogate issues associated with disability and technology, the subject of my research activities over the last two years. While I will draw on the insights given to me by the participants in these investigations, in this chapter I plan to put myself into the picture. While I am involved in collecting data from others, I am concurrently engaging with technology myself—a woman researcher with a disability using technology to engage in research with people with disabilities who use technology.

THE ROLE OF THE RESEARCHER

[. . .]

Focusing on the lives of "other people" obscures the researcher's own experiences and concerns. While quantitative methodologies have traditionally been incriminated in this practice, women researchers may also be inclined to approach research in this way, because detachment—the notion of taking oneself out of the picture in order to focus on the concerns of others—conforms to traditional gendered behaviour. The primacy of other people's concerns is established by the diminishment of one's own. Although covert, this practice reflects a view that the researcher is merely a technician who records, documents, and publishes the material of others. However well meaning, this practice is far from neutral.

While the relationship between researcher and the researched is always difficult, disability research has provoked vigorous argument that research which sees the disabled as the objects of research, rather than its authors, exacerbates their sense of exclusion and oppression. These arguments imply that only people with disabilities should research issues related to disability (Bury 1996, pp. 34–5). In examining my own experiences with disability and technology, I am engaging transparent research practices in order to establish a more egalitarian, reciprocal research agenda.

Although some people may dismiss the activity of self-research as mere egocentricity, it is never an easy task to reflect on one's own experience or behaviour. However, neglecting this issue, or failing to engage in the activity, could be seen as both churlish and methodologically reprehensible (Seymour 1998a, p. xi).

The researcher is open to criticism for expecting others to participate in an activity in which he or she chooses not to engage, but more importantly, the researcher hides or obscures the role he or she plays in the definition, development, and outcome of the project. What is written is displayed as if it were disconnected from the processes that made it possible (Wynne 1988, p. 103).

A researcher's ability to establish rapport and a trusting relationship with the person who is being interviewed is a critical component of research success. In collecting data for an earlier, more general study, the informants made it clear to me that my visible disability legitimated my right to conduct the research. In their eyes, the additional fact that I had worked and conducted previous research in the area confirmed that I had paid my dues in terms of commitment (Seymour 1998a, pp. 27–8). All researchers are centrally implicated in the knowledge process, in the writing of culture (Game 1991, p. 7). In terms of this research it is clear that I am far from a neutral component. It is imperative that I "write myself" into the project. In this chapter, I will identify issues related to my own experiences of technological engagement.

RESEARCH AND SELF-RESEARCH

People with disabled bodies are vulnerable to exploitation by others in many aspects of their lives (Albrecht 1992; Deegan & Brooks 1985; Dovey & Gaffram 1987; Lonsdale 1990; Oliver 1990; Smith & Smith 1991). . . . While people with disabilities may engage in a range of strategies to deflect attention from aspects of their bodies, their body is, in effect, "given" to the world for evaluation. Because the body is visible, others feel free to judge and appraise the person without notice or negotiation. When they become the subjects of scholarly inquiry, physical disabilities, with their conspicuous nature, and many specific disabling conditions, because of their rarity, act to heighten the possibility of identification and compromise the possibility of confidentiality. Vulnerability is thus a key issue in disability research.

Only seldom does the researcher experience the process of "being researched." I clearly remember a personal experience of being researched by others. Because of my disability I was asked to participate in a history-taking assessment activity undertaken by health professional students. I had been briefed by the lecturer to answer all questions truthfully, to expand on points if warranted, but not to introduce new topics or lines of inquiry. At the end of the lengthy process of data collection, the students were required to report verbally on what they had found out about me, "the patient," in my presence. Undertaken with serious intention and with much thoughtfulness and good will on the part of both the interviewers and the interviewee, this exercise remains vivid in my memory as an example of the distortions, misinterpretations, and incorrect reportage that may come to constitute a "case history"—the collection of information social scientists call data.

Moreover, as Williams points out (1988, p. 110), the dangers of exploitation may be heightened, not eradicated, by an attempt to create a more equal relationship between the researcher and the researched. Research participants are not dummies; they do not merely comply with our wishes or dutifully respond to our questions. . . . They are capable of subverting and resisting the process by withholding or distorting information, or by using the project to further their own personal or political needs. The dearth of studies that engage social scientists as research subjects may reflect reluctance to engage in work with people who are perceived to have highly developed skills in disruption and subversive activities!

[. . .]

Yet while self-research can be very illuminating, the activity only approximates the experience of being researched by someone else. The researcher remains the information gatekeeper. As with autobiographical writing in general, control remains in the hands of the author, no matter how "revealing" or "insightful" the work purports to be.

[. . .]

DISABILITY AND TECHNOLOGY

Research involving the topic of disability evokes a range of issues other than the issue of vulnerability discussed earlier. People with disabilities make other people feel uncomfortable. Bodily pain and dysfunction are "one's own business" to be managed in silence unless some specific information is required—perhaps by a clinician to confirm a diagnosis or by a social scientist to substantiate a point. People should not speak about their disability unless spoken to: they should remain stoic and silent unless requested to supply specific information about the "problem." Moreover, people with disabilities who are employed full time or who hold responsible positions in the workplace are "not really disabled"—their work status somehow eradicates the disability. Employability still conflicts with the old personal-tragedy model of disability (Oliver 1990, p. 10), and the participation of women with disabilities in public space significantly compounds this stereotype (Seymour 1998b, pp. 164–5).

Living with disability is living a life of constant management, adjustment, and compromise. If the disability is progressive or involves periods of exacerbation and remission, the person must constantly juggle those activities that can be accommodated, and discard or abandon those things that can no longer be accomplished. Making deals with the body—weighing up the losses and gains, trading this for that, pleading a special case, promising to rest up if you can just finish whatever—draws a line between coping and not coping that is fine, and must be continually negotiated; it offers flimsy and precarious support for identity and self-esteem. Living with a disability involves ongoing processes of disembodiment and re-embodiment in response to the challenge of risk, uncertainty, and vulnerability. While not essentially different from the processes by which everyone manages himself or herself in everyday life (Nettleton & Watson 1998), these activities assume heightened importance in the lives of people with physical disabilities.

Augmenting damaged organs with mechanical devices, supplementing strength in muscles and bones, and substituting bodily activities disrupted by blockage, dysfunction, or neural loss have become almost routine techniques of medical practice. Biotechnology now offers a wide range of procedures for bodily restoration and repair. The accelerated development of technology in recent years presents a less comfortable spectre. While promising boundless opportunities for novel bodily experience, sensation, function, and performance, medical technologies expose the body to the risks of surveillance, disembodiment, refabrication, and transcendence (Seymour 1998a, pp. 180–5).

In terms of current practice and use, however, technology offers tantalising opportunities to people with disabilities. Reducing the effect of disease fluctuations, ameliorating pain, and preventing further deformity and destruction must be seen as high priorities in this precarious context. Controlling the physical manifestations of the disease process by invoking the large range of medical, pharmacological, or technical interventions now available will result in a more durable, reliable body. Bodily harmony may be restored by prosthetic substitution and organ bypass. Managing weakness and pain will eliminate the fine line of uncertainty and unpredictability that people with disabilities must constantly negotiate.

Many people feel that technology has taken them by surprise. In fact, technology has been taking us by stealth for a very long time. None of us is immune from technology, though we seldom stop to consider the extent of our immersion and reliance. Workplace restructuring and economic rationalist practices have forced all but the most resistant among us to engage with computer technology. For some, conducting a simple banking transaction through a machine may evoke fear and trepidation. Others may feel that committing personal information to a database for medical, economic, legal, or other "legitimate" purposes effectively strips them of autonomy, knowledge, and control. Anxieties over the "millennium bug" may well be a thinly veiled resentment about our involuntary conscription into the techno-world. Resentment about some technological developments must be tempered by recognition of the enormous potential of others.

PUTTING MYSELF IN THE PICTURE

For me, the computer seemed like my salvation. An inflammatory joint condition since middle adolescence has had a strong impact on my body. While scarcely a joint has escaped the destructive progress of the disease, the major impact has been in my upper limbs, particularly in the joints of my wrists and fingers. The disease has provoked several significant career changes to accommodate deteriorating function and prolong my working life. The relatively sedentary life of an academic seemed ideal, the advent of the computer heaven sent.

Writing a book in 1988 (Seymour 1989) was a painstaking process of handwriting and laborious rewriting. Construction and placement of elements of the argument involved cutting the written work with scissors and inserting sections into more appropriate locations in the text with clear tape. Once relocated, the selection seldom fitted the developing argument as well as expected, thus requiring another cut, move, fix, and repair of the site, as well as the new location. Paragraphs usually needed reconstruction to accommodate the new material; introductory preamble and concluding comments added to situate the point into the larger argument. Margin notes and other scribbled instructions identified additional tasks to be done and indicated where they should be inserted: direct and instructional, but greatly adding to the visual confusion of the developing manuscript. Correction fluid and an eraser were constantly utilised in an effort to avoid more wholesale change, mostly unsuccessfully. A much-thumbed dictionary averted humiliation, and a thesaurus suggested a range of ways to express the same thing. Photocopying preserved the day's effort and protected the ongoing work. Cluttered, uneven pages cobbled together with sticky tape, additions crabbed between the lines; an expanding pile of paper filled with asterisks, dashes, and other editorial hieroglyphs was the product of my labours. Scissors, sticky tape, correction fluid, erasers, a mountain of pens, and piles of writing pads were the tools of this production. Finding the correct coins for the photocopy machine became a daily obsession. The meaning of "manuscript" is "a handwritten document," and in 1988 this is exactly what I did.

In 1997, a new book (Seymour 1998a). By now there was a computer on every desk. Moving text, trying it out in a new context, inserting a section from another document, locating words or sections easily, committing common phrases or references to memory for future use, spell checks and a thesaurus were basic functions of the new technology. Neat, clean copies could be printed at will, allowing easy identification of issues requiring further work. Automatic back-up ensured document security. For the nervous writer, three floppy discs upgraded daily guaranteed a good night's sleep. The "manuscript" was now a machine-produced document.

Yet despite the indisputable advantages of word-processor computing, the manuscript is still a handwritten document. While the dominant hand no longer guides the pen over the paper, directs the scissor blades, secures the tape, or searches the pages of the dictionary or thesaurus, word processing is an intensely manual activity. Both hands are now required to activate the keyboard. Fingertips, previously little utilised, now interface between body and machine. The smooth, sinuous actions of handwriting learned at school are replaced by the rapid, repetitive, hammer thrusts required to produce typescript. While replacing the pen with the keyboard has dramatically changed the bodily functions and activities required to produce academic work, the hands are no less implicated in this process. Hands remain central to the production of academic capital.

GENDERED WORK

Transforming the work of others to tidy typescript has long been seen as women's work. Girls who were deemed unsuited for serious positions in the workplace, or who, not surprisingly, saw themselves in these terms, were encouraged to "do typing." The "tidying-up" nature of this activity fitted well with the gendered construction of women's work in serving the needs of others (Pringle 1988).

Secretarial colleges were filled with girls who "chose" this option because it promised a place in an office, a public space in the world of business, rather than the more deeply gendered work of caring for others involved in nursing, kindergarten, and primary teaching. Men created the ideas, women produced the documents. While presentation greatly enhanced the impact of the ideas, essentially the work could be done by any number of women. Secretarial pools attest to the non-personal nature of the work, with the quality of the typewriter often as important as the skills of the typist. Although the work was mechanical, poorly paid, and presented few real opportunities for advancement, office work offered women an alternative to even more traditional women's occupations.

The advent of word-processor technology disrupted the gendered relationship between boss and secretary—between the man as creator of office capital and the woman as producer of clean typescript. Seen almost solely as the preserve of women, typing quite suddenly became everybody's business. Secretaries lost their jobs as men's hands hit the keyboards. While computer hardware was expensive, it represented clear opportunities to "downsize" the workforce. Those secretaries who could reinvent themselves in terms of new workplace directions stayed on; the rest left and were not replaced.

While secretarial work remained the domain of low-paid women workers, the conditions under which the work was conducted received relatively little attention. Compared to some other work, the nine-to-five routine, sedentary, and single-task characteristics of office labour were seen as easy work. Like migrant women workers involved in assembly-line production, the bodily damage caused by repetitive work conducted at the behest of others, over many hours each day, often in cramped conditions, was seldom considered (Julian & Easthope 1996, pp. 115–16; Lin & Pearse 1990, pp. 234–7; Petersen 1994, pp. 80–2; White 1994, p. 51). The design of office equipment compounded the deleterious effects of long hours of static back, neck, and upper-limb posture required to facilitate the continual hammering of fingers on a keyboard (Freund & McGuire 1991, pp. 55–8). The long-term effects on muscles, nerves, and joints were obscured by the transitory nature of women's working life.

The pain experienced by relatively powerless migrant women factory workers was only recognised when middle-class, more politically powerful, women began to use the new computer technology and experience for themselves the pain caused by rapid, repetitive movement. Recognition of the condition resulted in the naming of the syndrome repetitive strain injury, though the medical profession remained sceptical of pain that was often unaccompanied by clear clinical evidence. Since a high incidence of the condition was recorded in Australia, the pejorative term "kangaroo paw" became associated with the condition, denoting a political rather than clinical aetiology (Lin & Pearse 1990, pp. 234–7; Willis 1986).

Similarly, the dramatic increase in men's keyboard usage has provoked concern and presaged major changes to computer design. While non-secretarially trained men and women have taken to the keyboard like lemmings in many workplaces, it is the traditional areas of men's work that are receiving particular attention from computer corporations. Law and medicine, for example, have been high employers of female secretarial labour. To reduce the high cost of labour and construct a lean workforce responsive to change, doctors and lawyers have appropriated the keyboard. If professional workers produce their own documents, significant savings can be made in filing, retrieval, and turnaround time, as well as in salaries. While typewriters were strongly associated with women's work, the new technology is not seen to compromise men's integrity.

The keyboard that activated the new technology was the same design as that used by secretaries to operate the old technology, the typewriter of yesteryear. Not surprisingly, new users began to experience pain and subsequent dysfunction. Compelled to address the concerns of their new clientele in order to protect the burgeoning market, computer companies have focused energy on the development of new and less damaging ways to access the computer. Voice-recognition technology has been developed to bypass the keyboard, to replace hand function with the voice. "Hands-free" technology will protect the new user from the consequences of pain and lost productivity that have bedevilled women workers in the past. Targeted at men in particular parts of the workforce, promotional material for early voice-recognition software highlighted the labour-saving advantages of doing the job yourself while, implicitly, protecting the body from damage. A man used to dictating a letter or a report to a secretary could now dictate directly to a computer using the voice-recognition software. A machine replaces a woman; the potential savings are enormous. As long as there is no bodily cost to the user, the technology promises to reconfigure the workplace dramatically.

PROGRESS REPORT

[. . .]

The change from keyboard to voice activation is comparable to the change from pen to computer. Voice activation involves a lengthy process of training the computer to recognise your voice. As with training a dog, "letting the machine get away with it" will result in a lifetime of bad habits. . . .

While I worked hard for many months to fit voice-activation training into my crowded academic workload, I have abandoned the task. Although the deterioration of my hands greatly heightened my motivation to succeed, I gave up. While technological adoption is usually conspicuous, abandonment is often invisible. Why did I do this?

I gave up because the process was difficult and extremely time consuming. I worked long into the night and at weekends to make up the work I had been unable to complete during the training process—invisible, body-tiring labour. I was not resistant to change; indeed I recognised the absolute necessity to adopt new ways of doing work in order to prolong my working life. I gave up as a result of careful analysis and conscious choices—the context of critical compromise within which women manage their lives. In truth, the greatly extended working hours were

endangering the very joints I was endeavouring to spare in order to extend my working life. Yet despite the analytical decision-making process, I felt guilty. People with disabilities are judged by how well they can prove to others that they are trying to help themselves. I felt that in failing to master the technology I had failed to help myself. Both gender and age compounded my sense of failure: I felt that I was acting out the stereotypical script associated with older women and, as if this was not enough, I felt guilty about the financial cost to my employer. I now use an old wooden coat-hanger I discovered at the back of a cupboard, a "technology" from a much earlier time. By removing the central hook, I am able to use the curved remaining section to prod the computer keys into life, one by one and slowly. My joints are less painful and I can continue to write. It works for me.

CONCLUSION

[. . .]

In terms of disability, technology can be seen to reproduce some of the characteristics of medicine. While it seems highly desirable to substitute technology for lost function, this seductive solution is underpinned by a mechanistic view of the body, long associated with the "medical model" (Freund & McGuire 1991, pp. 203–29; Petersen 1994, pp. 20–1; Seymour 1989, chapter 4; White 1996, pp. 38–9). In this perspective, the body is viewed in terms of a machine, parts of which may malfunction or wear out. Identification of the problem and isolation of the part prepares the way for remedial intervention. Just as the plumber turns off the water at the meter to work on the kitchen tap, the doctor also assumes that work on a part of the body will have no more than temporary impact on the body as a whole. As the medical model reduced the body to a machine, so too may the technology—machine model compromise and reduce the body.

Technology is not neutral; it is not simply a functional aid. Technology is highly political; it is gendered and intrusive. While seemingly pragmatic and solution driven, technology is capable of reproducing the problems associated with medicine in the past. It may not only be body denying but also threaten the embodied self.

[. . .]

My disability has not only directed my research in particular ways, but the insights of the research participants have helped me to understand my own experiences and frustrations. The participants have enabled me to see that my problems are not located in personal failure or ineptitude, but in the structures of technological production, marketing, and training. Shared experiences, shared fears, reciprocal understandings. Not *my* concerns and *their* concerns, but *our* concerns. We share a range of joys and sorrows. As Wynne suggests, putting oneself in the picture may well raise a Pandora's box of "methodological horrors" (1988, p. 114), but omitting to acknowledge the invisible factors that influence and constitute a research project is to commit a greater sin.

---

75. • *Kimberly A. Williams*

WOMEN@WEB:
Cyber Sexual Violence in Canada (New)

Kimberly A. Williams is the director of Women's & Gender Studies at Mount Royal University (MRU) in Calgary, Alberta. Her book *Imagining Russia* won the 2009 SUNY Press First Book Prize in Women's & Gender Studies. The following article, written especially for this collection, is the result of a course on the interconnectedness of Internet communications technologies and men's violence against women that Williams piloted as part of the Gender, Technology & Human Rights Learning Community at MRU.

Men's violence against women has historically been conceptualized as physical/sexual violence affecting the corporeal body. Over the course of the past two decades, however, the ways in which sexualized and gender-based violence is typically inflicted on women and girls has expanded to include cyberspace. The United Nations estimates that 95 percent of abusive behavior in online spaces targets women and comes from their current or former male partners (Fascendini and Fialová 1), and reports indicate that although women and men in the United States have been using the Internet in equal numbers since 2000, "the vilest communications are still disproportionately lobbed at women." A 2006 study on chat rooms conducted by researchers at the University of Maryland found that "[a]ccounts with feminine user names incurred an average of 100 sexually explicit or threatening messages a day" while "[m]asculine names received 3.7" (Hess par. 8). The high-profile media attention given to several teenage girls across Canada who have taken their own lives after experiencing a deadly combination of physical sexual assault plus online sexual coercion, sexual comments or advances, and slut-shaming has recently prompted a national conversation about the role of Internet communications technologies (ICTs), particularly social media outlets, in Canada's already startlingly high rates of violence against women.

In this essay, I provide an overview of the types, causes, and consequences of technology-related violence against women (eVAW) and explore the conditions and structures that have facilitated its sharp increase over the course of the past decade. I close with a discussion of feminist efforts to turn the structural misogyny of ICTs on its head by harnessing them to eradicate eVAW, expand gender equality, and advance social justice.

EVAW: TYPES, CAUSES, AND CONSEQUENCES

While the causes of technology-related sexualized and gender-based violence are, like those of conventional physical/sexual violence against women, rooted in sexism and misogyny, researchers at the University of Western Ontario have demonstrated that "technology extends the reach [of that violence] and creates new forms of abusive behavior" that would not be possible without ICTs. They have identified six broad categories of eVAW, arguing that eVAW is distinguishable from more conventional forms of violence against women due to not only its mode(s) but also its scope and potential for longevity and re-victimization:

1. Hacking: The use of technology to gather and/ or modify private information. This can include stealing passwords or unauthorized editing of a website.
2. Surveillance/Tracking: The use of technology to monitor a victim's activities and behaviors, through, for example, GPS tracking on a mobile phone.
3. Impersonating: The use of technology to assume the identity of the victim or someone else as a means to access private information. This can include sending unauthorized emails from the victim's email account, calling the victim from unknown number, or creating fake identity documents.

4. Harassment/Spamming: The use of technology to continuously contact, annoy, threaten, and/or scare the victim.
5. Recruitment: The use of technology to lure potential victims into violent situations through, for example, fraudulent postings and advertisements on dating or employment sites, chat rooms, or message boards.
6. Malicious Distribution: The use of technology to distribute denigrating and illegal materials related to the victim and/or organizations, e.g., leaking (or threatening to leak) intimate photos/ video or using technology as a propaganda tool to promote violence against women. (Learning Network 2)

With the development over the past three decades of increasingly sophisticated and accessible technologies, ICTs have made it possible not only for abusers to remain anonymous to the victim/survivor but also for the abuse to be committed from a distance. According to Flavia Fascendini and Kateřina Fialová at the Association for Progressive Communications (APC), because sexual harassers are now able to send abusive messages from anywhere in the world to anyone, anywhere in the world, it is much more difficult for survivors to identify and take legal action against perpetrators (27). Additionally, increased automation (e.g., the reduced time and effort humans spend on particular tasks) enables digital surveillance and stalking by "allow[ing] abusers to check their partners' mobile phones for SMS messages, monitor social networking activity, check their browser history and log into their personal accounts with little effort" (26–27). ICTs are also increasingly accessible and affordable. This makes possible the immeasurable scope of eVAW, and the potentially unending cycle of re-victimization as "the propagation of texts and images [. . .] can follow victims/survivors everywhere—at home, work and school, whenever their computer or mobile phone is turned on, without a break or relief" (APC 27).

Feminist researchers have noted that the potential consequences of eVAW "appear to be similar or amplified when compared to violence not involving technology" and can include "psychological impacts (e.g., sadness, shame, depression, stress/anxiety, fear); health impacts (e.g., health concerns related to stress); privacy concerns (e.g., embarrassment or fear associated with the belief that one is or has been watched or monitored; use of a woman's personal information against her); and social effects (e.g., compromised sense of security; social withdrawal; isolation; compromised productivity at work; loss of income; loss of reputation)" (Learning Network 2). Additionally, young women who participated in a May 2015 workshop on cyber-violence in Toronto pointed out that the "harms of unwanted harassment, sexual bullying and spreading of sexual rumours [. . .] are regarded as common occurrences online" and that eVAW "could lead to depression, anxiety, emotional trauma, lowered self-esteem and confidence, and self-harm and suicide" (metracadmin pars. 2-3).

The obvious question, often leveled at girls and women by everyone, from their harassers to the police officers they call in to stop the abuse, is, "If you're being harassed, why don't you simply get off the Internet?" The inherent problem with such a suggestion is that, just as men do, women use the Internet for work and play, and it has become a constitutive part of most of our lives. In fact, the girls who participated in the Toronto workshop on cyber-violence back in May 2015 said that it would be impossible to disengage with the Internet, "as it might mean missing out on important dialogues, events and news" (metracadmin par. 3). The suggestion, then, that women should get offline in order to avoid being the victim of eVAW is akin to warning them to stay home in order to avoid being raped.

UNPACKING INTERNET GOVERNANCE, LAW ENFORCEMENT, AND STEM

So what's going on? The answer to this question is at least fourfold. First, there's the ubiquity of men's violence against women: Gender norms, stereotypes, and hierarchical power relations between men and women that exist offline are clearly being replicated online. Second, although slightly more women than men are using social media (Dickey par. 5), the leaders, decision-makers, and designers behind the scenes at companies like Twitter, LinkedIn, Facebook, and Google are, according to those companies' own internal diversity reports, overwhelmingly white men. According to *Forbes*, women comprise, on average, only about one-third of the tech workforce (Marcus par. 3). That gap expands the higher up one goes in an organization, with the best ICT company, Facebook, showing women holding just 23.1 percent of leadership jobs (Jones and Trop par. 8). Most of those reports also gathered statistics about gender and ethnicity for technical jobs, finding (not surprisingly) that white and Asian men tend to dominate in technical jobs like coding and programming, while women and other people of color are clustered in administrative support and service work. These results confirm that the sphere of Internet governance is heavily patriarchal. Not only does it ascribe to the "five men and a whiteboard" model in which men outnumber women as decision-makers, but it also means that men's bodies, perspectives, concerns, and ways of doing things are assumed to be normal and natural, thus resulting in the framing of issues and agendas that looks universal and gender-neutral but that is actually "indebted to privileged positions in the hierarchy between men and women as well as the hierarchy among different groups of men" (Jensen 55).

The third answer to the question of what's going on is that the understanding of what actually counts as men's violence against women among policymakers and law enforcement officials has not caught up with the eVAW made possible by ICTs. For example, when one female journalist reported bomb threats made against her via Twitter, the officers sent to investigate the case "thought usernames were secret codes and didn't seem to know what an IP address was" (Hess par. 24). Adding to their confusion, at least in Canada, is the myth that there are no existing laws that make cyber sexual violence a crime. But Toronto-based feminist bloggers Jessica Spence and Steph Guthrie argue that Canada's Criminal Code includes "more than a few laws which prohibit" behaviors ranging from stalking and hate speech to counseling suicide (e.g., telling someone to kill themselves) and advocating genocide (e.g., suggesting that all feminists should be killed) (par. 34). The problem, then, is not that laws against eVAW do not exist but that police are stuck in conventional notions of what counts as "violence against women" that "require that victims feel tangible, immediate, and sustained fear" (Hess par. 29). They do not know how to apply existing laws to online activities that they interpret as not real, harmless, and/or inevitable (Hess par. 31).

The fourth concern is that, although girls and women are the majority of social media users, there is a widespread lack of knowledge among them regarding the mechanics of the Internet, especially in terms of how to maintain their privacy in cyberspace. This lack of knowledge is likely directly related to the dramatic underenrollment around the world of girls and women in sciences, technology, engineering, and math (STEM), all of which are considered the domain of men. In Canada, women comprise the majority of university graduates in education, health sciences, humanities, visual and performing arts, communications, social and behavioral sciences, and law, but men represent the overwhelming majority (67.4 percent) of STEM graduates (*Violence* par. 31). The upshot, then, is that even though women *use* technology, they are not participating in its creation, design, and implementation. Nor do they tend to know how it works, which, given the increasing ubiquity of eVAW, could well be fatal.

ERADICATING EVAW: HARNESSING ICTS FOR GENDER JUSTICE

Feminists in Canada have been quick to respond productively and proactively to the rapid expansion into cyberspace of sexualized violence over the past two decades. They are making extensive use of ICTs to support victims/survivors and prevent men's violence against women. Brick-and-mortar anti-VAW organizations across the country maintain websites that provide information and connect survivors to service providers, and some now also offer free online anti-VAW training that specifically addresses how technology has transformed what counts as "violence against women." Additionally, several Facebook groups not only deliver information on anti-VAW tools, resources, and upcoming events, but they also facilitate discussion forums that enable survivors to connect with each other, raise awareness, and call out online violence as unacceptable. Last, a plethora of new mobile apps "can help locate, identify, respond to, and support victims of violence and reduce their risk of further harm" (Learning Network 3).

This work has served as a catalyst for several educational programs that help get girls into STEM and keep them there and/or teach girls and women to be savvy tech users, especially of ICTs. It has also been at the heart of a national push to (re)educate and train Canadian law enforcement officials to recognize and take seriously eVAW cases and the applicability to them of existing laws. The pioneering work of Canadian feminists against eVAW has also made possible the creation of a new national legal framework to address what Canadian lawmakers term "cyber sexual violence," resulting in the passage by Parliament of Bill C-13 in October 2014. Unfortunately, Bill C-13 has been the source of much controversy, as feminists have argued that it will be relatively ineffectual in protecting survivors of eVAW because it fails to address the root causes of sexual violence. Additionally, the legislation does not acknowledge the fact that people of color, women, and member of the LGBTQ+ community are more likely to experience online violence.

Feminist antiviolence research projects like APC, GenderIT.org, and the University of Western Ontario's Learning Network, along with a few individual feminist tech journalists and bloggers, have repeatedly demanded increased research and reporting on cybersexism and eVAW. In addition to their demand for the collection of gender-disaggregated data about the male-dominated tech industry (which resulted, finally, in the gender and racial diversity reporting by so many technology companies in 2014), they advocate improving women's access to ICT governance by addressing the inherent sexism and racism in the tech industry, arguing that nondiscrimination, gender equality, and women's empowerment must be guiding principles.

The next feminist eVAW frontier, then, will be to decide how to best proceed with the unsurprising information that ICTs such as YouTube, Facebook, and Twitter are fairly transparently white supremacist, patriarchal structures that have not only excluded women and most people of color from governance and high-level technology jobs but also facilitated a culture of systemic misogyny that legitimates, and even enables, the mobilization of sexism and sexist exploitation in cyberspace, resulting in eVAW.

WORKS CITED

Dickey, Megan Rose. "23 Statistics That Prove Men Dominate the Tech World." *Business Insider,* 15 July 2013, www.businessinsider.com.au/statistics-prove-men-dominate-tech-world-2013-7.

Fascendini, Flavia, and Kateřina Fialová. *Voices from Digital Spaces: Technology Related Violence Against Women.* Association for Progressive Communications, Dec. 2011, www.genderit.org/sites/default/upload/apcwnsp_mdg3advocacypaper_full_2011_en_0.pdf.

Guthrie, Steph and Jessica Spence. "The 7 Deadly Myths of Online Violence Against Women." *Witopoli: Women in Toronto Politics,* 11 Oct. 2013, witopoli.com/2013/10/11/the-7-deadly-myths-of-online-violence-against-women/.

Hess, Amanda. "Why Women Aren't Welcome on the Internet." *Pacific Standard,* 6 Jan. 2014, psmag.com/why-women-aren-t-welcome-on-the-internet-aa21fdbc8d6#.v7o0auqxd.

Jensen, Heike. "Whose Internet Is It Anyway? Shaping the Internet—Feminist Voices in Governance and Decision Making." *Global Information Society Watch,* 2013, www.giswatch.org/institutional-overview/womens-rights-gender/whose-internet-it-anyway-shaping-internet-feminist-voice.

Jones, Stacy and Jocelyn Trope. "See How the Big Tech Companies Compare on Employee Diversity." *Fortune,* 30 July 2015, fortune.com/2015/07/30/tech-companies-diversity/.

Learning Network. *Technology-Related Violence Against Women.* Centre for Research and Education on Violence Against Women and Children, April 2013, www.vawlearningnetwork.ca/network-areas/technology-related-violence.

Marcus, Bonnie. "The Lack of Diversity in Tech is a Cultural Issue." *Forbes.* 12 Aug. 2015, www.forbes.com/sites/bonniemarcus/2015/08/12/the-lack-of-diversity-in-tech-is-a-cultural-issue/#37e4bc453577.

metracadmin. "How do young women experience cyber sexual violence?" *METRAC,* 12 June 2015, www.metrac.org/how-do-young-women-experience-cyber-sexual-violence/.

Violence Against Women Survey. Statistics Canada, 1993, http://www23.statcan.gc.ca/ imdb-bmdi/pub/3896-eng.htm.

76. • *Jason Whitesel*

GAY MEN'S USE OF ONLINE PICTURES IN FAT-AFFIRMING GROUPS[1] (2010)

Jason Whitesel is an assistant professor in Women's & Gender Studies at Pace University. He is the author of *Fat Gay Men: Girth, Mirth, and the Politics of Stigma.* The following essay was previously published in an anthology, *LGBT Identity and Online New Media.*

The Internet has occasioned a new relationship between gay identity and body symbolism, in reworked commercial images for men who are inadequately represented by advertising and other forms of media. Cyberspace offers fat gay men a forum where they can reconfigure imagery and text, to signal issues of personal, collective, and gender identity.[2] Though the counseling community has discussed how advertisements negatively affect gay consumers' perceptions of their bodies (Matthews 2005; Shernoff 2002), few have considered advertisements as part of an interactive process that provides an opportunity for gay men to re-evaluate their body images in virtual and actual experiences. To develop a larger model for understanding visibility politics and virtual body images, this chapter examines how the subject of fat gay men trying to gain a presence in existing advertising offers evidence of resistant cultural practices. Building on studies that unpack the complex semiotics of advertisements and media images (Bordo 1997; Goffman 1979), the chapter discusses how reworking the images can provide a site for both critique and reinstatement of conformity.

Two visual case studies—*Absolut Beefy* and the "fat morph"—provide physically inventive images that challenge conventional portrayals of fat in an effort to enhance fat's visibility to a number of supportive enthusiasts. The first is a remake of a vodka advertisement, and the second is a digital remake of an underwear advertisement, both introduce fat into advertising. Regarding semiotic structures, fat gay men emerge as "inveterate and promiscuous producers of signs" (Hawkes 1977, 134). Visual semiotics involves continuous dismantling and reassembling of visual texts, recognizing that visual communication represents "not the mere 'embroidery' of 'reality,' but a way of knowing it, of coping with it, and of changing it" (Hawkes 1977, p. 143). This chapter asks, "In what ways do emerging visual technologies reshape fat politics for gay men?"

This discussion focuses on work by an artist who recreates commercial images and another who digitally alters them, both doing something similar to "subvertisements" (a subversive form of re-appropriating advertising images (see Ironkite 2009)). Both artists mimic the "look and feel" of the originals while incorporating fat-affirming themes (Lasn 2000, p. 131). Both also "poach" basic visual elements from widely circulated ad campaigns, convert them into a vehicle for reclaiming a fat gay male identity, and recirculate the new images among members of online subcultures. Since these artists actively participate in online fat-friendly groups, their works "speak from a position of collective identity, to forge an alliance with a community of others in defense of tastes" (Jenkins 1992, p. 23).

GAY BODIES WITHIN THE BOUNDS

Like heterosexual women, gay men experience conflict with their appearance, physique, and relationship to food more than heterosexual men do. Gay men do not retain the benefits of fatness that heterosexual men have historically. They also negatively associate fat with effeminacy. It is important therefore to identify boundaries, the role of advertising, and the historical context of fatness and body image, including its gendered implications for gay men. Folding in social history, this chapter situates the images in the context of developing gay social trends, referencing events like HIV/AIDS that influence gay men's current and everyday understandings of fatness and their bodies. Gay men revisit their relationships to fat subsequent to diseased bodies and recognize that their adherence to the norms and physicality of hegemonic masculinity remains under constant surveillance. Thus, gay men live in historically constituted and highly gendered communities. For the contemporary generation of gay men, loosening the restrictions on their waistlines signifies a reconfiguring of gay body concepts.

Body image influences boundary marking: "conceptions of bodily boundaries and social order" raise "consciousness about how fundamental body imagery is to worldview and so to political language" (Haraway 1986, p. 520). Commercialized images reify body boundaries. Most gay personals, for instance, reflect these persistent images and separate bodies with the usual seeker's request that one should be in shape and "please, *NO* fats or femmes!" Following the personal ad lingo, failure to be "height-weight proportionate" exceeds the bounds of how a gay body "ought to *look*" (Goode 2005, p. 328). Gay men marginalize those who don't conform to strict bodily standards and use these boundaries to create inequality, the most salient of which is gender (Giles 1998). Heterosexism perpetuates the myth that gay men are effeminate and that effeminate men must be gay; simultaneously, it assumes that same-sex relationships include a masculine role and feminine complement. Fat produces stereotypical feminized features that threaten masculinity and its archetype of the disciplined, muscular body (Bell and McNaughton 2007; Durgadas 1998). It reinforces the effeminate label when men develop breasts or hips and diminishes the visibility of their genitals (Millman 1980). To gain acceptance, gay men often adopt rigid gender roles, such as the straight-acting, masculine male, to create a border between themselves and the stigma surrounding the "fats" and the "femmes" (Bergling 2001; Connell 1992). Thus, gay men use gendered dimensions of the body to make in- and out-group distinctions.

Advertising plays an irresponsible role in the construction of boundaries, seducing gay men to subordinate their bodies to systems of commercial oppression. Similar to female beauty standards, gay men feel compelled to purchase products and procedures that market physical "perfection" (Signorile 1997). Thus, advertising as a boundary-ordering device implicates gay men in financing industries that contribute to their body dissatisfaction. Like other body aesthetics, the gay male aesthetic rewards those with a lean, taut, and muscular upper body, and visual elements of gay culture such as clubs and commercial representations reinforce this standard. The oppressive content of gay visual culture centers on body worship of male models in homoerotic media like pornography and magazines about physique and fashion. Because many gay men prioritize personal appearance, they spend an inordinate amount of time and resources trying to change their appearance through gyms, cosmetic surgery, tanning, and hair restoration and removal

(Blotcher 1998; Drummond 2005; Feraios 1998; Padva 2002). Commercial images exclude imperfect gay bodies, namely fat, old, or disabled, and divide men along these lines.

ONLINE AUDIENCES FOR GAY- AND FAT-AFFIRMING IMAGES

Web transformation of commercialized images is a proliferating phenomenon defined by its instability. The image analysis in this chapter comes from two personal profile websites that cater exclusively to fat gay men and their admirers.[3] The first, targeted at young adults, is marketed by a young network administrator from Florida, who is stereotypically handsome and "well built" (over 6 feet tall, about 190 lbs, with an athletic build). Since the site was started from his standpoint as an outsider who admires big-and-beefy college gays, objectification was central to this site's inception. Started in early 2003 as a fraternity with international membership mostly from North America, the site invites members to post personal profile images that provide pleasure to members who largely assume them to be authentic.

Affirming fellow gay men of larger stature, the second site was started by an insider, a big man from Ohio, and his supportive partner, in 1996 when the Internet was taking off (Textor 1999). On the main page, there was a clickable link to galleries featuring members' fat-and-gay fantasy and erotic folkart (Wright cited in Campbell 2004). The gallery contained everything from sketches and animation to digital artwork. This site went down in 2006 with hopes of moving to a new server.

Gay- and fat-affirming images on these sites resurface as numerous moderated e-mail groups pick up where the websites leave off. For example, one of the largest storehouses of images displayed a series of nine *Yahoo!* groups inspired by homoerotic pictures of beer-drinking college men proudly showing off their guts. Here members posted individual photo albums, but the archives mostly contained images collected by the moderator for admirers to consume. Now there are videos on YouTube that evoke responses from enthusiasts such as "I wish I looked like that!" Cross-posting provides images with broader coverage. Furthermore, each site sorts and catalogues images differently, so the categorization of different "types" varies depending on the group's specialization (Hacking 1986; Textor 1999). The appeal of appropriated images online comes from giving them a new twist under a fat-affirming framework. Members of fat interest groups negotiate and transform meanings of mainstream images by reading them both with and "against the grain," (Benjamin 1968, p. 257) taking what the image-maker originally intended and then recasting it in a playful "key" (Goffman 1974, p. 44; Hall 1998 [originally 1981]). Groups organize around similar viewing habits, reinforcing alternative visual codes that eroticize the fat male body.

NEW MEDIA: AN APPARATUS FOR SOCIAL CHANGE

Online groups of fat gay men construct a sense of community based on asserting the visibility of the body and they rely heavily on the stylized repetition of images to build their communities.[4] Based on conceptual interest, two image exemplars from these communities are discussed here, and interpreted in close relation to the analytical and theoretical frameworks of semiotics and boundary work.

During HBO's final season of the series, *Sex and the City* (Home Box Office 1998–2004, USA), Samantha's love interest, Smith Jared, appears in a vodka campaign with the slogan *Absolut Hunk.* Peter Gehrke, who takes pictures for the real vodka company, produced the fake ad (Atkinson 2003). The simulation, inspired by 70s pinups, features Smith nude with a vodka bottle carefully positioned in front of his genitals. In this iconic sign, Smith, the object of the advertisement, boasts a smooth, tanned and muscled physique, a sprinkling of facial scruff and surfer hair, all signifying sexual desirability. The bottle's placement associates vodka with sexual opportunity: removing it would fully expose the model, supplying sex plus the goods (Schroeder

2002). The ad was such a highly successful product placement that several viewers, even men, requested copies of the image (Atkinson 2003).

The glorious image of *Absolut Hunk* soon took on a new meaning. Following the episode, "celebrity fat" became a theme in the press and popular imagination surrounding the ad, appealing to gay men in fat-affirming groups. Was Smith fat? Absolutely not: as he drew in his abdominal muscles, viewers could see his ribcage. However, ad executives reported having digitally airbrushed the original photo to remove Smith's "love handles" (Atkinson 2003). Then a week into the media hype over the advertisement and its production, a fat gay artist decided to remake the ad by visually substituting his own body for Smith's and naming it *Absolut Beefy . . .* From his double vantage point of artist *and* model, the artist reflexively inserted himself into a narrow image of beauty, thereby redefining body politics through an alternative representation. This fatvertisement challenged the dominant one that the television producers had conveyed. Thus, in defense of fat identity, *Absolut beefy* borrowed and changed the meaning *of Absolut Hunk* from that intended by its fat-phobic creators. The artist posted this subcultural image, with the similar slogan, on the first website mentioned above, where male spectators go to view profiles of fat men.

The fatvertisement appropriates the homoerotic content of the original, while imagining a popular culture inclusive of fat men. It resembles the original ad and demands that the beefy character be equivalent to the hunk. Even though elsewhere, the artist usually reveals body hair, he chose to mimic the original image in this fatvertisement, thereby commenting only on fat vs. thin. Had he left his body hairy in his fatvertisement, viewers might have missed his point about body size or been led to imagine a hairy *Absolut Bear.* Like the original, the parody retains a soft focus produced by the natural light and white bedding enveloping the model. However, the fat model's posture and gaze differ. The poached ad uses "self-flaunting" to re-signify Smith's languid posture and bedroom eyes used to entice the spectator (Joanisse and Synnott cited in Monaghan 2005, p. 101). It projects attitude: the model cocks his head and challenges the viewer with his dead-on stare, making no effort to "suck in" his stomach.[5] Nevertheless, the remake subtly pays "homage to the phallic power of masculinity" evident in the original, in which the positioning of the bottle substitutes for an erection (Hennen 2005, p. 35). In the remake, the artist/model intentionally positions the bottleneck to intersect the crease under his stomach and the cap directs the viewer to a cavernous navel surrounded by handfuls of flab. The fat model's swollen (which may be read as phallic) body contrasts with Smith's trim, muscular frame, shifting the sexual focus away from the penis and redirecting it across the entire upper body (Kulick 2005). Overall, *Absolut Beefy* sexualizes a body typically left out of both popular culture and gay men's media.

Similar to *Absolut's* campaign, advertisements for Calvin Klein underwear accentuate the homoerotic aspects of the brand. It was in the early 1990s that icons modeling them became enormously popular: Mark Wahlberg began modeling underwear with Kate Moss in one of Klein's most widely distributed campaigns in 1992. Today, male models, who strike classically inspired poses in their contemporary boxer briefs, represent a mainstay of consumer culture. Such advertisements commodify (and sometimes domesticate) macho men like Wahlberg in order to persuade consumers to buy underwear.

One of the ads, taken by gay photographer Herb Ritts, features Wahlberg in his underwear against a vacant background, unaccompanied by models or props. In this mainstream underwear promotion, also cross-marketed to gay men, the hairless and ripped male body signifies an object to be consumed. The spatial organization of this three-quarter length, black-and-white portrait of Wahlberg standing and facing front creates a subordinate effect: the bad boy is now held captive for the viewer. The model's manner also communicates a related message: like a child, the model is clowning around naked, playfully tugging the hem of his underpants, euphorically throwing his head back, while appeasing the viewer with his irresistible smile, being vulnerable in a stereotypically feminine way (Bordo 1999; Goffman 1974).

Like the *Absolut Beefy* fatvertisement, a computer artist remade the Wahlberg image by morphing it. . . . The artist uses the process of "tweening" photographs, in which he morphs two images by computer, often stretching, distorting, and twisting them. Through this process he wreaks havoc on commercialized images of men, porn being the most popular (though male celebrities and sport stars come in close second) as targets of his use of transformative technology. The morph of the CK underwear ad parodies how advertisers signify a "real man's" body and appears on at least two fat-affirming websites and one moderated e-mail group. It disrupts the dominant visual system by distorting the original image and spoofing the written text of the ad. In the original, pleasure comes from imagining the genitals underneath the model's briefs, while the morph shifts the focus to another part of the body, that is, the bloated stomach now stretched tightly across the model's midsection with the help of computer technology.

The fat morph represents another way that gay men in fat-affirming groups can transform homoerotic commercial representations of the male body. Warping life-like images by computer, morphing plays upon notions of essential identity and confronts viewers with spectacles of unstable identity (Alcalay 1998). Such creative agency made possible by computers is especially popular among the youth culture whose members like to re-envision themselves by altering their appearance. It emphasizes the mutability of the body, corresponding with the "amodern" body concept put forth by cyberfeminists (Haraway 2004 [originally 1992]). In this way, morphs epitomize queer politics that mark the instability of identity.[6] Rather than completely overturning dominant images, they float between mainstream depictions and marginalized representations (Alcalay 1998). Morphs play with relationships between the body and technology, thus creating new virtual beings with no real human referent (Sturken and Cartwright 2001). For gay men in online fat communities, morphs superimpose fat onto idealized male bodies in homoerotic media. . . .

A deconstructionist reading reveals disconnect: in the original, the face and upper body project an air of confidence. In the morph, this runs counter to how fat gay men are thought to carry themselves in a fat-phobic community, thereby making an implicit social commentary on how gay men typically define themselves and their happiness. The morph suggests that men who might otherwise be weight-conscious in private could come to pose self-confidently in public images, particularly those intended for fat admirers.

Finally, the disconnection between the upper body and the abdomen makes the morph look artificial, and not completely register as a "real" body. Unlike *Absolut Beefy* with its life-like softer fat distribution, the distended stomach in the morph invokes "hard fat" where the exaggerated midsection almost resembles another muscle, gendering it "masculine" (Moffet 2002). Members of fat-affirming groups often desire men with paunches because to them, it suggests masculinity. The morph signifies their attempt to reclaim beerguts and potbellies despite the gay community's aversion to them. Considering that many fat gay men feel denied gender prescriptions and relationship roles typically accorded to gay men with idealized physiques, this redeeming image is not surprising.

MIXED MODES OF RESISTANCE

[. . .]

What do people do when the dominant sign systems do not represent them? Gay men in fat-affirming groups interpret dominant images differently, and some members actively rework them. The fat morph refigures what constitutes a pleasing body; in this way, visual technology affects fat politics. A fat stomach in both images discussed in this chapter no longer represents an undesirable feature, but symbolizes the "intimate experience of boundaries, their construction and deconstruction" (Haraway 1986, p. 525). The artists discussed in this chapter pattern their work after the social norms, aesthetic conventions, and interpretive practices of the larger online fat-affirming community. However, they do not avoid the trappings of the men's media or resolve the feminization of fat gay men without partially appealing to the hegemonic masculinity that works against them. *Absolut Beefy* is arguably the more powerful of the two images because it provides pleasure in its presumed authenticity and engages softer styles of masculinity. Nevertheless, the *Beefy* and *Burger King* slogans both serve to recoup masculinity and the morph still relies on idealized male qualities such as broad shoulders, strong arms, and a babyface.

For morphing to work, it has to keep some aspects of the sampled image recognizable. In the case of the fat morph, it alters the weight and size aspect of extreme body worship, while retaining the various idealized male qualities. This suggests that gay men in fat-affirming communities may still require other dominant drivers of ideal beauty. Men in these groups do occasionally marginalize other men for being too old or too thin, which implies that they may just exchange one rigid body ideal for another. There appears to be a conundrum if one explanation for concerns with body image focuses on social approval and acceptance in the gay community. Gay men in the "circuit" emphasize a desire for slender physiques, and leathermen prefer muscular bodies, while other gay subcultures emphasize alternatives. "Bears" admire larger hairy bodies, while "Chasers" prefer "Chubbies." Body type remains a significant criterion for inclusion in all of these subcultures.

Buying into conformity (or the rejection of it) often represents a mixed mode of resistance. Gay men in online fat-affirming groups seem to be involved in social protest, though not the same activities in which female fat activists engage. These may include scale-tossing/scale-smashing, ice cream socials in front of weight loss centers, or returning advertisements to magazines with decals that read, "Feed this woman!" (LeBesco 2004, p. 107). . . .

Fatvertisements provide a site for both conformity and resistance, ironically even at times when resistance is still conforming. Feminists face the same challenge in thinking about fat women who demanded stylish, sexy fashion only to embrace their consumer niche recognition as a feminist victory (LeBesco 2004).

Should feminists recuperate fat-affirming beauty shows and pageants as "feminism"? Like fatvertisements, this is not an either/or proposition. Modes of resistance in commercialized contexts create strange bedfellows; they incorporate outcasts from the cult of beauty back into a questionable system, as does the question of eroticism, which leads to objectification sometimes as well. Perhaps a Foucaultian (see Foucault 1977) analysis can bring us closer to answering this question of eroticizing fat responsibly. Making this new set of associations with fat equating to sexy goes beyond fetishism, not eliminating sexual desirability as the system, but transforming its standards for what qualifies as "desirable." Then of course, one is obligated to consider the consequences of embracing sexual objectification. . . .

What are some next steps and key questions in examining gay men's online negotiation of fat bodies? The thrust of most existing research is on obesity. Obesity researchers consider how subcultures influence their members' eating habits and body mass. However, their focus can lead one to believe that perhaps fat-affirming groups would increase the number of fat people. A more useful research approach would be not to confuse real bodies with the various negative appraisals of them and instead ask, what produces a new subjectivity from fat-hating to fat-admiring (Butler 1990)? While doctors both measure and calibrate body mass, Fat Studies scholars (such as LeBesco 2001 and 2004; Wann 1998) like me are interested in how some people can reconfigure

negative perceptions and characterizations of fat, so that they can assume a livable fat identity. Most of the existing work along these lines, however, focuses on how women come to body acceptance.

Fat is a "spoiled identity"; yet, how do individuals reshuffle a stigma like this (Goffman 1963)? This is important to consider when one's sullied identity surrounding one's size becomes an object of desire. The point, therefore, would be to look at shifts from shame to pride. In the context of a society where bodies are subjected to intervention, even to surgery, tremendous self-consciousness surrounds fat bodies, especially gay bodies that are often held accountable to such an unforgiving standard (predominantly apparent within the "gay scene"). Unlike celebrities obsessed with perpetual youth, who therefore use concealment strategies, gay men in fat-affirming groups use fatvertisements to create visibility markers, having a field day with our body-conscious culture. If advertisements represent a paradigm that can be destabilized in multiple ways (e.g., AIDS or fatness destabilizing thin), then what would restabilization look like? My analysis of the two fatvertisements in this chapter identifies not only resistance to thin, but also the need to retain some semblance of recognizable features, such as a babyfaced boy with muscular shoulders and a smooth torso, juxtaposed against a fat belly. In cyberspace, these recognizable features, coupled with the abject fatness, work to create and sustain new paradigms for the range of acceptable and desirable gay bodies.

NOTES

1. This is a revised version of an earlier work (Whitesel 2007), permission granted by *Limina*. Thanks to M. Cooper, M. Galin, C. Pullen, and A. Shuman for editing advice.
2. "Fat," "big," "beefy," and "chubby" are terms used by men in these groups.
3. For ethical reasons, I have chosen not to reveal the names of these two "safe-sites" that restrict access only to those that agree to the terms and conditions. To give some indication of user context, new members must

create a username and password to log on to these websites. Once authenticated, they have access to personals, stories, chat and messaging—most free, though some accounts can be "upgraded" for a nominal fee.
4. Similarly, see Ferreday 2001.
5. For discussion of "face-off masculinity," see Bordo 1999, pp. 186-188. For description of the sensuous pleasures of abandoning restraint on the abdominal muscles, see Stoltenberg 1998, p. 406.
6. On "queering" fatness, see LeBesco 2001.

REFERENCES

Alcalay, R. 1998. Morphing out of identity politics: Black or white and terminator 2. In *Bad subjects: Political education for everyday life,* edited by Bad Subjects Production Team. New York: New York University Press, 136–142.

Atkinson, C. 2003. Absolut nabs sexy HBO role: "Sex and the city" features fake ad, *Ad Age,* http://www.oaaa.org/presscenter/release.asp?RELEASE_ID=1368 [Accessed September 25, 2008]

Baudrillard, J. 2001[1988]. Simulacra and simulations. In *Jean Baudrillard: Selected writings,* edited by M. Poster. Palo Alto, CA: Stanford University Press.

Bell, K. and McNaughton, D. 2007. Feminism and the invisible fat man. *Body and Society* 13: 107–131.

Benjamin, W. 1968. *Illuminations,* translated by H. Zohn, edited by H. Arendt. New York: Schocken Books.

Bergling, T. 2001. *Sissyphobia: Gay men and effeminate behavior.* Binghamton, NY: Haworth Press.

Blotcher, J. 1998. Justify my love handles: How the queer community trims the fat. In *Looking queer: Body image and identity in lesbian, bisexual, gay and transgender communities,* edited by D. Atkins. Binghamton, NY: Haworth Press, 359–366.

Bordo, S. 1997. *Twilight zones: The hidden life of cultural images from Plato to O.J.* Berkeley: University of California Press.

Bordo, S. 1999. *The male body: A new look at men in public and private.* New York: Farrar, Straus & Giroux.

Bulkmale. 2009. http://www.bulkmale.com/store/ [Accessed August 23, 2009]

Butler, J. 1990. *Gender trouble: Feminism and the subversion of identity.* New York: Routledge.

Campbell, J. 2004. *Getting it on online: Cyberspace, gay male sexuality, and embodied identity.* New York: Harrington Park Press.

Connell, R. W. 1992. A very straight gay: Masculinity, homosexual experience, and the dynamics of gender. *American Sociological Review* 57: 735–751.

Drummond, M. 2005. Men's bodies: Listening to the voices of young gay men. *Men and Masculinities* 7: 270–290.

Durgadas, G. 1998. Fatness and the feminized man. In *Looking queer: Body image and identity in lesbian, bisexual, gay and transgender communities,* edited by D. Atkins. Binghamton, NY: Haworth Press, pp. 367–371.

Feraios, A. 1998. If only I were cute: Looksism and internalized homophobia in the gay male community. In *Looking queer: Body image and identity in lesbian, bisexual, gay and transgender communities,* edited by D. Atkins. Binghamton: Haworth Press, 415–429.

Ferreday, D. 2001. Unspeakable bodies: Erasure, embodiment and the pro-ana community. *International Journal of Cultural Studies* 6: 277–295.

Foucault, M. 1977. *The History of Sexuality Vol. 1.,* trans. Robert Hurley. London: Penguin.

Giles, P. 1998. A matter of size. *In Looking queer: Body image and identity in lesbian, bisexual, gay and transgender communities,* edited by D. Atkins. Binghamton, NY: Haworth Press, pp. 355–357.

Goffman, E. 1963. *Stigma: Notes on the management of spoiled identity.* Englewood Cliffs, NJ: Prentice-Hall.

Goffman, E. 1974. *Frame analysis: An essay on the organization of experience.* Cambridge, MA: Harvard University Press.

Goffman, E. 1979. *Gender advertisements.* Cambridge, MA: Harvard University Press.

Goode, E. 2005. *Deviant behavior,* 7th ed. Upper Saddle River, NJ: Pearson.

Graham, M. 2005. Chaos. In *Fat: The anthropology of an obsession,* edited by D. Kulick and A. Meneley. New York: Penguin Group, 169–184.

Hacking, I. 1986. Making up people. *In Reconstructing individualism: Autonomy, individuality, and the self in western thought,* edited by T. Heller, M. Sosna, and D. Wellbery. Palo Alto, CA: Stanford University Press, 222–236.

Hall, S. 1998 [1981]. Notes on deconstructing "the popular." In *Cultural theory and popular culture,* edited by J. Storey. Athens: University of Georgia Press, 442–453.

Haraway, D. 1986. A manifesto for cyborgs: Science, technology, and socialist feminism in the 1980s. In *Feminist Social Thought: A Reader* (1997), edited by D. Meyers. New York: Routledge, 502–531.

Haraway, D. 2004. [1992]. The promises of monsters: A regenerative politics for inappropriate/d others. In *The Haraway reader,* edited by D. Haraway. New York: Routledge.

Hawkes, T. 1977. *Structuralism and semiotics.* London: Methuen, 63–124.

Hennen, P. 2005. Bear bodies, bear masculinity: Recuperation, resistance or retreat? *Gender and Society* 19: 25–43.

hooks, b. 1992. *Black looks: Race and representation.* London: Turnaround Press, 21–39.

Ironkite, 2009. Subvertisements. http://ironkite.smugmug.com/gallery/1521_QfrTR#4323S_JdGh3 [Accessed August 23, 2009]

Jenkins, H. 1992. *Textual poachers: Television fans and participatory culture.* New York: Routledge.

Kruger, S. 1998. Get fat, don't die!: Eating and AIDS in gay men's culture. In *Eating culture,* edited by R. Scapp and B. Seitz. New York: State University of New York Press, 36–59.

Kulick, D. 2005. Porn. In *Fat: The anthropology of an obsession,* edited by D. Kulick and A. Menely. New York: Penguin Group, 77–92.

Lasn, K. 2000. *Culture jam: The uncooling of America.* New York: William Morrow & Co.

LeBesco, K. 2001. Queering fat bodies/politics. In *Bodies out of bounds: Fatness and transgression,* edited by J. E. Braziel and K. LeBesco. Berkeley: University of California Press, 74–87.

LeBesco, K. 2004. *Revolting bodies: The struggle to redefine fat identity.* Amherst: University of Massachusetts Press.

Matthews, T. 2005. Video. *Do I look fat? Gay men, body image and eating disorders.* Blah Blah Blah Productions, USA.

McGann, P. 2002. Eating muscle: Material semiotics and a manly appetite. In *Revealing male bodies,* edited by N. Tuana, G. Johnson, M. Hamington, and W. Cowling. Bloomington: Indiana University Press, 83–99.

Millman, M. 1980. *Such a pretty face: Being fat in America.* New York: W. W. Norton.

Moffet, F. 2002. Video. *Hard fat: An exploration of desire, masculinity and size.* Vidéographe Production, Canada.

Monaghan, L. 2005. Big handsome men, bears and others: Virtual constructions of 'fat male embodiment'. *Body and Society* 11: 81–111.

Padva, G. 2002. Heavenly monsters: Politics of the male body in the naked issue of attitude magazine. *International Journal of Sexuality and Gender Studies* 7: 281–292.

Schroeder, J. 2002. *Visual consumption.* New York: Routledge.

Shernoff, M. 2002. Body image, working out and therapy. *Journal of Gay and Lesbian Social Services* 14: 89–94.

Signorile, M. 1997. *Life outside—The Signorile report on gay men: Sex, drugs, muscles, and the passages of life.* New York: HarperCollins.

Stoltenberg, J. 1998. Learning the F words. In *Looking queer: Body image and identity in lesbian, bisexual, gay and transgender communities,* edited by D. Atkins. Binghamton, NY: Haworth Press, 393–411.

Sturken, M. and Cartwright, L. 2001. *Practices of looking: An introduction to visual culture.* New York: Oxford University Press.

Textor, A. 1999. Organization, specialization, and desires in the big men's movement: Preliminary research in the study of subculture-formation. *Journal of Gay, Lesbian, and Bisexual Identity* 4: 217–239.

Wann, M. 1998. *Fat! So?: Because you don't have to apologize for your size.* Berkeley: Ten Speed Press.

Whitesel, J. 2007. Fatvertising: Refiguring fat gay men in cyberspace. *Limina* 13: 92-102.

77. • *Farida Vis, Liesbet van Zoonen, and Sabina Mihelj*

WOMEN RESPONDING TO THE ANTI-ISLAM FILM *FITNA*:
Voices and Acts of Citizenship on YouTube (2011)

Farida Vis is a research fellow at the University of Sheffield. Her research interests include online responses of the aftermath of Hurricane Katrina, relationships between newspaper articles and photojournalism, and media representation of the peace process. Liesbet van Zoonen is professor of popular culture and dean of the Erasmus Graduate School of Social Sciences and Humanities at Erasmus University Rotterdam. She is also a part-time professor in Communication and Media Studies at Loughborough University. Her research focuses on media, popular culture, and gender. Sabina Mihelj is a lecturer in the Department of Social Sciences at Lough-borough University. Her areas of expertise are media and nationalism, eastern and central European media, and television studies. Their collaborative work here was first published in Feminist Review.

INTRODUCTION

In early March 2008, Dutch anti-Islam Member of Parliament Geert Wilders produced a sixteen-minute short video called *Fitna* to express in visual form his argument that Islam is a dangerous religion, and that the Netherlands is under the threat of a "tsunami of Muslims."[1] As no Dutch broadcaster wished to show it, the film, a compilation of existing audio-visual material, was released on the internet (on Live Leak) and caused immense debate in the Netherlands and abroad, comparable to the fall-out from the Danish cartoon crisis. Wilders' opponents accused him of visual demagogy, while his supporters praised him for having the courage to speak his mind. The debate was intense and focused primarily on the film itself, Wilders' motives and the question of whether or not *Fitna* should be banned (Ruigrok *et al.*, 2008). . . .

[. . .]

Missing from these debates was and is a discussion of the way in which Wilders exploits images of gender and female bodies in particular to make his point against Islam. In this article we will first examine how Wilders' stereotypes of women and men come directly from traditional Orientalist discourse. The more important point of the article, however, is our analysis of the response videos that were produced and uploaded to YouTube by women from around the globe: in some cases to express their annoyance with Wilders; in other cases to show their own understanding of Islam. . . .

[. . .]

FITNA AND ORIENTALIST DISCOURSE

To understand how gender is exploited in *Fitna*, we first need to examine how women and men from Muslim and non-Muslim backgrounds are cast in the different roles of victim, perpetrator and hero.

Muslim women are shown in three ways in *Fitna*:

- as victims of extreme violence (there are short sequences on genital mutilation, showing a screaming woman and pool of blood at her feet, we see the still veiled head of a beheaded woman, a woman kneeling in front of group of men, one of whom points a machine gun at her head);
- as complicit in the encouragement of anti-Semitism and anti-Western feelings; for example three-and-half-year-old Basmallah, a little Palestinian girl wearing hijab, who proudly declares, encouraged by a woman out of view, that the Quran says that Jews are pigs and apes. We are shown a still of a smiling woman, also in hijab, holding up her blood soaked toddler following a religious ceremony. Finally, there are shots of women at demonstrations in full black niqab holding up radical slogans in praise of Hitler;
- as part of the allegedly changing Dutch landscape, the film includes shots of Muslim women wearing different kinds of headscarves, most notably black niqab, in everyday settings: with toddlers in pushchairs around town, in the park, at the market and so on.

In stark contrast, non-Muslim women are shown exclusively as victims or as aid workers, and the film contains an especially harrowing sequence of a phone conversation between a woman stuck in one of the Twin Towers describing to the 911 operator that she is burning up and the emergency woman comforting her calmly and telling her to say her prayers.

Muslim men are either shown as radical preachers—such as the London-based Imam Abu Hamza al Masrior or Iraqi Sheik Bakr Al Samarai[2]—or as part of large groups, making it difficult to identify individuals (see Moore *et al.* (2008) for similar findings in recent coverage in the British national print media). These large groups of Muslim men include Hizbollah supporters, who collectively make what looks like the Nazi salute, shout at demonstrations with kaffiyehs covering their faces, hold up placards with slogans such as "You will pay with your blood" and "Freedom go to Hell!" In a short sequence men wave bloody daggers in the air, images of hands, blood and daggers. A group of Muslim men talk about Islam being the best religion, saying that anyone who converts to Christianity deserves to die. The most excessive example of the portrayal of Muslim men as violent aggressors concerns a sequence where five men with machine guns dressed in black decapitate American journalist Daniel Pearl (the actual beheading is not shown, but Pearl's bloodcurdling cries are audible). Finally, Muslim men are also, albeit indirectly, presented as the perpetrators of violence against women (and homosexuals), as highlighted above.

Non-Muslim men are exclusively shown as actual or possible victims of Islam. The film shows five such images: the blood stained face of a young man after the Madrid bombings; the killing of Daniel Pearl; footage of the murdered Dutch film director Theo van Gogh, with the voice of his murderer, Mohammed B, played as part of the footage, in which he declares that if he had the chance to repeat the murder, with the help of God, he would. Finally, Wilders himself appears in the film in the form of newspaper items concerning a jihad against him.

The narrative that articulates these roles into a coherent traditional gender discourse of male activity versus female passivity is that of men fighting over the control of women and femininity: Muslim men as individuals or as collective are shown as perpetrators who preach and enact violence, oppress and abuse Muslim women; non-Muslim women

and some men, especially homosexuals, are cast as real or future victims of this aggression, specifically within the Dutch national context. White Dutch male heroes, embodied in the figures of Theo van Gogh and Geert Wilders himself, are seen to come to the rescue of non-Muslim women and (homosexual) men, as well as of those Muslims supposedly directly oppressed by Islam. This imagery and narrative are similar to the representation of Islam and Muslim women in more mainstream media, in which their oppression is a key trope, articulated in recurrent coverage of, among other things, forced marriage, honour violence, female genital mutilation and Sharia law (Poole, 2002). . . .

In addition, while Islam is not tied to one particular ethnicity, the representation of Islamic "Others" as a tied knot of male perpetrators and female victims is part of a particular racist discourse that comes in various forms: it is a reworking of Spivak's well-known expression of a protection scenario where the white male hero has to save the "brown" women from the "brown" men (as summarized in Stabile and Kumar, 2005). Leila Ahmed (1992) has demonstrated how a similar scenario was used to justify the occupation of Egypt in the 1880s by Britain: superior Christian invaders had to rescue and liberate Muslim women from Muslim men. More recently Stabile and Kumar (2005: 771) have shown that the American invasion of Afghanistan was premised on comparable arguments, namely the noble ideal of protecting women combined with a civilizing mission brought into "an uneasy alliance to justify the destruction of a country's infrastructure in order to protect women." These analyses more generally draw on Edward Said's understanding of "Orientalism" as a stereotypical representation of the peoples of the Middle East that unmistakably helped to legitimate Western imperialist occupation and oppression.

[. . .]

In its extreme repetition of existing stereotypes and prejudice about Islam, *Fitna* hardly merits special analysis. Yet, the video had an unexpectedly poignant side-effect that is more worthwhile: thousands of people from around the globe, a number of whom were women, responded by producing and uploading their own videos to YouTube. These videos contain the views of Muslims and non-Muslims, and some include their experiences and understanding of Islam. They thus offer the opportunity to focus on how women themselves articulate their position in relation to Islam, thus recognizing them as independent actors and hearing their voices.

METHOD

Videos on YouTube seem to produce easy data that allow for non-obtrusive measures. Yet, as a data-archive it is in constant flux, with new videos constantly added, others taken down, and posters sometimes suspended all together. Our initial search for videos resulting from the search terms "*Fitna* Wilders," kept throwing up changing numbers of relevant videos (around 3,000), with many double counts as well. To counter the variability of the material, the problems with manually coding the metadata associated with each video and the unreliability of the poster information as displayed on their channel, a customized e-research tool was developed for us by Mike Thelwall of the University of Wolverhampton. . . .

We conducted a quantitative and qualitative content analysis of these videos that was meant to answer our overall research question, namely whether and how the representation of gender and Islam in these videos differs from the representation of gender and Islam in *Fitna*. We were especially interested to find out whether and how the female posters presented an alternative discourse about gender and Islam, in which women are shown as active agents of their own lives, rather than as victims in need of rescue. We divided this question into four sub-questions that informed our quantitative and qualitative coding of *Fitna* and the response videos:

1. *What are the socio-demographic characteristics of the women uploading the response videos (age, nationality, religion)?. . .*

2. *What are the generic and ideological characteristics of Fitna and the videos uploaded by women?. . .*

3. *How are women and men from Muslim and non-Muslim backgrounds represented in Fitna and in the response videos? . . .*

4. *What kind of alternative stories do female posters tell about Islam?. . .*

FEMALE POSTERS ON YOUTUBE

When we collected our data at the end of September 2009, female posters had uploaded 200 video responses to *Fitna*. While a few of them had responded as early as February, linked to the widely circulating rumours about the film, most of them uploaded their video around the time of its release in March 2008 and in the months immediately after. . . .

Most of the posters were younger than thirty, with an average age of 28.9, according to their registration. While the quranmiracles poster was listed as 55 years old, this was an evident exception. While listing your religion is not part of the YouTube registration, a few posters provided other kinds of indicative information (for instance listing the Quran as their favourite book), but of those few that did refer to their religion mentioned Islam more than Christianity.

In comparison to the coverage of *Fitna* in the Dutch and the British press, these data suggest that YouTube offers a space for the kinds of citizens that are regularly ignored in mainstream debate: an analysis of Dutch press coverage found that the sources and voices talking about *Fitna* consisted by and large of national experts, political actors and Wilders himself. Ordinary citizens were relatively absent from the debates (Ruigrok *et al.*, 2008). Research about British news coverage of Wilders and his film produced similar outcomes: English cabinet members, politicians and experts dominated the press coverage, while the voices of Muslims were mostly absent (Knott *et al.*, 2010). In contrast, the YouTube videos offer a more international perspective, and allow younger women to speak and offer a voice to Muslims.

THE VIDEOS

The sixty-three videos were widely different in content and form, as can be expected in an open platform like YouTube. Among them were seven videos of *Fitna* itself (or parts thereof), including Polish and Farsi translations. Other videos (fourteen) were simply "cut-and-paste" productions in which the poster did not add her own material, but simply uploaded copies of news items, current affairs programmes, documentaries, cartoons or other existing audiovisual work. Most of the videos, however, were amateur videos in the form of cut-and-mix productions (eighteen) that used existing still and moving images in combination with text and music to make an original statement. A recurring theme in these cut-and-mix videos is imitation of *Fitna*, but with Christianity replacing Islam, for instance using violent texts from the Bible, illustrated by sounds and images.[3] Other examples include, for instance, a fairly simple one minute and nineteen seconds video without sound, which is titled "Anti-Wildersfilm," and described in the channel section as "a film about the super awful stupid nasty Geert Wilders." It is a sequence of images of handwritten texts on a white background (e.g. "Geert Wilders sucks"), original and morphed pictures and cartoons of Wilders, which ends with "made by anonymous."[4] Other such videos also contain pictures of Wilders morphed into singing strange songs, or fragments of texts (for instance from the Quran) on a simple unicolour or picture background. The organized response from a group of Egyptian Muslim women was constructed in this way. . . .

Other home-made videos could be typified as testimonials of women talking to camera and commenting on *Fitna* and/or Islam. One of them was the response of a British girl to the famous YouTube call from Queen Rania of Jordan to "send me your stereotypes" of Muslims which she would then try to counter (Jones, 2008). . . .

The majority of these videos (forty) demonstrate a clear critical position towards *Fitna*: they criticize and make fun of Wilders, analyse the visual rhetoric of the film, or offer alternative readings of Islam. The cut-and-paste videos of existing news and current affairs footage are generally neutral. Only two videos (apart from the seven reloads of *Fitna* itself) express univocal support for Wilders: a poster called inbenproWilders (including a typo, this probably means "I am pro Wilders"), uploaded one 2.51-minute silent video, showing white English and Dutch texts on a blue background, opening with the sentence: "Geert Wilders, is he right or wrong?", and then presenting a range of presumably relevant "facts," provided without offering any evidence. . . .

This part of our analysis thus demonstrates that YouTube offers an alternative space to express one's opinions in different formats than those of mainstream media coverage; cut-and-paste and testimonials are the typical YouTube genres that young women from Muslim and non-Muslim backgrounds (otherwise marginalized actors) used to criticize Geert Wilders and his film. Looking at the total number of views for these videos, it is also clear that this is not a marginal space: 677,125 views were registered for all videos and the average number of views per video was 12,311.[5] The first ten minutes of De Tegenfilm (The Counterfilm), for instance, drew 140,000 views; the videos of the Egyptian girls were accessed over 9,000 times in total. On the other hand, a video by rosefire18, text on background about the wonders of Islam, was accessed twenty-eight times only. This was exceptionally low, however, and the only video that attracted less than hundred views. [. . .]

DIFFERENT REPRESENTATIONS OF WOMEN?

A number of the YouTube cut-and-mix videos did not portray individual people at all, but simply presented written text on static background. Most of the people that do appear in these videos are male; 71.3 per cent. In addition, while the majority of people in the videos appear in their role as citizens, twice as many men as women appear as public officials.[6] Yet, within this overall, seemingly stereotypical context, there are remarkable differences between the representation of women and men that also demonstrate a clear alternative to the Orientalist extremism of *Fitna*.

(A) VISUAL IDENTIFICATION

An important difference between *Fitna* and the You-Tube videos of women concerns the presence of the headscarf and other Islamic headwear. . . .

We saw in the description of *Fitna* above that the sartorial indicators of Islam function as a key visual marker of "Otherness," for Muslim women and men alike. The headscarf specifically operates in *Fitna* as a sign of the alleged oppression of women in Islam. The relative absence of such visual markers in the videos of women themselves suggests that such an easy construction of difference between women and men, and between Muslims and non-Muslims is less feasible. The videos that they uploaded contain more diverse sartorial images of men and women.

(B) SOCIAL PRESENCE

The extremist image of Islam in *Fitna* is constructed by portraying Muslims in the particular social contexts of religious hate speech and terrorism, and presenting non-Muslim men and women as victims, as we described above. This observation also emerges from the quantitative comparisons of social contexts in which women and men appear in *Fitna*. . . . A third of the women shown in *Fitna* occur in conflict situations (as victims as we described above), and a third in public spaces (with their bodies and faces more or less covered and functioning as icons of Otherness). In contrast, the women and men shown in the You-Tube videos of women appear in the more everyday settings of work, and in religious contexts. The excessive association in *Fitna* of Islam with terrorism and conflict is largely absent from the YouTube videos.

(C) AUDIO AND VISUAL PRESENCE

The audio and visual presence of women and men in *Fitna* and the YouTube videos of female posters clearly differed. . . . The majority of men in *Fitna* appeared as moving and speaking image, with the fragments from extremist Islamist preachers dominant, contributing to the impression of male Muslims as aggressors. The overall presence of women and men in the YouTube videos is almost the complete opposite: although there were fewer women than men appearing in the videos, their presence was much stronger in terms of the length and audiovisual importance of their appearance. The majority of women in the films appear as moving and speaking image, or are portrayed through a combination of text, still image, voice over and moving image. Half of the images of men in the videos, on the other hand, are brief "image bites" of less than ten seconds (50.2), whereas the images of women generally lasted some ten seconds longer. Moreover, more women than men were given a sustained and long presence in the videos: 15 per cent of the women versus 12.5 per cent of the men were shown longer than three and a half minutes.[7]

THE VOICE OF MUSLIM WOMEN

In the YouTube videos, we found a number of instances in which Muslim women took or were given a voice to speak about *Fitna* or Islam. A first and very brief one, from mainstream media coverage, comes from a cut-and-paste video of a Dutch discussion programme in which Yassmina El Ksaihi, speaking on behalf of an organization working with Dutch citizens of Moroccan heritage, and wearing a bright pink hijab, summarizes in nine seconds that if Wilders' goal was for Dutch non-Muslims to turn against their fellow Muslim citizens she thought he had failed.[8] In The Countermovie, set in the Netherlands, a fictitious female Muslim newsreader wearing a light blue hijab reads the "News of Yesterday" announcing among other things that it has been five years ago since the Sharia was introduced in the Netherlands, and that Geert Wilders failed his civics exam "I am Halal," for the fifth time. As part of the testimonial genre, we found a voice-only video (without images) from a young Muslim woman speaking out against *Fitna* arguing that Wilders took Quranic verses out of context, herself highlighting their meaning in the clip, and furthermore questioning his authority to interpret them at all.[9]

Of all the uploaded videos the concerted effort of a group of young Egyptian women is the most elaborate and consequential example of Muslim women speaking for themselves. They produced two videos (one of 9.37 minutes and one of 9.59 minutes) to respond to *Fitna* and uploaded them around the end of April 2008, using different YouTube accounts, some of which were clearly set up for this purpose alone. Users with names such as TruthAbout-*Fitna*08, ZTruthAbout*Fitna* and *Fitna*movie2008 only uploaded these response videos and their channels have since ceased to be active. After its opening sequence addressing Wilders and stating the purpose of the film ("to clear up the misconceptions that you have," see above), the film then proceeds to go through the Quranic verses used in *Fitna*. A female voice-over reads the verse, which is followed by written texts of different colours on black background explaining their meaning and putting them in the context of the complete verse they were taken from.[10] With this approach, the makers of the video identify the 9/11 perpetrators as sinners in the eyes of Islam. Apart from being an exceptional reaction to *Fitna*, the video is also a rather unique intervention of women with respect to religious authority that may be typical of the Egyptian women's mosque movement (see Mahmood, 2005). First, the pure act of women reading out verses from the Quran in the semi-public and mixed gender space that YouTube constructs is a performance of religious identity that is hardly feasible in the offline context, where it is highly contested whether women are allowed such acts outside of women-only groups. Second, the additional act of women interpreting the true meaning of the Quranic verses is also rather uncommon and puts these videos right at the heart of liberal modern Islam. Whether these Egyptian posters consider themselves part of a wider movement is, however, a question for further research.[11]

In the second film (starting with "Hello again"), the women pick up on their assessment of terrorists as sinners, and try to clarify "why some Muslims Interpret Qu'ran verses in a wrong way and act upon it."[12] They do this by showing a series of pictures and clips about the violent treatment of Muslims around the world. The invasion of Iraq, Abu Ghraib and the occupation of Palestine provide strong images, especially of Muslim women as victims of violence—this time not of Islam as in the Wilders film—but of Western and Israeli war crimes. They end this sequence of harrowing images with the promise of a third film and the text:

> Those were some scenes from life in Palestine, Iraq and Lebanon. Where there's a 9/11 everyday . . . Now, put yourself in their shoes. Invaders killing your kids in front of your eyes, torturing your brothers and destroying your home. EVERYDAY!

> Would you be psychologically and emotionally stable? How would you deal with this life? If you have strong faith . . . Resort to God's help praying him to get rid of those invaders for you! [Or] else . . . lose control. Muslims who lose control . . . are those who try to give themselves the right to take "revenge." So they start interpreting Quran verses in a way, which gives them this right. Now you're starting to see the whole picture. Never hear a story from one side. Think about it.

All versions of these two videos were watched over 9,000 times in total and evoked 169 text comments on YouTube. Strikingly, the different uploads of the same film evoked widely different kinds of discussion. The makers of the videos regularly reacted to the comments of the viewers, thanking for positive comments, explaining their motives and discussing different interpretations of the Quranic verses they used.[13]

CONCLUSION AND THEORETICAL REFLECTIONS

. . . Our analysis of the YouTube videos uploaded by women showed that YouTube clearly offers an alternative and an important space to discuss *Fitna* and Islam. Firstly, the women uploading their videos are a different kind of actor in public debate than the ones participating in mainstream media discussions: they come from across the globe, they are relatively young and many of them are active Muslims. Secondly, while many of them express their ideas by copying and pasting footage from existing media, the majority of the women uploading their videos produced their own material by cutting and mixing images, sound and texts or by speaking directly to the camera in a testimonial. In these alternative expressions, there was only rare support for Geert Wilders or a staunch anti-Islam standpoint. On the contrary, direct criticism and ridicule of Wilders were common, as were serious and committed explanations of Islam and how Muslim women themselves interpret their religion. Overall, the portrayals of women and men in the videos were radically different from those in *Fitna*; although relatively few women appeared in the videos, they were not typified in terms of "us" versus "them" through headwear or other sartorial markers; they also received lengthy attention, spoke for themselves and were shown in ordinary work contexts or in everyday religious settings, instead of as victims of conflict, as in *Fitna*. Women also actively explained and discussed their understanding of Islam, thus not only taking on Wilders, but also claiming their right to speak within Islam.

It thus seems justified to conclude that women, Muslim and non-Muslim, have used YouTube to give themselves both a political and a religious voice in the global Islam debate, in which *Fitna* presents an extremist position. It also seems legitimate to say that these voices are heard, given the significant amount of views that the total and most individual videos received. Without knowing too much about the background of the posters, our data nevertheless demonstrate how these women constituted themselves as global citizens through their act of copying or making videos and uploading them to YouTube. Notwithstanding the absence of a global polity in which to claim citizen rights and perform citizen duties, their videos are typical "acts of citizenship," as Isin and Nielsen (2008) have called it, by women claiming their right to speak to wider audiences, and to political and religious actors that have often prevented them from speaking or have not bothered to listen to them.

. . . In the global Islam debate, of which *Fitna* and the YouTube videos are a part, there is no authority to speak to, and the questions thus remain—to whom is voice directed and who is listening (see Bickford, 1996)? Our data did show that women's voices are certainly "heard" and seen, but we got little information about how exactly they are listened to and made sense of, with the exception—again—of the videos

of the Egyptian women. Following Crawford's (2009) analysis of listening in social media, a form of reciprocal listening occurred there, involving a two-way process between speaking and listening, clearly visible in the comment threads sparked by the videos uploaded by Egyptian posters. Still, we could argue that other videos in our sample also constituted voices that were acknowledged. According to Mitra and Watts' (2002: 484) theorizing of the notion of "voice" in cyberspace, "the moment in which voice is actualized as an event, when it becomes an answerable phenomenon, is when it is acknowledged." Following that logic, the pure act of uploading your video to YouTube produces by definition an acknowledged voice, because the technological capabilities of the platform (the options to respond with text and new videos) make it immediately into an answerable phenomenon, whether actually listened to or not. And so, we come back full circle to the act of citizenship: whether typified as deliberation or as voice, in both cases the simple act of uploading a video to intervene in the global Islam debate, has constituted those women as citizens— albeit temporarily—thus countering the debilitating discourse of Orientalism, and rendering them simultaneously answerable and accountable to others who hold different or similar opinions.

To sceptics, such online acts of citizenship and alternative voices may seem inconsequential. Indeed, these voices and acts so far failed to provoke repercussions in mainstream debates, and instead remained enclosed in the "public sphericules" created by alternative communicative platforms, thus contributing to "two-tier" society and a segmented public sphere (Gitlin, 1998). Yet whose responsibility is it to establish the feedback loops that would allow such alternative voices and acts of citizenship to partake in an active encounter with voices in the mainstream, and thus establish a truly public and democratic debate capable of reaching across identity barriers and social and ideological differences? In line with recent work on the politics of voice and listening (see Couldry and Dreher, 2007), surely we cannot blame the fragmentation and polarization of public debates about Islam in the West on the alternative communicative platforms and their participants themselves, or expect all solutions to come from them. In the case of *Fitna*, ordinary citizens posting their videos on You Tube did their bit. The onus is now on the mainstream gatekeepers of the mainstream public spheres in the West to allow these voices to be heard on a wider scale, and counter the fragmentation and polarization of debate they have themselves helped create.

REFERENCES

Ahmed, L. (1992) *Women and Gender in Islam: Historical Roots of a Modern Debate*, New Haven: Yale University Press.

Aly, A. (2009) "Media hegemony, activism and identity: Muslim women representing Muslim women" in Ho, C and Dreher T. (2009) editors, *Beyond the Hijab Debates: New Conversations on Gender, Race and Religion*, Newcastle: Cambridge Scholars Publishing.

Bickford, S. (1996) *The Dissonance of Democracy: Listening, Conflict and Citizenship*, Ithaca, NY: Cornell University Press.

Chalmers, S. and Dreher, T. (2009) "Safeguarding masculinity, protecting "our" borders: the banality of sexual violence in the public sphere in Australia" in Ho, C and Dreher T. (2009) editors, *Beyond the Hijab Debates: New Conversations on Gender, Race and Religion*, Newcastle: Cambridge Scholars Publishing.

Choua, N. and Kranenberg, A. (2008) "*Fitna* ontleed: de film beeld voor beeld" Volkskrant, 15 April, http://www.volkskrant.nl/binnenland/article527366.ece/Fitna_ontleed, (accessed 6 July 2010).

Couldry, N. and Dreher, T. (2007) "Globalization and the public sphere: exploring the space of community media in Sydney" *Global Media and Communications*, Vol. 3, No. 1: 79–100.

Crawford, K. (2009) "Following you: disciplines for listening in social media" *Continuum: Journal of Media and Cultural Studies*, Vol. 23, No. 4: 525–535.

Duits, L. and van Zoonen, L. (2006) "Headscarves and porno-chic: disciplining girls' dress in the European multicultural society" *The European Journal of Women's Studies*, Vol. 13, No. 2: 103–117.

Elster, J. (1998) editor, *Deliberative Democracy*, Cambridge: Cambridge University Press.

Gitlin, T. (1998) "Public sphere or public sphericules?" in Liebes, T. and Curran, J. (1998) editors, *Media, Ritual and Identity*, London: Routledge.

Hirschman, A. (1970) *Exit, Voice and Loyalty: Responses to Decline of Firms, Organizations and States*, Cambridge, MA: Harvard University Press.

Isin, E.F. and Nielsen, G.M. (2008) editors, *Acts of Citizenship*, London: Zed Books.

Jaggar, A. (2000) "Multicultural democracy" in Chambers, S. and Costain, A. (2000) editors, *Deliberation, Democracy and the Media*. Lanham, MD: Rowman & Littlefield.

Jones, B. (2008) "Queen Rania takes on stereotypes" BBC NEWS, Friday 25 July 2008, http://news.bbc.co.uk/2/hi/middle_east/7524933.stm (accessed 8 March 2010).

Kabeer, S. (2008) "Geert wilders, '*Fitna*,' and the last refuge of the bigoted" Global Comment, where the world thinks out loud, 14 April 2008, http://globalcomment.com/2008/geert-wildersFitna-and-the-last-refuge-of-the-bigoted/ (accessed 5 March 2010).

Knott, K., Poole, E. and Taira, T. (2010) "Media portrayals and the secular sacred" Presentation to Loughborough University, Department of Social Sciences, 5 March 2010.

Mahmood, S. (2005) *Politics of Piety: The Islamic Revival and the Feminist Subject*, Princeton, NJ: Princeton University Press.

Meer, D., Dwyer, C. and Modood, T. (2010) "Embodying nationhood? Conceptions of British national identity, citizenship, and gender in the "veil affair" *The Sociological Review*, Vol. 58, No. 1: 84–111.

Mitra, A. and Watts, E. (2002) "Theorizing cyberspace: the idea of voice applied to the internet discourse" *New Media and Society*, Vol. 4, No. 4: 479–498.

Moore, K., Mason, P. and Lewis, J. (2008) "Images of Islam in the UK: the representation of British Muslims in the national print media 2000–2008" Cardiff, Cardiff School of Journalism, Media and Cultural Studies.

Poole, E. (2002) *Reporting Islam. Media Representations of British Muslims*, London: I.B. Tauris.

Poole, E. and Richardson, J.E. (2006) editors, *Muslims in the News Media*, London: I.B. Tauris.

Richardson, J.E. (2006) "Who gets to speak? A study of sources in the broadsheet press" in Poole, E. and Richardson, J.E. (2006) editors, *Muslims in the News Media*, London: I.B. Tauris.

Ruigrok, N., Scholten, O., Krijt, M., Schaper, J. and Paanakker, H. (2008) *Fitna en de media: Een onderzoek naar aandacht en rolpatronen. {Fitna and the Media: A Research into Attention and Source Roles}*, Amsterdam: Dutch New Monitor, http://www.nieuwsmonitor.net/list, (English summary available, accessed 6 July 2010).

Stabile, C.A. and Kumar, D. (2005) "Unveiling imperialism: media, gender and the war in Afghanistan" *Media, Culture and Society*, Vol. 27, No. 5: 765–782.

Vis, F. and Thelwall, M. (2010) "Challenging dominant representations of Islam online: innovative methods for studying YouTube" Innovative Methods in the Study of Religion Conference, London, 29–30 March 2010.

Zoonen, L., van, Müller, F. and Hirzalla, F. (2009) "De slag om Fitna [Fitna, the video battle]" in Aarts, M. and van der Haak, M. (2009) editors, *Popvirus: popularization of religion and culture*, Amsterdam: Aksant Publishers.

NOTES

1. Wilders said this in an interview with a Dutch newspaper, *Volkskrant*, 7 October 2006. Retrieved on 6 July 2010, http://www.volkskrant.nl/binnenland/ article577161.ece/

2. Abu Hamza al Masri was detained by the British authorities in 2004 on allegations of terrorism; Al Samarai was a supporter of Saddam Hussein who has not been seen since 2003.

3. For example http://www.youtube.com/watch?v=Nen318ns3OU, accessed on 8 March 2010, see also Van Zoonen *et al.* (2009).

4. All translations from Dutch by the authors, URL: http://www.youtube.com/watch?V=0AkRAG6Yyfs, accessed on 8 March 2010.

5. Calculated on the basis of viewing numbers on 9 March 2010. Excluding the reloads of *Fitna*, the call of Queen Rania which attracted over a million views by itself, and three videos that were removed by that day because of copyright issues.

6. The significance of the coded differences was tested with the X^2 test for association of nominal variables ($X^2 = 32$, $p = 0.01$).

7. Ibid ($X^2 = 55.5$, $p = 0.05$).

8. http://www.youtube.com/watch?v=frZmIZTHC04, accessed 12 February 2010.

9. Title: Re *Fitna* the movie. URL: http://www.youtube.com/watch?v=pF0AANuODOU.

10. http://www.youtube.com/watch?v=Kw4TjTtlWCU, accessed 8 March 2010.

11. We analysed the motives and aims of the posters in another part of the research. See http://www.lboro.ac.uk/departments/ss/research/FITNAindex.html.

12. http://www.youtube.com/watch?v=qK2VErvUHww, accessed 12 February 2010.

13. We cover the discussions that followed these and other videos that were uploaded in response to *Fitna* in: Van Zoonen, L. Mihelj, S. and Vis, F. (under review), "YouTube interactions between agonism, antagonism and dialogue: video responses to the anti-Islam film *Fitna*." See http://www.lboro.ac.uk/departments/ss/research/FITNA/index.html.

78. • *Aliette de Bodard*

IMMERSION (2012)

Aliette de Bodard is a Franco-Vietnamese writer of fantasy and science fiction. She has written various novels and short stories on artificial intelligence, alternative (Xuva) universe, and Aztec mystery-fantasy. The short story included here has won a Nebula and a Locus award.

In the morning, you're no longer quite sure who you are.

You stand in front of the mirror—it shifts and trembles, reflecting only what you want to see— eyes that feel too wide, skin that feels too pale, an odd, distant smell wafting from the compartment's ambient system that is neither incense nor garlic, but something else, something elusive that you once knew.

You're dressed, already—not on your skin, but outside, where it matters, your avatar sporting blue and black and gold, the stylish clothes of a well-traveled, well-connected woman. For a moment, as you turn away from the mirror, the glass shimmers out of focus; and another woman in a dull silk gown stares back at you: smaller, squatter and in every way diminished—a stranger, a distant memory that has ceased to have any meaning.

Quy was on the docks, watching the spaceships arrive. She could, of course, have been anywhere on Longevity Station, and requested the feed from the network to be patched to her router—and watched, superimposed on her field of vision, the slow dance of ships slipping into their pod cradles like births watched in reverse. But there was something about standing on the spaceport's concourse—a feeling of closeness that she just couldn't replicate by standing in Golden Carp Gardens or Azure Dragon Temple. Because here—here, separated by only a few measures of sheet metal from the cradle pods, she could feel herself teetering on the edge of the vacuum, submerged in cold and breathing in neither air nor oxygen. She could almost imagine herself rootless, finally returned to the source of everything.

Most ships those days were Galactic—you'd have thought Longevity's ex-masters would have been unhappy about the station's independence, but now that the war was over Longevity was a tidy source of profit. The ships came; and disgorged a steady stream of tourists—their eyes too round and straight, their jaws too square; their faces an unhealthy shade of pink, like undercooked meat left too long in the sun. They walked with the easy confidence of people with immersers: pausing to admire the suggested highlights for a second or so before moving on to the transport station, where they haggled in schoolbook Rong for a ride to their recommended hotels—a sickeningly familiar ballet Quy had been seeing most of her life, a unison of foreigners descending on the station like a plague of centipedes or leeches.

Still, Quy watched them. They reminded her of her own time on Prime, her heady schooldays filled with raucous bars and wild weekends, and late minute revisions for exams, a carefree time she'd never have again in her life. She both longed for those days back, and hated herself for her weakness. Her education on Prime, which should have been her path into the higher strata of the station's society, had brought her nothing but a sense of disconnection from her family; a growing solitude, and a dissatisfaction, an aimlessness she couldn't put in words.

She might not have moved all day—had a sign not blinked, superimposed by her router on the edge of her field of vision. A message from Second Uncle.

"Child." His face was pale and worn, his eyes underlined by dark circles, as if he hadn't slept. He probably hadn't—the last Quy had seen of him, he had been closeted with Quy's sister Tam, trying to organize a delivery for a wedding—five hundred winter melons, and six barrels of Prosper's Station best fish sauce. "Come back to the restaurant."

"I'm on my day of rest," Quy said; it came out as more peevish and childish than she'd intended.

Second Uncle's face twisted, in what might have been a smile, though he had very little sense of humor. The scar he'd got in the Independence War shone white against the grainy background—twisting back and forth, as if it still pained him. "I know, but I need you. We have an important customer."

"Galactic," Quy said. That was the only reason he'd be calling her, and not one of her brothers or cousins. Because the family somehow thought that her studies on Prime gave her insight into the Galactics' way of thought—something useful, if not the success they'd hoped for.

"Yes. An important man, head of a local trading company." Second Uncle did not move on her field of vision. Quy could *see* the ships moving through his face, slowly aligning themselves in front of their pods, the hole in front of them opening like an orchid flower. And she knew everything there was to know about Grandmother's restaurant; she was Tam's sister, after all; and she'd seen the accounts, the slow decline of their clientele as their more genteel clients moved to better areas of the station; the influx of tourists on a budget, with little time for expensive dishes prepared with the best ingredients.

"Fine," she said. "I'll come."

At breakfast, you stare at the food spread out on the table: bread and jam and some colored liquid—you come up blank for a moment, before your immerser kicks in, reminding you that it's coffee, served strong and black, just as you always take it.

Yes. Coffee.

You raise the cup to your lips—your immerser gently prompts you, reminding you of where to grasp, how to lift, how to be in every possible way graceful and elegant, always an effortless model.

"It's a bit strong," your husband says, apologetically. He watches you from the other end of the table, an expression you can't interpret on his face—and isn't this odd, because shouldn't you know all there is to know about expressions—shouldn't the immerser have everything about Galactic culture recorded into its database, shouldn't it prompt you? But it's strangely silent, and this scares you, more than anything. Immersers never fail.

"Shall we go?" your husband says—and, for a moment, you come up blank on his name, before you remember—Galen, it's Galen, named after some physician on Old Earth. He's tall, with dark hair and pale skin—his immerser avatar isn't much different from his real self, Galactic avatars seldom are. It's people like you who have to work the hardest to adjust, because so much about you draws attention to itself—the stretched eyes that crinkle in the shape of moths, the darker skin, the smaller, squatter shape more reminiscent of jackfruits than swaying fronds. But no matter: you can be made perfect; you can put on the immerser and become someone else, someone pale-skinned and tall and beautiful.

Though, really, it's been such a long time since you took off the immerser, isn't it? It's just a thought—a suspended moment that is soon erased by the immerser's flow of information, the little arrows drawing your attention to the bread and the kitchen, and the polished metal of the table—giving you context about everything, opening up the universe like a lotus flower.

"Yes," you say. "Let's go." Your tongue trips over the word—there's a structure you should have used, a pronoun you should have said instead of the lapidary Galactic sentence. But nothing will come, and you feel like a field of sugar canes after the harvest—burnt out, all cutting edges with no sweetness left inside.

Of course, Second Uncle insisted on Quy getting her immerser for the interview—just in case, he said, soothingly and diplomatically as always. Trouble was, it wasn't where Quy had last left it. After putting out a message to the rest of the family, the best information Quy got was from Cousin Khanh, who thought he'd seen Tam sweep through the living quarters, gathering every piece of Galactic tech she could get her hands on. Third Aunt, who caught Khanh's message on the family's communication channel, tutted disapprovingly. "Tam. Always with her mind lost in the mountains, that girl. Dreams have never husked rice."

Quy said nothing. Her own dreams had shriveled and died after she came back from Prime and failed Longevity's mandarin exams; but it was good to have Tam around—to have someone who saw beyond the restaurant, beyond the narrow circle of family interests. Besides, if she didn't stick with her sister, who would?

Tam wasn't in the communal areas on the upper floors; Quy threw a glance towards the lift to Grandmother's closeted rooms, but she was doubtful Tam would have gathered Galactic tech just so she could pay her respects to Grandmother. Instead, she went straight to the lower floor, the one she and Tam shared with the children of their generation.

It was right next to the kitchen, and the smells of garlic and fish sauce seemed to be everywhere—of course, the youngest generation always got the lower floor, the one with all the smells and the noises of a legion of waitresses bringing food over to the dining room.

Tam was there, sitting in the little compartment that served as the floor's communal area. She'd spread out the tech on the floor—two immersers (Tam and Quy were possibly the only family members who cared so little about immersers they left them lying around), a remote entertainment set that was busy broadcasting some stories of children running on terraformed planets, and something Quy couldn't quite identify, because Tam had taken it apart into small components: it lay on the table like a gutted fish, all metals and optical parts.

But, at some point, Tam had obviously got bored with the entire process, because she was currently finishing her breakfast, slurping noodles from her soup bowl. She must have got it from the kitchen's leftovers, because Quy knew the smell, could taste the spiciness of the broth on her tongue—Mother's cooking, enough to make her stomach growl although she'd had rolled rice cakes for breakfast.

"You're at it again," Quy said with a sigh. "Could you not take my immerser for your experiments, please?"

Tam didn't even look surprised. "You don't seem very keen on using it, big sis."

"That I don't use it doesn't mean it's yours," Quy said, though that wasn't a real reason. She didn't mind Tam borrowing her stuff, and actually would have been glad to never put on an immerser again—she hated the feeling they gave her, the vague sensation of the system rooting around in her brain to find the best body cues to give her. But there were times when she was expected to wear an immerser: whenever dealing with customers, whether she was waiting at tables or in preparation meetings for large occasions.

Tam, of course, didn't wait at tables—she'd made herself so good at logistics and anything to do with the station's system that she spent most of her time in front of a screen, or connected to the station's network.

"Lil' sis?" Quy said.

Tam set her chopsticks by the side of the bowl, and made an expansive gesture with her hands. "Fine. Have it back. I can always use mine."

Quy stared at the things spread on the table, and asked the inevitable question. "How's progress?"

Tam's work was network connections and network maintenance within the restaurant; her hobby was tech. Galactic tech. She took things apart to see what made them tick; and rebuilt them. Her foray into entertainment units had helped the restaurant set up ambient sounds—old-fashioned Rong music for Galactic customers, recitation of the newest poems for locals.

But immersers had her stumped: the things had nasty safeguards to them. You could open them in half, to replace the battery; but you went no further. ·Tam's previous attempt had almost lost her the use of her hands.

By Tam's face, she didn't feel ready to try again. "It's got to be the same logic."

"As what?" Quy couldn't help asking. She picked up her own immerser from the table, briefly checking that it did indeed bear her serial number.

Tam gestured to the splayed components on the table. "Artificial Literature Writer. Little gadget that composes light entertainment novels."

"That's not the same—" Quy checked herself, and waited for Tam to explain.

"Takes existing cultural norms, and puts them into a cohesive, satisfying narrative. Like people forging their own path and fighting aliens for possession of a planet, that sort of stuff that barely speaks to us on Longevity. I mean, we've never even seen a planet." Tam exhaled, sharply—her eyes half on the dismembered Artificial Literature Writer, half on some overlay of her vision. "Just like immersers take a given culture and parcel it out to you in a form you can relate to: language, gestures, customs, the whole package. They've got to have the same architecture."

"I'm still not sure what you want to do with it." Quy put on her immerser, adjusting the thin metal mesh around her head until it fitted. She winced as the interface synced with her brain. She moved her hands, adjusting some settings lower than the factory ones—darn thing always reset itself to factory, which she suspected was no accident. A shimmering lattice surrounded her: her avatar, slowly taking shape around her. She could still see the room—the lattice was only faintly opaque—but ancestors, how she hated the feeling of not quite being there. "How do I look?"

"Horrible. Your avatar looks like it's died or something."

"Ha ha ha," Quy said. Her avatar was paler than her, and taller: it made her look beautiful, most customers agreed. In those moments, Quy was glad she had an avatar, so they wouldn't see the anger on her face. "You haven't answered my question."

Tam's eyes glinted. "Just think of the things we couldn't do. This is the best piece of tech Galactics have ever brought us."

Which wasn't much, but Quy didn't need to say it aloud. Tam knew exactly how Quy felt about Galactics and their hollow promises.

"It's their weapon, too." Tam pushed at the entertainment unit. "Just like their books and their holos and their live games. It's fine for them—they put the immersers on tourist settings, they get just what they need to navigate a foreign environment from whatever idiot's written the Rong script for that thing. But we—we worship them. We wear the immersers on Galactic all the time. We make ourselves like them, because they push, and because we're naive enough to give in."

"And you think you can make this better?" Quy couldn't help it. It wasn't that she needed to be convinced: on Prime, she'd never seen immersers. They were tourist stuff, and even while travelling from one city to another, the citizens just assumed they'd know enough to get by. But the stations, their ex-colonies were flooded with immersers.

Tam's eyes glinted, as savage as those of the rebels in the history holos. "If I can take them apart, I can rebuild them and disconnect the logical circuits. I can give us the language and the tools to deal with them without being swallowed by them."

Mind lost in the mountains, Third Aunt said. No one had ever accused Tam of thinking small. Or of not achieving what she set her mind on, come to think of it. And every revolution had to start somewhere—hadn't Longevity's War of Independence started over a single poem, and the unfair imprisonment of the poet who'd written it?

Quy nodded. She believed Tam, though she didn't know how far. "Fair point. Have to go now, or Second Uncle will skin me. See you later, lil' sis."

As you walk under the wide arch of the restaurant with your husband, you glance upwards, at the calligraphy that forms its sign. The immerser translates it for you into "Sister Hai's Kitchen," and starts giving you a detailed background of the place: the menu and the most recommended dishes—as you walk past the various tables, it highlights items it thinks you would like, from rolled-up rice dumplings to fried shrimps. It warns you about the more exotic dishes, like the pickled pig's ears, the fermented meat (you have to be careful about that one, because its name changes depending on which station dialect you order in), or the reeking durian fruit that the natives so love.

It feels . . . not quite right, you think, as you struggle to follow Galen, who is already far away, striding ahead with the same confidence he always exudes in life. People part before him; a waitress with a young, pretty avatar bows before him, though Galen himself takes no notice. You know that such obsequiousness unnerves him; he always rants about the outdated customs aboard Longevity, the inequalities and the lack of democratic government—he thinks it's only a matter of time before they change, adapt themselves to fit into Galactic society. You—you have a faint memory of arguing with him, a long time ago, but now you can't find the words, anymore, or even the reason why—it makes sense, it all makes sense. The Galactics rose against the tyranny of Old Earth and overthrew their shackles, and won the right to determine their own destiny; and every other station and planet will do the same, eventually, rise against the dictatorships that hold them away from progress. It's right; it's always been right.

Unbidden, you stop at a table, and watch two young women pick at a dish of chicken with chopsticks—the smell of fish sauce and lemongrass rises in the air, as pungent and as unbearable as rotten meat—no, no, that's not it, you have an image of a dark-skinned woman, bringing a dish of steamed rice to the table, her hands filled with that same smell, and your mouth watering in anticipation . . .

The young women are looking at you: they both wear standard-issue avatars, the bottom-of-the-line kind—their clothes are a garish mix of red and yellow, with the odd, uneasy cut of cheap designers; and their faces waver, letting you glimpse a hint of darker skin beneath the red flush of their cheeks. Cheap and tawdry, and altogether inappropriate; and you're glad you're not one of them.

"Can I help you, older sister?" one of them asks.

Older sister. A pronoun you were looking for, earlier; one of the things that seem to have vanished from your mind. You struggle for words; but all the immerser seems to suggest to you is a neutral and impersonal pronoun, one that you instinctively know is wrong—it's one only foreigners and outsiders would use in those circumstances. "Older sister," you repeat, finally, because you can't think of anything else.

"Agnes!"

Galen's voice, calling from far away—for a brief moment the immerser seems to fail you again, because you *know* that you have many names, that Agnes is the one they gave you in Galactic school, the one neither Galen nor his friends can mangle when they pronounce it. You remember the Rong names your mother gave you on Longevity, the childhood endearments and your adult style name.

Be-Nho, Be-Yeu. Thu—Autumn, like a memory of red maple leaves on a planet you never knew.

You pull away from the table, disguising the tremor in your hands.

Second Uncle was already waiting when Quy arrived; and so were the customers.

"You're late," Second Uncle sent on the private channel, though he made the comment half-heartedly, as if he'd expected it all along. As if he'd never really believed he could rely on her—that stung.

"Let me introduce my niece Quy to you," Second Uncle said, in Galactic, to the man beside him.

"Quy," the man said, his immerser perfectly taking up the nuances of her name in Rong. He was everything she'd expected; tall, with only a thin layer of avatar, a little something that narrowed his chin and eyes, and made his chest slightly larger. Cosmetic enhancements: he was good-looking for a Galactic, all things considered. He went on, in Galactic, "My name is Galen Santos. Pleased to meet you. This is my wife, Agnes."

Agnes. Quy turned, and looked at the woman for the first time—and flinched. There was no one here: just a thick layer of avatar, so dense and so complex that she couldn't even guess at the body hidden within.

"Pleased to meet you." On a hunch, Quy bowed, from younger to elder, with both hands brought together—Rong-style, not Galactic—and saw a shudder run through Agnes' body, barely perceptible; but Quy was observant, she'd always been. Her immerser was screaming at her, telling her to hold out both hands, palms up, in the Galactic fashion. She tuned it out: she

was still at the stage where she could tell the difference between her thoughts and the immerser's thoughts.

Second Uncle was talking again—his own avatar was light, a paler version of him. "I understand you're looking for a venue for a banquet."

"We are, yes." Galen pulled a chair to him, sank into it. They all followed suit, though not with the same fluid, arrogant ease. When Agnes sat, Quy saw her flinch, as though she'd just remembered something unpleasant. "We'll be celebrating our fifth marriage anniversary, and we both felt we wanted to mark the occasion with something suitable."

Second Uncle nodded. "I see," he said, scratching his chin. "My congratulations to you."

Galen nodded. "We thought—" he paused, threw a glance at his wife that Quy couldn't quite interpret—her immerser came up blank, but there was something oddly familiar about it, something she ought to have been able to name. "Something Rong," he said at last. "A large banquet for a hundred people, with the traditional dishes."

Quy could almost feel Second Uncle's satisfaction. A banquet of that size would be awful logistics, but it would keep the restaurant afloat for a year or more, if they could get the price right. But something was wrong—something—

"What did you have in mind?" Quy asked, not to Galen, but to his wife. The wife—Agnes, which probably wasn't the name she'd been born with—who wore a thick avatar, and didn't seem to be answering or ever speaking up. An awful picture was coming together in Quy's mind.

Agnes didn't answer. Predictable.

Second Uncle took over, smoothing over the moment of awkwardness with expansive hand gestures. "The whole hog, yes?" Second Uncle said. He rubbed his hands, an odd gesture that Quy had never seen from him—a Galactic expression of satisfaction. "Bitter melon soup, Dragon-Phoenix plates, Roast Pig, Jade Under the Mountain . . ." He was citing all the traditional dishes for a wedding banquet—unsure of how far the foreigner wanted to take it. He left out the odder stuff, like Shark Fin or Sweet Red Bean Soup.

"Yes, that's what we would like. Wouldn't we, darling?" Galen's wife neither moved nor spoke. Galen's head turned towards her, and Quy caught his expression at last. She'd thought it would be contempt, or hatred; but no; it was anguish. He genuinely loved her, and he couldn't understand what was going on.

Galactics. Couldn't he recognize an immerser junkie when he saw one? But then Galactics, as Tam said, seldom had the problem—they didn't put on the immersers for more than a few days on low settings, if they ever went that far. Most were flat-out convinced Galactic would get them anywhere.

Second Uncle and Galen were haggling, arguing prices and features; Second Uncle sounding more and more like a Galactic tourist as the conversation went on, more and more aggressive for lower and lower gains. Quy didn't care anymore: she watched Agnes. Watched the impenetrable avatar—a red-headed woman in the latest style from Prime, with freckles on her skin and a hint of a star-tan on her face. But that wasn't what she was, inside; what the immerser had dug deep into.

Wasn't who she was at all. Tam was right; all immersers should be taken apart, and did it matter if they exploded? They'd done enough harm as it was.

Quy wanted to get up, to tear away her own immerser, but she couldn't, not in the middle of the negotiation. Instead, she rose, and walked closer to Agnes; the two men barely glanced at her, too busy agreeing on a price. "You're not alone," she said, in Rong, low enough that it didn't carry.

Again, that odd, disjointed flash. "You have to take it off," Quy said, but got no further response. As an impulse, she grabbed the other woman's arm; felt her hands go right through the immerser's avatar, connect with warm, solid flesh.

You hear them negotiating, in the background—it's tough going, because the Rong man sticks to his guns stubbornly, refusing to give ground to Galen's onslaught. It's all very distant, a subject of intellectual study; the immerser reminds you from time to time, interpreting this and this body cue, nudging you this way and that—you must sit straight and silent, and support your husband—and so you smile through a mouth that feels gummed together.

You feel, all the while, the Rong girl's gaze on you, burning like ice water, like the gaze of a dragon. She won't move away from you; and her hand rests on you, gripping your arm with a strength you didn't think she had in her body. Her avatar is but a thin layer, and you can see her beneath it: a round, moon-shaped face with skin the color of cinnamon—no, not spices, not chocolate, but simply a color you've seen all your life.

"You have to take it off," she says. You don't move; but you wonder what she's talking about.

Take it off. Take it off. Take what off?

The immerser.

Abruptly, you remember—a dinner with Galen's friends, when they laughed at jokes that had gone by too fast for you to understand. You came home battling tears; and found yourself reaching for the immerser on your bedside table, feeling its cool weight in your hands. You thought it would please Galen if you spoke his language; that he would be less ashamed of how uncultured you sounded to his friends. And then you found out that everything was fine, as long as you kept the settings on maximum and didn't remove it. And then . . . and then you walked with it and slept with it, and showed the world nothing but the avatar it had designed—saw nothing it hadn't tagged and labelled for you. Then . . .

Then it all slid down, didn't it? You couldn't program the network anymore, couldn't look at the guts of machines; you lost your job with the tech company, and came to Galen's compartment, wandering in the room like a hollow shell, a ghost of yourself— as if you'd already died, far away from home and all that it means to you. Then—then the immerser wouldn't come off, anymore.

"What do you think you're doing, young woman?"

Second Uncle had risen, turning towards Quy— his avatar flushed with anger, the pale skin mottled with an unsightly red. "We adults are in the middle of negotiating something very important, if you don't mind." It might have made Quy quail in other circumstances, but his voice and his body language were wholly Galactic; and he sounded like a stranger to her—an angry foreigner whose food order she'd misunderstood—whom she'd mock later, sitting in Tam's room with a cup of tea in her lap, and the familiar patter of her sister's musings.

"I apologize," Quy said, meaning none of it.

"That's all right," Galen said. "I didn't mean to—" he paused, looked at his wife. "I shouldn't have brought her here."

"You should take her to see a physician," Quy said, surprised at her own boldness.

"Do you think I haven't tried?" His voice was bitter. "I've even taken her to the best hospitals on Prime. They look at her, and say they can't take it off. That the shock of it would kill her. And even if it didn't . . ." He spread his hands, letting air fall between them like specks of dust. "Who knows if she'd come back?"

Quy felt herself blush. "I'm sorry." And she meant it this time.

Galen waved her away, negligently, airily, but she could see the pain he was struggling to hide. Galactics didn't think tears were manly, she remembered. "So we're agreed?" Galen asked Second Uncle. "For a million credits?"

Quy thought of the banquet; of the food on the tables, of Galen thinking it would remind Agnes of home. Of how, in the end, it was doomed to fail, because everything would be filtered through the immerser, leaving Agnes with nothing but an exotic feast of unfamiliar flavors. "I'm sorry," she said, again, but no one was listening; and she turned away from Agnes with rage in her heart—with the growing feeling that it had all been for nothing in the end.

"I'm sorry," the girl says—she stands, removing her hand from your arm, and you feel like a tearing inside, as if something within you was struggling to claw free from your body. Don't go, you want to say. Please don't go. Please don't leave me here.

But they're all shaking hands; smiling, pleased at a deal they've struck—like sharks, you think, like tigers. Even the Rong girl has turned away from you; giving you up as hopeless. She and her uncle are walking away, taking separate paths back to the inner areas of the restaurant, back to their home.

Please don't go.

It's as if something else were taking control of your body; a strength that you didn't know you possessed. As Galen walks back into the restaurant's main room, back into the hubbub and the tantalizing smells of food—of lemongrass chicken and steamed rice, just as your mother used to make—you turn away from your husband, and follow the girl. Slowly, and from a distance; and then running, so that no one will stop you. She's walking fast—you see her tear her immerser away from her face, and slam it down onto a side table with disgust. You see her enter a room; and you follow her inside.

They're watching you, both girls, the one you followed in; and another, younger one, rising from the table she was sitting at—both terribly alien and terribly familiar at once. Their mouths are open, but no sound comes out.

In that one moment—staring at each other, suspended in time—you see the guts of Galactic machines spread on the table. You see the mass of tools; the dismantled machines; and the immerser, half spread-out before them, its two halves open like a cracked egg. And you understand that they've been trying to open them and reverse-engineer them; and you know that they'll never, ever succeed. Not because of the safeguards, of the Galactic encryptions to preserve their fabled intellectual property; but rather, because of something far more fundamental.

This is a Galactic toy, conceived by a Galactic mind—every layer of it, every logical connection within it exudes a mindset that might as well be alien to these girls. It takes a Galactic to believe that you can take a whole culture and reduce it to algorithms; that language and customs can be boiled to just a simple set of rules. For these girls, things are so much more complex than this; and they will never understand how an immerser works, because they can't think like a Galactic, they'll never ever think like that. You can't think like a Galactic unless you've been born in the culture.

Or drugged yourself, senseless, into it, year after year.

You raise a hand—it feels like moving through honey. You speak—struggling to shape words through layer after layer of immerser thoughts.

"I know about this," you say, and your voice comes out hoarse, and the words fall into place one by one like a laser stroke, and they feel right, in a way that nothing else has for five years. "Let me help you, younger sisters."

SECTION SIX

Activist Frontiers: Agency and Resistance

TABLE OF CONTENTS

LEARNING OBJECTIVES

By the end of this section, you will have a better understanding of:

1. Some of the many and varied strategies activists use to make social change.

2. The importance of intersectional approaches in activist work.

3. The challenges of working across social and cultural differences.

What is activism, and what forms of activism can we take part in? How can feminist, queer, and other marginalized communities transgress dominant cultural norms in the movement toward social justice? Why is intersectionality important in activist work? In this section, we explore these questions by focusing on different activist strategies. Activists use a wide range of strategies, and what follows is only a partial list, intended to be suggestive rather than definitive. We have selected the following to explore in greater depth: knowledge production, digital activism, community activist organizations, nonviolent direct action, humor, creative expression, safer spaces, and speak-outs and testimonials. Within each section there are specific examples of how the strategy has been used by activists.

INTERSECTIONALITY AND COALITIONS

Intersectional approaches are essential to activism in feminist and queer movements because without them there is a danger of reinforcing certain oppressive social hierarchies even as you try to dismantle others. For example, if feminist activism focuses only on straight women, it can reproduce heterosexual privilege while trying to dismantle male privilege. The activists highlighted in this section are not without criticism. Some have been accused of being myopic in their focus on one issue at the expense of others, or of supporting social hierarchy while they dismantle another. All activist work must be attentive to the ways in which it defines its goals, recognizing, as Lila Abu-Lughod explains in her essay, "Do Muslim Women Really Need Saving? Anthropological Reflections on Cultural Relativism and Its Others" (included in this section), that there is a danger of becoming complicit in divisive us/them narratives. In her discussion of transnational activism focused on women in the Muslim world, particularly in conjunction with the post-9/11 rhetoric of salvation and the use of the veil as oppressive symbol, Abu-Lughod reminds us that "[p]rojects of saving other women depend on and reinforce a sense of superiority by Westerners, a form of arrogance that deserves to be challenged" (p. 556).

It is important for feminist and queer activists to reflect on their motivations for their work as well as their complicity in the issues, the ways in which they benefit from the status quo or the ways in which they might benefit from a change. In her article, "Not Your Indian Eco-Princess: Indigenous Women's Resistance to Environmental Degradation," Beenash Jafri points to the failure of some transnational environmental activists to acknowledge the **neocolonial** relationships that nation-states like the United States, Canada, Australia, and New Zealand maintain with indigenous peoples. She warns that using indigenous women as symbols of an idealized relationship between women

Neocolonial: The relationship of power developed countries exercise over developing countries using economic relationships and cultural influence instead of military or political control. Neocolonialsim is a new form of colonialism, which is a practice whereby European countries conquered, occupied, and exploited countries in Africa, Asia, and the Americas.

TRANSNATIONAL CONNECTIONS

In Section III you read about female circumcision (also known as female genital cutting or female genital mutilation). Western feminists who are active in campaigns to end female circumcision in Africa, Asia, and the Middle East frequently argue that the practice stems from efforts to control female sexuality.

1. Research female circumcision. Where is it practiced? What are the arguments given in support of the practice? What are the arguments against it?

2. Research male circumcision. Compare the information you find to what you learned about female circumcision. What are the arguments made for and against male circumcision? How do these arguments compare to those made around female circumcision?

3. Male circumcision is common in the United States. If Western feminists advocate for the abolition of female circumcision, should they also try to end male circumcision?

4. How does this example demonstrate important concerns over transnational activist work?

and nature without a critical examination of the history and ongoing effects of colonialism can make invisible the ways in which nonindigenous people have benefitted from this oppression.

Abu-Lughod and Jafri point to problems in some activist work and underscore the importance of intersectionality. These critiques are important so that activists can learn from others' missteps. We can't let a fear of making mistakes prevent us from engaging in activism, but at the same time we should see openness and responsiveness to others' critiques as a necessary part of the activist process.

An important component of activist work is **coalition** building. Coalitions are fundamental to social justice, but these collaborations can be difficult because they require working across difference. Feminist activist and musician Bernice Johnson Reagon argues that acknowledging difference within coalitions is essential. Pretending that everyone is the same, and has come to the table for the same reasons, blocks the transformative potential of coalitions. In their article, "Making Coalitions Work: Solidarity Across Difference within US Feminism" (included in this section), Elizabeth R. Cole and Zakiya T. Luna build on this argument by looking at coalition work in action. They interviewed activists and analyzed their responses to investigate the ways in which coalitions come together and remain strong, as well as the challenges they face around differing interests and agendas.

Coalition: An association of individuals and/ or groups who come together around a shared interest or value.

KNOWLEDGE PRODUCTION: BOOKS, MAGAZINES, AND ZINES

Knowledge production is an integral part of activist work. As Charlotte Bunch explains in her essay, "Not by Degrees: Feminist Theory and Education," theory and organizing inform each other: in order to address discrimination, you need a framework for understanding it, and those frameworks need to respond to on-the-ground realities (12). Prior to the online revolution, which democratized publishing by allowing many more people to disseminate their writing at low cost, the production of knowledge was largely limited to those who could get their work published in print. The gatekeepers in the print publishing world represented dominant groups in society, and thus the experience of privileged white men were overrepresented in print media. People from marginalized groups had difficulty getting their work published, which served to maintain their marginalization as their experiences remained outside of mainstream visibility. Furthermore, when marginalized groups don't have access to knowledge production, their stories may be seen only or primarily through the eyes of the dominant group whose privilege may produce a distorted and self-serving narrative. Writer DaMaris B. Hill's work is attentive to these issues of self-representation and memory. Her memoir, "Concrete" (included in this section), engages with race, gender, and the construction of identity. Providing access to publishing is an essential component to social change because it democratizes knowledge production. Citing an early slogan of the **women in print movement**—"freedom of the press belongs to those who own the press"—Barbara Smith explains that because women, and particularly women of color and lesbians, have had less power in our society, they have had minimal access to publishing, meaning the stories about them were told by others (11). Smith and other activists created Kitchen Table: Women of Color Press in 1980 to respond to the dearth of publications by women of color and published influential texts like *This Bridge Called My Back: Writings By Radical Women of Color* and *Home Girls: A Black Feminist Anthology*. While Kitchen Table was an important intervention in the publishing world, limited access for marginalized groups remains a problem. Similarly, while the Internet has opened up tremendous opportunities for self-publishing, media companies maintain significant influence over what information we are exposed to online, and so the question of whose opinions are known and whose experiences are visible remains central to knowledge production.

Women in print movement: The activist efforts emerging in the late 1960s to increase the amount of published information by and about heterosexual women and lesbians based on the premise that access to information was empowering.

The Boston Women's Health Book Collective demonstrates the transformational capacity of publishing as an activist strategy engaged around a particular social justice issue. The group first met in 1969 to talk about their anger with the medical industry and particularly with "doctors who were condescending, paternalistic, judgmental and non-informative" ("Preface"). Through those discussions, they decided that in order to improve women's experiences with doctors and the medical community, women needed more information about their bodies and their health, because ignorance detracted from their ability to make informed decisions.

Because increasing women's knowledge about their bodies and their health was the primary goal of the Boston Women's Health Book Collective, they initially created a course that they offered locally in schools, churches, and homes. The course was so successful, and the demand for information was so great, that they decided to publish a book based on the course, *Our Bodies, Ourselves*, which was first published in 1971. In addition to providing information about women's bodies, the Boston Women's Health Book Collective wanted to change the narrative around women's health. For example, cultural norms around menstruation and masturbation were often couched in patriarchal and religious narratives that caused women to feel shame about their bodies. *Our Bodies, Ourselves* sought to reframe these topics in positive terms. The book has been republished in many new editions and translated into at least twenty-nine languages, selling millions of copies. After more than forty years, it is still going strong—now with an accompanying website and blog—and was included in the Library of Congress's 2012 exhibit "Books that Shaped America." The story of *Our Bodies, Ourselves* proves that individuals can make a difference: A small group of women created a book that questioned the medical establishment's views on women's bodies and in the process has educated and empowered millions of women globally.

In the preface to her 2014 book, *Trans Bodies, Trans Selves: A Resource for the Transgender Community*, Laura Erickson-Schroth says that she was twelve years old when she first looked at her mother's copy of *Our Bodies, Ourselves*. She was inspired by the women who wrote it and hopes that *her* book is just as radical as its predecessor, providing information about trans health and challenging the pathologization of trans identities (xi).

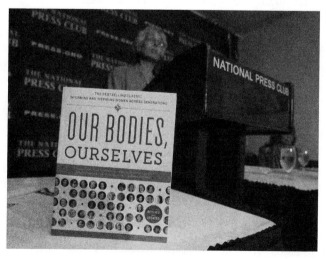

***Our Bodies, Ourselves* distributed to every member of Congress.** Judy Norsigian, co-founder of Our Bodies Ourselves (formerly the Boston Women's Health Book Collective), stands behind a copy of *Our Bodies, Ourselves* at the National Press Club in Washington, DC on October 22, 2012 where she announced the new initiative, Educate Congress, which aims to ensure that Representatives and Senators are educated about women's bodies and health. The initiative began as a response to Rep. Todd Akin's 2012 statement about "legitimate rape" and pregnancy.

Trans Bodies, Trans Selves emphasizes the importance of trans visibility by including many first-person narratives like those of prominent trans activists Dallas Denny and Jamison Green. Born in 1949, Denny says, "When I was in my early teens, I could find absolutely nothing about transgender issues. Nada. Zip. There were no zines, blogs, vlogs, Webs sites, or radio shows. There was no Internet . . . Libraries and bookstores offered no help. I was alone" (xix). Born a year earlier, Green agrees, explaining, "I had no idea that others like me existed until the mid-1970s, and I was unable to find reliable information that was reassuring—rather than pathologizing and insulting—until the late 1980s" (xx). *Trans Bodies, Trans Selves* addresses this deficit with information around many aspects of trans lives with a focus on terminology, identification documents, employment protections, guidelines and inclusion policies for sports, the processes involved in hormone therapy, and immigration policies. It provides strategies for dealing with challenges in employment, a sample doctor's care/carry letter explaining the transitioning process, and tips for how to organize activist groups. The book takes an intersectional approach, with sections like "On Top Surgery, Chests and Race/Class Privilege," "Working for LGBTQ Youth of Color," and "Liberation Doesn't Leave People Behind: Ableism, Transphobia, Classism, and Racism." *Trans Bodies, Trans Selves* provides the type of information that wasn't available to Denny and Green when they were coming of age.

Print and online magazines are also important sources of knowledge production. *BUST* is an example of a magazine (and now a website) that has challenged the status quo within the publishing industry. *BUST* got its start in 1993 when three friends, Marcelle Karp, Laurie Henzel, and Debbie Stoller, saw the need for a women's magazine that appealed to women like them, young feminists "who couldn't relate to the body-sculpting tips of *Cosmo* or the eyebrow tweezing directions of *Glamour*" (Karp and Stoller xiii). As young twenty-somethings, they had no money and no experience in publishing, but they had a vision for a new type of publication that would empower women to focus less on beauty and more on critically engaging with the world around them. The first issue of *BUST* was a self-published twenty-nine-page zine that they photocopied and stapled themselves. The print magazine is still being published more than twenty years later, now with a companion website, and the content continues to address topics that are too radical for more mainstream publications. Traditional media still encourages women to obsess over their appearance with damaging effects on female self-esteem, and this obsession with beauty also detracts from the time and energy that women could devote to other interests. Activist publications like *BUST* are important because they send a different message. They encourage a more empowering narrative about femininity and inspire a range of interests that move beyond traditional gender roles for women.

While zines can lead to more formal publications like magazines, as was the case with *BUST*, they don't have to. In fact, the DIY ethic is an important hallmark of zine culture, which emerged in conjunction with the Riot Grrrl movement (discussed later) with its questioning of power structures and encouragement of personal expression. Zinemakers take the power of publication out of the hands of the traditional publishing industry and put it into the hands of individuals, a democratizing force in the production of knowledge. What generally defines a zine (as opposed to a magazine) is its small circulation (between 100 and 1,000 copies), the fact that it's usually self-published (often via photocopier or online), and its irreverent challenging of traditional genres. Mainstream publications often stay away from controversial issues because they worry about upsetting readers and thereby lowering profits. In contrast, zines often take on these issues directly. Zines might contain personal essays, artwork, graphic novels, or poetry and might address topics like gender bending, body shaming, rape culture, trans history, alternative masculinities, aging, dis/ability rights, parenting, or animal rights. For example, in "Empower Yoself Before You Wreck Yoself: Native American Feminist Musings" (included in this section), creators Melanie Fey, Amber McCrary, and Bradly Werley include a range of genres from letters to short stories to address feminism and Native American rights from both historical and personal perspectives. Zine creators see their work as an outlet for creative expression, a channel for voicing anger, and a means of communicating to an audience directly, affectively, and passionately. Therefore, zines are political acts that inform, engage, and persuade.

DIGITAL ACTIVISM

The online revolution is important because it has created greater access to publishing and therefore to knowledge production. It has also created new tools for organizing and an unprecedented level of communication. Feministing. com and Everydayfeminism.com are two popular examples that demonstrate the way that websites can raise awareness, create community, and inspire action. In 2004, sisters Jessica and Vanessa Valenti started Feministing, a website offering a feminist take on a range of issues from popular culture to politics. Touting themselves as a "gateway to the feminist movement for young people," Feministing fosters dialogue around complex issues, encourages and publishes young writers, and promotes activism with information about grassroots initiatives and feminist organizations ("About Feministing"). In 2012 Sandra Kim started Everyday Feminism with similar goals. The site is grounded in intersectional analysis, an approach she hopes will encourage personal growth and activism. (See Section V for other examples of online feminism and a discussion of the ways in which women face violence and harassment in cyberspace.)

Mobile phone technologies like GPS mapping and photo and video recording create unprecedented possibilities for activists. For example,

INTERSECTIONAL ANALYSIS

Social media hashtag campaigns are an important component to digital activism. Beginning in July 2013, the Black Lives Matter hashtag (#blacklivesmatter) emerged as a grassroots reaction to shooting deaths of young black men at the hands of police officers or their stand-ins. In 2014, after a man killed six people motivated in part by his hatred of women, activists began using #yesallwomen to raise awareness about gendered violence. The hashtag was also a response to the earlier hashtag #notallmen, which was seen by many feminists as a defensive argument that prevented an honest dialogue around men's role in addressing the issue of violence against women.

QUESTIONS

1. Search on the Internet for information on these hashtags. Explain some of the strategies of the Black Lives Matter movement. How are they trying to make change? Explore the relationship between the #yesallwomen and the #notallmen campaigns. What point is each side trying to make?

2. Do you think this form of identity politics is useful in light of what you've learned about intersectional theory? Why or why not? For example, much of the media coverage of the Black Lives Matter campaign has focused on the experience of black men. Does this marginalize the violence experienced by black women? Is there enough focus on the violence experienced by queer black men? Similarly, does #yesallwomen suggest that all women are at equal risk for gendered violence? Which women's experiences are erased in these discussions?

3. When asked by protesters how he would address police killings of black men and women, former Baltimore Mayor and 2016 Presidential candidate, Martin O'Malley said, "Black lives matter. White lives matter. All lives matter." Critics argued that O'Malley's comment is "missing the point." What do you think they mean? What is lost in changing "black lives matter" to "all lives matter"?

Activists protest the deaths of Michael Brown and Eric Garner. First emerging after George Zimmerman was acquitted of murder charges in the shooting death of black teenager Trayvon Martin, the Black Lives Matter movement has increased public attention to the issues of racial discrimination and police brutality. Slogans, "Hands Up! Don't Shoot!" and "I Can't Breathe," used here by activists in New York City in January 2015, have arisen in response to the killing of black men by police officers.

Hashtags are an important part of social media activism. Here activists highlight the names of individual women at a 2015 event, #SayHerName: A Vigil in Memory of Black Women and Girls Killed by the Police. The hashtag #SayHerName was created by the African American Policy Forum to focus attention on black women's stories in discussions of race and policing.

Hollaback! is a crowd-sourced, application-based initiative that documents **street harassment**. Although street harassment is a common form of gender-based violence, it is rarely reported and almost never prosecuted. Hollaback! aims to change this by collecting the stories of women and LGBTQ folks who have been harassed. By downloading an application to their mobile phones, people can document harassment that they see or experience. Documenting the harassment does several things. First, it allows the targets of street harassment to take back the power. Harassers want to make their target scared or uncomfortable, but "[b]y holla'ing back you are transforming an experience that is lonely and isolating into one that is sharable. You change the power dynamic by flipping the lens off of you and onto the harasser. And you enter a worldwide community of people who've got your back" ("About"). Second, sharing individual stories creates awareness and empathy, which can be harnessed into political action. And finally, because all incidents are mapped, data is collected documenting areas with high levels of harassment.

> **Street harassment:** A form of sexual harassment in public places that includes unwanted comments, gestures, whistles, catcalls, or other unwanted attention by strangers.

Online games are another tool that activists have used to raise awareness and create empathy. Urban Ministries of Durham, a North Carolina organization fighting poverty and homelessness, co-created a game called Spent (playspent. org) to dramatize the tough decisions and experiences that many in their community face. Players are given $1,000 and challenged to make it to the end of the month without going broke while negotiating things like changes in employment, unforeseen medical costs, and the lack of affordable housing. As the player progresses through the game and makes difficult choices, the game provides contextual information about the structural causes of poverty and homelessness. Another online game, The Migrant Trail (themigranttrail.com), educates and engages around the pressing social issue of immigration. Players simulate the experience of either a migrant or a border-control agent on the US–Mexico border, encouraging a greater understanding into the migrants' motivations and the brutal experience of trying to cross the border, as well as the complexities of the job for border agents. It is important that these types of critiques emerge in the gaming world because gaming culture has historically privileged the experiences of the dominant group—telling their stories and showing the world through their eyes. It has therefore been less welcoming for women, people of color, and other marginalized groups (see Section V for more discussion of women and gaming). Games like Spent and The Migrant Trail encourage us to understand multiple perspectives around one issue.

COMMUNITY ACTIVIST ORGANIZATIONS

Community-serving activist organizations are usually designated as nonprofits or nongovernmental organizations (NGOs) because, unlike for-profit businesses, they are not designed to make a profit for owners or shareholders and/or because they operate in civil society outside of governmental structures. Helping Individual Prostitutes Survive (HIPS), a support and advocacy organization for male, female, and transgender sex workers in Washington, DC, is an example of community-based activism. HIPS helps with basic needs (such as food and housing) and provides crisis intervention for victims of abuse. The organization also offers physical and mental health services. What defines the organization is their nonjudgmental, respectful, and compassionate outreach to and with sex workers, an approach that makes their mobile van services so successful. On Thursday, Friday, and Saturday nights from 11 PM to 5 AM, HIPS workers drive through the streets of Washington, DC, distributing safer sex materials, candy, and water to sex workers (Montague). They also hand out "Bad Date Sheets," which provide information about individuals who have recently hurt sex workers in the area (Montague). HIPS demonstrates the need for community activist organizations, particularly around issues where government intervention is limited or complicated. Because prostitution is illegal in most places, it is difficult to imagine government services being provided with the same nonpunitive approach.

However, while HIPS demonstrates the value of community-activist organizations, critics worry that the neoliberal trend toward the increased privatization of social services (moving social programs outside of government) may actually have a negative effect on social justice (see Section III for more discussion of neoliberalism). For example, as Hannah E. Britton and Taylor Price discuss in their article, "'If Good Food is Cooked in One Country, We Will All Eat from It': Women and Civil Society in Africa" (included in this section), the **NGOization** of women's activism discourages more radical activism and can contain or even co-opt advocacy through grant-funded financing.

NGOization: The movement of social services from government to civil society as a result of neoliberal policies that favor privatization over government intervention.

Nonviolent direct action: Acts of protest or civil disobedience intended to raise awareness through disruption or spectacle.

NONVIOLENT DIRECT ACTION

Nonviolent direct action is an essential strategy for activists because it disrupts the lives and thoughts of those it targets, forcing them to take notice. Nonviolent direct action refers to acts of protest or civil disobedience designed to raise awareness, express outrage, and garner attention. It can include a range of activities including marches, sit-ins, hunger strikes, performances, and acts of civil disobedience. Nonviolent direct action may be used to get people's attention, make people feel uncomfortable, expose people to information, or incite anger, all in the name of making social change. Feminist and queer activists have successfully used nonviolent direct action to disrupt normative narratives and spur critical thinking around social justice issues.

Early AIDS activists often used nonviolent direct action to challenge stereotypes and prejudices about gay men as well as gay sex. In the early 1980s, AIDS was a terrifying epidemic that wasn't well understood by the medical community because of an inadequate amount of funding for research. There weren't enough beds in hospitals, treatments were experimental and ineffective, and ignorance about how the disease spread led to fear and paranoia. Gay activist Larry Kramer insisted that the only reason the public wasn't demanding more action to address the epidemic (and the only reason the public wasn't outraged at the number of deaths) was because of who the disease was primarily affecting: gay men and drug users. In his 1983 essay, "1,112 and Counting," Kramer pled for a larger activist response. He said, "If this article doesn't rouse you to anger, fury, rage, and action, gay men may have no future on this earth. Our continued existence depends on just how angry you can get."

Responding to this urgent need and harnessing the anger that Kramer encouraged, the AIDS Coalition to Unleash Power (ACT UP) emerged in 1987. ACT UP's first event was to disrupt traffic on Wall Street. Activists distributed handouts listing a series of demands and highlighting their slogan, "SILENCE = DEATH." Seventeen activists were arrested, and the newspapers featured pictures of the protesters being carried away on stretchers (Hirshman 197). The following year, ACT UP produced another major protest outside the headquarters of the Federal Drug Administration (FDA): "Wrapped in red tape, bearing fake tombstones, sporting black T-shirts with the signature triangles, for eight hours they surrounded the building. They chanted, stickered the walls of the building, lay down like corpses, and got arrested" (Hirshman 204). The activists achieved their objectives. Shortly after the protest, the FDA agreed to expedite the development and approval of new AIDS drugs (204). The success of ACT UP's activists was due in large part to their careful research and preparation. They created a media plan before their protests, they distributed handouts with specific information about how to support their cause, and they made clear demands. Their slogans were memorable: "Know Your Scumbag; The Government Has Blood On Its Hands" and "Kissing Doesn't Kill: Greed and Indifference Do" (200). Dr. Anthony Fauci, the head of the National Institutes of Health's National Institute of Allergy and Infectious Diseases, described his admiration for ACT UP: "They beautifully combined extraordinarily dramatic, provocative, and theatrical ways to get attention and once they got your attention they were able to talk to you like they were experts in the field" (qtd. in 208).

The frequently theatrical techniques of nonviolent direct action were also important tools in the disability rights movement. In the late 1970s, disability rights activists began a campaign to get wheelchair accessible lifts on public transportation by blocking the movement of buses with their wheelchairs. They also used nonviolent direct action tactics in a 1990 event called "The Capitol Crawl." At that event, ADAPT activists left their wheelchairs at the foot of the steps of the United States Capitol building in Washington, DC, and struggled to move themselves up the stairs, dramatizing how inaccessible public buildings (as the Capitol was at that time) limited their civil rights. In his essay, "I Was There" (included in this section), Michael Winter describes his participation in disability rights activism and his motivation for civil disobedience. Thanks in large part to ADAPT activists like Winter, the Americans with Disabilities Act was passed in 1990, requiring public transportation, public buildings, and other sites and goods (such as teaching materials for schools and universities) to be made accessible to people with disabilities.

As with the AIDS crisis and accessibility, nonviolent direct action has also been used to respond to gender-based state violence. As discussed in Section III, gender-based state violence is often premised on oppressive cultural norms. The transnational activist movement SlutWalk emerged in Toronto in 2011 as a response to comments from a police officer that reflected the unfair treatment that many rape survivors face in the criminal justice system. During a presentation on crime prevention at York University and in reference to the issue of campus rape, one of the invited speakers, Officer Michael Sanguinetti, said, "Women should avoid dressing like sluts to not be victimized" (qtd. in Pilkington). His words both revictimized the rape survivor by putting her behavior on trial and shifted the focus off the rapist, the real cause of the crime. SlutWalk emerged as a response to Sanguinetti's words and to rape culture in general. The first march in Toronto drew an estimated three thousand people, many of whom carried signs that said things like "Met a slut today? Don't assault her" and "We're here, we're sluts, get used to it" (Pilkington). The event was followed by marches around the world designed to expose and undermine the narrative by which women are blamed for being victims of sexual violence. Some marchers reclaimed the pejorative term "slut"

ACTIVISM AND CIVIC ENGAGEMENT

Become a "radical cheerleader." Radical cheerleading subverts the model of traditional cheerleading by using costumes, props, and chants in unexpected and irreverent ways. The cheers embrace irony, wordplay, and sarcasm while emphasizing social justice issues. For example, for Coming Out Day, the University of Colorado Boulder Campus Crusade for Queers used a cheer that included the following lines: "Just boy or girl is what they are trying to sew, That silly binary has got to go. If I wanna wear whitey-tighties with my dress, Who are you messing with my happiness? If I wanna wear high heels and I got a dick, Leave me alone, don't be a gender prick. So I've got short hair and a big strap-on, You have no right saying it's wrong. Gender, gender, f*** it we say. Life's more fun with gender play."

1. Get into groups of three or four and choose a social justice issue that you want to cheer about. Pick three points that you want to make about that issue. A point could be a fact that you want people to know, a misconception you want to correct, or a stereotype you want to challenge.

2. Come up with a cheer that incorporates the three points. Because cheers are chanted, keep the number of words down and try to use rhythm, rhyme, and other creative techniques to make the cheer memorable. Have fun, but be mindful of how various audiences might perceive your words.

3. Share your cheer with the class.

4. As a class, discuss whether there are upcoming campus events where you can put your radical cheerleading skills to use to raise awareness around social justice issues.

by dressing "slutty," wearing things like fishnet stockings and short skirts. Katt Schott-Mancini, one of the organizers of the Boston SlutWalk, explains the way the narrative of victim blaming causes us to lose our focus on the real culprit: "What you are wearing doesn't cause rape—the rapist causes it" (qtd. in Pilkington). Marches like that used by SlutWalk are a tried and true form of nonviolent direct action. They create a public spectacle that raises awareness and incites dialogue, and they can draw media attention that can pressure those in power to act.

HUMOR

While humor can be used in a disparaging way to legitimate and justify discrimination, humor also has the power to be subversive because it can destabilize what appears self-evidently true. As Sarah E. Fryett notes in her article, "Laudable Laughter: Feminism and Female Comedians" (included in this section), laughter can be a useful political tool by "radically [challenging] binaries of natural/unnatural and normal/deviant" (p. 593). Indeed, good comedy encourages us to think critically by uncovering contradiction and exposing absurdity, allowing us to look at something with fresh eyes. This becomes a political act when it is used to reveal the assumptions underlying prejudice and discrimination. For feminist and queer activists, comedy has been a particularly useful strategy for challenging discriminatory beliefs around gender, sexuality, race, religion, and other constructions of difference, thereby providing the space for oppressed groups to create new narratives.

One way in which comedians use their comedy to make social change is by addressing uncomfortable topics in a way that diffuses tension. In 2012 at a stand-up show in Los Angeles, comedian Tig Notaro started her performance by waving to the crowd and saying, "Good evening! Hello. I have cancer! How are you?" (Brownstone). Notaro says that she thought the contrast between the up-beat presentation and the fear inherent in the diagnosis was funny, "trying to make it sound like I'm saying, 'Are there any birthdays tonight, what are you celebrating?' but saying something really horrifying" (qtd. in Brownstone). For Notaro, the relentless positivity that well-intentioned people often impose on cancer patients is problematic, which the contrast in her performance helps expose (Brownstone). Bringing up cancer in a comedy act makes us address an uncomfortable topic by using humor to lower our guard and allow us to listen.

Humor can also create an entry point for the dominant group to engage with the experience of marginalized groups. Amy Schumer, a feminist comedian, has been successful with male audiences. Her TV show, *Inside Amy Schumer*, airs on Comedy Central, which has an audience that is 60 percent male (Dockterman 98). By making men laugh at "women's issues," she creates a level of consciousness about the role men play in systems of sexism. In one sketch she takes on sexual violence. She's playing a video game (that looks similar to *Call of Duty*) and her female avatar is raped by a superior officer. The game then offers the following prompt: "You were just assaulted by a fellow soldier. Do you wish to report?" "Yes." "Are you sure? Did you know he has a family? Does that change your mind about reporting?" (qtd. in Dockterman). In the context of a game, these questions seem ridiculous—would we ask that question about any other type of crime? With our laughter comes a recognition of the ways in which sexual violence is often trivialized in our culture. Schumer's work demonstrates the way in which comedy can be used to engage with the dominant group.

Negin Farsad and Dean Obeidallah, creators of the 2013 documentary film *The Muslims Are Coming!*, use a similar strategy to address Islamophobia. The film follows Farsad, Obeidallah, and a group of other Muslim comics as they tour the United States offering free stand-up comedy. In addition to their performances, they created conversation and engagement with non-Muslims through witty games like "Name that Religion" and activities like "Hug a Muslim." The documentary includes clips from their performances and activities as well as interviews from comics, celebrities, activists, and religious leaders. Farsad and Obeidallah use humor to address the fear inherent in Islamophobia and to create a less threatening environment for non-Muslims to engage with Muslims. Furthermore, they use satire and irony to expose the irrational assumptions that fuel anti-Muslim discrimination. When we laugh at stereotypes, we acknowledge their constructedness and lessen their power. Farsad and Obeidallah promise that by the end of the movie "you're gonna love the pants out of Muslims" ("A Longer Synopsis").

Comedy can also be a fruitful space for intersectional analysis. The comedian Margaret Cho uses humor to engage with social topics including beauty image, sexual violence, racism, LGBT rights, and sex work. In the film of her stand-up comedy show, *I'm the One That I Want* (2000), Cho addresses the racism and sexism she experienced during the production of her 1994 TV Show, *All-American Girl*, a sit-com about an Asian American family. She uses her comedy to expose the fetishized constructions of race, explaining how she was coached to act more "Asian." She also talks about the intense pressure to conform to Hollywood beauty standards. After being told to lose thirty pounds, Cho dieted herself into kidney failure. She has since, however, challenged such a beauty standard and now revels in empowering others to embrace their bodies and sexualities. Cho's comedy demonstrates the value of intersectionality as her humor is often produced at the intersection of cultural norms around gender, race, and sexuality.

CREATIVE EXPRESSION: ARTISTS AS ACTIVISTS

The Guerrilla Girls, an activist collective of women artists, reframe the question that has been asked too often and for too long: "Why haven't there been more great women artists?" They ask, instead, "Why haven't more women been *considered* great artists throughout Western history?" (7). To answer their question, they highlight how prejudice, restricted access, and biased art critics and historians have both stifled and dismissed the art of women and people of color. Calling themselves "the conscience of the art world," the Guerrilla Girls use posters, billboards, stickers, books, and nonviolent direct action to challenge racism and sexism in the art world. They frequently use humor to make their point. For example, in their poster, "The Advantages of Being a Woman Artist," they list things like "Working without the pressure of success," "Not having to be in shows with men," and "Having an escape from the art world in your 4 free-lance jobs" (9). In their 1989 poster "When Racism & Sexism Are No Longer Fashionable" (included in this section), they turn their gaze on the art collectors, emphasizing the ways in which race and gender affect the art market. The women who make up the Guerrilla Girls want us to question what counts as art, who's included in museums, and which artists are studied in school and encourage those who feel that women and people of color are inadequately represented in those places, to "[w]rite letters, make posters, make trouble" (91).

Despite the limitations placed on subordinate groups, women and LGBTQPAI+ folks often use creative expression for activist purposes, including (but not limited to) art installations, story quilts, musical performance (all discussed later), as well as creative writing, dance, and theater. Creativity is an accessible type of activism and can engage people who otherwise don't consider themselves political. Like nonviolent direct action, art can grab our attention; like humor, it can reframe social justice issues in ways that encourage critical thinking. Art can also produce aesthetic pleasure and elicit strong emotional responses, engaging our consciousness in a different way than other forms of activism.

COMMUNITY ART PROJECTS

The AIDS Memorial Quilt demonstrates the power of community art projects to create community, provide healing, raise awareness, and incite action. In 1985, gay rights activist Cleve Jones had an idea for a large quilt including individual squares for each person who had died of AIDS. He envisioned the quilt as a way of memorializing the victims and raising awareness around the devastating effects of the disease on individuals as well as their family and friends. The NAMES Project emerged in 1987 to organize the production and maintenance of the quilt, which, as of 2015, was comprised of 48,000 3-by-6 foot panels, each honoring an individual who succumbed to the disease. The fabric panels are decorated with paint, appliques, needlepoint, text, and photos. Two of the squares read: "The Best Daddy in the World Died of AIDS on March 2, 1987. I Love You Forever Daddy" and "I have decorated this banner to honor my

AIDS Memorial Quilt exhibited in Washington, D.C. In 2012 pieces of the quilt were displayed on the National Mall to mark the 25th anniversary of the beginning of the project. With 48,000 3-by-6 foot panels which each commemorate an individual who has died of the disease, the AIDS Memorial Quilt is the largest community art project in the world.

brother. Our parents did not want his name used publicly. The omission of his name represents the fear of oppression that AIDS victims and their families feel" (Rutledge 287). Many of the panels include just a name or imagery.

The first showing of the quilt was during the National March on Washington for Lesbian and Gay Rights on October 11, 1987. At that time, the quilt was larger than a football field, and half a million people came to look at it that first weekend ("The AIDS Memorial Quilt"). In 1988 the quilt was taken to cities across the United States, adding panels and collecting donations at each stop. The quilt has been displayed numerous times since, and it remains the largest community art project in the world ("The AIDS Memorial Quilt"). The NAMES Project continues to add to the quilt with new panels. Images of the quilt are featured on the project's website. The NAMES Project also preserves other submitted information about those that have been memorialized in the quilt, which is archived for future generations. What started with Cleve Jones and a small group of friends has grown into an international activist project raising money and awareness and forever changing the face of AIDS. The Quilt has been healing for friends and family members who make panels for their loved one, and it has drawn attention to the epidemic, helping activists to demand greater research funding.

VISUAL ART

Faith Ringgold is an artist who works in many media, and her work demonstrates the ability of activist art to challenge dominant narratives as well as aesthetic norms within the art industry. Beginning in the 1960s, Ringgold challenged the prevailing norms within the art world. Ringgold was a leader in the **black arts movement** and the **feminist art movement** and has spent many years advocating for the recognition of black and female artists. She has organized protests at major museums to draw attention to the exclusion of these artists and created organizations to encourage and foster black and female artists. The activism she is most well known for comes through her artwork, particularly her story quilts. These quilts use both words and imagery to tell a story, often one of political significance. Ringgold uses materials that challenge the historical subordination of women and people of color in the art world by contesting the traditional distinction between art and craft. While "art" has traditionally involved working with expensive materials (such as oil paints, marble, or bronze) as well as the implied leisure to produce something without secondary use value, the art that marginalized groups have historically created made use of inexpensive, common materials and usually had a secondary use value. Quilts, for example, were long dismissed by the art world as "low art" or craft and were rarely included in museums. By using fabric in her work and making quilts, Ringgold challenges the definition of "art" in a way that highlights how social hierarchies intersect with the construction of aesthetic value.

Black arts movement: The movement in the 1960s and 1970s to highlight and inspire African American contributions in literature, music, theater, dance, and visual art and to develop a black aesthetic.

Feminist art movement: Activism beginning in the 1960s and 1970s that promoted female artists, encouraged better representation of women's lives in art, and challenged aesthetic values within the art world, including the privileging of particular media.

Ringgold's work also plays with historical narratives in ways that present alternative views of familiar stories. For example, in her story quilt *Who's Afraid of Aunt Jemima?*, Ringgold alternates squares of imagery, patterns, and text to retell the story of Aunt Jemima, a character first emerging in the late nineteenth-century racist minstrel shows that used exaggerated racial stereotypes to legitimate and perpetuate white supremacy. The Aunt Jemima character was later appropriated to sell pancake mix, advertised in ways that perpetuated the mammy archetype. In Ringgold's retelling of the story, Aunt Jemima is a successful businesswoman named Jemima Blakey. While the minstrel imaginings of Aunt Jemima positioned her as a servant understood only in relation to her white employers, Ringgold gives Jemima Blakey her own story. Blakey and her husband open a restaurant and catering business in Harlem, and they have a mixed-race family. The quilt tells Blakey's story through African American vernacular. Using dialect in her art, Ringgold celebrates the value of oral storytelling.

MUSIC

Feminist and queer musicians alike must find their way in a male-dominated industry that both creates and reinforces oppressive narratives around sex and sexuality. However, music, like other creative expression, also creates space for resistance. One strategy has been to create feminist and queer independent record labels like Olivia Records, formed in 1973 to promote women's music. While major music labels still control most of the music that we are exposed to, new forms of self-publishing (including social media) have created new possibilities for music distribution. Musicians can use their work to make social change in a variety of ways. They can use lyrics and imagery to challenge and disrupt dominant narratives, they can challenge norms and tropes within particular musical genres, and they can use their celebrity to create community and raise awareness.

Many feminist musicians have contributed to feminist activism. One of the more well-known feminist movements in music is the Riot Grrrl revolution. The feminist punk band Bikini Kill (1990–1997) was credited with starting the Riot Grrrl revolution by centering their music on feminist lyrics and by using their fame to create feminist community in the punk scene and beyond. The four-member band included three women—lead singer Kathleen Hanna, bassist Kathi Wilcox, and drummer Tobi Vail—and one male, guitarist Billy Karren. Hanna was drawn to music as a space that embraced contradiction and ambiguity, but even in the punk rock scene she was disappointed to find that most people didn't consider feminism relevant anymore (Marcus 42). Bikini Kill used their lyrics to encourage women to come together and get politically active, to speak up, and to make change.

Other groups that were influential in the early years included Heavens to Betsy and Bratmobile (credited, in part, with coining the term "Riot Grrrl" in their zine). Forming later, bands like Sleater-Kinney and Le Tigre show the enduring influence of early Riot Grrrl bands. The Russian feminist punk group Pussy Riot, which cites Bikini Kill as one of its influences, was founded in 2011 and is known for its guerrilla performances that focus on feminism and LGBT rights. In 2012 Pussy Riot performed at the Christ the Savior Cathedral in Moscow where they railed against the Russian Orthodox Church and its support of Russian President Putin, whom Pussy Riot criticizes for, among other things, his campaign against gay rights. In response to the performance, three members of the group, Nadezhda Tolokonnikova, Maria Alyokhina, and Yekaterina Samutsevich, were arrested and convicted of hooliganism intended to incite religious hatred. They were sentenced to two years in prison, though they were all released before that period. Demonstrations were held around the world in support of Pussy Riot.

Inasmuch as the Riot Grrrl revolution transformed the punk scene, feminist activism is also an important current in other musical genres like rap and hip-hop. Prominent sociologist and scholar Patricia Hill Collins points to the ways in which black female musicians demonstrate a feminist ethic, noting that "artists such as Salt-n-Pepa, Lauryn Hill, Queen Latifah, India/Arie, and Alicia

Keys routinely argue that Black women have the right to be respected, to be loved by their families and partners, to express themselves freely (artistically and sexually), and not to be mistaken for the stereotypes that have been applied to them" (192). While images that legitimate female sexual desire can be emancipatory, particularly for women of color these images are always in tension with what scholar Evelyn Brooks Higginbotham calls the **politics of respectability** which accords women value based on perceived notions of sexual restraint.

Hip-hop feminist Joan Morgan argues that although rap is often presented as misogynistic, it's essential for women to engage with it because "it takes us straight to the battlefield" (72). Morgan maintains that sexism in rap is a mask that African American men wear, one that allows them to deal with the pain that is a product of their oppression (74). Therefore, because hip-hop has the capacity to articulate the collective pain of the African American community, it can be an effective tool for analyzing gender, race, and power (80). This tension between the sexist images of mostly black women and the liberatory potential of hip-hop as a musical genre has prompted the Crunk Feminist Collective (CFC), a group of hip-hop activists, to invoke percussion as a metaphor. Playing on the importance of percussion in Southern rap, the CRC observes "that the tension between competing and often contradictory political and cultural projects like hip-hop and feminism is percussive in that it is both disruptive and generative" (Durham et al. 724).

Musicians can use their art to teach, engage, and incite action, but consumers also play an important role. Supporting feminist and queer musicians by buying their music and attending their concerts creates a market for their work that finances further projects and encourages others to engage with music in political ways. The reverse is also true: when we buy music that supports ideas we *don't* agree with (e.g., songs with lyrics that trivialize sexual violence or encourage homophobia), we are implicitly encouraging a market that contributes to discrimination.

Politics of respectability: A term coined by Evelyn Brooks Higginbotham to describe efforts by those in marginalized groups to police the behavior of their community to encourage conformity with the dominant group's norms as a strategy for gaining greater acceptance.

SAFER SPACES

Physical and virtual spaces where people from marginalized groups can expect to be safer from hatred, hostility, and rejection—often called **safe spaces,** or **safer spaces**—are important because they create communities that can be healing, energizing, and informative. In her article, "On Lesbian-Feminism and Lesbian Separatism: A New Intersectional History" (included in this section), Julie R. Enszer points out that "[s]eparation provides people with time and space to explore the nature of their oppression with others who share similar experiences and without intrusions from individuals who benefit from structural power" (p. 599). This has been an

Safe space/safer space: A physical or virtual location where marginalized people are sheltered from the prejudice and discrimination that they may face outside the space.

Engaged Learning

Create a social justice playlist.

1. Think about the music you listen to and explore artists who define themselves as activists.
2. Select five songs that you believe have a positive message related to an issue that you care about. The songs can all be from one artist or from a combination of different artists. The songs can be new or old.
3. Look up the lyrics of the songs and do a close reading of the wording. Mark passages that are meaningful to you.
4. Make a one-page handout for your playlist. On the handout, explain how the songs engage in activism around a particular issue. You can talk about the lyrics, the music video for the song, and/or information from the artist(s) themselves. Feel free to add artwork or images of the artist. Be creative!
5. Share your list with your classmates. Make enough copies of your playlist to give a copy to each of your classmates. Read through your classmates' playlists and listen to the songs that interest you.

essential tool for creating queer communities as LGBTQPAI+ people have historically been excluded, formally and informally, from communities, organizations, and families. However, separatist strategies raise issues over who is included (e.g., see Tina Vasquez's discussion of the exclusion of trans women from the Michigan Womyn's Music Festival in her essay, "It's Time to End the Long History of Feminism Failing Transgender Women" in Section II).

Bluestockings, an independent bookstore in New York, is an example of the legacy of separatism that Enszer describes. They carry books, journals, magazines, and zines related to feminist and queer topics, and they use a radical nonprofit business model to run the store (Bluestockings is collectively owned and run by volunteers). It also offers community space for activist events and educational programs that promote "centered, strategic, and visionary thinking, towards the realization of a society that is infinitely creative, truly democratic, equitable, ecological, and free" ("Our History").

Women's centers on college campuses are another example of safer space activism. In her article, "Campus-Based Women's and Gender Equity Centers: Enacting Feminist Theories, Creating Social Change" (included in this section), Amber L. Vlasnik notes how they emerged on campuses in the 1960s and 1970s in conjunction with the women's movement and to support the increasing number of female students. Vlasnik provides tips on how to get involved with a women's or gender equity center on campus as well as how to start one.

SPEAK-OUTS AND TESTIMONIALS

Testimonials have historically been a powerful tool in social justice activism by giving voice to members of marginalized groups. Feeling silenced is part of the experience of marginalization: a person's story (and experience) isn't valued because it isn't heard. Creating space for people to vocalize their unique experience empowers them because it asserts the legitimacy of their experience and it gives the community a more complex, multifaceted understanding of an issue. Speak-outs are events where people come together to share their stories, usually around a particular social justice issue. Testimonials may also be shared as a part of a larger event. For example, student activists at colleges around the world organize Take Back the Night events to draw attention to sexual violence by using a variety of strategies, including marches, rallies, and candlelight vigils. These events often feature testimonials where survivors share their stories showing the real people behind the statistics and allowing survivors to see that they are not alone.

The Truth Telling Project is a speak-out that emerged as a response to the protests surrounding the August 9, 2014, killing of black teenager Michael Brown by white police officer Darren Wilson in Ferguson, Missouri. While Wilson was not indicted for the shooting, Brown's death spurred a nationwide discussion about African American experiences with police brutality and systemic racism. The goal of the Truth Telling Project is to record and broadcast first-person narratives of Ferguson residents or others who have experienced police violence in order to promote a dialogue that brings about change: "Giving voice to the voiceless through the power of storytelling will humanize persons in a manner that no Commission report, visual representation or media interview can" ("Declaration of Intent").

A social media version of the speak-out can be seen in the hashtag that emerged in response to the 2015 controversy over Planned Parenthood, the women's health care provider. After Amelia Bonow posted the story of her abortion on her Facebook page, Seattle writer Lindy West tweeted her story, adding the hashtag #ShoutYourAbortion (Pearson). West explained that she wanted to share Bonow's story, and encourage others to share their stories, saying, "It's about destigmatization, normalization, and putting an end to shame" (qtd. in Pearson). The people who used the hashtag to tell the story of their experience discussed the reasons for their choice, their belief that life doesn't begin at conception, the positive ways that abortion affected their lives, and their reasons for sharing their story, among other topics. Bonow said that she was motivated to talk about her experience because "abortion is still something to be whispered about" (qtd. in Pearson). Testimonials like hers have the potential to challenge misconceptions and offer support to people who may feel alone in their experience.

Speak-outs and testimonials have the power to challenge the dominant narrative and create space for feminist, queer, and other marginalized communities to push for social justice. Like the other strategies described here, they can be useful for raising awareness, encouraging critical thinking, and inciting action.

Critical Thinking Questions

1. Thinking about Abu-Lughod's essay, "Do Muslim Women Really Need Saving? Anthropological Reflections on Cultural Relativism and Its Others," what is the best approach for determining the need for international intervention while respecting cultural difference?

2. What activist strategies would you add to this section?

3. Nonviolent direct action is often successful because it involves acts that are disruptive or make people uncomfortable. Do you think there should be limits on this approach and, if so, what kinds of limits? Is breaking the law appropriate? Is inconveniencing people appropriate?

GLOSSARY

Black arts movement 541
Coalition 527
Feminist art movement 541
Neocolonial 526

NGOization 534
Nonviolent direct action 534
Politics of respectability 543
Safe space/safer space 543

Street harassment 533
Women in print movement 528

WORKS CITED

"About." *Hollaback!* 2016, www.ihollaback.org/about/.

"About Feministing." *Feministing.* 2016, feministing.com/about/.

"The AIDS Memorial Quilt." *NAMES Project Foundation.* 2016, www.aidsquilt.org/about/the-aids-memorial-quilt.

Brownstone, Sydney. "Tig Notaro: You'll Laugh, You'll Cry." *Mother Jones*, May/June 2013, www.motherjones.com/media/2013/04/interview-tig-notaro-cancer-professor-blastoff-inside-amy-schumer.

Bunch, Charolotte. "Not by Degrees: Feminist Theory and Education." *Feminist Theory: A Reader*, edited by Wendy K. Kolmar and Frances Bartkowski. 2nd ed., McGraw Hill, 2005, pp. 12–15.

CU Boulder Campus Crusade for Queers. "Coming Out Day Cheer." *Radical Cheerleaders of Santa Cruz.* archive.qzap.org/index.php/Detail/Object/Show/object_id/164. Accessed 3 June 2016.

"Declaration of Intent." *The Truth-Telling Project.* Center for Educational Equity, 2016, thetruthtellingproject.org/wp-content/uploads/2015/10/The-Declaration.pdf.

Dockterman, Eliana. "How Amy Schumer Gets Guys To Think Feminists Are Funny." *Time*, 1 April 2014, time.com/45771/

how-amy-schumer-got-guys-to-think-feminists-are -funny/.

Durham, Aisha, et al. "The Stage Hip-Hop Feminism Built: A New Directions Essay." *Signs: Journal of Women in Culture and Society*, vol. 38, no. 3, 2013, pp. 721–37. *JSTOR*, doi:10.1086/668843.

Erickson-Schroth, Laura. *Trans Bodies, Trans Selves: A Resource for the Transgender Community*. Oxford UP, 2014.

Guerrilla Girls. *The Guerrilla Girls' Bedside Companion to the History of Western Art*. Penguin Books, 1998.

Hill Collins, Patricia. *From Black Power to Hip Hop: Racism, Nationalism, and Feminism*. Temple UP, 2006.

Higginbotham, Evelyn Brooks. *Righteous Discontent: The Women's Movement in the Black Baptist Church, 1880– 1920*. Harvard UP, 1993.

Hirshman, Linda. *Victory: The Triumphant Gay Revolution*. HarperCollins Publishers, 2012.

HIPS: Reducing Harm in the Nation's Capital Since 1993. www.hips.org/. Accessed 3 June 2016.

Karp, Marcelle and Debbie Stoller. "The Birth of *BUST*." *The* BUST *Guide to the New Girl Order*, edited by Marcelle Karp and Debbie Stoller, Penguin Books, 1999.

Kramer, Larry, "1,112 and Counting." *The New York Native*, no. 59, 14 March 1983. *Indymedia UK*, 3 May 2003, www.indymedia.org.uk/en/2003/05/66488. html.

"A Longer Synopsis." *The Muslims Are Coming!* Written and directed by Negin Farsad and Dean Obeidallah, 2011, themuslimsarecoming.com/ about/a-longer-synopsis/.

Marcus, Sara. *Girls to the Front: The True Story of the Riot Grrrl Revolution*. HarperCollins Publishers, 2010.

Montague, Candace Y.A. "Helping Individual Prostitutes Survive: On The Van—Part One." *The Body: The Complete HIV/AIDS Resource*, Remedy Health Media, 27 Dec. 2010, www.thebody.com/content/ art59998.html.

Morgan, Joan. *When Chickenheads Come Home to Roost*. Touchstone, 1999.

"Our History." *Bluestockings*. bluestockings.com/about/ history/. Accessed 10 October 2016.

Pearson, Michael. "Women Embrace, Criticize #ShoutYourAbortion." *CNN,* Turner Broadcasting, 29 Sep. 2015, www.cnn.com/2015/09/22/living/ shout-your-abortion-feat/.

Pilkington, Ed. "SlutWalking Gets Rolling After Cop's Loose Talk about Provocative Clothing." *The Guardian*, 6 May 2011, www.theguardian.com/world/ 2011/ may/06/slutwalking-policeman-talk-clothing.

"Preface to the 1973 Edition of 'Our Bodies, Ourselves.'" *Our Bodies, Ourselves*. 2016, www.ourbodiesourselves.org/history/ preface-to-the-1973-edition-of-our-bodies-ourselves/.

Reagon, Bernice Johnson. "Coalition Politics: Turning the Century." *Home Girls: A Black Feminist Anthology*, edited by Barbara Smith, Kitchen Table: Women of Color Press, 1983. pp. 356–68.

Rutledge, Leigh W. *The Gay Decades: From Stonewall to the Present; The People and Events that Shaped Gay Lives*. Plume, 1992.

Smith, Barbara. "A Press of Our Own Kitchen Table: Women of Color Press." *Frontiers: A Journal of Women's Studies*, vol. 10, no. 3, 1989, pp. 11–13. *JSTOR*, doi:10.2307/3346433.

79. • *Lila Abu-Lughod*

DO MUSLIM WOMEN REALLY NEED SAVING? ANTHROPOLOGICAL REFLECTIONS ON CULTURAL RELATIVISM AND ITS OTHERS (2002)

Lila Abu-Lughod is a professor of anthropology and women's and gender studies at Columbia University. Her research focuses on gender in the Middle East, particularly on the ways in which representation and cultural productions affect politics, and the tensions around universalist arguments in human rights discourse. Her books include *Writing Women's Worlds: Bedouin Stories*, *Dramas of Nationhood: The Politics of Television in Egypt*, and *Veiled Sentiments: Honor and Poetry in a Bedouin Society*. In "Do Muslim Women Really Need Saving? Anthropological Reflections on Cultural Relativism and Its Others," Abu-Lughod explores the cultural narratives around Muslim women and the role these narratives play in foreign policy. Specifically, she argues that the image of the oppressed Muslim woman has been used to justify post-9/11 military intervention in Afghanistan.

What are the ethics of the current "War on Terrorism," a war that justifies itself by purporting to liberate, or save, Afghan women? Does anthropology have anything to offer in our search for a viable position to take regarding this rationale for war?

I was led to pose the question of my title in part because of the way I personally experienced the response to the U.S. war in Afghanistan. Like many colleagues whose work has focused on women and gender in the Middle East, I was deluged with invitations to speak—not just on news programs but also to various departments at colleges and universities, especially women's studies programs. Why did this not please me, a scholar who has devoted more than 20 years of her life to this subject and who has some complicated personal connection to this identity? Here was an opportunity to spread the word, disseminate my knowledge, and

correct misunderstandings. The urgent search for knowledge about our sister "women of cover" (as President George Bush so marvelously called them) is laudable and when it comes from women's studies programs where "transnational feminism" is now being taken seriously, it has a certain integrity (see Safire 2001).

My discomfort led me to reflect on why, as feminists in or from the West, or simply as people who have concerns about women's lives, we need to be wary of this response to the events and aftermath of September 11, 2001. I want to point out the minefields—a metaphor that is sadly too apt for a country like Afghanistan, with the world's highest number of mines per capita—of this obsession with the plight of Muslim women. I hope to show some way through them using insights from anthropology, the discipline whose charge has been to understand

and manage cultural difference. At the same time, I want to remain critical of anthropology's complicity in the reification of cultural difference.

CULTURAL EXPLANATIONS AND THE MOBILIZATION OF WOMEN

It is easier to see why one should be skeptical about the focus on the "Muslim woman" if one begins with the U.S. public response. I will analyze two manifestations of this response: some conversations I had with a reporter from the PBS *NewsHour with Jim Lehrer* and First Lady Laura Bush's radio address to the nation on November 17, 2001. The presenter from the *NewsHour* show first contacted me in October to see if I was willing to give some background for a segment on Women and Islam. I mischievously asked whether she had done segments on the women of Guatemala, Ireland, Palestine, or Bosnia when the show covered wars in those regions; but I finally agreed to look at the questions she was going to pose to panelists. The questions were hopelessly general. Do Muslim women believe "x"? Are Muslim women "y"? Does Islam allow "z" for women? I asked her: If you were to substitute Christian or Jewish wherever you have Muslim, would these questions make sense? I did not imagine she would call me back. But she did, twice, once with an idea for a segment on the meaning of Ramadan and another time on Muslim women in politics. One was in response to the bombing and the other to the speeches by Laura Bush and Cherie Blair, wife of the British Prime Minister.

What is striking about these three ideas for news programs is that there was a consistent resort to the cultural, as if knowing something about women and Islam or the meaning of a religious ritual would help one understand the tragic attack on New York's World Trade Center and the U.S. Pentagon, or how Afghanistan had come to be ruled by the Taliban, or what interests might have fueled U.S. and other interventions in the region over the past 25 years, or what the history of American support

for conservative groups funded to undermine the Soviets might have been, or why the caves and bunkers out of which Bin Laden was to be smoked "dead or alive," as President Bush announced on television, were paid for and built by the CIA.

In other words, the question is why knowing about the "culture" of the region, and particularly its religious beliefs and treatment of women, was more urgent than exploring the history of the development of repressive regimes in the region and the U.S. role in this history. Such cultural framing, it seemed to me, prevented the serious exploration of the roots and nature of human suffering in this part of the world. Instead of political and historical explanations, experts were being asked to give religio-cultural ones. Instead of questions that might lead to the exploration of global interconnections, we were offered ones that worked to artificially divide the world into separate spheres—recreating an imaginative geography of West versus East, us versus Muslims, cultures in which First Ladies give speeches versus others where women shuffle around silently in burqas.

Most pressing for me was why the Muslim woman in general, and the Afghan woman in particular, were so crucial to this cultural mode of explanation, which ignored the complex entanglements in which we are all implicated, in sometimes surprising alignments. Why were these female symbols being mobilized in this "War against Terrorism" in a way they were not in other conflicts? Laura Bush's radio address on November 17 reveals the political work such mobilization accomplishes. On the one hand, her address collapsed important distinctions that should have been maintained. There was a constant slippage between the Taliban and the terrorists, so that they became almost one word—a kind of hyphenated monster identity: the Taliban-and-the-terrorists. Then there was the blurring of the very separate causes in Afghanistan of women's continuing malnutrition, poverty, and ill health, and their more recent exclusion under the Taliban from employment, schooling, and the joys of wearing nail polish. On the other hand, her speech reinforced chasmic divides, primarily between the "civilized people throughout the world" whose hearts break for the women and children of Afghanistan and the Taliban-and-the-terrorists, the cultural monsters who want to, as she put it, "impose their world on the rest of us."

Most revealingly, the speech enlisted women to justify American bombing and intervention in Afghanistan and to make a case for the "War on Terrorism" of which it was allegedly a part. As Laura Bush said, "Because of our recent military gains in much of Afghanistan, women are no longer imprisoned in their homes. They can listen to music and teach their daughters without fear of punishment. The fight against terrorism is also a fight for the rights and dignity of women" (U.S. Government 2002).

These words have haunting resonances for anyone who has studied colonial history. Many who have worked on British colonialism in South Asia have noted the use of the woman question in colonial policies where intervention into sati (the practice of widows immolating themselves on their husbands' funeral pyres), child marriage, and other practices was used to justify rule. As Gayatri Chakravorty Spivak (1988) has cynically put it: white men saving brown women from brown men. The historical record is full of similar cases, including in the Middle East. In Turn of the Century Egypt, what Leila Ahmed (1992) has called "colonial feminism" was hard at work. This was a selective concern about the plight of Egyptian women that focused on the veil as a sign of oppression but gave no support to women's education and was professed loudly by the same Englishman, Lord Cromer, who opposed women's suffrage back home.

Sociologist Marnia Lazreg (1994) has offered some vivid examples of how French colonialism enlisted women to its cause in Algeria. She writes:

> Perhaps the most spectacular example of the colonial appropriation of women's voices, and the silencing of those among them who had begun to take women revolutionaries . . . as role models by not donning the veil, was the event of May 16, 1958 [just four years before Algeria finally gained its independence from France after a long bloody struggle and 130 years of French control—L.A.]. On that day a demonstration was organized by rebellious French generals in Algiers to show their determination to keep Algeria French. To give the government of France evidence that Algerians were in agreement with them, the generals had a few thousand native men bused in from nearby villages, along with a few women who were solemnly unveiled by French women . . . Rounding up Algerians and bringing them to demonstrations of loyalty to France was not in itself an unusual act during the colonial era. But to unveil women at a well-choreographed ceremony added to the event a symbolic dimension that dramatized the one constant feature of the Algerian occupation by France: its obsession with women. [Lazreg 1994:135]

Lazreg (1994) also gives memorable examples of the way in which the French had earlier sought to transform Arab women and girls. She describes skits at awards ceremonies at the Muslim Girls' School in Algiers in 1851 and 1852. In the first skit, written by "a French lady from Algiers," two Algerian Arab girls reminisced about their trip to France with words including the following:

> Oh! Protective France: Oh! Hospitable France! . . .
>
> Noble land, where I felt free
>
> Under Christian skies to pray to our God: . . .
>
> God bless you for the happiness you bring us!
>
> And you, adoptive mother, who taught us
>
> That we have a share of this world,
>
> We will cherish you forever! [Lazreg 1994:68–69]

These girls are made to invoke the gift of a share of this world, a world where freedom reigns under Christian skies. This is not the world the Taliban-and-the-terrorists would "like to impose on the rest of us."

Just as I argued above that we need to be suspicious when neat cultural icons are plastered over messier historical and political narratives, so we need to be wary when Lord Cromer in British-ruled Egypt, French ladies in Algeria, and Laura Bush, all with military troops behind them, claim to be saving or liberating Muslim women.

POLITICS OF THE VEIL

I want now to look more closely at those Afghan women Laura Bush claimed were "rejoicing" at their liberation by the Americans. This necessitates a discussion of the veil, or the burqa, because it is so central to contemporary concerns about Muslim women. This will set the stage for a discussion of how anthropologists, feminist anthropologists in particular, contend with the problem of difference in a global world. In the conclusion, I will return to the rhetoric of saving Muslim women and offer an alternative.

It is common popular knowledge that the ultimate sign of the oppression of Afghan women under the Taliban-and-the-terrorists is that they were forced to wear the burqa. Liberals sometimes confess their surprise that even though Afghanistan has been liberated from the Taliban, women do not seem to be throwing off their burqas. Someone who has worked in Muslim regions must ask why this is so surprising. Did we expect that once "free" from the Taliban they would go "back" to belly shirts and blue jeans, or dust off their Chanel suits? We need to be more sensible about the clothing of "women of cover," and so there is perhaps a need to make some basic points about veiling.

First, it should be recalled that the Taliban did not invent the burqa. It was the local form of covering that Pashtun women in one region wore when they went out. The Pashtun are one of several ethnic groups in Afghanistan and the burqa was one of many forms of covering in the subcontinent and Southwest Asia that has developed as a convention for symbolizing women's modesty or respectability. The burqa, like some other forms of "cover" has, in many settings, marked the symbolic separation of men's and women's spheres, as part of the general association of women with family and home, not with public space where strangers mingled.

Twenty years ago the anthropologist Hanna Papanek (1982), who worked in Pakistan, described the burqa as "portable seclusion." She noted that many saw it as a liberating invention because it enabled women to move out of segregated living spaces while still observing the basic moral requirements of separating and protecting women from unrelated men. Ever since I came across her phrase "portable seclusion," I have thought of these enveloping robes as "mobile homes." Everywhere, such veiling signifies belonging to a particular community and participating in a moral way of life in which families are paramount in the organization of communities and the home is associated with the sanctity of women.

The obvious question that follows is this: If this were the case, why would women suddenly become immodest? Why would they suddenly throw off the markers of their respectability, markers, whether burqas or other forms of cover, which were supposed to assure their protection in the public sphere from the harassment of strange men by symbolically signaling to all that they were still in the inviolable space of their homes, even though moving in the public realm? Especially when these are forms of dress that had become so conventional that most women gave little thought to their meaning.

To draw some analogies, none of them perfect, why are we surprised that Afghan women do not throw off their burqas when we know perfectly well that it would not be appropriate to wear shorts to the opera? At the time these discussions of Afghan women's burqas were raging, a friend of mine was chided by her husband for suggesting she wanted to wear a pantsuit to a fancy wedding: "You know you don't wear pants to a WASP wedding," he reminded her. New Yorkers know that the beautifully coiffed Hasidic women, who look so fashionable next to their dour husbands in black coats and hats, are wearing wigs. This is because religious belief and community standards of propriety require the covering of the hair.

They also alter boutique fashions to include high necks and long sleeves. As anthropologists know perfectly well, people wear the appropriate form of dress for their social communities and are guided by socially shared standards, religious beliefs, and moral ideals, unless they deliberately transgress to make a point or are unable to afford proper cover. If we think that U.S. women live in a world of choice regarding clothing, all we need to do is remind ourselves of the expression, "the tyranny of fashion."

What had happened in Afghanistan under the Taliban is that one regional style of covering or veiling, associated with a certain respectable but not elite class, was imposed on everyone as "religiously" appropriate, even though previously there had been many different styles, popular or traditional with different groups and classes—different ways to mark women's propriety, or, in more recent times, religious piety. Although I am not an expert on Afghanistan, I imagine that the majority of women left in Afghanistan by the time the Taliban took control were the rural or less educated, from nonelite families, since they were the only ones who could not emigrate to escape the hardship and violence that has marked Afghanistan's recent history. If liberated from the enforced wearing of burqas, most of these women would choose some other form of modest headcovering, like all those living nearby who were not under the Taliban—their rural Hindu counterparts in the North of India (who cover their heads and veil their faces from affines) or their Muslim sisters in Pakistan.

Even *The New York Times* carried an article about Afghan women refugees in Pakistan that attempted to educate readers about this local variety (Fremson 2001). The article describes and pictures everything from the now-iconic burqa with the embroidered eyeholes, which a Pashtun woman explains is the proper dress for her community, to large scarves they call chadors, to the new Islamic modest dress that wearers refer to as *hijab*. Those in the new Islamic dress are characteristically students heading for professional careers, especially in medicine, just like their counterparts from Egypt

to Malaysia. One wearing the large scarf was a school principal; the other was a poor street vendor. The telling quote from the young street vendor is, "If I did [wear the burqa] the refugees would tease me because the burqa is for 'good women' who stay inside the home" (Fremson 2001:14). Here you can see the local status associated with the burqa—it is for good respectable women from strong families who are not forced to make a living selling on the street.

The British newspaper *The Guardian* published an interview in January 2002 with Dr. Suheila Siddiqi, a respected surgeon in Afghanistan who holds the rank of lieutenant general in the Afghan medical corps (Goldenberg 2002). A woman in her sixties, she comes from an elite family and, like her sisters, was educated. Unlike most women of her class, she chose not to go into exile. She is presented in the article as "the woman who stood up to the Taliban" because she refused to wear the burqa. She had made it a condition of returning to her post as head of a major hospital when the Taliban came begging in 1996, just eight months after firing her along with other women. Siddiqi is described as thin, glamorous, and confident. But further into the article it is noted that her graying bouffant hair is covered in a gauzy veil. This is a reminder that though she refused the burqa, she had no question about wearing the chador or scarf.

Finally, I need to make a crucial point about veiling. Not only are there many forms of covering, which themselves have different meanings in the communities in which they are used, but also veiling itself must not be confused with, or made to stand for, lack of agency. As I have argued in my ethnography of a Bedouin community in Egypt in the late 1970s and 1980s (1986), pulling the black head cloth over the face in front of older respected men is considered a voluntary act by women who are deeply committed to being moral and have a sense of honor tied to family. One of the ways they show their standing is by covering their faces in certain contexts. They decide for whom they feel it is appropriate to veil.

To take a very different case, the modern Islamic modest dress that many educated women across the Muslim world have taken on since the mid-1970s now both publicly marks piety and can be read as a sign of educated urban sophistication, a sort of modernity (e.g., Abu-Lughod 1995, 1998; Brenner 1996; El Guindi 1999; MacLeod 1991; Ong 1990). As Saba Mahmood (2001) has so brilliantly shown in her ethnography of women in the mosque movement in Egypt, this new form of dress is also perceived by many of the women who adopt it as part of a bodily means to cultivate virtue, the outcome of their professed desire to be close to God.

Two points emerge from this fairly basic discussion of the meanings of veiling in the contemporary Muslim world. First, we need to work against the reductive interpretation of veiling as the quintessential sign of women's unfreedom, even if we object to state imposition of this form, as in Iran or with the Taliban. (It must be recalled that the modernizing states of Turkey and Iran had earlier in the century banned veiling and required men, except religious clerics, to adopt Western dress.) What does freedom mean if we accept the fundamental premise that humans are social beings, always raised in certain social and historical contexts and belonging to particular communities that shape their desires and understandings of the world? Is it not a gross violation of women's own understandings of what they are doing to simply denounce the burqa as a medieval imposition? Second, we must take care not to reduce the diverse situations and attitudes of millions of Muslim women to a single item of clothing. Perhaps it is time to give up the Western obsession with the veil and focus on some serious issues with which feminists and others should indeed be concerned.

Ultimately, the significant political–ethical problem the burqa raises is how to deal with cultural "others." How are we to deal with difference without accepting the passivity implied by the cultural relativism for which anthropologists are justly famous—a relativism that says it's their culture and it's not my business to judge or interfere, only to try to understand. Cultural relativism is certainly an improvement on ethnocentrism and the racism, cultural imperialism, and imperiousness that underlie it; the problem is that it is too late not to interfere. The forms of lives we find around the world are already products of long histories of interactions.

I want to explore the issues of women, cultural relativism, and the problems of "difference" from three angles. First, I want to consider what feminist anthropologists (those stuck in that awkward relationship, as Strathern [1987] has claimed) are to do with strange political bedfellows. I used to feel torn when I received the e-mail petitions circulating for the last few years in defense of Afghan women under the Taliban. I was not sympathetic to the dogmatism of the Taliban; I do not support the oppression of women. But the provenance of the campaign worried me. I do not usually find myself in political company with the likes of Hollywood celebrities (see Hirschkind and Mahmood 2002). I had never received a petition from such women defending the right of Palestinian women to safety from Israeli bombing or daily harassment at checkpoints, asking the United States to reconsider its support for a government that had dispossessed them, closed them out from work and citizenship rights, refused them the most basic freedoms. Maybe some of these same people might be signing petitions to save African women from genital cutting, or Indian women from dowry deaths. However, I do not think that it would be as easy to mobilize so many of these American and European women if it were not a case of Muslim men oppressing Muslim women—women of cover for whom they can feel sorry and in relation to whom they can feel smugly superior. Would television diva Oprah Winfrey host the Women in Black, the women's peace group from Israel, as she did RAWA, the Revolutionary Association of Women of Afghanistan, who were also granted the *Glamour Magazine* Women of the Year Award? What are we to make of post-Taliban "Reality Tours" such as the one advertised on the internet by Global Exchange for March 2002 under the title "Courage and Tenacity: A Women's Delegation to Afghanistan"? The rationale for the $1,400 tour is that "with the removal of the Taliban government, Afghan women, for the first time in the past decade, have the opportunity to reclaim their basic human rights and establish their role as equal citizens by participating in the rebuilding of their nation." The tour's objective, to celebrate International Women's Week, is "to develop awareness of the concerns and issues the Afghan women are facing as well as to witness the changing political, economic, and social conditions which have created new opportunities for the women of Afghanistan" (Global Exchange 2002).

To be critical of this celebration of women's rights in Afghanistan is not to pass judgment on any local women's organizations, such as RAWA, whose members have courageously worked since 1977 for a democratic secular Afghanistan in which women's human rights are respected, against Soviet-backed regimes or U.S.- Saudi-, and Pakistani-supported conservatives. Their documentation of abuse and their work through clinics and schools have been enormously important.

It is also not to fault the campaigns that exposed the dreadful conditions under which the Taliban placed women. The Feminist Majority campaign helped put a stop to a secret oil pipeline deal between the Taliban and the U.S. multinational Unocal that was going forward with U.S. administration support. Western feminist campaigns must not be confused with the hypocrisies of the new colonial feminism of a Republican president who was not elected for his progressive stance on feminist issues or of administrations that played down the terrible record of violations of women by the United States' allies in the Northern Alliance, as documented by Human Rights Watch and Amnesty International, among others. Rapes and assaults were widespread in the period of infighting that devastated Afghanistan before the Taliban came in to restore order.

It is, however, to suggest that we need to look closely at what we are supporting (and what we are not) and to think carefully about why. How should we manage the complicated politics and ethics of finding ourselves in agreement with those with whom we normally disagree? I do not know how many feminists who felt good about saving Afghan women from the Taliban are also asking for a global redistribution of wealth or contemplating sacrificing their own consumption radically so that African or Afghan women could have some chance of having what I do believe should be a universal human right—the right to freedom from the structural violence of global inequality and from the ravages of war, the everyday rights of having enough to eat, having homes for their families in which to live and thrive, having ways to make decent livings so their children can grow, and having the strength and security to work out, within their communities and with whatever alliances they want, how to live a good life, which might very well include changing the ways those communities are organized.

Suspicion about bedfellows is only a first step; it will not give us a way to think more positively about what to do or where to stand. For that, we need to confront two more big issues. First is the acceptance of the possibility of difference. Can we only free Afghan women to be like us or might we have to recognize that even after "liberation" from the Taliban, they might want different things than we would want for them? What do we do about that? Second, we need to be vigilant about the rhetoric of saving people because of what it implies about our attitudes.

Again, when I talk about accepting difference, I am not implying that we should resign ourselves to being cultural relativists who respect whatever goes on elsewhere as "just their culture." I have already discussed the dangers of "cultural" explanations; "their" cultures are just as much part of history and an interconnected world as ours are. What I am advocating is the hard work involved in recognizing and respecting differences—precisely as products of different histories, as expressions of different circumstances, and as manifestations of differently structured desires. We may want justice for women, but can we accept that there might be different ideas about justice and that different women might want, or choose, different futures from what we envision as best (see Ong 1988)? We must consider that they might be called to personhood, so to speak, in a different language.

Reports from the Bonn peace conference held in late November to discuss the rebuilding of Afghanistan revealed significant differences among the few Afghan women feminists and activists present. RAWA's position was to reject any conciliatory approach to Islamic governance. According to one report I read, most women activists, especially those based in Afghanistan who are aware of the realities on the ground, agreed that Islam had to be the starting point for reform. Fatima Gailani, a U.S.-based advisor to one of the delegations, is quoted as saying, "If I go to Afghanistan today and ask women for votes on the promise to bring them secularism, they are going to tell me to go to hell." Instead, according to one report, most of these women looked for inspiration on how to fight for equality to a place that might seem surprising. They looked to Iran as a country in which they saw women making significant gains within an Islamic framework—in part through an Islamically oriented feminist movement that is challenging injustices and reinterpreting the religious tradition.

The situation in Iran is itself the subject of heated debate within feminist circles, especially among Iranian feminists in the West (e.g., Mir-Hosseini 1999; Moghissi 1999; Najmabadi 1998, 2000). It is not clear whether and in what ways women have made gains and whether the great increases in literacy, decreases in birthrates, presence of women in the professions and government, and a feminist flourishing in cultural fields like writing and filmmaking are because of or despite the establishment of a so-called Islamic Republic. The concept of an Islamic feminism itself is also controversial. Is it an oxymoron or does it refer to a viable movement forged by brave women who want a third way?

One of the things we have to be most careful about in thinking about Third World feminisms, and feminism in different parts of the Muslim world, is how not to fall into polarizations that place feminism on the side of the West. I have written about the dilemmas faced by Arab feminists when Western feminists initiate campaigns that make them vulnerable to local denunciations by conservatives of various sorts, whether Islamist or nationalist, of being traitors (Abu-Lughod 2001). As some like Afsaneh Najmabadi are now arguing, not only is it wrong to see history simplistically in terms of a putative opposition between Islam and the West (as is happening in the United States now and has happened in parallel in the Muslim world), but it is also strategically dangerous to accept this cultural opposition between Islam and the West, between fundamentalism and feminism, because those many people within Muslim countries who are trying to find alternatives to present injustices, those who might want to refuse the divide and take from different histories and cultures, who do not accept that being feminist means being Western, will be under pressure to choose, just as we are: Are you with us or against us?

My point is to remind us to be aware of differences, respectful of other paths toward social change that might give women better lives. Can there be a liberation that is Islamic? And, beyond this, is liberation even a goal for which all women or people strive? Are emancipation, equality, and rights part of a universal language we must use? To quote Saba Mahmood, writing about the women in Egypt who are seeking to become pious Muslims, "The desire for freedom and liberation is a historically situated desire whose motivational force cannot be assumed a priori, but needs to be reconsidered in light of other desires, aspirations, and capacities that inhere in a culturally and historically located subject" (2001:223). In other words, might other desires be more meaningful for different groups of people? Living in close families? Living in a godly way? Living without war? I have done fieldwork in Egypt over more than 20 years and I cannot think of a single woman I know, from the poorest rural to the most educated cosmopolitan, who has ever expressed envy of U.S. women, women they tend to perceive as bereft of community, vulnerable to sexual violence and social anomie, driven by individual success rather than morality, or strangely disrespectful of God.

Mahmood (2001) has pointed out a disturbing thing that happens when one argues for a respect for other traditions. She notes that there seems to be a difference in the political demands made on those who work on or are trying to understand Muslims and Islamists and those who work on secular-humanist projects. She, who studies the piety movement in Egypt, is consistently pressed to denounce all the harm done by Islamic movements around the world—otherwise she is accused of being an apologist. But there never seems to be a parallel demand for those who study secular humanism and its projects, despite the terrible violences that have been associated with it over the last couple of centuries, from world wars to colonialism, from genocides to slavery. We need to have as little dogmatic faith in secular humanism as in Islamism, and as open a mind to the complex possibilities of human projects undertaken in one tradition as the other.

BEYOND THE RHETORIC OF SALVATION

Let us return, finally, to my title, "Do Muslim Women Need Saving?" The discussion of culture, veiling, and how one can navigate the shoals of cultural difference should put Laura Bush's self-congratulation about the rejoicing of Afghan women liberated by American troops in a different light. It is deeply problematic to construct the Afghan woman as someone in need of saving. When you save someone, you imply that you are saving her from something. You are also saving her *to* something. What violences are entailed in this transformation, and what presumptions are being

made about the superiority of that to which you are saving her? Projects of saving other women depend on and reinforce a sense of superiority by Westerners, a form of arrogance that deserves to be challenged. All one needs to do to appreciate the patronizing quality of the rhetoric of saving women is to imagine using it today in the United States about disadvantaged groups such as African American women or working-class women. We now understand them as suffering from structural violence. We have become politicized about race and class, but not culture.

As anthropologists, feminists, or concerned citizens, we should be wary of taking on the mantles of those 19th-century Christian missionary women who devoted their lives to saving their Muslim sisters. One of my favorite documents from that period is a collection called *Our Moslem Sisters,* the proceedings of a conference of women missionaries held in Cairo in 1906 (Van Sommer and Zwemer 1907). The subtitle of the book is *A Cry of Need from the Lands of Darkness Interpreted by Those Who Heard It.* Speaking of the ignorance, seclusion, polygamy, and veiling that blighted women's lives across the Muslim world, the missionary women spoke of their responsibility to make these women's voices heard. As the introduction states, "They will never cry for themselves, for they are down under the yoke of centuries of oppression" (Van Sommer and Zwemer 1907:15). "This book," it begins, "with its sad, reiterated story of wrong and oppression is an indictment and an appeal. . . . It is an appeal to Christian womanhood to right these wrongs and enlighten this darkness by sacrifice and service" (Van Sommer and Zwemer 1907:5).

One can hear uncanny echoes of their virtuous goals today, even though the language is secular, the appeals not to Jesus but to human rights or the liberal West. The continuing currency of such imagery and sentiments can be seen in their deployment for perfectly good humanitarian causes. In February 2002, I received an invitation to a reception honoring an international medical humanitarian network called Médecins du Monde/Doctors of the World (MdM). Under the sponsorship of the French Ambassador to the United States, the Head of the delegation of the European Commission to the United Nations, and a member of the European Parliament, the cocktail reception was to feature an exhibition of photographs under the clichéd title "Afghan Women: Behind the Veil."

The invitation was remarkable not just for the colorful photograph of women in flowing burqas walking across the barren mountains of Afghanistan but also for the text, a portion of which I quote:

> For 20 years MdM has been ceaselessly struggling to help those who are most vulnerable. But increasingly, thick veils cover the victims of the war. When the Taliban came to power in 1996, Afghan Women became faceless. To unveil one's face while receiving medical care was to achieve a sort of intimacy, find a brief space for secret freedom and recover a little of one's dignity. In a country where women had no access to basic medical care because they did not have the right to appear in public, where women had no right to practice medicine, MdM's program stood as a stubborn reminder of human rights. . . . Please join us in helping to lift the veil.

Although I cannot take up here the fantasies of intimacy associated with unveiling, fantasies reminiscent of the French colonial obsessions so brilliantly unmasked by Alloula in *The Colonial Harem* (1986), I can ask why humanitarian projects and human rights discourse in the 21st century need rely on such constructions of Muslim women.

Could we not leave veils and vocations of saving others behind and instead train our sights on ways to make the world a more just place? The reason respect for difference should not be confused with cultural relativism is that it does not preclude asking how we, living in this privileged and powerful part of the world, might examine our own responsibilities for the situations in which others in distant places have found themselves. We do not stand outside the world, looking out over this sea of poor benighted people, living under the shadow— or veil—of oppressive cultures; we are part of that

world. Islamic movements themselves have arisen in a world shaped by the intense engagements of Western powers in Middle Eastern lives.

A more productive approach, it seems to me, is to ask how we might contribute to making the world a more just place. A world not organized around strategic military and economic demands; a place where certain kinds of forces and values that we may still consider important could have an appeal and where there is the peace necessary for discussions, debates, and transformations to occur within communities. We need to ask ourselves what kinds of world conditions we could contribute to making such that popular desires will not be overdetermined by an overwhelming sense of helplessness in the face of forms of global injustice. Where we seek to be active in the affairs of distant places, can we do so in the spirit of support for those within those communities whose goals are to make women's (and men's) lives better (as Walley has argued in relation to practices of genital cutting in Africa, [1997])? Can we use a more egalitarian language of alliances, coalitions, and solidarity, instead of salvation?

Even RAWA, the now celebrated Revolutionary Association of the Women of Afghanistan, which was so instrumental in bringing to U.S. women's attention the excesses of the Taliban, has opposed the U.S. bombing from the beginning. They do not see in it Afghan women's salvation but increased hardship and loss. They have long called for disarmament and for peacekeeping forces. Spokespersons point out the dangers of confusing governments with people, the Taliban with innocent Afghans who will be most harmed. They consistently remind audiences to take a close look at the ways policies are being organized around oil interests, the arms industry, and the international drug trade. They are not obsessed with the veil, even though they are the most radical feminists working for a secular democratic Afghanistan. Unfortunately, only their messages about the excesses of the Taliban have been heard, even though their criticisms of those in power in Afghanistan have included previous regimes.

A first step in hearing their wider message is to break with the language of alien cultures, whether to understand or eliminate them. Missionary work and colonial feminism belong in the past. Our task is to critically explore what we might do to help create a world in which those poor Afghan women, for whom "the hearts of those in the civilized world break," can have safety and decent lives.

NOTES

1. *Acknowledgments.* I want to thank Page Jackson, Fran Mascia-Lees, Tim Mitchell, Rosalind Morris, Anupama Rao, and members of the audience at the symposium "Responding to War," sponsored by Columbia University's Institute for Research on Women and Gender (where I presented an earlier version), for helpful comments, references, clippings, and encouragement.

REFERENCES CITED

Abu-Lughod, Lila
   1986 Veiled Sentiments: Honor and Poetry in a Bedouin Society. Berkeley: University of California Press.
   1995 Movie Stars and Islamic Moralism in Egypt. Social Text 42:53–67.
   1998 Remaking Women: Feminism and Modernity in the Middle East. Princeton: Princeton University Press.
   2001 Orientalism and Middle East Feminist Studies. Feminist Studies 27(1):101–113.
Ahmed, Leila
   1992 Women and Gender in Islam. New Haven, CT: Yale University Press.
Alloula, Malek
   1986 The Colonial Harem. Minneapolis: University of Minnesota Press.
Brenner, Suzanne
   1996 Reconstructing Self and Society: Javanese Muslim Women and "the Veil." American Ethnologist 23(4):673–697.
El Guindi, Fadwa
   1999 Veil: Modesty, Privacy and Resistance. Oxford: Berg.
Fremson, Ruth
   2001 Allure Must Be Covered. Individuality Peeks Through. New York Times, November 4: 14.
Global Exchange
   2002 Courage and Tenacity: A Women's Delegation to Afghanistan. Electronic document, http://www.globalexchange.org/tours/auto/2002-03-05_CourageandTenacityAWomensDele.html. Accessed February 11.
Goldenberg, Suzanne
   2002 The Woman Who Stood Up to the Taliban. The Guardian, January 24. Electronic document, http://222.guardian.co.uk/afghanistan/story/0,1284,63840.
Hirschkind, Charles, and Saba Mahmood
   2002 Feminism, the Taliban, and the Politics of Counter-Insurgency. Anthropological Quarterly, Volume 75(2):107–122.
Lazreg, Marnia
   1994 The Eloquence of Silence: Algerian Women in Question. New York: Routledge.
MacLeod, Arlene
   1991 Accommodating Protest. New York: Columbia University Press.
Mahmood, Saba
   2001 Feminist Theory, Embodiment, and the Docile Agent: Some Reflections on the Egyptian Islamic Revival. Cultural Anthropology 16(2):202–235.

Mir-Hosseini, Ziba
    1999 Islam and Gender: The Religious Debate in Con-
        temporary Iran. Princeton: Princeton University
        Press.
Moghissi, Haideh
    1999 Feminism and Islamic Fundamentalism. London:
        Zed Books.
Najmabadi, Afsaneh.
    1998 Feminism in an Islamic Republic. *In* Islam, Gender
        and Social Change. Yvonne Haddad and John Es-
        posito, eds. Pp. 59–84. New York: Oxford University
        Press.
    2000 (Un)Veiling Feminism. Social Text 64:29–15.
Ong, Aihwa
    1988 Colonialism and Modernity: Feminist Re-
        Presentations of Women in Non-Western Societies.
        Inscriptions 3–4:79–93.
    1990 State Versus Islam: Malay Families, Women's
        Bodies, and the Body Politic in Malaysia. American
        Ethnologist 17(2):258–276.
Papanek, Hanna
    1982 Purdah in Pakistan: Seclusion and Modem Occupa-
        tions for Women. *In* Separate Worlds. Hanna Papa-
        nek and Gail Minault, eds. Pp. 190–216. Columbus,
        MO: South Asia Books.

Safire, William
    2001 "On Language." New York Times Magazine,
        October 28: 22.
Spivak, Gayatri Chakravorty
    1988 Can the Subaltern Speak? *In* Marxism and the In-
        terpretation of Culture. Cary Nelson and Lawrence
        Grossberg, eds. Pp. 271–313. Urbana: University of
        Illinois Press.
Strathern, Marilyn
    1987 An Awkward Relationship: The Case of Feminism
        and Anthropology. Signs 12:276–292.
U.S. Government
    1907 Our Moslem Sisters: A Cry of Need from Lands of
        Darkness Interpreted by Those Who Heard It. New
        York: Fleming H. Revell Co.
    2002 Electronic document, http://www.whitehouse.gov/
        news/releases/200l/11/20011117. Accessed January
        10.
Walley, Christine
    1997 Searching for "Voices": Feminism, Anthropology,
        and the Global Debate over Female Genital Opera-
        tions. Cultural Anthropology 12(3):405–438.

80. • *Beenash Jafri*

NOT YOUR INDIAN ECO-PRINCESS:
Indigenous Women's Resistance to Environmental Degradation (new)

Beenash Jafri is assistant professor of crime and justice studies at the University of
Massachusetts Dartmouth. Her research centers on issues of race, gender, ethnicity,
and culture. Her writing has been published in journals including *American Indian
Culture & Research Journal* and *Critical Race and Whiteness Studies* and the anthologies
The Settler Complex: Recuperating Binarism in Colonial Studies, *Alliances: Re/Envisioning
Indigenous-Non-Indigenous Relationships*, and *Speaking for Ourselves: Environmental Justice
in Canada*. In "Not Your Indian Eco-Princess: Indigenous Women's Resistance to
Environmental Degradation," Jafri analyzes the use of essentialist representations of
indigenous women in feminist discourse.

In November 2012, the Idle No More movement sparked a series of cross-country protests against the Canadian government's plans to pass legislation that would drastically impact First Nations treaty rights, while facilitating resource extraction industries' access to Native land. The movement was led by a group of predominantly Native women: Sylvia McAdam (Cree), Nina Wilson (Nakota and Plains Cree), Jessica Gordon (Cree and Anishnaabe), and Sheelah McLean (non-Native). Also prominent in the movement was Chief Theresa Spence of the Attawapiskat Nation, who went on a hunger fast to demand a meeting about indigenous rights with the Canadian prime minister. These women are not alone: indigenous women have been at the forefront of growing transnational movements for climate justice and against exploitative resource extraction industries. Why has this been the case?

It might be tempting to explain the prominence of indigenous women in climate justice movements as flowing naturally from their identities as indigenous women. Popular culture certainly suggests as much: from Disney's *Pocahontas* (1995) to Sacagawea in *Night at the Museum* (2006) and Neytiri in *Avatar* (2009), movie audiences are saturated with representations of indigenous women who have close affinities with the natural world and nonhuman animals. These representations reflect a long-standing assumption that Native women—solely by virtue of being Native—are more in tune with nature than their white, non-Native counterparts. It isn't just popular culture that participates in the production and distribution of these stereotypes, however. Feminist writers, scholars, and activists have participated in this process as well. This was especially true of ecofeminism, a branch of feminist scholarship and activism that emerged in the late 1970s to address the environmental movement's failure to tackle issues of gender. Its proponents examined the connections between women and nature, with some suggesting that women had intrinsic affinities with nature and others focusing on capitalism's exploitation of both women and natural resources.

A contemporary example of ecofeminist discourse appears in *Mad Max: Fury Road* (2015), which features the Vuvalini, a tribe of wise older women who have saved seeds from the past in the hopes of reviving green life in the postapocalyptic desert setting of the film. The film's celebration of feminine power—while refreshing—also implies that these women hold these seeds and knowledge due to their gendered connections to the earth.

Indigenous peoples—and indigenous women in particular—have featured prominently in the work of many ecofeminists. As Noel Sturgeon argues in *Ecofeminist Natures: Race, Gender, Feminist Theory and Political Action,* many ecofeminists—particularly those writing in the late 1980s—essentialized the relationship between women and nature while holding up indigenous women as exemplary models of this relationship. For example, Sturgeon cites contributors to the edited collection *Reweaving the Web: The Emergence of Ecofeminism,* who frequently make reference to "the symbols and practices of Native-American cultures" (Diamond and Orenstein xi) as inspiration for ecofeminist thought. Those endorsing the myth that indigenous women are intrinsically connected to nature overlook two important points: first, that indigenous women's social, historical, and political relationships to land are dynamic and shifting, rather than fixed or intrinsic; and second, that colonization has a profound impact on those relationships. I examine each of these points in turn before reflecting on an alternative way to understand indigenous women's leadership within environmental movements.

I. INDIGENOUS WOMEN'S RELATIONSHIPS TO LAND

Indigenous women are not naturally inclined to be environmental stewards. It is true that indigenous societies on Turtle Island (North America)—many of which were traditionally matrifocal, centering the leadership of indigenous women—have historically had far more symbiotic relationships with nature than Western societies. However, these are the result of complex indigenous philosophies and knowledge systems, cultivated over centuries, that contrast Western ways of knowing and understanding concepts such as "land," "nature," and "culture." These philosophies and traditions did not emerge out of thin air, nor are they static or unchanging. Rather, as described by scholars such as Vine Deloria Jr. (Standing Rock Sioux), they emerge from dynamic *practices* of relating to and interacting with land, water, plants, and nonhuman animals that have been passed down from one generation to the next. Indigenous philosophies and traditions have also shifted and transformed over time, in response to changing political and environmental conditions. For example, in "Land as Pedagogy," indigenous writer Leanne Simpson, of Michi Saagiig Nishnaabeg ancestry, writes about the grounded, holistic, community-based knowledge system that is tied to making maple syrup in her community in the North shore of Lake Huron near Ontario, Canada (2 fn2). Simpson anchors her argument through a story about Kwezens (translation: girl), whose participation in maple tapping teaches and reinforces many lessons: for example, how to learn from nonhuman animal teachers such as squirrels, who model ways to collect maple sap; how to creatively adapt squirrel strategies; trusting that her work collecting sap will be recognized by her elders in loving ways; and learning how to prepare the sap for cooking and eating by observing elders (6–7). Simpson describes maple tapping not as a process of resource extraction and production but as part of a process of learning about self, community, and relationships "both *from* the land and *with* the land" (7, original emphasis). She further asserts that:

> It is critical to avoid the assumption that this story takes place in pre-colonial times because Nishnaabeg conceptualizations of time and space present an on-going intervention to linear thinking—this story

happens in various incarnations all over our territory every year in March when the Nishnaabeg return to the sugar bush. Kwezen's presence . . . is complicated by her fraught relationality to the tenacity of settler colonialism, and her very presence simultaneously shatters the disappearance of Indigenous women and girls from settler consciousness. (8)

The active, dynamic Nishnaabeg practice of maple tapping that Simpson describes is a form of resistance to settler colonialism. Settler colonialism refers to the ongoing colonialism that structure nation-states such as the United States, Canada, Australia, and New Zealand. In these white settler states, indigenous peoples continue to be subject to colonial laws, policies, and regulations that restrict access to land, modes of governance and social organization, spirituality, language, and medicine. Resistance to ongoing colonialism, including that described by Simpson, also persists: indigenous peoples across the world engage in acts of what Anishnaabe scholar Gerald Vizenor refers to in his book, *Manifest Manners,* as *survivance.* Beyond mere survival, *survivance* signals indigenous modes of actively being in the world. It refers to "moving beyond our [Native] basic survival in the face of overwhelming cultural genocide to create spaces of synthesis and renewal" (Vizenor 53).

II. LAND, ENVIRONMENT AND COLONIZATION

When popular films, ecofeminist theories/activism, and others uncritically celebrate indigenous women's relationships to land/nature without paying heed to the context of colonialism, they make invisible an entire system of land dispossession that enabled the establishment of white settler societies. For example, in the classic ecofeminist text, *Woman and Nature,* Susan Griffin frames Sacagawea as a woman highly attuned to her natural surroundings, who is subject to patriarchal oppression by Lewis and Clark, as well as her father, her husband

and Shoshone community (52–53). Yet by failing to examine the constitutive impact of colonialism on Sacagawea's experiences—and by positing patriarchy as the primary source of the marginalization and oppression Sacagawea experienced—Griffin fails to take into account the way in which patriarchy works in conjunction with colonialism, as well as other systems of oppression, including racism, capitalism, and heteronormativity. As Maile Arvin, Eve Tuck and Angie Morrill write, "Native men are not the root cause of Native women's problems; rather, Native women's critiques implicate the historical and ongoing imposition of colonial, heteropatriarchal structures onto their societies" (18).

The impact of colonialism on indigenous women's lives cannot be understated. For example, colonialism affected the ways in which indigenous women experienced relationships to land. As Tonawanda Seneca scholar Mishuana Goeman recounts in *Mark My Words: Native Women Mapping Our Nations,* colonization drastically transformed the landscape of the places we now refer to as the United States, Canada, Australia, and New Zealand. Colonization did not only involve the physical displacement of indigenous peoples. It also introduced and implemented European modes of imagining, organizing, and relating to space, land, and nature, which relied on scientific knowledge and devalued indigenous ways of knowing and relating to land. Whereas diverse Native nations had local, often matrifocal, place-based knowledge derived from centuries of caring and cultivating relationships with land, the systematic imposition of European modes of thought through colonial policies and regulations—for instance, through the transformation of matrilineal and/or matrifocal governance into patriarchal governance through the Indian Act in Canada—disrupted these relationships. Colonial constructions of nature and the environment—that is to say, dominant constructions—view these as objects that are fundamentally separate from humans or culture. For instance, the notion that land can be

"owned" and made the property of humans relies on the presumption that land is an object or commodity meant to be managed and controlled by humans. This colonial discourse is also gendered: just as patriarchy objectifies women as the property of men, colonial discourse *feminizes* land and nature, framing them as objects belonging to men (e.g., see McClintock, *Imperial Leather*). The notion that Europeans were better equipped to manage and control land and women has been a salient feature of colonial discourses, one that has been used to mark indigenous populations as "savage" in relation to "civilized" Europeans and European men as more properly masculine than Native men. Its effects have been violent, as European colonizers were threatened by the relative egalitarianism and matrifocal organization of the indigenous societies they encountered. Correspondingly, as Andrea Smith argues in *Conquest: Sexual Violence and American Indian Genocide*, the conquest of Native women specifically, via rape and sexual violence, was central to colonialist ventures. The preponderance of sexual violence combined with the imposition of patriarchal forms of social organization has meant that colonization has been particularly devastating for Native women. Thus the stakes for decolonizing have arguably been higher for Native women than Native men, for whom colonialism has expanded access to patriarchal power.

Resource extraction industries—including mining, oil and gas drilling, and forestry—follow the same logic as their earlier colonial predecessors. These industries, which are fueled by the demands of global capitalist markets, view natural resources as just that: as resources meant to be located, extracted, processed, sold to, and consumed by people. Extractive industries, and their corporate and government supporters, prioritize economic growth above social concerns. The toxic wastes and environmental degradation that extractive processes produce are thus dealt with by these industries as an afterthought. The effects of this toxicity and degradation are experienced unevenly, with distribution largely determined by structural factors shaped by racism, patriarchy, colonialism, and capitalism. As scholars and activists in the environmental justice movement have persuasively demonstrated (e.g., Bullard, *Confronting Environmental Racism;* LaDuke, *All Our Relations*), it is poor people of color and indigenous peoples across the world who are most vulnerable to environmental risk. For example, in North America, extractive industries have targeted First Nations reserves (Canada) and Indian reservations (United States); organizations such as the Indigenous Environmental Network were formed in direct response to that targeting ("About"). Colonial policies support these practices: as I mentioned at the start of this essay, in Canada, the federal government passed a series of bills in 2012 that would facilitate resource extraction practices while diminishing First Nations access and authority over their own lands.

III. UNDERSTANDING INDIGENOUS WOMEN'S RESISTANCE TO ENVIRONMENTAL DEGRADATION

I return now to the question I posed earlier in this essay: Why have indigenous women figured so predominantly in movements for climate justice? To reiterate an earlier point, indigenous women's leadership on these issues flows from neither their gender nor their ancestry. Rather, this leadership is borne of colonialism's impact on

indigenous communities and nations, which—due to colonialism's disruption of women's leadership within traditional indigenous societies—has affected indigenous women in particular. As Freda Huson, spokesperson for the Unist'ot'en Clan, says in relation to addressing the colonial, patriarchal systems supported by Canadian governments and the Indian Chiefs whom they empower through the Indian Act:

> The true traditional decision-making is carried through the clans and through the women who carry the clans. . . . For us, it has been a dual struggle—against government and industry and also against Indian Act chiefs. These male Indian Act chiefs are imposing top-down decisions. That is why we pulled out of the political negotiations and the treaty process. . . . These Chiefs are so worried about funding. The resources being extracted from our territories are worth billions of dollars, and while the government is getting wealthy we are fighting over crumbs. So we are taking action through our hereditary clan system and building awareness and unity through our actions. (qtd. in Walia)

Huson's emphasis on the ways that colonialism and patriarchy mutually reinforce one another is instructive. For non-Native feminists and others wishing to express support and solidarity for Native women, it is crucial that we listen closely to these articulations. Otherwise—if we focus singularly on the impact of patriarchy on Native women's lives—we risk erasing the colonization that is at the root of violence against Native women.

WORKS CITED

"About." *Indigenous Environmental Network,* www.ienearth.org/about/. Accessed 29 October 2015.

Arvin, Maile, et al. "Decolonizing Feminism: Challenging Connections Between Settler Colonialism and Heteropatriarchy." *Feminist Formations,* vol. 25, no.1, 2013, pp. 8–34.

Avatar. Directed by James Cameron. 20th Century Fox, 2009.

Bullard, Robert. *Confronting Environmental Racism: Voices From the Grassroots.* South End Press, 1993.

Deloria, Vine Jr. *God Is Red: A Native View of Religion.* Fulcrum Publishing, 2003.

Diamond, Irene, and Gloria Orenstein, editors. *Reweaving the Web: The Emergence of Ecofeminism.* Sierra Club Books, 1990.

Goeman, Mishuana. *Mark My Words: Native Women Mapping Our Nations.* U of Minnesota P, 2013.

Griffin, Susan. *Woman and Nature: The Roaring Inside Her.* Sierra Club Books, 1978.

LaDuke, Winona. *All Our Relations: Native Struggles for Land and Life.* South End Press, 1999.

Mad Max: Fury Road. Directed by George Miller. Warner Brothers, 2015.

McClintock, Anne. *Imperial Leather: Race, Gender and Sexuality in the Colonial Contest.* Routledge, 1995.

Night at the Museum. Directed by Shawn Levy. 20th Century Fox, 2006.

Pocahontas. Directed by Eric Goldberg and Mike Gabriel. Buena Vista Pictures, 1995.

Simpson, Leanne Betasamosake. "Land as Pedagogy: Nishnaabeg Intelligence and Rebellious Transformation."

Decolonization: Indigeneity, Education and Society, vol. 3, no. 3, 2014, pp. 1–25. decolonization.org/index.php/des/article/view/22170/17985.

Smith, Andrea. *Conquest: Sexual Violence and American Indian Genocide.* South End Press, 2005.

Sturgeon, Noel. *Ecofeminist Natures: Race, Gender, Feminist Theory and Political Action.* Routledge, 1997.

Vizenor, Gerald Robert. *Manifest Manners: Narratives on Postindian Survivance.* U of Nebraska P, 1994.

Walia, Harsha. "Indigenous Sovereigntists Speak." *Rabble.ca.*, 8 February 2013, abble.ca/news/2013/02/indigenous-sovereigntists-speak.

81. • *Elizabeth R. Cole and Zakiya T. Luna*

MAKING COALITIONS WORK:
Solidarity across Difference within US Feminism (2010)

Elizabeth R. Cole is the associate dean for social sciences and a professor of women's studies, psychology, and Afroamerican and African studies at the University of Michigan. Her research focuses on intersectionality and the construction of race, class, and gender. Her work has been published in *Psychology of Women Quarterly*, *Feminism & Psychology*, *Sex Roles*, and *Feminist Studies*, where this article was originally published. Zakiya T. Luna is assistant professor of sociology at University of California, Santa Barbara. Her research interests included reproductive justice, social movements, and inequality. She is coeditor of the University of California Press book series, *Reproductive Justice: A New Vision for the 21st Century*, and has had articles published in *Sociological Inquiry*, *Research in Social Movements, Conflicts and Change*, and *Societies without Borders: Social Science and Human Rights*. In "Making Coalitions Work: Solidarity across Difference within US Feminism," Cole and Luna analyze feminist activists who successfully participated in coalition work.

The importance of working in coalition, that is, the process through which groups that define themselves as different work together politically, either long or short term, in the service of some mutually valued end, is a frequent refrain in the writing of feminists of color. In the twenty-five years since Bernice Johnson Reagon addressed the West Coast Women's Music Festival on the importance of coalitions, many feminists— both scholars and activists—have argued for the centrality of coalitional strategies for feminist social change. Feminist coalition work has been variously described as an imperative, an opportunity, and an inevitability, given that difference is culturally constructed and all groups contain heterogeneity.[1] Yet relatively little work has looked at the way these theoretical premises play out in activists' political work. This article aims to bring our models of theorizing coalition into dialogue with practice by listening to activists' own reflections on their work.

[. . .]

. . . What, other than perceptions of basic self-interest, motivates groups that define themselves as different to work together? How do diverse groups conceptualize identity, belonging, and solidarity across difference—what Scott A. Hunt and Robert D. Benford call "external solidarity"[2]—in order to come together in the first place? . . . How do groups work together productively across power asymmetries to achieve common goals, and what practices are necessary to ensure meaningful participation by the most disempowered constituencies?

This article engages these questions based on a reading of the feminist literature on coalitions and activists' narratives recorded as part of a larger project collecting oral history interviews with feminist scholar-activists in four countries. A description of the project, including the US Site Booklet of interview transcripts, from which quotations in this article are taken, is available at "Global Feminisms: Comparative Case Studies of Women's Activism and Scholarship," http://www. umich.edu/~glblfem/. The US-based segment of this project was planned and implemented by an interdisciplinary team of faculty and students. We chose activists whose work addressed sites of intersection between feminist social movements and other axes of oppression such as race/ethnicity, sexual orientation, social class, and ability status. Our selection strategy was intended to generate a sample that could illuminate important fault

lines within the women's movement in the United States. Potential participants were told that it was not necessary to identify with the label "feminist" in order to take part and that the interview would include an opportunity to discuss their thoughts about the term. Interviews were conducted at the authors' university, and participants' travel expenses were funded by the project. Despite the substantial demands of participation, only one invitee declined to participate, due to scheduling constraints.

[. . .]

BUILDING SOLIDARITY ACROSS GROUPS: NARRATIVES OF IDENTITY AND BELONGING

Repeatedly the literature within feminist theory on coalitions suggests that women of color are exceptionally well positioned to apprehend opportunities for, and possibilities presented by, coalitional work because they belong to multiple oppressed communities defined by gender, race, and often class. Of course every individual occupies specific positions with respect to gender, race, class, sexuality, and other socially constructed distinctions associated with political and economic stratification. However, those who claim multiple subordinated identities may be particularly attuned to the ways that organizations, social movements, and public policies based on social identities often frame their analysis to address primarily the concerns of individuals who, but for one marginalized status, are otherwise privileged.[3]

For example, Diane L. Fowlkes observed that when the Combahee River Collective grounded their political analysis in terms of their lived experiences of racism, sexism, and homophobia, they reconstructed their own identities within a social and historical environment in which issues of sexuality were rarely mentioned and issues of gender were often overlooked. In doing so, not only did the collective reveal implicit aspects of the construction of others' identities (e.g., that the concept of "woman" was often assumed to be white and heterosexual), but they also argued that coalitions were necessary because of complex interlocking structures of oppression and privilege. Later work by Chela Sandoval and Gloria Anzaldúa suggested some of the concrete ways that individuals marginalized by multiple statuses might serve as catalysts for such political linkages. Specifically, Anzaldúa argued that her socially marginal position as a lesbian of color rendered her identity inherently hybrid, or *mestiza:* being at once homeless and at home everywhere positioned her to shift between communities and constituencies.[4] Fowlkes observed that in making this argument, Anzaldúa used "complex identity narration" as a tool of struggle. In this reading, women of color scholar/activists have deployed their analysis of the complex layering of their oppression to construct meaningful identities that are themselves tools for social change.[5] Indeed, scholars of the "new social movements," that is, the non-class-based social movements that emerged beginning in the 1960s, emphasized the central importance of identity construction and redefinition to mobilization in these organizations. Importantly then, because identities are constructed categories, so too are solidarity and connection, and therefore alliances are potentially fluid.

However, other theorists, including Chandra Talpade Mohanty and Judith Butler reject identity as the basis of coalition, worrying that such an approach contributes to the reification and normalization of certain identities. Butler argued that when activists premise a coalition on the assertion of an ideal association between identity and action ("we'll all join hands as women!"), they impose fixed and normative identities on the actors. Kimberlé Crenshaw also argued that identity politics is flawed, however, not because of its emphasis on differences between groups but rather because it is premised on turning a blind eye to differences within groups.[6] For similar reasons, Mohanty urged activists to engage difference, rather than to attempt to transcend it.[7] Although the claim to a common identity may be motivated by the desire for unity within a movement, Butler

encouraged those undertaking coalitional politics to embrace fractures and ruptures in identity in order to make the broadest possible movement:

> Without the goal of "unity" . . . provisional unities might emerge in the context of concrete actions that have purposes other than the articulation of identity. Without the compulsory expectation that feminist actions must be instituted from some stable, unified and agreed upon identity, those actions might well get a quicker start and seem more congenial to a number of "women" for whom the category is permanently moot.[8]

Similarly, Floya Anthias argued that any attempt to describe membership or belonging simultaneously implies a boundary indicating which groups are different or "other."[9] Thus, within the literature on identities and coalition, there is a tension between those who claim that an appreciation for the complexity of identity is a central tool for struggle and those who caution that as a political tool, any identity claim simultaneously engages otherness and exclusion and thus may be an obstacle to successful coalition.

[. . .]

DEFINING SOCIAL IDENTITIES

Several of the activists explicitly discussed their experiences redefining the social identities that had been ascribed to them in ways that were consistent with their own sense of the meaning of their social locations. For example, Grace Lee Boggs, a community organizer in her late eighties, discussed how she became a part of the predominantly Black community in south Chicago where she lived and worked. Her involvement with a tenants' union led to her participation in organizing a delegation for a national march to protest discrimination in defense plants. Even though the march did not materialize, Boggs became more active in the larger struggles of African Americans, which led her to Detroit where she resides today. The daughter of Chinese immigrants, Boggs perceived the definition of community in that time and place not to have been constrained by racial ancestry. She argued that people from generations after hers

> who remember the nationalist phase of the Black movement and the extreme race consciousness that has developed ever since, say, 1960, find it difficult to recall that in the 1940s and 1950s there was not that sense of color consciousness in the Black community. . . . And I was strange to people. I mean, they . . . considered me a person of color, but I wasn't Black, and kids used to come up and touch my hair and say, you know, "What nice hair you have," because it was so straight, and black. . . . People, I think, accepted me. Particularly, because, you know, I was married to Jimmy [Boggs, who was Black] and we lived in the Black community. And I had a wonderful time. It was the first community I had ever really belonged to.

Later in the interview she elaborated on the extent of her involvement with that community. "I became so active in the Black Movement that the FBI, its records say, 'She's probably Afro-Chinese.' But that's how closely I became identified." However, when the eighty-eight-year-old Boggs reflected on identity explicitly, she commented with humor that "if I were to characterize myself as something particular, I would say I'm old!"

> I don't believe in getting stuck in any one identity. I think that our tendency . . . it's so easy to become fragmented because we live in a fragmented . . . fragmenting society. It's so difficult to be whole, to see yourself as many faceted, to see how many possibilities there are in who we are . . . you know, here I've been Afro-Chinese, I've been Asian American. I've had the opportunity to know so many different people and work with so many different people of all ethnicities and all ages, and of all classes.

Thus, Boggs saw a potential danger in the idea of social identity, in that it can constrain both one's sense of self and the ability to see meaningful connections

with others. Her story also pointed to the importance of context as she later reminded the audience that a movement to empower Asian Americans did not exist during her early years of activism. She did not have the option to organize around her racial identity, but, instead of avoiding political action, she became an active ally. Boggs established her commitment to racial justice and local community empowerment over decades. She continued to move beyond activism around obvious identity categories when she founded the Boggs Center, in Detroit, Michigan, which offers community programs, many of which are aimed at youth.

If Boggs's many identifications were grounded locally, Rabab Abdulhadi, an activist who was instrumental in founding the Union of Palestinian Women's Associations, described how, for diasporic Palestinian women, Palestine transcends a specific geographical location to shape their identities and daily lives.

> Thinking about how Palestinian women who are living in the Diaspora, in exile, in the US, people like me and others, have the transnational networks and connections and belongings and identifications with a place called Palestine that is always transnationally imagined. . . . There is a physical place . . . called Palestine . . . geography. At the same time, people are not there, but there is this kind of connection that has . . . that shapes the identity, the thinking, the psyche, everyday life of your existence, and a lot of the women I would call [Palestinian], they have these transnational relations and networks and so on, [but they] are not living actually here and there. They're living here and here. It's always here and here. It's . . . you could be physically here or you could be physically there, but there is this kind of . . . I don't want to call it divided loyalty. I think there is this kind of connection, and I think it is transnational.

In Abdulhadi's reckoning, this transnational experience is so profound that both Palestine and the place of exile may simultaneously be experienced as "here." This view of the world, she argued, allows the transnational feminist living in exile to appreciate the power of borders but also to envision a world in which borders are not fixed in time or space. From this vantage point, Abdulhadi observed that commonalities between women who are widely geographically dispersed may come into view:

> I would say, well, "Global South" is right there in New York City-in the Bronx and in Harlem and in El Barrio, and in Brooklyn, and right there in the streets of NYU, which is supposed to be very fancy, but. . . . You know, so it's . . . everywhere, always when we think . . . if we think about South and North, we don't think about them as like, um, forcefully divided geographically . . . and distinct and discrete units, that there is all . . . a lot of fluidity in them, but we recognize how they are structured . . . in terms of oppression.

In contrast, Cathy J. Cohen, whose political and academic work has mainly addressed queer issues within communities of color, particularly their early disavowal of people with HIV/AIDS, envisaged a shared identity based not on a real or imagined location but on a complete reconceptualization of the ways that the state attempts to control sexuality. Early in her interview, she described her political coming-of-age as a graduate student who became a leader in campus antiracism movements in the 1980s. Many women played leadership roles in her organization; in response, members of older Black organizations sought to discredit them through lesbian-baiting. Cohen recalled that these criticisms led members of her group "to kind of debate and talk about what was the importance of having a broad and inclusive agenda. It meant going back and reading things that we hadn't read." This return to theory led the group to a more nuanced understanding of group identity and its political implications. Cohen recalled, "It wasn't about kind of running away in any way from race, because we are all kind of strong, proud Black women. But it also meant understanding that just because someone shared

a racial identity with us didn't mean that they also shared a political identity with us. . . . And it was kind of an important and growing moment in understanding the distinction between the two."

Cohen, who is African American and a lesbian, has worked to explain and challenge how the interests of subordinated constituencies within a minority group may experience a political "secondary marginalization."[10] Her thinking has resulted in a new way to understand the concept of "queer" in structural terms that transcend a straight/gay binary. In her interview she noted that

> queer sexuality for me is sexuality that really challenges hetero-normative expectations and assumptions. And what I mean by that [is] it's people who are marginalized on the basis of their sexuality. So you can undoubtedly include lesbian-gay-bisexual-transgender folks in that category. I would also argue that women who are resource-poor and have children are marginalized by their sexual decisions and might be considered queer. Now, I want to be careful because a lot of people will say, "Oh, that's a nice academic argument." And I think at some level it is an academic argument. It's about kind of how do we conceptualize this category "queer." But for me it then becomes, are there political unities between these groups of people that organizers can start to think about how would you build a base for political mobilization?

In Cohen's re-vision of queer identity, mothers who are low-income and people who identify as sexual minorities are not merely potential allies. Because they share political interests by virtue of their common social experience of marginalization in relation to dominant groups, they potentially share an identity as well. Her reconceptualization of "queer" as a very broad politicized identity recalls Anthias's observation that "unities and divisions are constructions rather than representing actual and fixed groupings of people."[11] Cohen's narrative highlights the ways that activists' political work and theory building challenges those who might assume that collective identities are essential, fixed, or ascribed and demonstrates the creative ways identity may be used to generate social change.

These narratives illustrate how feminist activists who occupy multiple subordinated identities have developed from their social locations a complex understanding of the ways that identities are crafted through lived experience, the personal meaning attached to experience, and the power of these identities to generate political alliances. Boggs, Abdulhadi, and Cohen described the development of nuanced understandings of their social locations in ways that suggested their identities were built through reflection (as in Abdulhadi's conceptualization of geography and time), carefully nurtured alliances (as in Boggs's relation to Black communities in Chicago and Detroit), and expansive imagination (as in Cohen's re-envisioning of the category "queer").

EARLY EXPERIENCES AND IMAGINED COMMUNITIES

Many activists recall that early experiences and influences encouraged them to see connections across difference. A common theme in these interviews is the impact of childhood experiences that pushed interviewees to feel empathy toward people whose social identity categories were different from theirs. These examples highlight the flexible and constructed nature of social identity. For example, bioethicist Adrienne Asch recalled how her parents created a social life for their family that included people from diverse backgrounds; moreover, they also refused to define their daughter primarily in terms of the way some others saw her—disabled—thus allowing Asch to recognize that marginalized identities were one part of a person but not a defining feature. Later, Asch would challenge feminists whose work implicitly suggested that women with disabilities were not among the women whose interests the women's movements sought to advance. She took feminists to task both for excluding the experiences of

women with disabilities from their theorizing and for their failure to acknowledge the implications of women choosing abortion in cases of fetal genetic anomalies, which Asch argued implicitly devalues the lives of people with disabilities, many of whom are women.

In these interviews, respondents also recalled formative experiences that led them to feel connections with people from outside their own ascribed groups, people whom others might have viewed as stigmatized or marked by difference. Loretta Ross vividly described daily experiences that required her to empathize across difference. One of her sisters was severely disabled, and at times Ross recalled resenting the caretaking role she often had to assume. Looking back, Ross felt the responsibility for her sister that her mother compelled her to take on instilled in her a capacity to empathize with Vietnam veterans with whom she interacted during her work as a hospital volunteer. Later, Ross protested the war, having witnessed firsthand its effects on people she claimed as members of her community.

Verónica Giménez is a member of Sista II Sista, a Brooklyn-based collective of young Latinas and Black women who work to end violence in their community. She recalled that when she first emigrated to the United States she was bused to a school in racially segregated Howard Beach. When white students suggested she could "pass" as Italian American due to her last name, rather than accept the privileges that might come with such an identity, she chose to identify with her less-privileged national identity. Although it had happened years before, a vicious racist attack on a young Black man in that town was foremost in her mind as she actively chose to embrace her racial consciousnesses as a member of an oppressed group.

> So my racial consciousness really became blown when I was not willing to be accepted under the Italian . . . auspice. They were willing to say, well, since my father's last name has an Italian descendency, they were

like, "well, you're Italian too." And I was like "No, I'm not, I'm not Italian, I'm not Italian-American," and I related more to being Venezolana and bringing up my identity that way.

Rather than accepting white privilege, which she felt would make her complicit in racial oppression, Giménez worked to challenge oppression on multiple fronts.

Before activists enter into coalition, they have to consider the possibility as not only viable to some degree but also desirable. Many of the activists described how they imagined connections that helped create a worldview in which links across difference were expected and cultivated. Abdulhadi recalled that when she was growing up in Palestine, her mother emphasized the importance of connections with people beyond one's geographic location. Seeing a newspaper picture of Angela Davis, who was on trial in connection with George Jackson's prison break, her mother insisted Davis was a friend to the Palestinians. Her mother's views led Abdulhadi to develop a sense of solidarity with the African American struggle taking place on a faraway continent, "Because in Palestine you're not interacting with a whole lot of other people from other countries. Little by little you start connecting, and you start seeing the intersections . . . the similarities." In a setting where restrictions on their movement rarely allowed Palestinians to interact with people from other backgrounds, these small moments added up to major changes in her ability to imagine connections. Seeing Davis's picture in newspapers evoked a sense of connection for Abdulhadi's mother who then used the opportunity to teach her daughter about links among oppressed peoples. Although the political contexts were in many ways different for African American and Palestinian women, the understanding of similarities in their experiences of oppression marked an opportunity for feelings of solidarity. Similarly, community organizer and civil rights activist Boggs recalled that upon the

start of the Greensboro, North Carolina, lunch counter sit-ins in 1960, Black activists in Detroit held sympathy strikes, even though the right to service in public accommodations had already been secured in the Northern states.

[. . .]

WORKING ACROSS POWER ASYMMETRIES

Activists who described collaborating with groups with greater access to material resources and other kinds of power and privilege recounted the difficulties of what was essentially a translation or cross-cultural understanding. Ross spoke of her years of work as an African American woman in mainstream, predominantly white feminist organizations. In her view, these organizations were fraught with competitiveness and unspoken class conflicts. Ross argued that these group dynamics are very difficult to apprehend, but this understanding was critical to working successfully in such an environment.

> And so for a Black woman, you constantly have to try to figure out what's the normal treatment with which they treat white women versus how they treat me. Is it racism or is this just politics as usual? . . . So I mean, we tend to paint all white women with the same broad brush without understanding the conflicts and tensions within them. We don't understand the role of anti-Semitism in dividing white women, you know, old forms of European nationalism that are still being played out among white people. We don't even understand the construction of whiteness and what goes into that. And so we're not as sharp as I'd like us to be in understanding how to use and manipulate power within the mainstream movement.

But such sensitivity to these dynamics resulted only from years of working within the organization. After she left the organization, Ross continued to act as a bridge even when Black women questioned her engagement with white feminists. Twenty years later Ross was able to use her position to help her organization, SisterSong Women of Color Reproductive Health Collective, gain seats on the steering committing of the 2004 March for Women's Lives. When asked to endorse the march, rather than accept outright, SisterSong set its own terms to reduce the effects of unequal resources between mainstream organizations and smaller women of color organizations. Due to widespread organizing efforts, the march had over one million participants and garnered cosponsors from organizations in multiple movements, not just women's organizations. For example, the National Association for the Advancement of Colored People and the Sierra Club endorsed the march, the first time either group had supported a major pro-choice event. Despite the short-term success of the coalition, Ross expressed her frustration with that kind of work: "It's exhausting to try to study [those dynamics], I mean,

getting into that. Not everybody is prepared to be a bridge."

[. . .]

These interviews suggest some of the challenges faced by organizations attempting to work across differences of power. Powerful groups may assume that their practices and internal dynamics are universal and thus should be transparent to all. Such assumptions may pose an additional burden for coalition partners with less power and privilege. Not only must they do the political work, but they must also struggle to decode what is unsaid and then communicate that information back to their coalition partners, who may not be eager to receive feedback reminding them of their blind spots. Activists who recounted such narratives invariably commented on the toll this "double shift" can take. For this reason, some strategically chose only short-term alliances across differences of power.

[. . .]

NOTES

The interviews discussed in this article were funded by a University of Michigan Rackham Interdisciplinary Collaboration Research Grant. Additional support was provided by the College of Literature, Science, and the Arts; the International Institute; Institute for Research on Women and Gender; Women's Studies Program; Humanities Institute; Center for South Asian Studies; the Herman Family Fund; the Center for African and Afroamerican Studies; and the Office of the Provost at the University of Michigan.

1. Bernice Johnson Reagon, "Coalition Politics: Turning the Century" in *Home Girls: A Black Feminist Anthology,* ed. Barbara Smith (New York: Kitchen Table/Women of Color Press, 1983), 3 (imperative); Gloria Anzaldúa, "Bridge, Drawbridge, Sandbar or Island: Lesbians-of-Color Hacienda Alianzas," in *Bridges of Power: Women's Multicultural Alliances,* ed. Lisa Albrecht and Rose M. Brewer (Philadelphia: New Society Publishers, 1990), 220 (opportunity); Kimberlé Crenshaw, "Mapping the Margins: Intersectionality, Identity Politics, and Violence against Women of Color," in *The Public Nature of Private Violence,* ed. Martha Albertson Fineman and Roxanne Mykitiuk (New York: Routledge, 1994), 114 (inevitability); Cathy J. Cohen, "Punks, Bulldaggers, and Welfare Queens: The Radical Potential of Queer Politics?" in *Feminist Frontiers,* 8th ed., ed. Verta Taylor, Nancy E. Whittier, and Leila Rupp (Boston: McGraw Hill, 2004), 608 (heterogeneity).

2. Scott A. Hunt and Robert D. Benford, "Collective Identity, Solidarity, and Commitment," in *Blackwell Companion to Social Movements,* ed. David A. Snow, Sarah A. Soule, and Hanspeter Kriesi (Malden, MA: Blackwell, 2004), 433-57. The authors make a distinction between internal solidarity, which links the members of a social movement organization to one another, and external solidarity, which is the "identification with groups to which one does not belong" (439).

3. Deborah K. King, "Multiple Jeopardy, Multiple Consciousness: The Context of a Black Feminist Ideology," *Signs* 14 (Autumn 1988): 42.

4. Diane L. Fowlkes, "Moving from Feminist Identity Politics to Coalition Politics through a Feminist Materialist Standpoint of Intersubjectivity in Gloria Anzaldúa's *Borderlands/La Frontera: The New Mestiza,*" *Hypatia* 12 (Spring 1997): 105; Chela Sandoval, *Methodology of the Oppressed* (Minneapolis: University of Minnesota Press, 2000), 57; Anzaldúa, "Bridge, Drawbridge, Sandbar," *222.*

5. Gloria Anzaldúa, cited in Fowlkes, "Moving from Feminist Identity Politics," 108.

6. Chandra Talpade Mohanty, *Feminism without Borders: Decolonizing Theory, Practicing Solidarity* (Durham, NC: Duke University Press, 2003), 300; Judith Butler, *Gender Trouble: Feminism and the Subversion of Identity*

(New York: Routledge, 1990), 172; Crenshaw, "Mapping the Margins," 114.

7. *Mohanty, Feminism without Borders,* 300.

8. Butler, *Gender Trouble,* 21.

9. Floya Anthias, "Beyond Feminism and Multiculturalism: Locating Difference and the Politics of Location," *Women's Studies International Forum* 25 (May-June 2002): 275-86.

10. Cathy J. Cohen, *The Boundaries of Blackness: AIDS and the Breakdown of Black Politics* (Chicago: University of Chicago Press, 1999), 70.

11. Anthias, "Beyond Feminism and Multiculturalism," 277.

82. • DaMaris B. Hill

CONCRETE (NEW)

DaMaris B. Hill is an assistant professor of creative writing and African American and Africana studies at the University of Kentucky. Her work examines the individual and collective realities of the human experience and includes fiction, poetry, and criticism. The anxieties of the contemporary world and representation in popular narratives are themes in her work; She explains, "I belong to a generation of people who do not fear death but are afraid that we may be forgotten." Hill won the Zora Neale Hurston/Richard Wright Creative Writing Award for Short Fiction in 2003 for her story "On the Other Side of Heaven –1957," and she is the 2016 Scholar in Residence for Critical Conversations Concerning Race and Teaching for the Center for the Enhancement of Learning and Teaching at the University of Kentucky. "Concrete" is a memoir that explores ideas of spirituality and citizenship within the context of black girlhood.

My Granddad was Captain America, but my father was just a man. He was not the defender of democracy that his father was, nor was he a flower. He wasn't the feminine lilac luster of bee balm like his mother, but weedy, maybe like the lush leaf of wild cane. Granddad raised him tough like a tin can of seasoned tobacco, taught him to lock away savory scents of life. He was something like his beard, soft

and prickly. There was nothing left for him to be but a preacher. My daddy taught me to breathe, the power of the voice, and commanded me to have my say. So when I threatened Robert with death, I most likely meant it. I was nine.

Riley Curry is my favorite person on TV. She is much lighter than a paper bag and only little girls the color of Oreo cookies qualify as "cute" to me, but Riley's smile is well worth me ignoring my prejudice; she is stunning. She is loud in her laughter and loved, black girl magic. Her skin must be a soufflé mixture of honey and stardust. I know that her Afro puff acts as her human helmet. It allows her to breathe on this planet. She is something like an angel. I bet, she only looks like flesh and dense matter. I bet her daddy can't hold her still without her permission. Like if he reached for her, she would become ethereal and float away.

I may look like a sweet confection, some blend of *Werther's* hard caramel candy, the kind with a special space in the center to rest your tongue, but I am a concrete woman, something like a fountain among the cityscape. I am all phosphates and resin, the kind that gives the wet look to lush rough of rock. I lived a long time in Charm City, where divas chime in the voices of church bells. You know us when you see us; we carry our beauty like an heirloom. In Baltimore, we fancy and prettier than the women who powder their faces like porcelain.

All daddy's girls get an extra portion of "don't-do-right" when they leave Heaven for the birth canal. And this "don't-do-right" is nurtured from forgiving hugs, a daddy's arms can cover us from any evil like the wings of Michael the Archangel. So by the time we are in the world, we have forgotten all the instructions, the dos, the don'ts and the never forgets. We don't know the boundaries, can't recall the expectations. How was I ignorant to the fact that I could frighten a bully, a boney white boy named Robert, into working with his worst enemy? I heard that the vice principal's office was a palace of punishments. She was a tall white woman with short hair, and she was rumored to have rulers ready for wristing in her right hand drawer.

Riley Curry is my role model. She is like the love child of Ma Rainey and The Beastie Boys, but her and her grandmother look like Anna Julia Cooper, the black woman that couldn't get a PhD at Columbia University so she sailed to France to study at the Sorbonne. She stunned them. Curtains and table clothes must hide the pixie dust trailing behind Riley; those reporters treat her ratchet. Are they mad that she is blessed? She is a Gabriel kind of girl. She already has enough money to buy them and the networks.

Baltimore is a land where the river and seas meet. It can't keep quiet or still. So when people tried to bind it in legal contracts, they had no right. They couldn't keep it there. Next, they steamed rolled it, prisoned it in tar and rocked it over. They were bent on paving it into submission. They tried to fix it by plaquering it with people names. Jailed it in fencing and blasted it with basketballs, like loose confetti. These balls keep the Baltimore seagulls at bay. No nesting or chicks near the courts, places where basketballs ricochet from backboard to black man to white guy to lesser known women to ghostly reporters to microphones across fiber optics and cameras that crowd around Steph Curry and the fluid swish of his satin shorts—and capture the glimmer image of an American hero, the man—until she stops it, this renegade role model Riley.

I had no choice and righteous words. Anna Julia Cooper said "Bullies are always cowards at heart and may be credited with a pretty safe instinct in scenting their prey." I didn't know her, but she was AME like me and my daddy was a local celebrity, a preacher, so church was all I knew. I wish my daddy would have known that my mighty words were perfumed in the moral right, not anger. They be from a fire shut up in my bones. The Old Testament is full of legacy and justice. Then, they were the only stories I knew. And, like my daddy, I was good with words. I could wield them like the sleeves of a wide satin robe and gold lined sash or like my daddy did silly church ladies that were easily moved by piano chords.

Robert had no business reaching for Lisa's hind parts, making her out to be the wrong kind of girl for me to play with. She was the only girl on the block, besides my sister. Her mamma looked like a Greek Janet Jackson, the kind of white woman that could be called pretty in public, and her step-daddy hung nude pictures on the wall, you know art, where a woman's lady parts would be apples or something. The kind that gave you an idea about what you will look like when you became a woman, somewhere around sixteen and Lisa had a big brother named Niko, who looked like Tarzan and taught us how to swing trees and one day when I became a woman I was going to kiss him and that bully Robert had no business touching "some body" that wasn't his.

I was just warning him, giving him a chance to choose righteousness. Anna Julia Cooper calls for us to be women who are so sure of our own social footing that we need not fear leaning to lend a hand to a falling sister. This, I remembered. So right there in the middle of recess, between Four Square and the basketball games, I stopped discussing all the mysteries of the sun with a boy named Daniel who had a special talent for setting ants on fire with a magnifying glass, to write Robert, the bully, a warning letter. I wasted no righteousness. I decorated it with expletives and illustrations. I stabbed it up, the note, to encourage him not to lay a finger on my friend. The bastard, bastard being the word that I am sure I misspelled in the letter, he ratted me out and ran to the vice-principal, a woman who promptly conspired with her enemy, the bully Robert, and called my daddy with their stories.

Daddy Curry is a believer; some think he is saintly. But everybody knows that calling out for Jesus doesn't make a black man bullet proof, so it's best to be a celebrity. The fans, some of them preachers and policemen, will recognize this kind of man as a citizen. They praise him because they believe he loves the game of basketball. False. Daddy Curry loves his daughter Riley and basketball protects them both, pads Daddy Curry and Riley from basic bias like the gear of an ice hockey goalie. Basketball celebrity is mighty, but it barely protects her from angry reporters, who tell us all about how disruptive she is. They want to shame her for having her say just like they did Jarena Lee, Sojourner Truth, Frances Harper, Anna Julia Cooper, Billie Holiday, Shirley Chisholm, Vashti McKenzie, Sandra Bland. . . .

In the city, concrete springs up like trees. From New York to DC, we have five story brownstones that are made of marble, some are rust colored or have gray faces. They line the streets in groves, up and down town. We have penthouses; they are the tree houses of the heavens. Sometimes they are so near to the sun that the rays threaten to bleach and scorch every fabric in the place. We use thick drapes and layer in curtains to protect all that is inside from damage.

I bet Daddy Curry likes high rises and thinks a penthouse is the closest thing on earth to living in Heaven. I bet Riley has heard about angels and their wings. I bet they are the inspiration for the way she wears them. You know, dressing the curtains over her like a cape. I bet when she is home, she flies around freely. I bet her smile is a blinding sunbeam in her daddy's face. Or maybe he forgets to look for her in the curtains, because he is busy with a reporter's request? Maybe Riley is a little too comfortable and close to getting burnt by her environment. They are both full of promise like a new beam of dawn, living miracles, but her daddy's skin is deep yellow and tough like a brass tobacco can and he doesn't know that Riley is lilac soft in her skin and sensitive to all types of things. He is a daddy and maybe he forgets that even girls that are the magic you made them will need protection from the elements that are harmless in isolation, but sting when collected against her.

Robert, the white boy, the bully, the boney one with the coffee cup haircut, did not die. He was rescued. I was beaten for not behaving. My daddy became something that resembled a man. He stormed in the house like he was pure lightning wearing a weather coat and wool hat. Not much for zoot suits, I'm sure all was nicely tailored underneath. I wouldn't know. Never taking off his coat or hat, he darted toward me with his belt in hand and cut me. I screamed. And in the chaos and commotion of him defending the common good, my protests were fleeting. I wanted to remind him that I only had confections for skin, wanted to remind him how sweet I was, not the soft chew of a tootsie roll, but I was dazzled like rock candy on a stick. I wanted him to remember that I was one of those good gifts.

Riley Curry retired from news reporting at age two. The night her father won it all in basketball. So when I hear that nine AME church members have been murdered while studying the Old Testament, I wish for Riley's smile. I wish she was in the way of the day-to-day of our lives, singing how blessed she is over top the funeral bells and sirens. Without her, there is nothing left to smile about on TV. Anna Julia Cooper said, "Let woman's claim be as broad in the concrete as the abstract." Susie Jackson was probably praying for the killer when she was shot. I know this and wonder; what is to be gained by staring into the sun? "Life must be something more than dilettante speculation."

Icarus flies too high. Some think the same of black women, particularly of those from Baltimore, who wear their grandmother's prayers and collected histories like bustles. They boast about a league of black women geniuses, brag on how blessed they are, saying things like "we raise our women from stars, not soil." Baltimore ain't got an earthy clutch of women. We are gilded, all waxed and wonderful, glossy. Even old women sparkle like glass in the streets. We take care, scrub our steps clean without dirtying our knees. We avoid the company of water rats. A kitchen table community, we feed folks with our politics, steam crabs and corn. Then we weight them with cake. We sweet and sweat. Even when we spit in your face, it tastes like salt water taffy.

I am hard-headed and mouthy. My Granddad was Captain America—he knew how this country worked. He knew my opinion was only worth cents on the dollar. He knew that I was made of light, but my life would be murky. My daddy knew I needed a bit of faith to see my way through. Who knew that "don't-do-right" was some sort

of a nickname for "don't-do-righteous"? A black woman being able to have her say was a calculated concern, a risk. Captain America kept warning my daddy about me, this grown mouth girl, lush with guts and giggles. He was the first to tell my daddy that nothing good could come from it and how he should reel me in on the edge of a whip. Zora Neale Hurston, another black woman they denied a PhD from both Columbia or Northwestern Universities, she too was determined to have her say. She traveled the world and wrote it all down. She say women be the mules of the world. I believe her.

Riley Curry put on your curtains and come to the rescue, fly by to see about me. The impossible is beginning to happen, the world is dressing me in a saddle and calling it a bodice. They keep telling me that it is all right and that it pinches because it is cased in coins. I say, I can't breathe. They tell me not to worry, stay pretty as a gypsy, but the harness at my mouth is a fancy cut of lace, the cheap kind made of recycled credit cards and plastic promises. It bites me in the corners of my mouth leaving blood in my words.

Be more careful. In Baltimore two young men got it wrong. They wrestled a black girl to the ground. They whipped her. Reports say rape. And while we celebrate Riley for being our heartbeat and number one, black women are keeping count of democracy's debt, staking our claims early, tacking the sidewalk with big chalk. When it looks like hopscotch, we are dancing and calling out for the drums. This is one of the ways black women pray, boldly in broad daylight, giggly and all up in your face, but some ain't no wiser. They smug and just one way, like them streets designed to slow you down at the Inner Harbor. It is like the whole world has abandoned their feet and has taken to those rental boats. They lack faith. They are paddling backwards and crashing into one another. They never notice the schools of mermaids below the tides or the light riding the water. Maybe all of this is hard to see, because the trash floats and white foams in caps of waves.

EMPOWER YOSELF BEFORE YOU WRECK YOSELF:
Native American Feminist Musings (2014)

In "Empower Yoself Before You Wreck Yoself: Native American Feminist Musings," Fey, McCrary, and Werley use a variety of genres to address feminism and the Native American experience. The zine discusses topics important to Native American history like the American Indian Movement (AIM), a civil rights organization that emerged to fight racism and discrimination and address sovereignty issues, as well as issues of cultural appropriation like the use of Native American mascots.

Yá'át'ééh!

Thanks for picking up a copy of **Empower Yoself Before You Wreck Yoself!** We're two Navajo women hoping to fashion a space where other Native women can join in to create, examine and define what's important to us. We're here to fight back against assimilation caused by a patriarchal and predominately white male run society. We're here to encourage participation and to encourage women to confront their insecurities. We're here to say that Native women have a place in counter-cultures such as the Riot Grrrl scene, Hip Hop, Punk, Psychobilly, etc. We want to create a community not only for Native women but women of color, LGBTQ folk and those who are generally intrigued with counter-cultures. We fancy decolonization, not elitism. We fancy disrupting the status-quo.

Most of all, we're here to offer support and open up discourse between Native Women. That means we would like to hear from you! Feel like submitting a piece to our zine or sending us hate mail? Then please email us at NAfeministmusings@gmail.com.

Please enjoy our zine debut and ahéhee' !

Fondly,

EYBYWY crew

ROMANCE ME AT WOUNDED KNEE

"Hey, Annie Mae, check this bad boy out." Annie Mae was sitting on the remnants of an old, battered wall when she turned around to look at Nogeeshik and was alarmed to see him holding an old pogo stick. The smile that was plastered across his face glittered in the metal reflection of the old toy.

"Have you lost your mind?" She laughed as she moved her long tresses of black hair behind her ears.

"What? Are you kidding me? This is going to be my new war pony. But I am curious, have you lost your mind?" Nogeeshik replied while he adjusted his belt buckle.

"I've been searching for peace of mind my entire life," Annie Mae cooed. She took the rifle that was sitting across her lap, placed it against the wall on which she sat. A dry South Dakota breeze blew dust through the air of Wounded Knee. "What are you going to do with that mighty steed?"

"Well, I figure I'm going to ride her all around this town and fight the white man. Yup," Nogeeshik continued, "I'll have one hand on the handle and the other will be holding a rifle and the gods will be hootin' and hollerin' in the background, applauding my valiance."

"Oh I'm sure. And where did you find your war pony?"

My own manifesto

To me Feminism is empowerment. Empowerment for me comes in many different forms whether it be music, books, friends, actions, words, laughter. It can be as something as simple as a phone call from my best friend uplifting me to go to work the next day. Or it can be as complicated as decolonizing my lifestyle i.e. diet, relationships or literature. But I feel these all tie into my everyday life and I try to live my own manifesto and although I live in a small border town where most times I feel lonely and alienated the women around me help me keep going i.e. empower me to live another day to encourage my love ones that it will get better.

Hold on. Hold on.
Hold on. hold on.
Hold on. hold on.
Hold on. reserve.

Break the Silence

When it comes to Native issues most times I hear, "break the stereotype." Don't be a stereotype! Sometimes, I wonder what does that even mean? If I act a certain way, I will embarrass a whole culture? I don't want to act a certain way in front of people that are non-natives. Obsessively thinking "Oh no, am I acting this way, that way?" But I feel this is a warped state of mind. Who enjoys not being themselves? Instead of hearing the DONT'S of what I shouldn't be as a an Indigenous person. Sometimes the encouragement of what we can DO as a culture seems more pro active than reactive such as breaking the silence. Speaking the unspoken.

Let go. let go.
Let go. let go
Let go. let go
Let go. let go.

"I found it in a shed, next to some shovels. Yup, this is my new warrior woman. Don't be jealous." Annie Mae scratched at her nose and smiled.

"I don't know man; your new pony looks noisy and lame. You'll be an easy shot for sure. And you say you found her in a shack? You can keep your war beast."

"Hey," Nogeeshik wrapped his arms around the pogo stick like it was his Saturday night date, "don't talk about my new pony like that. You might hurt her feelings." Annie Mae looked around her to see if anyone else was watching this spectacle. Some other Natives were in the background, making a fire and glancing at them with suspicious eyes.

"Watch this," said the man in the black brimmed hat. He put the pogo stick on the ground and began to roll up the bottoms of his jeans. Annie Mae marveled at his skinny ankles and big feet. He picked up the pogo stick, got a small pinch of dirt, and sprinkled it over the handlebars.

"Now what are you doing?" Annie Mae asked, feet dangling gently in the air.

"I'm saying a prayer. May she soar like our grandfather Eagle!" He placed one foot on the wing of his new pony, looked seriously at Annie Mae and then yelled, "Onward, beast!" The pogo stick leapt into the air, dust covering Nogeeshik's boots, his long black hair flying around like disoriented black birds. Annie Mae clutched at her stomach to control her giggles.

"This is how we are going to win the war," Nogeeshik exclaimed as he bounced up and down. A stiff breeze was punctuated by the sound of gun fire in the background but they paid no attention.

"Certainly," Annie Mae said, "one look at you and you'll win all of the white men's hearts, just like you've won mine." Nogeeshik suddenly lost his balance, his large feet unable to break his fall and he landed hip first into the dirt. At this Annie Mae fell over laughing, her big cheek bones round just like the little moons.

"Really?" Nogeeshik dusted off his hat.

"Yeah, who doesn't love a man who has such a manly steed?" Annie Mae picked up her gun, placed it over her shoulders, and rested her hands off the ends. Nogeeshik, still in the dirt, rubbed his chin in contemplation.

"In that case, would you like to marry me?" he asked, sly and doe-eyed. Annie Mae grinned, tilted her head to the side and looked at the disheveled man still clinging tightly to his pogo stick. She smiled as more bullets went flying through the air, striking innumerable but unseen targets.

"Okay, let's get married."

BRIEF HISTORY

*It was in a Native American Women Writers class during college that I learned about Annie Mae for the first time. Her story immediately resonated with me, so much in fact that I found myself dedicating a lot of personal time to learning more about why she had come to be seen as a sort of Native American martyr. Although the internet is rampant with photos of her, some where she looks incredibly stunning and others where she is being led away in handcuffs, this one is my absolute favorite. The photo was taken during the 71 day reoccupation of Wounded Knee during 1973 where she did in fact marry her second husband Nogeeshik Aquash.

I absolutely love this photo because she looks genuinely happy, even though the reoccupation was incredibly dangerous. To me, the picture says that it's important to find the time to laugh even in the most hostile of environments. It's what inspired me to write the piece of flash fiction on the previous pages.

For those who are unfamiliar with her short but very significant life, Annie Mae was a Mi'kmaq Indian born in 1945 Nova Scotia. At the age of 17, she married and had two daughters but shortly thereafter, separated from her husband and joined the American Indian Movement (AIM). She became one of the most active and prominent female figures in AIM, taking part in historical events such as the 1972 Trail of Broken Treaties march on Washington D.C. that led to the occupation of the Bureau of Indian Affairs Headquarters. She also played an integral role in the armed reoccupation of Wounded Knee in 1973. It was here that she began her short and tumultuous marriage with Nogeeshik.

The events that led to her death have been shrouded in mystery and controversy, even to this day. In 1975, she went into hiding as she was suspected of being an FBI informant by other AIM members. Sometime during the month of December Annie Mae was abducted, taken to the outskirts of the Pine Ridge Reservation in South Dakota and shot, execution style, in the back of the head. Her body wasn't discovered until February 1976 and was deemed unidentifiable. An autopsy was conducted by a BIA coroner who stated that she had died of exposure. The coroner was ordered to cut off her hands and send them to Washington D.C. for fingerprint testing. She was initially buried under the name of Jane Doe but after she was identified, her family wanted her body exhumed for a second autopsy. It was discovered that she was shot with a .32 caliber. It wasn't until numerous decades later that several AIM members were indicted for her murder and found guilty.

EAST FLG (BORDERTOWN BLUES)

Welcome to Idiocracy the land of sweet hypocrisy
Smiles that hide behind hidden racism
So apparent I taste them
Your mama taught you this
Your papa taught you dis
The natives that come from the hood, our rural hood
Where our parents weren't treated so good
Taken from their mamas
Then let the boarding school set the trauma
Now they tell us to calm down
They don't understand the history behind these frowns
Have you ever met a Native? Well let me introduce myself
My name is Amber
And I love to love
and I hate to hate
But growing up an Indigenous girl in a not so
Indigenous world
Seems to be my fate

TUBA CITY BLUES

The rez night air is crisp, stars cast against an inky black sky, open space for miles and miles. I hold hands with my white boyfriend, still feeling the shakes from a ghastly hangover. Wind blows sand in through the cracks of this double-wide trailer and I feel the Milky Way in the pit of my stomach.

I analyze the faces surrounding me. An older, beautiful Navajo woman with hair and eyes as black as a raven's wing laughs and sips from her coffee spiked with Brandy. A Caucasian man joins in with her, a weathered cowboy hat on his head, cowboy boots on his feet, and a heavy beige coat with Native designs on his shoulders. And beside him, a quiet old Navajo war veteran, hair pulled back into a loose pony tail, rubs his voluptuous belly. "For a fifth of whiskey 7 Navajo men put electricity into this trailer for me. They dug the trenches for 3 days, ran the wires," says the beautiful Navajo woman, the wrinkles around her eyes pulled tight from smiling. Noticing the expression on my face she says firmly, "Hey, but now I have electricity in THIS home." The trailer shakes subtly from the wind.

I eye her Brandy; ask if I can have a taste. She disregards me. I look at the door for any sign of my friend who has abandoned me, left me with her family so that she can snag somebody at the local rodeo.

"I know what you are," the Caucasian man tells me casually, a triumphant grin on his thin, dry lips. "You're one of those *white* Natives." He eyeballs his Native flute, brings it to his reedy pout to play a few random notes. I say nothing. My white boyfriend says nothing. The War Veteran swigs on Brandy and I ponder his liver run thin from Hepatitis C. The beautiful Navajo woman closes her eyes and breaks into reverie, "Before the People transitioned into this world, Melanie, this glittering world, men and women were at odds, not only with their fists but with their hearts. Stubbornness and rage led to disownment. So on the banks of a mighty river, the men and women separated themselves onto different sides, to remain as foes. But . . ." says the raven-haired woman as she sips again from her coffee stained cup, "difficulties did occur and it was soon realized that men and women were only being unreasonable, were actually destined for one another. This separation is upon us yet again. You see men courting men, women dating women, men in high heels and women growing beards. It's happening right before your beady little eyes, Melanie. Disunion. And it's wrong," she slurs, the sound of sand still blowing in through all the cracks of her household. "It is a sign. This world of ours is going to meet its end and the new world waits. But not everyone is going to make it." She laughs deeply and grabs onto my shoulders hard, pulls me closer to her, her raucous laugh and hair smothering me.

As she pulls away I feel the Milky Way spill out of my belly in opulent waves and I fall into inky black tides. And in the heavens exist all of the faces of all the women I have ever loved and will love. In this galaxy fixed with a multitude of luminous points, there is weightlessness, concord, all borders removed. Intolerance is moot. It's neither the beautiful Navajo woman's bony fingers nor my boyfriend's thick hand that fills me with gravity, brings me back to the small trailer positioned in the wild landscape on the Navajo reservation. It's the overly eager voice of the Caucasian man that returns me from the stars. "I'm perfectly fine sleeping in the back of my truck. Got all the Pendletons I need back there," he says, continuing to fiddle with his flute. I am overcome by the desire to ruin, to become a great flood, to become a mighty asteroid that might destroy the earth. I want to stand up on table of the table, smash that Native flute, smash the Brandy, and scream at the top of my lungs that the warmest place I have ever been is a woman's bosom. I want to roar that the end of the world isn't going to be brought on by so-called unconventional means of finding love and happiness but rather through ignorance and the segregation of people from different backgrounds!

But I don't.

I sit in silence with my white boyfriend, lost in an ocean of blowing sand. And I go to bed early that night and don't sleep at all.

MY LETTER TO THE GOVERNOR OF OREGON

✓ Cultural Appropriation:
"Taking intellectual property, traditional knowledge, cultural expressions, or artifacts from someone else's culture without permission. This can include unauthorized use of another culture's dance, dress, music, language, folklore, cuisine, traditional medicine, religious symbols, etc. It's most likely to be harmful when the source community is a *minority group* that has been oppressed or exploited in other ways or when the object of appropriation is particularly sensitive, e.g. sacred objects."

—Susan Scafidi (a law professor at Fordham University, *Jezebel.com*)

There's been a lot of talk lately about cultural appropriation in the Native American community, much to the displeasure of those found guilty. The use of traditional Native attire for contemporary fashion aesthetics hasn't been this popular since the 1960's. But for whatever reason, Native American headdresses, prints, moccasins, dream catchers, etc. are "in" these days, much to the chagrin of countless Natives. First and foremost, let's take a look back in history, to that of the boarding school. Natives of all backgrounds essentially had their native customs, language, and culture beaten out of them in these schools, literally. The motto was *Kill the Indian, Save the Man,* originally coined by Richard Henry Pratt. Children were forcibly taken from their parents and put in these schools where they were subject to corporal punishment for speaking their language or practicing their religion. What this amounted to can be seen of as a sort of cultural genocide, and whatever was retained by young Native students was done so in secret. Those who refused to be fully assimilated had to use cunning and wit to hold onto what was traditionally dear to them.

Nowadays, there has been a noticeable shift in public perception regarding Native culture/customs. There are innumerable people prancing around in Native American headdresses at music festivals and/or claiming Native ancestry ("My great, great, great grandma was a Cherokee princesses.")

etc. The colonizers sought to take away and now their descendants stereotype and exploit. I bet the colonizers never saw this irony coming. Let's take a look at pop culture, just for some examples: No Doubt, some of those Kardashian sisters, Pharrell, Katy Perry, that one chick who's the daughter of the governor of Oklahoma, etc. Some offer up apologies, such as No Doubt and Pharrell, but others openly continue to be culturally insensitive, citing that they're either showing an appreciation for the culture or can't really figure out what people are making a big fuss about. What many seem to lack is the knowledgeable difference between appreciation and appropriation.

Another form of cultural appropriation is that of the Native American mascot. There has been some leeway in the matter with the US Patent Office recently cancelling the trademarks of the Washington Redskins because the name was found to be "disparaging to Native Americans". But there's still a considerable populace who firmly believe that Native American mascots aren't offensive. To further complicate matters, there are some tribes, such as the Seminoles, who publicly condone the use of Native American mascots. One has to wonder where this drift between tribes is spawning from.

Others that condone the use of the Native American mascot are the Confederated Tribes of the Grand Ronde. In Oregon this year, <u>Senate Bill 1509</u> was passed: <u>Allows district school board to enter into approved written agreement with federally recognized Native American tribes in Oregon for use of mascot that represents, is associated with or is significant to tribe</u> (gov.oregonlive.com). Interestingly, in May of 2012, <u>the Oregon State Board of Education issued a state wide ban on Native American mascots.</u> Apparently the bill surpasses that ban? One must wonder why this tribe would accept such a deal, when the state board has stated that Native American mascots are detrimental to Native American students in regards to self-esteem and self-image. (Native American Mascot Ban, www.oregonlive.com) Examples of detriment include: rival teams invoking racist stereotypes and

making references to the Trail of Tears, scalping, and rampant alcoholism. The fans of teams that have Native American names or mascots often wear things such as headdresses, which in traditional culture is an honored item that must be earned by its wearer through acts of bravery.

I wrote a letter to Oregon's governor John Kitzhaber before the voting of SB 1509. In 2013, he had vetoed the bill and in hopes of him vetoing it again, I sent the letter. However, the bill was still passed, which I found disheartening. I thought I'd share the letter that I wrote to him and the response that I was given several months later from one of his "specialists". The response was rather generic, which leads me to believe that the letter was probably never even read.

February 27, 2014

Dear Governor John Kitzhaber,

I am writing you today because I find the use of Native American mascots incredibly offensive. I am part of the Navajo tribe and take great pride in my culture and heritage. Native American mascots are culturally and racially insensitive, serving only to further enforce a stereotype. The noble savage, the romantic brave on a mighty steed, the Indian princess, etc. are all discriminatory. The truth is that Native Americans are a colonized people and the use of Native American mascots by our colonizers not only dictates our image but also dehumanizes us. I believe there would be outrage if teams and high schools existed with mascots like the Jews, the Blackfaces, etc., so why should Natives be treated any differently?

I understand that people are greatly attached and territorial when it comes to their mascots, especially when these mascots have been around for many generations. But it's also important to understand that several generations of social conditioning have occurred as well (i.e. being programmed to believe that parading around images of indigenous peoples like caricatures is acceptable and not racist.)

I am originally from Arizona but have been living in Portland for 3 years. I was excited to move here because I saw Oregon as an innovative state with a close knit community. This could be our chance to set a new precedent, to be a model for the rest of the country. I believe that one day we will look back and be surprised that this blatant racism was still occurring with the support of many Americans in 2014. Please, for people of color and for the Native American community, please veto SB 1509.

Thank you for your time and consideration.

Best,

Melanie Fey

May 2, 2014

Dear Mrs. Fey:

Thank you for contacting Governor Kitzhaber's office about Senate Bill 1509.

On March 6 2014, Governor Kitzhaber signed Senate Bill 1509. The Governor's decision followed careful consideration about this important issue. Tribal representatives, lawmakers, and other interested parties worked together to draft legislation that passed both chambers of the Oregon legislature, and that legislation was signed by Governor Kitzhaber.

Thank you again for contacting our office.

Sincerely,

Brandon Goldner

Constituent Affairs Specialist

Office of Governor John A. Kitzhaber, M.D.

Yá'át'ééh!

BIOS

Shi éí Melanie Fey yinishyé!

Melanie is an interesting concoction of Navajo, German, Italian and hopeful writer that was spawned in Tuba City, AZ. She grew up in Flagstaff, pursued a Bachelor's degree in English from Arizona State, had a brief stint in Japan and now resides in Portland, Oregon. Whenever in doubt, she asks herself, what would Lord Byron do? Or better yet, w would Frida Kahlo do?

Naakaii Diné'é nishłį.
Italian báshíshchíín.
Táchii'nii dashicheii.
German dashinali.

T'áá ákódí.

Ahéhee'!

Yá'át'ééh,
Shí éí Amber yinishyé.
Kinłichíi'nii nishłį.
Naakai
Dine'e
báshíshchíin

Ashįįhí dashicheii.
Ta'neeszahnii dashináli.
Ahéhee'.

My name is Amber. I like to listen to Mazzy Star, write and sometimes feel sorry for myself in my room with my humidifier on full blast. I enjoy a good cup of tea and a cute dress. Also this side project would not be possible without my mom, the works of Kathleen Hanna and the book that changed my life "Colonize this! Young women of color on today's feminism." Thanks.

84. • *Hannah E. Britton and Taylor Price*

"IF GOOD FOOD IS COOKED IN ONE COUNTRY, WE WILL ALL EAT FROM IT":
Women and Civil Society in Africa (new)

Hannah E. Britton is an associate professor of political science and women, gender, and sexuality studies at the University of Kansas. She has published extensively in the field of African politics, gender and politics, and gender-based violence. Her recent work examines strategies for preventing labor and sexual exploitation. Taylor Price is a Ph.D. candidate in political science at the University of Wisconsin-Madison. Her dissertation examines the conditions under which traditional leaders will participate in the implementation of women's rights policies in Namibia. In "If Good Food is Cooked in One Country, We Will All Eat From It': Women and Civil Society in Africa," Britton and Price analyze women's activism in Africa. An earlier version of this piece was published in *The Handbook of Civil Society in Africa,* edited by Ebenezer Obadare and published by Springer-Verlag (2004).

There is no singular way to describe the shape, composition, and strategies of African women working in society. Across the continent, women have utilized spaces and organizations outside the state—in what is called civil society—as sites for economic and social advancement, as areas to mobilize for national liberation, as places to rebuild after conflict, and as networks for transnational mobilization. Sometimes this space can facilitate confrontational and direct action. Other times women may use the space more covertly, to activate their "slivers of agency" (Enloe) in the face of colonial rule, religious fundamentalism, or authoritarian dictators. In times of democratic openings and national transformations, women may use their organizations and social groups to demand greater political representation and state recognition of their rights.

Most of the recent national advancements for women have resulted from the collective action of women's organizations and social movements pressuring states for change. The upsurge of African women in national offices is the result of intentional, strategic organizing of women in civil society to foster support for women's representation. The international norms of women's rights and women's representation have diffused not only down from the global community but also from within Africa itself (Tripp et. al; Bauer and Britton).

Despite these advances, new challenges threaten to stall the progress made by women in civil society. Political parties are beginning to co-opt women's seats in national legislatures so that they become loyal votes that legitimize otherwise draconian rulers. The global economic restructuring around neoliberal policies threatens social structures, welfare policies, health systems, and educational frameworks that often affect women first and most directly. Rates of human trafficking, gender-based violence, and gender discrimination continue to undermine the safety and advancement of women, girls and LGBT citizens across the continent.

To counteract these challenges and further advance their rights, women are initiating new efforts to utilize their collective resources within civil society. Transnational action and mobilization across borders ensure that successful policies and programs no longer stop at the border's edge. As Gladys Mutukwa, head of Namibia's Ministry of Information and Broadcasting, stated at the 2007 National Conference to End Gender-Based Violence, "if good food is cooked in one country, we will all eat from it."

POST-COLONIAL AND POST-CONFLICT PERIOD

While the end of colonial domination and civil conflict meant new openings for women to participate in civil society and public life, the imprint of pre-colonial and colonial ruling patterns often dictated the confines within which women could act and speak. Countries that gained independence early in the decolonization period often saw very limited changes in women's roles following the cessation of conflict. In part, this was because the rulers left in place by exiting colonial powers were authoritarian or because the liberation forces or military rulers that took power often dealt with dissent harshly. Women's political participation and agitation for representation was regarded as threatening and unpatriotic because it challenged their former liberation struggle allies who were now in office. Despite women's crucial roles in independence struggles as soldiers and activists, women's re-subordination was evident across the continent, from Mozambique (Sheldon) to Angola (Scott), from Zimbabwe (Ranchod-Nilson) to Eritrea (Hale).

Sometimes women in these states were able to slowly mobilize for change around a specific issue over a period of years. Literacy, health care, and violence against women—these topics necessitated

targeted action, and women were able to develop civil society groups around these issues. Rather than working in familiar coalitions from the liberation struggle that would garner attention from the authoritarian state, women felt "the need to protect their own interests . . . working in smaller enclaves in order to safeguard their resources" (Fallon 68-69). Women were often able to work toward these strategic needs without challenging the power and masculinity of the state. By carefully navigating their activities, women could argue they were working for the interests of the state by assisting in the welfare of society and by supplementing the work of government. Over time, these civil society groups often developed into more confrontational associations and coalitions demanding both recognition from political leaders and transformation in the state. Women's organizations became increasingly bold as the democratic openings continued to appear.

A process of political learning transpired between the earlier (1960-1990) and later (after 1990) waves of democratization. This second wave of democratization corresponded with what is now commonly called the second African independence or the African Renaissance. Women learned that changes in the public sphere had to be seized quickly, or political leaders would demand that women return to their place in the domestic sphere. Unlike countries that achieved national liberation early and then had a gradual march toward increasingly autonomous women's movements, such as Ghana (Fallon), countries gaining independence later often had women poised to take large, quick strides toward women's advancement in the state as we saw in placed like South African and Namibia (Bauer and Britton). For example, women in South Africa looked toward their allies in Zimbabwe and learned that if they did not pressure for representation in national office, they would be asked to leave politics for the men. Women's groups worked to secure constitutional protection, electoral systems, and legislative advancements to ensure their seats at the table of national politics. These organizations recognized that changes in the economy and social structure were also needed, but these groups worked quickly to ensure that insider strategies for change in the government were secure so that other sectors could follow (Bauer and Britton).

In the 1990s and 2000s, a number of African countries followed suit. There was a cascading effect of national leaders and political parties adopting some form of quotas or reserved seats to increase women's representation in politics including Burundi, Rwanda, Tanzania, Eritrea, Mauritania, Angola, Djibouti, Liberia, Niger, Burkina Faso, Democratic Republic of Cong, Ethiopia, Senegal, Zimbabwe, and Swaziland to name a few (Tripp et al.). Governments may have been motivated by a desire to appear more democratic than they actually were. Women often became the physical markers and visible symbols for government ideologies. As a government turns toward fundamentalism, women are pressured to dress and behave in scripted 'traditional' ways. Many states remained semi-authoritarian, and the act of putting women into positions of national prominence was a visible way to claim legitimacy for their governments. But women often had limited power even though they held national office, as they had to remain loyal to their leaders or risk losing office.

NGOIZATION OF WOMEN'S ACTIVISM

Despite the energy of African countries after the African Renaissance in the 1990s, contemporary patterns of women's participation in civil society are more institutionalized and less revolutionary. As women across Africa have started to take their place in parliaments, the revolutionary fervor of grassroots politics has transformed into more pragmatic, less confrontational, and more institutionalized processes. While this may be a useful strategy for sustaining more systematic change, many worry this shift has depoliticized the movements and minimized the goals of advancing women. Instead of broad-based social movements, we see a new cadre of individual women operating as gender consultants and advocates within institutionalized organizations. Africa is part of the global trend of women's organizations and movements converting themselves into non-governmental organizations (NGOs).

The NGOization (Alverez) of women's civil society groups is part of a global restructuring in response to neo-liberal policies as well as the professionalization and privatization of activist movements. This trend corresponds to the surge of neo-liberal economic policies that encouraged the downsizing of the state and the outsourcing of government programs to civil society. At the same time, Africa has seen the expansion of the international donor and development regime into the state. There is a push to formalize community-based organizations and activist networks into non-governmental organizations that can be recognized by, registered with, and regulated by the government.

NGOization involves a transformation from movement politics, characterized by oppositional politics and volunteer staff, to professionalized NGOs with paid staff and access to donors and grants. The NGOization was also, in some ways, a recipe for survival for overworked and under-resourced activists. As Tamale states, "the fact that most of us work double- or even triple-shifts (inside and outside the home), the fact that our work is under-resourced, we were forced to turn to the development industry" (39). The promise of grant funding and international support was a key factor in the turn of African organizations to the NGO model.

NGOs have been a site of effective policy initiation and program implementation. NGOs are ideally positioned to assist with implementation of government policies because they often have strong relationships with local communities. They are an inexpensive option for governments, because governments can just fund the programs and not the staff or overhead. The result is that governments across Africa are outsourcing key functions to feminist and women-centered NGOs. NGOs often provide legal advice, public health and community education, skills and job training, microfinance and economic development projects, rape and domestic violence support, and rights-based education.

This NGOization has been necessary to continue to attract domestic and foreign funding, as donors have become more likely to fund institutionalized, formalized groups that can demonstrate an absorptive capacity to receive, administer, and distribute grants. Although the pattern of NGOization has taken away some of the activist nature of the organizations, most continue to be the bedrock for creating an informed and self-sufficient civil society. In some instances, this NGO-state collaboration can be a positive strategy, creating a hybrid form of engagement and cooperation, where government programs are more targeted and where NGOs can shape the nature of implementation and policy creation.

There is very little research on how these structures and networks perform over time. High turnover rates for staff members that "NGO hop", tensions inherent in state-civil society collaborations, and the mission creep of NGOs—all of these factors make it difficult to assess their effectiveness and collaboration in the long-term. There are significant concerns about the long-term effects of NGOization, especially among those working in activist networks. The process of formalizing a movement into an NGO structure often means that more radical strategies and viewpoints become sidelined or erased. Groups become more focused on their existence, their ability to survive and secure funds. Their activist agendas then become replaced with more mainstream programs. Tamale, in particular, has voiced the concern that the professionalization of the women's movement signals a shift from *feminists and activists* to *femocrats and careerists* that are more concerned with personal advancement than the movement itself. She argues that the "government's tight control of non-governmental organizations' work . . . has depoliticized the women's movement" (39).

Given the dependence on donors and governments, many fear that women's movements are being co-opted by government agendas. They may become merely bureaucratic handmaidens who lose their autonomy and critical edge (Britton). But there are also some useful and progressive changes that have resulted from the growing influence of the international development regime. Most donor agencies and international organizations stress women's rights as human rights (Tripp). This is a powerful hook utilized by many local women's groups when they challenge their leaders and political parties to realize women's rights.

CONCLUSION

There is a persistent tension in the experiences of women in civil society across Africa. While women have succeeded in altering constitutions, legislation, and patterns of representation, they still face several obstacles. Women in civil society are now struggling to ensure that these voices are authentic and substantive—and not just window-dressing for authoritarian leaders or political parties. New challenges of HIV/AIDS, constrictions of state support due to economic pressures of the global economic recession, migratory pressures caused by economics and the environment, and continued civil unrest and authoritarianism all place significant burdens on women in civil society. Women must continue to develop new tools to sustain their families and their countries.

The new push for inclusionary feminism, in which women gain access to and influence on the state, continues to blur the arbitrarily rigid boundaries between the state and civil society. This has been a conscious, pragmatic strategy on the part of women across Africa to harness the state as yet another tool to transform women's lives in civil society. One key point of consistency across the history of women in Africa is their ability to employ civil society as a resource for collective action and as a resource for nurturing coalition building across differences and borders. As women continue to agitate for their needs and interests, this cross-national collaboration ensures that women can share their models of good practices across borders.

WORKS CITED

Alvarez, Sonia E. "Advocating Feminism: The Latin American Feminist NGO 'Boom.'" *International Feminist Journal of Politics*, 1(2) 1999: 181–209. Print.

Bauer, Gretchen and Hannah Britton. *Women in African Parliaments.* Boulder: Lynne Rienner Publisher, 2006. Print.

Britton, Hannah. "Organizing Against Gender Violence in South Africa." *Journal of Southern African Studies*, 32(1) 2006: 145-163. Print.

Enloe, Cynthia. *Maneuvers: The International Politics of Militarizing Women's Lives.* Los Angeles: University of California Press, 2000. Print.

Fallon, Kathleen. *Democracy and the Rise of Women's Movement in Sub-Saharan Africa.* Baltimore: Johns Hopkins University Press, 2008. Print.

Hale, Sondra. "The Solider and the State: Post-Liberation Women: The Case of Eritrea." *Frontline Feminisms: Women, War, and Resistance.* Eds. Marguerite Waller and Jennifer Rycenga. New York: Garland Publishing, 2001. 349–370. Print.

Ranchod-Nilsson, Sita. "'This Too Is a Way of Fighting': Rural Women's Participation in Zimbabwe's Liberation War." *Women and Revolution in Africa, Asia, and the New World.* Ed. Mary Ann Tetreault. Columbia, South Carolina: University of South Carolina Press, 1994. 62–88. Print.

Scott, Catherine. "'Men in our Country Behave Like Chiefs': Women and the Angolan Revolution." *Women and Revolution in Africa, Asia, and the New World.* Ed. Mary Ann Tetreault. Columbia, South Carolina: University of South Carolina Press, 1994. 89–108. Print.

Sheldon, Kathleen. "Women and Revolution in Mozambique: A Luta Continua." *Women and Revolution in Africa, Asia, and the New World.* Ed. Mary Ann Tetreault. Columbia, South Carolina: University of South Carolina Press, 1994. 33–61. Print.

Tamale, Sylvia. "African Feminism: How Should We Change?" *Development*, 49.1 (2006): 38–41. Print.

Tripp, Aili Mari, Isabel Casimiro, Joy Kwesiga, Alice Mungwa. *African Women's Movements: Transforming Political Landscapes.* Cambridge: Cambridge UP, 2009. Print.

Tripp, Aili Mari. "Women in Movement: Transformations in African Political Landscapes." *Gender and Civil Society: Transcending Boundaries.* Eds. Jude Howell and Diane Mulligan. London: Routledge, 2005. 78–100. Print.

85. • *Michael Winter*

I WAS THERE (2008)

Michael Winter was a disability rights activist who served as president of the National Council on Independent Living. In "I Was There" he describes his participation in nonviolent direct action in support of the Americans with Disabilities Act (ADA), the landmark civil rights law passed in 1990 that provides protections against discrimination for people with disabilities. His first-person account of civil disobedience demonstrates how the work of activists in the disability rights movement raised awareness about the barriers faced by those with disabilities.

On the afternoon of March 11th, I was very excited as I thought about the next day's activities. I had been elected President of the National Council on Independent Living and had dedicated myself and the organization to working with ADAPT to ensure that we do anything and everything necessary to get the Americans with Disabilities Act

signed. At the same time, I was on a Transit Board and the Executive Director of the Berkley Center for Independent Living. I felt very fortunate that I was able to participate in this historical event.

The next morning, I thought about the many times that I had been discriminated against: being forced to go to a "special" segregated school instead of integrated ones, not being allowed on a Continental Trailways bus because of my disability, and being told in a restaurant that "We don't serve disabled people." But I also had very positive thoughts about what a great life and great opportunities I had to that point. I was determined to work to overcome the injustices of discrimination and create more positive opportunities for myself and for others with disabilities.

As I listened to the speakers on that day, I considered how life had prepared me for this moment of civil disobedience. Although I had taken part in such "street theatre" before, this seemed like the crowning glory of them all.

After the speeches, we started chanting "What do we want?" "ADA!" "When do we want it?" "NOW!" The chants became louder and louder, and ultimately my good friend Monica Hall told me that it was time to get out of my wheelchair and crawl up the steps to the Capitol Building. Monica took my wheelchair, smiled and said, "I'll meet you at the top!" I started to climb step by step towards the top.

At the very beginning, I looked up and thought that I would never make it. But right below me was a seven year old girl who was making the same climb, step by step, her wheelchair left somewhere below or whisked somewhere above. This was Tom Olin's young niece. I felt an obligation to be a role model for this girl and we ultimately made it to the top together.

Some people may have thought that it was undignified for people in wheelchairs to crawl in that manner, but I felt that it was necessary to show the country what kinds of things people with disabilities have to face on a day-to-day basis. We had to be willing to fight for what we believed in.

The next day, we visited the Capitol under the pretense of wanting to go on a tour. I was one of the only demonstrators wearing a tie; my Board of Directors insisted that as the CEO of a nonprofit organization, I might as well look professional if I was going to get arrested. There was a lovely young woman who was volunteering at the Capitol to give tours over the summer, and as more and more people arrived she approached me and shared her excitement at giving a tour to so many people with disabilities.

A few minutes later we all began chanting, and Congressmen came to assure us that the ADA would be passed. These individuals included House Speaker Foley, Republican leader Michel, and Congressman Hoyer. We got louder and louder and all of a sudden, chains came out and people began to chain themselves in a circle. The young volunteer came up to me and asked, "Do you think they're ready for their tour now?" I was sorry and somewhat amused to be the one to tell her that no one would be touring on that day and that many individuals would probably be arrested.

Soon after this, the Capitol police began arresting people and cutting chains. The whole process took 2-3 hours and resulted in my own arrest. We were all sent to the Capitol jail and were scheduled to appear before a judge late that evening. In jail, I had the honor of being with Wade Blank, Michael Auberger, and many other disabled activists. It is ironic and perhaps fitting that I now oversee the implementation and compliance to the transportation provisions of the ADA, the law that we all fought so hard for.

I remember Evan Kemp watching the proceedings very closely from the back of the courtroom, and I remember our attorney, Tim Cook, informing the judge that we all pled guilty, that all of the defendants were part of the "Wheels of Justice" campaign to end the segregation of and the discrimination towards people who use wheelchairs. All of the defendants were released on our own recognizance and were given one year of probation.

I was the only one who was fined, because I held a job with significant income, and I was proud to "donate" $100.00 to the cause of justice and equality. Those few days and the passing of the ADA were monumental for me as an individual and an activist, but also for people across the United States of America. We now have taken steps to move towards inclusion and away from segregation and discrimination of people with disabilities.

I often think of these days and the lessons and power that they brought me in my current job as Director of the Office of Civil Rights at the Federal Transit Administration. It is important to keep these memories fresh in our minds and to avoid complacency in the face of injustice.

86. • *Sarah E. Fryett*

LAUDABLE LAUGHTER:
Feminism and Female Comedians (new)

Sarah E. Fryett is a visiting assistant professor in the department of English and writing at the University of Tampa. Her work revolves around feminist and queer theory, as well as philosophy, first-year writing pedagogy, and media studies. Her recent publications include a forthcoming essay on the representation of lesbian identity in the Netflix drama *Orange Is the New Black*. In "Laudable Laughter: Feminism and Female Comedians," Fryett argues that female comedians challenge reigning normative discourses surrounding sexuality and gender through humorous reversals, incongruity, and frankness.

Comedian Elvira Kurt—imagining an audience member's thoughts in one of her skits—inquires: "If you're a lesbian, and we are laughing at you, does this mean we're gay?" She responds, after a pause and a widening of the eyes: "Yes, yes, it does. Let the parade begin" ("Elvira")! Titters, guffaws, and clapping follow this bit. Why is the audience laughing? Why do I laugh each and every time I hear this piece (which is a lot, after all, as I am writing an essay on it)? The answer is simple: Kurt's comedy challenges a number of stereotypes—being gay is contagious/gays and lesbians love parades—that pervade our heteronormative culture. This observation led me to contemplate comedic performance as critical of cultural norms, and if, as Kathleen Rowe notes, our culture prefers "women's tears over their laughter," we must ask what might laughter enable (214)?

In thinking about female comedians, the following question comes to mind: Is comedy a viable arena for a feminist critique of patriarchy and heteronormativity? Yes. Laughter is political in its capacity to be critical and creative through a challenge to the institutions of patriarchy and heteronormativity. Though there are many forms of laughter such as nervous laughter and laughter at awkward moments, here I am referring to the physical and mental laughing moment elicited from a comedic performance. Using the nineteenth-century German philosopher Friedrich Nietzsche in conjunction with an interspersing of feminist theorists, I construct a framework for theorizing the transformative power of comedy and its potential ramifications. Focusing on Elvira Kurt, Wanda Sykes, and Amy Schumer, I offer an interdisciplinary textual analysis that demonstrates how female comedians challenge reigning normative discourses surrounding sexuality and gender through humorous reversals, incongruity, and frankness.

I first look to Nietzsche because, though not explicit, a close reading of his works advances a conceptualization of laughter as a transformative practice or, as he would phrase it, a practice of transvaluation. Transvaluation is a process whereby concepts are forced into a rigorous examination—challenged and destroyed. Through that challenge and destruction, an opening is created to allow for new possibilities/new ways of thinking. Though Nietzsche was responding, in his conceptualization of transvaluation, to what he saw as societal problems of the nineteenth century, the process can be applied to any structure of values that portends to construct the *truth*. I borrow his term to articulate a twenty-first-century feminist practice of laughter that radically challenges binaries of natural/unnatural and normal/deviant.

Often overlooked is *how* transvaluation occurs, and I argue that one possibility is laughter. In Nietzsche's *Thus Spoke Zarathustra*, he makes apparent this idea. *Thus Spoke Zarathustra* offers a variety of critiques concerning religious values such as morality, good and bad, and notions of the body, using an odd amalgamation of philosophy and narrative. The text chronicles the character Zarathustra as he travels through the countryside. Zarathustra, remembering his own council, notes, "I told them to overthrow their old professorial chairs wherever that old conceit [good and evil] had sat; I told them to laugh at their great masters of virtue and their saints and poets and world redeemers" (157). Laughter, a physical and mental phenomenon, functions as a method and a tool to overcome the old conceits of the great masters. That is, laughter—allowing a lightness of mood to infiltrate the serious—forces a questioning of what is conceived to be truth, the supposed natural and innate. Toward the end of this section, Nietzsche writes: "let each truth be false to us which was not greeted by one laugh" (169). Each "truth" must be greeted with a laugh because the laugh challenges foundations and refuses closure and sedimentation; it is the catalyst for change and revision. This Nietzschean laugh of transvaluation is essential to a feminist practice that is rooted in destabilizing the institutions of patriarchy and heteronormativity and the narratives that maintain those systems.

Feminist theorists less than a hundred years later interested in challenging the institutions of patriarchy and heteronormativity are many, but only a small sampling engage with the notion of laughter. Hélène Cixous is one of them, and she tackles the discourse of psychoanalysis—a direct corollary of the institution of patriarchy—within her essay "The Laugh of the Medusa." She interrogates structures of language, specifically phallocentric (privileging of the masculine) language, among other discursive practices, which erase and silence women and

women's sexuality. Though not employing the Nietzschean term "transvaluation," Cixous transvalues the narrative of psychoanalysis, through a laughing, parodic revisioning of the Medusa myth. Medusa, a Greek mythological figure beheaded for supposedly desecrating a temple, is conceptualized as a female monster. Cixous questions and answers:

> Wouldn't the worst be, isn't the worst, in truth, that women aren't castrated, that they have only to stop listening to the Sirens (for the Sirens were men) for history to change its meaning? You only have to look at the Medusa straight on to see her. And she's not deadly. She's beautiful and *she's laughing*. (my emphasis, 885)

By transforming the raging snake-haired woman into a laughing beauty, Cixous accomplishes two actions. On one level, this reimagining destabilizes the mythological Medusa (of Ovid, of Freud), thereby focusing a critique on how narratives manipulate images and characters for specific purposes. On another level, her laughter challenges a tradition that erases and silences, physically and mentally, women and their bodies. Medusa's laugh conceptualizes an alternative possibility, a bodily practice of disruptive laughter that momentarily "speaks." This "speaking" laughter transvalues the logic of phallocentrism. The laugh as critical engagement, a method for a feminism of the twenty-first century, at once demonstrates the pitfalls of a language entrenched in patriarchal and heteronormative narratives while simultaneously and creatively offering a new space to think that is inextricably linked to the body's sensations.

Informed by these theories, I turn to Kurt's performances because they play with and reverse heternormative narratives. In the following example, homosexuality replaces heterosexuality as the natural/normal sexuality—calling into question this very divide. She says, somewhat playfully: "The more I hang around straight people the more I find them like me. As long as they keep it to themselves. As long as they don't flaunt it. [Pause] Stay away from my kids" ("Elvira Kurt Giggles")! In this controversial time period with the repeal of Don't Ask, Don't Tell, the recent Supreme Court ruling on same-sex marriage, among other controversial issues, the traditional narrative goes: "If gays and lesbians keep their sexuality to themselves, I'm okay with them." Kurt's humorous statement reverses that narrative to demonstrate the absurdity of that common sentiment. She also implicitly interrogates heterosexuality as the norm, what Adrienne Rich refers to as "compulsory heterosexuality." Rich defines compulsory heterosexuality as "a political institution which disempowers women" because it supports the male/female binary, keeping intact hierarchical understandings of gender relations (203). Compulsory heterosexuality is reinforced on every level from Disney narratives to advertisements to history books. Rich observes:

> The lie of compulsory female heterosexuality today afflicts not just feminist scholarship, but every profession, every reference work, every curriculum, every organizing attempt, every relationship or conversation over which it hovers. It creates [. . .] a profound falseness, hypocrisy, and hysteria in the heterosexual dialogue. (221)

Kurt's reversal in this example encourages a critical examination of that "falseness, hypocrisy, and hysteria"—a transvaluation of heteronormativity. Kurt, by substituting "straight people" into a derogatory statement usually reserved for gays and lesbians creates a reflective moment where we recognize the institution of normative sexuality.

In another moment of transvaluation through sarcastic humor, Kurt tackles her mother's disappointment upon learning that she is a lesbian. In Kurt's skit from "Giggles Comedy," she flips the pages of an invisible album, imitates her mother's voice, and points to pictures saying: "This was the university she was supposed to go to. This was the guy she was supposed to marry. This was her first girlfriend, Brenda. They said they were roommates." Applause and laughter follow this bit. A similar routine that Kurt often concludes with centers on her mother meeting a friend in the supermarket

and, as they compare their children, Kurt, impersonating her mother's Hungarian accent, says, "My daughter, she's a comedian and a lesbian. Both at the same time. Oh yeah, like a dream come true." Kurt brings these erased encounters into the open, creating awareness and recognition. In relating her experiences with parental disappointment, she turns these shameful, rarely discussed encounters into an occasion for comedy; in doing so, Kurt advocates for lesbian voices and visibility. This cultural commentary steeped in humor transvalues the institution of heternormativity.

The next skit I turn to that offers a similar critical commentary is from Wanda Sykes's HBO performance *I'ma Be Me*. Sykes poses a poignant reimagining of the "coming out" narrative— coming out black instead of coming out gay. This reimagining functions on a number of levels as it: (a) offers a humorous yet critical space from which to view the "coming out" narrative and the concept of the closet, (b) showcases the absurdity of heterosexist responses to "coming out," and (c) challenges the institution of heteronormativity. As Eve Kosofsky Sedgwick notes in *Epistemology of the Closet*, "The closet is the defining structure for gay oppression in this century," and though Sedgwick is referring to the twentieth century, the closet still functions as a limiting structure today, in the twenty-first century (71). Sykes—acknowledging these structures—begins the routine with: "It's harder to be gay than black [. . .] *I didn't have to come out black*." Without delving into whether this is an accurate statement regarding oppression, Sykes does offer a poignant observation concerning the coming out process. She continues—pausing after each word—with: "I didn't have to sit my parents down and tell them about my blackness." In this juxtaposition, Sykes challenges the audience to examine the relationship between discriminatory practices and (in)visibility, thereby casting light on the proverbial skeletons in the closet.

In the remainder of this short piece, Sykes relates a conversation with her mother that humorously brings the coming out story to the stage, prompting transvaluation. Sykes—taking a deep breath—says: "I hope you still love me. Mom, Dad, I'm black." What follows is Sykes intoning her mother in a heartbroken, slightly hysterical voice: "Oh, lawd. [. . .] Anything but black, Jesus. Give her cancer. Anything but black. [. . .]." Saying something of this ilk is unimaginable; no one would dream of articulating this thought as it relates to race. Why, then, is it okay to mutter it in relation to being gay or lesbian? It is in the incongruity of Sykes's statement that a critique emerges. Continuing in her mother's voice, she blurts: "You've been hanging around black people, and there you go thinking you're black. What did I do? I knew I shouldn't have let you watch *Soul Train*." Here the notion that hanging out with black folks will somehow make one black pokes fun at the idea that being gay is somehow contagious—similar to the Kurt quote that opened the essay. There is also the infamous self-blaming that Sykes's mother does, which again emphasizes the ridiculousness of these comments. Her mother's final comment is: "Oh, you weren't born black. The Bible says Adam and Eve not Adam and Mary J. Blige." The decry of "not being born" and the resemblance to an anti-LGBT slogan that emerged in the late 1970s (Adam and Eve not Adam and Steve) create a further contrast between the narrative of coming out black and coming out gay. Through this reversal, Sykes critically tackles the space of the closet and the coming out narrative, cementing a practice of transvaluation.

In a slightly different—but no less powerful—humorous moment, Amy Schumer substantiates a transvaluation of patriarchy in her sketch "Last F**kable Day." The blunt and ironic comedy skit, which opened the third season of her show *Inside Amy Schumer* on Comedy Central, confronts unrealistic female beauty ideals that pervade Hollywood. The skit begins with Schumer jogging through the woods when she happens upon a picnic attended by Julia Louis-Dreyfus, Tina Fey, and Patricia Arquette. Schumer is invited to join the party and asks: "Is it someone's birthday here?" Arquette answers: "The opposite. We are celebrating Julia's last

f**kable day." Schumer's confused look prompts Louis-Dreyfus to add: "In every actress' life, the media decides when you're not believably f**kable anymore." The irony of celebrating, as one would a birthday, Louis-Dreyfus's last "f**kable day generates the humor in this sketch, and that humor elucidates Hollywood's fetishistic standards for female actresses. When you reach a certain age, your appeal dramatically plummets. Anti-aging advertisements from antiwrinkle creams to surgical procedures saturate our world, and the imperative is: *you must stay young*. Hollywood maintains this discriminatory practice, which silences and erases older female voices and bodies. Schumer's sketch, however, names this practice of erasure, and by naming, initiates transvaluation and a Cixousean "speaking" moment.

The next part of the conversation encourages transvaluation by unearthing the contradictory nature of these female beauty standards. Schumer inquires: "Well, how do you know [that you are not f**kable]? Who tells you?" Fey replies: "No one really tells you. There are signs, though. Like, when Sally Fields was Tom Hanks's love interest in *Punchline* and twenty minutes later she was his mom in *Forest Gump*." Arquette also observes: "Another common sign is when they start remaking your best movies with younger and more f**kable actresses." These responses show how Hollywood determines a woman's worth based on age. The clearest critique, though, occurs when Schumer asks: "Wait, what about men? Who tells men when it's their last f**kable day?" Raucous laughter ensues, and Arquette plainly states: "Honey, men don't have that day." This comment calls attention to the double standard that exists in Hollywood and patriarchy's control of female beauty standards. Passivity, weakness, and submissiveness are the female beauty ideals; activity, strength, and power are the male beauty ideals. These sexist standards of beauty pervade Hollywood and firmly sustain a gendered binary: male = active/female = passive. The sketch however, through frank humor, destabilizes these ideals of female attractiveness—cementing a transvaluation of patriarchy.

Kurt, Sykes, and Schumer challenge the institutions of patriarchy and heteronormativity through humorous reversals, incongruity, and candor. They advance a critique by contesting traditional norms of sexuality and gender. Kurt and Sykes tackle heteronormativity by insisting on visibility and creating stark, laughable contrasts; Schumer confronts patriarchy through an embrace of strong language and candid observations. All three comedians destabilize the all-encompassing narratives that disallow difference and create false hierarchical dichotomies. These comedic moments break through the silenced and erased bodies—undermining the institutions' truth. By laughing at these false truths, as Nietzsche and Cixous enjoin us to do, we substantiate transvaluation. A feminist practice for the twenty-first century must embrace this *laudable laughter*.

WORKS CITED

Cixous, Hélène. "The Laugh of the Medusa." Edited by Keith and Paula Cohen. *Signs: Journal of Women in Culture and Society*, vol. 1, no. 4, 1976, pp. 875–93.

"Elvira Kurt—Giggles Comedy Agency." *YouTube*, uploaded by WE Talent Group, 17 Apr. 2009, www.youtube.com/watch?v=DCI5maHosiU.

"Elvira Kurt—Stand Up." *YouTube*, uploaded by fr-mtransguy, 11 May 2015, www.youtube.com/watch?v=H6qVzyr4yhY.

Nietzsche, Friedrich. *Thus Spoke Zarathustra*. Edited by Adrian Del Caro and Robert Pippen, Cambridge UP, 2006.

Rich, Adrienne. "Compulsory Heterosexuality and the Lesbian Existence." *Adrienne Rich's Poetry and Prose*, edited by Barbara Charlesworth Gelpi and Albert Gelpi, W.W. Norton, 1993.

Rowe, Kathleen. *The Unruly Woman: Gender and the Genres of Laughter*. U of Texas P, 1995.

Schumer, Amy. "Last F**kable Day." *Inside Amy Schumer*, season 3, episode 1, Comedy Central, 21 April 2015. *YouTube*, 22 Apr. 2015, www.youtube.com/watch?v=XPpsI8mWKmg.

Sedgwick, Eve Kosofsky. *Epistemology of the Closet*. U of California P, 1990.

"Wanda Sykes: I'ma Be Me—Gay vs. Black." *YouTube*, uploaded by HBO, 1 Feb. 2010, www.youtube.com/watch?v=1_wWJ-_4uSY.

87. • Guerrilla Girls

WHEN RACISM & SEXISM ARE NO LONGER FASHIONABLE (1989)

The Guerrilla Girls are a group of anonymous feminist artists who use humor to fight discrimination in the art world. They wear gorilla masks in public to keep their identities secret. Their name references the unconventional tactics of guerrilla warfare that influence their protest art, which includes provocative posters and billboards designed to raise awareness and incite conversation. The group had its start in 1985 as a reaction to the Museum of Modern Art's 1984 exhibition of contemporary art where only 13 of the 169 artists included were female. When they realized that just protesting in front of the museum wasn't effective, they started their first poster campaign. Since then they've used other strategies to get their message out, including publishing books like *The Guerrilla Girls' Bedside Companion to the History of Western Art* and *The Guerrilla Girls' Art Museum Activity Book.* "When Racism & Sexism Are No Longer Fashionable" is one of their most well-known posters.

---

88. • *Kathleen Hanna/Bikini Kill*

RIOT GRRRL MANIFESTO (1992)

Bikini Kill is a punk band that was a major contributor to the Riot Grrrl movement, a feminist subculture emerging out of the punk music scene and focusing on political activism around issues like rape, domestic violence, and gender inequality. The Riot Grrrl movement also espoused a DIY ethic that gave rise to a vibrant zine culture. Bikini Kill began in Olympia, Washington, in 1990 and became known for their feminist lyrics and for encouraging a more welcoming environment for women in the sometimes hostile punk scene. Kathleen Hanna was the lead singer for Bikini Kill, and her "Riot Grrrl Manifesto" evokes the energy and ethos of the movement, particularly its focus on female empowerment.

BECAUSE us girls crave records and books and fanzines that speak to US that WE feel included in and can understand in our own ways.

BECAUSE we wanna make it easier for girls to see/hear each other's work so that we can share strategies and criticize-applaud each other.

BECAUSE we must take over the means of production in order to create our own meanings.

BECAUSE viewing our work as being connected to our girlfriends-politics-real-lives is essential if we are gonna figure out how what we are doing impacts, reflects, perpetuates, or DISRUPTS the status quo.

BECAUSE we recognize fantasies of Instant Macho Gun Revolution as impractical lies meant to keep us simply dreaming instead of becoming our dreams AND THUS seek to create revolution in our own lives every single day by envisioning and creating alternatives to the bullshit christian capitalist way of doing things.

BECAUSE we want and need to encourage and be encouraged in the face of all our own insecurities, in the face of beergutboyrock that tells us we can't play our instruments, in the face of "authorities" who say our bands/zines/etc are the worst in the US and

BECAUSE we don't wanna assimilate to someone else's (boy) standards of what is or isn't cool.

BECAUSE we are unwilling to falter under claims that we are reactionary "reverse sexists" AND NOT THE TRUEPUNKROCKSOULCRU-SADERS THAT WE KNOW we really are.

BECAUSE we know that life is much more than physical survival and are patently aware that the punk rock "you can do anything" idea is crucial to the coming angry grrrl rock revolution which seeks to save the psychic and cultural lives of girls and women everywhere, according to their own terms, not ours.

BECAUSE we are interested in creating non-hierarchical ways of being AND making music, friends, and scenes based on communication + understanding, instead of competition + good/bad categorizations.

BECAUSE doing/reading/seeing/hearing cool things that validate and challenge us can help us gain the strength and sense of community that we need in order to figure out how bullshit like racism, able-bodieism, ageism, speciesism, classism, thinism, sexism, anti-semitism and heterosexism figures in our own lives.

BECAUSE we see fostering and supporting girl scenes and girl artists of all kinds as integral to this process.

BECAUSE we hate capitalism in all its forms and see our main goal as sharing information and staying alive, instead of making profits or being cool according to traditional standards.

BECAUSE we are angry at a society that tells us Girl = Dumb, Girl = Bad, Girl = Weak.

BECAUSE we are unwilling to let our real and valid anger be diffused and/or turned against us via the internalization of sexism as witnessed in girl/girl jealousy and self defeating girltype behaviors.

BECAUSE I believe with my wholeheartmindbody that girls constitute a revolutionary soul force that can, and will change the world for real.

89. • *Julie R. Enszer*

ON LESBIAN-FEMINISM AND LESBIAN SEPARATISM:
A New Intersectional History (new)

Julie R. Enszer is a scholar and a poet. Her book manuscript, *A Fine Bind*, is a history of lesbian-feminist presses from 1969 until 2009. Her scholarly work has appeared or is forthcoming in *Southern Cultures*, *Journal of Lesbian Studies*, *American Periodicals*, *WSQ*, and *Frontiers*. She is the author of two poetry collections, *Sisterhood* and *Handmade Love*, and she is editor of *Milk & Honey: A Celebration of Jewish Lesbian Poetry* and *Sinister Wisdom*, a multicultural lesbian literary and art journal. She is also a regular book reviewer for the *Lambda Book Report* and *Calyx*. In "On Lesbian-Feminism and Lesbian Separatism: A New Intersectional History," Enszer analyzes the legacy of the lesbian separatist movement.

Have you benefited from an all-woman support group? Received a scholarship reserved exclusively for women or people of color? Does your favorite hair salon serve only women? Have you enjoyed a musical event with all women performers? These opportunities exist because of separatism.

What is separatism? Separatism is a theory and practice in which a group of people, often people who have suffered the effects of structural oppression, create separate spaces, often to achieve revolutionary outcomes. Within political and social movements, oppressed people separate from dominant cultures or colonizing forces for various reasons. Separation provides people with time and space to explore the nature of their oppression with others who share similar experiences and without intrusions from individuals who benefit from structural power. Through separation, oppressed people build strength without having their ideas and experienced invalidated by power structures designed to support systems of domination. In addition, people sometimes experience emotional and spiritual healing from temporary or permanent withdrawals from oppressive systems.

Many activists use separatism as an organizing strategy for movement building. During the twentieth century, separatism has been a key practice for a variety of political and social movements. For instance, various religious groups have practiced separatism as a way to preserve religious and cultural practices; Malcolm X advocated separatism as a part of his strategy to build the Nation of Islam and to promote liberation and economic independence for African Americans in the United States. During the women's liberation movement and the gay liberation movement of the late 1960s and early 1970s, lesbians and gay men advocated separating from various groups to work through questions about gender and sexuality. All-women consciousness raising groups provided a forum for women to understand sexism and its effects on their lives. Gay male spaces, whether in urban, suburban, or rural settings, allowed men to explore stigmatized elements of male–male sexuality and create experiences that celebrated gay men's sexualities.

For a period during the 1970s and 1980s, lesbianism and feminism became interlocking ideologies for various activist formations, expanding on the quip attributed to Ti-Grace Atkinson: "Feminism is the theory; lesbianism is the practice" (Koedt). Lesbian-feminism linked radical sex, gender, and sexuality analyses into a transformative social movement with broad effects on politics, culture, and the material conditions of women's lives. An important element of lesbian-feminist thinking and activism was lesbian separatism. Lesbian separatism, a political philosophy of dedicating one's time and resources only to women, took many forms during the 1970s and 1980s. The projects of lesbian separatism and its philosophy continue to shape the lives of feminists—women and men—today.

A brief history of theorizing about lesbian separatism in conjunction with how women created different separatist practices invites a variety of questions. What does it mean to be a lesbian? Can someone choose to be a lesbian? What are the political implications of sexual orientation? What does it mean to choose to work only with women, or only with lesbians? Where do people stake primary allegiances for political, social, and cultural work? These questions through the lens of lesbian separatism invite new examinations of sex, gender, sexuality, and race.

EARLY THEORIZING

Lesbian-feminists elaborated ideas about lesbian separatism, including what it means and how it should be practiced throughout the 1970s in a variety of geographic locations, including New York City; Washington, DC; Ann Arbor, Michigan; Seattle, Washington; Oakland, California; and other places. In all of these cities, lesbian separatism emerged as a strategy for women's liberation. For many women, lesbian separatism was an exciting theory and practice, although, like other philosophies, ideas about lesbian separatism accreted slowly as women thought intensively about what lesbian means and what comprises separatist practices. In other words, lesbian separatism evolved—and continues to evolve—through practical applications.

In 1970, the Radicalesbians, a New York City–based group, issued a statement titled "The Woman-Identified Woman." They called on women to focus on "the primacy of women relating to women, of women creating a new consciousness of and with each other." This statement is one of the earliest articulations of lesbian separatism. A year later, two women in Ann Arbor, Michigan, calling themselves Revolutionary Lesbians, published a paper named *Spectre*. They advocated separatism in a piece titled, "How to Stop Choking to Death." For these women, patriarchy, or systemic male dominance, caused women to nearly choke to death. The way for lesbians to breathe freely was to separate from men. Thus separatism was how women could "stop choking to death." Revolutionary Lesbians posited that separatism was "working directly only with women."

In Chicago, Vernita Gray, an African American lesbian, recalls, "Lesbian separatism was really springing up in that era. . . . I called myself a separatist. . . . I felt and feel to this day that it's important for women to have power. That's so important because once you take and claim your own power it's very difficult for people to oppress you" (Baim and Keehnen 62). If the Revolutionary Lesbians defined separatism as "working directly with only women," Gray captures its significance: claiming power.

In Washington, DC, a group of women who called themselves "The Furies" began experimenting with implementing the ideas of lesbian separatism in their political and personal lives. They lived collectively and reported on their living experiences in their newspaper, *The Furies*. The Furies believed that women could choose to be lesbians—and that by making the choice to be lesbians, women rejected heteropatriarchy. The Furies theorized that heterosexuality put women in too much close contact with male oppressors, whereas being a lesbian was "a choice for women and against oppression" (Reid 6). The Furies discovered, however, that the choice for women and against oppression was only a beginning. Many more choices followed. Members of the collective debated about the nature of personal property. For example, they wondered, could people in the collective own anything individually, or was everything community property? What about toothbrushes? Could they be owned individually? Members of The Furies also debated how to organize their lives together: How often should they meet formally? What types of outside jobs should they work? It was a fertile environment for thinking explicitly about how to live lesbian-feminist principles and articulate values of lesbian separatism. The Furies collective eventually folded, but it made important contributions to theorizing about lesbian separatism—and through the newspaper, The Furies spread the ideas of lesbian separatism widely.

In Seattle, lesbian separatists published a manifesto titled *Lesbian Separatism: An Amazon Analysis* (1973). These women believed that lesbian separatism was the only viable ideology to "destroy patriarchy and male supremacy and build an egalitarian matriarchal society" (Amazon 43). They imagined that by dismantling patriarchy, women would replace it with a society based on the investment of power in women, a matriarchy, and that this change from men to women would create more equality. The Seattle women conceived separatism as "long term struggles with racism, classism, ageism, etc" (Amazon 43). Central to all of the early theorizing about lesbian separatism is the idea that lesbian separatist practices should address centrally issues of women of color. Lesbian separatists imagined it as an ideology that could simultaneously address homophobia, sexism, and racism.

SEPARATIST PRACTICES

In spite of the fact that early theorizing about separatism considered challenging racism, as well as sexism, homophobia, and classism, as central to the project, some women of color and white women criticize lesbian separatism as only for white women. One of the most significant criticisms of separatism came in 1977 from an iconic statement by the Combahee River Collective. In the section "What We Believe" of the Combahee River Collective Statement, members of the collective write, "Although we are feminists and lesbians, we feel solidarity with progressive Black men and do not advocate the fractionalization that white women who are separatists demand" (Moraga and Anzaldúa 213). The collective continues, "[W]e reject the stance of lesbian separatism because it is not a viable political analysis or strategy for us. It leaves out far too much and far too many people, particularly Black men, women, and children" (Moraga and Anzaldúa 214). Many skirmishes around lesbian separatism centered on men of color and commitments to addressing racism through bigender coalitions. In addition, the role of male children in separatist communities, events, and organizations was hotly debated. These debates occurred in a variety of lesbian and feminist communities with different valences and shades of meaning.

The critique of lesbian separatism by the Combahee River Collective does not diminish the significance of separatist practices for lesbians of color. Separatist projects that center women of color were a vital component of feminism during the 1980s. Lesbians of color organized conferences and gatherings like the first black lesbian conference held in October 1980 at the San Francisco Women's Building and published journals like *Azalea* (1977–1983), based in New York City, and *Onyx* (1982–1984) and *Aché* (1989–1993), both based in the San Francisco Bay area. These projects were part of a vibrant network of lesbian-feminist and lesbian separatist projects during the 1970s, 1980s, and 1990s. Women built a variety of different organizations and activist projects that embodied and experimented with theories about lesbian separatism. Lesbian separatism inspired the creation of feminist record company Olivia Records, as well as feminist publishers like Diana Press, Daughters Publishing Company, Inc., and the Women's Press Collective; print shops like Tower Press in New York City and Sojourner Press in Atlanta, Georgia; book distributors like Women in Distribution and Diaspora Distribution; innumerable coffee houses in communities across the United States; and entertainment companies like We Want the Music, the producer of the Michigan Womyn's Music Festival. The Womyn of Color tent at the Michigan Womyn's Music Festival operated as a space for generating and nurturing projects by, for, and about lesbians of color.

In 1981, the iconic book *This Bridge Called My Back* helped to articulate the identity formation of women of color, linking various nonwhite identities under one rubric. *This Bridge* circulated widely in feminist communities. Persephone Press, a publishing company owned and operated by two white women, one gentile and one Jewish, originally published *This Bridge*. When Persephone Press went out of business, a new publishing company spearheaded by women of color, including Audre Lorde, Barbara Smith, Cherrie Moraga, hattie gosset, and others, took over *This Bridge*. Kitchen Table: Women of Color Press became one of the most influential feminist publishers of the 1980s and 1990s, bringing to feminist readers many influential books and pamphlets. Kitchen Table: Women of Color Press published only books by women of color and emphasized the control of all aspects of the material production of the books by women of color. For instance, in the second edition of *This Bridge*, published by Kitchen Table: Women of Color Press, the authors wrote that this edition was "conceived of and produced entirely by women of color." *This Bridge* not only elaborated the identity formation of woman of color by ensuring that the material production of the book was done by women of color and benefitted women of color, Kitchen Table: Women of Color Press expressed solidarity with separatist ideas and demonstrated their significance to lesbians of color.

In addition to cultural production organizations, lesbian separatism inspired land communities where women bought large land tracts, some to create sustainable farms and others to create retreats for women and vacation destinations. Land communities inspired publications like *Country Women* and *Maize* where lesbian separatists shared information about rural and country life. Two land communities in the south were explicitly for women of color: Maat Dompim in Buckingham County, Virginia, founded by Blanche Jackson and Amoja Three Rivers, and Arco Iris, in Arkansas, founded by Águila (Maria Christina Moroles) and her lover. Lesbian separatism as a theory animated many women to imagine remaking the world in a variety of realms—cultural, economic, social, and political. The vision translated into material practices was of women controlling their own lives and building their own communities.

PROVOCATIVE QUESTIONS

While the ideas of women's autonomy and lesbian solidarity seem commonsense, critics often attack lesbian separatism. Why? What does lesbian and feminist separatism challenge in the world? What benefits accrue to different people and power structures in dismantling separate spaces and attacking organizations that promote lesbian and feminist separatism?

One of the things that characterized developing theories about lesbian separatism is the idea that sexual orientation is something that women can choose. This notion may seem an anathema in current conversations about sexual orientation where popular views of sexual orientation see it as innate and immutable—including Lady Gaga's popular anthem "Born This Way." Yet seeing sexual orientation as neither innate nor immutable opens possibilities for various people. What benefits can you imagine for the ability to choose or change one's sexual orientation?

Finally, the Combahee River Collective was itself a formation of only women, which, in spite of the critique of separatism, may be seen as a separatist formation. Does a group need to explicitly identify as lesbian separatist? Or is the behavior of being a group of only women or only lesbians enough in and of itself to carry the label separatist? What are the stakes in naming a group, organization, or political practice as lesbian separatist?

The project of social transformation, political revolutions, and reforms require multiple strategies to achieve visions that activists imagine. Separatism is one strategy that appeals to activists at different historical moments. What benefits from separatism do you see? What benefits can you imagine? Where might separatist strategies serve people today? What limits might separatism encounter today in social movements? In addition to analyzing how separatism might operate in the world today based on this brief history, think about the key values that lesbian separatists sought to enact in their work. What are your underlying values? How do you express them on a daily basis? What communities have your primary allegiance? How do you express those allegiances? In addition to the spaces and opportunities that lesbian separatism creates for women—and men—today, one legacy of lesbian separatism is a commitment to examination of the material conditions of women's lives. By making your values and allegiances transparent through daily action, your life honors the values of lesbian separatists.

EXPLORE MORE

Interested in learning more about how lesbian separatists saw the world around them and organized their work? Here are a few resources to explore:

- Hoagland, Sarah Lucia, and Julia Penelope. *For Lesbians Only: A Separatist Anthology.* Onlywomen Press, 1988.
- "The Woman-Identified Woman." *Radicalesbians,* Know, 1970, library.duke.edu/digitalcollections/wlmpc_wlmms01011/.
- All of the issues of *The Furies* are available online at the *Rainbow History Project*: rainbowhistory.omeka.net/items/browse?tags=furies&page=1.
- An interview with Barbara Smith, the publisher of Kitchen Table: Women of Color Press and a member of the Combahee River Collective, at www.makers.com/barbara-smith.
- Moraga, Cherríe and Gloria Anzaldúa, *This Bridge Called My Back*, (New York: Kitchen Table Women of Color Press, 1981, 1983; SUNY-Albany Press, 2015).

WORKS CITED

Alice, Debbie, Gordon, and Mary. *Lesbian Separatism: An Amazon Analysis*. Lesbian Separatist Group at It's About Time, 1973.

Baim, Tracy, and Owen Keehnen. *Vernita Gray: From Woodstock to the White House*. Prairie Avenue Productions, 2014.

Koedt, Anne. "Lesbianism and Feminism." *Chicago Women's Liberation Union Herstory Website Archive*, 1971. *The* www.cwluherstory.org/lesbianism-and-feminism.html.

Moraga, Cherríe, and Gloria Anzaldúa. *This Bridge Called My Back*. Kitchen Table: Women of Color Press, 1983.

Reid, Coletta. "Ideology: Guide to Action." *The Furies*, vol. 1, no. 3, 1972, p. 6.

90. • *Amber L. Vlasnik*

CAMPUS-BASED WOMEN'S AND GENDER EQUITY CENTERS:
Enacting Feminist Theories, Creating Social Change (new)

Amber L. Vlasnik is the assistant dean of student affairs at the University of California San Diego's Thurgood Marshall College. Previously, she worked in the field of campus-based women's centers for over twelve years, leading the centers at Wright State University and Louisiana State University, and serving as affiliate faculty in women's studies at both institutions. In "Campus-Based Women's and Gender Equity Centers: Enacting Feminist Theories, Creating Social Change," Vlasnik explains the evolution of women's and gender equity centers at colleges and universities and the role they play in higher education.

What's a women's or gender equity center?
Are centers still necessary? What do they do?
Where's the men's center?
How can I get involved?

Questions such as these are common when students first learn about a women's or gender equity center. Perhaps a professor or academic advisor tells a student about the campus's center, or a student discovers the center's physical space while navigating campus or attends a center-sponsored program. Faculty, staff, administrators, alumni, and community members may also ask these questions, particularly if they previously worked or studied at a campus *without* a center. While each women's or gender equity center is slightly different in name, mission, and activities, this chapter explains some of the common questions about centers and also explores how students interested in feminism, intersectionality, and social justice can get involved in their campus's center, identify campus services related to women's and gender equity centers, or even

work to build a center on their campus, if their college or university does not yet have one.

WHAT'S A WOMEN'S OR GENDER EQUITY CENTER?

Women's and gender equity centers have been a part of US higher education since the first campus-based women's center opened at the University of Minnesota in 1960 (Bonebright et al. 80). Prior to the 1960s, institutional structures to serve women would have consisted of a Dean of Women (Brooks 17–18; Schwartz 504–5) or a continuing education for women program (Rice with Meyer 553–54). In the late 1960s and early 1970s, centers were founded in large numbers as a "direct response to the growth of the women's movement and an acknowledgement of the need for a new kind of support for women" (Chamberlain 83). Centers started during this period were often closely tied with the women's movement (Clevenger 3), the establishment of women's studies programs (Chamberlain 90–91), and activism for the rights and status of women that was concurrently happening on campuses and in the community (Chamberlain 85). As a result of these close relationships, early centers shared commitments to changing their institutions as well as society.

Today, approximately five hundred women's and gender equity centers serve their institutions (National Women's Studies Association, qtd. in Vlasnik 1), and they have differing missions, names, and activities based on the needs and cultures of their institutions (Davie, "A Journey" 5; Marine 16). While there is no standard definition of a women's center, their initial missions and activities often focused on equality between women and men, as well as safety, support, community, and resources for women (Kunkel, "Women's Needs on Campus" 16–20; Kunkel, "Starting a Women's Center" 67). In the twenty-first century, women's centers have expanded their missions in critical ways, now including a focus on leadership development, technology, and international issues (Davie, "Drawing New Maps" 448–49). In addition to the original focus on women, centers now strive to serve men, trans* and gender nonconforming individuals, and other groups that may not have been an explicit part of the original missions or activities of women's centers (e.g., Nicolazzo and Harris 6–7; Goettsch et al., "Contextual Statement" 489–90). Importantly, centers today often utilize intersectionality as a framework for analysis and action on their campuses and in their local communities (Goettsch et al., "Structural Issues" 8). For example, centers may examine interlocking identities such as race and gender in order to better serve women of color, as well as explore how racism and sexism simultaneously shape opportunities

for students in the classroom or in campus leadership positions. As a symbol of these evolving commitments, some centers have changed their names to include the term "gender" (Goettsch et al., "Contextual Statement" 489) and have formalized programs, partnerships, and coalition with campus counterparts such as multicultural, LGBT+, international, disability services, and other campus and community partners dedicated to serving minoritized or marginalized populations (Goettsch et al., "Contextual Statement" 490; Marine 23–24). The staff, volunteers, and supporters of women's/gender centers work collaboratively to initiate change on their campuses and in their communities to advance gender equity, dismantle gender-based oppression and discrimination, create opportunities for individuals and groups across their differences, and educate and empower allies.

ARE CENTERS STILL NECESSARY? WHAT DO THEY DO?

Where do conversations and programs about gender, gender equity, feminism, and social justice happen on your campus? What staff person or office advocates for women or to eliminate gender-based barriers? While women compose the numerical majority of students in US higher education (National Center for Education Statistics), sexism, gender-based harassment and violence, and misogyny have not been eradicated in the academy or in society. In recent years, women's and gender equity centers have played a pivotal role in providing survivor-centered advocacy and expertise about gender-based violence prevention and education (particularly as related to new regulatory requirements for Title IX), as well as preparing "members of the university community to engage successfully with an increasingly complex world" (Vlasnik 5). Through creating safe space for dialogue across difference, providing educational programming and leadership opportunities, and advocating for the elimination of gender-based barriers, centers are often the only place on campus where discussions and action related to gender equity, feminism, and social change occur.

During the past half century, women's and gender equity centers have worked collaboratively with campus partners—multicultural centers, LGBT+ centers, academic programs, student activities and organizations, and many other allied offices and organizations—to make campuses more inclusive, with a special focus on and expertise in gender-related issues. Centers have been responsible for a variety of tangible changes on their campuses, among them the creation of childcare centers; survivor-centered sexual assault prevention education for women, men, genderqueer, and trans* individuals; annual gender-related programming that enhances the curriculum and the cocurriculum; and the broadening, reshaping, and creation of policies to better protect and serve the needs of an increasingly diverse student population and workforce. They are also responsible for the education—and often transformation—of students as they learn and practice vital skills and thinking through center programming, employment, internships, and volunteering (Murray and Vlasnik 124). Centers are often close collaborators with academic programs, particularly women's/gender studies programs (Chamberlain 90; Zaytoun Byrne 50). Through center internships, volunteering, and programming, students can apply the feminist and gender-related theories learned in their coursework (e.g., creating a tabling event in the student center about consent or the wage gap) and then return to the classroom with firsthand experiences and knowledge to share with their professors and classmates (e.g., the process of creating materials, how people responded to the topic). This model of theory to practice is one of the foundations of women's/gender equity centers in the academy (Zaytoun Byrne 48).

WHERE'S THE MEN'S CENTER?

Sometimes it is asked in earnest, sometimes to deflect discomfort or as a joke, and other times to suggest that women's centers are not needed, but the question "Where's the men's center?" is common for women's center staff and volunteers. Women's and gender equity centers were founded because of the disparate educational opportunities and experiences between women and men in US higher education, and centers continue to exist because members of college communities—in all their diversity—continue to face significant gender-based barriers. In reality, almost all centers are open to men, and many do specialized programming and educational discussions that explore the social construction of gender, gender roles, and masculinities. While some men's centers/programs exist in higher education, they are few in number since the missions and expertise of women's and gender equity centers are almost always broad enough to encompass programs and services related to men and masculinities. In recent years, women's centers have formally expanded their missions, activities, and—in some cases—their names, to demonstrate their commitment to inclusion and their exploration of gender and masculinities. In 2015, the Council for the Advancement of Standards in Higher Education (CAS) voted to change the name of its twelve-prong standards (493–501) for these programs from "Women Student Programs and Services" to "Women's and Gender Programs and Services" (Goettsch et al., "Contextual Statement" 489–90). While not all centers utilize the CAS standards, the change served as an important landmark for the field of women's and gender equity centers.

Men are critical allies in the work for gender justice and feminist community. In particular, men who are willing to examine their male privilege and to talk with other men about how to challenge sexism and misogyny can find community in a campus-based women's or gender equity center. Centers have long served as safe spaces in which difficult dialogues can occur, and center employees are almost always trained diversity educators and facilitators of formal and informal discussions that explore privilege and oppression. Campus-based centers seek to engage all interested members in discussions about gender, feminism, and sexism and about how sexism intersects with oppressions such as racism, heterosexism, ableism, classism, and cisgenderism, among others. The goal of these discussions is to increase understanding and enact social change. Men are necessary for this work, both on the college campus and in the community.

HOW CAN I GET INVOLVED?

Since women's and gender equity centers are not membership-based clubs or organizations, many people are unsure of how to utilize or support the center. The following three lists of critical questions will help you get started.

If your campus has a women's or gender equity center:

- What are the mission, vision, and goals of your campus's center?
- What are its unique services or programs?
- What is the center's upcoming programming schedule? Can you attend?
- Do the center's employees supervise internships or volunteer experiences? Can you get involved?
- Does the center have physical space for you and your friends to study or gather?
- What, if any, student organizations do the center staff advise?

If your campus does not have a women's or gender equity center and you are looking for center-like services and programs:

- Where does diversity programming happen on your campus? Do they include gender-related and/or feminist topics?
- Are there feminist student organizations or organizations focused on gender issues?
- Where do students go for campus services or referrals to address gender-based concerns in their academic, career, or personal lives?
- Who makes policy recommendations on your campus?
- Who is the chief diversity officer of your institution?

- Do any academic programs—such as women's and gender studies—plan lectures and events related to women, gender, feminism, and social justice? Can you attend?

If you want to start discussions about a women's or gender equity center on your campus:

- Have there been any women- or gender-related initiatives, offices, or organizations on your campus in the past? What did they do, and why don't they exist anymore?
- What gender-related issues are currently happening on your campus, and who is working to address them?
- Are there other students who share your concerns and would be willing to work with you? How can you identify and engage them?
- What campus offices or organizations might be allies in the creation of a center? What about community-based allies or organizations (e.g., alumni, local women's groups, or a small group of donors)?
- Is there a campus administrator (employee) who would be supportive of a women's or gender equity center, and can you meet to discuss your interest?
- To what institutions does your campus compare itself? How many of these peer institutions have women's centers, and what services do they offer?
- Will your student government support your efforts? In what tangible ways?

ENVISIONING AND WORKING FOR A DIFFERENT TOMORROW

Women's and gender equity centers can be a disruptive presence in the academy. They ask difficult questions about what gender means on campus and in society, discover and address injustices on behalf of individuals and groups, and challenge their institutions to become more inclusive and diverse. Like many administrative units in higher education, student involvement is critical to maximize the center's impact and grow its scope and resources. Additionally, the thoughtful participation of students pushes centers to expand their work and imagine new possibilities for the future. Together, women's and gender equity centers and students can reshape their institutions and the world around them. Your ideas and contributions are welcome, so get involved and engaged!

WORKS CITED

Bonebright, Denise A., et al. "Developing Women Leaders on Campus: A Human Resources-Women's Center Partnership at the University of Minnesota." *Advances in Developing Human Resources*, vol. 14, no. 1, 2012, pp. 79–95.

Brooks, Kathryn H. "The Women's Center: The New Dean of Women?" *Initiatives*, vol. 51, no. 2/3, 1988, pp. 17–21.

Chamberlain, Mariam K., editor. *Women in Academe: Progress and Prospects.* Russell Sage Foundation, 1988.

Clevenger, Bonnie Mason. "Women's Centers on Campus: A Profile." *Initiatives*, vol. 51, no. 2/3, 1988, pp. 3–9.

Davie, Sharon L. "Drawing New Maps." *University and College Women's Centers: A Journey toward Equity*, edited by Sharon L. Davie. Greenwood, 2002, pp. 447–58.

Davie, Sharon L. "A Journey toward Equity." *University and College Women's Centers: A Journey toward Equity*, edited by Sharon L. Davie. Greenwood, 2002, pp. 3–16.

Goettsch, Jane, et al. *Campus Women's Centers for the Twenty-First Century: Structural Issues and Trends.* Issue Brief no. 3, Greater Cincinnati Consortium of Colleges and Universities / Southwestern Ohio Council for Higher Education, June 2012, corescholar.libraries.wright.edu/womensctr_bib/84.

Goettsch, Jane, et al. "Women's and Gender Programs and Services: CAS Contextual Statement." *CAS Professional Standards for Higher Education*, edited by Jennifer B. Wells, 9th ed., Council for the Advancement of Standards in Higher Education, 2015, pp. 489–92.

Kunkel, Charlotte A. "Starting a Women's Center: Key Issues." *University and College Women's Centers: A Journey toward Equity*, edited by Sharon L. Davie, Greenwood Publishing, 2002, pp. 65–78.

Kunkel, Charlotte A. "Women's Needs on Campus: How Universities Meet Them." *Initiatives*, vol. 56, no. 2, 1994, pp. 15–28.

Marine, Susan. "Reflections from 'Professional Feminists' in Higher Education: Women's and Gender Centers at the Start of the Twenty-First Century." *Empowering Women in Higher Education and Student Affairs: Theory, Research, Narratives, and Practice from Feminist Perspectives*, edited by Penny A. Pasque and Shelley Errington Nicholson, Stylus Publishing, 2011, pp. 15–31.

Murray, Margaret A., and Amber L. Vlasnik. "Women's Center Volunteer Intern Program: Building Community While Advancing Social and Gender Justice." *NASPA Journal about Women in Higher Education*, vol. 8, no. 2, 2015, pp. 123–24.

National Center for Education Statistics. "Table 303.45. Total Fall Enrollment in Degree-Granting Postsecondary Institutions, by Level of Enrollment, Sex, Attendance Status, and Age of Student: 2009, 2011, and 2013." *Digest of Education Statistics*, 2014, nces.ed.gov/programs/digest/d14/tables/dt14_303.45.asp.

Nicolazzo, Z, and Crystal Harris. "This is What a Feminist (Space) Looks Like: (Re)conceptualizing Women's Centers as Feminist Spaces in Higher Education." *About Campus*, vol. 18, no. 6, 2014, pp. 2–9.

Rice, Joy K., with Susan Meyer. *Continuing Education for Women.* Edited by Sharan B. Merriam and Phyllis M. Cunningham, Jossey-Bass, 1989, pp. 550–68.

Schwartz, Robert A. "Reconceptualizing the Leadership Roles of Women in Higher Education: A Brief History on the Importance of Deans of Women." *The Journal of Higher Education*, vol. 68, no. 5, 1997, pp. 502–22.

Vlasnik, Amber L. *Ohio Women's Centers: Statement of Philosophy.* Issue Brief no. 1, Greater Cincinnati Consortium of Colleges and Universities / Southwestern Ohio Council for Higher Education, May 2010, www.gcccu.org/committees/documents/ WCC.Issue.Brief.01.pdf.

"Women's and Gender Programs and Services: CAS Standards and Guidelines." *CAS Professional Standards for Higher Education*, edited by Jennifer B. Wells, 9th ed., Council for the Advancement of Standards in Higher Education, 2015, pp. 493–501.

Zaytoun Byrne, Kelli. "The Roles of Campus-Based Women's Centers." *Feminist Teacher*, vol. 13, no. 1, 2000, pp. 48–60.

Index